Fodor's

NEW ENGLAND

WELCOME TO NEW ENGLAND

New England's distinctive sights and landscapes make it a classic American destination. Vermont's and New Hampshire's blazing fall foliage, Connecticut's Colonial towns, and Maine's rocky coast are just a few regional icons. Massachusetts, home to Boston's stirring Revolutionary-era sites, is one of many places where history comes alive. You can sample the good life too, with visits to Newport's Gilded Age mansions in Rhode Island or a stay in a sleek country inn. Enjoy nature's bounty, whether you're skiing, hiking, or simply taking in a magnificent view.

TOP REASONS TO GO

★ **Fall Foliage:** Scenic drives and walks reveal America's best festival of colors.

★ **History:** The Freedom Trail, Mystic Seaport, and more preserve a fascinating past.

★ **Small Towns:** A perfect day includes strolling a town green and locavore dining.

★ **The Coast:** Towering lighthouses and pristine beaches, plus whale-watching and sailing.

★ **Outdoor Fun:** Top draws are Acadia National Park, Cape Cod, and the Appalachian Trail.

★ **Regional Food:** Maine lobster and blueberries, Vermont maple syrup and cheese.

Fodor's NEW ENGLAND

Publisher: Amanda D'Acierno, *Senior Vice President*

Editorial: Arabella Bowen, *Editor in Chief*; Linda Cabasin, *Editorial Director*

Design: Tina Malaney, *Associate Art Director*; Chie Ushio, *Senior Designer*; Erica Cuoco, *Production Designer*

Photography: Jennifer Arnow, *Senior Photo Editor*; Mary Robnett, *Photo Researcher*

Production: Linda Schmidt, *Managing Editor*; Evangelos Vasilakis, *Associate Managing Editor*; Angela L. McLean, *Senior Production Manager*

Maps: Rebecca Baer, *Senior Map Editor*; Mark Stroud (Moon Street Cartography) and David Lindroth, *Cartographers*

Sales: Jacqueline Lebow, *Sales Director*

Marketing & Publicity: Heather Dalton, *Marketing Director*; Katherine Punia, *Publicity Director*

Business & Operations: Susan Livingston, *Vice President, Strategic Business Planning*; Sue Daulton, *Vice President, Operations*

Fodors.com: Megan Bell, *Executive Director, Revenue & Business Development*; Yasmin Marinaro, *Senior Director, Marketing & Partnerships*

Writers: Kara Baskin, Bethany Cassin Beckerlegge, Fred Bouchard, Seth Brown, Liz Boardman, Grace-Yvette Gemmell, Debbie Hagan, Megan Johnson, Kim Foley MacKinnon, Victoria Abbott Riccardi, Mary Ruoff, Laura V. Scheel, Aaron Starmer

Editors: Salwa Jabado (lead editor), Daniel Mangin, Kristan Schiller (Boston editor); Luke Epplin, Teddy Minford, Amanda Sadlowski, Doug Stallings, Eric Wechter (editorial contributors)

Production Editor: Jennifer DePrima

32nd Edition

ISBN 978-1-101-87991-7

ISSN 0192–3412

SPECIAL SALES

This book is available at special discounts for bulk purchases for sales promotions or premiums. For more information, e-mail specialmarkets@penguinrandomhouse.com.

PRINTED IN THE UNITED STATES OF AMERICA

10 9 8 7 6 5 4 3 2 1

CONTENTS

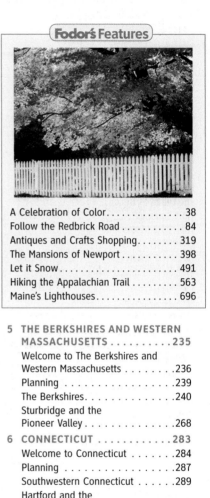

Fodor's Features

MAPS

ABOUT
THIS GUIDE

Fodor's Recommendations

Everything in this guide is worth doing—we don't cover what isn't—but exceptional sights, hotels, and restaurants are recognized with additional accolades. **Fodor's** Choice★ indicates our top recommendations. Care to nominate a new place? Visit Fodors.com/contact-us.

Trip Costs

We list prices wherever possible to help you budget well. Hotel and restaurant price categories from $ to $$$$ are noted alongside each recommendation. For hotels, we include the lowest cost of a standard double room in high season. For restaurants, we cite the average price of a main course at dinner or, if dinner isn't served, at lunch. For attractions, we always list adult admission fees; discounts are usually available for children, students, and senior citizens.

Hotels

Our local writers vet every hotel to recommend the best overnights in each price category, from budget to expensive. Unless otherwise specified, you can expect private bath, phone, and TV in your room. ⇨ *For expanded hotel reviews, facilities, and deals, visit Fodors.com.*

Top Picks	Hotels &
★ **Fodor's** Choice	**Restaurants**
	☒ Hotel
Listings	⬐ Number of
✉ Address	rooms
✉ Branch address	⏃⏃ Meal plans
☎ Telephone	✗ Restaurant
🖷 Fax	⟁ Reservations
⊕ Website	⋔ Dress code
✉ E-mail	▭ No credit cards
✍ Admission fee	$ Price
⊘ Open/closed	
times	**Other**
Ⓜ Subway	⇨ See also
⊹ Directions or	☞ Take note
Map coordinates	⚐ Golf facilities

Restaurants

Unless we state otherwise, restaurants are open for lunch and dinner daily. We mention dress code only when there's a specific requirement and reservations only when they're essential or not accepted. To make restaurant reservations, visit Fodors.com.

Credit Cards

The hotels and restaurants in this guide typically accept credit cards. If not, we'll say so.

EUGENE FODOR

Hungarian-born Eugene Fodor (1905–91) began his travel career as an interpreter on a French cruise ship. The experience inspired him to write *On the Continent* (1936), the first guidebook to receive annual updates and discuss a country's way of life as well as its sights. Fodor later joined the U.S. Army and worked for the OSS in World War II. After the war, he kept up his intelligence work while expanding his guidebook series. During the Cold War, many guides were written by fellow agents who understood the value of insider information. Today's guides continue Fodor's legacy by providing travelers with timely coverage, insider tips, and cultural context.

EXPERIENCE
NEW ENGLAND

WHAT'S WHERE

1 Boston. Massachusetts's capital city is also New England's hub. Boston's many universities lend it a cosmopolitan air, yet its blue-collar roots are still visible. This is the cradle of American democracy, a place where soaring skyscrapers cast shadows on Colonial graveyards.

2 Cape Cod, Nantucket, and Martha's Vineyard. Great beaches, delicious seafood, and artsy shopping districts fill scenic Cape Cod, chic Martha's Vineyard, and remote Nantucket.

3 The Berkshires and Western Massachusetts. The mountainous Berkshires live up to the storybook image of rural New England while supporting a thriving arts scene. Farther east, the Pioneer Valley is home to a string of historic settlements.

4 Connecticut. The bustling southwest contrasts with the Quiet Corner in the northeast, known as an antiquing destination. Small villages line the southeastern coast, within reach of a pair of casinos. The Connecticut River Valley and Litchfield Hills boast grand old inns, rolling farmlands, and state parks.

5 Rhode Island. The smallest New England state is home to great sailing and glitzy mansions in Newport.

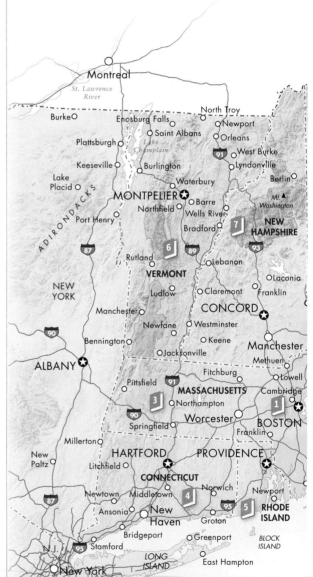

South County has sparsely populated beaches and fertile countryside; scenic Block Island is a short ferry ride away.

6 **Vermont.** Vermont has farms, freshly starched towns and small cities, quiet country lanes, and bustling ski resorts. The Green Mountain state is synonymous with cheese and maple syrup, and its billboard-free back roads may be the most scenic in the region.

7 **New Hampshire.** Portsmouth is the star of the state's 18-mile coastline. The Lakes Region is a popular summertime escape, and the White Mountains' dramatic vistas attract photographers and adventurous hikers farther north.

8 **Inland Maine.** The largest New England state's rugged interior—including the Western Lakes and vast North Woods regions—attracts skiers, hikers, campers, anglers, and other outdoors enthusiasts.

9 **The Maine Coast.** Classic villages, rocky shorelines, and picturesque Main Streets draw scores of vacationers to Maine. Acadia National Park is where majestic mountains meet the coast; Bar Harbor is the park's gateway town.

NEW ENGLAND PLANNER

When to Go

All six New England states are year-round destinations. Winter is popular with skiers, summer draws beach lovers, and fall delights those who love the bursts of autumnal color. Spring can also be a great time, with sugar shacks transforming maple sap into all sorts of tasty things. ■TIP➜ **You'll probably want to avoid rural areas during mud season (April) and black fly season (mid-May to mid-June).**

Memorial Day sets off the great migration to the beaches and the mountains, and summer begins in earnest on July 4. Those who want to drive to Cape Cod in July or August, beware: on Friday and Sunday, weekenders clog the overburdened U.S. 6. The same applies to the Maine Coast and its feeder roads, Interstate 95 and U.S. 1.

In the fall, a rainbow of reds, oranges, yellows, purples, and other vibrant hues emerges. The first scarlet and gold colors appear in mid-September in northern areas; "peak" color occurs at different times from year to year. Generally, it's best to visit the northern reaches in late September and early October and move south as October progresses.

CLIMATE

In winter, coastal New England is cold and damp; inland temperatures may be lower, but generally drier conditions make them easier to bear. Snowfall is heaviest in the interior mountains and can range up to several hundred inches per year in northern Maine, New Hampshire, and Vermont. Spring is often windy and rainy; in some years it feels as if winter tumbles directly into summer. Coastal areas can be quite humid in summer, while inland, particularly at higher elevations, there's a prevalence of cool summer nights. Autumn temperatures can be mild even into October.

Getting Here and Around

For more information, see Travel Smart New England.

Air Travel: The main gateway to New England is Boston's Logan International Airport (BOS). Other New England airports include Bradley International Airport (BDL, 12 miles north of Hartford), T. F. Green Airport (PVD, just outside Providence), Manchester Boston Regional Airport (MHT, in New Hampshire), Portland International Jetport (PWM, in Maine), and Burlington International Airport (BTV, in Vermont).

Car Travel: New England is best explored by car. Areas in the interior are largely free of heavy traffic and congestion, and parking is consistently easy to find. Coastal New England is considerably more congested, and parking can be scarce or expensive in Boston, Providence, and many smaller resort towns along the coast. Still, a car is typically the best way to get around, even on the coast—though once you arrive, you may want to explore on foot, on a bike, or by public transportation. In New England's interior, public transportation options are more limited and a car is nearly essential.

Train Travel: Amtrak offers frequent daily service to several New England destinations, including Boston; Portland, Maine; coastal New Hampshire; several points in Vermont; and Pittsfield, Springfield, Worcester, and Framingham, Massachusetts. The Massachusetts Bay Transportation Authority (MBTA) connects Boston with outlying areas.

1

TRAVEL TIMES FROM BOSTON TO:	BY AIR	BY CAR	BY BUS	BY TRAIN
Acadia National Park (ME)	1 hour	5 hours	not applicable	not applicable
Burlington, VT	no direct flight	3½ hours	4½–5 hours	8¾ hours
Hartford, CT	no direct flight	1¾ hours	2–2¾ hours	4–4½ hours
New York, NY	¾–1 hour	4 hours	4½–7 hours	3½–4¼ hours
Portland, ME	no direct flight	2 hours	2¼ hours	2½ hours
Providence, RI	no direct flight	1 hour	1 hour	½–¾ hour
Provincetown, MA	½ hour	2¼ hours	3–3½ hours	not applicable

Visitor Information

Each New England state provides a helpful free information kit, including a guidebook, a map, and listings of attractions and events; all include listings and advertisements for lodging and dining. Each state (as well as the city of Boston) also has an official website with material on sights and lodgings; most of these sites have a calendar of events and other special features.

Contacts Connecticut Commission on Culture & Tourism. ☎ *888/288–4748* ⊕ *www. ctvisit.com.* **Greater Boston Convention & Visitors Bureau.** ☎ *888/733–2678, 617/ 536–4100* ⊕ *www.bostonusa.com.* **Maine Office of Tourism.** ☎ *888/624–6345* ⊕ *www. visitmaine.com.* **Massachusetts Office of Travel and Tourism.** ☎ *800/227–6277, 617/973–8500* ⊕ *www.massvacation.com.* **New Hampshire Division of Travel and Tourism Development.** ☎ *800/386–4664* ⊕ *www.visitnh. gov.* **Rhode Island Tourism Division.** ☎ *800/ 556–2484* ⊕ *www.visitrhodeisland.com.* **Vermont Department of Tourism and Marketing.** ☎ *800/837–6668, 802/828–3237* ⊕ *www. vermontvacation.com.*

New England on the Big Screen

New England has long served as a backdrop for movies, sometimes the setting is just as integral to the film as its leading actors. Think of *Jaws, Mystic Pizza, The Great Gatsby, The Perfect Storm, What About Bob, The Departed,* and *The Social Network,* and you'll immediately think of place as much as plot. It's easy enough to visit locations like Newport, RI, Cambridge, MA, Lake Winnipesaukee, NH, and Mystic, CT and see where some of these iconic movies scenes were set. In fact, many towns have tour guides who specialize in visiting the sights. Watching these movies, and so many others set in the region, is a fun way to get excited about your trip.

NEW ENGLAND TODAY

The People

The idea of the self-reliant, thrifty, and often stoic New England Yankee has taken on almost mythic proportions in American folklore, but in some parts of New England—especially in rural Maine, New Hampshire, and Vermont—there still is some truth to this image, which shouldn't come as a surprise. You need to be independent if you farm an isolated field, live in the middle of a vast forest, or work a fishing boat miles off the coast. As in any part of the country, there are stark differences between the city mice and the country mice of New England. Both, however, are usually well educated and fiercely proud of the region, its rugged beauty, and its contributions to the nation.

Demographically, Vermont, Maine, and New Hampshire are three of the nation's four whitest states. African American and Asian populations are more common in Massachusetts and Connecticut. In northern Maine there is a heavy French Canadian influence from nearby Québec.

The Politics

Though they're often portrayed as liberal states, the political makeup of New England is actually more complex. The region's representation in both the U. S. Senate and in the House of Representatives skews heavily Democratic. That said, there is also a conservative tendency of a distinctly libertarian character among rural New Englanders and in New Hampshire, which hosts the nation's first primary each presidential election season.

The Economy

Long gone are the days when New England's shoe and textile industries sailed overseas, when many a mill town suffered blows to employment and self-image, and in recent years the unemployment rate has fallen below the national average.

According to the Federal Reserve Bank of Boston's New England Public Policy Center, economic indicators improved modestly across the region in 2015. It experienced the fastest rate of year-over-year job gains since 2001, as well as persistent declines in unemployment rates. Within the region, Massachusetts was the only state to experience year-over-year job growth above the regional and national rates, growing 2.6% between August 2014 and August 2015. Connecticut was right behind it, with an increase of 2%. In comparison, other New England states had more modest gains ranging from 1.7% in New Hampshire to 1.1% in Maine.

Exports are a major part of the modern New England economy, consisting heavily of computers and other electronics, chemicals, and specialized machinery. The Boston area is home to a thriving biotech industry. The service industries are also strong, especially in the insurance and financial sectors, which have a long history in Hartford. Some towns are known for a particular export: Groton, Connecticut, and Bath, Maine, both have naval shipyards supplying the military with high-tech ships and submarines; Springfield, Massachusetts, is a gun-manufacturing center; and Barre, Vermont, quarries granite. Assorted foods produced include maple syrup, blueberries, cranberries, lobster, and other seafood.

Sports

Fans from all five states follow Massachusetts's sports teams as if they were their own. Boston is home to three of the region's four major sports teams—Red Sox baseball, Bruins hockey, and Celtics basketball. The New England Patriots (football) play in the small suburb of Foxboro, about 30 miles southwest of Downtown Boston.

New England is currently enjoying a period of unprecedented success, as the region's teams have racked up nine titles since 2002. The Patriots charged into the 21st century, winning three out of four Super Bowls 2002–2005, then losing in both 2008 and 2012 to the New York Giants, only to reclaim the title in 2015 against the Seattle Seahawks. Red Sox fans, often referred to as Red Sox Nation, are some of the most fanatical in the country. The 2004 season was the pinnacle of bliss for many New Englanders, as they witnessed their beloved "BoSox" win the World Series, ending an 86-year drought. The Sox would do it again three years later, in 2007, and yet again in 2013. The Boston Bruins bested the Vancouver Canucks in the 2011 Stanley Cup Finals to win their first trophy since 1972, but lost it in 2013 to the Chicago Blackhawks. Not to be left out, the Celtics advanced their status as one of basketball's marquee franchises, capturing an NBA record 17th title in 2008 (the Los Angeles Lakers have since equaled the Celtics' title bounty, with their victory over Boston in the 2010 Finals).

Held each spring, the Boston Marathon is New England's largest sporting event, attracting more than 500,000 spectators. Started in 1897, the world's oldest annual marathon attracts more than 30,000 competitors.

The Language

As people move around, local accents have begun to blend together, creating a broader New England accent. In some urban areas, you may not in fact detect any accent, but linguistic differences are still evident in some places, especially close to the coast.

Boston's distinct accent is similar in tone to that of New York City's Bronx, and is noted by the dropping of the "R" in certain places, as in the pronunciation of the famous sports arena, "the Gahden." Bostonians also lengthen their vowels, so chowder sounds like "chowdah." Town names in Massachusetts are often spoken very differently than they are spelled; Gloucester, for example, becomes "Glawstuh." Bostonians also rush their speech, so "Hi, how are you?" is "hihawaya?" and "Did you eat?" sounds like "Jeet?"

Connecticut, Maine, and Rhode Island also have a Boston-like accent with nuanced differences. Rhode Islanders drop their R's at the end of words and use an "aw" sound for the O or A in words like "coffee" or "talk" but an "ah" sound for the short O's in words like "Providence" and "mom." In Connecticut and New Hampshire, the accent is not nearly as strong, but it comes out in certain words, like how locals pronounce Concord ("Cahn-cuhd"). Meanwhile, true Mainers drop or soften their R's—making their favorite dish "lobstah"; they also often accentuate the vowel, so a one-word syllable can be pronounced like two, meaning "here" may become "hee-yuh."

QUINTESSENTIAL NEW ENGLAND

Fall Foliage

It's impossible to discuss New England without mentioning the time of year when the region's deciduous (leaf-shedding) trees—maples, oaks, birches, and beeches—explode in reds, yellows, oranges, and other rich hues. Autumn is the most colorful season in New England, but it can be finicky, defined as much by the weather as it is by the species of tree—a single rainstorm, for instance, can strip trees of their grandeur. No two parts of the region undergo the transition at the same time, and you can actually follow the colors from one area to the next, if you have a little time. No matter where you find yourself, be sure to book lodging early: you'll be competing with thousands of other like-minded leaf peepers. Keep in mind that all that advance preparation will pay off on that first drive down a winding country road aflame in the bright sun of a New England autumn day.

The Coast

The coast of New England is both workplace and playground. In the 17th century, boatbuilders began to spring up in town after town to support the burgeoning maritime trades. Today, shipyards are fewer and farther between than they once were, but shipping—and especially fishing—remains important to the economy on the coast and beyond. It's not all work and no play: classic wooden sailboats now serve cruise goers, and some fishermen have traded in their lobster boats for whale-watching vessels. On shore, the coast's lighthouses are a New England staple, and more than 60 of these beacons of light line Maine's jagged coast, standing sentinel along the shore. In Massachusetts, Cape Cod is a beachcombers' paradise, and the relatively chilly waters of the North Atlantic don't scare away swimmers come summertime.

New Englanders are a diverse group joined by a shared past and pride in their roots. It should therefore come as no surprise that, although New England offers diverse activities across its six states, it gives visitors and residents distinct experiences that perfectly define the region.

Food, Glorious Food

Lobster and wild blueberries from Maine, Grade A maple syrup from Vermont, Portuguese sausage from Cape Cod, and dishes from every region of Italy in Boston's North End or Providence's Federal Hill: this is just a sampling to whet your appetite. New England dining is truly a gastronomic journey, spanning both simple preparations and truly artistic culinary creations, from blueberry pie just like Grandma used to make to world-class molecular gastronomy in an upscale Boston dining room. Local ingredients and sustainable methods are commonplace in Vermont and in foodie-centric cities throughout the region. Native chefs often leave the region to perfect their trade, only to return to enrich the dining scene with their experiences, while the region's undeniable bounty attracts newcomers from all over.

Artists and Artisans

New England's independent artisans have built up a thriving cottage industry. Some of the finest potters spin their wheels on the coast, and one-of-a-kind jewelry is wrought in silver, pewter, and other metals. Modern furniture makers take simple, classic New England designs, like those of the Shakers and Quakers, and refine them for buyers eager to pay for expert craftsmanship. Perhaps the greatest inspiration has been taken from the land itself—the Green and White mountain ranges of Vermont and New Hampshire, respectively; the historic coast of Massachusetts, or its Berkshire Mountains and Pioneer Valley; the southern shore of Connecticut; and the oceanfront cliffs of Rhode Island—having sat patiently for thousands of painters, whose canvases are sold in small shops and local museums everywhere.

IF YOU LIKE

Architecture

From classic Colonial homes to stunning Victorian estates, New England exhibits a range of architectural sensibilities dating from its 16th-century settlers to its 19th-century aristocrats.

Benefit Street, Providence, Rhode Island. This street boasts an enormous collection of stunningly preserved Colonial architecture, thanks to its place as the former home to the city's wealthiest families in the 18th and early 19th centuries.

High Street, Newburyport, Massachusetts. Once a leading port and shipbuilding center, Newburyport's High Street is still lined with some of the finest examples of Federal-period (roughly 1790–1810) mansions in New England, originally built for wealthy sea captains.

Lockwood-Mathews Mansion Museum, Norwalk, Connecticut. Built in 1864, this is one of the oldest (and finest) surviving Second Empire–style country homes in the United States. The Victorian decor, explained in detail by guides, is something to behold.

Museums of Old York, York, Maine. Nine historic 18th- and 19th-century buildings make up these museums, which tell the story of York's history from early Colonial times.

Strawbery Banke Museum, Portsmouth, New Hampshire. Settled in 1623, Strawbery Banke was a prosperous port before the Revolutionary War, and today the harbor city is still bustling. The museum is an outdoor collection of 40-plus historic buildings, staffed by costumed interpreters.

Vermont State House, Montpelier, Vermont. This is the country's oldest legislative chambers still in their original condition. The building is topped by a gleaming dome, and its Barre-granite columns are quite impressive.

Picturesque Towns

Keep your camera handy: New England has a seemingly endless supply of picture-perfect towns.

The "Quiet Corner," Connecticut. You'll find quaint shops, local restaurants, and Colonial homes in this series of charming villages that include Woodstock, Pomfret, and Putnam.

Penobscot Bay, Maine. Visitors meander through classic coastal towns like Camden, where historic homes line the streets and the quaint harbor is as scenic as it gets.

Deerfield, Massachusetts. Head to the main street in historic Deerfield to see 12 museum houses, all built between 1720 and 1850. Visitors can take a guided or self-guided tour, depending on the house.

Tamworth, New Hampshire. This was President Grover Cleveland's chosen spot for summer holidays, and with good reason: the town is simply irresistible, no matter the season.

Wickford, Rhode Island. This harborside village is packed with gorgeous 18th- and 19th-century homes, historic churches, and small shops, making it a great spot to spend awhile exploring.

Wilmington, Vermont. The main village near Mount Snow is filled with 18th- and 19th-century buildings and its classic Main Street is a hub of shops and cafés.

Art

The breadth and depth of art in New England is staggering. You can see everything from ancient Egyptian mummies to paintings by Impressionist masters to contemporary works by leading artists.

Currier Museum of Art, New Hampshire. The museum in Manchester has an amazing permanent collection of works by European and American masters like Claude Monet, Edward Hopper, Winslow Homer, John Marin, and Andrew Wyeth.

Farnsworth Art Museum, Maine. Farnsworth may be small, but it's impressive, with most of its collection devoted to the Maine-inspired works of the famous Wyeth family.

Museum of Art, Rhode Island School of Design, Rhode Island. Highlights include Impressionist paintings, Gorham silver, Newport furniture, an ancient Egyptian mummy, and the largest historic Japanese wooden sculpture in the United States, a 12th-century Buddha.

Museum of Fine Arts, Boston. You can easily spend a day (if not a week) at this world-class museum, which houses almost half a million objects, including Impressionist treasures, African masks, Native American pottery, and so much more.

New Britain Museum of American Art, Connecticut. In this museum's collection there are more than 10,000 works dating from 1740 to the present, including paintings by John Singer Sargent, Winslow Homer, and Georgia O'Keeffe, as well as a selection of Impressionist artists, including Mary Cassatt, William Merritt Chase, Childe Hassam, and John Henry Twachtman.

Southern Vermont Arts Center, Vermont. Ten galleries with works by more than 600 artists, many of them from Vermont, make up the permanent collection.

Shopping

From local crafts and antiques to factory outlets and boutique shops, New England is a shopping paradise no matter what kind of souvenir you want to bring home.

Boston and Cambridge, Massachusetts. For antiques in Boston, head to Charles Street; for a bustling, if not unique shopping area, check out the old Quincy Market (now Faneuil Hall Marketplace); and Newbury Street is Boston's version of Rodeo Drive. In Cambridge, Harvard Square is chock-a-block with clothing, book, and specialty stores.

Burlington, Vermont. You'll find all sorts of shopping opportunities in Burlington, especially along Main Street and at the Church Street Marketplace—a busy pedestrian mall with trendy shops, crafts vendors, street performers, and sidewalk cafés.

Exeter, New Hampshire. Wander Exeter's town center and browse its many shops for special handcrafted souvenirs by local artists.

Kittery, Maine. With more than 120 factory outlets and shops in close proximity, Kittery is a major shopping destination and a bargain-hunter's dream.

New Haven, Connecticut. Home to Yale University, New Haven is a charming town to explore, and its historic district is filled with unique boutique shops.

Newport, Rhode Island. Chock-a-block with upscale shops, waterfront restaurants, and tasty ice-cream parlors, Newport has a compact downtown area perfect for exploring on foot.

Putnam, Connecticut. Over 400 antiques dealers cluster around cute Main Street, Putnam, in the Quiet Corner of Connecticut.

NEW ENGLAND TOP ATTRACTIONS

Acadia National Park

(A) This wonder of the Maine Coast was the first national park established east of the Mississippi River. Hosting more than 2 million visitors annually, it is regularly one of the most popular in the United States. In the warmer months, take a drive around Mount Desert Island's 27-mile Park Loop Road to acquaint yourself with the area while indulging in spectacular views of the mountains and the sea. Head to the top of Cadillac Mountain for amazing 360-degree views (especially popular at sunrise) or bike the scenic 45-mile carriage-road system, inspecting each of the 17 stone bridges along the way. Go on a ranger-led boat trip in search of local wildlife, such as porpoises, seals, and seabirds, or cruise to the fjordlike bay of Somes Sound, where steep, rocky cliffs jut out of the sea. Adorable Bar Harbor is the park's gateway town.

Appalachian Trail

(B) The 2,180-mile Appalachian Trail, running from Springer Mountain, Georgia, to Mt. Katahdin, Maine, cuts through five New England states: Connecticut, Massachusetts, Vermont, New Hampshire, and Maine. The trail is best known as a weeks-long endurance test for expert hikers, but many stretches can be walked in a few hours. "AT" terrain in New Hampshire and Maine can be quite challenging; the trail is more manageable in southern New England. If you're a novice, you can also drive to many of the trailheads—if only to say you've set foot on the country's most famous trail.

Baxter State Park

(C) Between 1930 and 1962, former Maine governor Percival Baxter bought and then donated parcels of land with the goal of preserving the wilds of northern Maine. The result is Baxter State Park: more than 200,000 acres with countless

lakes and streams, plus Mt. Katahdin, Maine's tallest peak and the northern terminus of the Appalachian Trail. Offering frequent sightings of moose, white-tailed deer, and black bear, and attracting only 60,000 visitors a year, Baxter State Park provides a wilderness experience unparalleled in New England.

Boston

(D) New England's largest and most cosmopolitan city is the region's hub for modern commerce, education, and culture, where early United States history is never far from view. Orient yourself with a 360-degree survey from the Prudential Skywalk Observation Deck before hitting the streets to explore. The 50-acre Boston Common is the oldest city park in the nation; across the street is the Public Garden, where a ride on a Swan Boat has been a popular pastime—a harbinger of spring—since 1877. Two lanterns hung from the Old North Church kicked off the

Revolutionary War and made Paul Revere a legend; the Freedom Trail is a 2½-mile route that winds past 16 of the city's most historic landmarks. Be sure to include a visit to the Museum of Fine Arts, containing more than 450,000 works of art from almost every corner of the world, including Egyptian mummies and Asian scrolls.

Cape Cod National Seashore

(E) Comprising 40 miles of sandy beaches and nearly 44,000 acres of a landscape that has inspired countless artists, the Cape Cod National Seashore features the best of what New England has to offer. Since its designation in 1961 by President John F. Kennedy, it has become the perfect place for explorers looking for an untouched stretch of coast. Numerous programs—from guided bird walks to surf rescue demonstrations to snorkeling in Wellfleet's kettle ponds—take place year-round; most are free.

Green Mountains

(F) Vermont takes both its nickname (the Green Mountain State) and its actual name (*verts monts,* or "green mountains" in French) from this 250-mile-long mountain range that forms the spine of the state. Part of the Appalachian Mountain system, the Green Mountains are a wild paradise filled with rugged hiking trails (most notably the Long Trail and the Appalachian Trail), unspoiled forests, quaint towns, and some of the East Coast's best ski resorts. About 400,000 acres are protected in Green Mountain National Forest.

Lake Winnipesaukee

(G) As fun to fish as it is to pronounce, the largest and longest lake in New Hampshire is home to three species of trout, small- and largemouth bass, bluegill, and more. The 72-square-mile lake and its more than 250 islands also contain beaches, arcades, water parks, and countless other fun family diversions. In summer, Winnipesaukee buzzes with activity as travelers flock to resort towns like Wolfeboro, Weirs Beach, and Meredith.

Maine Coast

(H) Counting all its nooks, crannies, and crags, Maine's coast would stretch for thousands of miles if you could pull it straight. The Southern Coast is the most visited section, stretching north from Kittery to just outside Portland, but don't let that stop you from heading farther "Down East" (Maine-speak for "up the coast"). Despite the cold North Atlantic waters, beachgoers enjoy miles of sandy— or, more frequently, rocky—beaches, with sweeping views of lighthouses, forested islands, and the wide-open sea.

Mt. Washington

(I) New England's highest mountain, this New Hampshire peak has been scaled by many a car (as the classic bumper stickers attest). You can also take a cog railway to

the top or, if you're an intrepid hiker, navigate a maze of trails. The weather station here recorded a wind gust of 231 mph in April 1934, the highest wind speed ever recorded at a surface station until it was surpassed in 1996 by a 253 mph gust on Australia's Barrow Island. Bundle up if you make the trek: the average temperature at the summit is below freezing.

Mystic

(J) Home to two great museums—Mystic Seaport, known for its collection of historic ships and re-creation of a 19th-century seaside village, and the Mystic Aquarium and Institute for Exploration—this Connecticut seaside town is one of the state's biggest draws. When you finish touring the town's two impressive institutions, peruse its boutiques and galleries downtown.

Newport

(K) Rhode Island's treasure trove contains a bounty of preserved Colonial buildings and Gilded Age mansions unlike any other in the country. Here you'll find more than 200 pre-Revolutionary structures and scores of jaw-dropping, over-the-top castles from the late 19th century. Newport is also a picturesque seaside town and one of the world's great sailing capitals.

Portland Head Light

(L) One of the most photographed lighthouses in the nation, the historic white-stone Portland Head Light was commissioned by George Washington and completed in 1791 for the whopping sum of $2,250. It welcomes nearly 1 million visitors each year and features an informative museum in the Victorian-style innkeeper's cottage. The lighthouse is located in Fort Williams Park, about 2 miles from the town center of Cape Elizabeth, at the southwest entrance of Portland harbor.

NEW ENGLAND WITH KIDS

From beachside amusement parks to fantastic children's museums, there's no end of activities and attractions for kids and families all over New England.

Massachusetts

Children's Museum, Boston Make bubbles, climb through a maze, and while away the hours in the "Adventure Zone" at this fun museum just for tykes in Downtown Boston. A special play area for those under three lets them run around in a safe environment. There are seasonal festivals throughout the year.

Magic Wings Butterfly Conservatory & Gardens, Deerfield. Almost 4,000 free-flying native and tropical butterflies are the star attraction here, contained within an 8,000-square-foot glassed enclosure that keeps the temperature upward of 80°F year-round. Relax around the Japanese koi pond on one of numerous benches and watch the kids chase the colorful creatures as they flit about. Or walk outside to the Iron Butterfly Outdoor Gardens, where flowers attract still more butterflies.

Massachusetts Audubon Wellfleet Bay Wildlife Sanctuary, South Wellfleet. With its numerous programs and its beautiful salt-marsh surroundings, this is a favorite stop for Cape vacationers year-round. Five miles of nature trails weave throughout the sanctuary's 1,100 acres of marsh, beach, and woods. If you're careful and quiet, you may be able to get close to sunbathing seals or birds like the great blue heron. Naturalists are on hand for guided walks and lectures.

Plimoth Plantation, Plymouth. Want to know what life was like in Colonial America? A visit to this living-history museum is like stepping into a time machine and zooming back to the year 1627. Guides dress in period costume and act like early-17th-century Pilgrims.

Connecticut

Connecticut Science Center, Hartford. With unique, high-quality, and highly interactive exhibits, this science center is a must. It's geared toward older kids, but there is a kids space for the under-seven set. There's also a 3-D theater.

Dinosaur State Park, Rocky Hill. Dinosaur lovers can explore a 200-million-year-old fossil trackway, take in interactive exhibits, and even cast a dinosaur footprint to take home.

Mystic Aquarium and Institute for Exploration, Mystic. This aquarium and research institute is one of only four North American facilities to feature endangered Steller sea lions; it's also home to New England's only beluga whale. You'll also see African penguins, harbor seals, graceful sea horses, Pacific octopuses, and sand tiger sharks—kids can even touch a cownose ray. Nearby Mystic Seaport is another great attraction for families.

Rhode Island

Block Island. Hop on the ferry at Port Judith and head to Block Island for an easy and scenic bike ride or just to spend the day at one of its many gorgeous, and often uncrowded, beaches.

Providence Children's Museum. Aimed at children ages 1–11, PCM explores arts, culture, history, and science. Exhibits are based on the developmental needs of children and embrace a wide range of learning styles.

Roger Williams Park and Zoo, Providence. Home to more than 100 species of animals from around the world, Roger Williams Park has more than 40 acres to explore. One highlight is Marco Polo's

Adventure Trek, with camels, moon bears, snow leopards, red crowned cranes, and red pandas. Look for interactive educational programs.

Vermont

ECHO Leahy Center for Lake Champlain, Burlington. Lots of activities and hands-on exhibits make learning about the geology and ecology of Lake Champlain an engaging experience.

Montshire Museum of Science, Norwich. This interactive museum uses more than 60 hands-on exhibits to explore nature and technology. The building sits amid 110 acres of nature trails and woodlands, where live animals roam freely.

Shelburne Farms, Shelburne. This working dairy farm is also an educational and cultural resource center. Visitors can watch artisans make the farm's famous cheddar cheese from the milk of more than 100 purebred and registered Brown Swiss cows. A children's farmyard and walking trails round out the experience.

New Hampshire

Hampton Beach. This seaside diversion draws families to its almost Coney Island–like fun. Along the boardwalk, kids enjoy arcade games, parasailing, live music, and an annual children's festival. They can even learn how saltwater taffy is made.

Lake Winnipesaukee, Weirs Beach. The largest lake in the state, Lake Winnipesaukee provides plenty of family-friendly fun. Base yourself in Weirs Beach and the kids can swim, play arcade games, cruise the lake, take a scenic railroad along the shoreline, and even see a drive-in movie.

SEE Science Center, Manchester. For kids who love LEGO, the models of old Manchester and the millyard are sure to impress.

There are also rotating exhibits and science demonstrations

Maine

Acadia National Park, Mount Desert Island. Head out on a whale- and puffin-watching trip from Bar Harbor, drive up scenic Cadillac Mountain, swim at Echo Lake Beach, hike one of the many easy trails, and don't forget to sample some wild blueberry pie.

Maine Discovery Museum, Bangor. There are three floors of fun, educational activities at the Maine Discovery Museum. Exhibits include Nature Trails; Booktown; Sounds Abound; Artscape; and Body Journey.

Maine Narrow Gauge Railroad Museum, Portland. For train fans, check out the scenic rides on these narrow-gauge trains. In the winter, they have *Polar Express*–themed trips.

FLAVORS OF NEW ENGLAND

The locavore movement has officially hit New England. New farms, greenmarkets, and gourmet food shops are sprouting up every day and chefs are exploring more farm-to-table options.

FOOD FESTIVALS

New England has a plethora of food festivals that celebrate local offerings ranging from blueberries to cheese. The following is a small sample of the celebrations honoring regional cuisine.

Chowderfest, Boston, Massachusetts. Thousands gather at City Hall Plaza for the annual Chowderfest (⊕ *www.bostonharborfest. com*) in early July. The chowder cook-off is part of Harborfest, Boston's yearly festivities centered around Independence Day.

Maine Lobster Festival, Rockland, Maine. Stuff your face with lobster tails and claws during this "lobstravaganza" (⊕ *www. mainelobsterfestival.com*) in late July and early August. With almost 20,000 pounds of delicious crustacean at your finger tips, leaving hungry is unthinkable.

New Hampshire Pumpkin Festival, Laconia, New Hampshire. Formerly located in Keene, the newly renamed and relocated festival (as of 2015) tries to outdo itself each October for most lighted pumpkins (⊕ *www.pumpkinfestival2015.org*). Enjoy hayrides and contests ranging from pie eating to pumpkin-seed spitting.

Vermont Cheesemakers Festival, Shelburne, Vermont. Artisanal cheeses and local beer and wine highlight this daylong festival (⊕ *www.vtcheesefest.com*) in late July. Sample more than 200 cheese varieties from 40 local cheese makers in the Coach Barn of Shelburne Farms.

Wilton Blueberry Festival, Wilton, Maine. You can pick your own wild blueberries and sample baked goods from pancakes to pies at the annual Wilton Blueberry Festival (⊕ *www.wiltonbbf.com*), which takes place in early August.

SPECIALTIES BY STATE

Massachusetts

Concord grapes started growing in their namesake Massachusetts village in 1849, and **cranberries** are cultivated on marshy bogs. Known as "Little Italy," Boston's North End boasts almost 90 Italian restaurants; you'll find everything from hole-in-the-wall pizza joints to elegant eateries serving regional cuisine from every corner of "the boot"; no trip here is complete without a **cannoli** from Mike's Pastry. For more than 100 years fisherman and whalers of Portuguese and Azorean decent have called Provincetown home; some say Provincetown Portuguese Bakery's decadent *malassadas* (fried dough dusted with sugar) are alone worth the trip to the end of Cape Cod.

Connecticut

New Haven–style pizza, a decidedly thin-crust pie cooked in a brick oven, can be found at several pizzerias in town. The original creator, Frank Pepe Pizzeria Napoletana, has been around since 1925, while two blocks away is Sally's Apizza, established in 1938. If you prefer a newcomer, try BAR, a nightclub-cum-microbrewery popular with the college crowd. At any of the above, ask for fresh "mootz" (mozzarella in East Coast speak). **Connecticut-style lobster rolls,** warm lobster meat served on a bun doused with drawn butter, are another state specialty.

Over the past decade the state has also become known for its **wines**. Chardonnay,

Riesling, Cabernet Sauvignon, and many other varietals are grown throughout New England, but Connecticut's wine production stands out. The Connecticut Wine Trail is a collection of 25 vineyards, divided between the Western Trail in the Litchfield Hills and the Eastern Trail near the southeastern shore. Hopkins Vineyard (Western Trail), overlooking Lake Waramaug, and Jonathan Edwards Winery (Eastern Trail) are two of the most admired stops along the trail.

Rhode Island

Rhode Islanders are partial to **johnnycakes,** a cornmeal flatbread that was once a staple of Early American gastronomy. They also like to sip **cabinets,** or milk shakes, often made with coffee and celery salt (also known as frappés in other parts of New England).

The Ocean State may be small, but its capital's food reputation is big, thanks to its status as the home of Johnson & Wales, a prestigious culinary academy. Some of its graduates have opened restaurants in Providence, drawing discriminating diners from near and far. Savor Italian food along Providence's Atwells Avenue in the Federal Hill neighborhood or nosh with the posh at upscale river-view establishments in downtown Providence.

Vermont

Vermonters are big on **maple syrup** straight-up and in candy, but dairy products take top billing in this state. Milk and cream from the region's dairy farms are used in cheeses, like the famous **cheddar;** and in **ice cream,** from the likes of Ben & Jerry's. Willow Hill Farm in Milton, Vermont, is famous for its sheep's milk cheeses; try the savory Vaquero Blue, a blue cheese made from both sheep and cow's milk. For a family-friendly stop, check out Shelburne

Farms' children's farmyard. Located on the shore of Lake Champlain, Shelburne Farms uses only Brown Swiss cows to make its famous cheddar. In addition to the Vermont Cheesemakers Festival, Shelburne attracts visitors year-round to taste cheeses and explore walking trails.

New Hampshire

Northern New Hampshire's cuisine carries a heavy French Canadian influence. One of the most enticing francophone creations is *poutine* (french fries covered with cheese curds and gravy). The local **corn chowder** substitutes corn for clams and bacon, putting a twist on a Northeastern classic. The Smuttynose Brewing Company, a craft brewery in Portsmouth, offers tours and tastings.

Maine

Lobster classics include **boiled lobster**—a staple at picnic-bench-and-paper-plate spots along the Maine Coast—and **lobster rolls,** a lobster meat and mayo (or melted butter) preparation served in a toasted hot dog bun. **Blueberries, strawberries, raspberries,** and **blackberries** grow wild (and on farms) all over the Northeast in the summer. Blueberry pancakes with maple syrup, blueberry muffins, and blueberry pies are popular, especially along the coast. Mainers also love **whoopie pies,** cakelike cookies sandwiched together with frosting.

Portland's waterfront Commercial Street is bookended by two typical Maine diners, Gilbert's Chowderhouse and Becky's Diner. The former has one of the state's finest lobster rolls and homemade clam cakes; the latter opens for breakfast at 4 am to feed fishermen before they head out to sea. Order a slice of fresh pie or buy one whole to take with you.

OUTDOOR ADVENTURES

BEACHCOMBING AND SWIMMING

Long, wide beaches line the New England coast from southern Maine to southern Connecticut, with dozens dotting the shores of Cape Cod, Martha's Vineyard, and Nantucket. Many beaches have lifeguards on duty in season; some have picnic facilities, restrooms, changing facilities, and concession stands. Depending on the locale, you may need a parking sticker to use the lot.

When to Go

The waters are at their warmest in August, though they're cold even at the height of summer along much of Maine, New Hampshire, and Massachusetts. Inland, small lake beaches abound, most notably in New Hampshire and Vermont. The best time to beachcomb is after the tide has gone out, when the retreating water has left behind its treasures. Early spring is an especially good time to see sand dollars washed up on beaches.

What to Look For

The best part of beachcombing is that you never quite know what you'll find at your feet. Sea glass—nothing more than man-made glass worn smooth from its seaward journeys—is common and most prized in rare shades of blue. You'll also find shells in abundance: blue mussels, tiny periwinkles, razor (or "jackknife") clams, ridged scallops, and briny oysters, with their rough outside shell and lovely mother-of-pearl interiors.

Best Beaches

Block Island, Rhode Island. Twelve miles off Rhode Island's coast, this 10-square-mile island has 17 miles of shoreline, 365 freshwater ponds, and plenty of hiking trails. Some liken it to Ireland, on account of its rolling green hills. Take the hour-long ferry from Port Judith.

Cape Cod National Seashore, Massachusetts. With more than 150 beaches (roughly 40 miles worth), Cape Cod has enough to keep any beachcomber happy and sandy year-round. They range from the tourist-packed strand in Dennis to the almost untouched stretches of coast protected by the Cape Cod National Seashore. Favorite activities include swimming, bicycling, and even dune-buggy excursions.

Gloucester Beaches, Massachusetts. Situated on the North Shore, Gloucester is the oldest seaport in the nation. Its trio of beaches—Good Harbor Beach, Long Beach, and Wingaersheek Beach—offer a haven for those journeying north of Boston for sun and sand. For a peek at a lighthouse, head to Wingaersheek; for excellent sunbathing, Long Beach is your best bet; for crowds, showers, and a snack bar, enjoy sizable Good Harbor Beach—all three have dunes.

Hampton Beach State Park, New Hampshire. The Granite State's ocean shore is short, but this state park along historic Route 1 takes full advantage of the space it has. In addition to swimming and fishing, there are campsites with full hookups for RVs, as well as an amphitheater with a bandshell for outdoor concerts.

Joseph A. Sylvia State Beach, Martha's Vineyard, Massachusetts. It's best to bike, walk, or shuttle to this 2-mile stretch of sand and get there early, but once you're there you'll be rewarded with relatively warm water and views of Cape Cod across the sound.

Popham Beach State Park, Maine. At low tide, you can explore the tidal flats and tide pools at this state park. There are also lifeguards and bathhouses.

BICYCLING

Biking on a road through New England's countryside is an idyllic way to spend a day. Many ski resorts accommodate mountain bikes in summer.

Bike Tours

There are a multitude of tour operators and magnificent trails throughout New England, and many bike shops rent and repair bicycles. Urban Adventours in Downtown Boston provides both tours and rentals complete with helmet, lock, and Boston bike map. Bike New England offers cycling routes and maps throughout the Northeast.

Safety

On the road, watch for trucks and stay as close as possible to the side of the road, in single file. On the trail, ride within your limits and keep your eyes peeled for hikers and horses (both of which have the right of way), as well as dogs. Always wear a helmet and carry plenty of water.

Best Rides

Acadia National Park, Maine. At the heart of this popular park is the 45-mile network of historic carriage roads covered in crushed rock that cyclists share with equestrians and hikers. Mountain bikes (or hybrids) are the way to go here, so leave your road bike at home. Fit and experienced riders can ascend the road to the top of Cadillac Mountain, but take caution: heavy traffic in high season can make this a dangerous proposition.

All Along the Coast. U.S. 1, Maine. The major road that travels along the Maine Coast is just a narrow two-lane highway most of the way, but it is still one of the country's most historic highways. As a result, it's very popular in spring, summer, and fall with serious long-distance cyclists.

Boston, Massachusetts. Commuters and hard-core cyclists alike buzz along the streets and bike paths of New England's largest city. For a scenic ride, the 17-mile-long Dr. Paul Dudley White Bike Path can't be beat. It hugs the Charles River, with great views of crew teams at practice, the spires of Harvard University, and the city skyline. Or, for a bit of history with your ride, hop on the 10-mile-long Minuteman Bikeway, which runs from the Alewife T stop (on the Red Line, in North Cambridge) through Lexington all the way to Bedford. From here you can cycle to Concord, following the path the minutemen traveled on the first day of the American Revolution.

Cape Cod, Massachusetts. Cape Cod has miles of bike trails, some following the national seashore and most on level terrain. On either side of the Cape Cod Canal is a straight, easy, 7-mile trail with views of canal traffic. Extending 22 miles from South Dennis to Wellfleet, the Cape Cod Rail Trail is a converted railbed that is now a paved, mostly flat bike path passing through a handful of the Cape's scenic towns, offering ample opportunity for side trips.

Killington Resort, Vermont. Following the lead of many ski resorts in the western United States, Killington allows fat-tire riders on many of its ski trails after the snow has melted. Stunt riders can enjoy the jumps and bumps of the mountain-bike park.

Portland, Maine. The paved Eastern Prom Trail extends from the edge of the Old Port to East End Beach, then to Back Bay for a 6-mile loop, before returning.

BOATING

Along many of New England's larger lakes, sailboats, rowboats, canoes, kayaks, and outboards are available for rent at local marinas. Rentals are available at a number of seacoast locations, but you may be required to prove your own seaworthiness before setting sail. Lessons are commonly available.

What to Wear

It can get cold on the water, especially while sailing, so dress in layers and bring along a windbreaker and fleece even if it's warm on land. Don't wear cotton or jeans: once they get wet, they stay wet and will leave you chilled. Sunscreen, sunglasses (with Croakies so they don't fall overboard), and a hat are also musts, as are drinking water and high-energy snacks, especially for canoe and kayak expeditions.

Best Boating

Allagash Wilderness Waterway, Maine. This scenic and remote waterway (92 miles of lakes, ponds, rivers, and streams) is part of the 740-mile Northern Forest Canoe Trail, which also floats through New York, Vermont, and New Hampshire.

Lake Champlain, Vermont. Called by some the sixth Great Lake, 435-square-mile Lake Champlain is bordered by Vermont's Green Mountains to the east and the Adirondacks of New York to the west. Burlington, Vermont, is the largest lakeside city and a good bet for boat rentals—be it a canoe, kayak, rowboat, skiff, or motorboat. Attractions include numerous islands and deep-blue water often brushed by pleasant New England breezes.

Lakes Region, New Hampshire. Lake Winnipesaukee is the largest lake in New Hampshire, but there are plenty of other puddles, both large and small, worth dipping a paddle into. Squam Lake is a tranquil area made famous by *On Golden Pond,* and Lake Wentworth has a state park with a boat launch, bathhouse, and picnic tables.

Mystic, Connecticut. The world's largest maritime museum, Mystic Seaport, is also a good place to get out on the water. A wide variety of sailing programs are offered—including lessons on a 61-foot schooner—as well as instruction on powerboating. If you're eager to test your skills against other sailors, there's also a weekly race series.

Newport and Block Island, Rhode Island. Narragansett Bay, Newport Harbor, and Block Island Sound are among the premier sailing areas in the world. Newport hosted the America's Cup, yachting's most prestigious race, from 1930 to 1983. Numerous outfitters provide public and private sailing tours, sailing lessons, and boat rentals.

Rockland, Maine. For a guided trip on the water, consider a windjammer excursion out of Rockland, Camden, or Rockport. From day sails to multiday cruises, trips run $50–$1,000 and include meals. Check The Maine Windjammer Association (⊕ *www. sailmainecoast.com*) or Windjammer Cruises (⊕ *www.mainewindjammercruises. com*) for more information.

HIKING

Probably the most famous trails in the region are the 270-mile Long Trail, which runs north–south through the center of Vermont, and the Maine-to-Georgia Appalachian Trail, which runs through New England on private and public land. The Appalachian Mountain Club (AMC) maintains a system of staffed huts in New Hampshire's Presidential Range, with bunk space and meals available by reservation. There's plenty of good hiking at state parks throughout the region.

Safety

There are few real hazards to hiking, but a little preparedness goes a long way. Know your limits, and make sure the terrain you are about to embark on doesn't exceed your abilities. Check the trail map carefully and pay attention to elevation changes, which make a huge difference in the difficulty of a hike: a steep mile is much tougher to negotiate and takes longer than a flat 2- or even 3-mile stretch. Bring layers of clothing to accommodate changes in weather, and always carry enough drinking water. Before you go, be sure to tell someone where you're going and how long you expect to be gone.

Best Hikes

Acadia National Park, Maine. Acadia's network of old carriage roads make for great, relatively flat hiking through the woods where you can often spot wildlife. If you're up for a challenge, hike up Cadillac Mountain or Acadia Mountain; both provide steep climbs and breathtaking views. The Ocean Path Trail has spectacular seaside views and leads to not-to-be-missed Thunder Hole, where waves crash spectacularly.

Appalachian Trail, Connecticut, Massachusetts, Vermont, New Hampshire, Maine. The New England section of the trail, which reaches south to Georgia, provides the opportunity for a great day hike or for the start of a challenging six-month endurance test. The popular trail is marked by rectangular white blazes which are well maintained and relatively easy to follow.

Mt. Washington, New Hampshire. The cog railroad and the auto road to the summit are both popular routes up New England's highest mountain, but for those with stamina and legs of steel, it's one heck of a hike. Of the handful of trails to the top, the most popular begins at the Pinkham Notch Visitor Center. Be sure to dress in layers and pack warm clothing for the frequent winds toward the peak.

The Long Trail, Vermont. Following the main ridge of the Green Mountains from one end of Vermont to the other, this is the nation's oldest long-distance trail. In fact, some say it was the inspiration for the Appalachian Trail. Hardy backpackers make a go of its full 270 miles, but day hikers can drop in and out at many places along the way.

HISTORY YOU CAN SEE

From Pilgrims to pirates, witches to whalers, the American Revolution to the Industrial Revolution, history lies thick as autumn leaves on the ground in New England.

Pilgrim's Progress

The story of the Pilgrims comes alive when you visit New England. From Province-town, where the *Mayflower* actually first landed, to Plymouth and throughout Cape Cod, these early New England settlers left an indelible mark on the region. Their contemporaries, the Puritans, founded the city of Boston. Both groups, seeking religious freedom, planted the seeds for the founding of the United States.

What to See:

In Plymouth (south of Boston) you can visit **Plimoth Plantation**, *Mayflower II*, and, of course, **Plymouth Rock** itself. On Cape Cod, visit **First Encounter Beach** in Eastham and the **Pilgrim Monument** in Provincetown.

Talkin' 'Bout a Revolution

New England is the cradle of democracy. Home to many of the patriots who launched the American Revolution and the war's first battles, here you can see real evidence of the events you read about in school. From historic battle-fields to the re-created Boston Tea Party ships, New England—and Massachusetts especially—is filled with touchstones of our national story.

What to See:

In Boston, walk the **Freedom Trail** or just be on the lookout for markers and plaques as you walk around Downtown—you can literally trip over history wherever you step. Outside the city, **Lexington** and **Concord** make easy side trips for a quick primer on the start of the American Revolution.

Sea to Shining Sea

New England has a long and proud maritime history. From the *Mayflower* to the Maine shipwrights still at work today, you'll feel New England's seafaring tradition up and down the coastline. Many museums tell the story of the region's contributions to shipbuilding, nautical exploration, and whaling. Although the latter is no longer a pillar of the local economy, today you can visit Earth's largest mammals on whale-watching expeditions departing any number of ports along the New England coast.

What to See:

One of the nation's most famous ships, the USS *Constitution,* is docked in Charlestown, Massachusetts, just outside of Boston (it's in drydock through 2017). The **Maine Maritime Museum** in Bath, Maine, is the last remaining intact shipyard in the United States to have built large wooden sailing vessels. But the granddaddy of New England maritime experiences is undoubtedly **Mystic Seaport** in Connecticut, where almost 500 vessels are preserved.

Frozen in Time

New England preserves its past like no other region of the United States. In addition to countless museums, historic sites, refurbished homes, and historical markers, the area has several wonderfully preserved villages, each trying to capture a specific moment in time.

What to See:

A mile-long stretch of Main Street in Deerfield, Massachusetts, contains a remarkably well-preserved portion of an 18th-century village. **Historic Deerfield** contains more than a dozen homes built between 1730 and 1850, all maintained as interpretive museums. Together, they house more than 25,000 artifacts harking back to the archetypal New England village.

One of the country's finest re-creations of a Colonial-era village, **Old Sturbridge Village,** in Massachusetts, emulates an early-19th-century New England town, with more than 40 historic buildings moved here from other communities. Guides clad in period costumes do the sort of activities that villagers did back in the day: farmers plow, blacksmiths pound, and bakers bake. A slice of New England life in the early days of America, the village represents a period of transition brought about by the growing significance of commerce and manufacturing, improvements in agriculture and transportation, and various social changes.

Near Lake Champlain, the **Shelburne Museum** spans 39 exhibition halls—many of which are restored 18th- and 19th-century buildings relocated here from throughout New England and New York. The sheer size and breadth of the museum's collections are dizzying. On display are more than 150,000 artifacts and works of art, as well as period structures that include a one-room schoolhouse, a lighthouse, a covered bridge, and even the 220-foot steamboat *Ticonderoga,* which once sailed Lake Champlain and is the last side-wheel steamboat of its kind. The landscaping recalls a classic New England village and features more than 400 lilac trees and various gardens.

Writing the Story of America

The list of New England writers who have shaped American culture is long indeed. Massachusetts alone has produced great poets in every generation: Anne Bradstreet, Phillis Wheatley, Emily Dickinson, Henry Wadsworth Longfellow, William Cullen Bryant, e.e. cummings, Robert Lowell, Elizabeth Bishop, Sylvia Plath, and Anne Sexton. Bay State writers include Louisa May Alcott, author of the enduring classic *Little Women*; Nathaniel Hawthorne, who re-created the Salem of his Puritan ancestors in *The Scarlet Letter*; Herman Melville, who wrote *Moby-Dick* in a house at the foot of Mt. Greylock; Eugene O'Neill, whose early plays were produced at a makeshift theater in Provincetown on Cape Cod; Lowell native Jack Kerouac, author of *On the Road*; and John Cheever, chronicler of suburban angst. Mark Twain, arguably the most famous American author of all time, lived in Connecticut for much of his writing career (in Hartford and later Redding).

What to See:

Many homes of famous New England writers are well preserved. An especially rich stop is **Concord, Massachusetts,** where you can see the homes of Alcott, Emerson, Thoreau (as well as his Walden Pond), and Hawthorne. You can visit their graves (and those of other authors) in the Author's Ridge section of the town's **Sleepy Hollow Cemetery.** Another favorite stop is the **Mark Twain House** in Hartford, Connecticut.

TOP EXPERIENCES

Peep a Leaf

Tourist season in most of New England is concentrated in late spring and summer, with a reprise in September and October, especially in the northern states, when leaf peepers from all over descend by the car- and busload to see the leaves turn red, yellow, orange, and all shades in between. Foliage season can be fragile and unpredictable—temperature, winds, and rain all influence when the leaves turn and how long they remain on the trees—but that makes the season even more precious. Apple picking at a local orchard and searching for the perfect pumpkin for a jack-o'-lantern amid the falling leaves are quintessential New England experiences.

Comb a Beach

Whether sandy or rocky, New England beaches can be filled with flotsam and jetsam. Anything from crab traps unmoored by heavy waves to colored sea glass worn smooth by the water to lost watches, jewelry, and the like can appear at your feet. Also common are the shells of sea urchins, clams, and other bivalves. During certain times of the year sand dollars of all sizes and colors are plentiful—you may even find one still whole.

Take Yourself Out to a Ballgame

Fenway Park, the oldest ballpark in the major leagues, has been the home of the Boston Red Sox since it opened in 1912. Though the bleachers are the cheapest seats and the farthest from the field, they're quite popular with a loyal crowd of fans, who gather to drink beer in plastic cups and watch as batters attempt to clear the 37-foot-tall left-field wall known as the Green Monster. Seat 21 of Section 42, Row 37 in the right-field bleachers is painted red in honor of the longest measurable home run ever hit at Fenway,

Ted Williams's legendary 502-foot blast on June 9, 1946. To get an up-close and inexpensive look at some of the game's next rising stars, visit the Red Sox triple-A farm team, the Paw Sox, located in Pawtucket, Rhode Island. During the summer, the Cape Cod Baseball League features some of the nation's best young collegiate talent.

Hit the Slopes

The mountain snow in New England may not be as legendarily fine as the powder out west—in fact, it can be downright unpleasant when packed snow becomes crusty ice—but skiing is quite popular here. Vermont has several ski areas, with Killington ranking among the largest resorts in the Northeast: its nearly 200 trails span seven mountains. New Hampshire's White Mountains and Massachusetts's Berkshires also cater to snow-sports lovers, while Sunday River and Sugarloaf in Maine are perennial favorites with advanced-intermediate and expert skiers. Beginners (and lift-ticket bargain hunters) can choose from a number of small but fun hills throughout northern New England.

Eat a Maine Lobster

Maine lobsters are world renowned, and lobstermen and fish markets all along the coast will pack a live lobster in seaweed for overnight shipment to almost anywhere nationwide. These delectable crustaceans are available throughout New England, but without a doubt the best place to eat them is near their waters of origin. Lobster meat is sweet (especially the claws), and most agree that a simple preparation is the best way to go: steamed and eaten with drawn butter, or pulled into chunks and placed in a toasted hot dog bun—the famous New

England lobster roll. There are two types of lobster rolls to try: traditional Maine-style features a cold lobster salad with a leaf of lettuce and the barest amount of mayonnaise, while the Connecticut lobster roll is served warm with drawn butter (no mayo). Don't forget to save room for New England's other culinary treasure: *chowdah*. No two clam chowders taste the same, but they're all delicious.

Rise and Shine at a B&B

New England's distinctive architecture, much of it originating in the 18th and 19th centuries, has resulted in beautiful buildings of all shapes and sizes, many of which have been restored as bed-and-breakfasts. These inns typify the cozy, down-home, historic feel of New England, and are an ideal lodging choice. This is especially true when the weather is cold, and the warm ambience of many of these inns more than justifies their slightly steeper rates.

Watch a Whale

The deep, cold waters of the North Atlantic serve as feeding grounds and migration routes for a variety of whales, including fin and humpback whales, the occasional blue whale, and the rare, endangered white whale. Cape Cod and Maine's Southern Coast and Mid-Coast regions are the best places to hop aboard a whale-watching boat, but tours also depart Boston Harbor. Boats head to whale feeding grounds about 20 miles offshore, where the majestic animals are numerous. Some captains go so far as to guarantee at least a single sighting or they'll give you a ticket for a second tour. Whale-watching season varies by tour skipper, but generally runs April–October.

Fair Thee Well

New Englanders love their fairs and festivals. "Maine-iacs" celebrate the moose, clam, lobster, and blueberry. Maple sugar and maple syrup are feted in Vermont, while "live free or die" New Hampshire honors American independence. Newport, Rhode Island, hosts two highly regarded music festivals, one for folk music and one for jazz. Many rural communities throughout New England hold agricultural fairs in late August and September.

Find the Perfect Souvenir

Artists and craftspeople abound in New England, meaning that finding the perfect souvenir of your vacation will be an enjoyable hunt. Whether you choose a watercolor of a picturesque fishing village, a functional and beautiful piece of handmade pottery, or a handcrafted piece of jewelry, you'll be supporting the local economy while taking a little piece of the region home with you.

Get Up Close and Personal with Nature

New England may be known for its flashy foliage in the fall and spectacular slopes in the winter, but the outdoors in spring and summer delights all the senses as well. Breathe in the ocean air as you drive along the Maine Coast or amble on Newport's 3½-mile Cliff Walk. Revel in the fragrance of the mountains and forests in the Berkshires, Vermont's Green Mountains, and New Hampshire's White Mountains while hiking the Appalachian Trail. Observe moose and bear in their natural habitat, or spot birds, seals, dolphins, and whales in theirs.

Savor Sweet Stuff

Summer vacations in New England go hand in hand with sweet treats; it's difficult to visit without sampling homemade fudge at an old-fashioned candy store, buying an ice cream for your sweetie, or bringing some saltwater taffy to share with the folks back home. Be sure to try one Maine specialty: the whoopie pie. Made from two chocolate circles of cake with vanilla-cream filling in between, it's a delectable Maine tradition. If you are visiting Maine when the tiny wild blueberry is in season, take every opportunity to savor this flavorful fruit—in pie, muffin, or pancake form—and you'll understand its legendary culinary status. In Vermont, go on a factory tour at Ben & Jerry's, and have a delicious cone afterward. You can even have dessert for breakfast when you top your pancakes with Vermont's maple syrup. The Green Mountain state's favorite sons by no means have the market cornered on ice cream goodness; you'll find excellent frozen treats in every corner of the region (Cape Cod is especially blessed in this regard). In Boston, head to the Italian North End for legendary cannoli.

Check Out Lighthouses

Maine's long and jagged coastline is home to more than 60 lighthouses, perched high on rocky ledges or on the tips of wayward islands. Though modern navigational technology has made many of the lights obsolete, various preservation groups restore and maintain them, often making them accessible to the public. Some of the state's more famous include the Portland Head Light, commissioned by President George Washington in 1787 and immortalized in one of Edward Hopper's paintings; Two Lights, a few miles down the coast in Cape Elizabeth; and West Quoddy Head, on the easternmost tip of land in the United States. Some lighthouses are privately owned and others accessible only by boat, but plenty are within easy reach and open to the public, some with museums and tours. At the Maine Lighthouse Museum in Rockland, visitors can view a collection of Fresnel lenses and Coast Guard artifacts.

Sail the Coast

The coastline of northern New England is a sailor's paradise, with its hidden coves, windswept islands, and picture-perfect harbors where you can pick up a mooring for the night. With nearly 3,500 miles of undulating, rocky shoreline, you could spend a lifetime of summers sailing the waters off the Maine Coast and never see it all. If you're not one of the lucky few with a sailboat to call your own, there are many companies that offer sailboat charters, whether for day trips or weeklong excursions. It might sound like an expensive getaway, but as meals and drinks are usually included, an overnight sailing charter might not cost any more than a seaside hotel room—plus you'll be accompanied by an experienced captain to provide history and insight along the voyage.

Get the First Sight of First Light

At 1,530 feet, Cadillac Mountain, in Maine's Acadia National Park, is the highest mountain on the New England coast: what better place to view the sunrise? Drive the narrow, winding, 3½-mile road to the summit before dawn (not accessible when the Loop Road is closed in the winter), and you could be the first person in the United States to see the summer sun's rays. (Depending on the time of year: sometimes the first sunrise is at West Quoddy Head Lighthouse in Lubec, Maine.)

BEST FALL FOLIAGE DRIVES & ROAD TRIPS

A CELEBRATION

Picture this: one scarlet maple offset by the stark white spire of a country church, a whole hillside of brilliant foliage foregrounded by a vintage barn or perhaps a covered bridge that straddles a cobalt river. Such iconic scenes have launched a thousand postcards and turned New England into the ultimate fall destination for leaf peepers.

OF COLOR

By Susan MacCallum-Whitcomb

Mother Nature, of course, puts on an annual autumn performance elsewhere, but this one is a showstopper. Like the landscape, the mix of deciduous (leaf-shedding) trees is remarkably varied here and creates a broader than usual palette. New England's abundant evergreens lend contrast, making the display even more vivid. Every September and October, leaf peepers arrive to cruise along country lanes, join outdoor adventures, or simply stroll on town greens.

Did you know the brilliant shades actually lurk in the leaves all year long? Leaves contain three pigments. The green chlorophyll, so dominant in summer that it obscures the red anthocyanins and orangey-yellow carotenoids, decreases in fall and reveals a crayon box of color.

Above, Vermont's Green Mountains are multicolored in the fall (and often white in winter).

PREDICTING THE PEAK

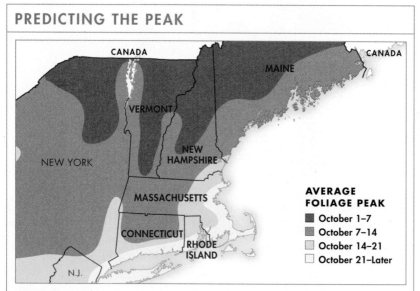

AVERAGE FOLIAGE PEAK
- ■ October 1–7
- ■ October 7–14
- ■ October 14–21
- □ October 21–Later

LOCATION

Pinning down precisely when colors will appear remains an inexact science, although location plays a major role. Typically, the transformation begins in the highest and northernmost parts of New England in mid-September, then moves steadily into lower altitudes and southern sectors throughout October.

For trip planning, think in terms of regions rather than states. In Maine (a huge state that runs north–south) leaf color can peak anytime from the fourth week of September to the third week of October, depending on the locale.

WEATHER

Early September weather is another deciding factor. From the foliage aficionado's perspective, the ideal scenario is calm, temperate days capped by nights that are cool but still above freezing. If the weather is too warm, it delays the onset of the season. If it's too dry or windy, the leaves shrivel up or blow off.

COLOR CHECK RESOURCES

Curious about current conditions? In season, each state maintains a dedicated website reporting on foliage conditions. Weather Channel has peak viewing maps and Foliage Network uses a network of spotters to chart changes.

- ■ **Connecticut:** ☎ 800/282–6863 ⊕ www.ct.gov/dep
- ■ **Foliage Network:** ⊕ www.foliagenetwork.com
- ■ **Maine:** ☎ 888/624–6345 ⊕ www.mainefoliage.com
- ■ **Massachusetts:** ☎ 800/227–6277 ⊕ www.massvacation.com
- ■ **New Hampshire:** ☎ 800/258–3608 ⊕ www.visitnh.gov
- ■ **Rhode Island:** ☎ 800/556–2484 ⊕ www.visitrhodeisland.com
- ■ **Vermont:** ☎ 800/837–6668 ⊕ www.vermontvacation.com
- ■ **Weather Channel:** ⊕ www.weather.com

TOP TREES FOR COLOR

A AMERICAN BEECH. This tree's smooth, steel-gray trunk is crowned with gold, copper, and bronze-tinted leaves in autumn, giving it a metallic sheen. Though the elliptical leaves sometimes hang on all winter, its "fruit" goes fast because beechnuts are a popular snack for birds, squirrels, and even bears.

B NORTHERN RED OAK. The upside of oaks is that they retain their fall shading until late in the season—the downside is that, for most species, that color is a boring brown. Happily, the northern red isn't like other members of the oak family. Its elongated, flame-shaped leaves turn fiery crimson and incandescent orange.

C QUAKING ASPEN. Eyes and ears both prove useful when identifying this aspen. Look for small, ovate leaves that usually become almost flaxen. Or listen for the leaves' quake: a sound, audible in even a gentle breeze, which the U.S. Forest Service likens to that made by "thousands of fluttering butterfly wings."

D SUGAR MAPLE. The leaf of the largest North American maple species is so lovely that Canada put it on its national flag. Each generally has five multi-pointed lobes—plus enough anthocyanin to produce a deep red color. The tree itself produces plentiful sap and is the cornerstone of New England's syrup industry.

E WHITE ASH. This tall tree typically grows to between 65 to 100 feet. Baseball enthusiasts admire the wood (which is used to craft bats); while foliage fans admire the compound leaves, each consisting of five to nine slightly serrated, tapering leaflets. They range in hue from burgundy and purple to amber.

F WHITE BIRCH. A papery, light, bright bark makes this slender hardwood easily recognizable. Centuries ago, Native Americans used birch wood to make everything from canoes to medicinal teas. Today's photographers know the bark also makes great pictures since it provides a sharp contrast to the tree's vibrant yellow leaves.

FANTASTIC FALL ITINERARY

The Berkshires

Fall is the perfect time to visit New England—country roads wind through dense forests exploding into reds, oranges, yellows, and purples. For inspiration, here is an itinerary for the truly ambitious that links the most stunning foliage areas; choose a section to explore more closely. Like autumn itself, this route works its way south from northern Vermont into Connecticut, with one or two days in each area.

VERMONT

NORTHWEST VERMONT

In Burlington, the elms will be turning colors on the University of Vermont campus. You can ride the ferry across Lake Champlain for great views of Vermont's Green Mountains and New York's Adirondacks. After visiting the resort town of Stowe, detour off Route 100 beneath the cliffs of Smugglers' Notch. The north country's palette unfolds in Newport, where the blue waters of Lake Memphremagog reflect the foliage.

NORTHEAST KINGDOM

After a side trip along Lake Willoughby, explore St. Johnsbury, where the Fairbanks Museum and St. Johnsbury Athenaeum reveal Victorian tastes in art and natural-history collecting. In Peacham, stock up for a picnic at the Peacham Store.

NEW HAMPSHIRE

WHITE MOUNTAINS AND LAKES REGION

In New Hampshire, Interstate 93 narrows as it winds through craggy Franconia Notch. Get off the interstate for the sinuous Kancamagus Highway portion of Route 112 that passes through the mountains to Conway. In Center Harbor, in the Lakes Region, you can ride the *MS Mount Washington* for views of the Lake Winnipesaukee shoreline, or ascend to Moultonborough's Castle in the Clouds for a falcon's-eye look at the colors.

MT. MONADNOCK

In Concord, stop at the Museum of New Hampshire History and the State House. Several trails climb Mt. Monadnock, near Jaffrey Center, and colorful vistas extend as far as Boston.

⇨ For local drives perfect for an afternoon, also see our Fall Foliage Drive Spotlights on Western Massachusetts, Connecticut, Rhode Island, Vermont, New Hampshire, and Inland Maine.

THE MOOSE IS LOOSE!

Take "Moose Crossing" signs seriously because things won't end well if you hit an animal that stands six feet tall and weighs 1,200 pounds. Some 40,000 reside in northern New England. To search out these ungainly creatures in the wild, consider an organized moose safari in northern New Hampshire or Maine.

MASSACHUSETTS

THE MOHAWK TRAIL

In Shelburne Falls, Massachusetts, the Bridge of Flowers displays the last of autumn's blossoms. Follow the Mohawk Trail section of Route 2 as it ascends into the Berkshire Hills—and stop to take in the view at the hairpin turn just east of North Adams (or drive up Mt. Greylock, the tallest peak in New England, for more stunning vistas). In Williamstown, the Clark Art Institute houses a collection of impressionist works.

THE BERKSHIRES

The scenery around Lenox, Stockbridge, and Great Barrington has long attracted the talented and the wealthy. Near U.S. 7, you can visit the homes of novelist Edith Wharton (the Mount, in Lenox), sculptor Daniel Chester French (Chesterwood, in Stockbridge), and diplomat Joseph Choate (Naumkeag, in Stockbridge).

CONNECTICUT

THE LITCHFIELD HILLS

This area of Connecticut combines the feel of upcountry New England with exclusive urban polish. The wooded shores of Lake Waramaug are home to country inns and wineries in pretty towns. Litchfield has a perfect village green—an idealized New England town center.

FOLIAGE PHOTO HINT
Don't just snap the big panoramic views. Look for single, brilliantly colored trees with interesting elements nearby, like a weathered gray stone wall or a freshly painted white church. These images are often more evocative than big blobs of color or panoramic shots.

LEAF PEEPER PLANNER

Hot-air balloons and ski-lift rides give a different perspective on fall's color.

Enjoying fall doesn't necessarily require a multistate road trip. If you are short on time (or energy), a simple autumnal stroll might be just the ticket: many state parks even offer free short ranger-led rambles.

HIKE AND BIKE ON A TOUR

You can sign on for foliage-focused hiking holidays with **Country Walkers** (☎ 800/234–6900 ⊕ www.countrywalkers.com) and **Boundless Journeys** (☎ 800/941–8010 ⊕ www.boundlessjourneys.com); or cycling ones with **Discovery Bicycle Tours** (☎ 800/257–2226 ⊕ www.discoverybicycletours.com) and **VBT Bicycling Vacations** (☎ 800/245–3868, ⊕ www.vbt.com). Individual state tourism boards list similar operators elsewhere.

SOAR ABOVE THE CROWDS

New Hampshire's **Cannon Mountain** (☎ 603/823–8800 ⊕ www.cannonmt.com) is only one of several New England ski resorts that provides gondola or aerial tram rides during foliage season. Area hot-air balloon operators, like **Balloons of Vermont, LLC** (☎ 802/369–0213 ⊕ www.balloonsofvermont.com), help you take it in from the top.

ROOM AT THE INN?

Accommodations fill quickly in autumn. Vermont's top lodgings sell out months in advance for the first two weeks in October. So book early and expect a two-night minimum stay requirement. If you can't find a quaint inn, try basing yourself at a B&B or off-season ski resort. Also, be prepared for some sticker shock; if you can travel midweek, you'll often save quite a bit.

RIDE THE RAILS OR THE CURRENT

Board the **Essex Steam Train** for a ride through the Connecticut countryside (☎ 800/377–3987 ⊕ www.essexsteamtrain.com) or float through northern Rhode Island on the **Blackstone Valley Explorer** riverboat (☎ 401/724–2200 ⊕ www.rivertourblackstone.com).

MASSACHUSETTS FALL FOLIAGE DRIVE

When fall foliage season arrives, the Berkshires are the place to appreciate the autumnal grandeur. Winding roads lined with dramatic trees ablaze—notably maples, birches, and beeches—pass alongside meadows, pasture, farmland, mountains, rivers, and lakes.

Although this complete scenic loop is only about 35 miles, you could easily spend the day making your way leisurely along the circuit. Begin in North Adams, a city transformed by art, and spend some time at the Massachusetts Museum of Contemporary Art (MASS MoCA). Just west of downtown off Route 2, the Notch Road leads into the **Mt. Greylock State Reservation,** ambling upward to the summit. At 3,491 feet, it's the state's highest point and affords expansive views of the countryside. Hike any of the many trails throughout the park, picnic at the peak, or stay for a meal at the rustic **Bascom Lodge.** Continue your descent on the Notch Road to Rockwell Road to exit the park and join Route 7 South.

BEST TIME TO GO

Peak season for leaf viewing in the Berkshires generally happens in mid-October. Trees growing near waterways—and they are plentiful in the area—tend to have more vibrant colors that peak a bit sooner. The state regularly updates fall foliage information by phone and online (*800/632-8038* ⊕ *www.massvacation.com*).

Follow Route 7 South into the small town center of Lanesborough, where you'll turn left onto Summer Street. Horse farms and wide-open pastures make up the landscape, with distant mountain peaks hovering grandly in the background. If you want to pick your own apples, take a 1½-mile detour off Summer Street and stop at **Lakeview Orchard**.

Summer Street continues to tiny Berkshire Village, where you'll pick up Route 8 heading back toward North Adams. Running parallel to Route 8 from Lanesborough to Adams, is the paved **Ashuwillticook Rail Trail** for biking and walking. Right in the midst of two mountain ranges, the trail abuts wetlands, mixed woodland (including beech, birch, and maple trees), the Hoosac River, and the Cheshire Reservoir. In Cheshire, **Whitney's Farm Market** is busy on fall weekends with pony rides, pumpkin picking, a corn maze, and hayrides; plus it sells baked goods like the pumpkin whoopie pie.

Continuing on Route 8, you'll start to leave farm country as you make your way back to North Adams. Once a part of its much larger neighbor, the town of Adams still has active mills and the **Susan B. Anthony Birthplace Museum**. The 1817 Federal home of her birth has been fully restored.

NEED A BREAK?

Bascom Lodge. Built in the 1930s, this mountaintop lodge retains its rustic charm with comfortable, no-frills lodging and a restaurant in a stunning setting. ⊠ *Mt. Greylock State Reservation, Adams* 🕾 *413/743–1591* ⊕ *www.bascomlodge.net* ⊘ *Closed Nov.–May.*

Lakeview Orchard. Here you can pick your own bushel of apples (and other fall fruit) and sip on freshly pressed cider. The friendly farmers also sell homemade pies and pastries, but make sure to sample their singular (and superb) cider doughnuts. ⊠ *94 Old Cheshire Rd., Lanesboro* 🕾 *413/448–6009* ⊕ *www.lakevieworchard. com* ⊘ *Early July–Oct., Tues.–Sun. 9–5.*

Whitney's Farm Market. Whitney's Farm has a large market with baked goods and a deli; you can also pick your own seasonal fruit. The fun Pumpkin Fest takes place on weekends, mid-September–October. ⊠ *1775 S. State Rd., Cheshire* 🕾 *413/442–4749* ⊕ *www.whitneysfarm.com* ⊘ *Apr.–Dec., daily 9–6.*

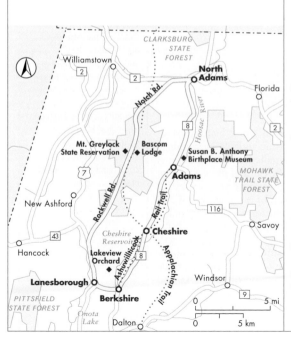

CONNECTICUT FALL FOLIAGE DRIVE

Hidden in the heart of Litchfield County, the crossroads village of New Preston perches above a 40-foot waterfall on the Aspetuck River. Just north of here you'll find Lake Waramaug nestled in the rolling foothills and Mt. Tom, both ablaze with rich color every fall.

Start in New Milford and stroll along historic Main Street. Here you'll find New England's longest village green, as well as many shops, galleries, and restaurants within a short walk. Hop in the car and drive south on Main Street, then turn left to head north on wooded Route 202. About 4 miles north of the green you'll find the **Silo at Hunt Hill Farm Trust.** The former property of the late Skitch Henderson, onetime music director of NBC and the New York Pops, the farm trust consists of a gallery, cooking school, and gift store housed in the buildings of two farms, which date to the 1700s. Continue north on Route 202 to the junction of Route 45 and follow signs for Lake Waramaug.

BEST TIME TO GO

Peak foliage in Connecticut occurs early October–mid-November, according to the state's Department of Environmental Protection. In season, the website (⊕ *www.ct.gov/dep*) includes daily updates on leaf color. Hope for a wet spring, warmer fall days, and cool (but not too cool) nights for the most dramatic display.

2

Route 45 will bring you through the tiny village center of New Preston; stop here for a bit of shopping at **Dawn Hill Antiques.** Take 45 north and follow signs for Lake Waramaug. The 8-mile drive around the lake is stunning in autumn with the fiery foliage of red maples, rusty brown oaks, and yellow birches reflected in the water. The beach area of **Lake Waramaug State Park,** about halfway around the lake, is a great place for a picnic, or perhaps even a quick dip on a warm fall day. **Hopkins Vineyard** is open daily for tastings; head to its Hayloft Wine Bar to enjoy a glass of wine and the spectacular lake views.

After completing a loop of Lake Waramaug, head back to Route 202 North toward Litchfield. Another excellent leaf-peeping locale is **Mt. Tom State Park,** about 3 miles or so from the junction of Routes 45 and 202. Here you can hike the mile-long trail to the summit and climb to the top of a stone tower that provides 360-degree views of the countryside's colors—the vibrant magenta-reds of the sugar maples are always among the most dazzling. After your hike, continue north on Route 202, ending your journey in the quintessential New England town of Litchfield. Peruse the shops and galleries in the town center and end the day with a dinner at the chic **West Street Grill.**

It's only about 30 miles from New Milford to the center of Litchfield, but with stops at the Silo at Hunt Hill, Lake Waramaug, and Mt. Tom you could easily spend half the day just enjoying the scenery.

NEED A BREAK?

Dawn Hill Antiques. This shop is filled with antiques discovered by the owners on their regular trips to Europe. ⊠ *11 Main St., New Preston* ☏ *860/868–0066* ⊕ *www. dawnhillantiques.com.*
Hopkins Vineyard. This winery produces more than 13 different wines, from sparkling to dessert. Tastings are available, and a wine bar in the hayloft with views of the lake serves a fine cheese-and-pâté board. ⊠ *25 Hopkins Rd., off N. Shore Rd., New Preston* ☏ *860/868–7954* ⊕ *www.hopkinsvineyard. com* 🍽 *Tours $14* ⊙ *Call for hrs.*

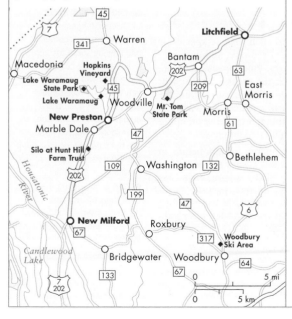

RHODE ISLAND FALL FOLIAGE DRIVE

The Rhode Island State Tree is the red maple, which turns up in shades of gold, purple, and scarlet in fall.

This tiny state is also home to such diverse species as scarlet oak, white oak, northern red oak, yellow birch, gray birch, ash, and black cherry. Pine forests dominate southern woodlands, reserving the most dramatic leaf peeping for the northern and western regions. Along the way, you'll find dense forests, rolling meadows with centuries-old stone walls, an occasional orchard or pumpkin patch, and archetypal New England country stores.

This tour through the state's quieter corners begins in Providence, where you can stroll across **Brown University's** handsome campus of dignified academic buildings and towering shade trees. Drive north from Providence on Route 122 and then Route 114 north for about 12 miles to Cumberland, a small town with undulating woodland crowned by a canopy of sugar maple, scarlet oak, and birch trees. Stop at **Diamond Hill Vineyards**, whose grapevines and apple trees yield an intriguing selection of wines, including some sweet varieties made from fruits and berries grown on-site—perfect on a cool October day.

BEST TIME TO GO

Foliage peaks in most of Rhode Island in the second and third weeks of October, beginning in the northwestern corner and moving south to the coast. Color can last more than two weeks in years with no big storms and plenty of cool, crisp autumn nights. If you don't have long to linger, check out the stunning views from Prospect Terrace, on Providence's East Side, or take a walk along the rural trails of Tiverton's Weetamoo Woods and Little Compton's Wilbour Woods.

The rest of the tour meanders through some of Rhode Island's most pastoral countryside. Drive west about 12 miles on Route 116 through Greenville, turning west on U.S. 44 for 7 miles to the hamlet of Chepachet, where Colonial and Victorian buildings contain antiques shops and quirky stores. Don't miss **Brown & Hopkins,** one of the country's oldest continuously operating general stores—complete with nostalgia-inducing candy counter—or the **Tavern on Main,** a rambling 18th-century restaurant some say is haunted.

Follow U.S. 44 west 5 miles through the burst of changing leaves in **Pulaski Memorial State Forest.** Turn left onto Route 94 and follow this for about 13 miles to Route 102, then continue southeast another 20 miles to Exeter. This mostly undeveloped route from Chepachet to Exeter is lined with pristine hardwood forests, with an abundance of red maple, white oak, beech, elm, and poplar trees.

From Route 102, continue east to the Colonial seaport of Wickford, whose pretty harbor opens to Narragansett Bay. The town's oak- and beech-shaded lanes are perfect for a late-afternoon stroll among the galleries and boutiques.

The drive totals about 80 miles and takes four–eight hours, depending on stops.

NEED A BREAK?

Brown & Hopkins Country Store. Opened in 1809, this store carries candles, reproduction antiques, penny candy, and handmade soaps. ⊠ *1179 Putnam Pike, Chepachet* ☎ *401/568-4830* ⊕ *www.brownandhopkins. com* ⊗ *Mon.–Sat. 10–5, Sun. 11–5.*

Diamond Hill Vineyards. This winery produces Pinot Noir from grapes grown on-site, as well as wines made from local apples, blueberries, and other fruit. ⊠ *3145 Diamond Hill Rd., Cumberland* ☎ *401/333-2751* ⊕ *www. diamondhillvineyards. com* ⊠ *Free* ⊗ *Thurs.–Sat. noon–5, Sun. noon–3.*

Tavern on Main. For lunch, try the homemade seafood stuffies or the lobster roll. ⊠ *1157 Putnam Pike, Chepachet* ☎ *401/710-9788* ⊕ *www.tavernonmainri. com* ⊗ *Closed Mon. and Tues.*

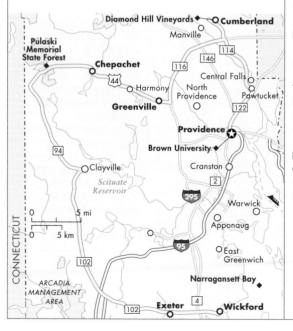

VERMONT FALL FOLIAGE DRIVE

Nearly 80% of Vermont is forested, with cities few and far between. The state's interior is a rural playground for leaf peepers, and it's widely considered to exhibit the most intense range of colors anywhere on the continent. Its tiny towns and hamlets—the few distractions from the dark reds, yellows, oranges, and russets—are as pristine as nature itself.

Begin this drive in Manchester Village, along the old-fashioned, well-to-do homes lining Main Street, and continue south to Arlington, North Bennington, and Old Bennington. Stop just a mile south along Route 7A at **Hildene.** The 412 acres of explorable grounds at the estate of Abraham Lincoln's son are ablaze with color, and the views over the Battenkill Valley are as good as any you can find. Drive south another mile along 7A to the **Equinox Valley Nursery,** where you can sample delicious apple cider and doughnuts amid views of the arresting countryside. A few more miles south along 7A is the small town of Arlington.

BEST TIME TO GO

Late September and early October are the times to go, with the southern area peaking about a week later than the north. Remember to book hotels in advance. The state has a Fall Foliage Hotline and an online interactive map (*802/828–3239* ⊕ *www.foliage-vermont. com*). The drive from Manchester to Bennington outlined here takes just 30 minutes, but a relaxed pace is best suited to taking in all the sights.

From Route 7A in Arlington you can take two adventurous and stunning detours. One is pure foliage: follow Route 313 west a few miles to the New York State border for more beautiful views. Or head east 1 mile to East Arlington, where delightful stores await, including a chocolate emporium. (You can continue even farther east from this spot to Kelly Stand Road leading into the Green Mountains—a little-known route that can't be beat.) Back on 7A South in Arlington, stop at the **Cheese House,** the delightfully cheesy roadside attraction.

Farther south in Shaftsbury is **Clear Brook Farm,** a brilliant place for fresh produce and pumpkins. Robert Frost spent much of his life in South Shaftsbury, and you can learn about his life at his former home, the **Stone House.** From South Shaftsbury take Route 67 through North Bennington and continue on to Route 67A in Old Bennington. Ride the elevator up the 306-foot-high **Bennington Battle Monument** to survey the season's progress across four states. Back down from the clouds, walk a few serene blocks to the cemetery of the **Old First Church,** where Robert Frost is buried, and contemplate his autumnal poem, "Nothing Gold Can Stay."

NEED A BREAK?

Equinox Valley Nursery. This nursery carries fresh produce, seasonal snacks, cider doughnuts, and is full of family-friendly fall activities: a corn maze, hayrides, and pumpkin carving. Kids especially will appreciate the 300-odd scarecrows scattered throughout the property. ⊠ *1158 Main St., Manchester* ☎ *802/362–2610* ⊕ *www.equinoxvalleynursery.com* 🖃 *Free.*

Clear Brook Farm. Set on more than 25 acres, this certified organic farm sells its own produce, in addition to plants, baked goods, and other seasonal treats. ⊠ *47 Hidden Valley Rd., Manchester* ☎ *802/442–4273* ⊕ *www.clearbrookfarm.com* ☉ *Late Apr.–mid-May, daily 10–5; mid-May–Aug., Mon.–Sat. 9–6, Sun. 9–5; Sept. and Oct., Mon.–Sat. 10–6, Sun. 10–5.*

The Cheese House. Get your Vermont cheddar fix at this shop shaped like a cheese wheel. It also sells maple syrup, chocolate, wine, and other local products and gifts. ⊠ *5187 Rte. 7A, Arlington* ☎ *802/375–9033* ⊕ *www.thevermontcheesehouse.com* 🖃 *Free* ☉ *Closed Tues.*

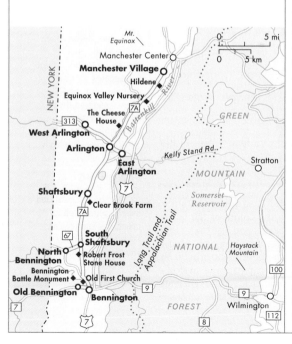

NEW HAMPSHIRE FALL FOLIAGE DRIVE

Quaint villages graced with green commons, white town halls, and covered bridges: southwestern New Hampshire is dominated by the imposing rocky summit of Mt. Monadnock and the brilliant colors of autumn. Kancamagus Highway is another classic foliage route, but for more solitude and less traffic, try this more accessible route that peaks a few weeks later than the state's far north.

The Granite State is the second-most-forested state in the nation; by Columbus Day the colors of the leaves of its maple, birch, elm, oak, beech, and ash trees range from green to gold, purple to red, and orange to auburn. Routes 12, 101, 202, and 124 compose a loop around **Mt. Monadnock**. Start in Keene with a cup of coffee at Prime Roast; for New Hampshire–made products, take a walk on Main Street or detour west on Route 9 to reach **Stonewall Farm** for something more country.

BEST TIME TO GO

The best time to view foliage in southern New Hampshire is generally early October, but it can vary by up to four weeks. For updates about leaf changes, visit the Foliage Tracker page on the website of **Visit New Hampshire** (*800/258–3608* ⊕ *www.visitnh.gov*).

PLANNING YOUR TIME

Expect to travel about 55 miles. The journey can take up to a full day if you stop to explore along the way.

From Keene, travel east on Route 101 through Dublin. In **Peterborough,** browse the local stores, whose attitudes and selections mirror the state's independent spirit.

Then turn south on Route 202 toward Jaffrey Village. Just west on Route 124, in historic Jaffrey Center, be sure to visit the **Meeting House Cemetery,** where author Willa Cather is buried. One side trip, 4 miles south on Route 202, leads to the majestic **Cathedral of the Pines** in Rindge, one of the best places in the region for foliage viewing because evergreens offset the brilliant shades of red.

Heading west on Route 124, you can take Dublin Road to the main entrance of **Monadnock State Park** or continue along to the Old Toll Road parking area for one of the most popular routes up the mountain, the **Halfway House Trail.** All the hiking trails have great views, including the area's many lakes. Continuing on Route 124, head southwest on Fitzwilliam Road to Fitzwilliam, then turn north on Route 12 back to Keene.

NEED A BREAK?

Stonewall Farm. This nonprofit working farm teaches about the importance of agriculture. The only working dairy farm in the region open to the public, Stonewall presents an active schedule of events, including maple sugaring and seasonal horse-drawn hayrides. Walking trails wind throughout the farm. There's fine hiking in good weather, and in winter you can borrow snowshoes for free. Young children love the discovery room, and the interactive greenhouse is geared for all ages.
✉ *242 Chesterfield Rd., Keene* ☎ *603/357-7278*
⊕ *www.stonewallfarm.org*
☉ *Farm Store daily 9–4:30; Discovery Room Tues., Thurs., and weekends 9–4:30; daily milkings at 4:30 am and 4:30 pm.*

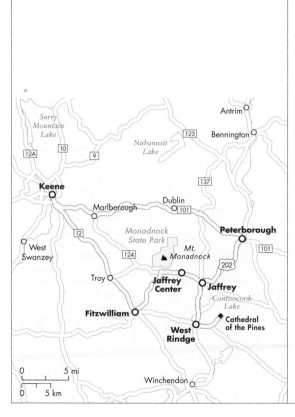

INLAND MAINE FALL FOLIAGE DRIVE

Swaths of pine, spruce, and fir trees offset the red, orange, and yellow of maples and birches along this popular foliage drive through western Maine's mountains, but hardwoods largely dominate the landscape.

Wending its way to the four-season resort town of Rangeley, near its northern terminus, the route passes stunning overlooks, forest-lined lakes, waterfalls, hiking trails, and a state park. Mountain vistas are reflected in the many (often connected) lakes, ponds, rivers, and streams.

From U.S. 2 in Mexico, Route 17 heads north past old homesteads and fields along the Swift River Valley before making a mountainous switchback ascent to **Height of Land,** the drive's literal pinnacle. The must-stop overlook here has off-road parking, interpretive panels, stone seating, and a short path to the **Appalachian Trail.** On a clear day, you can look west to New Hampshire and Canada. **Mooselookmeguntic Lake** and **Upper Richardson Lake** seem to float amid the forestland below. A few miles north of here is an overlook for Rangeley Lake, also with interpretive panels.

BEST TIME TO GO

Fall color usually peaks in the Rangeley area in the first or second week of October. Get fall foliage updates at ⊕ *www.mainefoliage.com.*

PLANNING YOUR TIME

The Rangeley Lakes National Scenic Byway (⊕ *www.byways.org*) makes up much of this 59-mile drive (1½ hours without stops), but plan for a relaxed full day of exploring.

2

In tiny, welcoming Oquossoc, where Routes 17 and 4 meet, stop at the **Gingerbread House Restaurant** for a meal, or for just baked goods or an ice cream. The hamlet is also home to the **Rangeley Outdoor Sporting Heritage Museum,** where you can learn why visitors have come here to fish, hunt, and enjoy the outdoors since the mid-1800s.

Rangeley, 7 miles east on Route 4, has restaurants, inns, a waterfront park, and outdoorsy shops. The countryside sweeps into view along public hiking trails at both **Saddleback Maine** ski resort and the 175-acre **Wilhelm Reich Museum.**

The road to **Rangeley Lake State Park** is accessible from both Routes 4 and 17, as is the **Appalachian Trail.** Overhanging foliage frames waterfalls at the scenic rest areas at each end of the drive: at Coos Canyon on Route 17 en route to Height of Land, and at Smalls Falls on Route 4 near Madrid, the terminus. Both spots have swimming holes, several falls, and paths with views of their drops. Coos Canyon is along the Swift River, a destination for recreational gold panning. You can rent or buy panning equipment at **Coos Canyon Rock and Gift,** across from its namesake. It also sells sandwiches and snacks.

NEED A BREAK?

Rangeley Lakes Heritage Trust. The trust protects about 13,000 acres of land in the Rangeley Lakes area. Both online and at its Oquossoc office, the trust has maps and descriptions of its 35 miles of recreational trails, along with information about fishing, hunting, snowmobiling, picnicking, and other outdoor activities. ✉ *52 Carry Rd., Oquossoc* ☎ *207/864–7311* ⊕ *www.rlht.org.* **Wilhelm Reich Museum.** This museum showcases the life and work of controversial physician-scientist Wilhelm Reich (1897–1957). There are magnificent views from the observatory, and great trails throughout the 175-acre property. ✉ *19 Orgonon Circle, off Rte. 4, Rangeley* ☎ *207/864-3443* ⊕ *www.wilhelmreichtrust. org* 🖼 *Museum $6, grounds free* ⊙ *Museum: July and Aug., Wed.– Sun. 1–5; Sept., Sat. 1–5. Grounds daily 9–5.*

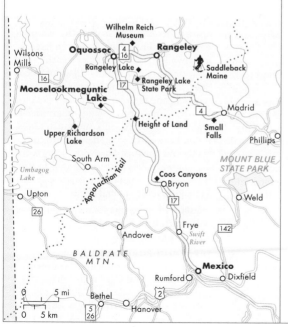

GREAT ITINERARIES

Whether it's your first trip to New England or you vacation here every year, these itineraries will help you explore charming seaside towns and bustling cities, eat at cutting-edge restaurants and the best seafood shacks, and experience both popular spots and hidden gems. Mix and match the itineraries, or use them as a jumping-off point for your own adventure.

CAPE COD BEACHES AND VILLAGES, 7 DAYS

Cape Cod can be all things to all visitors, with quiet villages and lively resorts, gentle bay-side wavelets and crashing surf. A car is the best way to meander along Massachusetts's beach-lined, arm-shape peninsula, but in busy town centers—such as Falmouth, Hyannis, Chatham, and Provincetown—you can get around quite easily on foot. Keep in mind that Cape-bound traffic is particularly bad on Friday late afternoon–evening and Saturday morning–afternoon (most house rentals are Saturday to Saturday), and traffic in the other direction is rough on Sunday, especially in the afternoon. Cross as early in the day as possible or wait until well after rush hour. For most visitors, time at the beach is key, but there is plenty to do and see once you've had enough sun and surf or if the weather doesn't cooperate. And about those beaches: be prepared to pay for day passes—most beach parking lots charge a sometimes-hefty fee.

Fly in: Logan International Airport (BOS), Boston

Fly out: Logan International Airport (BOS), Boston

DAY 1: HYANNIS
The best way to spend a week on the Cape is to pick a central location and use it as a launching point to explore. Begin by

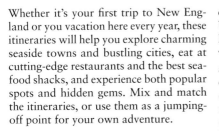

crossing the Bourne Bridge and head east on U.S. 6 toward Hyannis: make this centrally located, larger town your headquarters.

The crowded Mid Cape is a center of activity, and its heart is **Hyannis.** Here you can cruise around the harbor or go on a deep-sea fishing trip. There are shops and restaurants along Main Street and plenty of kid-friendly amusements. Fans of John F. Kennedy shouldn't miss the museum in his honor. End the day with a concert at the **Cape Cod Melody Tent** (open seasonally) or the Cotuit Center for the Arts.

Logistics: 72 miles; via I-90 W, I-93 S, Rte. 3 S, U.S. 6 E, and Rte. 132 S; 1½ hours from Logan airport.

DAY 2: FALMOUTH
For your first excursion, wander along Route 28 until you reach **Falmouth** in the Upper Cape. Here you can stroll around the village green, duck into some of the historic houses, and stop at the Waquoit Bay National Estuarine Research Reserve for a walk along the barrier beach. Take some time to check out the village of **Woods Hole,** a center for international marine research, and the year-round ferry port for Martha's Vineyard. A small aquarium has regional sea-life exhibits and touch tanks. If you have extra time, head north to the lovely old town of **Sandwich,** known for the **Sandwich Glass Museum,** and the beautiful grounds and collection of antique cars at **Heritage Museums and Gardens.**

Logistics: 21 miles; via Rte. 28 N; 48 minutes, starting in Hyannis.

DAY 3: BARNSTABLE, YARMOUTH PORT, DENNIS
Spend your day exploring the northern reaches of the Mid Cape with a drive along scenic Route 6A, which passes through the charming, slow-paced villages of **Barnstable, Yarmouth Port,** and **Dennis.** There are

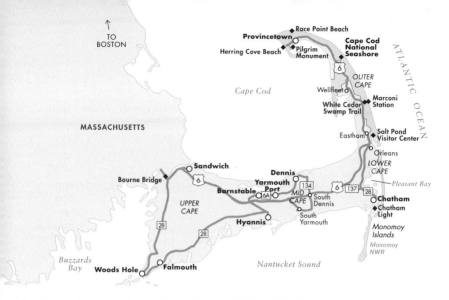

beaches and salt marshes, antiques shops and galleries, and old cemeteries along this route. Yarmouth Port's **Bass Hole Boardwalk** makes for a particularly beautiful stroll. In Dennis there are historic houses to tour, and the **Cape Cod Museum of Art** merits a stop. End the day by climbing 30-foot Scargo Tower to watch the sun set. At night you can catch a film at the Cape Cinema, on the grounds of the **Cape Playhouse.**

If you're traveling with kids, spend some time in the southern sections of Yarmouth and Dennis, where Route 28 passes by countless amusement centers and minia-ture-golf courses.

Logistics: 9 miles; via Rte. 6A E; 20 min-utes, starting in Hyannis.

DAY 4: CHATHAM

Chatham, with its handsome Main Street, is a perfect destination for strolling, shop-ping, and dining. A trip to the nearby **Monomoy Islands** is a must for bird-watch-ers and nature lovers. Back in town, you can watch glassblowing at the **Chatham Glass Company,** visit the **Atwood House Museum,** and drive over to take in the view from **Chatham Light.**

Logistics: 19½ miles; via U.S. 6 E; 35 min-utes, starting in Hyannis.

DAY 5: CAPE COD NATIONAL SEASHORE

On Day 5, leave your Hyannis hub and head for the farther reaches of Cape Cod. Take U.S. 6 east, before making a slight detour onto the less commercial end of Route 28. On the way north toward Orleans you'll drive past sailboat-speck-led views of Pleasant Bay.

Stop in Eastham at the Cape Cod National Seashore's **Salt Pond Visitor Center.** Take time to stroll along one of the beaches—there are more than 40 miles of pristine sand from which to choose—or bike on the many pic-turesque trails. Head slightly farther north to historic **Marconi Station,** which was the landing point for the transatlantic telegraph early in the 20th century, or park your car in **Wellfleet**'s historic downtown area, where you'll find a bounty of intriguing shops and galleries. It's also worth walking the short but stunning White Cedar Swamp Trail. Continue on to Provincetown to spend two nights at the tip of the Cape.

Logistics: 47 miles; via U.S. 6 E; 1¼ hours, starting in Hyannis.

DAYS 6 AND 7: PROVINCETOWN

Bustling **Provincetown** sits at the very end of the Cape, and there's a lot to see and do here. You can park the car and forget about it until you leave town, as everything is easily walkable. Catch a whale-watching boat and take a trolley tour through town, or bike through the **Cape Cod National Seashore** on its miles of trails. Climb the **Pilgrim Monument** for a spectacular view of the area—on an exceptionally clear day you can see the Boston skyline. Visit museums, shops, and art galleries, or spend the afternoon swimming and sunning on the beaches at **Herring Cove** or **Race Point**.

Logistics: 116 miles; via U.S. 6 W, Rte. 3 N and I–93 N; 2½ hours, starting in Provincetown and ending in Boston.

NEW HAVEN, BOSTON, AND PROVIDENCE IN 5 DAYS

These three cities all have some of the best dining the northeast has to offer, and each makes a case for having the finest Italian cuisine in the region, leaving you to judge whose cuisine reigns supreme. In addition, history buffs can get their fill while exploring New England's Colonial and maritime past.

Fly in: Bradley International Airport (BDA), Hartford

Fly out: Logan International Airport (BOS), Boston

DAY 1: NEW HAVEN

Start your journey in **New Haven**, Connecticut. The Constitution State's second-largest city is home to **Yale University,** named for British shipping merchant Elihu Yale. Take an hour-long walking tour with one of the university's guides and feast your eyes on the iconic Gothic-style structures that adorn the campus. After you've worked up an appetite, a stop for New Haven–style pizza is a must. Less than a mile from campus are two institutions known for thin-crust pies cooked in brick ovens: **Pepe's Pizzeria** and **Sally's Apizza.** For the burger enthusiast, there's **Louis' Lunch** on Crown Street. Don't ask for ketchup: it's been taboo here since they opened in 1895. Spend your first night in New Haven.

Logistics: 53 miles; via I–91 S; 1 hour staring at Bradley airport.

DAY 2: NEW HAVEN TO PROVIDENCE

On your second day, get an early start, and head north on Interstate 95 to make your way toward Providence, Rhode Island. There are plenty of small towns bursting with New England's maritime history along Connecticut's shoreline. Stop in New London, Niantic, or **Stonington** and explore the region's rich seafaring history. If you're planning on making one stop on the way to Rhode Island, the seaside village of **Mystic** is worth at least a half day to explore the seaport or to take a boat out on the water. **Mystic Seaport,** with its nearly 500 ships and more than 60 preserved historic buildings, will transport you back to 19th-century New England. For those looking to try their luck at a game of chance, take a slight detour north on Interstate 395 to either of Connecticut's two casinos, **Foxwoods Resort Casino** or **Mohegan Sun.** Overnight in Providence or in any of the seaside towns along the way.

Logistics: 103 miles; via I–95 N; 1 hour 42 minutes, starting in New Haven.

DAY 3: PROVIDENCE

Rhode Island's capital holds treasures like **Benefit Street,** with its Federal-era homes, and the **Museum of Art, Rhode Island School of Design.** Be sure to savor a knockout Italian meal on Atwells Avenue in **Federal Hill—Pane e Vino** is a popular choice. For dessert, it's hard to top the cannoli at **Scialo Bros. Bakery.** If you're visiting in early June, sample authentic eats from all over Italy, while live music fills the streets, during the Federal Hill Stroll. On summer nights, catch a Paw Sox baseball game at McCoy Stadium in the neighboring town of **Pawtucket,** home of the beloved Triple-A farm team for the Boston Red Sox. Also in the warmer months, typically late May–early November, Providence hosts **WaterFire,** a public celebration of art and performance. The festival's 100 bonfires on the rivers of downtown Providence

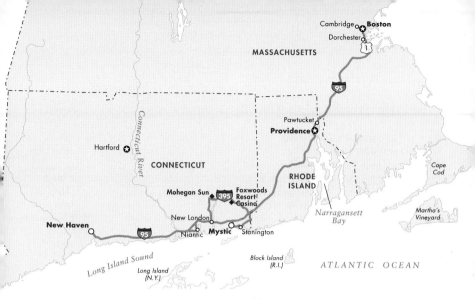

Cambridge Boston
Dorchester

MASSACHUSETTS

Pawtucket
Providence

Hartford

CONNECTICUT

RHODE
ISLAND

Cape
Cod

Connecticut River

Mohegan Sun 395 Foxwoods
Resort Casino

Narragansett
Bay

Martha's
Vineyard

New Haven

New London

95 Niantic Mystic Stonington

Long Island Sound

Block Island
(R.I.)

ATLANTIC OCEAN

Long Island
(N.Y.)

attracts tens of thousands of viewers each year for the popular annual event. Spend the night in a downtown Providence hotel for easy access to sights and restaurants.

DAYS 4 AND 5: BOSTON

A short drive north on Interstate 95 will bring you to **Boston**, New England's cultural and commercial hub. To savor Boston's centuries-old ties to the sea, take a half-day stroll past **Faneuil Hall** and **Quincy Market** or a boat tour of the harbor (you can even head out on a whale-watching tour from here). In Boston, famous buildings such as Faneuil Hall are not merely civic landmarks, but national icons. From the **Boston Common**, the 2.5-mile **Freedom Trail** links treasures of America's struggle for independence, such as the **USS Constitution** (better known as "Old Ironsides") and the **Old North Church** (of "one if by land, two if by sea" fame). Be sure to walk the gas-lighted streets of **Beacon Hill**, too. Boston's **North End** is the oldest residential neighborhood in the city, and has great dining options like **Antico Forno**, which offers pizza baked in a wood-burning brick oven.

The following day, either explore the massive **Museum of Fine Arts** and the grand boulevards and shops of **Back Bay**, or visit colorful **Cambridge**, home of **Harvard University** and the **Massachusetts Institute of Technology (MIT)**. Lively **Harvard Square** is a perfect place to do some people-watching or catch a street performance; the **All Star Sandwich Bar** is an excellent choice for lunch. For an experience unique to the Boston area, head a few miles south of the city along U.S. 1 to Dorchester's **Boston Bowl** to cap off your trip with candlepin bowling. Here, at all hours of the night, Bay Staters play a smaller version of 10-pin bowling that uses balls weighing less than 3 pounds and allows participants to bowl three balls per frame instead of two.

Logistics: 50 miles; via I–95 N and I–93 N; 1 hour, starting in Providence.

MASSACHUSETTS, NEW HAMPSHIRE, AND MAINE, 7 DAYS

Revel in the coast beauty of three New England states—Massachusetts, New Hampshire, and Maine—on the path from the region's largest city, Boston, to the its highest peak, Mt. Washington. An assortment of New England's treasures are at your fingertips as you negotiate the ins and outs of the jagged northeastern coastline, before ascending the heights of the White Mountains.

Fly in: Logan International Airport (BOS), Boston

Fly out: Logan International Airport (BOS), Boston

DAY 1: THE NORTH SHORE AND NEW HAMPSHIRE COAST

After flying into Boston, pick up a rental car and head for the North Shore of Massachusetts. In **Salem**, the **Peabody Essex Museum** and the **Salem Maritime National Historic Site** chronicle the evolution of the country's early shipping fortunes. Spend some time exploring more of the North Shore, including the old fishing port of **Gloucester**, and **Rockport**, a great place to find that seascape rendered in oils. **Newburyport**, with its Federal-style ship-owners' homes, is home to the **Parker River National Wildlife Refuge**, beloved by birders and beach walkers.

New Hampshire fronts the Atlantic for a scant 18 miles, but its coastal landmarks range from honky-tonk **Hampton Beach** to quiet **Odiorne Point State Park** in Rye and pretty Portsmouth, where the cream of pre-Revolutionary society built Georgian- and Federal-style mansions—visit a few at the **Strawbery Banke Museum.** Stay the night in **Portsmouth** at the centrally located **Ale House Inn.**

Logistics: 64 miles; via I–95 N; 1 hour 10 minutes, starting at Logan airport.

DAY 2: THE YORKS

Much of the appeal of the Maine Coast lies in geographical contrast—from its long stretches of swimming and walking beaches in the south to the rugged, rocky cliffs in the north. As the shoreline physically evolves, each town along the way reveals a slightly different character, starting with **York.**

In **York Village** take a leisurely stroll through the buildings of the **Museums of Old York** getting a glimpse of 18th-century life in this gentrified town. Spend time wandering between shops or walking nature trails and beaches around York

Harbor. There are several grand lodging options here, most with views of the harbor. If you prefer a livelier pace, continue on to **York Beach,** a haven for families with plenty of entertainment venues. Stop at Fox's Lobster House after visiting **Nubble Light** for a seaside lunch or dinner.

Logistics: 10 miles; via I–95 N; 15 minutes, starting in Portsmouth.

DAY 3: OGUNQUIT AND THE KENNEBUNKS

For well over a century, **Ogunquit** has been a favorite vacation spot for those looking to combine the natural beauty of the ocean with a sophisticated environment. Take a morning walk along the Marginal Way to see the waves crashing against the rocks. In **Perkins Cove,** have lunch, stroll the shopping areas, or sign on with a lobster-boat cruise to learn about Maine's most important fishery—the state's

2

lobster industry satisfies more than 90% of the world's appetite.

Head north to the Kennebunks, allowing at least two hours to wander through the shops and historic homes of Dock Square in **Kennebunkport**. This is an ideal place to rent a bike and ramble around backstreets, head out Ocean Avenue past large mansions, or ride to one of several beaches to relax awhile. Spend your third night in Kennebunkport.

Logistics: 22 miles; via I–95 N and Rte. 9 E; 30 minutes, starting in York.

DAYS 4 AND 5: PORTLAND

If you have time, you can easily spend several days in **Portland**, Maine's largest city, exploring its historic neighborhoods, shopping and eating in the **Old Port**, or visiting one of several excellent museums. A brief side trip to **Cape Elizabeth** takes you to **Portland Head Light**, Maine's first lighthouse, which was commissioned by George Washington in 1787. The lighthouse is on the grounds of Fort Williams Park and is an excellent place for a picnic; be sure to spend some time wandering the ample grounds. There are also excellent walking trails (and views) at nearby Two Lights State Park. If you want to take a boat tour while in Portland, get a ticket for Casco Bay Lines and see some of the islands that dot the bay. Spend two nights in Portland.

Logistics: 28 miles; via I–95 N; 40 minutes, starting in Kennebunkport.

DAY 6: BRETTON WOODS

Wake up early and drive to **Bretton Woods**, New Hampshire where you will spend nights six and seven. The driving time from Portland to Bretton Woods is approximately three hours, due to steep two-lane mountain roads. ■TIP→ **Be sure to take a four-wheel-drive vehicle in winter.** Drive northwest along U.S. 302 toward Sebago Lake, a popular watersports area in the summer, and continue on toward the time-honored New England towns of Naples and Bridgton. Just

15 miles from the border of New Hampshire, and nearing Crawford Notch, U.S. 302 begins to thread through New Hampshire's **White Mountains,** passing beneath brooding **Mt. Washington** before arriving in Bretton Woods.

Logistics: 98 miles; via Rte. 113 N and U.S. 302 W; 3 hours, starting from Portland.

DAY 7: THE WHITE MOUNTAINS

In Bretton Woods, the **Mount Washington Cog Railway** still chugs to the summit, and the **Omni Mount Washington Resort** recalls the glory days of White Mountain resorts. Beloved winter activities here include snowshoeing and skiing on the grounds; you can even zip-line. Afterward, defrost with a cup of steaming hot cider while checking out vintage photos of the International Monetary Conference (held here in 1944), or head to the Cave, a Prohibition-era speakeasy, for a drink.

Logistics: 159 miles; via I–93 S; 2½ hours, starting at the Omni Mount Washington Resort and ending in Boston.

MAINE'S NORTHERN COAST: PORTLAND TO ACADIA NATIONAL PARK, 6 DAYS

Lighthouses, beaches, lobster rolls, and water sports—Maine's northern coast has something for everyone. Quaint seaside villages and towns line the shore as U.S. 1 winds its way toward the easternmost swath of land in the United States at Quoddy Head State Park. Antiquing is a major draw, so keep an eye out for roadside shops crammed with gems. Maine's only national park, Acadia, is a highlight of the tour, drawing more than 2 million visitors per year.

Fly in: Portland International Jetport (PWM), Portland

Fly out: Bangor International Airport, (BGR), Bangor

DAY 1: PORTLAND TO BRUNSWICK

Use Maine's maritime capital as your jumping-off point to head farther up the Maine Coast, or, as Mainers call it, "Down East." Plan to spend half of your first day in Portland, then head to Brunswick for the night.

Portland shows off its restored waterfront at the **Old Port**. From there, before you depart, you can grab a bite at either of two classic Maine eateries: **Gilbert's Chowder House** or **Becky's Diner**, or check out what's new in the buzzy restaurant scene here. For a peek at the freshest catch of the day, wander over to the **Harbor Fish Market**, a Portland institution since 1968, and gaze upon Maine lobsters and other delectable seafood. Two lighthouses on nearby **Cape Elizabeth, Two Lights** and **Portland Head**, still stand vigil.

Following U.S. 1, travel northeast along the ragged, island-strewn coast of Down East Maine and make your first stop at the retail outlets of **Freeport**, home of **L.L. Bean**. Almost 3 million people visit the massive flagship store every year, where you can find everything from outerwear to camping equipment. Just 10 miles north of Freeport on U.S. 1, **Brunswick** is home to the campus of **Bowdoin College** and also features a superb coastline for kayaking. Spend the night in Brunswick at one of the many inns that line U.S. 1.

Logistics: 30 miles; via U.S. 1 N; 30 minutes from Portland airport.

DAY 2: BATH

From Brunswick, head to **Bath**, Maine's shipbuilding capital, and tour the **Maine Maritime Museum**, stopping for lunch on the waterfront. Check out the boutiques and antiques shops, or take in the plenitude of beautiful homes. From here it's a 30-minute detour down Route 127 to Georgetown Island and Reid State Park, where you will find a quiet beach lining Sheepscot Bay—and maybe even a sand dollar or two to take home, if you arrive at low tide. For a stunning vista, make your way to Griffith Head.

Drive north and reconnect with U.S. 1. Continue through the towns of **Wiscasset** and **Damariscotta**, where you may find yourself pulling over to stop at the outdoor flea markets and intriguing antiques shops that line the road. Another hour from here is **Rockland**, where you'll spend your second night.

Logistics: 52 miles; via U.S. 1 N; 1 hour 15 minutes, starting in Brunswick.

DAY 3: ROCKLAND, CAMDEN, AND CASTINE

From Rockland, spend the day cruising on a majestic schooner or reserve a tee time at Somerset Resorts'18-hole championship course that overlooks the Rockland Harbor. If you're an art lover, save some time for Rockland's **Farnsworth Art Museum** and the **Wyeth Center**.

In **Camden** and **Castine**, exquisite inns occupy homes built from inland Maine's gold and timber. Camden is an ideal place to stay overnight as you make your way closer to Acadia National Park; it is a beautiful seaside town with hundreds of boats bobbing in the harbor, immaculately kept antique homes, streets lined with boutiques and specialty stores, and restaurants serving lobster at every turn. The modest hills (by Maine standards, anyway) of nearby Mt. Battie offer good hiking and a great spot from which to picnic and view the surrounding area. It is also one of the hubs for the beloved and historic windjammer fleet—there is no better way to see the area than from the deck of one of these graceful beauties.

Logistics: 62 miles; via U.S. 1 N and Rte. 166 S; 1½ hours, starting in Rockland.

DAYS 4 AND 5: MOUNT DESERT ISLAND AND ACADIA NATIONAL PARK

On Day 4, head out early for **Bar Harbor** and plan to spend two nights here, using the bustling village as jumping-off point for the park—Bar Harbor is less than 5

miles from the entrance to **Mount Desert Island**'s 27-mile Park Loop Road. Spend at least a day exploring **Acadia National Park,** Maine's only national park and its most popular tourist destination. Enjoy the island's natural beauty by kayaking its coast, biking the 45-mile, historic, unpaved, carriage-road system, and driving to the summit of **Cadillac Mountain** for a stunning panorama.

Logistics: 52 miles; via Rte. 166 N, U.S. 1 N and Rte. 3 E; 1¼ hours, starting in Castine.

DAY 6: BAR HARBOR TO QUODDY HEAD STATE PARK

About 100 miles farther along U.S. 1 and "Way Down East" is Quoddy Head State Park in Lubec, Maine. Here, on the easternmost tip of land in the United States, sits the **West Quoddy Head Light,** one of 60 lighthouses that dot Maine's rugged coastline. Depending on the time of year (and your willingness to get up very early), you may be lucky enough to catch the East Coast's first sunrise here.

Logistics: 103 miles; via U.S. 1 N; 2½ hours, starting in Bar Harbor. From the park, it is 119 miles (2½ hours) to the Bangor airport via Rte. 9 W.

CONNECTICUT WINERIES AND RHODE ISLAND MANSIONS, 5 DAYS

Travel Connecticut's Lower River Valleys as you meander toward the eastern section of the state's Wine Trail. While you sample varietals from the area's best wineries, get a taste of New England's literary and maritime history along the way. Stay overnight in seaside Mystic, another highlight, and then finish your tour by gawking at Newport's grand mansions and strolling the gorgeous Cliff Walk.

Fly in: Bradley International Airport (BGR), Hartford

Fly out: T. F. Green Airport (PVD), Warwick

DAY 1: HARTFORD

Start your journey in **Hartford,** Connecticut. The **Mark Twain House and Museum,** which Samuel Clemens and his wife built, resembles a Mississippi steamboat beached in a Victorian neighborhood; it's adjacent to the **Harriet Beecher Stowe Center,** which is also worth a visit. Downtown, you can visit the Nutmeg State's ornate **State Capitol** and the **Wadsworth Atheneum Museum of Art,** which houses fine Impressionist and Hudson River School paintings. Sports fans, take note: the **Naismith**

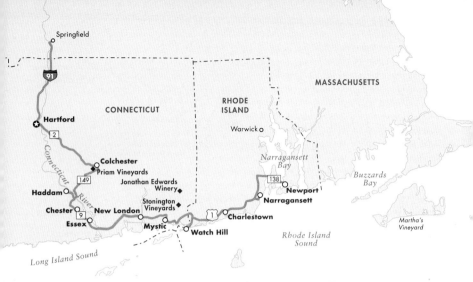

Memorial Basketball Hall of Fame is only a quick detour up Interstate 91, in **Springfield**, Massachusetts, where Dr. James Naismith invented basketball in 1891. Spend your first night in Hartford.

DAY 2: CONNECTICUT RIVER VALLEY AND SOUTHEASTERN SHORE

Just a half-hour southeast of Hartford along Route 2 is your first wine stop, Priam Vineyards, in Colchester. Sample any of the boutique wines before bearing south to explore the centuries-old towns of **Essex**, Chester, and **East Haddam**, which dot the banks of the Connecticut River. In Essex, take a ride on the **Essex Steam Train**—the 12-mile excursion showcases the area's well-preserved countryside.

Continue on to **Mystic**, where the days of wooden ships and whaling adventures live on at **Mystic Seaport**. This world-class museum offers a peek into the past with restored vessels, figureheads, ship carvings, and vintage photography. Spend your second night in Mystic.

Logistics: 60 miles; via Rte. 2 E; 1 hour, starting in Hartford.

DAY 3: CONNECTICUT WINE TRAIL

A patchwork of six wineries—the heart of the eastern section of the **Connecticut Wine Trail**—sit in this tiny southeastern corner of the state. Taste through the

portfolio at each of the picturesque vineyards until you find the perfect bottle to take home; many wineries offer self-guided walks through peaceful vineyards, allowing you to roam on your own. **Stonington Vineyards** has daily guided tours, and Jonathan Edwards Winery, perched above the Atlantic, is a serene setting for picnics. Cap off the day by crossing the state line into Rhode Island and spend the night in **Watch Hill**. If you're there on a weekday, you can pop into the **Watch Hill Lighthouse** to see the original Fresnal light, a binnacle, mariners' sea chests, and historical documents and photos about the lighthouse and the area.

Logistics: 13½ miles; via U.S. 1 N; 25 minutes, starting in Mystic.

DAYS 4 AND 5: RHODE ISLAND'S BEACHES AND NEWPORT'S MANSIONS

En route to Newport along U.S. 1 from **Watch Hill**, sandy beaches dot the coast in **Charlestown** and **Narragansett**. If it's summer and the weather is fine, spend the afternoon at the beach before continuing on to Newport. Despite its Colonial downtown and seaside parks, to most people **Newport** means mansions—the most opulent enclave of private homes ever built in the United States. Turn-of-the-20th-century "summer cottages" such as the **Breakers** and **Marble House** are must-sees. Embark on the scenic **Cliff Walk** for remarkable views of these great houses on one side and the Atlantic on the other. Newport's downtown is excellent for window-shopping, and there are plenty of places to enjoy fresh seafood.

Newport is known to many as the sailing capital of the East Coast, and you may get the best feel for it from the deck of a schooner cruising its famous harbor. Tours generally last around 90 minutes, and some offer beverages and snacks. Tennis enthusiasts can visit the **International Tennis Hall of Fame & Museum,** which, along with exhibits focusing on the legends of the game, has a unique interior designed by architect Stanford White. You can easily spend a few days exploring Newport.

Logistics: 39½ miles; via U.S. 1 N; 1 hour, starting in Watch Hill. From Newport, it is 26 miles (30 minutes) to T. F Green Airport via RI 138 W and RI 4 N.

BEST OF VERMONT, 7 DAYS

Following roads that weave through the Green Mountains and charming towns, this 200-mile journey is ideal at any time of year and covers Vermont from top to bottom.

Fly in: Bradley International Airport (BDL), Hartford

Fly out: Burlington International Airport (BTV), Burlington

DAY 1: BRATTLEBORO

Artsy **Brattleboro** is the perfect place to begin a tour of Vermont, and it's worth taking a day to do some shopping and exploring. Catch a movie at the art deco **Latchis Theatre,** browse in a bookstore, or simply grab a cup of joe and people-watch. For dinner, make a reservation well in advance at tiny **T.J. Buckley's,** one of the best restaurants in the state. Spend your first night in Brattleboro.

Logistics: 78 miles; via I–91 N; 1 hour and 15 minutes from Bradley airport.

DAYS 2-4: KILLINGTON

Depart Brattleboro heading west on Route 9 and link up with Route 100 in Wilmington. As you travel north along the eastern edge of **Green Mountain National Forest,** you'll pass a plethora of panoramic overlooks and delightful ski towns. Stop to snap a photo, or take a moment to peruse the selection at a funky general store, as you make your way toward gigantic Killington Peak. Spend the next three nights in **Killington,** the largest ski resort in Vermont, and an outdoor playground year-round. A tip for skiers: one of the closest places to the slopes to stay is **The Mountain Top Inn & Resort.**

Wake up early to carve the mountain's fresh powder in winter. Nonskiers can still enjoy the snow, whether at the tubing park, on a snowmobile adventure, or in snowshoes on one of several trails. In summer, long after the ground has thawed, those trails are opened to mountain bikers and hikers. For a more leisurely activity, try your hand at the 18-hole disc-golf course. The excellent Grand Spa is also a lovely way to spend the day.

Logistics: 94 miles; via Rte. 9 W, Rte. 100 N, 2½ hours, starting in Brattleboro.

DAY 5: KILLINGTON TO BURLINGTON

Continue on Route 100 north until you reach Hancock, then head west on Route 125. Welcome to the land of poet Robert Frost, who spent almost 40 years living in Vermont, summering in the nearby tiny mountain town of Ripton, where he wrote numerous poems. Plaques along the 1.2-mile **Robert Frost Interpretive Trail**, a quiet woodland walk that takes about 30 minutes, display commemorative quotes from his poems, including his classic, "The Road Not Taken." After your stroll, head north on U.S. 7 until you hit Burlington.

Burlington, Vermont's largest city and home to the **University of Vermont,** is located on the eastern shore of Lake Champlain. Bustling in the summer and fall, the **Burlington Farmers' Market** is filled with everything from organic meats and cheeses to freshly cut flowers and maple syrup. Spend the night in Burlington. In the evening, check out **Nectar's,** where the band Phish played their first bar gig, or wander into any of the many other pubs and cafés that attract local musicians.

Logistics: 84 miles; via Rte. 100 N, Rte. 125 W, and U.S. 7 N; 2½ hours, starting in Killington.

DAY 6: SHELBURNE AND LAKE CHAMPLAIN

On your second day in Burlington, you can take a day trip south to the **Magic Hat Brewing Company;** established in 1994, it was at the forefront of Vermont's microbrewery explosion. Take a free half-hour guided or self-guided tour of the Artifactory (even dogs are welcome), and fill a growler from one of the 48 taps pumping out year-round, seasonal, and experimental brews. A stone's throw down U.S. 7, in **Shelburne,** is family-friendly **Shelburne Farms.** Watch the process of making cheese from start to

finish, or wander the gorgeous 1,400-acre estate designed by Frederick Law Olmsted, co-designer of New York's Central Park. The grounds overlook beautiful **Lake Champlain** and make the perfect setting for a picnic. In winter Shelburne Farms offers sleigh rides and other themed activities; if you're visiting in late July, don't miss the **Vermont Cheesemakers Festival,** showcasing more than 200 varieties of cheese crafted by 40 local purveyors. If you can't get enough, you can opt to spend the night here.

Logistics: 3.6 miles, via U.S. 7 to Magic Hat; another 3.4 miles to Shelburne Farms; 40 minutes round-trip altogether.

DAY 7: STOWE

A 30-minute drive down Interstate 89 from Burlington reunites you with Route 100 in the small town of Waterbury. Head north in the direction of Stowe, and in under 2 miles you can make the obligatory pit stop at **Ben & Jerry's Ice Cream Factory.** The factory tour offers a lively behind-the-scenes look at how their ice cream is made; at the end of the tour, you get to taste limited-release creations only available at the factory before voting on your favorites.

Next, set out for the village of **Stowe.** Its proximity to Mt. Mansfield (Vermont's highest peak at 4,395 feet) has made Stowe a popular ski destination since the 1930s. If there's snow on the ground, hit the slopes, hitch a ride on a one-horse open sleigh, or simply put your feet up by the fire and enjoy a Heady Topper (an unfiltered, hoppy, American Double IPA beloved by Vermonters). In warmer weather, pop into the cute shops and art galleries that line the town's main street and sample some of the finest cheddar cheese and maple syrup that Vermont has to offer. Rejuvenate yourself at **Topnotch Resort,** which offers more than 100 different treatments. Spend your final night here.

Logistics: 36 miles; via I–89 S and Rte. 100 N; 45 minutes, starting in Burlington. From Stowe to the Burlington airport: 33 miles; via Rte. 100 and I–89 N; 41 minutes.

BOSTON AND
ENVIRONS

WELCOME TO BOSTON AND ENVIRONS

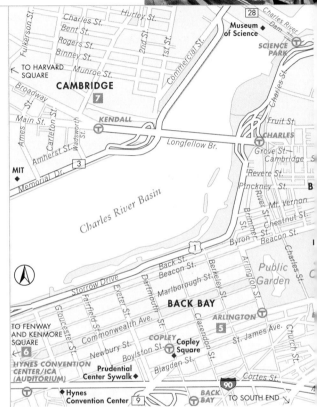

TOP REASONS TO GO

★ **Freedom's Ring:** Walk through America's early history on the 2½-mile Freedom Trail that snakes through town.

★ **Ivy-Draped Campus:** Hang in Harvard Square like a collegiate or hit the university's museums: the Sackler (ancient art), the Botanical Museum, the Peabody (archaeology), and the Natural History Museum.

★ **Posh Purchases:** Strap on some stilettos and join the quest for fashionable finds on Newbury Street, Boston's answer to Manhattan's 5th Avenue.

★ **Sacred Ground:** Root for (or boo) the Red Sox at baseball's most hallowed shrine, Fenway Park.

★ **Tea Time:** Interact with the city's history at the Boston Tea Party Ships & Museum: greet reenactors and explore replicas of the ships at the actual spot where the tea met the sea.

1 Beacon Hill, Boston Common, and the Old West End. The Brahmins' old stomping ground has many landmarks (Boston Common and the State House among them). The Old West End has the Museum of Science and TD Garden.

2 Government Center and the North End. The sterile Government Center area is home to lovely Faneuil Hall and the trio of restored buildings that share its name. The small North End is full of history and a strong Italian influence.

3 Charlestown. Charlestown's Freedom Trail sights can't be missed—literally. The Bunker Hill Monument is a towering tribute to a pivotal 1775 battle; the USS *Constitution*, a towering tangle of masts and rigging, highlights the neighborhood's naval heritage.

GETTING ORIENTED

With such a complex identity, it's no surprise that Boston, despite its relatively small size, offers visitors a diverse set of experiences. History buffs—and just about everyone else—will spend a day or more following the thick red line of the Freedom Trail and tracing Revolutionary history through town. Shopaholics can join the quest for fashionable finds on Newbury Street, while sports fiends gravitate toward Fenway Park for a tour (or if very lucky, a game) of the beloved Boston Red Sox's home. The Museum of Fine Art's expansive catalog of French Impressionists and American painters, the Isabella Stewart Gardner Museum's palazzo of painting masters, and the Institute of Contemporary Art's modern works satisfy any artistic taste.

4 Downtown. This maze-like section of central Boston encompasses the Financial District and Downtown Crossing (a retail zone); as well as Chinatown, the revived Theater District, plus portions of the Freedom Trail and HarborWalk.

5 The Back Bay. Back Bay's chichi shops, upscale restaurants, and deluxe lodgings sit alongside attractions like the Public Garden and Public Library.

6 The Fenway. Sox fans, art lovers, and college students all frequent the Fens. Fenway Park, the Museum of Fine Arts, and the Isabella Stewart Gardner Museum are here.

7 Cambridge. A separate city across the Charles River, Cambridge has long been a haven for intellectuals and iconoclasts. Along with Harvard and MIT, you'll find bookstores, cafés, and funky boutiques.

FENWAY PARK

For baseball fans Fenway Park is Mecca: a trip there is a religious pilgrimage to the home of former baseball greats such as Ted Williams and Carl Yastrzemski. The Boston Red Sox have played here since 1912, making Fenway the oldest Major League ballpark. The scoreboard is still operated by hand, and fans still clamor for cramped, uncomfortable seats.

(above) Take yourself out to a ballgame at legendary Fenway Park. (lower right) Iconic sox mark the park walls. (upper right) Flags adorn the epicenter of Red Sox Nation.

For much of the ballpark's history Babe Ruth's specter loomed large. After winning five titles by 1918 (including the first World Series in 1903), the team endured an 86-year title drought after trading away the Sultan of Swat. The team vexed generations of fans with colossal late-season collapses, post-season bungles, and losses to the hated New York Yankees. The Sox snapped the spell in 2004, defeating the Yanks in the American League Championship Series after being down 3–0 and sweeping the St. Louis Cardinals in the World Series. The Red Sox won it all again in 2007, completely exorcising "The Curse" in 2013.

FUN FACT

A lone red seat in the right-field bleachers marks where Ted Williams' 502-foot shot—the longest measurable home run hit inside Fenway Park—landed on June 9, 1946.

TICKET TIPS

Can't get tickets? At Gate E two hours before the game, a handful of tickets are sold. There's a one-ticket limit, so everyone must be in line.

THE NATION

The Red Sox have the most rabid fan base in baseball. They follow the team with an intensity usually seen in religious cults. The Pats and Celtics may be champion-caliber teams, too, but this is first and foremost a Red Sox town.

THE MONSTER

Fenway's most dominant feature is the 37-foot-high "Green Monster," the wall that looms over left field. It's just over 300 feet from home plate and in the field of play, so deep fly balls that would have been outs in other parks sometimes become home runs. The Monster also stops line drives that would have been over the walls of other stadiums.

THE MUSIC

Fans sing "Take Me Out to the Ballgame " during the 7th inning stretch in every ballpark...but at Fenway they also sing Neil Diamond's "Sweet Caroline" in the middle of the 8th. If the Sox win, the Standell's "Dirty Water " blasts over the loudspeakers at the game's end.

THE CURSE

In 1920 the Red Sox traded pitcher Babe Ruth to the Yankees, where he became a home-run-hitting baseball legend. Some fans—most famously *Boston Globe* columnist Dan Shaughnessy, who wrote a book called *The Curse of the Bambino*—blamed this move for the team's 86-year title drought, but others will claim that "The Curse" was just a media-driven storyline used to explain the team's past woes. Still, fans who watched a ground ball roll between Bill Buckner's legs in the 1986 World Series or saw Aaron Boone's winning home run in the 2003 American League Division Series swear the curse was real.

THE SPORTS GUY

For an in-depth view of the psyche of a die-hard Red Sox fan, pick up a copy of Bill Simmons's book *Now I Can Die in Peace*. Simmons, a native New Englander, writes for ESPN.com and is the editor-in-chief of Grantland.com.

VISIT THE NATION

Can't get tickets but still want to experience the excitement of a Red Sox game? Then head down to the park and hang out on Yawkey Way, which borders the stadium. On game days it's closed to cars and filled with vendors, creating a street-fair atmosphere. Duck into a nearby sports bar (there are many) and enjoy the game with other fans who couldn't secure seats. A favorite is the Cask 'n Flagon, at Brookline Avenue and Lansdowne Street, across the street from Fenway.

The closest you can get to Fenway without buying a ticket is the **Bleacher Bar** (*82A Lansdowne St.*), which actually has a huge window in the center-field wall overlooking the field. If you want to see a game from this unique vantage point, get here early—it starts filling up a few hours before game time.

Updated by
Kara Baskin

There's history and culture around every bend in Boston — skyscrapers nestle next to historic hotels, while modern marketplaces line the antique cobblestone streets. But to Bostonians, living in a city that blends yesterday and today is just another day in their beloved Beantown.

It's difficult to fit Boston into a stereotype because of the city's many layers. The deepest is the historical one, the place where musket-bearing revolutionaries vowed to hang together or hang separately. The next tier, a dense spread of Brahmin fortune and fortitude, might be labeled the Hub. It was this elite caste of Boston society, descended from wealthy English Protestants who first settled the state, that funded and patronized the city's universities and cultural institutions, gaining Boston the label "the Athens of America" and felt only pride in the slogan "Banned in Boston." Over that layer lies Beantown, home to the Red Sox faithful and the raucous Bruins fans who crowded the old Boston "*Gah*-den"; this is the city whose ethnic loyalties account for its many distinct neighborhoods. Crowning these layers are the students who converge on the area's universities and colleges every fall.

PLANNING

WHEN TO GO

Summer brings reliable sunshine, sailboats to Boston Harbor, concerts to the Esplanade, and café tables to assorted sidewalks. If you're dreaming of a classic shore vacation, summer is prime.

Weather-wise, late spring and fall are the optimal times to visit Boston. Aside from mild temperatures, the former offers blooming gardens throughout the city and the latter sees the surrounding countryside ablaze with brilliantly colored foliage. At both times expect crowds.

Autumn attracts hordes of leaf peepers, and more than 250,000 students flood into the area each September, then pull out in May and June. Hotels and restaurants fill up quickly on move-in, move-out, and graduation weekends.

Winters are cold and windy.

PLANNING YOUR TIME

If you have a couple of days, hit Boston's highlights—Beacon Hill, the Freedom Trail, and the Public Garden—the first day, and then check out the Museum of Fine Arts or the Isabella Stewart Gardner Museum the morning of the second day. Reserve day two's afternoon for an excursion to Harvard or shopping on Newbury Street.

GETTING HERE AND AROUND

AIR TRAVEL

Boston's major airport, Logan International (BOS), is across the harbor from Downtown, about 2 miles outside the city center, and can be reached by taxi, water taxi, or bus/subway via MBTA's Silver or Blue line. Logan has four passenger terminals, identified by letters A, B, C, and E. A free airport shuttle runs between the terminals and airport hotels. Some airlines use different terminals for international and domestic flights; most international flights arrive at Terminal E. A visitor center in Terminal C offers tourist information. T. F. Green Airport, in Providence, Rhode Island, and the Manchester Boston Regional Airport in Manchester, New Hampshire, are both about an hour from Boston.

Airport Information Logan International Airport (Boston). ⊠ *I–90 east to Ted Williams Tunnel, Boston* ☎ *800/235–6426* ⊕ *www.massport.com/logan* Ⓜ *Airport.* **Manchester Boston Regional Airport.** ⊠ *Off I–293/Rte. 101, Exit 2, Manchester* ☎ *603/624–6556* ⊕ *www.flymanchester.com.* **T.F. Green Airport.** ⊠ *2000 Post Rd., Off I–95, Exit 13, Warwick* ☎ *888/268–7222, 401/737–4000* ⊕ *www.pvdairport.com.*

CAR TRAVEL

In a place where roads often evolved from cow paths, driving is no simple task. A surfeit of one-way streets and inconsistent signage add to the confusion. Street parking is hard to come by, as much of it is resident-permit-only. Your own car is helpful if you're taking side trips, but for exploring the city it will only be a burden. Also, Bostonians give terrible directions, since few of them actually drive.

PUBLIC TRANSIT

The "T," as the Massachusetts Bay Transportation Authority's subway system is nicknamed, is the cornerstone of an efficient, far-reaching public transit network that also includes aboveground trains, buses, and ferries. Its five color-coded lines will put you within a block of almost anywhere you want to go. Subways operate from about 5:30 am to 12:30 pm, as do buses, which crisscross the city and reach into suburbia.

A standard adult subway fare is $1.70 with a CharlieCard or $2 with a ticket or cash. For buses it's $1.25 with a CharlieCard or $1.50 with a ticket or cash (more if you are using an Inner or Outer Express bus). Commuter rail and ferry fares vary by route; yet all options charge seniors and students reduced prices, and kids under 12 ride free with a paying adult. Contact the MBTA (☎ *617/222–3200 or 800/392–6100* ⊕ *www.mbta.com*) for schedules, routes, and rates.

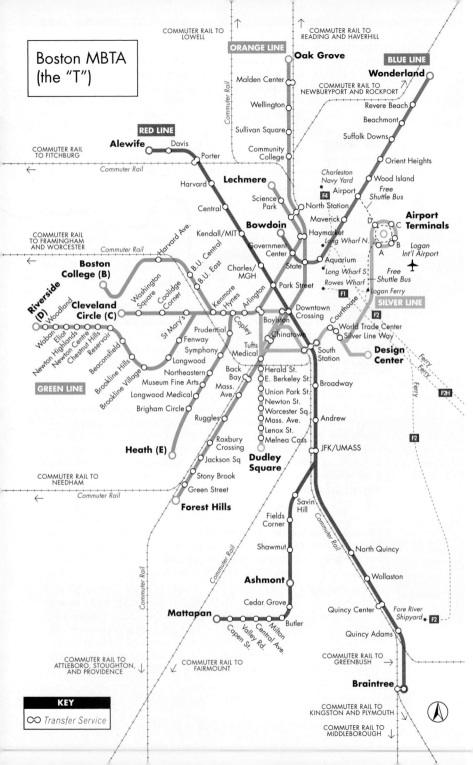

TAXI TRAVEL

Cabs are available 24/7. Rides within the city cost $2.60 for the first 1/7 mile and 40¢ for each 1/7 mile thereafter (tolls, where applicable, are extra).

VISITOR INFORMATION

Contact the city and state tourism offices for details about seasonal events, discount passes, trip planning, and attraction information. The National Park Service has a Boston office for Boston's historic sites that provides maps and directions. The Welcome Center and Boston Common Visitor Information Center offer general information. The Cambridge Tourism Office's information booth is in Harvard Square, near the main entrance to the Harvard T stop.

Contacts Boston Common Visitor Information Center. ⊠ *139 Tremont St., On the Common, Downtown* ☎ *617/536–4100* ⊕ *www.bostonusa.com/visit/planyourtrip/resources/vic/.* **Cambridge Tourism Office.** ⊠ *4 Brattle St., Harvard Square* ☎ *800/862–5678, 617/441–2884* ⊕ *www.cambridge-usa.org.* **Greater Boston Convention and Visitors Bureau.** ⊠ *2 Copley Pl., Suite 105, Back Bay* ☎ *888/733–2678, 617/536–4100* ⊕ *www.bostonusa.com.* **Massachusetts Office of Travel and Tourism.** ⊠ *State Transportation Bldg., 10 Park Plaza, Suite 4510, Back Bay* ☎ *800/227–6277, 617/973–8500* ⊕ *www.massvacation.com.* **National Parks Service Visitor Center.** ⊠ *Faneuil Hall, Downtown* ☎ *617/242–5642* ⊕ *www.nps.gov/bost.*

ONLINE RESOURCES

Boston.com, home of the *Boston Globe* online, has news and feature articles, ample travel information, and links to towns throughout Massachusetts. The site for Boston's arts and entertainment weekly, the *Boston Phoenix* (⊕ *www.bostonphoenix.com*) has nightlife, movie, restaurant, and arts listings. The Bostonian Society (⊕ *bostonhistory.org*) answers some frequently asked questions about Beantown history on their website. The iBoston (⊕ *www.iboston.org*) page has wonderful photographs of architecturally and historically important buildings. *The Improper Bostonian* (⊕ *www.improper.com*) and *WickedLocal* (⊕ *www.wickedlocal.com*) provide a more relaxed (and irreverent) take on Boston news and information.

EXPLORING

BEACON HILL AND BOSTON COMMON

Updated by
Kim Foley
MacKinnon

Past and present home of the old-money elite, contender for the "Most Beautiful" award among the city's neighborhoods, and hallowed address for many literary lights, Beacon Hill is Boston at its most Bostonian. The redbrick elegance of its narrow streets sends you back to the 19th century just as surely as if you had stumbled into a time machine. But Beacon Hill residents would never make the social faux pas of being out of date. The neighborhood is home to hip boutiques and trendy restaurants frequented by young, affluent professionals rather than DAR (Daughters of the American Revolution) matrons.

Boston Common. Nothing is more central to Boston than the Common, the oldest public park in the United States and undoubtedly the largest and most famous of the town commons around which New England settlements were traditionally arranged. Dating from 1634, Boston Common started as 50 acres where the freemen of Boston could graze their cattle. (Cows were banned in 1830.) Latin names are affixed to many of the Common's trees; it was once expected that proper Boston schoolchildren be able to translate them.

On Tremont Street near Boylston stands the 1888 **Boston Massacre Memorial**; the sculpted hand of one of the victims has a distinct shine from years of sightseers' caresses. The Common's highest ground, near the park's Parkman Bandstand, was once called Flagstaff Hill. It's now surmounted by the **Soldiers and Sailors Monument,** honoring Civil War troops. The Common's only body of water is the **Frog Pond,** a tame and frog-free concrete depression used as a children's wading pool and spray fountain during steamy summer days and for ice-skating in winter. It marks the original site of a natural pond that inspired Edgar Allan Poe to call Bostonians "Frogpondians." In 1848 a gushing fountain of piped-in water was created to inaugurate Boston's municipal water system.

On the Beacon Street side of the Common sits the splendidly restored **Robert Gould Shaw 54th Regiment Memorial,** executed in deep-relief bronze by Augustus Saint-Gaudens in 1897. It commemorates the 54th Massachusetts Regiment, the first Civil War unit made up of free black people, led by the young Brahmin Robert Gould Shaw. He and half of his troops died in an assault on South Carolina's Fort Wagner; their story inspired the 1989 movie *Glory.* The monument—first intended to depict only Shaw until his abolitionist family demanded it honor his regiment as well—figures in works by the poets John Berryman and Robert Lowell, both of whom lived on the north slope of Beacon Hill in the 1940s. This magnificent memorial makes a fitting first stop on the Black Heritage Trail. ⊠ *Bounded by Beacon, Charles, Tremont, and Park Sts., Beacon Hill* ⊕ *www.cityofboston.gov/freedomtrail/ bostoncommon.asp* Ⓜ *Park St., Boylston.*

Central Burying Ground. The Central Burying Ground may seem an odd feature for a public park, but remember that in 1756, when the land was set aside, this was a lonely corner of the Common. It's the final resting place of Tories and Patriots alike, as well as many British casualties of the Battle of Bunker Hill. The most famous person buried here is Gilbert Stuart, the portraitist best known for his likenesses of George and Martha Washington; he died a poor man in 1828. The Burying Ground is open daily 9–5. ⊠ *Boylston St. near Tremont, Beacon Hill* ⊕ *www.cityofboston.gov/parks/hbgi/CentralBuryingCentral. asp* Ⓜ *Park St., Boylston.*

Louisburg Square. One of Beacon Hill's most charming corners, Louisburg Square (proper Bostonians always pronounce the "s") was an 1840s model for a town-house development that was never built on the Hill because of space restrictions. Today, the grassy square, enclosed by a wrought-iron fence, belongs collectively to the owners of the houses

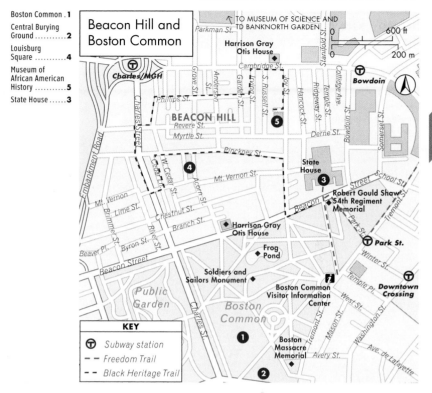

facing it. The statue at the north end of the green is of Columbus, the one at the south end of Aristides the Just; both were donated in 1850 by a Greek merchant who lived on the square. The houses, most of which are now divided into apartments and condominiums, have seen their share of famous tenants, including author and critic William Dean Howells at Nos. 4 and 16, and the Alcotts at No. 10 (Louisa May not only lived but also died here, on the day of her father's funeral). In 1852 the singer Jenny Lind was married in the parlor of No. 20. Louisburg Square is also the current home of U.S. Secretary of State John Kerry.

There's a legend that Louisburg Square was the location of the Rev. William Blaxton's spring, although there's no water there today. Blaxton, or Blackstone, was one of the first Bostonians, having come to the Shawmut Peninsula in the mid-1620s. When the Puritans, who had settled in Charlestown, found their water supply inadequate, Blaxton invited them to move across the river, where he assured them they would find an "excellent spring." Just a few years later, he sold them all but 6 acres of the peninsula he had bought from the Native Americans and decamped to Rhode Island, seeking greater seclusion; a plaque at 50 Beacon Street commemorates him. ⊠ *Between Mt. Vernon and Pickney Sts., Beacon Hill* Ⓜ *Park St.*

DID YOU KNOW?

Quincy Market, now known as Faneuil Hall Marketplace first opened in 1826. It was renovated in 1976 and now offers one of the best spots for grazing in the city.

FAMILY
Fodor's Choice
★
Museum of African American History.
Ever since runaway slave Crispus
Attucks became one of the famous
victims of the Boston Massacre of
1770, the African American community of Boston has played an
important part in the city's history.
Throughout the 19th century, abolition was the cause célèbre for Boston's intellectual elite, and during
that time, blacks came to thrive in
neighborhoods throughout the city.
The Museum of African American
History was established in 1964 to

> **DID YOU KNOW?**
>
> Beacon Hill's north slope played
> a key part in African American
> history. A community of free blacks
> lived here in the 1800s; many
> worshipped at the African Meeting
> House, established in 1805 and
> still standing. It came to be known
> as the "Black Faneuil Hall" for the
> fervent antislavery activism that
> started within its walls.

promote this history. The umbrella organization includes a trio of historic sites: the Abiel Smith School, the first public school in the nation
built specifically for black children; the African Meeting House, where
in 1832 the New England Anti-Slavery Society was formed under the
leadership of William Lloyd Garrison; and the African Meeting House
on the island of Nantucket, off the coast of Cape Cod. Park Service
personnel lead tours of the **Black Heritage Trail**, starting from the Shaw
Memorial on Boston Common. The museum is the site of activities,
including lectures, children's storytelling, and concerts focusing on
black composers. ⊠ *46 Joy St., Beacon Hill* ☎ *617/725–0022* ⊕ *www.
afroammuseum.org* ⊠ *$5* ⊗ *Sept.–May, Mon.–Sat. 10–4; June–Aug.,
Mon.–Sat. 9:30–5* Ⓜ *Park St.*

FAMILY
Fodor's Choice
★
State House. On July 4, 1795, the surviving fathers of the Revolution
were on hand to enshrine the ideals of their new Commonwealth in a
graceful seat of government designed by Charles Bulfinch. Governor
Samuel Adams and Paul Revere laid the cornerstone; Revere would later
roll the copper sheathing for the dome.

Bulfinch's neoclassical design is poised between Georgian and Federal;
its finest features are the delicate Corinthian columns of the portico,
the graceful pediment and window arches, and the vast yet visually
weightless golden dome (gilded in 1874 and again in 1997). During
World War II the dome was painted gray so that it would not reflect
moonlight during blackouts and thereby offer a target to anticipated
Axis bombers. It's capped with a pinecone, a symbol of the importance
of pinewood, which was integral to the construction of Boston's early
houses and churches; it also serves as a reminder of the state's early
connection to Maine, once part of Massachusetts.

Inside the building are Doric Hall, with its statuary and portraits; the
Hall of Flags, where an exhibit shows the battle flags from all the wars
in which Massachusetts regiments have participated; the Great Hall, an
open space used for state functions that houses 351 flags from the cities
and towns of Massachusetts; the governor's office; and the chambers
of the House and Senate. The Great Hall contains a giant, modernistic
clock designed by New York artist R. M. Fischer. Its installation in 1986
at a cost of $100,000 was roundly slammed as a symbol of legislative

extravagance. There's also a wealth of statuary, including figures of Horace Mann, Daniel Webster, and a youthful-looking President John F. Kennedy in full stride. Just outside Doric Hall is *Hear Us,* a series of six bronze busts honoring the contributions of women to public life in Massachusetts. But perhaps the best-known piece of artwork in the building is the carved wooden *Sacred Cod,* mounted in the Old State House in 1784 as a symbol of the commonwealth's maritime wealth. It was moved, with much fanfare, to Bulfinch's structure in 1798. By 1895, when it was hung in the new House chambers, the representatives had begun to consider the Cod their unofficial mascot—so much so that when *Harvard Lampoon* wags "codnapped" it in 1933, the House refused to meet in session until the fish was returned, three days later. You can take a guided tour or do a self-guided tour. ⊠ *Beacon St. between Hancock and Bowdoin Sts., Beacon Hill* ☎ 617/727–3676 ⊕ *www.sec.state.ma.us/trs/trsidx.htm* ⊡ *Free* ☉ *Weekdays 8:45–5. 30-min guided tours 10–3:30. Advance reservations requested* Ⓜ *Park St.*

THE OLD WEST END

A few decades ago this district—separated from Beacon Hill by Cambridge Street—resembled a typical medieval city: thoroughfares that twisted and turned, maddening one-way lanes, and streets that were a veritable hive of people. Today little remains of the *old* Old West End except for a few brick tenements and a handful of monuments, including the first house built for Harrison Gray Otis. The biggest surviving structures with any real history are two public institutions, Massachusetts General Hospital and the former Suffolk County Jail, which dates from 1849. The onetime prison is now part of the luxurious, and wryly named, Liberty Hotel. Here you'll also find TD Banknorth Garden, the home away from home for loyal Bruins and Celtics fans. In addition, the innovative Museum of Science is one of the neighborhood's more modern attractions. The newest addition to the skyline here is the Leonard P. Zakim Bunker Hill Bridge, which spans the Charles River just across from the TD Banknorth Garden.

FAMILY
Fodor'sChoice
★
Museum of Science. With 15-foot lightning bolts in the Theater of Electricity and a 20-foot-long Tyrannosaurus rex model, this is just the place to ignite any child's scientific curiosity. Located just north of Massachusetts General Hospital, the museum sits astride the Charles River Dam. More than 550 exhibits cover astronomy, astrophysics, anthropology, medical progress, computers, the organic and inorganic earth sciences, and much more. The emphasis is on hands-on education.

At the "Investigate!" exhibit, there are no wrong answers, only discoveries. Children explore such scientific principles as gravity by balancing objects. They learn the physics behind everyday play activities such as swinging and bumping up and down on a teeter-totter in the "Science in the Park" exhibit. Other displays include "Light House," where you can experiment with color and light, and the perennial favorite, "Dinosaurs: Modeling the Mesozoic," which lets kids become paleontologists and examine dinosaur bones, fossils, and tracks.

Continued on page 91

FOLLOW THE REDBRICK ROAD

BOSTON'S FREEDOM TRAIL

by Mike Nalepa

Paul Revere

Samuel Adams

Benjamin Franklin

John Hancock

Paul Revere's ride

The Freedom Trail is more than a collection of historic sites related to the American Revolution or a suggested itinerary connecting Boston's unique neighborhoods. It's a chance to walk in the footsteps of our forefathers—literally, by following a crimson path on public sidewalks—and pay tribute to the figures all school kids know, like Paul Revere, John Hancock, and Ben Franklin. In history-proud Boston, past and present intersect before your eyes not as a re-creation but as living history accessible to all.

Boston played a key role in the dramatic events leading up to the American Revolution. Many of the founding fathers called the city home, and many of the initial meetings and actions that sparked the fight against the British took place here. In one day, you can visit Faneuil Hall—the "Cradle of Liberty"—where outraged colonial radicals met to oppose British authority; the site of the incendiary Boston Massacre; and the Old North Church, where lanterns hung to signal Paul Revere on his thrilling midnight ride. Colonists may have originally landed in Jamestown and Plymouth, but if you really want to see where America began, come to Boston.

Boston Common, Founder's Statue

⊕ www.nps.gov/bost
⊕ www.thefreedomtrail.org

☏ 617/242-5642

🎟 Admission to the Freedom Trail itself is free. Several museum sites charge for admission. However, most attractions are free monuments, parks, and landmarks.

The 1729 Old South Meeting House, where many protesters gathered during the American Revolution.

PLANNING YOUR TRAIL TRIP

THE ROUTE

The 2½-mi Freedom Trail begins at Boston Common, winds through Downtown, Government Center, and the North End, and ends in Charlestown at the USS *Constitution*. The entire Freedom Trail is marked by a red line on the sidewalk; it's made of paint or brick at various points on the Trail. ⇨ *For more information on Freedom Trail sites, see listings in Neighborhood chapters.*

GETTING HERE AND BACK

The route starts near the Park Street T stop. When you've completed the Freedom Trail, head for the nearby Charlestown water shuttle, which goes directly to the downtown area. For schedules and maps, visit ⊕ *www.mbta.com.*

TIMING

If you're stopping at a few (or all) of the 16 sites, it takes a full day to complete the route comfortably. ■TIP➔ If you have children in tow, you may want to split the trail into two or more days.

VISITOR CENTERS

There are Freedom Trail information centers in Boston Common (Tremont Street), at 15 State Street (near the Old State House), and at the Charlestown Navy Yard Visitor Center (in Building 5).

TOURS

The National Park Service's free 90-minute Freedom Trail walking tours begin at the Boston National Historical Park Visitor Center at 15 State Street and cover sites from the Old South Meeting House to the Old North Church. Check online for times; it's a good idea to show up at least 30 minutes early, as the popular tours are limited to 30 people.

Half-hour tours of the USS *Constitution* are offered Tuesday through Sunday. Note that visitors to the ship must go through security screening.

FUEL UP

The trail winds through the heart of Downtown Boston, so finding a quick bite or a nice sit-down meal isn't difficult. Quincy Market, near Faneuil Hall, is packed with cafés and eateries. Another good lunch choice is one of the North End's wonderful Italian restaurants.

WHAT'S NEARBY

For a short break from revolutionary history, be sure to check out the major attractions nearby, including the Boston Public Garden, New England Aquarium, and Union Oyster House.

Above: In front of the Old State House a cobblestone circle marks the site of the Boston Massacre.

TOP SIGHTS

Boston Common

Benjamin Franklin Statue

The Granary Burial Grounds

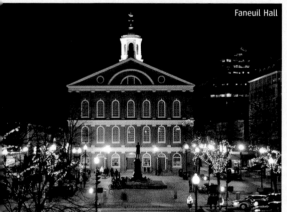
Faneuil Hall

Park Street Church

Old North Church

Bunker Hill Monument

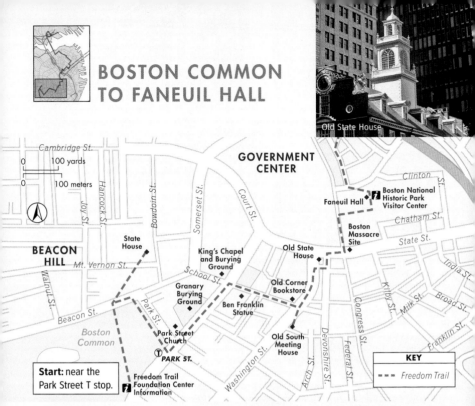

BOSTON COMMON TO FANEUIL HALL

Old State House

GOVERNMENT CENTER

Cambridge St.

0   100 yards
0   100 meters

Hancock St.
Joy St.
Bowdoin St.
Somerset St.
Court St.
Clinton St.
Chatham St.
State St.
India St.
Kilby St.
Broad St.
Milk St.
Franklin St.
Congress St.
Devonshire St.
Federal St.
Arch St.
Washington St.
Walnut St.
Beacon St.
Mt. Vernon St.
Park St.
School St.

BEACON HILL

State House

King's Chapel and Burying Ground

Granary Burying Ground

Ben Franklin Statue

Old State House

Old Corner Bookstore

Boston Massacre Site

Faneuil Hall

Boston National Historic Park Visitor Center

Old South Meeting House

Park Street Church

Boston Common

🅣 PARK ST.

Start: near the Park Street T stop.

🄵 Freedom Trail Foundation Center Information

KEY

- - - *Freedom Trail*

Many of the Freedom Trail sites between Boston Common and the North End are close together. Walking this 1-mile segment of the trail makes for a pleasant morning.

THE ROUTE

Begin at ★ **Boston Common,** then head for the **State House,** Boston's finest example of Federal architecture. Several blocks away is the **Park Street Church,** whose 217-foot steeple is considered to be the most beautiful in New England. The church was actually founded in 1809, and it played a key role in the movement to abolish slavery.

Reposing in the church's shadows is the ★ **Granary Burying Ground,** final resting place of Samuel Adams, John Hancock, and Paul Revere. A short stroll to Downtown brings you to **King's Chapel,** founded in 1686 by King James II for the Church of England.

Follow the trail past the **Benjamin Franklin statue** to the **Old Corner Bookstore** site, where Hawthorne, Emerson, and Longfellow were published. Nearby is the **Old South Meeting House,** where arguments in 1773 led to the Boston Tea Party. Overlooking the site of the Boston Massacre is the city's oldest public building, the **Old State House,** a Georgian beauty.

In 1770 the Boston Massacre occurred directly in front of here—look for the commemorative stone circle.

Cross the plaza to ★ **Faneuil Hall** and explore where Samuel Adams railed against "taxation without representation." ■ **TIP**➔ A good mid-trail break is the shops and eateries of Faneuil Hall Marketplace, which includes Quincy Market.

Old Corner Book Store Site

★ = **Fodor's** Choice   ★ = Highly Recommended   ℭ = Family Friendly

NORTH END TO CHARLESTOWN

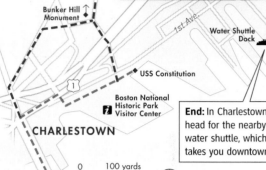

USS Constitution

Freedom Trail sites between Faneuil Hall and Charlestown are more spread out along 1½ miles. The sites here, though more difficult to reach, are certainly worth the walk.

THE ROUTE

When you depart Faneuil Hall, follow the red stripe to the North End, Boston's Little Italy.

The ☙ **Paul Revere House** takes you back 200 years—here are the hero's own saddlebags, a toddy warmer, and a pine cradle made from a molasses cask. It's also air-conditioned in the summer, so try to stop here in mid-afternoon to escape the heat. Next to the Paul Revere House is one of the city's oldest brick buildings, the **Pierce-Hichborn House**.

Next, peek inside a place guaranteed to trigger a wave of patriotism: the ★ **Old North Church** of "One if by land, two if by sea" fame. Then head toward **Copp's**

Paul Revere House

Hill Burying Ground, where you can view graves from the late 17th century through the early 19th century. Afterward, cross the bridge over the Charles and check out that revered icon, the ☙ **USS Constitution,** "Old Ironsides." It's open until 6 PM (4 PM November through March), and you'll need about an hour for a visit, so plan accordingly.

The perfect ending to the trail? A walk to the top of the ☙ **Bunker Hill Monument** for the incomparable vistas. The hill was the site of one of the first battles of the Revolutionary War. Though the colonial rebels actually lost, they inflicted large casualties on the better-trained British, proving themselves against the empire.

Bunker Hill Monument ↑

Water Shuttle Dock ⛴

• **USS Constitution**

🅱 Boston National Historic Park Visitor Center

CHARLESTOWN

End: In Charlestown head for the nearby water shuttle, which takes you downtown

1st Ave.

Charlestown Bridge

0 — 100 yards
0 — 100 meters

NORTH END

Commercial St.

Copp's Hill Burying Ground •

Hull St.   Charter St.

Snow St.   Salem St.   Tileston St.

• **Old North Church**

Prince St.

Endicott St.   Margin St.

Pierce-Hichborn House •   • **Paul Revere House**

Hanover St.

North St.   Richmond St.

John F. Fitzgerald   Cross St.

GOVERNMENT CENTER   Surface Rd.

Clinton St.

♦ **Faneuil Hall**

State St.

DID YOU KNOW?

If the Freedom Trail leaves you eager to see more Revolutionary War sites, drive about 30 minutes to Lexington and Concord, where the "shot heard 'round the world" launched the first battles in 1775.

The **Charles Hayden Planetarium,** with its sophisticated multimedia system based on a Zeiss planetarium projector, produces exciting programs on astronomical discoveries. Laser light shows, with laser graphics and computer animation, are scheduled Thursday through Sunday evenings. The museum also includes the **Mugar Omni Theater,** a five-story dome screen. The theater's state-of-the-art sound system provides extra-sharp acoustics, and the huge projection allows the audience to practically experience the action on-screen. Try to get tickets in advance online or by phone. The planetarium shows are best for children older than five.

After touring the museum, refuel the family at one of the six eateries in the Riverview Cafe located in the Red Wing on the first level.

From April through November, you can catch a Duck Tour from the first level of the museum. You'll need a reservation, so plan ahead. You might be in the mood to sit and tour the city after spending a morning on your feet walking through the exhibit halls. ■TIP→ **Combine your admission with tickets to either the planetarium or Omni Theater and save $4 overall.** ✉ *Science Park at Charles River Dam, Old West End* ☎ *617/723–2500* ⊕ *www.mos.org* ✏ *$23* ☉ *July 5–Labor Day, Sat.– Thurs. 9–7, Fri. 9–9; after Labor Day–July 4, Sat.–Thurs. 9–5, Fri. 9–9* Ⓜ *Science Park.*

FAMILY **Sports Museum of New England.** The fifth and sixth levels of the TD Garden house the Sports Museum of New England, where displays of memorabilia and photographs showcase local sports history and legends. Take a tour of the locker and interview rooms (off-season only), test your sports knowledge with interactive games, and see how you stand up to life-size statues of heroes Carl Yastrzemski and Larry Bird. The museum is generally open Monday to Saturday 10–5 and Sunday 11–5, but call ahead to confirm because it closes often for events. "Behind the Scenes" tours of TD Garden are offered every hour on the hour between 10 and 4. ✉ *TD Garden, 100 Legends Way, Old West End* ⊹ *Use west premium seating entrance* ☎ *617/624–1234* ⊕ *www. sportsmuseum.org* ✏ *$12* Ⓜ *North Station.*

FAMILY **TD Garden.** Diehards may still moan about the loss of the old Boston Garden, a much more intimate venue than this mammoth facility, which opened in 1995. Regardless, the home of the Celtics (basketball) and Bruins (hockey) is still known as the good old "Gah-den," and its air-conditioning, comfier seats, improved food selection, 1,200-vehicle parking garage, and nearly double number of bathrooms, has won grudging acceptance. The Garden also serves as a concert venue, featuring big-name acts, like Justin Timberlake and U2. On occasion, there are public-skating events in winter; call ahead for information. ✉ *100 Legends Way, Old West End* ☎ *617/624–1050* ⊕ *www.tdbanknorthgarden. com* Ⓜ *North Station.*

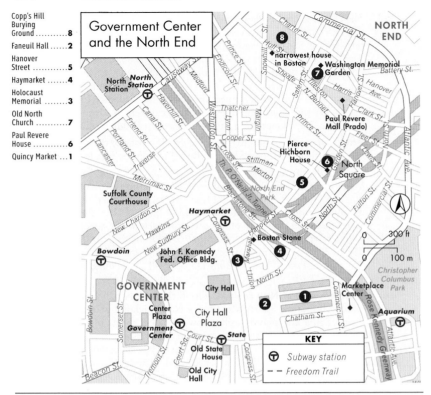

GOVERNMENT CENTER

This is a section of town Bostonians love to hate. Not only does Government Center house what they can't fight—City Hall—but it also contains some of the bleakest architecture since the advent of poured concrete. But though the stark, treeless plain surrounding City Hall has been roundly jeered, the expanse is enlivened by feisty political rallies, free summer concerts, and the occasional festival.

FAMILY
Fodor'sChoice
★

Faneuil Hall. The single building facing Congress Street is the real Faneuil Hall, though locals often give that name to all five buildings in this shopping complex. Bostonians pronounce it *Fan*-yoo'uhl or *Fan*-yuhl. Like other Boston landmarks, Faneuil Hall has evolved over many years. It was erected in 1742, the gift of wealthy merchant Peter Faneuil, who wanted the hall to serve as both a place for town meetings and a public market. It burned in 1761 and was immediately reconstructed according to the original plan of its designer, the Scottish portrait painter John Smibert (who lies in the Granary Burying Ground). In 1763 the political leader James Otis helped inaugurate the era that culminated in American independence when he dedicated the rebuilt hall to the cause of liberty.

In 1772 Samuel Adams stood here and first suggested that Massachusetts and the other colonies organize a Committee of Correspondence to maintain semiclandestine lines of communication in the face of hardening British repression. In later years the hall again lived up to Otis's dedication when the abolitionists Wendell Phillips and Charles Sumner pleaded for support from its podium. The tradition continues to this day: in presidential-election years the hall is the site of debates between contenders in the Massachusetts primary.

Faneuil Hall was substantially enlarged and remodeled in 1805 according to a Greek Revival design of the noted architect Charles Bulfinch; this is the building you see today. Its purposes remain the same: the balconied Great Hall is available to citizens' groups on presentation of a request signed by a required number of responsible parties; it also plays host to regular concerts.

Inside Faneuil Hall are dozens of paintings of famous Americans, including the mural *Webster's Reply to Hayne* and Gilbert Stuart's portrait of Washington at Dorchester Heights. Park rangers give informational talks about the history and importance of Faneuil Hall every half hour. There are interactive displays about Boston sights and National Park Service rangers at the visitor center on the first floor can provide maps and other information.

On the building's top floors are the headquarters and museum and library of the **Ancient & Honorable Artillery Company of Massachusetts.** Founded in 1638, it's the oldest militia in the Western Hemisphere, and the third oldest in the world, after the Swiss Guard and the Honorable Artillery Company of London. Its status is now strictly ceremonial, but it's justly proud of the arms, uniforms, and other artifacts on display. Admission is free. The museum is open weekdays 9 to 3.

Faneuil Hall has always sat in the middle of Boston's main marketplace. When such men as Andrew Jackson and Daniel Webster debated the future of the Republic here, the fragrances of bacon and snuff—sold by merchants in **Quincy Market** across the road—greeted their noses. Today the aroma of coffee wafts through the hall from a snack bar. The shops at ground level sell New England bric-a-brac. ⊠ *Faneuil Hall Sq., Government Center* ☎ *617/523–1300* ⊕ *www.cityofboston. gov/freedomtrail/faneuilhall.asp* ⊠ *Free* ⊙ *Great Hall daily 9–5; informational talks every ½ hr. Shops Mon.–Sat. 10–9, Sun. noon–6. Visitor center daily 9–6* Ⓜ *Government Center, Aquarium, State.*

Haymarket. Loud, self-promoting vendors pack this exuberant maze of a marketplace at Marshall and Blackstone streets on Friday and Saturday from dawn to dusk (most vendors are usually gone by 5). Pushcart vendors hawk fruits and vegetables against a backdrop of fish, meat, and cheese shops. The accumulation of debris left every evening has been celebrated in a whimsical 1976 public-art project—Mags Harries's *Asaroton*, a Greek word meaning "unswept floors"—consisting of bronze fruit peels and other detritus smashed into pavement. Another Harries piece, a bronze depiction of a gathering of stray gloves, tumbles down between the escalators in the Porter Square T station in

Cambridge. At Creek Square, near the Haymarket, is the **Boston Stone.** Set into a brick wall, this was allegedly a marker used as milepost zero in measuring distances from Boston. ⊠ *Marshall and Blackstone Sts., Government Center* ⊘ *Fri. and Sat. dawn–dusk* Ⓜ *Government Center.*

FodorśChoice
★

Holocaust Memorial. At night its six 50-foot-high glass-and-steel towers glow like ghosts. During the day the monument seems at odds with the 18th-century streetscape of Blackstone Square behind it. Located at the north end of Union Park, the Holocaust Memorial is the work of Stanley Saitowitz, whose design was selected through an international competition; the finished memorial was dedicated in 1995. Recollections by Holocaust survivors are set into the glass-and-granite walls; the upper levels of the towers are etched with 6 million numbers in random sequence, symbolizing the Jewish victims of the Nazi horror. Manufactured steam from grates in the granite base makes for a particularly haunting scene after dark. ⊠ *Union St. near Hanover St., Government Center* ☏ *617/457–8755* ⊕ *www.nehm.org* Ⓜ *Haymarket, Government Center, State.*

FAMILY
FodorśChoice
★

Quincy Market. Quincy Market, also known as Faneuil Hall Marketplace, is not everyone's cup of tea; some people prefer grit to polish, and disdain the shiny cafés and boutiques. But there's no denying that this pioneer effort at urban recycling set the tone for many similar projects throughout the country, and that it has brought tremendous vitality to a once-tired corner of Boston. Quincy Market attracts huge crowds of tourists and locals throughout the year. In the early '70s, demolition was a distinct possibility for the decrepit buildings. Fortunately, with the participation of the Boston Redevelopment Authority, architect Benjamin Thompson planned a renovation of Quincy Market, and the Rouse Corporation of Baltimore undertook its restoration, which was completed in 1976. Try to look beyond the shop windows to the grand design of the market buildings themselves; they represent a vision of the market as urban centerpiece, an idea whose time has certainly come again.

The market consists of three block-long annexes: **Quincy Market, North Market,** and **South Market,** each 535 feet long and across a plaza from Faneuil Hall. The structures were designed in 1826 by Alexander Parris as part of a public-works project instituted by Boston's second mayor, Josiah Quincy, to alleviate the cramped conditions of Faneuil Hall and clean up the refuse that collected in Town Dock, the pond behind it. The central structure, made of granite, with a Doric colonnade at either end and topped by a classical dome and rotunda, has kept its traditional market-stall layout, but the stalls now purvey international and specialty foods: sushi, frozen yogurt, bagels, calzones, sausage-on-a-stick, Chinese noodles, barbecue, and baklava, plus all the boutique chocolate-chip cookies your heart desires. This is perhaps Boston's best locale for grazing.

Along the arcades on either side of the Central Market are vendors selling sweatshirts, photographs of Boston, and arts and crafts—some schlocky, some not—alongside a couple of patioed bars and restaurants.

The North and South markets house a mixture of chain stores and specialty boutiques. Quintessential Boston remains here only in Durgin Park, opened in 1826 and known for its plain interior, brassy waitresses, and large portions of traditional New England fare.

A greenhouse flower market on the north side of Faneuil Hall provides a splash of color; during the winter holidays, trees along the cobblestone walks are strung with thousands of sparkling lights. In summer up to 50,000 people a day descend on the market; the outdoor cafés are an excellent spot to watch the hordes if you can find a seat. Year-round the pedestrian walkways draw street performers, and rings of strollers form around magicians and musicians. ✉ *Bordered by Clinton, Commercial, and Chatham Sts., Government Center* ☎ *617/523–1300* ⊕ *www.faneuilhallmarketplace.com* ⊙ *Mon.–Sat. 10–9, Sun. 11–6. Restaurants and bars generally open daily 11 am–2 am; food stalls open earlier* Ⓜ *Government Center, Aquarium, State.*

THE NORTH END

The warren of small streets on the northeast side of Government Center is the North End, Boston's Little Italy. In the 17th century the North End *was* Boston, as much of the rest of the peninsula was still under water or had yet to be cleared. Here the town grew rich for a century and a half before the birth of American independence. The quarter's dwindling ethnic character lingers along Salem or Hanover Street, where you can still hear people speaking with Abruzzese accents.

Copp's Hill Burying Ground. An ancient and melancholy air hovers like a fine mist over this Colonial-era burial ground. The North End graveyard incorporates four cemeteries established between 1660 and 1819. Near the Charter Street gate is the tomb of the Mather family, the dynasty of church divines (Cotton and Increase were the most famous sons) who held sway in Boston during the heyday of the old theocracy. Also buried here is Robert Newman, who crept into the steeple of the Old North Church to hang the lanterns warning of the British attack the night of Paul Revere's ride. Look for the tombstone of Captain Daniel Malcolm; it's pockmarked with musket-ball fire from British soldiers, who used the stones for target practice. Across the street at 44 Hull is the **narrowest house in Boston**—it's a mere 10 feet across. ✉ *Intersection of Hull and Snowhill Sts., North End* ⊕ *www.cityofboston.gov/freedomtrail/coppshill.asp* ⊙ *Daily 10–5* Ⓜ *North Station.*

FAMILY **Hanover Street.** This is the North End's main thoroughfare, along with the smaller and narrower Salem Street. It was named for the ruling dynasty of 18th- and 19th-century England; the label was retained after the Revolution, despite a flurry of patriotic renaming (King Street became State Street, for example). Hanover's business center is thick with restaurants, pastry shops, and Italian cafés; on weekends, Italian immigrants who have moved to the suburbs return to share an espresso with old friends and maybe catch a soccer game broadcast via satellite. Hanover is one of Boston's oldest public roads, once the site of the residences of the Rev. Cotton Mather and the Colonial-era patriot

Dr. Joseph Warren, as well as a small dry-goods store run by Eben D. Jordan—who went on to launch the Jordan Marsh department stores. ⊠ *Between Commercial and Congress Sts., North End* Ⓜ *Haymarket, North Station.*

Fodor's Choice
★

Old North Church. At one end of the **Paul Revere Mall** is a church famous not only for being the oldest standing church building in Boston (built in 1723) but for housing the two lanterns that glimmered from its steeple on the night of April 18, 1775. This is Christ, or Old North, Church, where Paul Revere and the young sexton Robert Newman managed that night to signal the departure by water of the British regulars to Lexington and Concord.

Although William Price designed the structure after studying Christopher Wren's London churches, Old North—which still has an active Episcopal congregation (including descendants of the Reveres)—is an impressive building in its own right. Inside, note the gallery and the graceful arrangement of pews; the bust of George Washington, pronounced by the Marquis de Lafayette to be the truest likeness of the general he ever saw; the brass chandeliers, made in Amsterdam in 1700 and installed here in 1724; and the clock, the oldest still running in an American public building. Try to visit when changes are rung on the bells, after the 11 am Sunday service; they bear the inscription, "We are the first ring of bells cast for the British Empire in North America." On the Sunday closest to April 18, descendants of the patriots reenact the raising of the lanterns in the church belfry during a special evening service. Visitors are welcome to drop in, but to see the bell-ringing chamber and the crypts, take the 30-minute behind-the-scenes tour offered Monday to Saturday ($3 ticket).

Behind the church is the **Washington Memorial Garden,** where volunteers cultivate a plot devoted to plants and flowers favored in the 18th century. ⊠ *193 Salem St., North End* ☎ *617/858–8231* ⊕ *www. oldnorth.com* ⊙ *Jan. and Feb., daily 10–4; Mar.–May, daily 9–5; June–Oct., daily 9–6; Nov. and Dec., daily 9–5. Sun. services at 9 and 11 am* Ⓜ *Haymarket, North Station.*

FAMILY

Paul Revere House. Originally on the site was the parsonage of the Second Church of Boston, home to the Rev. Increase Mather, the Second Church's minister. Mather's house burned in the great fire of 1676, and the house that Revere was to occupy was built on its location about four years later, nearly 100 years before Revere's 1775 midnight ride through Middlesex County. Revere owned it from 1770 until 1800, although he lived there for only 10 years and rented it out for the next two decades. Pre-1900 photographs show it as a shabby warren of storefronts and apartments. The clapboard sheathing is a replacement, but 90% of the framework is original; note the Elizabethan-style overhang and leaded windowpanes. A few Revere furnishings are on display here, and just gazing at his silverwork—much more of which is displayed at the Museum of Fine Arts—brings the man alive. Special events are scheduled throughout the year, many designed with children in mind.

The immediate neighborhood also has Revere associations. The little park in North Square is named after Rachel Revere, his second wife, and the adjacent brick **Pierce-Hichborn House** once belonged to relatives of Revere. The garden connecting the Revere house and the Pierce-Hichborn House is planted with flowers and medicinal herbs favored in Revere's day. ⊠ *19 North Sq., North End* ☎ *617/523–2338* ⊕ *www. paulreverehouse.org* ✑ *$3.50, $5.50 with Pierce-Hichborn House* ☉ *Mid-Apr.–Oct., daily 9:30–5:15; Nov.–mid-Apr., daily 9:30–4:15. Closed Mon. Jan.–Mar.* Ⓜ *Haymarket, Aquarium, Government Center.*

3

CHARLESTOWN

Boston started here. Charlestown was a thriving settlement a year before Colonials headed across the Charles River at William Blaxton's invitation to found the city proper. Today the district's attractions include two of the most visible—and vertical—monuments in Boston: the Bunker Hill Monument, which commemorates the grisly battle that became a symbol of patriotic resistance against the British, and the USS *Constitution,* whose masts continue to tower over the waterfront where she was built more than 200 years ago.

Fodor'sChoice
★
Bunker Hill Monument. Three misunderstandings surround this famous monument. First, the Battle of Bunker Hill was actually fought on Breed's Hill, which is where the monument sits today. (The real Bunker Hill is about ½ mile to the north of the monument; it's slightly taller than Breed's Hill.) Bunker was the original planned locale for the battle, and for that reason its name stuck. Second, although the battle is generally considered a Colonial success, the Americans lost. It was a Pyrrhic victory for the British Redcoats, who sacrificed nearly half of their 2,200 men; American casualties numbered 400–600. And third: the famous war cry "Don't fire until you see the whites of their eyes" may never have been uttered by American Colonel William Prescott or General Israel Putnam, but if either one did shout it, he was quoting an old Prussian command made necessary by the notorious inaccuracy of the musket. No matter. The Americans did employ a deadly delayed-action strategy on June 17, 1775, and conclusively proved themselves worthy fighters, capable of defeating the forces of the British Empire.

Among the dead were the brilliant young American doctor and political activist Joseph Warren, recently commissioned as a major general but fighting as a private, and the British Major John Pitcairn, who two months before had led the Redcoats into Lexington. Pitcairn is believed to be buried in the crypt of Old North Church.

In 1823 the committee formed to construct a monument on the site of the battle chose the form of an Egyptian obelisk. Architect Solomon Willard designed a 221-foot-tall granite obelisk, a tremendous feat of engineering for its day. The Marquis de Lafayette laid the cornerstone of the monument in 1825, but because of a lack of funds, it wasn't dedicated until 1843. Daniel Webster's stirring words at the ceremony commemorating the laying of its cornerstone have gone down in history:

"Let it rise! Let it rise, till it meets the sun in his coming. Let the earliest light of the morning gild it, and parting day linger and play upon its summit."

The monument's zenith is reached by a flight of 294 steps. There's no elevator, but the views from the observatory are worth the effort of the arduous climb. From April through June, due to high numbers, all visitors who wish to climb must first obtain a pass from the Bunker Hill Museum at 43 Monument Square. Climbing passes are free, but limited in number and offered on a first-come, first-served basis. The museum's artifacts and exhibits tell the story of the battle, while a detailed diorama shows the action in miniature. ⊠ *Monument Sq., Charlestown* ☎ *617/242–5641* ⊕ *www.nps.gov/bost/historyculture/bhm.htm* ✉ *Free* ☉ *Museum daily 9–5, monument daily 9–4:30* Ⓜ *Community College.*

FAMILY
Fodor's Choice
★

USS *Constitution*. Better known as "Old Ironsides," the USS *Constitution* usually rides proudly at anchor in her berth at the Charlestown Navy Yard. From 2015 through late 2017, however, the ship will be out of the water at Dry Dock 1 (also in the Navy Yard) for repairs, though visitors can still visit the top deck and get a rare view of its hull. The oldest commissioned ship in the U.S. fleet is a battlewagon of the old school, of the days of "wooden ships and iron men"—when she and her crew of 200 succeeded at the perilous task of asserting the sovereignty of an improbable new nation. Every July 4, she's towed out for a turnabout in Boston Harbor, the very place her keel was laid in 1797.

The venerable craft has narrowly escaped the scrap heap several times in her long history. She was launched on October 21, 1797, as part of the nation's fledgling navy. Her hull was made of live oak, the toughest wood grown in North America; her bottom was sheathed in copper, provided by Paul Revere at a nominal cost. Her principal service was during Thomas Jefferson's campaign against the Barbary pirates, off the coast of North Africa, and in the War of 1812. In 42 engagements her record was 42–0.

The nickname "Old Ironsides" was acquired during the War of 1812, when shots from the British warship *Guerrière* appeared to bounce off her hull. Talk of scrapping the ship began as early as 1830, but she was saved by a public campaign sparked by Oliver Wendell Holmes's poem "Old Ironsides." She underwent a major restoration in the early 1990s. Today she continues, the oldest commissioned warship afloat in the world, to be a part of the U.S. Navy.

The navy personnel who look after the *Constitution* maintain a 24-hour watch. Instead of taking the T, you can get closer to the ship by taking MBTA Bus 93 to Chelsea Street from Haymarket. Or you can take the Boston Harbor Cruise water shuttle from Long Wharf to Pier 4. ⊠ *Charlestown Navy Yard, 55 Constitution Rd., Charlestown* ☎ *617/242–7511* ⊕ *www.navy.mil/local/constitution/* ✉ *Free* ☉ *While in dry dock, Tues.–Sun. 10–6; Oct., Tues.–Fri. 2–6, weekends 10–6* Ⓜ *North Station.*

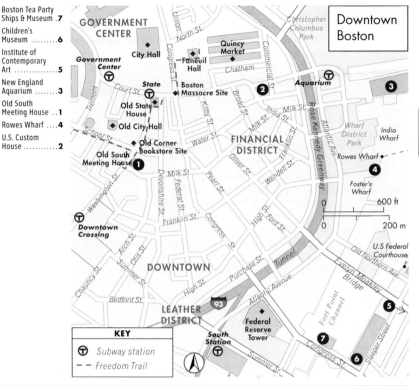

DOWNTOWN

Boston's commercial and financial districts—the area commonly called Downtown—are in a maze of streets that seem to have been laid out with little logic; they are village lanes now lined with modern 40-story office towers. Just as the Great Fire of 1872 swept the old Financial District clear, the Downtown construction in more recent times has obliterated many of the buildings where 19th-century Boston businessmen sat in front of their rolltop desks. Yet historic sites remain tucked among the skyscrapers; a number of them have been linked together to make up a fascinating section of the Freedom Trail.

The area is bordered by State Street on the north and by South Station and Chinatown on the south. Tremont Street and the Common form the west boundary, and the harbor wharves the eastern edge. Locals navigate the tangle of thoroughfares in between, but few of them manage to give intelligible directions, so carry a map.

FAMILY

Fodor's Choice

★

Boston Tea Party Ships & Museum. Located at the Congress Street Bridge where Griffin's Wharf once was, the museum is as close as possible to the actual spot where the Boston Tea Party took place on December 16, 1773. Visitors can check out *The Beaver II*, a historic reproduction of one of the ships forcibly boarded and unloaded the night Boston Harbor became a teapot, along with a reproduction of the *Eleanor,* another of the ships (the third ship, the *Dartmouth,* is under construction with no firm date set for opening). The museum is big on interaction. Actors in period costumes greet patrons, and after assigning them a Colonial persona, ask a few people to heave boxes of tea into the water. Inside, there are 3-D holograms, talking portraits, and even the Robinson Half Tea Chest, one of two original tea chests known to exist. Outside, you can explore the replicas of the ships, meet reenactors, or drink a cup of tea in Abigail's Tea Room, which has one of the best views around. ⊠ *Fort Point Channel at Congress St. Bridge, Downtown* ⊕ *www. bostonteapartyship.com* ✉ *$25 (check website for discounts)* ⊘ *Daily 10–5* Ⓜ *South Station.*

FAMILY **Children's Museum.** Most children have so much fun here that they don't
Fodor's Choice realize they're actually learning something. Creative hands-on exhibits
★ demonstrate scientific laws, cultural diversity, and problem solving. Some of the most popular stops are also the simplest, like the bubble-making machinery and the two-story climbing maze. At the Japanese House you're invited to take off your shoes and step inside a two-story silk merchant's home from Kyoto. The "Boston Black" exhibit stimulates dialogue about ethnicity and community, and children can play at a Cape Verdean restaurant and the African Queen Beauty Salon. In the toddler PlaySpace, children under three can run free in a safe environment. There's also a full schedule of special exhibits, festivals, and performances. ⊠ *308 Congress St., Downtown* ☏ *617/426–6500* ⊕ *www.bostonkids. org* ✉ *$14, Fri. 5–9 $1* ⊘ *Sat.–Thurs. 10–5, Fri. 10–9* Ⓜ *South Station.*

Fodor's Choice **Institute of Contemporary Art.** Housed in a breathtaking cantilevered edi-
★ fice that juts out over the Boston waterfront, the ICA moved to this site in 2006 as part of a massive reinvention that has made the museum one of Boston's most exciting attractions. Since its founding in 1936, the institute has cultivated its cutting-edge status: it's played host to works by Edvard Munch, Egon Schiele, and Oskar Kokoschka. Early in their careers, Andy Warhol, Robert Rauschenberg, and Roy Lichtenstein each mounted pivotal exhibitions here. The ICA's permanent collection showcases work by contemporary artists featured in ICA exhibitions, many at seminal moments in their careers. ⊠ *100 Northern Ave., South Boston* ☏ *617/478–3100* ⊕ *www.icaboston.org* ✉ *$15, free Thurs. 5–9, free for families last Sat. of every month (except Dec.)* ⊘ *Tues. and Wed. 10–5, Thurs. and Fri. 10–9, weekends 10–5. Tours on select weekends at 1 and select Thurs. at 6* Ⓜ *Courthouse.*

FAMILY **New England Aquarium.** This aquarium challenges you to imagine life
Fodor's Choice under and around the sea. Its glass-and-steel exterior is constructed to
★ mimic fish scales, and seals bark outside. Inside the main facility you'll see penguins, sea otters, sharks, and other exotic sea creatures—more than 30,000 animals, with 800 different species.

In the semi-enclosed outdoor space of the New Balance Foundation Marine Mammal Center, visitors can enjoy the antics of northern fur seals and sea lions while gazing out at Boston Harbor.

The real showstopper, though, is the four-story, 200,000-gallon ocean-reef tank, one of the largest of its kind in the world, which was renovated in 2013. Ramps winding around the tank lead to the top level and allow you to view the inhabitants from many vantage points. Up top, the new Yawkey Coral Reef Center features a seven-tank exhibit gallery that gives a close-up look at animals that might not be easily seen on the reef. Don't miss the five-times-a-day feedings; each lasts nearly an hour and takes divers 24 feet into the tank.

The aquarium has one of the largest exhibits of jellies in the country, with thousands of jellyfish (some grown in the museum's labs).

Get up close to sharks and rays at the Trust Family Foundation Shark and Ray Touch Tank, the largest of its kind on the East Coast. The Blue Planet Action Center is an interactive educational experience where visitors have the chance to see shark and lobster nurseries.

At the Edge of the Sea exhibit children can gingerly pick up starfish and other creatures. Whale-watch cruises leave from the aquarium's dock from April to October, and cost $45. The 6½-story-high IMAX theater takes you on virtual journeys from the bottom of the sea to the depths of outer space with its 3-D films.

If you are planning to see an IMAX show as well as check out the aquarium, buy a combo ticket; you'll save $5 for the adult ticket. Similarly, you'll save $12 with a combo ticket for the Aquarium and the whale-watch. ■ TIP➔ **Save yourself the torture of waiting in long weekend or summer season lines, and purchase your timed tickets in advance; you can even print them at home.** ⊠ *1 Central Wharf, between Central and Milk Sts., Downtown* ☎ *617/973–5200* ⊕ *www.neaq.org* 🎫 *$26.95, IMAX $9.95* ☉ *July–early Sept., Sun.–Thurs. 9–6, Fri. and Sat. 9–7; early Sept.–June, weekdays 9–5, weekends 9–6* Ⓜ *Aquarium, State.*

Old South Meeting House. This is the second-oldest church building in Boston, and were it not for Longfellow's celebration of the Old North in "Paul Revere's Ride," it might well be the most famous. Some of the fiercest of the town meetings that led to the Revolution were held here, culminating in the gathering of December 16, 1773, which was called by Samuel Adams to confront the crisis of three ships, laden with dutiable tea, anchored at Griffin's Wharf. The activists wanted the tea returned to England, but the governor would not permit it—and the rest is history. To cries of "Boston Harbor a teapot tonight!" and John Hancock's "Let every man do what is right in his own eyes," the protesters poured out of the Old South, headed to the wharf with their waiting comrades, and dumped 18,000 pounds' worth of tea into the water.

One of the earliest members of the congregation was an African slave named Phillis Wheatley, who had been educated by her owners. In 1773 a book of her poems was printed (by a London publisher), making her the first published African American poet. She later traveled to London, where she was received as a celebrity, but was again overtaken by poverty and died in obscurity at age 31.

The church suffered no small amount of indignity in the Revolution: its pews were ripped out by occupying British troops, and the interior was used for riding exercises by General John Burgoyne's light dragoons. A century later it escaped destruction in the Great Fire of 1872, only to be threatened with demolition by developers. Interestingly, it was the first successful preservation effort in New England. The building opened as an independent, nonprofit museum in 1877 and contains the last remaining example of a two-tiered gallery in a New England meetinghouse. The pulpit is a combination of two pulpits that were both original to the meetinghouse during points in the Victorian era. The white barrel portion of the pulpit dates from 1858 and the mahogany wine glass portion in the front dates from 1808.

The **Voices of Protest** exhibit celebrates Old South as a forum for free speech from Revolutionary days to the present. ⊠ *310 Washington St., Downtown* ☎ *617/482–6439* ⊕ *www.oldsouthmeetinghouse. org* 🎟 *$6* ☉ *Apr.–Oct., daily 9:30–5; Nov.–Mar., daily 10–4* Ⓜ *State, Downtown Crossing.*

Rowes Wharf. Take a Beacon Hill redbrick town house, blow it up to the *n*th power, and you get this 15-story Skidmore, Owings & Merrill extravaganza from 1987, one of the more welcome additions to the Boston Harbor skyline. From under the complex's gateway six-story arch, you can get great views of Boston Harbor and the yachts docked at the marina. Water shuttles pull up here from Logan Airport—the most intriguing way to enter the city. A windswept stroll along the HarborWalk waterfront promenade at dusk makes for an unforgettable sunset on clear days. ⊠ *Atlantic Ave. south of India Wharf, Waterfront* Ⓜ *Aquarium.*

U.S. Custom House. This 1847 structure resembles a Greek Revival temple that appears to have sprouted a tower. It's just that. This is the work of architects Ammi Young and Isaiah Rogers—at least, the bottom part is. The tower was added in 1915, at which time the Custom House became Boston's tallest building. It remains one of the most visible and best-loved structures in the city's skyline. To appreciate the grafting job, go inside and look at the domed rotunda. The outer surface of that dome was once the roof of the building, but now the dome is embedded in the base of the tower.

The federal government moved out of the Custom House in 1987 and sold it to the city of Boston, which, in turn, sold it to the Marriott Corporation, which has converted the building into hotel space and luxury time-share units, a move that disturbed some historical purists. You can now sip a cocktail in the hotel's Counting Room Lounge after 6 pm, or visit the 26th-floor observation deck for a fee at 2 pm. The magnificent Rotunda Room sports maritime prints and antique artifacts, courtesy of the Peabody Essex Museum in Salem. ⊠ *3 McKinley Sq., Downtown* ☎ *617/310–6300* 🎟 *$5* Ⓜ *State, Aquarium.*

THE BACK BAY

In the folklore of American neighborhoods, the Back Bay stands as a symbol of propriety and high social standing. Before the 1850s it really was a bay, a tidal flat that formed the south bank of a distended Charles River. The filling in of land along the isthmus that joined Boston to the mainland (the Neck) began in 1850, and resulted in the creation of the South End. To the north a narrow causeway called the Mill Dam (later Beacon Street) was built in 1814 to separate the Back Bay from the Charles. By the late 1800s Bostonians had filled in the shallows to as far as the marshland known as the Fenway, and the original 783-acre peninsula had been expanded by about 450 acres. Thus the waters of Back Bay became the neighborhood of Back Bay.

Heavily influenced by the then-recent rebuilding of Paris according to the plans of Baron Georges-Eugène Haussmann, the Back Bay planners created thoroughfares that resemble Parisian boulevards. Almost immediately, fashionable families began to decamp from Beacon Hill and South End and establish themselves in the Back Bay's brick and brownstone row houses. By 1900 the streets between the Public Garden and Massachusetts Avenue had become the smartest, most desirable neighborhood in all of Boston.

Today the area retains its posh spirit, but mansions are no longer the main draw. Locals and tourists flock to the commercial streets of Boylston and Newbury to shop at boutiques, galleries, and the usual mall stores. Many of the bars and restaurants have patio seating and bay windows. The Boston Public Library, Symphony Hall, and numerous churches ensure that high culture is not lost amid the frenzy of consumerism.

TOP ATTRACTIONS

FAMILY
Fodor's Choice
★

Boston Public Garden. Keep in mind that the Boston Public Garden and Boston Common (not Commons!) are two separate entities with different histories and purposes and a distinct boundary between them at Charles Street. The Common has been public land since Boston was founded in 1630, whereas the Public Garden belongs to a newer Boston, occupying what had been salt marshes on the edge of the Common. By 1837 the tract was covered with an abundance of ornamental plantings donated by a group of private citizens. The area was defined in 1856 by the building of Arlington Street, and in 1860 the architect George Meacham was commissioned to plan the park.

The central feature of the Public Garden is its irregularly shaped pond, intended to appear, from any vantage point along its banks, much larger than its nearly 4 acres. The pond has been famous since 1877 for its foot-pedal-powered (by a captain) **Swan Boats** (⊕ *swanboats.com*), which make leisurely cruises during warm months. The pond is favored by ducks and swans, and for the modest price of a few boat rides you can amuse children here for an hour or more. Near the Swan Boat dock is what has been described as the world's smallest suspension bridge, designed in 1867 to cross the pond at its narrowest point.

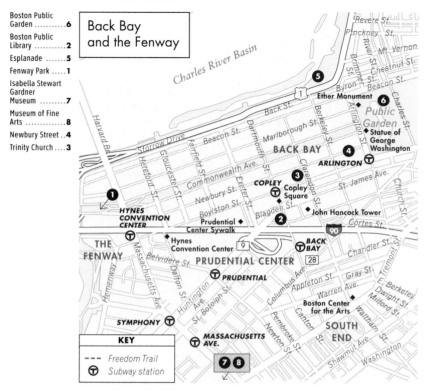

Back Bay
and the Fenway

The Public Garden is America's oldest botanical garden, and is replete with gorgeous formal plantings. The beds along the main walkways are replanted for spring and summer. The tulips during the first two weeks of May are especially colorful, and there's a sampling of native and European tree species.

The dominant work among the park's statuary is Thomas Ball's equestrian **George Washington** (1869), which faces the head of Commonwealth Avenue at the Arlington Street gate. This is Washington in a triumphant pose as liberator, surveying a scene that, from where he stood with his cannons at Dorchester Heights, would have included an immense stretch of blue water. Several dozen yards to the north of Washington (to the right if you're facing Commonwealth Avenue) is the granite-and-red-marble **Ether Monument,** donated in 1866 by Thomas Lee to commemorate the advent of anesthesia 20 years earlier at nearby Massachusetts General Hospital (you can visit the hospital to this day and see the famous Ether Dome). Other Public Garden monuments include statues of the Unitarian preacher and transcendentalist William Ellery Channing, at the corner opposite his Arlington Street Church; Edward Everett Hale, the author (*The Man Without a Country*) and philanthropist, at the Charles Street Gate; and the abolitionist senator

Charles Sumner and the Civil War hero Colonel Thomas Cass, along Boylston Street.

The park contains a special delight for the young at heart; follow the children quack-quacking along the pathway between the pond and the park entrance at Charles and Beacon streets to the *Make Way for Ducklings* bronzes sculpted by Nancy Schön, a tribute to the 1941 classic children's story by Robert McCloskey. ⊠ *Bounded by Arlington, Boylston, Charles, and Beacon Sts., Back Bay* ☎ 617/522–1966 *Swan Boats* ⊕ *friendsofthepublicgarden.org/* 🎟 *Swan Boats $3.50* ☉ *Swan Boats mid-Apr.–June 20, daily 10–4; June 21–Labor Day, daily 10–5; day after Labor Day–mid-Sept., weekdays noon–4, weekends 10–4* Ⓜ *Arlington.*

Fodor'sChoice
★ **Boston Public Library.** This venerable institution is a handsome temple to literature and a valuable research library. The Renaissance Revival building was opened in 1895; a 1972 addition emulates the mass and proportion of the original, though not its extraordinary detail; this skylighted annex houses the library's circulating collections.

You don't need a library card to enjoy the magnificent art. The murals at the head of the staircase, depicting the nine muses, are the work of the French artist Puvis de Chavannes; those in the book-request processing room to the right are Edwin Abbey's interpretations of the Holy Grail legend. Upstairs, in the public areas leading to the fine-arts, music, and rare-books collections, is John Singer Sargent's mural series on the *Triumph of Religion,* shining with renewed color after its cleaning and restoration in 2003. The corridor leading from the annex opens onto the Renaissance-style **courtyard**—an exact copy of the one in Rome's Palazzo della Cancelleria—around which the original library is built. A covered arcade furnished with chairs rings a fountain; you can bring books or lunch into the courtyard, which is open all the hours the library is open, and escape the bustle of the city. Beyond the courtyard is the main entrance hall of the 1895 building, with its immense stone lions by Louis St. Gaudens, vaulted ceiling, and marble staircase. The corridor at the top of the stairs leads to **Bates Hall,** one of Boston's most sumptuous interior spaces. This is the main reference reading room, 218 feet long with a barrel-arch ceiling 50 feet high. ⊠ *700 Boylston St., at Copley Sq., Back Bay* ☎ 617/536–5400 ⊕ *www.bpl.org* ☉ *Mon.–Thurs. 9–9, Fri. and Sat. 9–5, Sun. 1–5. Free guided art and architecture tours Mon. at 2:30, Tues. and Thurs. at 6, Wed., Fri., and Sat. at 11, Sun. at 2* Ⓜ *Copley.*

QUICK BITES
Courtyard. You can take a lunch break at the Courtyard or the MapRoom Café, adjoining restaurants in the Boston Public Library. Breakfast and lunch are served in the 1895 map room, and the main restaurant, which overlooks the courtyard, is open for lunch and afternoon tea. ⊠ *700 Boylston St., at Copley Sq., Back Bay* ☎ *617/859–2251* ⊕ *www. thecateredaffair.com/bpl/courtyard* ☉ *Courtyard: weekdays 11:30–2:30 for lunch, Wed.–Fri. 2–4 for tea. MapRoom Café: Mon.–Sat. 9–5.*

Shoppers take a break at a Newbury Street café.

Museum of Fine Arts. Count on staying a while if you have any hope of seeing what's here. Eclecticism and thoroughness, often an incompatible pair, have coexisted agreeably at the MFA since its earliest days. From Renaissance and baroque masters to Impressionist marvels, African masks and sublime samples of Native American pottery to contemporary crafts, the collections are happily shorn of both cultural snobbery and shortsighted trendiness.

The MFA's collection of approximately 450,000 objects was built from a core of paintings and sculpture from the Boston Athenaeum, historical portraits from the city of Boston, and donations by area universities. The MFA has more than 70 works by John Singleton Copley; major paintings by Winslow Homer, John Singer Sargent, Fitz Henry Lane, and Edward Hopper; and a wealth of American works ranging from native New England folk art and Colonial portraiture to New York abstract expressionism of the 1950s and 1960s.

More than 30 galleries contain the MFA's European painting and sculpture collection, dating from the 11th century to the 20th. Contemporary art has a dynamic home in the MFA's dramatic I. M. Pei–designed building.

The year-round cocktail party "MFA First Fridays," from 6 to 9:30—held monthly—has become quite the social event. Stop by to admire the art in a festive atmosphere. A fun midweek event called "Winedays," held on the last Wednesday of the month from 5:30 to 7:30, is offered February through October, when you can sample wine and snacks for $25. ■ TIP→ The museum requires you to check any bag larger than 11 inches by 15 inches (even purses). ⊠ *465 Huntington Ave., The Fenway*

☎ *617/267–9300* ⊕ *www.mfa.org* ✉ *$25 (good for 2 days in a 10-day period)* ☉ *Sat.–Tues. 10–4:45, Wed.–Fri. 10–9:45. 1-hr tours daily; call for scheduled times* Ⓜ *Museum.*

Fodor's Choice **Trinity Church.** In his 1877 masterpiece, architect Henry Hobson Richard-
★ son brought his Romanesque Revival style to maturity; all the aesthetic elements for which he was famous come together magnificently—bold polychromatic masonry, careful arrangement of masses, sumptuously carved interior woodwork—in this crowning centerpiece of Copley Square. A full appreciation of its architecture requires an understanding of the logistical problems of building it here. The Back Bay is a reclaimed wetland with a high water table. Bedrock, or at least stable glacial till, lies far beneath wet clay. Like all older Back Bay buildings, Trinity Church sits on submerged wooden pilings. But its central tower weighs 9,500 tons, and most of the 4,500 pilings beneath the building are under that tremendous central mass. The pilings are checked regularly for sinkage by means of a hatch in the basement.

Richardson engaged some of the best artists of his day—John LaFarge, William Morris, and Edward Burne-Jones among them—to execute the paintings and stained glass that make this a monument to everything that was right about the pre-Raphaelite spirit and the nascent aesthetic of Morris's Arts and Crafts movement. LaFarge's intricate paintings and ornamented ceilings received a much-needed overhaul during the extensive renovations completed in 2005. Along the north side of the church, note the Augustus Saint-Gaudens statue of Phillips Brooks—the most charismatic rector in New England, who almost single-handedly got Trinity built and furnished. Shining light of Harvard's religious community and lyricist of "O Little Town of Bethlehem," Brooks is shown here with Christ touching his shoulder in approval. For a nice respite, try to catch one of the Friday organ concerts beginning at 12:15. The 11:15 Sunday service is usually followed by a free guided tour. ✉ *206 Clarendon St., Back Bay* ☎ *617/536–0944* ⊕ *trinitychurchboston.org* ✉ *Entrance free, guided and self-guided tours $7* ☉ *Sept.–June, Mon., Fri., and Sat. 9–5, Tues.–Thurs. 9–6, Sun. 1–6; services Sun. at 7:45, 9, and 11:15 am and 6 pm. Self-guided tours ongoing; guided tours take place several times daily; call to confirm times. Last admission 30 mins prior to closing. Hrs change slightly in summer* Ⓜ *Copley.*

WORTH NOTING

FAMILY **Esplanade.** Near the corner of Beacon and Arlington streets, the Arthur Fiedler Footbridge crosses Storrow Drive to the 3-mile-long Esplanade and the **Hatch Memorial Shell**. The free concerts here in summer include the Boston Pops' immensely popular televised July 4 performance. For shows like this, Bostonians haul lawn chairs and blankets to the lawn in front of the shell; so bring a takeout lunch from a nearby restaurant, find an empty spot—no mean feat, so come early—and you'll feel right at home. An impressive stone bust of the late maestro Arthur Fiedler watches over the walkers, joggers, picnickers, and sunbathers who fill the Esplanade's paths on pleasant days. Here, too, is the turn-of-the-20th-century **Union Boat Club Boathouse,** headquarters

for the country's oldest private rowing club. ⊠ *Back Bay* ⊕ *www. esplanadeassociation.org.*

Newbury Street. Eight-block-long Newbury Street has been compared to New York's 5th Avenue, and certainly this is the city's poshest shopping area, with branches of Chanel, Diane von Furstenberg, Burberry, Jack Spade, Marc Jacobs, and other top names in fashion. But here the pricey boutiques are more intimate than grand, and people live above the trendy restaurants and ubiquitous hair salons, giving the place a neighborhood feel. Toward the Massachusetts Avenue end, cafés proliferate and the stores get funkier, ending with Newbury Comics and Urban Outfitters. ⊠ *From Arlington St. to Massachusetts Ave., Back Bay* ⊕ *www.newbury-st.com/* Ⓜ *Hynes, Copley.*

THE FENWAY

The marshland known as the Back Bay Fens gave this section of Boston its name, but two quirky institutions give it its character: Fenway Park, home of Boston's beloved Red Sox, and the Isabella Stewart Gardner Museum, the legacy of a high-living Brahmin who attended a concert at Symphony Hall in 1912 wearing a headband that read, "Oh, You Red Sox." Not far from the Gardner is another major cultural magnet: the Museum of Fine Arts. Kenmore Square, a favorite haunt for Boston University students, adds a bit of funky flavor to the mix.

Fodor's Choice ★ **Fenway Park.** For 86 years, the Boston Red Sox suffered a World Series dry spell, a streak of bad luck that fans attributed to the "Curse of the Bambino," which, stories have it, struck the team in 1920 when they sold Babe Ruth (the "Bambino") to the New York Yankees. All that changed in 2004, when a maverick squad broke the curse in a thrilling seven-game series against the team's nemesis in the series semifinals. This win against the Yankees was followed by a four-game sweep of St. Louis in the finals. Boston, and its citizens' ingrained sense of pessimism, hasn't been the same since. The repeat World Series win in 2007, and again in 2013, cemented Bostonians' sense that the universe had finally begun working correctly and made Red Sox caps the residents' semiofficial uniform. ⊠ *4 Yawkey Way, between Van Ness and Lansdowne Sts., The Fenway* ☎ *877/733–7699 box office, 617/226–6666 tours* ⊕ *www.redsox.com* 🎫 *Tours $18* ⊗ *Tours run daily 9–5, on the hr. Tickets are sold first-come, first served* Ⓜ *Kenmore.*

Fodor's Choice ★ **Isabella Stewart Gardner Museum.** A spirited society woman, Isabella Stewart came in 1860 from New York to marry John Lowell Gardner, one of Boston's leading citizens. "Mrs. Jack" promptly set about becoming the most un-Bostonian of the Proper Bostonians. She built a Venetian palazzo to hold her collected arts in one of Boston's newest neighborhoods. Her will stipulated that the building remain exactly as she left it—paintings, furniture, and the smallest object in a hall cabinet—and that is as it has remained.

Gardner's palazzo includes such masterpieces as Titian's *Europa*, Giotto's *Presentation of Christ in the Temple*, Piero della Francesca's *Hercules*, and John Singer Sargent's *El Jaleo*. Spanish leather panels,

Renaissance hooded fireplaces, and Gothic tapestries accent salons; eight balconies adorn the majestic Venetian courtyard. There's a Raphael Room, Spanish Cloister, Gothic Room, Chinese Loggia, and a magnificent Tapestry Room for concerts, where Gardner entertained Henry James and Edith Wharton.

On March 18, 1990, the Gardner was the target of a sensational art heist. Thieves disguised as police officers stole 12 works, including Vermeer's *The Concert*. None of the art has been recovered, despite a $5 million reward. Because Mrs. Gardner's will prohibited substituting other works for any stolen art, empty expanses of wall identify spots where the paintings once hung.

An addition to the museum opened in 2012. The Renzo Piano–designed building houses a music hall, exhibit space, and conservation labs, where Gardner's works can be repaired and preserved.

A quirk of the museum's admission policy waives entrance fees to anyone named Isabella and on your birthday. And if you've visited the MFA in the two days prior to your trip here, there's a $2 admission-fee discount.

Allot two hours to tour the museum properly, and note that the collections generally appeal to a "grown-up" audience, so there isn't much for young children here. If you're looking for a light lunch after your tour, visit Cafe G near the gift shop. ⊠ *280 The Fenway, The Fenway* ☎ *617/566–1401, 617/566–1088 café* ⊕ *www.gardnermuseum. org* 🎫 *$15* ⊘ *Museum Wed. and Fri.–Mon. 11–5, Thurs. 11–9; café Tues.–Fri. 11:30–4, weekends 11–4* Ⓜ *Museum.*

CAMBRIDGE

Across the Charles River is the überliberal academic enclave of Cambridge. The city is punctuated at one end by the funky tech-noids of MIT and at the other by the grand academic fortress that is Harvard University. Civic life connects the two camps into an urban stew of 100,000 residents who represent nearly every nationality in the world, work at every kind of job from tenured professor to taxi driver, and are passionate about living on this side of the river.

The Charles River is the Cantabrigians' backyard, and there's virtually no place in Cambridge more than a 10-minute walk from its banks. Strolling, running, or biking here is one of the great pleasures of Cambridge, and views include graceful bridges, the distant Boston skyline, crew teams rowing through the calm water, and the elegant spires of Harvard soaring into the sky.

No visit to Cambridge is complete without an afternoon in Harvard Square. It's home to every variation of the human condition; Nobel laureates, homeless buskers, trust-fund babies, and working-class Joes mill around the same piece of real estate. Walk down Brattle Street past Henry Wadsworth Longfellow's house. Farther along Massachusetts Avenue is Central Square, an ethnic melting pot of people and restaurants. Ten minutes more brings you to MIT, with its eclectic architecture from postwar pedestrian to Frank Gehry's futuristic fantasyland. In

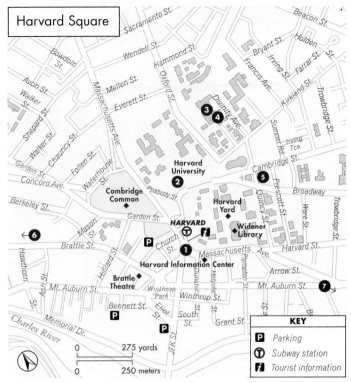

addition to providing a stellar view, the Massachusetts Avenue Bridge, spanning the Charles from Cambridge to Boston, is also notorious in MIT lore for its Smoot measurements.

Fodor's Choice ★ **Harvard Art Museums.** In late 2014, the combined collections of the Busch-Reisinger and Fogg museums (which closed in 2008) and the Arthur M. Sackler Museum (which closed in 2013) reopened under one glorious mostly glass roof, under the umbrella name Harvard Art Museums. Housed in a facility designed by award-winning architect Renzo Piano, the 204,000-square-foot museum is spread over seven levels, allowing more of Harvard's 250,000-piece art collection to be seen in one place. Highlights include American and European paintings, sculptures, and decorative arts from the Fogg Museum; and works by German expressionists, materials related to the Bauhaus, and postwar contemporary art from German-speaking Europe from the Busch-Reisinger Museum. In addition to the gallery spaces, there's a 300-seat theater, a café, plus conservation and research labs. ⊠ *32 Quincy St., Harvard Square* ☎ *617/495–9400* ⊕ *www.harvardartmuseums.org* ☑ *$15* ⊙ *Daily 10–5* Ⓜ *Harvard.*

FAMILY
Fodor's Choice ★ **Harvard Museum of Natural History.** In 2012, Harvard University created a new consortium, the Harvard Museums of Science & Culture, uniting under one administration several of its most visited public museums.

DID YOU KNOW?

The Harvard Museum of Natural History's collection includes 21 million specimens, but only a small sample is on display. An active lecture and family program means there's plenty of opportunity to interact with another local species— the Harvard researcher.

The Harvard Museum of Natural History (which exhibits specimens from the Museum of Comparative Zoology, Harvard University Herbaria, and the Mineralogical and Geological Museum) displays some 12,000 specimens, including dinosaurs, rare minerals, hundreds of mammals and birds, and Harvard's world-famous Blaschka Glass Flowers. The museum combines historic exhibits drawn from the university's vast collections with new and changing multimedia exhibitions such as *New England Forests and Mollusks: Shelled Masters of the Marine Realm,* and the renovated Earth & Planetary Sciences gallery. ⊠ *26 Oxford St., Harvard Square* ☎ *617/495–3045* ⊕ *www.hmnh.harvard. edu* ✉ *$12; ticket includes admission to adjacent Peabody Museum* ⊗ *Daily 9–5* Ⓜ *Harvard.*

FAMILY

Fodor's Choice

★

Harvard Square. Tides of students, tourists, political-cause proponents, and bizarre street creatures are all part of the nonstop pedestrian flow at this most celebrated of Cambridge crossroads.

Harvard Square is where Massachusetts Avenue, coming from Boston, turns and widens into a triangle broad enough to accommodate a brick peninsula (above the T station). The restored 1928 kiosk in the center of the square once served as the entrance to the MBTA station. Harvard Yard, with its lecture halls, residential houses, libraries, and museums, is one long border of the square; the other three are composed of clusters of banks and a wide variety of restaurants and shops.

On an average afternoon you'll hear earnest conversations in dozens of foreign languages; see every kind of youthful uniform from Goth to impeccable prep; wander by street musicians playing Andean flutes, and doing excellent Stevie Wonder or Edith Piaf imitations; and watch an outdoor game of pickup chess between a street-tough kid and an older gent wearing a beret. An afternoon in the square is people-watching raised to high art.

The historic buildings are worth noting. It's a thrill to walk though the big brick-and-wrought-iron gates to Harvard Yard on up to Widener Library.

Across Garden Street, through an ornamental arch, is **Cambridge Common,** decreed a public pasture in 1631. It's said that under a large tree that once stood in this meadow George Washington took command of the Continental Army on July 3, 1775. A stone memorial now marks the site of the "Washington Elm." Also on the Common is the Irish Famine Memorial by Derry artist Maurice Herron, unveiled in 1997 to coincide with the 150th anniversary of "Black '47," the deadliest year of the potato famine. At the center of the Common a large memorial commemorates the Union soldiers who lost their lives in the Civil War. On the far side of the Common is a fantastic park. ⊠ *Harvard Square* ⊕ *www.harvardsquare.com* Ⓜ *Harvard.*

QUICK BITES

Broadway Marketplace. The Broadway Marketplace is just around the corner from Harvard Yard. Besides the excellent fresh produce, there's a selection of sandwiches and prepared meals; choose one to be heated up and then grab a seat for a quick, delicious (if pricey) bite. Every Thursday (5–7 pm), there's a wine, beer, or liquor tasting, a great way to mingle with locals. ✉ *468 Broadway, Harvard Square* ☎ *617/547–2334* ⊕ *www. broadwaymarketplace.com* ⊘ *Mon.–Sat. 7 am–9 pm, Sun. 8:30–8* Ⓜ *Harvard.*

Harvard University. The tree-studded, shady, and redbrick expanse of Harvard Yard—the very center of Harvard University—has weathered the footsteps of Harvard students for hundreds of years. In 1636 the Great and General Court of the Massachusetts Bay Colony voted funds to establish the colony's first college, and a year later chose Cambridge as the site. Named in 1639 for John Harvard, a young Charlestown clergyman who died in 1638 and left the college his entire library and half his estate, Harvard remained the only college in the New World until 1693, by which time it was firmly established as a respected center of learning. Local wags refer to Harvard as WGU—World's Greatest University—and it's certainly the oldest and most famous American university.

Although the college dates from the 17th century, the oldest buildings in Harvard Yard are from the 18th century (though you'll sometimes see archaeologists digging here for evidence of older structures). Together the buildings chronicle American architecture from the Colonial era to the present. **Holden Chapel,** completed in 1744, is a Georgian gem. The graceful **University Hall** was designed in 1815 by Charles Bulfinch. An 1884 statue of John Harvard by Daniel Chester French stands outside; ironically for a school with the motto of "Veritas" ("Truth"), the model for the statue was a member of the class of 1882 and not Harvard himself. **Sever Hall,** completed in 1880 and designed by Henry Hobson Richardson, represents the Romanesque revival that was followed by the neoclassical (note the pillared facade of Widener Library) and the neo-Georgian, represented by the sumptuous brick houses along the Charles River, many of which are now undergraduate residences. **Memorial Church,** a graceful steepled edifice of modified Colonial Revival design, was dedicated in 1932. Just north of the Yard is **Memorial Hall,** completed in 1878 as a memorial to Harvard men who died in the Union cause; it's High Victorian both inside and out. It also contains the 1,166-seat Sanders Theatre, which serves as the university's largest lecture hall, site of year-round concerts by students and professionals, and the venue for the festive Christmas Revels.

Many of Harvard's cultural and scholarly facilities are important sights in themselves, but most campus buildings, other than museums and concert halls, are off-limits to the general public.

The **Harvard Information Center,** in the Smith Campus Centre, has a small exhibit space, distributes maps of the university area, and offers free student-led tours of Harvard Yard. The tour doesn't include visits to museums, and it doesn't take you into campus buildings, but it provides a fine orientation. The information center is open year-round (except during spring recess and other semester breaks). From the end of June through August, guides offer tours every half hour; however, it's best to call ahead to confirm times. ✉ *Bounded by Massachusetts Ave. and Mt. Auburn, Holyoke, and Dunster Sts., 1350 Massachusetts Ave., Harvard Square* ☎ *617/495–1573 Information Center* ⊕ *www.harvard.edu*

⊙ *Information Center: Mon.–Sat. 9–5 (except during school breaks). Tours: Sept.–May, Mon.–Sat. 10–4* Ⓜ *Harvard.*

Longfellow House-Washington's Headquarters. If there's one historic house to visit in Cambridge, this is it. Henry Wadsworth Longfellow, the poet whose stirring tales of the Village Blacksmith, Evangeline, Hiawatha, and Paul Revere's midnight ride thrilled 19th-century America, once lived in this elegant mansion. One of several original Tory Row homes on Brattle Street, the house was built in 1759 by John Vassall Jr., and George Washington lived (and slept!) here during the Siege of Boston from July 1775 to April 1776. Longfellow first boarded here in 1837 and later received the house as a gift from his father-in-law on his marriage to Frances Appleton, who burned to death here in an accident in 1861. For 45 years Longfellow wrote his famous verses here and filled the house with the exuberant spirit of his own work and that of his literary circle, which included Ralph Waldo Emerson, Nathaniel Hawthorne, and Charles Sumner, an abolitionist senator. Longfellow died in 1882, but his presence in the house lives on—from the Longfellow family furniture to the wallpaper to the books on the shelves (many the poet's own). The home is preserved and run by the National Park Service; free 45-minute guided tours of the house are offered hourly. The formal garden is the perfect place to relax. Longfellow Park, across the street, is the place to stand to take photos of the house. The park was created to preserve the view immortalized in the poet's "To the River Charles." ✉ *105 Brattle St., Harvard Square* ☎ *617/876–4491* ⊕ *www. nps.gov/long* 🎫 *Free* ⊙ *Grounds daily dawn–dusk; house Memorial Day–Labor Day, Wed.–Sun. 9:30–5. Last tour at 4* Ⓜ *Harvard.*

Massachusetts Institute of Technology. Founded in 1861, MIT moved to Cambridge from Copley Square in the Back Bay in 1916. Once dissed as "the factory," particularly by its Ivy League neighbor, Harvard University, MIT mints graduates that are the sharp blades on the edge of the information revolution. It's perennially in the top five of U.S. News and World Report's college rankings. It has long since fulfilled the predictions of its founder, the geologist William Barton Rogers, that it would surpass "the universities of the land in the accuracy and the extent of its teachings in all branches of positive science." Its emphasis shifted in the 1930s from practical engineering and mechanics to the outer limits of scientific fields.

Architecture is important at MIT. Although the original buildings were obviously designed by and for scientists, many represent pioneering designs of their times. The **Kresge Auditorium,** designed by Eero Saarinen, with a curving roof and unusual thrust, rests on three, instead of four, points. The nondenominational **MIT Chapel,** a circular Saarinen design, is lighted primarily by a roof oculus that focuses natural light on the altar and by reflections from the water in a small surrounding moat; it's topped by an aluminum sculpture by Theodore Roszak. The serpentine **Baker House,** now a dormitory, was designed in 1947 by the Finnish architect Alvar Aalto in such a way as to provide every room with a view of the Charles River. Sculptures by Henry Moore and other notable artists dot the campus. The latest addition is the newly minted

Green Center, punctuated by the splash of color that is Sol Lewitt's 5,500-square-foot mosaic floor.

The East Campus, which has grown around the university's original neoclassical buildings of 1916, also has outstanding modern architecture and sculpture, including the stark high-rise **Green Building** by I. M. Pei, housing the Earth Science Center. Just outside is Alexander Calder's giant stabile (a stationary mobile) *The Big Sail*. Another Pei work on the East Campus is the **Wiesner Building,** designed in 1985, which houses the **List Visual Arts Center.** Architect Frank Gehry made his mark on the campus with the cockeyed, improbable **Ray & Maria Stata Center,** a complex of buildings on Vassar Street. The center houses computer, artificial intelligence, and information systems laboratories, and is reputedly as confusing to navigate on the inside as it is to follow on the outside. East Campus's **Great Dome,** which looms over neoclassical Killian Court, has often been the target of student "hacks" and has at various times supported a telephone booth with a ringing phone, a life-size statue of a cow, and a campus police cruiser. Nearby, the domed **Rogers Building** has earned unusual notoriety as the center of a series of hallways and tunnels dubbed "the infinite corridor." Twice each winter the sun's path lines up perfectly with the corridor's axis, and at dusk students line the third-floor hallway to watch the sun set through the westernmost window. The phenomenon is known as "MIT-henge."

MIT maintains an information center in the Rogers Building, and offers free tours of the campus weekdays at 11 and 3. Check the schedule, as the tours are often suspended during school holidays. General hours for the information center are weekdays 9–5. ⊠ *77 Massachusetts Ave., Kendall Square* ☎ *617/253–4795* ⊕ *www.mit.edu* Ⓜ *Kendall/MIT.*

Peabody Museum of Archaeology & Ethnology. With one of the world's outstanding anthropological collections, the Peabody focuses on Native American and Central and South American cultures. The Hall of the North American Indian is particularly outstanding, with art, textiles, and models of traditional dwellings from across the continent. The Mesoamerican room juxtaposes ancient relief carvings and weavings with contemporary works from the Maya and other peoples. ⊠ *11 Divinity Ave., Harvard Square* ☎ *617/496–1027* ⊕ *www.peabody. harvard.edu* 💲 *$12, includes admission to Harvard Museum of Natural History, accessible through the museum; free for Massachusetts residents on Sun. 9–noon year-round and Wed. 3–5 Sept.–May (excluding commercial groups)* ⊙ *Daily 9–5* Ⓜ *Harvard.*

WHERE TO EAT

Updated by Victoria Abbott Riccardi

In a city synonymous with tradition, Boston chefs have spent recent years rewriting culinary history. The stuffy, wood-paneled formality is gone; the endless renditions of chowdah, lobster, and cod have retired. A crop of young chefs has ascended, opening small, upscale neighborhood spots that use New England ingredients to delicious effect.

Traditional eats can still be found (Durgin-Park remains as the best place to get baked beans), but many diners now gravitate toward innovative food in understated environs. Whether you're looking for casual French, down-home Southern cooking, some of the best sushi in the country, or Vietnamese *banh mi* sandwiches, Boston restaurants are ready to deliver. The fish and shellfish brought in from nearby shores continue to inform the regional cuisine: expect to see several seafood options on local menus, but don't expect them to be boiled or dumped into the lobster stew that JFK loved. Instead, you might be offered swordfish with salsa verde, cornmeal-crusted scallops, or lobster cassoulet with black truffles.

In many ways, though, Boston remains solidly skeptical of trends. If you close your eyes in the North End, Boston's Little Italy, you can easily imagine you're in Rome circa 1955. And over in the university culture of Cambridge, places like East Coast Grill and Oleana espoused the locavore and slow-food movements before they became buzzwords. *Prices in the reviews are for the average price of a main course at dinner, or if dinner is not served, at lunch.*

WHAT IT COSTS IN BOSTON

	$	$$	$$$	$$$$
AT DINNER	under $18	$18–$24	$25–$35	over $35

Use the coordinate (⊕ B2) at the end of each listing to locate a site on the Where to Eat and Stay in Boston map.

BACK BAY AND SOUTH END

$$$ SEAFOOD Fodor's Choice ★

🍴 **Atlantic Fish Co.** Designed to look like an ocean vessel with gorgeous wood finishes and nautical artwork, this local seafood restaurant delivers first-class fish, so fresh that the extensive menus are printed daily to reflect the day's catch served broiled, baked, blackened, fried, grilled, or pan-seared. Unsnap your starched napkin and begin with a platter of chilled seafood (lobster, little necks, oysters, crab, and shrimp), followed by any one of the specialties ranging from simple fried Ipswich clams to pan-seared bass with lobster ravioli in an unctuous lobster cream sauce. The sea bass chowder with bacon is a delectable alternative to the common clam-based versions around town. Steak and chicken are available for culinary landlubbers. [$] *Average main: $31* ✉ *761 Boylston St., Back Bay* ☎ *617/267–4000* 🌐 *www.atlanticfishco.com* 💳 *No credit cards* [M] *Copley* ⊕ *C5.*

$$$$ AMERICAN

🍴 **The Butcher Shop.** Chef Barbara Lynch has remade the classic meat market as a polished wine bar–cum–hangout, and it's just the kind of high-quality, low-pretense spot every neighborhood could use. Stop in for a glass of wine and a casual, quick snack of homemade prosciutto and salami or a plate of artisanal cheeses. Or, linger longer over dinner specials like tagliatelle Bolognese or a juicy prime rib eye, a hefty investment at $59, but one of the best in the city. Reservations are accepted for parties of six or more. [$] *Average main: $37* ✉ *552 Tremont St., South End* ☎ *617/423–4800* 🌐 *www.thebutchershopboston.com* [M] *Back Bay* ⊕ *E6.*

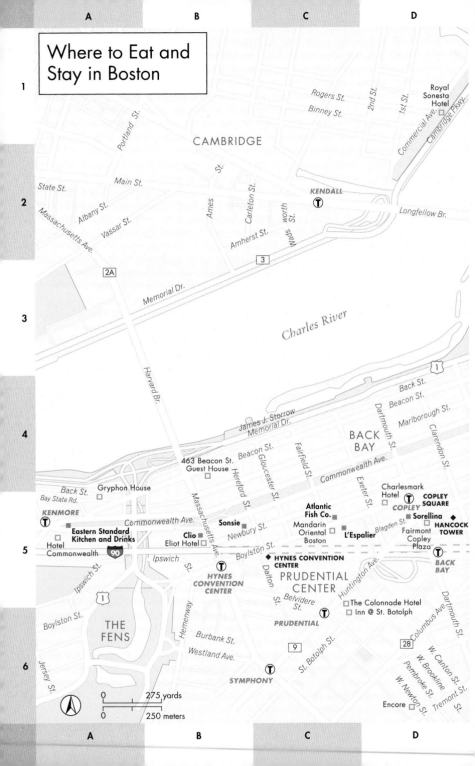

Where to Eat and Stay in Boston

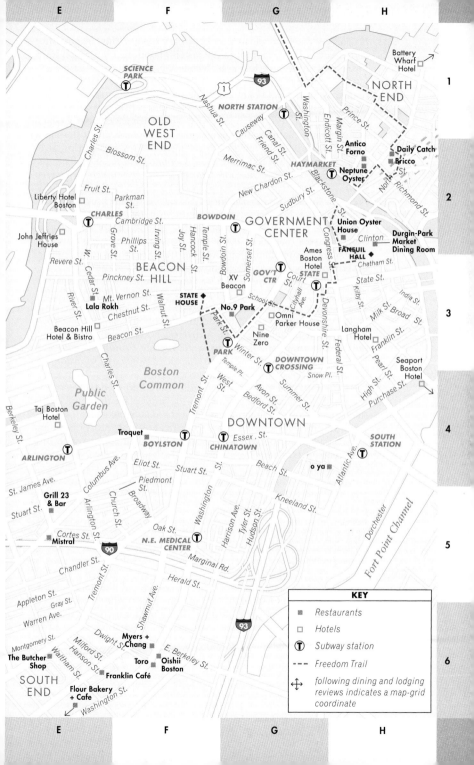

$$$$ FRENCH Fodor's Choice ★ 🍴 **Clio.** A magnet for romantics and diehard foodies, this elegant toffee-and-cream-color restaurant in the tasteful boutique Eliot Hotel transforms ingredients like foie gras, Maine lobster, and Kobe sirloin into fanciful masterpieces that appear almost too good to eat. Flavor-rich foams, emulsions, and bubbles still dominate the hyper-seasonal menu, which in addition to à la carte offerings, has a five-course ($79) and nine-course ($124) tasting menu with wine pairing available. Cocktail aficionados will appreciate the creative and sophisticated offerings at the comfy bar overlooking the tiny sister sashimi restaurant, Uni. [$] *Average main: $39* ✉ *Eliot Hotel, 370 Commonwealth Ave., Back Bay* ☎ *617/536–7200* 🌐 *www.cliorestaurant.com* ⊗ *No lunch* ✍ *Reservations essential* [M] *Hynes* ✥ *B5.*

$$$ AMERICAN Fodor's Choice ★ 🍴 **Eastern Standard Kitchen and Drinks.** A vivid red awning beckons patrons of this spacious brasserie-style restaurant open for breakfast, lunch, and dinner. The bar area and red banquettes fill most nights with Boston's power players (members of the Red Sox management are known to stop in), thirtysomethings, and students from the nearby universities all noshing on raw-bar specialties and comfort dishes such as lamb-sausage rigatoni, rib eye, and burgers. It's a Sunday brunch hot spot, especially on game days (the Big Green Monster is a very short walk away). The cocktail list ranks as one of the best in town, filled with old classics and new concoctions, and in addition to a boutique wine list you'll find a reserve list for rare beers. A covered, heated patio offers alfresco dining year-round. [$] *Average main: $25* ✉ *528 Commonwealth Ave., Kenmore Square* ☎ *617/532–9100* 🌐 *www.easternstandardboston.com* [M] *Kenmore* ✥ *A5.*

$ AMERICAN FAMILY Fodor's Choice ★ 🍴 **Flour Bakery + Café.** When folks in the South End need coffee, a great sandwich, or a raspberry crumb bar—or just a place to sit and chat—they come here. A communal table in the middle acts as a gathering spot, around which diners enjoy homemade soups, hearty bean and grain salads, and specialty sandwiches like grilled chicken with Brie, roasted peppers, caramelized onions, and arugula, or a BLT with applewood-smoked bacon. Of course, it's the irresistible sweets, like pecan sticky buns, lemon tarts, and double chocolate cookies that require a trip to Flour, which has proven so popular that owner Joanne Chang has opened three more locations—in the Fort Point Channel neighborhood, Cambridge (by MIT), and Back Bay. [$] *Average main: $9* ✉ *1595 Washington St., South End* ☎ *617/267–4300* 🌐 *www.flourbakery.com* ✍ *Reservations not accepted* [M] *Massachusetts Ave.* ✥ *E6.*

$$ AMERICAN 🍴 **The Franklin Café.** This place has jumped to the head of the class by keeping things simple yet effective. (The litmus test: local chefs gather here to wind down after work.) You can't go wrong with the skillet smoked mussels, succulent turkey meat loaf, or homey corned beef with cabbage. The vibe tends to feel more like a bar than a restaurant (hence the many bartender awards), so be forewarned that it can get loud. The wait for a table (there are only seven booths and two tables) can be downright impossible on weekend nights, and desserts are not served. On the upside, you'll be pleasantly surprised by the prices and the fact that a full menu is served until 1:30 am and cocktails until 2 am. [$] *Average main: $18*

CLOSE UP

Refueling

If you're on the go, you might want to try a local chain restaurant where you can stop for a quick bite or get some takeout. The places listed below are fairly priced, committed to quality, and use decent, fresh ingredients.

B.Good. This chainlet's avocado-and-salsa-topped veggie burgers, baked sweet-potato fries, and sesame-ginger chicken salad are redefining fast food in Boston.

Bertucci's. Thin-crust pizzas fly fast from the brick ovens here, along with pastas and a decent tiramisu.

BoLoCo. For quick, cheap, healthful, and high-quality wraps and burritos, this is easily the city's most

dependable (and also locally based) chain. BoLoCo's menu also includes smoothies and breakfast options, and its hours are some of the longest in this notoriously early-to-bed city.

Finagle A Bagel. Find fresh, doughy bagels in flavors from jalapeño cheddar to triple chocolate, plus sandwiches and salads. Service is swift and efficient.

UBurger. Better-than-average burgers with toppings that lean toward the gourmet (sautéed mushrooms, blue cheese) and a great chocolate frappe (Boston-ese for milk shake) make this spot the East Coast's answer to California's much-loved In-n-Out.

✉ *278 Shawmut Ave., South End* ☎ *617/350–0010* ⊕ *www.franklincafe. com* ⊘ *No lunch* ⊜ *Reservations not accepted* Ⓜ *Union Park* ✛ *E6.*

$$$$
STEAKHOUSE

✕ **Grill 23 & Bar.** Pinstripe suits, dark paneling, Persian rugs, and waiters in white jackets give this single-location steak house a posh tone with a big, buzzing bar overlooking Berkeley Street and a quieter, smaller one on the second floor by the cozy fireplace. Both bars serve excellent drinks, specialty Scotches, and bar bites, along with the full menu, which places a premium on seasonal, organic, sustainable, and humanely raised meats and ingredients. In addition to seasonally dressed tartares (steak and tuna) and weekly cuts of all-natural beef like the 14-ounce dry-aged New York sirloin, you'll find seafood specialties such as spicy native halibut with chimichurri that give beef sales a run for their money. Desserts, such as the decadent Valrhona chocolate layer cake, rank far above those of the average steak house. Make sure to leave room. Ⓢ *Average main: $40* ✉ *161 Berkeley St., Back Bay* ☎ *617/542–2255* ⊕ *grill23.com* ⊘ *No lunch* Ⓜ *Back Bay/ South End* ✛ *E5.*

$$$$
FRENCH
Fodor'sChoice
★

✕ **L'Espalier.** In 2008 L'Espalier left its longtime home in a Back Bay town house, reopening beside the Mandarin Oriental Hotel. The new locale, with its floor-to-ceiling windows and modern decor, looks decidedly different. But chef-owner Frank McClelland's dishes—from caviar and roasted foie gras to garlicky beef tenderloin and deconstructed lobster potpie—are as elegant as ever. In the evening, a three-course prix-fixe and various tasting menus, including a vegetarian one, tempt discriminating diners. A budget-minded power lunch as well as à la carte options are available weekday afternoons. Finger sandwiches and sublime sweets are served for weekend tea; the salon menu hits the spot for postwork drinks and nibbles, like a perfectly ripe from-age flight from the city's premier cheese trolley. $ *Average main: $150* ✉ *774 Boylston St., Back Bay* ☎ *617/262–3023* ⊕ *www.lespalier.com* ⌂ *Reservations essential* Ⓜ *Copley* ✛ *C5.*

$$$$
FRENCH
Fodor's Choice
★

✕ **Mistral.** Polished service and upscale yet unpretentious dishes, like beef-tenderloin pizza topped with mashed potatoes and white-truffle oil, make Mistral a perennial South End hot spot. Grab a table by the arched, floor-to-ceiling windows or a seat at the always-buzzing bar—either way, there'll be plenty to see in this airy white room with a Provençal-theme decor. Boston's fashionable set has been coming here for years, which speaks to chef Jamie Mammano's consistently excellent French-Mediterranean cuisine with fail-safe favorites like tuna tartare, duck with cherries, and French Dover sole. The seasonally tweaked menu rarely changes—but no one's complaining. Unlike many trendy restaurants, Mistral sticks to what it does best. A luxurious à la carte brunch is served on Sunday. $ *Average main: $36* ✉ *223 Columbus Ave., South End* ☎ *617/867–9300* ⊕ *mistralbistro.com* ☾ *No lunch* Ⓜ *Back Bay* ✛ *E5.*

$
CHINESE

✕ **Myers + Chang.** Pink and orange dragon decals cover the windows of this all-day Chinese café, where Joanne Chang (of Flour fame) has returned to her familial cooking roots. Sharable platters of creative dumplings, wok-charred udon noodles, and stir-fries brim with fresh ingredients and addictive, pungent flavors from China, Japan, Taiwan, Thailand, and Vietnam, thanks to plenty of hot chili peppers, garlic, fresh herbs, crushed peanuts, and lime. The staff is young and hip, and the crowd generally follows suit. $ *Average main: $16* ✉ *1145 Washington St., South End* ☎ *617/542–5200* ⊕ *www.myersandchang.com* Ⓜ *Back Bay* ✛ *F6.*

$$$
JAPANESE

✕ **Oishii Boston.** Although the entrance to this superb sushi restaurant may elude you, simply follow the crowds of raw fish fans streaming into the sleek, gray industrial space, where sushi chef–owner Ting Yen turns succulent morsels of seafood into edible enchantment. From tuna tartare with sesame oil and golden caviar to crunchy tempura oysters, from lobster salad maki to grilled Wagyu beef with shallot-sake sauce, this larger, tonier incarnation of Yen's überpopular 14-seat restaurant Oishii in Chestnut Hill allows him to spread his wings. The vibe is hip and so are the diners. While the delectable nine-course *omakase* (chef's tasting) is quite a splurge ($150 and $225 paired with sake), the set lunch specials (*kaiseki*) offer fabulous value. $ *Average main: $30* ✉ *1166 Washington St., South End* ☎ *617/482–8868* ⊕ *www.oishiiboston.com* ⊟ *No credit cards* ☾ *Closed Mon.* Ⓜ *East Berkeley* ✛ *F6.*

$$$
AMERICAN

✕ **Sonsie.** Café society blossoms along Newbury Street, particularly at Sonsie, where a well-heeled crowd sips coffee up front or angles for places at the bar. Lunch and dinner dishes, such as grilled pork chop with creamy hominy and pickled fruit are basic bistro fare with an American twist. The restaurant is a terrific place for weekend brunch, when the light pours through the long windows, and is at its most vibrant in warm weather, when the open doors make for colorful people-watching. A downstairs wine room, meanwhile, offers more intimacy. The late-night pizza and dessert menu (nightly until 12:30 am) is perfect for after-hours cravings. $ *Average main: $25* ⊠ *327 Newbury St., Back Bay* ☎ *617/351–2500* ⊕ *sonsieboston.com* Ⓜ *Hynes* ✛ *B5.*

$$$$
ITALIAN
✕ **Sorellina.** Everything about this upscale Italian spot is oversized, from its space near Copley Square to its portions. The sexy, all-white dining room is filled with well-heeled locals (some live in the gorgeous apartment building above it) who come for the modern twist on basic Italian dishes. Grilled octopus with squid-ink couscous, various versions of carpaccio, and the signature tuna tartare dot the list of starters, while veal saltimbocca with wild mushrooms and truffled whipped potato takes the spotlight for entrées. Just save room for dessert: it's always a highlight here. $ *Average main: $41* ⊠ *1 Huntington Ave., Back Bay* ☎ *617/412–4600* ⊕ *www.sorellinaboston.com* ☉ *No lunch* Ⓜ *Copley, Back Bay* ✛ *D5.*

$$$
SPANISH
Fodor'sChoice
★
✕ **Toro.** The opening buzz from chefs Ken Oringer and Jamie Bissonnette's tapas joint, which now has an outpost in Manhattan, still remains loud—for good reason. Small plates such as grilled corn with aioli and cotija cheese are hefty enough to make a meal out of a few, or you can share the regular or vegetarian paella with a group. A predominantly Spanish wine list complements the plates. Crowds have been known to wait it out for more than an hour for dinner, which is on a first-come, first-served basis. Aim to go for lunch during the week for a less hectic, but just as satisfying experience. $ *Average main: $35* ⊠ *1704 Washington St., South End* ☎ *617/536–4300* ⊕ *www.toro-restaurant.com* ⌲ *Reservations not accepted* Ⓜ *Massachusetts Ave.* ✛ *F6.*

$$$
FRENCH FUSION
Fodor'sChoice
★
✕ **Troquet.** Despite boasting what might well be Boston's longest wine list, with nearly 500 vintages (more than 45 of which are available by the glass), plus an unobstructed view of the Common, this French fusion spot flies somewhat under the radar. Still, locals know that Troquet offers all the ingredients for a lovely and delectable evening: a quietly elegant dining room, a knowledgeable yet unpretentious staff, and decadent fare, beginning with chewy rolls and farm-churned butter scooped from a bucket, and entrées like roasted suckling pig and beef with a bordelaise sauce. The menu includes by-the-glass wine recommendations after each entrée, so you're sure to sip something delicious and appropriate. $ *Average main: $32* ⊠ *140 Boylston St., Back Bay* ☎ *617/695–9463* ⊕ *troquetboston.com* ☉ *Closed Sun. and Mon. No lunch* Ⓜ *Boylston* ✛ *F4.*

BEACON HILL

$$$
MIDDLE EASTERN
✕ **Lala Rokh.** A rotating gallery of Persian art, ranging from miniatures and medieval maps to modern photographs, adorns the walls of this recently renovated fantasy of food and art now sporting a new coat of pearl-gray paint, a wraparound bar, dark-wood tables, and leather banquettes. The cuisine remains just as authentic as ever, however, and encompasses all of Iran. Along with classics such as *fesejan,* duck leg in a satiny pomegranate-walnut sauce, you'll find brain fritters, smoky eggplant puree, *pollo* (rice dishes), kebabs, and richly spiced lamb stews, including one seasoned with dried lime. The staff obviously enjoys explaining the menu, and the wine list is well selected for foods that often defy wine matches. $ *Average main: $26* ⊠ *97 Mt. Vernon St., Beacon Hill* ☎ *617/720–5511* ⊕ *www.lalarokh.com* ☉ *No lunch* Ⓜ *Charles/MGH* ✛ *E3.*

$$$$ EUROPEAN Fodor's Choice ★ 🍴 **No. 9 Park.** The stellar cuisine at chef Barbara Lynch's first restaurant continues to draw plenty of well-deserved attention from its place in the shadow of the State House's golden dome. Settle into the plush but unpretentious dining room and indulge in pumpkin risotto with rare lamb or the memorably rich prune-stuffed gnocchi drizzled with bits of foie gras, the latter of which is always offered even if you don't see it on the menu. The wine list bobs and weaves into new territory, but is always well chosen, and the savvy bartenders are of the classic ilk, so you'll find plenty of classics and very few cloying, dessertlike sips here. [$] *Average main: $39* ✉ *9 Park St., Beacon Hill* ☎ *617/742–9991* 🌐 *www.no9park.com* [M] *Park St.* ✣ *G3.*

DOWNTOWN

$$$$ JAPANESE Fodor's Choice ★ 🍴 **o ya.** Despite its side-street location and hidden door, o ya isn't exactly a secret: dining critics from the *New York Times, Bon Appetit,* and *Food & Wine* have all named this tiny, improvisational sushi spot among the best in the country. Chef Tim Cushman's *nigiri* menu features squid-ink bubbles, homemade potato chips—even foie gras. Other dishes offer a nod to New England, such as the braised pork with Boston baked beans and "legs and eggs," lobster legs and caviar. For a hauntingly spectacular evening, indulge in the *omakase* tasting menu featuring either 17 courses ($185, or $265 with wine) or 20-plus courses ($285 or $465 with wine). Yes, that's a lot to drop on one dinner, but compared to the cost of flying to Japan, it's a bargain. Cushman's wife Nancy oversees an extensive sake list that includes sparkling and aged varieties. [$] *Average main: $60* ✉ *9 East St., Downtown* ☎ *617/654–9900* 🌐 *www.oyarestaurantboston.com* ⏲ *Closed Sun. and Mon. No lunch* [M] *South Station* ✣ *G4.*

GOVERNMENT CENTER/FANEUIL HALL

$$ AMERICAN 🍴 **Durgin-Park Market Dining Room.** You should be hungry enough to cope with enormous portions, yet not so hungry you can't tolerate a long wait (or sharing a table with others). Durgin-Park was serving its same hearty New England fare (Indian pudding, baked beans, corned beef and cabbage, and a prime rib that hangs over the edge of the plate) back when Faneuil Hall was a working market instead of a tourist attraction. The service is as brusque as it was when fishmongers and boat captains dined here, but that's just part of its charm. [$] *Average main: $20* ✉ *340 Faneuil Hall Market Pl., North Market Bldg., Boston* ☎ *617/227–2038* 🌐 *www.arkrestaurants.com/durgin_park.html* [M] *Government Center* ✣ *H2.*

$$$ SEAFOOD 🍴 **Union Oyster House.** Established in 1826, this is Boston's oldest continuing restaurant, and almost every tourist considers it a must-see. If you like, you can have what Daniel Webster had—oysters on the half shell at the ground-floor raw bar, which is the oldest part of the restaurant and still the best. The rooms at the top of the narrow staircase are dark and have low ceilings—very Ye Olde New England—and plenty of nonrestaurant history. The small tables and chairs (as well as the endless lines and kitschy nostalgia) are as much a part of the charm as

the simple and decent (albeit pricey) food. On weekends, especially in summer, make reservations a few days ahead or risk enduring waits of historic proportions. One cautionary note: locals hardly ever eat here. [$] *Average main: $28* ✉ *41 Union St., Government Center* ☎ *617/227–2750* 🌐 *www.unionoysterhouse.com* [M] *Haymarket* ✥ *H2.*

NORTH END

$$ ITALIAN Fodor's Choice ★ 🍴 **Antico Forno.** Many of the menu choices here come from the eponymous wood-burning brick oven, which turns out surprisingly delicate pizzas simply topped with tomato and fresh buffalo mozzarella. Though its pizzas receive top billing, Antico excels at a variety of Italian country dishes. Don't overlook the hearty baked dishes and handmade pastas; the specialty, gnocchi, is rich and creamy but light. The joint is cramped and noisy, but also homey and comfortable—which means that your meal will resemble a raucous dinner with an adopted Italian family. [$] *Average main: $18* ✉ *93 Salem St., North End* ☎ *617/723–6733* 🌐 *www.anticofornoboston.com* [M] *Haymarket* ✥ *H2.*

$$$$ ITALIAN 🍴 **Bricco.** A sophisticated but unpretentious enclave of nouveau Italian, Bricco has carved out quite a following. And no wonder: the handmade pastas alone are argument for a reservation. Simple but well-balanced main courses such as roast chicken marinated in seven spices and a brimming *brodetto* (fish stew) with half a lobster and a pile of seafood may linger in your memory. You're likely to want to linger in the warm room, too, gazing through the floor-to-ceiling windows while sipping a glass of Sangiovese from the Italian and American wine list. [$] *Average main: $44* ✉ *241 Hanover St., North End* ☎ *617/248–6800* 🌐 *www.bricco.com* ⏲ *No lunch* ✍ *Reservations essential* [M] *Haymarket* ✥ *H2.*

$$ SEAFOOD Fodor's Choice ★ 🍴 **Daily Catch.** You've just got to love this shoebox-size place—for the noise, the intimacy, the complete absence of pretense, and, above all, the food, which proved so popular, it spawned two other locations (one in Brookline and another in Boston's Seaport area). Compact and brightly lighted, this storefront restaurant has been a local staple for more than 40 years and for good reason. With garlic and olive oil forming the foundation for almost every dish, this cheerful, bustling spot specializes in big skillets of calamari dishes, black squid-ink pastas, and linguine with clam sauce, that all would seem less perfect if served on fine white china versus the actual cooking pan that's placed in front of you with an efficient flourish as soon as it leaves the stove. [$] *Average main: $21* ✉ *323 Hanover St., North End* ☎ *617/523–8567* 🌐 *www.thedailycatch.com* 💳 *No credit cards* ✍ *Reservations not accepted* [M] *Haymarket* ✥ *H2.*

$$$ SEAFOOD Fodor's Choice ★ 🍴 **Neptune Oyster.** This *piccolo* oyster bar, the first of its kind in the neighborhood, has only 22 chairs, but the long marble bar adorned with mirrors has extra seating for 15 more patrons, who can watch the oyster shuckers deftly undo handfuls of more than a dozen different kinds of bivalves to savor as an appetizer or on a *plateau di frutti di mare,* a gleaming tower of oysters and other raw-bar items piled over ice that you can order from the slip of paper they pass out listing each day's crustacean options. Dishes change seasonally, but a couple of year-round favorites include the North End Cioppino (fish stew)

and the signature lobster roll that, hot or cold, overflows with meat. Service is prompt even when it gets busy (as it is most of the time). Go early to avoid a long wait. $ *Average main: $32* ⊠ *63 Salem St., North End* ☎ *617/742–3474* ⊕ *www.neptuneoyster.com* ⌲ *Reservations not accepted* Ⓜ *Haymarket* ✛ *H2.*

CAMBRIDGE

Use the coordinate (✛ B2) at the end of each listing to locate a site on the Where to Eat and Stay in Cambridge map.

$ ✕ **All Star Sandwich Bar.** This brightly colored place with about a dozen tables has a strict definition of what makes a sandwich: no wraps. The owners have put together a list of classics, like crispy, overstuffed Reubens and beef on weck (a jumbo caraway-and-salt-topped roll), which are served quickly from an open kitchen. Their famous Atomic Meatloaf Meltdown has been highlighted on a number of foodie networks. Not into sandwiches? Soups, salads, a burger, and chili are available, along with a small selection of beer and wine. If pies are more your thing, sister restaurant All-Star Pizza Bar is just across the street. $ *Average main: $11* ⊠ *1245 Cambridge St., Cambridge* ☎ *617/868–3065* ⊕ *www.allstarsandwichbar.com* ⌲ *Reservations not accepted* Ⓜ *Central/Inman* ✛ *A4.*

AMERICAN
Fodor's Choice
★

$$ ✕ **Area Four.** A bona fide hit from day one, everything at this glass-enclosed eatery in the avant-garde Technology Square area is scrumptious—from the morning sticky buns and excellent dark coffee at the café to the clam-bacon pizza in the casual dining room. A central wood-fired oven turns out chewy-crusted pies and small skillets of mac and cheese with croissant crumbs and crackly skinned chicken over wilted greens. You will find only local, seasonal, and sustainable cooking here. $ *Average main: $18* ⊠ *500 Technology Sq., Cambridge* ☎ *617/758–4444* ⊕ *www.areafour.com* ▭ *No credit cards* ✛ *C6.*

MODERN
AMERICAN
Fodor's Choice
★

$$$ ✕ **Oleana.** With three restaurants (including Sofra in Cambridge and Sarma in Somerville), and a cookbook to her name, chef-owner Ana Sortun is one of the city's culinary treasures. So is Oleana, which specializes in zesty Eastern Mediterranean *meze* (small plates) plumped up with fresh-picked produce from her husband's nearby Siena Farms. Although the menu changes often, look for the hot, crispy fried mussels starter and the smoky eggplant puree beside tamarind-glazed beef. Lamb gets jacked up with Turkish spices, while duck gets accented with garlic and hazelnuts. In warm weather the back patio garden is a hidden utopia. $ *Average main: $26* ⊠ *134 Hampshire St., Cambridge* ☎ *617/661–0505* ⊕ *www.oleanarestaurant.com* ☾ *No lunch* ⌲ *Reservations essential* Ⓜ *Central* ✛ *B5.*

MEDITERRANEAN
Fodor's Choice
★

$ ✕ **Orinoco.** It's easy to miss this red clapboard, Latin American restaurant located down an alleyway in Harvard Square. Don't. Owner Andres Banger's dream to bring bountiful plates of superfresh family fare from his home country of Venezuela to Cambridge (as well as Brookline and the South End), will reward you with delectable, palm-sized *arepas,* or crispy, hot, corn-flour pockets stuffed with beans, cheese, and pork; *pabellon criollo,* moist shredded beef with stewed

LATIN AMERICAN
Fodor's Choice
★

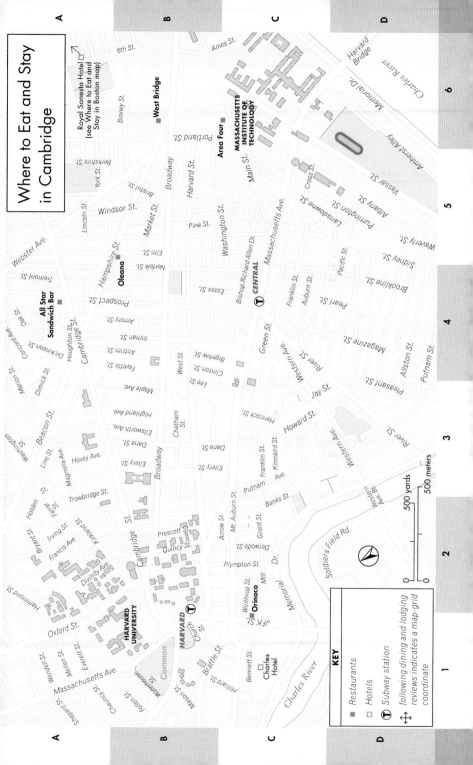

beans, rice, and plantains; and red chili adobo–marinated, charred *pollo* (chicken). Empanadas, hearty salads, and stuffed French-bread sandwiches at lunch, along with a small selection of wine and beer, round out the very affordable menu at this casual eatery. When weather permits, ask for a seat on the hidden back patio, a quiet flower-and-fountain-filled oasis that makes the rest of the world feel very far away. $ *Average main: $17* ⊠ *56 JFK St., Harvard Square* ☎ *617/354–6900* ⊕ *www.orinocokitchen.com* ⊟ *No credit cards* ⊗ *Closed Mon.* ⌒ *Reservations not accepted* ⊹ *C1.*

$$$　✕ **West Bridge.** Expertly crafted cocktails may draw area techies, MIT
MODERN　folks, and neighborhood hipsters into this happening white, window-
AMERICAN　filled room with exposed ceiling pipes in Kendall Square, but it's the
Fodor'sChoice　small and large plates of lusty, flavor-rich food, like the gooey duck egg
★　in a jar served over potato puree with crisp duck skin that keeps them lingering. While the menu changes often, you'll always find creatively prepared meats, seafood, and veggies invigorated with additions like guanciale (cured pork jowl), verjus (vinegary juice from unripe grapes), miso, sambal (spicy Asian paste), and salsa verde. A broad selection of unusual beers and wines by the glass means every bite will have a great sip to match. $ *Average main: $26* ⊠ *1 Kendall Sq., Kendall Square* ☎ *617/945–0221* ⊕ *www.westbridgerestaurant.com* ⊟ *No credit cards* ⊗ *No lunch weekends* ⊹ *B6.*

WHERE TO STAY

Updated
by Megan
Johnson

At one time great lodging was scarce in Boston. If you were a persnickety blue blood in town to visit relatives, you checked into the Charles or the old Ritz on Newbury. If you were a parent in town to see your kid graduate from one of the city's many universities, you suffered through a stay at a run-down chain. And if you were a young couple in town for a little romance, well, you could just forget it. A dearth of suitable rooms practically defined Boston. Oh, how things have changed.

In the early 2000s, Boston finally got wise to modernization, and a rush of new construction took the local hotel scene by storm. Sleek, boutique accommodations began inviting guests to Cambridge and Downtown, areas once relegated to alumni and business traveler sets. New, mega-luxury lodgings like the Mandarin Oriental and the Taj (the latter, in that old Ritz spot) infiltrated posh Back Bay, while high-end, hipster-friendly spots like the W Boston and Ames are drawing visitors to up-and-coming areas in Downtown. Even mostly residential areas like the South End now draw discerning boarders, thanks to the revamped Chandler and the nearby Inn@St. Botolph.

Speaking of revamped, it seems that nearly every hotel in town just got a face-lift. From spruced up decor (good-bye, grandma's bedspread; hello, puffy white duvets) to hopping restaurant-bars to new spas and fitness centers, Boston's lodgings are feeling the competitive heat and acting accordingly. You don't just get a room anymore—you get an experience.

Many properties have stellar weekend deals, so you may be able to try an upscale Fodor's Choice even if you thought it was out of your budget.

Prices in the reviews are the lowest cost of a standard double room in high season.

Use the coordinate (✛ B2) at the end of each listing to locate a site on the Where to Eat and Stay in Boston map.

WHAT IT COSTS				
	$	$$	$$$	$$$$
FOR TWO PEOPLE	under $200	$200–$299	$300–$399	over $399

3

BACK BAY

$$
HOTEL
Fodor'sChoice
★
Charlesmark Hotel. Hipsters and romantics who'd rather spend their cash on a great meal than a hotel bill have put this late-19th-century former residential row house on the map. **Pros:** fantastic price for the location; free Wi-Fi. **Cons:** some might feel crowded by compact rooms and hallways. $ *Rooms from: $239* ✉ *655 Boylston St., Back Bay* ☎ *617/247–1212* ⊕ *www.thecharlesmarkhotel.com* ⤷ *40 rooms* ❑ *Breakfast* Ⓜ *Copley* ✛ *D5.*

$$$$
HOTEL
FAMILY
Colonnade Hotel. Following a recent makeover, the Colonnade showcases clean, modern environs injected with hues of khaki, chocolate, and chrome. **Pros:** roof-deck pool; across from Prudential Center shopping; good Red Sox packages. **Cons:** Huntington Avenue can get clogged with rush-hour traffic; on summer days the pool is packed by 11 am. $ *Rooms from: $479* ✉ *120 Huntington Ave., Back Bay* ☎ *617/424–7000, 800/962–3030* ⊕ *www.colonnadehotel.com* ⤷ *276 rooms, 9 suites* ❑ *No meals* Ⓜ *Back Bay, Prudential Center* ✛ *C5.*

$$$$
HOTEL
Fodor'sChoice
★
Eliot Hotel. One of the city's best small hotels is on posh Commonwealth Avenue, modeled after Paris's epic Champs Élysées, and it expertly merges the old blue-blood Boston aesthetic with modern flair (like zebra-print rugs mingling with crystal chandeliers); everyone from well-heeled Sox fans to traveling CEOs to tony college parents has noticed. **Pros:** super location; top-notch restaurants; pet friendly; beautiful rooms. **Cons:** very expensive; some complain of elevator noise. $ *Rooms from: $485* ✉ *370 Commonwealth Ave., Back Bay* ☎ *617/267–1607, 800/443–5468* ⊕ *www.eliothotel.com* ⤷ *16 rooms, 79 suites* ❑ *No meals* Ⓜ *Hynes* ✛ *B5.*

$$$
HOTEL
FAMILY
Fodor'sChoice
★
Fairmont Copley Plaza. Past guests, including one Judy Garland, felt at home in this decadent, unabashedly romantic hotel that underwent a $20 million renovation in early 2012. **Pros:** very elegant; luxurious gym. **Cons:** tiny bathrooms with scratchy towels; charge for Internet access (no charge on Fairmont President's Club level). $ *Rooms from: $369* ✉ *138 St. James Ave., Back Bay* ☎ *617/267–5300, 866/540–4417* ⊕ *www.fairmont.com/copley-plaza-boston* ⤷ *366 rooms, 17 suites* ❑ *No meals* Ⓜ *Copley, Back Bay* ✛ *D5.*

$
B&B/INN
463 Beacon Street Guest House. Though there's no sign on the door of this handsome brownstone, international visitors and college students have discovered the rooming house—and quickly warmed to its slightly quirky, old-auntie charm. **Pros:** Newbury Street is three blocks away; the

	NEIGHBORHOOD VIBE	PROS	CONS
Beacon Hill and Boston Common	Old brick and stone buildings host luxe boutique hotels and B&Bs on the hill or along busy, preppy Charles Street; some skyscraper lodging right on Boston Common.	Safe, quaint area with lamp-lit streets; chain-free upscale shopping and dining; outdoor fun abounds in the park; good T access.	Street parking is extremely hard to come by; not budget friendly; very close to noisy hospital; hills can be very steep.
Downtown	The city's financial center hums with activity and busy hotels during the week; new boutique lodging is moving in to compete with the big-box chains.	Excellent area for business travelers; frequent low weekend rates; good T and bus access; walking distance to Theater District and some museums.	All but dead at night; expensive garage parking during the day; Downtown Crossing is mobbed at lunchtime and on weekends; poorly marked streets.
The Back Bay	High-priced hotels in the city's poshest neighbor-hood, home to excellent shops, restaurants, bars, spas, and salons. Commonwealth Avenue is lined with historic mansions.	Easy, central location; safe, beautiful area to walk around at night; ample T access; excellent people-watching.	Rooms, shopping, and eating can be ridiculously expensive; Newbury Street is overcrowded with tourists on weekends.
The South End	Small, funky lodgings in a very hip and happening (and gay-friendly) area packed with awesome independent restaurants and shops.	The city's best dining scene; easy T and bus access; myriad parks; walking distance from the Back Bay and Downtown; safe along the main avenues at night.	Some bordering blocks turn seedy after dusk; difficult street parking (and few garages); only a handful of hotel options.
The Fenway and Kenmore Square	A sampling of large and small hotels and inns, plus two hostels; the area is a mix of students, young professionals, and die-hard Sox fans.	Close to Fenway Park (home of the Red Sox); up-and-coming dining scene; less expensive than most 'hoods; very accessible by T.	Impossible street parking on game days (and pricey garages); expect big crowds for concert and sporting events; some bars are loud and tacky.
Boston Outskirts	Mostly midsize chain hotels in student neighborhoods full of coffee shops, convenience stores, and rowdy college bars.	Serviceable airport lodging near Logan; cheap rates on rooms in Brighton, Allston, and parts of Brookline; easier driving than Downtown.	No overnight street parking in Brookline; far from Boston center and museums, shopping, and the river; some areas get dicey at night; T rides into the city proper can take an hour.
Cambridge	A mix of grand and small hotels pepper the hip, multi-university neighborhood; expect loads of young freethinkers and efficient (if laid-back) service.	Hallowed academia; verdant squares; good low- and high-cost eating and lodging; excellent neighborhood restaurants; very few chain anythings.	Spotty T access; less of a city feel; a few areas can be very quiet and slightly dodgy at night; lots of one-way streets make driving difficult.

Charles River and Esplanade are one block in the other direction. **Cons:** some rooms have a two-person occupancy limit, and because of the layout, the house isn't appropriate for children under seven. $ *Rooms from: $169* ✉ *463 Beacon St., Back Bay* ☎ *617/536–1302* ⊕ *www.463beacon. com* ⬅ *18 rooms, 14 with bath* ⏺ *No meals* Ⓜ *Hynes* ✛ *B4.*

$$ ⏹ **Inn@St. Botolph.** The posh yet homey 16-room Inn@St. Botolph follows a groundbreaking new hotel model—no front desk, no restaurant, and no valet (there is, however, an office on-site that is staffed 24/7). **Pros:** affordable style; free satellite TV and Wi-Fi; free transit to top area restaurants, where guests also get "preferred" pricing. **Cons:** DIY parking; for those who need hand-holding, there's no front desk. $ *Rooms from: $299* ✉ *99 St. Botolph St., Back Bay* ☎ *617/236–8099* ⊕ *www. innatstbotolph.com* ⬅ *16 rooms* ⏺ *Breakfast* Ⓜ *Prudential* ✛ *C6.*

B&B/INN
FAMILY
Fodor's Choice
★

$$$$ ⏹ **Mandarin Oriental Boston.** With too many amenities to list, the 148-room hotel has helped redefine luxury in town (pay attention, Ritz and Four Seasons) since opening in 2008, and it offers services many guests are calling "out of this world." Need your pants hemmed in 30 minutes? No problem. **Pros:** amazing service; very quiet; good-size rooms. **Cons:** small fitness center; exorbitantly expensive; average views. $ *Rooms from: $545* ✉ *776 Boylston St., Back Bay* ☎ *617/535–8888* ⊕ *www. mandarinoriental.com/boston* ⬅ *136 rooms, 12 suites* ⏺ *No meals* Ⓜ *Prudential, Copley* ✛ *C5.*

HOTEL

$$ ⏹ **Taj Boston Hotel.** Standing guard at the corner of fashionable Newbury Street and the Public Garden, the old-school elegant Taj features plush new robes and towels in guest rooms, new carpets, Molton Brown bath amenities, and vibrant floral displays in the lobby. **Pros:** white-glove service; amazing views; proximity to shopping, dining, and the park. **Cons:** all this luxury will cost you. $ *Rooms from: $299* ✉ *15 Arlington St., Back Bay* ☎ *617/536–5700* ⊕ *www.tajhotels.com* ⬅ *273 rooms, 44 suites* ⏺ *No meals* Ⓜ *Arlington* ✛ *E4.*

HOTEL
FAMILY

BEACON HILL

$$$ ⏹ **Beacon Hill Hotel & Bistro.** This home away from home—or, rather, full-service version of home where you hardly have to lift a finger (unless it's to dial room service)—is within walking distance of the Public Garden, Back Bay, Government Center, and the river Esplanade. **Pros:** free Wi-Fi; many nearby shops and restaurants; executive-chef Lucas Sousa's decadent Sunday brunch at the ground-floor bistro. **Cons:** neighborhood parking is nonexistent; the rooms are somewhat small. $ *Rooms from: $325* ✉ *25 Charles St., Beacon Hill* ☎ *617/723–7575* ⊕ *www. beaconhillhotel.com* ⬅ *12 rooms, 1 suite* ⏺ *Breakfast* Ⓜ *Arlington, Charles/MGH* ✛ *E3.*

HOTEL

$ ⏹ **John Jeffries House.** Right next to the Charles/MGH stop, the John Jeffries isn't only easily accessible, it's affordable—a veritable home run in this city. **Pros:** great Beacon Hill location; free Wi-Fi; good value. **Cons:** there's a busy (and noisy) hospital across the street; no spa or gym facilities. $ *Rooms from: $125* ✉ *14 David G. Mugar Way, Beacon Hill* ☎ *617/367–1866* ⊕ *www.johnjeffrieshouse.com* ⬅ *46 rooms, about half are suites* ⏺ *Breakfast* Ⓜ *Charles/MGH* ✛ *E2.*

B&B/INN

$$$$
HOTEL
Fodor's Choice
★
Liberty Hotel Boston. Since it opened in late 2007, the buzz surrounding the chic Liberty—formerly Boston's Charles Street Jail—was at first deafening, with bankers, tech geeks, foreign playboys, and fashionistas all scrambling to call it their own; a few years later, the hype has thankfully died down, though it's still part retreat, part nightclub. **Pros:** Lydia Shire's popular restaurant Scampo is on the first floor; bustling nightlife; proximity to the river and Beacon Hill. **Cons:** loud in-house nightlife; long waits at bars and restaurants. $ *Rooms from: $699* ✉ *215 Charles St., Beacon Hill* ☎ *617/224–4000* ⊕ *www.libertyhotel.com* ⬚ *288 rooms, 10 suites* ❚◯❙ *No meals* Ⓜ *Charles/MGH* ✛ *E2.*

$$$$
HOTEL
Fodor's Choice
★
XV Beacon. The 1903 beaux arts exterior of one of the city's first small luxury hotels is a study in understated class and elegance. **Pros:** in-room massages; chef Jamie Mammano's steak house, Mooo; free pet stays. **Cons:** some rooms are very small; can be expensive on weekends during peak months (May, June, September, October). $ *Rooms from: $575* ✉ *15 Beacon St., Beacon Hill* ☎ *617/670–1500, 877/982–3226* ⊕ *www.xvbeacon.com* ⬚ *63 rooms* ❚◯❙ *No meals* Ⓜ *Government Center, Park St.* ✛ *G3.*

DOWNTOWN

$$$
HOTEL
Ames Boston Hotel. One of the newer players on the Boston scene, the 114-room Ames is all New England modernity. **Pros:** very cool design; cushy beds; limo service. **Cons:** far from South End and Back Bay shopping. $ *Rooms from: $375* ✉ *1 Court St., Downtown* ☎ *617/979–8100, 888/697–1791* ⊕ *www.ameshotel.com* ⬚ *114 rooms, 11 suites, 1 apartment* ❚◯❙ *No meals* Ⓜ *State, Government Center* ✛ *G3.*

$$$$
HOTEL
FAMILY
Battery Wharf Hotel. One of the growing number of lodgings clustered along Boston's ever-expanding Harborwalk—a pretty pedestrian path that runs from Charlestown to Dorchester—the Battery Wharf Hotel looks more like a gated community than a chain hotel. **Pros:** great water views; access to Harborwalk; close to the North End. **Cons:** far from Newbury Street and South End shopping; 15- to 20-minute walk to nearest T stations. $ *Rooms from: $499* ✉ *3 Battery Wharf, North End* ☎ *877/794–6218* ⊕ *www.batterywharfhotelboston.com* ⬚ *120 rooms, 30 suites* ❚◯❙ *No meals* Ⓜ *Haymarket, North Station* ✛ *H1.*

$$$
HOTEL
Langham Hotel. This 1922 Renaissance Revival landmark (the former Federal Reserve Building) strikes an admirable balance between historic, old-world charm and sleek, modern appointments. **Pros:** ideal spot for business travelers; fabulous Sunday brunch and weekend Chocolate Bar at Café Fleuri; the beautiful Post Office Square park adjacent to the Langham is a quiet oasis. **Cons:** Downtown location feels remote on weekends; pricey during the week; expensive valet parking. $ *Rooms from: $395* ✉ *250 Franklin St., Downtown* ☎ *617/451–1900, 800/543–4300* ⊕ *www.boston.langhamhotels.com* ⬚ *318 rooms, 17 suites* ❚◯❙ *No meals* Ⓜ *South Station* ✛ *H3.*

$$
HOTEL
FAMILY
Fodor's Choice
★
Nine Zero. Hotel rooms can get a little lonely, and that's why this Downtown spot instated its "guppy love" program; yes, that's right, you get a pet fish on loan. **Pros:** pet and kid friendly; lobby wine tasting every evening (from 5 to 6); Etro bath products. **Cons:** smallish rooms; high parking fees. $ *Rooms from: $249* ✉ *90 Tremont St., Downtown*

☎ *617/772–5800, 866/906–9090 ⊕ www.ninezero.com ↘185 rooms,
5 suites* ⦿*No meals* Ⓜ *Park St., Government Center ✛ G3.*

$$$ 🏨 **Omni Parker House.** If any hotel says "Boston," it's this one, where JFK
HOTEL proposed to Jackie, and Charles Dickens gave his first reading of "A
FAMILY Christmas Carol"—in fact, you may well see a Dickens impersonator in
the lobby, since history tours always include the Parker House on their
routes. **Pros:** historic property; near Downtown Crossing on the Free-
dom Trail. **Cons:** small rooms, some quite dark; thin-walled rooms can
be noisy. $ *Rooms from: $339* ✉ *60 School St., Downtown* ☎ *617/227–
8600, 800/843–6664* ⊕ *www.omniparkerhouse.com* ↘*551 rooms, 21
suites* ⦿*No meals* Ⓜ *Government Center, Park St. ✛ G3.*

$$ 🏨 **Seaport Boston Hotel.** Chances are, if you've ever been to Boston on
HOTEL business, you've already stayed at the Seaport, where guest rooms are
among the biggest in the city. **Pros:** beautiful on-site Wave Health &
Fitness Club; close to a newly developed restaurant scene offering 20
dining options; free Wi-Fi. **Cons:** far from city center. $ *Rooms from:
$209* ✉ *World Trade Center, 1 Seaport La., Waterfront* ☎ *617/385–
4000, 800/440–3318* ⊕ *www.seaportboston.com* ↘*428 rooms* ⦿*No
meals* Ⓜ *World Trade Center ✛ H4.*

SOUTH END

$ 🏨 **Encore.** Innkeepers Reinhold Mahler and David Miller, who are a
B&B/INN retired architect and creative set designer, respectively, have pooled their
creative energies into this South End lodging gem, proving that they know
a thing or two about ambience. **Pros:** trendy South End location; free
Wi-Fi; Bang & Olufsen sound systems. **Cons:** small breakfast nook; two-
night minimums on weekends in July and August, three-night minimum
in September and October; no elevator. $ *Rooms from: $155* ✉ *116 W.
Newton St., South End* ☎ *617/247–3425* ⊕ *www.encorebandb.com* ↘*4
rooms* ⦿*Breakfast* Ⓜ *Back Bay, Massachusetts Ave. ✛ D6.*

KENMORE SQUARE

$$$ 🏨 **Gryphon House.** The staff in this value-packed, four-story 19th-cen-
B&B/INN tury brownstone is helpful and friendly, and the suites are thematically
Fodor'sChoice decorated: one evokes rustic Italy; another is inspired by neo-Gothic art.
★ **Pros:** elegant suites are lush and spacious; gas fireplaces in all rooms;
free Wi-Fi. **Cons:** may be too fussy for some; there's no elevator or
wheelchair access. $ *Rooms from: $300* ✉ *9 Bay State Rd., Kenmore
Square* ☎ *617/375–9003, 877/375–9003* ⊕ *www.innboston.com* ↘*8
suites* ⦿*Breakfast* Ⓜ *A5.*

$$$ 🏨 **Hotel Commonwealth.** Luxury and service without pretense makes this
HOTEL hip spot a solid choice. **Pros:** down bedding; perfect locale for Red Sox
Fodor'sChoice fans; happening bar scene at Eastern Standard; free Wi-Fi. **Cons:** area
★ is mobbed during Sox games; small gym. $ *Rooms from: $399* ✉ *500
Commonwealth Ave., Kenmore Square* ☎ *617/933–5000, 866/784–
4000* ⊕ *www.hotelcommonwealth.com* ↘*149 rooms, 5 suites* ⦿*No
meals* Ⓜ *Kenmore ✛ A5.*

CAMBRIDGE

Use the coordinate (✛ B2) at the end of each listing to locate a site on the Where to Eat and Stay in Cambridge map.

$$$
HOTEL
FAMILY
Fodor's Choice
★

Charles Hotel. It used to be that the Charles was *the* place to stay in Cambridge, and while other luxury hotels have since arrived to give it a little healthy competition, this Harvard Square staple is standing strong. **Pros:** two blocks from the T Red Line to Boston; on-site jazz club and hip Noir bar; outdoor skating rink in winter. **Cons:** luxury comes at a price. $ *Rooms from: $399* ⊠ *1 Bennett St., Cambridge* ☎ *617/864–1200, 800/882–1818* ⊕ *www.charleshotel.com* ⊃ *249 rooms, 45 suites* ❙⊙❙ *No meals* Ⓜ *Harvard* ✛ *C1.*

$$$
HOTEL
FAMILY

Royal Sonesta Hotel. Right next to the Charles River, the certified-green Sonesta has one of the best city skyline and sunset views in Boston. **Pros:** walk to Museum of Science and T to Downtown Boston; complimentary shuttle to Cambridge-area attractions; nice pool. **Cons:** parking is not free. $ *Rooms from: $379* ⊠ *40 Edwin Land Blvd., off Memorial Dr., Cambridge* ☎ *617/806–4200, 800/766–3782* ⊕ *www.sonesta.com/boston* ⊃ *381 rooms, 19 suites* ❙⊙❙ *No meals* Ⓜ *Lechmere* ✛ *A6.*

NIGHTLIFE AND PERFORMING ARTS

NIGHTLIFE

Updated by
Fred Bouchard

BEACON HILL

BARS

Cheers. The upstairs pub—dismantled in England, shipped to Boston, and reassembled—later became the inspiration for the now-classic TV series *Cheers*. Enjoy a quality burger at the model bar of the Hollywood set and imagine Sam and Diane walking in the door and calling your name. ⊠ *Hampshire House, 84 Beacon St., Beacon Hill* ☎ *617/227–9605* ⊕ *www.cheersboston.com* Ⓜ *Park St., Charles/MGH.*

Fodor's Choice
★

The Sevens Ale House. This vintage bar is an easygoing alternative to Beacon Hill's tony stuffiness, with its dark tones, simple bar setup, well-peppered dartboard, perfectly poured pints, and decent wines. It's pleasantly untrendy. ⊠ *77 Charles St., Beacon Hill* ☎ *617/523–9074* Ⓜ *Charles/MGH.*

GOVERNMENT CENTER

BARS

Fodor's Choice
★

Black Rose. Hung with 20 bright county banners, decorated with pictures of Ireland and portraits of Samuel Beckett, Lady Gregory, and James Joyce, the Rose draws as many tourists as locals. Friendly Irish bartenders serve up pints, blarney, and far more Irish whiskeys (21) than Scotches (14). Nightly shows by traditional Irish and contemporary musicians confirm its abiding Gaelic good cheer, or *craic*. ⊠ *160 State St., Boston* ☎ *617/742–2286* ⊕ *www.blackroseboston.com* Ⓜ *Aquarium, State.*

CHARLESTOWN
BARS

Warren Tavern. This venerable Colonial-era watering hole, rebuilt in 1780, was frequented by Paul Revere; even George Washington had a few drinks here. Today tourists and locals stop by for a glass and passable grub en route to the historic Navy Yard. Try the house-made potato chips with your ale of choice. Singers pipe up Wednesday and Thursday around 9 pm. ⊠ 2 *Pleasant St., Charlestown* ☎ *617/ 241–8142* ⊕ *www.warrentavern. com* Ⓜ *Community College.*

DOWNTOWN
DANCE CLUBS

Whiskey Saigon. With its rich red velvet and crystal chandeliers, this recent upgrade to the former Gypsy Bar calls to mind the decadence of a dark European castle. Rows of video screens broadcast the Fashion Network, adding a sexier, more modern touch. Thirtysomething revelers and European students snack on lime-and-ginger-marinated tiger shrimp and sip "See You in Church" martinis (vodka with fresh marmalade) while the trendy dance floor throbs to Top 40 and EDM. ⊠ *116 Boylston St., Theater District* ☎ *617/482–7799* ⊕ *www.whiskysaigon. com* Ⓜ *Boylston.*

BACK BAY
MUSIC CLUBS

Red Room @ Cafe 939. By day a Berklee College coffee and snack bar, the Cafe by night opens its tidy, scarlet, 150-seat concert space. Run, booked, and played by students, it's an ideal all-ages venue for aspiring student bands and indies on the rise. Refreshments are light (soft drinks, noodles), and so is the cover charge, $0–$16. There are a dozen eateries within 200 yards. ⊠ *939 Boylston St., Back Bay* ☎ *617/747–2261* ⊕ *www.cafe939.com* Ⓜ *Hynes.*

THE SOUTH END
BARS

Franklin Café. A neighborhood institution for 20 years, The Franklin's renowned for creative cocktails, local microbrews, fine wines, and upscale pub food. There's no sign: just look for the white martini logo (or folks waiting for a dinner table) to know you're there. ⊠ *278 Shawmut Ave., South End* ☎ *617/350–0010* ⊕ *www.franklincafe.com* Ⓜ *Back Bay/South End.*

THE FENWAY
BARS
Boston Beer Works. Standing opposite Fenway Park since 1992, this brewery has all its works exposed—the tanks, pipes, and gleaming stainless-steel and copper kettles. Seasonal brews, in addition to 20 microbrews on tap, draw students, young adults, and tourists alike to the original location (its sibling by the TD Garden is popular, too). The atmosphere is too electric and noisy for quiet chats, and good luck trying to get in on a Sox game day. There are 20 small screens to view sports events, but the real action here is the busy brewers. Full bar service features West Coast wines. ⊠ *61 Brookline Ave., The Fenway* ☎ *617/536–2337* ⊕ *www.beerworks.net* Ⓜ *Kenmore.*

ALLSTON
ROCK CLUBS
Fodor'sChoice **Paradise Rock Club.** This iconic bandbox near Boston University is famed
★ for bringing up big-name talent (think U2), hosting Coldplay, and nurturing local rock and hip-hop acts. Two tiers of booths provide good sight lines from all angles, even some intimate, out-of-the-way corners. Four bars quench the crowd's thirst, and food is available. Some shows are for 18-plus only; many sell out. The newer Paradise Lounge next door is a more intimate space to catch local (often acoustic) songsters, literary readings, poetry slams, and other artsy events. Most tickets run $20–$30. ⊠ *967–969 Commonwealth Ave., Allston* ☎ *617/562–8800* ⊕ *crossroadspresents.com/paradise-rock-club* Ⓜ *Pleasant St.*

Fodor'sChoice **Scullers Jazz Club.** Since 1989, this intimate and amiable venue over-
★ looking the Charles River has presented top names in jazz, Latin, and contemporary, but also blues, soul, R&B, cabaret, and world music. Impresario Fred Taylor continues into his sixth decade hosting musical greats, like Gary Burton, Michael Bublé, Lisa Fischer, Terence Blanchard, Ronnie Earl, and Acoustic Alchemy. Performances are Wednesday through Saturday 8 and 10 pm; tickets range from $25 to $50—discounted with dinner next door in The Doubletree Suites by Hilton Hotel's Green Room. Advance purchase is recommended. ⊠ *Doubletree Suites by Hilton Hotel, 400 Soldiers Field Rd., Allston* ☎ *617/562–4111* ⊕ *www.scullersjazz.com* Ⓜ *BU West, Bus 47, or CT2.*

SOMERVILLE
MUSIC CLUBS
Fodor'sChoice **Johnny D's Uptown.** This is as close as Boston gets to a rural roadhouse:
★ good eats and good music, where every seat is a good seat. The diverse lineup sweeps into Cajun, country, rockabilly, blues, roots, world, jazz, Latin, and poetry. Come early for Southern and Mediterranean bistro food, local craft brews, or on weekends enjoy a jazz brunch from 8:30 am to 2:30 pm, and Sunday open blues jams. Minors may visit with a parent or guardian. ⊠ *17 Holland St., Somerville* ☎ *617/776–9667 recorded info, 617/776–2004* ⊕ *johnnyds.com* Ⓜ *Davis.*

CAMBRIDGE

BLUES AND R&B CLUBS

Cantab Lounge. This place hums every night with live bands cranking out rhythm and blues, soul, funk, rock, or bluegrass. The theme-driven bar downstairs hosts open-mike performers (Monday) bluegrass (Tuesday), poetry slams (Wednesday), and Club Bohemia. Its diverse twenties to forties crowd is friendly and informal. ⊠ *738 Massachusetts Ave., Cambridge* ☎ *617/354–2685* ⊕ *www.cantab-lounge.com* Ⓜ *Central.*

JAZZ CLUBS

Regattabar. Though the venerable Regattabar has lately scaled back its jazz roster to host private events, regular favorites include leading men (Ron Carter, Joe Lovano, Lee Konitz), top guitarists (John Scofield, Mike Stern, Pat Martino), and local favorites. Tickets for shows run about $20–$40. The dimly lit 220-seat club with subtle nautical decor offers tasty fare and drinks. ⊠ *Charles Hotel, 1 Bennett St., Cambridge* ☎ *617/661–5000 calendar, 617/395–7757 tickets* ⊕ *www. regattabarjazz.com* Ⓜ *Harvard.*

Ryles Jazz Club. Soft lights, mirrors, and good barbecue set the mood for fine jazz on the ground-floor main stage, host to a steady showcase since the 1960s of new bands, favored locals, and national stars. Ryles's upstairs dance hall has earned its spurs as a sizzling Latin dancers' destination, with DJs spinning salsa, merengue, bachata, kizomba (with lessons from 7 pm). There's world music, Brazilian, and open mike for jazz singers. Sunday jazz brunch requires reservations. Covers vary ($10–$20) and there is free parking for patrons. ⊠ *212 Hampshire St., Cambridge* ☎ *617/876–9330* ⊕ *www.ryles.com* Ⓜ *Bus 69, 83, or 91.*

MUSIC CLUBS

The Sinclair. Bringing a long-awaited sophisticated rock music and dining venue to Harvard Square, The Sinclair's adventurous, near-nightly lineup of indie rock—with enticing flings into world, electronica, and jazz—often sells out. Its adjacent but quite separate restaurant and bar, with wanderlusty train and highway decor, serious beverage list, creative mixology, and cuisine inspired by regional Americana, is proving to be a winning formula. Accommodating 500, here's a party made to order for transient, academic, and streetwise grown-ups. ⊠ *52 Church St., Harvard Square* ☎ *617/547–5200* ⊕ *www.sinclaircambridge.com* Ⓜ *Harvard.*

ROCK CLUBS

Middle East & ZuZu Restaurant & Nightclub. This nightclub has balanced its kebab-and-falafel menu with three ever-active performance spaces to carve its niche as one of New England's most eclectic alternative-rock venues. National and local acts vie for the large upstairs and cavernous downstairs rooms, while intimate combos play ZuZu's and the tiny Corner. Phenoms like the Mighty Mighty Bosstones got their start here. Music-world celebs drop by when playing town. There's also belly dancing, folk, jazz, country-rock, and dancing at ZuZu. Nightly shows at 8 pm usually run $10–$20. ⊠ *472–480 Massachusetts Ave., Cambridge* ☎ *617/497–0576, 617/864–3278 recorded line* ⊕ *www.mideastoffers. com* Ⓜ *Central.*

PERFORMING ARTS

BEACON HILL
CONCERTS

Hatch Memorial Shell. On the bank of the Charles River, this wonderful acoustic shell, 100 feet wide and wood inlaid, is home to Boston Pops' famous Fourth of July concert and dozens of other free summer classical-orchestra concerts, zumba dance shows, and other events. Local radio stations air music shows and festivals here from April through October. Friday Flicks, often animated for children, are screened at sunset. ⊠ *Off Storrow Dr. at embankment, Beacon Hill* ☏ *617/626–4970* ⊕ *www.mass.gov/* Ⓜ *Charles/MGH, Arlington.*

DOWNTOWN AND SOUTH BOSTON
CONCERTS

Blue Hills Bank Pavilion. Up to 5,000 people gather on the waterfront in a huge white tent for breathtaking summertime concerts. National headliners—such as Florence & The Machine, Widespread Panic, Barenaked Ladies, Umphrey's McGee, Modest Mouse—play here from June through September. In chilly months, the scene turns to presenter Live Nation's Xfinity Center. Purchase tickets at Orpheum Theater or Ticketmaster. ⊠ *290 Northern Ave., South Boston* ☏ *617/728–1600* ⊕ *www. livenation.com/venues/14347/blue-hills-bank-pavilion* Ⓜ *South Station.*

Boston Opera House. The glittering, regilded Boston Opera House hosts plays, musicals, and traveling Broadway shows (long runs for *Wicked, Once*) and has also booked performers as diverse as Sarah Brightman, Pat Metheny, and the late B.B. King. The magnificent building, constructed in 1926, also hosts Boston Ballet's iconic holiday sellout, Tchaikovsky's *Nutcracker.* ⊠ *539 Washington St., Downtown* ☏ *617/259–3400* ⊕ *www.bostonoperahouseonline.com* Ⓜ *Boylston, Chinatown, Downtown Crossing, Park St.*

BACK BAY
CONCERTS

Berklee Performance Center. The main stage for the internationally renowned Berklee College of Music, the "BPC" is best known for its jazz and pop programs, but also hosts folk, world, and rock acts, and pop stars like Talking Heads, Aimee Mann, Snarky Puppy, and Melody Gardot. Bargain alert: BPC stages a wealth of excellent student and faculty shows, and showcases sets and clinics by visiting artists that cost next to nothing. ⊠ *136 Massachusetts Ave., Back Bay* ☏ *617/266–7455 box office* ⊕ *www.berklee.edu/BPC* Ⓜ *Hynes.*

New England Conservatory's Jordan Hall. One of the world's acoustic treasures, New England Conservatory's Jordan Hall is ideal for solo and string quartet recitals yet spacious enough for chamber and full orchestras. The pin-drop intimacy of this all-wood, 1,000-seat hall is in demand year-round for ensembles visiting and local. Boston Philharmonic and Boston Baroque perform here regularly. Dozens of free faculty and student concerts, jazz and classical, are a best-kept secret. ⊠ *30 Gainsborough St., Back Bay* ☏ *617/585–1260 box office* ⊕ *necmusic. edu/calendar_event* Ⓜ *Symphony.*

Symphony Hall. While Boston's Symphony Hall—the home of the Boston Symphony Orchestra and the Boston Pops—is considered among the best in the world for its sublime acoustics, it's also worth visiting to enjoy its other merits. The stage is framed by an enormous organ facade and an intricate golden proscenium. Above the second balcony are 16 replicas of Greek and Roman statues, which, like the rest of the Hall, marry the acoustic and aesthetic by creating niches and uneven surfaces to enhance the acoustics of the space. Although acoustical science was a brand-new field of research when Professor Wallace Sabine planned the interior, not one of the 2,500 seats is a bad one—the secret is the box-within-a-box design. ⊠ *301 Massachusetts Ave., Back Bay* ☎ *888/266–1200 box office, 617/638–9390 tours* ⊕ *www.bso.org* ☉ *Free walk-up tours Oct.–May, Wed. at 4 and some Sat. at 2. Call to confirm hrs* Ⓜ *Symphony.*

OPERA
Boston Lyric Opera. At Citi Performing Arts Center's Schubert Theater, the Boston Lyric Opera stages four full productions each season—three classics and a 20th-century work. Recent operas performed were Massenet's *Werther*, Mozart's *Don Giovanni*, and Puccini's *La Bohème*. ⊠ *11 Ave. de Lafayette, Downtown* ☎ *617/542–4912, 617/542–6772 audience services office* ⊕ *blo.org* Ⓜ *Boylston.*

THEATER
Huntington Theatre Company. Boston's largest resident theater company consistently performs a high-quality mix of 21th-century plays and classics under the artistic direction of Peter DuBois, and commissions playwrights to produce original dramas. The Huntington performs at two locations: Boston University Theatre and the Calderwood Theatre Pavilion in the South End. ⊠ *Boston University Theatre, 264 Huntington Ave., Back Bay* ☎ *617/266–0800 box office* ⊕ *www.huntingtontheatre. org* Ⓜ *Symphony.*

THE SOUTH END
BALLET
Boston Ballet. The city's premier dance company performs at the Boston Opera House. In addition to a world-class repertory of choreographed classical (Mahler's Third Symphony) and high-spirited modern works, Boston Ballet presents an elaborate signature *Nutcracker* during the holidays. ⊠ *19 Clarendon St., South End* ☎ *617/695–6955* ⊕ *www. bostonballet.org* Ⓜ *Back Bay.*

THEATER
Boston Center for the Arts. Of Boston's multiple arts organizations, this nonprofit arts-and-culture complex is one of the most lively and diverse. Here you can see the work of budding playwrights, check out rotating exhibits from contemporary artists, or stop in for a curator's talk and other special events. The BCA houses six performance spaces, a community music center, the Mills Art Gallery, and studio space for some 40 Boston-based contemporary artists. ⊠ *539 Tremont St., South End* ☎ *617/426–5000* ⊕ *www.bcaonline.org* ▭ *Free* ☉ *Weekdays 9–5; Mills Gallery Wed. and Sun. noon–5, Thurs.–Sat. noon–9* Ⓜ *Back Bay/ South End.*

CAMBRIDGE

BALLET

José Mateo's Ballet Theatre. This troupe is building an exciting, contemporary repertory under Cuban-born José Mateo, the resident artistic director-choreographer. Performances, which include an original *Nutcracker,* take place October through April at the **Sanctuary Theatre,** a beautifully converted former church at Massachusetts Avenue and Harvard Street in Harvard Square. ✉ *400 Harvard St., Cambridge* ☎ *617/354–7467* ⊕ *www.ballettheatre.org* Ⓜ *Harvard.*

FILM

Brattle Theatre. A classic moviegoer's iconic den with 230 seats, Brattle Theatre shows classic movies, new foreign and indie films, theme series, and directors' cuts. Tickets sell out for its Valentine's Day screenings of *Casablanca*; the Bugs Bunny Film Festival in February; *Trailer Treats,* an annual fundraiser featuring classic and modern movie previews; and DocYard, a stunning series of documentaries. At Christmastime, expect seasonal movies like *It's a Wonderful Life* and *Holiday Inn.* Enjoy a rotating selection of local beers and wines. ✉ *40 Brattle St., Harvard Sq., Cambridge* ☎ *617/876–6837* ⊕ *brattlefilm.org* Ⓜ *Harvard.*

Harvard Film Archive. Screening independent, foreign, classic, and experimental films rarely seen in commercial cinemas, Harvard Film Archive is open to the public Friday through Monday. The 200-seat theater, with pristine film and digital projection, is located in the basement of the stunning brick-and-glass Carpenter Visual Arts Center, Le Corbusier's only American building. Tickets are $9, seniors and students, $7. ✉ *Carpenter Center for the Visual Arts, 24 Quincy St., Cambridge* ☎ *617/495–4700* ⊕ *hcl.harvard.edu/hfa* Ⓜ *Harvard.*

THEATER

Fodor's Choice
★ **American Repertory Theater.** Founded by Robert Brustein and since 2009 under the helm of Tony Award–winning director Diane Paulus, the ART is one of America's most celebrated regional theaters, recently winning Tonys for Broadway originals *All the Way* and *Once* and revivals of *The Glass Menagerie, Pippin,* and *The Gershwins' Porgy and Bess.* Loeb Drama Center houses two theaters; the smaller black box often stages productions by the irreverent Harvard-Radcliffe Dramatic Club. OBERON, the ART's "club theater" with flexible stage design, engages young audiences in immersive theater (and has attracted national acclaim for its groundbreaking model), like Paulus's "disco-ball and hustle queen" extravaganza, *The Donkey Show,* on Saturday night. ✉ *64 Brattle St., Harvard Sq., Cambridge* ☎ *617/547–8300* ⊕ *americanrepertorytheater.org* Ⓜ *Harvard.*

SPORTS AND THE OUTDOORS

Updated by
Kim Foley
MacKinnon

Everything you've heard about the zeal of Boston fans is true; you cheer, and you pray, and you root some more. "Red Sox Nation" witnessed a miracle in 2004, with the reverse of the curse and the team's first World Series victory since 1918.

Then in 2007 and 2013 they proved it wasn't just a fluke with two more Series wins. In 2008 the Celtics ended their 18-year NBA championship drought with a victory over longtime rivals the LA Lakers. And three-time champions the New England Patriots are still a force to be reckoned with.

Bostonians' fervor for sports is equally evident in their leisure-time activities. Harsh winters keep locals wrapped up for months, only to emerge at the earliest sign of oncoming spring. Once the mercury tops freezing and the snows begin to melt, Boston's extensive parks, paths, woods, and waterways teem with sun worshippers and athletes.

BASEBALL

See the Fenway Park spotlight.

BASKETBALL

Boston Celtics. One of the most storied franchises in the National Basketball Association, the Boston Celtics have won the NBA championship 17 times since 1957, more than any other team in the league. The last title came in 2008, after a solid defeat of longtime rivals (the LA Lakers) ended an 18-year championship dry spell. Basketball season runs from late October to April, and playoffs last until mid-June. ⊠ *TD Garden, 100 Legends Way, Old West End* ☎ *866/423–5849* ⊕ *www.celtics.com* Ⓜ *North Station.*

BICYCLING

It's common to see suited-up doctors, lawyers, and businessmen commuting on two wheels through Downtown; unfortunately, bike lanes are few and far between. Boston's dedicated bike paths are well used, as much by joggers and in-line skaters as by bicyclists.

Back Bay Bicycles. Road bikes rent here for $65 per day (weekly rates are also available)—cash only. City bikes rent for $35. ⊠ *362 Commonwealth Ave., Back Bay* ☎ *617/247–2336* ⊕ *www.backbaybicycles.com.*

Community Bicycle Supply. This South End place rents cycles from April through October. Their $25 daily rate also includes a helmet and lock. ⊠ *496 Tremont St., at E. Berkeley St., South End* ☎ *617/542–8623* ⊕ *www.communitybicycle.com* Ⓜ *Back Bay.*

Dr. Paul Dudley White Bike Path. This 17-mile-long path follows both banks of the Charles River as it winds from Watertown Square to the Museum of Science. ⊠ *Watertown* ⊕ *www.eot.state.ma.us/default.asp?pgid=../common/downloads/bikemaps/dudley&sid=about* Ⓜ *Science Park.*

BOWLING

Back in 1880 Justin White adjusted the size of his pins at his Worcester, Massachusetts, bowling hall, giving birth to candlepin bowling, a highly popular pint-sized version of 10-pin bowling. Now played almost exclusively in northern New England and in the Canadian Maritime Provinces, candlepin bowling is a game of power and accuracy.

Paradoxically, candlepin bowling is both much easier and far more difficult than regular bowling. The balls are significantly smaller, weighing less than 3 pounds. There are no finger holes, and players of all ages and abilities can whip the ball down the alley. But because both the ball and the pins are lighter, it is far more difficult to bowl strikes and spares. Players are allowed three throws per frame, and bowlers may hit fallen pins (called wood) to knock down other pins. There has never been a perfect "300" score. The top score is 245. Good players score around 100 to 110, and novice players should be content with a score of 90.

A handful of alleys are in and around Boston, and many of them maintain their own quirky charm and history.

Boston Bowl. Open 24 hours a day, Boston Bowl attracts a more adult crowd. It has pool tables, a game room, both 10-pin and candlestick bowling, and a restaurant and new full-service bar. ☒ *820 Morrissey Blvd., Dorchester* ☎ *617/825–3800* ⊕ *www.bostonbowl.com.*

Needham Bowlaway. Founded in 1917, this tiny alley's eight cramped lanes are tucked away down a flight of stairs. Fans say Bowlaway is like bowling in your own basement. The charge is $25 per lane per hour. Note that this is a drive-to destination, though it's a short walk from Needham Center train station. ☒ *16 Chestnut St., Needham* ☎ *781/449–4060* ⊕ *www.needhambowl.com.*

Sacco's Bowl Haven. The '50s decor here "makes bowling the way it was, the way it is." Run by the Sacco family until 2010, the building and alleys were bought and are maintained by Flatbread Company pizzeria. Its 10 lanes are open daily until midnight (11 pm Sunday), and cost $25 per hour. You can bowl away and enjoy organic pizza. ☒ *45 Day St., Somerville* ☎ *617/776–0552.*

FOOTBALL

New England Patriots. Boston has been building a football dynasty over the past decade, starting with the New England Patriots come-from-behind victory against the favored St. Louis Rams in the 2002 Super Bowl. Coach Bill Belichick and heartthrob quarterback Tom Brady then brought the team three more championship rings in 2004, 2005, and 2014, and have made Patriots fans as zealous as their baseball counterparts. Exhibition football games begin in August, and the season runs through the playoffs in January. The state-of-the-art Gillette Stadium is in Foxborough, 30 miles southwest of Boston. ☒ *Gillette Stadium, Rte. 1, off I–95 Exit 9, Foxborough* ☎ *508/543–1776 Ticketmaster* ⊕ *www.patriots.com* Ⓜ *Gillette Stadium.*

Many of the local University teams row on the Charles River.

HOCKEY

Boston Bruins. Beantown's hockey team is on the ice from September until April, frequently on Thursday and Saturday evenings. Playoffs last through early June. ✉ *TD Garden, 100 Legends Way, Old West End* ☎ *617/624–2327* ⊕ *www.bostonbruins.com* Ⓜ *North Station.*

PARKS AND BEACHES

FAMILY
Fodor's Choice
★

Arnold Arboretum. The sumptuously landscaped Arnold Arboretum is open all year to walkers, nature lovers, and joggers. Volunteer docents give free walking tours in spring, summer, and fall. ✉ *125 Arborway, Jamaica Plain* ☎ *617/524–1718* ⊕ *www.arboretum.harvard.edu* Ⓜ *Forest Hills.*

Boston Harbor Cruises. Boston Harbor Cruises offers ferries to the Harbor Islands from Long Wharf (Downtown) with limited service in spring and fall. Service expands in June with additional departures from Hingham and Hull to six island destinations. High-speed catamarans run daily from May through mid-October and cost $17 round-trip. Other islands can be reached by the free inter-island water shuttles that depart from Georges Island. ✉ *Long Wharf, Waterfront* ☎ *617/227–4321* ⊕ *bostonsbestcruises.com* Ⓜ *Aquarium.*

FAMILY
Fodor's Choice
★

Boston Harbor Islands National Park Area. Comprising 34 islands and peninsulas, the Boston Harbor Islands National Park Area is something of a hidden gem for nature lovers and history buffs, with miles of lightly traveled trails and shoreline and several little-visited historic sites to explore. The focal point of the national park is 39-acre Georges Island, where you'll find the partially restored pre–Civil War Fort Warren that once held Confederate prisoners. Other islands worth visiting include Peddocks Island, which holds the remains of Fort Andrews, and Spectacle Island, a popular destination for swimming (with lifeguards). Lovells, Peddocks, Grape, and Bumpkin islands all allow camping with a permit from late June through Labor Day. Peddocks also has yurts available. Pets and alcohol are not allowed on the Harbor Islands. ✉ *Visitor Pavilion, 191 W. Atlantic Ave., Downtown* ☎ *617/223–8666* ⊕ *www.bostonislands.com* Ⓜ *Aquarium.*

FAMILY

Fodor's Choice

★

Emerald Necklace. The nine large public parks known as Boston's Emerald Necklace stretch 7 miles from the Back Bay Fens to Franklin Park in Dorchester, and include Arnold Arboretum, Jamaica Pond, Olmsted Park, and the Riverway. The linear parks, designed by master landscape architect Frederick Law Olmsted more than 100 years ago, remain a well-groomed urban masterpiece. Locals take pride in and happily make use of its open spaces and its pathways and bridges connecting rivers and ponds. ✉ *Boston* ⊕ *www.emeraldnecklace.org.*

Rose Fitzgerald Kennedy Greenway. After Boston's Central Artery (I–93) was moved underground as part of the Big Dig project, the state transformed the footprint of the former highway into the Rose Fitzgerald Kennedy Greenway, a gorgeous 1½-mile-long ribbon of parks boasting fountains, organically maintained lawns and landscapes, hundreds of trees, and chairs, tables, and umbrellas for the public's use. The Greenway stretches from the North End (New Sudbury and Cross streets) to Chinatown (Kneeland and Hudson streets), curving through the heart of Downtown, just a few blocks from the harbor in most places.

The Conservancy, a nonprofit foundation, operates, maintains, and programs the park with more than 350 events each year, including concerts, exercise classes, and farmers' and artisan markets. A mobile food program features more than 20 food trucks and carts operating seasonally in several locations on the Greenway, with the heart of the activity at Dewey Square Park. In 2013, a one-of-a-kind carousel was installed, with 36 seats featuring 14 characters native to the Boston area, including a lobster, rabbit, grasshopper, and falcon. ✉ *Downtown* ☎ *617/292–0020* ⊕ *www.rosekennedygreenway.org* Ⓜ *South Station, North Station, Aquarium, Haymarket.*

RUNNING

Fodor's Choice

★

Boston Marathon. Every Patriots' Day (the third Monday in April), fans gather along the Hopkinton-to-Boston route of the Boston Marathon to cheer on more than 25,000 runners from all over the world. The race ends near Copley Square in the Back Bay. ✉ *Copley Square, Back Bay* ⊕ *www.baa.org* Ⓜ *Copley, Arlington.*

SHOPPING

Updated by
Victoria Abbott
Riccardi

Boston's shops are generally open Monday through Saturday from 10 or 11 until 6 or 7 and Sunday noon to 5. Many stay open until 8 pm one night a week, usually Thursday. Malls are open Monday through Saturday from 9 or 10 until 8 or 9 and Sunday noon to 6.

MAJOR SHOPPING DISTRICTS

Boston's shops and department stores are concentrated in the area bounded by Quincy Market, the Back Bay, and Downtown. There are plenty of bargains in the Downtown Crossing area. The South End's gentrification creates its own kind of consumerist milieus, from housewares shops to avant-garde art galleries. In Cambridge you can find lots of shopping around Harvard and Central squares, with independent boutiques migrating west along Massachusetts Avenue (or Mass Ave., as almost everyone else calls it) toward Porter Square and beyond.

Boylston Street. Parallel to Newbury Street is Boylston Street, where you'll find a few standout shops such as Pompanoosuc Mills (handcrafted furnishing) scattered among the other chains and restaurants. ⊠ *Boston.*

Brattle Street. A handful of chains and independent boutiques are clustered on Brattle Street. ⊠ *Behind Harvard Sq., Cambridge* Ⓜ *Harvard.*

Charles Street. Pretty Charles Street, running north to south, abounds with top-notch antiques stores such as Eugene Galleries and Devonia, as well as plenty of independently owned fashion boutiques and homegoods stores whose prices reflect their high Beacon Hill rents. River Street, parallel to Charles Street, is also an excellent source for antiques. Both are easy walks from the Charles Street T stop on the Red Line. ⊠ *Boston* Ⓜ *Charles/MGH.*

Copley Place. Two modern structures dominate Copley Square—the **John Hancock Tower** off the southeast corner and the even more assertive Copley Place skyscraper on the southwest. An upscale, glass-and-brass urban mall built between 1980 and 1984, Copley Place includes two major hotels: the high-rise Westin and the Marriott Copley Place. Dozens of shops, restaurants, and offices are attractively grouped on several levels, surrounding bright, open indoor spaces. ⊠ *100 Huntington Ave., Back Bay* ⊕ *www.simon.com/mall/copley-place* ⊙ *Shopping galleries Mon.–Sat. 10–8, Sun. noon–6* Ⓜ *Copley.*

Faneuil Hall Marketplace. This complex is both huge and hugely popular (drawing 18 million people a year), but not necessarily unique—most of its independent shops have given way to Banana Republic, Urban Outfitters, and other chains. Founded in 1742 as a market for crops and livestock, the place has plenty of history and offers one of the area's great à la carte casual dining experiences (Quincy Market). Pushcarts sell everything from apparel to jewelry to candy to Boston souvenirs and buskers perform crowd-pleasing feats such as break dancing. ⊠ *Bounded by Congress St., Atlantic Ave., the Waterfront, and Government Center, Downtown* ☎ *617/523–1300* ⊕ *www.faneuilhallmarketplace.com* Ⓜ *Government Center.*

Harvard Square. Harvard Square takes up just a few blocks but holds more than 150 stores selling clothes, books, records, furnishings, and specialty items. ✉ *Cambridge* Ⓜ *Harvard.*

Newbury Street. Boston's version of LA's Rodeo Drive, all of Newbury Street is a shoppers' paradise, from high-end names such as Brooks Brothers to tiny specialty shops such as the Fish and Bone. Upscale clothing stores, up-to-the-minute art galleries, and dazzling jewelers line the street near the Public Garden. As you head toward Massachusetts Avenue, Newbury gets funkier and the cacophony builds, with skate-boarders zipping through traffic and garbage-pail drummers burning licks outside hip boutiques. The big-name stores run from Arlington Street to the Prudential Center. ✉ *Boston* ⊕ *www.newbury-st.com* Ⓜ *Arlington, Copley, Hynes.*

Porter Square. This spot in north Cambridge has distinctive clothing stores, as well as crafts shops, coffee shops, natural-foods stores, restaurants, and bars with live music. ✉ *West on Massachusetts Ave. from Harvard Sq., Cambridge* Ⓜ *Porter Square.*

Prudential Center. A skywalk connects Copley Place to the Prudential Center. The Pru, as it's often called, contains moderately priced chain stores such as Ann Taylor and the Body Shop, and is anchored by Saks Fifth Avenue and Lord and Taylor. ✉ *800 Boylston St., Back Bay* ☎ *800/746–7778* ⊕ *www.prudentialcenter.com* Ⓜ *Prudential.*

South End. Merchants here are benefiting from the ongoing gentrification that has brought high real-estate prices and trendy restaurants to the area. Explore the chic home-furnishings and gift shops that line Tremont Street, starting at Berkeley Street. The MBTA's Silver Line bus runs through the South End. ✉ *Boston* ⊕ *www.south-end-boston. com* Ⓜ *Back Bay.*

BEACON HILL

CLOTHING AND SHOES

Crush Boutique. Step down to this subterranean shop to find weekend casual outfits, jeans, silky shifts, and even party-girl attire. You'll also find affordable jewelry and handbags to dress up any ensemble. Crush's Newbury Street shop (between Fairfield and Gloucester streets) has a more LA vibe to it. ✉ *131 Charles St., Beacon Hill* ☎ *617/720–0010* ⊕ *www.shopcrushboutique.com* Ⓜ *Charles/MGH.*

Helen's Leather Shop. Channel your inner cowgirl (or -boy) at this family-owned shop specializing in Western wear, including hand-tooled boots embroidered, dyed, and crafted from leather and exotic skins. Choose from half a dozen brands of boots (Lucchese, Nocona, Dan Post, Tony Lama, Justin, and Frye); then browse through the leather sandals, jackets, briefcases, luggage, and accessories. ✉ *110 Charles St., Beacon Hill* ☎ *617/742–2077* ⊕ *www.helensleather.com* ☉ *Closed Tues. May–Oct.* Ⓜ *Charles/MGH.*

Moxie. Shoe fanatics will swoon over the personal service and tightly curated selection of fashion-forward flats, sandals, heels, and boots at this friendly, neighborhood boutique, which also carries a reliable assortment of galoshes, in the event of a sudden downpour. ✉ *51 Charles St., Beacon Hill* ☎ *617/557–9991* ⊕ *www.moxieboston.com* Ⓜ *Charles/MGH.*

Wish. This contemporary women's boutique can outfit you for a stylish weekend in the country or a sultry soiree in the city. You'll find beloved brands like Diane von Furstenberg, Theory, and Joie, along with an otherworldly, cool-weather cashmere collection that has earned a cult following. ✉ *49 Charles St., Beacon Hill* ☎ *617/227–4441* ⊕ *www. wishboston.com* Ⓜ *Charles/MGH.*

3

BACK BAY

ART GALLERIES

Copley Society of Art. After more than a century, this nonprofit membership organization continues to present the works of well-known and aspiring New England artists. ✉ *158 Newbury St., Back Bay* ☎ *617/536–5049* ⊕ *www.copleysociety.org* ☉ *Closed Mon. except by appointment* Ⓜ *Copley.*

CLOTHING AND SHOES

Alan Bilzerian. Satisfying the Euro crowd, this store sells luxe men's and women's clothing by such fashion darlings as Yohji Yamamoto and Ann Demeulemeester. ✉ *34 Newbury St., Back Bay* ☎ *617/536–1001* ⊕ *www.alanbilzerian.com* ☉ *Closed Sun.* Ⓜ *Arlington.*

Anne Fontaine. You can never have too many white shirts—especially if they're designed by this Parisienne. The simple, sophisticated designs are mostly executed in cotton and priced around $295. Complete your outfit with the store's selection of sleek skirts, slacks, and accessories. ✉ *280 Boylston St., Back Bay* ☎ *617/423–0366* ⊕ *www.annefontaine. com* Ⓜ *Arlington, Boylston.*

Jos. A. Bank Clothiers. Founded in 1907, this national men's chain with two other locations, 70 Franklin Street and 84 State Street, has crisp suits, dress shirts, and leather shoes for the conservatively well-dressed male everywhere. And gents, should you need a tuxedo at the last minute, rest assured. The store rents them. ✉ *399 Boylston St., Back Bay* ☎ *617/536–5050* ⊕ *www.josbank.com* Ⓜ *Arlington.*

DEPARTMENT STORES

Barneys New York. The hoopla (not to mention the party) generated by this store's arrival was surprising in a city where everything new is viewed with trepidation. But clearly Boston's denizens have embraced the lofty, two-story space because it's filled with cutting-edge lines like Comme des Garçons and Nina Ricci, as well as a few bargains in the second-level Co-op section. ✉ *100 Huntington Ave., Back Bay* ☎ *617/385–3300* ⊕ *www.barneys.com* Ⓜ *Copley.*

Lord & Taylor. Somewhat overstuffed with merchandise for men, women, children and infants, this Boston branch of the popular national chain stocks classic clothing by such designers as Anne Klein and Ralph Lauren, along with accessories, cosmetics, and jewelry. ✉ *760 Boylston St., Back Bay* ☎ *617/262–6000* ⊕ *www.lordandtaylor.com* Ⓜ *Prudential Center.*

Neiman Marcus. At its Back Bay location, the flashy Texas-based retailer jokingly referred to by some as "Needless Markup" has three levels of swank designers and a jaw-dropping shoe section, as well as cosmetics and housewares. ⊠ *5 Copley Pl., Back Bay* ☎ *617/536–3660* ⊕ *www. neimanmarcus.com* Ⓜ *Back Bay.*

SPECIALTY STORES

The Fish and Bone. This boutique is dedicated to all things cat and dog. Choose from the enormous selection of collars, toys, and food. ⊠ *217 Newbury St., Back Bay* ☎ *857/753–4176* ⊕ *www.thefishandbone.com* Ⓜ *Arlington.*

THRIFT SHOPS

Second Time Around. Okay, so $700 isn't all that cheap for a used suit—but what if it's Chanel? Many of the items here, from jeans to fur coats, are new merchandise; the rest is on consignment. The staff makes periodic markdowns, ranging from 20% to 50% over a 90-day period. If nothing strikes you at this location, keep walking down Newbury Street, where you'll have two more chances—219 Newbury and 324 Newbury—to ferret out that perfect piece. ⊠ *176 Newbury St., Back Bay* ☎ *617/247–3504* ⊕ *www.secondtimearound.net* Ⓜ *Copley.*

DOWNTOWN

BOOKS

Brattle Book Shop. The late George Gloss built this into Boston's best used- and rare-book shop. Today his son Kenneth fields queries from passionate book lovers. If the book you want is out of print, Brattle has it or can probably find it. The store has been in operation since 1825. ⊠ *9 West St., Downtown* ☎ *617/542–0210, 800/447–9595* ⊕ *www. brattlebookshop.com* ⊙ *Closed Sun.* Ⓜ *Downtown Crossing.*

DEPARTMENT STORES

Macy's. Three floors offer men's and women's clothing and shoes, housewares, and cosmetics. Although top designers and a fur salon constitute part of the mix, Macy's Boston location doesn't feel exclusive; instead, it's a popular source for family basics. ⊠ *450 Washington St., Downtown* ☎ *617/357–3000* ⊕ *www.macys.com* Ⓜ *Downtown Crossing.*

SOUTH END

CRAFTS

Gracie Finn's. You'll never know what you'll find at this trendy South End shop packed with whatever strikes the owner's fancy, like colorful canvas bags, unusual cards, luxurious soaps, feather-light merino wool scarves, and not-your-dime-store party hats in hot pink with silver glitter. ⊠ *50 Concord Sq., South End* ☎ *617/357–0321* ⊕ *www.graciefinn. com* Ⓜ *Back Bay.*

TOYS

Tadpole. This is a treasure trove of educational games, dolls, trucks, blocks, and every other necessity for a kid's toy chest. Stock up on baby gear and essentials as well. ✉ *58 Clarendon St., South End* ☎ *617/778–1788* ⊕ *www.shoptadpole.com* Ⓜ *Back Bay.*

CAMBRIDGE

ANTIQUES

Cambridge Antique Market. Off the beaten track, this antiques hot spot has a selection bordering on overwhelming: five floors of goods from over 150 dealers ranging from 19th-century furniture to vintage clothing, much of it reasonably priced. Head to the basement for a large selection of secondhand bikes. For those with four wheels, two parking lots sit next to the building. ✉ *201 Monsignor O'Brien Hwy., Cambridge* ☎ *617/868–9655* ⊕ *www.marketantique.com* ◷ *Closed Mon.* Ⓜ *Lechmere.*

BOOKS

Harvard Book Store. Time disappears as you browse the tables and shelves of this always-busy bookstore packed with new titles upstairs and used and remaindered books downstairs. The collection's diversity has made the store a favored destination for academics. ✉ *1256 Massachusetts Ave., Cambridge* ☎ *617/661–1515* ⊕ *www.harvard.com* Ⓜ *Harvard.*

Schoenhof's. Since 1856 a friendly staff has been helping patrons navigate through thousands of foreign books, including ones in French, German, Italian, and Spanish. The store also excels in printed materials for learning more than 500 different foreign languages and has a nice selection of foreign books for children. ✉ *76-A Mount Auburn St., Cambridge* ☎ *617/547–8855* ⊕ *www.schoenhofs.com* ◷ *Closed Sun.* Ⓜ *Harvard.*

CLOTHING AND SHOES

Mint Julep. Cute dresses, playful skirts, and form-fitting tops make up the selection here. The Cambridge location is a little larger and easier to navigate, but Brookline houses the original. ✉ *6 Church St., Cambridge* ☎ *617/576–6468* ⊕ *www.shopmintjulep.com* Ⓜ *Harvard.*

TOYS

FAMILY **The World's Only Curious George Store.** Time can really slip away from you in this jungle of kids' books and gifts. Decorated with tropical plants, a fake hut, and tot-size chairs, and equipped with puzzles, toys, activity sets, and books of all kinds for all ages, this store is a wonderland for kids and a parent's salvation on a rainy day. ✉ *1 JFK St., Harvard Sq., Cambridge* ☎ *617/498–0062* ⊕ *thecuriousgeorgestore.com* Ⓜ *Harvard.*

SIDE TRIPS FROM BOSTON

Updated by Megan Johnson

LEXINGTON

16 miles northwest of Boston.

Discontented with the British, American Colonials burst into action in Lexington in April 1775. On April 18, patriot leader Paul Revere alerted the town that British soldiers were approaching. The next day, as the British advance troops arrived in Lexington on their march toward Concord, the Minutemen were waiting to confront the Redcoats in what became the first skirmish of the Revolutionary War.

These first military encounters of the American Revolution are very much a part of present-day Lexington, a modern suburban town that sprawls out from the historic sites near its center. Although the downtown area is generally lively, with ice cream and coffee shops, boutiques, and a great little movie theater, the town becomes especially animated each Patriots' Day (April 19, but celebrated on the third Monday in April), when costume-clad groups re-create the Minutemen's battle maneuvers and Paul Revere rides again.

To learn more about the city and the 1775 clash, stop by the **Lexington Visitor Center.**

GETTING HERE AND AROUND

Massachusetts Bay Transportation Authority (MBTA) operates bus service in the greater Boston area and serves Lexington.

Contacts MBTA. ☎ *800/392–6100, 617/222–3200, 617/222–5146 TTY* ⊕ *www.mbta.com.*

VISITOR INFORMATION

Contacts Lexington Visitors Center. ⊠ *1875 Massachusetts Ave.* ☎ *781/862–1450* ⊕ *www.lexingtonchamber.org.*

TOURS

Contacts Liberty Ride. ⊠ *1875 Massachusetts Ave.* ☎ *781/698–4586* ⊕ *tourlexington.us/libertyride.html.*

EXPLORING

Battle Green. It was on this 2-acre triangle of land, on April 19, 1775, that the first confrontation between British soldiers, who were marching from Boston toward Concord, and the Colonial militia known as the Minutemen took place. The Minutemen—so called because they were able to prepare themselves at a moment's notice—were led by Captain John Parker, whose role in the American Revolution is commemorated in Henry Hudson Kitson's renowned 1900 *Minuteman* statue. Facing downtown Lexington at the tip of Battle Green, the statue's in a traffic island, and therefore makes for a difficult photo op. ⊠ *Junction of Massachusetts Ave. and Bedford St.* ⊡ *Free.*

Buckman Tavern. While waiting for the arrival of the British on the morning of April 19, 1775, the Minutemen gathered at this 1690 tavern. A half-hour tour takes in the tavern's seven rooms, which have been

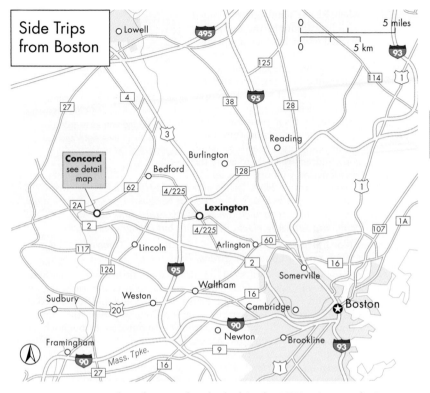

Side Trips
from Boston

restored to the way they looked in the 1770s. Among the items on display is an old front door with a hole made by a British musket ball. ✉ *1 Bedford St.* 📞 *781/862–1703* ⊕ *www.lexingtonhistory.org* 🎫 *First Shot! Package (Buckman Tavern, Munroe Tavern, and Hancock-Clarke House): $15. One house: $8* 🕑 *Mar. 15–Nov. 28, daily 10–4.*

Hancock-Clarke House. On April 18, 1775, Paul Revere came here to warn patriots John Hancock and Sam Adams (who were staying at the house while attending the Provincial Congress in nearby Concord) of the advance of British troops. Hancock and Adams, on whose heads the British king had put a price, fled to avoid capture. The house, a parsonage built in 1698, is a 10-minute walk from Lexington Common. Inside are the pistols of the British major John Pitcairn, as well as period furnishings and portraits. ✉ *36 Hancock St.* 📞 *781/862–1703* ⊕ *www.lexingtonhistory. org* 🎫 *$8; $15 combination ticket includes Buckman Tavern and Munroe Tavern* 🕑 *Apr. 11–May 25, weekends 10–4; May 26–Nov. 1, daily 10–4.*

FAMILY **Minute Man National Historical Park.** West of Lexington's center stretches this 1,000-acre, three-parcel park that also extends into nearby Lincoln and Concord. Begin your park visit at Lincoln's **Minute Man Visitor Center** to see its free multimedia presentation, "The Road to Revolution," a captivating introduction to the events of April 1775. Then, continuing along Highway 2A toward Concord, you pass the point where Revere's midnight ride ended with his capture by the British; it's marked with a boulder and plaque, as well as an enclosure where rangers sometimes give educational presentations. You can also visit the 1732 **Hartwell Tavern,** a restored drover's (driver's) tavern staffed by park employees in period costume; they frequently demonstrate musket firing or open-hearth cooking, and children are likely to enjoy the reproduction Colonial toys. ⊠ *250 North Great Rd. (Hwy. 2A), ¼ mile west of Hwy. 128* ☎ *978/369–6993* ⊕ *www.nps.gov/mima* ⊘ *Minute Man National Historical Park daily, sunrise–sunset. Hartwell Tavern Wed.–Sun., June 21–Aug. 16, and Mon. and Sat., Aug.–Oct., 9:30–5:30, but changes may occur.*

North Bridge Visitor Center. ⊠ *174 Liberty St., Concord* ☎ *978/369–6993* ⊕ *www.nps.gov/mima* ⊘ *Mar., Tues.–Sat. 11–3; Apr.–Oct., daily 9–5.*

Munroe Tavern. As April 19, 1775, dragged on, British forces met fierce resistance in Concord. Dazed and demoralized after the battle at Concord's Old North Bridge, the British backtracked and regrouped at this 1695 tavern 1 mile east of Lexington Common, while the Munroe family hid in nearby woods. The troops then retreated through what is now the town of Arlington. After a bloody battle there, they returned to Boston. Tours of the tavern last about 30 minutes. ⊠ *1332 Massachusetts Ave.* ☎ *781/862–1703* ⊕ *www.lexingtonhistory.org* ▧ *$8; $15 combination ticket includes Hancock-Clarke House and Buckman Tavern* ⊘ *Apr. 11–Memorial Day, weekends noon–4; Memorial Day–Nov. 1, daily noon–4* ☞ *Part of Lexington Historical Society.*

National Heritage Museum. View artifacts from all facets of American life, put in social and political context. Specializing in the history of American Freemasonry and Fraternalism, the changing exhibits and lectures also focus on local events leading up to April 1775 and illustrate Revolutionary-era life through everyday objects such as blacksmithing tools, bloodletting paraphernalia, and dental instruments, including a "tooth key" used to extract teeth. ⊠ *33 Marrett Rd., Hwy. 2A at Massachusetts Ave.* ☎ *781/861–6559* ⊕ *www.monh. org* ▧ *Donations accepted* ⊘ *Wed.–Sat. 10–4.*

CONCORD

About 10 miles west of Lexington, 21 miles northwest of Boston.

The Concord of today is a modern suburb with a busy center filled with arty shops, places to eat, and (recalling the literary history made here) old bookstores. Autumn lovers, take note: Concord is a great place to start a fall foliage tour. From Boston, head west along Route 2 to Concord, and then continue on to find harvest stands and apple picking around Harvard and Stow.

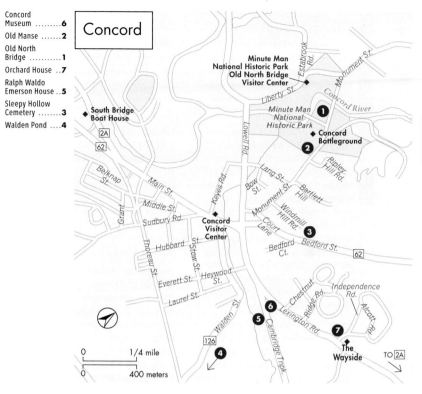

Concord

3

GETTING HERE AND AROUND

The MBTA runs buses to Concord. On the MBTA Commuter Rail, Concord is a 40-minute ride on the Fitchburg Line, which departs from Boston's North Station.

Contacts MBTA. ☎ *617/222–3200, 800/392–6100* ⊕ *www.mbta.com.*

VISITOR INFORMATION

Contacts Concord Visitor Center. ✉ *58 Main St.* ☎ *978/369–3120* ⊕ *www.concordchamberofcommerce.org.*

EXPLORING

FAMILY **Concord Museum.** The original contents of Emerson's private study, as well as the world's largest collection of Thoreau artifacts, reside in this 1930 Colonial Revival building just east of the town center. The museum provides a good overview of the town's history, from its original American Indian settlement to the present. Highlights include American Indian artifacts, furnishings from Thoreau's Walden Pond cabin (there's a replica of the cabin itself on the museum's lawn), and one of the two lanterns hung at Boston's Old North Church to signal that the British were coming by sea. If you've brought children, ask for a free family activity pack. ✉ *200 Lexington Rd., entrance on Cambridge Tpke.* ☎ *978/369–9763* ⊕ *www.concordmuseum.org* 🖼 *$10*

CLOSE UP

Literary Concord

The first wholly American literary movement was born in Concord, the tiny town west of Boston that, quite coincidentally, also witnessed the beginning of the American Revolution.

Under the influence of essayist and poet Ralph Waldo Emerson, a group eventually known as the Transcendental Club (but called the Hedges Club at the time) assembled regularly in Emerson's Concord home. Henry David Thoreau, a fellow townsman and famous proponent of self-reliance, was an integral club member, along with such others as pioneering feminist Margaret Fuller and poet Ellery Channing, both drawn to Concord simply because of Emerson's presence.

These are the names that have become indelible bylines in high school anthologies and college syllabi, but Concord also produced beloved authors outside the Transcendentalist movement. These writers include Louisa May Alcott of *Little Women* fame and children's book author Harriet Lothrop, pseudonymously known as Margaret Sydney. Even Nathaniel Hawthorne, whose various temporary homes around

Massachusetts constitute a literary trail all their own, resided in Concord during the early and later portions of his career.

The cumulative inkwells of these authors have bestowed upon Concord a literary legacy unique in the United States, both for its influence on literature in general and for the quantity of related sights packed within such a small radius. From Alcott's Orchard House to Hawthorne's Old Manse, nearly all of their houses remain standing, well preserved and open for tours.

The Thoreau Institute, within walking distance of a reconstruction of Thoreau's famous cabin in the woods at Walden Pond, is a repository of his papers and original editions. Emerson's study sits in the Concord Museum, across the street from his house. Even their final resting places are here, on Authors Ridge in Sleepy Hollow Cemetery, a few short blocks from the town common. **Concord Bike Tours** (☎ *978/697–1897* ⊕ *www.concordbiketours.com*) will guide you through the sites on two wheels, usually April through November (weather permitting).

⊗ *Jan.–Mar., Mon.–Sat. 11–4, Sun. 1–4; Apr., May, and Sept.–Dec., Mon.–Sat. 9–5, Sun. noon–5; June–Aug., daily 9–5.*

Old Manse. The Reverend William Emerson, grandfather of Ralph Waldo Emerson, watched rebels and Redcoats battle from behind his home, which was within sight of the Old North Bridge. The house, built in 1770, was occupied continuously by the Emerson family for almost two centuries, except for a 3½-year period during which Nathaniel Hawthorne rented it. Furnishings date from the late 18th century. Tours run throughout the day and last 45 minutes, with a new tour starting within 15 minutes of when the first person signs up. ⊠ *269 Monument St.* ☎ *978/369–3909* ⊕ *www.thetrustees.org/places-to-visit/greater-boston/old-manse.html* ⊡ *Grounds free; house tours $10* ⊗ *Grounds daily sunrise–sunset. House walk-in tours: Mar. 16–-Apr. 19, weekends* *noon–5; Apr. 19–Oct. 31, noon–5 weekends; Nov. 1–Dec. 29, week-ends noon–5. Prebooked, by prior appointment tours are available daily year-round.*

Old North Bridge. A half mile from Concord center, at this bridge, the Concord Minutemen turned the tables on the British on the morning of April 19, 1775. The Americans didn't fire first, but when two of their own fell dead from a Redcoat volley, Major John Buttrick of Concord roared, "Fire, fellow soldiers, for God's sake, fire." The Minutemen released volley after volley, and the Redcoats fled. Daniel Chester French's famous statue *The Minuteman* (1875) honors the country's first freedom fighters. Inscribed at the foot of the statue are words Ralph Waldo Emerson wrote in 1837 describing the confrontation: "By the rude bridge that arched the flood / Their flag to April's breeze unfurled / Here once the embattled farmers stood / And fired the shot heard round the world." The lovely wooded surroundings give a sense of what the landscape was like in more rural times. Guests who take the Liberty Ride trolley tour from Lexington Center will be treated to a quick stop at the bridge. ⊠ *Concord Center, near Minute Man Monument* ⊕ *www.nps.gov/mima.*

Orchard House. The dark brown exterior of Louisa May Alcott's family home sharply contrasts with the light, wit, and energy so much in evidence within. Named for the apple orchard that once surrounded it, Orchard House was the Alcott family home from 1857 to 1877. Here Louisa wrote *Little Women,* based in part on her life with her three sisters; and her father, Bronson, founded the Concord School of Philosophy—the building remains behind the house. Because Orchard House had just one owner after the Alcotts left, and because it became a museum in 1911, more than 75% of the original furnishings remain, including the semicircular shelf-desk where Louisa wrote *Little Women.* ⊠ *399 Lexington Rd.* ☎ *978/369–4118* ⊕ *www.louisamayalcott.org* ☞ *$10* ⊙ *Apr.–Oct., Mon.–Sat. 10–4:30, Sun. 1–4:30; Nov.–Mar., weekdays 11–3, Sat. 10–4:30, Sun. 1–4:30. Tours usually every 30 mins Apr.–Oct.; less frequently in winter.*

Ralph Waldo Emerson House. The 19th-century essayist and poet Ralph Waldo Emerson lived briefly in the Old Manse in 1834–35, then moved to this home, where he lived until his death in 1882. Here he wrote the *Essays.* Except for artifacts from Emerson's study, now at the nearby Concord Museum, the Emerson House furnishings have been preserved as the writer left them, down to his hat resting on the newel post. You must join one of the half-hour-long tours to see the interior. ⊠ *28 Cambridge Tpke., at Lexington Rd.* ☎ *978/369–2236* ⊕ *www. nps.gov/nr/travel/massachusetts_conservation/ralph_waldo_emerson_ house.html#plan* ☞ *$8* ⊙ *Mid-Apr.–Oct., Thurs.–Sun. 10–4:30. Call for tour schedule.*

Sleepy Hollow Cemetery. This garden cemetery on the National Registry of Historic Places serves as a home to the graves of American literary greats like Louisa May Alcott, Ralph Waldo Emerson, Henry David Thoreau, and Nathaniel Hawthorne. Each Memorial Day Alcott's grave

Retrace Henry David Thoreau's steps at Walden Pond.

is decorated in commemoration of her death. ⊠ *Bedford St. (Hwy. 62)* ☎ *978/318–3233* ⊘ *Daily dawn–dusk.*

Fodor'sChoice
★

Walden Pond. For lovers of Early American literature, a trip to Concord isn't complete without a pilgrimage to Henry David Thoreau's most famous residence. Here, in 1845, at age 28, Thoreau moved into a one-room cabin—built for $28.12—on the shore of this 100-foot-deep kettle hole formed by the retreat of an ancient glacier. Living alone for the next two years, Thoreau discovered the benefits of solitude and the beauties of nature. *Walden,* published in 1854, is a mixture of philosophy, nature writing, and proto-ecology. The site of the original house is staked out in stone. A full-size, authentically furnished replica of the cabin stands about ½ mile from the original site, near the Walden Pond State Reservation parking lot. To get to Walden Pond State Reservation from the center of Concord—a trip of only 1½ miles—take Concord's Main Street a block west from Monument Square, turn left onto Walden Street, and head for the intersection of Highways 2 and 126. Cross over Highway 2 onto Highway 126, heading south for ½ mile. ⊠ *915 Walden St. (Hwy. 126)* ☎ *978/369–3254* ⊕ *www.mass.gov/ dcr/parks/walden* ⊠ *Free, $8 for vehicles with Massachusetts plates, $10 for vehicles with non-Massachusetts plates* ⊘ *Daily 8 am–sunset weather permitting.*

WHERE TO EAT

$$
AMERICAN

✕ **Main Streets Market & Cafe.** Cyclists, families, and sightseers pack into this brick building, which was used to store munitions during the Revolutionary War. Wood floors and blackboard menus add a touch of nostalgia, but the extensive menu includes many modern hits. Breakfast offerings include a quiche and breakfast sandwich of the day. At lunch, the grilled panini are excellent; they also serve flatbread pizza and pub fare. At night heartier offerings dominate the menu, including baked lobster mac and cheese, scallop and shrimp risotto, and a Yankee pot roast dinner. There's a full bar, live music six nights a week, and in summer the small alley outside leads to a counter that serves ice cream. It's open late on Friday and Saturday night. $ *Average main: $18* ⊠ *42 Main St.* ☎ *978/369–9948* ⊕ *www.mainstreetsmarketandcafe.com* ▭ *No credit cards.*

3

THE NORTH SHORE

The slice of Massachusetts's Atlantic Coast known as the North Shore extends past Boston to the Cape Ann region just shy of the New Hampshire border. In addition to miles of woods and beaches, the North Shore's highlights include Marblehead, a classic New England sea town; Salem, which thrives on a history of witches, writers, and maritime trades; Gloucester, the oldest seaport in America; Rockport, rich with crafts shops and artists' studios; and Newburyport, with its redbrick center and clapboard mansions, and a handful of typical New England towns in between. Bustling during the short summer season and breathtaking during the autumn foliage, the North Shore is calmer (and colder) between November and June. Many restaurants, inns, and attractions operate on reduced hours during the off-season.

MARBLEHEAD

17 miles north of Boston.

Marblehead, with its narrow and winding streets, beautifully preserved clapboard homes, sea captains' mansions, and harbor, looks much as it must have when it was founded in 1629 by fishermen from Cornwall and the Channel Islands. One of New England's premier sailing capitals, Marblehead attracts boats from along the Eastern Seaboard each July during Race Week—first held in 1889. Parking in town can be difficult; lots at the end of Front Street or on State Street by the Landing restaurant are the best options.

VISITOR INFORMATION

Contacts Marblehead Chamber of Commerce Information Booth. ⊠ *62 Pleasant St.* ☎ *781/631–2868* ⊕ *www.visitmarblehead.com.*

EXPLORING

Abbott Hall. The town's Victorian-era municipal building, built in 1876, displays Archibald Willard's painting *The Spirit of '76.* Many visitors, familiar since childhood with this image of the three Revolutionary veterans with fife, drum, and flag, are surprised to find the original in an otherwise unassuming town hall. Also on-site is a small naval museum exploring Marblehead's maritime past. ⊠ *188 Washington St.* ☎ *781/631–0000* ▭ *Free* ☉ *Call for hrs.*

Fort Sewall. Magnificent views of Marblehead, of the harbor, the Misery Islands, and the Atlantic are best enjoyed from this fort built in 1644 atop the rocky cliffs of the harbor. Used as a defense against the French in 1742 as well as during the War of 1812, Fort Sewall is today open to the public as community parkland. Barracks and underground quarters can still be seen, and Revolutionary War reenactments by members of the modern-day Glover's Marblehead Regiment are staged at the fort annually. ⊠ *End of Front St.* ☎ *781/631–1000* ⊕ *www.marblehead.org/ index.aspx?NID=1012* ⊠ *Free* ☉ *Daily sunrise–sunset.*

The 1768 Jeremiah Lee Mansion. Marblehead's 18th-century high society is exemplified in this mansion run by the Marblehead Museum and historical society. Colonel Lee was the wealthiest merchant and ship owner in Massachusetts in 1768, and although few original furnishings remain, the unique hand-painted wallpaper and fine collection of traditional North Shore furniture provide clues to the life of an American gentleman. Across the street at the main museum (open year-round), the J.O.J. Frost Folk Art Gallery pays tribute to the town's talented 19th-century native son; there are also exhibits focusing on the Civil War. ⊠ *161 Washington St.* ☎ *781/631–1768* ⊕ *www.marbleheadmuseum. org/properties/lee-mansion/* ⊠ *$10* ☉ *June–Oct., Tues.–Sat. 10–4.*

WHERE TO EAT AND STAY

$

SEAFOOD

✕ **The Landing.** Decorated in nautical blues and whites, this pleasant restaurant sits right on Marblehead harbor, with a deck that's nearly in the water. The restaurant offers classic New England fare like clam chowder and broiled scrod, and serves brunch on Sunday. The pub area has a lighter menu and a local feel. $ *Average main: $12* ⊠ *81 Front St.* ☎ *781/639–1266* ⊕ *www.thelandingrestaurant.com* ⊟ *No credit cards.*

$$

B&B/INN

Fodor's Choice

★

⊡ **Harbor Light Inn.** Housed in a pair of adjoining 18th-century mansions in the heart of Old Town Marblehead, this elegant inn, which is now honored as one of the Distinguished Inns of New England, features many rooms with canopy beds, brick fireplaces, and Jacuzzis. **Pros:** nice location amid period homes; on-site tavern with pub menu; outdoor heated swimming pool. **Cons:** many one-way and narrow streets make this town somewhat confusing to get around in by car and the inn tricky to find. $ *Rooms from: $169* ⊠ *58 Washington St.* ☎ *781/631–2186* ⊕ *www.harborlightinn.com* ⇆ *20 rooms, 3 apartments* ⍨ *Breakfast.*

SALEM

16 miles northeast of Boston, 4 miles west of Marblehead.

Known for years as the Witch City, Salem is redefining itself. Though numerous witch-related attractions and shops still draw tourists, there's much more to the city. But first, a bit on its bewitched past . . .

The witchcraft hysteria emerged from the trials of 1692, when several Salem-area girls fell ill and accused some of the townspeople of casting spells on them. More than 150 men and women were charged with practicing witchcraft, a crime punishable by death. After the trials later that year, 19 people were hanged and one man was crushed to death.

Though the witch trials might have built Salem's infamy, it'd be a mistake to ignore the town's rich maritime and creative traditions, which played integral roles in the country's evolution. Frigates out of Salem

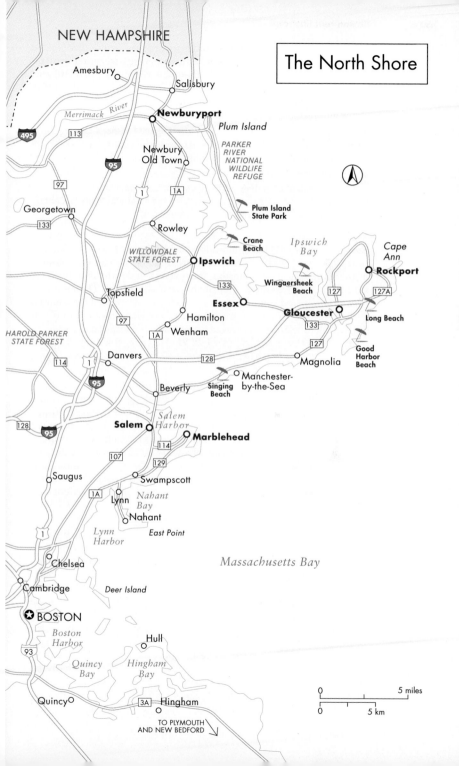

The North Shore

NEW HAMPSHIRE

Amesbury
Salisbury
Newburyport
Merrimack River
Plum Island
495
113
Newbury
Old Town
PARKER
RIVER
NATIONAL
WILDLIFE
REFUGE
95
97
1
1A
Georgetown
Plum Island
State Park
133
Rowley
Crane
Beach
Ipswich
Bay
Cape
Ann
WILLOWDALE
STATE FOREST
Ipswich
Rockport
133
Wingaersheek
Beach
127
127A
Topsfield
Essex
Gloucester
97
Hamilton
133
Long Beach
HAROLD PARKER
STATE FOREST
1A
Wenham
127
114
1
Danvers
128
Magnolia
Good
Harbor
Beach
95
Beverly
Manchester-
by-the-Sea
Singing
Beach
128
Salem
Harbor
95
Salem
Marblehead
114
107
129
Saugus
Swampscott
1A
Lynn
Nahant
Bay
Nahant
Lynn
Harbor
East Point
Massachusetts Bay
Chelsea
Cambridge
Deer Island
BOSTON
Boston
Harbor
Hull
93
Quincy
Bay
Hingham
Bay
Quincy
3A
Hingham
TO PLYMOUTH
AND NEW BEDFORD

0   5 miles
0   5 km

opened the Far East trade routes and generated the wealth that created America's first millionaires. Among its native talents are writer Nathaniel Hawthorne, the intellectual Peabody Sisters, navigator Nathaniel Bowditch, and architect Samuel McIntire. This creative spirit is today celebrated in Salem's internationally recognized museums, waterfront shops and restaurants, galleries, and wide common.

To learn more on the area, stop by the **Regional Visitor's Center**. Innovatively designed in the Old Salem Armory, the center has exhibits, a 27-minute film, maps, and a gift shop.

VISITOR INFORMATION

Contacts Destination Salem. ⊠ *93 Washington St. (Salem City Hall)* ☎ *978/744–3663, 877/725–3662* ⊕ *www.salem.org.* **Regional Visitor's Center.** ⊠ *2 New Liberty St.* ☎ *978/740–1650* ⊕ *www.nps.gov/ner/sama.*

EXPLORING

House of the Seven Gables. Immortalized in Nathaniel Hawthorne's classic novel, this site is itself a historic treasure. Built in 1668 and also known as the Turner-Ingersoll Mansion, the house includes the famous secret staircase, a re-creation of Hepzibah's cent shop from *The House of Seven Gables*, and some of the finest Georgian interiors in the country. Also on the property is the small house where Hawthorne was born in 1804; built in 1750, it was moved from its original location a few blocks away. ⊠ *115 Derby St.* ☎ *978/744–0991* ⊕ *www.7gables.org* ⌨ *$12.50* ⊙ *Nov., Dec., and mid-Jan.–June, daily 10–5; July–Oct., daily 10–7.*

Fodor'sChoice ★ **Peabody Essex Museum.** Salem's world-class museum celebrates superlative works from around the globe and across time, including American art and architecture, Asian export art, photography, maritime art and history, as well as Native American, Oceanic, and African art. Its 30 galleries, housed in a contemplative blend of modern design, represent a diverse range of styles; exhibits include pieces ranging from American decorative and seamen's art to an interactive Art & Nature Center and photography. While there be sure to tour the Yin Yu Tang house. This fabulous 200-year-old house dates to the Qing Dynasty (1644–1911) of China. The museum brought it over from China in sections and reassembled it here. ⊠ *East India Sq.* ☎ *978/745–9500, 866/745–1876* ⊕ *www.pem.org* ⌨ *$18* ⊙ *Tues.–Sun. (and Mon. holidays) 10–5.*

Salem Maritime National Historic Site. Near Derby Wharf, this 9¼-acre site focuses on Salem's heritage as a major seaport with a thriving overseas trade. It includes the 1762 home of Elias Derby, America's first millionaire; the 1819 Customs House, made famous in Nathaniel Hawthorne's *The Scarlet Letter*; and a replica of the *Friendship*, a 171-foot, three-masted 1797 merchant vessel. There's also an active lighthouse dating from 1871, as well as the nation's last surviving 18th-century wharves. The West India Goods Store, across the street, is still a working 19th-century store, with glass jars of spices, teas, and coffees. New to the site is the 1770 Pedrick Store House, moved from nearby Marblehead and reassembled right on Derby Wharf; the two-story structure once played a vital role in the lucrative merchant seaside trade. ⊠ *193 Derby St.* ☎ *978/740–1650* ⊕ *www.nps.gov/sama* ⌨ *Site and tours free* ⊙ *Hrs vary.*

Salem Witch Museum. An informative and fun introduction to the 1692 witchcraft hysteria, this museum has a 15-minute guided tour through their exhibit, "Witches: Evolving Perceptions," that describes witch hunts through the years. ✉ *19½ N. Washington Sq.* ☎ *978/744–1692* 🌐 *www.salemwitchmuseum.com* 🎟 *$10* 🕑 *Sept.–June, daily 10–5; July and Aug., daily 10–7.*

WHERE TO EAT AND STAY

$$ SEAFOOD 🍴 **Finz Seafood & Grill.** This contemporary seafood restaurant on Pickering Wharf treats patrons to prime canal views. Seafood potpie and lobster rolls highlight the lunch menu, while sesame-crusted tuna or steamed lobster are dinner favorites. Nab a seat on the outdoor deck when the weather's fine and eat practically among the boats. There's also live music on occasional weeknights. [$] *Average main: $21* ✉ *76 Wharf St.* ☎ *978/744–8485* 🌐 *www.hipfinz.com.*

$ B&B/INN 🏨 **Amelia Payson House.** Built in 1845, this Greek Revival house is a comfortable bed-and-breakfast near all the historic attractions. **Pros:** spotless; cozy; decorated in period furniture. **Cons:** no children under 14. [$] *Rooms from: $145* ✉ *16 Winter St.* ☎ *978/744–8304* 🌐 *www.ameliapaysonhouse.com* 💳 *No credit cards* 🕑 *Closed Dec.–Apr.* 🛏 *3 rooms* 🍽 *Breakfast.*

$$ HOTEL 🏨 **The Hawthorne Hotel.** Elegantly restored, this full-service landmark hotel celebrates the town's most famous writer and is within walking distance from the town common, museums, and waterfront. **Pros:** lovely, historic lobby; parking available behind hotel; easy walking access to all the town's features. **Cons:** many rooms are small. [$] *Rooms from: $159* ✉ *18 Washington Sq. W* ☎ *978/744–4080, 800/729–7829* 🌐 *www.hawthornehotel.com* 🛏 *93 rooms (89 in main building, and 4 in guesthouse)* 🍽 *No meals* ☞ *$25 charge per room per night for pets.*

PERFORMING ARTS

THEATER

Cry Innocent: The People versus Bridget Bishop. This show, the longest continuously running play north of Boston, transports audience members to Bridget Bishop's trial of 1692. After hearing historical testimonies, the audience cross-examines the witnesses and must then decide the verdict. Actors respond in character revealing much about the Puritan frame of mind. Each show is different and allows audience members to play their "part" in history. ✉ *Old Town Hall, 32 Derby Sq.* ☎ *978/867–4767* 🌐 *www.cryinnocentsalem.com* 🎟 *$12* 🕑 *July–Oct., showtimes vary.*

GLOUCESTER

37 miles northeast of Boston, 8 miles northeast of Manchester-by-the-Sea.

On Gloucester's fine seaside promenade is a famous statue of a man steering a ship's wheel, his eyes searching the horizon. The statue, which honors those who go down to the sea in ships, was commissioned by the town citizens in celebration of Gloucester's 300th anniversary in 1923. The oldest seaport in the nation (with some of the North Shore's best beaches) is still a major fishing port. Sebastian Junger's 1997 book *A Perfect Storm* was an account of the fate of the *Andrea*

The First Witch Trial

It was in Danvers, not Salem, that the first witch trial was held, originating with the family of Samuel Parris, a minister who moved to the area in 1680 from Barbados, bringing with him two slaves, including one named Tituba. In 1691 Samuel's daughter, Betty, and niece, Abigail, began having "fits." Tituba, who had told Betty and Abigail stories of magic and witchcraft from her homeland, baked a "witch cake" to identify the witches who were harming the girls. The girls in turn accused Tituba of witchcraft.

After three days of "questioning," which included beatings from Samuel and a promise from him to free her if she cooperated, Tituba confessed to meeting the devil (in the form of a black hog or dog). She also claimed there were other witches in the village, confirming the girls' accusations against Sarah Good and Sarah Osborne, but she refused to name any others. Tituba's trial prompted the frenzy that led to the deaths of 20 accused "witches."

Gail, a Gloucester fishing boat caught in the storm of the century in October 1991. In 2000 the book was made into a movie, filmed on location in Gloucester.

VISITOR INFORMATION

Contacts Cape Ann Chamber of Commerce. ✉ *33 Commercial St.* ☎ *978/283–1601* ⊕ *www.capeannchamber.com.*

EXPLORING

Cape Ann Museum. The recently renovated Cape Ann Museum celebrates the art, history, and culture of Cape Ann. The museum's collections include fine art from the 19th century to the present, artifacts from the fishing, maritime, and granite-quarrying industries, as well as textiles, furniture, a library-archives, and two historic houses. ✉ *27 Pleasant St.* ☎ *978/283–0455* ⊕ *www.capeannmuseum.org* 🗎 *$10* ⊙ *Tues.–Sat. 10–5, Sun. 1–4.*

Hammond Castle Museum. Inventor John Hays Hammond Jr. built this structure in 1926 to resemble a "medieval" stone castle. Hammond is credited with more than 500 patents, including inventions associated with the organ that bears his name. The museum contains medieval-style furnishings and paintings, and the Great Hall houses an impressive 8,200-pipe organ. From the castle you can see Norman's Woe Rock, made famous by Longfellow in his poem "The Wreck of the Hesperus." ✉ *80 Hesperus Ave., south side of Gloucester off Rte. 127* ☎ *978/283–2080, 978/283–7673* ⊕ *www.hammondcastle.org* 🗎 *$10* ⊙ *Tues.–Sun. 10–4, last ticket sold at 3:30* ☞ *Closed in winter.*

Rocky Neck. The town's creative side thrives in this neighborhood, one of the oldest continuously working artists' colonies in the United States. Its alumni include Winslow Homer, Maurice Prendergast, Jane Peter, and Cecilia Beaux. ✉ *6 Wonson St.* ☎ *978/515–7005* ⊕ *www. rockyneckartcolony.org* ⊙ *Cultural Center: June–Aug., Thurs.–Sun.*

noon–6; Sept.–May, Thurs.–Sun. noon–4. Gallery 53: May–Oct., daily 10–6. Call for winter hrs.

BEACHES

Gloucester has some of the best beaches on the North Shore. From Memorial Day through mid-September, parking costs $20 on weekdays and $25 on weekends, when the lots often fill by 10 am.

Good Harbor Beach. This beach has calm, waveless waters and soft sand, and is surrounded by grassy dunes, making it perfect any time of year. In summer (June, July, and August), it is lifeguard patrolled and there is a snack bar if you don't feel like packing in food. The restrooms and showers are wheelchair accessible, and you can pick up beach toys at the concessions. On weekdays parking is plentiful, but the lot fills by 10 am on weekends. In June, green flies can be bothersome. **Amenities:** ood and drink; lifeguards; parking (fee); showers; toilets. **Best for:** swimming and playing on the shore. ⊠ *Clearly signposted from Rte. 127A* *Parking $20 per car; $25 on weekends and holidays.*

Long Beach. Just as its name implies, this soft-sand beach that is half in Rockport, half in Gloucester is long, and it's also broad. It draws crowds from the houses that border it, particularly on weekends. Pay attention to the tide schedule, or you may find there's no beach to sit on. Cape Ann Motor Inn is nearby. Very limited parking. Don't even think of parking on neighborhood streets if you don't have a town parking sticker—you will be towed. However, there is a lot on the Gloucester side. **Amenities:** none. **Best for:** swimming; walking. ⊠ *Off Rte. 127A on Gloucester-Rockport town line, off Rockport Rd.*

Wingaersheek Beach. With white sand and dunes, Wingaersheek Beach is a well-protected cove with both a beach side and a boat side. The white Annisquam lighthouse is in the bay. The beach is known for its miles of white sand and calm waters. On weekends arrive early. The parking lot generally fills up by mid-morning. **Amenities:** food and drink; parking (fee); toilets. **Best for:** swimming; walking. ⊠ *Exit 13 off Rte. 128* *Limited parking, $20 per car; $25 on weekends and holidays.*

WHERE TO EAT AND STAY

$$ ✕ **The Franklin Cafe.** This contemporary nightspot offers bistro-style AMERICAN chicken, roast cod, and steak frites, perfect for the late-night crowd (it's open until midnight during the summer). Live jazz is on tap every other Tuesday, and every Friday evening. Look for the signature martini glass over the door. $ *Average main: $20* ⊠ *118 Main St.* ☎ *978/283–7888* ⊕ *www.franklincafe.com* ⊗ *No lunch.*

$$ ✕ **Passports.** With an eclectic lunch and dinner menu—hence the name— ECLECTIC Passports is a bright and airy café with French, Spanish, and Thai dishes, as well as lobster sandwiches. The fried oysters and house haddock are favorites here, and there's always local art hanging on the walls for patrons to buy. Occasionally there are wine tastings. $ *Average main: $15* ⊠ *110 Main St.* ☎ *978/281–3680.*

$$ **Cape Ann Motor Inn.** On the sands of Long Beach, this three-story, HOTEL shingled motel has no-frills rooms except for the balconies and ocean views. **Pros:** exceptional view from every room; kids under five stay free. **Cons:** thin walls; motel quality; summer season can be loud and

crowded. [$] *Rooms from: $180* ✉ *33 Rockport Rd.* ☎ *978/281–2900, 800/464–8439* 🌐 *www.capeannmotorinn.com* 💳 *No credit cards* 🛏 *30 rooms, 1 suite* 🍴 *Breakfast.*

$ RESORT FAMILY 🏨 **Cape Ann's Marina Resort & Spa.** This year-round hotel less than a mile from downtown Gloucester comes alive in summer. **Pros:** free Wi-Fi. **Cons:** "resort" is a misnomer—the hotel is surrounded by parking lots; expect motel quality. [$] *Rooms from: $145* ✉ *75 Essex Ave.* ☎ *978/283–2116, 800/626–7660* 🌐 *www.capeannmarina.com* 🛏 *31 rooms* 🍴 *No meals.*

ROCKPORT

41 miles northeast of Boston, 4 miles northeast of Gloucester on Rte. 127.

Rockport, at the very tip of Cape Ann, derives its name from the local granite formations. Many Boston-area structures are made of stone cut from its long-gone quarries. Today the town is a tourist center with a well-marked, centralized downtown that is easy to navigate and access on foot. Unlike typical tourist-trap landmarks, Rockport's shops sell quality arts, clothing, and gifts, and its restaurants serve seafood or home-baked cookies rather than fast food. Walk past shops and colorful clapboard houses to the end of Bearskin Neck for an impressive view of the Atlantic Ocean and the old, weather-beaten lobster shack known as Motif No. 1 because of its popularity as a subject for amateur painters and photographers.

VISITOR INFORMATION

Contacts Cape Ann Chamber of Commerce, Rockport Division. ✉ *33 Commercial St., Gloucester* ☎ *978/283–1601* 🌐 *www.rockportusa.com.*

WHERE TO EAT AND STAY

$$ SEAFOOD 🍴 **Brackett's Ocean View.** A big bay window in this quiet, homey restaurant provides an excellent view across Sandy Bay. The menu includes chowders, fish cakes, and other seafood dishes. [$] *Average main: $18* ✉ *25 Main St.* ☎ *978/546–2797* 🌐 *www.bracketts.com* 💳 *No credit cards* 🕒 *Closed Nov.–Mar.*

$ B&B/INN Fodor's Choice ★ 🏨 **Sally Webster Inn.** This historic inn, which is within walking range of shops, restaurants, and beaches, was named for a member of Hannah Jumper's "Hatchet Gang," teetotalers who smashed up the town's liquor stores in 1856 and turned Rockport into the dry town it remained until as recently as 2008. **Pros:** homey atmosphere in an excellent location with attentive staff. **Cons:** some rooms accessed via second-floor stairs. [$] *Rooms from: $150* ✉ *34 Mt. Pleasant St.* ☎ *978/546–9251* 🌐 *www.sallywebster.com* 💳 *No credit cards* 🛏 *7 rooms* 🍴 *Breakfast.*

ESSEX

35 miles northeast of Boston, 12 miles west of Rockport.

The small seafaring town of Essex, once an important shipbuilding center, is surrounded by salt marshes and is filled with antiques stores and seafood restaurants.

GETTING HERE AND AROUND

Head west out of Cape Ann on Rte. 128, turning north on Rte. 133.

VISITOR INFORMATION

Contacts Escape to Essex. 🌐 *www.visitessexma.com.*

EXPLORING

FAMILY **Essex Shipbuilding Museum.** At what is still an active shipyard, this museum chronicles over 300 years of wooden shipbuilding. Essex launched approximately 400 vessels, most of them two-masted fishing schooners for the Gloucester fleet. The museum offers shipbuilding demonstrations, events, and self- and fully guided tours. The collection includes ship models on loan from the Smithsonian, as well as the 83-foot *Evelina M. Goulart*—one of only seven remaining Essex-built schooners. ✉ *66 Main St. (Rte. 133)* ☎ *978/768–7541* 🌐 *www.essexshipbuildingmuseum.org* 🎟 *Self-guided tour $7; guided tour $10* 🕒 *Mid-May–mid-Oct., Wed.–Sun. 10–5; early spring/late fall, weekends 10–5.*

WHERE TO EAT

$$ SEAFOOD FAMILY Fodor's Choice ★ 🍴 **Woodman's of Essex.** According to local legend, this is where Lawrence "Chubby" Woodman invented the first fried clam back in 1916. Today this sprawling wooden shack with indoor booths and outdoor picnic tables is *the* place for seafood in the rough. Besides fried clams, you can tuck into clam chowder, lobster rolls, or the popular "down-river" lobster combination plate. [$] *Average main: $16* ✉ *121 Main St. (Rte. 133)* ☎ *978/768–2559, 800/649–1773* 🌐 *www.woodmans.com* 💳 *No credit cards.*

IPSWICH

30 miles north of Boston, 6 miles northwest of Essex.

Quiet little Ipswich, settled in 1633 and famous for its clams, is said to have more 17th-century houses standing and occupied than any other place in America; more than 40 were built before 1725. Information and a booklet with a suggested walking tour are available at the **Ipswich Visitor Information Center.**

VISITOR INFORMATION

Contacts Ipswich Visitor Information Center. ✉ *36 S. Main St. (Rte. 1A)* ☎ *978/356–8540* 🌐 *www.ipswichvisitorcenter.org.*

EXPLORING

Castle Hill on the Crane Estate. This 59-room Stuart-style mansion, built in 1927 for Richard Crane—of the Crane plumbing company—and his family, is part of the Crane Estate, a stretch of more than 2,100 acres along the Essex and Ipswich rivers, encompassing Castle Hill, Crane Beach, and the Crane Wildlife Refuge. Although the original furnishings were sold at auction, the mansion has been elaborately refurnished in period style; photographs in most of the rooms show their original appearance. The Great House is open for one-hour tours and also hosts concerts and other events. Inquire about seasonal programs like fly-fishing or kayaking. If you're looking for an opulent and exquisite overnight stay, book a room at the on-site Inn at Castle Hill. ✉ *Argilla Rd.* ☎ *978/356–4351* 🎟 *Grounds: $10 per car; $2 per bicycle; $4 per motorcycle. Tours: prices vary* 🕒 *Memorial Day–Columbus Day weekends, Wed.–Sat., call for hrs.*

BEACHES

FAMILY **Crane Beach.** Crane Beach, one of New England's most beautiful beaches, is a sandy, 4-mile-long stretch backed by dunes and a nature trail. Public parking is available, but on a nice summer weekend it's usually full before lunch. There are lifeguards, a snack bar, and changing rooms. Check ahead before visiting mid-July to early August, when greenhead flies terrorize sunbathers. The Ipswich Essex Explorer bus runs between the Ipswich train station and Crane Beach weekends and holidays from June to September; the $5 pass includes round-trip bus fare and beach admission. Contact the Ipswich Visitor Information Center for information. **Amenities:** food and drink; lifeguards; parking (fee); toilets; showers. **Best for:** swimming; walking. ✉ *310 Argilla Rd.* ☎ *978/356–4354* 🎟 *In summer, $20/car weekdays, $25/car weekends* 🕒 *Daily 8–sunset.*

SPORTS AND THE OUTDOORS

FAMILY **Ipswich River Wildlife Sanctuary.** The Massachusetts Audubon Society's Ipswich River Wildlife Sanctuary has trails through marshland hills, where there are remains of early Colonial settlements as well as abundant wildlife. Make sure to grab some birdseed and get a trail map from the office. Enjoy bridges, man-made rock structures, and other surprises on the Rockery Trail. ✉ *87 Perkins Row, southwest of Ipswich, 1 mile off Rte. 97, Topsfield* ☎ *978/887–9264* 🌐 *www.massaudubon.org* 🎟 *$4* 🕒 *Tues.–Sun. dawn–dusk. Visitor center hrs vary.*

WHERE TO EAT

$$ SEAFOOD FAMILY Fodor's Choice ★ 🍴 **Clam Box.** Shaped like a giant fried-clam box, this small roadside stand is the best place to sample Ipswich's famous bivalves. Since 1935 locals and tourists have been lining up for clams, oysters, scallops, and onion rings. [$] *Average main: $18* ✉ *246 High St. (Rte. 1A)* ☎ *978/356–9707* 🌐 *www.ipswichma.com/clambox* 🕒 *Closed late Nov.–Feb.* ✍ *Reservations not accepted* ☞ *$10 credit card minimum.*

NEWBURYPORT

38 miles north of Boston, 12 miles north of Ipswich on Rte. 1A.

Newburyport's High Street is lined with some of the finest examples of Federal-period (roughly, 1790–1810) mansions in New England. The city was once a leading port and shipbuilding center; the houses were built for prosperous sea captains. Although Newburyport's maritime significance ended with the decline of the clipper ships, the town was revived in the 1970s. Today the town has shops, restaurants, galleries, and a waterfront park and boardwalk. Newburyport is walker friendly, with well-marked restrooms and free parking all day down by the water.

A stroll through the **Waterfront Park and Promenade** offers a view of the harbor as well as the fishing and pleasure boats that moor here.

A causeway leads from Newburyport to a narrow piece of land known as Plum Island, which harbors a summer colony at one end.

EXPLORING

Custom House Maritime Museum. Built in 1835 in Greek Revival style, this museum contains exhibits on maritime history, ship models, tools, and paintings. ✉ *25 Water St.* ☎ *978/462–8681* 🌐 *www.customhousemaritimemuseum.org* 🎟 *$7* 🕒 *Hrs vary seasonally, check the website or call ahead.*

WHERE TO STAY

$$ B&B/INN 🏨 **Clark Currier Inn.** Once the home of the 19th-century sea captain Thomas March Clark, this 1803 Federal mansion has been beautifully restored. **Pros:** easy to find; close to shopping and the oceanfront; good for couples looking for a peaceful and quiet experience. **Cons:** children under 10 not allowed. [$] *Rooms from: $185* ✉ *45 Green St.* ☎ *978/465–8363* 🌐 *www.clarkcurrierinn.com* 🛏 *11 rooms* 🍴 *Breakfast.*

3

SPORTS AND THE OUTDOORS

FAMILY **Parker River National Wildlife Refuge.** On Plum Island, this 4,662-acre refuge of salt marsh, freshwater marsh, beaches, and dunes is one of the few natural barrier beach, dune, and salt-marsh complexes left on the Northeast coast. Here you can bird-watch, fish, swim, and pick plums and cranberries. The refuge is a popular place in summer, especially on weekends; cars begin to line up at the gate before 7 am. There's no restriction on the number of people using the beach, but only a limited number of cars are let in; no pets are allowed in the refuge. ✉ *6 Plum Island Tpke.* ☎ *978/465–5753* 🌐 *www.fws.gov/refuge/parker_river* 🎟 *$5 per car; bicycles and walk-ins $2* 🕒 *Daily dawn–dusk. Beach usually closed during nesting season in spring and early summer.*

FAMILY Fodor'sChoice ★ **Salisbury Beach State Reservation.** Relax at the long sandy beach, launch a boat, or just enjoy the water. From Newburyport center, follow Bridge Road north, take a right on Beach Road, and follow it until you reach State Reservation Road. The park is popular with campers; reservations in summer are made many months ahead to ensure a spot. ✉ *Rte. 1A, 5 miles northeast of Newburyport, Beach Rd., Rte. 1A, Salisbury* ☎ *978/462–4481* 🌐 *www.mass.gov/dcr* 🎟 *Beach free, parking $9.*

SHOPPING

Todd Farm Flea Market. A New England tradition since 1973, the Todd Farm Flea Market features up to 240 vendors from all over New England and New York. It's open every Sunday from mid-April through late November, though its busiest months are May, June, September, and October. Merchandise varies from antique furniture, clocks, jewelry, recordings, and tools to fishing rods, golf accessories, cedar fencing, vintage toys, and seasonal plants and flowers. Antiques hunters often arrive before the sun comes up for the best deals. ✉ *283 Main St., Rte. 1A, Rowley* ☎ *978/948–3300* 🌐 *www.toddfarm.com* 🕒 *Apr.–Nov., Sun. 5 am–1 pm.*

SOUTH OF BOSTON

People from all over the world travel south of Boston to visit Plymouth for a glimpse into the country's earliest beginnings. The two main stops are the Plimoth Plantation, which re-creates the everyday life of the Pilgrims; and the *Mayflower II,* which gives you an idea of how frightening the journey across the Atlantic must have been. As you may guess, November in Plymouth brings special events focused on Thanksgiving. Farther south, New Bedford recalls the world of whaling.

EN
ROUTE

Adams National Historic Park. Take a guided tour of the birthplace and homes of Presidents John Adams and his son John Quincy Adams, as well as "Peace field," the Stone Library, and Adams Crypt, where the Adams presidents and their wives are buried in Quincy's Church of the Presidents. Tours begin at the NPS Visitor Center at 1250 Hancock Street, with trolley transportation to all sites. Get your parking validated adjacent to the visitor center on Saville Road. ⊠ *135 Adams St., Quincy* ☎ *617/770–1175* ⊕ *www.nps.gov/adam* ⊠ *$10* ⊘ *Apr.–Nov. 10 tours daily 9–5; last tour at 3:15.*

PLYMOUTH

40 miles south of Boston.

On December 26, 1620, 102 weary men, women, and children disembarked from the *Mayflower* to found the first permanent European settlement north of Virginia. Today Plymouth is characterized by narrow streets, clapboard mansions, shops, antiques stores, and a scenic waterfront. To mark Thanksgiving, the town holds a parade, historic-house tours, and other activities. Historic statues dot the town, including depictions of William Bradford, Pilgrim leader and governor of Plymouth Colony for more than 30 years, on Water Street; a Pilgrim maiden in Brewster Gardens; and Massasoit, the Wampanoag chief who helped the Pilgrims survive, on Carver Street.

VISITOR INFORMATION

Contacts Plymouth Visitor Information Center. ⊠ *130 Water St., at Hwy. 44* ☎ *508/747–7525, 800/872–1620* ⊕ *seeplymouth.com/.*

EXPLORING

FAMILY **Mayflower II.** This seaworthy replica of the 1620 *Mayflower* was built in England through research and a bit of guesswork, then sailed across the Atlantic in 1957. As you explore the interior and exterior of the ship, sailors in modern dress answer your questions about both the reproduction and the original ship, while costumed guides provide a 17th-century perspective. Plymouth Rock is nearby. ⊠ *State Pier* ☎ *508/746–1622* ⊕ *www.plimoth.org* ⊠ *$12* ⊘ *Late Mar.–Nov., daily 9–5.*

FAMILY **Pilgrim Hall Museum.** From the waterfront sights, it's a short walk to one of the country's oldest public museums. Established in 1824, Pilgrim Hall Museum transports you back to the time of the Pilgrims' landing with objects carried by those weary travelers to the New World. Historic items on display include a carved chest, a remarkably well-preserved wicker cradle, Myles Standish's sword, and John Alden's Bible. ⊠ *75 Court St. (Rte. 3A)* ☎ *508/746–1620* ⊕ *www.pilgrimhall. org* ⊠ *$8* ⊘ *Feb.–Dec., daily 9:30–4:30 including Thanksgiving Day.*

FAMILY
Fodor'sChoice
★ **Plimoth Plantation.** Over the entrance to this popular attraction is the caution: you are now entering 1627. Believe it. Against the backdrop of the Atlantic Ocean, and 3 miles south of downtown Plymouth, this Pilgrim village has been carefully re-created, from the thatch roofs, cramped

quarters, and open fireplaces to the long-horned livestock. Throw away your preconception of white collars and funny hats; through ongoing research, the Plimoth staff has developed a portrait of the Pilgrims that's more complex than the dour folk in school textbooks. Listen to the accents of the "residents," who never break out of character. You might see them plucking ducks, cooking rabbit stew, or tending gardens. Feel free to engage them in conversation about their life, but expect only curious looks if you ask about anything that happened after 1627. "Thanksgiving: Memory, Myth & Meaning," an exhibit in the visitor center, offers a fresh perspective on the 1621 harvest celebration that is now known as "the first Thanksgiving." Note that there's not a lot of shade here in summer. ✉ *137 Warren Ave. (Hwy. 3A)* ☎ *508/746–1622* ⊕ *www.plimoth.org* 🖂 *$25.95* ⊙ *Daily 9–5, but call ahead.*

WHERE TO EAT AND STAY

$$
SEAFOOD
✕ **Blue-eyed Crab Grille & Raw Bar.** Grab a seat on the outside deck overlooking the water at this friendly, somewhat funky (plastic fish dangling from the ceiling), fresh-fish shack. If the local Island Creek raw oysters are on the menu, go for them! Otherwise start with thick crab bisque full of hunks of floating crabmeat or the steamed mussels. Dinner entrées include seafood stew with chorizo and sweet potatoes and the classic fish-and-chips. Locals come for the brunch specials, too, like grilled shrimp and poached eggs over red-pepper grits, the lobster omelet, and banana-ginger pancakes. $ *Average main: $22* ✉ *170 Water St.* ☎ *508/747–6776* ⊕ *www.blueeyedcrab.com* ▭ *No credit cards.*

$
HOTEL
FAMILY
🏨 **Best Western Cold Spring.** Walk to the waterfront and downtown Plymouth from this clean, family-friendly motel. **Pros:** free parking; ½ mile from Plymouth Rock and Mayflower II; some of the best wallet-pleasing rates in the area. **Cons:** basic rooms without much character. $ *Rooms from: $140* ✉ *188 Court St.* ☎ *508/746–2222, 800/678–8667* ⊕ *www.bestwesternmassachusetts.com* ⤳ *57 rooms* ⅋ *Breakfast.*

NEW BEDFORD

45 miles southwest of Plymouth, 50 miles south of Boston.

In 1652 colonists from Plymouth settled in the area that now includes the city of New Bedford. The city has a long maritime tradition, beginning as a shipbuilding center and small whaling port in the late 1700s. By the mid-1800s it had developed into a center of North American whaling. Today New Bedford has the largest fishing fleet on the East Coast. Although much of the town is industrial, the restored historic district near the water is a delight. It was here that Herman Melville set his masterpiece, *Moby-Dick,* a novel about whaling.

VISITOR INFORMATION

Contacts Destination New Bedford/City of New Bedford Tourism. ✉ *133 William St., Room 119* ☎ *800/508–5353, 508/979–1745* ⊕ *www.destinationnewbedford.org.*

EXPLORING

FAMILY **New Bedford Whaling Museum.** Established in 1903, this is the world's largest museum of its kind. A highlight is the skeleton of a 66-foot blue whale, one of only three on view anywhere. An interactive exhibit lets you listen to the underwater sounds of whales, dolphins, and other sea life—plus the sounds of a thunderstorm and a whale-watching boat—as a whale might hear them. You can also peruse the collection of scrimshaw, visit exhibits on regional history, and climb aboard an 89-foot, half-scale model of the 1826 whaling ship *Lagoda*—the world's largest ship model. A small chapel across the street from the museum is the one described in *Moby-Dick*. ✉ *18 Johnny Cake Hill* ☎ *508/997–0046* 🌐 *www.whalingmuseum.org* 🎟 *$14* 🕓 *Apr.–Dec., daily 9–5; Jan.–Mar., Tues.–Sat. 9–4, Sun. 11–4.*

FAMILY **New Bedford Whaling National Historical Park.** The city's whaling tradition is commemorated at this park that takes up 13 blocks of the waterfront historic district. The park visitor center, housed in an 1853 Greek Revival building that was once a bank, provides maps and information about whaling-related sites. Free walking tours of the park leave from the visitor center at 10:30 and 2:30 in July and August. ✉ *33 William St.* ☎ *508/996–4095* 🌐 *www.nps.gov/nebe* 🎟 *Free* 🕓 *Apr.–Dec. daily 9–5; Jan.–March Wed.–Sun. 9–5.*

Rotch-Jones-Duff House & Garden Museum. The only whaling-era mansion on its original grounds open to the public, the Rotch-Jones-Duff (RJD) House and Garden Museum chronicles the economic, social, and political evolution of the city. Originally built in 1834, the Greek Revival mansion, which is located on a full city block of gardens a half-mile south of downtown, tells the story of the three prominent families who called it home in the 1800s. The museum is filled with elegant furnishings from the era, including a mahogany piano, a massive marble-top sideboard, and portraits of the house's occupants. A free self-guided audio tour is available. ✉ *396 County St.* ☎ *508/997–1401* 🌐 *www.rjdmuseum.org* 🎟 *$6* 🕓 *Mon.–Sat. 10–4, Sun. noon–4.*

WHERE TO EAT

$$ PORTUGUESE 🍴 **Antonio's.** Expect the wait to be long and the dining room to be loud, but it's worth the hassle to sample the traditional fare of New Bedford's large Portuguese population at this friendly, unadorned restaurant. Dishes include hearty portions of pork and shellfish stew, *bacalau* (salt cod), and grilled sardines, often on plates piled high with crispy fried potatoes and rice. [$] *Average main: $15* ✉ *267 Coggeshall St., near intersection of I–195 and Hwy. 18* ☎ *508/990–3636* 🌐 *www.antoniosnewbedford.com* 💳 *No credit cards.*

CAPE COD,
MARTHA'S VINEYARD,
AND NANTUCKET

WELCOME TO CAPE COD, MARTHA'S VINEYARD, AND NANTUCKET

TOP REASONS TO GO

★ **Beaches:** Cape Cod's picturesque beaches are the ultimate reason to go. The high sand dunes, gorgeous sunsets, and never-ending sea will get you every time.

★ **Visiting Lighthouses:** Lighthouses rise along Cape Cod's coast like architectural exclamation points. Highlights include Eastham's beautiful Nauset Light and Chatham and Nobska Lights for their spectacular views.

★ **Biking the Trails:** Martha's Vineyard and Nantucket each have dedicated bike paths, but the Cape Cod Rail Trail from South Dennis to south Wellfleet (with a spur out to Chatham) is the definitive route, with over 25 miles of relatively flat terrain.

★ **Setting Sail:** Area tour operators offer everything from sunset schooner cruises to charter fishing expeditions. Whale-watching adventures are popular mid-April–October.

★ **Browsing the Galleries:** The Cape was a prominent art colony in the 19th century, and today it has a number of galleries.

1 Cape Cod. Cape Cod is a place of many moods. The Upper Cape (closest to the bridges) has the oldest towns, plus fine beaches and fascinating little museums. The Mid Cape has sophisticated Colonial-era hamlets but also motels and miniature golf courses. In the midst of it all sits Hyannis, the Cape's unofficial capital. The Lower Cape has casual clam shacks, lovely lighthouses, funky art galleries, and stellar natural attractions. The narrow forearm of the Outer Cape is famous for sand dunes, crashing surf, and scrubby pines. Frenetic and fun-loving Provincetown is a leading gay getaway.

2 Martha's Vineyard. The Vineyard lies 7 miles off the Cape's southwest tip. The Down-Island towns are the most popular and most populous, but much of what makes this island special is found in its rural Up-Island reaches, where dirt roads lead past crystalline ponds, cranberry bogs, and conservation lands.

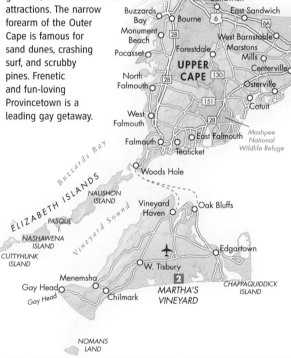

3 **Nantucket.** Nantucket, or "Far Away Island" in the Wampanoag tongue, is nearly 30 miles south of Hyannis. Ferries dock in pretty Nantucket Town, where tourism services are concentrated. The rest of the island is mostly residential—trophy houses abound—and nearly all roads terminate in tiny beach communities.

GETTING ORIENTED

The Cape is divided into four major areas and is shaped roughly like an arm bent at the elbow: the Upper Cape (the shoulder); the Mid Cape (the upper arm); the Lower Cape (the bicep and forearm); and the Outer Cape (the wrist and hand), with Provincetown at the very end. Each of the Cape's 15 towns is further broken up into smaller villages; the town of Barnstable, for example, consists of Barnstable, West Barnstable, Cotuit, Marston Mills, Osterville, Centerville, and Hyannis. The islands, Martha's Vineyard and Nantucket, lie to the south. Martha's Vineyard is about 7 miles off the Cape's southwest tip, while Nantucket is some 30 miles south of Hyannis. Both are connected to the Cape by ferries, and both also have air service.

4

CAPE COD NATIONAL SEASHORE

John F. Kennedy certainly knew a good thing when he saw it. During his presidency, Kennedy marked off a magnificent 40-mile swath of the Massachusetts coast, protecting it for future generations. Today the Cape Cod National Seashore remains the Cape's signature site.

Encompassing more than 44,000 acres of coastline from Chatham to Provincetown, the park is truly a national treasure. Without protection, such expansive beauty would surely have been lost to rampant overdevelopment long ago. Within its borders are extraordinary ocean beaches, dramatic dunes, ancient swamps, salt marshes, and wetlands; pitch-pine and scrub-oak forest; much wildlife; and a number of historic structures open for touring.

There's no question that the National Seashore's beaches are the main attractions for sunbathers, swimmers, and surfers. It's not at all uncommon for the parking lots to fill up by 11 am on hot, sunny days. Arrive early to find your spot on the sand, or venture out on some of the less-traveled trails to find solitude in high season.

BEST TIME TO GO

Swimming is best in summer; the park becomes sublime in the fall with golden salt-marsh grasses and ruby-red cranberry bogs. Winter and early spring nearly guarantee you'll have the place to yourself.

CONTACT INFO

Cape Cod National Seashore ⊠ *Doane Rd. off U.S. 6 02642* ☎ *508/255-3421* ⊕ *www.nps.gov/caco* 🎫 *Free* ⊘ *Daily 9–4:30.*

BEST WAYS TO EXPLORE

TAKE A WALK

Walking the marked trails, beaches, and wooded fire roads is an excellent way to truly experience the diverse natural splendor within the park. There are 11 self-guided trails that begin at various points, leading through shaded swamps, alongside marshes, and through meadows, forest, and dunes. Most of the terrain is flat and sometimes sandy.

RIDE A BIKE

Three well-maintained bicycle trails run through parts of the park. In Eastham, the short Nauset Trail heads from the Salt Pond Visitor Center through the woods and out to Coast Guard Beach. Truro's Head, off the Meadow Trail, edges a large salt meadow that's an ideal place for birding. The most physically demanding—and most dramatic—of the park's bike trails is the Province Lands Trail, more than 7 miles of steep hills and hairpin curves through forest and sand dunes. Mountain bikers can make their own trails on the miles of fire roads.

SEE THE SIGHTS

Several historic homes and sites are open for touring, and there are also a few notable overlooks easily accessible by car. Climb the steep steps of lighthouses in Eastham and Truro or see rescue reenactments at the Old Harbor Life-Saving Station in Provincetown. Scenic overlooks include Eastham's exquisite Fort Hill area; Wellfleet's Marconi Station Site, where the first transatlantic wireless message was sent in 1903; Truro's Pilgrim Heights; and Provincetown's scenic 2-mile Race Point Road.

TOUR WITH A RANGER

There is a full schedule of mostly free ranger-guided activities mid-April–Thanksgiving. Combining history, folklore, science, and nature, rangers take visitors right to the source, whether for a full-moon hike in the dunes, a campfire on the beach, a paddling trip, or a photography workshop.

SHIFTING SANDS

Forged by massive moving glaciers more than 20,000 years ago, Cape Cod's landscape is still in perpetual motion, continually shaped by the powerful forces of sand, wind, and water. The Cape's land is slowly giving way to rising ocean levels and erosion, losing an average of nearly 4 feet of outer beach per year. Many a home or structure has succumbed to the unrelenting ocean over the years; some—like Truro's Highland Light and Eastham's Nauset Light—have been moved to safety. Eventually Cape Cod will likely be lost to the sea, but not for thousands of years. You'll see many signs on beaches and trails asking walkers to keep off the dunes. Take heed, for much of the fragile landscape of the outer Cape is held together by its dune formations and the vegetation that grows within them.

4

THE CAPE'S BEST BEACHES

Blessed by a great variety of surrounding waters, Cape Cod, Martha's Vineyard, and Nantucket boast some of the world's best beaches. They face the wild, bracing surf of the Atlantic Ocean on one side, while the warmer and gentler waters of Cape Cod Bay or the Nantucket Sound sweep the opposite shores.

Cape Cod alone has more than 150 beaches—enough to keep the most inveterate beachcomber busy all year long. One can still capture that sense of adventure that enchanted Thoreau so long ago while walking the isolated stretches of towering dune-backed beaches from Eastham to Provincetown. Families love the easy access and more placid beaches of the bay and sound, which in turn tend to be more crowded. If saltwater isn't your thing, the Cape has dozens of freshwater kettle holes inland that were carved in the far-distant past by receding glaciers. Aside from warm, salt-free water, some—like Scargo Lake in Dennis—are also blessed with sandy beaches.

HISTORY LESSON

In this centuries-old area even a fun-in-the-sun day can double as a history lesson. In the Lower Cape, Eastham's popular **First Encounter Beach** has a bronze plaque that marks the spot where Myles Standish and his *Mayflower* buddies first encountered Native Americans in 1620.

UPPER CAPE

For Families: Parents love North Falmouth's **Old Silver**—a long crescent of soft white sand—for its comparatively calm, warm water, and kids enjoy poking around the shallow tidal pools full of sea life.

MID CAPE

For Wanderers: Stretching some 6 miles across a peninsula that ends at Sandy Neck Light, **Sandy Neck Beach** in West Barnstable offers a spectacular combination of sand, sea, and dunes perfect for strolling and watching the plentiful birdlife.

For Active Types: Encompassing 1½ miles of soft, white sand on Nantucket Sound, busy West Dennis Beach has plenty of space to try windsurfing, play a game of beach volleyball, or just sit back and enjoy the people-watching.

LOWER CAPE

For Traditionalists: Locals contend that Eastham's **Nauset Light Beach** and **Coast Guard Beach,** both set within the Cape Cod National Seashore, are the quintessential beaches. Combining serious surf, sweeping expanses of sand, magnificent dunes, and mesmerizing views, these spots deliver on the wow factor.

For Bird-Watchers: On the barrier beaches of the **Monomoy National Wildlife Refuge,** accessible by boat tours from Chatham, you're bound to see more

4

sandpipers and plovers than people. Summer through early fall, shorebirds and waterfowl flock here to nest, rest, and feast in tidal flats.

OUTER CAPE

For Views: After the winding drive amid the dunes and scrub in the National Seashore, **Race Point Beach** in Provincetown literally is the end of the road. Cape Cod Bay and the Atlantic meet here in a powerful tumbling of waves; views are vast and include extraordinary sunsets as well whale sightings.

For Night Owls: After-hours, it's tough to beat **Cahoon Hollow Beach** in Wellfleet. The water here is chilly but the music at the Beachcomber bar and restaurant is hot.

MARTHA'S VINEYARD

For Photographers: Perhaps no beach in this camera-ready region is more photogenic than that below the **Aquinnah Cliffs.** The multicolored clay cliffs face west, allowing for gorgeous photos at sunset.

NANTUCKET

For Sand Castle Connoisseurs: Jetties Beach has the finest sand castle–building material: hordes gather to prove it during Sandcastle & Sculpture Day, held annually in mid-August.

Updated by Laura V. Scheel

Even if you haven't visited Cape Cod and islands, you can likely—and accurately—imagine "sand dunes and salty air, quaint little villages here and there." As that 1950s Patti Page song promises, "you're sure to fall in love with old Cape Cod."

Cape Codders are fiercely protective of the environment. Despite some occasionally rampant development, planners have been careful to preserve nature and encourage responsible, eco-conscious building. Nearly 30% of the Cape's 412 square miles is protected from development, and another 35% has not yet been developed (on Nantucket and Martha's Vineyard, percentages of protected land are far higher). Opportunities for sports and recreation abound, as the region is rife with biking and hiking trails, serene beaches, and waterways for boating and fishing. One somewhat controversial potential development has been a large-scale "wind farm" in Nantucket Sound, comprising some 130 turbines, each about 260 feet tall and several miles offshore.

The area is also rich in history. Many don't realize that the Pilgrims landed here first: in November 1620, the lost and travel-weary sailors dropped anchor in what is now Provincetown Harbor and spent five weeks here, scouring the area for food and possible settlement. Were it not for the aid of the resident Native Americans, the strangers would barely have survived. Even so, they set sail again for fairer lands, ending up across Cape Cod Bay in Plymouth.

Virtually every period style of residential American architecture is well represented on Cape Cod, including—of course—that seminal form named for the region, the Cape Cod–style house. These low, 1½-story domiciles with clapboard or shingle siding—more traditionally the latter in these parts—and gable roofs have been a fixture throughout Cape Cod since the late 17th century. You'll also find grand Georgian and Federal mansions from the Colonial era, as well as handsome Greek Revival, Italianate, and Second Empire houses that date to Victorian times. Many of the most prominent residences were built for ship captains and sea merchants. In recent decades, the region has seen an influx of angular, glassy, contemporary homes, many with soaring windows and skylights, and massive wraparound porches that take advantage of their enviable sea views.

PLANNING

WHEN TO GO

The Cape and islands teem with activity during high season: roughly late June to Labor Day. If you're dreaming of a classic shore vacation, this is prime time. However, along with the dream come daunting crowds and high costs. Fall has begun to rival summer in popularity, at least on weekends through late October, when the weather is temperate and the scenery remarkable. Many restaurants, shops, and hotels remain open in winter, too, making the area desirable even during the coldest months. The region enjoys fairly moderate weather most of the year, with highs typically in the upper 70s and 80s in summer, and in the upper 30s and lower 40s in winter. Snow and rain are not uncommon during the cooler months, and it can be windy any time.

PLANNING YOUR TIME

The region can be enjoyed for a few days or a few weeks, depending on the nature of your trip. As the towns are all quite distinct on Cape Cod, it's best to organize your trip based on your interests: an outdoors enthusiast would want to head to the National Seashore region, for example; those who prefer shopping and amusements would do better in the Mid-Cape area. As one Fodors.com forum member noted, the Cape is generally "not something to see . . . instead, people go to spend a few days or weeks, relax, go to the beach . . . that sort of thing." A day trip to Nantucket to wander the historic downtown is manageable; several days is best to appreciate Martha's Vineyard's diversity.

GETTING HERE AND AROUND

AIR TRAVEL

The major air gateways are Boston's Logan International Airport and Providence's T. F. Green International Airport. Most major airlines fly to Boston; several fly to Providence; even fewer fly directly to the Cape and islands, and many of those flights are seasonal. Smaller municipal airports are in Barnstable, Martha's Vineyard, Nantucket, and Provincetown.

CAR TRAVEL

Cape Cod is easily reached from Boston via Route 3 and from Providence via I–195. Once you cross Cape Cod Canal, you can follow U.S. 6. Without any traffic, it takes about an hour to 90 minutes to reach the canal from either Boston or Providence. Allow an extra 30–60 minutes' travel time in peak periods.

Parking, in general, can be a challenge in summer, especially in congested downtowns and at popular beaches. If you can walk, bike, carpool, or cab it somewhere, do so. But unless you are planning to focus your attention on a single community, you'll probably need a car on the Cape. Authorities on both Nantucket and Martha's Vineyard strongly encourage visitors to leave their cars on the mainland: taking a vehicle onto the island ferries is expensive and requires reservations (another option is renting upon arrival), and there is ample and efficient transportation once you arrive.

FERRY TRAVEL

Martha's Vineyard and Nantucket are easily reached by passenger ferries (traditional and high-speed boats) from several Cape towns; some of this service runs year-round while other is seasonal. Even parking for the ferries must be reserved during the busy season, but passenger reservations are rarely necessary. Trip times vary from as little as 45 minutes to about two hours and run $8.50–$38 one way; bicycles can be taken aboard many ferries for $4, while cars cost $43.50–$68 one way (reservations required and very limited).

TRAIN TRAVEL

For the first time since the late 1980s, seasonal train travel to Cape Cod from Boston has returned. The train runs only on weekends (Friday–Sunday) from Boston's South Station, Memorial Day–Labor Day. The 2½-hour trip makes stops in Braintree, Middleborough, Buzzards Bay, and Hyannis. Round-trip fare from Boston is $40; bring your bike for no extra fee.

Contact Cape Flyer. ✉ *Hyannis Transportation Center, 215 Iyannough Rd., Barnstable* ☎ *508/775–8504* ⊕ *www.capeflyer.com.*

RESTAURANTS

Cape Cod kitchens have long been closely associated with seafood: the waters off the Cape and islands yield a bounty of lobsters, clams, oysters, scallops, and myriad fish that make their way onto local menus. In addition to the region's strong Portuguese influence, globally inspired and contemporary fare commonly turn up among restaurant offerings. Also gaining in popularity is the use of locally, and often organically, raised produce, meat, and dairy.

Note that ordering an expensive lobster dinner may push your meal into a higher price category than this guide's price range shows for the restaurant. You can indulge in fresh local seafood and clambakes at seat-yourself shanties for a lower price than at their fine-dining counterparts. Often, the tackier the decor (plastic fish on the walls), the better the seafood. Such laid-back local haunts usually operate a fish market on the premises and can be found in every town on the Cape. *Prices in the reviews are the average cost of a main course at dinner or, if dinner is not served, at lunch.*

HOTELS

B&Bs are king in the cape, so you can bed down in a former sea captain's home or even a converted church. However, there are also a few larger resorts and even a handful of chain hotels. You'll want to make reservations for inns well in advance during peak summer periods. Smoking is prohibited in all Massachusetts hotels. *Prices in the hotel reviews are the lowest cost of a standard double room in high season, excluding 12.45% taxes and service charges. Prices for rentals are the lowest per-night cost for a one-bedroom unit in high season.*

CONDO AND HOUSE RENTALS

Many travelers to the Cape and the islands rent a house if they're going to stay for a week or longer. Many local real-estate agencies deal with rentals. Be sure to book a property well in advance of your trip: prime properties are often rented out to the same people year after year. Expect rentals on both Martha's Vineyard and Nantucket to be significantly higher than those on the Cape, simply because there are fewer options.

WHAT IT COSTS				
	$	$$	$$$	$$$$
Restaurants	under $18	$18–$24	$25–$35	over $35
Hotels	under $200	$200–$299	$300–$399	over $399

4

CAPE COD

Continually shaped by ocean currents, this windswept land of sandy beaches and dunes has compelling natural beauty. Everyone comes for the seaside, yet the crimson cranberry bogs, birch and beech forests, freshwater ponds, and interior marshlands are just as splendid. Local history is fascinating; whale-watching provides an exhilarating experience of the natural world; cycling trails lace the landscape; shops purvey everything from antiques to pure kitsch; and you can dine on simple, fresh seafood, creative contemporary cuisine, or most anything in between.

Henry David Thoreau, who famously traveled the sparsely populated mid-19th-century Cape Cod, likened the peninsula to "a bare and bended arm." Indeed, looking at a map the outline is obvious, and many people hold their own arm aloft and point to various places from shoulder to fist when asked for directions.

Separated from the Massachusetts mainland by the 17½-mile Cape Cod Canal—at 480 feet, the world's widest sea-level canal—and linked to it by two heavily trafficked bridges, the Cape is surrounded by water that defines the peninsula's land and seascapes: just off the mainland to the southeast are the gentler, warmer waters of Buzzards Bay, Vineyard Sound, and Nantucket Sound. Cape Cod Bay extends north to the tip of Provincetown, where it meets the Atlantic Ocean.

There are three main roads that travel, more or less, the entire Cape: U.S. Highway 6, Route 28, and Route 6A, a designated historic road also called the Old King's Highway. Most visitors stick to these main byways, though the back roads can save time and aggravation in summer. *The towns have been arranged geographically in this guide, starting with the Upper Cape and ending with the Outer Cape.*

SANDWICH

3 miles east of Sagamore Bridge, 11 miles west of Barnstable.

Fodor's Choice ★ The oldest town on Cape Cod, Sandwich was established in 1637 by some of the Plymouth Pilgrims and incorporated on March 6, 1638.

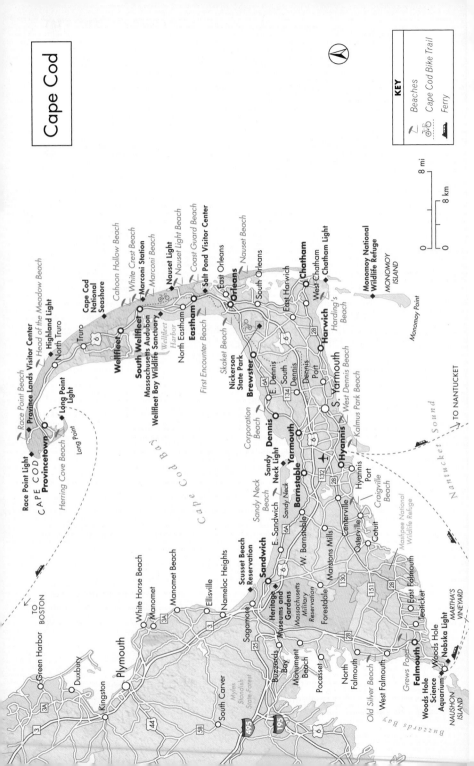

Cape Cod

KEY

Beaches
Cape Cod Bike Trail
Ferry

8 mi
8 km

CAPE COD
Provincetown
Race Point Light
Race Point Beach
Province Lands Visitor Center
Herring Cove Beach
Long Point
Long Point Light
Highland Light
Head of the Meadow Beach
North Truro
Truro
Cape Cod National Seashore
Cahoon Hollow Beach
White Crest Beach
Marconi Station
Marconi Beach
Wellfleet
South Wellfleet
Massachusetts Audubon
Wellfleet Bay Wildlife Sanctuary
Wellfleet Harbor
Nauset Light
Nauset Light Beach
Coast Guard Beach
Salt Pond Visitor Center
Eastham
North Eastham
First Encounter Beach
Skaket Beach
Nickerson State Park
Brewster
Corporation Beach
Dennis
E. Dennis
South Dennis
Dennis Port
134
Orleans
East Orleans
South Orleans
Nauset Beach
East Harwich
West Chatham
Chatham
Chatham Light
Harwich
Harding's Beach
Monomoy National Wildlife Refuge
MONOMOY ISLAND
Monomoy Point
S. Yarmouth
West Dennis Beach
Kalmus Park Beach
Hyannis
Hyannis Port
Craigville Beach
Yarmouth
Barnstable
Sandy Neck Light
Sandy Neck
Sandy Neck Beach
E. Sandwich
W. Barnstable
6A
Centerville
Osterville
Cotuit
Marstons Mills
132
28
Mashpee National Wildlife Refuge
Sandwich
Scusset Beach Reservation
Sagamore
Heritage Museums and Gardens
Massachusetts Military Reservation
Forestdale
130
151
28
North Falmouth
West Falmouth
Old Silver Beach
Grews Pond
Falmouth
East Falmouth
Teaticket
Woods Hole
Nobska Light
Woods Hole Science Aquarium
NAUSHON ISLAND
MARTHA'S VINEYARD
NASHON ISLAND
Buzzards Bay
Monument Beach
Pocasset
Myles Standish State Forest
White Horse Beach
Manomet
Manomet Beach
Ellisville
Namequoit Heights
3A
Plymouth
Kingston
Duxbury
Green Harbor
TO BOSTON
South Carver
44
58
3
495
195
6
28
25
TO NANTUCKET

Cape Cod Bay
Nantucket Sound
Buzzards Bay

N

Today, it is a well-preserved, quintessential New England village with a white-columned town hall and streets lined with 18th- and 19th-century houses.

VISITOR INFORMATION

Contacts Sandwich Chamber of Commerce. ✉ *128 Rte. 6A, Sandwich Center* ☎ *508/833–9755* ⊕ *www.sandwichchamber.com.*

EXPLORING

FAMILY

Fodor'sChoice

★

Heritage Museums and Gardens. These 100 beautifully landscaped acres overlooking the upper end of Shawme Pond are one of the region's top draws. Paths crisscross the grounds, which include gardens planted with hostas, heather, herbs, and fruit trees. Rhododendrons are in full glory mid-May–mid-June, and daylilies reach their peak mid-July–early August. In 1967, pharmaceuticals magnate Josiah K. Lilly III purchased the estate and turned it into a nonprofit museum. One highlight is the reproduction Shaker Round Barn, which showcases classic and historic cars—including a 1919 Pierce-Arrow, a 1915 Milburn Light Electric, a 1911 Stanley Steamer, and a 1930 yellow-and-green Duesenberg built for movie star Gary Cooper. The art museum has an extraordinary collection of New England folk art, including paintings, weather vanes, Nantucket baskets, and scrimshaw. Both adults and children can enjoy riding on a Coney Island–style carousel dating to the early 20th century. Other features include Hidden Hollow, an outdoor activity center for families with children.

A shuttle bus, equipped with a wheelchair lift and space to stow baby strollers, transports visitors on certain days. In summer, concerts are held in the gardens, often on Wednesday or Saturday evening or on Sunday afternoon. The center of the complex is about ¾ mile on foot from the in-town end of Shawme Pond. ✉ *67 Grove St., Sandwich Center* ☎ *508/888–3300* ⊕ *www.heritagemuseumsandgardens.org* ✑ *$18* ☉ *Apr.–June and Sept.–Nov., daily 10–5; July and Aug., Thurs.–Tues. 10–5, Wed. 10–8.*

FAMILY

Sandwich Boardwalk. The long sweep of Cape Cod Bay stretches out around the beach at the end of the Sandwich Boardwalk, where a platform provides fine views, especially at sunset. You can look out toward Sandy Neck, Wellfleet, and Provincetown or toward the white cliffs beyond Sagamore. Near this mostly rocky beach are dunes covered with rugosa roses, which have a delicious fragrance; this is a good place for birding. The creeks running through the salt marsh make for great canoeing. From the town center it's about a mile to the boardwalk; cross Route 6A on Jarves Street, and at its end turn left, then right, and continue to the boardwalk parking lot. ✉ *End of Jarves St., Sandwich Center.*

Sandwich Glass Museum. Shimmering glass was manufactured here more than a century ago, and the Sandwich Glass Museum shows you what the factory looked in its heyday. There's an "ingredient room" showcasing a wide spectrum of glass colors, along with the minerals added to the sand to obtain them, and an outstanding collection of blown and pressed glass in many shapes and hues. Large lamps, vases, and pitchers are impressive, as are the hundreds of candlesticks on display.

4

There are glassblowing demonstrations daily 10–3. The extensive gift shop sells some handsome reproductions, including some made by local and national artisans. Also home to the Sandwich Historical Society, the museum hosts historic walking tours on certain days June–October. ✉ *129 Main St., Sandwich Center* ☎ *508/888–0251* 🌐 *www.sandwichglassmuseum.org* 🎟 *$9* 🕒 *Apr.–Dec., daily 9:30–5; Feb. and Mar., Wed.–Sun. 9:30–4.*

WHERE TO EAT

$$ SEAFOOD 🍴 **Pilot House.** Views of the bustling Cape Cod Canal abound from this casual spot's enviable waterside perch. Seafood is the main catch here, though there are a few alternatives in the form of hefty burgers, steaks, and prime rib. Scallops, clams, oysters, and mussels get top billing, usually served fried among heaps of steaming french fries. For something a bit healthier, opt for anything broiled or baked. There's a pianist in the dining room every Friday and Saturday, and live music, a fire pit, and lots of prime seating on the grounds outside in warmer months. [$] *Average main: $23* ✉ *14 Gallo Rd., Sandwich Center* ☎ *508/888–8889* 🌐 *www.pilothousecapecod.com* 🕒 *Closed Mon. and Tues. Nov.–Apr.*

WHERE TO STAY

$ B&B/INN Fodor's Choice ★ 🏨 **Belfry Inne & Bistro.** This one-of-a-kind inn comprises a 1901 former church, an ornate wood-frame 1882 Victorian, and an 1827 Federal-style house. **Pros:** great in-town location; bright, beautiful, and spacious rooms. **Cons:** some steep stairs. [$] *Rooms from: $189* ✉ *6 Jarves St.* ☎ *508/888–8550, 800/844–4542* 🌐 *www.belfryinn.com* 🛏 *23 rooms* 🍽 *Breakfast.*

$ B&B/INN 🏨 **1750 Inn at Sandwich Center.** Gracious hosts Jan and Charlie Preus have created a warm and inviting inn that's appealing whether you seek quiet seclusion or the opportunity to mingle with fellow guests. **Pros:** easy access to town center; innkeepers really know the area; appealing package options. **Cons:** some steep, narrow stairs. [$] *Rooms from: $179* ✉ *118 Tupper Rd.* ☎ *508/888–6958, 800/249–6949* 🌐 *www.innatsandwich.com* 🛏 *5 rooms* 🍽 *Breakfast.*

NIGHTLIFE

British Beer Company. This traditional British "public house" has a great menu that includes fish, ribs, and pizza. Entertainment options throughout the week include karaoke, trivia night, and a variety of bands that perform Thursday–Saturday. There are two other Cape locations in Falmouth and Hyannis. ✉ *46 Rte. 6A* ☎ *508/833–9590* 🌐 *www.britishbeer.com.*

SHOPPING

Downtown Sandwich has quite a few specialty shops, as well as several good antiques co-ops, boutiques, and galleries. Along Route 6A, you'll find more of the same, just spread out along the miles.

Fodor's Choice ★ **Titcomb's Bookshop.** You'll find used, rare, and new books here, including a large collection of Americana. There's also an extensive selection of children's books. Look for frequent author events and book signings. ✉ *432 Rte. 6A, East Sandwich* ☎ *508/888–2331* 🌐 *www.titcombsbookshop.com.*

FALMOUTH

15 miles south of Bourne Bridge, 20 miles South of Sandwich.

Falmouth, the Cape's second-largest town, was settled in 1660. Today it is largely suburban, with a mix of old and new developments and a sizable year-round population. Many residents commute to other towns on the Cape, to southeastern Massachusetts, and even to Boston. The town has a quaint downtown area, with a typically old New England village green and a shop-lined Main Street. South of town center, Falmouth faces Nantucket Sound and has several often-crowded beaches popular with families. To the east, the Falmouth Heights neighborhood mixes inns, B&Bs, and private homes, nestled close together on residential streets leading to the sea. Bustling Grand Avenue, the main drag in Falmouth Heights, hugs the shore and the beach.

The village of Woods Hole, part of Falmouth, is home to several major scientific institutions—the National Marine Fisheries Service, the Marine Biological Laboratory (MBL), the Woods Hole Oceanographic Institution, and the U.S. Geological Survey's Branch of Marine Geology—and is a departure point for ferries to Martha's Vineyard.

VISITOR INFORMATION

Contacts Falmouth Chamber of Commerce and Visitor Center. ✉ *20 Academy La.* ☎ *508/548–8500, 800/526–8532* ⊕ *www.falmouthchamber.com.*

EXPLORING

FAMILY **Woods Hole Science Aquarium.** This impressive facility displays 16 large
Fodor'sChoice tanks and many more smaller ones filled with regional fish and shellfish.
★ Rooms are small, but they are crammed with stuff to see. Magnifying glasses and a dissecting scope help you examine marine life. Several hands-on pools hold banded lobsters, crabs, snails, starfish, and other creatures. The stars of the show are two harbor seals, on view in the outdoor pool near the entrance; watch their feedings, most days, at 11 and 4. ✉ *166 Water St., Woods Hole* ☎ *508/495–2001* ⊕ *aquarium. nefsc.noaa.gov* ✉ *Free* ☉ *Tues.–Sat. 11–4.*

BEACHES

FAMILY **Old Silver Beach.** This long, beautiful crescent of soft white sand is anchored by the Sea Crest Beach Resort at one end. It's especially good for small children because a sandbar keeps it shallow at the southern end and creates tidal pools full of crabs and minnows. Very popular, this beach has its share of crowds on nice, sunny days. **Amenities:** food and drink; lifeguards; parking (fee); showers; toilets. **Best for:** swimming; walking. ✉ *296 Quaker Rd., North Falmouth* ⊕ *www.falmouthmass. us* ✉ *$20 daily parking.*

WHERE TO EAT

$$$ ✗ **C Salt Wine Bar & Grille.** With an open kitchen that turns out some
AMERICAN excellent and artful dishes and a notable wine list, this tiny place keeps its tables full and its guests happy. Fine service by a friendly and knowledgeable staff adds greatly to the overall atmosphere. Favorite starters include the crispy Thai calamari and the oyster selection at the raw bar; for dinner the succulent root beer–braised short ribs more than satisfy. There are several seafood options to choose from as well, including New

Bedford sea scallops, halibut, and mussels. Do save room for dessert: the resident pastry chef makes a magical crème brûlée. $ *Average main: $31* ✉ *75 Davis Straits (Rte. 28)* ☎ *774/763–2954* ⊕ *www.csaltfalmouth. com* ✍ *Reservations essential.*

$

SEAFOOD

✗ **The Clam Shack.** Fried clams are crisp and fresh at this basic seafood joint right on Falmouth Harbor; the meaty lobster roll and the fish 'n' chips platter are good choices, too. Place your order at the counter, and then take your tray to the picnic tables on the roof deck for the best views. More tables are on the dock in back, or you can squeeze into the tiny dining room. Just don't plan on a late night here—the Shack closes most evenings around 8. $ *Average main: $16* ✉ *227 Clinton Ave., Falmouth Harbor* ☎ *508/540–7758* ▭ *No credit cards* ⊙ *Closed early Sept.–mid-May.*

$$$

ITALIAN

Fodor'sChoice

★

✗ **La Cucina Sul Mare.** Northern Italian and Mediterranean cooking distinguishes this classy, popular place. The staff are friendly, and the setting is both intimate and festive, if a bit crowded. The *zuppa de pesce*, a medley of seafood sautéed in olive oil and garlic and finished in a white-wine, herb-and-tomato broth, is a specialty. Make sure to come hungry—portions here are huge—and expect a long wait during prime hours in season (reservations are accepted only for parties of five-plus); however, you can use the call-ahead waitlist to get a jump on the line. $ *Average main: $25* ✉ *237 Main St., Falmouth Center* ☎ *508/548–5600* ⊕ *www.lacucinasulmare.com* ✍ *Reservations not accepted.*

WHERE TO STAY

$$

B&B/INN

🛏 **The Captain's Manor Inn.** With its expansive landscaped grounds ringed by a wrought-iron fence, this elegant 1849 Italianate inn with a wraparound porch resembles a private estate. **Pros:** walk to town center; elegant setting. **Cons:** not for those with small children; long stairway to second-floor rooms. $ *Rooms from: $259* ✉ *27 W. Main St., Falmouth Center* ☎ *508/388–7336* ⊕ *www.captainsmanorinn.com* ⇄ *8 rooms* ⦿ *Breakfast.*

$$

B&B/INN

🛏 **Coonamessett Inn.** At this delightful inn, five buildings of one- and two-bedroom suites ring a landscaped lawn that leads to a scenic wooded pond. **Pros:** lush grounds; high marks in romantic-dining setting. **Cons:** constant weddings. $ *Rooms from: $280* ✉ *311 Gifford St., at Jones Rd.* ☎ *508/548–2300* ⊕ *www.coonamessettinn.com* ⇄ *28 suites, 1 cottage* ⦿ *Breakfast.*

$$

B&B/INN

Fodor'sChoice

★

🛏 **Inn on the Sound.** At this understated and serene but stylish inn, perched on a bluff overlooking Vineyard Sound, the living room and most guest rooms face the water. **Pros:** grand water views; elegant setting. **Cons:** not an in-town location; not for those with small children. $ *Rooms from: $279* ✉ *313 Grand Ave., Falmouth Heights* ☎ *508/457–9666, 800/564–9668* ⊕ *www.innonthesound.com* ⇄ *11 rooms* ⦿ *Breakfast.*

SPORTS AND THE OUTDOORS
BIKING

Fodor'sChoice

★

Shining Sea Bikeway. The wonderful Shining Sea Bikeway is almost 11 miles of paved bike path through four of Falmouth's villages, running from Woods Hole to North Falmouth. It follows the shore of Buzzards Bay, providing water views, and dips into oak and pine woods; a detour

DID YOU KNOW?

Frappé is Massachusetts speak for milk shake. Try a frappé or get the scoop on the best ice cream flavors from your server at a local take-out window.

onto Church Street takes you to Nobska Light. A brochure is available at the trailheads. If you're taking your bike to Martha's Vineyard, park in one of Falmouth's Steamship Authority lots and ride to the ferry. Free shuttles from Falmouth to the Woods Hole ferry dock have bike carriers. There's also a parking area near Depot Avenue, on County Road at the other end. ⊠ *Falmouth.*

FISHING

Eastman's Sport & Tackle. Freshwater ponds are good for perch, pickerel, trout, and more; get the required license (along with rental gear) at Eastman's Sport & Tackle. It's a good resource if you are looking for local guides. ⊠ *783 Main St., Falmouth Center* ☎ *508/548–6900* ⊕ *www. eastmanstackle.com.*

SHOPPING

Falmouth Village has an easily walkable and attractive Main Street, lined with specialty shops—you won't find major chain stores here—and an assortment of good restaurants. The pretty Margaret E. Noonan Park is home to many events, including an impressive Thursday afternoon Farmers' Market held mid-May–mid-October.

Bean & Cod. This specialty food shop sells cheeses, breads, great sandwiches, and picnic fixings, along with coffees and teas. They also pack and ship gift baskets. ⊠ *140 Main St., Falmouth Center* ☎ *508/548–8840.*

HYANNIS

23 miles east of the Bourne Bridge, 21 miles northeast of Falmouth.

Perhaps best known for its association with the Kennedy clan, the Hyannis area was also a vacation site for President Ulysses S. Grant in 1874 and later for President Grover Cleveland. A bustling year-round hub of activity, Hyannis has the Cape's largest concentration of businesses, shops, malls, hotels and motels, restaurants, and entertainment venues.

VISITOR INFORMATION

Contacts Hyannis Chamber of Commerce. ⊠ *397 Main St.* ☎ *508/775–2201* ⊕ *www.hyannis.com.*

EXPLORING

John F. Kennedy Hyannis Museum. In Main Street's Old Town Hall, this museum explores JFK's Cape years (1934–63) through enlarged and annotated photographs culled from the archives of the JFK Library near Boston, as well as a seven-minute video narrated by Walter Cronkite. Also on-site is the **Cape Cod Baseball League Hall of Fame and Museum,** housed in several rooms in the basement of the JFK museum (appropriately referred to as "the Dugout"). Plaques of Hall of Famers, autographed items from former players who went on to play professional ball, and other Cape League memorabilia are on view; several films about the league and baseball itself play continuously. ⊠ *397 Main St.* ☎ *508/790–3077* ⊕ *www.jfkhyannismuseum.org* ⊠ *$10, includes baseball museum* ⊙ *Mid-Apr.–May and Nov., Mon.–Sat. 10–4, Sun. noon–4; June–Oct., Mon.–Sat. 9–5, Sun. noon–5.*

BEACHES

FAMILY **Kalmus Park Beach.** This wide, sandy beach has an area set aside for windsurfers and a sheltered area that's good for kids. It's a great spot for watching boats go in and out of the harbor. **Amenities:** food and drink; lifeguards; parking (fee); showers; toilets. **Best for:** swimming; walking; windsurfing. ✉ *End of Ocean St.* 🌐 *www.townofbarnstable.us* 🎫 *Parking $20.*

WHERE TO EAT

$$$ BRAZILIAN Fodor's Choice ★ 🍴 **Brazilian Grill.** The Cape has a large Brazilian population, and you can find many of these residents, plus plenty of satisfied visitors, at this all-you-can-eat churrascaria. Be prepared for some serious feasting; this experience is not for nibblers or vegetarians. Waiters circulate through the dining room offering more than a dozen grilled meats—beef, pork, chicken, sausage, and even quail—on swordlike skewers. You can help yourself to a buffet of soups, salads, and side dishes, including *farofa* (a couscous-like dish made of manioc), plantains, rice, and beans. The atmosphere is often loud and jovial. For dessert, the homemade flan is your best bet. [$] *Average main: $33* ✉ *680 Main St.* ☎ *508/771–0109* 🌐 *www.braziliangrill-capecod.com* 🕒 *No lunch weekends.*

$$$ ECLECTIC Fodor's Choice ★ 🍴 **Naked Oyster Bistro & Raw Bar.** With its own oyster farm in nearby Barnstable, this restaurant—as well as its clientele—benefits from near-daily deliveries of the succulent bivalves. More than 1,000 oysters are eaten here on an average summer weekend. You'll always find close to two dozen raw and "dressed" oyster dishes, such as barbecue oysters on the half shell with blue cheese, caramelized onions, and bacon. The oyster stew is out of this world. There's also a nice range of non-oyster entrées, salads, and appetizers. Exposed-brick walls inside and a few street-side tables outside add to the pleasurable dining experience. [$] *Average main: $28* ✉ *410 Main St.* ☎ *508/778–6500* 🌐 *www.nakedoyster.com* 🕒 *Closed Sun. mid-Oct.–mid-Apr.*

WHERE TO STAY

$$$ HOTEL Fodor's Choice ★ 🏨 **Anchor-In.** Most rooms at this small-scale motel on the north end of Hyannis Harbor have harbor views and small balconies overlooking the water, and its simple street-side appearance belies its spacious and immaculate accommodations, extensive grounds, and warm, B&B-style personal service from Lisa and Skip Simpson. **Pros:** easy walk downtown; great harbor views. **Cons:** no elevator—second-floor rooms accessed via stairs. [$] *Rooms from: $319* ✉ *1 South St.* ☎ *508/775–0357* 🌐 *www.anchorin.com* 🛏 *42 rooms* 🍽 *Breakfast.*

NIGHTLIFE AND PERFORMING ARTS

FAMILY **Cape Cod Melody Tent.** In 1950, actress Gertrude Lawrence and her husband, producer-manager Richard Aldrich, opened the Cape Cod Melody Tent to showcase Broadway musicals and concerts. Today, it's the region's top venue for pop concerts and comedy shows. Performers who have played here in the round include the Indigo Girls, Lyle Lovett, Tony Bennett, Diana Krall, and Crosby, Stills & Nash. The Tent also holds a children's theater series in July and August, Wednesday at 11 am. ✉ *21 W. Main St.* ☎ *508/775–5630* 🌐 *www.melodytent.org.*

CLOSE UP

Cape Cod Clam Shacks

Cape Codders have been clamming for generations, and the iconic mollusks are a celebrated part of the culture here. Classic clam shacks are known for their bountiful baskets of crispy fried clams, which, according to Cape Codders, should always be ordered "whole"—that is, with the bellies. Fried clams are never the only item on the menu: a typical menu also includes clam chowder, lobster rolls, fried fish, scallops, shrimp, coleslaw, fries, potato salad, and other nonseafood items. The quintessential experience usually involves ordering at one window, picking up at another, and eating at a picnic table—hopefully one with a beach or harbor view! A few of our favorites on Cape Cod include the Clam Shack in Falmouth, Mac's Seafood in Wellfleet, and Arnold's Lobster & Clam Bar in Eastham. The Bite in Menemsha on Martha's Vineyard is also worth a try.

BARNSTABLE

4 miles north of Hyannis.

With nearly 50,000 year-round residents, Barnstable is the largest town on the Cape. It's also the second oldest, founded in 1639. You can get a feeling for its age in Barnstable Village, on and near Main Street (Route 6A), a lovely area of large old homes.

BEACHES

FAMILY **Sandy Neck Beach.** Sandy Neck Beach stretches some 6 miles across a peninsula that ends at **Sandy Neck Light.** The beach is one of the Cape's most beautiful—dunes, sand, and bay spread endlessly east, west, and north. The marsh used to be harvested for salt hay; now it's a haven for birds, which are out and about in the greatest numbers in morning and evening. The lighthouse, standing a few feet from the eroding shoreline at the tip of the neck, has been out of commission since 1952. It was built in 1857 to replace an 1827 light, and it used to run on acetylene gas. As you travel east along Route 6A from Sandwich, Sandy Neck Road is just before the Barnstable line, although the beach itself is in West Barnstable. **Amenities:** food and drink; lifeguards; parking (fee); showers; toilets. **Best for:** sunset; swimming; walking. ⊠ *Sandy Neck Rd., West Barnstable* 🅿 *Parking $20* ⊘ *Daily 8 am–9 pm (staffed until 5 pm).*

WHERE TO STAY

$ 🏠 **Beechwood Inn.** This lovely yellow-and-pale-green 1853 Queen Anne
B&B/INN house, named for its two magnificent and aged beech trees, has gingerbread trim and is wrapped by a wide porch with wicker furniture and a glider swing. **Pros:** afternoon tea; seven beaches within a 5-mile radius. **Cons:** narrow, curved stairs. $ *Rooms from: $189* ⊠ *2839 Rte. 6A* 🕾 *508/362–6618, 800/609–6618* ⊕ *www.beechwoodinn.com* 🛏 *6 rooms* ⊗ *Breakfast.*

$ 🏠 **Honeysuckle Hill.** Innkeepers Rick Kowarek and Nancy Hunter-Young
B&B/INN provide plenty of thoughtful touches at this 1810 Queen Anne–style
Fodor's Choice cottage: fresh flowers in every room, refrigerators stocked with bever-
★ ages, and beach chairs with umbrellas (perfect for nearby Sandy Neck

Beach). **Pros:** lush gardens on the grounds; tasteful, large rooms; very short drive to Sandy Neck Beach. **Cons:** most rooms are accessed via steep stairs. $ *Rooms from: $199* ⊠ *591 Rte. 6A, West Barnstable* ☎ *508/362–8418, 866/444–5522* ⊕ *www.honeysucklehill.com* ➳ *4 rooms, 1 suite* ❑ *Breakfast.*

YARMOUTH

Yarmouth Port is 3 miles east of Barnstable Village; West Yarmouth is 2 miles east of Hyannis.

Once known as Mattacheese, or "the planting lands," Yarmouth was settled in 1639 by farmers from the Plymouth Bay Colony. By then the Cape had begun a thriving maritime industry, and men turned to the sea to make their fortunes. Many impressive sea captains' houses—some now B&Bs and museums—still line enchanting Route 6A and nearby side streets, and Yarmouth Port has some real old-time stores in town. West Yarmouth has a very different atmosphere, stretched on busy commercial Route 28 south of Yarmouth Port.

VISITOR INFORMATION

Contacts Yarmouth Chamber of Commerce. ⊠ *424 Rte. 28, West Yarmouth* ☎ *508/778–1008, 800/732–1008* ⊕ *www.yarmouthcapecod.com.*

EXPLORING

FAMILY **Bass Hole Boardwalk.** Taking in one of Yarmouth Port's most beautiful areas, Bass Hole Boardwalk extends over a swampy creek, crosses salt marshes, and winds around vegetated wetlands and upland woods. Gray's Beach is a little crescent of sand with still water that's good for kids inside the roped-in swimming area. At the end of the boardwalk, benches provide a place to relax and look out over abundant marsh life and, across the creek, the beautiful, sandy shores of Dennis's Chapin Beach. At low tide you can walk out on the flats for almost a mile. ⊠ *Center St., near Gray's Beach parking lot, Yarmouth Port.*

Edward Gorey House. Explore the eccentric doodlings and offbeat humor of the late acclaimed artist and illustrator. Regularly changing exhibitions, arranged in the downstairs rooms of Gorey's former home, include drawings of his oddball characters and reveal the mysterious psyche of the sometimes dark but always playful illustrator. ⊠ *8 Strawberry La., Yarmouth Port* ☎ *508/362–3909* ⊕ *www.edwardgoreyhouse.org* ☒ *$8* ◷ *Mid-Apr.–June, Thurs.–Sat. 11–4, Sun. noon–4; July–mid-Oct., Wed.– Sat. 11–4, Sun. noon–4; mid-Oct.–Dec. Fri. and Sat. 11–4, Sun. noon–4.*

QUICK
BITES

Jerry's Seafood. Open year-round, this simple shack serves fried clams and onion rings, along with thick frappés (milk shakes), frozen yogurt, and soft-serve ice cream, at good prices. ⊠ *654 Rte. 28, West Yarmouth* ☎ *508/775–9752* ⊕ *www.jerryscapecod.com.*

WHERE TO EAT

$$$
JAPANESE
Fodor'sChoice
★

✕ **Inaho.** Yuji Watanabe, chef-owner of the Cape's best Japanese restaurant, makes early-morning journeys to Boston's fish markets to shop for the freshest local catch. His selection of sushi and sashimi is vast and artful, and vegetable and seafood tempura come out of the kitchen fluffy and light. If you're a teriyaki lover, you can't do any better than the chicken's beautiful blend of sweet and sour. Can't decide what to order? He's happy to design a varied and generous tasting menu. One remarkable element of the restaurant is its artful lighting: small pinpoint lights on the food accentuate the presentation in a dramatic way. The serene and simple Japanese garden out back has a traditional koi pond. [$] *Average main: $29* ✉ *157 Main St., Yarmouth Port* ☎ *508/362–5522* 🌐 *www.inahocapecod.com* ⏲ *Closed Sun. No lunch.*

$ BRITISH 🍴 **The Optimist Café.** From the outside, this bold Gothic Victorian looks like something out of a Brothers Grimm tale, with its steeply pitched roof, fanciful turrets, frilly gingerbread trim, and deep rose-and-green paint job. There is a great selection for breakfast (served all day) and lunch, featuring traditional English fare like smoked fish dishes, curries, scones, and crumpets. Treat yourself to a ploughman's lunch, consisting of cheeses, chutney, and crusty bread. [$] *Average main: $11* ✉ *134 Rte. 6A, Yarmouth Port* ☎ *508/362–1024* 🌐 *www.optimistcafe.com* ⏲ *No dinner.*

WHERE TO STAY

$$ HOTEL FAMILY 🏨 **Bayside Resort.** A bit more upscale than most properties along Route 28, the Bayside overlooks pristine salt marshes and Lewis Bay. Although it's not right on the water, there's a small beach and a large outdoor pool with a café (there's also an indoor pool, which kids enjoy). **Pros:** ideal for families with children; close to attractions of busy Rte. 28. **Cons:** no beach swimming; not for those seeking intimate surroundings. [$] *Rooms from: $259* ✉ *225 Rte. 28, West Yarmouth* ☎ *508/775–5669, 800/243–1114* 🌐 *www.baysideresort.com* 🛏 *128 rooms* 🍽 *Breakfast.*

$$ B&B/INN Fodor's Choice ★ 🏨 **Capt. Farris House.** A short hop off congested Route 28 sits this imposing 1845 Greek Revival home. **Pros:** beautiful grounds; ideal location for exploring Mid Cape area; close to area restaurants and attractions. **Cons:** no elevator; not close to the beach. [$] *Rooms from: $210* ✉ *308 Old Main St., Bass River Village* ☎ *508/760–2818* 🌐 *www.captainfarris.com* 🛏 *6 rooms, 3 suites* 🍽 *Breakfast.*

$ B&B/INN Fodor's Choice ★ 🏨 **Liberty Hill Inn.** Smartly and traditionally furnished common areas—including the high-ceiling parlor, the formal dining room, and the wraparound porch—are a major draw to this dignified 1825 Greek Revival house. **Pros:** tasteful surroundings; beautiful grounds. **Cons:** some steep stairs; some bathrooms have only small shower stalls. [$] *Rooms from: $195* ✉ *77 Rte. 6A, Yarmouth Port* ☎ *508/362–3976* 🌐 *www.libertyhillinn.com* ⏲ *Closed Feb.–mid-Mar.* 🛏 *8 rooms, 1 suite* 🍽 *Breakfast.*

NIGHTLIFE AND PERFORMING ARTS

Oliver's & Planck's Tavern. Fish tanks illuminate this friendly bar, which hosts live music in a variety of genres on weekends throughout the year. There's also a midweek trivia night. ✉ *6 Bray Farm Rd., off Rte. 6A, Yarmouth Port* ☎ *508/362–6062* 🌐 *www.oliverscapecod.com.*

DENNIS

Dennis Village is 4 miles east of Yarmouth Port; West Dennis is 1 mile east of South Yarmouth.

The backstreets of Dennis Village still retain the Colonial charm of its seafaring days. The town, which was incorporated in 1793, was named for the Reverend Josiah Dennis. There were 379 sea captains living here when fishing, salt making, and shipbuilding were the main industries, and the elegant houses they constructed—now museums and B&Bs—still line the streets.

VISITOR INFORMATION

Contacts Dennis Chamber of Commerce. ⊠ *238 Swan River Rd., West Dennis* ☎ *508/398–3568, 800/243–9920* ⊕ *www.dennischamber.com.*

EXPLORING

Fodor's Choice **Cape Cod Museum of Art.** This museum on the grounds of the Cape Play-
★ house has a permanent collection of more than 850 works by Cape-associated artists. Important pieces include a portrait of a fisherman's wife by Charles Hawthorne, the father of the Provincetown art colony; a 1924 portrait of a Portuguese fisherman's daughter by William Paxton, one of the first artists to summer in Provincetown; a collection of wood-block prints by Varujan Boghosian, a member of Provincetown's Long Point Gallery cooperative; an oil sketch by Karl Knaths, who painted in Provincetown from 1919 until his death in 1971; and works by abstract expressionist Hans Hofmann. Throughout the year are special events, workshops, and classes. ⊠ *60 Hope La., Dennis Village* ☎ *508/385–4477* ⊕ *www.ccmoa.org* ⊠ *$9* ⊙ *Tues.–Sat. 10–5, Sun. noon–5.*

BEACHES

Parking at all Dennis beaches is $20 per day in season ($25 on weekends) for nonresidents.

FAMILY **Corporation Beach.** Once a privately owned packet landing, the beautiful crescent of white sand backed by low dunes now serves a decidedly noncorporate purpose as a public beach. **Amenities:** food and drink; lifeguards; parking (fee); showers; toilets. **Best for:** sunset; swimming; walking. ⊠ *Corporation Rd., Dennis Village* ⊠ *Parking $20 weekdays, $25 weekends.*

WHERE TO EAT

$ ✕**Captain Frosty's.** A great stop after the beach, this barn-shaped sea-
SEAFOOD food shack is where locals go to get their fried seafood. This mod-
FAMILY est joint has a regular menu supplemented by specials posted on the
Fodor's Choice board and a counter where you order and take a number written on a
★ french-fries box. The staff are young and hardworking, pumping out fresh fried clams and fish 'n' chips on paper plates. All frying is done in heart-healthy canola oil, and rice pilaf is offered as a substitute for fries. There's seating inside as well as outside on a shady brick patio. $ *Average main: $15* ⊠ *219 Rte. 6A, Dennis Village* ☎ *508/385–8548* ⊕ *www.captainfrosty.com* ⊙ *Closed early Sept.–mid-Apr.* ⊛ *Reservations not accepted.*

$$$
AMERICAN
Fodor's Choice
★

✕ **Red Pheasant.** This is one of the Cape's best cozy country restaurants, with a consistently good kitchen where creative American food, much of it locally sourced and organic, is prepared with elaborate sauces and herb combinations. The sauteed dayboat scallops, for example, are served with butternut squash risotto, pumpkin seeds, and a ginger syrup. The exquisitely roasted rack of lamb Persillade is local favorite; in fall, look for game dishes like venison and quail. Try to reserve a table in the more intimate Garden Room. The expansive wine list is excellent. $ *Average main: $30* ✉ *905 Rte. 6A, Dennis Village* ☎ *508/385–2133* ⊕ *www.redpheasantinn.com* ⊘ *No lunch* ⚖ *Reservations essential.*

WHERE TO STAY

$
B&B/INN
Fodor's Choice
★

⌂ **Isaiah Hall B&B Inn.** Lilacs and pink roses trail the white-picket fence outside this 1857 Greek Revival farmhouse on a quiet residential road near the bay, where innkeepers Jerry and Judy Neal set the scene for a romantic getaway with guest rooms that have country antiques, floral-print wallpapers, fluffy quilts, and Priscilla curtains. **Pros:** beautiful grounds; near beaches and attractions. **Cons:** not for those with children under seven; some very steep steps; some rooms are on the small side. $ *Rooms from: $175* ✉ *152 Whig St., Box 1007, Dennis Village* ☎ *508/385–9928* ⊕ *www.isaiahhallinn.com* ⇄ *10 rooms, 2 suites* ⏻⏐ *Breakfast.*

NIGHTLIFE AND PERFORMING ARTS

FAMILY
Fodor's Choice
★

Cape Playhouse. For Broadway-style dramas, comedies, and musicals, attend a production at the Cape Playhouse, the country's oldest professional summer theater. In 1927 Raymond Moore, who had been working with a theatrical troupe in Provincetown, bought an 1838 Unitarian meetinghouse and converted it into a theater, where the original pews still serve as seats. The opening performance was *The Guardsman,* starring Basil Rathbone. Other stars who performed here in the early days—some in their professional stage debuts—include Bette Davis (who first worked here as an usher), Gregory Peck, Lana Turner, Ginger Rogers, Humphrey Bogart, Tallulah Bankhead, and Henry Fonda, who appeared with his then-unknown 20-year-old daughter, Jane. Behind-the-scenes tours are available. The playhouse offers children's theater on Friday mornings in July and August. The 26-acre property includes a restaurant, the Cape Cod Museum of Art, and the Cape Cinema. ✉ *820 Rte. 6A, Dennis Village* ☎ *508/385–3911, 877/385–3911* ⊕ *www.capeplayhouse.com* ⊘ *June–Sept.*

Harvest Gallery Wine Bar. Near the Cape Playhouse, this friendly place has an extensive wine list, a good variety of hors d'oeuvres and other nibbles, eclectic artwork, and live music. ✉ *776 Main St., Dennis Village* ☎ *508/385–2444* ⊕ *www.harvestgallerywinebar.com* ⊘ *Closed Mon., and mid-Jan.–early Apr.*

BREWSTER

7 miles northeast of Dennis, 20 miles east of Sandwich.

Brewster's location on Cape Cod Bay makes it a perfect place to learn about the region's ecology. The Cape Cod Museum of Natural History

Learn more about the Cape's marshlands, forests, and ponds at the Cape Cod Museum of Natural History in Brewster.

is here, and the area is rich in conservation lands, state parks, forests, freshwater ponds, and brackish marshes. When the tide is low in Cape Cod Bay, you can stroll the beaches and explore tidal pools up to 2 miles from the shore on the Brewster flats.

VISITOR INFORMATION

Contacts Brewster Chamber of Commerce. ✉ *Town Hall, 2198 Rte. 6A* ☎ *508/896–3500* ⊕ *www.brewster-capecod.org.*

EXPLORING

Brewster Store. Built in 1852 as a church, this local landmark is a typical New England general store with such essentials as daily newspapers, penny candy, groceries, and benches out front for conversation. They specialize in oil lamps and antique lanterns of all types. Out back, the Brewster Scoop serves ice cream mid-June–early September. Upstairs, memorabilia from antique toys to World War II bond posters is displayed. Downstairs there's a working antique nickelodeon; locals warm themselves by the old coal stove in colder months. ✉ *1935 Rte. 6A* ☎ *508/896–3744* ⊕ *www.brewsterstore.com.*

FAMILY
Fodor'sChoice
★

Cape Cod Museum of Natural History. A short drive west from the heart of Brewster, this spacious museum and its pristine grounds include a shop, a natural-history library, and exhibits such as a working beehive and a pond- and sea-life room with live specimens. Walking trails wind through 80 acres of forest, marshland, and ponds, all rich in birds and other wildlife. The exhibit hall upstairs has a wall display of aerial photographs documenting the process by which the famous Chatham sandbar was split in two. In summer there are guided field walks, nature programs, and art classes for preschoolers through ninth graders. ✉ *869 Rte. 6A, West Brewster* ☎ *508/896–3867* 🌐 *www.ccmnh.org* 🎟 *$10* ⏲ *June–Sept., daily 9:30–4; Feb. and Mar., Thurs.–Sun. 11–3; Oct.–Dec., Apr., and May, Wed.–Sun. 11–3. Trails open year-round.*

FAMILY **Nickerson State Park.** These 1,961 acres were once part of a vast estate belonging to Roland C. Nickerson, son of Samuel Nickerson, a Chatham native who founded the First National Bank of Chicago. Roland and his wife, Addie, lavishly entertained such visitors as President Grover Cleveland at their private beach and hunting lodge in English country-house style, with coachmen dressed in tails and top hats and a bugler announcing carriages entering the front gates. In 1934 Addie donated the land for the state park in memory of Roland and their son, who died during the 1918 flu epidemic.

4

The park consists of acres of oak, pitch-pine, hemlock, and spruce forest speckled with seven freshwater kettle ponds formed by glaciers. Some ponds are stocked with trout for fishing. You can swim, canoe, sail, and kayak in the ponds, and bicycle along 8 miles of paved trails that have access to the Cape Cod Rail Trail. Bird-watchers seek out the thrushes, wrens, warblers, woodpeckers, finches, larks, cormorants, great blue herons, hawks, owls, and ospreys. Red foxes and white-tailed deer are occasionally spotted in the woods. ✉ *3488 Rte. 6A, East Brewster* ☎ *508/896–3491* 🌐 *www.mass.gov/eea/agencies/dcr* 🎟 *$5* ⏲ *Daily dawn–dusk.*

WHERE TO EAT

$$$$ ECLECTIC 🍴 **Bramble Inn.** Inside an inviting 1860s white house in Brewster's historic village center, this romantic property presents well-crafted, globally inspired contemporary fare in four dining rooms. During the warmer months, dine on a patio amid fragrant flower beds. The menu changes often but always includes the assorted seafood curry—the house favorite—which combines lobster, shrimp, scallops, and cod in a light curry sauce with grilled banana, toasted coconut, sliced almonds, and house chutney. If you'd rather graze, opt for the "Bramble Bites"—choose from risottos, skillet-roasted mussels, salmon Niçoise, and the like—served in the bar as well as on the garden patios. There are also four lovely rooms for overnight guests. [$] *Average main: $35* ✉ *2019 Rte. 6A, East Brewster* ☎ *508/896–7644* 🌐 *www.brambleinn.com* ⏲ *Closed Mon. and Tues. No lunch.*

$$$$ FRENCH Fodor's Choice ★ 🍴 **Chillingsworth.** One of the crown jewels of Cape restaurants, Chillingsworth combines formal presentation with an excellent French menu and a diverse wine cellar to create a memorable dining experience. Superrich risotto, roasted lobster, and grilled Angus sirloin are favorites. Dinner in the main dining rooms is prix fixe and includes seven courses—appetizer, soup, salad, sorbet, entrée, "amusements," and dessert, plus coffee or tea. Less expensive à la carte options for lunch, dinner, and Sunday brunch are served in the more casual, patio-style Chill's Bistro. There are also a few guest rooms here for overnighting. [$] *Average main: $70* ✉ *2449 Rte. 6A, East Brewster* ☎ *508/896–3640* 🌐 *www.chillingsworth.com* ⏲ *Closed Thanksgiving–mid-May* ✍ *Reservations essential.*

WHERE TO STAY

$$ B&B/INN Fodor's Choice ★ 🏨 **Captain Freeman Inn.** Named for the sea captain who had the home built in 1866, this gracious inn retains its aged elegance with original ornate plaster ceiling medallions, marble fireplaces, and sturdy yet graceful construction. **Pros:** authentic historic lodging with modern amenities; short walk to town center. **Cons:** not for those with children. [$] *Rooms from: $259* ✉ *15 Breakwater Rd.* ☎ *508/896–7481* 🌐 *www.captainfreemaninn.com* 🛏 *11 rooms* 🍴 *Breakfast.*

$ B&B/INN FAMILY Fodor's Choice ★ 🏨 **Old Sea Pines Inn.** With its white-column portico and wraparound veranda overlooking a broad lawn, Old Sea Pines, which housed a "charm and personality" school in the early 1900s, resembles a vintage summer estate. **Pros:** welcomes families; beautiful grounds; reasonable rates. **Cons:** no TV in main building; steep stairway to upper floors. [$] *Rooms from: $170* ✉ *2553 Rte. 6A* ☎ *508/896–6114* 🌐 *www.oldseapinesinn.com* 🕒 *Closed Dec.–mid-Apr.* 🛏 *24 rooms (19 with bath), 5 suites* 🍴 *Breakfast.*

NIGHTLIFE AND PERFORMING ARTS

FAMILY **Cape Cod Repertory Theatre Co.** Several impressive productions, from original works to the classics, are staged every year in this indoor Arts and Crafts–style theater set way back in the woods. There are mesmerizing outdoor shows for kids offered on weekday mornings during the summer, as well as hour-long puppet shows. ✉ *3299 Rte. 6A, west of Nickerson State Park, East Brewster* ☎ *508/896–1888* 🌐 *www.caperep.org* 🕒 *Closed Dec.–Apr.*

SPORTS AND THE OUTDOORS

Jack's Boat Rentals. Choose from among canoes, kayaks, pedal boats, sailboats, stand-up paddleboards, and sailboards at the location in Nickerson State Park (at Flax Pond). ✉ *Nickerson State Park, Rte. 6A, at Flax Pond, East Brewster* ☎ *508/896–8556* 🌐 *www.jacksboatrental.com.*

SHOPPING

With Brewster's abundant historic and natural appeal, it's no surprise that shoppers will benefit from the bounty of antiques shops, art galleries, and specialty shops here.

FAMILY Fodor's Choice ★ **Brewster Book Store.** A special place, Brewster Book Store is filled to the rafters with all manner of books by local and international authors, with an extensive fiction selection and kids' section. Author signings and children's story times take place year-round. ✉ *2648 Rte. 6A, East Brewster* ☎ *508/896–6543, 800/823–6543* 🌐 *www.brewsterbookstore.com.*

Satucket Farm Stand. This real old-fashioned farm stand offers plenty of local produce, flowers, herbs, homemade baked goods, and other treats. The stand is open daily Memorial Day–Labor Day. ✉ *76 Harwich Rd.* ☎ *508/896–5540* 🌐 *www.satucketfarm.com.*

HARWICH

6 miles south of Brewster, 5 miles east of Dennis.

The Cape's famous cranberry industry took off in Harwich in 1844, when Alvin Cahoon was its principal grower. Today you'll still find working cranberry bogs throughout Harwich. Three naturally sheltered harbors on Nantucket Sound make the town, like its English namesake, popular with boaters. You'll find dozens of elegant sailboats and elaborate yachts in Harwich's harbors, plus plenty of charter fishing boats. Every August the town pays celebratory homage to its large boating population with a grand regatta, Sails Around the Cape.

VISITOR INFORMATION

Contacts Harwich Chamber of Commerce. ✉ *1 Schoolhouse Rd., at Rte. 28, Harwich Port* ☎ *508/432–1600, 800/442–7942* 🌐 *www.harwichcc.com.*

WHERE TO EAT

$$$ ITALIAN Fodor's Choice ★ 🍴 **Buca's Tuscan Roadhouse.** This romantic roadhouse near the Chatham border, adorned with tiny white lights, wine bottles, and warm-hue walls, might just transport you to Italy—and if it doesn't, the food will. From the baby arugula, goat cheese, pancetta, and pistachio salad to veal with red wine, balsamic butter, sun-dried cherries, and roasted tomatoes, this is mouthwatering Italian fare taken far beyond traditional home cooking. There are always excellent specials added to the menu; in the fall and winter, look for value-priced entrées. Save room for the signature three-tier chocolate cake with a coconut-chocolate sauce. [$] *Average main: $27* ✉ *4 Depot Rd.* ☎ *508/432–6900* 🌐 *www.bucasroadhouse.com* 🕒 *No lunch* ✍ *Reservations essential.*

$$$ AMERICAN Fodor's Choice ★ 🍴 **Cape Sea Grille.** Sitting primly inside a dashing Gothic Victorian house on a side street off hectic Route 28, this gem with distant sea views cultivates a refined ambience with fresh flowers, white linens, and a vibrant, welcoming atmosphere. Chef-owner Douglas Ramler relies on the freshest ingredients. Specialties from the seasonal menu may include pan-seared lobster with pancetta, potatoes, grilled asparagus, and a Calvados-saffron reduction, or grilled Atlantic halibut with smoked bacon, fennel, and basil tart. There are also generous wine, martini, and drink lists. [$] *Average main: $32* ✉ *31 Sea St., Harwich Port* ☎ *508/432–4745* 🌐 *www.capeseagrille.com* 🕒 *Closed Mon.–Wed. Columbus Day–early Dec. and mid-Dec.–early Apr. No lunch* ✍ *Reservations essential.*

WHERE TO STAY

$$$$ RESORT FAMILY Fodor's Choice ★ 🏨 **Wequassett Inn Resort and Golf Club.** Twenty Cape-style cottages and an attractive hotel make up this traditionally elegant resort by the sea. **Pros:** waterfront setting; activities and programs for all ages; babysitting services. **Cons:** rates are very steep; not an in-town location. [$] *Rooms from: $595* ✉ *2173 Orleans Rd. (Rte. 28)*\ ☎ *508/432–5400, 800/225–7125* 🌐 *www.wequassett.com* 🕒 *Closed Nov.–Mar.* 🛏 *115 rooms, 7 suites* 🍽 *No meals.*

$$$$ B&B/INN 🏨 **Winstead Village Inn.** With its graceful columns and welcoming front veranda, the regal Winstead Inn sits along a quiet street on the edge of downtown Harwich. **Pros:** spacious, elegant rooms; pretty pool area. **Cons:** numerous stairs; not for those on a budget; ½ mile from the beach (the Beach House is a separate property). [$] *Rooms from: $410* ✉ *114 Parallel St.* ☎ *508/432–4444, 800/870–4405* 🌐 *www.winsteadinn.com* 🕒 *Closed Nov.–Easter* 🛏 *15 rooms* 🍽 *Breakfast.*

CHATHAM

5 miles east of Harwich.

Fodor's Choice
★

At the bent elbow of the Cape, with water nearly surrounding it, Chatham has all the charm of a quietly posh seaside resort, with plenty of shops but none of the crass commercialism that plagues some other towns on the Cape. The town has gray-shingle houses—many improbably large and grandiose—with tidy awnings and cheerful flower gardens, an attractive Main Street with crafts and antiques stores alongside dapper cafés, and a five-and-dime. Although it can get crowded in high season—and even on weekends during shoulder seasons—Chatham remains a true New England village.

VISITOR INFORMATION

Contacts Chatham Chamber of Commerce. ✉ *2377 Main St.* ☎ *508/945–5199, 800/715–5567* ⊕ *www.chathaminfo.com.*

EXPLORING

Atwood House Museum. Built by sea captain Joseph C. Atwood in 1752, this museum has a gambrel roof, hand-hewn floor planks, an old kitchen with a wide hearth and a beehive oven, and some antique dolls and toys. The New Gallery displays portraits of local sea captains. The Joseph C. Lincoln Room has the manuscripts, first editions, and mementos of the Chatham writer, and antique tools are displayed in a room in the basement. There's also a local commercial fishing gallery. The 1974 Durand Wing has collections of seashells from around the world, as well as threaded Sandwich glass, Parian-ware figures, unglazed porcelain vases, figurines, and busts. In a remodeled freight shed are the stunning and provocative murals (1932–45) by Alice Stallknecht Wight portraying religious scenes in Chatham settings. On the grounds are an herb garden, the old turret and lens from the Chatham Light, and a simple camp house rescued from eroding North Beach. ✉ *347 Stage Harbor Rd., West Chatham* ☎ *508/945–2493* ⊕ *www.chathamhistoricalsociety. org* ✉ *$6* ⊙ *July and Aug., Tues.–Fri. 10–4, Sat. 1–4; June and Sept.–mid-Oct., Tues.–Sat. 1–4.*

Chatham Light. The view from this lighthouse—of the harbor, the sandbars, and the ocean beyond—justifies the crowds. The lighthouse is especially dramatic on a foggy night, as the beacon's light pierces the mist. Coin-operated telescopes allow a close look at the famous "Chatham Break," the result of a fierce 1987 nor'easter that blasted a channel through a barrier beach just off the coast. The U.S. Coast Guard auxiliary, which supervises the lighthouse, offers free tours May–October on most Wednesdays; otherwise, the interior is off-limits. There is free parking in front of the lighthouse—the 30-minute limit is strictly monitored. ✉ *Main St., near Bridge St., West Chatham* ☎ *508/945–3830* ⊕ *www.uscg.mil/d1/staChatham* ✉ *Free* ⊙ *May–Oct., Wed. by appointment only.*

Fodor's Choice
★

Monomoy National Wildlife Refuge. This 2,500-acre preserve includes the Monomoy Islands, a fragile 9-mile-long barrier-beach area south of Chatham. Monomoy's North and South islands were created when a storm divided the former Monomoy Island in 1978. A haven for bird-watchers, the refuge is an important stop along the North Atlantic Flyway for migratory waterfowl and shorebirds—peak migration times are May and late July. It also provides nesting and resting grounds for 285 species, including gulls—great black-backed, herring, and laughing—and several tern species. White-tailed deer wander the islands, and harbor and gray seals frequent the shores in winter. The only structure on the islands is the **South Monomoy Lighthouse**, built in 1849. ⊠ *Wikis Way, Morris Island* ☎ *508/945–0594* ⊕ *www.fws.gov/refuge/ Monomoy* ⊡ *Free.*

BEACHES

FAMILY **Harding's Beach.** West of Chatham center, on the calmer and warmer waters of Nantucket Sound, Harding's Beach is very popular with families. It can get crowded, so plan to arrive earlier or later in the day. **Amenities:** food and drink; lifeguards; parking (fee); showers; toilets. **Best for:** swimming; walking; windsurfing. ⊠ *Harding's Beach Rd., off Barn Hill Rd., West Chatham* ⊡ *Parking $15.*

WHERE TO EAT

$$$ ✕**Impudent Oyster.** This cozy, festive tavern with an unfailingly cheerful
SEAFOOD staff and superb but reasonably priced seafood occupies a dapper house just off Main Street. It's a great place for a romantic meal or dinner with the kids, and the menu offers light burgers and sandwiches, as well as more-substantial fare. The mussels with white-wine sauce is a local favorite. The dining room is split-level, with a bar in back. It's always packed, and there's not a ton of seating, so reserve on weekends. $ *Average main: $27* ⊠ *15 Chatham Bars Ave.* ☎ *508/945–3545.*

$$$ ✕**Pisces.** An intimate dining room inside a simple yellow house, Pisces
SEAFOOD serves coastal-inspired fare. If it swims in local waters, you can probably sample it here. A rich chowder of lobster, white truffle oil, and corn is a terrific way to start your meal. Move on to Mediterranean-style fisherman's stew in saffron-lobster broth, or local cod with lemon-caper aioli. Complement your dinner with a selection from the extensive wine list, which offers more than 20 glass pours. $ *Average main: $28* ⊠ *2653 Main St., South Chatham* ☎ *508/432–4600* ⊕ *www.piscesofchatham. com* ⊙ *Closed mid-Oct.–mid-Apr. No lunch* ⚲ *Reservations essential.*

NIGHTLIFE AND PERFORMING ARTS

Chatham Squire. Boasting four bars (including a raw bar), this is a rollicking year-round local hangout, drawing a young crowd to the bar side and a mixed crowd of locals to the restaurant. There's live entertainment on weekends. ⊠ *487 Main St.* ☎ *508/945–0945* ⊕ *www.thesquire.com.*

SHOPPING

Chatham Jam and Jelly Shop. This shop sells delicious concoctions like rose-petal jelly, apple-lavender chutney, and wild beach plum jelly, as well as all the old standbys. All preserves are made on-site in small batches, and about 75 of the 120-plus varieties are available for sampling (which is encouraged). ⊠ *16 Seaquanset Rd., at Rte. 28, West Chatham* ☎ *508/945–3052* ⊕ *www.chathamjamandjellyshop.com.*

Yankee Ingenuity. Here you'll find a varied selection of unique jewelry and lamps and a wide assortment of unusual, beautiful trinkets at reasonable prices (especially for Chatham). ⊠ *525 Main St.* ☎ *508/945–1288* ⊕ *www.yankee-ingenuity.com.*

ORLEANS

8 miles north of Chatham, 35 miles east of Sagamore Bridge.

Orleans has a long heritage in fishing and seafaring, and many beautifully preserved homes from the Colonial era can still be seen in the small village of East Orleans, home of the town's Historical Society and Museum. In other areas of town, such as down by Rock Harbor, more modestly grand homes stand near the water's edge.

VISITOR INFORMATION

Contacts Orleans Chamber of Commerce. ⊠ *44 Main St.* ☎ *508/255–1386, 508/255–1386* ⊕ *www.orleanscapecod.org.*

EXPLORING

FAMILY **Rock Harbor.** This harbor was the site of a War of 1812 skirmish in which the Orleans militia kept a British warship from docking. In the 19th century Orleans had an active saltworks, and a flourishing packet service between Rock Harbor and Boston developed. Today it's the base of charter-fishing and party boats in season, as well as of a small commercial fishing fleet. Sunsets over the harbor are spectacular, and it's a great place to watch the boats float past. Parking is free. ⊠ *Rock Harbor Rd.*

QUICK BITES

Cottage St. Bakery. Delicious artisanal breads, pastries, cakes, and sweets are made here, as well as healthful breakfast and lunch fare, from homemade granola to hearty soups and hefty sandwiches. ⊠ *5 Cottage St.* ☎ *508/255–2821* ⊕ *www.cottagestreetbakery.com.*

BEACHES

There is a daily parking fee for both beaches mid-June–Labor Day.

FAMILY **Nauset Beach.** This town-managed beach—not to be confused with Nauset Light Beach on the National Seashore—is a 10-mile sweep of sandy ocean beach with low dunes and large waves good for bodysurfing or board surfing. Despite its size, the massive parking lot often fills up on sunny days; arrive quite early or in the late afternoon if you want to claim a spot. The beach gets extremely crowded in summer; unless you walk a ways, expect to feel very close to your neighbors on the sand. **Amenities:** food and drink; lifeguards; parking (fee); showers; toilets. **Best for:** sunrise; surfing; swimming; walking. ⊠ *Beach Rd., Nauset Heights* ☎ *508/240–3780* ⊠ *Parkin $15 mid-June–Labor Day.*

FAMILY **Skaket Beach.** On Cape Cod Bay, Skaket Beach is a sandy stretch with calm, warm water good for children. When the tide is out, you can walk seemingly endlessly on the sandy flats. The parking lot fills up fast on hot July and August days; try to arrive before 11 or after 2. The many tide pools make this a favorite spot for families. Sunsets here draw a good crowd. **Amenities:** food and drink; lifeguards; parking (fee); showers; toilets. **Best for:** sunset; swimming; walking. ⊠ *Skaket Beach Rd.* ☎ *508/240–3775* ⊠ *Parking $15 mid-June–Labor Day.*

WHERE TO EAT

$$$ MEDITERRANEAN Fodor's Choice ★ 🍴 **Abba.** In an elegant and intimate setting, Abba serves inspired pan-Mediterranean cuisine. Chef and co-owner Erez Pinhas skillfully combines Middle Eastern, Asian, and southern European flavors in such dishes as herb-crusted rack of venison with shiitake risotto and asparagus in port sauce, and grilled tuna with vegetable nori roll tempura in a balsamic miso-mustard sauce. Cushy pillows on the banquettes and soft candlelight flickering from Moroccan glass votives add a touch of opulence. [$] *Average main: $27* ✉ *89 Old Colony Way* ☎ *508/255–8144* 🌐 *www.abbarestaurant.com* 🕒 *No lunch* ✍ *Reservations essential.*

WHERE TO STAY

$$$ B&B/INN Fodor's Choice ★ 🏨 **A Little Inn on Pleasant Bay.** This gorgeously decorated inn occupies a 1798 building on a bluff beside a cranberry bog, and many of the rooms look clear out to the bay for which it's named (others face the lush gardens). **Pros:** great water views; abundant buffet breakfast; spacious baths. **Cons:** not an in-town location; not for those traveling with small children. [$] *Rooms from: $378* ✉ *654 S. Orleans Rd., South Orleans* ☎ *508/255–0780, 888/332–3351* 🌐 *www.alittleinnonpleasantbay.com* 🕒 *Closed Oct.–mid-May* 🛏 *9 rooms* 🍽 *Breakfast.*

SPORTS AND THE OUTDOORS

Many of Orleans's freshwater ponds offer good fishing for perch, pickerel, trout, and more.

Arey's Pond Boat Yard. There's a sailing school here offering individual and group lessons. The company also rents sailboats, kayaks, row boats, and stand-up paddleboards. ✉ *45 Arey's La., off Rte. 28, South Orleans* ☎ *508/255–0994* 🌐 *www.areyspondboatyard.com.*

Goose Hummock Shop. Fishing licenses and gear are available at the Goose Hummock Shop, which also rents canoes, paddleboards, and kayaks. Lessons and tours are available. ✉ *15 Rte. 6A* ☎ *508/255–0455* 🌐 *www.goose.com.*

EASTHAM

3 miles north of Orleans, 6 miles south of Wellfleet.

Often overlooked on the speedy drive up toward Provincetown on U.S. 6, Eastham is a town full of hidden treasures. Unlike other towns on the Cape, it has no official town center or Main Street; the highway bisects it, and the town touches both Cape Cod Bay and the Atlantic. Amid the gas stations, convenience stores, restaurants, and large motel complexes, Eastham's wealth of natural beauty takes a little exploring to find.

VISITOR INFORMATION

Contacts Eastham Chamber of Commerce. ✉ *1700 Rte. 6, at Governor Prence Rd.* ☎ *508/240–7211* 🌐 *www.easthamchamber.com.*

EXPLORING

FAMILY Fodor's Choice ★ **Cape Cod National Seashore.** The region's most expansive national treasure, Cape Cod National Seashore was established in 1961 by President John F. Kennedy, for whom Cape Cod was home and haven. The

27,000-acre park, extending from Chatham to Provincetown, protects 30 miles of superb beaches; great rolling dunes; swamps, marshes, and wetlands; and pitch-pine and scrub-oak forest. Self-guided nature trails, as well as biking and horse trails, lace through these landscapes. Hiking trails lead to a red-maple swamp, Nauset Marsh, and to Salt Pond, in which breeding shellfish are suspended from floating "nurseries"; their offspring will later be used to seed the flats. Also in the seashore is the Buttonbush Trail, a nature path for people with vision impairments. A hike or bike ride to Coast Guard Beach leads to a turnout looking out over marsh and sea. A section of the cliff here was washed away in 1990, revealing the remains of a prehistoric dwelling. The national seashore has two visitor centers, one in Eastham and one in Provincetown.

Salt Pond Visitor Center, at the southern end of the Cape, offers guided walks, boat tours, demonstrations, and lectures mid-April–Thanksgiving, as well as evening beach walks, campfire talks, and other programs (many are free) in summer. The center includes a museum with displays on whaling and the old saltworks, as well as early Cape Cod artifacts including scrimshaw, the journal that Mrs. Penniman kept while on a whaling voyage with her husband, and some of the Pennimans' possessions, such as their tea service and the captain's top hat. An air-conditioned auditorium shows films on geology, sea rescues, whaling, Henry David Thoreau, and Guglielmo Marconi. ⊠ *Salt Pond Visitor Center, 50 Doane Rd.* ☎ *508/255–3421 for Salt Pond Visitor Center* ⊕ *www.nps.gov/caco* ⊠ *Free* ☉ *Visitor Center daily 9–4:30 (hrs extended slightly in summer).*

Nauset Light. Moved 350 feet back from its perch at cliff's edge in 1996, this much-photographed red-and-white lighthouse tops the bluff where the Three Sisters Lighthouses once stood. (The Sisters themselves can be seen in a little landlocked park surrounded by trees; they're reached by paved walkways off Nauset Light Beach's parking lot.) How the lighthouses got there is a long story. In 1838 three brick lighthouses were built 150 feet apart on the bluffs in Eastham overlooking a particularly dangerous area of shoals (shifting underwater sandbars). In 1892, after the eroding cliff dropped the towers into the ocean, they were replaced with three wooden towers. In 1918, two were moved away, as was the third in 1923. Eventually the National Park Service acquired the Three Sisters and brought them together in the inland park, where they would be safe. Lectures on and guided tours of the lighthouses (free, donations accepted) are conducted Sunday early May–October, as well as Wednesday in July and August. ⊠ *Ocean View Dr. and Cable Rd.* ☎ *508/240–2612* ⊕ *www.nausetlight.org* ⊠ *Free.*

BEACHES

FAMILY **First Encounter Beach.** A great spot for watching sunsets over Cape Cod Bay, First Encounter Beach is rich in history. Near the parking lot, a bronze marker commemorates the first encounter between local Native Americans and passengers from the *Mayflower,* led by Captain Myles Standish, who explored the entire area for five weeks in 1620 before moving on to Plymouth. The beach is popular with families who favor its warmer, calmer waters and tide pools. **Amenities:** parking (fee); showers; toilets. **Best for:** sunset; swimming; walking;

DID YOU KNOW?

With 40 miles of beach along the National Seashore, lifeguards are on duty only at certain sections. Coast Guard Beach is one area that also has practical facilities, making it popular with families.

windsurfing. ✉ *End of Samoset Rd., off U.S. 6* 🎟 *Parking $15 weekdays, $18 weekends.*

Fodor's Choice ★ **Nauset Light Beach.** Adjacent to Coast Guard Beach, this long, sandy beach is backed by tall dunes, frilly grasses, and heathland. The trail to the Three Sisters lighthouses takes you through a pitch-pine forest. Parking here fills up very quickly in summer; plan to arrive early or you may have to go elsewhere. ■ **TIP→ Daily parking is expensive; the annual seashore pass grants access to all six National Park beaches and costs the same as three days of parking.** **Amenities:** lifeguards; parking (fee); showers; toilets. **Best for:** sunrise; surfing; swimming; walking. ✉ *Off Ocean View Dr.* 🌐 *www.nps.gov/caco/index.htm* 🎟 *Parking $20.*

WHERE TO EAT

$$ SEAFOOD FAMILY 🍴 **Arnold's Lobster & Clam Bar.** You can't miss this hot spot on the side of Route 6: look for the riot of colorful flowers lining the road and the patient folks waiting in long lines in the parking lot. That crowd is testament to the freshness and flavors that come out of this busy kitchen for lunch, dinner, and takeout, putting forth everything from grilled burgers to 3-pound lobsters. Unusual for a clam shack like this is the full bar, offering beer, wine, mixed drinks, and the house specialty: margaritas. There's ice cream and an artfully designed miniature-golf course to keep the kids happy. [$] *Average main: $21* ✉ *3580 State Hwy.* ☎ *508/255–2575* 🌐 *www.arnoldsrestaurant.com* 💳 *No credit cards* ⏲ *Closed Nov.–Apr.* ✍ *Reservations not accepted.*

$ ITALIAN FAMILY 🍴 **Fairway Restaurant and Pizzeria.** The friendly, family-run Fairway specializes in Italian comfort food—try the eggplant Parmesan, fettuccine and meatballs, or a well-stuffed calzone—but also has a very popular breakfast. Attached to the Hole in One Donut Shop—a favorite among locals for early-morning coffee and exceptional doughnuts and muffins—the Fairway puts a jar of crayons on every paper-covered table and sells its own brand of root beer. The pizzas are hearty and filling, rather than the thin-crust variety. [$] *Average main: $18* ✉ *4295 U.S. Rte. 6, North Eastham* ☎ *508/255–3893* 🌐 *www.fairwaycapecod.com* 💳 *No credit cards* ⏲ *No lunch.*

WHERE TO STAY

$$ B&B/INN Fodor's Choice ★ 🏨 **Fort Hill Bed and Breakfast.** Gordon and Jean Avery run this enchanting, adults-only B&B in an 1864 Greek Revival farmhouse nestled in the tranquil Fort Hill area—the only lodging within the National Seashore. **Pros:** pastoral setting; close to nature trails; private and elegant lodging. **Cons:** not for those traveling with children. [$] *Rooms from: $290* ✉ *75 Fort Hill Rd.* ☎ *508/240–2870* 🌐 *www.forthillbedandbreakfast.com* ⏲ *Closed mid-Oct.–May* 🛏 *2 suites, 1 cottage* 🍽 *Breakfast.*

$$ B&B/INN 🏨 **Penny House Inn & Spa.** Tucked behind a wave of privet hedges, this rambling gray-shingled inn's spacious rooms are filled with antiques, collectibles, and wicker furnishings. **Pros:** private and secluded; ideal for a romantic getaway; full range of spa services. **Cons:** off busy U.S. 6; no water views or beachfront. [$] *Rooms from: $245* ✉ *4885 County Rd.* ☎ *508/255–6632, 800/554–1751* 🌐 *www.pennyhouseinn.com* 🛏 *3 rooms, 9 suites* 🍽 *Breakfast.*

$$
B&B/INN
Fodor's Choice
★

Whalewalk Inn & Spa. Set amid three landscaped acres, this 1830 whaling master's home has wide-plank pine floors, fireplaces, and 19th-century country antiques to provide historical appeal. **Pros:** beautiful grounds; elegantly appointed rooms; decadent spa treatments. **Cons:** not for those traveling with small children. $ *Rooms from: $230* ⊠ *220 Bridge Rd.* ☎ *508/255–0617, 800/440–1281* ⊕ *www.whalewalkinn. com* ☾ *Closed Dec.–Mar.* ⇗ *11 rooms, 6 suites* ⦿ *Breakfast.*

WELLFLEET AND SOUTH WELLFLEET

6 miles north of Eastham, 13 miles southeast of Provincetown.

Fodor's Choice
★

Still famous for its world-renowned and succulent namesake oysters, Wellfleet is today a tranquil community; many artists and writers call it home. Less than 2 miles wide, it's one of the most attractively developed Cape resort towns, with a number of fine restaurants, historic houses, and art galleries, and a good old Main Street in the village proper.

VISITOR INFORMATION

Contacts Wellfleet Beach Sticker Office. ⊠ *255 Commercial St., Wellfleet* ☎ *508/349-9818* ⊕ *www.wellfleetma.org.* **Wellfleet Chamber of Commerce.** ⊠ *1410 Rte. 6, near the post office, South Wellfleet* ☎ *508/349-2510* ⊕ *www. wellfleetchamber.com.*

EXPLORING

Marconi Station. On the Atlantic side of the Cape is the site of the first transatlantic wireless station erected on the U.S. mainland. It was from here on January 18, 1903, that Italian radio and wireless-telegraphy pioneer Guglielmo Marconi sent the first American wireless message to Europe: "most cordial greetings and good wishes" from President Theodore Roosevelt to King Edward VII of England. There's a lookout deck that offers a vantage point of both the Atlantic and Cape Cod Bay. Off the parking lot, a 1½-mile trail and boardwalk lead through the Atlantic White Cedar Swamp, one of the most beautiful trails on the seashore; free maps and guides are available at the trailhead. Marconi Beach, south of the Marconi Station on Marconi Beach Road, is one of the National Seashore's lovely ocean beaches. ⊠ *Marconi Site Rd., South Wellfleet* ☎ *508/349-3785* ⊕ *www.nps.gov/caco* ⊡ *Free* ☾ *Daily dawn–dusk.*

FAMILY
Fodor's Choice
★

Massachusetts Audubon Wellfleet Bay Wildlife Sanctuary. Encompassing nearly 1,000 acres, this reserve is home to more than 250 species of birds. The jewel of the Massachusetts Audubon Society, the sanctuary is a superb place for walking, birding, and watching the sun set over the salt marsh and bay. The **Esther Underwood Johnson Nature Center** contains two 700-gallon aquariums that offer an up-close look at marine life common to the region's tidal flats and marshlands. From the center you can hike five short nature trails, including a fascinating boardwalk trail that leads over a salt marsh to a small beach, or you can wander through the butterfly garden. The sanctuary offers camps for children in July and August, as well as weeklong field schools for adults. ⊠ *291 U.S. 6, South Wellfleet* ☎ *508/349-2615* ⊕ *www.massaudubon.*

org/wellfleetbay 🎟 *$5* ⏲ *Trails daily 8 am–dusk. Nature center: late May–mid-Oct., daily 8:30–5; mid-Oct.–late May, Tues.–Sun. 8:30–5.*

BEACHES

Cahoon Hollow Beach. The restaurant and music club on top of the dune are the main attractions at Cahoon Hollow Beach, which tends to draw younger and slightly rowdier crowds. It's a big Sunday-afternoon party place. The Beachcomber restaurant has paid parking, which is reimbursed when you buy something to eat or drink. Erosion has made getting to the beach a steep climb. **Amenities:** food and drink; lifeguards; parking (fee); toilets. **Best for:** partiers; surfing; swimming; walking. ✉ *Ocean View Dr., Greater Wellfleet* 🎟 *Parking $20.*

Fodor's Choice ★ **Marconi Beach.** Marconi Beach, part of the Cape Cod National Seashore, is accessed via a very long and steep series of stairs lead down to the beach. It's also popular with both surfers and surf casters looking for striped bass or bluefish. Erosion from fierce storms has compromised beach access. ■ **TIP→ Daily parking is expensive; the annual seashore pass grants access to all six National Park beaches and costs the same as three days of parking.** **Amenities**: lifeguards; parking (fee); showers; toilets. **Best for:** sunrise; surfing; swimming; walking. ✉ *Marconi Beach Rd., off U.S. 6, South Wellfleet* 🌐 *www.nps.gov/caco* 🎟 *Parking $20.*

White Crest Beach. White Crest Beach is a prime surfer hangout where the dudes often spend more time waiting for waves than actually riding them. If you're up to the challenge, join one of the spontaneous volleyball games. The other challenge will be working your way down (and then up) to the water: Mother Nature and her fury have made this a steep trek. **Amenities:** lifeguards; parking (fee); toilets. **Best for:** sunrise; surfing; swimming; walking. ✉ *Ocean View Dr., Greater Wellfleet* 🎟 *Parking $20.*

WHERE TO EAT

$ SEAFOOD FAMILY 🍴 **Mac's Seafood.** Right at Wellfleet Harbor, this ambitious little spot serves some of the freshest seafood around. You can always sit along the pier and soak up the great water views while you chow down. Mac's serves a vast variety of local fish dishes, plus globe-trotting fare like sushi, grilled-scallop burritos, and linguiça sausage sandwiches. There's also a selection of smoked fish, pâtés, lobster, and fish you can take home to grill yourself. Nearby is **Mac's Shack** (91 Commercial St., $$$), a funky sit-down restaurant in a rambling mid-19th-century barn overlooking Duck Creek. Come here for the finest sushi, the tasty coconut curry scallops, fantastic seafood, and the lobster mashed potatoes. Look for the lobster boat on the roof. [$] *Average main: $18* ✉ *Wellfleet Town Pier, 265 Commercial St., Wellfleet Harbor* ☎ *508/349–9611* 🌐 *www.macsseafood.com* ⏲ *Closed mid-Sept.–late May.*

$$ AMERICAN Fodor's Choice ★ 🍴 **Wicked Oyster.** In a rambling, gray clapboard house, the Wicked Oyster serves up the most innovative fare in Wellfleet. It's farmhouse-sparse inside, with brightly painted walls accented with paintings by local artists. Try the pan-roasted catch of the day with littleneck clams, leeks, bacon, and fingerling potatoes. Oyster stew and the open-face burger (with blue-cheese aioli and applewood-smoked bacon) are among the top lunch dishes. Breakfast is a favorite here: try the smoked-salmon Benedict.

There's also an outstanding wine list. Parking is tight at this popular spot in summer. $\boxed{\$}$ *Average main: $25* ⊠ *50 Main St., Downtown Wellfleet* ☎ *508/349–3455* ⊕ *www.thewickedo.com* ☺ *Closed Wed.*

WHERE TO STAY

$\$$ 🏨 **Even'tide.** Long a summer favorite, this motel is set back from the main road, surrounded by 5 acres of trees and lawns; it has direct access to the Cape Cod Rail Trail. **Pros:** short drive or bike ride from beach; suites are a bargain for families. **Cons:** need a car to get downtown; motel-style rooms. $\boxed{\$}$ *Rooms from: $169* ⊠ *650 U.S. 6, South Wellfleet* ☎ *508/349–3410, 800/368–0007* ⊕ *www.eventidemotel.com* ☺ *Closed Nov.–Apr.* ⌫ *31 units, 10 cottages* ❏ *No meals* ☞ *1- or 2-wk minimum for cottages in summer.*

HOTEL
FAMILY

$\$$ 🏨 **Inn at Duck Creeke.** Set on 5 wooded acres by a pond, a creek, and a salt marsh, this old inn consists of a circa-1815 main building and two other houses from the same era. **Pros:** relatively low rates; walking distance to downtown. **Cons:** some units share a bath; not all rooms have Wi-Fi. $\boxed{\$}$ *Rooms from: $150* ⊠ *70 Main St., Downtown Wellfleet* ☎ *508/349–9333* ⊕ *www.innatduckcreeke.com* ☺ *Closed mid-Oct.– early May* ⌫ *22 rooms (19 with bath)* ❏ *Breakfast.*

B&B/INN

NIGHTLIFE AND PERFORMING ARTS

FAMILY
Fodor's Choice
★

Wellfleet Drive-In Theater. A classic Cape experience is the Wellfleet Drive-In Theater, located near the Eastham town line. Regulars spend the night in style: chairs, blankets, and picnic baskets. Films start at dusk nightly May–September, and there's also a standard indoor cinema with four screens, a miniature-golf course, and a bar and grill. It's also the home of the beloved Wellfleet Flea Market, held weekends late spring–mid-October. ⊠ *51 U.S. 6, South Wellfleet* ☎ *508/349–7176* ⊕ *www.wellfleetcinemas.com.*

SPORTS AND THE OUTDOORS

BOATING

Jack's Boat Rental. Jack's rents canoes, kayaks, pedal boats, sailboats, surfboards, boogie boards, and sailboards. Delivery is available for three-plus-day rentals for a fee. ⊠ *2616 U.S. 6, at Cahoon Hollow Rd., Greater Wellfleet* ☎ *508/349–9808, 508/349–7553* ⊕ *www. jacksboatrental.com.*

SHOPPING

Downtown Wellfleet is best approached on foot; along the way you'll find many art galleries and clothing boutiques. You'll pay a handsome premium for fresh fruits, vegetables, and flowers behind the Town Hall at Hatch's—but what a beautiful display. There's also the Wellfleet Marketplace for groceries, books, beer, and wine. In the height of summer, the price is worth not having to drive 15 miles to Orleans. A recent and much welcomed addition is the Wednesday morning Wellfleet Farmers' Market, held behind Preservation Hall on Main Street. The Wellfleet Flea Market draws people from all over the Cape who drive the distance to find the bargains.

4

FLEA MARKET

Fodor'sChoice **Wellfleet Flea Market.** The giant Wellfleet Flea Market sets up shop in
★ the parking lot of the Wellfleet Drive-In Theater mid-April–June, September, and October, weekends and holiday Mondays 8–4; July and
August, Wednesday, Thursday, weekends, and holiday Mondays 8–4.
You'll find antiques, cosmetics, kitchen supplies, socks, old advertising
posters, books, plants, trinkets, and plenty more among the many vendors. On Monday and Tuesday in July and August the vendors make
way for large arts-and-crafts shows. A snack bar and playground keep
fatigue at bay. ⊠ *51 U.S. 6, South Wellfleet* ☎ *508/349–0541* ⊕ *www.
wellfleetcinemas.com/flea-market.*

PROVINCETOWN

9 miles northwest of Wellfleet, 62 miles from Sagamore Bridge.

Many people know that the Pilgrims stopped here at the curved tip of
Cape Cod before proceeding to Plymouth. Historical records suggest
that an earlier visitor, Thorvald, brother of Viking Leif Erikson, came
ashore here in AD 1004 to repair the keel of his boat and consequently
named the area Kjalarness, or Cape of the Keel. In 1602, Bartholomew
Gosnold came to Provincetown and named the area Cape Cod after the
abundant codfish he found in the local waters.

Incorporated as a town in 1727, Provincetown was for many decades
a bustling seaport, with fishing and whaling as its major industries.
In the late 19th century, groups of Portuguese fishermen and whalers
began to settle here, lending their expertise and culture to an already
cosmopolitan town. Fishing is still an important source of income for
many Provincetown locals, but today the town ranks among the world's
leading whale-watching—rather than whale-hunting—outposts.

Artists began to arrive in the late 1890s to take advantage of the unusual
Cape Cod light; in fact, Provincetown is the nation's oldest continuous
art colony. By 1916, with five art schools flourishing here, painters'
easels were nearly as common as shells on the beach. This bohemian
community, along with the availability of inexpensive summer lodgings,
attracted young rebels, as well as writers like John Reed (*Ten Days That
Shook the World*) and Mary Heaton Vorse (*Footnote to Folly*), who in
1915 began the Cape's first significant theater group, the Provincetown
Players. The young, then unknown Eugene O'Neill joined them in 1916,
when his *Bound East for Cardiff* premiered in a tiny wharf-side East
End fish house.

America's original gay resort, Provincetown today is as appealing to
artists as it is to gay and lesbian—as well as straight—tourists. The
awareness brought by the AIDS crisis and, more recently, Massachusetts's legalization of same-sex marriage has turned the town into the
most visibly gay vacation community in America.

GETTING HERE AND AROUND

You're at the end of the line here, which means driving to Provincetown
in the height of summer often means slogging through slow traffic. Congestion is heaviest around Wellfleet and it can be slow going. Driving the
3 miles of Provincetown's main downtown thoroughfare, Commercial

Artists and birders flock to the Wellfleet Bay Wildlife Sanctuary, protected by the Massachusetts Audubon Society.

Street, in season could take forever. No matter, there are plenty of pretty vistas on the way along U.S. 6 and Route 6A. Parking is not one of Provincetown's better amenities (there are two large, paid central parking lots if you can find a space), so bike and foot are the best and most popular ways to explore the downtown area. But Provincetown can also be reached by air (year-round via Cape Air from Boston) or ferry (multiple options from Boston in season).

The Provincetown/North Truro Shuttle, run by the Cape Cod Regional Transit Authority, provides a much-needed seasonal transportation boost in season (mid-June–mid-September). Once in Provincetown, the shuttle heads up Bradford Street, with alternating trips to Herring Cove Beach, Race Point Beach, Pilgrim Park, and the Provincetown Airport. Bikes are accommodated.

Bus Contacts Cape Cod Regional Transit Authority. ☎ *800/352-7155* ⊕ *www.capecodtransit.org.*

VISITOR INFORMATION
Contacts Provincetown Chamber of Commerce. ⊠ *Information booth, 307 Commercial St., Downtown Center* ☎ *508/487-3424* ⊕ *www.ptownchamber.com.* **Provincetown Business Guild.** ⊠ *3 Freeman St., Unit #2, Downtown Center* ☎ *508/487-2313, 800/637-8696* ⊕ *www.ptown.org.*

EXPLORING
Fodor'sChoice ★ **Commercial Street.** Take a casual stroll by the many architectural styles— Greek Revival, Victorian, Second Empire, and Gothic, to name a few— used in the design of the impressive houses for wealthy sea captains and merchants. The Provincetown Historical Society's walking-tour

pamphlet is available for $1 at many shops. The center of town is where you'll find the crowds and the best people-watching, especially if you try to find an empty spot on the benches in front of the exquisitely renovated Town Hall. The East End has a number of nationally renowned galleries; the West End has a number of small inns with neat lawns and elaborate gardens. Commercial Street runs parallel to the water, so there is always a patch of sand close at hand, should you need a break. ⊠ *Provincetown.*

✕ **Spiritus.** Local bars close at 1 am, at which point this pizza joint becomes the town's epicenter. It's the ultimate place to see and be seen, slice in hand and witty banter at the ready. The same counter serves delectable ice cream from Emack & Bolios, Häagen-Dazs, and Giffords of Maine. ⊠ *190 Commercial St., Downtown Center* ☎ *508/487–2808* ⊕ *www.spirituspizza. com* ⊙ *Closed Nov.–Apr.*

Pilgrim Monument. The first thing you'll see in Provincetown is this grandiose edifice, somewhat out of proportion to the rest of the low-rise town. The monument commemorates the Pilgrims' first landing in the New World and their signing of the Mayflower Compact (the first Colonial American rules of self-governance) before they set off to explore the mainland. Climb the 116 steps and 60 short ramps of the 252-foot-high tower for a panoramic view—dunes on one side, harbor on the other, and the entire bay side of Cape Cod beyond. At the tower's base is a museum of Lower Cape and Provincetown history, with exhibits on whaling, shipwrecks, and scrimshaw. ⊠ *1 High Pole Hill Rd., Downtown Center* ☎ *508/487–1310* ⊕ *www.pilgrim-monument.org* ⊠ *$12* ⊙ *Apr.–Memorial Day and Labor Day–Nov., daily 9–5; Memorial Day–Labor Day, daily 9–7.*

Fodor's Choice
★

Province Lands Visitor Center. Part of the Cape Cod National Seashore, the Province Lands stretch from High Head in Truro to the tip of Provincetown and are scattered with ponds, cranberry bogs, and scrub. More than 7 miles of bike and walking trails lace through forests of stunted pines, beech, and oak and across desertlike expanses of rolling dunes. At the visitor center you'll find short films on local geology and exhibits on the life of the dunes and the shore. You can also pick up information on guided walks, birding trips, lectures, and other programs, as well as on the Province Lands' pristine beaches, Race Point and Herring Cove, and walking, biking, and horse trails. Don't miss the awe-inspiring panoramic view of the dunes and the surrounding ocean from the observation deck. This terrain provides optimal conditions for the deer tick, which can cause Lyme disease, so use extra caution. ⊠ *Race Point Rd., east of U.S. 6, Greater Provincetown* ☎ *508/487–1256* ⊕ *www.nps.gov/caco* ⊠ *Free* ⊙ *Early May–late Oct., daily 9–5.*

Fodor's Choice
★

Provincetown Art Association and Museum. Founded in 1914 to collect and exhibit the works of artists with Provincetown connections, this facility has a 1,650-piece permanent collection, displayed in changing exhibitions that mix up-and-comers with established 20th-century figures like Milton Avery, Philip Evergood, William Gropper, Charles Hawthorne, Robert Motherwell, Claes Oldenburg, Man Ray, John Singer Sargent, Andy

Warhol, and Agnes Weinrich. A stunning contemporary wing has greatly expanded the exhibit space. The museum store carries books of local interest, including works by or about area artists and authors, as well as posters, crafts, cards, and gift items. Art classes (single day and longer) offer the opportunity to study under such talents as Hilda Neily, Selina Trieff, and Doug Ritter. ✉ *460 Commercial St., East End* ☎ *508/487–1750* 🌐 *www.paam.org* 🎟 *$10* 🕒 *Late May–Sept., Mon.–Thurs. 11–8, Fri. 11–10, weekends 11–5; Oct.–late May, Thurs.–Sun. noon–5.*

BEACHES

FAMILY **Herring Cove Beach.** Herring Cove Beach is relatively calm and warm for a National Seashore beach, but it's not as pretty as some because its parking lot isn't hidden behind dunes. It's close to town, so in warm weather it's always crowded. The lot to the right of the bathhouse is a great place to watch the sunset. ■ **TIP→ Daily parking is expensive; the annual seashore pass grants access to all six National Park beaches and costs the same as three days of parking.** **Amenities:** food and drink; lifeguards; parking (fee); toilets; showers. **Best for:** sunset; swimming; walking. ✉ *Provincetown* 🌐 *www.nps.gov/caco* 🎟 *Parking $20.*

Fodor's Choice ★ **Race Point Beach.** Race Point Beach, one of the Cape Cod National Seashore beaches in Provincetown, has a wide swath of sand stretching far off into the distance around the point and Coast Guard station. Because of its position facing north, the beach gets sun all day long. Keep an eye out for whales off-shore; it's also a popular fishing spot. ■ **TIP→ Daily parking is expensive; the annual seashore pass grants access to all six National Park beaches and costs the same as three days of parking.** **Amenities:** lifeguards; parking (fee); showers; toilets. **Best for:** sunrise; sunset; surfing; swimming; walking. ✉ *Race Point Rd., east of U.S. 6* ☎ *508/487–1256* 🌐 *www.nps.gov/caco/index.htm* 🎟 *Parking $20.*

WHERE TO EAT

$ AMERICAN Fodor's Choice ★ 🍴 **The Canteen.** Bustling from lunch until close, this casual newcomer has made a big impression on P-Town in just a couple of years. Order at the counter, then grab a seat at one of the picnic tables inside or out and wait for your smashing lobster roll, crispy fish 'n' chips, steaming bowl of New England clam chowder, or juicy shrimp sliders to come out of the kitchen, which specializes in remaking Cape Cod classics with locally sourced, delicious ingredients. Don't forget to order a side of crispy brussels sprouts. There's also a large beer menu, a good selection of wines, and delicious house-made lemonade and iced tea. Coffee is by Stumptown, as it always should be. [$] *Average main: $12* ✉ *225 Commercial St., Downtown Center* ☎ *508/487–3800* 🌐 *www.thecanteenptown.com.*

$$$ AMERICAN Fodor's Choice ★ 🍴 **Devon's.** Now that this local favorite has relocated to a larger space, maybe the wait for tables won't be so long. Specialties from the oft-changing menu include brown-butter pan-seared halibut or Provincetown day-boat scallops. Sampling the small plates and bites is an adventure: choose from such variety as Mexican street tacos, fried buttermilk whole quail to a steaming bowl of homemade ramen noodles. Save some room for knockout desserts like the flourless chipotle chocolate torte with raspberry coulis. Devon's is also a good spot for

breakfast. $ *Average main: $30* ⊠ *31 Bradford St., Downtown Center* ☎ *508/487-4773* ⊕ *www.devons.org* ⊙ *Closed Wed., and Nov.–mid-May. No lunch* ⚭ *Reservations essential.*

$$$
SEAFOOD

✕ **Lobster Pot.** Provincetown's Lobster Pot is fit to do battle with all the lobster shanties anywhere (and everywhere) else on the Cape; although it's often jammed with tourists, the crowds reflect the generally high quality. The hardworking kitchen turns out classic New England cooking: lobsters, generous and filling seafood platters, and some of the best chowder around. Eat like a local and try the barbecue pepper shrimp. $ *Average main: $27* ⊠ *321 Commercial St., Downtown Center* ☎ *508/487-0842* ⊕ *www.ptownlobsterpot.com* ⊙ *Closed Jan.* ⚭ *Reservations not accepted.*

$$$
AMERICAN
Fodor's Choice
★

✕ **The Mews.** This perennial favorite with magnificent harbor views focuses on seafood and grilled meats with a cross-cultural flair: popular entrées include roasted vegetable and polenta lasagna with a tomato-olive sauce and "shaking beef," a Vietnamese-inspired dish of beef tenderloin sautéed with scallions and red onions and a lime-black pepper sauce. (There's also a lighter bistro menu for smaller appetites.) The view of the bay from the bar is nearly perfect, and the gentle lighting makes this a romantic spot to have a drink. The restaurant claims its vodka bar is New England's largest, with more than 275 varieties. Sunday brunch is served Mother's Day–Columbus Day; in fall and winter, Monday night gets lively with the very popular open-mike coffeehouse. It's one restaurant that's open year-round. $ *Average main: $27* ⊠ *429 Commercial St., East End* ☎ *508/487-1500* ⊕ *www.mews.com* ⊙ *No lunch Mon.–Sat.* ⚭ *Reservations essential.*

$$$
AMERICAN
Fodor's Choice
★

✕ **The Pointe.** Inside the snazzy Crowne Pointe Inn, this intimate, casually handsome restaurant occupies the parlor and sunroom of a grand sea captain's mansion. The kitchen serves finely crafted, healthful, modern American food, such as local cheeses, grass-fed sirloin, and several local seafood options. The wine list is substantial, with well over a hundred selections to choose from. You may fall in love with the intimate bar and dining area and the welcoming staff. $ *Average main: $27* ⊠ *Crowne Pointe Inn, 82 Bradford St., Downtown Center* ☎ *508/487-2365* ⊕ *www.provincetown-restaurant.com* ⊙ *No lunch* ⚭ *Reservations essential.*

WHERE TO STAY

$$$
B&B/INN
Fodor's Choice
★

⛨ **Brass Key.** One of the Cape's most luxurious small resorts, this meticulously kept year-round getaway comprises a beautifully restored main house—originally a sea captain's home built in 1828—and several other carefully groomed buildings and cottages. **Pros:** ultraposh rooms; beautiful and secluded grounds; pool on-site. **Cons:** among the highest rates in town; not for those with children; significant minimum-stay requirements in summer. $ *Rooms from: $349* ⊠ *67 Bradford St., Downtown Center* ☎ *508/487-9005, 800/842-9858* ⊕ *www.brasskey.com* ⇆ *43 rooms* ⎮⍾⎮ *Breakfast* ☞ *Pets are only allowed in certain rooms.*

$$
B&B/INN
Fodor's Choice
★

⛨ **Crowne Pointe Historic Inn and Spa.** Created meticulously from six different buildings, this inn hasn't a single detail left unattended. **Pros:** great on-site amenities; posh and luxurious room decor; professional and well-trained staff. **Cons:** among the highest rates in town; significant minimum-stay requirements in summer. $ *Rooms from: $249* ✉ *82 Bradford St., Downtown Center* ☎ *508/487–6767, 877/276–9631* ⊕ *www.crownepointe.com* ⟿ *37 rooms, 3 suites* ⎟○⎟ *Breakfast.*

$$
B&B/INN

☷ **Eben House.** Owners David Bowd and Kevin O'Shea (he's the talented designer) completed a rigorous interior renovation on this 1776 property—one of the oldest and few remaining brick colonials in town—that have taken it from sad to chic. **Pros:** simple, stunning interior design; exceptional service; complimentary parking. **Cons:** some rooms accessed via steep stairs. $ *Rooms from: $200* ✉ *90 Bradford St., Downtown Center* ☎ *508/487–0386* ⊕ *www.ebenhouse.com* ☾ *Closed weeknights Nov.–Apr.* ⟿ *11 rooms, 3 suites* ⎟○⎟ *Breakfast.*

$
HOTEL

☷ **Harbor Hotel Provincetown.** A former drab and run-down property on the eastern edge of town has been transformed into a hip and sleek hotel directly across the street from the bay. **Pros:** fresh, fun decor; great views and easy access to bay beach; great amenities. **Cons:** very long walk to town center; bay-view rooms closed in winter. $ *Rooms from: $179* ✉ *698 Commercial St., Greater Provincetown* ☎ *800/422–4224* ⊕ *www.harborhotelptown.com* ▭ *No credit cards* ⟿ *119 rooms, 10 suites* ⎟○⎟ *No meals.*

$$
B&B/INN
Fodor's Choice
★

☷ **White Porch Inn.** This sterling, light-filled B&B offers a soothing respite from the bustle of town. **Pros:** fresh and immaculate; steps from East End shopping and dining; enthusiastic and friendly staff. **Cons:** somewhat long walk to West End shopping and businesses. $ *Rooms from: $299* ✉ *7 Johnson St., Downtown Center* ☎ *508/364–2549, 508/487–0592* ⊕ *www.whiteporchinn.com* ▭ *No credit cards* ⟿ *10 rooms* ⎟○⎟ *Breakfast.*

NIGHTLIFE AND PERFORMING ARTS

Provincetown is a party town. During the busy summer season, hawkers in full-on drag or wearing very little at all compete with the din on Commercial Street to announce showtimes of the evening's performances. Pick your pleasure: dancing poolside at a few big nightclubs; watching talented drag performers strut their stuff; enjoying in excellent live theater; strolling between art galleries; or sipping colorful cocktails at the water's edge. While the nightclub scene is decidedly gay, in most venues there is a clear "straight-friendly" welcome. And much of the summer entertainment is first-class, drawing top Broadway and cabaret performers from New York City and beyond, offered at prices that would be a bargain back home.

NIGHTLIFE

Governor Bradford Restaurant. If you think the Governor Bradford looks a bit like a locals' dive bar, that wouldn't be too far from the truth: it's dark and rustic, and lacks the glittering lights of some of the other town nightspots. It's on a busy corner of Commercial and Standish streets, where you can sit at tables with windows open to the street or inside at the long bar. Late-night fun includes drag karaoke, a great time and wildly popular; downstairs are multiple pool tables, darts, and a jukebox. ✉ *312 Commercial St., Downtown Center* ☎ *508/487–2781.*

Paramount. Part of the Crown & Anchor complex of entertainment options, the Paramount is the hotel's main nightlife venue, offering poolside dancing to skilled DJs—including many names from the top international dance scene—on many nights. It's also host to cabaret performances and live theater. Next door is a video bar and a male-only leather bar, The Vault. Cover charges vary. ✉ *247 Commercial St., Downtown Center* ☎ *508/487–1430* ⊕ *www.onlyatthecrown.com/paramount.*

PERFORMING ARTS

Crown & Anchor. A huge presence in Provincetown, the Crown & Anchor has several different performance venues, adding much to the heady pulse of the nightlife scene here. In addition to the Paramount dance club (which sometimes hosts live performances) and the men-only leather bar (aptly named The Vault), the complex holds court with a venue for raucous cabaret and a piano bar. Bigger-draw entertainers often appear at the nearby Provincetown Town Hall auditorium. ✉ *247 Commercial St., Downtown Center* ☎ *508/487–1430* ⊕ *www.onlyatthecrown.com.*

The Provincetown Theater. This year-round venue provides excellent theater, showcasing many new works, as well as more unusual fare. In addition, there are dance performances, readings by playwrights, and workshops. ✉ *238 Bradford St.* ☎ *508/487–7487* ⊕ *www.provincetowntheater.org.*

SPORTS AND THE OUTDOORS

TOURS

Fodor's Choice
★

Art's Dune Tours. Art's Dune Tours has been taking eager passengers into the dunes of Province Lands since 1946. A bumpy but controlled ride (about one hour) transports you through sometimes surreal sandy vistas peppered with beach grass, along a shoreline patrolled by seagulls and sandpipers. Head out at sunset for a stunning ride, available with or without a clambake feast; on Sunday there is a special Race Point Lighthouse Tour. ✉ *4 Standish St., Downtown Center* ☎ *508/487–1950, 800/894–1951* ⊕ *www.artsdunetours.com* 🎟 *From $28.*

WHALE-WATCHING

FAMILY
Fodor's Choice
★

Dolphin Fleet. Tours are led by scientists from the Center for Coastal Studies in Provincetown, who provide commentary while collecting data on the whales they've been monitoring for years. They know many of them by name and will tell you about their habits and histories. These trips are most often exciting and incredibly thrilling with close-up encounters. ■ **TIP→ Look for discount coupons in local free brochures and publications.** ✉ *Chamber of Commerce Bldg., MacMillan Wharf, Downtown Center* ☎ *508/240–3636, 800/826–9300* ⊕ *www.whalewatch.com* 🎟 *From $46* ⊙ *Tours mid-Apr.–Oct.*

SHOPPING

Provincetown shopping can be artistic, sophisticated, whimsical, and even downright tawdry—a perfect reflection of the town's very character. There is also a wide selection of touristy schlock. You'll find exquisite original art galleries primarily on the east end but also next to taffy and fudge shops, high-end home decor and designer clothing boutiques next to tattoo parlors and T-shirt shops, and even boutiques specializing in alternative interests (think leather and adult novelties). Most shopping is concentrated along Commercial Street.

ART GALLERIES

★
Julie Heller Gallery. Julie Heller Gallery has contemporary artists as well as some Provincetown icons. The gallery has works from the Sol Wilson and Milton Avery estates, as well as from such greats as Robert Motherwell, Agnes Weinrich, and Blanche Lazzell. There's another location at 465 Commercial Street. ⊠ *2 Gosnold St., Downtown Center* ☎ *508/487–2169* ⊕ *www.juliehellergallery.com.*

SPECIALTY STORES

Marine Specialties. Marine Specialties is full of treasures, knickknacks, and clothing. Here you can purchase some very reasonably priced casual- and military-style clothing, as well as seashells, marine supplies, stained-glass lamps, candles, rubber sharks (you get the idea), and prints of old advertisements. ⊠ *235 Commercial St., Downtown Center* ☎ *508/487–1730.*

4

MARTHA'S VINEYARD

Far less developed than Cape Cod—thanks to a few local conservation organizations—yet more cosmopolitan than neighboring Nantucket, Martha's Vineyard is an island with a double life. From Memorial Day through Labor Day, the quieter (some might say the real) Vineyard quickens into a vibrant, star-studded place.

The busy main port, Vineyard Haven, welcomes day-trippers fresh off ferries and private yachts to browse in its array of shops. Oak Bluffs, where pizza and ice cream emporiums reign supreme, has the air of a Victorian boardwalk. Edgartown is flooded with seekers of chic who wander tiny streets that hold boutiques, stately whaling captains' homes, and charming inns.

Summer regulars have included a host of celebrities over the years, among them Oprah Winfrey, Carly Simon, Ted Danson, Spike Lee, and Diane Sawyer; President Barack Obama and his family vacationed here nearly every summer of his two terms in the Oval Office. If you're planning to stay overnight on a summer weekend, be sure to make reservations well in advance; spring is not too early. Things stay busy on September and October weekends, a favorite time for weddings, but begin to slow down soon after. In many ways the Vineyard's off-season persona is even more appealing than its summer self, with more time to linger over pastoral and ocean vistas, free from the throngs of cars, bicycles, and mopeds.

Except for Oak Bluffs and Edgartown, the Vineyard is "dry," but many restaurants allow you to bring your own beer or wine. The town of Vineyard Haven allows beer and wine—but no liquor—sales in restaurants only.

GETTING HERE AND AROUND

AIR TRAVEL

Cape Air has regular, year-round flight service to the island from Hyannis, Boston, and Providence's T. F. Green Airport and seasonal service (starting mid-June) from White Plains, NY (including a bus transfer to and from Manhattan). From New York's LaGuardia Airport,

Philadelphia, and Washington, D.C., U.S. Airways Express provides seasonal service. JetBlue provides seasonal nonstop service from New York–JFK.

BUS TRAVEL

Once on the island, the Martha's Vineyard Transit Authority (VTA) provides regular service to all six towns on the island, including stops at all ferry landings and the airport. The buses can accommodate a limited number of bicycles, and the island has an excellent network of well-maintained bike trails. The VTA also has free in-town shuttle-bus routes in Edgartown and Vineyard Haven. You can also get around by bicycle (rentals are available) and by taxi (an expensive option).

Bus Contacts Martha's Vineyard Transit Authority (VTA). ☎ 508/693–9940 ⊕ www.vineyardtransit.com.

CAR TRAVEL

Although traffic can be bad during the season, it can be handy to have a car in order to see all of Martha's Vineyard and travel freely. Instead of bringing one over on the Steamship Authority ferry from Woods Hole (the only ferry service that transports cars—expensively), it's sometimes easier and more economical to rent one once you're on the island for a few days of exploring, particularly during the busy season when car reservations on the ferry are hard to come by. Don't expect a bargain for on-island rentals either; you'll pay about $180 per day for a Jeep. The island does its best to discourage extra automobile traffic.

Contacts A-A Island Auto Rental. ⊠ 5 Corners, 4 Water St., Vineyard Haven ☎ 508/696–5300 ⊕ www.mvautorental.com. **Sun 'n' Fun Rentals.** ⊠ 28 Lake Ave., Oak Bluffs ☎ 508/693–5457 ⊕ www.sunnfunrentals.com.

FERRY TRAVEL

The Steamship Authority is the main ferry (operating year-round) heading to Martha's Vineyard from Woods Hole. Other ferries leave from Falmouth Harbor (Island Queen); North Kingstown, RI (Vineyard Fast Ferry); Hyannis (Hy-Line); New Bedford (Seastreak); New York City (Seastreak, seasonally).

VISITOR INFORMATION

Contacts Martha's Vineyard Chamber of Commerce. ⊠ 24 Beach St., Vineyard Haven ☎ 508/693–0085, 800/505–4815 ⊕ www.mvy.com.

VINEYARD HAVEN (TISBURY)

7 miles southeast of Woods Hole, 3½ miles west of Oak Bluffs, 8 miles northwest of Edgartown.

Most people call this town Vineyard Haven because of the name of the port where ferries arrive, but its official name is Tisbury. Not as high-toned as Edgartown or as honky-tonk as Oak Bluffs, Vineyard Haven blends the past and present with a touch of the bohemian. Visitors step off the ferry right into the bustle of the harbor, one block from the shops and restaurants of Main Street.

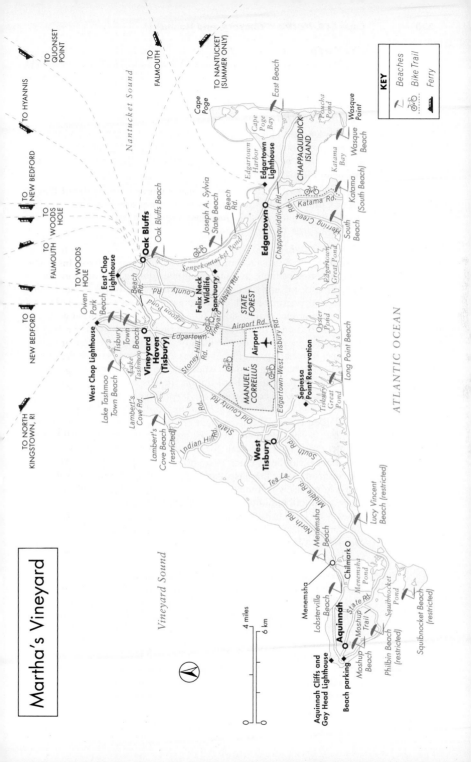

Martha's Vineyard

TO QUONSET POINT

TO HYANNIS

TO NANTUCKET (SUMMER ONLY)

TO FALMOUTH

TO NEW BEDFORD

TO WOODS HOLE

TO WOODS HOLE

TO FALMOUTH

TO NEW BEDFORD

TO NORTH KINGSTOWN, RI

Nantucket Sound

Vineyard Sound

ATLANTIC OCEAN

KEY

Beaches

Bike Trail

Ferry

Oak Bluffs

East Chop Lighthouse

West Chop Lighthouse

Owen Park Beach

Vineyard Haven (Tisbury)

Lake Tashmoo Town Beach

Lambert's Cove Beach (restricted)

Lambert's Cove Rd.

Indian Hill Rd.

State Rd.

Old County Rd.

Lagoon Pond

Tashmoo Town Beach

Lake Tashmoo

Beach Rd.

County Rd.

Edgartown–Vineyard Haven Rd.

Felix Neck Wildlife Sanctuary

Sengekontacket Pond

Oak Bluffs Beach

Joseph A. Sylvia State Beach

Beach Rd.

Airport Rd.

Airport

MANUEL F. CORRELLUS STATE FOREST

Stoney Hill Rd.

Edgartown–West Tisbury Rd.

West Tisbury

Sepiessa Point Reservation

Tisbury Great Pond

Oyster Pond

Long Point Beach

South Rd.

Tea La.

Middle Rd.

Menemsha Rd.

North Rd.

State Rd.

Chilmark

Menemsha

Menemsha Beach

Lobsterville Beach

Menemsha Pond

Aquinnah

Moshup Trail

Moshup Beach

Squibnocket Pond

Squibnocket Beach (restricted)

Philbin Beach (restricted)

Aquinnah Cliffs and Gay Head Lighthouse

Beach parking

Lucy Vincent Beach (restricted)

Edgartown

Edgartown Lighthouse

Edgartown Harbor

Edgartown Great Pond

Katama Rd.

Chappaquiddick Rd.

Herring Creek Rd.

South Beach

Katama (South Beach)

CHAPPAQUIDDICK ISLAND

Cape Poge

Cape Poge Bay

Poucha Pond

East Beach

Katama Bay

Wasque Beach

Wasque Point

4 miles

6 km

BEACHES

FAMILY **Lake Tashmoo Town Beach.** Swimmers have access to the warm, relatively shallow, brackish Lake Tashmoo from this beach—or cooler, gentler Vineyard Sound. It's a favorite spot for surf casters. **Amenities:** lifeguards; parking (no fee); toilets. **Best for:** sunset; swimming. ✉ *End of Herring Creek Rd.*

FAMILY **Owen Park Beach.** This small, sandy harbor beach is just steps away from the ferry terminal in Vineyard Haven, making it a great spot to catch some last rays before heading home. **Amenities:** lifeguards; toilets. **Best for:** swimming. ✉ *Off Main St.*

Tisbury Town Beach. This public beach is next to the Vineyard Haven Yacht Club. It is only accessed by foot or bike: no parking here. But it's a nice place for a picnic. **Amenities:** none. **Best for:** swimming. ✉ *End of Owen Little Way, off Main St.*

WHERE TO EAT

$$$ SEAFOOD 🍴 **Beach Road.** With its ample windows looking out to the serene lagoon, lofted ceilings, and mellow globe lighting held aloft by sturdy ropes, the decor aptly reflects the kitchen's "sea-to-table" theme for its seasonally inspired and locally sourced offerings. The varied scope of the menu encourages sampling, and there is a surprising mix of elements to choose from. It's not often that a house-made, prime beef hot dog shares space with the likes of lamb osso buco and squid-ink linguine. But that's part of what makes dining here a savory adventure. The massive bar is a popular spot for dining and cocktails; despite town bylaws forbidding hard liquor, there is a creative and unusual selection of alcohol concoctions. [$] *Average main: $25* ✉ *79 Beach Rd.* ☎ *508/693–8582* 🌐 *www.beachroadmv.com* 🕒 *Closed Mon.*

$$$ AMERICAN FAMILY 🍴 **Black Dog Tavern.** This island landmark—more popular with tourists than locals—lies just steps from the ferry terminal in Vineyard Haven. In July and August, the wait for breakfast (with an expansive omelet assortment) can be as much as an hour. Why? Partly because the dining room—roaring fireplace, dark-wood walls, maritime memorabilia, and a grand view of the water—makes everyone feel so at home. But diners also spill out onto the patio when the weather allows. The menu is heavy on local fish, chowders, and chops. [$] *Average main: $25* ✉ *20 Beach St. Ext.* ☎ *508/693–9223* 🌐 *www.theblackdog.com* 🕒 *No dinner Sun.–Wed. Oct.–May* ✍ *Reservations not accepted.*

WHERE TO STAY

$$$ B&B/INN 🏨 **Crocker House Inn.** This casual 1890 farmhouse-style inn is tucked into a quiet lane off Main Street, minutes from the ferries and Owen Park Beach. **Pros:** great owners; short walk from town; easygoing vibe. **Cons:** not for those with small children; books up quickly in summer. [$] *Rooms from: $295* ✉ *12 Crocker Ave.* ☎ *508/693–1151, 800/772–0206* 🌐 *www.crockerhouseinn.com* 🛏 *8 rooms* 🍽 *Breakfast.*

$$$ B&B/INN FAMILY 🏨 **Twin Oaks Inn.** On a half acre of landscaped lawn within walking distance of the ferry, this family-friendly inn is part classic, home-style B&B, part country inn. **Pros:** good value; five-minute walk to shops and dining. **Cons:** on busy road; no water or beach views from most units. [$] *Rooms*

from: $315 ⊠ 28 Edgartown Rd. ☎ 508/693–1066, 800/696–8633 ⊕ www.hanoverhouseinn.com ⇨ 22 rooms in 2 buildings ⍾⃝ Breakfast.

NIGHTLIFE AND PERFORMING ARTS

Vineyard Playhouse. The Vineyard Playhouse has a year-round schedule of professional productions. From mid-June through early September, a troupe performs drama, classics, and comedies on the air-conditioned main stage. Summer Shakespeare and other productions take place at the natural amphitheater at Tashmoo Overlook on State Road in Vineyard Haven—bring insect repellent and a blanket or lawn chair. The theater is wheelchair accessible and provides hearing devices. ⊠ *24 Church St. ☎ 508/696–6300 ⊕ www.vineyardplayhouse.org.*

SHOPPING

Vineyard Haven has a nice concentration of shopping along Main Street, which is intersected with several shorter streets that also hold shops of interest. Conveniently, since many people arrive by ferry without their vehicles, the majority of shopping is easily accessible right from the ferry docks. You won't find any large-scale chain stores here—rather, a good variety of upscale clothing shops, galleries, and other independently owned businesses selling everything from kitchen ware to luxury bath products.

Fodor's Choice ★ **Rainy Day.** As the name suggests, Rainy Day carries gifts and amusements perfect for one of the island's gloomy afternoons when you just need a warm, dry diversion. You'll find toys, crafts, cards, soaps, home accessories, gifts, and more. ⊠ *66 Main St. ☎ 508/693–1830 ⊕ www.rainydaymv.com.*

OAK BLUFFS

3½ miles east of Vineyard Haven.

Circuit Avenue is the bustling center of the Oak Bluffs action, with most of the town's shops, bars, and restaurants. Colorful gingerbread-trimmed guesthouses and food and souvenir joints enliven Oak Bluffs Harbor, once the setting for several grand hotels. This small town is more high-spirited than haute, more fun than refined. ∎ **TIP→ Look for the yellow tourist information booth at the bottom of Circuit Avenue. It's open June–mid-October and is staffed with helpful folks from the area.**

EXPLORING

FAMILY **Flying Horses Carousel.** A National Historic Landmark, this is the nation's oldest continuously operating merry-go-round. Handcrafted in 1876—the horses have real horsehair and glass eyes—and brought from Coney Island in 1884, the ride gives children a taste of entertainment from an era before smartphones. ⊠ *15 Lake Ave. ☎ 508/693–9481 ⊕ www.mvpreservation.org ⍾ $2.50 ⊗ Easter–late May, weekends 10–5; late May–early Sept., daily 10–10; early Sept.–mid-Oct., weekdays 11–4:30, weekends 10–5.*

Fodor's Choice ★ **Oak Bluffs Campground.** This 34-acre warren of streets is tightly packed with more than 300 gaily painted Carpenter Gothic Victorian cottages with wedding-cake trim; they date mainly to the 1860s and '70s, when visitors coming for Methodist revivalist services began to lease lots and build houses for summer use. As you wander through this fairy-tale setting, imagine it on a balmy summer evening, lighted by the warm glow of paper lanterns hung from every cottage porch. This describes the scene on Illumination Night at the end of the Camp Meeting season, which is attended these days by some fourth- and fifth-generation cottagers—and newcomers: some houses do change hands, and some are rented. Attendees mark the occasion as they have for more than a century, with lights, song, and open houses for families and friends. Ninety-minute tours of the area are conducted at 10 am on Tuesday and Thursday in July and August; join Community Sings on Wednesday evenings. ✉ *Off Circuit Ave.* ☎ *508/693–0525* 🌐 *www.mvcma.org* 🎟 *Tour $10.*

BEACHES

FAMILY **Joseph A. Sylvia State Beach.** This 2-mile-long sandy beach has a view of Cape Cod across Nantucket Sound. Occasional food vendors and calm, warm waters make it a popular spot for families. Arrive early or late in high summer: the parking spots fill up quickly. It's best to bike, walk, or take the shuttle here. **Amenities:** parking (no fee). **Best for:** swimming. ✉ *Off Beach Rd., between Oak Bluffs and Edgartown.*

WHERE TO EAT

$$$$ AMERICAN Fodor's Choice ★

🍴 **Sweet Life Café.** Housed in a charming Victorian house, this island favorite's warm hues, low lighting, and handsome antique furniture will make you feel like you've entered someone's home. The cooking is more sophisticated than home style, however: dishes are prepared in inventive ways and change often with the seasons. Sautéed halibut is served with sweet-pea risotto, pine nuts, and a marjoram beurre blanc, while the white gazpacho is filled with steamed clams, toasted almonds, sliced red grapes, and paprika oil. The desserts are superb; try the warm chocolate fondant with toasted-almond ice cream. There's outdoor dining by candlelight in a shrub-enclosed garden. [$] *Average main: $37* ✉ *63 Upper Circuit Ave.* ☎ *508/696–0200* 🌐 *www.sweetlifemv.com* 🕒 *Closed Jan.–Mar. No lunch* ✍ *Reservations essential.*

WHERE TO STAY

$$ B&B/INN

🏨 **Pequot Hotel.** In this casual cedar-shingle inn on a tree-lined street, the first floor has a wide porch with rocking chairs—perfect for enjoying coffee or tea with the cookies that are set out in the afternoon. **Pros:** steps from shops and dining; reasonable rates; charmingly offbeat. **Cons:** some rooms are small. [$] *Rooms from: $225* ✉ *19 Pequot Ave.* ☎ *508/693–5087, 800/947–8704* 🌐 *www.pequothotel.com* 🕒 *Closed mid-Oct.–Apr.* 🛏 *31 rooms, 1 apartment* 🍽 *Breakfast.*

NIGHTLIFE

Loft. This adults-only venu makes its home in the vast space above the MV Chowder Co. and has long historic roots. Today it's home to an over-21 "playground" consisting of numerous pool tables, Ping-Pong, darts, shuffleboard, foosball, video games, a full bar, and frequent live music and DJ-led dance parties. A full menu is available in the restaurant below. ✉ *9 Oak Bluffs Ave.* ☎ *508/696–3000* 🌐 *www.loftob.com.*

Sacred to the Wampanoag Tribe, the red-hued Aquinnah Cliffs are a popular attraction on Martha's Vineyard.

SPORTS AND THE OUTDOORS
FISHING
Dick's Bait & Tackle. You can buy fishing accessories and bait, and check out a current copy of the fishing regulations here. ⊠ *108 New York Ave.* ☎ *508/693–7669.*

EDGARTOWN

6 miles southeast of Oak Bluffs.

Fodor's Choice
★ Once a well-to-do whaling center, Edgartown remains the Vineyard's toniest town and has preserved parts of its elegant past. Sea captains' houses from the 18th and 19th centuries, with well-manicured gardens and lawns, line the streets.

A sparsely populated area with many nature preserves, where you can fish, Chappaquiddick Island, 1 mile southeast of Edgartown, makes for a pleasant day trip or bike ride on a sunny day. The "island" is actually connected to the Vineyard by a long sand spit that begins in South Beach in Katama. It's a spectacular 2¾-mile walk, or you can take the ferry, which departs about every five minutes.

EXPLORING
FAMILY **Felix Neck Wildlife Sanctuary.** The 350-acre Massachusetts Audubon Society preserve, 3 miles outside Edgartown toward Oak Bluffs and Vineyard Haven, has 4 miles of hiking trails traversing marshland, fields, woods, seashore, and waterfowl and reptile ponds. Naturalist-led events include sunset hikes, stargazing, snake or bird walks, and canoeing. ⊠ *100 Felix Neck Rd., off Edgartown–Vineyard Haven Rd.*

☎ 508/627–4850 🌐 www.massaudubon.org 🎟 $4 🕓 June–Aug., Mon.–Sat. 9–4, Sun. 10–3; Sept.–May, weekdays 9–4, Sat. 10–3, Sun. noon–3. Trails daily sunrise–dusk.

QUICK BITES

Espresso Love. When you need a pick-me-up, pop into Espresso Love for a cappuccino and a homemade raspberry scone or blueberry muffin. If you prefer something cold, the staff also makes fruit smoothies. Light lunch fare is served: bagel sandwiches, burgers, salads, soups, and delicious pastries and cookies—all homemade, of course. ✉ *17 Church St.* ☎ *508/627–9211* 🌐 *www.espressolove.com.*

Fodor's Choice ★ **Mytoi.** The Trustees of Reservations' 14-acre preserve is a serene, beautifully tended, Japanese-inspired garden with a creek-fed pool spanned by a bridge and rimmed with Japanese maples, azaleas, bamboo, and irises. A boardwalk runs through part of the grounds, where you're apt to see box turtles and hear the sounds of songbirds. There are few more enchanting spots on the island. Restrooms are available. ✉ *56 Dike Bridge Rd., 2 miles from Chappaquiddick Rd., Chappaquiddick Island* ☎ *508/627–7689* 🌐 *www.thetrustees.org/places-to-visit/cape-cod-islands/mytoi.html* 🎟 *Free* 🕓 *Daily sunrise–sunset.*

WHERE TO EAT

$$$$ FRENCH 🍴 **Alchemy Bistro and Bar.** According to the menu, the definition of *alchemy* is "a magic power having as its asserted aim the discovery of a panacea and the preparation of the elixir of longevity"—lofty goals for a French-style bistro. This high-class version has elegant gray wainscoting, classic paper-covered white tablecloths, old wooden floors, and an opening cut into the ceiling to reveal second-floor tables. The only things missing are the patina of age and experience—and French working-folks' prices—but you can expect quality and imagination. The alcohol list, long and complete, includes cognacs, grappas, and beers. On balmy evenings, the half-dozen outdoor tables on the candlelit brick patio are highly coveted. [$] *Average main: $36* ✉ *71 Main St.* ☎ *508/627–9999* 🌐 *www.alchemyedgartown.com* 🕓 *No lunch* ✍ *Reservations essential.*

$$$$ AMERICAN Fodor's Choice ★ 🍴 **Détente.** A dark, intimate wine bar and restaurant with hardwood floors and richly colored banquette seating, Détente serves more than a dozen wines by the glass as well as numerous half bottles. Even if you're not much of an oenophile, it's worth a trip just for the innovative food, much of it from local farms and seafood purveyors. Start with a foie gras or tuna tartare, followed by such choice entrées as roasted monkfish, local scallops, or grass-fed beef. [$] *Average main: $35* ✉ *15 Winter St.* ☎ *508/627–8810* 🌐 *www.detentemv.com* 🕓 *Closed Tues., and Nov.–late Apr. No lunch* ✍ *Reservations essential.*

$$$$ SEAFOOD FAMILY 🍴 **The Dunes.** The airy restaurant at Winnetu Oceanside Resort draws plenty of discerning diners to sample some of the island's most exquisite and creatively prepared seafood. It's the only dining room with a south-facing water view, and a stunning one at that—especially if you're lucky enough to sit outside on the large dining and drinking area. Locally caught fluke with littleneck clams, leeks, smoked bacon, and a rich chowder broth is another star. If you've got children in tow, you'll

appreciate the back dining area, complete with separate play area; you can actually have dinner with the little ones along—without the angry glares from your neighbors. There is a free water taxi from Edgartown to the restaurant; call ahead. [$] *Average main: $37* ✉ *Winnetu Oceanside Resort, 31 Dunes Rd.* ☎ *508/627–3663* 🌐 *www.winnetu.com* 🕒 *Closed mid-Oct.–mid-Apr. No lunch.*

$ AMERICAN Fodor's Choice ★ 🍴 **Morning Glory Farm.** This farm store is full of incredible goodies, most made or grown on the premises, including fresh farm greens in the salads and vegetables in the soups, and homemade pies, breads, quiches, cookies, and cakes. A picnic table and grass to sit on while you eat make this an ideal place for a simple country lunch. [$] *Average main: $6* ✉ *W. Tisbury Rd.* ☎ *508/627–9003* 🌐 *www.morninggloryfarm.com* 🕒 *Closed late Dec.–early May.*

WHERE TO STAY

$$$$ B&B/INN Fodor's Choice ★ 🏨 **Hob Knob.** This 19th-century Gothic Revival boutique hotel blends the amenities and service of a luxury property with the ambience and charm of a small B&B. **Pros:** spacious rooms; on-site spa; removed from crowds. **Cons:** steep rates; not overlooking harbor; not for those with small children. [$] *Rooms from: $485* ✉ *128 Main St.* ☎ *508/627–9510, 800/696–2723* 🌐 *www.hobknob.com* 🛏 *16 rooms, 1 suite* 🍽 *Breakfast.*

$$$$ RESORT FAMILY Fodor's Choice ★ 🏨 **Winnetu Oceanside Resort.** A departure from most properties on the island, the contemporary Winnetu—styled after the grand multistory resorts of the Gilded Age—has successfully struck a fine balance in that it both encourages families and provides a contemporary seaside-resort experience for couples. **Pros:** outstanding staff; tons of activities; fantastic restaurant. **Cons:** not an in-town location; lots of kids in summer. [$] *Rooms from: $495* ✉ *31 Dunes Rd.* ☎ *866/335–1133, 508/310–1733* 🌐 *www.winnetu.com* 🕒 *Closed late Oct.–mid-Apr.* 🛏 *58 suites, 80 homes* 🍽 *No meals.*

SHOPPING

Edgartown Books. This longtime island favorite carries a large selection of island-related titles and periodicals, and the staff will be happy to make a summer reading recommendation. ✉ *44 Main St.* ☎ *508/627–8463* 🕒 *Closed Nov.–Apr.*

WEST TISBURY

8 miles west of Edgartown, 6½ miles south of Vineyard Haven.

West Tisbury retains its rural appeal and maintains its agricultural tradition at several active horse and produce farms. The town center looks very much like a small New England village, complete with a white-steepled church.

EXPLORING

Sepiessa Point Reservation. A paradise for bird-watchers, Sepiessa Point Reservation consists of 164 acres on splendid Tisbury Great Pond. There are expansive pond and ocean views, walking trails around coves and saltwater marshes, horse trails, swimming areas, and a boat launch. ✉ *Tiah's Cove Rd.* ☎ *508/627–7141* 🌐 *www.mvlandbank.com* 🎟 *Free* 🕒 *Daily sunrise–sunset.*

WHERE TO EAT

$$$$ ✕ **State Road Restaurant.** High ceilings, exposed beams, and a beauti-
AMERICAN ful stone fireplace make for a warm and light-filled meal. The menu
Fodor'sChoice takes advantage of local and organic products, creating memorable
★ dishes like pan-roasted duck breast or prosciutto-wrapped monkfish.
Sunday brunch is a favorite (no reservations accepted); try the bacon
cheddar jalapeño grits, served with wilted spinach, roasted shallots,
and eggs the way you like them. $ *Average main: $35* ⊠ *688 State Rd.*
☎ *508/693–8582* ⊕ *www.stateroadrestaurant.com.*

WHERE TO STAY

$$ ⊡ **Lambert's Cove Inn, Farm & Restaurant.** A narrow road winds through
B&B/INN pine woods and beside creeper-covered stone walls to this posh,
Fodor'sChoice handsomely designed inn surrounded by extraordinary gardens and
★ old stone walls. **Pros:** tasteful and eclectic decor; fantastic restau-
rant; serene grounds. **Cons:** need a car to explore island; far from the
action. $ *Rooms from: $275* ⊠ *90 Manaquayak Rd., off Lambert's
Cove Rd.* ☎ *508/693–2298* ⊕ *www.lambertscoveinn.com* ⊅ *15 rooms*
⊺◯⊦ *Breakfast.*

SHOPPING

FAMILY **Alley's General Store.** Step back in time with a visit to Alley's General
Store, a local landmark since 1858. Alley's sells a truly general variety
of goods: everything from hammers to housewares and dill pickles to
sweet muffins as well as great things you find only in a country store.
There's even a post office inside. ⊠ *299 State Rd.* ☎ *508/693–0088.*

AQUINNAH

*6½ miles west of Menemsha, 10 miles southwest of West Tisbury, 17
miles southwest of Vineyard Haven.*

Aquinnah, called Gay Head until the town voted to change its name in
1997, is an official Native American township. The Wampanoag tribe
is the guardian of the 420 acres that constitute the Aquinnah Native
American Reservation. Aquinnah (pronounced a- *kwih*-nah) is Wampa-
noag for "land under the hill." You can get a good view of Menemsha
and Nashaquitsa ponds, the woods, and the ocean beyond from Quitsa
Pond Lookout on State Road. The town is best known for the red-hued
Aquinnah Cliffs. This is the end of the world, or so it seems when you're
standing on the edge of the cliff looking out over the ocean.

EXPLORING

Fodor'sChoice **Aquinnah Cliffs.** A National Historic Landmark, the spectacular Aquin-
★ nah Cliffs are part of the Wampanoag Reservation land. These dra-
matically striated walls of red clay are the island's major attraction, as
evinced by the tour bus–filled parking lot. Native American crafts and
food shops line the short approach to the overlook, from which you
can see the Elizabeth Islands to the northeast across Vineyard Sound
and Nomans Land Island, a wildlife preserve, 3 miles off the Vineyard's
southern coast. ⊠ *State Rd.*

Gay Head Lighthouse. This brick lighthouse (also called the Aquinnah
Lighthouse) was successfully moved back from its precarious perch

atop the rapidly eroding cliffs in spring 2015. Bad weather may affect its hours. Parking can be limited here. ☒ *9 Aquinnah Circle* ☎ *508/627–4441* ⊕ *www.mvmuseum.org* 🗂 *$5* ☽ *July–mid-Oct., daily 11–4.*

NANTUCKET

At the height of its prosperity in the early 19th century, the little island of Nantucket was the foremost whaling port in the world. Its harbor bustled with whaling ships and merchant vessels; chandleries, cooperages, and other shops crowded the wharves. Burly ship hands loaded barrels of whale oil onto wagons, which they wheeled along cobblestone streets to refineries and candle factories. Sea breezes carried the smoke and smells of booming industry through town as its inhabitants eagerly took care of business. Shipowners and sea captains built elegant mansions, which today remain remarkably unchanged, thanks to a very strict building code initiated in the 1950s. The entire town of Nantucket is now an official National Historic District encompassing more than 800 pre-1850 structures within 1 square mile.

Day-trippers usually take in the architecture and historical sites, dine at one of the many delightful restaurants, and browse in the pricey boutiques, most of which stay open mid-April–December. Signature items include Nantucket lightship baskets, originally crafted by sailors whiling away a long watch; artisans who continue the tradition now command prices of $700 and up, and antiques are exponentially more expensive.

GETTING HERE AND AROUND

Year-round flight service to Nantucket from Boston and Hyannis is provided by Cape Air and Nantucket Airlines. American Airlines offers seasonal service to the island from Washington, D.C., Philadelphia, and New York's LaGuardia; from Newark Airport, American Airlines also provides seasonal service.

Arriving by ferry puts you in the center of town, and several ferry companies offer service to Nantucket from two different ports, either year-round or seasonally. You can board in Hyannis (Hy-Line, Steamship Authority) or Harwich Port (Freedom Cruise Line). The only company that carries cars is Steamship Authority; car service is very expensive, and reservations must be made far in advance.

There is little need for a car here to explore; ample public transportation and smoothly paved bike paths can take you to the further reaches with ease. The Nantucket Regional Transit Authority (NRTA) runs shuttle buses from in town to most areas of the island. Service is generally available late May–mid-October. If you're still determined to rent a car while on Nantucket, book early—and expect to spend at least $95 a day during high season. If your car is low-slung, don't attempt the dirt roads. Some are deeply pocked with puddles, and some are virtual sandpits, challenging even to four-wheel-drive vehicles.

Bus Contacts Nantucket Regional Transit Authority. ☒ *3 E. Chestnut St.* ☎ *508/228–7025* ⊕ *www.nrtawave.com.*

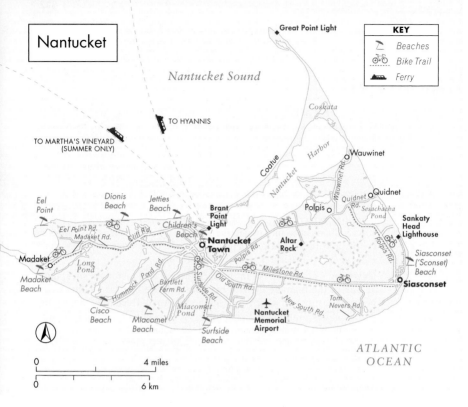

Nantucket

Nantucket Sound

Great Point Light

Coskata

TO HYANNIS

TO MARTHA'S VINEYARD
(SUMMER ONLY)

Wauwinet

Harbor

Coatue

Nantucket

Eel
Point

Dionis
Beach

Jetties
Beach

Brant
Point
Light

Quidnet Quidnet

Polpis

Rd. Sesachacha
Pond

Sankaty
Head
Lighthouse

Eel Point Rd.
Madaket Rd.

Children's
Beach

Cliff Rd.

**Nantucket
Town**

Altar
Rock

Polpis Rd.

Siasconset
('Sconset)
Beach

Madaket

Long
Pond

Pond Rd.

Polpis Rd.

Siasconset

Madaket
Beach

Bartlett
Farm Rd.

Milestone Rd.

Old South Rd.

Surfside Rd.

Hummock Pond Rd.

Cisco
Beach

Miacomet
Beach

Miacomet
Pond

New South Rd.

Tom
Nevers Rd.

Surfside
Beach

**Nantucket
Memorial
Airport**

*ATLANTIC
OCEAN*

0   4 miles

0   6 km

Car Rental Contacts Nantucket Island Rent-a-Car. ⊠ *Nantucket Memorial Airport, 14 Airport Rd.* ☎ *508/228—9989, 800/508—9972* ⊕ *www.nantucketislandrentacar.com.* **Nantucket Windmill Auto Rental.** ⊠ *Nantucket Memorial Airport, 14 Airport Rd.* ☎ *508/228–1227, 800/228–1227* ⊕ *www.nantucketautorental.com.*

VISITOR INFORMATION

Contacts Nantucket Chamber of Commerce. ⊠ *Zero Main St.* ☎ *508/228–1700* ⊕ *www.nantucketchamber.org.* **Nantucket Visitor Services and Information Bureau.** ⊠ *25 Federal St.* ☎ *508/228-0925* ⊕ *www.nantucket-ma.gov.*

NANTUCKET TOWN

30 miles southeast of Hyannis, 107 miles southeast of Boston.

Fodor's Choice
★

At the height of its prosperity in the early 19th century, the little town of Nantucket was the foremost whaling port in the world. Shipowners and sea captains built elegant mansions, which today remain remarkably unchanged, thanks to a very strict building code initiated in the 1950s. The entire town of Nantucket is now an official National Historic District encompassing more than 800 pre-1840 structures within 1 square mile.

TOURS

Fodor's Choice ★ **Nantucket Historical Association** (*NHA*). This association maintains an assortment of venerable properties in town. A $20 pass gets you into all of the association's sites, including the glorious Whaling Museum. A cheaper $6 pass excludes the Whaling Museum but includes the Oldest House, Old Mill, Old Gaol, Greater Light, and the Fire Hose Cart House. Reserve in advance for two very popular walking tours, which depart daily late May–early November: a 60-minute downtown tour and an 80-minute historic house tour. Both cost $10. ⊠ *13 Broad St., Nantucket* ☎ *508/228–1894* ⊕ *www.nha.org.*

EXPLORING

African Meeting House. When the island abolished slavery in 1773, Nantucket became a destination for free blacks and escaping slaves. The African Meeting House was built in the 1820s as a schoolhouse, and it functioned as such until 1846, when the island's schools were integrated. A complete restoration has returned the site to its authentic 19th-century appearance. Next door is the late 18th-century Florence Higginbotham house, originally purchased by Seneca Boston, a former slave and weaver. ⊠ *29 York St.* ☎ *508/228–9833* ⊕ *www.afroammuseum.org* ⊠ *$5* ⊙ *June–Oct., weekdays 11–3, Sat. 11–1, Sun. 1–3.*

Brant Point Light. The promontory where this 26-foot-tall, white-painted beauty stands offers views of the harbor and town. The point was once the site of the second-oldest lighthouse in the country (1746); the present, much-photographed light was built in 1901. ⊠ *End of Easton St., across the footbridge.*

First Congregational Church. The tower of this church provides the best view of Nantucket—for those willing to climb its 94 steps. Rising 120 feet, the tower is capped by a weather vane depicting a whale catch. Peek in at the church's 1852 trompe-l'oeil ceiling. ⊠ *62 Centre St.* ☎ *508/228–0950* ⊕ *www.nantucketfcc.org* ⊠ *Tower tour $5* ⊙ *Mid-June–mid-Oct., Mon.–Sat. 10–4; services Sun. at 10 am.*

FAMILY Fodor's Choice ★ **Whaling Museum.** With exhibits that include a fully rigged whaleboat and a skeleton of a 46-foot sperm whale, this must-see museum—a complex that includes a restored 1846 spermaceti candle factory—offers a crash course in the island's colorful history. Items on display include harpoons and other whale-hunting implements; portraits of whaling captains and their wives (a few of whom went whaling as well); the South Seas curiosities they brought home; a large collection of sailors' crafts; a full-size tryworks once used to process whale oil; and the original 16-foot-high 1850 lens from Sankaty Head Lighthouse. The Children's Discovery Room provides interactive-learning opportunities. Be sure to climb—or take the elevator—up to the observation deck for a view of the harbor. ⊠ *13–15 Broad St.* ☎ *508/228–1894* ⊕ *www.nha.org* ⊠ *$20, includes other historic sites* ⊙ *Mid-Feb.– early Apr., weekends 11–3; mid-Apr.– late May, daily 11–4; late May–Oct., daily 10–5; Nov., weekends 11–4.*

BEACHES

FAMILY **Jetties Beach.** A short bike or shuttle-bus ride from town, Jetties Beach is popular with families because of its calm surf. It's also a good place to try out kayaks and sailboards. The shore is a lively scene, with a

Each beach on Nantucket has a unique approach—sometimes getting there is half the fun.

playground and volleyball nets on the beach and adjacent public tennis courts. There is a boardwalk to the beach (special wheelchairs are available). You'll have a good view of passing ferries—and an even better one if you clamber out on the jetty itself. (Careful, it's slippery.) **Amenities:** food and drink; lifeguards; parking (fee); showers; toilets; water sports. **Best for:** swimming; windsurfing. ✉ *Bathing Beach Rd., 1½ miles northwest of Straight Wharf* 🚗 *Parking $15.*

Fodor's Choice
★

Surfside Beach. Surfside Beach, accessible via the Surfside Bike Path (3 miles) or by shuttle bus, is the island's most popular surf beach. This wide strand of sand comes fully equipped with conveniences. It draws teens and young adults as well as families and is great for kite flying and, after 5 pm, surf casting. **Amenities:** food and drink; lifeguards; parking (fee); showers; toilets. **Best for:** surfing; swimming; walking. ✉ *Surfside Rd., South Shore.*

WHERE TO EAT

$$$$
MODERN
AMERICAN
Fodor's Choice
★

✕ **American Seasons.** Picture a farmhouse gone sexy: that's the mood—wholesome yet seductive—at this candlelit hideaway decorated with Rufus Porter–style murals. Highlights of chef Neil Ferguson's artistic menu include roasted day-boat scallops with salsify purée and pickled grapes, and oven-roasted guinea hen with caramelized sauerkraut, lentils, and sherry vinegar. The patio bar draws aficionados eager to sample the rich array à la carte. 💲 *Average main: $38* ✉ *80 Centre St.* ☎ *508/228–7111* ⊕ *www.americanseasons.com* ☉ *Closed mid-Dec.–mid-Apr. No lunch* ⚄ *Reservations essential.*

$ AMERICAN FAMILY 🍴 **Fog Island Café.** Cherished year-round for its exceptional breakfasts (try the pesto scrambled eggs), Fog Island is just as fine a spot for lunch. The storefront space is cheerily decked out in a fresh country style, and chef-owners Mark and Anne Dawson—both Culinary Institute of America grads—seem determined to provide the best possible service to visitors and locals alike. [$] *Average main: $14* ✉ *7 S. Water St.* ☎ *508/228–1818* 🌐 *www.fogisland.com* 🕑 *No dinner. No lunch Sun.*

$$$ ECLECTIC Fodor's Choice ★ 🍴 **Lola 41 degrees.** By extending Nantucket's longitude and latitude, you'll not only strike this hit restaurant's namesake but also some of the territory that its menu covers. Sushi and sake are specialties, but so are globe-trotting treats like a chili-fired Spanish shrimp salad, grilled wild salmon with tabbouleh and Greek yogurt sauce, or Maine lobster with morel spaghettini and lemon-chive mascarpone. Everywhere this restaurant ventures is good—especially when it ends up heading south for a killer tres leches cake. The place started out as (and remains) a superpopular watering hole for the chic set. [$] *Average main: $26* ✉ *15 S. Beach St.* ☎ *508/325–4001* 🌐 *www.lola41.com* 🕑 *No lunch mid-Apr.–mid-Oct.*

$$$$ ASIAN 🍴 **The Pearl.** With its white onyx bar illuminated a Curaçao blue and its walls awash in flowing voile, this ultracool space—a sophisticated upstairs cousin to the Boarding House—would seem right at home in South Beach. The cushy white-leather banquettes tucked behind the aquarium are the power seats. Executive chef Seth Raynor has great enthusiasm for the bold flavors of Asian cuisine, especially in its street-wise guise. You may have a tough time choosing between the beef barbecue with piquant Thai chili-lime sauce and the signature wok-fried lobster—so do yourself a favor and order both. Asian-themed restaurants often disappoint in the dessert round, but not so here. Pace yourself for some esoteric dazzlers such as the mascarpone-and-chèvre cheesecake with cherry syrup and beet sorbet. [$] *Average main: $37* ✉ *12 Federal St.* ☎ *508/228–9701* 🌐 *www.thepearlnantucket.com* 🕑 *Closed Jan.–Apr. No lunch* ✍ *Reservations essential.*

$$$$ MODERN AMERICAN Fodor's Choice ★ 🍴 **Straight Wharf.** This loftlike restaurant with a harborside deck has enjoyed legendary status since the mid-1970s, when chef Marion Morash used to get a helping hand from culinary buddy Julia Child. The couple now in command—Gabriel Frasca and Amanda Lydon—were fast-rising stars on the Boston restaurant scene, but their approach here is the antithesis of flashy; if anything, they have lent this venerable institution a more barefoot air, appropriate to the place and season. Hurricane lamps lend a soft glow to well-spaced tables lined with butcher paper, and dish towels serve as napkins. Intense champions of local crops and catches, the chefs concoct stellar dishes like oysters with Meyer lemon granita, and line-caught halibut with garlic-chive spaetzle. [$] *Average main: $42* ✉ *6 Harbor Sq.* ☎ *508/228–4499* 🌐 *www.straightwharfrestaurant.com* 🕑 *Closed mid-Oct.–mid-May* ✍ *Reservations essential.*

WHERE TO STAY

$$$$ RESORT FAMILY Fodor's Choice ★ 🏨 **The Nantucket Hotel and Resort.** Although this modern, nautically themed beauty opened only in 2012, the structure itself dates back to 1891 and the golden age of grand seaside hotels. **Pros:** immaculate and large rooms, many with kitchens; ideal for families; full-service restaurant. **Cons:** can be noisy in summer. [$] *Rooms from: $850* ✉ 77

When farmers flood cranberry fields during harvest season, the ripe crimson fruit floats to the surface.

Easton St. ☎ *508/228–4747, 866/807–6011* 🌐 *www.thenantuckethotel.com* ⏲ *Closed Feb.* 🛏 *16 rooms, 26 suites, 2 cottages* 🍴 *Breakfast.*

$$$$ B&B/INN Fodor's Choice ★ 🏨 **Union Street Inn.** Ken Withrow worked in the hotel business, Deborah Withrow in high-end retail display, and guests get the best of both worlds in this 1770 house, a stone's throw from the bustle of Main Street. **Pros:** pampering by pros; pervasive good taste. **Cons:** bustle of town; some small rooms; not for those with children. [$] *Rooms from: $589* ✉ *7 Union St.* ☎ *888/517–0707* 🌐 *www.unioninn.com* ⏲ *Closed Nov.–late Apr., except for Christmas stroll weekend in early Dec.* 🛏 *11 rooms, 1 suite* 🍴 *Breakfast.*

NIGHTLIFE AND PERFORMING ARTS

Chicken Box (*The Box*). Live music—including some big-name bands—plays six nights a week in season, and weekends year-round. ✉ *16 Dave St.* ☎ *508/228–9717* 🌐 *www.thechickenbox.com.*

Muse. This is a year-round venue hosting live bands, including the occasional big-name act. The crowd—the barnlike space can accommodate nearly 400—can get pretty wild. There's also an eatery serving great pizza, burgers, and other bar-type snacks. ✉ *44 Surfside Rd.* ☎ *508/228–6873* 🌐 *www.themusenantucket.com.*

SPORTS AND THE OUTDOORS

BOATING

FAMILY **Nantucket Community Sailing.** Renting sailboats, sailboards, and kayaks at Jetties Beach, NCS also offers youth and adult sailing classes and water-sport clinics for disabled athletes. Its Outrigger Canoe

Club—a Polynesian tradition—heads out several evenings a week in season. ✉ *Jetties Beach, Bathing Beach Rd.* ☎ *508/228–6600* 🌐 *www.nantucketcommunitysailing.org.*

SHOPPING

CRAFTS

Nantucket Looms. Luscious textiles woven on the premises and chunky Susan Lister Locke jewelry are the focus of Nantucket Looms. You can also find beautiful serving ware and high-end local crafts. ✉ *51 Main St.* ☎ *508/228–1908* 🌐 *www.nantucketlooms.com.*

MARKETS

Fodor's Choice ★ **Bartlett's Farm.** Bartlett's Farm encompasses 100 acres overseen by eighth-generation Bartletts. Healthy, tasty prepared foods—within a minisupermarket—are added incentive to make the trek out. If you're not up it, however, a produce truck is parked on Main Street through the summer. ✉ *33 Bartlett Farm Rd.* ☎ *508/228–9403* 🌐 *www.bartlettsfarm.com.*

4

SIASCONSET

7 miles east of Nantucket Town.

First a fishing outpost and then an artists' colony—Broadway actors favored it in the late 19th century—Siasconset (or 'Sconset, in local vernacular) is a charming cluster of rose-covered cottages linked by driveways of crushed clamshells; at the edges of town, the former fishing shacks give way to magnificent sea-view mansions. The small town center consists of a market, post office, café, lunchroom, and a combination liquor store–lending library.

EXPLORING

Altar Rock. A dirt track leads to the island's highest point, Altar Rock (101 feet), and the view is spectacular. The hill overlooks approximately 4,000 acres of rare coastal heathland laced with paths leading in every direction. ✉ *Altar Rock Rd., 3 miles west of Milestone Rd. rotary on Polpis Rd.*

WHERE TO EAT

$$$$ MODERN AMERICAN 🍴 **Topper's.** The Wauwinet, a lavishly restored 19th-century inn on Nantucket's northeastern shore, is where islanders and visitors alike go to experience utmost luxury—and that includes the food. In the creamy-white dining room, awash in lush linens and glorious flowers, you can choose from a three-course prix-fixe menu or order à la carte, and more casual fare is on offer out on the deck. Many visitors take advantage of the *Wauwinet Lady* (a complimentary launch docked at the White Elephant, a sister property) to frame the journey with a scenic harbor tour; jitney service is also offered so you don't have to drive. [$] *Average main: $39* ✉ *The Wauwinet, 120 Wauwinet Rd., Wauwinet* ☎ *508/228–8768* 🌐 *www.wauwinet.com* 🕒 *Closed Nov.–Apr. No dinner Sun.* ✍ *Reservations essential.*

WHERE TO STAY

$$$$

RESORT

Fodor's Choice

★

▦ **The Wauwinet.** This resplendently updated 1850 resort straddles a "haulover" poised between ocean and bay (think beaches on both sides), and you can head out by complimentary van or launch to enjoy ultimate pampering (the staff-to-guest ratio exceeds one-to-one). **Pros:** solicitous staff; dual beaches; peaceful setting. **Cons:** not for those with small children; distance from town; overly chichi. $ *Rooms from: $925* ✉ *120 Wauwinet Rd., Wauwinet* ☎ *508/228–0145* ⊕ *www.wauwinet. com* ⊗ *Closed Nov.–Apr.* ➪ *32 rooms, 4 cottages* ❙❍❙ *Breakfast.*

SPORTS AND THE OUTDOORS

BIKING

'Sconset Bike Path. This 6½-mile bike path starts at the rotary east of Nantucket Town and parallels Milestone Road, ending in 'Sconset. It is mostly level, with some gentle hills. Slightly longer (and dippier), the 9-mile **Polpis Road Path,** veering off to the northeast, is far more scenic and leads to the turnoff to Wauwinet. ✉ *Off Milestone Rd.*

THE BERKSHIRES AND WESTERN MASSACHUSETTS

WELCOME TO THE BERKSHIRES AND WESTERN MASSACHUSETTS

TOP REASONS TO GO

★ **The Countryside:**
Rolling hills, dense stands of forest, open pastures, and scenic valleys greet your eye at every turn.

★ **Early American History:**
Visit preserved villages, homes, and inns, where memories of Colonial history and personalities are kept alive.

★ **Summer Festivals:**
Watch renowned dance companies perform against a Berkshire backdrop at Jacob's Pillow, or listen to the Boston Symphony Orchestra at Tanglewood in Lenox.

★ **Under-the-Radar Museums:** Western Massachusetts has an eclectic assortment of institutions, from the Eric Carle Museum of Picture Book Art to the Basketball Hall of Fame.

★ **Pioneer Valley College Towns:** Three academic centers—Amherst (University of Massachusetts, Amherst College, and Hampshire College), Northampton (Smith College), and South Hadley (Mount Holyoke College)—pulse with cultural activity and youthful energy.

1 The Berkshires. The "hills" you'll see here are actually the beginnings of the Green Mountains of Vermont. Though it'll only cost you a few hours' drive from Boston or New York City, a trip to the Berkshires is a complete escape from all things urban: this is a place of ski resorts and winding forest drives, leaf peeping and gallery browsing, extreme sports and extreme spas. If you're looking for a place to recharge your batteries and your soul, you'll be hard-pressed to find a better option in the Northeast— even the Boston Symphony Orchestra comes here for their summer break.

2 Sturbridge and the Pioneer Valley. Overshadowed somewhat by Boston to the east and the Berkshires to the west, the Pioneer Valley is home to historic settlements, unique museums, college towns, and natural treasures. Old Sturbridge Village—a re-created early-19th-century village with restored buildings, reenactments, and activities—is the premier attraction here. The principal city here is Springfield, home to the Naismith Memorial Basketball Hall of Fame, but most of the area is quite rural—this is where the idyllic New England countryside of the imagination comes to life.

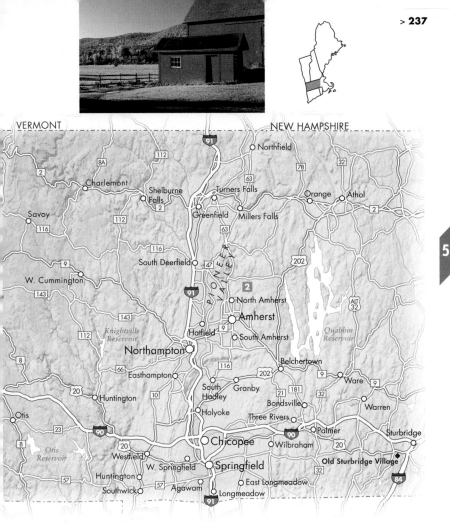

GETTING ORIENTED

Interstate 90, the Massachusetts Turnpike, leads west from Boston to the Berkshires. The main north–south road within the Berkshires is U.S. 7. Route 2 runs from the northern Berkshires to Greenfield at the head of the Pioneer Valley and continues across Massachusetts into Boston; the scenic section known as the Mohawk Trail runs from Williamstown to Orange. Interstate 91 runs north–south in the Pioneer Valley in Western Massachusetts.

Updated by
Seth Brown

Rolling terrain defines the Western Massachusetts landscape. The Bay State's most westerly portion consists of the Berkshires, a bucolic highland region filled with winding mountain roads. Just east, the Pioneer Valley runs north–south through the state's heart, home to the elite "Five College Consortium" of institutions: Amherst, Hampshire, Mount Hollyhock, Smith, and U Mass Amherst. In addition to their natural advantages, the Berkshires and the Pioneer Valley support dynamic cultural venues and risk-taking restaurants—in short, a happening' place with lots to offer.

The burgeoning Berkshires arts community arose from the ruins of a manufacturing economy—aging mills having been converted into artist lofts and a former electric plant morphing into a contemporary art museum. Smaller museums can be found throughout the region, and you can view the creations of its myriad artists and craftspeople at their studios or in local galleries. Hikers, from the casual wanderer to the intrepid trailblazer, also have plenty to experience. In autumn, leaf peepers descend to explore this area renowned for fall foliage whose vibrant oranges, yellows, and reds typify the harvest season.

Though it might be presumptuous to proclaim a "renaissance," it can't be denied that the concentration of arts and culture in the Berkshires has reinvigorated the whole region. Following the artistic explosion, boutique shopping and international cuisine have transformed a formerly depressed postindustrial area into a hot spot for festivals celebrating everything from ice sculptures to the spoken word. The trend continues in the Pioneer Valley, especially in college towns like Northampton, propelled forward by the youthful energy of a large student population.

PLANNING

WHEN TO GO

The dazzling foliage and cool temperatures make fall the best time to visit Western Massachusetts, but the Berkshires and the Pioneer Valley are evolving into a year-round destination. Visit in spring, and witness the burst of color that signals winter's end. Summer is a time of festivals, adventure sports, and outdoor concerts. Many towns save their best for winter, when inns open their doors to carolers and shops serve eggnog. Though usually considered the off-season, it's the perfect time to try cross-country skiing or to spend a night by the fireplace, tucked under a quilt while catching up on books by Nathaniel Hawthorne or Henry David Thoreau.

GETTING HERE AND AROUND

AIR TRAVEL

Most travelers arrive at Boston's Logan International Airport, the state's major airline hub. From Boston you can reach most parts of the Pioneer Valley in less than two hours by car, the Berkshires in about three.

Bradley International Airport in Windsor Locks, Connecticut, 18 miles south of Springfield, Massachusetts, on Interstate 91, serves the Pioneer Valley and the Berkshires. Another alternative—and actually closer to the area than Logan—is T. F. Green International Airport in Providence, Rhode Island.

CAR TRAVEL

Public transportation can be spotty in this region, with buses that don't run on Sunday or in the evening, so you'll almost certainly need a car. But you'll want one anyway so you can take leisurely drives to see the fall foliage. Be warned, though, that the winding mountain roads here are not for the fainthearted.

TRAIN TRAVEL

The Northeast Corridor and high-speed Acela services of Amtrak link Boston with the principal cities between it and Washington, D.C. Amtrak's *Lake Shore Limited,* which stops at Springfield and Pittsfield in the Berkshires, carries passengers from Chicago to Boston. For destinations north and west of Boston, trains depart from Boston's North Station.

Train Information Amtrak. ☎ *800/872–7245* ⊕ *www.amtrak.com.*

RESTAURANTS

At country inns in the Southern Berkshires and the Pioneer Valley, you can find dishes strongly reminiscent of old England—double-cut pork chops, rack of lamb, and game—as well as traditional New England fare like Boston baked beans, Indian pudding, and the dubiously glorified "New England boiled dinner" (slow-boiled meat and vegetables). For those who come to the Berkshires for a taste of history, you'll find plenty of it on the menu.

If you prefer more creative contemporary fare, though, you will not be disappointed. Modern cafés and trendy restaurants serving everything from fusion cuisine to pizza with inspired toppings also do business here.

Perhaps most enticingly, an influx of multiculturalism to the Berkshires has resulted in a number of excellent international food options, especially in the Northern/Central region. In addition to the standard Chinese, Indian, and Thai, visitors can now partake of a wider range of cuisines—including Peruvian, Spanish, Colombian, Malaysian, and more. *Restaurant prices are the average cost of a main course at dinner or, if dinner is not served, at lunch.*

HOTELS

The signature accommodation outside Boston is the country inn; in the Berkshires, where magnificent mansions have been converted into luxury lodgings, these inns have reached a very grand scale indeed. Less extravagant and less expensive are bed-and-breakfast establishments, many in private homes. Make reservations for inns well ahead during peak periods (summer through winter in the Berkshires). Smoking is banned in all Massachusetts hotels.

Campers can pitch their tents amid acres of pine forest dotted with rivers and lakes or in the shadows of the rolling Berkshire Hills. The camping season in Massachusetts generally runs late May–mid-October. For more about camping, contact the Massachusetts Department of Conservation and Recreation (☎ 617/626–1250 ⊕ *www.mass.gov/portal/transportation-recreation/camping/*). *Hotel prices are the lowest cost of a standard double room in high season, excluding 12.45% tax and service charges. Hotel reviews have been shortened. For full information, visit Fodors.com.*

WHAT IT COSTS				
	$	$$	$$$	$$$$
Restaurants	under $18	$18–$24	$25–$35	over $35
Hotels	under $200	$200–$299	$300–$399	over $399

VISITOR INFORMATION

Visitor Information Massachusetts Department of Fish and Game. ✉ *251 Causeway St., Suite 400, Boston* ☎ *617/626–1500* ⊕ *www.mass.gov/eea/agencies/dfg.* **Massachusetts Office of Travel & Tourism.** ✉ *10 Park Plaza, Suite 4510, Boston* ☎ *617/973–8500* ⊕ *www.massvacation.com.*

THE BERKSHIRES

Occupying the far western end of the state, the Berkshires are only about three hours by car from Boston or New York City, yet the region lives up to the storybook picture of rural New England: wooded hills, narrow winding roads, and compact historic villages. Skiing is popular in winter, and sugar-maple sap runs in the spring. Summer brings cultural events, like the renowned Tanglewood classical music festival in Lenox. And fall foliage blazes along the scenic Mohawk Trail, running east to west across the northern Berkshires.

ESSENTIALS

Bus Information Berkshire Regional Transit Authority. ⊠ *North Adams* ☎ *800/292–2782, 413/499–2782* ⊕ *www.berkshirerta.com.*

Visitor Information Berkshires Visitors Bureau. ⊠ *66 Allen St., Pittsfield* ☎ *413/743–4500, 800/237–5747* ⊕ *www.berkshires.org.*

NORTH ADAMS

130 miles northwest of Boston; 73 miles northwest of Springfield; 20 miles south of Bennington, Vermont.

If you're looking for a Berkshires getaway that combines culture with outdoor fun and a cool place to stay, put North Adams on your short list. In addition to the Massachusetts Museum of Contemporary Arts (Mass MoCA), North Adams has mills and factory buildings that have been converted into artist studios. The Porches Inn, a row of eye-catching multihue Victorians, has added "hip" to downtown. The 11-mile Ashuwillticook Rail Trail is accessible in nearby Adams, as is Mt. Greylock State Reservation, if you venture there on foot via one of the local trailheads.

5

GETTING HERE AND AROUND

Arrive North Adams from Pittsfield in the south via Route 8, or from Williamstown in the west via Route 2. Once in town you can see everything on foot in good weather, with most of the action within a few blocks of Main Street. Natural Bridge State Park is the exception, but it's still a reasonable walk.

EXPLORING
TOP ATTRACTIONS

FAMILY
Fodor'sChoice
★

Massachusetts Museum of Contemporary Arts (*Mass MoCA*). It's not just its dimensions—27 buildings over 13 acres, with more than 250,000 square feet of gallery space—that are impressive at Mass MoCA. The nation's largest center for contemporary visual and performing arts is one of the finest such facilities in the world, a major draw for its art shows, music and dance presentations, and film screenings. The enormous space in the main gallery allows for massive exhibits that wouldn't fit anywhere else, like Xu Bing's *Phoenix*: two gigantic birds with 90-foot wingspans. The building, formerly the home of the Sprague Electrical Company and still a worthwhile sight itself, also includes studios, cafés, shops, and the inspiring Kidspace gallery and studio. ⊠ *87 Marshall St.* ☎ *413/664–4111* ⊕ *www.massmoca.org* ⊡ *$16* ⊙ *July and Aug., daily 10–6; Sept.–June, Wed.–Mon. 11–5.*

Natural Bridge State Park. The 30-foot span that gives this 48-acre park its name crosses Hudson Brook, yielding appealing views of rocky chasms. The marble arch at the park's center rises in what functioned as a marble quarry from the early 1880s to the mid-1900s. Natural Bridge has picnic sites, hiking trails, and well-maintained restrooms. In winter the area is popular for cross-country skiing. ⊠ *McCauley Rd., off Rte. 8* ☎ *413/663–6392* ⊕ *www.mass.gov/eea/agencies/dcr/massparks/region-west/natural-bridge-state-park-generic.html.*

FAMILY **North Adams Museum of History & Science.** North Adams's best-kept secret, this museum boasts more than 25 permanent exhibits between three floors, including a kid-friendly science discovery room, a model train, and a full-size reproduction of the Ft. Massachusetts Barracks Room. Military and railroad history are among the many topics covered; the museum building itself was once part of a railroad yard. ✉ *Western Gateway Heritage State Park, State St., Bldg. 5A* ☎ *413/664–4700* 🌐 *www.northadamshistory.org* 🎟 *Free* ⏲ *Nov.–Apr., Sat. 10–4, Sun. 1–4; May–Oct., Thurs.–Sat. 10–4, Sun. 1–4.*

Susan B. Anthony Birthplace Museum. This museum celebrates the extraordinary life and legacy of Susan B. Anthony, who played a pivotal role in winning women the right to vote. In addition to viewing suffrage mementos, you can learn about the abolition and temperance movements, in which she also participated. Definitely worth a look is the collection of 19th-century postcards supporting these three campaigns. ✉ *67 East Rd., Adams* ☎ *413/743–7121* 🌐 *www.susanbanthonybirthplace.com* 🎟 *$6* ⏲ *Late May–mid-Oct., Thurs.–Mon. 10–4; mid-Oct.–late May, Fri. and Sat. 10–4, Sun. 11:30–4.*

WORTH NOTING

Down Street Art. This public-arts project includes 31 galleries in downtown North Adams. From late June through September, DSA presents visual and performing arts events including exhibitions, video screenings, site-specific installations, and, on the last Thursday of the month, opening galas and performances. ✉ *51 Main St.* ☎ *413/663–5253* 🌐 *www.downstreetart.org.*

QUICK BITES

Jack's Hot Dog Stand. A family-owned institution since 1917, Jack's is where locals go for wieners and hamburgers, plain or topped with chili, cheese, or both. This hole-in-the-wall also serves sweet sausages, as well as onion rings and fries. The place only takes cash and closes at 7 pm, and during lunch hour a free stool at the counter is hard to find. ✉ ***12 Eagle St.*** ☎ ***413/664–9006*** 🌐 ***www.jackshotdogstand.com*** ⏲ ***Closed Sun.***

FAMILY **Western Gateway Heritage State Park.** The old Boston & Maine Railroad yard is the site of this park whose visitor center's exhibits trace the impact of train travel on the region. A 30-minute film documents the intense labor required to construct the nearby Hoosac Tunnel. One block from the park, a pedestrian bridge affords a good view of tracks as they disappear into the tunnel. ✉ *115 State St.* ☎ *413/663–6312* 🌐 *www.mass.gov/eea/agencies/dcr/massparks/region-west/western-gateway-heritage-state-park-generic.html* 🎟 *Free* ⏲ *Visitor center Thurs.–Mon. 10–4.*

WHERE TO EAT

$$ FRENCH FUSION ✕ **Gramercy Bistro.** Within the Mass MoCA complex, this upscale-casual eatery serves everything from chicken-liver mousse to seafood paella. Chef-owner Alexander Smith relies on organic meats and locally grown produce when possible, adding serious zip with sauces made from wasabi and saffron. Drop by on Sunday for their memorable brunch. [$] *Average main: $24* ✉ *87 Marshall St.* ☎ *413/663–5300* 🌐 *www.gramercybistro.com* ⏲ *Closed Tues. No lunch Mon.*

$ ✕ **The Parlor Cafe.** This cozy coffeehouse serves sandwiches and baked
AMERICAN goods; the place also pours draft beer, as well as interesting local drinks
Fodor'sChoice like the popular "ginger libation" (ginger beer). The location across
★ from the Massachusetts College of Liberal Arts pulls in students, along
with the laptop crowd looking for a place to work while sipping organic
loose-leaf tea or having coffee and a bagel. More substantial fare ranges
from quesadillas to specialty sandwiches like the Goat Figure (grilled
multigrain bread with goat cheese and fig preserves). On weekends,
the café often hosts live music and the occasional spoken word performance. $ *Average main: $7* ✉ *303 Ashland St.* ☎ *413/346–4279*
⊕ *www.theparlorcafe.com* ▭ *No credit cards.*

$ ✕ **The Sushi House.** Right on the main drag, this pan-Asian restaurant
ASIAN serves Chinese, Thai, Korean, and Japanese classics. Start with seaweed
salad, then consider a noodle dish like pad thai or *pad see ew* (wide, flat
noodles with meat and Chinese broccoli). Hot clay pots contain wonderful dishes like sweet *massaman* curry (a peanut and potato concoc-
tion) and spicy *bibim bap* (a bowl of rice and vegetables topped with
meat, a fried egg, and hot chili sauce). $ *Average main: $15* ✉ *45 Main
St.* ☎ *413/664–9388.*

WHERE TO STAY

$$ 🏨 **Porches Inn.** Dilapidated mill-workers' houses dating to the 1890s have
B&B/INN been restored and connected with one long porch—complete with rock-
Fodor'sChoice ing chairs—to become one of New England's quirkiest hotels. **Pros:** out-
★ door heated pool and hot tub; large guest rooms; free Wi-Fi. **Cons:** small
breakfast room. $ *Rooms from: $289* ✉ *231 River St.* ☎ *413/664–0400*
⊕ *www.porches.com* ⟿ *47 rooms, 18 suites* ❘❘ *Breakfast.*

$$ 🏨 **Topia Inn.** Innkeepers Nana Simopoulos and Caryn Heilman have
B&B/INN transformed a derelict downtown building into an eco-friendly marvel,
with solar panels, biofuel heating, and natural clay walls. **Pros:** artsy
rooms; organic breakfasts; steam showers and spa tubs. **Cons:** next door
to a bar. $ *Rooms from: $250* ✉ *10 Pleasant St., Adams* ☎ *413/743–
9600* ⊕ *www.topiainn.com* ⟿ *7 rooms* ❘❘ *Breakfast.*

SPORTS AND THE OUTDOORS
KAYAKING
Berkshire Outfitters. If you're itching to explore the Cheshire lakes by
kayak, the Ashuwillticook Rail Trail by bike, or Mt. Greylock's summit on snowshoes, visit Berkshire Outfitters. Just 300 yards from the
trail, this shop rents bicycles, kayaks, canoes, snowshoes, and cross-
country skis. The knowledgeable staff are happy to dispense advice
and trail maps. ✉ *169 Grove St., Adams* ☎ *413/743–5900* ⊕ *www.
berkshireoutfitters.com.*

WILLIAMSTOWN

5 miles west of North Adams.

Williamstown is largely built around the prestigious Williams College,
a smallish but verdant campus bisected by Route 2. Williams is one of
the "Little Ivies," and indeed there are ivy-covered buildings, a Gothic-
style chapel, marble columns, and various other architectural features.

Winslow Homer's *West Point, Prout's Neck* is among the notable paintings at Williamstown's Clark Art Institute.

Although "downtown" consists of just a few streets, two noteworthy art museums can be found near the town center, and there are enough upscale shops and restaurants offering international cuisine. In summertime, theatregoers replace college students for the **Williamstown Theatre Festival**; if you're lucky, you may catch a famous actor at a local bar.

GETTING HERE AND AROUND

Williamstown encompasses the surrounding farms and rolling hills, but the town proper straddles Route 2. On the Williams College campus you can walk to Spring Street and Water Street, and anything else you want to see is probably just a short drive off Route 2 (or you can a hop onto the BRTA bus).

EXPLORING

Fodor'sChoice
★

Clark Art Institute. One of the nation's notable small art museums, the Clark has won numerous architectural awards for its recent redesign by Reed Hilderbrand and for the new Clark Center by Pritzker Prize–winning architect Tadao Ando. The polished concrete of the latter visually connects it to the landscape through glass windows and open spaces. The museum has a large collection of Impressionist works, in particular many significant Renoir paintings. Other strengths include English silver, European and American photography 1840–1920, and 17th- and 18th-century Flemish and Dutch masterworks. ⊠ *225 South St.* 🕾 *413/458–2303* ⊕ *www.clarkart.edu* 🎟 *$20* ⊗ *Tues.–Sun. 10–5.*

FAMILY
Fodor'sChoice
★

Williams College Museum of Art. The collection at this fine museum spans a range of eras and cultures, with American and 20th-century art two major focuses. The original octagonal structure facing Main Street was built as a library in 1846, and the painted wall above the stairs is by Sol

LeWitt—actually the third mural to occupy the wall. Special events take place on the outdoor patio on Thursday night in summer. ✉ *15 Lawrence Hall Dr.* ☎ *413/597–2376* 🌐 *wcma.williams.edu* 🎫 *Free* 🕓 *Sept.–May, Fri.–Tues. 10–5, Thurs. 10–8; June–Aug., Fri.–Wed. 10–5, Thurs. 10–8.*

WORD OF MOUTH

"There are many choices for a stroll, one of the most interesting being the Williams College campus. This college, established in 1798, has lovely historical buildings, an excellent art museum, and a large, modern theater space." —partypoet1

WHERE TO EAT

$ BAKERY Fodor's Choice ★ 🍴 **A-Frame Bakery.** The tiny A-frame at the intersection of U.S. 7 and Route 2 isn't much to look at, but the bakery within sells delectable goods that inspire loyalty in locals and visitors alike. The babka—especially the chocolate, though there's also a cinnamon edition—is second to none and must be ordered a day ahead. It's worth the wait, but be aware that there is no place to sit inside and enjoy it. [$] *Average main: $3* ✉ *1194 Cold Spring Rd.* ☎ *413/458–3600* 🕓 *Closed Mon. and Tues.* 💳 *No credit cards.*

$ MEXICAN Fodor's Choice ★ 🍴 **Coyote Flaco.** The best Mexican food in the Berkshires can be found at this unassuming spot where traditional cuisine meets local ingredients. The Enchilada Oaxaca is a good bet, with blue corn tortillas stuffed with your choice of meat and topped with mole. Side dishes often come in cute little tortilla cups, and margarita options are plentiful. Service can be slow on busy nights, but it's worth it. [$] *Average main: $16* ✉ *505 Cold Spring Rd.* ☎ *413/458–4240* 🌐 *www.coyoteflacomas.com* 🕓 *Closed Mon.*

$$ ECLECTIC 🍴 **Mezze Bistro & Bar.** With a beautiful hilltop location and charming grounds, the bistro can get crowded in summer, when everyone wants to rub elbows with stars from the Williamstown Theatre Festival. With an emphasis on local and seasonal ingredients, the menu is always in a state of flux, but it's bound to contain roast veal with duck-fat potatoes, hanger steak with hen-of-the-woods mushrooms, and the like. [$] *Average main: $22* ✉ *777 Cold Spring Rd.* ☎ *413/458–0123* 🌐 *www.mezzerestaurant.com* 🕓 *No lunch* ✍ *Reservations essential.*

$$ AMERICAN Fodor's Choice ★ 🍴 **'6 House Pub.** Set in an old cow barn, this rustic, wood-paneled pub has buckets of character and an interesting array of upholstered furniture—you can nestle into an old wing chair to dine if you like. Chef Matt Schilling's extensive menu runs the gamut from traditional pub food to upscale vegetarian fare, such as wild-mushroom-and-cheese ravioli alfredo, and grilled plum salad with Granny Smith apples, Gorgonzola, and glazed walnuts. If you love seafood, order the "lobster martini" appetizer or the lobster roll. Daily specials include prime-rib-and-pasta combos, but there's plenty to try on the standard menu. [$] *Average main: $19* ✉ *1896 House Inn, 910 Cold Spring Rd.* ☎ *413/458–1896, 888/999–1896* 🌐 *www.6housepub.com* 🕓 *No lunch Mon.–Thurs.*

WHERE TO STAY

$ B&B/INN 🏨 **Guest House at Field Farm.** Built in 1948, this guesthouse contains a fine collection of art on loan from Williams College and the Whitney Museum. **Pros:** great views of the Berkshires; wonderful art collection;

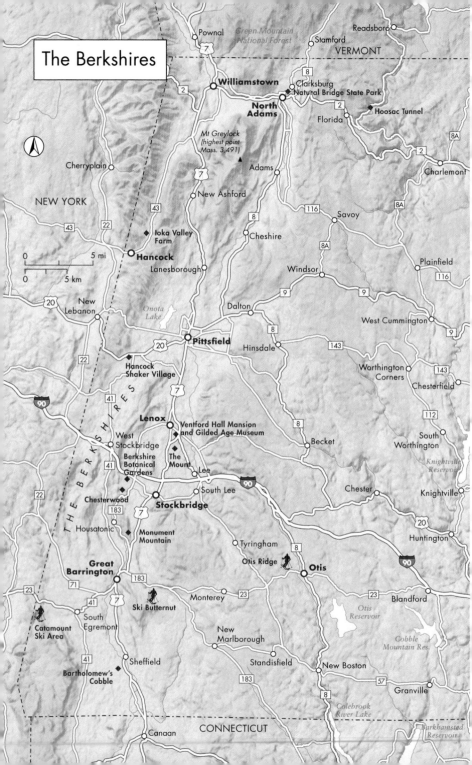

luxurious robes and towels; seasonal swimming pool; free Wi-Fi. **Cons:** no TV in rooms; not an option for families with young children. [$] *Rooms from: $195* ✉ *554 Sloan Rd.* ☎ *413/458–3135* 🌐 *www.guesthouseatfieldfarm.org* 🕒 *Closed Jan.–Mar.* 🛏 *6 rooms* 🍴 *Breakfast.*

$$ HOTEL 🏨 **Orchards Hotel.** Although it's near Route 2 and surrounded by parking lots, this thoroughly proper hostelry compensates with a courtyard filled with fruit trees and a pond stocked with koi. **Pros:** elegant rooms; flat-screen TVs; good alternative to chain hotels and bed-and-breakfasts. **Cons:** no in-room coffeemakers; some service lapses; minor wear and tear visible. [$] *Rooms from: $259* ✉ *222 Adams Rd.* ☎ *413/458–9611, 800/225–1517* 🌐 *www.orchardshotel.com* 🛏 *49 rooms* 🍴 *No meals.*

$ B&B/INN 🏨 **River Bend Farm.** Listed on the National Register of Historic Places, this 1770 Georgian Colonial is neither on a river nor is it a farm, but it is a rustic place to discover simpler times. **Pros:** lovely furnishings; good breakfast; friendly innkeepers. **Cons:** on a busy road; shared bathrooms. [$] *Rooms from: $120* ✉ *643 Simonds Rd.* ☎ *413/458–3121* 🌐 *www.riverbendfarmbb.com* 💳 *No credit cards* 🕒 *Closed Nov.–Mar.* 🛏 *3 rooms without bath* 🍴 *Breakfast.*

PERFORMING ARTS

Fodor's Choice ★ **Williamstown Theatre Festival.** The festival, a past Tony Award winner for outstanding regional theater, is Williamstown's hottest summer ticket. From June through August, the long-running event presents well-known theatrical works featuring famous performers on the Main Stage and contemporary works on the Nikos Stage. ✉ *Williams College, '62 Center for Theatre and Dance, 1000 Main St.* ☎ *413/597–3400, 413/458–3200 (off-season)* 🌐 *www.wtfestival.org.*

SPORTS AND THE OUTDOORS

Mt. Greylock State Reservation. The centerpiece of this 10,327-acre reservation south of Williamstown is Mt. Greylock, the highest point in Massachusetts at 3,491 feet. The reservation has facilities for cycling, fishing, horseback riding, camping, and snowmobiling. Many treks—including a portion of the Appalachian Trail—start from the parking lot at the summit, an 8-mile drive from the mountain's base. ✉ *Visitor center, 30 Rockwell Rd., Lanesboro* ☎ *413/499–4262* 🌐 *www.mass.gov/eea/agencies/dcr/massparks/region-west/mt-greylock-state-reservation-generic.html.*

SHOPPING

Shops at the Library. On downtown Williamstown's main drag, minishops sell clothing, gifts, and antiques. The most attractive find amid the old clocks and bookends may well be their "We ship anything anywhere" policy. ✉ *70 Spring St.* ☎ *413/458–3436* 🌐 *www.shopsatthelibrary.com.*

The Store at 5 Corners. This store's 239-year streak of continual operation ended in 2011, when it closed for the first time since the 1770s. In addition to being a gift shop and small market for fresh fruits and cheeses, its reincarnation doubles as a café, with a large wooden table and benches where you can have breakfast, fancy baked goods, or just coffee. ✉ *6 New Ashford Rd., U.S. 7 at Rte. 43* ☎ *413/458–6105* 🌐 *www.thestoreatfivecorners.com* 🕒 *Closed Tues.*

5

Toonerville Trolley CDs and Records. Some people consider this tiny place to be the best music store in the world for its hard-to-find jazz, rock, and classical recordings—many on vinyl. The same friendly and knowledgeable owner has curated the selection for nearly four decades. ✉ *131 Water St.* ☎ *413/458–5229* 🌐 *www.toonervilletrolleycds.com* 🕒 *Closed Sun.*

FAMILY Fodor's Choice ★ **Where'd You Get That?** Jam-packed with toys, games, and more bizarre novelty items than you could possibly imagine, this store benefits from the enthusiasm of owners Ken and Michele Gietz. Grab an offbeat gift for a friend (and some of the interesting candies for yourself). ✉ *100 Spring St.* ☎ *413/458–2206* 🌐 *www.wygt.com.*

HANCOCK

15 miles south of Williamstown.

Tiny Hancock, the village closest to the Jiminy Peak ski resort, really comes into its own in winter, though it's also a great base for outdoors enthusiasts year-round, with biking, hiking, and other options in summer.

GETTING HERE AND AROUND

You can take Route 43 from Williamstown, U.S. 7 north from Pittsfield to Bailey Road west in Lanesborough, or the BRTA bus from Lanesborough, with plenty of mountain views and trees along the way.

EXPLORING

FAMILY **Ioka Valley Farm.** Bring the kids to this 600-acre farm whose family-friendly activities include games and tractor rides. Seasonal offerings range from pick-your-own pumpkins (mid-September–October) to cut-your-own Christmas trees (late November–late December) and a petting farm in June and July. For a real treat, catch a weekend brunch (late February–early April) with homemade maple syrup atop pancakes, waffles, and French toast. ✉ *3475 Rte. 43* ☎ *413/738–5915* 🌐 *www.iokavalleyfarm.com.*

WHERE TO STAY

$ RESORT 🏨 **Country Inn at Jiminy Peak.** Massive stone fireplaces in the lobby and lounge lend this hotel a ski-lodge atmosphere, and the condo-style suites (privately owned but put into a rental pool) can accommodate up to four people. **Pros:** restaurant; nice bathrooms; eat-in kitchenettes; lodging-and-skiing package deals. **Cons:** hallways are a bit dark; outdoor pool is small. [$] *Rooms from: $135* ✉ *37 Corey Rd.* ☎ *413/738–5500, 800/882–8859* 🌐 *www.jiminypeak.com* 🛏 *105 suites* 🍴 *No meals.*

SPORTS AND THE OUTDOORS

SKIING

Jiminy Peak. The only full-service ski and snowboard resort in the Berkshires, Jiminy Peak is also the largest in southern New England. This is mostly a cruising mountain. Trails are groomed daily, though some small moguls are left to build up along the slope sides. The steepest black-diamond runs are on the upper head walls; longer, outer runs make for good intermediate terrain. There's night skiing daily, and snowmaking capacity can cover 93% of skiable terrain. Jiminy has three terrain parks, as well as a weekends-only mountain coaster: a two-person cart that shoots down the mountain at speeds of up to 25 mph. During the summer, the resort transforms into an adventure park. **Facilities:** 45 trails; 170 acres; 1,150-foot vertical drop; 9 lifts. ✉ 37 *Corey Rd.* ☎ *413/738–5500, 888/454–6469* ⊕ *www.jiminypeak.com* 🎫 *Lift ticket: $71.*

PITTSFIELD

21 miles south of Williamstown, 11 miles southeast of Hancock.

Pittsfield is a workaday city without the quaint, rural demeanor of the comparatively small Colonial towns that surround it. There's a positive buzz in Pittsfield these days, though, thanks to a resurgence of sorts: the beautifully restored Colonial Theatre hosts 250 performances every year, and a number of new shops and restaurants have appeared along North Street. City-sponsored art walks and a major renovation of the Berkshire Museum are additional evidence of Pittsfield's comeback.

5

GETTING HERE AND AROUND

U.S. 7 (1st Street, in town), U.S. 20 (South Street), and Route 9 (East Street) all converge on Pittsfield. Trains and buses stop at the Intermodal Transportation Center, one block from North Street, along which you can walk to museums, interesting stores, and all sorts of restaurants. Buses service the mall and Allendale, but to get elsewhere you'll need to drive.

EXPLORING

FAMILY

Fodor's Choice

★

Berkshire Museum. Opened in 1903, this "universal" museum has a little bit of everything: paintings from the Hudson River School, Alexander Calder mobiles, local artifacts, and natural history specimens both animal and mineral. The Hall of Innovation showcases Berkshires innovators whose creations range from special effects for *Star Wars* to the paper used for U.S. currency. The 10-foot-high stegosaurus outside the museum advertises the dinosaur gallery, where families can sift through the dig pit for bones, but don't miss the ancient gallery with its Egyptian mummy, or the aquarium with a touch tank in the basement. The museum's cinema screens American independent and foreign films. ✉ *39 South St.* ☎ *413/443–7171* ⊕ *www.berkshiremuseum.org* 🎫 *$13* ⊗ *Mon.–Sat. 10–5, Sun. noon–5.*

Fodor's Choice

★

Hancock Shaker Village. America's third Shaker community, Hancock was founded in the 1790s. At its peak in the 1840s, the village had almost 300 inhabitants who made their living farming, selling seeds and herbs, making medicines, and producing crafts. The religious community officially closed in 1960, but visitors today can still see demonstrations of blacksmithing, woodworking, and more. Many examples of Shaker ingenuity are on display: the Round Stone Barn and the Laundry and Machine Shop are two of the most interesting buildings. The Shaker focus on sustainability has been maintained in the form of water turbines, sustainable gardens, and a solar array. There's also a farm (with a wonderful barn), some period gardens, a museum shop with reproduction Shaker furniture, a picnic area, and a café. Visit in April to catch the baby animals at the farm, or in September for the country fair. Reserve early if you want a spot at the Shaker-inspired suppers in

Many of New England's back roads are lined with historic split-rail fences or stone walls.

October. ✉ *34 Lebanon Mountain Rd., off U.S. 20 at Rte. 41, Hancock* ☎ *413/443–0188, 800/817–1137* 🌐 *www.hancockshakervillage.org* 🎟 *$18* 🕒 *Apr.–June, daily 10–4; July–Oct., daily 10–5.*

WHERE TO EAT

$ AMERICAN 🍴 **Dottie's Coffee Lounge.** The raised seating area by the windows somehow adds a touch of class to this quintessential coffee shop where the art crowd hangs out. In addition to fine coffee, friendly barristas serve soups and sandwiches. If you're late for the theater, grab a prewrapped meal to go. [$] *Average main: $8* ✉ *444 North St.* ☎ *413/443–1792* 🌐 *www.dottiescoffeelounge.com* 🕒 *Kitchen closed Sat.*

$$ ITALIAN Fodor's Choice ★ 🍴 **Elizabeth's.** You'd never guess this little white house was a restaurant, let alone one serving such superb Italian fare. The cuisine at Elizabeth's, where you feel like you're having dinner at a friend's house, emphasizes high-quality ingredients. From the four-cheese lasagna with caramelized onions to the classic pasta puttanesca (olives, garlic, capers, hot pepper), all the richly flavored entrées are accompanied by salads resplendent with seasonal greens, vegetables, fruits, and cheeses. Don't pass up the *bagna cauda,* a hot dipping sauce of anchovies, garlic, and olive oil. Credit cards aren't accepted, though personal checks are—and in some cases an IOU will do. With giant portions and a gracious atmosphere, it's hard not to feel at home. [$] *Average main: $22* ✉ *1264 East St., off Rte. 9* ☎ *413/448–8244* 💳 *No credit cards* 🕒 *Closed Mon. and Tues., and Sun. in summer. No lunch* ✍ *Reservations essential.*

$$ ASIAN Fodor's Choice ★ 🍴 **Enso.** Don't be fooled by the giant log-cabin exterior: this former steak house is now an Asian bistro with a full hibachi grill and sushi bar. The menu incorporates typical favorites but also innovative concoctions such as the must-try Treasure Island, a spicy mélange of various types of fish layered with avocado, lobster, roe, and the chef's special sauce. Lanterns add warmth to the spacious interior, where seating options include the colorful bar, the large dining room, and an intimate side room. The sake selection is broad and impressive. [$] *Average main: $21* ✉ *1035 South St.* ☎ *413/499–7900* 🌐 *www.ensobistro.com* 💳 *No credit cards.*

$ SOUTH AMERICAN 🍴 **La Fogata.** The open kitchen looks almost like a lunch counter at this no-frills corner restaurant known for good, honest Colombian food. Unless you're a vegetarian, it's hard to go wrong here: all the meats are delicious, from the thin, perfectly seasoned chicken to the pork rind that bacon aspires to be. Serious meat lovers will appreciate the Picada La Fogata, an array of the best meats served with chimichurri and plantains. It's worth ordering one of the Latin American soft drinks if you've never tried one. [$] *Average main: $15* ✉ *770 Tyler St.* ☎ *413/443–6969* ⏲ *Closed Mon.*

5

PERFORMING ARTS

Colonial Theatre. Back in the day, stars such as Helen Hayes and Al Jolson appeared at this 780-seat 1903 theater; now restored, it hosts the likes of Audra McDonald and James Taylor. A second stage, the Garage, hosts comedy acts and programs for children. ✉ *111 South St.* ☎ *413/997–4444* 🌐 *www.berkshiretheatregroup.org.*

South Mountain Concerts. One of the country's most distinguished chamber music series presents concerts every Sunday in September at 3 pm on South Mountain's wooded slope. ✉ *New S. Mountain Rd., 720 South St., off U.S. 20, 2 miles south of town* ☎ *413/442–2106* 🌐 *www.southmountainconcerts.org.*

SPORTS AND THE OUTDOORS

HIKING

Ashuwillticook Rail Trail. Passing through the Hoosac River Valley, the paved 11-mile Ashuwillticook (pronounced *Ash*-oo-will-ti-cook) trail links Adams with Lanesborough. The trail follows an old railroad, passing through rugged woodland and alongside Cheshire Lake. Walkers, joggers, cyclists, in-line skaters, and cross-country skiers all enjoy this route. ✉ *3 Hoosac St., Adams* ☎ *413/442–8928* 🌐 *www.mass.gov/eea/agencies/dcr/massparks/region-west/ashuwillticook-rail-trail.html.*

SKIING

FAMILY **Bousquet Ski Area.** On the tamer side of Berkshire ski options, Bousquet has 23 trails if you count merging slopes separately. Experts will probably wish to go elsewhere: Bousquet has a few steeper pitches, but it's focused mainly on good beginner and intermediate runs. There are three double chairlifts, two carpet lifts, and a small terrain park. In summer, Bousquet offers waterslides, a large activity pool, a miniature golf course, a climbing wall, an adventure park, and a zip line. **Facilities:** 23 trails; 200 acres; 750-foot vertical drop; 5 lifts. ✉ *101 Dan Fox Dr., off U.S. 7* ☎ *413/442–8316, 413/442–2436 for snow conditions* 🌐 *www.bousquets.com* 🎫 *Lift ticket: $45* ⏲ *June–Sept. and Dec.–Mar.*

ZIP-LINING

FAMILY **Ramblewild.** The Northeast's largest tree-to-tree adventure park has eight trails of climbing, swinging, leaping, and zip-lining derring-do. Difficulty levels range from beginner to expert. Ramblewild's staff are friendly, and the philosophy here is environmentally conscientious. ⊠ *110 Brodie Mountain Rd., Lanesboro* ☎ *413/499–9914* ⊕ *www.ramblewild.com* ☞ *$48.*

SHOPPING

Bartlett's Orchard. The smell of freshly baked cider doughnuts greets you upon entering this orchard's market. You'll find many apple varieties bagged for purchase, but it's more fun to head into the orchard and pick your own. If you come between September and mid-October, you can pick raspberries and flowers as well. ⊠ *575 Swamp Rd., Richmond* ☎ *413/698–2559* ⊕ *www.berkshires.org/member/bartletts-orchard.*

Whitney's Farm. In addition to offering pick-your-own blueberries, tomatoes, peppers, and pumpkins on a seasonal basis, Whitney's sells fresh produce, herbs, and dairy products. A deli and a bakery are also on-site. ⊠ *1775 S. State Rd., Cheshire* ☎ *413/442–4749* ⊕ *www. whitneysfarm.com.*

LENOX

10 miles south of Pittsfield, 130 miles west of Boston.

The famed Tanglewood music festival has been a fixture in upscale Lenox for decades, and it's one of the reasons the town remains fiercely popular in summer. Booking a room here or in any of the nearby communities can set you back dearly during musical or theatrical events. Many of the town's most impressive homes are downtown; others you can only see by setting off on the curving back roads that thread the region. In the center of the village, a few blocks of shabby-chic Colonial buildings contain shops and eateries. Five miles south of Lenox is **Lee**, famous for its harder-than-average marble, quarried in 19th century for use in the cottages of the Vanderbilts and their ilk. Today the bustling downtown area has a mix of touristy and workaday shops and restaurants.

GETTING HERE AND AROUND

Just off Interstate 90, Lenox is south of Pittsfield. During the summer Tanglewood season, traffic in Lenox and environs often moves at a slow pace.

ESSENTIALS

Visitor Information Lenox Chamber of Commerce. ⊠ *Lenox Library, 18 Main St.* ☎ *413/637–3646* ⊕ *www.lenox.org.*

EXPLORING

TOP ATTRACTIONS

Frelinghuysen Morris House & Studio. This modernist property on a 46-acre site exhibits the works of American abstract artists Suzy Frelinghuysen and George L. K. Morris, as well as those of their contemporaries, including Pablo Picasso, Georges Braque, and Juan Gris. In addition to the paintings, frescoes, and sculptures on display, a 57-minute documentary on Frelinghuysen and Morris plays on a continuous loop. Tours are offered on the hour—just be aware that it's a long walk to the house. Painting demonstrations and workshops occasionally take place. ☒ *92 Hawthorne St.* ☎ *413/637–0166* ⊕ *www.frelinghuysen.org* ▣ *$15* ☉ *Late June–early Sept., Thurs.–Sun. 10–3; early Sept.–mid-Oct., Thurs.–Sat. 10–3.*

FodorśChoice ★ **The Mount.** This 1902 mansion with myriad classical influences was the summer home of novelist Edith Wharton. The 42-room house and 3 acres of formal gardens were designed by Wharton, who is considered by many to have set the standard for 20th-century interior decoration. In designing the Mount, she followed the principles set forth in her book *The Decoration of Houses* (1897), creating a calm and well-ordered home. To date, nearly $15 million has been spent on an ongoing project that most recently restored the third-floor bedroom suite. Summer is a fine time to enjoy the informal café and occasional free concerts on the terrace. Guided tours take place during regular hours, the private "ghost tour" after hours. ☒ *2 Plunkett St.* ☎ *413/551–5111, 888/637–1902* ⊕ *www.edithwharton.org* ▣ *$18* ☉ *Grounds daily sunrise–sunset. House: May–Oct., daily 10–5.*

FodorśChoice ★ **Schantz Galleries.** Jim Schantz's gallery is small and tucked behind a bank, but it displays some of the finest glasswork in the world. With items from nearly five dozen contemporary artists—including Dale Chihuly and Lino Tagliapietra—the museum-quality collection is truly stunning. ☒ *3 Elm St., Stockbridge* ☎ *413/298–3044* ⊕ *www.schantzgalleries.com* ☉ *Daily 10–5:30.*

Ventfort Hall Mansion and Gilded Age Museum. Built in 1893, Ventfort Hall was the summer "cottage" of Sarah Morgan, the sister of financier J. P. Morgan. Lively tours offer a peek into the lifestyles of Lenox's super-rich "cottage class." Although the property is being restored and some rooms are closed, the many that are open reveal the original stained-glass windows and hand-carved woodwork. The museum's temporary exhibits explore the role of Lenox and the Berkshires as the era's definitive mountain retreat. Victorian high tea is among the highlights. ☒ *104 Walker St.* ☎ *413/637–3206* ⊕ *www.gildedage.org* ▣ *$18* ☉ *May–Oct., weekdays 10–5, weekends 10–3; Nov.–Apr., weekdays 10–4.*

FodorśChoice ★ **The Wit Gallery.** If you walked past this gallery, you'd inevitably end up ducking in for a closer inspection of the stunning glassworks in the windows. The expertly curated selection inside has more to offer, however, including everything from wooden sculptures to cold-cast metal faces, almost every piece demanding attention. ☒ *27 Church St.* ☎ *413/637–8808* ⊕ *www.thewitgallery.com* ▣ *Free* ☉ *Daily 10–5.*

WORTH NOTING

FAMILY **Berkshire Scenic Railway Museum.** Antique rail equipment, vintage items, and a large working model railway are in the collection of this museum in a restored 1903 railroad station. In late 2015, Hoosac Valley Service began hour-long train rides, making the 10-mile journey between Adams and North Adams in restored historic cars; call or check the website for the schedule. ☒ *10 Willow Creek Rd.* ☎ *413/637–2210* ⊕ *www.berkshirescenicrailroad.org* ▣ *Free* ☉ *Late May–Oct., Sat. 9–4.*

5

DeVries Fine Art. This sculpture gallery features the work of one man: Andrew DeVries. The evocative detail of his bronze figurative pieces makes them worth a look. ✉ *62 Church St.* ☎ *413/637–3462* 🌐 *www.andrewdevries.com* 🕒 *May–Oct., Fri.–Sun. 11–4, and by appt.*

WHERE TO EAT

$ PERUVIAN Fodor's Choice ★ 🍴 **Alpamayo.** Don't let the no-frills decor fool you: what this place lacks in style it more than makes up for in inventive flavors, especially at dinner. Start with an appetizer of beef heart or ceviche before moving on to the pile of fried seafood known as *jalea,* or the delectable mishmash that is *lomo saltado* (Angus beef, onions, tomatoes, and french fries, all sautéed together)—though not much to look at, the latter entrée is satisfyingly rich. For dessert, two can easily share the generous caramel custard. If you're up for something new, order a pitcher of *chicha morada,* a purple corn drink that defies description. [$] *Average main: $18* ✉ *60 Main St., Lee* ☎ *413/243–6000* 🌐 *www.alpamayorestaurant.com* 🕒 *Closed Mon.*

$ SOUTHWESTERN 🍴 **Baja Charlie's.** For a quick bite to break up a full day of sightseeing, grab a seat in the tiny Baja Charlie's dining area, or on the pleasant patio. The menu covers the Cal-Mex basics—nachos, tacos, burritos, chimichangas, enchiladas, and quesadillas—and the chef doesn't skimp on the meat. You can also order take-out. [$] *Average main: $12* ✉ *62A W. Center St., Lee* ☎ *413/243–4322* 🕒 *Closed Sun. and Mon.*

$$$ FRENCH 🍴 **Bistro Zinc.** Pastel-yellow walls, tall windows, a pressed-metal ceiling, and small-tile floors set an inviting tone at this stylishly modern French bistro that from certain angles evokes a country place in Provence. The kitchen turns out expertly prepared and refreshingly simple classics, from steak frites to coq au vin. The long zinc-top bar, always full and determinedly sophisticated, is the best Lenox has to offer for nightlife. [$] *Average main: $25* ✉ *56 Church St.* ☎ *413/637–8800* 🌐 *www.bistrozinc.com.*

$ INDIAN 🍴 **Bombay Bar and Grill.** This little eatery with views of Laurel Lake through the full-wall windows is quite a find. After some complimentary papadam bread with chutney, try an appetizer sampler with samosas and either fried vegetables or yogurt-cooked chicken. Signature dishes include fish steamed in banana leaf, shrimp with curry leaves, tender chicken *tikka masala* (in a tomato-cream sauce), and lamb *rogan josh* (flavored with ginger, tomato, and onion). Everything looks as good as it smells. Vegan options are available, and there's a full bar. The weekend lunch buffet is a bargain. [$] *Average main: $17* ✉ *Black Swan Inn, 435 Laurel St., Lee* ☎ *413/243–6731* 🌐 *www.bombaylee.com* 🕒 *Closed Mon.* ✍ *Reservations not accepted.*

$$$ ITALIAN 🍴 **Café Lucia.** The menus change with the seasons at this northern Italian restaurant, so you might find anything from veal piccata with anchovies, lemons, and capers in summer to osso buco in winter. The porch is one of the best places to take everything in. Weekend reservations are essential, especially when there's a concert at Tanglewood. [$] *Average main: $30* ✉ *80 Church St.* ☎ *413/637–2640* 🌐 *www.cafelucialenox.com* 🕒 *Closed Sun. and Mon. No lunch* ✍ *Reservations essential.*

$ BAKERY Fodor's Choice ★ 🍴 **Chocolate Springs Cafe.** Escape into chocolate bliss here, where even the aromas are intoxicating. This award-winning chocolatier offers wedges of decadent cakes, ice creams, and sorbets, and dazzling chocolates all made on-site. Whether you like your chocolate dark and pure, sugar-free—even with a chipotle filling—you can't go wrong. You can eat at one of a handful of leather couches or wooden chairs and tables, but don't expect so much as a salad or a wrap: it's all chocolate, all the time. [$] *Average main: $6* ✉ *Lenox Commons, 55 Pittsfield/Lenox Rd.* ☎ *413/637–9820* 🌐 *www.chocolatesprings.com.*

$$$ CAFÉ 🍴 **Church Street Café.** A bit more laid-back than its nearby competitors but not much cheaper, this café with hardwood floors, recycled metal chairs, and black-and-white photos has a rustic-minimalist aesthetic. From the cod en papillote to the butternut squash ravioli, the globally inspired, seasonally changing dishes served here pair well with selections from the extensive wine list. In warm weather you can dine on a shaded outdoor deck. [$] *Average main: $25* ✉ *65 Church St.* ☎ *413/637–2745* 🌐 *www.churchstreetlenox.com* ⏲ *Closed Tues. and Wed. No lunch weekdays.*

5

WHERE TO STAY

$$ B&B/INN 🏨 **Applegate Inn.** This 1925 Georgian Revival mansion sits at the end of a regal circular drive, overlooking 6 acres of lush lawns and apple trees. **Pros:** charming dining room; delicious breakfast; heated pool. **Cons:** some traffic noise. [$] *Rooms from: $210* ✉ *279 W. Park St.* ☎ *413/243–4451* 🌐 *www.applegateinn.com* 🛏 *5 rooms, 6 suites* 🍽 *Breakfast.*

$$$$ B&B/INN 🏨 **Blantyre.** Modeled after a castle in Scotland, this supremely elegant 1902 manor house sits amid nearly 117 acres of manicured lawns and woodlands. **Pros:** stunning hot tub at spa; high-end toiletries; exquisitely maintained property. **Cons:** some rooms have quirky configurations. [$] *Rooms from: $675* ✉ *16 Blantyre Rd., off U.S. 20* ☎ *413/637–3556* 🌐 *www.blantyre.com* 🛏 *23 rooms, 9 suites, 4 cottages* 🍽 *Breakfast.*

$ B&B/INN 🏨 **Brook Farm Inn.** Tucked away in a wooded glen a short distance from Tanglewood, this 1880s inn often has classical music playing in the fireplace-lighted library. **Pros:** attentive innkeepers; delicious breakfasts; proximity to Tanglewood; wooded setting. **Cons:** books up fast. [$] *Rooms from: $189* ✉ *15 Hawthorne St.* ☎ *413/637–3013, 800/285–7638* 🌐 *www.brookfarm.com* 🛏 *14 rooms, 1 suite* 🍽 *Breakfast.*

$$$$ RESORT FAMILY 🏨 **Cranwell Resort, Spa, and Golf Club.** This 380-acre resort is tastefully upscale, as you'll see from the guest rooms in the Mansion; all are furnished with ornate antiques and have marble bathrooms, as well as refrigerators and flat-screen TVs. **Pros:** golfing with a view; many activities; nice swimming pool; good for families. **Cons:** extra cost for some amenities; some complaints of housekeeping issues. [$] *Rooms from: $495* ✉ *55 Lee Rd., Rte. 20* ☎ *413/637–1364, 800/272–6935* 🌐 *www.cranwell.com* 🛏 *114 rooms* 🍽 *No meals.*

$$ B&B/INN Fodor's Choice ★ 🏨 **Devonfield Inn.** Occupying a grand Federal house, the Devonfield sits atop a birch-shaded hillside overlooking 32 acres of rolling meadows. **Pros:** good breakfasts; separate cottage available; nice pool and lawn. **Cons:** not for families with young children. [$] *Rooms from: $265* ✉ *85 Stockbridge Rd., Lee* ☎ *413/243–3298, 800/664–0880* 🌐 *www.devonfield.com* 🛏 *6 rooms, 3 suites, 1 cottage* 🍽 *Breakfast.*

$$$ B&B/INN Fodor's Choice ★ **Gateways Inn and Restaurant.** The 1912 summer cottage of Harley Procter (as in, Procter & Gamble) has had numerous owners during its tenure as a country inn. **Pros:** well-appointed rooms; great location in the heart of Lenox; late-night nibbles in the piano bar. **Cons:** lots of stairs; weddings sometimes take over the lobby. [$] *Rooms from: $300* ✉ *51 Walker St.* ☎ *413/637–2532* 🌐 *www.gatewaysinn.com* 🛏 *9 rooms, 2 suites* 🍴 *Breakfast.*

PERFORMING ARTS

Shakespeare and Company. The works of William Shakespeare and other writers are performed between three theaters. The Tina Packer Playhouse and Elayne P. Bernstein Theatre are both indoors, so you can enjoy productions throughout much of the year. The outdoor Rose Footprint Theatre reflects the dimensions of Shakespeare's first performance space in London: the Rose. ✉ *70 Kemble St.* ☎ *413/637–3353* 🌐 *www.shakespeare.org.*

Fodor's Choice ★ **Tanglewood.** The 200-acre summer home of the Boston Symphony Orchestra, Tanglewood attracts thousands every summer to concerts by world-famous musicians. The 5,000-seat main shed hosts larger concerts; the more intimate Seiji Ozawa Hall seats around 1,200 and is used for chamber music and solo performances. The hall is named for the renowned conductor, for years the BSO's music director, a job now held by the Latvian-born Andris Nelsons. Among the most rewarding ways to experience Tanglewood is to purchase lawn tickets, arrive early with blankets or lawn chairs, and enjoy a picnic under the stars. Except for the occasional big-name concert, lawn tickets cost only $20. Inside the shed, tickets vary in price, with most of the good seats costing $38–$120. You can hear the same music for much less by attending an open rehearsal. ✉ *297 West St., off Rte. 183* ☎ *617/266–1492, 888/266–1492* 🌐 *www.tanglewood.org.*

SPORTS AND THE OUTDOORS

HIKING

FAMILY **Pleasant Valley Wildlife Sanctuary.** Beaver ponds, hardwood forests, and sun-dappled meadows abound at this preserve run by the Massachusetts Audubon Society. Recent wildlife sightings are noted on whiteboards at the entrance and the visitor center, so you'll know what to watch for on the 7 miles of trails. These include loops that range in difficulty from a half-hour stroll around a pond to a three-hour mountain hike. Trails are also open in winter for snowshoeing. At the visitor center there's a nature play area for children. ✉ *472 W. Mountain Rd.* ☎ *413/637–0320* 🌐 *www.massaudubon.org* 🎟 *$5* 🕒 *Nature center: Aug.–mid-Oct., Tues.–Fri. 9–4, Sat.–Mon. 10–4; mid-Oct.–July, Tues.–Fri. 9–4.*

HORSEBACK RIDING

Berkshire Horseback Adventures. Travel along the shaded trails of Kennedy Park and Lenox Mountain and enjoy breathtaking views of Berkshire County when you book rides lasting anywhere from an hour to a whole day. ✉ *293 Main St.* ☎ *413/637–9090* 🌐 *www.berkshirehorseback.net.*

SPAS

Canyon Ranch. The Berkshires' outpost of the Arizona resort couldn't be more elegantly old-fashioned. The holistic spa is set in Bellefontaine Mansion, an 1897 replica of Le Petit Trianon in Versailles. Looks can be deceiving, though: housed within is a state-of-the-art fitness center, with the latest classes and the best equipment—perfect for gym junkies. Choose from more than 40 fitness classes per day, plus lifestyle-management workshops and private consultations with wellness experts in the fields of medicine, nutrition, behavior, and physiology, while trying new fitness techniques, eating healthful cuisine—even chocolate sauce, craftily made from white grape juice and cocoa—and enjoying the Berkshires countryside on hikes and paddling excursions. ⊠ *165 Kemble St.* ☎ *800/742–9000, 413/637–4400* ⊕ *www.canyonranch.com.*

OTIS

20 miles southeast of Lenox.

With a ski area and 20 lakes and ponds, Otis supplies plenty of what made the Berkshires desirable in the first place: the great outdoors. Nearby Becket hosts the outstanding Jacob's Pillow Dance Festival in summer. Dining and lodging options are slim in Otis, but plentiful in Great Barrington (16 miles west) and Lenox (20 miles northwest).

GETTING HERE AND AROUND

Otis lies at the intersection of Route 8 and Route 23. The town has no public transportation, so you'll need a car to get around.

EXPLORING

Fodor's Choice
★

Jacob's Pillow Dance Festival. For 10 weeks every summer, the tiny town of Becket, 8 miles north of Otis, becomes a hub of the dance world. The Jacob's Pillow Dance Festival showcases world-renowned performers of ballet, modern, and international dance. Before the main events, works in progress and even some of the final productions are staged outdoors, often free of charge. ⊠ *358 George Carter Rd., at U.S. 20, Becket* ☎ *413/243–0745* ⊕ *www.jacobspillow.org.*

SPORTS AND THE OUTDOORS

SKI AREA

Otis Ridge. The least expensive ski area in New England, Otis Ridge is a haven for beginners and families, but black-diamond skiers can still choose between a wide-open straight shot downwards and a more challenging wooded path. The remote location is stunning, and the vibe is friendly. Two lifts are tiny tows serving dedicated beginner slopes; the other two are a chairlift and a T-bar. Try night skiing for a cheap ticket. **Facilities:** 10 trails; 60 acres; 400-foot vertical drop; 4 lifts. ⊠ *159 Monterey Rd. (Rte. 23), off Rte. 8* ☎ *413/269–4444* ⊕ *www.otisridge.com* ☜ *Lift ticket: $40* ☾ *Closed Mon. and Tues.*

STOCKBRIDGE

20 miles northwest of Otis, 7 miles south of Lenox.

The quintessence of small-town New England charm, Stockbridge is untainted by large-scale development. It is also the blueprint for small-town America as represented on the covers of the *Saturday Evening Post* by painter Norman Rockwell, the official state artist of Massachusetts. From 1953 until his death in 1978, Rockwell lived in Stockbridge and painted the simple charm of its buildings and residents. James Taylor sang about the town in his hit "Sweet Baby James," as did balladeer Arlo Guthrie in his famous Thanksgiving anthem "Alice's Restaurant," in which he tells what ensued when he tossed some garbage out the back of his Volkswagen bus down a Stockbridge hillside.

Indeed, Stockbridge is the stuff of legend. Travelers have been checking into the Red Lion Inn on Main Street since the 18th century, and Stockbridge has only slightly altered in appearance since that time. The 18th- and 19th-century buildings surrounding the inn contain engaging shops and eateries. The rest of Stockbridge is best appreciated on a country drive or bike ride along its hilly, narrow lanes.

GETTING HERE AND AROUND

Stockbridge is accessible from West Stockbridge or Lee, both of which are exits off the Massachusetts Turnpike (Interstate 90). Once here, you can easily walk around the village and drive around the larger area.

ESSENTIALS

Visitor Information Stockbridge Chamber of Commerce. ⊠ *50 Main St.* ☎ *413/298–5200, 413/298–5200* ⊕ *www.stockbridgechamber.org.*

EXPLORING

Berkshire Botanical Gardens. These gardens' 15 acres contain extensive plantings of exotic and native flora—some 2,500 varieties in all—plus greenhouses, ponds, and nature trails. A guided tour, included with admission, leaves Monday–Saturday at 10 am. October's Harvest Festival is by far the biggest of the facility's annual events. ⊠ *5 W. Stockbridge Rd.* ☎ *413/298–3926* ⊕ *www.berkshirebotanical.org* ⊠ *$15* ⊗ *May–Oct., daily 9–5.*

Fodor'sChoice
★ **Chesterwood.** For 33 years, this was the summer home of the sculptor Daniel Chester French (1850–1931), who created *The Minute Man* in Concord and the Lincoln Memorial's famous seated statue of the president in Washington, D.C. Occasional tours are given of the house, which is maintained in the style of the 1920s, but the real prize is the studio, where you can view the casts and models French used to create the Lincoln Memorial. The beautifully landscaped 122-acre grounds make for an enchanting stroll or bucolic picnic. ⊠ *4 Williamsville Rd., off Rte. 183* ☎ *413/298–3579* ⊕ *www.chesterwood.org* ⊠ *$17.50 ($10 grounds only)* ⊗ *May–Oct., daily 10–5.*

Naumkeag. The Berkshire cottage of Joseph Choate (1832–1917), an influential New York City lawyer and the ambassador to Great Britain during President William McKinley's administration, provides a glimpse into the Gilded Age lifestyle. The 44-room gabled mansion, designed by Stanford White and completed in 1887, sits atop Prospect Hill. Its

CLOSE UP

Norman Rockwell: Illustrating America

I was showing the America I knew and observed to others who might not have noticed. My fundamental purpose is to interpret the typical American. I am a storyteller.

—Norman Rockwell

If you've ever seen old copies of the *Saturday Evening Post,* no doubt you're familiar with American artist Norman Rockwell. He created 321 covers for the well-regarded magazine, and the *Post* always sold more copies when one of Rockwell's drawings was on the front page. The accomplished artist also illustrated Boy Scouts of America calendars, Christmas cards, children's books, and even a few stamps for the U.S. Postal Service—in 1994 a stamp bearing his image came out in his honor. His illustrations tended to fit the theme of Americana, family, or patriotism.

Born in New York City in 1894, the talented designer had a knack for art early on but strengthened his talent with instruction at the National Academy of Design and the Art Students League. He was only 22 when he sold his first cover to the *Post.* He married three times and had three sons by his second wife. He died in 1978 in Stockbridge, Massachusetts, where he had lived since 1953.

Famous Rockwell works include his *Triple Self-Portrait* and the *Four Freedoms,* illustrations done during World War II. The latter series of oil paintings represents freedom of speech, freedom of worship, freedom from want, and freedom from fear. In a poetic turn, in 1977, President Gerald R. Ford bestowed on Rockwell the Presidential Medal of Freedom, the highest civilian honor a U.S. citizen can be given. Ford praised Rockwell for his "vivid and affectionate portraits of our country."

5

many original furnishings and artworks span three centuries; the collection of Chinese porcelain is particularly noteworthy. The meticulously kept 8 acres of formal gardens, a three-decade project of Choate's daughter, Mabel, and landscape designer Fletcher Steele, alone make this site worth a visit. ⊠ *5 Prospect Hill Rd.* ☎ *413/298–8138* ⊕ *www. thetrustees.org/places-to-visit/berkshires/naumkeag.html* ⊠ *$15* ⊗ *Late May–mid-Oct., daily 10–5; mid-Oct.–early Dec., weekends 10–4 (call or check website to confirm late-fall hrs).*

Norman Rockwell Museum. This charming museum traces the career of one of America's most beloved illustrators, beginning with his first *Saturday Evening Post* cover in 1916. The crown jewel of the 570 Rockwell illustrations is the famed Four Freedoms gallery, although various works—including his self-portraits—are equally charming. The museum also mounts exhibits of work by other artists. Rockwell's studio was moved to the museum grounds and is complete in every detail. Stroll the 36-acre site, picnic on the grounds, or relax at the outdoor café (late May–mid-October). There's a children's version of the audio tour and a scavenger hunt, as well as a creativity center with art materials. ⊠ *9 Rte. 183* ☎ *413/298–4100* ⊕ *www.nrm.org* ⊠ *$18* ⊗ *May–Oct., daily 10–5; Nov.–Apr., weekdays 10–4, weekends 10–5.*

Stockbridge's churches are among the charming buildings on Main Street.

WHERE TO EAT AND STAY

$$$ ECLECTIC 🍴 **Once Upon a Table.** They picked a cute little name for a cute little restaurant in the mews off Stockbridge's Main Street. And the owners of this upscale eatery picked a menu to match: a small but appealing selection of Continental and contemporary American cuisine. After a sourdough rosemary roll, you can try escargot potpie (a puff pastry over a few snails in garlic butter), or entrées such as seared crab cakes with capers, rack of lamb with garlic mashed potatoes, and duck in raspberry sauce. [$] *Average main: $25* ✉ *36 Main St.* ☎ *413/298–3870* 🌐 *www.onceuponatablebistro.com* ✍ *Reservations essential.*

$$$ FRENCH 🍴 **Rouge.** In West Stockbridge (5 miles northwest), this French restaurant has been such a success that it has expanded to include a bar and a larger dining area. Owner-chef William Merelle is from Provence, where he met his American wife and co-owner, Maggie, formerly a wine merchant. Try the steak au poivre with arugula or the braised duck with shredded potato cake. [$] *Average main: $30* ✉ *3 Center St., West Stockbridge* ☎ *413/232–4111* 🌐 *www.rougerestaurant.com* 🕒 *Closed Mon. and Tues. No lunch* ✍ *Reservations essential.*

$$ VIETNAMESE 🍴 **Truc Orient Express.** Mixed in among shops filled with arts and crafts, this homey restaurant has been serving up authentic Vietnamese food for more than 30 years. *Bánh xèo* (rice pancakes) figure prominently on the menu, among other favorites, but owners Trai Duong and Luy Nguyen go playful with adventurous fare such as *ca chien* (whole fried flounder in a pungent fish sauce). [$] *Average main: $21* ✉ *3 Harris St.* ☎ *413/232–4204* 🕒 *Closed Tues. No lunch.*

$$$
B&B/INN
Fodor's Choice
★
The Inn at Stockbridge. Antique furnishings and feather comforters are among the accents in the guest rooms of this 1906 Georgian Revival inn. **Pros:** beautiful grounds; good breakfast; lovely furniture. **Cons:** noise from highway (most noticeable in suites); not within walking distance of town. $ *Rooms from: $320* ⊠ *30 East St.* ☎ *413/298–3337, 888/466–7865* ⊕ *www.stockbridgeinn.com* ⤳ *7 rooms, 8 suites* |◎| *Breakfast.*

$$$
B&B/INN
Fodor's Choice
★
The Red Lion Inn. An inn since 1773, the Red Lion has hosted presidents, senators, and other celebrities, these days between a large main building and nine annexes. **Pros:** inviting lobby with fireplace; rocking chairs on porch; quaintly romantic. **Cons:** pricey dining; minuscule fitness center; no mobile reception. $ *Rooms from: $304* ⊠ *30 Main St.* ☎ *413/298–5545, 413/298–1690* ⊕ *www.redlioninn.com* ⤳ *125 rooms, 25 suites* |◎| *No meals.*

PERFORMING ARTS

Berkshire Theatre Festival. This summerlong festival has presented plays since 1929. Those on the Main Stage tend to be better-known works with established actors. A smaller theater mounts more experimental works, and the outdoor stage favors family-friendly shows. Festival productions also take place at the Colonial Theatre in Pittsfield. ⊠ *6 Main St.* ☎ *413/298–5576* ⊕ *www.berkshiretheatregroup.org.*

SPAS

Kripalu Center. You'll see many people sitting peacefully on the grounds as you approach this health and yoga retreat proficient at helping patrons achieve a heightened state of grace. Meals always include gluten-free items in addition to more standard fare. ⊠ *57 Interlaken Rd.* ☎ *866/200–5203, 800/741–7353* ⊕ *www.kripalu.org.*

SHOPPING

FAMILY **Williams and Sons Country Store.** Well-worn wooden floors and old-time music provide an authentic feel that pairs well with the country-store staples for sale here: toys, maple goodies, jams, and an abundance of candy. Williams and Sons remains the best general store in the Berkshires. ⊠ *38 Main St.* ☎ *413/298–3016.*

GREAT BARRINGTON

7 miles southwest of Stockbridge; 13 miles north of Canaan, Connecticut.

The largest town in South County became, in 1781, the first place in the United States to free a slave under due process of law and was also the birthplace, in 1868, of W. E. B. DuBois, the civil rights leader, author, and educator. The many ex–New Yorkers who live in Great Barrington expect great food and service, and the restaurants here accordingly deliver complex, delicious fare. The town is also a favorite of antiques hunters, as are the nearby villages of South Egremont and Sheffield. On U.S. 7 alone, dozens of antiques shops await your discerning eye.

GETTING HERE AND AROUND

The nearest international airports are Bradley International Airport in Windsor Locks, Connecticut, and Albany International Airport in Albany, New York, but you are better off driving in on U.S. 7 from either Stockbridge or Canaan, Connecticut. Great Barrington is

CLOSE UP

Massachusetts Farm Stands

Living like a locavore is easy in the Berkshires and Western Massachusetts. The area's many farms produce everything from fruits, vegetables, dairy products, and meat to maple syrup, flowers, and Christmas trees. And you can find any of the above at farm stands throughout the region. Look for spinach, asparagus, maple syrup, and flowers in the spring, an endless array of produce in summer, and apples, cranberries, pumpkins, and squash that seem to mimic the palette of the fall foliage.

FARM STANDS

A great place to find farm stands is south on Route 7 and Route 8. More than 30 can be found along or just off these roads.

YOU-PICK FARMS

Farms where you pick your own produce are popular in Massachusetts. Berry farms and fruit orchards predominate, but there are also pick-your-own pumpkin patches, cornfields, and others.

FOR MORE INFORMATION

Berkshire Grown. To learn more about the region's farms, dairies, and farm-to-table restaurants, check out Berkshire Grown. ⊠ *Great Barrington* ☎ *413/528–0041* ⊕ *www.berkshiregrown.org.*

Northeast Organic Farming Association. This group has information about all things organic in Massachusetts. ⊠ *Barre* ☎ *978/355–2853* ⊕ *www.nofamass.org.*

also on the BRTA bus line from Stockbridge. There's plenty of parking in town, most of which is walkable as well.

ESSENTIALS

Visitor Information Southern Berkshire Chamber of Commerce. ⊠ *362 Main St.* ☎ *413/528–1510, 800/269–4825* ⊕ *www.southernberkshirechamber.com.*

EXPLORING

Fodor'sChoice ★ **Berkshire Mountain Distillers.** The sweet scent of the country's premier craft gin permeates the Berkshires' first legal distillery since prohibition. The retail store, open every afternoon, sells Greylock Gin, a multiple gold-medal winner, and Ethereal Gin, whose ingredients are reimagined every season, among other spirits. Hour-long distillery tours take place on Friday and Saturday. The head distiller, Jon, is friendly, knowledgeable, and happy to pour a taste of a gin, whiskey, or even maple syrup aged in a bourbon cask. ⊠ *356 S. Main St., Sheffield* ☎ *413/229–0219* ⊕ *www.berkshiremountaindistillers.com* 🎟 *Tour $10.*

WHERE TO EAT

$ ✕ **Aroma Bar and Grill.** Popular with college students for its reasonable
INDIAN prices, this restaurant with a green-and-burgundy color scheme serves up good deals at lunch and at Sunday's brunch buffet. The cooks do well with everything from tandoori chicken and other standards to less common dishes such as the moist minced-lamb *seekh* kebab. If you miss the buffet, order a combo appetizer platter or the Raja Thali dinner special to experience the full range of tastes. The naan is so flavorful—especially the stuffed varieties—that you'll almost feel guilty

dousing it with the trio of flavorful chutneys provided. $ *Average main: $15* ⊠ *485 Main St.* ☎ *413/528–3116* ⊕ *www.aromabarandgrill.com* ⊗ *No lunch Mon.*

$ ✕ **Baba Louie's Sourdough Pizza Co.** Is the pizza here good enough to
PIZZA merit the long lines that sometimes stretch out the door? Possibly. Specialty pizzas go far beyond the usual toppings, from the roasted sweet potatoes, parsnips, and fennel on the Isabella Pizzarella to the mozzarella, ricotta, shrimp, pineapple, Canadian bacon, and dried coconut on the Hannah Jo. Weird, but tasty. Baba Louie's fires up sourdough ground wheat, spelt-berry, and gluten-free crusts. Pasta and salads are served, too, but you really ought to order a pizza. Enjoy the trattoria's rustic interior, and try to ignore the din of the crowd. $ *Average main: $13* ⊠ *286 Main St.* ☎ *413/528–8100* ⊕ *www.babalouiespizza.com* ⌲ *Reservations not accepted.*

$$ ✕ **Bizen.** Expect crowds—and, on busy nights, a wait—at this Railroad
JAPANESE Street mainstay for Japanese fare ranging from *robata* (charcoal-grill) to katsu and tempura. Dining room tables wrap around three sides of the large central sushi bar. If not ordering from the extensive sushi menu, try the *harumaki* (deep-fried lobster and fish in rice paper) or the *una jyu* (grilled river eel in a sweet sauce). Many of the dishes are organic. For a special treat, reserve a week ahead for a tea ceremony or to experience the 10-course *kaiseki* tasting menu. $ *Average main: $21* ⊠ *17 Railroad St.* ☎ *413/528–4343* ⊟ *No credit cards.*

$$ ✕ **Castle Street Café.** Chef-owner Michael Ballon wins raves for his
CAFÉ simple but elegant cuisine and masterful hand with fresh area produce. Local artworks, hardwood floors, and sleek furnishings create an understated interior—a perfect backdrop for oysters on the half shell or duck with black-currant sauce. The wine list has smart selections in all price ranges, and the bread basket's warm offerings are the work of the Berkshire Mountain Bakery. The frequent evening jazz may seem ear-splittingly loud if you aren't a fan. $ *Average main: $23* ⊠ *10 Castle St.* ☎ *413/528–5244* ⊕ *www.castlestreetcafe.com* ⊗ *Closed Tues. No lunch.*

WHERE TO STAY

$$ ▦ **The Barrington.** As a third-floor bed-and-breakfast above retail
B&B/INN frontage, the Barrington may lack the exterior aesthetic appeal of its Berkshire peers, but it more than compensates for this by its central Main Street location and spacious, eclectically furnished guest rooms. **Pros:** clean, spacious rooms; conscientious innkeepers; central location; flat-screen TVs; free Wi-Fi. **Cons:** no guest lobby; dismal exterior and hallway; pricey for the setting. $ *Rooms from: $250* ⊠ *281 Main St., 3rd fl.* ☎ *413/528–6159* ⊕ *www.thebarringtongb.com* ⥻ *6 rooms* ⦚○⦚ *Breakfast.*

$ ▦ **Wainright Inn.** Built in 1766 as the Troy Tavern & Inn, this well-run
B&B/INN lodging has wraparound porches on two levels; the ground-floor porch leads into an antiques-filled parlor and a dining room with flowers on the sideboards. **Pros:** good breakfast; within walking distance of downtown; lots of charm. **Cons:** Main Street traffic; no room TVs. $ *Rooms from: $179* ⊠ *518 S. Main St.* ☎ *413/528–2062* ⊕ *www.wainwrightinn. com* ⥻ *8 rooms, 1 suite* ⦚○⦚ *Breakfast.*

PERFORMING ARTS

Mahaiwe Performing Arts Center. Catch a performance by Arlo Guthrie or Béla Fleck at the center's stunning 1905 theater. The year-round schedule includes theater, music, dance, comedy, and film. ⊠ *14 Castle St.* ☎ *413/528–0100* ⊕ *www.mahaiwe.org.*

SPORTS AND THE OUTDOORS

HIKING

A 90-mile swath of the Appalachian Trail cuts through the Berkshires. You'll also find hundreds of miles of trails elsewhere throughout the area's forests and parks.

Appalachian Trail. You can walk part of the Appalachian Trail on a moderately strenuous stretch that leads to Ice Gulch, a gorge so deep and cold that there is often ice in it, even in summer. Follow the Ice Gulch ridge to the shelter and a large, flat rock from which you can enjoy a panoramic view of the valley. The hike takes about 45 minutes one way. ⊠ *Trailhead on Lake Buel Rd., about 100 feet northwest of Deerwood Park Dr.* ⊕ *www.appalachiantrail.org.*

Bartholomew's Cobble. This rock garden beside the Housatonic River (the Native American name means "river beyond the mountains") is a National Natural Landmark, with 5 miles of hiking trails passing through fields of wildflowers. The 277-acre site has a visitor center and a museum, as well as the state's largest cottonwood trees. ⊠ *105 Weatogue Rd., Sheffield* ☎ *413/229–8600* ⊕ *www.thetrustees.org/ places-to-visit/berkshires/bartholomews-cobble.html* ⊠ *$5* ⊙ *Daily dawn–dusk.*

Monument Mountain. For great views with minimal effort, hike Monument Mountain, famous as a spot for literary inspiration. Nathaniel Hawthorne and Herman Melville trekked it on August 5, 1850, seeking shelter in a cave during a thunderstorm. There they discussed ideas that would become part of a novel called *Moby-Dick*. While poet William Cullen Bryant stayed in the area, he penned a lyrical poem, "Monument Mountain," about a lovesick Mohican maiden who jumped to her death from the cliffs. Most hikers find the 2½-mile loop an easy stroll. ⊠ *Trailhead at parking lot on west side of U.S. 7, 3 miles north of Rte. 183* ☎ *413/298–3239* ⊕ *www.thetrustees.org/places-to-visit/berkshires/ monument-mountain.html.*

SKI AREAS

Catamount Ski Area. Skiers seeking a family experience often end up here. Although it's not the biggest mountain in the area, Catamount can be less crowded than other options when it's not a holiday weekend, and the terrain is varied. The Sidewinder, an intermediate cruising trail, is more than 1 mile from top to bottom. Just watch out for ice on the tougher trails. There's also night skiing and snowboarding, plus three terrain parks for snowboarders and others. **Facilities:** 36 trails; 130 acres; 1,000-foot vertical drop; 7 lifts. ⊠ *3290 Rte. 23, South Egremont* ☎ *413/528–1262, 413/528–1262 for snow conditions* ⊕ *www.catamountski.com* ⊠ *Lift ticket: $35.*

Ski Butternut. With a variety of trails and slopes, including a 1½-mile run, Ski Butternut is good for skiers of all ability levels. There are a few beginner and advanced trails, and more than half the mountain is mellow intermediate terrain. For snowboarders there are top-to-bottom terrain parks and a beginner park, and eight lanes are available for snow tubing. Eleven lifts, including four carpet lifts and the longest quad in the Berkshires, keep traffic spread out. **Facilities:** 22 trails; 110 acres; 1,000-foot vertical drop; 11 lifts. ⊠ *380 State Rd.* ☎ *413/528–2000, 413/528–4433 for ski school, 800/438–7669 for snow conditions* ⊕ *www.skibutternut.com* 🎟 *Lift ticket: $60.*

SHOPPING

ANTIQUES

The Great Barrington area, including the small towns of Sheffield and South Egremont, has the Berkshires' greatest concentration of antiques stores. Some shops are open sporadically, and many are closed on Tuesday.

Elise Abrams Antiques. The owner of this store selling dining-related antique porcelain, glassware, and tabletop accessories is an expert in the field. The prices match the high quality of her selections. ⊠ *11 Stockbridge Rd., near Rte. 183* ☎ *413/528–3201* ⊕ *www.eliseabramsantiques. com* ☉ *Closed Tues. and Wed.*

Great Barrington Antiques Center. The feeling is "indoor flea market" in this space, where 30-plus dealers sell Oriental rugs, vintage furniture, and smaller decorative pieces. ⊠ *964 S. Main St.* ☎ *413/644–8848* ⊕ *www.greatbarringtonantiquescenter.com.*

CRAFTS

Sheffield Pottery. Many of the roughly 100 local potters whose creative output can be found here use native Sheffield clay to fashion their vases, birdbaths, colorful dinner platters, and other ceramics. The resident shop cat adds to the down-home ambience. In addition to the diverse pottery, ceramics supplies are available for purchase. ⊠ *995 N. Main St., Sheffield* ☎ *888/774–2529* ⊕ *www.americanmadepottery.com.*

FOOD

Bizalion. This French specialty food shop carries imported cheeses, cured meats, and olive oils from local producers, who also sell their wares to fancy restaurants in New York City and Martha's Vineyard. Bizalion doubles as an informal eatery; on their small menu are some appealing sandwiches, including one with arugula, pine nuts, prosciutto, goat cheese, and olive oil on toasted bread. ⊠ *684 Main St.* ☎ *413/644–9988* ⊕ *www.bizalions.com.*

Blueberry Hill Farm. Organic blueberries are ripe for the picking here on midsummer weekends. Bring your own container; payment is by cash or check only. ⊠ *100 East St., about 10 miles southwest of Great Barrington, Mount Washington* ☎ *413/528–1479* ⊕ *www.austinfarm. com* 🎟 *Free.*

Boardman's Farm Stand. Known for its sweet corn, Boardman's makes a fine quick stop to pick up fresh fruits and vegetables, from pumpkins and peppers to peaches and nectarines. ⊠ *64 Hewins St., off Maple Ave., southeast from U.S. 7, Sheffield* ☎ *413/229–8554.*

Howden Farm. About 4 miles south of the town center, you can pick raspberries mid-August–mid-October and pumpkins late September–October. Locals have snatched up the farm's sweet corn for decades. ⊠ *303 Rannapo Rd., off Rte. 7A, Sheffield* ☎ *413/229–8481* ⊕ *www.howdenfarm.com.*

FAMILY **Taft Farms.** Raspberries ripen here early July–mid-October, and you can pick your own pumpkin September–October. Grab a roast turkey (or other) sandwich, served on freshly baked bread, for a fine homemade lunch. If you have time to linger, check out the small turtle pond in the plant nursery. ⊠ *119 Park St. N* ☎ *413/528–1515* ⊕ *www.taftfarms.com.*

HOME DECOR

Fodor's Choice **Asia Barong.** The eye-catching sculptures visible from the roadside only
★ hint at the vast spectacle inside what bills itself as America's largest Asian art store. Carvings of every conceivable material (from wood to whalebone), size (from half an inch to 8 feet tall), and subject matter (albeit heavy on the gods and dragons) can be found here. The sheer volume of art outstrips many museums, but you can still buy a traditional sarong or a gift from the $5 shelves. Humorous signs throughout the store add a touch of character. ⊠ *199 Stockbridge Rd.* ☎ *413/528–5091* ⊕ *www.asiabarong.com.*

STURBRIDGE AND THE PIONEER VALLEY

Historic settlements line the majestic Connecticut River, the wide and winding waterway that runs through Western Massachusetts. Springfield, known for its family-friendly attractions and museums, and a cluster of college towns and quaint, rural villages, form a highly visible portion of the Pioneer Valley.

Educational pioneers established major colleges, including Mount Holyoke, Amherst, Smith, Hampshire, and the University of Massachusetts. Northampton and Amherst serve as cultural hubs; both have become desirable places to live, drawing former city dwellers who relish the ample natural scenery, sophisticated cultural venues, and lively dining and shopping.

SPRINGFIELD

90 miles west of Boston; 30 miles north of Hartford, Connecticut.

Springfield is the busy hub of the Pioneer Valley. Known as the birthplace of basketball—the game was devised here in 1891 as a gym instructor's last-ditch attempt to keep a group of unruly teenagers occupied in winter—the city also has a cluster of fine museums and family attractions.

GETTING HERE AND AROUND

Springfield is roughly the center of Massachusetts, accessible by bus, train, and Interstates 90 and 91. Parts of Springfield are walkable, but you're better off driving or using the local PVTA buses.

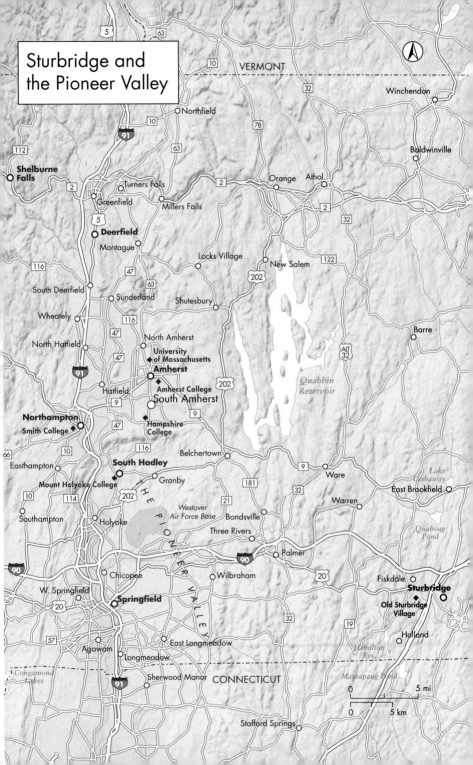

Sturbridge and the Pioneer Valley

VERMONT

Winchendon

Northfield

Boldwinville

Shelburne Falls

Turners Falls

Orange Athol

Greenfield

Millers Falls

Deerfield

Montague

Locks Village

New Salem

South Deerfield

Sunderland

Shutesbury

Barre

Wheately

North Amherst

North Hatfield

University of Massachusetts

Amherst

Quabbin Reservoir

Hatfield

Amherst College

South Amherst

Northampton

Hampshire College

Smith College

Belchertown

Ware

Lake Lashaway

Easthampton

South Hadley

Granby

East Brookfield

Mount Holyoke College

Westover Air Force Base

Warren

Quaboag Pond

Southampton

Holyoke

Bondsville

Three Rivers

Palmer

THE PIONEER VALLEY

Chicopee

Wilbraham

Fiskdale

Sturbridge

W. Springfield

Old Sturbridge Village

Springfield

Holland

Agawam

East Longmeadow

Hamilton Res.

Congamond Lakes

Longmeadow

Mashapaug Pond

Sherwood Manor

CONNECTICUT

0   5 mi

0   5 km

Stafford Springs

ESSENTIALS

Visitor Information Greater Springfield Convention & Visitors Bureau.
✉ *1441 Main St.* ☎ *413/787–1548, 800/723–1548* ⊕ *www.valleyvisitor.com.*
Sturbridge Area Tourist Association. ✉ *380 Main St., Sturbridge* ☎ *800/628-8379, 508/347–2761* ⊕ *www.sturbridgetownships.com.*

EXPLORING

FAMILY
Fodor's Choice
★
Naismith Memorial Basketball Hall of Fame. Along the banks of the Connecticut River, this 80,000-square-foot facility is named for Dr. James Naismith, the Canadian phys-ed instructor who invented the game of basketball in 1891 during his five years at Springfield's YMCA Training Center. High-profile players such as Michael Jordan and Kareem Abdul-Jabbar of the NBA and Nancy Lieberman of the WNBA are among the nearly 300 enshrinees, but the hall celebrates the accomplishments of players, coaches, and others at all levels of the sport. In addition to displays chronicling basketball history, the hall has a soaring domed arena where you can practice jumpers, walls of inspirational quotes you can view, dozens of interactive exhibits, and video footage and interviews with former players. The hall is easy to find: look for the 15-story spire with an illuminated basketball on top. ✉ *1000 W. Columbus Ave.* ☎ *413/781–6500, 877/446–6752* ⊕ *www.hoophall.com* 🎟 *$22* ◷ *Sun.–Fri. 10–4, Sat. 10–5.*

FAMILY
Six Flags New England. With more than 160 rides and shows, this massive attraction is the region's largest theme and water park. You can visit Looney Tunes town and climb aboard DC Superhero rides such as Batman: The Dark Knight and Superman: The Ride, which is more than 20 stories tall and has a top speed of 77 mph. New rides are added frequently, like the Wicked Cyclone, a hybrid wooden structure with a steel track, and the Fireball, a seven-story loop coaster. Visit in autumn to catch Fright Fest haunted events and attractions. ✉ *1623 Main St., Agawam* ☎ *413/786–9300* ⊕ *www.sixflags.com/newengland* 🎟 *$60* ◷ *Hrs vary.*

> **QUICK BITES**
>
> **La Fiorentina Pastry Shop.** Springfield's South End is home to a lively Little Italy, including this shop that has doled out heavenly pastries and coffees since the 1940s. The chocolate-covered cannoli, complete with gilded lilies, are especially good. ✉ *883 Main St.* ☎ *413/732–3151* ⊕ *www.lafiorentinapastry.com* ◷ *Mon.–Sat. 8–6, Sun. 8–2.*

FAMILY
Springfield Museums. This complex of museums in what's known as the Quadrangle includes four impressive facilities (single admission), plus a free sculpture garden. The must-see **George Walter Vincent Smith Art Museum** houses a fascinating private art collection that includes a salon gallery with 19th-century American paintings by Frederic Church and Albert Bierstadt. The Japanese antiquities room is filled with armor, textiles, and porcelain, as well as carved jade and rock-crystal snuff bottles. The **Museum of Fine Arts** has paintings by Paul Gauguin, Claude Monet, Pierre-Auguste Renoir, Edgar Degas, Winslow Homer, and J. Alden Weir, as well as 18th-century American paintings and contemporary works by Georgia O'Keeffe, Frank Stella, and George Bellows. The **Springfield Science Museum** has an Exploration Center of touchable

displays, the oldest operating planetarium in the United States, dinosaur exhibits, an extensive collection of stuffed and mounted animals, and the African Hall, through which you can take an interactive tour of that continent's flora and fauna. The **Museum of Springfield History** tells the story of the town's manufacturing heritage. Springfield was home to the former Indian Motorcycle Company, and the museum has a rich collection of Indian bikes and memorabilia.

Also amid the Quadrangle is the free **Dr. Seuss National Memorial Sculpture Garden,** an installation of bronze statues depicting scenes from Theodor Geisel's famously whimsical children's books. Born in Springfield in 1904, Geisel was inspired by the animals at the Zoo in Forest Park, where his father served as director. The first phase of **The Amazing World of Dr. Seuss Museum** is set to open here in 2016. ⊠ *220 State St.* ☎ *413/263–6800* ⊕ *www.springfieldmuseums.org* ⊠ *$18* ⊙ *Tues.–Sat. 10–5, Sun. 11–5.*

FAMILY **Zoo in Forest Park and Education Center.** At this leafy, 735-acre retreat, hiking paths wind through the trees, paddleboats navigate Porter Lake, and hungry ducks float on a small pond. The zoo, where Theodor Geisel—better known as Dr. Seuss—found inspiration for his children's books, is home to nearly 200 animals, from black bears and bobcats to lemurs and wallabies. It's manageable in size, and spotting animals in the exhibits is fairly easy, which makes this an especially good stop for families with small children. Another plus: you can purchase small bags of food from the gift shop and feed many of the animals. Leave time to explore the park after you finish the zoo. ⊠ *302 Sumner Ave.* ☎ *413/733–2251* ⊕ *www.forestparkzoo.org* ⊠ *$9* ⊙ *Weekdays 10–3, weekends 10–4.*

OFF THE BEATEN PATH **Old Sturbridge Village.** A re-creation of a New England village circa 1790–1840, this site contains more than 40 historic buildings moved here from other towns. There are several industrial buildings, including a working sawmill, and guides in period costumes demonstrate home-based crafts like spinning, weaving, and shoemaking. In season, take an informative stagecoach ride, or cruise the Quinebaug River while learning about river life in 19th-century New England and catching glimpses of ducks, geese, turtles, and other local wildlife. Other popular seasonal events include Christmas by Candlelight during the last week of December, and summer's Redcoats to Rebels reenactment brigade. ⊠ *1 Old Sturbridge Village Rd.* ☎ *508/347–3362, 800/733–1830* ⊕ *www. osv.org* ⊠ *$28* ⊙ *May–Oct., daily 9:30–5; Nov., Wed.–Sun. 9:30–4; early Dec.–late Dec., Fri.–Sun. 4–9; late Dec.–Feb., weekends 9:30–4.*

WHERE TO EAT

$ CAJUN Fodor's Choice ★ ✕ **Big Mamou.** This casual joint serves up some seriously good Louisiana grub. Their only room can get loud and crowded: at a table for two, you may find yourself chatting with the next table over, but it will likely be about how good the food is. Owner-chef Wayne Booker's hometown recipes, among them sausage and chicken ya-ya (chicken breast wrapped around andouille sausage with creole spices) never fail to satisfy. Other favorites include shrimp-and-sausage jambalaya, barbecue pulled pork, and the namesake "Big Mamou," a blend of shrimp and

Costumed historians are part of the 19th-century Old Sturbridge Village.

crayfish in a lobster-brandy cream sauce. Added bonus: you can bring your own bottle. [$] *Average main: $16* ✉ *63 Liberty St.* ☎ *413/732–1011* 🌐 *www.chefwaynes-bigmamou.com* 🕓 *No dinner Sun. No lunch Sun. June–Sept.* ✍ *Reservations not accepted.*

$ VIETNAMESE 🍴 **Pho Saigon.** A little out of the way, this understated eatery serves authentic Vietnamese cuisine at wallet-pleasing prices. Enjoy the made-from-scratch soups and the shrimp cakes with shredded yams. House specialties include beef pho, fried soft-shell crab, and the "happy pancake," a rice-batter crêpe stuffed with shrimp and chicken. There are many vegetarian options, too. Don't park in the lot across the street or you may get towed; if the restaurant lot is full, park on the street. [$] *Average main: $10* ✉ *400 Dickinson St.* ☎ *413/781–4488* 🌐 *www.phosaigonspringfield.com* 🕓 *Closed Wed.*

$ ITALIAN 🍴 **Red Rose.** Featuring massive chandeliers, an open kitchen, and a large dining area, this half-century-old family restaurant is a big, brassy eatery where everyone from canoodling couples to huge parties can feel right at home. The eggplant is exquisite, whether you get crispy-light baked pieces along with ricotta cheese atop a Primavera pizza, or a full meal of sumptuous eggplant Parmesan. The rest of the menu runs to typical Italian favorites, from heaping platters of pasta to pizzas served atop giant tomato cans. [$] *Average main: $17* ✉ *1060 Main St.* ☎ *413/739–8510* 🌐 *www.redrosepizzeria.com* 🕓 *Closed Mon.* ✍ *Reservations essential.*

$$ GERMAN Fodor's Choice ★ 🍴 **Student Prince.** Impressive beer-stein and corkscrew collections and dark-wood paneling lend this restaurant inside an old fort the feel of convivial hunting lodge. The fried Camembert and a few salads notwithstanding, the menu is decidedly meat-centric—beef, chicken, veal,

lamb, pork, and sausage—with a nod to Bay State fish and seafood. The main attractions are German dishes such as *hoppel poppel* ("farmer's omelet," with eggs, onion, potato, bacon, and hot dogs), *jaeger schnitzel* (veal steak), sauerbraten served with potato dumplings and cabbage, *eisbein* (pig knuckle), and very good sauerkraut. In winter, try the *weisswurst* (sausage made with veal and fresh pork bacon). $ *Average main: $21* ⊠ *8 Fort St.* ☎ *413/734–7475* ⊕ *www.studentprince.com.*

WHERE TO STAY

$
B&B/INN
Naomi's Inn. This elegantly restored house in a residential neighborhood has individually decorated suites, all with lush comfort and artistic flair. **Pros:** elegantly designed; luxe linens and other fabrics; warm and knowledgeable hosts. **Cons:** near a hospital, so you may hear sirens. $ *Rooms from: $150* ⊠ *20 Springfield St.* ☎ *413/433–6019, 888/762–6647* ⊕ *www.naomisinn.net* ⤳ *6 suites* �‖ *Breakfast.*

$
B&B/INN
Fodor's Choice
★
The Publick House. Step back in time at this rambling 1771 inn, whose guest rooms have wide plank floors and a few period antiques and reproductions. **Pros:** Colonial ambience and architecture; historical significance; free Wi-Fi; flat-screen TVs. **Cons:** slanted hallway floor; thin walls, loud pipes; small step-up bathrooms. $ *Rooms from: $185* ⊠ *277 Main St., Sturbridge* ☎ *508/347–3313, 800/782–5425* ⊕ *www.publickhouse.com* ⤳ *14 rooms, 3 suites in main inn* �‖ *No meals.*

$
B&B/INN
Sturbridge Country Inn. This homey 1840s Greek Revival farmhouse on Sturbridge's busy Main Street is an ideal option for visitors looking for modest accommodations in a friendly, come-as-you-are atmosphere. **Pros:** welcoming vibe; large lobby with board games and a player piano; free Wi-Fi; flat-screen TVs in some rooms. **Cons:** unsophisticated interiors; some rooms have old TVs and furniture. $ *Rooms from: $99* ⊠ *530 Main St., Sturbridge* ☎ *508/347–5503* ⊕ *www.sturbridgecountryinn. com* ⤳ *12 rooms, 4 suites* �‖ *No meals.*

SOUTH HADLEY

12 miles north of Springfield.

A quiet college town with a cluster of Main Street cafés and stores, South Hadley is surrounded by rolling hills and farmland. It's best known for the Mount Holyoke College Art Museum, one of the region's finest cultural facilities.

GETTING HERE AND AROUND

With Bradley International Airport and the Springfield Amtrak station to the south, South Hadley is easy to access. By car, it's east of Interstate 91 and north of U.S. 202 at the intersection of Route 47 and Route 116. You can walk around the Mount Holyoke campus, but you'll need to drive to get most anywhere else.

EXPLORING

Mount Holyoke College. Founded in 1837, Mount Holyoke was the first women's college in the United States. Among its alumnae are poet Emily Dickinson and playwright Wendy Wasserstein. The handsome wooded campus, encompassing two lakes and lovely walking or riding trails, was landscaped by Frederick Law Olmsted, the co-designer of Manhattan's Central Park. ✉ *50 College St.* ☎ *413/538–2000* 🌐 *www.mtholyoke.edu.*

Mount Holyoke College Art Museum. The 24,000 works in the college's collection include Asian, European, and American paintings, as well as sculpture and contemporary art from around the world. The coins and numismatics exhibit is definitely worth a look. ✉ *Lower Lake Rd., 3 blocks north of Morgan St.* ☎ *413/538–2245* 🌐 *www.mtholyoke.edu/artmuseum* 🎟 *Free* 🕒 *Tues.–Fri. 11–5, weekends 1–5.*

WHERE TO EAT AND STAY

$ AMERICAN FAMILY 🍴 **Flayvors of Cook Farm.** The main advantage of stopping for the delicious homemade ice cream at this family farm is that you can see the dairy cows from the dining tables—and even pet them, if you are brave. [$] *Average main: $5* ✉ *Cook Farm, 129 S. Maple St., Hadley* ☎ *413/584–2224* 🌐 *www.flayvors.com.*

$$$ ECLECTIC 🍴 **Food 101 Bar & Bistro.** There's nothing basic about this popular, candlelit restaurant across from the Mount Holyoke campus. Dishes are complicated but mostly successful: try the upscale *pommes frites* (french fries) with spicy ketchup and wasabi mayonnaise, the pan-seared sea scallops with cauliflower risotto, or the beet, chèvre, and mâche salad in warm curry oil. This spot is a magnet for foodies, yuppies, and college students on their parents' tabs. From the fancy plating to the nice lighting, the atmosphere almost justifies the high prices. [$] *Average main: $25* ✉ *19 College St.* ☎ *413/535–3101* 🌐 *www.food101bistro.com* 🕒 *Closed Mon. No lunch.*

$ B&B/INN 🏨 **Daniel Stebbins House Bed & Breakfast.** Within walking distance of downtown and Mount Holyoke, this 1795 Federal-style inn has been elegantly renovated to include four second-floor guest rooms, all with period antiques, fine reproductions, and gas fireplaces. **Pros:** the most elegant choice in town; lush linens and bed coverings; pretty landscaping; free Wi-Fi. **Cons:** thin walls; close quarters. [$] *Rooms from: $135* ✉ *25 Woodbridge St.* ☎ *413/533–2149* 🌐 *www.danielstebbinsbedandbreakfast.com* 🛏 *4 rooms* 🍽 *Breakfast.*

SHOPPING

The Odyssey Bookshop. In addition to stocking 50,000 new and used titles, Odyssey has readings and book signings by locally (and sometimes nationally) known authors. There's a special event nearly every night. ✉ *9 College St.* ☎ *413/534–7307* 🌐 *www.odysseybks.com.*

NORTHAMPTON

10 miles northeast of South Hadley.

The cultural center of Western Massachusetts is without a doubt the city of Northampton (nicknamed "Noho"), whose vibrant downtown is packed with interesting restaurants, lively clubs, and offbeat boutiques. The city attracts artsy types, academics, activists, lesbians and gays, and just about anyone else seeking the culture and sophistication of a big metropolis but the conviviality and easy pace of a small town.

GETTING HERE AND AROUND

Amtrak's *Vermonter* train, which travels between Washington, D.C., and St. Albans, Vermont, stops in Northampton. The city is also served by buses from nearby Springfield's train station, although most people arrive by car on Interstate 91. Downtown is crossed by Routes 5, 9, and 10, and walking to most downtown locations is not only possible, but an excellent way to spend an afternoon. Local PVTA buses are also available.

ESSENTIALS

Visitor Information Greater Northampton Chamber of Commerce. ⊠ *99 Pleasant St.* ☎ *413/584–1900, 800/238–6869* ⊕ *www.explorenorthampton.com.*

EXPLORING

Calvin Coolidge Presidential Library and Museum. Opened in 1894, the Romanesque-style Forbes Library is one of the city's most distinguished buildings. The Hosmer Gallery on the upper floor has some artwork, but the main draw is the Calvin Coolidge Presidential Library and Museum, within the Forbes Library. Northampton was the 30th president's Massachusetts home, where he practiced law and served as mayor (1910–1911). Some of his papers and memorabilia are collected here, at the only public library in the United States to hold a presidential collection. ⊠ *20 West St.* ☎ *413/587–1011* ⊕ *www.forbeslibrary.org* ⊗ *Mon. 9–5, Tues. and Thurs. 1–5, Wed. 4–9.*

QUICK BITES
Herrell's Ice Cream. On the lower level of Thornes Marketplace, Herrell's is famous for its chocolate pudding, vanilla malt, and cinnamon nutmeg flavors, as well as for its delicious homemade hot fudge. ⊠ *8 Old South St.* ☎ *413/586–9700* ⊕ *www.herrells.com.*

FAMILY
Fodor's Choice
★
R. Michelson Galleries. In an unassuming former bank lies a rich gallery of works by dozens of children's book illustrators, from Maurice Sendak to Mo Willems. You can also view photos by Leonard Nimoy, and there's a Dr. Seuss area with a few sculptures along with his illustrations. ⊠ *132 Main St.* ☎ *413/586–3964* ⊕ *www.rmichelson.com* ⊗ *Mon.–Wed. 10–6, Thurs.–Sat. 10–9, Sun. noon–5.*

Smith College. The nation's largest liberal arts college for women opened its doors in 1875, funded by a bequest from Sophia Smith, a local heiress. Renowned for its School of Social Work, Smith has a long list of distinguished alumnae, among them activist Gloria Steinem, chef Julia Child, and writer Margaret Mitchell. One of New England's most serene campuses, Smith is a leading center of political and cultural activity. The on-campus **Lyman Plant House** is worth a visit. The flourishing **Botanic Garden of Smith College** covers the entire 150-acre campus. ⊠ *College La.* ☎ *413/584–2700* ⊕ *www.smith.edu.*

Smith College Museum of Art. A floor of skylighted galleries, an enclosed courtyard, and a high-tech library make up this museum, whose permanent collection's highlights include pivotal paintings by Mary Cassatt, Paul Cézanne, Edgar Degas, Georgia O'Keeffe, Auguste Rodin, and Georges Seurat. More recent acquisitions include African, Asian, and Islamic art. ⊠ *Brown Fine Arts Center, 22 Elm St., at Bedford Terr.*

☎ *413/585–2760* 🌐 *www.smith.edu/artmuseum* 🎫 *$5 (free 2nd Fri. of month 4–8)* ⏲ *Tues.–Sat. 10–4, Sun. noon–4.*

WHERE TO EAT

$ ITALIAN 🍴 **Mulino's Restaurant.** In sleek second-floor quarters, this modern trattoria carefully serves home-style Italian food. You'll rarely taste a better carbonara sauce on this side of the Atlantic, but don't overlook the melt-in-your-mouth veal saltimbocca. Portions are huge, and the wine list is varied, making this a popular destination for college kids with their families. [$] *Average main: $18* ✉ *41 Strong Ave., 2nd fl.* ☎ *413/586–8900* 🌐 *www.mulinosrestaurant.com* ⏲ *No lunch.*

$ AMERICAN 🍴 **Northampton Brewery.** In a rambling building in Brewster Court, this noisy and often-packed pub has extensive outdoor seating on a deck. The kitchen turns out sandwiches and comfort food, including stuffed peppers and burgers with blue cheese and caramelized onions. The main draws here, though, are the local and international brews, best enjoyed with some appetizers to wash down. [$] *Average main: $18* ✉ *11 Brewster Ct., near Hampton Ave.* ☎ *413/584–9903* 🌐 *www.northamptonbrewery.com* ✍ *Reservations not accepted.*

$$ ITALIAN Fodor's Choice ★ 🍴 **Spoleto.** Local favorite Spoleto offers a something-for-everyone menu: beef, chicken, and seafood dishes served with flair and flavor. Pizza and pasta are mainstays, but there are adventurous choices as well, among them the house-made wild boar sausage. Service can be spotty, especially on busy nights, but you can console yourself with a glass of wine from the extensive list. [$] *Average main: $24* ✉ *1 Bridge St.* ☎ *413/586–6313* 🌐 *www.spoletorestaurants.com* ⏲ *No lunch.*

NIGHTLIFE AND PERFORMING ARTS

Bishop's Lounge. Depending on the night, the lineup here might include live music, DJ sets, stand-up comedy, or even karaoke. There's sometimes a small cover charge, sometimes not. ✉ *41 Strong Ave., 3rd fl.* ☎ *413/586–8900.*

Diva's Nightclub. This spacious club serves the region's sizable lesbian and gay community with great music that fills the cavernous dance floor. ✉ *492 Pleasant St.* ☎ *413/586–8161* 🌐 *www.divasofnoho.com* ⏲ *Closed Mon. and Tues.*

Fitzwilly's. A reliable choice for a night out, Fitzwilly's draws a friendly mix of locals and tourists for drinks and tasty pub fare. (Try the sliders.) ✉ *23 Main St.* ☎ *413/584–8666* 🌐 *www.fitzwillys.com.*

Hugo's. A bit of a dive, the dimly lighted Hugo's has cheap beer, affordable pool, a rocking jukebox, and all the local color you could want. ✉ *315 Pleasant St.* ☎ *413/387–6023.*

SPORTS AND THE OUTDOORS

FAMILY **Norwottuck Rail Trail.** Part of the Connecticut River Greenway State Park, this paved 10-mile path links Northampton with Belchertown by way of Amherst. Great for biking, rollerblading, jogging, and cross-country skiing, it runs along the old Boston & Maine Railroad route. Free trail maps are available on the Mass.gov website. ✉ *446 Damon Rd., at Rte. 9* ☎ *413/586–8706* 🌐 *www.mass.gov/eea/agencies/dcr/massparks/region-west/norwottuck-rail-trail.html.*

SHOPPING

Ten Thousand Villages. Purchasing this shop's fair-trade crafts—including home-decor items and very stylish jewelry, scarves, and handbags—supports artisans in developing countries. ⊠ *82 Main St.* ☎ *413/582–9338* ⊕ *northampton.tenthousandvillages.com.*

Fodor's Choice
★
Thornes Marketplace. A quintessential stop on any Northampton visit—and not just because the market's centrally located garage is your best bet for convenient parking—Thornes contains an eclectic lineup of shops, among them **Cedar Chest** for home goods, **Glimpse of Tibet** for Tibetan handicrafts, and **Herrell's Ice Cream** and **Captain Candy** for sweets and desserts. Also here are **Booklink Booksellers,** a yoga studio, a chair-massage parlor, and clothing and jewelry stores. ⊠ *150 Main St.* ☎ *413/584–5582* ⊕ *www.thornesmarketplace.com.*

AMHERST

5

8 miles northeast of Northampton.

Fodor's Choice
★
One of New England's most visited spots, Amherst is known for its scores of world-renowned authors, poets, and artists. The above-average intelligence quotient of its population is no accident, as Amherst is home to a trio of colleges, Amherst, Hampshire, and the University of Massachusetts. Art galleries, book and music stores, and several downtown cultural venues tickle the intellectual fancy of the college-age crowd, the locals, and the profs.

GETTING HERE AND AROUND

The closest airport is Bradley International in Connecticut. Amtrak's *Vermonter* train stops in nearby Northampton. From there you can take a PVTA bus into town, where the buses are also a good way to get around. If driving, reduce hassle by bringing change for the parking kiosks.

ESSENTIALS

Visitor Information Amherst Area Chamber of Commerce. ⊠ *28 Amity St.* ☎ *413/253–0700* ⊕ *www.amherstarea.com.*

EXPLORING

Emily Dickinson Museum. The famed Amherst poet lived and wrote in this brick Federal-style home. Admission is by guided tour only, and to say that the tour guides are knowledgeable would be a massive understatement; the highlight of the tour is the sunlit bedroom where the poet wrote many of her works. Next door is **The Evergreens,** the imposing Italianate Victorian mansion in which Emily's brother Austin and his family resided for more than 50 years. ⊠ *280 Main St.* ☎ *413/542–8161* ⊕ *www.emilydickinsonmuseum.org* 🎟 *$12* ⊗ *Mar.–May and Sept.–Dec., Wed.–Sun. 11–4; June–Aug., Wed.–Sun. 10–5.*

QUICK BITES

The Black Sheep. Newspapers are strewn about the tables at this funky downtown café specializing in creative sandwiches, salads, and soups. Baked goods are impressive in both size and taste. This is a great place to pick up on the college vibe, enjoy a cup of coffee, and take advantage of free Wi-Fi. The Black Sheep is unabashedly political, not only with the signs

in the windows, but also the naming of some menu items, which will likely amuse liberals more than conservatives. ✉ ***79 Main St.*** ☎ ***413/253–3442*** 🌐 ***www.blacksheepdeli.com*** 🕑 ***Daily 7–7.***

FAMILY Fodor's Choice ★ **Eric Carle Museum of Picture Book Art.** If you have kids in tow—or if you just love children's book illustrations—"the Carle" is a must-see. This light-filled museum celebrates and preserves not only the works of renowned children's book author Eric Carle, who penned *The Very Hungry Caterpillar,* but also original picture-book art by Maurice Sendak, William Steig, Chris Van Allsburg, and many others. Puppet shows and storytelling events are among the museum's ongoing programs. Children are invited to create their own works of art in the studio or read classics or discover new authors in the library. ✉ *125 W. Bay Rd.* ☎ *413/658–1100* 🌐 *www.picturebookart.org* 🎟 *$9* 🕑 *Tues.–Fri. 10–4, Sat. 10–5, Sun. noon–5.*

Yiddish Book Center. Founded in 1980, this nonprofit organization received a National Medal for Museum and Library Service for its role in preserving the Yiddish language and Jewish culture. The award recognized the center's rescue of more than a million Yiddish books that might otherwise have been lost. Housed in a cool, contemporary structure that mimics a traditional Eastern European *shtetl,* or village, the collection comprises more than 100,000 volumes. Special programs take place throughout the year. The biggest is Yidstock, a mid-July festival celebrating klezmer and other Jewish music. ✉ *Hampshire College, 1021 West St.* ☎ *413/256–4900* 🌐 *www.yiddishbookcenter.org* 🎟 *$8* 🕑 *Sun.–Fri. 10–4; tours Sun. at 11 and 1. Closed Jewish holidays.*

WHERE TO EAT AND STAY

$ BARBECUE 🍴 **Bub's Bar-B-Q.** You can smell the sweet and tangy homemade barbecue sauce even before you enter this down-home rib joint. Your eyes may wander to the sides bar filled with orange-glazed sweet potatoes and spicy ranch beans, but the main attraction is the heaping platters of falling-off-the-bone ribs and pulled pork. Then again, who can turn down fried gator tail and hush puppies? The atmosphere is low on pretension and high on charm, from the free jukebox and table trivia cards to the stuffed-monkey ordering system. There's plenty of outdoor seating when the weather cooperates. [$] *Average main: $14* ✉ *676 Amherst Rd., Sunderland* ☎ *413/548–9630* 🌐 *www.bubsbbq.com* 🕑 *Closed Mon. No lunch Tues.–Fri.*

$$ AMERICAN Fodor's Choice ★ 🍴 **Judie's.** Since 1977, academic types have crowded around small tables on Judie's glassed-in porch, ordering traditional dishes like grilled chicken with lobster ravioli, steak and potatoes, seafood gumbo, and a marvelous French onion soup. Your best bet? Try the more creative popover specials in flavors such as gumbo and shrimp scampi. The atmosphere is hip and artsy; a painting covers each tabletop. [$] *Average main: $23* ✉ *51 N. Pleasant St.* ☎ *413/253–3491* 🌐 *www.judiesrestaurant.com* ✍ *Reservations not accepted.*

$ MEXICAN 🍴 **Mission Cantina.** Diners pack this cantina daily to enjoy Mexican food at reasonable prices. What the single-page menu lacks in variety, it makes up for in reliability: everything from the crispy fish tacos to the mole enchiladas is worth trying. If the giant sangria doesn't seem perky enough, order one of the offbeat margaritas such as hibiscus or grilled pineapple. Show up early for dinner to avoid a long wait. [$] *Average main: $13* ✉ *485 West St.* ☎ *413/230–3580* 🌐 *missioncantinaamherst.com* 🕒 *No lunch weekends.*

$ B&B/INN Fodor'sChoice ★ 🏨 **Allen House Inn.** Meticulous attention to detail distinguishes this late-19th-century inn owned by a husband-and-wife team. **Pros:** charm and elegance; great linens; free parking. **Cons:** ornate furnishings may be a bit much for some; tiny baths. [$] *Rooms from: $175* ✉ *599 Main St.* ☎ *413/253–5000* 🌐 *www.allenhouse.com* 🛏 *14 rooms* 🍴 *Breakfast.*

$$$ B&B/INN 🏨 **The Lord Jeffery Inn at Amherst College.** On the town common of downtown Amherst, this rambling 1926 inn owned by Amherst College is a favorite among visiting parents and professors. **Pros:** great location on the town common. **Cons:** some baths are closet-size; many wedding, school, and graduation celebrations are held here. [$] *Rooms from: $315* ✉ *30 Boltwood Ave.* ☎ *413/253–2576* 🌐 *www.lordjefferyinn.com* 🛏 *36 rooms, 13 suites* 🍴 *No meals.*

5

NIGHTLIFE AND PERFORMING ARTS

Hangar Pub and Grill. Beers brewed on the premises are among the draws at this evening hangout with a game room. ✉ *10 University Dr.* ☎ *413/253–4400* 🌐 *www.amherstbrewing.com.*

SHOPPING

Atkins Farms Country Market. An institution in the Pioneer Valley, this market sells produce, baked goods, and specialty foods—try a cider doughnut to sample the best of all three. ✉ *1150 West St.* ☎ *413/253–9528* 🌐 *www.atkinsfarms.com.*

DEERFIELD

10 miles northwest of Amherst.

In Deerfield a horse pulling a carriage clip-clops past perfectly maintained 18th-century homes, neighbors tip their hats to strangers, kids play ball in fields by the river, and the bell of the impossibly beautiful brick church peals from a white steeple. This is the perfect New England village, though not without a past darkened by tragedy. Its original Native American inhabitants, the Pocumtucks, were all but wiped out by deadly epidemics and a war with the Mohawks. English pioneers eagerly settled into this frontier outpost in the 1660s and '70s, but two bloody massacres at the hands of Native Americans and the French prompted them to abandon it until 1707, when construction began on the buildings that remain today.

GETTING HERE AND AROUND

You can take the train to Springfield, but the most direct public transportation to Deerfield is a Peter Pan bus. If you're driving, take Route 10 from the south or Route 2 from the west. Aside from walking around Historic Deerfield, however, you won't get far without a car.

EXPLORING

Fodor'sChoice ★ **Historic Deerfield.** With 52 buildings on 93 acres, Historic Deerfield provides a vivid glimpse into 18th- and 19th-century America. Along the tree-lined main street are 12 museum houses, built between 1720

Historic Deerfield is one of many places in the region to experience America's past through living history.

and 1850. Four are open to the public on self-guided tours, and the remainder can be seen on guided tours that begin on the hour. At the **Wells-Thorn House,** various rooms depict life as it changed from 1725 to 1850. The adjacent **Frary House** displays arts and crafts from the 1900s; the attached Barnard Tavern was the main meeting place for Deerfield's villagers. The **Wright House** contains furniture from the era. Also of note is the **Williams House,** the stately home of an affluent early New England couple.

The **Flynt Center of Early New England Life** contains needlework, textiles, and clothing dating back to the 1600s. The visitor center is located at Hall Tavern, 80 Old Main Street. Plan to spend at least one full day at Historic Deerfield. ⊠ *Old Main St.* ☎ *413/775–7214* ⊕ *www.historic-deerfield.org* ⊠ *$14* ⊙ *Apr.–Dec., daily 9:30–4:30. Flynt Center: Apr.–Dec., daily 9:30–4:30; Jan.–Mar., weekends 9:30–4:30.*

QUICK BITES
Richardson's Candy Kitchen. The name is no joke: the back half of this store is a kitchen where you can see delectable chocolates being made. A short drive from Historic Deerfield, Richardson's sells luscious cream-filled chocolates, truffles, and other handmade confections—try an almond acorn. ⊠ *500 Greenfield Rd.* ☎ *413/772–0443* ⊕ *www.richardsonscandy.com.*

FAMILY **Magic Wings Butterfly Conservatory and Gardens.** This glass conservatory glitters with more than 4,000 butterflies. Kids love the butterfly nursery, where newborns first take flight. Outside is a three-season garden filled with plants that attract local species. There's also a snack bar, a gift shop, and a butterfly-theme restaurant. ✉ *281 Greenfield Rd., South Deerfield* ☎ *413/665–2805* 🌐 *www.magicwings.net* 🎟 *$14* 🕒 *Daily 9–5.*

OFF THE BEATEN PATH

The Montague Bookmill. This old mill complex along the Saw Mill River—since converted into a quintet of businesses—exudes old New England. **The Bookmill** is a quirky secondhand bookshop whose comfortable chairs make it easy to curl up with a book. The good-humored staffers at the adjoining **Lady Killigrew** café serve beer, coffee, and bagels; there's free Wi-Fi, too. The fantastic waterfall views from the deck of **Alvah Stone,** which serves lunch and dinner, justify its slightly elevated prices. From Thursday to Sunday, you can visit **Turn It Up** for music and movies, and the **Sawmill River Arts** crafts gallery for items by local artists. The complex is incredibly picturesque, if not entirely wheelchair accessible. ✉ *440 Greenfield Rd., Montague* ✥ *¼ mile past village green over a small bridge* ☎ *413/367–9206* 🌐 *www.montaguebookmill.com.*

WHERE TO EAT AND STAY

$$$ AMERICAN Fodor's Choice ★

🍴 **Chandler's.** The soft glow of candlelight gives one of the area's best restaurants an intimate feel. Start out with a pan-seared crab cake with a spicy remoulade, then enjoy entrées like grilled salmon with basil pesto risotto and duck breast in a sesame honey-soy glaze. Even though this is fine dining, Chandler's also has an excellent children's menu. The staff could not be more attentive. [$] *Average main: $28* ✉ *Yankee Candle Village, 25 Greenfield Rd., South Deerfield* ☎ *413/665–1277* 🌐 *chandlers.yankeecandle.com* 🕒 *No dinner Mon. and Tues.*

$$ B&B/INN

🏨 **Deerfield Inn.** Period wallpaper and handsome fireplaces contribute to the aura of authenticity of this historic 1884 inn and tavern. **Pros:** gorgeous architecture; tavern oozes atmosphere; surrounded by museums. **Cons:** bathrooms are basic and tiny; sounds travel through halls and into rooms. [$] *Rooms from: $210* ✉ *81 Old Main St.* ☎ *413/774–5587, 800/926–3865* 🌐 *www.deerfieldinn.com* 🛏 *24 rooms* 🍽 *Breakfast.*

SHELBURNE FALLS

18 miles northwest of Deerfield.

A tour of New England's fall foliage wouldn't be complete without a trek across the famed Mohawk Trail, a 63-mile section of Route 2 that runs past Shelburne Falls. The community, separated from neighboring Buckland by the Deerfield River, is filled with little art galleries and surrounded by orchards, farm stands, and sugar houses.

GETTING HERE AND AROUND

Shelburne Falls lies on Route 2, otherwise known as the Mohawk Trail, useful not only for driving through town, but for setting off to the Berkshires as well.

EXPLORING

Bridge of Flowers. From April to October, an arched, 400-foot trolley bridge is transformed into this promenade bursting with color and a wide variety of flowers. ✉ *Water St.* ☎ *413/625–2544* 🌐 *www.bridgeofflowersmass.org.*

Shelburne Falls Trolley Museum. Take a ride on an old-fashioned trolley at this tribute to the old Colrain Street Railway Combine No. 10, which served businesses in and around Shelburne during the early 20th century. ✉ *14 Depot St.* ☎ *413/625–9443* ⊕ *www.sftm.org* ✉ *All-day trolley pass $4* ☉ *Late May–Oct., weekends 11–5; July and Aug., weekends 11–5 and Mon. 1–5.*

SPORTS AND THE OUTDOORS

RAFTING

Zoar Outdoor. White-water rafting, canoeing, and kayaking in the Class II–III rapids of the Deerfield River are popular summer activities. From April to October, Zoar Outdoor conducts kid-friendly rafting trips along 10 miles of challenging rapids, as well as floats along gentler sections of the river. Zip-line tours and rock climbing are also offered in season. ✉ *7 Main St., off Rte. 2, Charlemont* ☎ *800/532–7483* ⊕ *www.zoaroutdoor.com.*

SHOPPING

Sidehill Farm. This farm sells yogurt, raw milk, and cheese, as well as beef, from grass-fed cows. Vegetables and fruits are generally available throughout the year. ✉ *58 Forget Rd., Hawley* ☎ *413/339–0033* ⊕ *www.sidehillfarm.net.*

6

CONNECTICUT

WELCOME TO CONNECTICUT

TOP REASONS TO GO

★ **Country Driving:** Follow the rolling, twisting roads of Litchfield County through the charming villages of Kent, Salisbury, and Litchfield.

★ **Maritime History:** The town of Mystic is packed with interesting nautical attractions related to Connecticut's rich seafaring history.

★ **Urban Exploring:** Anchored by Yale University, downtown New Haven buzzes with hip restaurants, smart boutiques, and acclaimed theaters.

★ **Literary Giants:** In one historic Hartford neighborhood, you can explore the homes— and legacies—of Mark Twain and Harriett Beecher Stowe.

★ **Antiques Hunting:** You'll find numerous fine shops, galleries, and auction houses specializing in antiques all over the state, but two towns in particular stand out: Woodbury and Putnam.

1 Southwestern Connecticut. Enjoy a mix of moneyed bedroom communities and small, dynamic cities, with miles of gorgeous Long Island Sound shoreline. Shop Greenwich Avenue's boutiques, catch a show at the Westport Playhouse, and end with a nightcap in Norwalk's lively SoNo neighborhood.

2 Hartford and the Connecticut River Valley. Get your arts-and-culture fix in Hartford with a visit to the historic Old State House, the Connecticut Science Center, or the Wadsworth Atheneum. Drive south through the Connecticut River Valley for a scenic, small-town New England experience.

3 The Litchfield Hills. Litchfield County's pastoral countryside is the perfect

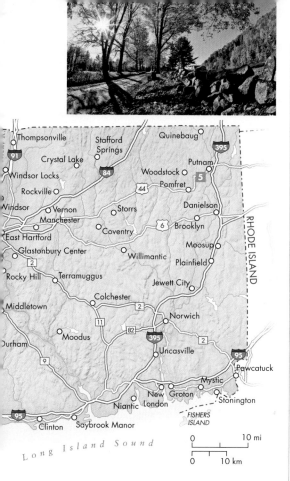

GETTING ORIENTED

Connecticut's coastline runs east–west, from the towns of Stonington and Mystic at the Rhode Island border, down to Greenwich in the southwest corner of the state. Head north from Greenwich and vicinity to the hills of Litchfield County in the northwest, bordered by New York and Massachusetts. In the center of the state, you'll find the capital, Hartford; travel south from here to tour the small towns of the Connecticut River Valley. Northeast of Hartford is the less-traveled Quiet Corner, whose rural towns abut Massachusetts and Rhode Island.

setting for an autumn weekend: nestle into a romantic country inn, leaf peep around Lake Waramaug, and hunt for undiscovered treasures in the antiques shops of Woodbury.

4 New Haven, Mystic, and the Coast. Wander through Yale's campus or visit the dinosaurs at the Peabody Museum of Natural History before dining at a classic New Haven pizzeria. Head east along the coastline for one unspoiled seaside

town after the next, or roll the dice and head inland to the casinos at Foxwoods or Mohegan Sun.

5 The Quiet Corner. The scenic drive along Route 169 through Brooklyn toward Woodstock affords glimpses of authentic Colonial homes, rolling hills, and bucolic views. Try the local wines at Sharpe Hill Vineyard in Pomfret, or go antiquing in downtown Putnam.

Updated
by Bethany
Cassin
Beckerlegge

You can travel from just about any point in Connecticut to any other in less than two hours, yet the land you traverse—fewer than 60 miles top to bottom and 100 miles across—is as varied as a drive across the country.

Connecticut's 253 miles of shoreline blows salty sea air over beach communities like Old Lyme and Stonington, while patchwork hills and peaked mountains fill the state's northwestern corner, and once-upon-a-time mill towns line rivers such as the Housatonic. Connecticut has seemingly endless farmland in the northeast, where cows might just outnumber people, as well as chic New York City bedroom communities such as Greenwich and New Canaan, where boutique shopping bags are the dominant species.

Just as diverse as the landscape are the state's residents, who numbered more than 3½ million at last count. There really is no such thing as the definitive "Connecticut Yankee." Yes, families can trace their roots back to the 1600s, when Connecticut was founded as one of the 13 original colonies, but the state motto is "He who transplanted still sustains." And so the face of the Nutmegger is that of the family from Naples now making pizza in New Haven and the farmer in Norfolk whose land dates back five generations, the grandmother in New Britain who makes the state's best pierogi and the ladies who lunch in Westport, the celebrity nestled in the Litchfield Hills and the Bridgeport entrepreneur working to close the gap between Connecticut's struggling cities and its affluent suburbs.

One quality all Connecticut Yankees have in common, however, is inventiveness; Nutmeggers are historically known for both their intellect and their desire to have a little fun. The nation's first public library opened in New Haven in 1656 and its first state house in Hartford in 1776. Tapping Reeve developed America's first law school in Litchfield in 1784, and West Hartford's Noah Webster published the first dictionary in 1806. On the fun side, Lake Compounce in Bristol was the country's first amusement park; Bethel's P. T. Barnum staged the first three-ring circus; and the hamburger, the lollipop, the Frisbee, and the Erector Set were all invented here.

Not surprisingly, Nutmeggers have a healthy respect for their history. For decades, Mystic Seaport, which traces the state's rich maritime past, has been the premier tourist attraction. Today, however, Foxwoods Casino near Ledyard, run by the Mashantucket Pequots, is North America's largest casino, drawing more than 40,000 visitors per day. Thanks in large part to these lures, not to mention rich cultural destinations, cutting-edge restaurants, shopping outlets, first-rate lodgings, and abundant natural beauty (including 92 state parks and 30 state forests), tourism is one of the state's leading industries. Exploring Connecticut reveals a small state that's big in appeal.

PLANNING

WHEN TO GO

Connecticut is lovely year-round, but fall and spring are particularly appealing times to visit. A fall drive along the state's back roads or the Merritt Parkway, a National Scenic Byway, is a memorable experience. Spots of yellow, orange, and red dot the fall landscape, but the state blooms in springtime, too: town greens are painted with daffodils and tulips, and dogwoods punctuate the rich green countryside. The prime time for attractions is, of course, summer, when travelers have the most options but also plenty of company, especially along the shore.

PLANNING YOUR TIME

The Nutmeg State is a confluence of different worlds, where farm country meets country homes, and fans of the New York Yankees and Red Sox can (quasi)peacefully coexist. To get a true sense of this variety, start in the scenic Litchfield Hills, where you can see historic town greens and trendy cafés. Head south, if you have a bit more time, to the wealthy southwestern corner of the state and then over to New Haven, with its cultural pleasures. If you have five days or a week, take in the capital city of Hartford, the surrounding towns of the Connecticut River Valley, and on down to the southeastern shoreline.

GETTING HERE AND AROUND

AIR TRAVEL

People visiting Connecticut from afar can fly into New York City, Boston, or Providence, or into smaller airports in or near Hartford and New Haven.

Airport Contacts Bradley International Airport. ⊠ *11 Schoephoester Rd., Windsor Locks* ☎ *860/292–2000* ⊕ *www.bradleyairport.com.* **Tweed New Haven Airport.** ⊠ *155 Burr St., New Haven* ☎ *203/466–8833* ⊕ *www.flytweed.com.*

CAR TRAVEL

Interstates are the quickest routes between many points in Connecticut, but they can be busy and unattractive. From New York City, head north on Interstate 95, which hugs the Connecticut shoreline into Rhode Island, or, for Hartford and the Litchfield Hills, head north on Interstate 684, then east on Interstate 84. From central New England, go south on Interstate 91, which intersects Interstate 84 in Hartford and Interstate 95 in New Haven. From Boston, take Interstate 95 south through Providence or take the Massachusetts Turnpike west to Interstate 84. Interstate 395 runs north–south from southeastern Connecticut to Massachusetts.

Often faster because of less traffic, the historic Merritt Parkway (Route 15) winds its way between Greenwich and Middletown; U.S. 7 and Route 8 extend between Interstate 95 and the Litchfield Hills; Route 9 heads south from Hartford through the Connecticut River Valley to Old Saybrook; and scenic Route 169 meanders through the Quiet Corner.

TRAIN TRAVEL

Amtrak runs from New York to Boston, stopping in Stamford, Bridgeport, and New Haven, before heading either north through Hartford and several other towns or east to Old Saybrook and Mystic. Metro-North runs from New York to several towns on the southeastern coastline (including Stamford, Greenwich, and South Norwalk) and ending in New Haven.

Train Contacts Amtrak. ☎ 800/872–7245 ⊕ www.amtrak.com. **Metro-North Railroad.** ☎ 877/690–5114 ⊕ www.mta.info.

RESTAURANTS

Call it the fennel factor or the arugula influx: southern New England has witnessed a gastronomic revolution. Preparation and ingredients reflect the culinary trends of nearby Manhattan and Boston; indeed, the quality and diversity of Connecticut restaurants now rival those of sophisticated metropolitan areas. Although traditional favorites remain—New England clam chowder, buttery lobster rolls, and fish 'n' chips—you may also find that sliced duck is wrapped in phyllo, served with a ginger-plum sauce (the orange glaze decidedly absent), and that everything from lavender to fresh figs is used to season and complement dishes. Dining is also increasingly international: you'll find Indian, Vietnamese, Thai, Malaysian, South American, and Japanese restaurants—even Spanish tapas bars—in cities and suburbs. The farm-to-table movement influences what appears on your plate in many establishments, with conscientious chefs partnering up with local producers to provide the best seasonal ingredients. The one drawback of this turn toward sophistication is that finding a dinner entrée for less than $10 is difficult. *Restaurant prices are the average cost of a main course at dinner, or if dinner is not served, at lunch.*

HOTELS

Connecticut has plenty of business-oriented chain hotels and low-budget motels, along with many of the more unusual and atmospheric inns, resorts, bed-and-breakfasts, and country hotels that are typical of New England. You'll pay dearly for rooms on the coast in summer and in the hills in autumn, when thousands of visitors peep the changing leaves. Rates are lowest in winter but so are the temperatures, making spring the best season for bargain seekers. *Hotel prices are the lowest cost of a standard double room in high season. Reviews have been shortened. For full information, visit Fodors.com.*

WHAT IT COSTS				
	$	$$	$$$	$$$$
Restaurants	under $18	$18–$24	$25–$35	over $35
Hotels	under $200	$200–$299	$300–$399	over $399

TOURS

Connecticut Art Trail. This self-guided tour takes you through 18 museums and historic sites statewide, where you can experience European and American art, culture, and history. ⊠ *Hartford* ⊕ *www.arttrail. org* 🖃 *$25.*

Connecticut Freedom Trail. The state's African American heritage can be found on the trail, which covers more than 130 historic sights across 50 towns. ☎ *860/256–2800* ⊕ *www.ctfreedomtrail.org.*

Connecticut Wine Trail. The trail guides you through 25 member wineries. ⊕ *www.ctwine.com.*

VISITOR INFORMATION

Visitor Contacts Connecticut Commission on Culture & Tourism. ⊠ *1 Constitution Plaza, 2nd fl., Hartford* ☎ *888/288–4748* ⊕ *www.ctvisit.com.*

SOUTHWESTERN CONNECTICUT

Southwestern Connecticut is a rich swirl of old New England and new New York, a region that consistently reports the highest cost of living and the most expensive homes of any area in the country. Its commuter towns are home primarily to white-collar executives. Some still make the hour-plus dash to and from New York City, but many drive to Stamford, which is reputed to have more corporate headquarters per square mile than any other U.S. city.

Venture away from the wealthy bedroom communities, and you'll discover cities struggling through various stages of urban renewal: Stamford, Norwalk, Bridgeport, and Danbury. These four have some of the region's best cultural and shopping opportunities, but the economic disparity between Connecticut's troubled cities and its upscale towns is perhaps most visible in Fairfield County.

ESSENTIALS

Visitor Information Visit Fairfield County. ☎ *800/663–1273* ⊕ *www.visitfairfieldcountyct.com.*

GREENWICH

28 miles northeast of New York City, 64 miles southwest of Hartford.

Lush forests, rolling hills, sandy beaches overlooking sparkling Long Island Sound, and a picture-perfect downtown area filled with chic boutiques and trendsetting restaurants: welcome to Greenwich. It's easy to see why this ritzy enclave has become a haven for Fairfield County's rich and famous. Soak up some history and culture at the

Bruce Museum, then head to Greenwich Avenue for excellent (expensive) shopping and dining.

GETTING HERE AND AROUND

If you are traveling north from New York City, Greenwich will be the first town in Connecticut once you cross the state border. It's easily accessible from Interstate 95 or the Merritt Parkway if you are coming by car, and is also serviced by Metro-North commuter trains.

EXPLORING

FAMILY **Audubon Greenwich.** Established in 1942 as the National Audubon Society's first nature-education facility, this center in northern Greenwich is the best location in the area for bird-watching. During the Fall Hawk Watch Festival you can spot more than 16 species of hawks, eagles, and vultures. Other events include the Spring into Audubon Festival and the semiannual bird counts in summer and winter. The center is filled with interactive exhibits, galleries, and classrooms, a wildlife observation room, and a deck with sweeping views of wildlife activity. Outside are 7 miles of hiking trails passing through 285 acres of woodland, wetland, and meadow. ✉ *613 Riversville Rd.* ☎ *203/869–5272* 🌐 *greenwich.audubon.org* 🎟 *$3* 🕒 *Daily 10–5.*

FAMILY Fodor's Choice ★ **Bruce Museum of Arts and Science.** The owner of this 19th-century home, wealthy textile merchant Robert Moffat Bruce, bequeathed it to the town of Greenwich in 1908 with the stipulation that it be used "as a natural history, historical, and art museum." Today this diversity remains, reflected in the museum's collection of some 15,000 objects in fine and decorative arts, natural history, and anthropology, including paintings by Childe Hassam, sculptures by Auguste Rodin, and stained glass by Dale Chihuly. On permanent display is a spectacular mineral collection. Kids enjoy the touchable meteorite and glow-in-the-dark minerals, as well as the fossilized dinosaur tracks. ✉ *1 Museum Dr., off I–95* ☎ *203/869–0376* 🌐 *www.brucemuseum.org* 🎟 *$7 (free Tues.)* 🕒 *Tues.–Sun. 10–5.*

WHERE TO EAT AND STAY

$$ SOUTHWESTERN 🍴 **Boxcar Cantina.** If it's Southwestern food you're craving, Boxcar Cantina delivers, with the freshest and most authentic dishes in the area. Diners rave about their margaritas, pairing them happily with fish tacos, quesadillas, enchiladas, and burritos. The chefs take special care to source their organic ingredients locally. You can also grab some guac and tamales from their stand at the Westport Farmers Market in nearby Westport, on Thursday 10–2. [$] *Average main: $23* ✉ *44 Old Field Point Rd.* ☎ *203/661–4774* 🌐 *www.boxcarcantina.com* 🕒 *No lunch weekends.*

$$$ SEAFOOD 🍴 **Elm Street Oyster House.** Locals come here for outstanding oysters and the freshest fish in town. The colorful artwork gives the slightly cramped dining room a certain cheerfulness; expect an equally lively crowd on weekends. Menu standouts include the varied selection of fresh oysters from all over the country, classic lobster rolls, and outstanding seafood chili. [$] *Average main: $34* ✉ *11 W. Elm St.* ☎ *203/629–5795* 🌐 *www.elmstreetoysterhouse.com.*

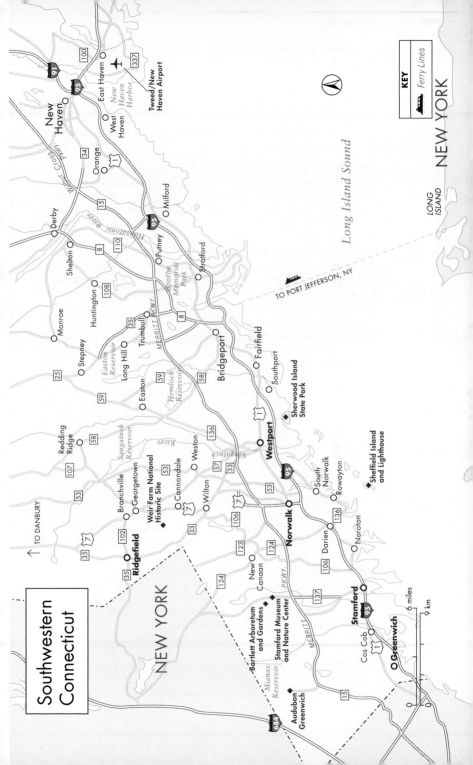

$$$ HOTEL Fodor's Choice ★ **Delamar Greenwich Harbor Hotel.** This three-story luxury hotel just blocks from downtown Greenwich resembles a villa on the Italian Riviera. **Pros:** waterfront location; posh spa; easy walk to downtown restaurants and shopping. **Cons:** super pricey. *[$] Rooms from: $349 ✉ 500 Steamboat Rd. ☎ 203/661–9800, 866/335–2627 🌐 www.thedelamar.com 🛏 74 rooms, 8 suites 🍴 No meals.*

STAMFORD

6 miles northeast of Greenwich, 38 miles southwest of New Haven.

While business is often what brings people to Stamford, what keeps them here are the quality restaurants, nightclubs, and shops that line Atlantic and lower Summer streets. Weekenders have plenty of options beyond the downtown canyons: beaches, boating on the sound, and hiking are only minutes away.

GETTING HERE AND AROUND

Stamford is easily accessible from Interstate 95 and the Merritt Parkway. It is also a major rail hub for Metro-North commuter trains and Amtrak; the high-speed Acela makes a stop here on its route from Boston to Washington, D.C.

EXPLORING

Bartlett Arboretum and Gardens. This 93-acre arboretum is home to more than 2,000 varieties of annuals, perennials, wildflowers, and woody plants. There's also a greenhouse, marked ecology trails, a pretty pond, and a boardwalk through a red maple swamp. Brilliant, bold colors make the wildflower garden stunning in spring. Sunday afternoon is the time to visit for a guided walk. *✉ 151 Brookdale Rd., off High Ridge Rd. ☎ 203/322–6971 🌐 www.bartlettarboretum.org 🎟 $6 ⏲ Grounds daily 9–dusk.*

FAMILY **Stamford Museum and Nature Center.** Oxen, sheep, pigs, and other animals roam this 118-acre New England farmstead. Once the estate of Henri Bendel, the property includes a Tudor-revival stone mansion housing exhibits on natural history, art, and Americana. An observatory has a 22-inch research telescope—perfect for stargazing—and nature trails wind through the woods. *✉ 39 Scofieldtown Rd. ☎ 203/322–1646 🌐 www.stamfordmuseum.org 🎟 Grounds $10, observatory $5 ⏲ Grounds daily 9–5. Observatory: Sept.–May, Fri. 8 pm–10 pm; June–Aug., Fri. 8:30 pm–10:30 pm.*

WHERE TO EAT

$$$$ STEAKHOUSE ✕ **Capital Grille.** This swanky and splurge-worthy steak house serves up impeccable fillets (beef and salmon alike), along with a host of other well-crafted entrées in the dimly lit dining room with an old-school gentleman's club feel. Though dry-aged steaks are their specialty, Capital Grille also excels at seafood: pan-seared scallops, Maine lobster, and sushi-grade seared sesame tuna are equally delicious choices. Don't forget to add a side of truffle fries or lobster mac 'n' cheese. *[$] Average main: $52 ✉ 230 Tressor Blvd. ☎ 203/967–0000 🌐 www.thecapitalgrille.com ⏲ No lunch weekends.*

$ AMERICAN 🍴 **City Limits Diner.** This art deco–style diner, alive with bright colors and shiny chrome, touts its food as running the gamut from "haute to homespun." Roughly translated, this is the place for everything from hot pastrami on rye served with an egg cream to pan-roasted Atlantic salmon with Israeli couscous and shiitake mushrooms. All breads, pastries, and ice cream are made in-house and available for purchase. [$] *Average main: $15* ✉ *135 Harvard Ave.* ☎ *203/348–7000* 🌐 *www.citylimitsdiner.com.*

$$$ AMERICAN 🍴 **Harlan Social.** It's all about the food at this lively gastropub. In the industrial-chic dining room and bar, you can sample their small plates—short-rib empanadas, steamed P.E.I. mussels, and poached lobster and avocado salad are all on offer—or choose some charcuterie or a selection from the mozzarella bar. Main courses range from burgers and homemade gnocchi to pan-seared salmon; chances are there's something for everyone here. Cap off your meal with homemade doughnuts or chocolate ganache tart—both worth every calorie. [$] *Average main: $32* ✉ *121 Towne St.* ☎ *203/883–8000* 🌐 *www.harlansocial.com.*

NIGHTLIFE AND PERFORMING ARTS

NIGHTLIFE

Tigín Pub. Stop in for the perfect pint at this Irish pub with an authentic atmosphere. ✉ *175 Bedford St.* ☎ *203/353–8444* 🌐 *www.tiginirishpub.com.*

PERFORMING ARTS

The Palace Theatre. Plays, comedy shows, musicals, and film festivals are presented at the Palace, which is owned and operated by the Stamford Center for the Arts. ✉ *61 Atlantic St.* ☎ *203/325–4466* 🌐 *www.palacestamford.org.*

FAMILY **Stamford Symphony Orchestra.** Performing at the Palace Theatre October–April, this orchestra offers a popular family concert series. ✉ *263 Tresser Blvd.* ☎ *203/325–1407* 🌐 *www.stamfordsymphony.org.*

NORWALK

14 miles northeast of Stamford, 47 miles northeast of New York City.

In the 19th century, Norwalk became a major New England port and manufacturing center, which produced pottery, clocks, watches, shingle nails, and paper. It later fell into neglect, in which it remained for much of the 20th century. In the early 1990s, however, Norwalk's coastal business district was the focus of major redevelopment, which has since turned it into a hot spot for trendy shopping, culture, and dining, much of it along the main drag, Washington Street. The stretch is known as SoNo (South Norwalk), and in the evening it is the place to be seen if you're young, single, and living it up in Fairfield County.

GETTING HERE AND AROUND

If you are traveling by car, Norwalk is most easily reached by Interstate 95 and the Merritt Parkway. Metro-North commuter trains also stop here. Exit at the South Norwalk stop to put yourself within walking distance of SoNo shops, restaurants, and bars.

Norwalk's Maritime Aquarium is a great way to get eye-to-eye with animals endemic to Long Island Sound, like loggerhead turtles.

EXPLORING

Lockwood-Mathews Mansion Museum. This ornate tribute to Victorian decorating was built in 1864 as the summer home of LeGrand Lockwood. It remains one the oldest (and finest) surviving Second Empire–style country homes in the United States; it's hard not to be impressed by its octagonal skylighted rotunda and more than 50 rooms of gilt, frescoes, marble, intricate woodwork, and etched glass. ⊠ *295 West Ave.* ☎ *203/838–9799* ⊕ *www.lockwoodmathewsmansion.com* ✉ *$10* ⊗ *Apr.–Jan., Wed.–Sun. noon–4.*

FAMILY

Fodor's Choice

★

Maritime Aquarium at Norwalk. This 5-acre waterfront center, the cornerstone of the SoNo district, explores the marine life and maritime culture of Long Island Sound. The aquarium's more than 20 habitats include some 1,000 creatures indigenous to the sound, including stately loggerhead sea turtles, happy harbor seals, and the dozens of jellyfish that perform their ghostly ballet in "Jellyfish Encounter." You can see toothy bluefish and sand tiger sharks in the 110,000-gallon Ocean Beyond the Sound aquarium. The aquarium also operates an Environmental Education Center and leads marine-mammal cruises aboard the *Spirit of the Sound,* and has a towering IMAX theater. ⊠ *10 N. Water St.* ☎ *203/852–0700* ⊕ *www.maritimeaquarium.org* ✉ *Aquarium $19.95, IMAX $9.50; combination ticket $24.95* ⊗ *Labor Day–June, daily 10–5; July–Labor Day, daily 10–6.*

Sheffield Island and Lighthouse. Adjacent to the Stewart B. McKinney National Wildlife Refuge, this 3-acre park is a prime spot for a picnic. The 1868 lighthouse has 10 rooms to explore between four levels. Clambakes are held Thursday evenings June–September. To get here, take a ferry from the Sheffield Island Dock. ✉ *Sheffield Island Dock, Washington and N. Water Sts.* ☎ *203/838–9444* 🌐 *www.seaport.org* 🎟 *Round-trip ferry service and lighthouse tour $22* ⏲ *Ferry: Memorial Day–Labor Day, Mon., Thurs., and Fri. at 11 and 3, Tues. and Wed. at 11, weekends and holidays at 11, 2, and 3:30.*

WHERE TO EAT AND STAY

$$$ MODERN AMERICAN Fodor's Choice ★

🍴 **Match.** Nestled in the heart of SoNo, Match uses fresh, local ingredients in inventive American dishes. High ceilings, exposed brick, and industrial fixtures provide a sleek, urban look. Indulge in one of the signature wood-fired pizzas straight out of the oven, or savor the light-as-air gnocchi in a beef, pork, and veal ragù. Complete your meal with a melt-in-your-mouth hot chocolate soufflé topped with raspberries and vanilla gelato. [$] *Average main: $28* ✉ *98 Washington St.* ☎ *203/852–1088* 🌐 *www.matchsono.com.*

$ HOTEL

🏨 **Hotel Zero Degrees Norwalk.** This ultramodern boutique lodging is a great addition to a region choked with lackluster chain hotels. **Pros:** best choice in the area; tasty restaurant; free shuttle service. **Cons:** noise from the nearby train tracks; not walking distance to downtown. [$] *Rooms from: $180* ✉ *353 Main Ave.* ☎ *203/750–9800* 🌐 *www.hotelzerodegrees.com/hotels/norwalk* 🛏 *96 rooms* 🍽 *Breakfast.*

NIGHTLIFE

Barcelona. This wine bar serves exceptional Spanish-style tapas. ✉ *63 N. Main St.* ☎ *203/899–0088* 🌐 *www.barcelonawinebar.com.*

Local Kitchen and Craft Beer Bar. Exposed brick, rustic wooden booths, and metal accents give this pub in the heart of bustling SoNo an industrial feel. Pair one of the 30-plus craft beers on tap with their to-die-for burger. ✉ *68 Washington St.* ☎ *203/957–3352* 🌐 *www.sonolocal.com.*

RIDGEFIELD

11 miles north of New Canaan, 43 miles west of New Haven.

In Ridgefield, you'll find an outstanding contemporary art museum nestled in a rustic atmosphere within an hour of Manhattan. The inviting town center is a largely residential sweep of lawns and majestic homes, with a feel more reminiscent of the peaceful Litchfield Hills, even though the town is in the northern reaches of Fairfield County.

GETTING HERE AND AROUND

From Interstate 95 or the Merritt Parkway, head north on Route 7 to Route 33 to reach Ridgefield, or take Metro-North to the Branchville station.

EXPLORING

Fodor's Choice ★

Aldrich Contemporary Art Museum. Cutting-edge art is not necessarily what you'd expect to find in a stately 18th-century structure that by turns served as a general store, a post office, and, for 35 years, a church. Nicknamed "Old Hundred," this historic building is just part of the vast facility, which includes a 17,000-square-foot exhibition space that puts its own twist on traditional New England architecture. The white-clapboard-and-granite structure houses 12 galleries, a screening room, a sound gallery, a 22-foot-high project space for large installations, a 100-seat performance space, and an education center. Outside is a 2-acre sculpture garden. ■ **TIP→ Every third Saturday admission is free.** ✉ *258 Main St.* ☎ *203/438–4519* 🌐 *www.aldrichart.org* 🎫 *$10* ⏲ *Mon. and Wed.–Sat. 10–5, Sun. noon–5.*

Weir Farm National Historic Site. These 153 wooded acres on the Ridgefield–Wilton border are where the noted American Impressionist painter J. Alden Weir (1852–1919) lived and worked from the early 1880s. Rangers give tours of the Weir home, studio, outbuildings, gardens, and grounds, where the artist set many of his paintings and congregated with such notable fellow painters as Childe Hassam and John Singer Sargent. ✉ *735 Nod Hill Rd.* ☎ *203/834–1896* 🌐 *www.nps.gov/wefa* 🎫 *Free* ⏲ *Grounds: daily sunrise–sunset. Visitor center: May–Oct., Wed.–Sun. 10–4. Tours: May–Oct., Wed.–Sun. at 11, 1, 2, and 3.*

WHERE TO EAT

$$ FRENCH 🍴 **Luc's Café and Restaurant.** A cozy bistro set inside a stone building with low ceilings and closely spaced tables, Luc's takes full advantage of its handy location in Ridgefield's quaint downtown. The place charms patrons with carefully prepared food and low-key, friendly service. You can opt for a simple salade niçoise or *croque monsieur* (hot ham-and-cheese sandwich) or enjoy a classic steak au poivre with a velvety Roquefort sauce and crispy frites. There's an extensive wine list, plus a range of aperitifs and single-malt whiskies. Enjoy live jazz on some evenings. [$] *Average main: $22* ✉ *3 Big Shop La.* ☎ *203/894–8522* 🌐 *www.lucscafe.com* ⏲ *Closed Sun.*

WESTPORT

15 miles southeast of Ridgefield, 47 miles northeast of New York City.

Westport, an artists' community since the turn of the 20th century, continues to attract creative types. Despite commuters and corporations, the town remains more artsy and cultured than its neighbors.

GETTING HERE AND AROUND

You can reach Westport by car via Interstate 95 (Exit 17 will put you closest to the center of town and main shopping areas) or the Merritt Parkway. Metro-North also has two stops here: Westport (closer to town) and Greens Farms (farther east).

EXPLORING

OFF THE BEATEN PATH

Connecticut's Beardsley Zoo. The indoor, walk-through South American rain forest alone justifies a visit to this zoo. It comes alive with dozens of species, some rare and endangered, such as keel-billed toucans, broad-snouted caimans, and black-and-gold howler monkeys living in a lush environment of waterfalls, ponds, greenery, and bamboo. The zoo itself has 36 acres of exhibits featuring bison, tigers, timber wolves, and proud peacocks that freely roam the property right along with you. There's also a working carousel and a New England farmyard. ✉ *1875 Noble Ave., Bridgeport* ☎ *203/394–6565* 🌐 *www.beardsleyzoo.org* 🎫 *$14* ⏲ *Daily 9–4.*

FAMILY **Sherwood Island State Park.** Summer visitors congregate at this state park, which has a 1½-mile sweep of sandy beach, two picnic areas on the water's edge, sports fields, and several food stands (open seasonally). The on-site nature center offers various programs from bird-watching to nature walks. Note that there's a parking fee Memorial Day–Labor Day. ✉ *Sherwood Island Connector* ☎ *203/226–6983* 🌐 *www.ct.gov/deep/sherwoodisland* 🎟 *Free* 🕒 *Daily 8 am–sunset.*

WHERE TO EAT

$$$ AMERICAN 🍴 **Westport Garden Café.** Within the garden store Terrain, you'll find a quaint café that offers exquisitely prepared cuisine using locally sourced organic produce so fresh you'll want to become a gardener yourself. Entrées like line-caught Atlantic cod with squash risotto, or the braised beef short ribs are served with a delicious (and frankly adorable) terracotta pot of baked bread. The delectable Terrain burger usually comes on either a crosssection of a tree trunk or a thin slab of slate. The bonus? You can browse the store and its home accessories, plants, and garden supplies while you wait for your table. [$] *Average main: $28* ✉ *561 Post Rd. E* ☎ *203/226–2750* 🌐 *www.shopterrain.com/westport-restaurant* 🕒 *No dinner Mon. and Tues.*

$$$ SEAFOOD 🍴 **The Whelk.** This upscale seafood bar serves straight-from-the-sea clams, oysters, and fish inventively prepared and exquisitely presented. The clean lines of the dining room give the nearly always crowded restaurant a maritime feel that perfectly complements the food. [$] *Average main: $35* ✉ *575 Riverside Ave.* ☎ *203/557–0902* 🌐 *www.thewhelkwestport.com* 🕒 *Closed Sun. and Mon.*

PERFORMING ARTS

FAMILY **Levitt Pavilion for the Performing Arts.** Enjoy an excellent series of mostly free summer concerts here that range from jazz to classical, folk to blues. ✉ *40 Jesup Rd.* ☎ *203/221–2153* 🌐 *www.levittpavilion.com.*

Westport Country Playhouse. Long associated with benefactors Joanne Woodward and Paul Newman, the venerable and intimate Westport Country Playhouse presents high-quality plays throughout the year. ✉ *25 Powers Ct.* ☎ *203/227–4177* 🌐 *www.westportplayhouse.org.*

HARTFORD AND THE CONNECTICUT RIVER VALLEY

Less touristy than the coast and the northwest hills, the Connecticut River Valley is a swath of small towns and uncrowded state parks punctuated by a few small cities and one large one: the capital city of Hartford. South of Hartford, with the exception of industrial Middletown, genuinely quaint hamlets vie for attention with antiques shops, scenic drives, and romantic restaurants and country inns.

Westward expansion in the New World began along the meandering Connecticut River. Dutch explorer Adrian Block first explored the area in 1614, and in 1633 a trading post was established at what is now Hartford. Within five years, throngs of restive Massachusetts Bay colonists had settled in this fertile valley. What followed were more than three centuries of shipbuilding, shad hauling, and river trade with ports as far away as the West Indies and the Mediterranean.

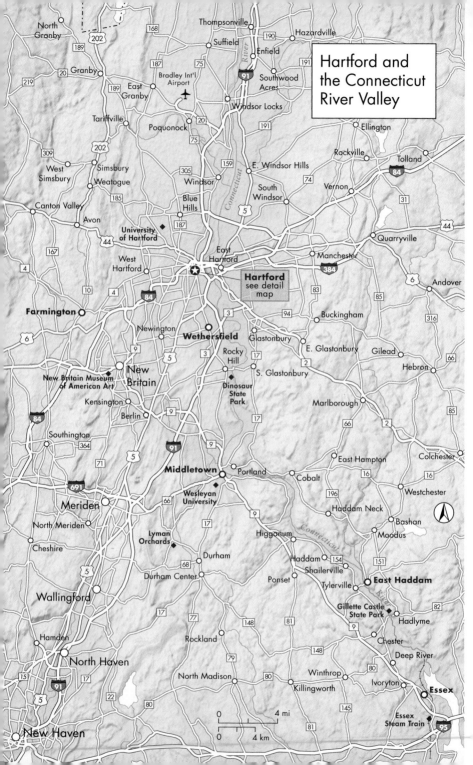

Hartford and
the Connecticut
River Valley

Ride through the Connecticut River Valley on a vintage Essex Steam Train.

ESSENTIALS
Visitor Information Central Regional Tourism District. ✉ *1 Constitution Plaza, 2nd fl., Hartford* ☎ *860/787-9640* ⊕ *www.visitctriver.com.*

ESSEX

29 miles east of New Haven.

Essex, consistently named one of the best small towns in the United States, looks much like it did in the mid-19th century, at the height of its shipbuilding prosperity. Essex's boat manufacturing was so important to the early United States that the British burned more than 40 ships here during the War of 1812. Gone are the days of steady trade with the West Indies, when the aroma of imported rum, molasses, and spices hung in the air. Whitewashed houses—many the former roosts of sea captains—line Main Street, which has shops that sell clothing, antiques, paintings and prints, and sweets.

GETTING HERE AND AROUND
The best way to reach Essex is by car; take Interstate 95 to Route 9 north.

EXPLORING
FAMILY
Fodor'sChoice
★
Connecticut River Museum. In an 1878 steamboat warehouse, this museum tells the story of the Connecticut River through maritime artifacts, interactive displays, and ship models. The riverfront museum even has a full-size working reproduction of the world's first submarine, the *American Turtle*; the original was built by David Bushnell in 1775 as a "secret weapon" to win the Revolutionary War. ✉ *67 Main St.* ☎ *860/767-8269*

⊕ *www.ctrivermuseum.org* ✉ *$9* ⊗ *Memorial Day–Columbus Day, daily 10–5; Columbus Day–Memorial Day, Tues.–Sun. 10–5.*

FAMILY
Fodor'sChoice
★

Essex Steam Train and Riverboat. This ride offers some of the best views of the Connecticut River valley from 1920s-era coaches pulled by a vintage steam locomotive and an old-fashioned riverboat. The train, traveling along the Connecticut River through the lower valley, makes a 12-mile round-trip from Essex Station to Deep River Station; from there, if you wish to continue, you board the riverboat for a ride to East Haddam (the open promenade deck on the third level has the best views). The train also hosts seasonal events such as the North Pole Express, a nighttime trip to pick up Santa, and Day Out with Thomas, perfect for little ones who love the *Thomas & Friends* television show. ✉ *Valley Railroad Company, 1 Railroad Ave.* ☎ *860/767–0103* ⊕ *www.essexsteamtrain.com* ✉ *Train $19, train and boat $29* ⊗ *May–Dec., hrs vary.*

EAST HADDAM

15 miles north of Essex, 28 miles southeast of Hartford.

Fishing, shipping, and musket making were the chief enterprises of East Haddam, the only town in the state that occupies both banks of the Connecticut River. This lovely community still retains much of its old-fashioned charm, most of it centered around its historic downtown.

GETTING HERE AND AROUND

The best way to reach East Haddam is by car. From Interstate 95, take Route 9 north to Route 82 east to Route 154 north.

EXPLORING

FAMILY
Fodor'sChoice
★

Gillette Castle State Park. The outrageous 24-room oak-and-fieldstone hilltop castle, modeled after medieval castles of the Rhineland and built between 1914 and 1919 by the eccentric actor and dramatist William Gillette, is the park's main attraction. You can tour the castle and hike trails near the remains of a 3-mile private railroad, which chugged about the property until the owner's death in 1937. Gillette, who was born in Hartford, wrote two famous plays about the Civil War and was especially beloved for his play *Sherlock Holmes* (in which he performed the title role). In his will, he demanded that the castle not fall into the hands of "some blithering saphead who has no conception of where he is or with what surrounded." ✉ *67 River Rd., off Rte. 82* ☎ *860/526–2336* ⊕ *www.ct.gov/deep/gillettecastle* ✉ *Park free, castle $6* ⊗ *Park daily 8–sunset.*

Fodor'sChoice
★

Goodspeed Opera House. This magnificent 1876 Victorian-gingerbread "wedding cake" theater on the Connecticut River—so called for its turrets, mansard roof, and grand filigree—is widely recognized for its role in the preservation and development of American musical theater. Well over a dozen Goodspeed productions have gone on to Broadway, including *Annie.* Performances take place April–early December. ✉ *6 Main St.* ☎ *860/873–8668* ⊕ *www.goodspeed.org* ✉ *Tours $5* ⊗ *Tours June–Oct., Sat. 11–1.*

MIDDLETOWN

15 miles northwest of East Haddam, 24 miles northeast of New Haven.

With its Connecticut River setting, easy access to major highways, and historic architecture, Middletown is a popular destination for recreational boaters and tourists alike. The town's High Street is an architecturally eclectic thoroughfare—Charles Dickens once called it "the loveliest Main Street in America" (Middletown's actual Main Street runs parallel to it a few blocks east). Students from nearby Wesleyan University add a youthful vigor to the town when school is in session.

GETTING HERE AND AROUND

Middletown is best reached by car. From Hartford, follow Interstate 91 south to Route 9 south. From the coast, take Interstate 95 to Route 9 north.

EXPLORING

FAMILY **Dinosaur State Park.** See some 500 tracks left by the dinosaurs that once roamed the area around this park north of Middletown. The tracks are preserved under a giant geodesic dome. You can even make plaster casts of tracks on a special area of the property; call ahead to learn what materials you need to bring. ✉ *400 West St., east of I–91, Rocky Hill* ☎ *860/529–8423* 🌐 *www.dinosaurstatepark.org* 🎟 *$6* 🕒 *Trails daily 9–4, exhibits Tues.–Sun. 9–4:30.*

6

Wesleyan University. Founded in 1831, Wesleyan University is one of the oldest Methodist institutions of higher education in the country. There are roughly 2,800 undergraduates, which gives Middletown a contemporary, college-town feel. Note the massive, fluted Corinthian columns of the 1828 Greek Revival Russell House at the corner of Washington Street, across from the pink Mediterranean-style Davison Art Center, built 15 years later. Farther along you'll find gingerbreads, towering brownstones, Tudors, and Queen Annes. A few hundred yards up on Church Street, which intersects High Street, is the Olin Library. This 1928 structure was designed by Henry Bacon, architect of the Lincoln Memorial. ✉ *45 Wyllys Ave., off High St.* ☎ *860/685–2000* 🌐 *www.wesleyan.edu.*

OFF THE BEATEN PATH

Lyman Orchards. Looking for a quintessential New England outing? These orchards just south of Middletown are not to be missed. Get lost in the sunflower maze, then pick your own fruits and vegetables—berries, peaches, pears, apples, and even pumpkins—from June to October. ✉ *Rtes. 147 and 157, Middlefield* ☎ *860/349–1793* 🌐 *www.lymanorchards.com* 🕒 *Nov.–Aug., daily 9–6; Sept. and Oct., daily 9–7.*

WHERE TO EAT AND STAY

$ AMERICAN 🍴 **O'Rourke's Diner.** This glass-and-steel classic is the place to go for top-notch diner fare, including creative specialties like the omelet stuffed with roasted portobello mushrooms, Brie, and asparagus. The steamed cheeseburgers are another favorite. Arrive early for lunch, as the lines often file out the door. [$] *Average main: $13* ✉ *728 Main St.* ☎ *860/346–6101* 🌐 *www.orourkesmiddletown.com* 🕒 *No dinner.*

$ HOTEL 🏨 **Inn at Middletown.** The Inn is centrally located in a historic former National Guard Armory in the heart of downtown Middletown. **Pros:**

Connecticut's Historic Gardens

These extraordinary Connecticut gardens form Connecticut's Historic Gardens, a "trail" of natural beauties across the state. For more information on each of the gardens, visit ⊕ www.cthistoricgardens.org.

Bellamy-Ferriday House & Garden, Bethlehem. Highlights of this garden include an apple orchard and a circa-1915 formal parterre garden that blossoms with peonies, roses, and lilacs.

Butler-McCook House & Garden, Hartford. Landscape architect Jacob Weidenmann created a Victorian garden that serves as an amazing respite from downtown city life.

Florence Griswold Museum, Old Lyme. The gardens at the historic Florence Griswold Museum, once the home of a prominent Old Lyme family and later a haven for artists, have been restored to their 1910 appearance and feature hollyhocks and black-eyed Susans.

Glebe House Museum, Woodbury. Legendary British garden writer and designer Gertrude Jekyll designed only three gardens in the United States, and the one at the Glebe House Museum is the only one still in existence. It is a classic example of Jekyll's ideas about color harmony and plant combinations; a hedge of mixed shrubs encloses a mix of perennials.

Harriet Beecher Stowe Center, Hartford. The grounds at the Harriet Beecher Stowe Center feature Connecticut's largest magnolia tree, a 100-year-old pink dogwood, an antique rose garden, a wildflower meadow, and a blue cottage garden.

Hill-Stead Museum, Farmington. The centerpiece of the Hill-Stead Museum is a circa-1920 sunken garden enclosed in a yew hedge and surrounded by a wall of rough stone. At the center of the octagonal design is a summerhouse with 36 flowerbeds and brick walkways radiating outward.

Promisek Beatrix Farrand Garden, Bridgewater. The prolific Beatrix Farrand designed the garden at Promisek Beatrix Farrand Garden, which overflows with beds of annuals and perennials such as hollyhocks, peonies, and always-dashing delphiniums.

Roseland Cottage, Woodstock. At Roseland Cottage, the boxwood parterre garden includes 21 flowerbeds surrounded by boxwood hedges.

Webb-Deane-Stevens Museum, Wethersfield. This Colonial Revival garden is filled with such old-fashioned flowers as peonies, pinks, phlox, hollyhocks, and larkspur, as well as a profusion of roses.

---

close to Wesleyan campus and steps from downtown shopping; grand old building; large rooms. **Cons:** no real grounds to speak of; rather expensive on weekends when Wesleyan is in session. $ *Rooms from: $159* ✉ *70 Main St.* ☎ *860/854–6300* ⊕ *www.innatmiddletown.com* ⌂ *88 rooms, 12 suites* ❘◯❘ *No meals.*

NIGHTLIFE AND PERFORMING ARTS
NIGHTLIFE
Eli Cannon's. At last count, the cozy Eli Cannon's had more than 35 beers on tap, as well as an extensive selection of bottled beers. ✉ *695 Main St.* ☎ *860/347–3547* ⊕ *www.elicannons.com.*

PERFORMING ARTS
Wesleyan University Center for the Arts. See modern dance or a provocative new play, hear top playwrights and actors discuss their craft, or take in an art exhibit or concert at this college arts center. ✉ *283 Washington Terr.* ☎ *860/685–3355* ⊕ *www.wesleyan.edu/cfa.*

SHOPPING
Wesleyan Potters. There's more to this place than just pottery: the non-profit guild also makes jewelry, clothing, and weavings. ✉ *350 S. Main St.* ☎ *860/347–5925 for office, 860/344–0039 for shop* ⊕ *www. wesleyanpotters.com* ☽ *Closed Mon. and Tues.*

WETHERSFIELD

32 miles northeast of New Haven.

6

Wethersfield, a vast Hartford suburb, dates to 1634 and has the state's largest—and, some say, the most picturesque—historic district, with more than 100 pre-1849 buildings. Old Wethersfield has the oldest firehouse in the state, the oldest historic district in the state, and the oldest continuously operating seed company. Today, this "dated" community has new parks and new shops, but history is still its main draw.

GETTING HERE AND AROUND
Wethersfield is only a few miles south of Hartford, and most easily reachable by car. From Hartford, take Interstate 91 south to Route 3 south.

EXPLORING
Fodor$Choice **New Britain Museum of American Art.** An important stop for art lovers, ★ this 100-year-old museum's collection of more than 10,000 works from 1740 to the present focuses solely on American art. Among its treasures number paintings by John Singer Sargent, Winslow Homer, and Georgia O'Keeffe, as well as sculpture by Isamu Noguchi. Of particular note is the selection of Impressionist artists, including Mary Cassatt, William Merritt Chase, Childe Hassam, and John Henry Twachtman, as well as Thomas Hart Benton's five-panel mural *The Arts of Life in America.* The museum also has a café, a large shop, and a library of art books. ✉ *56 Lexington St., 8 miles west of Wethersfield, New Britain* ☎ *860/229–0257* ⊕ *www.nbmaa.org* 💲*$15 (free Sat. 10–noon)* ☽ *Sun.–Wed. and Fri. 11–5, Thurs. 11–8, Sat. 10–5.*

Webb-Deane-Stevens Museum. For a true sample of Wethersfield's historic past, stop by the Joseph Webb House, the Silas Deane House, and the Isaac Stevens House, next door to each other along Main Street and all built in the mid- to late 1700s. These well-preserved examples of Georgian architecture reflect their owners' lifestyles as, respectively, a merchant, a diplomat, and a tradesman. The Webb House, a registered National Historic Landmark, was the site of the strategy conference between George Washington and the French general Jean-Baptiste Rochambeau that led to the British defeat at Yorktown. ✉ *211 Main St., off I–91* ☎ *860/529–0612* ⊕ *webb-deane-stevens.org* ⊠ *$12* ◌ *May–Oct., Mon. and Wed.–Sat. 10–4, Sun. 1–4; Apr. and Nov., Sat. 10–4, Sun. 1–4; other times by appt.*

HARTFORD

4 miles north of Wethersfield, 45 miles northwest of New London, 81 miles northeast of Stamford.

Midway between New York City and Boston, Hartford is Connecticut's capital city and the former insurance capital of the United States. Founded in 1635 on the banks of the Connecticut River, Hartford was at various times home to authors Mark Twain and Harriet Beecher Stowe, inventors Samuel and Elizabeth Colt, landscape architect Frederick Law Olmsted, and Ella Grasso, the first woman to be elected a state governor. Today Hartford is poised for change, with a revitalized downtown core featuring a bustling convention center and a top-notch science museum, the Connecticut Science Center. The city is a destination on the verge of discovery.

GETTING HERE AND AROUND

Hartford is located in the middle of the state, at the intersection of two main highways: Interstate 91, which runs north–south from Western Massachusetts straight through Hartford and on to the Connecticut coastline, and Interstate 84, which runs generally east–west from Union at the northeast border with Massachusetts to near Danbury at the New York border. Amtrak serves Hartford on the Northeast Regional line. Bradley International Airport in Windsor Locks, 15 minutes north of Hartford, offers flights to more than 30 destinations in the United States, Canada, and the Caribbean.

EXPLORING

TOP ATTRACTIONS

FAMILY

Fodor's Choice

★

Connecticut Science Center. This strikingly modern building, designed by world-renowned architect César Pelli, houses 40,000 square feet of exhibit space under a wavelike roof that appears to float over the structure. Dive into a black hole and examine the moon's craters in the Exploring Space exhibit, race mini-sailboats and magnetic trains at Forces in Motion, and discover your hidden athletic talents in the Sports Lab. Kid Space is perfect for ages three–six. Complete your visit by taking in a movie in the 3-D digital theater. ✉ *250 Columbus Blvd.* ☎ *860/724–3623* ⊕ *www.ctsciencecenter.org* ⊠ *$21.95* ◌ *Tues.–Sun. 10–5.*

Harriet Beecher Stowe Center. Abolitionist and author Harriet Beecher Stowe (1811–96) spent her final years at this 1871 Victorian Gothic cottage, now a popular stop on the Connecticut Freedom Trail. The center was built around the cottage in tribute to the author of the anti-slavery novel *Uncle Tom's Cabin*. Stowe's personal writing table and effects are housed inside. ✉ *77 Forest St.* ☎ *860/522–9258* ⊕ *www.harrietbeecherstowecenter.org* ⊠ *$14* ◌ *Mon.–Sat. 9:30–5, Sun. noon–5.*

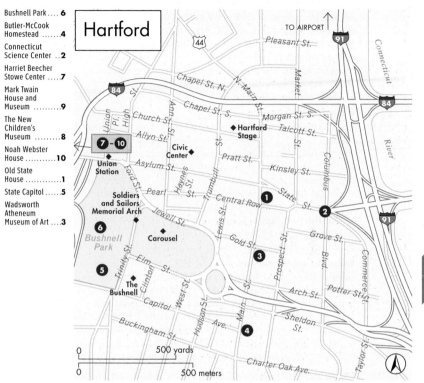

Fodor's Choice
★ **Mark Twain House and Museum.** Built in 1874, this building was the home of Samuel Langhorne Clemens (better known as Mark Twain) until 1891. In the time he and his family lived in this 25-room Victorian mansion, Twain published seven major novels, including *Tom Sawyer, Huckleberry Finn,* and *The Prince and the Pauper.* The home is one of only two Louis Comfort Tiffany–designed domestic interiors open to the public. A contemporary museum on the grounds presents an up-close look at the author and screens an outstanding Ken Burns documentary on his life. ⊠ *351 Farmington Ave., at Woodland St.* ☎ *860/247–0998* ⊕ *www.marktwainhouse.org* 🎟 *$19* ⊙ *Daily 9:30–5:30.*

FAMILY **The New Children's Museum.** A life-size walk-through replica of a 60-foot sperm whale greets patrons at this museum. Located in West Hartford, the museum also has a wildlife sanctuary and real-life images of outer space beamed in from NASA, as well as an exhibit that encourages would-be engineers to build a city and solve for real-world problems like natural disasters and traffic. ⊠ *950 Trout Brook Dr., 5 miles west of downtown, West Hartford* ☎ *860/231–2824* ⊕ *www. thechildrensmuseumct.org* 🎟 *$14.75* ⊙ *Tues.–Sat. 9–4, Sun. 11–4.*

Fodor's Choice
★ **Wadsworth Atheneum Museum of Art.** Following a five-year, $33 million renovation project (completed in 2015), the nation's oldest public art museum now has a fresh face. The first American museum to acquire

works by Salvador Dalí and Italian Renaissance artist Caravaggio, it houses more than 50,000 artworks and artifacts spanning 5,000 years, along with 7,000 items documenting African-American history and culture in partnership with the Amistad Foundation. Particularly impressive are the museum's baroque, Impressionist, and Hudson River School collections. ⊠ *600 Main St.* ☎ *860/278–2670* ⊕ *www. wadsworthatheneum.org* 🖃 *$10* ☉ *Wed.–Fri. 11–5, weekends 10–5.*

WORTH NOTING

FAMILY **Bushnell Park.** Fanning out from the State Capitol building, this city park, created in 1850, was the first public space in the country with natural landscaping. The original designer, a Swiss-born landscape architect and botanist named Jacob Weidenmann, planted 157 varieties of trees and shrubs to create an urban arboretum. Kids love the Bushnell Park Carousel (open May–September), intricately hand-carved in 1914 by the Artistic Carousel Company of Brooklyn, New York. An oasis of green, the park has a pond and about 750 trees, including four state-champion trees. ⊠ *Asylum and Trinity Sts.* ☎ *860/232–6710* ⊕ *www. bushnellpark.org.*

Butler-McCook Homestead. Built in 1782, this was home to four generations of Butlers and McCooks until it became a museum in 1971. Today, it houses Hartford's oldest intact collection of art and antiques, including furnishings, family possessions, and Victorian-era toys that show the evolution of American tastes over nearly 200 years. The beautifully restored Victorian garden was originally designed by Jacob Weidenmann. ⊠ *396 Main St.* ☎ *860/522–1806* ⊕ *www.ctlandmarks.org* 🖃 *$10* ☉ *Oct.–Dec., weekends noon–4; May–Sept.,Thurs.–Sun. noon–4.*

QUICK
BITES

Mozzicato–De Pasquale's Bakery, Pastry Shop & Caffé. Located on Franklin Avenue in Hartford's Little Italy neighborhood, this shop serves delectable Italian pastries in the bakery, and espresso, cappuccino, and gelato in the café. ⊠ *329 Franklin Ave.* ☎ *860/296–0426* ⊕ *www.mozzicatobakery.com.*

Old State House. This Federal-style house with an elaborate cupola and roof balustrade was designed in the early 1700s by Charles Bulfinch, architect of the U.S. Capitol. It served as Connecticut's state capitol until a new building opened in 1879, when it became Hartford's city hall until 1915. In the 1820 Senate Chamber, where everyone from Abraham Lincoln to George Bush has spoken, you can view a portrait of George Washington by Gilbert Stuart, and in the Courtroom you can find out about the trial of the *Amistad* Africans in the very place it began. In summer, enjoy concerts and a farmers' market; don't forget to stop by the Museum of Natural and Other Curiosities. ⊠ *800 Main St.* ☎ *860/522–6766* ⊕ *www.ctosh.org* 🖃 *$6* ☉ *Mid-Oct.–June, weekdays 10–5; July–mid-Oct., Tues.–Sat. 10–5.*

State Capitol. The gold-leaf dome of the State Capitol rises above Bushnell Park. Built in 1878, the building houses the state's executive offices and legislative chamber, as well as historical memorabilia. On a tour, you can walk through the Hall of Flags, see a statue of Connecticut state hero Nathan Hale, and observe the proceedings of the General Assembly, when in session, from the public galleries. ⊠ *210 Capitol*

Connecticut's Victorian Gothic state capitol rises from Hartford's Bushnell Park.

Ave. ☎ *860/240–0222* 🌐 *www.cga.ct.gov/capitoltours* 🎟 *Free* 🕓 *Building weekdays 9–3. Tours hourly: Sept.–June, weekdays 9:15–1:15; July and Aug., weekdays 9:15–2:15.*

OFF THE BEATEN PATH

Noah Webster House. This 18th-century farmhouse is the birthplace of the famed author (1758–1843) of the *American Dictionary.* Inside you'll find Webster memorabilia and period furnishings; outside, there is a garden planted with herbs, vegetables, and flowers that would have been available to the Websters when they lived here. ✉ *227 S. Main St., West Hartford* ☎ *860/521–5362* 🌐 *www.noahwebsterhouse.org* 🎟 *$7* 🕓 *Daily 1–4.*

WHERE TO EAT

$$ PIZZA

🍴 **First and Last Tavern.** What looks to be a simple neighborhood joint south of downtown is actually one of the state's most hallowed pizza parlors, serving superb thin-crust pies (locals love the puttanesca) since 1936. The old-fashioned wooden bar in one room is jammed most evenings with suburbia-bound daily-grinders. The main dining room, which is just as noisy, has a brick outer wall covered with celebrity photos. [$] *Average main: $18* ✉ *939 Maple Ave.* ☎ *860/956–6000* 🌐 *www.firstandlasttavern.com* ✍ *Reservations not accepted.*

$$$$ AMERICAN Fodor's Choice ★

🍴 **Max Downtown.** With its contemporary design, extensive martini list, and sophisticated cuisine, Max Downtown is a favorite among the city's well-heeled, as well as a popular after-work spot. Creative entrées include sesame-crusted ahi tuna with a ginger-scallion ponzu sauce; seared sea scallops with coconut-whipped carrots, glazed turnip, and sweet potato; and a wide range of perfectly prepared steaks with toppings like foie gras butter and Maytag bleu cheese sauce. Don't skip dessert—not with options like chocolate-chip ice cream cake or s'mores crème brûlée. Max Downtown is part of a small empire of excellent Hartford-area restaurants. [$] *Average main: $40* ✉ *185 Asylum St.* ☎ *860/522–2530* 🌐 *www.maxrestaurantgroup.com/downtown* 🕘 *No lunch weekends* ✍ *Reservations essential.*

$$ ITALIAN 🍴 **Salute.** Packed every night, Salute is *the* downtown spot for consistently delicious Italian fare and excellent service. The kitchen serves up a lengthy list of pasta dishes: try the chicken gnocchi with pesto cream or the perfectly executed fettuccine with clams. The rib-eye steak and filet mignon are always on point, as are the house seafood specialties like sesame-crusted ahi tuna with veggie spring rolls or the scallops with shrimp fried rice. Traditional Italian desserts like tiramisu and gelato are available for after dinner. [$] *Average main: $24* ✉ *100 Trumbull St.* ☎ *860/899–1350* 🌐 *www.salutect.com* 🕘 *No lunch Sun.*

WHERE TO STAY

$$$ HOTEL 🏨 **Hartford Marriott Downtown.** This upscale hotel is connected to the Connecticut Convention Center and conveniently located within walking distance of the Connecticut Science Center, the Wadsworth Atheneum, the Old State House, and other attractions. **Pros:** close to major attractions; in the heart of downtown. **Cons:** convenient location comes at a price. [$] *Rooms from: $349* ✉ *200 Columbus Blvd.* ☎ *860/249–8000* 🌐 *www.marriott.com* 🛏 *401 rooms, 8 suites* 🍽 *No meals.*

$$ HOTEL 🏨 **Residence Inn Hartford-Downtown.** In the historic Richardson Building, the all-suites Residence Inn is convenient to Pratt Street, the Hartford Stage, and the Old State House. **Pros:** spacious rooms; right in middle of downtown. **Cons:** rather dull furnishings. [$] *Rooms from: $249* ✉ *942 Main St.* ☎ *860/524–5550* 🌐 *www.marriott.com* 🛏 *120 suites* 🍽 *Breakfast.*

NIGHTLIFE AND PERFORMING ARTS

NIGHTLIFE

Black-Eyed Sally's. For barbecue and blues, head to laid-back Black-Eyed Sally's. ✉ *350 Asylum St.* ☎ *860/278–7427* 🌐 *www.blackeyedsallys.com.*

PERFORMING ARTS

Bushnell. In addition to national tours of major musicals, the Bushnell is home to the Hartford Symphony Orchestra. ✉ *166 Capitol Ave.* ☎ *860/987–5900, 888/824–2874* 🌐 *www.bushnell.org.*

Hartford Stage Company. The Tony Award–winning Hartford Stage Company puts on new and classic plays from around the world. ✉ *50 Church St.* ☎ *860/527–5151* 🌐 *www.hartfordstage.org.*

Real Art Ways. Modern and experimental musical compositions are presented here, as well as avant-garde and foreign films. ✉ *56 Arbor St.* ☎ *860/232–1006* 🌐 *www.realartways.org.*

TheatreWorks. This is the Hartford equivalent of "Off-Broadway," where experimental new dramas are presented. ✉ *233 Pearl St.* ☎ *860/527–7838* 🌐 *www.theaterworkshartford.org.*

FARMINGTON

9 miles southwest of Hartford.

Farmington, incorporated in 1645, is a classic river town with a perfectly preserved main street. This bucolic and affluent suburb of Hartford oozes historical charm. Antiques shops are near the intersection of Routes 4 and 10, along with some excellent house museums.

GETTING HERE AND AROUND

Farmington is most easily reachable by car. From Hartford, take Interstate 84 west to Route 4 west.

EXPLORING

Hill-Stead Museum. Converted from a private home into a museum by its talented owner, Theodate Pope, a turn-of-the-20th-century architect, the house has a superb collection of French Impressionist art displayed in situ, including Claude Monet's haystacks and Edouard Manet's *Guitar Player* hanging in the drawing room. Poetry readings take place in the elaborate Beatrix Farrand–designed sunken garden every other week in summer. ✉ *35 Mountain Rd.* ☎ *860/677–4787* 🌐 *www.hillstead.org* 🎫 *$15* 🕓 *Tues.–Sat. 10–4.*

6

OFF THE BEATEN PATH

Lake Compounce. Opened in 1846, the country's oldest amusement park is known to locals simply as "the Lake." Today's attractions include a lakefront beach; a water park; and a clipper ship with a 300-gallon bucket of water that gives unsuspecting guests a good dousing. There are also such hair-raising rides as the Sky Coaster, the Boulder Dash, and the Zoomerang. ✉ *822 Lake Ave., off I–84, Bristol* ☎ *860/583–3631* 🌐 *www.lakecompounce.com* 🎫 *$38.99* 🕓 *Memorial Day–Oct. (call for hrs).*

WHERE TO EAT AND STAY

$$ ITALIAN

🍴 **Joey Garlic's.** Come to this Italian eatery for huge portions of classic dishes and a family-friendly atmosphere. Patrons rave about the eggplant fries and the meatball salad. Specialty pizzas and overstuffed grinders are crowd-pleasers as well. [$] *Average main: $19* ✉ *372 Scott Swamp Rd.* ☎ *860/678–7231* 🌐 *www.joeygarlics.com.*

$ HOTEL

🏨 **Avon Old Farms Hotel.** A country hotel at the base of Avon Mountain, this 20-acre compound of Colonial-style buildings with manicured grounds sits midway between Farmington and Simsbury. **Pros:** attractive pool area; central location. **Cons:** furniture somewhat dated; rooms in the annex are motel style. [$] *Rooms from: $164* ✉ *279 Avon Mountain Rd., Avon* ☎ *860/677–1651* 🌐 *www.avonoldfarmshotel.com* 🛏 *160 rooms* 🍽 *Breakfast.*

THE LITCHFIELD HILLS

Fodor's Choice ★

The foothills of the Berkshire Mountains are some of the most spectacular and unspoiled scenery in Connecticut. Two highways, Interstate 84 and Route 8, form the southern and eastern boundaries of the region. New York, to the west, and Massachusetts, to the north, complete the rectangle. Grand old inns and sophisticated eateries are plentiful. Rolling farmlands abut thick forests, and trails—including a section of the

Appalachian Trail—traverse state parks and forests. Two rivers, the Housatonic and the Farmington, attract anglers and canoers, and the state's three largest natural lakes, Waramaug, Bantam, and Twin, are here. Sweeping town greens and stately homes anchor Litchfield and New Milford. Kent, New Preston, and Woodbury draw avid antiquers, and Washington and Norfolk provide a glimpse into New England village life as it might have existed two centuries ago.

ESSENTIALS

Visitor Information Litchfield Hills–Northwest Connecticut Convention and Visitors Bureau. ☎ *800/663–1273* 🌐 *www.northwestct.com.*

NEW MILFORD

28 miles west of Waterbury, 46 miles northeast of Greenwich.

If you're approaching the Litchfield Hills from the south, New Milford is a practical starting point to begin a visit. It was also a starting point for a young cobbler named Roger Sherman, who opened his shop in 1743 at the corner of Main and Church streets. A Declaration of Independence signatory, Sherman also helped draft the Articles of Confederation and the Constitution. You'll find shops, galleries, and eateries all within a short stroll of the New Milford green.

GETTING HERE AND AROUND

New Milford is best visited by car. From Danbury and points south, take Route 7 to Route 202 to reach the town.

EXPLORING

Silo at Hunt Hill Farm Trust. Once the property of Skitch Henderson, former music director of the New York Pops, this unusual attraction consists of several farm buildings dating back to the 1700s. The Skitch Henderson Living Museum focuses on his collections of musical memorabilia, including rare recordings and scores. Inside a barn is the Silo Store, packed with crafts, cooking supplies, and assorted goodies and sauces. The Silo Gallery presents art shows and literary readings; you can also enroll in a class at the on-site cooking school. ✉ *44 Upland Rd.* ☎ *860/355–0300* 🌐 *www.thesilo.com* 🎟 *Suggested donation* 🕒 *Wed.–Sat. 10–5, Sun. noon–5.*

WHERE TO EAT

$$ BARBECUE 🍴 **The Cookhouse.** Stop here for some of the best "slow-smoked" barbecue in Connecticut. The casual, family-friendly spot offers a wide variety of comfort-food staples. Try the chicken-fried steak, cookhouse meat loaf, or the delicious baby back ribs. Come hungry on Thursday night: it's all-you-can-eat barbecue for $21, and it comes with a free pint of beer. [$] *Average main: $20* ✉ *31 Danbury Rd.* ☎ *860/355–4111* 🌐 *www.thecookhouse.com.*

KENT

14 miles northwest of New Milford.

Kent once held many ironworks, and today boasts the area's greatest concentration of art galleries—some nationally renowned—as well as

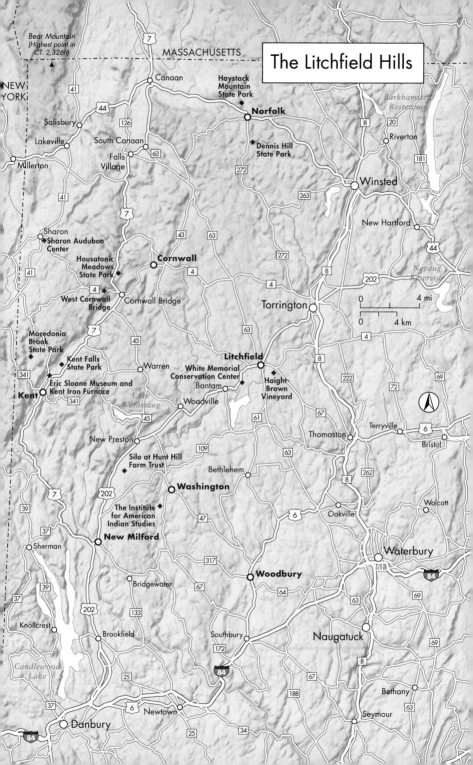

a prep school of the same name. The Schaghticoke Indian Reservation is also here: during the Revolutionary War, 100 Schaghticokes helped defend the colonies by transmitting messages of army intelligence from the Litchfield Hills to Long Island Sound along the hilltops by way of shouts and drumbeats.

GETTING HERE AND AROUND

To reach Kent by car, travel north from New Milford on Route 7.

EXPLORING

Eric Sloane Museum and Kent Iron Furnace. Hardware-store buffs and vintage-tool aficionados will feel right at home at this museum. Artist and author Eric Sloane (1905–85) was fascinated by Early American woodworking tools, and his collection showcases examples of American craftsmanship from the 17th to the 19th century. The museum contains a re-creation of Sloane's last studio and also encompasses the ruins of a 19th-century iron furnace. Sloane's books and prints, which celebrate vanishing aspects of Americana such as barns and covered bridges, are available for sale here. ✉ *31 Kent–Cornwall Rd.* ☎ *860/927–3849* 🌐 *www.ct.gov/cct/cwp/view.asp?a=2127&q=302262* 🎟 *$8* 🕒 *May–Oct., Thurs.–Sun. 10–4.*

Macedonia Brook State Park. Early-season trout fishing is superb at 2,300-acre Macedonia Brook State Park, where you can also hike and cross-country ski. ✉ *159 Macedonia Brook Rd., off Rte. 341* ☎ *860/927–3238* 🌐 *www.ct.gov/deep/macedoniabrook* 🎟 *Free* 🕒 *Daily 8–sunset.*

WHERE TO STAY

$$$ B&B/INN Fodor's Choice ★

🏨 **The Inn at Kent Falls.** This 18th-century Colonial carefully preserves the charm of the past while providing every convenience today's travelers expect. **Pros:** stylish rooms; country setting; excellent breakfasts. **Cons:** queen rooms are on the small side. [$] *Rooms from: $350* ✉ *107 Kent Cornwall Rd.* ☎ *860/927–3197* 🌐 *www.theinnatkentfalls.com* 🛏 *6 rooms* 🍴 *Breakfast.*

SPORTS AND THE OUTDOORS

Appalachian Trail. The Appalachian Trail's longest river walk, off Route 341, is this nearly 8-mile hike from Kent to Cornwall Bridge along the Housatonic River. ✉ *Kent.*

EN ROUTE

Kent Falls State Park. Heading north from Kent toward Cornwall, you'll pass the entrance to 295-acre Kent Falls State Park, where you can hike a short way to one of the most impressive waterfalls in the state and picnic in the green meadows at the base of the falls. On weekends, there's a $15 fee for parking. ✉ *U.S. 7* ☎ *860/927–3238* 🌐 *www.ct.gov/deep/kentfalls* 🎟 *Free* 🕒 *Daily 8–7.*

SHOPPING

House of Books. Stop in here for a great selection of books for readers of all ages, along with local maps, cards, and art supplies. ✉ *10 N. Main St.* ☎ *860/927–4104* 🌐 *www.hobooks.com.*

Kent Coffee and Chocolate Company. This shop sells delicious organic chocolates, and many of the homemade varieties are filled with roasted nuts and fruits. It's also a great place to stop for coffee and tea. ✉ *8 N. Main St.* ☎ *860/927–1445* 🌐 *www.kentcoffee.com.*

6

CORNWALL

12 miles northeast of Kent.

Connecticut's Cornwalls can get confusing: there's Cornwall, Cornwall Bridge, West Cornwall, Cornwall Hollow, East Cornwall, and North Cornwall. This quiet part of the Litchfield Hills is known for its fantastic vistas of woods and mountains and for its covered bridge, which spans the Housatonic.

GETTING HERE AND AROUND

Head north from Kent on Route 7 to reach Cornwall.

EXPLORING

Housatonic Meadows State Park. The park is marked by its tall pine trees near the Housatonic River and has terrific riverside campsites. Fly-fishers consider this 2-mile stretch of the river among the best places in New England to test their skills against trout and bass. ✉ *U.S. 7, Cornwall Bridge* ☎ *860/927–3238* 🌐 *www.ct.gov/deep/housatonicmeadows.*

FAMILY **Sharon Audubon Center.** With 11 miles of hiking trails, this 1,147-acre property—a mixture of forests, meadows, wetlands, ponds, and streams—provides myriad hiking opportunities. It's also home to Princess, an American crow, who shares the visitor center with small hawks, an owl, and other animals in a live-animal display. Also here is a natural-history museum and children's adventure center. An aviary houses a bald eagle, a red-tailed hawk, and two turkey vultures. ✉ *325 Cornwall Bridge Rd., Sharon* ☎ *860/364–0520* 🌐 *www.sharon.audubon.org* 🎟 *$3* 🕓 *Tues.–Sat. 9–5, Sun. 1–5. Trails daily dawn–dusk.*

West Cornwall Bridge. A romantic reminder of the past, this single-lane bridge is several miles up U.S. 7 on Route 128 in West Cornwall. The bridge was built in 1841 and incorporates strut techniques that were later copied by bridge builders around the country. ✉ *Junction of Rtes. 7 and 128.*

WHERE TO STAY

$ B&B/INN 🏨 **Cornwall Inn.** This 19th-century inn combines country charm with contemporary elegance; eight rustic guest rooms in the adjacent lodge are slightly more private and have cedar-post beds. **Pros:** tranquil setting; lovely grounds; welcoming to kids and pets. **Cons:** a bit far from neighboring towns. [$] *Rooms from: $199* ✉ *270 Kent Rd. S* ☎ *860/672–6884* 🌐 *www.cornwallinn.com* 🛏 *12 rooms, 1 suite* 🍴 *Breakfast.*

SPORTS AND THE OUTDOORS

CANOEING AND KAYAKING

Clarke Outdoors. This outfitter rents canoes, kayaks, and rafts, and operates 10-mile trips from Falls Village to Housatonic Meadows State Park. ✉ *163 Rte. 7, 1 mile south of covered bridge, West Cornwall* ☎ *860/672–6365* 🌐 *www.clarkeoutdoors.com.*

FISHING

Housatonic Anglers. Enjoy a half- or full-day fishing trip on the Housatonic River and its tributaries with this company. You can also take fly-fishing lessons. ✉ *26 Bolton Hill Rd.* ☎ *860/672–4457* 🌐 *www.housatonicanglers.com.*

Be patient on back roads: many covered bridges, like this one in West Cornwall, are single-lane only.

Housatonic River Outfitters. This outfitter operates a full-service fly shop, leads guided trips of the region, conducts classes in fly-fishing, and stocks a good selection of vintage and antique gear. ⊠ *24 Kent Rd., Cornwall Bridge* ☎ *860/672–1010* ⊕ *www.dryflies.com.*

SKIING

FAMILY **Mohawk Mountain.** The trails at Mohawk Mountain, ranging down 650 vertical feet, include plenty of intermediate terrain, with a few trails for beginners and a few steeper sections for more advanced skiers toward the top of the mountain. A small section is devoted to snowboarders. Trails are serviced by five triple lifts and three magic carpets; 12 trails are lighted for night skiing. The base lodge has munchies and a retail shop, and halfway up the slope the Pine Lodge Restaurant has an outdoor patio. **Facilities:** 25 trails; 112 acres; 650-foot vertical drop; 7 lifts ⊠ *46 Great Hollow Rd., off Rte. 4* ☎ *860/672–6100, 800/895–5222* ⊕ *www.mohawkmtn.com* ▨ *Lift ticket $60.*

NORFOLK

23 miles northeast of Cornwall, 59 miles north of New Haven.

Thanks to its severe climate and terrain, Norfolk has resisted development and stands as one of the best-preserved villages in the Northeast. Notable industrialists have been summering here for two centuries, and many enormous homesteads still exist. The striking town green, at the junction of Route 272 and U.S. 44, has a fountain designed by Augustus Saint-Gaudens (executed by Stanford White) at its southern corner. It stands as a memorial to Joseph Battell, who turned Norfolk into a major trading center.

GETTING HERE AND AROUND

To reach Norfolk by car from points north or south, use Route 272.

EXPLORING

Dennis Hill State Park. Dr. Frederick Shepard Dennis, the former owner of these 240 acres, lavishly entertained his guests—among them President William Howard Taft and several Connecticut governors—in the stone pavilion at the summit of the estate. From its 1,627-foot height, you can see Haystack Mountain, New Hampshire, and, on a clear day, the New Haven harbor, all the way across the state. Picnic on the park's grounds or hike one of its many trails. ✉ *Rte. 272* ☎ *860/482–1817* 🌐 *www.ct.gov/deep/cwp/view.asp?A=2716&Q=325186* 🎟 *Free* 🕒 *Daily 8 am–dusk.*

Haystack Mountain State Park. One of the most spectacular views in the state can be seen from this park at the end of a challenging trail to the top. If you'd rather drive, a road will get you halfway there. ✉ *Rte. 272* ☎ *860/482–1817* 🌐 *www.ct.gov/deep/HaystackMountain* 🕒 *Daily 8–sunset.*

6

WHERE TO STAY

$$ B&B/INN 🏨 **Manor House Inn.** Among this 1898 Bavarian Tudor's remarkable appointments are its wood-beam ceilings, graceful arches, and antique beds—not to mention the 20 stained-glass windows designed by Louis Comfort Tiffany. **Pros:** sumptuous decor; lavish breakfasts; peaceful atmosphere. **Cons:** no phone or TV in guest rooms (and mobile reception is iffy in these parts). [$] *Rooms from: $215* ✉ *69 Maple Ave.* ☎ *866/542–5690* 🌐 *www.manorhouse-norfolk.com* 🛏 *8 rooms, 1 suite* 🍴 *Breakfast.*

$$ B&B/INN 🏨 **Mountain View Inn.** Perfectly restored, this gracious country retreat welcomes you with expansive lawns and a lovely wraparound porch. **Pros:** meticulously maintained; gracious innkeepers; great location. **Cons:** Victorian decor not everyone's cup of tea. [$] *Rooms from: $225* ✉ *67 Litchfield Rd.* ☎ *860/542–6991, 866/792–7812* 🌐 *www.mvinn.com* 🛏 *7 rooms, 1 cottage* 🍴 *Breakfast.*

PERFORMING ARTS

Infinity Music Hall. Built in 1883, this modernized 300-seat music hall hosts more than 200 shows a year by local performers as well as nationally known groups. ✉ *20 Greenwoods Rd.* ☎ *866/666–6306* 🌐 *www.infinityhall.com.*

Norfolk Chamber Music Festival. Held at the Music Shed on the 70-acre Ellen Battell Stoeckel Estate, the Norfolk Chamber Music Festival presents world-renowned artists and ensembles on Friday and Saturday evenings in summer. Students from the Yale School of Music perform on Thursday evening and Saturday morning. Stroll the 70-acre grounds or visit the art gallery. ✉ *Ellen Battell Stoeckel Estate, 20 Litchfield Rd.* ☎ *860/542–3000* 🌐 *www.yale.edu/norfolk.*

SHOPPING

Norfolk Artisans Guild. The shop carries works by more than 60 local artisans, from hand-stitched pillows to one-of-a-kind baskets. ⊠ *10 Station Pl.* ☎ *860/542–5055* ⊘ *Closed Mon. and Tues.*

LITCHFIELD

20 miles south of Norfolk, 34 miles west of Hartford.

Everything in Litchfield, the wealthiest and most noteworthy town in the Litchfield Hills, seems to exist on a larger scale than in neighboring burgs, especially the impressive Litchfield Green and the white Colonial and Greek Revival homes that line the broad elm-shaded streets. Harriet Beecher Stowe, author of *Uncle Tom's Cabin,* and her brother, abolitionist preacher Henry Ward Beecher, were born and raised in Litchfield, and many famous Americans earned their law degrees at the Litchfield Law School. Today lovely but expensive boutiques and restaurants line the downtown area.

GETTING HERE AND AROUND

To reach Litchfield by car from points north or south, take Route 8 to Route 118 west.

EXPLORING

Haight-Brown Vineyard. A founding member of the Connecticut Wine Trail, the state's oldest winery opened its doors in 1975. You can stop in for complimentary tastings and winery tours. Seasonal events include barrel tastings in April and a harvest festival in September. ⊠ *29 Chestnut Hill Rd., off Rte. 118* ☎ *860/567–4045* ⊕ *www.haightvineyards. com* ▱ *Tasting $9* ⊘ *Mon.–Thurs. noon–5, Fri.–Sun. noon–6.*

Litchfield History Museum. In this well-regarded museum, seven neatly organized galleries highlight family life and work during the 50 years following the American Revolution. The extensive reference library has information about the town's historic buildings, including the Sheldon Tavern, where George Washington slept on several occasions, and the Litchfield Female Academy, where in the late 1700s Sarah Pierce taught girls not only sewing and deportment but also mathematics and history. ⊠ *7 South St., at Rtes. 63 and 118* ☎ *860/567–4501* ⊕ *www.litchfieldhistoricalsociety.org* ▱ *$5, includes Tapping Reeve House and Litchfield Law School* ⊘ *Mid-Apr.–late Nov., Tues.–Sat. 11–5, Sun. 1–5.*

Tapping Reeve House and Litchfield Law School. In 1773, Judge Tapping Reeve enrolled his first student, Aaron Burr, in what became the first law school in the country. (Before Judge Reeve, students studied the law as apprentices, not in formal classes.) This school is dedicated to Reeve's achievement and to the notable students who passed through its halls, including three U.S. Supreme Court justices. This museum is one of the state's most worthy attractions, with multimedia exhibits, an excellent introductory film, and restored facilities. ⊠ *82 South St.* ☎ *860/567–4501* ⊕ *www.litchfieldhistoricalsociety.org* ▱ *$5, includes Litchfield History Museum* ⊘ *Mid-Apr.–late Nov., Tues.–Sat. 11–5, Sun. 1–5.*

Fodor's Choice ★ **White Memorial Conservation Center.** This 4,000-acre nature preserve houses top-notch natural-history exhibits. There are 30 bird-watching platforms, two self-guided nature trails, several boardwalks, boating facilities, and 35 miles of hiking, cross-country-skiing, and horseback-riding trails. ✉ *80 Whitehall Rd., off U.S. 202* ☎ *860/567–0857* 🌐 *www.whitememorialcc.org* 🎟 *Grounds free, conservation center $6* 🕓 *Grounds, daily dawn–dusk; conservation center, Mon.–Sat. 9–5, Sun. noon–5.*

WHERE TO EAT AND STAY

$$$ AMERICAN 🍴 **The Village.** Beloved among visitors and locals alike, this storefront eatery in a redbrick town house serves tasty, unfussy food—inexpensive pub grub in one room, updated contemporary American cuisine in the other. Whether you order a burger or horseradish-and-Parmesan-crusted salmon, you're bound to be pleased. [$] *Average main: $25* ✉ *25 West St.* ☎ *860/567–8307* 🌐 *www.village-litchfield.com.*

$$$$ AMERICAN 🍴 **West Street Grill.** This sophisticated dining room on the town green is *the* place to see and be seen. Dinner selections might include free-range chicken with potato puree and mushrooms, braised short ribs over a Gorgonzola-polenta cake, or organic Irish salmon with fingerling potatoes. Don't miss the house-made ice creams and sorbets either. [$] *Average main: $36* ✉ *43 West St.* ☎ *860/567–3885* 🌐 *www.weststreetgrill.com.*

$$$$ RESORT Fodor's Choice ★ 🏨 **Winvian.** This private 113-acre hideaway consists of 18 of the most imaginative and luxuriously outfitted cottages you'll ever lay eyes on. **Pros:** whimsical and superplush accommodations; outstanding cuisine; stunning setting. **Cons:** superpricey. [$] *Rooms from: $459* ✉ *155 Alain White Rd., Morris* ☎ *860/567–9600* 🌐 *www.winvian.com* 🛏 *18 cottages, 1 suite* 🍽 *Some meals.*

SPORTS AND THE OUTDOORS

HIKING

Mt. Tom State Park. Hike the mile-long trail to the stone tower atop Mt. Tom and enjoy expansive views, or take a swim in the pond below and picnic on the beach. ✉ *U.S. 202* ☎ *860/868–2592 (Labor Day–Memorial Day), 860/567–8870 (Memorial Day–Labor Day)* 🌐 *www.ct.gov/deep/mounttom* 🎟 *Parking: weekends $15, weekdays $10* 🕓 *Daily 8–sunset.*

HORSEBACK RIDING

Lee's Riding Stable. This stable leads trail and pony rides. Lessons are also available. ✉ *57 E. Litchfield Rd.* ☎ *860/567–0785* 🌐 *www.windfieldmorganfarm.com/lees.*

SHOPPING

Jeffrey Tillou Antiques. This antiques store specializes in 18th- and 19th-century American furniture and paintings. ✉ *39 West St.* ☎ *860/567–9693* 🌐 *www.tillouantiques.com.*

WASHINGTON

14 miles southwest of Litchfield.

The beautiful buildings of the Gunnery prep school mingle with stately Colonials and churches in Washington, one of the best-preserved Colonial towns in Connecticut. The Mayflower Inn, south of the Gunnery on Route 47, attracts an exclusive clientele. In 1779 Washington, which was settled in 1734, became the first town in the United States to be named for the first president.

GETTING HERE AND AROUND

Washington is best visited by car. Route 47 runs through town, connecting it with New Preston to the north and Woodbury to the south.

EXPLORING

The Institute for American Indian Studies. The exhibits in this small but excellent and thoughtfully arranged collection detail the history and continuing presence of more than 10,000 years of Native American life in New England. Highlights include nature trails, a simulated archaeological site, and an authentically constructed Algonquian Village with wigwams, a longhouse, a rock shelter, and more. A gift shop presents the work of some of the country's best Native American artists. ✉ *38 Curtis Rd., off Rte. 199* ☎ *860/868–0518* 🌐 *www.iaismuseum.org* 🎟 *$8* 🕒 *Mon.–Sat. 10–5, Sun. noon–5.*

WHERE TO EAT AND STAY

$$$$ AMERICAN 🍴 **The Mayflower Grille.** At the refined and romantic restaurant of the Mayflower Inn & Spa, gaze through the dining room's large windows—or from your seat on the terrace in warm weather—toward the formal English gardens while enjoying deftly prepared regional American cuisine. The menu changes seasonally, but may include Atlantic salmon roasted with fennel or Kobe-beef carpaccio with Parmesan aioli. After dinner, stop by the wood-paneled library for a glass of cognac. [$] *Average main: $37* ✉ *118 Woodbury Rd.* ☎ *860/868–9466* 🌐 *www.mayflowerinn.com.*

$$$$ RESORT Fodor's Choice ★ 🏨 **Mayflower Inn & Spa.** Though the most expensive suites at this inn run upwards of $1,000 per night, the elegant Mayflower is often booked months in advance. **Pros:** perfected landscaped grounds; solicitous but relaxed service; outstanding spa. **Cons:** very pricey. [$] *Rooms from: $690* ✉ *118 Woodbury Rd.* ☎ *860/868–9466* 🌐 *www.mayflowerinn.com* 🛏 *19 rooms, 11 suites* 🍽 *No meals.*

WOODBURY

10 miles southeast of Washington.

There may be more antiques shops in quickly growing Woodbury than in all other towns in the Litchfield Hills combined. Some of the best-preserved examples of Colonial religious architecture in New England can be found here along U.S. 6, including five magnificent churches and the Greek Revival King Solomon's Temple, formerly a Masonic lodge.

Continued on page 326

ANTIQUES AND CRAFTS SHOPPING
SOMETHING OLD, SOMETHING NEW

By Christina Valhouli

Forget the mall. In New England, shoppers can pick up serious antiques or quirky bric-a-brac in old mills and converted barns. Or hit funky galleries or annual craft fairs to meet artisans and buy one-of-a-kind products. Your souvenirs will be as memorable as the shopping experience.

Alongside New England's wealth of early American history is some of the best antique and craft shopping in the country—and often in beautiful settings perfect for browsing. You can explore galleries in converted farmhouses, craft shops clustered around the village green, or a picturesque Main Street (Woodstock, Vermont, or Camden, Maine, are good bets). Drive through historic coastal towns, like Essex, Massachusetts, where finds such as sun-bleached, centuries-old wooden tables or antique compasses evoke the area's maritime heritage. Picture-perfect towns like Blue Hill, Maine, and Chester, Connecticut, are home to plenty of contemporary artists' galleries and cooperatives, like the Connecticut River Artisans, which showcases handmade quilts, jewelry, and ceramics; or try your luck at the Frog Hollow Craft Center in Burlington, Vermont.

Top Left, Hand-blown glass. Top right, Brimfield Antique Show. Bottom, antique pocket watch.

GREAT FINDS: CRAFTS

When most people think of a typical New England look, the austere lines of a Shaker table or the colorful patterns in a quilt come to mind. Artisans here still make crafts the old-fashioned way, but a new generation of glassblowers, potters, and weavers is creating products that will appeal to modernistas.

QUILTS. Today's quilters continue to produce traditional quilts, but there are plenty of contemporary styles available. Instead of star patterns, go for bold stripes or blocky squares made from funky fabrics. Buy one for your bed or to hang; baby quilts start around $100.

SHAKER-STYLE FURNITURE. The Shakers believed that form must follow function, and a typical Shaker design is clean, straight-lined, and devoid of decoration. Carpenters still make Shaker-inspired furniture, including ladderback chairs, tables, and bookcases. Chairs start around $300.

FELT. Humble felt is simply unspun wool that has been rolled and beaten into a solid form, but it's one of the most versatile (and eco-friendly) products around. Contemporary artists fashion felt into handbags, rugs, and even lightweight sculptures. Handbags start at $60.

CERAMICS. Visit a pottery studio or an art gallery and choose from ceramic plates and mugs or sturdier stoneware products that can survive the dishwasher. Small ceramic pieces start at $25.

WOOD-TURNED BOWLS. Hand- or wood-turned bowls are individually shaped on a lathe from solid blocks of wood. Each piece has a unique size, shape, grain pattern, and color. Look for rare spalted wood bowls—highly valued for their patterns and rich contrasts. Bowls are around $40 and up.

BLOWN GLASS. It's worth a trip to a glass-blowing studio just to see the artisans blow a gob of molten glass into a beautiful object. Best bets include colorful vases, bowls, and sculptures; handblown glass is typically $100 to $500.

GREAT FINDS: ANTIQUES

Antiques can run the gamut from auction-worthy pieces to decorative trinkets and vintage items from the '40s, '50s and '60s. Antique trends come and go, but popular New England buys include "smalls" like old prints and glass bottles. Don't be put off if you don't know a lot about antiques—however, do keep in mind that a true antique must be at least 100 years old.

KITCHEN TOOLS. Although you won't be tempted to cook with an old iron cauldron, items like engraved stove plates, mortar and pestles, and spoon racks look great on display for about $40–$180.

■TIP→
Start a collection easily with two or more of the same item (salt and pepper shakers) or style (speckled graniteware).

PENS. Hardly anyone writes letters anymore, which makes collecting old pens even more special. Parker pens from the 1970s are airplane inspired, while antique fountain pens are sheathed in beautiful wood or mother of pearl (and a joy to use). Prices are $100 up to thousands.

MIRRORS. If your taste runs toward the ornate, browse for 19th-century Federal and Queen Anne–style gilt mirrors. For something smaller and more understated, try a concave or vintage sunburst mirror. Prices range from $200–$2,000.

JEWELRY. Cuff links, earrings, and brooches make great gifts and will take up little room in your luggage. Antique jewelry runs the gamut from fun beaded necklaces to delicate Art Deco pieces. Prices start at $20.

MAPS. Frame an old nautical chart or map of a town you vacationed in for a stylish memento. Reproductions are easier on the wallet but still look good. Prices start at $40 for prints and run up to the thousands for antiques.

AMERICANA. This can be anything from painted signs to photographs of historic villages or kitschy porcelain figurines that evoke what it means to be American. Items inspired by the Stars and Stripes make colorful decorative accents for a country home feel. Postcards and other small items start at $5.

6

IN FOCUS ANTIQUES AND CRAFTS SHOPPING

TOP SHOPPING ROUTES & SIGHTS

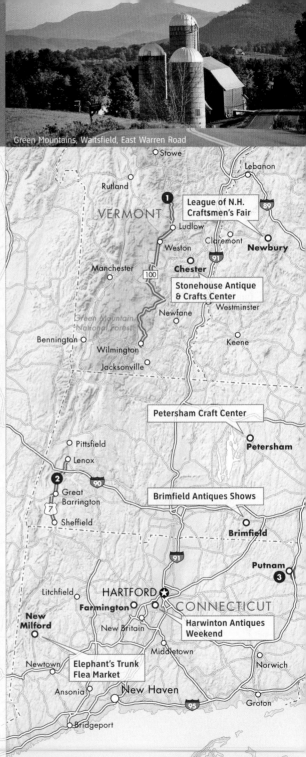

Green Mountains, Waitsfield, East Warren Road

One of the most effective and fun ways to shop is to hop in the car and drive through sleepy, scenic towns. On several key shopping routes in New England, stretches of road are absolutely packed with shops. Charles Street in Boston and downtown Providence and Portland are ideal, compact urban shopping areas for walking. If you do have wheels, try these routes.

❶ Route 100. One of the most picturesque drives in the Green Mountain State, this winding road goes from Wilmington north all the way up to Stowe. You'll pass craft studios, general stores like the Vermont Country Store in Weston, and plenty of red barns and covered bridges.

❷ Route 7, Berkshire County. Practically the entire route is chock-a-block with antiques stores. The Berkshire County Antiques and Art Dealers Association (⊕ www.bcaada.com) publishes a handy guide to the various shops. Key Western Massachusetts shopping towns include Great Barrington, Sheffield, and Lenox.

❸ Main Street, Putnam. Most of the town has a stuck-in-time quality, so it's a great place to spend the day the northeastern part of the state. The majority of antique stores are clustered around Main Street and its offshoots. Start your hunt at the massive Antiques Marketplace.

League of N.H. Craftsmen's Fair

Stonehouse Antique & Crafts Center

Petersham Craft Center

Brimfield Antiques Shows

Harwinton Antiques Weekend

Elephant's Trunk Flea Market

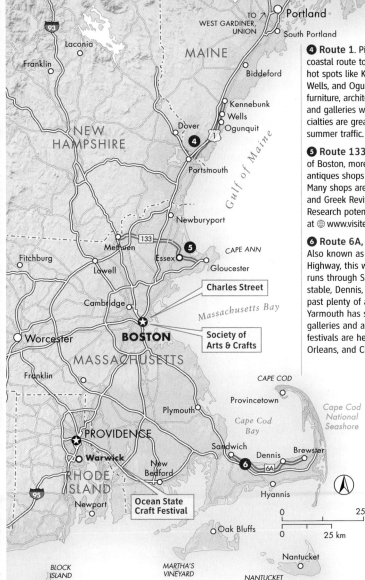

Antique Shop, Shefield, Berkshires | White Elephant Shop, Essex

4 Route 1. Pick up this Maine coastal route to hit shopping hot spots like Kennebunk, Wells, and Ogunquit. Colonial furniture, architectural antiques, and galleries with quirky specialties are great breaks from summer traffic.

5 Route 133, Essex. North of Boston, more than 30 antiques shops line this road. Many shops are in old Colonial and Greek Revival buildings. Research potential shops online at ⊕ www.visitessexma.com).

6 Route 6A, Cape Cod. Also known as the Old King's Highway, this winding route runs through Sandwich, Barnstable, Dennis, and Brewster past plenty of antiques shops. Yarmouth has several art galleries and annual crafts festivals are held in Falmouth, Orleans, and Chatham.

DID YOU KNOW?

Antiques can be more than just decoration: clocks can be fixed to tell time, dressers are great for storage, and old-fashioned oil lamps can illuminate today's homes, too.

WHERE TO GET THE GOODS

Depending on your budget, there are plenty of places to shop. Take your pick from artisan studios, art galleries, auction houses, and multi-dealer antique centers. Some antiques shops are one step above flea markets, so prices can vary widely. Antiques shows and craft fairs also offer excellent one-stop shopping opportunities.

TOP ANTIQUES SHOWS

★ **Brimfield Antique and Collectible Shows**, Brimfield, Massachusetts. May, July and September (⊕ *www.brimfieldshow.com*).
Connecticut Spring Antiques Show, Hartford, Connecticut. March (⊕ *www.ctspringantiquesshow.com*). June and September **Elephant's Trunk Country Flea Market,** New Milford, Connecticut. Most Sundays except in December and March (⊕ *www.etflea.com*).
Maine Antiques Festival, Union, Maine. August (⊕ *maineantiquesfestival.com*).

Top, Ceramics sold along Route 100, Vermont.

Right, antique rocking horse.

TOP CRAFT FAIRS AND CENTERS

Center for Maine Crafts
West Gardiner, Maine (⊕ *mainecrafts.org*).
★ **League of New Hampshire Craftsmen's Fair**, Newbury, New Hampshire. August (⊕ *www.nhcrafts.org*).
Ocean State Artisans Holiday Craft Festival, Warwick, Rhode Island. November (⊕ *www.oceanstateartisans.com*).
Petersham Craft Center, Petersham, Massachusetts (⊕ *www.petershamcraftcenter.org*).
Society of Arts and Crafts, Boston, Massachusetts (⊕ *www.societyofcrafts.org*).
Stonehouse Antique and Crafts Center, Chester, Vermont (☎ 802/875–4477).

6

IN FOCUS ANTIQUES AND CRAFTS SHOPPING

SHOPPING KNOW-HOW

Many shops are often closed on Sundays and Mondays. Call ahead to confirm. Before you whip out the credit card (or a wad of cash), there are a few other things to remember.

■ Unless you're an expert, it can be difficult to tell if an item is a reproduction or a genuine antique. Buy a price guide or a reference book like Miller's *Antiques & Collectibles* or *Kovel's* to have an idea of a fair value.

■ To ensure you are buying from a legitimate source, make sure the dealer belongs to a professional organization.

■ Think carefully about shipping costs for bulky items. It's also a good idea to carry with you some key measurements from your house.

■ If you find a piece that you love, check it carefully for any flaws. Point out any dings or scratches and use it as a bargaining chip when negotiating a price.

■ Always remember the golden rule: Buy what you love at a price you can afford.

GETTING HERE AND AROUND

To reach Woodbury by car from Washington, take Route 47 south to Route 6.

EXPLORING

Glebe House Museum and The Gertrude Jekyll Garden. This property consists of the large, antiques-filled, gambrel-roof Colonial home of Dr. Samuel Seabury, who, in 1783, was elected the first Episcopal bishop in the United States, and its historic garden. The latter was designed in the 1920s by renowned British horticulturist Gertrude Jekyll. Though small, it is a classic, old-fashioned English-style garden and the only one of the three Jekyll designed in the United States still in existence. ✉ *49 Hollow Rd.* ☎ *203/263–2855* 🌐 *www.theglebehouse.org* 🎟 *$5* 🕓 *May–Oct., Wed.–Sun. 1–4; Nov., weekends 1–4.*

WHERE TO EAT AND STAY

$$$ AMERICAN Fodor's Choice ★ 🍴 **Good News Café.** Carole Peck is a well-known name throughout New England, and, since this café opened in 1992, foodies have been flocking to Woodbury to sample her superb cuisine. The emphasis is on healthy, innovative, and surprisingly well-priced fare: wok-seared Gulf shrimp with new potatoes, grilled green beans, and a garlic aioli, and the Nantucket cod with spinach and matchstick potatoes are good choices. In the simpler room next to the bar, you can order from a less expensive café menu. [$] *Average main: $27* ✉ *694 Main St. S* ☎ *203/266–4663* 🌐 *www.good-news-cafe.com* 🕓 *Closed Tues.*

$$ B&B/INN 🏨 **Cornucopia at Oldfield.** A short drive from Woodbury antiques shops and restaurants, this Federal Colonial house has a bounty of pleasing comforts, from high-quality antiques and soft bedding to floral gardens and a pool surrounded by a private hedge. **Pros:** fine antiques; beautifully kept grounds; modern in-room amenities. **Cons:** on somewhat busy road. [$] *Rooms from: $225* ✉ *782 N. Main St., Southbury* ☎ *203/267–6772* 🌐 *www.cornucopiabnb.com* 🛏 *4 rooms, 1 suite* 🍽 *Breakfast.*

SHOPPING

Country Loft Antiques. This antiques shop specializes in 18th- and 19th-century French country antiques. ✉ *557 Main St. S* ☎ *203/266–4500* 🌐 *www.countryloftantiques.com.*

Mill House Antiques. The Mill House carries formal and country English and French furniture and decor. ✉ *1068 Main St. N* ☎ *203/263–3446* 🌐 *www.millhouseantiquesandgardens.com.*

Monique Shay Antiques & Designs. The six barns that make up Monique Shay's store are packed with French Canadian country antiques. ✉ *920 Main St. S* ☎ *203/263–3186* 🌐 *www.moniqueshay.com.*

NEW HAVEN, MYSTIC, AND THE COAST

As you drive northeast along Interstate 95, culturally rich New Haven is the final urban obstacle between southwestern Connecticut's overdeveloped coast and southeastern Connecticut's quiet shoreline. The remainder of the jagged coast, which stretches to Rhode Island, consists of small fishing villages, quiet hamlets, and relatively undisturbed beaches. The only interruptions along this seashore are the industry and piers of New London and Groton. Mystic, Stonington, Old Saybrook, Clinton, and Guilford are havens for fans of antiques and boutiques. The Mashantucket Pequot Reservation owns and operates the Foxwoods Casino and the Mashantucket Pequot Museum & Research Center, near the town of Ledyard north of Groton, and the Mohegan Tribe run the Mohegan Sun casino in Uncasville. These two properties have added noteworthy hotels and marquee restaurants in recent years.

NEW HAVEN

46 miles northeast of Greenwich.

Though the city is best known as the home of Yale University, New Haven's historic district, dating back to the 17th century, and the distinctive shops, prestigious museums, and highly respected theaters downtown are major draws. In recent years, the restaurant scene has also garnered considerable acclaim, and has become famous for its unique "apizza" legacy.

GETTING HERE AND AROUND

By car, New Haven is accessible from both Interstate 95 and Route 15. By rail, Amtrak's Northeast Regional and high-speed Acela trains stop here, and New Haven is also the end of the eponymous Metro-North commuter line from New York City. Shore Line East train service connects New Haven and New London.

ESSENTIALS

Visitor Information Greater New Haven Convention and Visitors Bureau. ✉ *195 Church St., 14th fl.* ☏ *203/777–8550, 800/777–8550* ⊕ *www.visitnewhaven.com.*

EXPLORING

TOP ATTRACTIONS

Fodor'sChoice
★

Yale Center for British Art. Featuring the largest collection of British art outside Britain, the center surveys the development of English art, life, and thought from the Elizabethan period to the present. The skylighted galleries of architect Louis I. Kahn's final work contain works by John Constable, William Hogarth, Thomas Gainsborough, Joshua Reynolds, and J. M. W. Turner, to name but a few. You'll also find rare books and paintings documenting English history. ✉ *1080 Chapel St.* ☏ *203/432–2800, 877/274–8278* ⊕ *britishart.yale.edu* ☚ *Free* ☉ *Tues.–Sat. 10–5, Sun. noon–5.*

QUICK
BITES

Sugar Bakery and Sweet Shop. Winning Food Network's Cupcake Wars put this little East Haven bakery on the map. Stop in to try one of 25 different kinds of cupcake rotated daily. With flavors like cannoli, cookie dough, and the Elvis (banana cupcake with peanut-butter-and-jelly buttercream frosting), you're bound to find one (or more) to fuel your perfect sugar high. ✉ *422 Main St., East Haven* ☏ *203/469–0851* ⊕ *www.thesugarbakery.com.*

6

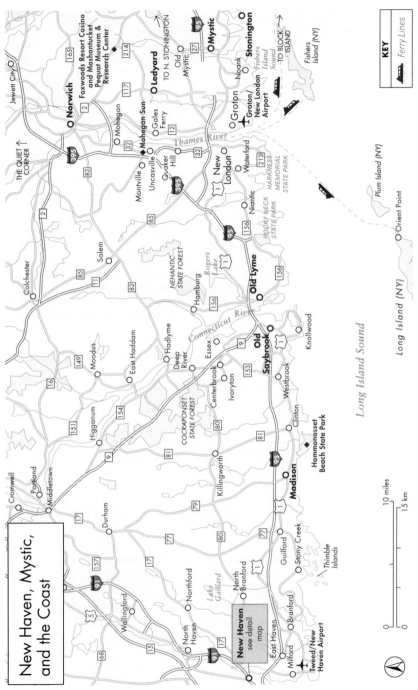

New Haven, Mystic, and the Coast

KEY

Ferry Lines

THE QUIET CORNER

Jewett City
Norwich
165
2
Foxwoods Resort Casino and Mashantucket Pequot Museum & Research Center
214
Ledyard
117
Mohegan
32
Mohegan Sun
Gales Ferry
12
Old Mystic
27
Mystic
Stonington
TO N. STONINGTON
Noank
Fishers Island Sound
Groton
New London Airport
Waterford
213
Fishers Island (NY)
TO BLOCK ISLAND

82
Montville
85
Uncasville
Quaker Hill
New London
11
Niantic
156
ROCKY NECK STATE PARK
HARKNESS MEMORIAL STATE PARK

2
Salem
11
82
NEHANTIC STATE FOREST
Rogers Lake
Hamburg
156
Old Lyme
156
Plum Island (NY)
Orient Point

Colchester
85
Moodus
149
East Haddam
Hadlyme
Deep River
Essex
9
Old Saybrook
Knollwood
11
Long Island (NY)

16
154
COCKAPONSET STATE FOREST
Centerbrook
Ivoryton
153
Westbrook
Clinton

151
Higganum
Cromwell
Portland
Middletown
9
81
Killingworth
80
81
Madison
Hammonasset Beach State Park
Long Island Sound

17
Durham
79
77
80
77
Guilford
Stony Creek
Thimble Islands

157
Northford
Lake Gaillard
North Branford
1
Wallingford
68
5
North Haven
17
15
Branford
East Haven
Milford
Tweed/New Haven Airport

New Haven see detail map

Thames River
Connecticut River

0   10 miles
0   15 km

Yale University. New Haven's manufacturing history dates to the 19th century, but the city owes its fame to merchant Elihu Yale. In 1718 his contributions enabled the Collegiate School, founded in 1701 at Saybrook, to settle in New Haven, where it changed its name to Yale University. This is one of the nation's great institutions of higher learning, and its campus holds some handsome neo-Gothic buildings and noteworthy museums. University guides conduct hour-long walking tours that include Connecticut Hall in the Old Campus, which has had a number of illustrious past residents. Tours start from 149 Elm Street on the north side of New Haven Green. ⊠ *Yale Visitor Center, 149 Elm St.* ☎ *203/432–2300* ⊕ *www.yale.edu/visitor* ◻ *Free* ☉ *Tours weekdays at 10:30 and 2, weekends at 1:30.*

WORTH NOTING

Beinecke Rare Book and Manuscript Library. The collections here include a Gutenberg Bible, illuminated manuscripts, and original Audubon bird prints. The building that houses them is an attraction in its own right: the walls are made of marble cut so thin that the light shines through, making the interior a breathtaking sight on sunny days. ⊠ *121 Wall St.* ☎ *203/432–2977* ⊕ *www.library.yale.edu/beinecke* ◻ *Free* ☉ *Mon.–Thurs. 9–7, Fri. 9–5, Sat. noon–5.*

New Haven Green. Bordered on its west side by the Yale campus, the green is a fine example of early urban planning. Village elders set aside the 16-acre plot as a town common as early as 1638. Three early-19th-century churches—the Gothic-style **Trinity Episcopal Church,** the Georgian-style **Center Congregational Church,** and the predominantly Federal-style **United Church**—have since contributed to its present appeal. ⊠ *Between Church and College Sts.*

FAMILY **Peabody Museum of Natural History.** Opened in 1876, the Peabody houses more than 11 million specimens, making it one of the largest natural history museums in the nation. In addition to exhibits on Andean, Mesoamerican, and Pacific cultures, the venerable museum has an excellent ornithology collection, including a stuffed dodo and passenger pigeon. The main attractions for both children and amateur paleontologists are some of the world's earliest reconstructions of dinosaur skeletons. ⊠ *170 Whitney Ave.* ☎ *203/432–5050* ⊕ *www.peabody.yale.edu* ◻ *$13* ☉ *Tues.–Sat. 10–5, Sun. noon–5.*

Yale University Art Gallery. Since its founding in 1832, this art gallery has amassed more than 200,000 works from around the world, dating from ancient Egypt to the present day. Highlights include works by Vincent van Gogh, Edouard Manet, Claude Monet, Pablo Picasso, Winslow Homer, and Thomas Eakins, as well as Etruscan and Greek vases, Chinese ceramics and bronzes, early Italian paintings, and a collection of American decorative arts that is considered one of the world's finest. The gallery's landmark main building is also of note: opened in 1953, it was Louis I. Kahn's first major commission and the first modernist building on the neo-Gothic Yale campus. ⊠ *1111 Chapel St.* ☎ *203/432–0600* ⊕ *www.yale.edu/artgallery* ◻ *Free* ☉ *July and Aug., Tues.–Fri. 10–5, weekends 11–5; Sept.–June, Tues., Wed, and Fri. 10–5, Thurs. 10–8, weekends 11–5.*

6

New Haven Pizza 101

New Haven has been on pizza lovers' radars for decades. The "apizza" (pronounced "ah-beetz" by locals) style is defined by its thin, chewy crust, which makes for a unique—and, some would argue, superior—pizza experience. From white clam pies to mashed potato–topped concoctions, here are the area's best *(see Where to Eat for more details)*.

It should come as no surprise that **BAR** *(see Nightlife)*, a nightclub-cum-microbrewery, feels right at home in a college town, and furthermore that its signature pie just happens to be bacon-and-mashed-potato-topped pizza—a college student's comfort-food dream. If you want to taste what this place does best, brush aside any nagging thoughts of carbs and calories, and go for the masterpiece: a slightly charred, crispy-crusted pizza, topped with a thin layer of creamy mashed potatoes and bits of bacon.

Pepe's Pizzeria is where it all began: in 1925 Frank Pepe opened his eponymous pizzeria and created what would become the iconic New Haven–style pizza. Eager customers line up for hours to get a taste of the famous thin-crust pies, in particular Frank Pepe's pièce de résistance— the white clam pizza. This masterful creation consists of olive oil, garlic, oregano, grated Parmesan cheese, and littleneck clams atop a thin crust.

Just two blocks from Pepe's on Wooster Street (New Haven's Little Italy) is **Sally's Apizza**, a rival of Frank Pepe's since 1938, when Pepe's nephew decided to open his own place. Now visitors to New Haven and Wooster Street must pledge their allegiance to just one of these famed pizzerias, although no one will blame you if you decide to be a double agent.

If you don't want to get involved with that feud, there's always **Modern Apizza,** which differentiates itself by offering New Haven–style pizza with no toppings. Serving its signature pies (plain with a layer of tomato sauce and just a sprinkling of Parmesan cheese) since 1934, they do let you add toppings if you want, including a clam, bacon, peppers, and mozzarella specialty.

WHERE TO EAT

$$$
SPANISH
✕**Barcelona.** There's no need to take a transatlantic flight for authentic Spanish cuisine when you can feast on tapas right here in New Haven. This place delivers in both dining and decor—think 2,000-bottle wine cellar, an open kitchen, and a massive mural of a Spanish bullfighter. There are entrées on the menu, but the tapas are a better bet: the chorizo with sweet-and-sour figs offers an intensely rich bite, the organic greens with goat-cheese croquetas nicely balances tastes and textures, and the *gambas al ajillo* (shrimp sautéed with garlic, sherry, and *guindilla* peppers) are full of flavor. $ *Average main: $30* ✉ *Omni New Haven Hotel, 155 Temple St.* ☎ *203/848–3000* ⊕ *www.barcelonawinebar.com* ⊘ *No lunch* ⚭ *Reservations essential.*

$$
AMERICAN
✕**Caseus Fromagerie Bistro.** The aroma of high-quality aged cheese will hit you as you walk into this bi-level bistro and fromagerie. On the ground floor you can buy cheeses to go, in addition to other goodies like artisanal chocolates, jams, and olive oils. Visit the upstairs bistro to

Beinecke Rare Book and Manuscript Library 5
New Haven Green 1
Peabody Museum of Natural History ...6
Yale Center for British Art 4
Yale University .. 2
Yale University Art Gallery 3

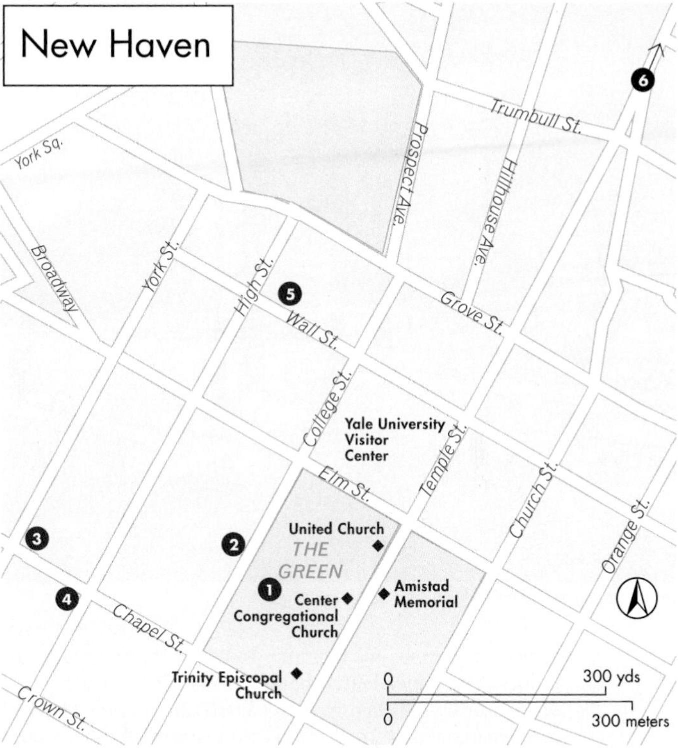

linger over decadent mac 'n' cheese (made in any of three different ways: chèvre, raclette, and Comté), the grilled cheese made with the bistro's "best melting cheeses," or the onion soup topped with no fewer than six cheeses. All ingredients used on their seasonal menu are all-natural and organic, and dishes that do not include cheese, like the half chicken roasted with fresh thyme butter or the seared scallops with heirloom tomatoes, are equally delightful. [$] *Average main: $20* ✉ *93 Whitney Ave.* ☎ *203/624–3373* 🌐 *www.caseusnewhaven.com* 🕓 *Closed Sun.*

$$$ **AMERICAN** 🍴 **Heirloom.** This isn't your typical hotel restaurant: occupying half of the lobby of the Study at Yale, this contemporary American eatery has a casually refined decor and a chalkboard menu. Dine during the day if you want to enjoy the sunlight pouring in through the floor-to-ceiling windows. A seasonal menu emphasizes the freshest locally sourced ingredients, with highlights like baked Connecticut clams with rosemary and pancetta, or an elevated version of chicken and dumplings: local ricotta gnocchi with vegetables in a chicken brodetto. The bar is great for a pre- or postdinner cocktail. [$] *Average main: $35* ✉ *The Study at Yale, 1157 Chapel St.* ☎ *203/503–3919* 🌐 *www.heirloomnewhaven.com.*

$ **AMERICAN** 🍴 **Louis' Lunch.** This all-American luncheonette on the National Register of Historic Places claims to be the birthplace of the hamburger. Its first-rate burgers are cooked in an old-fashioned upright broiler and served with either a slice of tomato or cheese on two pieces of toast. As most

Yale's leafy campus is home to many neo-Gothic buildings.

customers, who come from far and wide for these tasty morsels, agree: it doesn't get much better than that. The place is open until 2 am, Thursday–Saturday. $ *Average main: $10* ✉ *263 Crown St.* ☎ *203/562–5507* ⊕ *www.louislunch.com* ▭ *No credit cards* ☉ *Closed Sun. and Mon. No dinner Tues. and Wed.*

$$ ✕ **Modern Apizza.** It's not what Modern Apizza has that sets it apart
PIZZA from the rest, but what it doesn't have: toppings. The pizzeria's signature "plain" pie is a thin crust with a layer of tomato sauce and just a sprinkling of Parmesan cheese. If you want "mootz" (mozzarella in New Haven–speak), then you have to ask for it. But why mess with a classic? If it ain't broke, don't fix it: Modern Apizza has been serving its signature pies since 1934, and business is still booming. $ *Average main: $19* ✉ *874 State St.* ☎ *203/776–5306* ⊕ *www.modernapizza.com.*

$$ ✕ **Pepe's Pizzeria.** Does this place serve the best pizza in the world, as so
PIZZA many reviewers claim? If it doesn't, it sure comes close. Pizza is the only thing on the menu—try the justifiably famous white-clam pie (especially good topped with bacon). Expect to wait an hour or more for a table, or, on weekend evenings, come after 10. $ *Average main: $20* ✉ *157 Wooster St.* ☎ *203/865–5762* ⊕ *www.pepespizzeria.com* ▭ *No credit cards* ⌂ *Reservations not accepted.*

$$ ✕ **Sally's Apizza.** This place has been a rival of Frank Pepe's since 1938,
PIZZA when Salvatore Consiglio, Pepe's nephew, decided to break away from his relatives and open his own place. The result of this family feud is two competing pizzerias and a divided city: those who believe Frank Pepe's serves the best pizza and those who are devoted to Sally's. All pies here are hand tossed and baked in a coal-fired oven. Try a slice topped with

fresh tomato for a little taste of pizza heaven. [$] *Average main: $22* ✉ *237 Wooster St.* ☎ *203/624–5271* 🌐 *www.sallysapizza.com.*

$$$$ FRENCH 🍴 **Union League Cafe.** In a gorgeous Beaux-Arts dining room, this lively brasserie wins high marks for its updated French cuisine. Diners rave about the seared cod with potato and garlic confit, and wax poetic when describing the perfectly executed beef tenderloin with watercress and a whole-grain-mustard sauce. The knowledgeable staff are happy to recommend wine pairings to complement whatever dishes you select. Prices may be steep, but most think it's worth the splurge. [$] *Average main: $36* ✉ *1032 Chapel St.* ☎ *203/562–4299* 🌐 *www.unionleaguecafe.com.*

$$$ ECLECTIC 🍴 **Zinc.** In a sexy, dimly lighted storefront space looking toward the glorious New Haven green, Zinc turns heads with its artfully prepared and globally inspired farm-to-table cooking. You can't go wrong with starters like grilled shrimp with polenta grits, shiitake mushrooms, and bacon; or the Saigon beef lettuce wraps with peanuts, chili, and garlic. The sea scallops with barley risotto and roasted cauliflower is a standout among the entrées. [$] *Average main: $28* ✉ *964 Chapel St.* ☎ *203/624–0507* 🌐 *www.zincfood.com* 🕒 *Closed Sun. No lunch Sat.*

WHERE TO STAY

$$ HOTEL 🏨 **Omni Hotels & Resorts.** This comfortable hotel is near the heart of New Haven and outfitted with all the modern amenities. **Pros:** upscale furnishings; nice gym and spa; walking distance from many shops and restaurants. **Cons:** somewhat steep rates; in busy part of downtown. [$] *Rooms from: $235* ✉ *155 Temple St.* ☎ *203/772–6664* 🌐 *www.omnihotels.com/hotels/new-haven-yale* 🛏 *299 rooms, 7 suites* 🍽 *No meals.*

$$$ HOTEL 🏨 **The Study at Yale.** With bellhops dressed as newsies, a pair of spectacles emblazoned on all hotel signature items, and overflowing bookshelves in the hotel's lobby and suites, the Study is chic lodging for the scholarly set. **Pros:** destination restaurant; attentive staff; in the middle of the action. **Cons:** small gym; only one computer in the lobby. [$] *Rooms from: $300* ✉ *1157 Chapel St.* ☎ *203/503–3900* 🌐 *www.studyhotels.com* 🛏 *124 rooms, 9 suites* 🍽 *No meals.*

NIGHTLIFE AND PERFORMING ARTS

NIGHTLIFE

Anna Liffey's. This is one of the city's liveliest Irish pubs. ✉ *17 Whitney Ave.* ☎ *203/773–1776* 🌐 *www.annaliffeys.com.*

BAR. This spot is a cross between a nightclub, a brick-oven pizzeria, and a brewpub. ✉ *254 Crown St.* ☎ *203/495–1111* 🌐 *www.barnightclub.com.*

Toad's Place of New Haven. Alternative and traditional rock bands play at Toad's Place. ✉ *300 York St.* ☎ *203/624–8623* 🌐 *www.toadsplace.com.*

PERFORMING ARTS

Long Wharf Theatre. The well-regarded Long Wharf Theatre presents works by contemporary writers and revivals of neglected classics. ✉ *222 Sargent Dr.* ☎ *203/787–4282* 🌐 *www.longwharf.org.*

Shubert Performing Arts Center. Broadway musicals, dance performances, and classical music concerts are on the bill at the Shubert Performing Arts Center. ✉ *247 College St.* ☎ *203/624–1825* 🌐 *www.shubert.com.*

Woolsey Hall. Built in 1901 to commemorate Yale's bicentennial, Woolsey Hall hosts performances by the New Haven Symphony Orchestra and the Philharmonia Orchestra of Yale, as well as recitals on the Newberry Memorial Organ. ⊠ *500 College St., at Grove St.* ⊕ *www.yale.edu/woolsey.*

Yale Repertory Theatre. This theater stages both premiers and fresh interpretations of classics. ⊠ *1120 Chapel St.* ☎ *203/432–1234* ⊕ *www.yalerep.org.*

Yale School of Music. Most events in the impressive roster of performances by the Yale School of Music take place in Sprague Memorial Hall. ⊠ *470 College St.* ☎ *203/432–4158* ⊕ *music.yale.edu.*

SHOPPING

Atticus Bookstore & Café. This independent bookseller in the heart of the Yale campus offers a full café menu, which you can enjoy while devouring the latest bestseller. ⊠ *1082 Chapel St.* ☎ *203/776–4040* ⊕ *www.atticusbookstorecafe.com.*

SPORTS AND THE OUTDOORS

FAMILY **Connecticut Open.** This tennis tournament held in late August showcases some of the best players in the world of women's tennis. ⊠ *Connecticut Tennis Center at Yale, 45 Yale Ave.* ☎ *855/464–8366 for tickets* ⊕ *www.ctopen.org.*

MADISON

22 miles east of New Haven, 62 miles northeast of Greenwich.

Coastal Madison has an understated charm. Ice cream parlors, antiques stores, and quirky gift boutiques prosper along U.S. 1, the town's main street. Stately Colonial homes line the town green, site of many a summer antiques fair and arts-and-crafts festival. The Madison shoreline, particularly the white stretch of sand known as Hammonasset Beach and its parallel boardwalk, draws visitors year-round.

GETTING HERE AND AROUND

Madison is accessible by car and train. Drive north on Interstate 95 from New Haven, or take the Shore Line East train to the Madison stop.

BEACHES

FAMILY **Hammonasset Beach State Park.** The largest of the state's shoreline sanctuaries, Hammonasset Beach State Park has 2 miles of white sand beaches, a top-notch nature center, excellent birding, and a hugely popular campground with about 55 sites. **Amenities:** food and drink; lifeguards; showers; toilets. **Best for:** swimming; walking. ⊠ *1288 Boston Post Rd., off I–95* ☎ *203/245–2785 for park, 203/245–1817 for campground* ⊕ *www.ct.gov/deep/hammonasset* ≦ *Free.*

Fodor'sChoice
★

WHERE TO STAY AND EAT

$$ ✕ **Lenny and Joe's Fish Tale.** At Lenny and Joe's Fish Tale, kids of all
SEAFOOD ages love to eat their lobster rolls or fried seafood outdoors by a hand-carved Dentzel carousel with flying horses (and a whale, frog, lion, seal, and more), which the restaurant runs from early May through early

October. $ *Average main: $19* ✉ *1301 Boston Post Rd.* ☎ *203/245–7289* ⊕ *www.ljfishtale.com.*

$
B&B/INN
🏠 **Scranton Seahorse Inn.** In the heart of Madison, this historic inn run by pastry chef Michael Hafford offers a restful retreat within walking distance of the beach and shops. **Pros:** central location; gracious innkeeper; meticulous attention to detail. **Cons:** books up quickly. $ *Rooms from: $185* ✉ *818 Boston Post Rd.* ☎ *203/245–0550* ⊕ *www.scrantonseahorseinn.com* ⏎ *7 rooms* ⎮◎⎮ *Breakfast.*

OLD SAYBROOK

9 miles east of Madison, 29 miles east of New Haven.

Old Saybrook, once a lively shipbuilding and fishing town, bustles with summer vacationers and antiques shoppers. Its downtown is an especially pleasing place for a window-shopping stroll.

GETTING HERE AND AROUND
Drive north on Interstate 95 to Route 154 to reach Old Saybrook. The town is also served by Amtrak's Northeast Regional line, and the Shore Line East commuter trains.

WHERE TO EAT AND STAY

$$$
FRENCH
✗ **Café Routier.** Grilled hanger steak with cauliflower gratin and seared scallops with pancetta and butternut squash puree are among the favorites at this bistro, which specializes in regional favorites and seasonal dishes. Check out the Mood Lounge for smaller plates meant for sharing and excellent cocktails. $ *Average main: $26* ✉ *1353 Boston Post Rd., 5 miles west of Old Saybrook, Westbrook* ☎ *860/399–8700* ⊕ *www.caferoutier.com* ☾ *No lunch.*

$$$$
HOTEL
🏠 **Saybrook Point Inn & Spa.** Guest rooms at the cushy Saybrook Point Inn are done up in 18th-century style, with reproductions of British furnishings and Impressionist art; many have fireplaces, making them especially cozy on cool evenings. **Pros:** tasteful decor; great spa. **Cons:** pricey; you'll need a car to get downtown. $ *Rooms from: $436* ✉ *2 Bridge St.* ☎ *860/395–2000, 800/243–0212* ⊕ *www.saybrook.com* ⏎ *82 rooms, some condos* ⎮◎⎮ *No meals.*

SHOPPING
Old Saybrook Antiques Center. More than 125 dealers selling every type of antique imaginable operate out of the Old Saybrook Antiques Center. ✉ *756 Middlesex Tpke.* ☎ *860/388–1600* ⊕ *www.oldsaybrookantiques.com.*

Saybrook Country Barn. You'll find everything you need to outfit a home in country style, from tiger-maple dining room tables to hand-painted pottery. ✉ *2 Main St.* ☎ *860/388–0891* ⊕ *www.saybrookcountrybarn.com.*

OLD LYME

4 miles east of Old Saybrook, 40 miles south of Hartford.

Old Lyme, on the other side of the Connecticut River from Old Saybrook, is renowned among art lovers for its past as the home of the Lyme Art Colony, the most famous gathering of Impressionist painters in the United States. Artists continue to be attracted to the area for its lovely countryside and shoreline. The town also has handsome old houses, many built for sea captains.

GETTING HERE AND AROUND

Old Lyme is best reached by car. Drive north on Interstate 95 from Old Saybrook.

EXPLORING

Fodor's Choice ★ **Florence Griswold Museum.** Central to Old Lyme's artistic reputation is this grand late-Georgian-style mansion, which served as a boardinghouse for members of the Lyme Art Colony in the first decades of the 20th century. When artists like Willard Metcalf, Clark Voorhees, Childe Hassam, and Henry Ward Ranger flocked to the area to paint its varied landscape, Miss Florence Griswold offered housing as well as artistic encouragement. The house has been restored to its 1910 appearance, when the colony was in full flower (clues to the house's layout and decor were gleaned from members' paintings). The museum's 10,000-square-foot Krieble Gallery, on the riverfront, hosts changing exhibitions of American art. ✉ *96 Lyme St.* ☎ *860/434–5542* 🌐 *www.florencegriswoldmuseum.org* 🎫 *$10* 🕒 *Tues.–Sat. 10–5, Sun. 1–5.*

WHERE TO STAY

$$ B&B/INN Fodor's Choice ★ 🏨 **Bee and Thistle Inn and Lounge.** Behind a weathered stone wall in the historic district sits this three-story 1756 Colonial house with 5½ acres of broad lawns, formal gardens, and herbaceous borders. **Pros:** a short walk from Griswold Museum; lovely old home; fantastic restaurant. **Cons:** can hear noise from Interstate 95; lacks some modern amenities. [$] *Rooms from: $242* ✉ *100 Lyme St.* ☎ *860/434–1667* 🌐 *www.beeandthistleinn.com* 🛏 *11 rooms* 🍴 *Breakfast.*

NORWICH

27 miles northeast of Old Saybrook, 37 miles southeast of Hartford.

Outstanding Georgian and Victorian structures surround the triangular town green in Norwich, and more can be found downtown by the Thames River. The former mill town is hard at work on restoration and rehabilitation efforts. So eye-catching are these brightly colored structures that the Paint Quality Institute has designated the town one of the "Prettiest Painted Places in New England."

GETTING HERE AND AROUND

To reach Norwich from the coast by car, take Interstate 95 to Interstate 395 north to Route 82 east.

EXPLORING

Slater Memorial Museum & Converse Art Gallery. On the grounds of the Norwich Free Academy, this museum houses one of the country's largest collections of Greek, Roman, and Renaissance plaster casts of some of the world's greatest sculptures, including the Winged Victory, Venus de Milo, and Michelangelo's *Pietà*. The Converse Art Gallery, adjacent to the museum, hosts six to eight shows a year, many of which showcase Connecticut artists and craftsmen as well as student work. ✉ *108*

Crescent St. ☎ *860/887–2506* 🌐 *www.norwichfreeacademy.com* 🎟 *$3* 🕒 *Tues.–Fri. 9–4, weekends 1–4.*

WHERE TO STAY

$$$ B&B/INN 🏨 **Spa at Norwich Inn.** On 42 rolling acres right by the Thames River, this Georgian-style inn is best known for its spa, which offers the full range of skin-care regimens, body treatments, and fitness classes. **Pros:** expansive spa; beautiful grounds; excellent food. **Cons:** oriented toward spa guests; tired room decor in need of an upgrade. [$] *Rooms from: $325* ✉ *607 W. Thames St.* ☎ *860/425–3500, 800/275–4772* 🌐 *www.thespaatnorwichinn.com* 🛏 *49 rooms, 54 villas* 🍴 *No meals.*

LEDYARD

10 miles south of Norwich, 37 miles southeast of Hartford.

Located in the woods of southeastern Connecticut between Norwich and the coastline, Ledyard is known first and foremost for the vast Mashantucket Pequot Tribal Nation's Foxwoods Resort Casino. With the opening of the excellent Mashantucket Pequot Museum & Research Center, however, the tribe has moved beyond gaming to educating the public about their history, as well as that of other Northeast Woodland tribes. Nearby is Connecticut's other major casino, Mohegan Sun.

GETTING HERE AND AROUND

Driving is probably the best way to get to Ledyard: take Interstate 95 to Route 2 west. If you are only planning to visit Foxwoods, many bus companies run charter trips directly there; see 🌐 *www.foxwoods.com/bus* for more information.

EXPLORING

Foxwoods Resort Casino. Located on the Mashantucket Pequot Indian Reservation near Ledyard, Foxwoods is the largest resort casino in North America. The skylighted compound draws 40,000-plus visitors daily to its more than 6,200 slot machines, 380 gaming tables, and a 3,200-seat bingo parlor. This 4.7-million-square-foot complex includes the Grand Pequot Tower, the Great Cedar Hotel, and the Two Trees Inn, which have more than 1,400 guest rooms combined, as well as a full-service spa, retail concourse, food court, and numerous restaurants. The luxurious Fox Tower adds another 825 posh rooms and suites, plus several notable restaurants. ✉ *350 Trolley Line Blvd., Mashantucket* ☎ *800/369–9663* 🌐 *www.foxwoods.com* 🕒 *Daily 24 hrs.*

FAMILY Fodor's Choice ★ **Mashantucket Pequot Museum & Research Center.** Housed in a large complex 1 mile from Foxwoods, this museum brings to life the history and culture of the Northeastern Woodland tribes in general and the Pequots in particular with exquisite detail. Highlights include views of an 18,000-year-old glacial crevasse, a caribou hunt from 11,000 years ago, and a 17th-century fort. Perhaps most remarkable is a sprawling "immersion environment": a 16th-century village with more than 50 life-size figures and real smells and sounds. Audio devices provide detailed information about the sights. A full-service restaurant offers both Native and traditional American cuisine. ✉ *110 Pequot Tr., Mashantucket* ☎ *800/411–9671* 🌐 *www.pequotmuseum.org* 🎟 *$20* 🕒 *Apr.–Nov., Wed.–Sat. 10–4.*

Mohegan Sun. The Mohegan Tribe, known as the Wolf People, operate this casino west of Ledyard and just south of Norwich, which has more than 300,000 square feet of gaming space, including 6,000 slot machines and more than 250 gaming tables. Also part of the complex: the Kids Quest family-entertainment center, a 130,000-square-foot shopping mall, more than 40 restaurants and food-and-beverage suppliers, and a 34-story, 1,200-room luxury hotel with a full-service spa. A 10,000-seat arena, home to the WNBA's Connecticut Sun, draws major national acts, while a swanky 300-seat cabaret hosts intimate shows and comedy acts. Mohegan After Dark is a 22,000-square-foot complex with three nightclubs. ✉ *1 Mohegan Sun Blvd., off I–395, Uncasville* ☎ *888/226–7711* 🌐 *www.mohegansun.com* 🕒 *Daily 24 hrs.*

WHERE TO STAY

$$$$ HOTEL 🏨 **The Fox Tower.** This lavishly appointed hotel offers stylish accommodations just seconds away from the casino's action. **Pros:** elegant rooms; easy access to the casino; nice views from upper floors. **Cons:** if you're not a gambler, this might not be your scene. [$] *Rooms from: $399* ✉ *Foxwoods Resort Casino, 350 Trolley Line Blvd., Mashantucket* ☎ *800/369–9663* 🌐 *www.foxwoods.com* 🛏 *825 rooms* 🍴 *No meals.*

$$$$ HOTEL 🏨 **Grand Pequot Tower.** Mere steps from the gaming floors, this expansive 17-story showpiece contains deluxe rooms and suites updated with modern decor in pleasantly neutral tones. **Pros:** elegant rooms; easy access to the casino; nice views from upper floors. **Cons:** not much appeal if you're not gambling. [$] *Rooms from: $399* ✉ *Foxwoods Resort Casino, 350 Trolley Line Blvd., Mashantucket* ☎ *860/312–5044, 800/369–9663* 🌐 *www.foxwoods.com* 🛏 *824 rooms* 🍴 *No meals.*

$$$ HOTEL 🏨 **Mohegan Sun.** The emphasis of this 34-story hotel is on luxury. **Pros:** numerous fine restaurants are steps from lobby; incredible views from upper floors; excellent spa and fitness center. **Cons:** need to enjoy casinos. [$] *Rooms from: $299* ✉ *1 Mohegan Sun Blvd., Uncasville* ☎ *888/777–7922* 🌐 *www.mohegansun.com* 🛏 *1,020 rooms, 180 suites* 🍴 *No meals.*

$$ B&B/INN 🏨 **Stonecroft.** A sunny 1807 Georgian Colonial marks the center of Stonecroft: 6½ acres of green meadows, woodlands, and rambling stone walls. **Pros:** scenic and verdant grounds; cheerful service. **Cons:** secluded location requires a car to get around. [$] *Rooms from: $219* ✉ *515 Pumpkin Hill Rd.* ☎ *800/772–0774* 🌐 *www.stonecroft.com* 🛏 *10 rooms* 🍴 *Breakfast.*

MYSTIC

8 miles south of Ledyard.

Mystic has devoted itself to recapturing the seafaring spirit of the 18th and 19th centuries. Some of the nation's fastest clipper ships were built here in the mid-19th century; today, the 37-acre Mystic Seaport is the state's most popular museum. Downtown Mystic has an interesting collection of boutiques and galleries.

GETTING HERE AND AROUND

By car, take Interstate 95 to Route 27 south to reach Mystic. Amtrak's Northeast Regional train service also stops here.

Mystic Seaport exhibits a number of vessels you can tour, including the *Charles W. Morgan*.

ESSENTIALS

Visitor Information Mystic Country–Eastern Regional Tourism District.
✉ *27 Coogan Blvd., Bldg. 3A* ☎ *860/536-8822* ⊕ *www.mysticcountry.com.*

EXPLORING

FAMILY
Fodor'sChoice
★

Mystic Aquarium. The famous Arctic Coast exhibit—which holds 800,000 gallons of water, measures 165 feet at its longest point by 85 feet at its widest point, and ranges from just inches to 16½ feet deep—is just a small part of this revered establishment. Check out world-renowned ocean explorer Dr. Robert Ballard's Institute for Exploration and its Nautilus Live Theater which features a live video link with the E/V *Nautilus* as it explores wrecks. You can also see African penguins, harbor seals, graceful sea horses, Pacific octopuses, and sand tiger sharks. Don't miss feeding time at the Ray Touch Pool, where rays suction sand eels right out of your hand. The animals here go through 1,000 pounds of herring, capelin, and squid each day—Juno, a male beluga whale, is responsible for consuming 85 pounds of that himself. ■TIP→ For an up-close-and-personal experience with a beluga whale, take part in the Trainer for Day ($325) or Beluga Encounter ($165) program. Both allow you to touch and interact with these magnificent animals. ✉ *55 Coogan Blvd.* ☎ *860/572-5955* ⊕ *www.mysticaquarium.org* ✉ *$34.99* ☉ *Mar. and Sept.–Nov., daily 9–4:50; Apr.–Aug., daily 9–5:50; Dec.–Feb., daily 10–4:50.*

FAMILY
Fodor'sChoice
★

Mystic Seaport. The world's largest maritime museum, Mystic Seaport encompasses 37 acres of indoor and outdoor exhibits, with more than 1 million artifacts that provide a fascinating look at the area's rich ship-building and seafaring heritage. In narrow streets and historic homes and buildings (some moved here from other sites), craftspeople give demonstrations of skills like open-hearth cooking and weaving. The museum's more than 500 vessels include the *Charles W. Morgan,* the last remaining wooden whaling ship afloat, and the 1882 training ship *Joseph Conrad*; you can climb aboard for a look around, or for sail-setting demonstrations and reenactments of whale hunts. ■ TIP→ **Children under five are admitted free.** ⊠ *75 Greenmanville Ave., 1 mile south of I–95* 🕾 *860/572–0711* ⊕ *www.mysticseaport.org* ☞ *$25* 🕙 *Dec.–Mar., Thurs.–Sun. 10–4; Apr.–Oct., daily 9–5; Nov., daily 10–4.*

WHERE TO EAT

$$
SEAFOOD
Fodor's Choice
★

✕ **Abbott's Lobster in the Rough.** If you want some of the state's best lobsters, mussels, crabs, or clams on the half shell, head down to this unassuming seaside lobster shack in sleepy Noank, a few miles southwest of Mystic. Most seating is outdoors or on the dock, where the views of Noank Harbor are magnificent. 🖇 *Average main: $20* ⊠ *117 Pearl St., Noank* 🕾 *860/536–7719* ⊕ *www.abbotts-lobster.com* 🕙 *Closed Nov.–Mar., and weekdays early May, Sept., and Oct.*

$$$$
AMERICAN

✕ **Oyster Club.** Serving the freshest cuisine in the area, the Oyster Club has elevated the casual dining experience to an art form. Relax in the rustic barnlike dining room, and start your meal with a selection of oysters and clams from the raw bar or with a cup of the raved-about quohog chowder. Then move along to either surf or turf for an entrée: the seared yellowfin tuna with roasted sweet peppers, couscous, and capers; the tagliatelle with ragù of prime beef; or the luxurious butter-poached lobster roll. In summer the Treehouse, an open-air deck, offers another lively spot to enjoy food and drink. 🖇 *Average main: $35* ⊠ *13 Water St.* 🕾 *860/415–9266* ⊕ *www.oysterclubct.com* 🕙 *No lunch weekdays.*

WHERE TO STAY

$$
HOTEL

🏨 **Mystic Marriott Hotel and Spa.** This six-story hotel has Georgian-style architecture and modern rooms accented with old-world touches such as rich fabrics, gleaming wood furnishings, and elegant detailing. **Pros:** convenient to Mystic attractions; fine spa. **Cons:** on a busy road. 🖇 *Rooms from: $209* ⊠ *625 North Rd., Groton* 🕾 *860/446–2600, 860/446–2600* ⊕ *www.marriott.com* 🛏 *280 rooms, 4 suites* ⦿ *No meals.*

$
B&B/INN

🏨 **Old Mystic Inn.** This 1784 inn was once a well-regarded bookstore, so it's no surprise that guest rooms in the cozy main house and carriage house are named for New England authors. **Pros:** beautifully kept historic house; quiet neighborhood; friendly host. **Cons:** need a car to get downtown. 🖇 *Rooms from: $185* ⊠ *52 Main St.* 🕾 *860/572–9422* ⊕ *www.oldmysticinn.com* 🛏 *8 rooms* ⦿ *Breakfast.*

$$
HOTEL

🏨 **Whaler's Inn.** A perfect compromise between a chain motel and a country inn, this five-building complex with public rooms furnished with lovely antiques is one block from the Mystic River and downtown area. **Pros:** within walking distance of downtown shopping; excellent restaurant. **Cons:** rooms in some buildings have less character; on a busy street. 🖇 *Rooms from: $200* ⊠ *20 E. Main St.* 🕾 *860/536–1506* ⊕ *www.whalersinnmystic.com* 🛏 *49 rooms* ⦿ *Breakfast.*

SHOPPING

Finer Line Gallery. This gallery exhibits prints with nautical themes, including some local scenes. ✉ *48 W. Main St.* ☎ *860/536–8339* 🌐 *www.finerlinegallery.com.*

Olde Mistick Village. Resembling an early-1700s American village, Olde Mistick Village has more than 50 shops selling everything from crafts and clothing to souvenirs and munchies. ✉ *27 Coogan Blvd.* ☎ *860/536–4941* 🌐 *www.oldemistickvillage.com.*

STONINGTON

7 miles southeast of Mystic, 57 miles east of New Haven.

The pretty village of Stonington pokes into Fishers Island Sound. A quiet fishing community clustered around white-spired churches, Stonington is far less commercial than Mystic. In the 19th century, though, it was a busy whaling, sealing, and transportation center. Historic buildings line the town green and border both sides of Water Street up to the imposing Old Lighthouse Museum.

GETTING HERE AND AROUND

From Mystic by car, take Route 1 north (you'll actually be heading due east so don't be concerned) to Route 1A.

6

EXPLORING

Old Lighthouse Museum. This museum occupies a lighthouse originally built in 1823 and moved to higher ground 17 years later. Climb to the top of the tower for a spectacular view of Long Island Sound and three states. Six rooms of exhibits depict the varied history of the small coastal town. ✉ *7 Water St.* ☎ *860/535–1440* 🌐 *www.stoningtonhistory.org* 🎟 *$9* 🕒 *May–Oct., Thurs.–Tues. 10–5.*

Stonington Vineyards. At this small coastal winery, you can browse the works of local artists in the gallery or enjoy a picnic lunch on the grounds—the vineyard's Seaport White, a Vidal-Chardonnay blend, is a nice accompaniment. ✉ *523 Taugwonk Rd.* ☎ *860/535–1222* 🌐 *www.stoningtonvineyards.com* 🎟 *Tasting $12, tour free* 🕒 *Daily 11–5, tours at 2.*

WHERE TO STAY

$$$ B&B/INN Fodor's Choice ★

🏨 **Inn at Stonington.** The views of Stonington Harbor and Fishers Island Sound are spectacular from this waterfront inn in the heart of Stonington Village. **Pros:** smartly furnished rooms; walking distance from village shops and dining; great water views. **Cons:** no restaurant. [$] *Rooms from: $340* ✉ *60 Water St.* ☎ *860/535–2000* 🌐 *www.innatstonington.com* 🛏 *18 rooms* 🍴 *Breakfast.*

THE QUIET CORNER

Few visitors to Connecticut experience the old-fashioned ways of the "Quiet Corner," a vast patch of sparsely populated towns that seem a world away from the rest of the state. There's a reclusive allure here: whereas people once left New York City for the Litchfield Hills, many now leave for northeastern Connecticut. The cultural capital of the

Quiet Corner is Putnam, a small mill city on the Quinebaug River whose formerly industrial town center has been transformed into a year-round antiques mart. Smaller jewels are Pomfret and Woodstock—two towns where authentic Colonial homesteads still seem to outnumber the contemporary, charmless clones seen springing up all too rapidly across the state. The stretch of Route 169 from Brooklyn past Woodstock has been named a National Scenic Byway.

POMFRET

51 miles north of Stonington; 6 miles north of Brooklyn.

Pomfret, one of the grandest towns in the region, was once known as the inland Newport because it attracted the wealthy, who summered here in large "cottages." Today it is a quiet stop-off along Route 169, designated by the National Scenic Byway Program as one of the most picturesque in the country.

GETTING HERE AND AROUND

Pomfret is best visited by car; Route 169 runs right through the center of town. From Interstate 395, take Route 44 west to Route 169 south.

EXPLORING

Connecticut Audubon Society Center at Pomfret. Adjacent to more than 700 acres of rolling meadows, grasslands, and forests, this nature center organizes natural-history exhibits, as well as seasonal lectures and workshops. Miles of trails provide excellent birding: look for the ruby-crowned kinglet, yellow-rumped warbler, and blue-headed vireo. ✉ *218 Day Rd.* ☎ *860/928–4948* 🌐 *www.ctaudubon.org/center-at-pomfret* 🎟 *Free* ⏲ *Sanctuary, daily dawn–dusk; center, weekdays 9–4, weekends noon–4.*

Sharpe Hill Vineyard. Centered on an 18th-century-style barn in the hills of Pomfret, this vineyard offers tastings of its excellent wines, and serves lunch and dinner in a European-style wine garden and relaxed restaurant (reservations are essential). Try Ballet of Angels, a heavenly semidry white and one of the more popular wines from New England. ✉ *108 Wade Rd.* ☎ *860/974–3549* 🌐 *www.sharpehill.com* 🎟 *Tastings $10–$15* ⏲ *Fri.–Sun. 11–5.*

WHERE TO EAT

$$$$ AMERICAN Fodor's Choice ★

🍴 **Golden Lamb Buttery.** Connecticut's most unusual dining experience has achieved almost legendary status. Eating here, in a converted barn on a 1,000-acre farm, is far more than a chance to enjoy good Continental food: it's a social and gastronomical event. There is one seating each for lunch and dinner; choose from one of four entrées, which might include roast duck or chateaubriand. The prix-fixe dinner is $75; an à la carte menu is available at lunch. Before dinner, you can take a hay ride accompanied by a musician. [$] *Average main: $75* ✉ *499 Wolf Den Rd., off Rte. 169, Brooklyn* ☎ *860/774–4423* 🌐 *www.thegoldenlamb.com* ⏲ *Closed Sun. and Mon. No dinner Tues.–Thurs.* ✍ *Reservations essential* 👔 *Jacket and tie.*

$$ AMERICAN

🍴 **Vanilla Bean Café.** Homemade soups, sandwiches, and baked goods have long been a tradition at this café housed in a restored 19th-century

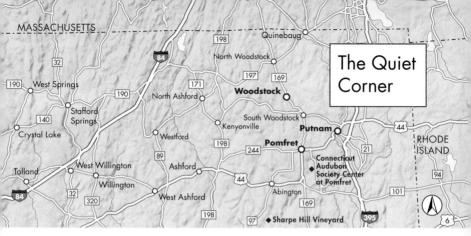

barn. Dinner specials might include pan-seared blackfish with local squash or wild mushroom mac 'n' cheese. Belgian waffles and blueberry pancakes are breakfast highlights. There are also an art gallery and live music. $ *Average main: $20* ⊠ *450 Deerfield Rd.* ☎ *860/928–1562* ⊕ *www.thevanillabeancafe.com* ☽ *No dinner Mon. and Tues.*

PUTNAM

5 miles northeast of Pomfret.

Ambitious antiques dealers have reinvented Putnam, a mill town 30 miles west of Providence, Rhode Island, that was neglected after the Depression. Putnam's downtown, with more than 400 antiques dealers, is today the heart of the Quiet Corner's antiques trade.

GETTING HERE AND AROUND
By car, take Route 44 east from Pomfret to reach Putnam.

WHERE TO EAT

$$$
AMERICAN
✕ **85 Main.** This stylish bistro is *the* place to go for a break from antiquing. Typical lunchtime offerings include roasted corn and clam chowder, pesto chicken salad, and burgers with fries; dinner could be maple-glazed sea scallops or veal Bolognese. There's also a raw bar and a full sushi bar. $ *Average main: $27* ⊠ *85 Main St.* ☎ *860/928–1660* ⊕ *www.85main.com.*

SHOPPING

Antiques Marketplace. This four-level emporium features more than 350 dealers selling everything from fine furniture to tchotchkes. ⊠ *109 Main St.* ☎ *860/928–0442* ⊕ *antiquesmarketplace.tumblr.com.*

Arts & Framing. Head here for antique art and for art restoration and framing services. ⊠ *112 Main St.* ☎ *860/963–0105* ⊕ *www. artsandframingputnam.com.*

WOODSTOCK

5 miles northwest of Putnam.

The landscape of this enchanting town is splendid in every season: the rolling hills seem to stretch for miles. Scenic roads lead past antiques shops, a country inn in the grand tradition, orchards, livestock grazing in grassy fields, and the fairgrounds of one of the state's oldest agricultural fairs, held each Labor Day weekend.

GETTING HERE AND AROUND

To reach Woodstock by car from Putnam, follow Route 171 west to Route 169 north.

EXPLORING

Roseland Cottage. This pink board-and-batten Gothic Revival house was built in 1846 as a summer home for New York silk merchant, publisher, and abolitionist Henry C. Bowen. The house and outbuildings (including a carriage house with private bowling alley) hold a prominent place in history, having hosted four U.S. presidents: Ulysses S. Grant, Rutherford B. Hayes, William Henry Harrison, and William McKinley. The parterre garden features 21 flower beds surrounded by 600 yards of boxwood hedge. ✉ *556 Rte. 169* ☎ *860/928–4074* 🌐 *www.historicnewengland.org/historic-properties/homes/roseland-cottage* 🎟 *$10* 🕒 *June–mid-Oct., Wed.–Sun. 11–4.*

WHERE TO STAY

$$ B&B/INN 🏨 **The Inn at Woodstock Hill.** Filled with antiques, this inn overlooking the countryside has guest rooms with four-poster beds, handsome fireplaces, pitched ceilings, and timber beams. **Pros:** beautiful grounds; pretty rooms. **Cons:** traditional decor feels very old-fashioned; somewhat remote; expensive restaurant. [$] *Rooms from: $207* ✉ *94 Plaine Hill Rd., South Woodstock* ☎ *860/928–0528* 🌐 *www.woodstockhill.com* 🛏 *21 rooms* 🍴 *Breakfast.*

SHOPPING

Christmas Barn. This country store has 12 rooms of holiday decorations. ✉ *835 Rte. 169* ☎ *860/928–7652.*

Scranton's Shops. This store sells the wares of 60 regional artisans. ✉ *300 Rte. 169* ☎ *860/928–3738* 🌐 *www.scrantonsshops.com.*

Whispering Hill Farm. Supplies for rug hooking and braiding, quilting, and needlework, plus an assortment of antiques are all on sale here. ✉ *18 Castle Rock Rd.* ☎ *860/928–0162* 🌐 *www.whispering-hill.com.*

RHODE ISLAND

7

Visit Fodors.com for advice, updates, and bookings

WELCOME TO RHODE ISLAND

TOP REASONS TO GO

★ **Mansions:** See how the social elite lived during Newport's Gilded Age on a tour of Cornelius Vanderbilt's opulent 70-room "summer cottage" known as The Breakers.

★ **Historic Street:** Follow Benefit Street on Providence's East Side for a mile-long walk through history, and see ornate homes built by leading Colonial merchants.

★ **Nature:** Block Island is one of the most serene spots on the Eastern Seaboard, especially at Rodman's Hollow, a glacial outwash basin, where winding paths lead to the sea.

★ **Sand:** Take your pick of South County's numerous sugar-white beaches, including East Matunuck State Beach in South Kingstown.

★ **Food Enclave:** From food trucks to upscale dining, Providence has an exciting culinary scene fueled in large part by young chefs trained at Johnson & Wales University.

1 Providence. Visit Rhode Island's capital city on an empty stomach, so you can fill up at its exciting culinary scene, anchored by one of New England's most treasured Little Italy neighborhoods: Federal Hill. Prestigious colleges give Providence intellectual and cultural vitality, while restored Colonial houses on the East Side preserve its history.

2 The Blackstone Valley. The Blackstone River powered the factories that led America's industrial revolution in the 19th century. A fascinating museum honors the laborers—children included—who worked in the mills. Today, nearly 16 miles of paved bike path follow the river's edge.

3 South County. Visit some of southern New England's most accessible and scenic stretches of beach, and you'll discover how warm and welcoming the ocean can be in summer. Explore nature preserves or take a fishing charter trip out of Galilee, Snug Harbor, or Jerusalem. Get off the beaten path to explore antiques shops and galleries in the villages along the way.

4 Newport County and East Bay. No socks required in this longtime yachting enclave, where boat crews unwind after a day on the water. Take in the beaches, elaborate mansions, professional tennis, world-renowned music festivals, and a burgeoning foodie scene. Go fly a kite in Brenton Point State Park.

5 Block Island. This laid-back island with 17 miles of beaches—including Crescent Beach, one of New England's best—offers a classic seaside escape in summer, even when the population swells from the regular 950 to nearly 15,000. Relax at one of the Victorian inns and bed-and-breakfasts, peruse the galleries and shops, and have a comfort-food lunch or haute-cuisine dinner.

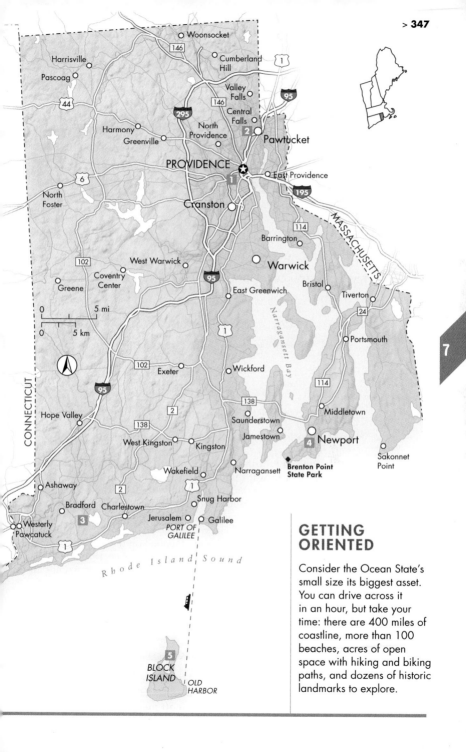

GETTING ORIENTED

Consider the Ocean State's small size its biggest asset. You can drive across it in an hour, but take your time: there are 400 miles of coastline, more than 100 beaches, acres of open space with hiking and biking paths, and dozens of historic landmarks to explore.

Updated by
Liz Boardman

"Rhode Island: 3% Bigger at Low Tide," reads a locally made T-shirt—an exaggeration, of course: the state geologist calculates it's actually more like 0.5%. But the smallest state's size is a source of pride, given all there is to do within its 1,500 square miles. You may find it hard to choose among so many experiences: historic walks, fine dining, and the WaterFire display in Providence; apple picking and riverboat cruises in the Blackstone Valley; fishing trips and beach excursions in South County and Block Island; pedaling along Bristol's bike path; and taking sunset sails in Newport and touring the Gilded Age mansions.

Rhode Island and Providence Plantations, the state's official name, has a long history of forward thinking and a spirit of determination and innovation embodied in the 11-foot-tall bronze Independent Man atop the marble-domed State House. The first of the 13 colonies to declare independence from Britain can also claim the first successful textile mill (in Pawtucket), America's oldest synagogue (in Newport), and the first lunch wagon (in Providence). A state founded on the principle of religious liberty drew Baptists, Jews, Quakers, and others throughout the 17th and 18th centuries, then flourished with factories, silver foundries, and jewelry companies, which brought workers from French Canada, Italy, Ireland, England, Portugal, and Eastern Europe.

Rhode Island remains an attractive, spirited place to live or visit. A public works project has opened up the river in Downtown Providence; infrastructural improvements at Fort Adams State Park in Newport allow it to host international yacht-racing events; extended commuter rail service makes it easier to travel between Providence, T. F. Green Airport, and Wickford; and bike-path expansions allow cyclists to traverse South County, East Bay, and Blackstone Valley. Rhode Island's 39 cities and towns—none more than 50 miles apart—offer natural beauty, inspired culinary artistry, and many opportunities to relax and enjoy its scenic vistas.

PLANNING

WHEN TO GO

With its arts and music festivals and gorgeous beach days, summer is high season in Rhode Island and a great time to visit, but there are fun and exciting things to do here year-round. Newport's Jazz and Folk festivals heat up the town in late July and early August, just after the Newport Music Festival for classical music fans in July. This is also the time to take the ferry to low-key, beach-ringed Block Island for a day trip or overnight stay.

The shoulder seasons (April–May and September–October) bring pleasant weather and more affordable accommodations. In early fall, the return of student life to Providence colleges gives the capital city energy and a youthful vibe. October is a good time to catch fall foliage in the Blackstone Valley, around the University of Rhode Island in Kingston, or in picturesque Tiverton and Little Compton.

Late fall, winter, and early spring each have their own charms, such as restaurant week in Providence, Newport, and Narragansett, when eateries join together to promote special three-course prix-fixe menus.

PLANNING YOUR TIME

By car, it's an hour or less from any one place in Rhode Island to another. Although distances are short, the state is densely populated, so allow extra time for traffic congestion.

Most sights in Providence can be seen in a day or two. The Blackstone Valley and Tiverton/Little Compton make good half-day side trips from Providence. Newport, though not even 12 square miles, offers enough to fill two days, and the same can be said for South County, with its superb beaches. If you have a full week, you can visit all four regions of the state, as well as Block Island.

GETTING HERE AND AROUND

AIR TRAVEL

Rhode Island's main airport is T. F. Green in Warwick, which is served by most domestic air carriers. There are smaller airports, with limited carriers, in Westerly and on Block Island. Boston's Logan Airport is an hour's drive from Providence.

Air Contacts T. F. Green Airport. ✉ *2000 Post Rd., off I–95, Warwick* ☎ *401/691–2471, 888/268–7222* ⊕ *www.pvdairport.com.*

CAR TRAVEL

New England's main highway, Interstate 95, cuts diagonally through Rhode Island, spanning 43 miles from Connecticut to Massachusetts.

Interstate 195 southeast from Providence leads to New Bedford, Massachusetts, and Cape Cod. Route 146 northwest from Providence leads to Worcester, Massachusetts, and to Interstate 90, which passes through the Blackstone Valley. U.S. 1 follows much of the Rhode Island coast east from Connecticut before turning north to Providence. Route 138 heads east from U.S. 1 to Jamestown, Newport, and Portsmouth, in easternmost Rhode Island. Route 114 leads south from East Providence down through the East Bay community of Bristol and then to Newport.

Once you're here, a car is your best way to get around the state, although parts of Providence and Newport are walkable and have reliable public buses. Parking is easy to find outside of cities, though challenging and sometimes expensive in Downtown Providence and Newport.

RESTAURANTS

The creative passion of award-winning chefs, many in their twenties and early thirties, fuels Rhode Island's vibrant restaurant scene. Abundant fresh seafood makes for outstanding variations on New England staples like fish 'n' chips, clam chowder, and stuffed quahogs (hard clams)—all best savored at a beachside clam shack. Then there's the more typically Rhode Island fare, such as the johnnycake (a thin corn pancake cooked on a griddle), coffee milk, Del's frozen lemonade, and Gray's Ice Cream. Authentic Italian-American restaurants can be found in Providence's Federal Hill neighborhood. *Restaurant prices are the average cost of a main course at dinner or, if dinner is not served, at lunch.*

HOTELS

Major chain hotels are certainly represented in Rhode Island, but boutique hotels, small bed-and-breakfasts, and historic inns provide a more intimate experience. Rates vary seasonally: in Newport, for example, a winter stay often costs half what it does in summer. Many inns in coastal towns are closed in winter. *Hotel prices are the lowest cost of a standard double room in high season, excluding service and 13% state hotel tax. Reviews have been shortened. For full information, visit Fodors.com.*

WHAT IT COSTS			
$	**$$**	**$$$**	**$$$$**
Restaurants	under $18	$18–$24	$25–$35	over $35
Hotels	under $200	$200–$299	$300–$399	over $399

OUTDOOR SPORTS

Department of Environmental Management's Division of Licensing. Contact the department for boating, fishing, and hunting information, regulations, and licenses. A three-day tourist hunting or freshwater fishing pass costs $16; a saltwater fishing license costs $10 and is good for a year. ☎ 401/222–6647 ⊕ *www.dem.ri.gov/programs/bpoladm/manserv/hfb.*

HIKING

Audubon Society of Rhode Island. The society leads interesting hikes and field expeditions around the state. ✉ *12 Sanderson Rd., Smithfield* ☎ *401/949–5454* ⊕ *www.asri.org.*

VISITOR INFORMATION

Rhode Island Commerce/Tourism. ☎ *800/556–2484* ⊕ *www.visitrhodeisland.com.*

PROVIDENCE

Big-city sophistication with small-city charm: Providence has the best of both worlds. A thriving arts community, prestigious academic institutions Brown University and the Rhode Island School of Design (RISD), an impressive restaurant scene, and a revitalized Downtown all help the city live up to its nickname: Creative Capital. Close (but not too close) to Boston—with a completely different sensibility—Providence is a worthy stop on any New England tour.

The Moshassuck and Woonasquatucket rivers merge just southeast of the Rhode Island State House to form the Providence River. Scenic Waterplace Park hosts WaterFire, a series of mesmerizing summer-evening bonfires on the Woonasquatucket just west of the confluence. This relatively recent tradition beloved by locals and visitors alike began in the 1990s, but Providence gives equal weight to its long history, celebrating everything from its wealth of Colonial architecture to its literary tradition. After all, H. P. Lovecraft was a son of Providence, and Edgar Allan Poe courted the poet Sarah Helen Whitman here.

GETTING ORIENTED

The narrow Providence River acts as a natural boundary between Downtown and the East Side, two major neighborhoods in the heart of the city. West of the river lies the Downtown business district, much of which the locals have dubbed Downcity. From here, Federal Hill, historically an Italian neighborhood, pushes west along Atwells Avenue. Just north of Downcity is the white-marble State House. On the East Side, South Main and Benefit streets run parallel to the Providence River. The western half of the East Side is known as College Hill, at the top of which Thayer Street runs north–south. (Don't confuse the city of East Providence with Providence's East Side.)

GETTING HERE AND AROUND

AIR TRAVEL T. F. Green Airport, 10 miles south of Providence in Warwick, is served by American, Cape Air, Condor, Delta, JetBlue, New England, Southwest, TACV Cabo Verde, and United. By cab, the ride from T. F. Green to Downcity hotels takes about 15 minutes and costs around $30. The Airport Taxi & Limousine Service shuttle, running from the airport to Downcity hotels, RISD, and Brown University, costs $11 one way. The Massachusetts Bay Transportation Authority (MBTA) commuter rail service connects T. F. Green and Providence on weekdays for $2.75.

BUS TRAVEL At Kennedy Plaza in Downcity you can board the local Rhode Island Public Transit Authority (RIPTA) buses or trolleys. The Route 92 trolley links Federal Hill to the East Side, and the Route 6 trolley links Downcity to the Roger Williams Park and Zoo. RIPTA fares are $2 per ride; an all-day pass is $6. Exact change is needed when boarding buses, or you'll get your change back in the form of a fare card. RIPTA buses also service T. F. Green; Route 14 links the airport to Kennedy Plaza.

TRAIN TRAVEL Amtrak trains between New York and Boston stop at Westerly, Kingston, and Providence. From Boston you can also take an MBTA commuter train to Providence.

TAXI TRAVEL   The basic taxi rate in Providence is $3 for the first mile, and $3.50 for each succeeding mile.

PARKING   Overnight parking is not generally allowed on Providence streets. During the day it can be difficult to find curbside parking, especially Downcity and on Federal and College hills. There is a large parking garage at Providence Place mall.

TOURS   **Providence Preservation Society.** The society publishes booklets (available at its headquarters) with self-guided walking tours of the city. Tours include Benefit Street, Downtown, and the Elmwood section. ✉ *21 Meeting St., at Benefit St.* ☎ *401/831–7440* ⊕ *www.ppsri.org/ppsresources* 🖅 *$3 each* ☉ *Weekdays 10–5.*

Fodor'sChoice   **Savoring Federal Hill.** For an insider's tour of "Little Italy," sign up for
★   Cindy Salvato's three-hour walking and tasting tour; you'll visit a bakery, an Italian specialty store, and other long-standing Federal Hill establishments. For St. Joseph's Day (March 19), her Zeppole Crawl introduces participants to festive Italian pastries, including some by Cindy herself. ✉ *Providence* ☎ *401/934–2149* ⊕ *www.savoringrhodeisland.com* 🖅 *From $50.*

ESSENTIALS

Transportation Contacts Airport Taxi & Limousine Service. ☎ *401/737–2868* ⊕ *www.airporttaxiri.com.* **Amtrak.** ☎ *800/872–7245* ⊕ *www.amtrak.com.* **Massachusetts Bay Transportation Authority** (*MBTA*). ☎ *617/222–3200, 800/392–6100* ⊕ *www.mbta.com.* **Rhode Island Public Transit Authority** (*RIPTA*). ✉ *Kennedy Plaza Passenger Terminal, 1 Kennedy Plaza, Downtown* ☎ *401/781–9400* ⊕ *www.ripta.com.*

Visitor Information Providence Warwick Convention & Visitors Bureau. ✉ *10 Memorial Blvd.* ☎ *401/456–0200, 800/233–1636* ⊕ *www.goprovidence.com.*

EXPLORING

DOWNTOWN

Providence contains about two dozen official neighborhoods and a handful of unofficial ones, each with its own identity. You may, for instance, hear locals refer to Downtown's artistic and financial core as Downcity. North of Downcity is the often-bustling Waterplace Park; west of Downcity is Federal Hill, long an Italian-American bastion but these days diversifying. It's definitely worth a stop, and, if you're traveling with kids, so is the Providence Children's Museum.

TOP ATTRACTIONS

Downcity. A highly walkable section of Downtown—and for some residents synonymous with it—Downcity contains a thriving mix of college buildings, restaurants, independent shops, theaters, hotels, and financial institutions. The Downcity merchants' association defines the neighborhood as encompassing the area west of the Providence River bordered by Memorial Boulevard and Empire, Sabin, and Pine streets, though others stake out slightly more territory. Technically outside Downcity but adjacent to it and aligned with it in spirit are Waterplace Park and the sprawling Providence Place shopping center and neighboring bus

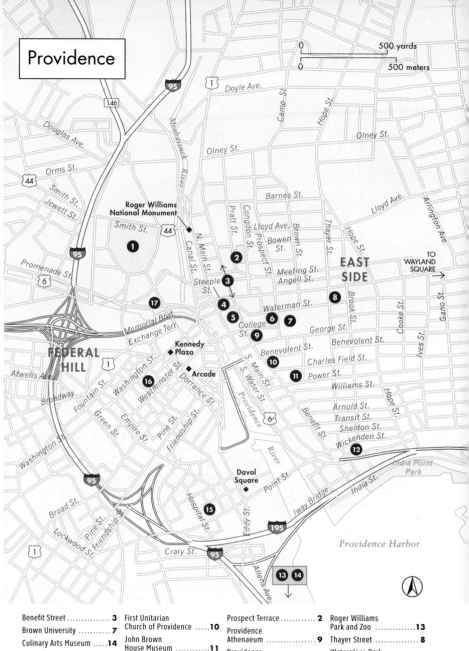

Providence

95			
146			

Doyle Ave.

Olney St.

Douglas Ave.

Orms St.

44 Smith St.

Jewett St.

Roger Williams
National Monument

44 Smith St.

❶

Promenade St.

6

95

FEDERAL
HILL

Atwells Ave.

1

Broadway

Fountain St.

Green St.

Empire St.

Washington St.

Broad St.

Pine St.

Lockwood St. Friendship St.

1

Crary St.

95

Memorial Blvd.

Exchange Terr.

Kennedy
◆ Plaza

❿

Washington St.

Westminster St.

Dorrance St.

Pine St.

Friendship St.

Hospital St.

❶⑤

Davol
Square ◆

Point St.

S. Eddy St.

Iway Bridge

Athens Ave.

195

❶③ ❶④

Providence Harbor

Moshassuck River

N. Main St.

Canal St.

Steeple St.

❷

❸

❹

❺

College St.

❾

Waterman St.

❻ ❼

S. Main St.

S. Water St.

Providence River

6

Barnes St.

Pratt St.

Congdon St.

Prospect St.

Lloyd Ave.

Bowen St.

Brown St.

Meeting St.

Angell St.

Benevolent St.

❿

Charles Field St.

⓫ Power St.

Williams St.

Arnold St.

Transit St.

Sheldon St.

Wickenden St.

⓬

Olney St.

Camp St.

Hope St.

Thayer St.

Hope St.

EAST
SIDE

Brook St.

❽

George St.

Benevolent St.

Cooke St.

Ives St.

Gano St.

TO
WAYLAND
SQUARE →

Lloyd Ave.

Arlington Ave.

Benefit St.

India Point
Park

India St.

Providence Harbor

0 ——— 500 yards
0 ——— 500 meters

The Providence River acts as a natural boundary between two major neighborhoods, Downtown and the East Side.

and train hubs. ✉ *Bordered by Memorial Boulevard and Empire, Sabin, and Pine Sts., Downtown* ⊕ *www.shopdowncity.com.*

FAMILY
Fodor's Choice
★

Providence Children's Museum. At Rhode Island's only hands-on children's museum, kids and their families play and learn in vibrant interactive environments. Favorites include Water Ways, an engaging hands-on playground of pumps, mazes, dams, and fountains, and Littlewoods, with a cave and a climbing tree for toddlers. Kids can also explore an outdoor climbing structure. ✉ *100 South St., Downtown* ☎ *401/273–5437* ⊕ *www.childrenmuseum.org* ⏰ *$9* ⏱ *Apr.–early Sept., daily 9–6; early Sept.–Mar., Tues.–Sun. 9–6; sometimes open Fri. until 8.*

FAMILY
Waterplace Park and River Walk. Venetian-style footbridges, cobblestone walkways, and an amphitheater encircling a tidal basin set the tone at this 4-acre tract along the Woonasquatucket River near where it joins the Moshassuck to form the Providence River. In summer the park is a gathering place for free concerts. It's also the site of **Water-Fire,** a multimedia installation featuring music and nearly 100 burning braziers that rise from the water between dusk and midnight on some nights spring–fall. WaterFire attracts nearly 1 million visitors annually. ✉ *Memorial Blvd., Steeple St., and Exchange St., Downcity, Downtown* ☎ *401/273–1155* ⊕ *www.waterfire.org.*

WORTH NOTING

Rhode Island State House. Designed by the noted architecture firm McKim, Mead & White, Rhode Island's beautiful 1904 capitol building has one of the world's largest self-supporting marble domes. The gilded Independent Man statue that tops the dome was struck by lightning 27 times before lightning rods were installed in 1975. The State Library on the

Roger Williams

It was an unthinkable idea: total separation of church and state. Break the tie between them, and where would the government get its authority? The answer threatened the Puritan way of life. And that's why in the winter of 1636 the Massachusetts Bay Colony banished a certain preacher with radical opinions named Roger Williams. He fled south into the wilderness, with the goal of establishing a new colony founded on religious tolerance, and arranged to buy land from the Narragansett sachems Canonicus and Miantonomo at the confluence of the Woonasquatucket and Moshassuck rivers. Word spread that this new settlement, which Williams had named Providence, was a place where civil power rested in the hands of the people. Those persecuted for their beliefs flocked there, and it thereafter grew into a prosperous Colonial shipping port. What started out as a radical experiment became the basis of American democracy.

The National Park Service runs the **Roger Williams National Memorial** (⊠ 282 N. Main St., Providence ☎ 401/521-7266 ⊕ www.nps.gov/rowi), a 4½-acre park. A five-minute film about Williams plays at the visitor center, where there are related exhibits. The park is on the east side of the Moshassuck River at North Main Street and Park Row West. From June through mid-October it's open daily 9–5, until 4:30 the rest of the year.

7

north side of the second floor contains the military accoutrements of Nathanael Greene, a Quaker who served as George Washington's second-in-command during the Revolutionary War, as well as the state flag on board Apollo 11's first lunar landing mission in 1969. In the State Room is a full-length portrait of Washington by Rhode Islander Gilbert Stuart, who also painted the portrait of Washington that appears on the $1 bill. The museum's centerpiece is the original 1663 parchment charter granted by King Charles II to the colony of Rhode Island. Look for the brooding, dark portrait of former Gov. Lincoln Chafee, who also served as U.S. senator. Guided tours lasting 50 minutes are offered on weekdays. ⊠ 82 Smith St., Downtown ☎ 401/222-3983 ⊕ www. sos.ri.gov/publicinfo/tours ⊗ Weekdays 8:30–4:30; tours weekdays at 9, 10, 11, 1, and 2.

EAST SIDE

Home to Brown University and the Rhode Island School of Design (RISD), the East Side is Providence's intellectual center. It includes Benefit Street, dubbed the "mile of history" for its high concentration of Colonial architecture; RISD's top-quality art museum; and Thayer Street, a gentrified mix of shops, restaurants, and an art-house cinema.

TOP ATTRACTIONS

Fodor'sChoice ★ **Benefit Street.** The city's wealthiest families lived along the "mile of history" during the 18th and early 19th centuries. Home to a high concentration of Colonial architecture, Benefit Street passes through the campuses of Brown University and the Rhode Island School of Design. Between mid-June and mid-October, the Rhode Island Historical

The Independent Man sculpture atop the State House symbolizes Rhode Island's free-thinking spirit.

Society conducts 90-minute tours ($14) of the area. Tours depart the John Brown House Museum Tuesday–Saturday at 11 am. ⊠ *Benefit St., Downtown* ☏ *401/273–7507* ⊕ *www.rihs.org.*

Brown University. Founded in 1764, this Ivy League institution is the nation's seventh-oldest college and has more than 40 academic departments. On a stroll through the College Hill campus, you'll encounter Gothic and Beaux-Arts structures, as well as the imposing Prospect Street gates, which open twice a year—in fall to welcome the students and spring to bid them farewell. On the ground floor of Manning Hall, the Haffenreffer Museum of Anthropology exhibits artifacts from around the world. The David Winton Bell Gallery in the List Art Center hosts several major art exhibitions a year. The Humanity-Centered Robotics Initiative's Robot Block Party, held in April, celebrates robots and how they are being used to solve the world's problems. ⊠ *Stephen Robert '62 Campus Center, 75 Waterman St., East Side* ☏ *401/863–2378* ⊕ *www.brown.edu.*

John Brown House Museum. Rhode Island's most famous 18th-century home was the stately residence of John Brown, a wealthy businessman, slave trader, politician, and China Trade merchant. John Quincy Adams called the home, designed in late-Georgian, early-Federal style, "the most magnificent and elegant private mansion that I have ever seen on this continent." An ardent patriot, Brown was a noteworthy participant in the burning of the British customs ship *Gaspee* in 1772. A variety of musical concerts are held on the lawn in summer. ⊠ *52 Power St., East Side* ☏ *401/273–7507* ⊕ *www.rihs.org/museums/john-brown-house* 🎟 *$10* ⊙ *Apr.–Nov., Tues.–Sat. 10–4; Dec.–Mar., Fri.*

and Sat. 10–4. Guided tours Apr.–Nov., Tues.–Fri. at 1:30 and 3, Sat. at 10:30, noon, 1:30, and 3; Dec.–Mar., Sat. 10:30, noon, 1:30, and 3.

FAMILY

Fodor's Choice

★

Museum of Art, Rhode Island School of Design. This museum houses more than 86,000 objects ranging from ancient art to work by contemporary artists from across the globe. Highlights include Impressionist paintings, Gorham silver, Newport furniture, an ancient Egyptian mummy, and a 12th-century Buddha—the largest historic Japanese wooden sculpture in the United States. Artists represented include major figures in the history of visual art and culture, including Cézanne, Chanel, Copley, Degas, Hirst, Homer, LeWitt, Matisse, Manet, Picasso, Rothko, Sargent, Turner, Twombly, van Gogh, and Warhol—to name a few. ⊠ *224 Benefit St., East Side* ☎ *401/454–6500* ⊕ *www.risdmuseum.org* ⊠ *$12* ⊘ *Tues., Wed., and Fri.–Sun. 10–5, Thurs. 10–9.*

Providence Athenaeum. Philadelphia architect William Strickland designed this 1838 Greek Revival building in which Edgar Allan Poe courted the poet Sarah Helen Whitman; the collection here includes a Poe-signed periodical containing a piece he published anonymously. An 1870s Manet print that illustrated Poe's "The Raven" hangs in the rare book room, which also contains two medieval illuminated manuscripts. Raven signs are posted at eight points of interest on a self-guided library tour. Among them is a special cabinet modeled after an Egyptian temple, which houses the library's multivolume imperial edition of *Description de l'Egypte* (1809–22), commissioned by Napoléon. ⊠ *251 Benefit St., East Side* ☎ *401/421–6970* ⊕ *www.providenceathenaeum.org* ⊠ *Free* ⊘ *Early Sept.–May, Mon.–Thurs. 9–7, Fri. and Sat. 9–5, Sun. 1–5; June 1–20, Mon.–Thurs. 9–7, Fri. 9–5, Sat. 9–1; June 21–early Sept., Mon.– Thurs. 10–6, Fri. 9–5, Sat. 10–2.*

7

Thayer Street. Bustling Thayer Street bears a proud old New England name and is very much a part of life at Brown University. Gentrification has resulted in an influx of chain stores, but in the blocks between Waterman and Bowen streets you'll still find fashion boutiques, shops selling funky gifts, the Avon Cinema art house, and restaurants serving every kind of cuisine from Greek to Korean. ⊠ *Thayer St., between Waterman and Bowen Sts., East Side* ⊕ *www.thayerstreetdistrict.com.*

WORTH NOTING

First Baptist Church in America. This historic house of worship was built in 1775 for a congregation originally established in 1638 by Roger Williams and his fellow Puritan dissenters. The writer H. P. Lovecraft attended Sunday school here briefly as a child, and the church now hosts the kickoff of NecronomiCon Providence, an international festival celebrating Lovecraft and other creators of "weird fiction, art, and academia." Architecture and design buffs will appreciate the 185-foot steeple, erected in 3½ days, as well as the auditorium's large crystal chandelier from Ireland, installed in 1792. Self-guided tour booklets are available in multiple languages. ⊠ *75 N. Main St., East Side* ☎ *401/454–3418* ⊕ *www.fbcia.org* ⊠ *$2* ⊘ *Weekdays 10–3. Guided tours late May–early Sept.*

First Unitarian Church of Providence. This Romanesque house of worship made of Rhode Island granite was built in 1816. Its steeple houses a

2,500-pound bell, the largest ever cast in Paul Revere's foundry. ✉ *1 Benevolent St., at Benefit St., East Side* ☎ *401/421–7970* ⊕ *www. firstunitarianprov.org* 🎫 *Free* ⊗ *Aug.–mid-July, weekdays 9–4.*

John Hay Library. Built in 1910 and named for Abraham Lincoln's secretary, "the Hay" houses Brown University Library's collections of rare books and manuscripts. World-class collections of Lincoln-related items, H. P. Lovecraft letters, and toy soldiers are of particular interest. The library is open to the public, but you need a photo ID to enter. ✉ *20 Prospect St., East Side* ☎ *401/863–2146* ⊕ *library.brown.edu/hay* 🎫 *Free* ⊗ *Sept.–mid-Dec. and Feb.–May, weekdays 10–5.*

FAMILY **Prospect Terrace.** This pocket park offers arguably the most scenic views of Downcity, particularly in the fall, when the surrounding foliage plays spectacularly off the urban backdrop. Prospect Terrace's centerpiece is a statue of Roger Williams, Rhode Island's forward-thinking founder—who here seems to be groovin' to the 1980s song "Walk Like an Egyptian."✉ *184 Pratt St., at Cushing St., East Side* ☎ *401/785– 9450* ⊕ *www.providenceri.com/parks-and-rec.*

Wickenden Street. Named for a Baptist minister who was one of Providence's first settlers, this main artery in the Fox Point district is home to antiques stores, art galleries, and trendy cafés. It also hosts the Coffee Exchange, one of the area's most popular gathering spots. Sidewalk sales are held in the spring and fall. Once a working-class Portuguese neighborhood, the Wickenden Street area has seen gentrification come and go over the years, but Our Lady of the Rosary Church on Traverse Street still conducts three weekend Masses in Portuguese. ✉ *Wickenden St., East Side.*

FEDERAL HILL

Popular Federal Hill may no longer be predominantly Italian-American, but the neighborhood remains infused with Italian charm and hospitality. The stripe down Atwells Avenue, the main thoroughfare, is painted in red, white, and green, and a huge *pignoli* (pine nut), an Italian symbol of abundance and quality, hangs on an arch soaring over the street. Grocers sell pasta, pastries, and hard-to-find Italian groceries. To get the full experience, take a seat near the fountain in DePasquale Square, especially during the Feast of St. Joseph in March; the Federal Hill Stroll in early in June; or the Columbus Day Festival and parade in October. The neighborhood lies to the west of Downtown, separated from Downtown by Interstate 95, and is bounded by Westminster Street to the south, and Route 6 to the west and north. For a look at what's on, check out ⊕ *www.federalhillprov.com.*

You're as likely to hear Italian as English in this neighborhood.

SOUTHERN PROVIDENCE

In the southern end of Providence, you'll find two interesting stops, the Culinary Arts Museum and the city's well-regarded zoo. Both are about 3½ miles south of Waterplace Park.

TOP ATTRACTIONS

OFF THE BEATEN PATH

Culinary Arts Museum. This offbeat gem on the Johnson & Wales University campus celebrates the joy of cooking and eating throughout human history. An authentic 1920s diner is one of the high points, and there are examples of cookbooks, menus, and restaurant advertising, along with exhibits about cooking in ancient times, eating in transit, and cooking competitions ranging from the county fair to the Culinary Olympics. ✉ *315 Harborside Blvd., off Narragansett Blvd. (U.S. 1A) on Providence–Cranston border* ☎ *401/598–2805* 🌐 *www.culinary.org* 🎟 *$7* 🕒 *Tues.–Sun. 10–5.*

FAMILY Fodor's Choice ★ **Roger Williams Park and Zoo.** Plan a full day to take in this regal 435-acre Victorian park where you can picnic, feed ducks in the lakes, rent a swan-shape paddleboat, and ride a Victorian-style carousel. The 40-acre zoo—one of the nation's oldest—has African elephants, Masai giraffes, zebras, red pandas, snow leopards, moon bears, gibbons, giant anteaters, giraffes, and river otters in natural settings. In October, more than 5,000 carved pumpkins line the Wetlands Trail for the well-attended Jack-O-Lantern Spectacular. The **Museum of Natural History** has a collection of more than 250,000 specimens, including preserved animals, plants, rocks, fossils, and ethnographic objects, in a setting that you will either find quaint or antiquated. The **Cormack Planetarium** has a 2 pm show on weekends year-round, daily in summer. The **Botanical Center** has two greenhouses and 12,000 square feet of indoor gardens. ✉ *1000 Elmwood Ave., Elmwood* ☎ *401/785–9450 for museum, 401/785–3510 for zoo* 🌐 *www.rwpzoo.org* 🎟 *Zoo $14.95, planetarium $2, museum $3, botanical center $5* 🕒 *Zoo and museum daily 10–4; botanical center Tues.–Sat. 11–4.*

WHERE TO EAT

The hard part about dining in Providence is choosing among its many superb restaurants. If you're in the mood for Italian, take a stroll through Federal Hill on Atwells Avenue; Downtown is home to excellent fine-dining establishments; and the East Side has great neighborhood and upscale-casual restaurants, as well as an assortment of spots with a hip ambience and an international menu.

DOWNTOWN

$$$$ AMERICAN 🍴 **Birch.** Benjamin Sukle, a nominee for the James Beard Foundation's best chef of the Northeast, serves creative, modern, four-course prix-fixe meals at his 18-seat restaurant. Over the course of two hours, you'll swoon over such dishes as picolino cucumber marinated in honey, herbs, and seaweed; grilled radishes; Rhode Island bluefish with caramelized sauerkraut; and, for dessert, warm plums. Seating in the minimalist, exposed-redbrick space is around a U-shape bar. [$] *Average main: $49* ✉ *200 Washington St., Downtown* ☎ *401/272–3105* 🌐 *www.birchrestaurant.com* 🕒 *Closed Tues. and Wed.* ✍ *Reservations essential* 💳 *No credit cards.*

$$$ MODERN AMERICAN 🍴 **The Dorrance Kitchen & Cocktails.** The opulent first floor of the former Union Trust Building is home to one of Providence's best-known purveyors of farm-to-table food. Siena marble, ornate plaster detailing, and

7

stained-glass windows lend the place a Newport-mansion vibe. The bar serves creative cocktails—the Up N' Cumber cocktail with cucumber vodka, elderflower liqueur, lime juice, and ginger beer is divine. Top picks among the small and large plates include curried cauliflower as a first course and, for the main event, pappardelle and lobster. [$] *Average main: $28* ⊠ *60 Dorrance St., Downcity, Downtown* ☎ *401/521–6000* ⊕ *www.thedorrance.com* ⊗ *Closed Sun. and Mon. No lunch.*

$$$
MODERN
AMERICAN
Fodor's Choice
★

✕ **Gracie's.** The city's best spot for a romantic meal is Table 21 in a private alcove at Ellen Slattery's stellar Downcity restaurant. Across the street from the Trinity Rep theater, Gracie's mixes sophistication with whimsy in the main dining room with star-theme decor. Executive chef Matthew Varga harvests many of his ingredients from the restaurant's rooftop garden. You can't go wrong with the seasonal, house-made gnocchi; Varga prepared a recent version with port-and-fennel sausage, stewed tomatoes, Swiss chard, and provolone. A three-course prix-fixe menu for $45 is available nightly, but for true excitement, opt for the five-, seven- or nine-course tasting menu ($85–$120) and see what pleasures come your way. [$] *Average main: $28* ⊠ *194 Washington St., Downcity, Downtown* ☎ *401/272–7811* ⊕ *www.graciesprov.com* ⊗ *Closed Sun. and Mon. No lunch.*

$$$
SEAFOOD

✕ **Hemenway's Seafood Grill & Oyster Bar.** In a city where culinary newcomers tend to garner all the attention, Hemenway's continues to be one of the best seafood restaurants. The menu includes New England staples like a perfectly cracked baked stuffed lobster with lump crab and scallop stuffing, fried whole-belly clams, and George's Bank sea scallops baked, fried, or grilled. The inspired chef's specialties include figs with goat cheese wrapped in bacon, and Portuguese-style littleneck clams with *chouriço* (spicy Portuguese sausage), tomatoes, and scallions. The wine list is extensive, and craft beer lovers will find a wealth of choices. The high-ceiling dining room's huge windows look out on Providence's World War II Memorial. In warm weather, dine outside on the front patio. [$] *Average main: $30* ⊠ *121 S. Main St., Downtown* ☎ *401/351–8570* ⊕ *www.hemenwaysrestaurant.com.*

$$$
MODERN
AMERICAN

✕ **Mill's Tavern.** Handsome brick walls and vaulted casement ceilings lend a cozy New England vibe to this contemporary French-influenced American restaurant. The menu includes selections from both a raw bar and a wood-burning oven and rotisserie. Dishes change quarterly to reflect what's in season locally. The chef might prepare a stuffed pork chop with fig, Brie, and walnuts, serving it with sweet potatoes and maple Dijon pork jus, or perhaps and crab-crusted day-boat scallops with farro and chorizo cream sauce. Take advantage of the three-course prix-fixe menu ($30), offered nightly except Saturday. [$] *Average main: $30* ⊠ *101 N. Main St., Downtown* ☎ *401/272–3331* ⊕ *www.millstavernrestaurant.com* ⊗ *No lunch.*

$
AMERICAN

✕ **Ogie's Trailer Park.** Fun and kitschy Ogie's bar and restaurant fuses trailer-park chic and *Jetsons*-style space-age decor. The menu emphasizes "gourmet comfort food," which translates into the likes of tater tots in béchamel sauce, grilled peanut butter and jelly, and mac 'n' cheese croquettes. The house favorite, Rhody Fried Chicken, involves a chicken breast encrusted with Cool Ranch Doritos. The patio, which has a fire pit—and a trailer built into the wall—is open year-round, if you care to brave the elements. When it's warm out, a tiki bar is open, though tiki drinks and other craft cocktails are poured year-round. $ *Average main: $8* ✉ *1155 Westminster St., Downtown* ☎ *401/383–8200* ⊕ *www.ogiestrailerpark.com* ⊗ *No lunch Mon.–Sat.*

$$$ ✕ **Red Fin Crudo + Kitchen.** Television celebrity chefs Julio Lazzarini
TAPAS Jenny Behm-Lazzarini—he's been on *Chopped,* and she's been on *Cutthroat Kitchen*—serve up the tastes of New England, northern Spain, the Mediterranean, and the Caribbean at their amazing tapas and cocktails restaurant. The crispy fried brussels sprouts with pork belly, Valdeón cheese, and a sherry glaze are definitely worth trying, as is the *jamón iberico de bellota,* four-year cured Iberico ham with Spanish olive oil and toast. The lobster mac 'n' cheese is more richly elegant than its name implies. On the last Sunday of the month, the place plays host to the Drag Brunch, which consists of cocktails, brunch, and what's billed as "a bold, brassy, and very risqué" drag show. $ *Average main: $25* ✉ *71 Washington St., Downcity, Downtown* ☎ *401/454–1335* ⊕ *www. redfincrudo.com* ⊗ *Closed Sun. and Mon.* ⌷ *Reservations essential* ▭ *No credit cards.*

EAST SIDE

$$$ ✕ **Al Forno.** When it opened in 1980, Al Forno put Providence on the
ITALIAN national dining map. Though its glory days may have passed, the restaurant retains a loyal following for its thin-crust pizzas with toppings like crispy fried calamari and pumpkin. There are also Italian specialties, including wood-grilled white wine–braised short ribs and handmade bread gnocchi with wild boar–sausage ragout. The city's movers and shakers gravitate to upstairs tables. $ *Average main: $30* ✉ *577 S. Main St., East Side* ☎ *401/273–9760* ⊕ *www.alforno.com* ⊗ *Closed Sun. and Mon. No lunch* ⌷ *Reservations not accepted.*

$$$$ ✕ **Bacaro.** The two levels of this lively Italian restaurant founded by
ITALIAN chef Brian Kingsford and partner Jennifer Matta offer unique dining experiences. The informal first floor has a deli case stocked with cured meats, cheeses, olives, and traditional Italian-style small plates; upstairs is a more traditional dining room with impressive views of the Providence River. There's also a beautiful garden patio. Every table receives a separate checklist of the cured meats and other items the deli sells, and selections come on a beautifully arranged board. The menu changes to emphasize seasonal, local ingredients, with offerings like pan-seared duck breast and confit of duck leg with roasted figs drizzled with wildflower honey. Save room for the house-made ice cream in Swiss chocolate almond, salted caramel, and other rich flavors. $ *Average main: $35* ✉ *262 S. Water St., East Side* ☎ *401/751–3700* ⊕ *www. bacarorestaurant.net* ⊗ *Closed Sun. and Mon. No lunch* ⌷ *Reservations essential.*

$$$ ✕ **Chez Pascal.** You can tell that this French bistro will be welcoming
FRENCH and unpretentious from its logo: a trio of pigs in striped shirts and berets. In a peaceful residential neighborhood, Chez Pascal seats 80, yet a dividing wall makes it feel intimate and romantic. The menu always includes escargot appetizer, baked in butter, garlic, and parsley, as well as a house-butchered pork entrée of the day, but the chef also works in

7

dishes based on locally available seasonal ingredients. Lunches featuring house-made sausages, hot dogs, and cured meats are served at two long tables in the open Wurst Kitchen, inside the main dining room. $ *Average main: $26* ⊠ *960 Hope St., East Side* ☎ *401/421–4422* ⊕ *www. chez-pascal.com* ⊗ *Closed Sun. No lunch Mon.*

$ × **The Duck & Bunny.** This creperie and café is a cool spot for brunch,
CAFÉ afternoon tea and sandwiches, or dessert. At brunch the "crepioli"
Fodor'sChoice (the restaurant's variation on ravioli) delight with seasonal trappings
★ like butternut squash stuffing and a sage butter sauce. The cupcakes get a lot of press (and deserve it), but the dessert crepes are standouts, too. The Angelina, a favorite of many patrons, consists of house-made chocolate, raspberry jam, Cloumage (curd-style cheese), fresh blueberries, and lemon zest. The menu includes gluten-free and vegan options. $ *Average main: $10* ⊠ *312 Wickenden St., Fox Point* ☎ *401/270– 3300* ⊕ *www.theduckandbunny.com* ⊗ *Closed Mon.* ⊜ *Reservations not accepted* ⊟ *No credit cards.*

$$ × **Red Stripe.** A giant fork hangs outside this neighborhood brasserie in
FRENCH Wayland Square, and the chefs do things big here—from the 10-ounce Angus burger to the everything-but-the-kitchen-sink chopped salad. Menu highlights include roasted half chicken with lemon and rosemary jus, and bacon and cheddar meat loaf. Prince Edward Island mussels come with a choice of savory broth and hand-cut fries, uncovered tableside with a steamy aromatic flourish. $ *Average main: $18* ⊠ *465 Angell St., East Side* ☎ *401/437–6950* ⊕ *www.redstriperestaurants.com.*

$$$ × **The Salted Slate.** Ben Lloyd, the chef-owner of this new American res-
AMERICAN taurant, is committed to honoring the origins of the food he prepares. He purchases meat, poultry, and fish whole from local vendors, butchers them in-house, and uses every part from nose to tail. In a simple, rustic setting, Lloyd wows with entrées such as lamb—raised on a farm just a few miles from the restaurant—with tomato torta, smoked marble potatoes, grilled mushrooms, and chimichurri. Another dish you might find on the ever-changing menu is sea scallops, braised red cabbage, crispy *guanciale* (cured pork cheek), charred cauliflower, and mushroom eggplant cream. $ *Average main: $27* ⊠ *Wayland Sq., 186 Wayland Ave., East Side* ☎ *401/270–3737* ⊕ *www.saltedslate.com* ⊗ *Closed Mon.*

FEDERAL HILL

$ × **Angelo's Civita Farnese.** Locals come to this third-generation, family-
ITALIAN owned restaurant in the heart of Federal Hill for the chicken or eggplant
FAMILY Parmesan, veal with peppers, and braciola like grandma used to make. The prices are reasonable, the atmosphere warm and casual. $ *Average main: $12* ⊠ *141 Atwells Ave., Federal Hill* ☎ *401/621–8171* ⊕ *www. angelosonthehill.com.*

$ × **Kitchen.** The lone chef and solitary waiter at this five-table restaurant
AMERICAN produce what some patrons describe as "breakfast nirvana." People wait in line for thick-cut bacon, Portuguese sweet-bread toast, and grilled blueberry corn muffins. Be patient—the meal is worth the time spent on line—and bring cash: Kitchen doesn't take credit. $ *Average main: $8* ⊠ *94 Carpenter St., Federal Hill* ☎ *401/272–1117* ⊗ *Closed Mon. and Tues.* ⊜ *Reservations not accepted* ⊟ *No credit cards.*

$$ MODERN AMERICAN Fodor's Choice ★ 🍴 **Nick's on Broadway.** Expect a wait for brunch at this trendy West End restaurant. Chef Derek Wagner entices his morning crowd with blueberry pancakes, poached eggs on a buttermilk biscuit with hollandaise and basil, and other well-prepared brunch fare. The restaurant also serves dinner, at which the chef's passionate embrace of farm-to-table precepts—not to mention his attention to detail—are even more in evidence. His outstanding homemade mustard may occupy a small place on the charcuterie plate, but its subtle composition speaks volumes. Ask for a seat at the polished wood counter for a front-row view of the open-kitchen choreography. [$] *Average main: $24* ✉ *500 Broadway, Federal Hill* ☎ *401/421–0286* 🌐 *www.nicksonbroadway.com* 🕓 *Closed Mon. and Tues. No dinner Sun.*

$$$ FUSION 🍴 **North.** Tucked away near Federal Hill, this nontraditional restaurant serves a creative menu that changes daily. You might find small-plate offerings like the irresistible tiny ham biscuits served with house-made mustard; Chinese noodles with mutton, squid, and fermented chili; or a five-spice cider doughnut. Fifty cents of every meal goes to support a local homeless shelter and food bank. [$] *Average main: $30* ✉ *3 Luongo Memorial Sq., Federal Hill* ☎ *401/ 421–1100* 🌐 *www.foodbynorth.com* 🕓 *No lunch* ✍ *Reservations not accepted* 💳 *No credit cards.*

$$$ ITALIAN 🍴 **Pane e Vino.** Portions are big in the Rhode Island comfort-food tradition at this Federal Hill spot whose name means "bread and wine" in Italian; count on fresh ingredients presented in a straightforward way. Appetizers include grilled octopus with fava beans and house-made meatballs. Share a pasta if you dare, but keep in mind that the veal chop could probably topple Fred Flintstone's footmobile. Gluten-free dishes are also available. A prix-fixe menu ($25) is offered on weekdays 5–7 and all day Sunday. The tables in front near the window are especially suited for a romantic dinner. [$] *Average main: $25* ✉ *365 Atwells Ave., Federal Hill* ☎ *401/223–2230* 🌐 *www.panevino.net* 🕓 *No lunch.*

$$ ITALIAN 🍴 **Siena.** This place generates well-deserved buzz for its *branzino* (sea bass) with scallops in a creamy scallion sauce and for its pasta with a rich Bolognese—both of which are legendary. It's best to split an appetizer, as portions are huge, though you may wish to keep the delicious *involtini di melanzane* (eggplant rolled with prosciutto and ricotta and baked in tangy marinara sauce) all to yourself. The silky-white *pasta e fagioli* under the menu's antipasti section is a meal in itself. The excellent wine list is usually augmented by special selections available by the bottle or glass, and the well-trained waitstaff can help you make the perfect pairing. **■ TIP→ Ask for a table by the large windows, as the stylish back dining room can get noisy.** [$] *Average main: $23* ✉ *238 Atwells Ave., Federal Hill* ☎ *401/521–3311* 🌐 *www.sienari.com* 🕓 *No lunch.*

WHERE TO STAY

DOWNTOWN

$ B&B/INN 🏨 **Christopher Dodge House.** Rooms on the east side of this three-story 1858 Italianate brick town house have direct views of the State House, though Interstate 95 lies between. **Pros:** huge windows in rooms; free passes to a nearby health club. **Cons:** I–95 may be too

7

close for light sleepers. $ *Rooms from: $149* ✉ *11 W. Park St., Downtown* ☎ *401/351–6111* ⊕ *www.providence-hotel.com* ↻ *14 rooms* ⦿ *Breakfast.*

$ ⛆ **The Dean.** A building that once housed a strip club is now a trendy
HOTEL   boutique hotel with a minimalist, masculine vibe and a sexy cocktail den. **Pros:** central location; minimalist design; trendy food and beverage options. **Cons:** central location can be noisy; masculine vibe may not appeal to everyone; European-size (smallish) rooms. $ *Rooms from: $129* ✉ *122 Fountain St., Downcity, Downtown* ☎ *401/455–3326* ⊕ *www.thedeanhotel.com* ↻ *44 rooms, 8 suites* ⦿ *No meals.*

$ ⛆ **Hotel Providence.** In the heart of the city's Arts and Entertainment
HOTEL   District, this intimate boutique hotel sets the standard for elegant decor and attentive service. **Pros:** attentive staff; plush rooms; "doggie lounge" has treats for pets. **Cons:** late risers may not appreciate the 8 am pealing of Grace Church's 16 bells. $ *Rooms from: $189* ✉ *139 Mathewson St., Downcity, Downtown* ☎ *401/861–8000, 800/861–8990* ⊕ *www.hotelprovidence.com* ↻ *64 rooms, 16 suites* ⦿ *No meals.*

$ ⛆ **Omni Providence.** Towering over Downcity, the Omni is steps from
HOTEL   restaurants, the Rhode Island Convention Center, the Dunkin Donuts
FAMILY   Center, and Waterplace Park, home of the WaterFire event. **Pros:** centrally located; beautiful views of the city from upper floors; child and pet friendly. **Cons:** elevators can be slow. $ *Rooms from: $159* ✉ *1 W. Exchange St., Downcity, Downtown* ☎ *800/578–2900* ⊕ *www.omnihotels.com/hotels/providence* ↻ *564 rooms* ⦿ *No meals.*

$ ⛆ **Providence Biltmore.** The city's beloved landmark since 1922, and now
HOTEL   part of the Hilton Curio Collection, the Biltmore has been treated to a multimillion-dollar renovation that has brought guest rooms well into the 21st century. **Pros:** spacious suites; great location; storied past; attention to service and detail. **Cons:** some bathrooms are cramped. $ *Rooms from: $179* ✉ *Kennedy Plaza, 11 Dorrance St., Downcity, Downtown* ☎ *401/421–0700, 800/294–7709* ⊕ *www.providencebiltmore.com* ↻ *109 rooms, 185 suites* ⦿ *No meals.*

$ ⛆ **Renaissance Providence Downtown Hotel.** This luxury hotel occupies one
HOTEL   of Providence's most mysterious addresses, a stately nine-story Neoclassical Revival building constructed as a Masonic temple between 1926 and 1928 but unoccupied for an inconceivable 75 years. **Pros:** terrific location next door to Providence Place Mall; supercomfortable linens and bedding. **Cons:** some rooms have small windows. $ *Rooms from: $178* ✉ *5 Ave. of the Arts, Downcity, Downtown* ☎ *401/919–5000, 800/468–3571* ⊕ *www.renaissanceprovidenceri.com* ↻ *264 rooms, 8 suites* ⦿ *No meals.*

EAST SIDE

$ ⛆ **The Old Court Bed and Breakfast.** Parents of Brown and RISD students
B&B/INN   book their stays in this three-story Italianate inn on historic Benefit Street a few years before graduation. **Pros:** on a regal residential street; elegant furnishings; friendly service. **Cons:** small bathrooms. $ *Rooms from: $155* ✉ *144 Benefit St., East Side* ☎ *401/751–2002* ⊕ *www.oldcourt.com* ↻ *10 rooms* ⦿ *Breakfast.*

NIGHTLIFE AND PERFORMING ARTS

For events listings, consult the daily *Providence Journal* or the website ⊕ *www.golocalprov.com*. The weekly *Motif* or *Providence Monthly* are both available (free) in restaurants and shops.

NIGHTLIFE
DOWNTOWN

BARS **The Magdalenae Room.** Dimly lit and oozing sex appeal, this intimate
Fodor's Choice speakeasy has first-rate bartenders who can make all the classics or
★ craft a trendy cocktail, whatever your whim. ⊠ *The Dean, 122 Fountain St., Downcity, Downtown* ☎ *401/455–3326* ⊕ *www.thedeanhotel.com/eat-and-drink.*

Mirabar. Long-running Mirabar is one of the most popular gay clubs in Providence. ⊠ *15 Elbow St., Downtown* ☎ *401/331–6761* ⊕ *www.mirabar.com.*

Red Fin Crudo + Kitchen. This place is known for creative cuisine, but its bar is worth a separate trip. The craft cocktail menu changes weekly to feature seasonal and local ingredients like Sons of Liberty Spirits Co.'s Pumpkin Spice Whiskey. ⊠ *71 Washington St., Downcity, Downtown* ☎ *401/454–1335* ⊕ *www.redfincrudo.com.*

MUSIC CLUBS **AS220.** Hear original music from techno-pop and hip-hop to folk and jazz at this gallery and performance space. Spoken word and poetry slams, comedy nights, and open mikes are also scheduled, and the venue hosts Foo Fest, an annual block party. The bar has a dozen beers on tap, many from New England breweries. ⊠ *115 Empire St., Downcity, Downtown* ☎ *401/861–9190* ⊕ *www.as220.org.*

Lupo's Heartbreak Hotel. A legendary music venue in a five-story theater, Lupo's hosts nationally known alternative, rock, blues, and punk bands. ⊠ *79 Washington St., Downcity, Downtown* ☎ *401/331–5876* ⊕ *www.lupos.com.*

Point Street Dueling Pianos. Two pianists play whatever the audience wants to hear—from "Happy Birthday" to "Piano Man" to an assortment of rock 'n' roll, heavy metal, and pop. If you're in the mood to sing, you may find yourself invited on stage. Reservations are taken for groups of three or more. ⊠ *3 Davol Sq., Downtown* ☎ *401/270–7828* ⊕ *www.pointstreetpianos.com* ☒ *$5 cover after 8:30 ($10 on Sat.).*

EAST SIDE

BARS **Hot Club.** For more than a quarter century, this place has been a hangout for young professionals, university professors, and politicians. On summer nights, you'll find a crowd on the outdoor deck overlooking the Providence River. For cheap eats, try local favorites like the saugy dog (hot dog) or the stuffed quahog. ⊠ *575 S. Water St., East Side* ☎ *401/861–9007* ⊕ *www.hotclubprov.com.*

FEDERAL HILL

BARS **Lili Marlene's.** Nondescript and easygoing, this bar with cozy booths has a loyal following among in-the-know locals who like martinis and beer, good burgers, and free pool. ⊠ *422 Atwells Ave., Federal Hill* ☎ *401/751–4996.*

7

PERFORMING ARTS

FILM

Cable Car Cinema & Cafe. This neighborhood art-house cinema and café screens foreign and independent films. Seating is on couches and old-school theater chairs. The concession stand sells beer and wine. ⊠ *204 S. Main St., Downtown* ☎ *401/272–3970* ⊕ *www.cablecarcinema.com* 🎫 *$9.75.*

GALLERY TOURS

Gallery Night Providence. During Gallery Night, held on the third Thursday of the month (March–November), many galleries and museums hold open houses and mount special exhibitions. ⊠ *Information Center, 1 Regency Plaza, Downtown* ☎ *401/490–2042* ⊕ *www.gallerynight.org.*

MUSIC

Providence Performing Arts Center. The 3,200-seat center, which opened in 1928 as a Loew's Movie Palace, hosts concerts, national tours of hit Broadway shows, and other large-scale events. Major renovations to this building, which is listed on the National Register of Historic Places, restored the stage, lobby, and arcade to their original splendor. The mighty Wurlitzer pipe organ is a source of pride. ⊠ *220 Weybosset St., Downcity, Downtown* ☎ *401/421–2787* ⊕ *www.ppacri.org.*

The Vets. This 1,900-seat auditorium has a proscenium stage and an exquisite interior; it hosts concerts, operas, and spoken word and dance performances. From September to May, the Vets is the home of the Rhode Island Philharmonic. ⊠ *1 Ave. of the Arts, Downcity, Downtown* ☎ *401/421–2787* ⊕ *www.vmari.com.*

THEATER

Trinity Repertory Company. A past Tony Award winner for best regional theater, this troupe presents classic plays, intimate musicals, and new works by young playwrights, as well as an annual version of *A Christmas Carol*—all in a renovated former vaudeville house. ⊠ *201 Washington St., Downcity, Downtown* ☎ *401/351–4242* ⊕ *www.trinityrep.com.*

SPORTS AND THE OUTDOORS

BIKING

FAMILY **East Bay Bicycle Path.** This 14½-mile path connects Providence's India Point Park to Independence Park in Bristol. Along the way, you pass eight parks and deck bridges with views of coves and saltwater marshes. The route is often congested on fine-weather weekends. ■ TIP→ **Check out the George Redman Linear Park on the Washington Bridge over the Seekonk River. It's accessible from India Point Park.** ⊠ *India Point Park, India St.* ☎ *401/253–7482* ⊕ *www.dot.ri.gov/community/bikeri/eastbay.php.*

BOATING

Prime boating areas include the Providence River, the Seekonk River, and Narragansett Bay.

Narragansett Boat Club. Experienced scullers can join a group for afternoon rowing on the Seekonk and Providence rivers. The club also offers beginner sculling and rowing classes. ⌧ *2 River Rd., East Side* ☏ *401/272–1838* ⊕ *www.rownbc.org.*

ICE-SKATING

FAMILY **Alex and Ani City Center.** The 14,000-square-foot outdoor ice rink is twice the size of the one at New York City's Rockefeller Plaza. The facility is open daily, late November–mid-March, and skate and helmet rentals are available. In the summer, it hosts concerts, festivals, and other events. ⌧ *2 Kennedy Plaza* ☏ *401/331–5544* ⊕ *www.alexandanicitycenter.com* ⌨ *$7.*

SHOPPING

Providence has a handful of small but engaging shopping areas. In Fox Point, Wickenden Street contains many antiques stores and several art galleries. Near Brown University, Thayer Street has a number of boutiques, though there has been an influx of chain stores. With its eclectic collection of specialty stores, Hope Street has branded itself as the East Side's "Main Street." Downtown's Westminster Street has morphed into a strip of independently owned fashion boutiques, galleries, and design stores.

DOWNTOWN

ANTIQUES AND HOME FURNISHINGS

Craftland. Etsy fans will be delighted by the arts and crafts at this colorful shop and gallery: jewelry, notecards, prints, silk-screened T-shirts, fashion accessories, bags, and other sparkly handmade objects by local artists are all for sale. ⌧ *212 Westminster St., Downcity, Downtown* ☏ *401/272–4285* ⊕ *www.craftlandshop.com* ⌐ *Validated parking in Grant's Block lot.*

HomeStyle. Drop by HomeStyle along increasingly gentrified Westminster Street for eye-catching objets d'art, stylish housewares, and other decorative items. ⌧ *229 Westminster St., Downtown* ☏ *401/277–1159* ⊕ *www.homestyleri.com* ⌐ *Validated parking at InTown Parking Lot on Weybosset St.*

risd|works. This shop has a selection of quirky kitchen gadgets, hand-blown glass, jewelry, and prints by Rhode Island School of Design faculty and alumni, including *Family Guy* creator Seth MacFarlane's custom RISD T-shirt. ⌧ *20 N. Main St., Downtown* ☏ *401/277–4949* ⊕ *www.risdworks.com.*

The Stanley Weiss Collection. The landmark 1895 Tilden Thurber Building houses the country's largest collection of fine classical and Colonial furniture and antiques, available for viewing Saturday 11–5. ⌧ *292 Westminster St., Downtown* ☏ *401/272–3200* ⊕ *www.stanleyweiss.com.*

JEWELRY

Copacetic Rudely Elegant Jewelry. Expect the unusual at this 30-year-old shop, which sells handmade jewelry, gadgets, and clocks created by more than 100 artists. ⌧ *17 Peck St., Downtown* ☏ *401/273–0470* ⊕ *www.copaceticjewelry.com.*

7

MALLS

Arcade. Built in 1828, the Arcade has shops and restaurants on its first floor, including **Camen & Ginger** for vintage and antique items, and the **Lovecraft Arts & Sciences Council** for books on the supernatural by H. P. Lovecraft and other authors. The Greek Revival building has entrances on Westminster and Weybosset streets. ⊠ *65 Weybosset St., Downtown* ☎ *401/454–4568* ⊕ *www.arcadeprovidence.com.*

Providence Place. Nordstrom, Macy's, and an Apple Store are among the anchor tenants at this large mall whose restaurants include the Cheesecake Factory and P. F. Chang's. Also here are Dave & Busters, and a 16-screen cinema and IMAX theater. Parking in the garage is discounted with validation. ⊠ *1 Providence Pl., at Francis and Hayes Sts., Downtown* ☎ *401/270–1000* ⊕ *www.providenceplace.com.*

EAST SIDE

ART GALLERIES

Bert Gallery. This gallery displays late-19th- and early-20th-century paintings by regional artists. ⊠ *24 Bridge St.* ☎ *401/751–2628* ⊕ *www. bertgallery.com.*

The Peaceable Kingdom. This gallery stocks folk art from around the world, including nativities, weavings and rugs, clothing, jewelry, masks, and musical instruments. In October, hundreds of colorful skeletons are on display leading up to the Mexican Day of the Dead. ⊠ *116 Ives St., East Side* ☎ *401/351–3472* ⊕ *www.pkgifts.com.*

HANDICRAFTS AND HOME FURNISHINGS

Frog + Toad. Clothing, housewares, fair trade handicrafts, and locally designed goods can all be found at this small curiosity shop and gift boutique. ⊠ *795 Hope St., East Side* ☎ *401/831–3434* ⊕ *www. frogandtoadstore.com.*

Stock Culinary Goods. Useful, whimsical, and always well-designed utensils, stemware, dishes, and culinary gifts are the specialty of this foodie paradise with an industrial kitchen vibe. ⊠ *756 Hope St., East Side* ☎ *401/521–0101* ⊕ *www.stockculinarygoods.com.*

FEDERAL HILL

FOOD

FAMILY
Fodor'sChoice
★

Constantino's Venda Ravioli. The sights, scents, and flavors of Italy surround you at Constantino's as you peruse the amazing selection of imported foods. The convivial banter between customers and employees adds to the atmosphere. Stop here for lunch, or grab an espresso or gelato at the bar; in the summer, enjoy the gelato at neighboring DePasquale Square's fountain. ⊠ *275 Atwells Ave., Federal Hill* ☎ *401/421–9105* ⊕ *www.vendaravioli.com.*

Scialo Bros. Bakery. Get your cannoli fix at this family-owned bakery in business since 1916. ⊠ *257 Atwells Ave.* ☎ *401/421–0986, 877/421–0986* ⊕ *www.scialobakery.com.*

Tony's Colonial Food. This superb grocery offers a family-friendly atmosphere in which to peruse the finest of Italian meats and cheeses; imported vinegars and olive oils; and candies and confections—all at reasonable prices. In addition, Tony's deli stocks freshly prepared foods to eat on the premises or take with you; try the Italian grinder, a Rhode Island lunchtime staple. ✉ *311 Atwells Ave., Federal Hill* ☎ *401/621–8675* ⊕ *tonyscolonial.mybigcommerce.com.*

THE BLACKSTONE VALLEY

In 1790, young British engineer Samuel Slater arrived in Providence with the knowledge he gained from apprenticing in English cotton mills. It was a crime to export machinery designs for cotton-cloth manufacture, but Slater had memorized much of what he saw. He found backers and partners, and three years later a mill opened at Pawtucket Falls in the Blackstone River. Eventually hundreds of mills were operating up and down the river from Worcester to Providence, transforming a young nation's agriculture-dominated economy and launching an industrial revolution. The Blackstone Valley helped make America the world's industrial powerhouse for a century and a half, luring immigrants to the region to work in its factories to make textiles, as well as barbed wire, space suits, and even Mr. Potato Head. Much of that industry is now gone, and many old mills have been renovated and converted to condominiums, offices, and gallery spaces. But the scenic river, the focus of ongoing environmental remediation efforts, remains a major attraction in this region, which includes the communities of Woonsocket, Pawtucket, Central Falls, Cumberland, Lincoln, North Smithfield, Smithfield, Glocester, and Burrillville. The Blackstone River Valley National Heritage Corridor designation aims to preserve and interpret the area's landscape and history.

TOURS

FAMILY **Blackstone Valley Explorer.** Narrated 45-minute Blackstone River tours aboard the 40-passenger riverboat *Blackstone Valley Explorer* take place on Sunday afternoon. Topics covered on this pretty ride include area ecology and industrial history. ✉ *Central Falls Landing, 45 Madeira Ave., Central Falls* ☎ *800/454–2882, 401/724–2200* ⊕ *www.rivertourblackstone.com* ▣ *From $10.*

PAWTUCKET

5 miles north of Providence.

Once a thriving mill town, Pawtucket went through tough times before artists discovered its old mills and low rents. The city remains the world headquarters of the toy manufacturer Hasbro, creator of Mr. Potato Head, and has a thriving arts and cultural scene. A visit to the engaging Slater Mill Museum, America's first successful water-powered factory, provides a sense of Pawtucket's pivotal role in the American industrial evolution. Inside a converted mill, the Hope Artiste Village hints at the future with its mix of art studios, lofts, retail shops, light-industrial workshops, and the Met music venue.

ESSENTIALS

Visitor Information Blackstone Valley Visitor Center. ✉ *175 Main St.* ☎ *401/724–2200, 800/454–2882* ⊕ *www.tourblackstone.com.*

EXPLORING

Hope Artiste Village. The surviving redbrick buildings of the former Hope Webbing Company's textile mill now hold artists' studios, galleries (including the always-interesting Candita Clayton Gallery), cafés, shops, the Met music venue, the marvelously retro Breaktime Bowl and Bar bowling alley, and a well-attended winter farmers' market on Saturday mornings, November–May. ⊠ *999 Main St.* ☎ *401/321–3850* ⊕ *www.hopeartistevillage.com.*

FAMILY **Slater Memorial Park.** Within the stately grounds of this park along Ten Mile River are picnic tables, tennis courts, a playground, a dog park, and a river walk. The park's **Looff Carousel**, built by Charles I. D. Looff in 1894, has 39 horses, three dogs, a lion, a camel, a giraffe, and two chariots that are the earliest examples of the Danish immigrant's work—rides cost 50¢. The Pawtucket chapter of the Daughters of the American Revolution gives tours by appointment of the park's **Daggett House**, which dates to 1685. ⊠ *825 Armistice Blvd.* ☎ *401/728–0500 park information* ⊕ *www.experiencepawtucket.org* ⊠ *Free* ☉ *Park daily sunrise–sunset. Carousel: Apr.–June, Sept., and Oct., weekends 11–5; July and Aug., daily 11–5.*

FAMILY **Slater Mill Museum.** Concord and Lexington may legitimately lay claim to
Fodor's Choice what Ralph Waldo Emerson called "the shot heard round the world"
★ in 1776, but Pawtucket's Slater Mill provided the necessary economic shot in the arm. Built in 1793, this National Historic Landmark was the first successful water-powered spinning mill in America; it touched off the industrial revolution that helped secure America's sovereign independence in early days of the republic. The museum complex explores this second revolution with expert interpretive guides dressed in period clothing, who demonstrate fiber-to-yarn and yarn-to-fabric processes and discuss how industrialization forever changed this nation. On-site are collections of hand-operated and -powered machinery, a 120-seat theater, two gift shops, a gallery, and a recreational park. ⊠ *67 Roosevelt Ave.* ☎ *401/725–8638* ⊕ *www.slatermill.org* ⊠ *$12* ☉ *Mar. and Apr., weekends 11–3; May and June, Tues.–Sun. 10–4; July–Oct., daily 10–4; Nov., weekends 10–4.*

WHERE TO EAT

$ ✕ **Modern Diner.** On weekends, the line often trails out the door for a
DINER seat in this 1941 Sterling Streamliner diner that's a beauty to behold.
FAMILY Lobster Benedict and cranberry-apple French toast are two good bets for breakfast, which is served all day (until this family-run diner closes at 2). The burgundy-and-tan railway-car simulation was the first diner to be listed on the National Register of Historic Places. There's a modern addition with retro counter seating. Ⓢ *Average main: $8* ⊠ *364 East Ave.* ☎ *401/726–8390* ⊕ *www.moderndinerri.com* ⊟ *No credit cards* ☉ *No dinner.*

$ ✕ **Rasoi.** Taking its name from the Hindi word for kitchen, this restau-
INDIAN rant just into Pawtucket from Providence serves cuisine from a staggering 27 regions of India. Young professionals flock here for the lamb *barra* kebab, vegetable and berry *kofta,* Madras chicken curry, and freshly baked breads. The menu includes numerous spicy, gluten-free, and vegan selections. There is a vegan lunch buffet on Saturday and a

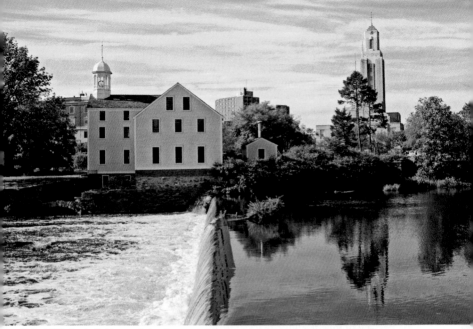

Slater Mill in Pawtucket is regarded as the country's first successful water-powered spinning mill.

regional lunch buffet on Sunday. The fetching dining room has a rectangular bar and warm orange walls, gold-specked blue floors, and red decorative panels. $ *Average main: $15* ✉ *727 East Ave.* ☎ *401/728–5500* ⊕ *www.indianrestaurantsri.com/rasoi.*

PERFORMING ARTS

The Met. This music venue books established and up-and-coming rock, folk, punk, and blues acts. Most concerts are open to all ages. ✉ *Hope Artiste Village, 1005 Main St.* ☎ *401/729–1005* ⊕ *www.themetri.com.*

Sandra Feinstein–Gamm Theatre. Known for its Shakespearean performances, the theater also presents edgy productions of classic and contemporary works in an intimate 137-seat setting. The season runs fall–spring. ✉ *172 Exchange St.* ☎ *401/723–4266* ⊕ *www.gammtheatre.org.*

SPORTS AND THE OUTDOORS

FAMILY **Pawtucket Red Sox.** The longtime minor-league affiliate of baseball's Boston Red Sox is looking to move elsewhere, but for at least 2016 will play its home games at the 10,000-seat McCoy Stadium. The season runs April–early September. ✉ *1 Ben Mondor Way* ☎ *401/724–7300* ⊕ *www.pawsox.com* ◫ *$8–$12.*

WOONSOCKET

10 miles north of Pawtucket, 15 miles north of Providence.

A former mill town struggling to gentrify, Woonsocket has a very fine museum about immigrant factory life and textile milling, as well as a jazz and blues club and a fish 'n' chips restaurant worthy of a special trip.

EXPLORING

FAMILY
Fodor's Choice ★
Museum of Work and Culture. In a former textile mill, this interactive museum examines the lives of American factory workers and owners during the Industrial Revolution. Focusing on French Canadian immigrants to Woonsocket's mills, the museum's cleverly laid-out walk-through exhibits begin with a 19th-century Québécois farmhouse, then continue with displays of life in a 20th-century tenement, a Catholic school, a church, and the shop floor. The genesis of the textile workers' union is described, as are the events that led to the National Textile Strike of 1934. There also an engaging presentation about child labor. ✉ *42 S. Main St.* ☎ *401/769–9675* 🌐 *www.rihs.org* 🎟 *$8* 🕒 *Tues.–Fri. 9:30–4, Sat. 10–4, Sun. 1–4.*

WHERE TO EAT AND STAY

$ SEAFOOD
🍴 **Ye Olde English Fish & Chips.** Folks come from all over to savor the affordable, fresh fried fish and hand-cut potatoes at this local institution in Market Square. The family-owned restaurant, which celebrated its 90th anniversary in 2012, serves up a casual and relaxed feast in a wood-paneled dining room. The clam chowder and clam cakes are very good. [$] *Average main: $10* ✉ *25 S. Main St.* ☎ *401/762–3637* 🌐 *www.yeoldeenglishfishandchips.com* 🕒 *Closed Sun. and Mon.*

$ B&B/INN
🏨 **The Pillsbury House Bed & Breakfast.** Tucked away on a historic street a half mile from the Blackstone River, this inn occupying an 1875 Victorian offers peace, quiet, and a splendid breakfast. **Pros:** stunning architecture; reasonable room rate; splendid breakfast. **Cons:** old-fashioned decor isn't for everyone. [$] *Rooms from: $95* ✉ *341 Prospect St.* ☎ *401/766–7983, 800/205–4112* 🌐 *www.pillsburyhouse.com* 🛏 *3 rooms, 1 suite* 🍽 *Breakfast.*

NIGHTLIFE AND PERFORMING ARTS

Chan's Fine Oriental Dining. Renowned blues and jazz performers are on the menu, along with folk, cabaret, and comedy acts. (Chan's also serves Chinese cuisine, but you're here for the music.) Reservations are recommended. ✉ *267 Main St.* ☎ *401/765–1900* 🌐 *www.chanseggrollsandjazz.com* 🎟 *$10–$25.*

SOUTH COUNTY

Officially called Washington County, the southwestern region of Rhode Island is home to beautiful seaside villages, unspoiled beaches, and parks and management areas with great hiking, kayaking, and running opportunities. More laid-back than Newport and Providence, the area has always been a summertime destination, but South County's 11 towns have grown into a region of year-round residents, many of whom can be found studying at the 1,200-acre main campus of the University of Rhode Island in Kingston. The university's Graduate School of Oceanography is in Narragansett, even closer to the coast.

ESSENTIALS

Visitor Information South County Tourism Council. ✉ *4808 Tower Hill Rd., Suite 101, Wakefield* ☎ *401/789–4422, 800/548–4662* 🌐 *www.southcountyri.com.*

WESTERLY

50 miles southwest of Providence, 100 miles southwest of Boston, 140 miles northeast of New York City.

The picturesque and thriving business district in this town of 18,000 people bordering Pawcatuck, Connecticut, has a lot going for it: galleries and artist studios, shops and restaurants, a Victorian strolling park, and more than 55 structures on the National Register of Historic Places. Once a busy little railroad town in the late 19th century, Westerly is now a stop on the New York–Boston Amtrak corridor. The town was known in the past for its red granite, which was used in monuments around the country. It has since sprawled out along U.S. 1 and grown to encompass seven villages in a 33-square-mile area: Westerly itself (also called downtown Westerly), along with Watch Hill, Dunn's Corners, Misquamicut, Bradford, Shelter Harbor, and Weekapaug.

GETTING HERE AND AROUND

When traveling between New York City and Boston, Amtrak makes stops at Westerly, Kingston, and Providence.

EXPLORING

FAMILY **Westerly Public Library and Wilcox Park.** Designed in 1898 by Warren Manning, an associate of Frederick Law Olmsted, co-creator of New York's Central Park, this 14½-acre Victorian strolling park in the heart of downtown Westerly has a pond, a meadow, an arboretum, a perennials garden, sculptures, fountains, and monuments. *The Runaway Bunny,* a sculpture inspired by the children's book of the same name, is popular with the little ones. A garden market, arts festivals, concerts, and Shakespeare-in-the-park productions are held periodically. The library's Hoxie Gallery holds monthly art exhibitions. ✉ *44 Broad St.* ☎ *401/596–2877* 🌐 *www.westerlylibrary.org* 🎟 *Free* 🕒 *Daily sunrise–9 pm.*

7

WHERE TO EAT

$ AMERICAN 🍴 **B&B Dockside.** It's all about breakfast and burgers at this café overlooking the Pawcatuck River. For breakfast, try the Portuguese toast, battered with cinnamon, vanilla, and cornflakes and served with maple syrup. (Live dangerously: add bacon and cream cheese.) Burgers rule the lunch menu, including the deliciously decadent Fat Elvis—with peanut butter, bacon, cheese, and caramelized bananas, it'll leave you saying, "Thank you, thankyouverymuch." [$] *Average main: $9* ✉ *19 Margin St.* ☎ *401/315–2520* 🌐 *www.bnbdockside.com* 🕒 *Closed Tues.*

$$ AMERICAN 🍴 **Bridge.** On the banks of the Pawcatuck River, this restaurant serves affordable American regional cuisine with an emphasis on local ingredients. There's a raw bar, and the menu includes lobster mac 'n' cheese, grilled lamb and pork chops, and grilled fish tacos. Gluten-free and vegan items are also available. The riverside bar and outdoor patio are great for taking in summer concerts in the park across the river, or for watching the annual Westerly-Pawcatuck Duck Race, during which 20,000 rubber duckies are cast into the river to raise money for local schools. [$] *Average main: $18* ✉ *37 Main St.* ☎ *401/348–9700* 🌐 *www.bridgeri.com.*

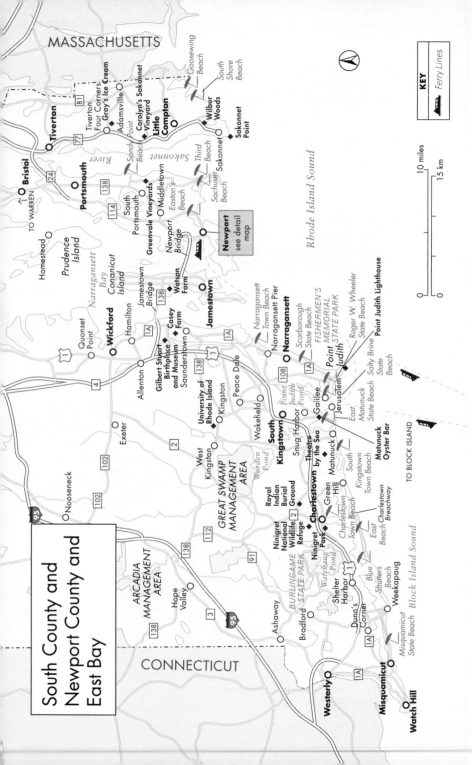

NIGHTLIFE

Knickerbocker Music Center. The band Roomful of Blues was born at "the Knick," and they still gig at this club near the Westerly train station. The venue hosts R&B, jazz, blues, and alt-country touring acts; local bands also perform, and there are open-mike nights. ✉ *35 Railroad Ave.* ☎ *401/315–5070* 🌐 *www.knickmusic.org.*

WATCH HILL

6 miles south of downtown Westerly.

For generations, this seaside village has attracted movers and shakers looking for a low-key getaway. Watch Hill has nearly 2 miles of gorgeous beaches, including Napatree Point Conservation Area, a great spot to see shorebirds and raptors and take in the sunset. Stargazers might catch a glimpse of Taylor Swift or Conan O'Brien, both of whom have homes here. The heart of the town is Bay Street, a seasonal business district with boutiques selling upscale beachwear, fashions, home goods, T-shirts, and souvenirs. There are also cafés and a historic carousel.

EXPLORING

FAMILY **Flying Horse Carousel.** At the beach end of Bay Street twirls one of the oldest carousels in America, built by the Charles W. F. Dare Company of New York City and part of a traveling carnival that came to Watch Hill before 1883. The carved wooden horses with real horsehair manes and leather saddles are suspended from chains attached to the ceiling, creating the impression the horses are flying. Riders must be under 12. ✉ *151 Bay St.* ☎ *401/348–6007* 🎟 *$1.50* 🕒 *Mid-June–early Sept., weekdays 10–9, weekends and holidays 9–9; late May–mid-June and early Sept.–mid-Oct., weekends 9–9.*

Watch Hill Lighthouse. A tiny museum at this 1808 lighthouse contains the original Fresnel light, letters and journals from lighthouse keepers, documentation of famous local shipwrecks, and photographs of the hurricane of 1938 and 19th- and early-20th-century sailing vessels off Watch Hill. Parking is for the handicapped and senior citizens only; everyone else must walk along a private road off Larkin Road. ✉ *14 Lighthouse Rd.* ☎ *401/596–7761* 🌐 *www.watchhilllighthousekeepers.org* 🎟 *Free* 🕒 *Grounds daily 8–sunset. Museum: July–early Sept., Tues.–Thurs. 1–3.*

WHERE TO EAT AND STAY

$$ AMERICAN Fodor's Choice ★

🍴 **Olympia Tea Room.** Overlooking the water since it first opened as an ice cream parlor in 1916, the Olympia is a century later one of South County's most sophisticated dining options. Varnished wood booths and a long marble counter echo the restaurant's rich history. The kitchen focuses on local and artisanal ingredients served with simple elegance, including whole roasted flounder and braised lamb shanks. The sommelier has curated a wine list with hundreds of selections—more than 40 available by the glass. [$] *Average main: $25* ✉ *74 Bay St.* ☎ *401/348–8211* 🌐 *www.olympiatearoom.com* 🕒 *Closed late Nov.–Apr., and Tues. in Sept. and Oct.* ✍ *Reservations not accepted.*

$$$$
RESORT
Fodor's Choice
★
Ocean House. High on bluffs overlooking Block Island Sound stands this extraordinary replica of the Victorian grande dame of the same name built here in 1868. **Pros:** exceptional service; beach with private cabanas; championship croquet lawn; spa with 25-meter lap pool; complimentary wine and cooking classes; no-tipping policy. **Cons:** expensive during high season; three-night minimum on weekends. $ *Rooms from: $1025* ⊠ *1 Bluff Ave.* ☎ *401/584–7000* ⊕ *www.oceanhouseri. com* ➦ *49 rooms, 18 suites* |○| *No meals.*

$$$$
RESORT
FAMILY
Watch Hill Inn Residences. Comprising an 1845 Victorian-style inn and a modern addition, this upscale inn has 20 suites, with kitchens and posh modern bathrooms, Apple TVs, Sonos Playbars, and iPads. **Pros:** steps from beaches and shops; many units have private decks; the latest in digital technology. **Cons:** three-night minimum stay. $ *Rooms from: $990* ⊠ *38–44 Bay St.* ☎ *401/348–6300* ⊕ *www.watchhillinn. com* ➦ *20 suites* |○| *Breakfast.*

$$$$
RESORT
Fodor's Choice
★
Weekapaug Inn. Guest rooms at this lovingly restored inn on Quonochontaug (Quonnie) Pond are furnished with luxury linens and the work of area artists. **Pros:** low-key luxury; serene pond views; charming, attentive service; no-tipping policy; guest pantry stocked with tasty treats; food for breakfast sourced locally. **Cons:** expensive; three-night minimum. $ *Rooms from: $690* ⊠ *25 Spray Rock Rd., Westerly* ☎ *401/637–7600* ⊕ *www.weekapauginn.com* ➦ *27 rooms, 4 suites* |○| *Breakfast.*

SHOPPING

Hope & Sundries. This welcoming general store with hipster-rustic design sells regional artisanal foods, home goods, toys, and gifts. Nearby at 147 Bay Street, the same owners operate Huxter, a clothing boutique inspired by the coastal New England lifestyle. ⊠ *103 Bay St.* ☎ *401/637–4686.*

MISQUAMICUT

2½ miles northeast of Watch Hill.

This family-oriented summer destination stretching 7 miles from Watch Hill to Weekapaug has a sandy beach the color of brown sugar. From waterslides to kiddie rides, the town's several amusement parks provide countless diversions. You can also hop on a Jet Ski, paddle a kayak, or find a spot for sunbathing. Evenings bring concerts and movies on the beach, and there are shore-side festivals in the spring and fall.

The Native American name for this sandy strip of beachfront means "Red Fish," referring to the Atlantic salmon common to the Pawcatuck River; the entire Westerly area, settled in 1661, once bore this name.

EXPLORING

FAMILY
Atlantic Beach Park. The largest and busiest of the several kid-oriented amusements along Misquamicut Beach, this facility offers old-fashioned fun for the entire family, including a carousel, bumper cars, a minigolf course, waterslides, batting cages, a roller coaster, a hurricane simulator, and a large arcade with more than 75 games. ⊠ *323 Atlantic Ave.* ☎ *401/322–0504* ⊕ *www.atlanticbeachpark.com* ➦ *Park free, $2 per*

ride; parking $15 ⏲ *Mid-June–early Sept., daily; mid-May–mid-June and early Sept.–mid-Oct., weekends; hrs vary.*

BEACHES

FAMILY **Misquamicut State Beach.** Part of the several-mile-long stretch of brown-sugar sand that makes up Misquamicut, this ½-mile state-run portion is Rhode Island's longest beach. Expect the 2,100-space parking lot to fill up on sunny summer holiday weekends. Bring your own chairs or blankets. **Amenities:** food and drink; lifeguards; parking (fee); showers; toilets. **Best for:** sunset; swimming; walking. ✉ *257 Atlantic Ave.* ☎ *401/596–9097* 🌐 *www.riparks.com/locations/locationmisquamicut.html* ⏲ *Early May–late May, weekends 9–6; late May–early Sept., daily 9–6.*

WHERE TO STAY

$ HOTEL 🏨 **Breezeway Resort.** A great choice for families, this well-maintained boutique motel is less than a quarter-mile from the ocean. **Pros:** nice range of room configurations; beach towels provided; on-site laundry; complimentary bicycles for adults. **Cons:** a bit noisy with so many kids; Wi-Fi in main lodge only. [$] *Rooms from: $189* ✉ *70 Winnapaug Rd.* ☎ *401/348–8953, 800/462–8872* 🌐 *www.breezewayresort.com* ⏲ *Closed late Oct.–early May* 🛏 *30 rooms, 22 suites, 2 villas, 1 cottage* 🍴 *Breakfast.*

7

CHARLESTOWN

12 miles northeast of Misquamicut.

Charlestown's secluded coastline makes it a great spot for swimming, sailing, surfing, beachcombing, bird-watching, and boating. Approximately 20% of Charlestown is conservation and recreation land, including Burlingame State Park, Ninigret Wildlife Refuge, Ninigret Park, and East Beach. The city regulates outdoor lighting to keep the night sky dark, so it's a fantastic place for sky watchers of all ages. Charlestown is also home to the Narragansett Indian Tribe Reservation, which holds the oldest recorded annual powwow in North America every August.

EXPLORING

FAMILY Fodor's Choice ★ **Frosty Drew Observatory and Sky Theatre.** In Ninigret Park but independently owned and managed, the observatory offers the state's best views of the night sky. Frosty Drew opens every Friday at sunset for stargazing and stays open until early Saturday morning if the skies are clear. It's also open on nights when meteor showers and other astronomical events are forecast. On cloudy nights, astronomers give presentations and offer tours. The place isn't heated, so dress for the season. ✉ *Ninigret Park, 61 Park La., off Old Post Rd.* ☎ *401/364–9508* 🌐 *www.frostydrew.org* 🎟 *Free* ⏲ *Fri. after sunset.*

FAMILY **Ninigret National Wildlife Refuge.** Spring brings opportunities to view the male American woodcock's mating ritual at this 400-acre sanctuary, but bird-watchers flock here year-round to commune with nature among 9 miles of trails and diverse upland and wetland habitats, including grasslands, shrublands, wooded swamps, and freshwater ponds. There's an abandoned naval air station on Ninigret Pond, the state's largest coastal salt pond and a fine place to watch the sunset. Hiking trails are closed in January, when bow hunters are allowed to cull white-tailed deer. Explore an impressive collection of wildlife and natural history displays at the Kettle Pond Visitor Center on the other side of U.S. 1 on Bend Road. ✉ *Ninigret Entrance Rd., off U.S. 1* ☎ *401/364–9124* 🌐 *www.fws.gov/ninigret* 🎫 *Free* 🕒 *Daily sunrise–sunset; visitor center daily 10–4.*

FAMILY **Ninigret Park.** This 227-acre park off Old Post Road was a World War II–era naval air training base, and now features picnic grounds, ball fields, a playground, a bike path, tennis and basketball courts, a criterium bicycle course, nature trails, a disc-golf course, a nature center, and a 3-acre spring-fed swimming pond. The Charlestown Seafood Festival is held here in August. ✉ *5 Park La., off U.S. 1* ☎ *401/364–1222* 🌐 *www.charlestownri.org* 🎫 *Free* 🕒 *Daily 8–sunset.*

BEACHES

FAMILY **Blue Shutters Beach.** Just west of the Ninigret Conservation Area with wonderful views of Block Island Sound, Blue Shutters is a popular escape for families, who enjoy building sandcastles, beachcombing, and bodysurfing the gentle waves. Beachgoers can see Block Island and Long Island from the shaded deck of the pavilion. Beach-accessible wheelchairs are available at no cost. **Amenities:** lifeguards; showers; toilets; parking (fee); food and drink. **Best for:** walking; sunsets; swimming. ✉ *469 East Beach Rd.* ☎ *401/364–1222* 🕒 *May–early Sept., weekdays 9–5, weekends and holidays 8–5.*

FAMILY **East Beach.** This tranquil and unspoiled barrier beach spans 3 narrow miles of shoreline that fronts and separates Ninigret Pond from the ocean. It stands in stark contrast to Narragansett's bustling Scarborough Beach. Parking is limited and fills up quickly. Be careful when swimming: the ocean side is known for riptides. **Amenities:** lifeguards; parking (fee); toilets. **Best for:** solitude; swimming; walking. ✉ *E. Beach Rd., off U.S. 1* ☎ *401/322–0450.*

WHERE TO EAT

$$ AMERICAN 🍴 **The Charlestown Rathskeller.** The hand-cut fries at this former speakeasy hidden in the woods are revered across southern New England, and steaks and burgers are big and cooked to perfection. For a lighter bite, try the locally sourced seafood and raw-bar options. [$] *Average main: $23* ✉ *489A Old Coach Rd.* ☎ *401/792–1000* 🌐 *www.thecharlestownrathskeller.com* ✍ *Reservations not accepted.*

SPORTS AND THE OUTDOORS

BOATING

Ocean House Marina. This full-service marina on scenic Ninigret Pond offers fuel, maintenance service, fishing supplies, and boat rentals. ✉ *60 Town Dock Rd., off U.S. 1* ☎ *401/364–6040* 🌐 *www.oceanhousemarina.com.*

PARKS

Burlingame State Park. This 2,100-acre park attracts many campers with its nature trails, picnic and swimming areas, and boating and fishing on crystal-clear Watchaug Pond. ✉ *1 Burlingame Rd.*

RHODE ISLAND TREATS

Clam Cakes. It's not summer for locals without a pilgrimage to a clam shack for these hunks of fried dough with briny, meaty clams inside. Pair them with the chowder of your choice.

Coffee Milk. The official state drink, coffee milk is like chocolate milk but made instead with coffee-flavored syrup, preferably Autocrat Coffee Syrup.

Del's Frozen Lemonade. You can get one of these refreshingly cold drinks from one of many Del's trucks making the rounds in the summer or at a Del's storefront.

NY System Wieners. Try a hot dog "done all the way": topped with meat sauce, mustard, onions, and celery salt. (They're said to be a great hangover cure.)

Rhode Island Style Calamari. This dish of lightly fried squid with hot cherry peppers and garlic is the official state appetizer for a good reason: the Port of Galilee in Narragansett processes millions of pounds of squid annually.

☎ 401/322–8910 ⊕ www.riparks.com/locations/locationburlingame.html ✉ Free ⊗ Mid-Apr.–mid-Oct.

SHOPPING

FAMILY **Fantastic Umbrella Factory.** With a hippie vibe, the kid- and first date–friendly Fantastic Umbrella Factory contains five rustic shops built around a wild garden and bamboo forest. Hardy, unusual daylilies and other plants are for sale, along with interesting clothing and jewelry, vintage eyewear, soy candles, creative pottery, blown glass, penny candy, and incense. In the South County Artisans Loft, a renovated second-floor barn space, you can meet local fine and craft artists and peruse their wares. For 50¢ you can scoop a cone full of seeds to feed the fenced-in emus, guinea hens, and ducks. The Small Axe Cafe (BYOB) serves an organic menu. ✉ 4820 Old Post Rd., off U.S. 1 ☎ 401/364–1060 ⊕ www.fantasticumbrellafactory.com.

SOUTH KINGSTOWN

10 miles northeast of Charlestown.

People often discover South Kingstown through the University of Rhode Island but return for its historic charm, arts-oriented community, great surfing beaches, and outdoors lifestyle. Almost a third of South Kingstown's 57 square miles is protected open space, allowing the town to maintain a rural character even as the population has doubled. There are two beaches, three rivers, several salt ponds, an 8-mile bike path, and numerous hiking trails, making it a great place for outdoors enthusiasts. ■ TIP→ Locals don't refer to it as South Kingstown. They use the names of its 14 distinct villages, which include Wakefield, Peace Dale, Matunuck, Snug Harbor, West Kingston, and Kingston, home of the University of Rhode Island's main campus.

BEACHES

Fodor's Choice ★ **East Matunuck State Beach.** Its vigorous waves, white sands, and picnic areas account for this 144-acre beach's popularity. Crabs, mussels, and starfish populate the rock reef that extends to the right of the strand, inspiring visitors to channel their inner marine biologist. A wind turbine provides power for the Daniel L. O'Brien Pavilion, named for a police officer killed in the line of duty while rescuing people stranded in this area during Hurricane Carol in 1954. ⚠ **Currents can be strong, so keep an eye on kids.** **Amenities:** food and drink; lifeguards; parking (fee); showers; toilets. **Best for:** surfing; swimming; walking; windsurfing. ✉ *950 Succotash Rd.* ☎ *401/789–8585* 🌐 *www.riparks.com/locations/locationeastmatunuck.html.*

FAMILY **South Kingstown Town Beach.** The ⅓-mile-long town beach—with a playground, a boardwalk, a volleyball court, and picnic tables—cannot be seen from the road and doesn't fill as quickly as the nearby state beaches. Surfers like this beach's waves; you can take lessons here in the summer. **Amenities:** lifeguards; parking (fee); toilets. **Best for:** sunset; surfing; swimming; walking. ✉ *719 Matunuck Beach Rd.* ☎ *401/789–9301* 🌐 *www.southkingstownri.com.*

WHERE TO EAT

$$ SEAFOOD Fodor's Choice ★ 🍴 **Matunuck Oyster Bar.** Shuckers are hard at work at the raw bar in this awesome waterside restaurant, an offshoot of the nearby Matunuck Oyster Farm. This year-round business committed to serving fresh, local produce and farm-raised, wild-caught seafood draws a crowd. (Thankfully, a free valet takes care of parking your vehicle.) Sunset is the best time to take in the view with a glass of wine while enjoying Point Judith calamari with cherry peppers and arugula, whole-belly fried clams, and different varieties of crisp, briny Rhode Island oysters, cherrystones, and littleneck clams. Lines are long, especially in summer. Snag a table outside if you can. [$] *Average main: $22* ✉ *629 Succotash Rd., Matunuck* ☎ *401/783–4202* 🌐 *www.rhodyoysters.com* ✍ *Reservations not accepted.*

$ AMERICAN 🍴 **Mews Tavern.** This cheery tavern always has several dozen beers on tap. Customers flock here for burgers and pizzas like the Salt Pond Oyster, which is topped with fried local oysters in a cornmeal crust. Also on the menu are Mexican dishes, chicken wings, and other comfort foods. Don't miss the downstairs bar, where patrons have written messages on dollar bills affixed to the ceiling and walls. [$] *Average main: $13* ✉ *456 Main St., Wakefield* ☎ *401/783–9370* 🌐 *www.mewstavern.com* ✍ *Reservations not accepted.*

NIGHTLIFE AND PERFORMING ARTS

For an extensive calendar of South County events pick up the free *South County Life* magazine or the weekly *Independent* newspaper.

Ocean Mist. The Ocean Mist has a beachfront deck where you can watch surfers on the point and catch some rays while enjoying a beer, a burger, or breakfast. Bands, including rock and reggae acts, perform nightly in summer and on weekends the rest of the year. Considered one of Rhode Island's best hangouts, "the Mist," as it's called by locals, is that cozy, worn sweatshirt of a beach bar that every coastal area wishes it had. ⊠ *895 Matunuck Beach Rd., Matunuck* ☎ *401/782–3740* ⊕ *www.oceanmist.net.*

Fodor's Choice
★

Theatre By The Sea. Directors, choreographers, and performers come from New York City to present a season of four summer musicals in an old 500-seat barn theater a quarter mile from the ocean. This is high-quality summer stock. Arrive early for dinner at the bistro on the property and to enjoy the stunning gardens. ⊠ *364 Cards Pond Rd., Matunuck* ☎ *401/782–8587* ⊕ *www.theatrebythesea.com* ✉ *Ticket prices vary* ☉ *Closed early Sept.–late May.*

SPORTS AND THE OUTDOORS

BIKING

FAMILY **William C. O'Neill Bike Path.** This scenic 8-mile paved path begins at Kingston Trail Station in West Kingston and travels through farmlands, the Great Swamp, and downtown Peace Dale and Wakefield to the border of Narragansett. Public art, including a sanctioned graffiti tunnel, decorates the path. Where it crosses Main Street in Wakefield, a comfort station with restrooms is open during daylight hours. ⊠ *1 Railroad Ave.* ☎ *401/789–9301* ⊕ *www.southcountybikepath.org.*

BOATING AND FISHING

Snug Harbor Marina. On the docks at Snug Harbor, an annual shark tournament takes place on the weekend after July 4th. You'll see mako, blue, and the occasional tiger shark being weighed in. The harbor is a fine spot for kayaking, and the marina has a fish market, arranges fishing charters, and sells bait. ⊠ *410 Gooseberry Rd., Wakefield* ☎ *401/783–7766* ⊕ *www.snugharbormarina.com.*

SHOPPING

The Purple Cow. Recognizable by its purple exterior, this funky shop carries home goods, jewelry, clothing, and gifts. It's been a favorite of locals since it opened in 1989. ⊠ *205 Main St.* ☎ *401/789–2389* ⊕ *www.thepurplecowco.net.*

NARRAGANSETT

5 miles east of Wakefield.

A summer resort destination during the Victorian era, Narragansett still has as its main landmark The Towers, the last remaining section of the 1886 Narragansett Pier Casino designed by McKim, Mead & White. The town is much quieter now, but it has beautiful beaches and remains home to a large commercial fishing fleet. Take a scenic drive down Route 1A to see the ocean and grand old shingle-style homes. You'll eventually wind up at Point Judith Lighthouse, which has been in continuous operation since the 19th century.

EXPLORING

TOP ATTRACTIONS

Block Island Ferry. If you're headed to Block Island, the Interstate Navigation Company offers two types of ferry service from Point Judith. Year-round, there's regular service, which takes 55 minutes and costs about $26 round-trip; late May–mid-October, there's high-speed service, which takes 30 minutes and costs $36 round-trip. Cars—which

Point Judith Lighthouse is just one of 21 such beacons in the Ocean State.

require an advance reservation—and bikes are only allowed on the regular service. ■TIP→ A Block Island Ferry Bloody Mary is a favorite beverage for some riders, but it's not recommended for the easily seasick. ⊠ *Galilee State Pier, 304 Great Island Rd.* ☎ *401/783–7996, 866/783–7996* ⊕ *www.blockislandferry.com.*

Point Judith Lighthouse. From the port of Galilee it's a short drive to this 1857 lighthouse with a beautiful ocean view. Because the lighthouse is an active Coast Guard Station, only the grounds are open to the public. Construction on the property has limited access to the grounds since Superstorm Sandy, but visitors can get good views from the adjoining Rose Nulman Park. ⊠ *1470 Ocean Rd.* ☎ *401/789–0444* ⊠ *Free* ⊙ *Daily sunrise–sunset.*

FAMILY   **South County Museum.** On part of early-19th-century Rhode Island governor William Sprague's former estate, now a town park, this museum founded in 1933 holds 25,000 artifacts dating from pre-European settlement to the mid-20th century. Six exhibit buildings include a printshop, a smithy, a carpentry shop, and a textile arts center. A living-history farm has Romney sheep, Nubian goats, and a flock of Rhode Island Red Heritage chickens, the state bird. ■TIP→ Attending the annual chick hatching is an Independence Day tradition for local families. ⊠ *115 Strathmore St., off Rte. 1A* ☎ *401/783–5400* ⊕ *www. southcountymuseum.org* ⊠ *$10* ⊙ *May, June, and Sept., Fri. and Sat. 10–4; July and Aug., Tues.–Sat. 10–4.*

WORTH NOTING

FAMILY **Adventureland of Narragansett.** Bumper boats, miniature golf, batting cages, and a go-cart track add up to great fun here. ✉ *112 Point Judith Rd. (Rte. 108)* ☎ *401/789–0030* ⊕ *www.adventurelandri.com* 💲 *$2–$8 depending on activity* ☉ *Late May–early Sept., daily; mid-Apr.–late May and early Sept.–Oct., weekends; hrs vary.*

FAMILY **Port of Galilee.** This little corner of Narragansett is a working fishing village, where you can eat at a fish shack, go for a swim at one of two state beaches, or just watch fishermen unload their catch. The port also offers year-round ferry service to Block Island. ✉ *Great Island Rd., off Galilee Escape Rd., west from Rte. 108* ☎ *401/789–1044* ⊕ *www. narragansettri.gov/383/port-of-galilee.*

BEACHES

Narragansett Town Beach. This crowded and lively beach is perfect for bodysurfing, sunbathing, people-watching, sandcastle making, crab hunting, and strolling its half-mile length. A sea wall (with free on-street parking) stretches along Ocean Road and attracts an eclectic crowd, including guitarists and motorcyclists. Covering approximately 19 acres, Narragansett Town Beach has a beautiful sandy beachfront, but is the only beach in the state that charges fees for both admission and parking. **Amenities:** food and drink; lifeguards; parking (fee); showers; toilets. **Best for:** surfing; swimming; walking. ✉ *39 Boston Neck Rd.* ☎ *401/783–6430* ⊕ *www.narragansettri.gov* 💲 *$8 (beach).*

Roger W. Wheeler State Beach. This beach—which some locals still call Sand Hill Cove, even though the name changed decades ago—has fine white sand, calm water, and a slight drop-off. It's a perennial favorite for parents with young children. **Amenities:** food and drink; lifeguards; parking (fee); showers; toilets. **Best for:** sunrise; sunset; swimming; walking. ✉ *100 Sand Hill Cove Rd.* ☎ *401/789–3563* ⊕ *www.riparks.com/ locations/locationrogerwheeler.html.*

FAMILY **Salty Brine State Beach.** Formerly known as Galilee State Beach, Salty Brine was renamed for a Rhode Island radio legend in 1990. It's a small but popular destination, especially for families with young children. Located near the state's largest commercial fishing port of Galilee, Salty Brine is permeated with the sights, sounds, and scents of Rhode Island's daily fishing culture. The beach, near bustling seafood restaurants, provides the best seat in the state for viewing the steady parade of ferries, fishing boats, and charters moving in and out of the channel. People flock to the beach for the annual Blessing of the Fleet parade of vessels on the last weekend in July. **Amenities:** food and drink; lifeguards; parking (fee); showers; toilets. **Best for:** sunrise; sunset; swimming; walking. ✉ *254 Great Rd.* ☎ *401/789–3563.*

FAMILY **Scarborough State Beach.** With generally moderate surf, this 42-acre beach has stunning views of where the Narragansett Bay empties into the ocean—although the scent of the neighboring wastewater treatment plant can mar the experience. There's a concrete boardwalk with gazebos and an observation tower. A grassy section on the southern end of the beach is good for kite flying and picnicking, and a trail connects it to Black Point, a scenic fishing and hiking area along the

7

rocky coastline. RIPTA buses service the beach, making it the easiest to access by transit. **Amenities:** food and drink; lifeguards; parking (fee); showers; toilets. **Best for:** surfing; swimming; walking; windsurfing. ✉ *870 Ocean Rd.* ☎ *401/789–2324* 🌐 *www.riparks.com/locations/locationScarborough.html.*

WHERE TO EAT

$$ SEAFOOD FAMILY Fodor's Choice ★

🍴 **Aunt Carrie's.** Family owned for four generations, this iconic Point Judith dining hall has been a must for Rhode Islanders every summer since it opened in 1920. Its peerless location and unpretentious atmosphere are the main draws, along with comfortable favorites like clam cakes, steamers, and fish 'n' chips. For a true native experience, try the Rhode Island Shore Dinner, an orgy of seafood served in several courses. The clam chowder comes three ways (red, white, and clear), and lobster figures in many dishes. Many of the recipes for namesake Carrie Cooper's pies are still in use, and some folks come from far away just for the Indian pudding, a traditional dessert made with cornmeal, molasses, and spices. Eat in the 125-seat dining hall or order at the take-out window and head to the picnic tables across the street—although the lines for both can get pretty long in the thick of summer. The restaurant serves beer and wine and operates an ice cream stand across the street. [$] *Average main: $19* ✉ *1240 Ocean Rd., Point Judith* ☎ *401/783–7930* 🌐 *www.auntcarriesri.com* ⏲ *Closed Oct.–Mar.* ✍ *Reservations not accepted.*

$$$ SEAFOOD Fodor's Choice ★

🍴 **Coast Guard House.** Built in 1888 as a U.S. Life Saving Service Station, this restaurant has been nearly destroyed twice by storms—by Hurricane Bob in 1991 and Superstorm Sandy in 2012. A renovation after Sandy relocated the dining area and gave it a minimalist design, affording diners an even more spectacular view of the ocean. The deck, a great hangout, remains, and a new terrace overlooks the ocean. The cuisine also was refreshed, the emphasis now on the raw bar and on local seafood dishes, with burgers, steaks, and pasta also on the menu. Parking can be difficult during high season, but there's free valet service. [$] *Average main: $25* ✉ *40 Ocean Rd.* ☎ *401/789–0700* 🌐 *www.thecoastguardhouse.com.*

$ ECLECTIC

🍴 **Crazy Burger Cafe & Juice Bar.** Vegetarians, vegans, and omnivores flock to this funky BYOB café not far from Narragansett Town Beach for smoothies, creative juice blends like pear-ginger-apple, eclectic burgers, and sweet-potato fries. Breakfast, served until 4 pm daily, features Mexican-style eggs, spinach crêpes, and cinnamon-bread French toast. White Christmas lights and colorful cloth napkins are part of the decor, as is a red phone booth behind the counter housing condiments (like the house-made ketchup). The waitstaff are friendly but usually very busy. Expect a bit of a wait until you can settle into a comfy booth and contemplate the extensive menu. [$] *Average main: $15* ✉ *144 Boon St.* ☎ *401/783–1810* 🌐 *www.crazyburger.com* ✍ *Reservations not accepted.*

$$ SEAFOOD

🍴 **George's of Galilee.** Owned by the same family since 1948, this local landmark near Salty Brine State Beach serves traditional Rhode Island favorites, including clambakes and "stuffies" (stuffed quahogs), and has a raw bar. Get your fried and broiled seafood here at reasonable prices: George's buys its ingredients directly from fishermen in Galilee, whom they list daily on their website. A recent renovation elevated the downstairs dining area and bar from beach-bar casual to low-key elegant, but summer traditions remain, including the takeout clam shack, live music on the deck on weekends, and beach volleyball on Monday night. $ *Average main: $19* ✉ *250 Sand Hill Cove Rd.* ☎ *401/783–2306* ⊕ *www.georgesofgalilee.com* ⊘ *Closed Jan.–mid-Feb. No dinner mid-Feb.–Mar., Mon.–Thurs.* ⬧ *Reservations not accepted.*

$$$

SPANISH

✕ **Spain of Narragansett.** This Spanish restaurant earns high marks for superbly prepared food and deft service. Worthy appetizers include grilled smoked chorizo and shrimp in garlic and olive oil. Entrées range from traditional paella to hefty *jefe* steak (sautéed tenderloin with artichoke hearts, mushrooms, and mustard-garlic sauce) for two. Daily specials such as roasted duck and shrimp wrapped with angel hair pasta tempt as well. There are few more impressive wine lists in the state, but don't overlook the sangria, which goes extremely well with the cuisine here. Arched entryways and tall plants help create a Mediterranean mood, and in summer you can dine on a patio anchored by a three-tier fountain. $ *Average main: $26* ✉ *1144 Ocean Rd.* ☎ *401/783–9770* ⊕ *www.spainri.com* ⊘ *Closed Mon. No lunch.*

$$$

SEAFOOD

✕ **Trio.** Close to Narragansett's best beaches, this welcoming place emphasizes seafood and classic comfort food favorites. The menu includes shrimp and scallops, and sole stuffed with crab and baby shrimp, along with grilled meats, baked oysters, and house-made pasta dishes. Trio also serves vegetarian and gluten-free dishes and artisanal pizzas. Vintage photos of turn-of-the-20th-century beachgoers decorate the walls of the cool-hued dining room and expansive bar area. The patio is open for dining in summer. $ *Average main: $25* ✉ *15 Kingstown Rd.* ☎ *401/792–4333* ⊕ *www.trio-ri.com* ⊘ *No lunch weekdays.*

WHERE TO STAY

$$

HOTEL

Fodor's Choice

★

🏨 **The Break.** Narragansett's first upscale boutique hotel has a laid-back boho surfer vibe—minus the feel of the cramped VW Vanagon. **Pros:** complimentary gourmet small-plates breakfast; saltwater fish tank in the lobby; spa services available. **Cons:** a hike to the beach; small signs, you might miss it the first drive by; two-night minimum on summer weekends. $ *Rooms from: $259* ✉ *1208 Ocean Rd.* ☎ *401/363–9800* ⊕ *www.thebreakhotel.com* 🛏 *12 rooms, 4 suites* ⦿*Breakfast* ⊟ *No credit cards.*

$

B&B/INN

🏨 **The Richards Bed and Breakfast.** Accomplished gardener Nancy Richards, who owns and operates this circa-1884 English-style stone mansion as a bed-and-breakfast with her husband, Steven, has created a lovely sanctuary for rest and relaxation. **Pros:** lots of quiet; remarkable architecture; great breakfast; walking path leads to rocky coast; hammock out back is the place to be in warm weather. **Cons:** a bit of a walk from the sandy beach; two-night minimum (four nights in August); credit cards not accepted. $ *Rooms from: $175* ✉ *144 Gibson Ave.* ☎ *401/789–7746* ⊕ *www.therichardsbnb.com* ⊟ *No credit cards* 🛏 *3 rooms, 1 suite* ⦿*Breakfast.*

7

SPORTS AND THE OUTDOORS

FISHING

Seven B's V. The 80-foot *Seven B's V* holds up to 120 passengers and offers daily fishing trips. ⊠ *Port of Galilee Dock RR, 30 State St.* ☎ *401/789–9250* ⊕ *www.sevenbs.com.*

SURFING

Narragansett Surf and Skate Shop. This shop rents surfboards, body-boards, and wet suits, and offers surfing and stand-up paddleboard lessons for individuals and groups. ⊠ *74 Narragansett Ave.* ☎ *401/789–7890* ⊕ *www.narragansettsurfandskate.com.*

WHALE-WATCHING

Lady Frances. In July and August, whale-watching excursions aboard the *Lady Frances* take you through warm waters where you'll get a chance to spot finback whales and other species. The company also conducts fishing trips. ■ TIP→ The family specials on Tuesday and Friday are a good deal. ⊠ *33 State St., Point Judith* ☎ *401/783–4988* ⊕ *www. francesfleet.com* ◪ *$48.*

WICKFORD

12 miles north of Narragansett Pier, 15 miles south of Providence.

A quaint village on a small harbor, Wickford has dozens of 18th- and 19th-century homes, some historical churches, and a handful of antiques shops and clothing boutiques. Wickford hosts Daffodil Days in the spring, the Wickford Arts festival in July, the Wicked Wickford Halloween festivities mid- to late October, and the Festival of Lights in December.

EXPLORING

Casey Farm. In the 19th century, this 1751 farmstead overlooking Narragansett Bay was the summer residence of the Casey family, who leased the land to tenant farmers. Today this community-supported farm is operated by resident managers who raise organic vegetables. Nearly 30 miles of stone walls surround the 300-acre farmstead. ■ TIP→ A weekly farmers' market takes place on Saturday, May–October. ⊠ *2325 Boston Neck Rd., Saunderstown* ☎ *401/295–1030* ⊕ *www.historicnewengland. org* ◪ *$4* ☉ *June–mid-Oct., Tues.–Thurs. 1–5, Sat. 9–2.*

Old Narragansett Church. Built in 1707—making it one of the oldest Episcopal churches in America—the Old Narragansett Church has no heat or electricity. But St. Paul's Parish continues to hold weekend services here and offers free 30-minute guided tours during summer months. One of the four Colonial parishes, the church has pew boxes, a wineglass pulpit, and an upstairs gallery where enslaved people were once welcomed to worship. The organ dates to 1680. ⊠ *62 Church La.* ☎ *401/294–4357* ⊕ *www.stpaulswickford.org* ☉ *July and Aug., Thurs.–Mon. 11–4.*

Smith's Castle. Originally the site of a trading post established by the state's founder, Roger Williams, the Smith's Castle grounds also include a marked mass grave, where 40 colonists killed in the Great Swamp battle of 1676 are buried. The land was part of a great plantation during the 18th century, spanning more than 3,000 acres worked by slaves and indentured laborers, and was later a large dairy farm. Saved from the wrecking ball by preservationists in 1949, the beautifully preserved saltbox plantation house appears much as it did in 1740. ✉ *55 Richard Smith Dr.* ☎ *401/294–3521* 🌐 *www.smithscastle.org* 🎟 *$8* 🕒 *May and Sept.–mid-Oct., Fri.–Sun. noon–4; June–Aug., Thurs.–Sun. noon–4; tours on the hr.*

EN ROUTE

Gilbert Stuart Birthplace and Museum. Built in 1751, the childhood home of one of America's foremost portrait artists—his image of George Washington graces the $1 bill—is set on 23 woodsy acres containing a scenic millpond and stream, Colonial herb gardens, nature trails, and a fish ladder. The fully restored gristmill here has the original granite millstones used to grind local whitecap flint corn into cornmeal. Stuart painted more than 1,000 portraits, including those of the first six U.S. presidents. The Welcome Center and Bell Art Gallery exhibits the works of Stuart and his daughter, also a painter, along with works by local and other artists. Guided tours take place on the hour. ✉ *815 Gilbert Stuart Rd., Saunderstown* ☎ *401/294–3001* 🌐 *www.gilbertstuartmuseum.com* 🎟 *$10* 🕒 *May–Oct., Mon., Tues., Fri., and Sat. 11–4, Sun. noon–4.*

WHERE TO EAT

$ CAFÉ 🍴 **Beach Rose Café.** This local favorite overlooking Wickford Harbor serves breakfast and lunch in a casual setting. The menu focuses on local fish and produce. Try the panino with house-made pesto, Asiago cheese, and chicken, or Fred's Scallop Roll on a grilled roll. The deck is dog friendly. [$] *Average main: $$8* ✉ *85 Brown St.* ☎ *401/295–2800* 🌐 *www.beachrosecafe.com* 💳 *No credit cards.*

SPORTS AND THE OUTDOORS

BOATING

Kayak Centre. Located in Wickford Harbor, the center rents kayaks and stand-up paddleboards, and gives lessons. ✉ *9 Phillips St.* ☎ *401/295–4400* 🌐 *www.kayakcentre.com.*

SHOPPING

ART GALLERIES

Five Main. This small fine-art gallery represents local and nationally known artists, photographers, and jewelry designers. You'll find inspired landscapes and seascapes as well as a collection of vintage pottery. ✉ *5 Main St.* ☎ *401/294–6280* 🌐 *www.fivemain.com.*

CRAFTS

The Mermaid's Purl. This welcoming yarn shop has a great selection of organic cotton, bamboo, alpaca, merino wool, and cashmere yarns, as well as felting supplies, beads and buttons, books and patterns, and knitting and crochet needles. Classes are offered so you know what to do with your purchases. For the Wednesday, Friday, and Saturday "knit-ins" you can bring your own work in progress and knit with the locals. ✉ *1 Main St.* ☎ *401/268–3899* 🌐 *www.themermaidspurl.com.*

NEWPORT COUNTY AND EAST BAY

Newport is one of the great sailing cities of the world and the host to world-class jazz, blues, folk, and classical music festivals. Colonial houses and Gilded Age mansions grace the city. Besides Newport itself, Newport County also encompasses the two other communities of Aquidneck Island—Middletown and Portsmouth—plus Conanicut Island (also known as Jamestown) to the west, and Tiverton and Little Compton, abutting Massachusetts to the east. Little Compton is a remote, idyllic town that presents a strong contrast to Newport's quick pace. Narrow and scenic Mount Hope Bridge carries traffic north from Aquidneck Island to Bristol, the most charming of the three towns that make up the East Bay region, which is entirely within Bristol County, one of the nation's smallest counties geographically.

GETTING HERE AND AROUND

You'll need to cross at least one of four major bridges to reach Newport County. The largest is the Newport Pell Bridge, spanning Narragansett Bay's East Passage via Route 138 and linking the island community of Jamestown with Newport. Motorists without a Rhode Island–issued EZ-Pass transponder have to pay $4 to cross it. Newport anchors Aquidneck Island, also home to the towns of Middletown and Portsmouth. From the north end of Portsmouth, Route 24 takes you across the Sakonnet River Bridge to Tiverton. Follow Route 77 south through Tiverton to reach quiet Little Compton. From the northwestern end of Portsmouth, you cross the Mount Hope Bridge to reach the charming town of Bristol in Bristol County, home to the oldest continuously held Independence Day parade in the country. The Jamestown Verrazzano Bridge connects Jamestown to North Kingstown over Narragansett Bay's West Passage.

FERRY TRAVEL Visitors headed to Newport from the west can save themselves the hassle of parking in Newport and the Newport Pell Bridge toll by parking their cars for free in Jamestown and boarding the Jamestown Newport Ferry. Conanicut Marine operates the 40-foot passenger ferry from One East Ferry Wharf in Jamestown and offers a free shuttle service to a large parking area at nearby Taylor Point. The ferry runs daily, mid-June–early September, and on weekends, late May–mid-June and late September–mid-October. The ferry links the village of Jamestown to Rose Island, Fort Adams State Park, Perrotti Park, and Ann Street Pier. An $23 round-trip rate is good for all day, but one-way passage rates and bicycle rates are available. Ferry service starts at 9:15 am in Jamestown, and the last run leaves Newport around 7:20 pm on weekdays and around 11 on weekends.

Oldport Marine Services operates a harbor shuttle service Monday–Thursday noon–6 and on Friday and weekends 11–7 ($10 all day; $6 round-trip, $3 one way). The shuttle lands at Perrotti Park, Bowen's Wharf, Ann Street Pier, International Yacht Restoration School, the Sail Newport dock, Fort Adams, and Goat Island.

TAXI TRAVEL Cozy Cab runs a daily shuttle service ($25 each way) between T. F. Green Airport in Warwick and the Newport Visitors' Information Center, as well as major hotels.

PARKING In Newport several lots around town offer pay parking. The largest and most economical is the garage behind the Newport Visitors' Information Center. Street parking can be difficult to find in summer.

ESSENTIALS

Transportation Contacts Jamestown Newport Ferry. ✉ *1 E. Ferry Wharf, Jamestown* ☎ *401/423–9900* ⊕ *www.jamestownnewportferry.com.* **Oldport Marine Services.** ✉ *1 Sayer's Wharf, Newport* ☎ *401/847–9109* ⊕ *www.oldportmarine.com.* **Orange Cab.** ✉ *Newport* ☎ *401/841–0021* ⊕ *www.newportshuttle.com.*

Visitor Information Discover Newport. ✉ *23 America's Cup Ave., Newport* ☎ *401/845–9123, 800/976–5122* ⊕ *www.gonewport.com.*

JAMESTOWN

25 miles south of Providence, 3 miles west of Newport.

Surrounded by Narragansett Bay's East and West passages, Conanicut Island comprises the town of Jamestown. About 9 miles long and 1 mile wide, the island is home to beautiful state parks, historic Beavertail Lighthouse, farmland, and a downtown village with a quaint mix of shops and restaurants.

EXPLORING

Jamestown Windmill. This English-designed smock windmill built in 1787 ground corn for more than 100 years. One of the most photographed sights on the island, the structure, named for its resemblance to farmers' smocks of yore, still works. In summer and early fall you can enter the three-story, octagonal structure and see the 18th-century technology. ✉ *North Rd., north of Weeden La.* ☎ *401/423–0784* ⊕ *www. jamestownhistoricalsociety.org* ☉ *Mid-June–mid-Oct., weekends 1–4.*

FAMILY **Watson Farm.** This historic New England farm has been in operation since 1789. Tenant farmers operate it, using sustainable practices to raise grass-fed beef and lamb, and producing wool blankets for local markets. They also host educational programs, like the annual Sheep Shearing Day on the second Saturday in May, when you can visit the baby lambs, see the flock being shorn by local shearers, and watch spinning and weaving demonstrations. You can also stroll 2 miles of trails and view seasonal farm activities. ✉ *455 North Rd.* ☎ *401/423–0005* ⊕ *www.historicnewengland.org/historic-properties/homes/watson-farm* 💵 *$4* ☉ *June–mid-Oct., Tues., Thurs., and Sun. 1–5.*

WHERE TO EAT AND STAY

$$$ ✗ **Jamestown FiSH.** This upscale Jamestown restaurant with a noteworthy wine list showcases the ocean's underappreciated species, like sable, char, and cuttlefish. The adventurous menu changes often to reflect available fresh seafood and produce. The spicy house-pureed soup made with fish, tomato, saffron, and fennel, garnished with a crusty Gruyère cracker, is a refreshing alternative to New England clam chowder, though you can get that here, too. The downstairs dining room is done up with white table linens and blue Italian water glasses, and has a gas fireplace. The upstairs bar area has a patio offering great views of

SEAFOOD

7

Newport Bridge when lighted at night. Patio seating is first-come, first-served, though you can make reservations for the indoor dining room. Area residents are big fans of the off-season Sunday brunch, served mid-October–late May. [$] *Average main: $28* ✉ *14 Narragansett Ave.* ☎ *401/423–3474* 🌐 *www.jamestownfishri.com* ⏲ *No lunch.*

$$$ AMERICAN Fodor's Choice ★ 🍴 **Simpatico Jamestown.** With nine dining rooms and a menu of seasonal classic American cuisine prepared with flair, it's tough to have a bad evening at this casually elegant restaurant. The lobster, tasso, and corn fritters; meaty Bolognese; and seafood entrées are all flavorfully complex. Couples looking for romance should seek out the Beech Tree room, a high-end adults-only tree fort, where seating is limited to parties of two; later, it becomes a hopping bar scene, with an incredible light show as the moon and stars sparkle through the tree leaves. [$] *Average main: $25* ✉ *13 Narragansett Ave.* ☎ *401/423–2000* 🌐 *www.simpaticojamestown.com* ⏲ *Closed Sun. and Mon. mid-Oct.–mid-May. No lunch.*

$ B&B/INN 🏨 **East Bay Bed & Breakfast.** This 1893 Victorian is peaceful day and night, even though it's only a block from Jamestown's two main streets and wharf. **Pros:** great value compared to Newport accommodations; large rooms; fireplace in common area. **Cons:** small showers; only three parking spaces; no kids under 12. [$] *Rooms from: $155* ✉ *14 Union St.* ☎ *401/423–0330, 800/243–1107* 🌐 *www.eastbaybnb.com* 🛏 *4 rooms* 🍽 *Breakfast.*

SPORTS AND THE OUTDOORS

PARKS

FAMILY **Beavertail State Park.** Water conditions range from tranquil to harrowing at this park straddling the southern tip of Conanicut Island. On a clear, calm day, however, the park's craggy shoreline seems intended for sunning, hiking, and climbing. There are restrooms with composting toilets open daily, year-round. On several dates (May–October), the Beavertail Lighthouse Museum Association opens the 1856 **Beavertail Lighthouse,** letting you climb 49 steps to enjoy the magnificent panorama from the observation deck. A museum occupies the lighthouse keeper's former quarters, and the old steam-engine room has a saltwater aquarium with local species. Both are open seasonally. ✉ *800 Beavertail Rd.* ☎ *401/423–3270* 🌐 *www.beavertaillight.org* 🎟 *Free* ⏲ *Museum: mid-June–early Sept., daily 10–4; late May–mid-June and early Sept.–mid-Oct., weekends noon–3.*

Fort Wetherill State Park. This outcropping of stone cliffs at the tip of the southeastern peninsula has 26 picnic tables and walking paths with scenic overlooks. A fort since the Revolutionary War era, it served as a top-secret German prisoner-of-war camp during World War II; it was declared government surplus in the 1970s and later turned into a state park. Scuba divers favor this spot, and it is a gathering point for viewing tall-ship parades and America's Cup races. There's also a boat ramp. Public restrooms are open daily, April–October. Some visitors may feel safer exploring the ruins in a group rather than solo. ✉ *3 Fort Wetherill Rd.* ☎ *401/423–1771* 🌐 *www.riparks.com/locations/locationfortwetherill.html* ⏲ *Daily sunrise–sunset.*

NEWPORT

30 miles south of Providence, 80 miles south of Boston.

The Gilded Age mansions of Bellevue Avenue are the go-to attraction for many Newport visitors. These ornately detailed late-19th-century homes, designed with a determined one-upmanship by the very wealthy, are almost obscenely grand. Their owners—Vanderbilts, Astors, Belmonts, and other budding aristocrats who made the city their playground for a mere six–eight summer weeks each year—helped establish the best young American architects and precipitated the arrival of the New York Yacht Club, which turned Newport into the sailing capital of the world.

Newport's music festivals are another draw: Bob Dylan famously went electric at the Newport Folk Festival, and in recent years, the outdoor festival has featured up-and-coming and internationally known indie and folk bands. In its earlier days, the Newport Jazz Festival hosted the likes of Miles Davis and Frank Sinatra; today it remains a showcase of traditional and avant-garde jazz. The Newport Music Festival brings classical music to the mansions, many of the artists and ensembles making their American debuts.

History buffs are enthralled by the large collection of Colonial-era architecture—Trinity Episcopal Church, Touro Synagogue, and the Colony House among them—reveling in these monuments to Newport's past as a haven for believers in religious freedom.

Pedestrian-friendly Newport has so much else to offer in such a relatively small geographical area—beaches, seafood restaurants, galleries, shopping, and cultural life. Summer can be extremely busy, but fall and spring are almost as nice and far less crowded.

FESTIVALS

Fodor's Choice
★

Newport Folk Festival. Held the last weekend in July, the festival books acts spanning folk, blues, country, bluegrass, folk rock, alt-country, indie folk, and folk punk. Lineups mix veteran performers like Jackson Browne, Patty Griffin, and Arlo Guthrie with younger stars like Conor Oberst, Brandi Carlile, and Nathaniel Rateliff & the Night Sweats. The festival is held rain or shine, and seating is general admission on a large uncovered lawn. Purchase tickets early: the last few festivals have sold out months in advance. ⊠ *Fort Adams State Park, Harrison Ave.* ☎ *401/848–5055* ⊕ *www.newportfolkfest.net* ☎ *$69–$90 per day.*

Newport Jazz Festival. The grandfather of all jazz festivals, founded in 1954, takes place on the first weekend in August. It showcases both jazz veterans and up-and-coming artists, playing traditional and avant-garde styles. Performers in recent years have included Esperanza Spalding, Wynton Marsalis, Dianne Reeves, Dr. John, the Maria Schneider Orchestra, and the Bad Plus with Bill Frisell. The festival is held rain or shine, with open-air lawn seating. ⊠ *Fort Adams State Park, Harrison Ave.* ☎ *401/848–5055, 800/745–3000* ⊕ *www.newportjazzfest. net* ☎ *$89 per day.*

Fodor's Choice
★

Newport Music Festival. A great way to experience one of the Newport mansions is at one of the 60 or so classical music concerts presented every July during the Newport Music Festival. Morning, afternoon, evening—even midnight—performances by world-class artists are scheduled at the Elms, the Breakers, and other venues. Selected works are chosen from 19th-century chamber music, vocal repertoire, and Romantic-era piano literature. Every year features at least one American debut and a tribute to a composer. ⊠ *Newport* ☎ *401/849–0700, 401/846–1133* ⊕ *www.newportmusic.org* ☜ *$20–$45.*

TOURS

BOAT TOURS More than a dozen yacht companies run tours of Newport Harbor and Narragansett Bay. Outings usually run two hours and cost about $25–$35 per person.

Classic Cruises of Newport. You have your choice of two vessels at Classic Cruises of Newport: the 19th-century *Madeleine* is a 72-foot schooner that cruises around the harbor, and the 1929 yacht *RumRunner II,* built for two New Jersey mobsters to carry "hooch," evokes the days of smuggling along the coast. Choose from a variety of tours, including gorgeous sunset sails. ⊠ *24 Bannister's Wharf* ☎ *401/847–0298* ⊕ *www.cruisenewport.com* ☜ *$25.*

Sightsailing of Newport. From May through mid-October, the 80-foot schooner *Aquidneck* and two sailboats depart Bowen's Wharf on up to two-hour tours of Newport Harbor and Narragansett Bay. ⊠ *Bowen's Wharf, America's Cup Ave.* ☎ *401/849–3333* ⊕ *www.sightsailing.com* ☜ *$30.*

TROLLEY **Viking Tours of Newport.** Take a trolley tour of Newport daily, April–
TOURS October and on Tuesday, Friday, and Saturday, November–March.
Fodor's Choice ⊠ *44 Long Wharf Mall* ☎ *401/847–6921* ⊕ *www.vikingtoursnewport.*
★ *com* ☜ *$39.*

WALKING **Newport Historical Society.** Various walking tours are available late
TOURS March–early January. ⊠ *127 Thames St.* ☎ *401/841–8770* ⊕ *www. newporthistorytours.org* ☜ *$8.*

EXPLORING

DOWNTOWN NEWPORT

Downtown Newport is the city's Colonial heart. More than 200 pre-Revolutionary buildings, mostly private residences, remain in Newport, but you'll also encounter landmarks such as St. Mary's Church, at the corner of Spring Street and Memorial Boulevard West, where John Fitzgerald Kennedy and Jacqueline Bouvier were married on September 12, 1953. The downtown waterfront is beautiful, and there are many boutiques and restaurants to occupy you. In summer traffic is thick, and the narrow one-way streets can be frustrating to navigate; consider parking in a pay lot and exploring the area on foot. The Ocean Drive and Bellevue Avenue are nice to see from a bicycle.

Colony House. Completed in 1741, this National Historic Landmark on Washington Square was the center of political activity in Colonial Newport. The Declaration of Independence was read from its steps on July 20, 1776, and British troops later used this structure as a barracks during their occupation of Newport. In 1781, George Washington met here with the French commander Count de Rochambeau, cementing an alliance that led to the American victory at Yorktown. The Newport Historical

Society manages the Colony House and offers guided tours. ⊠ *Washington Sq.* ☎ *401/841–8770* ⊕ *www.newporthistory.org* 🚶 *Walking tour $15, site tour $8* ☉ *June–Oct., daily 11–3 on the hr; Apr., May, Nov., and Dec. weekends 11–3 on the hr.*

Common Burial Ground. Among those buried in this graveyard, which dates to the 17th century, are several governors, a Declaration of Independence signatory, famous lighthouse keeper Ida Lewis, and Desire Tripp, whose unusual February 1786 gravestone commemorates the amputation of her arm. Many tombstones were made in the stone-carving shop of John Stevens, which opened in 1705 and still operates today. ⊠ *Farewell St.* ☎ *401/841–8770* ⊕ *www.newporthistory.org* 🚶 *Free.*

Great Friends Meeting House. The oldest house of worship in Rhode Island reflects the quiet reserve and steadfast faith of Colonial Quakers, who gathered here to discuss theology, peaceful alternatives to war, and the abolition of slavery. Built in 1699, the two-story shingle structure has wide-plank floors, simple benches, a balcony, and a wood-beam ceiling. ⊠ *29 Farewell St.* ☎ *401/841–8770* ⊕ *www.newporthistory.org* 🚶 *Tour $8* ☉ *June–Oct., daily 11–3 on the hr; Apr., May, Nov., and Dec. weekends 11–3 on the hr.*

Hunter House. The oldest house owned and maintained by the Preservation Society of Newport, the 1748 Hunter House served as the Revolutionary War headquarters of French admiral Charles Louis d'Arsac de Ternay after its Loyalist owner fled the city. Featuring a balustraded gambrel roof and heavy stud construction, it is an excellent example of an early Georgian frame residence. The carved pineapple over the doorway was a symbol of welcome throughout Colonial America. A collection of Colonial furniture includes pieces crafted by Newport's famed 18th-century Townsend-Goddard family of cabinetmakers and paintings by Cosmo Alexander, Gilbert Stuart, and Samuel King. The house is named after ambassador William Hunter, President Andrew Jackson's chargé d'affaires to Brazil. ⊠ *54 Washington St.* ☎ *401/847–1000* ⊕ *www.newportmansions.org* 🚶 *$30* ☉ *Late May–mid-Oct., daily 10–5.*

Newport Art Museum. More than a century old, the museum spans three buildings: the Cushing Gallery, the Coleman Center for Creative Studies, and the 1864 Griswold House, a National Historic Landmark designed by Richard Morris Hunt. In the museum's permanent collection are works by Fitz Henry Lane, George Inness, William Trost Richards, John La Farge, Nancy Elizabeth Prophet, Gilbert Stuart, and Helena Sturtevant, as well as contemporary artists like Dale Chihuly, Howard Ben Tré, and Joseph Norman. ⊠ *76 Bellevue Ave.* ☎ *401/848–8200* ⊕ *www.newportartmuseum.org* 🚶 *$10* ☉ *Tues.–Sat. 10–4, Sun. noon–4.*

Newport Historical Society Museum and Shop at Brick Market. Guided walking and site tours depart the Newport Historical Society's information center and museum in the 1762 Brick Market on Washington Square. Designed by Peter Harrison, the building houses a gift shop and a Newport history exhibit. Tour themes include Rogues and Scoundrels, about the history of pirates, criminals, and other unsavory types; and Road to Independence, a look at Newport's role in the American Revolution.

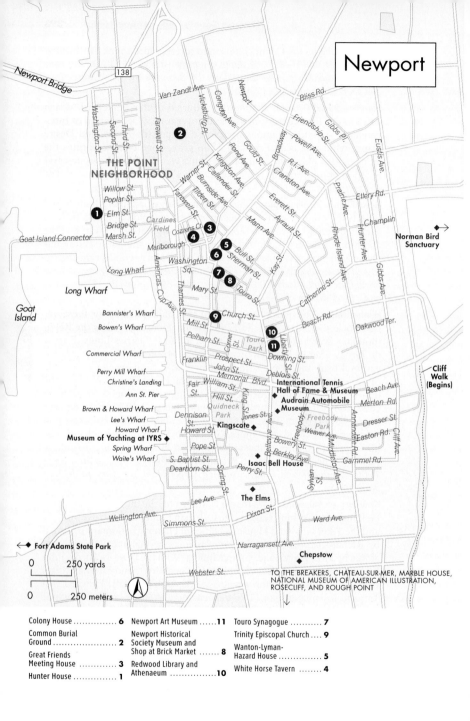

Newport

Colonial Newport

Established in 1639 by a small band of religious dissenters led by William Coddington and Nicholas Easton, Newport became a haven for those who believed in religious freedom. The deepwater harbor at the mouth of Narragansett Bay ensured its success as a leading Colonial port, and a building boom produced hundreds of houses and many landmarks that still survive today. These include the Wanton-Lyman-Hazard House and the White Horse Tavern, both built during the 17th century, plus Trinity Episcopal Church, Touro Synagogue, the Colony House, and the Redwood Library, all built in the 18th century.

WAR AND PEACE
British troops occupied Newport from 1776 to 1779, causing half the city's population to flee and ending a golden age of prosperity. The economic downturn that followed peace may not have been so great for its citizens, but it certainly played a part in preserving Newport's architectural heritage, as few owners had the capital to raze buildings and replace them with bigger and better ones.

✉ *127 Thames St.* ☎ *401/841–8770* ⊕ *www.newporthistory.org* 🖳 *Guided tours $15, self-guided tours $4* ⊙ *Daily 10–5.*

Redwood Library and Athenaeum. In 1747, Abraham Redwood gave 500 pounds sterling to found a library of arts and sciences; three years later, this Georgian Palladian–style building opened with 751 titles. More than half of the original collection vanished during the British occupation of Newport, though most of it has been recovered or replaced. Paintings on display include five portraits by Gilbert Stuart. Look for the portrait of the Colonial governor's wife, whose low neckline later led to the commissioning of Stuart's daughter Jane to paint a bouquet over her cleavage. A guided 35-minute tour is offered daily at 2 pm. The library presents talks by authors, musicians, and historians. ✉ *50 Bellevue Ave.* ☎ *401/847–0292* ⊕ *www.redwoodlibrary.org* 🖳 *Free, tour $5* ⊙ *Mon., Tues., and Thurs.–Sat. 9:30–5:30, Wed. 9:30–8, Sun. 1–5.*

Fodor's Choice
★

Touro Synagogue. In 1658, more than a dozen Jewish families, whose ancestors had fled Spain and Portugal during the Inquisition, founded a congregation in Newport. A century later, Peter Harrison designed this two-story Palladian house of worship for them. George Washington wrote a famous letter to the group in which he pledged the new American nation "would give to bigotry no sanction, to persecution no assistance." The oldest surviving synagogue in the country, Touro was dedicated in 1763 and its simple exterior and elegant interior remain virtually unchanged. A small trapdoor in the platform upon which the Torah is read symbolizes the days of persecution when Jews were forced to worship in secret. The John L. Loeb Visitors Center has two floors of state-of-the-art exhibits on early American Jewish life and Newport's Colonial history. ■**TIP→ The last synagogue tour is generally an hour before the visitor center closes.** ✉ *85 Touro St.* ☎ *401/847–4794* ⊕ *www.tourosynagogue.org* 🖳 *$12* ⊙ *Nov.–Apr., Sun. 11:30–2:30;*

May and June, Sun.–Fri. 11:30–2:30; July and Aug., Sun.–Fri. 9:30–4:30; Sept. and Oct., Sun.–Fri. 10–1:30 ☞ *No tours on Jewish holidays.*

QUICK
BITES

Rosemary & Thyme. The Brie, pear, and prosciutto on a grilled baguette—known affectionately to locals as the "BPP"—has earned a cult following at this little boulangerie and café. But you may have a hard time deciding between several outstanding European street food–inspired sandwiches. ✉ *382 Spring St.* ☎ *401/619–3338* ⊕ *www.rosemaryandthymecafe.com* ⊗ *Closed Mon.*

Trinity Episcopal Church. George Washington once sat in the distinguished visitor pew close to this church's distinctive three-tier wineglass pulpit. Completed in 1726, this structure is similar to Boston's Old North Church; both were inspired by the designs of Sir Christopher Wren. Trinity's 1733 London-made organ is believed to be the first big pipe organ in the 13 colonies. Among those buried in the churchyard's historic cemetery is French Admiral d'Arsac de Ternay, commander of the allied French Navy in Newport, who was buried with special permission in 1780 as there were then no Roman Catholic cemeteries in New England. ✉ *Queen Anne Sq., 145 Spring St.* ☎ *401/846–0660* ⊕ *www.trinitynewport.org* 🎫 *$5* ⊗ *Nov.–Apr., Sun. 11:30–12:30; May, Sun. 11:30–12:30, Sat. 10–3; June–Oct., Sun. 11:30–12:30, Mon.–Sat. 10–4* ☞ *No tours during parish events.*

Wanton-Lyman-Hazard House. As Newport's oldest house museum, this late-17th-century residence provides a glimpse of the city's Colonial and Revolutionary history. The dark-red building was the site of the city's Stamp Act riot of 1765. After the British Parliament levied a tax on most printed material, the Sons of Liberty stormed the house, which was then occupied by a prominent Loyalist. ✉ *17 Broadway* ☎ *401/846–0813* ⊕ *www.newporthistory.org* 🎫 *Site tour $8* ⊗ *Daily 11–3.*

GREATER NEWPORT

Just outside Downtown Newport you begin to discover stunning, opulent mansions. Along the waterfront, these "summer cottages" were built by wealthy families in the late 1800s and early 1900s as seasonal residences.

Audrain Automobile Museum. The museum's collection includes more than 160 rare, fully restored automobiles dating from the early 20th century to the present. The selection of vehicles on display varies—hot rods, super cars, and pre–World War II specimens are among the past exhibition topics. ✉ *222 Bellevue Ave.* ☎ *401/856–4420* ⊕ *www.audrainautomuseum.org* 🎫 *$12* ⊗ *Sun.–Thurs. 10–4, Fri. and Sat. 11–7.*

Fodor's Choice ★ **The Breakers.** The 70-room summer estate of Cornelius Vanderbilt II, president of the New York Central Railroad, was built in 1895. Architect Richard Morris Hunt modeled the four-story residence after 16th-century Italian Renaissance palaces. This mansion is not only big, but grand—be sure to look for the sculpted figures tucked above the pillars. The interior includes rare marble, alabaster, and gilded rooms with open-air terraces revealing magnificent ocean views. Noteworthy are a blue marble fireplace, rose alabaster pillars in the dining room, and a porch with a mosaic ceiling that took Italian artisans six months on their backs to install. ✉ *44 Ochre Point Ave.* ☎ *401/847–1000* ⊕ *www. newportmansions.org* ✉ *$21* ☉ *Mid-Mar.–June, Sept., and Oct., daily 9–5; July–early Sept., daily 9–7; Nov.–mid-Mar., daily 9–4.*

Chateau-sur-Mer. Built in 1852 as an Italianate-style villa for William Shepard Wetmore, a merchant in the China Trade, Chateau-sur-Mer was Newport's first grand residence. In 1857 Wetmore threw an extravagant, unprecedented gala for 2,500 people, ushering in the Gilded Age in Newport. The house is a treasure trove of Victorian architecture, furniture, wallpapers, ceramics, and stenciling; see hand-carved Italian woodwork, Chinese porcelains, and Japanese and Egyptian Revival wallpapers. The grounds contain rare trees from Mongolia. ✉ *474 Bellevue Ave.* ☎ *401/847–1000* ⊕ *www.newportmansions.org* ✉ *$16* ☉ *Mid-Mar.–mid-Nov., daily 10–5.*

Chepstow. Though not as grand as other Newport mansions, this Italianate-style villa with a mansard roof houses a remarkable collection of art and furniture gathered by the Morris family of New York City. Its significant 19th-century American paintings include Hudson River landscapes. Built in 1861, the home was designed by George Champlin Mason, a Newport architect. ✉ *120 Narragansett Ave.* ☎ *401/847–1000* ⊕ *www.newportmansions.org* ✉ *$16* ☉ *Late May–mid-Oct., daily 10–5.*

Cliff Walk. See the backyards of Newport's famous oceanfront Gilded Age mansions while strolling along this 3½-mile public walkway. The designated National Recreation Trail stretches from Memorial Boulevard at the western end of Easton's Beach (also called First Beach) south to the eastern end of Bailey's Beach. Along the way you'll pass Salve Regina University's Ochre Court, the Breakers, Forty Steps at Narragansett Avenue, Rosecliff, and Marble House and its Chinese Tea House. Park on either Memorial Boulevard or Narragansett Avenue. ✉ *Memorial Blvd.* ☎ *401/845–5300* ⊕ *www.cliffwalk.com* ✉ *Free.*

Fodor's Choice ★ **The Elms.** Architect Horace Trumbauer modeled this graceful 48-room French neoclassical home and its grounds after the Château d'Asnières near Paris. The Elms was built in 1901 for Edward Julius Berwind, a bituminous-coal baron. It was one of the first Newport mansions to be fully electrified. At the foot of the 10-acre estate is a spectacular sunken garden. The Behind the Scenes tour, which offers a glimpse into the lives of the Elms' staff members and the operation of facilities like the boiler room and kitchen, is one of the best of any of the mansion tours. ✉ *367 Bellevue Ave.* ☎ *401/847–1000* ⊕ *www.newportmansions.org* ✉ *$16* ☉ *Jan.–mid-May, daily 10–5; mid-May–Oct., daily 9–5; Nov.– early Jan., daily 9–4.*

FAMILY **Fort Adams State Park.** The largest coastal fortification in the United States can be found at this park, which hosts Newport's folk and jazz festivals and sailing events like the Volvo Ocean Race. From mid-May through mid-October, the nonprofit Fort Adams Trust offers daily tours of the fort, where soldiers lived from 1824 to 1950. Tours take in the fort's overlooks and tunnels, as well as its impressive walls. The views of Newport Harbor and Narragansett Bay are exquisite. The fort is reputed

Continued on page 404

Above left, stair hall of Château-sur-Mer, the first of the Bellevue Avenue mansions.

Opposite, Romantic Rosecliff's terracotta tiles look magical at dusk.

Below left, Statues of cherubs watch over the exterior of the Elms.

Right, Go behind the entrance gate on a tour of the Breakers.

The Mansions of Newport

GILDED AGE GEMS

By Andrew Collins, Debbie Harmsen, and Janine Weisman

Would you call a home with 70 rooms a cottage? If not, you're obviously not Cornelius Vanderbilt II. The Breakers, the "summer cottage" of the 19th-century multimillionaire, is one of a dozen mansions in Newport that are now by far the city's top attractions. Many of the homes are open to the public for tours, giving you a peek into the lives of the privileged.

THE SOCIAL SCENE

The Breakers dining room, just one of the opulent mansion's 70 rooms.

To truly appreciate a visit to Newport's mansions, you need to understand the times and the players—those who built these opulent homes and summered here for six weeks a year.

Newport at the turn of the 20th century was where the socialites of Boston, New York, and Philadelphia came for the summer. They were among the richest people in America at the time—from railroad tycoons and coal barons to plantation owners.

The era during which they lived here, the late 1800s up through the 1920s, is often referred to as the Gilded Age, a term coined by Mark Twain and co-author Charles Dudley Warner in a book by the same name. It was a time when who you knew was everything. Caroline Schermerhorn Astor was the queen of New York and Newport society; her list of the "Four Hundred" was the first social register. Three übersocialites were Alva Vanderbilt Belmont, Mary Ann (Mamie) Fish, and Tessie Oelrichs. These ladies who seriously lunched threw most of *the* parties in Newport.

While the women gossiped, planned soirees, and dressed and redressed thoughout the summer days, the men were usually off yachting.

In terms of the deepest pockets, the two heavyweight families during Newport's Gilded Age were the Vanderbilts and the Astors.

Madeleine Force was only 19 when she married John Jacob Astor IV at the Beechwood mansion in 1911; he was 47.

LEADING FAMILIES

Beechwood will soon be reinvented as an art museum.

Alva Vanderbilt Belmont

Cornelius Vanderbilt

John Jacob Astor IV

John Jacob Astor

THE VANDERBILTS Cornelius Vanderbilt I, called Commodore Cornelius Vanderbilt, built his empire on steamships and railroads. Cornelius had amassed almost $100 million before he died in 1877. He gave most of it to his son William Henry, who, also shrewd in the railroading business, nearly doubled the family fortune over the next decade. William Henry Vanderbilt willed $70 million to his son Cornelius Vanderbilt II, who became the chairman and president of New York Central Railroad; and $55 million to son William K. Vanderbilt, who also managed railroads for a while and saw his yacht, *The Defender*, win the America's Cup in 1895. One of Cornelius Vanderbilt II's sons, Alfred Gwynne Vanderbilt, died on the *Lusitania*, which sank three years after the *Titanic*. **Visit:** The Breakers, Marble House.

THE ASTORS Meanwhile, in the Astor camp, John Jacob Astor IV, who perished on the *Titanic*, had the riches his great-granddad had made in the fur trade as well as his own millions earned from successful real estate ventures, including New York City hotels such as the St. Regis and the Astoria (later the Waldorf–Astoria). His mother was Caroline Astor. Her mansion, Beechwood, is now owned by Oracle CEO Larry Ellison.

WHICH MANSION SHOULD I VISIT?

Even though the Newport "summer cottages" were inhabited for only six weeks each year, it would take you almost that long to explore all the grand rooms and manicured grounds. Each mansion has its own style and unique features. Here are the characteristics of each to help you choose those you'd like to visit:

★ **The Breakers:** The most opulent; enormous Italian Renaissance mansion built by Cornelius Vanderbilt II; tours are often big and very crowded; open most of the year.

Château-sur-Mer: The prettiest gardens and grounds; High Victorian–style mansion built in 1852; enlarged and modified in 1870s by Richard Morris Hunt.

Chepstow: Italianate villa with a fine collection of art; a bit less wow factor; summer hours only.

★ **The Elms:** A French chatea-style home with 10 acres of stunningly restored grounds; new guided servant quarters tour takes you into a hidden dormitory, roof, and basement; open most of the year.

Portrait of Mrs. Cornelius Vanderbilt II circa 1880, The Breakers.

Hunter House: Fantastic collection of Colonial furniture; downtown location, not on Bellevue Avenue; pricey admission; summer hours only.

Isaac Bell House: Currently undergoing restoration; less dramatic shingled Victorian displays an unusual mix of influences; less visited; summer hours only.

Kingscote: Gothic Revival–style home includes early Tiffany glass; one of the first summer cottages built in 1841; summer hours only.

★ **Marble House:** Outrageously opulent and sometimes crowded; former Vanderbilt home modeled on Petit Trianon in Versailles; tour at your own pace with digital audio tour; open most of the year.

Rosecliff: Romantic 1902 mansion; modeled after Grand Trianon in Versailles; somewhat crowded tours.

Rough Point: More contemporary perspective in 20th-century furniture; 1889 English manor–style home; tours are expensive and have limited availability.

MANSION TOURS

Preservation Society of Newport County. The Preservation Society maintains 11 historic properties and the Newport Mansions Store on Bannister's Wharf. Both guided tours and audio tours are available; you can purchase a combination ticket to see multiple properties for a substantial discount. The hours and days the houses are open in fall and winter vary. ☎ 401/847–1000 ⊕ www.newportmansions. org. ✉ The Newport Mansions Experience (admission to any 5 properties excluding Hunter House) $32.99.

Consider viewing mansions from the Cliff Walk for a different perspective.

Marble House at night.

TOP EXPERIENCE

★ **Cliff Walk.** See the backyards of Newport's famous oceanfront Gilded Age mansions while strolling along this 3½-mile public access walkway. The designated National Recreation Trail stretches from Memorial Boulevard at the west end of Easton's Beach (also called First Beach) southerly to the east end of Bailey's Beach. Along the way you'll pass the Breakers, Rosecliff, and Marble House and its Chinese Tea House. The north half of the walk is paved but the trail turns to large flat boulders south of Ruggles Avenue. Be prepared for increasingly rough terrain not suitable for small children, strollers, or people with mobility problems. Park on either Memorial Boulevard or Narragansett Avenue.

to be haunted and is often open for spooky ghost-hunting tours in the days leading up to Halloween. ⊠ *90 Fort Adams Dr.* ☎ *401/841–0707* ⊕ *www.fortadams.org* ⊠ *Park free; guided fort tour $12, self-guided tour $6* ⊗ *Daily 7:30–sunset.*

SCENIC DRIVE

Ocean Drive. There really isn't a street called Ocean Drive, but the name has come to indicate the roughly 10-mile scenic route from Bellevue Avenue at Memorial Boulevard south to Ocean Avenue and out to Castle Hill Avenue, Ridge Road, and Harrison Avenue. About halfway along, you'll come to the 89-acre Brenton Point State Park, a premiere destination for kite enthusiasts and picnickers. ⊠ *Bellevue Ave.*

FAMILY
Fodor's Choice
★
International Tennis Hall of Fame & Museum. Tennis fans and lovers of history, art, and architecture will enjoy a visiting the birthplace of American tournament tennis. The renovated museum contains interactive exhibits, a holographic theater that simulates being in a room with Roger Federer, displays of clothing worn by the sport's biggest stars, video highlights of great matches, and memorabilia that includes the 1874 patent from England's Queen Victoria for the game of lawn tennis. The 6-acre site is home to a grandstand, the shingle-style Newport Casino, which opened in 1880 and was designed by architects McKim, Mead & White, and the recently restored Casino Theatre. The 13 grass tennis courts, one clay court, and an indoor tennis facility are open to the public for play. In early July, the hall of fame hosts the prestigious Hall of Fame Tennis Championships. ⊠ *194 Bellevue Ave.* ☎ *401/849–3990* ⊕ *www.tennisfame.com* ⊠ *$15* ⊗ *Sept.–June, daily 10–5; July and Aug., daily 10–6.*

Isaac Bell House. Revolutionary in design when it was completed in 1883, the shingle-style Isaac Bell House combines Old English and European architecture with Colonial American and exotic details, such as a sweeping open floor plan and bamboo-style porch columns. McKim, Mead & White of New York City designed the home for Isaac Bell, a wealthy cotton broker. ⊠ *70 Perry St., at Bellevue Ave.* ☎ *401/847–1000* ⊕ *www. newportmansions.org* ⊠ *$16* ⊗ *Late May–mid-Oct., daily 10–5.*

Kingscote. Among Newport's first summer cottages, this 1841 Gothic Revival mansion designed by Richard Upjohn was built for George Noble Jones, a Georgia plantation owner. The house is named for its second owners, the King family, one of whose members hired McKim, Mead & White to expand and redesign it. The dining room, one of the 1881 additions, contains a cork ceiling and one of the first installations of Tiffany glass windows. Furnishings reflect the King family's involvement in the China Trade. ⊠ *253 Bellevue Ave.* ☎ *401/847–1000* ⊕ *www. newportmansions.org* ⊠ *$16* ⊗ *Late May–mid-Oct., daily 10–5.*

Fodor's Choice
★
Marble House. One of the most opulent of the Newport mansions, Marble House contains 500,000 cubic feet of marble. The house was built from 1888 to 1892 by William Vanderbilt, who gave it as a gift to his wife, Alva, for her 39th birthday. The house was designed by the architect Richard Morris Hunt who took inspiration from the Petit Trianon at Versailles. The Vanderbilts divorced in 1895 and Alva married Oliver

H. P. Belmont, moving down the street to Belcourt Castle. After his death, she reopened Marble House, and had the Chinese Tea House built on the back lawn, where she hosted "Votes for Women" rallies. ✉ *596 Bellevue Ave.* ☎ *401/847–1000* ⊕ *www.newportmansions.org* 💲*$16* 🕙 *Early Nov.–mid-May, daily 10–4; mid-May–Oct., daily 10–5.*

Museum of Yachting at IYRS. The 2½-acre campus the International Yachting Restoration School is home to the 1831 Aquidneck Mill, whose fourth floor houses the Museum of Yachting and the IYRS library. The museum's exhibits include yachting-related art and historical artifacts, and the maritime reference library contains more than 4,000 nautical titles, among them rare books, logbooks, yacht registers, and yacht club directories. From an elevated catwalk inside the adjacent Restoration Hall, a large brick building erected in 1903 and formerly an electric power plant, you can watch work being done on historically significant sailboats and powerboats. One big project taking place outside the hall these days is the ongoing restoration of the 1885 racing schooner *Coronet.* ✉ *Aquidneck Mill Building, 449 Thames St., 4th fl.* ☎ *401/848–5777* ⊕ *www.iyrs.edu/museum-yachting-iyrs* 🕙 *Wed.–Fri. noon–5.*

National Museum of American Illustration. This museum exhibits original work by Norman Rockwell, J. C. Leyendecker, Maxfield Parrish, N. C. Wyeth, and many others spanning the "Golden Age of American Illustration" (1895–1945). All 323 printed *Saturday Evening Post* covers are on display. The 1898 Beaux-Arts adaptation of an 18th-century French château was designed by the same architects responsible for the New York Public Library and other landmarks; Frederick Law Olmsted designed the adjacent grounds. ✉ *492 Bellevue Ave.* ☎ *401/851–8949* ⊕ *www.americanillustration.org* 💲*$18* 🕙 *Late May–early Sept., Thurs.–Sun. 11–5; early Sept.–late May, Fri. 11–5.*

FAMILY **Norman Bird Sanctuary.** Stroll through the woods or hike to the top of Hanging Rock for a spectacular view at this 325-acre sanctuary for more than 300 species of birds, plus deer, foxes, mink, turtles, and rabbits. The sanctuary has about 7 miles of trails. A 19th-century barn holds the visitor center, whose wildlife and ecosystem exhibits document Rhode Island's natural history. ■**TIP→ The raucous dawn chorus of birdsong in the spring is one of the great wildlife experiences in Rhode Island.** ✉ *583 Third Beach Rd., Middletown* ☎ *401/846–2577* ⊕ *www.normanbirdsanctuary.org* 💲*$7* 🕙 *Daily 9–5.*

Rosecliff. Newport's most romantic mansion was commissioned by Tessie Hermann Oelrichs, who inherited a Nevada silver fortune from her father. Stanford White modeled the 1902 palace after the Grand Trianon at Versailles. Rosecliff has a heart-shaped staircase and Newport's largest private ballroom. Rosecliff stayed in the Oelrichs family until 1941, went through several ownership changes, and then was purchased by Mr. and Mrs. J. Edgar Monroe of New Orleans in 1947. The Monroes were known for throwing big parties. Scenes from the films *The Great Gatsby* (1974), *True Lies* (1994), and *Amistad* (1997) were shot here. ✉ *548 Bellevue Ave.* ☎ *401/847–1000* ⊕ *www.newportmansions. org* 💲*$16* 🕙 *Mid-Mar.–late Nov., daily 10–4.*

Fodor'sChoice
★

Rough Point. Tobacco heiress and preservationist Doris Duke furnished her 39,000-square-foot English manorial–style house at the southern end of Bellevue Avenue with family treasures and fine art and antiques she purchased on her world travels. Highlights include paintings by Renoir, Van Dyck, and Gainsborough, numerous Chinese porcelains, Turkish carpets and Belgian tapestries, and a suite of Louis XVI chairs. Duke's two camels, Baby and Princess (who came with an airplane she had purchased from a Middle Eastern businessman), once summered here on the expansive grounds designed by landscape architect Frederick Law Olmsted. Duke bequeathed the oceanfront house with all its contents to the Newport Restoration Foundation to operate as a museum after her death. Each year, the foundation assembles an exhibit devoted to Duke's lifestyle and interests, which is included with a guided tour. ⊠ *680 Bellevue Ave.* ☎ *401/847–8344* ⊕ *www.newportrestoration.org* 🎫 *$25* ⊙ *Mid-Apr.–mid-May, Thurs.–Sat. 10–2; mid-May–early Nov., Tues.–Sat. 9:45–3:45.*

BEACHES

Easton's Beach (*First Beach*). A ¾-mile-long surfing beach, Easton's has a boardwalk, vintage carousel, aquarium, and playground. Public facilities include restrooms, indoor and outdoor showers, a skate park, an elevator, and beach wheelchairs for people with disabilities. The snack bar's twin lobster rolls are very popular (and a great deal). **Amenities:** food and drink; lifeguards; parking (fee); showers; toilets. **Best for:** sunrise; sunset; swimming; walking. ⊠ *175 Memorial Blvd.* ☎ *401/845–5810* ⊕ *www.cityofnewport.com/departments/easton-s-beach* ⊙ *Late May–early Sept., daily 9–6.*

Sachuest Beach (*Second Beach*). The western end of this 1¼-mile-long sandy beach attracts many surfers. Surfboard and stand-up paddleboard rentals are available. **Amenities:** food and drink; lifeguards; parking (fee); showers; toilets. **Best for:** surfing; swimming; walking; windsurfing. ⊠ *305 Sachuest Point Rd., Middletown* ☎ *401/849–2822* ⊙ *Late May–early Sept., daily 8–6.*

Third Beach. Located on the Sakonnet River, Third Beach is more peaceful than the nearby ocean beaches and a great spot for families. It has a boat ramp and is a favorite of windsurfers. You'll find a mobile concession stand on weekends. **Amenities:** parking (fee); lifeguards. **Best for:** swimming; walking; windsurfing. ⊠ *Third Beach Rd., Middletown* ☎ *401/849–2822.*

WHERE TO EAT

$$$$
AMERICAN
Fodor'sChoice
★

✕ **Castle Hill Inn.** No other restaurant in Newport can compete with the spectacular water views from the Sunset Room, one of four dining rooms inside the historic main inn. The three-course prix-fixe menu displays a passion for simple New England food done well, re-creating a clambake with littlenecks and plump *chouriço*-filled Georges Bank scallops. (There are also four- and six-course options.) A perfect spot for a romantic dinner, Castle Hill also serves lunch, allowing you to savor ethereal cuisine while watching sunlit clouds drift by. Favorites at the well-attended Sunday brunch include lobster hash and an omelet with fresh farm vegetables and artisanal cheeses. Produce comes from local growers listed on the various menus. $ *Average main: $80* ⊠ *590 Ocean Dr.* ☏ *888/466–1355, 401/849–3800* ⊕ *www.castlehillinn.com* ⌕ *Reservations essential.*

$$ ✕ **Flo's Clam Shack.** With an old boat in front, peeling paint, and a bam-
SEAFOOD boo-lined walkway leading to the order windows, this local institution across from Easton's Beach is as casual as they come. Lobster rolls, fried seafood, steamed clams, clam cakes, cold beer, and a great raw bar make for long lines in summer. An upstairs bar serves baked fish and seafood, chilled lobster, and other dishes; outside seating is available. $ *Average main: $18* ⊠ *4 Wave Ave., Middletown* ☏ *401/847–8141* ⊕ *www.flosclamshacks.com* ⊟ *No credit cards* ⊘ *Closed Dec.–Feb., and Mon.–Wed. Mar.–late May and early Sept.–Nov.* ⌕ *Reservations not accepted.*

$$$ ✕ **Fluke Wine, Bar & Kitchen.** Cocktails made with freshly pressed juices
WINE BAR are the best way to start your meal at this modern hot spot. Try the cool and refreshing Ocean Drive: named after Newport's scenic roadway, it's a blend of gin, muddled cucumber, mint, and lime juice. Plates of cheese and charcuterie and well-loved croquettes made with potato, bacon, and Swiss cheese are among the snack options. There are small-plate offerings such as tuna tartare; large-plate choices might include grilled local pork belly or skate with fries. $ *Average main: $30* ⊠ *41 Bowen's Wharf* ✢ *Entrance on Bannister's Wharf (look for blue and silver sign)* ☏ *401/849–7778* ⊕ *www.flukewinebar.com* ⊘ *Closed Sun.–Tues. mid-Nov.–Apr. No lunch* ⌕ *Reservations essential.*

$ ✕ **Franklin Spa.** A local landmark where the line trails out the door on
AMERICAN summer weekend mornings, this restaurant serves satisfying breakfasts worth the wait. The Portuguese Sailor (grilled chouriço and egg with melted cheese on sweet Portuguese bread) is a house specialty. Healthy options include egg-white omelets, fresh-squeezed orange juice, and fruit smoothies made with fat-free yogurt. The service is extremely friendly. $ *Average main: $8* ⊠ *229 Spring St.* ☏ *401/847–3540* ⊟ *No credit cards* ⌕ *Reservations not accepted.*

$ ✕ **Mission.** Head to this small, unpretentious redbrick restaurant for the
AMERICAN best burgers in town. Made from beef ground in-house, they come with lettuce, raw onion, and aioli ketchup, and you can add bacon, cheese, caramelized-onion sauerkraut, grilled jalapeños, and other toppings. The limited menu also includes hot dogs, falafels, and hand-cut fries. $ *Average main: $8* ⊠ *29 Marlborough St.* ☏ *401/619–5560* ⊕ *www. missionnpt.com* ⊘ *Closed. Mon.* ⌕ *Reservations not accepted* ⊟ *No credit cards.*

$$$$ ✕ **Restaurant Bouchard.** Regional variations on French cuisine are the
FRENCH focus at this upscale yet laid-back establishment inside a gambrel-roof 1785 Colonial. Nightly specials are based on the fresh catch from Rhode Island waters, which may include scallops, swordfish, and clams. Sautéed duck breast with a ground-coffee crust, finished with a brandy-balsamic sauce, might be among the meat selections. With New and Old World selections, there's something on the wine list to enhance every dish. ■ **TIP➜ Kids must be older than seven to enter the din-ing room.** $ *Average main: $35* ⊠ *505 Thames St.* ☏ *401/846–0123* ⊕ *www.bouchardnewport.com* ⊘ *Closed Tues. No lunch.*

$$ ✕ **Salvation Restaurant + Bar.** Vegetarians and red-meat fanatics alike can
CAFÉ easily find a dish to love at this funky lounge and eatery adored by local
hipsters for its lighthearted vibe. You could build a meal around start-
ers such as the roasted beet salad or shrimp and grits with applewood
bacon. The vegetarian pad thai is a solid entrée, as is the pork Bolognese
with fresh pasta. Colorful cocktails, like the Fruity Cougar (muddled
fresh raspberries and mint with Tito's Handmade Vodka and a splash
of fresh lime juice), and lavish desserts, such as chocolate-banana purses
with ginger ice cream, further stimulate the taste buds. Sit outside at
the tiki bar if weather permits. $ *Average main: $22* ⊠ *140 Broadway*
🕾 *401/847–2620* ⊕ *www.salvationcafe.com* ☾ *No lunch.*

$$$$ ✕ **Spiced Pear.** For atmosphere, service, and exceptional food, the
MODERN Spiced Pear is the ultimate fine-dining triple threat. Overlooking
AMERICAN Easton's Beach and the north end of the Cliff Walk, this refined open-
Fodor's Choice kitchen restaurant with attentive tuxedoed waiters and excellent wines
★ on an extensive list, serves creative New England cuisine with French
influences. Selections at dinner include butter-poached Maine lob-
ster and venison ravioli. For lunch you might try prime beef sirloin
or something else more straightforward. The Bar, which has lighter
fare and a signature martini, hosts a Friday-night jazz series. $ *Av-
erage main: $45* ⊠ *The Chanler at Cliff Walk, 117 Memorial Blvd.*
🕾 *401/847–2244* ⊕ *www.thechanler.com/dining.*

$$$ ✕ **Stoneacre Pantry.** A homey bistro with a seasonal approach, the
AMERICAN Stoneacre changes its menu frequently. Typical entrées may include
braised pork belly with apple puree, cider-braised cabbage and red
pearl onions, or wild Maine mussels with green curry and lime. Hardwood floors, exposed brick, unfinished wood paneling, and vintage
accents give this place a contemporary feel with rustic overtones. During the day, the wide storefront windows let in plenty of natural light.
$ *Average main: $28* ⊠ *515 Thames St.* 🕾 *401/619–7810* ⊕ *www.
stoneacrepantry.com* ⌁ *Reservations essential* ▤ *No credit cards.*

$$$$ ✕ **Tallulah on Thames.** The menu here changes a few times a week, so
MODERN that chefs can craft meals using the freshest locally sourced seafood and
AMERICAN produce. You can always count on imaginative, artistically presented
renditions of traditional New England fare—the only drawback being
that the portion sizes are small. The attentive staff offer expert advice
about the "create your own" four- and six-course prix-fixe options and
the restaurant's sterling lineup of boutique wines. End your meal on
an exquisite note with one of the intricate desserts. $ *Average main:
$68* ⊠ *464 Thames St.* 🕾 *401/849–2433* ⊕ *www.tallulahonthames.com*
☾ *Closed Mon. and Tues. No lunch* ⌁ *Reservations essential.*

$$$$ ✕ **22 Bowen's Wine Bar & Grille.** Excellent service, world-class steaks,
STEAKHOUSE and an extensive, award-winning wine list make dinner here a memorable experience. Although the restaurant is known for its steaks—and
it's impossible to go wrong ordering one—if you're in the mood for
something from the sea, consider the grilled swordfish or the seafood
pappardelle with shrimp, salmon, lobster, cremini mushrooms, tarra-
gon-brandy cream, and chervil gremolata. Floor-to-ceiling windows
allow you to watch the world go by on the wharf outside as you dine.

Gluten-free options are available. [$] *Average main: $38* ✉ *22 Bowen's Wharf* ☎ *401/841–8884* 🌐 *www.22bowens.com.*

$$$ AMERICAN 🍴 **White Horse Tavern.** The first tavern opened here in 1673, and ever since, almost without interruption, the premises have by turns served as a tavern, boardinghouse, or restaurant—at one time used as the meetinghouse for Colonial Rhode Island's General Assembly. Today, the tavern provides an intimate fine-dining experience, the mood set by the low dark-beam ceilings, cavernous fireplace, and uneven plank floors. The White Horse is known for its beef Wellington and wine list. [$] *Average main: $30* ✉ *26 Marlborough St.* ☎ *401/849–3600* 🌐 *www.whitehorsenewport.com* ✍ *Reservations essential.*

WHERE TO STAY

$ B&B/INN 🏨 **Architect's Inn.** Designed by George Champlin Mason, a Newport-based architect also responsible for the historic Chepstow mansion a mile away, this distinctive Swiss chalet–inspired house completed in 1873 has good-size guest rooms decorated in classic Victorian style. **Pros:** distinctive design; central but quiet location; friendly hosts cater to guests' dietary needs. **Cons:** guests asked to go shoeless to protect wood floors; one room is an anteroom that is not private. [$] *Rooms from: $165* ✉ *2 Sunnyside Pl., off Bellevue Ave.* ☎ *401/845–2547, 877/466–2547* 🌐 *www.architectsinn.com* 🛏 *3 rooms, 2 suites* 🍽 *Breakfast.*

$$$$ HOTEL Fodor's Choice ★ 🏨 **Castle Hill Inn and Resort.** Built as a summer house in 1874 for Alexander Agassiz, a scientist and explorer, this luxurious and romantic getaway on a 40-acre peninsula has its own private beach and trails to the Castle Hill Lighthouse. **Pros:** stunning views; superb restaurant; variety of rooms; pop-up spa. **Cons:** 3 miles from downtown Newport; expensive. [$] *Rooms from: $682* ✉ *590 Ocean Dr.* ☎ *401/849–3800, 888/466–1355* 🌐 *www.castlehillinn.com* 🛏 *35 rooms, 3 suites* 🍽 *Breakfast.*

$$$$ HOTEL Fodor's Choice ★ 🏨 **The Chanler at Cliff Walk.** The custom-designed rooms at this landmark boutique hotel on the Cliff Walk represent the most unique and luxurious accommodations in Newport. **Pros:** panoramic water views from many rooms; steps away from the Cliff Walk; great on-site restaurant. **Cons:** no elevator; some rooms have steps to access bathroom; traffic can be noisy. [$] *Rooms from: $659* ✉ *117 Memorial Blvd.* ☎ *401/847–1300, 401/847–1300* 🌐 *www.thechanler.com* 🛏 *14 rooms, 6 villas* 🍽 *Breakfast.*

$$ B&B/INN 🏨 **Francis Malbone House.** The design of the inn's main painted-brick house is attributed to Peter Harrison, the architect responsible for Touro Synagogue and the Redwood Library. **Pros:** steps from many restaurants and shops; highly professional service; fireplaces in most rooms; private courtyard. **Cons:** Thames Street abounds with tourists in summer. [$] *Rooms from: $275* ✉ *392 Thames St.* ☎ *401/846–0392, 800/846–0392* 🌐 *www.malbone.com* 🛏 *17 rooms, 3 suites* 🍽 *Breakfast.*

$$ HOTEL 🏨 **Hydrangea House Inn.** Rosie, the friendly house bichon, keeps watch at this mid-19th-century inn with decadent suites and guest rooms that exude romance. **Pros:** central location; huge rooms; highly personal service. **Cons:** slightly over-the-top decor. [$] *Rooms from: $295* ✉ *16 Bellevue Ave.* ☎ *401/846–4435, 800/945–4667* 🌐 *www.hydrangeahouse.com* 🛏 *3 rooms, 7 suites* 🍽 *Breakfast.*

$ B&B/INN 🏨 **Spring Street Inn.** This romantic bed-and-breakfast in a well-maintained 1858 Victorian is the real deal, offering some of the most attractive rates in downtown Newport. **Pros:** on a quiet but centrally located street; breakfast is terrific; attractive rates. **Cons:** small showers; two-night minimum on weekends (three on holidays and during festivals). [$] *Rooms from: $159* ✉ *353 Spring St.* ☎ *401/847–4767* 🌐 *www.springstreetinn.com* 🕒 *Closed late Nov.–mid-May* 🛏 *6 rooms, 1 suite* 🍴 *Breakfast.*

$$$$ HOTEL Fodor's Choice ★ 🏨 **Vanderbilt Grace.** Built in 1909 by Alfred Gwynne Vanderbilt for his mistress, Agnes O'Brien Ruiz, this Grace Hotels property aims to impress, and does. **Pros:** highly personalized service; full-service spa; indoor and outdoor pools; stylish snooker room. **Cons:** on a narrow street that's busy in summer; municipal parking lot next door; two-night minimum in high season. [$] *Rooms from: $595* ✉ *41 Mary St.* ☎ *401/846–6200* 🌐 *www.gracehotels.com/vanderbilt* 🛏 *33 rooms, 29 suites* 🍴 *No meals.*

NIGHTLIFE AND PERFORMING ARTS

To sample Newport's lively nightlife, you need only stroll down Thames Street or the southern end of Broadway after dark. Pick up the free *Newport Mercury* or *Newport This Week,* or visit 🌐 *www.newportri.com* for entertainment listings and news about featured events.

BARS

Candy Store. This is the best place to sip a dark and stormy and rub elbows with yacht crews. The walls are covered with photos from the halcyon days of Newport's America's Cup supremacy. If you're up for dancing, head downstairs to the Boom Boom Room. ✉ *Clarke Cooke House, Bannister's Wharf* ☎ *401/849–2900* 🌐 *www.bannistersnewport.com/clarke_candy_grill.html.*

Fastnet Pub. Named for the Fastnet Lighthouse off the coast of Cork, Ireland, this pub hosts Irish jam sessions on Sunday evening, when guest musicians, singers, and dancers familiar with traditional repertoire are invited to participate. ✉ *3 Broadway* ☎ *401/845–9311* 🌐 *www.thefastnetpub.com.*

FILM

FAMILY **newportFILM.** Enjoy sneak peeks of films before they open elsewhere thanks to this nonprofit group that hosts outdoor screenings and mini-festivals with programming for both adults and kids throughout the year. Founded in 2010, the group promotes documentary filmmaking to encourage community dialogue. ✉ *174 Bellevue Ave., Suite 314* ☎ *401/649–2784* 🌐 *www.newportfilm.com.*

SPORTS AND THE OUTDOORS

BASEBALL

FAMILY **Cardines Field.** One of America's oldest ballparks, with a circa-1908 original backdrop, is home to the Newport Gulls of the New England Collegiate Baseball League. Home games, June–early August, draw a family-friendly crowd. The field hosted barnstorming all-stars in the early 20th century, including the players of Negro League clubs. ✉ *20 America's Cup Ave.* 🌐 *www.newportgulls.com* 🎟 *$4.*

Newport's naturally protected harbor has made the city a sailing capital.

BIKING

The 12-mile swing down Bellevue Avenue to Ocean Drive and back offers amazing coastal views.

Ten Speed Spokes. This shop rents hybrid bikes for $35 per day, road bikes for $45. ✉ *18 Elm St.* ☎ *401/847–5609* ⊕ *www.tenspeedspokes.com.*

BOATING AND DIVING

The Dive Shop. This shop rents, sells, and services dive equipment, refills air tanks, and offers PADI instruction and certification. It also conducts group "fun dives" close to shore. ✉ *550 Thames St.* ☎ *401/847–9293* ⊕ *www.thediveshopnewport.com.*

Sail Newport. Take a private two-hour sailing lesson or rent a 19- or 22-foot sailboat or a kayak at Sail Newport, New England's largest public sailing center. ✉ *Ft. Adams State Park, 60 Ft. Adams Dr.* ☎ *401/846–1983* ⊕ *www.sailnewport.org.*

FISHING

The Saltwater Edge. This company gives lessons, and sells tackle for both fly-fishing and surf casting. ✉ *47 Valley Rd., Middletown* ☎ *401/842–0062, 866/793–6733* ⊕ *www.saltwateredge.com.*

POLO

FAMILY **Newport International Polo Series.** Teams from across the nation and around the world compete in Saturday matches in Portsmouth. Spectators are invited to stomp divots at the half and mingle with players and pet the horses after the match. Arrive early with your picnic lunch to get a choice tailgating spot. The concession stand has a bar and sells grilled fare. ⊠ *Glen Farm, 715 E. Main Rd., Portsmouth* ☎ *401/846–0200* ⊕ *www.nptpolo.com* ⊒ *$12–$50* ⊙ *June–Sept., Sat.; match times vary.*

SHOPPING

Many of Newport's shops and art and crafts galleries are on Thames Street, Spring Street, and at Bowen's and Bannister's wharves. The Brick Market area—between Thames Street and America's Cup Avenue—has more than 40 shops. Bellevue Avenue, just south of Memorial Boulevard near the International Tennis Hall of Fame, contains a strip of high-end fashion and home decor boutiques and gift shops.

ANTIQUES

Aardvark Antiques. This shop specializes in distinctive architectural salvage such as mantels, doors, stained glass, fountains, and garden statuary. ⊠ *9 Connell Hwy.* ☎ *401/849–7233, 800/446–1052* ⊕ *www. aardvarkantiques.com.*

Armory Antiques. The several dozen vendors in the vast Newport Armory, which dates to 1894, carry antiques, china, and estate jewelry. ⊠ *365 Thames St.* ☎ *401/848–2398* ⊕ *www.armoryantiquesnewport.com.*

The Drawing Room of Newport. Inside this shop, you'll find an extraordinary collection of Art Nouveau Zsolnay pottery from Hungary, as well as museum-quality lighting fixtures, antique glass, fine porcelain, and vintage Newport postcards from the 1890s through World War II. ⊠ *152 Spring St.* ☎ *401/841–5060* ⊕ *www.drawrm.com.*

ART AND CRAFTS GALLERIES

Arnold Art. This gallery exhibits original paintings and prints of landscapes and seascapes by Rhode Island artists. ⊠ *210 Thames St.* ☎ *401/847–2273* ⊕ *www.arnoldart.com.*

DeBlois Gallery. Paintings, photography, sculpture, ceramics, and works in other media by southern New England artists are this gallery's specialty. ⊠ *134 Aquidneck Ave., Middletown* ☎ *401/847–9977* ⊕ *www.debloisgallery.com* ⊙ *Closed Jan. and Feb.*

Spring Bull Gallery. This Rhode Island artists' cooperative, a working studio gallery, changes its shows monthly. One wall is dedicated to its members, who exhibit paintings, sculpture, and glasswork. ⊠ *55 Bellevue Ave.* ☎ *401/849–9166* ⊕ *www.springbullgallery.com.*

Fodor'sChoice ★ **Thames Glass.** Through a window in the gallery at Thames Glass, you can watch Matthew Buechner and his team making blown-glass gifts. Sign up for a lesson to make an ornament, paperweight, or vase out of molten glass. ⊠ *688 Thames St.* ☎ *401/846–0576* ⊕ *www.thamesglass.com.*

BEACH GEAR

Fodor'sChoice ★ **Water Brothers.** Come here for surf supplies, including bathing suits, wet suits, sunscreen, sunglasses, and surfboards. Owner Sid Abruzzi, a legend in the East Coast surf community, records a new surf report daily. ⊠ *23 Memorial Blvd.* ☎ *401/846–7873* ⊕ *www.originalwaterbrothers.com.*

CLOTHING

Angela Moore. Look to Angela Moore for stylish resort threads and signature hand-painted bead jewelry. ⊠ *190 Bellevue Ave.* ☎ *401/619–1900* ⊕ *www.angelamoore.com.*

JEWELRY

Alloy. At this shop, Tamar Kern displays her signature stackable cone rings, plus unique designs by other contemporary artists. ✉ *125 Bellevue Ave.* ☎ *401/619–2265* ⊕ *www.alloygallery.com.*

PORTSMOUTH

11 miles north of Newport.

Largely a bedroom community for Newport, Portsmouth attracts visitors for Newport Polo matches, its fanciful topiary garden, and the Greenvale winery. The town has an interesting history. A religious dissident named Anne Hutchinson led a group of settlers to the area in 1638 after being banished from the Massachusetts Bay Colony. The town was also the site of the Battle of Rhode Island on August 29, 1778, when American troops, including a locally recruited African American regiment, withdrew, leaving Aquidneck Island under British control.

EXPLORING

FAMILY **Green Animals Topiary Garden.** Fanciful animals, a sailing ship, and geometric shapes populate this large topiary garden on a Victorian estate that served as the summer residence of a Fall River, Massachusetts, textile mill owner. In addition to the topiaries, there are flower gardens, winding pathways, and a 1872 white clapboard house, which displays original family furnishings and an antique toy collection. ✉ *380 Cory's La., off Rte. 114* ☎ *401/683–1267* ⊕ *www.newportmansions.org* ☞ *$16* ⊙ *Mid-May–Oct., daily 10–6.*

Greenvale Vineyards. A restored stable on a farm owned by the same family for four generations houses the tasting room of this small producer. Two unusual wines, both whites, are the Stepping Stone, made mostly with the Cayuga grape, and the Vidal Blanc. Reds include the Merlot-dominant Elms Meritage blend. Tastings and a tour take place daily. On Saturdays, May–November, there are live jazz concerts. ✉ *582 Wapping Rd.* ☎ *401/847–3777* ⊕ *www.greenvale.com* ☞ *Tasting $12* ⊙ *Jan.–Mar., Mon.–Sat 11–4, Sun. noon–4; Apr.–Dec., Mon.–Sat. 10–5, Sun. noon–5. Tour daily at 2.*

BEACHES

FAMILY **Sandy Point Beach.** This Sakonnet River beach is a choice spot for families and beginning windsurfers because of its calm surf. Lifeguards are on duty on weekends, late May–mid-June, and daily mid-June–early September. **Amenities:** food and drink; lifeguards; parking (fee); showers; toilets. **Best for:** solitude; swimming; walking; windsurfing. ✉ *Sandy Point Ave.* ☎ *401/297–1263* ⊕ *www.portsmouthri.com/168/Beaches* ☞ *$10 weekdays, $15 weekends (free for residents).*

BRISTOL

5 miles north of Portsmouth, 20 miles southeast of Providence.

The home of the longest-running Fourth of July celebration—it began in 1785—Bristol shows off its patriotism with a red-white-and-blue center stripe down Hope Street, its charming business district, and flags flying from many homes and businesses. Midway between Newport and

Spend an afternoon wandering among living sculptures at the Green Animals Topiary Garden in Portsmouth.

Providence—each a 30-minute drive away—Bristol sits on a 10-square-mile peninsula between Narragansett Bay to the west and Mount Hope Bay to the east. Bristol was once a boatbuilding center; the Herreshoff Manufacturing Company built five consecutive America's Cup Defenders between 1893 and 1920. Independence Park marks the southern end of the East Bay Bike Path, which crosses the access road for Colt State Park, a great spot for picnicking and kite flying.

EXPLORING

FAMILY **Blithewold Mansion, Gardens, and Arboretum.** Starting with a sea of daffodils in April, this 33-acre estate on Bristol Harbor blooms all the way to fall. Highlights include fragrant pink chestnut roses and one of the largest giant sequoia trees on the East Coast. The 45-room English-style manor house is filled with original antiques and artworks. ✉ *101 Ferry Rd.* ☎ *401/253–2707* ⊕ *www.blithewold.org* ✉ *$12* ⊙ *Grounds daily 10–5. Mansion: mid-Apr.–mid-Oct., Tues.–Sun. 10–4.*

Herreshoff Marine Museum/America's Cup Hall of Fame. This maritime museum is devoted to the sport of yachting, and honors the Herreshoff Manufacturing Company, maker of yachts for eight consecutive America's Cup defenses. The museum's several dozen boats range from an 8½-foot dinghy to the *Defiant,* a 75-foot successful America's Cup defender. Halsey Herreshoff, a four-time cup defender and the grandson of yacht designer and company founder Nathanael Greene Herreshoff, established the hall of fame in 1992 as an arm of the museum, which hosts talks on yacht design and restoration, and operates a sailing school for kids and adults. ✉ *1 Burnside St.* ☎ *401/253–5000* ⊕ *www.*

herreshoff.org 🎟 *$12* 🕒 *Late Apr.–Sept., daily 10–5; Oct., Tues.–Sun. 10–5; Nov. and Dec., Fri.–Sun. 10–5.*

OFF THE BEATEN PATH

Warren. North of Bristol, Warren has the distinction of being the smallest town in the smallest county in the smallest state in the United States. Home to a thriving arts scene, the town is one of the state's nine Tax-Free Arts Districts, allowing gallery purchases free of sales tax. The town also claims the 2nd Story Theatre, which stages cutting-edge comedies and dramas. The East Bay Bike Path travels through Warren's commercial district, so stop for a Del's frozen lemonade. ✉ *Warren* 🌐 *www.discoverwarren.com.*

WHERE TO EAT AND STAY

$ CAFÉ 🍴 **Beehive Cafe.** This aptly named two-story café is abuzz with college students and foodies who appreciate the freshly baked bread, especially when it's used to make inventive sandwiches like roasted butternut squash with caramelized onions, Vermont cheddar, and tangy-sweet pesto. The breakfast menu (served daily until 3:30) includes banana-bread French toast, cornbread and granola made on-site, and a tasty side of fried chickpeas. [$] *Average main: $11* ✉ *10 Franklin St.* ☎ *401/396–9994* 🌐 *www.thebeehivecafe.com* 🕒 *No dinner Sun.–Wed.*

$$$ ECLECTIC 🍴 **DeWolf Tavern.** An 1818 rum distillery houses this distinctive restaurant—look for the timber ceilings, African granite from slave ship ballast in the walls, and framed sections of early-19th-century graffiti-covered plaster. Chef Sai Viswanath reinvents traditional New England fare by combining it with Indian preparations to create dishes like lobster roasted in a 900°F tandoor oven and seafood stew simmered in a coconut, coriander, star anise, and mustard-seed broth. Save room for the homemade ice cream. Alfresco dining on the second-story back deck at sunset is one of summer's great pleasures; in winter, ask to reserve Table 36 near the fireplace in the upstairs dining room. [$] *Average main: $28* ✉ *259 Thames St.* ☎ *401/254–2005* 🌐 *www.dewolftavern.com.*

$$$ MODERN AMERICAN Fodor's Choice ★ 🍴 **Persimmon.** This intimate neighborhood bistro just off the main street seats only 38 patrons, so reservations are essential on summer weekends. Neutral walls, white table linens, and simple but elegant china focus attention on the artfully composed dishes of chef and co-owner Champe Speidel, a four-time semifinalist for a James Beard Foundation Award. The meats, bacon, and sausage on the seasonal menu come from the restaurant's own butcher shop. Pan-seared Hudson Valley foie gras is an excellent appetizer, well followed by bread-crusted Atlantic halibut, if available, accompanied by a ragout of brussels sprouts, celery root, mussels, and clams. The wine list isn't huge, but it is impressive. [$] *Average main: $30* ✉ *31 State St.* ☎ *401/254–7474* 🌐 *www.persimmonri.com* 🕒 *Closed Mon., and Sun. Jan.–Apr. No lunch* ✍ *Reservations essential.*

$ HOTEL 🏨 **Bristol Harbor Inn.** Part of Thames Street Landing, this waterfront hotel was constructed with timber and architectural detailing from the 1818 rum distillery and warehouse that once occupied this site—you can still see the remnants of a giant rum keg in the building adjacent to the lobby. **Pros:** reasonably priced for a waterfront hotel; stellar restaurant; convenient location. **Cons:** other than shops and marina, there are no exterior grounds. [$] *Rooms from: $135* ✉ *259 Thames St.*

☎ *401/254–1444, 866/254–1444* 🌐 *www.bristolharborinn.com* 🛏 *40 rooms, 8 suites* 🍴 *Breakfast.*

$$ B&B/INN 🏨 **Point Pleasant Inn.** A regal East Bay estate set on a peninsula near Colt State Park, this rambling 1940 mansion anchors a gloriously situated 33-acre compound of well-tended lawns and manicured gardens. **Pros:** magnificent waterfront setting; huge rooms; gracious staff. **Cons:** pricey; not within walking distance of shopping and dining; site of many weddings and functions. [$] *Rooms from: $295* ✉ *333 Poppasquash Rd.* ☎ *401/253–0627* 🌐 *www.pointpleasantinn.com* ⏲ *Closed Dec.–Apr.* 🛏 *4 rooms, 3 suites* 🍴 *Breakfast.*

SPORTS AND THE OUTDOORS

BIKING

FAMILY **East Bay Bike Path.** Affording majestic views of Narragansett Bay, the flat 14½-mile East Bay Bike Path connects Providence to Bristol's historic downtown. ✉ *Colt State Park, Hope St.* ☎ *401/253–7482* 🌐 *www.riparks.com/Locations/LocationEastBay.html.*

SHOPPING

Woof! Woof! Pet Boutique and Biscuit Bar Stop here for locally made dog treats, high-quality dog food, toys for dogs and cats, and gifts for animal lovers. A fresh bowl of water and a dish of treats welcome dogs outside; dogs are welcome inside on leash. ✉ *31 Bradford St.* ☎ *401/289–2341* 🌐 *www.woofwoofboutique.com.*

TIVERTON AND LITTLE COMPTON

10 miles south of Bristol to Tiverton Four Corners.

This bucolic corner of Rhode Island, home to artists and working farms, is a pleasant afternoon drive from Newport or Bristol. Consider a hike in Tiverton's Weetamoo Woods or Little Compton's Wilbour Woods, or wander Tiverton Four Corners and check out the village's artist studios and arts center.

GETTING HERE AND AROUND

From Route 24 at the Sakonnet River Bridge, take Route 77 south for about 5¾ miles to reach historic Tiverton Four Corners. Continuing south to Little Compton you'll pass rolling estates, lovely homes, farmlands, woods, and a gentle western shoreline.

EXPLORING

Carolyn's Sakonnet Vineyard. White, red, and dessert wines are all in the portfolio of this winery founded in 1975. If you've ever wondered what a Rhode Island Pinot Noir might taste like, here's your chance to find out. Among the whites, the unoaked Chardonnay and the Vidal Blanc have won awards at recent competitions, as has the Blessed Blend Red (Cabernet Franc, Lemberger, Merlot, and Cabernet Sauvignon). In the winery's tasting room you can sample seven wines and keep the glass. ✉ *162 W. Main Rd., Little Compton* ☎ *401/635–8486* 🌐 *www.sakonnetwine.com* 🎟 *Tasting $14* ⏲ *Tastings: May–early Sept., Sun.–Wed. 10–6, Thurs.–Sat. 10–8; early Sept.–Apr., daily 11–5. Tours noon–3 on the hr.*

Rhode Island isn't just about regattas; working boats are common on the water, too.

FAMILY **Gray's Ice Cream.** A summertime pilgrimage destination for people from every corner of the state, this ice cream stop that's been around since 1923 sells more than 40 flavors of ice cream, all made on the premises. Coffee is the go-to flavor for most Rhode Islanders, but specialties such as Indian pudding and apple caramel spice have their adherents. ⊠ *16 East Rd., Tiverton* ☎ *401/624–4500* ⊕ *www.graysicecream.com* ⊗ *May–Oct., Mon.–Thurs. 6:30 am–9 pm, Fri.–Sun. 6:30 am–10 pm; Nov.–Apr., daily 6:30 am–7 pm.*

Little Compton Commons. This archetypal rural New England town square is actually more of a long triangle anchored by the Georgian-style United Congregational Church. Among the headstones in the nearby cemetery you'll find one for Elizabeth Pabodie, said to be the first white woman born in New England. Surrounding the green are a rock wall and all the elements of a small community: town hall, community center, police station, school, library, general store, and restaurant. ⊠ *40 Commons, Little Compton* ⊕ *www.little-compton.com.*

Sakonnet Point. A scenic drive down Route 77 ends at this quiet southeastern corner of Rhode Island. People like to fish off the Army Corps of Engineers breakwater, or walk along it to enjoy views of the harbor. The 1884 Sakonnet Lighthouse on Little Cormorant Rock is not open to the public. Parking is limited in the area. ⊠ *Sakonnet Point, 19 Bluff Head Ave., Little Compton.*

Tiverton Four Corners. From Route 24, head south on Route 77 to historic Tiverton Four Corners. The Four Corners Arts Center, in the historic Soule-Seabury House, hosts an annual antiques show, as well as art festivals and exhibits, concerts and dances, and other special events. ⊠ *Tiverton* ⊕ *www.tivertonfourcorners.com.*

SPORTS AND THE OUTDOORS

HIKING

FAMILY **Weetamoo Woods.** Weetamoo Woods takes its name from the last sachem of the Pocasset Tribe of Wampanoag Indians. There are more than 10 miles of walking trails in this 850-acre nature preserve, which encompasses a coastal oak-holly forest, an Atlantic white cedar swamp, two grassland meadows, early-American cellar holes, and the remains of a mid-19th-century village sawmill. The main entrance to Weetamoo Woods, a quarter-mile east of Tiverton Four Corners, has a parking area and a kiosk with maps. ⊠ *Rte. 179, Tiverton* ☎ *401/625–1300* ⊕ *www.tivertonlandtrust.org.*

FAMILY **Wilbour Woods.** This 30-acre hollow with picnic tables and a waterfall is a good place for a casual hike along a mile-long marked loop that winds along and over Dundery Brook. The trail passes a boulder dedicated to Queen Awashonks, who ruled the local Saugkonnates tribe during the early Colonial period. ⊠ *111 Swamp Rd., Little Compton.*

BLOCK ISLAND

Block Island, with its 950 year-round residents, is a laid-back community whose beauty is reminiscent of the coast of Scotland. About 12 miles off Rhode Island's southern coast, the island has 17 miles of beaches open to everyone. Despite the influx of summer visitors and thanks to the efforts of local conservationists, Block Island's beauty remains intact. More than 43% of the land is preserved, and the island's 365 freshwater ponds support thousands of bird species that migrate seasonally along the Atlantic Flyway.

Block Island is not all beaches and birds, however. Nightlife abounds in the summer at bars and restaurants, and it's casual—you can go anywhere in shorts and a T-shirt. The busiest season, when the population explodes to about 15,000, is May–mid-October. If you plan to stay overnight in the summer, make reservations well in advance: for weekends in July and August, calling in March is not too early. In the off-season, most restaurants, inns, stores, and visitor services close down, though some visitors brave the elements on Groundhog Day, to watch island residents gather at a local pub for an informal census.

Cell service and Internet can be spotty here, especially when it is raining and the entire island seems to be trying to stream content simultaneously. GPS isn't terribly useful, because street addresses aren't commonly used.

GETTING HERE AND AROUND

AIR TRAVEL New England Airlines operates scheduled flights from Westerly to Block Island State Airport year-round. Cape Air flies seasonally between Block Island and Providence's T. F. Green Airport.

FERRY TRAVEL There's year-round car-and-passenger ferry service to Block Island from the Port of Galilee, in the town of Narragansett in South County. Seasonal passenger-only ferry service is available from Newport; New

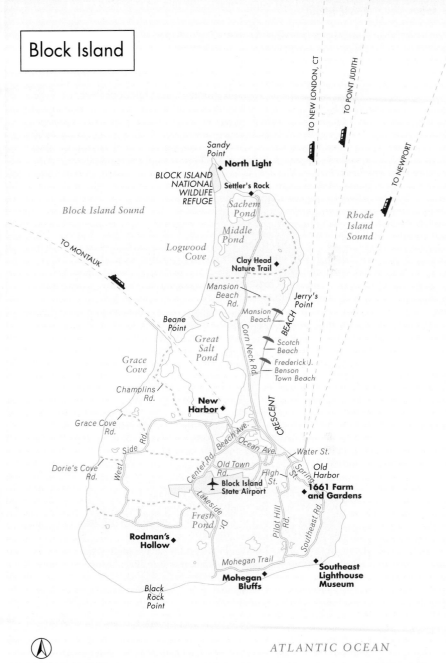

Block Island

BLOCK ISLAND NATIONAL WILDLIFE REFUGE

Block Island Sound

TO MONTAUK

TO NEW LONDON, CT

TO POINT JUDITH

TO NEWPORT

Rhode Island Sound

Sandy Point

North Light

Settler's Rock

Sachem Pond

Middle Pond

Logwood Cove

Clay Head Nature Trail

Mansion Beach Rd.

Mansion Beach

Jerry's Point

Beane Point

BEACH

Scotch Beach

Corn Neck Rd.

Frederick J. Benson Town Beach

Great Salt Pond

Grace Cove

Champlins Rd.

Grace Cove Rd.

New Harbor

CRESCENT

Beach Ave.

Ocean Ave.

Water St.

Side Rd.

Dorie's Cove Rd.

West Rd.

Center Rd.

Old Town Rd.

High St.

Spring St.

Old Harbor

✈ **Block Island State Airport**

1661 Farm and Gardens

Lakeside Dr.

Fresh Pond

Pilot Hill Rd.

Southeast Rd.

Rodman's Hollow

Mohegan Trail

Mohegan Bluffs

Southeast Lighthouse Museum

Black Rock Point

ATLANTIC OCEAN

0   1/2 mile
0   1 km

London, Connecticut; and Montauk, New York. Most ferry companies permit bicycles. The charge runs $3–$10 each way.

The most heavily trafficked route is Block Island Ferry's car-passenger service and high-speed passenger service between Block Island's Old Harbor and Galilee. By conventional ferry, the hour-long trip costs about $14 one way for passengers (rates fluctuate with oil prices) and $43 one way for automobiles. Ferries run from one or two times per day in winter to 10 times per day in summer. Make car reservations well ahead by telephone. Arrive 45 minutes ahead in high season to allow time to find parking in the pay lots ($10–$15 per day) that surround the docks. From early June to mid-October the high-speed service makes four to six daily 30-minute trips ($19 one way) along the same route. There is no auto or bicycle service on the high-speed ferry; passenger reservations are recommended.

Block Island Ferry also operates seasonal service from Newport's Perrotti Park to Old Harbor. The passengers-only ferry leaves Newport for Block Island once a day from July to early September at 9:15 am and leaves Block Island at 4:45 pm. One-way rates are about $25.50; no reservations or credit cards are accepted in Newport. Approximate sailing time is 70 minutes.

From late May to mid-October, a high-speed passenger-only ferry operated by Block Island Express runs between New London, Connecticut, and Old Harbor. The ferry departs from New London every three hours, three or four times a day, and takes a little more than an hour. Tickets are about $25 one way. Reservations are recommended.

Viking Fleet runs high-speed passenger service from Montauk, Long Island, to Block Island late May–mid-October. The boat departs from Montauk at 10 am and leaves Block Island at 5 pm, plus an additional trip on Sundays in July and August that departs from Block Island at 11:30 am and Montauk at 3:30 pm. The fare is $50 one way. Travel time is one hour; the ferry docks at New Harbor.

GETTING AROUND Block Island has two harbors, Old Harbor and New Harbor. Approaching the island by sea from New London, Newport, or Point Judith, you'll see Old Harbor, the island's only village, and its group of Victorian hotels. Most of the smaller inns, shops, and restaurants are also here. It's a short walk from the ferry landing to most of the interesting sights as well as many accommodations.

A car isn't necessary but can be helpful if you're staying far from Old Harbor or visiting for long. You can rent one at Block Island Car Rental.

ESSENTIALS

Air Travel Contacts Block Island State Airport. ⊠ *Center Rd., New Shoreham* ☎ *401/466–5511.* **Cape Air.** ☎ *800/227–3247, 508/771–6944* ⊕ *www.capeair. com.* **New England Airlines.** ⊠ *56 Airport Rd., Westerly* ☎ *800/243–2460* ⊕ *www.block-island.com/nea.*

Bike and Car Rental Contact Block Island Bike and Car Rental. ⊠ *Ocean Ave., New Shoreham* ☎ *401/466–2297.*

Boat and Ferry Contacts Block Island Express. ⊠ *2 Ferry St., New London* ☎ *401/466–2212, 860/444–4624* ⊕ *www.goblockisland.com.* **Block Island**

Ferry. ⊠ *304 Great Island Rd., Narragansett* ☎ *401/783–7996, 866/783–7996* ⊕ *www.blockislandferry.com.* **Viking Fleet.** ⊠ *462 West Lake Dr., Montauk* ☎ *631/668–5700* ⊕ *www.vikingfleet.com.*

Visitor Information Block Island Chamber of Commerce. ⊠ *1 Water St., New Shoreham* ☎ *401/466–2982, 800/383–2474* ⊕ *www.blockislandchamber.com.*

EXPLORING

TOP ATTRACTIONS

FAMILY
Fodor's Choice
★

Mohegan Bluffs. The dramatic 200-foot cliffs along Mohegan Trail, one of the island's top sights, offer a craggy beauty not found anywhere else in New England. On a clear day you can see all the way to Montauk Point on Long Island. The bluffs can be enjoyed from street level, but to access the beach below requires a descending a steep set of more than 100 stairs that lead almost to the bottom. Because of erosion, you have to scramble down the rock-strewn final yards to reach the beach. It is pebbly at the base of the stairs but sandy in the cove to the west, with wave action that attracts surfers. ■TIP➔ **Wear walking shoes, and don't attempt the descent unless you're in reasonably good shape.** ⊠ *Mohegan Trail, New Shoreham.*

FAMILY

North Light. An 1867 granite lighthouse on the northern tip of the Block Island National Wildlife Refuge, North Light serves as a maritime museum. The refuge is home to American oystercatchers, piping plovers, and other rare migrating birds. From a parking lot at the end of Corn Neck Road, it's a ¾-mile hike over sand to the lighthouse. Seals sun themselves on nearby Sandy Point in winter. ⊠ *Block Island National Wildlife Refuge, Corn Neck Rd., New Shoreham* ☎ *401/364–9124* ⊕ *www.fws.gov/refuge/block_island* ≌ *Suggested donation* ☉ *Early July–early Sept., Thurs.–Mon. 10–4.*

FAMILY
Fodor's Choice
★

Rodman's Hollow. This easy-to-find nature preserve is many people's first point of contact with the island's Greenway Trail system. The main trail runs south about 1 mile to clay bluffs with great ocean views, from which a winding path descends to the rocky beach below. Side trails cross the 50-acre hollow, offering longer hikes and the allure of getting mildly lost. The striking if muted natural beauty makes it easy to understand why, 40 years ago, this was the property that first awoke the local land conservation movement, now close to achieving its goal of preserving half the island. Geology buffs will appreciate this fine example of a glacial outwash basin. Nature lovers may enjoy looking for the Block Island meadow vole (field mouse), the northern harrier (an endangered raptor species), and the state insect, the (equally imperiled) American burying beetle. A small parking lot sits just south of Cooneymus Road near a stone marker. ⊠ *Cooneymus Rd., New Shoreham* ⊕ *www.nature.org.*

Southeast Lighthouse Museum. The small museum is housed inside an 1875 redbrick lighthouse with gingerbread detail that was moved back 360 feet from the eroded clay cliffs. The lighthouse is a National Historic Landmark; tours are offered during the summer. ⊠ *122 Mohegan Tr., New Shoreham* ☎ *401/ 466–5009* ≌ *Tours $10* ☉ *Late May–early Sept., daily 10–4.*

7

WORTH NOTING

FAMILY **1661 Farm and Gardens.** Animals you never knew existed—like the zedonk, a cross between a zebra and a donkey—are on display at this farm, as well as some you did. Camels, llamas, emus, kangaroos, and even fainting goats (whose legs stiffen when they get excited, causing them to keel over) will all gladly munch pellets out of your hand. Black swans stroll about, and lemurs leap around their own enclosure. A herd of gentle alpacas helps provide fibers for the adjacent North Light Fibers textile mill. ✉ *Off Spring St., New Shoreham* ☎ *401/466–2421* 🌐 *www.blockislandresorts.com* 🎟 *Free* 🕒 *Daily sunrise–sunset.*

New Harbor. The Great Salt Pond has a culture all its own, centered on the three marinas, two hotels, and five restaurants clustered along its southern shore that make up this commercial area about a 20-minute walk from Old Harbor. Up to 2,000 boats create a forest of masts on summer weekends, drawn by sail races and fishing tournaments. Over on the quiet north and east shores, clammers and windsurfers claim the tidal flats. The Montauk ferry docks at Champlin's, the largest of the marinas. ✉ *Great Salt Pond, New Shoreham.*

BEACHES

The eastern side of the island has several beaches with calm, warm waters ideal for swimming June–September.

Fodor's Choice ★ **Crescent Beach.** This 3-mile beach runs north from Old Harbor, and its white sands become wider and the crowds thinner the farther away from town you go. It is divided into smaller beaches with access points off Corn Neck Road. Farthest north is Mansion Beach: look for the sign, then follow the dirt road to the right. From the parking area, it's a short hike to reach what is easily one of New England's most beautiful beaches. In the morning, you might spot deer on the dunes; to the north, surfers can often be seen dotting Jerry's Point. Closer to Old Harbor, Scotch Beach, with its small parking lot directly off Corn Neck Road, attracts a lively crowd of young adults. **Amenities:** food and drink; lifeguards; parking (no fee); showers; toilets. **Best for:** sunrise; sunset; walking. ✉ *Corn Neck Rd., New Shoreham.*

WHERE TO EAT

$$ AMERICAN 🍴 **The Beachead.** The food—especially the Rhode Island clam chowder—is consistently great, the price is right, and you won't feel like a tourist at this local favorite. Catch ocean breezes on the patio, or in stormy weather sit at the bar and watch breakers roll in 30 feet away. The menu and service are unpretentious; stop in for a grilled tuna or chicken sandwich at lunch, or try more ambitious fare at dinner like Portuguese mussels linguiça or steak au poivre. The kitchen staff bring their reputation for reliability and quality to Payne's Dock, where it runs the Burger Bar at lunch and dinner during boating season. [$] *Average main: $18* ✉ *596 Corn Neck Rd., New Shoreham* ☎ *401/466–2249* 🌐 *www.thebeachead.com* 🕒 *Closed Dec.–Apr.* ✍ *Reservations not accepted.*

$$$
AMERICAN

$\times$**Eli's.** Creative cuisine inspired by Asian comfort food emerges from the kitchen of this intimate bistro. The fare changes seasonally but may include appetizers like steamed *bao* (buns), tuna nachos, and marinated lamb tartare. Roasted George's Bank scallops with charred eggplant puree might show up as a main course, along with the crowd-pleasing Eli's Surf & Turf burger, a short-rib-and-brisket burger topped with poached lobster and chorizo jam. Red-pepper risotto and roasted tofu "scallops" have been hits on the vegetarian menu. The pastry chef enjoys local fame for seasonal favorites like almond-berry cake and bread pudding. Wait times can be long in summer, when the tiny bar is prime real estate. $ *Average main: $28* $\boxtimes$ *456 Chapel St., New Shoreham* $\textcircled{\scriptsize{\textbf{m}}}$ *401/466–5230* $\oplus$ *www.elisblockisland.com* $\odot$ *Closed Nov.–Mar. No lunch* $\triangle$ *Reservations not accepted.*

$$$
SEAFOOD

$\times$**Finn's.** A Block Island institution, Finn's serves fresh, reliable fried and broiled seafood, and a wonderful smoked bluefish pâté. The island's best bet for simple steamed lobster, this is also the spot for an unfussy lunch like the Workman's Special, which includes a burger, coleslaw, and fries. The interior looks a little tired, so sit out on the deck, weather permitting, or get food to go from the takeout window and raw bar. Finn's Fish Market is in the same building; its lobster tanks and ice tables are the best source for local seafood to cook at home or over a beach fire. $ *Average main: $26* $\boxtimes$ *Ferry Landing, 212 Water St., New Shoreham* $\textcircled{\scriptsize{\textbf{m}}}$ *401/466–2473* $\oplus$ *www.finnsseafood.com* $\odot$ *Closed mid-Oct.–May* $\triangle$ *Reservations not accepted.*

$$$
AMERICAN

$\times$**Restaurant 1879 at the Atlantic Inn.** Because it shares an executive chef with popular Eli's, expectations are high for this casual Atlantic Inn restaurant, and it doesn't disappoint. The menu, which evolves daily, includes small and large plates, served à la carte or as part of the chef's reasonably priced tasting menu. Worth seeking out are the mac 'n' cheese fritters with a black-truffle cheese sauce, foie gras, and baby arugula, and the lobster sliders with white pear and kimchi. $ *Average main: $28* $\boxtimes$ *359 High St., New Shoreham* $\textcircled{\scriptsize{\textbf{m}}}$ *401/466–5883* $\oplus$ *www. atlanticinn.com.*

WHERE TO STAY

It's advisable to book accommodations well in advance, especially for weekends in July and August, when many hotels require a two-night minimum; the Chamber of Commerce runs a room reservation service that's handy for last-minute trips. Many visitors rent homes for stays of a week or more.

$$
HOTEL
Fodor'sChoice
★

$\boxed{\cdot}$**The Atlantic Inn.** Perched on a hill amid floral gardens and undulating lawns, away from the hubbub of the Old Harbor area, this long, white, classic 1879 Victorian resort dazzles guests with its big windows, high ceilings, sweeping staircase, and mesmerizing views. **Pros:** spectacular hilltop location; beautiful veranda for whiling away the afternoon; grand decor. **Cons:** no TVs or high-speed Internet in rooms. $ *Rooms from: $215* $\boxtimes$ *359 High St., New Shoreham* $\textcircled{\scriptsize{\textbf{m}}}$ *401/466–5883, 800/224–7422* $\oplus$ *www.atlanticinn.com* $\odot$ *Closed late Oct.–mid-Apr.* $\rightsquigarrow$ *20 rooms, 1 suite* $\textcircled{\tiny{O}}$ *Breakfast.*

$ 🖼 **Blue Dory Inn.** This Old Harbor district inn, with a main lodging and
B&B/INN three small shingle-and-clapboard outbuildings, has been a guesthouse since its construction in 1898. **Pros:** great in-town location; relatively affordable; pet friendly. **Cons:** some units are small. $ *Rooms from: $165* ✉ *61 Dodge St., New Shoreham* ☎ *401/466–5891, 800/992–7290* ⊕ *www.blockislandinns.com* ⤳ *11 rooms, 4 cottages, 3 suites* ⦿ *Breakfast.*

$$ 🖼 **Payne's Harbor View Inn.** This 2002 inn, designed to blend with the
B&B/INN island's historic architecture, occupies a breezy hillside overlooking the
Fodor'sChoice Great Salt Pond and is just minutes from Crescent Beach. **Pros:** rela-
★ tively inexpensive for luxurious feel; kayak rentals; Wi-Fi and TVs.
Cons: books up fast; children under 12 not permitted. $ *Rooms from: $235* ✉ *Ocean Ave. and Beach Ave., New Shoreham* ☎ *401/466–5758* ⊕ *www.paynesharborviewinn.com* ⤳ *10 rooms* ⦿ *Breakfast.*

$ 🖼 **The Rose Farm Inn.** With simple accommodations in a late-19th-century
B&B/INN farmhouse and more luxurious units in a more modern structure across a country lane, this property is set on a 20-acre pastoral farmstead. **Pros:** great spot for weddings; choice of accommodations; quiet setting yet easy walk to Old Harbor. **Cons:** bathrooms in Farm House a bit rustic; no TVs in rooms; no hot breakfast. $ *Rooms from: $199* ✉ *1005 High St., New Shoreham* ☎ *401/466–2034* ⊕ *www.rosefarminn.com* ⊙ *Closed mid-Oct.–early May* ⤳ *19 rooms* ⦿ *Breakfast.*

NIGHTLIFE

Nightlife, at least in season, is one of Block Island's highlights, and you have your pick of some two dozen places to grab a drink. Check the *Block Island Times* for band listings.

Captain Nick's. This place sets itself apart from the others by hosting June's Block Island Music Festival, a free roundup of soon-to-be-discovered bands from around the country. It has a bi-level bar, live music inside and out, and a suntanned crowd. Disco Monday has been an island tradition for more than two decades. The owner, a gifted pianist and singer, performs on Tuesday and Wednesday. Sushi is served Thursday–Sunday. ✉ *34 Ocean Ave., New Shoreham* ☎ *401/466–5670* ⊕ *www.captainnicks.com.*

Mahogany Shoals. A tiny shack built over the water at Payne's Dock, Mahogany Shoals is where Irish sea chanteys are the evening entertainment of choice. The place has expanded, gracefully, with an outdoor bar and an upper-level deck. It remains the best spot on the island to enjoy a quiet drink, peer at beautiful yachts, and catch a breeze on even the hottest of nights. ✉ *Payne's Dock, 133 Ocean Ave., New Shoreham* ☎ *401/466–5572.*

SPORTS AND THE OUTDOORS

BIKING

The best way to explore Block Island is by bicycle (about $20–$30 a day to rent) or moped (about $45 per hour, $85–$115 per day). Most rental places are open spring–fall and have child seats for bikes. All rent bicycles in various styles and sizes, including mountain bikes, hybrids, tandems, and children's bikes.

Island Moped and Bike Rentals. This shop has bikes of all kinds for daily and weekly rentals and mopeds for hourly to half-day rentals. ⊠ *41 Water St.* ☏ *401/741–2329* ⊕ *www.bimopeds.com.*

Old Harbor Bike Shop. Descend from the Block Island Ferry and climb on a bike at this shop that also has a location at the Boat Basin marina in New Harbor. ⊠ *Water St., south of ferry dock, New Shoreham* ☏ *401/466–2029* ⊕ *www.blockislandtransportation.com/about.htm.*

BOATING

FAMILY   **Aldo's Boat Rentals.** From no-skills-required pontoon boats to zippy sailboats, Aldo's offers all sorts of fun on the quiet waters of the Great Salt Pond. Bumper boats and paddleboats are fun for kids. ⊠ *Champlin's Marina, West Side Rd., Block Island, New Shoreham* ☏ *401/466–2700.*

FAMILY   **Pond and Beyond.** Guided wildlife kayak trips around the Great Salt Pond are a specialty here. Children ages 12 and older can join tours suited to their skill level, and younger kids can hang out at the sea-life touch tanks run nearby by the Block Island Maritime Institute. ⊠ *Ocean Ave., New Shoreham* ☏ *401/578–2773* ⊕ *www.pondandbeyondkayak.com* ⊘ *Closed mid-Oct.–late May.*

FISHING

Most of Rhode Island's record-setting fish have been caught on Block Island—in fact, it's held the striped bass record (currently a 77.4-pound whopper caught in 2011) since 1984. From almost any beach, skilled anglers can land tautog and bass. The New Harbor channel is a good spot to hook bonito and fluke. Shellfishing licenses ($20 per week) may be obtained at the harbormaster's building at the Boat Basin in New Harbor.

Block Island Fishworks. A tiny shop in New Harbor, Block Island Fishworks sells tackle, including hand-tied fly-fishing leaders. It also offers guide services, spearfishing lessons, and charter fishing trips—inshore for bass and blues, offshore for tuna and shark. ⊠ *40 Ocean Ave., New Shoreham* ☏ *401/742–3992* ⊕ *www.bifishworks.com.*

Twin Maples. For more than 60 years this shop has been selling bait and handmade lures, sophisticated fishing tackle, and coveted "Eat Fish" T-shirts from its salt-pond setting. ⊠ *Beach Ave., New Shoreham* ☏ *401/466–5547.*

HIKING

Fodor'sChoice   **Clay Head Nature Trail.** The outstanding Clay Head Nature Trail mean-
   ★   ders past Clay Head Swamp and along 150-foot clay bluffs. Songbirds chirp and flowers bloom along the paths; stick close to the ocean for a stunning hike that ends at Sachem Pond, or venture into the interior's intertwining paths for hours of wandering and blackberrying in an area called the Maze. The trailhead is recognizable by a simple white post marker on the east side of Corn Neck Road about 2 miles north of Old Harbor. ⊠ *Clay Head Trail Rd., New Shoreham.*

Greenway. The Block Island Chamber of Commerce distributes maps of this well-maintained trail system that meanders for 28 miles across the

Digging for clams is a fun pastime on Block Island's beaches.

island, crossing stone walls and reaching otherwise inaccessible places. ⊠ *Greenway, New Shoreham.*

WATER SPORTS

Block Island Parasail and Watersports. This outfitter will take you parasailing. It also rents five-person jet boats and 10-person banana boats. ⊠ *Old Harbor Basin, Water St., New Shoreham* ☎ *401/864–2474* ⊕ *www.blockislandparasail.com* ☉ *June–Oct., daily 9–sunset.*

Diamondblue Surf Shop. This shop stocks surf gear and offers kiteboarding lessons and stand-up paddleboard rentals. ⊠ *Bridgegate Square, 442 Dodge St., New Shoreham* ☎ *401/466–3145* ⊕ *www.diamondbluebi.com.*

Island Outfitters. Wet suits, spearguns, and scuba gear can be found here, along with beachwear and bathing suits. ⊠ *227 Weldon's Way, New Shoreham* ☎ *401/466–5502.*

SHOPPING

ANTIQUES AND COLLECTIBLES

Lazy Fish. The owner of this collection of home accessories is an interior designer who blends old with new to colorful but harmonious effect. ⊠ *235 Dodge St., New Shoreham* ☎ *401/466–2990.*

ART GALLERIES

Jessie Edwards Studios. This gallery exhibits photographs, sculptures, and contemporary American paintings, often with nautical themes. ⊠ *New Post Office Bldg., 30 Water St., 2nd fl., New Shoreham* ☎ *401/466– 5314* ⊕ *www.jessieedwardsgallery.com.*

Spring Street Gallery. The gallery exhibits paintings, photographs, stained glass, and serigraphs by island artists and artisans. ✉ *105 Spring St.* ☎ *401/466–5374* ⊕ *www.springstreetgallery.org.*

BOOKS

Island Bound Bookstore. Books about Block Island history are a specialty of this shop, which also has a good selection of fiction and nonfiction. There are also art supplies and crafts for adults and kids. ✉ *New Post Office Bldg., Water St., New Shoreham* ☎ *401/466–8878* ⊕ *www. islandboundbookstore.com.*

JEWELRY

Golddiggers. You can pick up handmade pendants, rings, charms, and bracelets with maritime themes at this jewelry store. ✉ *90 Chapel St., New Shoreham* ☎ *401/466–2611* ⊕ *www.blockislandgolddiggers.com.*

TEXTILES

North Light Fibers. The adjoining Abrams Animal Farm supplies wool from its alpacas, llamas, yaks, and sheep to make beautiful yarns, clothing, and blankets. Classes are offered in knitting, weaving, and felting. ✉ *10 Spring St., New Shoreham* ☎ *401/466–2050* ⊕ *www. northlightfibers.com.*

VERMONT

Visit Fodors.com for advice, updates, and bookings

WELCOME TO VERMONT

TOP REASONS TO GO

★ **Small-Town Charm:** Vermont rolls out a seemingly never-ending supply of tiny towns replete with white-steepled churches, town greens, red barns, general stores, and bed-and-breakfasts.

★ **Ski Resorts:** The East's best skiing can be found in well-managed, modern facilities with great views and lots and lots of fresh snow.

★ **Fall Foliage:** Perhaps the most vivid colors in North America wave from the trees in September and October, when the whole state is ablaze.

★ **Gorgeous Landscapes:** This sparsely populated, heavily forested state is an ideal place to find peace and quiet amid the mountains, valleys, and lakes.

★ **Tasty and Healthy Eats:** The rich soil and an emphasis on using local ingredients has led to great dairies, orchards, vineyards, specialty stores, and farm-to-table restaurants.

1 Southern Vermont. Most people's introduction to the state is southern Vermont, a relatively short drive from New York and Boston. As elsewhere across the state, you'll find unspoiled towns, romantic bed-and-breakfasts, lush farms, and pristine forests. There are two notable exceptions: sophisticated Manchester has upscale shopping, and independent Brattleboro remains a hippie enclave with an environmentally conscious disposition.

2 Central Vermont. Similar to southern Vermont in character and geography, central Vermont stretches from workaday Rutland in the south to the picturesque Mad River Valley in the north. Woodstock, Waitsfield, and Middlebury number among its inviting small towns.

3 Northern Vermont. The state's northernmost part is a place of contrasts. Burlington, with dramatic views of Lake Champlain and the Adirondacks, is the Vermont's most populous city, with around 60,000 residents; an arts-loving, laid-back college town, it has a sophisticated food scene. On the other side of Mount Mansfield is Stowe, the quintessential eastern ski town, beyond which the landscape becomes increasingly rural. Stupendous natural beauty and a sparse population make the Northeast Kingdom a refuge for nature lovers and for those who love getting away from it all.

GETTING ORIENTED

Vermont can be divided into three regions. The southern part of the state, flanked by Bennington on the west and Brattleboro on the east, played an important role in Vermont's Revolutionary War–era drive at independence—yes, there was once a Republic of Vermont—and eventual statehood. The central part is characterized by rugged mountains and the gently rolling dairy lands east of Lake Champlain's southern sliver. And northern Vermont is home to the state's capital, Montpelier, and its largest city, Burlington, as well as its most rural area, the Northeast Kingdom. The Green Mountains run north–south through the center of the state, covered in protected national forest.

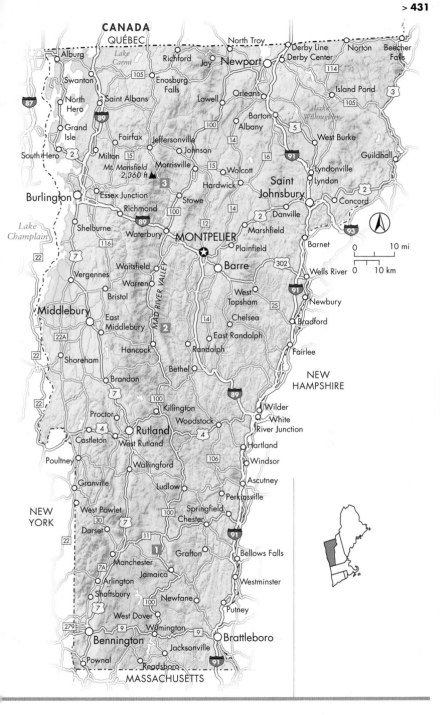

CANADA
QUÉBEC

North Troy

Alburg
Richford
Jay
Newport
Derby Line
Derby Center
Norton
Beecher Falls

Lake Carmi

Swanton
Enosburg Falls
105
114
Island Pond
3

North Hero
Saint Albans
Lowell
Orleans
105

87

Grand Isle
Fairfax
89
Barton
Albany
Lake Willoughby
West Burke

South Hero
Milton
15
Jeffersonville
Johnson
14
5
Lyndonville
Guildhall

2
Mt. Mansfield
2,360 ft
Morrisville
15
Wolcott
16
91
Lyndon

Essex Junction
3
Hardwick
Saint
Johnsbury
2
Concord

Burlington
Richmond
Stowe
14
Danville

89
100
12
Marshfield
93

Lake
Champlain
Shelburne
Waterbury
MONTPELIER
Plainfield
Barnet

116
Plainfield
10 mi

22
7
Waitsfield
Barre
302
Wells River
10 km

Vergennes
Warren
West
Topsham
25
91

Bristol
Chelsea
Newbury

Middlebury
East
Middlebury
14
Bradford

22A
East Randolph
Fairlee

22
Shoreham
Hancock
Randolph
NEW
HAMPSHIRE

Brandon
Bethel
89
8

22
100
Killington
Wilder

Proctor
Woodstock
White
River Junction

4
Castleton
West Rutland
Rutland
Hartland

Poultney
Wallingford
106
Windsor

Granville
Ludlow
Ascutney

NEW
YORK
West Pawlet
30
100
Springfield
Perkinsville

22
Dorset
7
Chester
91

11
Grafton
Bellows Falls

1
Manchester
Jamaica
Westminster

7A
Arlington
100
Newfane
Putney

Shaftsbury
West Dover
Wilmington

7
279
9
9
Brattleboro

Bennington
Jacksonville
91

Pownal
Readsboro

MASSACHUSETTS

Updated by
Aaron Starmer

Vermont is a land of hidden treasures and unspoiled scenery. Wander anywhere in the state—nearly 80% is forest—and you'll find pristine countryside dotted with farms and framed by mountains. Tiny towns with picturesque church steeples, village greens, and clapboard Colonial-era houses are perfect for exploring.

Sprawl has no place here. Highways are devoid of billboards by law, and on some roads cows still stop traffic twice a day en route to and from pasture. In spring, sap boils in sugarhouses, some built generations ago, while up the road a chef trained at the New England Culinary Institute in Montpelier might use the syrup to glaze a pork tenderloin.

It's the landscape, for the most part, that attracts people to Vermont. Rolling hills belie rugged terrain underneath the green canopy of forest growth. In summer, clear lakes and streams provide ample opportunities for swimming, boating, and fishing; hills attract hikers and mountain bikers. The more than 14,000 miles of roads, many of them only intermittently traveled by cars, are great for biking. In fall the leaves have their last hurrah, painting the mountainsides in yellow, gold, red, and orange. Vermont has the best ski resorts in the eastern United States, centered along the spine of the Green Mountains running north to south, and the traditional heart of skiing here is the town of Stowe. Almost anywhere you go, no matter what time of year, the Vermont countryside will make you reach for your camera.

Although Vermont may seem locked in time, technological sophistication appears where you least expect it: wireless Internet access in a 19th-century farmhouse-turned-inn and cell phone coverage from the state's highest peaks. Like an old farmhouse under renovation, though, the state's historic exterior is still the main attraction.

PLANNING

WHEN TO GO

In summer Vermont is lush and green, and in winter the hills and towns are blanketed white with snow, inspiring skiers to challenge the peaks at Stowe and elsewhere. Fall, however, is always the most amazing time to come. If you have never seen the state's kaleidoscope of autumn colors, it's well worth braving the slow-moving traffic and shelling out a few extra bucks for lodging. The only time things really slow down is during "mud season" in late spring, when even innkeepers counsel guests to come another time. Activities in the Champlain Islands essentially come to a halt in the winter, except for ice fishing and snowmobiling, and two of the biggest attractions, Shelburne Farms and the Shelburne Museum, are closed mid-October–April. Otherwise, Vermont is open for business year-round.

PLANNING YOUR TIME

There are many ways to take advantage of Vermont's beauty: skiing or hiking its mountains, biking or driving its back roads, fishing or sailing its waters, shopping for local products, visiting museums and sights, or simply finding the perfect inn and never leaving the front porch.

Distances are relatively short, yet the mountains and back roads will slow a traveler's pace. You can see a representative north–south cross-section of Vermont in a few days; if you have up to a week, you can really hit the highlights.

GETTING HERE AND AROUND

AIR TRAVEL

Allegiant, American, Delta, JetBlue, Porter, and United fly into Burlington International Airport. Rutland State Airport has daily service to and from Boston on Cape Air.

BOAT TRAVEL

Lake Champlain Ferries. This company operates ferries on three routes between Vermont and New York: from Grand Isle to Plattsburgh, New York; Burlington to Port Kent; and Charlotte to Essex. ☎ *802/864–9804* 🌐 *www.ferries.com* ⏲ *No Burlington–Port Kent service early Sept.–early June.*

CAR TRAVEL

Vermont is divided by a mountainous north–south middle, with a main highway on either side: scenic U.S. 7 on the western side and Interstate 91 (which begins in New Haven and runs through Hartford, central Massachusetts, and along the Connecticut River in Vermont to the Canadian border) on the east. Interstate 89 runs from New Hampshire across central Vermont from White River Junction to Burlington and up to the Canadian border. For current road conditions, check 🌐 *511VT.com* or call ☎ *511* in Vermont and ☎ *800/429–7623* from other states.

TRAIN TRAVEL

Amtrak. Amtrak has daytime service on the *Vermonter,* linking Washington, D.C., and New York City with Brattleboro, Bellows Falls, Windsor, White River Junction, Randolph, Montpelier, Waterbury, Essex Junction, and St. Albans. Amtrak's *Ethan Allen Express* connects New York City with Castleton and Rutland. ☎ *800/872–7245* 🌐 *www.amtrak.com.*

8

RESTAURANTS

Everything that makes Vermont good and wholesome is distilled in its restaurants. Many of them belong to the **Vermont Fresh Network** (⊕ *www. vermontfresh.net*), a partnership that encourages chefs to create menus emphasizing Vermont's wonderful bounty; especially in summer and early fall, the produce and meats are impeccable. The resulting Vermont cuisine is accordingly better defined than that found in neighboring states.

Great chefs come to Vermont for the quality of life, and the Montpelier-based New England Culinary Institute is a recruiting ground for new talent. Seasonal menus use local fresh herbs and vegetables along with native game. Look for imaginative approaches to native New England foods like maple syrup (Vermont is the largest U.S. producer), dairy products (cheese in particular), native fruits and berries, "new Vermont" products such as salsa and salad dressings, and venison, quail, pheasant, and other game.

Your chances of finding a table for dinner vary with the season: lengthy waits are common in tourist centers at peak times—a reservation is always advisable. Some of the best dining is at country inns. *Prices in the reviews are the average cost of a main course at dinner or, if dinner is not served, at lunch.*

HOTELS

Vermont's only large chain hotels are in Burlington and Rutland; elsewhere it's just inns, bed-and-breakfasts, and small motels. The inns and B&Bs, some of them quite luxurious, provide what many visitors consider the quintessential Vermont lodging experience. Most areas have traditional ski-base condos; at these you sacrifice charm for ski-and-stay deals and proximity to the lifts. Lodging rates are highest during foliage season, late September–mid-October, and lowest in late spring and November, although many properties close during these times. Winter is high season at ski resorts. *Prices in the reviews are the lowest cost of a standard double room in high season. Hotel reviews have been shortened. For full reviews visit Fodors.com.*

WHAT IT COSTS				
	$	$$	$$$	$$$$
Restaurants	under $18	$18–$24	$25–$35	over $35
Hotels	under $200	$200–$299	$300–$399	over $399

TOURS

Country Inns Along the Trail. This company arranges guided and self-guided hiking, skiing, and biking trips from inn to inn in Vermont. ⊠ *52 Park St., Brandon* ☏ *802/247–3300, 800/838–3301* ⊕ *www.inntoinn.com* ⊠ *From $545.*

P.O.M.G. Bike Tours of Vermont. The initials in this outfitter's name are short for "Peace Of Mind Guaranteed." The company leads weekend and multiday bike tours around the state. ☏ *802/434–2270, 888/635–2453* ⊕ *www.pomgbike.com* ⊠ *From $1,750.*

Vermont Bicycle Touring. This guide company leads bike tours across the state. ☎ *802/453–4811, 800/245–3868* ⊕ *www.vbt.com* ✉ *From $1,895.*

VISITOR INFORMATION

Statewide Ski Vermont/Vermont Ski Areas Association. ✉ *26 State St., Montpelier* ☎ *802/223-2439* ⊕ *www.skivermont.com.* **Vermont Department of Tourism and Marketing.** ✉ *1 National Life Dr., 6th fl., Montpelier* ☎ *802/828-3237, 800/837-6668* ⊕ *www.vermontvacation.com.* **Vermont Seasonal Hotline.** ☎ *802/828-3239 for foliage information, snow conditions, and events.*

Regional Northeast Kingdom Travel and Tourism Association. ☎ *802/626-8511* ⊕ *www.travelthekingdom.com.*

SOUTHERN VERMONT

Cross into the Green Mountain State from Massachusetts on Interstate 91, and you might feel as if you've entered another country. There isn't a town in sight: what you see are forested hills punctuated by rolling pastures. When you reach Brattleboro, no strip malls line the exits to signal your arrival at southeastern Vermont's gateway city, and en route downtown, you pass Victorian-era homes on tree-lined streets. From here, you can cross over the spine of the Green Mountains toward Bennington and Manchester.

The state's southwest corner is the southern terminus of the Green Mountain National Forest, dotted with lakes, threaded with trails and old forest roads, and home to three big ski resorts: Bromley, Stratton, and Mount Snow.

8

BRATTLEBORO

60 miles south of White River Junction.

Brattleboro has drawn political activists and earnest counterculturists since the 1960s. The arts-oriented town and environs (population 12,000) remains politically and culturally active; after Burlington, this is Vermont's most offbeat locale.

GETTING HERE AND AROUND

Brattleboro is near the intersection of Route 9, the principal east–west highway also known as the Molly Stark Byway, and Interstate 91. For downtown, take Exit 2 from Interstate 91.

ESSENTIALS

Visitor Information Brattleboro Area Chamber of Commerce. ✉ *180 Main St.* ☎ *802/254-4565, 877/254-4565* ⊕ *www.brattleborochamber.org.*

EXPLORING

Brattleboro Museum and Art Center. Downtown is the hub of Brattleboro's art scene, at the forefront of which is this museum in historic Union Station. It presents changing exhibitions of works by local, national, and international artists, and hosts lectures, readings, and musical performances. ✉ *10 Vernon St.* ☎ *802/257-0124* ⊕ *www.brattleboromuseum. org* ✉ *$8* ☉ *Thurs.–Mon. 11–5; 1st Fri. of month 11–8:30.*

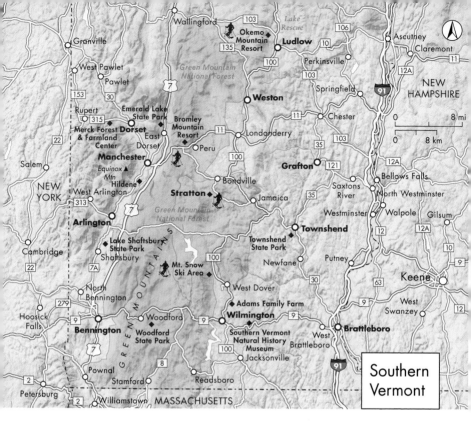

Southern Vermont

NEED A BREAK?

✕ **Mocha Joe's Cafe.** The team at this spot for coffee and conversation takes great pride in sourcing direct-trade beans from places like Kenya, Ethiopia, and Guatemala. Ground zero for Brattleboro's bohemian contingent and fellow travelers, the café is open until 9 on Friday and Saturday, closing at 8 the rest of the week. ✉ *82 Main St., at Elliot St.* ☎ *802/257–5637* ⊕ *www.mochajoes.com.*

OFF THE BEATEN PATH

Putney. Nine miles upriver, this town of fewer than 3,000 residents—the country cousin of bustling Brattleboro—is a haven for writers and fine and craft artists. There are many pottery studios to visit, the requisite general store, and a few orchards. Each November during the Putney Craft Tour, dozens of artisans open their studios and homes for live demonstrations and plenty of fun. ✉ *Putney* ⊕ *www.discoverputney.com.*

WHERE TO EAT

$
AMERICAN

✕ **Brattleboro Food Co-op.** Pick up a plate of chicken or beef *satay* (skewered grilled meat) at the deli counter of this hot spot for local and organic groceries, then find a seat in the glassed-in café area or out on the river-view patio. The deli also serves fabulous sandwiches, and there's a good beer and wine selection. The many fine products for sale in the store include a self-serve selection of varying grades of maple

OUTDOOR ACTIVITIES

Biking: Vermont, especially the often-deserted roads of the Northeast Kingdom, is great bicycle-touring country. Many companies lead weekend tours and weeklong trips throughout the state. If you'd like to go it on your own, most chambers of commerce have brochures highlighting the best cycling routes in their areas.

Canoeing and Kayaking: Getting on Vermont's many rivers and lakes is a great way to experience nature. Outfitters can be found almost anywhere there's water.

Fishing: Central Vermont is the heart of the state's warm-water lake and pond fishing area. Lake Champlain, stocked annually with salmon and lake trout, has become the state's ice-fishing capital.

Hiking: Vermont is an ideal state for hiking: nearly 80% of the state is forest, and trails are everywhere. The Long Trail runs the length of the state. It includes the first portion of the Appalachian Trail to be completed, an achievement that inspired the development of rest of that trail. Many bookstores carry guides about local hiking.

Skiing: The Green Mountains run through the middle of Vermont like a bumpy spine, visible from almost every point in the state; generous accumulations of snow make them ideal for skiing. Route 100, also known as Skier's Highway, paves the way to 13 ski areas.

syrup. $ *Average main: $8* ⊠ *2 Main St.* ☎ *802/257–0236* ⊕ *www. brattleborofoodcoop.com.*

$$
MODERN
AMERICAN
✕ **Duo.** A corner location in the historic Brooks House and huge, inviting windows make this stylish farm-to-table restaurant impossible to miss. The locally sourced fare changes with the season, but the menu always includes an innovative take on fritters and a winning pork dish. Brunch is a great way to sample what the owner calls "food you're familiar with, done better." $ *Average main: $22* ⊠ *136 Main St.* ☎ *802/254–4141* ⊕ *www.duorestaurants.com* ⊗ *No lunch weekdays* ⚑ *Reservations essential.*

$$
ITALIAN
✕ **Fireworks.** The airy and colorful Fireworks serves salads, pastas, and flatbread pizzas. Daily specials, often variations on the usual pizzas or pastas, are always worth considering, and cocktails are creatively mixed. In nice weather, check out the back patio. $ *Average main: $18* ⊠ *69–73 Main St.* ☎ *802/254–2073* ⊕ *www.fireworksrestaurant.net/ brattleboro* ⊗ *Closed Mon. No lunch.*

$$$
AMERICAN
Fodor'sChoice
★
✕ **Peter Havens.** A longtime Brattleboro favorite helmed since 2012 by chef Zachary Corbin, this chic little bistro is known for impeccably presented cuisine that draws heavily on local sources. One room is painted a warm red, another in sage, and a changing lineup of contemporary paintings adorns the walls of both rooms. Whatever your main dish, start off with the heavenly tuna tartare and a seasonal cocktail or glass of wine from a list that hits all the right notes. $ *Average main: $30* ⊠ *32 Elliot St.* ☎ *802/257–3333* ⊕ *www.peterhavens.com* ⊗ *Closed Mon. and Tues. No lunch Nov.–May.*

$$$$ AMERICAN Fodor's Choice ★ 🍴 **T.J. Buckley's.** It's easy to pass by this small place housed inside a converted 1925 lunch car (diner) built in Worcester, Massachusetts, but it's one of Vermont's most romantic restaurants. The sleek red and black space amounts to an intimate, candlelit theater with just 18 seats, its stage an open kitchen whose flames flare mere feet from enraptured patrons. Performing with aplomb under the whisper of jazz is the star of the show: Michael Fuller, the dashing owner and sole chef for more than three decades. The contemporary menu, conveyed verbally each day, is based on locally available ingredients. [$] *Average main: $40* ✉ *132 Elliot St.* ☎ *802/257–4922* 🌐 *www.tjbuckleysuptowndining.com* 🕒 *Closed Mon., Tues., and most Wed. No lunch* ✍ *Reservations essential.*

$ BARBECUE FAMILY 🍴 **Top of the Hill Grill.** Don't let the diminutive size of this roadside smokehouse deceive you. The place produces big flavors locals line up for: hickory-smoked ribs, apple-smoked turkey, beef brisket, and pulled pork, to name a few. Homemade pecan pie is the dessert of choice. The restaurant probably has the best view in town, with outdoor picnic tables and an enclosed area overlooking the West River. [$] *Average main: $15* ✉ *632 Putney Rd.* ☎ *802/258–9178* 🌐 *www.topofthehillgrill.com* 💳 *No credit cards* 🕒 *Closed Nov.–Mar.*

$ CAFÉ 🍴 **The Works Bakery Cafe.** Natural light fills this spot in the center of town, whose patrons work on laptops at long wooden tables or sit with a book and some coffee in one of the comfortable armchairs. Fresh-fruit smoothies, panini, wraps, and salads are among the menu highlights. This is a perfect breakfast or lunch stop, or just a great place to catch up on email. [$] *Average main: $7* ✉ *118 Main St.* ☎ *802/579–1851* 🌐 *www.worksbakerycafe.com.*

WHERE TO STAY

$$ B&B/INN Fodor's Choice ★ 🏨 **Forty Putney Road.** Realizing her dream to run an inn, Rhonda Calhoun took over this 1931 French-style manse and has added her own colorful touches to the original features. **Pros:** caring host makes you feel like a guest, not a customer; comforting details; fabulous breakfast. **Cons:** tight parking. [$] *Rooms from: $219* ✉ *192 Putney Rd.* ☎ *802/254–6268, 800/941–2413* 🌐 *www.fortyputneyroad.com* 🛏 *5 rooms, 1 suite* 🍽 *Breakfast.*

$ B&B/INN Fodor's Choice ★ 🏨 **Hickory Ridge House.** If you're looking for a relaxing country getaway, this 1808 Federal-style mansion on the wide meadow of a former sheep farm is a good bet. **Pros:** peaceful property; great breakfast; quintessential bed-and-breakfast experience. **Cons:** not within walking distance of town. [$] *Rooms from: $175* ✉ *53 Hickory Ridge Rd., 11 miles north of Brattleboro, Putney* ☎ *802/387–5709, 800/380–9218* 🌐 *www.hickoryridgehouse.com* 🛏 *6 rooms, 1 cottage* 🍽 *Breakfast.*

$ HOTEL 🏨 **Latchis Hotel.** To stay in the heart of town, you won't find a more economical option than this art-deco hotel. **Pros:** heart-of-town location; lots of personality; reasonable rates. **Cons:** limited breakfast. [$] *Rooms from: $100* ✉ *50 Main St.* ☎ *802/254–6300, 800/798–6301* 🌐 *www.latchis.com* 🛏 *30 rooms, 3 suites* 🍽 *Breakfast.*

The rolling green hills of Putney are home to many organic farm operations.

PERFORMING ARTS

Latchis Theatre. This movie theater's architecture represents a singular blending of art deco and Greek Revival style, complete with statues, columns, and 1938 murals by Louis Jambor (1884–1955), a noted artist and children's book illustrator. The Latchis hosts art exhibits, streams live events, and has four screening rooms. For a sense of the theater's original grandeur, buy a ticket for whatever is showing on the big screen. Though the space may lack state-of-the-art technology, watching a film here is far more memorable than at any multiplex. ✉ *50 Main St.* ☎ *802/254–6300, 800/798–6301* ⊕ *www.latchis.com.*

SPORTS AND THE OUTDOORS

BICYCLING

Brattleboro Bicycle Shop. This shop rents hybrid bikes (call ahead to reserve one), does repair work, and sells maps and equipment. ✉ *165 Main St.* ☎ *802/254–8644, 800/272–8245* ⊕ *www.bratbike.com.*

CANOEING

Vermont Canoe Touring Center. Canoes and kayaks are available for rent here. Payment is by cash or check only. ✉ *451 Putney Rd.* ☎ *802/257–5008* ⊕ *www.vermontcanoetouringcenter.com.*

HIKING

Fort Dummer State Park. You can hike and camp within the 217 acres of forest at this state park, the location of the first permanent white settlement in Vermont. That site is now submerged beneath the Connecticut River, but it is viewable from the northernmost scenic vista on Sunrise Trail. ✉ *517 Old Guilford Rd.* ☎ *802/254–2610* ⊕ *www.vtstateparks. com/htm/fortdummer.htm* 🎫 *$4* ⊙ *Facilities closed early Sept.–late May.*

MULTISPORTS OUTFITTERS

Sam's Outdoor Outfitters. At this labyrinthine two-story sports emporium you can find outerwear, shoes, and gear for all seasons and activities. Grab a bag of free popcorn while you're shopping. ⊠ *74 Main St.* ☎ *802/254–2933* ⊕ *www.samsoutfitters.com.*

SHOPPING

ART GALLERIES

Gallery in the Woods. This funky trilevel store sells art, jewelry, and light fixtures from around the world. Rotating shows take place in the upstairs and downstairs galleries. ⊠ *145 Main St.* ☎ *802/257–4777* ⊕ *www.galleryinthewoods.com.*

Gallery Walk. On this walk, you'll pass more than 30 galleries and other venues downtown and nearby that exhibit art; it takes place 5:30–8:30 on the first Friday evening of the month. ☎ *802/257–2616* ⊕ *www.gallerywalk.org.*

Vermont Artisan Designs. Artworks and functional items in ceramics, glass, wood, fiber, and other media created by more than 300 artists are on display at this gallery. ⊠ *106 Main St.* ☎ *802/257–7044* ⊕ *www.vtart.com.*

BOOKS

Everyone's Books. The literary (and literal) center of a bookish town, this is the place to pick up a best seller, a local classic, or a book on progressive politics or the environment. The shop hosts readings and author events. ⊠ *25 Elliot St.* ☎ *802/254–8160* ⊕ *www.everyonesbks.com.*

FOOD

Serenity Herbs and Teas. Even if you're not an avid tea drinker, it's hard not to admire the passion and expertise of the proprietors of this elegant shop; ask what makes a true Earl Grey and you'll learn more than you ever thought possible. All teas are hand blended in the back. ⊠ *60 Elliot St.* ☎ *802/246–1310* ⊕ *www.serenityherbsandteas.com* ⊘ *Closed Sun.–Tues.*

WILMINGTON

18 miles west of Brattleboro.

The village of Wilmington, with its classic Main Street lined with 18th- and 19th-century buildings, anchors the Mount Snow Valley. Most of the valley's lodging and dining establishments, however, can be found along Route 100, which travels 5 miles north to West Dover and Mount Snow, where skiers flock on winter weekends. The area abounds with cultural activity from concerts to art exhibits year-round.

GETTING HERE AND AROUND

Wilmington is at the junction of Route 9 and Route 100. West Dover and Mount Snow are a few miles to the north along Route 100.

ESSENTIALS

Visitor Information Southern Vermont Deerfield Valley Chamber of Commerce. ⊠ *21 W. Main St.* ☎ *802/464–8092, 877/887–6884* ⊕ *www.visitvermont.com.*

EXPLORING

FAMILY **Adams Family Farm.** At this working farm you can collect fresh eggs from the chicken coop, feed a rabbit, milk a goat, ride a tractor or a pony, catch a fish in the pond, or take a sleigh ride in winter. A livestock barn is open November–mid-June; the animals roam free the rest of the year. ✉ *15 Higley Hill Rd., off Rte. 100* ☎ *802/464–3762* 🌐 *www.adamsfamilyfarm.com* 🎟 *$6.95* 🕒 *Mid-June–Sept., daily 10–4; Oct.–mid-June, Tues.–Sun. 10–4.*

BILLBOARDLESS VERMONT

Did you know that there are no billboards in Vermont? The state banned them in 1967 (similar laws exist in Maine, Alaska, and Hawaii), and the last one came down in 1975, so when you look out your window, you see trees and other scenery—not advertisements.

FAMILY **Southern Vermont Natural History Museum.** This museum 5 miles east of Wilmington houses one of New England's largest collections of mounted birds, including three extinct species and a complete collection of mammals native to the Northeast. The museum also has exhibits with live hawks, owls, and reptiles, and there's an adjacent 600-acre nature preserve. ✉ *7599 Rte. 9, West Marlboro* ☎ *802/464–0048* 🌐 *www.vermontmuseum.org* 🎟 *$5* 🕒 *Weekdays 10–4, weekends 10–5.*

WHERE TO EAT

$ DINER FAMILY 🍴 **Dot's Restaurant.** Look for the classic red neon sign (one of only a handful still permitted in Vermont) at the main corner in downtown Wilmington: Dot's is a local landmark. After Hurricane Irene ravaged the building in 2011, the community rallied to save its traditional country diner. Donations poured in, the structure was entirely renovated and fortified against future flooding, and by 2013 Dot's was back in business. It remains a friendly place where locals and skiers pack the tables and counter to order favorites like chicken *cordon bleu* (stuffed with ham and cheese, then breaded and fried), barbecue ribs, and home-style roast beef. The Berry-Berry pancakes with four kinds of berries are de rigueur for breakfast, which starts at 5:30 am. A bowl of chili is perfect for lunch. [$] *Average main: $10* ✉ *3 W. Main St.* ☎ *802/464–7284* 🌐 *www.dotsofvermont.com.*

$$$ ITALIAN 🍴 **Nonna's.** Terrance Brannan, a James Beard–nominated consultant, crafted the menu at the haute-cuisine restaurant at Sawmill Farm. The focus is on traditional Italian dishes such as tuna carpaccio, fettuccine carbonara, lobster risotto, and saltimbocca. You can order à la carte, though the restaurant recommends the four-course prix-fixe presentation. [$] *Average main: $30* ✉ *Inn at Sawmill Farm, 7 Crosstown Rd., at Rte. 100, West Dover* ☎ *802/464–8131* 🌐 *www.theinnatsawmillfarm.com* 🕒 *Closed Tues. and Wed. No lunch.*

WHERE TO STAY

$ B&B/INN 🏨 **Deerhill Inn.** The restaurant at this quintessential New England inn is among the best in town. **Pros:** special place; great restaurant. **Cons:** must drive to town and resort. [$] *Rooms from: $185* ✉ *14 Valley View Rd., West Dover* ☎ *802/464–3100, 800/993–3379* 🌐 *www.deerhill.com* 🛏 *10 rooms, 3 suites* 🍽 *Breakfast.*

8

Vermont Maple Syrup

Vermont is the country's largest producer of maple syrup. A visit to a maple farm is a great way to learn all about sugaring, the process of extracting maple tree sap and making syrup. Sap is stored in a sugar maple tree's roots in the winter, and in the spring when conditions are just right, the sap runs up and can be tapped. Sugaring season runs March–April, which is when all maple syrup in the state is produced.

One of the best parts of visiting a maple farm is getting to taste and compare the four grades of syrup. As the sugaring season goes on and days become warmer, the sap becomes progressively darker and stronger in flavor. Grades are defined by color, clarity, and flavor. Is one grade better than another? Nope, it's just a question of taste. Sap drawn early in the season produces the lightest

color, and has the most delicate flavor: this is called Vermont Fancy. Vermont Grade A Medium Amber has a mellow flavor. Vermont Grade A Dark Amber is much more robust, and Vermont Grade B is the most flavorful, making it often the favorite of first-time tasters.

When visiting a maple farm, make sure they make their own syrup, as opposed to just bottling or selling someone else's. You'll learn more about the entire process that way. **Vermont Maple Syrup** (☎ 802/858–9444 ⊕ www.vermontmaple.org), a great resource, has a map of maple farms that host tours, a directory of producers open year-round, and a list of places from which you can order maple syrup by mail. You can also get the lowdown on events such as the annual Maple Open House Weekend, when sugarhouses throughout the state open their doors to visitors.

$$$ 🏨 **Grand Summit Hotel.** Mount Snow's comfortable main hotel is an easy
RESORT   choice for skiers whose main priority is getting on the slopes as quickly
FAMILY   as possible. **Pros:** easy ski access; modern property. **Cons:** somewhat bland decor. **$** *Rooms from: $380* ✉ *89 Grand Summit Way, West Dover* ☎ *800/498–0479* ⊕ *www.mountsnow.com* ⇆ *196 rooms, suites, and studios* ⦿l *No meals.*

SPORTS AND THE OUTDOORS
BOATING
Green Mountain Flagship Company. Canoes and kayaks are available for rent May–mid-October on Lake Whitingham. ✉ *389 Rte. 9, 2 miles west of Wilmington* ☎ *802/464–2975.*

SKI AREAS
Mount Snow. The closest major ski area to all of the Northeast's big cities, Mount Snow prides itself on its hundreds of snowmaking fan guns—more than any other resort in North America. There are four major downhill areas. The main mountain comprises mostly intermediate runs, while the north face has the majority of expert runs. The south face, Sunbrook, has wide, sunny trails. It connects to Carinthia, which is dedicated to terrain parks and glade skiing. In summer, the 800-acre resort has an 18-hole golf course, 45 miles of mountain-biking trails, and an extensive network of hiking trails. **Facilities:** 80 trails; 588

acres; 1,700-foot vertical drop; 30 lifts. ⊠ *39 Mount Snow Rd., West Dover* ☎ *802/464–3333, 802/464–2151 for snow conditions* ⊕ *www.mountsnow.com* ⊡ *Lift ticket: $90.*

Timber Creek. North of Mount Snow, this appealingly small cross-country skiing and snowshoeing center has 4½ miles of groomed loops. You can rent equipment and take lessons here. ⊠ *13 Tanglewood La., at Rte. 100, West Dover* ☎ *802/464–0999* ⊕ *www.timbercreekxc.com* ⊡ *$20.*

SNOWSHOE TRAIL

FAMILY **Molly Stark State Park.** This park is home to some of the state's most popular snowshoe trails. Mount Olga Trail is a relatively easy 1.7-mile loop culminating in a 360-degree view of southern Vermont and northern Massachusetts. ⊠ *705 Rte. 9 E* ☎ *802/464–5460* ⊕ *www.vtstateparks.com/htm/mollystark.htm.*

SHOPPING

Quaigh Design Centre. For half a century, this store has sold great pottery and artworks from Britain and New England, including woodcuts by Mary Azarian, a Vermont-based artist. Scottish woolens are also on offer. ⊠ *11 W. Main St.* ☎ *802/464–2780* ☉ *Closed Wed. July–Sept., and Mon.–Thurs. Oct.–June.*

WHO WAS MOLLY STARK?

In the heart of Wilmington beside the Crafts Inn stands a sculpture in honor of Molly Stark, the wife of the Revolutionary War general John Stark. The general was said to have roused his troops in the Battle of Bennington, vowing victory over the British: "They are ours, or this night Molly Stark sleeps a widow!" He lived, and hence the victory path across Vermont (now Route 9) is called the Molly Stark Trail (or Byway).

BENNINGTON

21 miles west of Wilmington.

Bennington is the commercial focus of Vermont's southwest corner and home to Bennington College. It's really three towns in one: Downtown Bennington, Old Bennington, and North Bennington. Downtown has retained much of the industrial character it developed in the 19th century, when paper mills, gristmills, and potteries formed the city's economic base. The outskirts of town are commercial and not worth a stop, so make your way right into Downtown and Old Bennington to appreciate the area's true charm.

GETTING HERE AND AROUND

The heart of modern Bennington is the intersection of U.S. 7 and Route 9. Old Bennington is a couple of miles west on Route 9, at Monument Avenue. North Bennington is a few miles north on Route 67A.

ESSENTIALS

Visitor Information Bennington Area Chamber of Commerce. ⊠ *100 Veterans Memorial Dr.* ☎ *802/447–3311* ⊕ *www.bennington.com.*

8

The poet Robert Frost is buried in Bennington at the Old First Church, "Vermont's Colonial Shrine."

EXPLORING
TOP ATTRACTIONS

FAMILY **Bennington Battle Monument.** This 306-foot stone obelisk with an elevator to the top commemorates General John Stark's Revolutionary War victory over the British, who attempted to capture Bennington's stockpile of supplies. Inside the monument you can learn all about the battle, which took place near Walloomsac Heights in New York State on August 16, 1777, and helped bring about the surrender of British commander "Gentleman Johnny" Burgoyne two months later. The top of the tower affords commanding views of the Massachusetts Berkshires, the New York Adirondacks, and the Vermont Green Mountains. ⊠ *15 Monument Circle, Old Bennington* ☎ *802/447–0550* ⊕ *www. benningtonbattlemonument.com* ✉ *$5* ☾ *Mid-Apr.–Oct., daily 9–5.*

Bennington Center for the Arts. The center mounts exhibitions by local and national artists in its galleries, and sculptures often dot the lawns. Permanent-collection highlights include wildlife paintings and Native American art and artifacts. ⊠ *44 Gypsy La.* ☎ *802/442–7158* ⊕ *www. thebennington.org* ✉ *$9* ☾ *Daily 10–5.*

Bennington Museum. The rich collections here feature military artifacts, early tools, dolls, and the Bennington Flag, one of the oldest of the Stars and Stripes in existence. Other areas of interest include early Bennington pottery, the Gilded Age in Vermont, mid-20th-century modernist painters who worked in or near Bennington, glass and metalwork by Lewis Comfort Tiffany, and photography, watercolors, and other works on paper. The highlight for many visitors, though, is the largest public collection of works by Grandma Moses (1860–1961), the popular self-taught artist who lived and painted in the area. ⊠ *75 Main St., Old Bennington* ☏ *802/447–1571* ⊕ *www.benningtonmuseum.com* ⊠ *$10* ⊙ *June–Oct., daily 10–5; Nov., Dec., and mid-Feb.–May, Thurs.–Tues. 10–5.*

Park-McCullough House. The architecturally significant Park-McCullough House is a 35-room classic French Empire–style mansion, built in 1865 and furnished with period pieces. Several restored flower gardens grace the landscaped grounds, and a stable holds some antique carriages. House tours are given on Friday in summer. The grounds are open daily year-round. ⊠ *1 Park St., at West St., North Bennington* ☏ *802/442–5441* ⊕ *www.parkmccullough.org* ⊠ *$10* ⊙ *House tours: June–Sept., Fri. 10–4; last tour at 3. Grounds daily sunrise–sunset.*

Robert Frost Stone House Museum. Robert Frost came to Shaftsbury in 1920, he wrote, "to plant a new Garden of Eden with a thousand apple trees of some unforbidden variety." The museum tells the story of the poet's life and highlights the nine years (1920–29) he spent living in the house with his wife and four children. It was here that he penned "Stopping by Woods on a Snowy Evening" and published two books of poetry. You can wander 7 of the Frost family's original 80 acres. Among the apple boughs you just might find inspiration of your own. ⊠ *121 Historic Rte. 7A, Shaftsbury* ☏ *802/447–6200* ⊕ *www.frostfriends.org* ⊠ *$6* ⊙ *Nov.–Sept., Wed.–Sun. 10–5; Oct., daily 10–5.*

WORTH NOTING

Bennington College. Contemporary stone sculpture and white-frame neo-Colonial dorms surrounded by acres of cornfields punctuate the green meadows of the placid campus of Bennington College. ⊠ *1 College Dr., off U.S. 7, North Bennington* ☏ *802/442–5401* ⊕ *www.bennington.edu.*

Old Bennington. West of downtown, this National Register Historic District is well endowed with stately Colonial and Victorian mansions. The Catamount Tavern, where Ethan Allen organized the Green Mountain Boys to capture Fort Ticonderoga in 1775, contains a bronze statue of Vermont's indigenous mountain lion, now extinct. ⊠ *Monument Ave., Old Bennington.*

The Old First Church. In the graveyard of this church, the tombstone of the poet Robert Frost proclaims, "I had a lover's quarrel with the world."⊠ *1 Monument Circle, at Monument Ave., Old Bennington* ☏ *802/447–1223* ⊕ *www.oldfirstchurchbenn.org* ⊠ *Free* ⊙ *Services: Sept.–June, Sun. at 11; July and Aug., Sun. at 9.*

WHERE TO EAT

$ × **Blue Benn Diner.** Breakfast is served all day in this authentic diner
DINER whose menu includes turkey hash and breakfast burritos with scrambled eggs, sausage, and chilies, plus pancakes of all imaginable varieties, and there are many vegetarian selections. The line may be long, especially on weekends: locals and tourists can't stay away. $ *Average main: $10* ⊠ *314 North St.* ☏ *802/442–5140* ▬ *No credit cards* ⌕ *Reservations not accepted.*

$ × **Pangaea Lounge.** Locals head here for affordable comfort food and
ECLECTIC excellent cocktails. The regionally sourced fare includes pulled-pork tacos, Cobb salad with Danish blue cheese, salmon burgers, and pork tenderloin with sweet potatoes and maple syrup. On warm-weather

weekends, follow the crowd out back to the deck. Next door is the restaurant's fancier, fine-dining twin, which is overpriced and not as intimate. [$] *Average main: $17* ✉ *3 Prospect St., 3 miles north of Bennington, North Bennington* ☎ *802/442–7171* 🌐 *www.vermontfinedining.com* ⏲ *No lunch.*

WHERE TO STAY

$ B&B/INN 🏨 **The Eddington House Inn.** A stay in this impeccably maintained, historic three-bedroom house is a great value. **Pros:** budget prices for a great bed-and-breakfast; privacy and gentle service; spotless and nicely updated. **Cons:** slightly off usual tourist track; only three rooms so it fills up fast. [$] *Rooms from: $159* ✉ *21 Main St., North Bennington* ☎ *802/442–1511* 🌐 *www.eddingtonhouseinn.com* 🛏 *3 suites* 🍴 *Breakfast.*

$ B&B/INN Fodor's Choice ★ 🏨 **Four Chimneys Inn.** One of the best inns in Vermont, this three-story 1915 neo-Georgian looks out over a substantial lawn and a wonderful old stone wall. **Pros:** stately mansion; nicely renovated rooms; extremely well kept. **Cons:** dinner only offered for special events. [$] *Rooms from: $159* ✉ *21 West Rd., Old Bennington* ☎ *802/447–3500* 🌐 *www.fourchimneys.com* 🛏 *9 rooms, 2 suites* 🍴 *Breakfast.*

PERFORMING ARTS

Basement Music Series. The Vermont Arts Exchange sponsors this fun and funky contemporary music series at the downtown Masonic Lodge. Some performances sell out, so it's wise to purchase tickets in advance. ✉ *504 Main St.* ☎ *800/838–3006 for ticket hotline* 🌐 *www.vtartxchange.org/bms.php.*

Oldcastle Theatre Company. This fine regional theater company focuses on American classics and crowd-pleasing musicals. The group's venue also hosts occasional concerts. ✉ *331 Main St.* ☎ *802/447–0564* 🌐 *www.oldcastletheatre.org* ⏲ *Closed Dec.–Mar.*

SPORTS AND THE OUTDOORS

FAMILY **Lake Shaftsbury State Park.** You'll find a swimming beach, nature trails, boat and canoe rentals, and a snack bar at this pretty park. ✉ *262 Shaftsbury State Park Rd., 10½ miles north of Bennington* ☎ *802/375–9978* 🌐 *www.vtstateparks.com/htm/shaftsbury.htm* ⏲ *Facilities closed early Sept.–mid-May.*

Long Trail. Four miles east of Bennington, the Long Trail crosses Route 9 and runs south to the top of Harmon Hill. Allot two or three hours for this steep hike. ✉ *Bennington.*

FAMILY **Woodford State Park.** This park has an activities center on Adams Reservoir, a playground, boat and canoe rentals, and nature trails. ✉ *142 State Park Rd., 10 miles east of Bennington* ☎ *802/447–7169* 🌐 *www.vtstateparks.com/htm/woodford.htm* ⏲ *Facilities closed mid-Oct.–mid-May.*

SHOPPING

FAMILY **The Apple Barn & Country Bake Shop.** Homemade baked goods, fresh cider, Vermont cheeses, maple syrup, and 30 varieties of apples are among the treats for sale here. There's berry picking in season, for a fun family stop, and on weekends you can watch the bakers make cider doughnuts. ✉ *604 Rte. 7S, 1½ miles south of downtown Bennington*

☎ *802/447–7780, 888/827–7537* 🌐 *www.theapplebarn.com* 🕒 *May–Nov., daily 8:30–5.*

The Bennington Bookshop. The state's oldest independent bookstore sells the latest new releases and hosts weekly readings, signings, and lectures. ✉ *467 Main St.* ☎ *802/442–5059* 🌐 *www.benningtonbookshop.com.*

Bennington Potters Yard. The yard's showroom stocks goods from the famed Bennington Potters. On a self-guided tour you can see the potters at work (except Sunday). ✉ *324 County St.* ☎ *802/447–7531, 800/205–8033* 🌐 *www.benningtonpotters.com.*

Now & Then Books. This great second-story bookstore stocks nearly 45,000 secondhand volumes. ✉ *439 Main St.* ☎ *802/442–5566* 🌐 *www.nowandthenbooksvt.com.*

ARLINGTON

15 miles north of Bennington.

Smaller than Bennington and more down-to-earth than upper-crust Manchester to the north, Arlington exudes a certain Rockwellian folksiness, and it should: the illustrator Norman Rockwell lived here from 1939 to 1953, and many neighbors served as models for his portraits of small-town life.

GETTING HERE AND AROUND

Arlington is at the intersection of Route 313 and Route 7A. Take Route 313 West to reach West Arlington.

EXPLORING

8

West Arlington. Norman Rockwell once lived in this place with a quaint town green. If you follow Route 313 west from Arlington, you'll pass by the Wayside Country Store, a slightly rickety charmer where you can pick up sandwiches and chat with locals. The store carries everything from ammo and sporting goods to toys, teas, and maple syrup. Continue on, and cross West Arlington's red covered bridge, which leads to the town green. To loop back to Route 7A, take River Road along the south side of the Battenkill River, a scenic drive. ✉ *West Arlington.*

WHERE TO STAY

$ B&B/INN 🏨 **The Arlington Inn.** The Greek Revival columns of this 1847 home lend it an imposing presence in the middle of town, but the atmosphere within is friendly and old-fashioned. **Pros:** heart-of-town location; friendly atmosphere. **Cons:** expensive dining. [$] *Rooms from: $199* ✉ *3904 VT Rte. 7A* ☎ *802/375–6532* 🌐 *www.arlingtoninn.com* 🛏 *13 rooms, 3 suites* 🍴 *Breakfast.*

$$ B&B/INN FAMILY 🏨 **Hill Farm Inn.** Simple cottages and the best views in the Manchester area make this former dairy farm a winner. **Pros:** glorious open meadow setting; innkeeper is a former private chef; updated rooms and bathrooms. **Cons:** books up on weekends with weddings. [$] *Rooms from: $215* ✉ *458 Hill Farm Rd., off Rte. 7A, Sunderland* ☎ *802/375–2269, 800/882–2545* 🌐 *www.hillfarminn.com* 🛏 *8 rooms, 3 suites, 1 farmhouse* 🍴 *Breakfast.*

$ B&B/INN FAMILY Fodor's Choice ★ **West Mountain Inn.** This 1810 farmhouse sits on 150 mountainside acres with hiking trails and easy access to the Battenkill River, where you can canoe or go tubing. **Pros:** mountainside location; lots of activities; great views. **Cons:** dining room not ideal for kids. [$] *Rooms from: $195* ✉ *144 West Mountain Inn Rd., at Rte. 313* ☎ *802/375–6516* 🌐 *www.westmountaininn.com* 🛏 *14 rooms, 6 suites* 🍴 *Some meals.*

SPORTS AND THE OUTDOORS

BattenKill Canoe. This outfitter rents canoes for trips along the Battenkill River, which runs directly behind the shop. If you're hooked, the company also conducts more involved white-water trips as well as inn-to-inn tours. ✉ *6328 Historic Rte. 7A* ☎ *802/362–2800, 800/421–5268* 🌐 *www.battenkill.com.*

SHOPPING

ANTIQUES

East Arlington Antiques Center. More than 70 dealers display their wares at the center, which occupies a converted 1930s movie theater. Among the finds is one of the country's best stoneware collections. ✉ *1152 East Arlington Rd., East Arlington* ☎ *802/375–6144.*

GIFTS

FAMILY **Village Peddler.** This shop has a "chocolatorium," where you can learn all about cocoa. It sells fudge and other candies and stocks a large collection of teddy bears. ✉ *261 Old Mill Rd., East Arlington* ☎ *802/375–6037* 🌐 *www.villagepeddlervt.com.*

MANCHESTER

9 miles northeast of Arlington.

Well-to-do Manchester has been a popular summer retreat since the mid-19th century, when city dwellers traveled north to take in the cool clean air at the base of 3,840-foot Mt. Equinox. Manchester Village's tree-shaded marble sidewalks and stately old homes—Main Street here could hardly be more picture-perfect—reflect the luxurious resort lifestyle of more than a century ago. A mile north on Route 7A, Manchester Center is the commercial twin to Colonial Manchester Village; it's also where you'll find the town's famed upscale factory outlets doing business in attractive faux-Colonial shops.

Manchester Village houses the world headquarters of Orvis, the outdoor-goods brand that was founded here in the 19th century and has greatly influenced the town ever since. The complex includes a fly-fishing school featuring lessons given in its casting ponds and the Battenkill River.

GETTING HERE AND AROUND

Manchester is the main town for the ski resorts of Stratton (a half-hour drive on Route 30) and Bromley (15 minutes to the northeast on Route 11). It's 15 minutes north of Arlington along scenic Route 7A.

The formal gardens and mansion at Robert Todd Lincoln's Hildene are a far cry from his father's log cabin.

ESSENTIALS

Visitor Information Green Mountain National Forest Visitor Center.
✉ *2538 Depot St.* ☎ *802/362–2307* ⊕ *www.fs.usda.gov/main/gmfl.* **Manchester and the Mountains Regional Chamber of Commerce.** ✉ *39 Bonnet St.*
☎ *802/362–6313* ⊕ *www.visitmanchestervt.com.*

EXPLORING

American Museum of Fly Fishing. This museum houses the world's largest collection of angling art and angling-related objects—more than 1,500 rods, 800 reels, 30,000 flies, including the tackle of Winslow Homer, Babe Ruth, Jimmy Carter, and other notables. Every August, vendors sell antique equipment at the museum's fly-fishing festival. You can also practice your casting out back. ✉ *4104 Main St.* ☎ *802/362–3300* ⊕ *www.amff.com* ✂ *$5* ⊘ *Nov.–May, Tues.–Sat. 10–4; June–Oct., Tues.–Sun. 10–4.*

FAMILY
Fodor'sChoice
★

Hildene. A twofold treat, the summer home of Abraham Lincoln's son Robert provides insight into the lives of the Lincoln family, as well as an introduction to the lavish Manchester life of the early 1900s. The only son of the president to survive into adulthood, Robert Lincoln served as secretary of war, U.S. ambassador to Great Britain, and general counsel and later president of the Pullman Palace Car Company. In 1905, Robert built a 24-room mansion where he and his descendants lived until 1975. The sturdy Georgian Revival house, the centerpiece of a beautifully preserved 412-acre estate, holds many of the family's prized possessions, including one of three surviving stovepipe hats owned by Abraham and a Lincoln Bible. When the 1,000-pipe Aeolian organ is played, the music reverberates as though from the mansion's very bones.

Rising from a 10-acre meadow, Hildene Farm, which opened in 2008, is magnificent. The agriculture center is built in a traditional style—post-and-beam construction of timber felled and milled on the estate. Best of all, you can meet the resident goats and watch goat cheese being made.

The highlight, though, may be the elaborate formal gardens, where a thousand peonies bloom every June. To get a glimpse of luxury travel in the Gilded Age, step aboard the restored 1903 Pullman car parked in a patch of forest north of the house. There is also a teaching green-house, a 600-foot floating boardwalk across the Battenkill wetlands, and more than 10 miles of walking trails. When conditions permit, you can cross-country ski and snowshoe on the property.

In good weather, a restored 1928 Franklin car once owned by Robert's daughter Jessie is parked in front of the carriage house, now occupied by a gorgeous museum store and welcome center. Allow at least half a day for exploring Hildene. ⊠ *1005 Hildene Rd., at Rte. 7A* ☎ *802/362–1788* ⊕ *www.hildene.org* ⛴ *Tour $18* ⊗ *Daily 9:30–4:30.*

Fodor's Choice   **Southern Vermont Arts Center.** Located at the end of a long, winding drive-
★   way, this center has a permanent collection of more than 800 19th- and 20th-century American artworks and presents temporary exhibitions. The original building, a Georgian mansion set on 100 acres, contains 10 galleries with works by more than 600 artists, many from Vermont. The building also hosts concerts, performances, and film screenings. In summer and fall, the views from the restaurant at lunchtime are magnificent. ⊠ *930 SVAC Dr., West Rd.* ☎ *802/362–1405* ⊕ *www.svac.org* ⛴ *$6* ⊗ *Tues.–Sat. 10–5, Sun. noon–5.*

WHERE TO EAT

$$$ ✕ **Bistro Henry.** The presence of chef-owner Henry Bronson accounts for
FRENCH   the popularity of this friendly place, as does the fact that dishes cost about $5 less than at Manchester's other upscale restaurants. Bistro classics include steak au poivre and medium-rare duck breast served with a crispy leg, but Bronson mixes things up with tuna wasabi accompanied by a spicy pad thai and Sicilian salmon served with couscous. Wines are well chosen, and the desserts made by Dina Bronson, Henry's wife, are memorable. (The couple met while working in Manhattan restaurants.) Indulge in the "gooey chocolate cake," a great molten treat paired with a homemade malted ice cream. $ *Average main: $25* ⊠ *1942 Depot St., 3 miles east of Manchester Center* ☎ *802/362–4982* ⊕ *www.bistrohenry.com* ⊗ *Closed Mon. No lunch.*

$$$$ ✕ **Chanteleer.** There is something wonderful about eating by candle-
EUROPEAN   light in an old barn, and with the rooster art above their rough-hewn wooden beams, Chanteleer's dining rooms are especially romantic. In winter, ask to sit by the great fieldstone fireplace. The menu runs to the Continental, with starters like escargot glazed with Pernod in a hazelnut and parsley butter. Crowd-pleasing entrées include Colorado rack of lamb and whole Dover sole filleted table-side. The Matterhorn choco-late sundae—vanilla ice cream covered with hazelnut nougatine and Toblerone chocolate sauce—makes a winning winter dessert. $ *Average main: $38* ⊠ *8 Reed Farm La., 3½ miles north of Manchester, East*

Dorset ☎ *802/362–1616* 🌐 *www.chantecleerrestaurant.com* 🕒 *Closed Mon. and Tues., and Nov. and Apr. No lunch* ✍ *Reservations essential.*

$$$$ STEAKHOUSE 🍴 **Chop House.** Walk to the very back room of the Equinox's Marsh Tavern, past a velvet curtain, to enter this special, very expensive steak house. The dining room has a bit of history: the marble above the fireplace is chiseled "L.L. ORVIS 1832," and way before he claimed the spot, the Green Mountain Boys gathered here to plan their Revolutionary War–era resistance. Today, you'll yield to aged corn- or grass-fed beef broiled at 1,700°F and finished with herb butter. The New York strip, rib eye, filet mignon, milk-fed veal chops, and seafood are delicious—a must for deep-pocketed carnivores. [$] *Average main: $47* ✉ *3567 Main St.* ☎ *802/362–4700* 🌐 *www.equinoxresort.com* 🕒 *Closed Mon. and Tues. No lunch.*

$$ PIZZA 🍴 **Depot 62 Cafe and Bistro.** The best pizzas in town are topped with terrific fresh ingredients and served in the middle of a high-end antiques showroom, making this Turkish-Mediterranean restaurant a local secret worth knowing about. The wood-fired oven yields masterful results—like the arugula pizza, a beehive of fresh greens atop a thin crust. This a great place for lunch or an inexpensive but satisfying dinner. Sit on your own or at the long communal table. [$] *Average main: $18* ✉ *515 Depot St.* ☎ *802/366–8181* 🌐 *www.depotbistro.com.*

$$$ FRENCH 🍴 **Mistral's at Toll Gate.** This classic French restaurant is tucked in a grotto on the climb to Bromley Mountain. The two dining rooms are perched over the Bromley Brook, and at night a small waterfall is magically illuminated—ask for a window table. Chef Dana Markey's specialties include chateaubriand béarnaise for two and crispy sweetbreads dijonnaise. [$] *Average main: $32* ✉ *10 Toll Gate Rd., off Rte. 11/30* ☎ *802/362–1779* 🌐 *www.mistralsattollgate.com* 🕒 *Closed Wed., and Tues. Nov.–June. No lunch.*

$$$ ECLECTIC Fodor's Choice ★ 🍴 **Perfect Wife.** Owner-chef Amy Chamberlain, a Manchester native, creates a fun, free-form atmosphere with dishes like Peking duck rolled in Mandarin pancakes and sesame-crusted yellowfin tuna topped with crispy rice sticks. Her establishment has two entrances: one to the restaurant on the lower level and another to the Other Woman Tavern above. The tavern, which is open more often in winter, is among the town's livelier spots, with Vermont microbrews on tap, live music on weekends, and a pub menu with burgers and potpies. [$] *Average main: $27* ✉ *2594 Depot St., 2½ miles east of Manchester Center* ☎ *802/362–2817* 🌐 *www.perfectwife.com* 🕒 *Closed Sun., and Mon.–Wed. in winter. No lunch.*

$$$$ AMERICAN 🍴 **The Reluctant Panther Inn & Restaurant.** The dining room at this luxurious inn is a large, modern space where rich woods and high ceilings meld into a kind of "nouveau Vermont" aesthetic. The contemporary American cuisine emphasizes farm-to-table ingredients and has earned the restaurant "Gold Barn" honors from the Vermont Fresh Network. You can pair your meal with a bottle from the award-winning wine list. When it's warm outside, sit on the landscaped patio, where there's a raw bar Thursday–Saturday evenings. [$] *Average main: $36* ✉ *39 West Rd.* ☎ *800/822–2331, 802/362–2568* 🌐 *www.reluctantpanther.com* 🕒 *No lunch.*

$$$
ECLECTIC
Fodor's Choice
★

✕ **The Silver Fork.** This intimate bistro with a Caribbean flair is owned by husband-and-wife team Mark and Melody French. They spent years in Puerto Rico, and the flavors of the island are reflected in their menu— it's certainly the only one in town to feature shrimp *mofongo* (with mashed plantains) alongside Wiener schnitzel, pulled pork empanadas, and warm apple-cinnamon beignets. Reserve one of the six tables ahead of time, or sit at the wine bar for a casual and romantic dinner with a maple martini or a bottle from the impressive wine list. $ *Average main: $30* ✉ *4201 Main St., across from Orvis Flagship Store* ☎ *802/768–8444* ⊕ *www.thesilverforkvt.com* ⊘ *Closed Sun. No lunch* ⌦ *Reservations essential.*

$$
AMERICAN

✕ **Ye Olde Tavern.** This circa-1790 Colonial inn dishes up Yankee favorites like pot roast and cheddar-and-ale onion soup, along with plenty of New England charm. A favorite of regulars and visitors alike, the tavern serves excellent food in a casual, colorful setting, and the mellow tap room is a nice stop for a drink and a taste of Vermont. $ *Average main: $22* ✉ *5183 Main St.* ☎ *802/362–0611* ⊕ *www.yeoldetavern.net.*

WHERE TO STAY

$$$
RESORT

🛏 **Equinox.** The Equinox defines the geographic center and historic heart of Manchester Village, and has been *the* fancy hotel in town—and in the state—since the 18th century. **Pros:** heart-of-town location; full-service hotel; great golf and spa. **Cons:** corporate feel; spotty service; overrun by New Yorkers on weekends. $ *Rooms from: $365* ✉ *3567 Main St.* ☎ *802/362–4700, 888/367–7625* ⊕ *www.equinoxresort.com* ⤹ *195 rooms and suites* ⦿ *No meals.*

$$$
HOTEL

🛏 **Taconic Hotel.** A fresh-faced Kimpton boutique venture in Manchester Village, the Taconic, which opened in late 2015, has public areas that include a wraparound porch and the Copper Grouse restaurant, run by a top Burlington chef known for upscale comfort food. **Pros:** contemporary Kimpton style; village location; Frette robes, Atelier Bloom bath products; fitness center open 24 hours; yoga mats in all rooms. **Cons:** perhaps too fresh-faced to feel truly "Vermont"; only chain's rewards members get free high-speed Internet/Wi-Fi. $ *Rooms from: $340* ✉ *3835 Main St.* ☎ *802/362–0147* ⊕ *www.taconichotel.com* ⤹ *87 rooms, 3 cottages* ⦿ *No meals.*

$
B&B/INN
Fodor's Choice
★

🛏 **Wilburton Inn.** Stepping into this hilltop 1902 Tudor-style mansion, you might think you've stumbled on a lavish film set: there's a palpably cinematic quality to the richly paneled guest rooms and the common rooms containing part of the owners' vast art collection. **Pros:** beautiful setting; easy access to Manchester; fine dining. **Cons:** limited indoor facilities; popular wedding site. $ *Rooms from: $190* ✉ *257 River Rd.* ☎ *802/362–2500, 800/648–4944* ⊕ *www.wilburton.com* ⤹ *30 rooms, 4 suites* ⦿ *Breakfast.*

NIGHTLIFE

Falcon Bar. This sophisticated bar has live music on weekends. In summer, don't miss the wonderful outdoor deck. In winter, the place to be is around the giant Vermont slate fire pit. ✉ *Equinox Resort, 3567 Main St.* ☎ *800/362–4747* ⊕ *www.equinoxresort.com.*

SPORTS AND THE OUTDOORS

BIKING

Battenkill Sports Bicycle Shop. This shop rents, sells, and repairs bikes and provides maps and route suggestions. ✉ *1240 Depot St., off U.S. 7* ☎ *802/362–2734, 800/340–2734* ⊕ *www.battenkillsports.com.*

FISHING

Battenkill Anglers. Teaching the art and science of fly-fishing, Battenkill Anglers offers both private and group lessons. ✉ *6204 Main St.* ☎ *802/379–1444* ⊕ *www.battenkillangler.com.*

HIKING

There are bountiful hiking trails in the Green Mountain National Forest. Shorter hikes begin at the Equinox Resort, which owns about 1,000 acres of forest and has a great trail system open to the public.

Long Trail. One of the most popular segments of Vermont's Long Trail leads to the top of Bromley Mountain. The strenuous 5.4-mile round-trip takes about four hours. ✉ *Rte. 11/30* ⊕ *www.greenmountainclub.org.*

Lye Brook Falls. This 4.6-mile hike starts off Glen Road and ends at Vermont's most impressive cataract, Lye Brook Falls. The moderately strenuous journey takes four hours. ✉ *Off Glen Rd., south from E. Manchester Rd. just east of U.S. 7* ⊕ *www.greenmountainclub.org.*

Mountain Goat. Stop here for hiking, cross-country-skiing, and snowshoeing equipment (some of which is available to rent), as well as a good selection of warm clothing. ✉ *4886 Main St.* ☎ *802/362–5159* ⊕ *www.mountaingoat.com.*

ICE-SKATING

FAMILY **Riley Rink at Hunter Park.** This Olympic-size indoor ice rink has skate rentals and a concession stand. ✉ *410 Hunter Park Rd.* ☎ *802/362–0150* ⊕ *www.rileyrink.com.*

SHOPPING

ART AND ANTIQUES

Long Ago & Far Away. This store specializes in fine indigenous artwork, including Inuit stone sculpture. ✉ *Green Mountain Village Shops, 4963 Main St.* ☎ *802/362–3435* ⊕ *www.longagoandfaraway.com.*

Tilting at Windmills Gallery. This large gallery displays the paintings and sculptures of nationally known artists. ✉ *24 Highland Ave., Manchester Center* ☎ *802/362–3022* ⊕ *www.tilting.com.*

BOOKS

FAMILY **Northshire Bookstore.** The heart of Manchester Center, this bookstore is adored by visitors and residents alike for its ambience, selection, and service. Up the iron staircase is a second floor dedicated to children's books, toys, and clothes. Connected to the store is the Spiral Press Café, where you can sit down to a grilled pesto-chicken sandwich or a latte and scone. ✉ *4869 Main St.* ☎ *802/362–2200, 800/437–3700* ⊕ *www.northshire.com.*

CLOTHING

Manchester Designer Outlets. This is the most upscale collection of stores in northern New England—and every store is a discount outlet. The architecture reflects the surrounding homes, so the place looks a bit

8

like a Colonial village. The long list of famous-brand clothiers here includes Kate Spade, Yves Delorme, Michael Kors, Ann Taylor, Tumi, BCBG, Armani, Coach, Polo Ralph Lauren, Brooks Brothers, and Theory. ⊠ 97 Depot St. ☎ 802/362–3736, 800/955–7467 ⊕ www. manchesterdesigneroutlets.com.

Orvis Flagship Store. The lodgelike Orvis store carries the company's latest clothing, fly-fishing gear, and pet supplies—there's even a trout pond. At this required shopping destination for many visitors—the Orvis name is pure Manchester—there are demonstrations of how fly rods are constructed and tested. You can attend fly-fishing school across the street. ⊠ 4200 Rte. 7A ☎ 802/362–3750 ⊕ www.orvis.com.

SPAS

Spa at Equinox. With mahogany doors and beadboard wainscoting, this spa feels like a country estate. At one end are an indoor pool and an outdoor hot tub; at the other end are the treatment rooms. The signature 100-minute Spirit of Vermont combines Reiki, reflexology, and massage. In the co-ed relaxation room, you can nestle into overstuffed chairs next to a two-sided fireplace made of Vermont gneiss. The locker rooms, with marble accents and pottery-bowl wash basins, have steam rooms and saunas. ⊠ Equinox Resort, 3567 Rte. 7A ☎ 802/362–4700, 800/362–4747 ⊕ www.equinoxresort.com.

DORSET

7 miles north of Manchester.

Lying at the foot of many mountains and with a village green surrounded by white clapboard homes and inns, Dorset has a solid claim to the title of Vermont's most picture-perfect town. Dorset has just 2,000 residents, but two of the state's best and oldest general stores.

The country's first commercial marble quarry opened here in 1785. Dozens followed suit, providing the marble for the main research branch of the New York Public Library and many Fifth Avenue mansions, among other notable landmarks, as well as the sidewalks here and in Manchester. A remarkable private home made entirely of marble can be seen on Dorset West Road, a beautiful residential road west of the town green. The marble Dorset Church on the green has two Tiffany stained-glass windows.

EXPLORING

FAMILY   **Dorset Quarry.** On hot summer days the sight of dozens of families jumping, swimming, and basking in the sun around this massive 60-foot-deep swimming hole makes it one of the most wholesome and picturesque recreational spots in the region. First mined in 1785, the stone from the country's oldest commercial marble quarry was used to build the main branch of the New York Public Library and the Montreal Museum of Fine Arts. ⊠ Rte. 30 ⊠ Free.

Fodor's Choice
★

FAMILY   **Merck Forest & Farmland Center.** This 3,100-acre educational center has 30 miles of nature trails for hiking, cross-country skiing, snowshoeing, and horseback riding. You can visit the 60-acre farm, which grows organic fruit and vegetables (sold at the farm stand), and check out the horses, cows, sheep, pigs, and chickens while you're there—you're even welcome to help out with the chores. ✉ *3270 Rte. 315, Rupert* ☎ *802/394–7836* 🌐 *www.merckforest.org* 🎫 *Free* 🕒 *Visitor center daily 9–4.*

WHERE TO EAT

$$$ AMERICAN 🍴 **The Dorset Inn.** Built in 1796, this inn has been continuously operating ever since. The comfortable tavern, which serves the same menu as the more formal dining room, is popular with locals, and Patrick, the amiable veteran bartender, will make you feel at home. Recent favorites include the Dorset Inn poutine and the maple-glazed duck breast. A member of the Vermont Fresh Network, the restaurant benefits greatly from its strong connections with local farmers. [$] *Average main: $25* ✉ *Dorset Green, 8 Church St.* ☎ *802/867–5500* 🌐 *www.dorsetinn.com* 🕒 *No lunch Mon. and Tues.*

$$$ ECLECTIC 🍴 **Inn at West View Farm.** Chef-owner Raymond Chen was the lead line cook at New York City's Mercer Kitchen before opening this restaurant. You'll find traditional floral wallpaper and soft classical music, but that's where the similarities to Dorset's other eateries end. Chen skillfully applies French techniques to Asian dishes crafted from fresh Vermont ingredients. You could make a meal out of the many small plates—think of them as a cross between tapas and dim sum. [$] *Average main: $30* ✉ *2928 Rte. 30* ☎ *802/867–5715, 800/769–4903* 🌐 *www.innatwestviewfarm.com* 🕒 *Closed Tues. and Wed.*

WHERE TO STAY

$$ HOTEL 🏨 **Barrows House.** If you've tired of the floral fabrics found in many New England inns, this renovated 19th-century manse, once the residence of the town's pastor, provides a pleasant alternative. **Pros:** good bar and restaurant; chintz-free decor. **Cons:** rooms can become drafty in cold weather. [$] *Rooms from: $275* ✉ *3156 Rte. 30* ☎ *802/867–4455* 🌐 *www.barrowshouse.com* 🛏 *18 rooms, 9 suites, 3 cottages* 🍽 *Breakfast.*

$$ B&B/INN 🏨 **Squire House Bed & Breakfast.** On a wonderfully quiet road, this inn has three guest rooms that combine modern comforts and antique fixtures. **Pros:** big estate feels like your own; well-maintained rooms; quiet. **Cons:** bathrooms less exciting than rooms. [$] *Rooms from: $210* ✉ *3395 Dorset West Rd.* ☎ *802/867–0281* 🌐 *www.squirehouse.com* 🛏 *2 rooms, 1 suite* 🍽 *Breakfast.*

PERFORMING ARTS

Dorset Players. The prestigious summer theater troupe presents the annual Dorset Theater Festival. Plays are staged in a wonderful converted pre-Revolutionary War barn. ✉ *Dorset Playhouse, 104 Cheney Rd.* ☎ *802/867–5777* 🌐 *www.dorsetplayers.org.*

SPORTS AND THE OUTDOORS

Emerald Lake State Park. This park has a well-marked nature trail, a small beach, boat rentals, and a snack bar. ✉ *65 Emerald Lake La., East Dorset* ☎ *802/362–1655* 🌐 *www.vtstateparks.com/htm/emerald.htm* 🎫 *$4* 🕒 *Facilities closed mid-Oct.–mid-May.*

SHOPPING

Dorset Union Store. Dating to 1816, this general store has good prepared dinners and a big wine selection. They also sell interesting gifts. ✉ *Dorset Green, Church St.* ☎ *802/867–4400.*

H. N. Williams General Store. Started in 1840 by William Williams, this trilevel country store has been run by the same family for six generations. This is one of those places where you can buy maple syrup and ammo, while catching up on posted town announcements. There's a deli on-site for sandwiches; a farmers' market is held outside on Sunday in summer. ✉ *2732 Rte. 30* ☎ *802/867–5353* 🌐 *www.hnwilliams.com.*

STRATTON

26 miles southeast of Dorset.

Stratton is really Stratton Mountain Resort, a mountaintop ski resort with a self-contained "town center" of shops, restaurants, and lodgings clustered at the base of the slopes. When the snow melts, golf, tennis, and a host of other summer activities are big attractions, but the ski village remains quiet.

GETTING HERE AND AROUND

From Manchester or U.S. 7, follow Route 11/30 east until they split. Route 11 continues past Bromley ski mountain, and Route 30 turns south 10 minutes toward Bondville, the town at the base of the mountain. At the junction of Routes 30 and 100 is the village of Jamaica, with its own cluster of inns and restaurants on the eastern side of the mountain.

WHERE TO EAT

$ AMERICAN FAMILY 🍴 **J.J. Hapgood General Store and Eatery.** You won't find a better meal at any other general store in the state. This is really more of a restaurant than a place to pick up the essentials, but like any good general store it's a friendly and relaxed gathering spot for locals. Breakfast is all about farm-fresh eggs and organic oatmeal. Lunch brings soups and sandwiches—in autumn, try a grilled cheese with local apple. After 3 pm, cooks fire up the pizza oven and crank out pies with Thai peanut sauce, pulled pork, kale, chickpeas, and other out-of-the-ordinary ingredients. [$] *Average main: $9* ✉ *305 Main St., Peru* ☎ *802/824–4800* 🌐 *www.jjhapgood.com.*

$$$ AMERICAN 🍴 **The Red Fox Inn.** This converted bi-level barn has the best nightlife in town and a fun dining room. The restaurant is on the upper level, where you'll see wagon wheels and a carriage suspended from the A-frame ceiling. Settle in near the huge fireplace for beef tenderloin, roasted half duckling, or penne alla vodka. Their apple pie was served at the inauguration of President Obama. Downstairs in the tavern (open year-round) there's Irish music, half-price Guinness, and fish 'n' chips on Wednesday. On the premises are some relaxed, no-frills accommodations. [$] *Average main: $26* ✉ *103 Winhall Hollow Rd., Bondville* ☎ *802/297–2488* 🌐 *www.redfoxinn.com* 🕒 *Closed Mon.–Wed. June–Oct. No lunch.*

WHERE TO STAY

$$$ ▦ **Long Trail House.** Directly across the street from the ski village, this
RENTAL   condo complex is one of the closest to the slopes. **Pros:** across from ski-
ing; reasonable rates for weekdays; outdoor heated pool. **Cons:** room
decor varies; two-night stay required on weekends. ⓢ *Rooms from:
$350* ⊠ *5 Village Lodge Rd.* ☎ *802/297–4000, 800/787–2886* ⊕ *www.
stratton.com* ↝ *100 units* ⦿| *No meals.*

$$ ▦ **Three Mountain Inn.** A 1780s tavern, this romantic inn in downtown
B&B/INN   Jamaica feels authentically Colonial, from the wide-plank paneling
Fodor'sChoice   to the low ceilings. **Pros:** romantic; well-kept rooms; great dinners.
★   **Cons:** 15-minute drive to skiing. ⓢ *Rooms from: $234* ⊠ *30 Depot
St., 10 miles northeast of Stratton, Jamaica* ☎ *802/874–4140* ⊕ *www.
threemountaininn.com* ↝ *8 rooms, 1 suite, 1 cottage* ⦿| *Breakfast.*

NIGHTLIFE

Mulligans. Popular Mulligans hosts bands and DJs in the downstairs
Green Door Pub on weekends. ⊠ *Village Sq., Stratton Mountain*
☎ *802/297–9293* ⊕ *www.green-door-pub.com.*

SPORTS AND THE OUTDOORS

SKI AREAS

FAMILY   **Bromley Mountain Resort.** About 20 minutes from Stratton, Bromley is
a favorite with families thanks to a child-care center for kids ages 6
weeks–6 years and programs for ages 3–17. The trails are evenly split
among beginner, intermediate, and advanced, with nothing too challenging. Beginning skiers and snowboarders have expanded access to
terrain-based training in the dedicated Learning Zone, and everyone
can unwind in the newly renovated base lodge. An added bonus: trails
face south, making for glorious spring skiing and warm winter days.
Facilities: 46 trails; 300 acres; 1,334-foot vertical drop; 9 lifts. ⊠ *3984
Rte. 11, Peru* ☎ *802/824–5522, 866/856–2201 for snow conditions*
⊕ *www.bromley.com* ▦ *Lift ticket: $71.*

Stratton Mountain. About 30 minutes from Manchester, and featuring an
entire faux Swiss village at its base, Stratton Mountain draws affluent
families and young professionals. Beginners will find more than 40%
of the mountain accessible to them, but that doesn't mean there aren't
some great steeps for the experts. The resort prides itself on its immaculate grooming and excellent cruising on all trails. An on-site day-care
center takes children ages 6 weeks–5 years for indoor activities and
outdoor excursions. Children also love careening down one of four
groomed lift-serviced lanes at the resort's Coca Cola Tube Park. Stratton has 11 miles of cross-country skiing, and in summer there are 15
outdoor clay tennis courts, 27 holes of golf, and hiking trails accessed
by a gondola. The sports complex (open year-round) has a 25-meter
indoor pool, a hot tub, a steam room, and a fitness center. **Facilities:** 97
trails; 670 acres; 2,003-foot vertical drop; 11 lifts. ⊠ *5 Village Lodge
Rd., Bondville* ☎ *802/297–4211 for snow conditions*, *800/787–2886*
⊕ *www.stratton.com* ▦ *Lift ticket: $99.*

8

WESTON

17 miles north of Stratton.

Best known as the home of the Vermont Country Store, Weston was one of the first Vermont towns to discover its own intrinsic loveliness—and marketability. With its summer theater, classic town green with Victorian bandstand, and an assortment of shops, the little village really lives up to its vaunted image.

WHERE TO STAY

$

B&B/INN

The Inn at Weston. A short walk from the town green and a stone's throw from four ski areas, this 1848 inn is run by Bob and Linda Aldrich, whose love of plants is evident from their immaculate gardens and on-site greenhouse. **Pros:** great rooms; terrific town location. **Cons:** high-end rooms are expensive. $ *Rooms from: $185* ⊠ *630 Main St.* ☎ *802/824–6789* ⊕ *www.innweston.com* ⊃ *13 rooms* ⦿ *Breakfast.*

PERFORMING ARTS

Weston Playhouse. The oldest professional theater in Vermont produces plays, musicals, and other works. The season runs late June–early September. ⊠ *703 Main St., off Rte. 100* ☎ *802/824–5288* ⊕ *www.westonplayhouse.org.*

SHOPPING

The Vermont Country Store. This store opened in 1946 and is still run by the Orton family, though it has become something of an empire, with a large catalog and online business. One room is set aside for Vermont Common Crackers and bins of fudge and copious candy. In others you'll find nearly forgotten items such as Lilac Vegetol aftershave, as well as practical items like sturdy outdoor clothing. Nostalgia-evoking implements dangle from the rafters. The associated Bryant House restaurant next door serves three country meals a day and if you can't get enough, there's a second store on Route 103 in Rockingham. ⊠ *657 Main St.* ☎ *802/824–3184* ⊕ *www.vermontcountrystore.com.*

LUDLOW

9 miles northeast of Weston.

Ludlow is a largely nondescript industrial town whose major draw is Okemo, one of Vermont's largest and most popular ski resorts.

GETTING HERE AND AROUND

Routes 100 and 103 join in northern Ludlow, separating about 2 miles south in the small downtown, where Route 103 becomes Main Street.

WHERE TO EAT

$$

AMERICAN

Coleman Brook Tavern. Slope-side at the Jackson Gore Inn, Coleman Brook is the fanciest and most expensive of Okemo's dozen or so places to eat, but it's not formal—you'll find diners wearing ski boots crowding the tables at lunch. Large wing chairs and big banquettes line window bays. Ask to sit in the Wine Room, a separate section where tables are surrounded by their noteworthy collection of bottles. Start with a pound of mussels steamed in butter, garlic, white wine, and fresh herbs. Then move on to the sesame seed–crusted ahi tuna served over green-tea

You never know what you'll find at a rambling general store like Weston's Vermont Country Store.

soba noodles in a ginger-miso broth. The s'mores dessert is cooked over a tabletop "campfire." $ *Average main: $24* ⊠ *Jackson Gore Inn, Okemo, 111 Jackson Gore Rd.* ☎ *802/228–1435* ⊕ *www.okemo.com/ dining/coleman-brook-tavern.*

$ ✕ **Goodman's American Pie.** This place has the best wood-fired pizza in
PIZZA town. It also has character to spare: sit in chairs from old ski lifts and
FAMILY order from a counter that was once a purple VW bus. Though Goodman's is on Main Street, it's set back and somewhat hidden. Locals and Okemo regulars in the know stop by to design their own pies from 27 ingredients. There are also six specials; one of these, the Rip Curl, has mozzarella, Asiago, ricotta, chicken, fresh garlic, and fresh tomatoes. Pizza is available by the slice, and there are arcade games in the back. $ *Average main: $10* ⊠ *5 Lamere Sq.* ☎ *802/228–4271* ⊕ *www.goodmansamericanpie.com.*

$$ ✕ **Harry's.** A local favorite across from the Jackson Gore access road,
ECLECTIC this casual restaurant has a number of international influences. Traditional contemporary entrées such as roast duck are at one end of the menu and Asian and Mexican dishes at the other. The large and tasty burrito, made with fresh cilantro and black beans, is one of the best bargains around. Chef-owner Trip Pearce often uses ingredients from his own garden. He also owns the equally popular Little Harry's in Rutland. $ *Average main: $24* ⊠ *68 Rte. 100 N, Mount Holly* ☎ *802/259–2996* ⊕ *www.harryscafe.com* ☉ *Closed Mon. and Tues. No lunch.*

$$$ ✕ **The Inn at Weathersfield.** One of Vermont's best restaurants, this culi-
ECLECTIC nary gem is part of an 18th-century countryside inn. A chalkboard
Fodor's Choice in the foyer lists the farms that grow the food patrons eat. Executive
★ chef Jean-Luc Matecap, who has extensive experience cooking for top

CLOSE UP

Vermont Artisanal Cheese

Vermont is the artisanal cheese capital of the country, with several dozen creameries open to the public churning out hundreds of different cheeses. Many creameries are "farmstead" operations, meaning that the animals whose milk is made into cheese are kept on-site. If you eat enough cheese during your time in the state, you may be able to differentiate between the many types of milk (cow, goat, sheep, or even water buffalo) and make associations between the geography and climate of where you are and the taste of local cheeses.

This is one of the reasons that taking a walk around a dairy is a great idea:

you can see the process in action, from grazing to aging to eating. The **Vermont Cheese Trail map**, which you can view or download on the website of the Vermont Cheese Council (☎ 866/261–8595 ⊕ www.vtcheese.com), has a comprehensive list of dairies, many of which you can visit. Though hours are given for some, it's generally recommended that you still call ahead.

At the **Vermont Cheesemakers Festival** (☎ 802/261–8595 ⊕ www.vtcheesefest.com), which takes place in July in Shelburne, cheese makers gather to sell their various cheeses. Beer and wine are served to wash it all down.

---

restaurants in France, Nantucket, and his native Vermont, is passionate about local ingredients. His farm-to-table cuisine can be enjoyed à la carte or prix fixe. Dishes on the latter menu include roasted Cavendish game birds and dry-aged Black Watch Farm sirloin. Service is excellent, and wines are reasonably priced. For a quicker bite, have a burger or some appetizers in the tavern. In summer, enjoy your meal on the patio. $ *Average main: $25* ⊠ *1342 Rte. 106, 15 miles east of Ludlow, Perkinsville* ☎ *802/263–9217* ⊕ *www.weathersfieldinn.com* ⊗ *Closed Mon. and Tues., and Apr. and early Nov. No lunch.*

WHERE TO STAY

$

B&B/INN

Inn at Water's Edge. Former Long Islanders Bruce and Tina Verdrager converted their old ski house and barns into this comfortably refined haven, perfect for those who want to ski but not stay in town. **Pros:** bucolic setting on a lakefront; interesting house. **Cons:** ordinary rooms. $ *Rooms from: $175* ⊠ *45 Kingdom Rd., 5 miles north of town* ☎ *802/228–8143, 888/706–9736* ⊕ *www.innatwatersedge.com* ⇆ *9 rooms, 2 suites* �‖ *Some meals.*

$

B&B/INN

Inn at Weathersfield. This is the kind of place where relaxation rules, unless you want to take advantage of seasonal activities like hiking, cross-country skiing, and apple picking. **Pros:** dynamite restaurant and tavern; laid-back inn; quiet setting. **Cons:** 15-mile drive from the Okemo slopes. $ *Rooms from: $149* ⊠ *1342 Rte. 106, Perkinsville* ☎ *802/263–9217* ⊕ *www.innatweathersfield.com* ⊗ *Closed first 2 wks in Nov.* ⇆ *12 rooms* �‖ *Breakfast.*

$$$

HOTEL

FAMILY

Jackson Gore Village. This slope-side base lodge is the place to stay if your aim is Okemo skiing. **Pros:** ski-in, ski-out access to mountain; good for families. **Cons:** chaotic and noisy on weekends;

expensive. $ *Rooms from: $355* ⊠ *111 Jackson Gore Rd., off Rte. 103* ☎ *802/228–1400, 800/786–5366* ⊕ *www.okemo.com* ⬎ *263 rooms and suites* ⦿ *No meals.*

SPORTS AND THE OUTDOORS
SKI AREAS

FAMILY **Okemo Mountain Resort.** Family fun is the focus of southern Vermont's biggest ski resort, which has dozens of beginner trails, some wide intermediate runs, terrain parks throughout, a tubing facility, a nursery, an ice-rink, indoor basketball and tennis courts, and a children's pool with slides. There's even Kids' Night Out child-care program on Saturday evening during the regular season, so parents can have date nights. The Okemo Valley Nordic Center has miles of cross-country and snowshoeing trails. Summer diversions include golfing, mountain biking, and activities and rides in the Adventure Zone. The newer Jackson Gore base features the latest (and fanciest) venues the resort has to offer. **Facilities:** 121 trails; 667 acres; 2,200-foot vertical drop; 20 lifts. ⊠ *77 Okemo Ridge Rd.* ☎ *802/228–4041, 802/228–5222 for snow conditions* ⊕ *www.okemo.com* ⬏ *Lift ticket: $92.*

GRAFTON

20 miles south of Ludlow.

Out-of-the-way Grafton is as much a historical museum as a town. During its heyday, citizens grazed 10,000 sheep and spun their wool into sturdy yarn for locally woven fabric. As the wool market declined, so did Grafton. In 1963 the Windham Foundation—Vermont's second-largest private foundation—commenced the town's rehabilitation. The Old Tavern (now called The Grafton Inn) was preserved, along with many other commercial and residential structures.

8

GETTING HERE AND AROUND
Routes 11, 35, and 103 intersect in Grafton.

EXPLORING
Historical Society Museum. This endearingly cluttered museum documents the town's history with photographs, soapstone displays, musical instruments, furniture, tools, and other artifacts. ⊠ *147 Main St.* ☎ *802/843–2584* ⊕ *www.graftonhistoricalsociety.com* ⬏ *$3* ⊙ *Late May–mid-Oct., Thurs.–Mon. 10–4.*

WHERE TO STAY
$$ 🏨 **The Grafton Inn.** One of the country's oldest operating inns, this
B&B/INN 1801 classic encourages you to linger on its wraparound porches, in its authentically Colonial common rooms, or with a book by the fire in its old-fashioned library. **Pros:** classic Vermont inn and tavern; professionally run; appealing common areas. **Cons:** rooms are attractive but not stellar. $ *Rooms from: $200* ⊠ *92 Main St.* ☎ *802/234–8689, 800/843–1801* ⊕ *www.graftoninnvermont.com* ⬎ *24 rooms, 6 suites, 5 houses* ⦿ *Breakfast.*

SHOPPING

Gallery North Star. Inside this restored 1877 home, original oil paintings, watercolors, lithographs, and sculptures by more than 30 New England artists are on display. ✉ *151 Townshend Rd.* ☎ *802/843–2465* 🌐 *www.gnsgrafton.com* 🕒 *Daily 10–5.*

Grafton Village Cheese Company. You can sample the best of Vermont cheddar at this downtown wine and cheese shop. ✉ *56 Townshend Rd.* ☎ *802/843–1062* 🌐 *www.graftonvillagecheese.com.*

TOWNSHEND

9 miles south of Grafton.

One of a string of attractive villages along the banks of the West River, Townshend embodies the Vermont ideal of a lush town green presided over by a gracefully proportioned church spire. The spire belongs to the 1790 Congregational Meeting House, one of the state's oldest houses of worship. North on Route 30 is the Scott Bridge, the state's longest single-span covered bridge. It makes for a pretty photo, though it's in a state of disrepair and therefore closed to foot and vehicle traffic.

GETTING HERE AND AROUND

Route 35 heading south from Grafton dead-ends into Route 30 at Townshend Common. Route 30 is the town's main drag.

EXPLORING

OFF THE BEATEN PATH

Newfane. With a village green surrounded by pristine white buildings, Newfane, 6 miles southeast of Townshend, is sometimes described as the quintessential New England small town. The 1839 First Congregational Church and the Windham County Court House, with green-shuttered windows and a rounded cupola, are often open. The building with the four-pointed spire is Union Hall, built in 1832. ✉ *Newfane* 🌐 *www.newfanevt.com.*

WHERE TO EAT

$ AMERICAN DINER

🍴 **Townshend Dam Diner.** Folks come from miles around to enjoy traditional fare such as meat loaf, roast beef, chili, and croquettes, as well as Townshend-raised bison burgers and creative daily specials. Breakfast, served all day, includes raspberry-chocolate-chip walnut pancakes and homemade French toast. You can sit at any of the 1930s enamel-top tables or in the big swivel chairs at the U-shaped counter. The diner is a few miles northwest of the village. [$] *Average main: $8* ✉ *5929 Rte. 30, West Townshend* ☎ *802/874–4107* 💳 *No credit cards* 🕒 *Closed Tues.*

WHERE TO STAY

$ B&B/INN

🏨 **Boardman House.** This handsome Greek Revival home on the town green combines modern comfort with the relaxed charm of a 19th-century farmhouse. **Pros:** inexpensive; perfect village green location. **Cons:** no phone, mobile reception is bad. [$] *Rooms from: $80* ✉ *Grafton Rd.* ☎ *802/365–4086* 💳 *No credit cards* 🛏 *4 rooms, 1 suite* 🍽 *Breakfast.*

$$ B&B/INN

🏨 **Four Columns Inn.** Rooms and suites in this white-columned, 1834 Greek Revival mansion were designed for luxurious romantic getaways. **Pros:** updated rooms; heart of town. **Cons:** little entertainment in these parts. $ *Rooms from: $225* ⊠ *21 West St., Newfane* ☎ *802/365–7713* ⊕ *www.fourcolumnsvt.com* ⮑ *15 rooms, 1 cottage* †○† *Breakfast.*

$$
B&B/INN

☷ **Windham Hill Inn.** As there's not too much to do nearby, you might find yourself sitting by a fire or swimming in the outdoor pool at this inn, part of the Relais & Châteaux collection. **Pros:** West River Valley views; exceedingly cozy spa. **Cons:** expensive; staff not always helpful. $ *Rooms from: $259* ⊠ *311 Lawrence Dr., West Townshend* ☎ *802/874–4080, 800/944–4080* ⊕ *www.windhamhill.com* ⮑ *11 rooms, 10 suites, 1 cottage* †○† *Breakfast.*

SPORTS AND THE OUTDOORS

Townshend State Park. At this park you'll find a sandy beach and a trail that climbs up a ravine full of small chutes and waterfalls. The hike here leads to views at the summit of 1,680-foot Bald Mountain. ⊠ *2755 State Forest Rd.* ☎ *802/365–7500* ⊕ *www.vtstateparks.com/htm/townshend. htm* ☾ *Facilities closed early Sept.–late May.*

CENTRAL VERMONT

Central Vermont's economy once centered on marble quarrying and mills. But today, as in much of the state, tourism drives the economic engine. The center of the dynamo is Killington, the East's largest downhill ski resort, but there's more to discover in central Vermont than high-speed chairlifts and slope-side condos. The old mills of Quechee and Middlebury now house restaurants and shops, with wonderful views of the waterfalls that once powered the mill turbines. Woodstock has upscale shops and a national historic park. Away from these settlements, the protected lands (except for occasional logging) of the Green Mountain National Forest are laced with hiking trails.

8

NORWICH

6 miles north of White River Junction.

On the bank of the Connecticut River, Norwich is graced with beautifully maintained 18th- and 19th-century homes set about a handsome green. Norwich is the Vermont sister town to sophisticated Hanover, New Hampshire (home of Dartmouth College), across the river.

GETTING HERE AND AROUND

Most attractions are off Interstate 91; the town sits a mile to the west.

EXPLORING

FAMILY
Fodor$Choice
★

Montshire Museum of Science. Numerous hands-on exhibits at this science museum explore nature and technology. Kids can make giant bubbles, see images from NASA space telescopes, watch marine life swim in aquariums, and explore a maze of outdoor trails by the river. Adults will happily join the fun. An ideal destination for a rainy day, this is one of the finest museums in New England. ⊠ *1 Montshire Rd.* ☎ *802/649–2200* ⊕ *www.montshire.org* ✉ *$16 mid-June–early Sept., $14 early Sept.–mid-June* ☾ *Daily 10–5.*

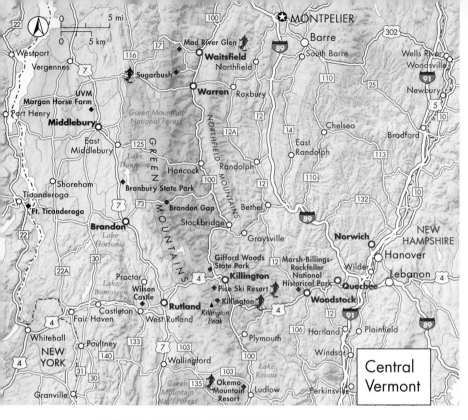

SPORTS AND THE OUTDOORS

Lake Morey Ice Skating Trail. For the most fun you can have on skates, head to American's longest ice-skating trail. From January to March, the frozen lake is groomed for ice-skating, providing a magical 4½-mile route amid forested hillsides. Bring your own skates or rent them at the Lake Morey Resort, which maintains the trail. ⊠ *1 Clubhouse Rd., Fairlee* ☎ *800/423–1211* ⊕ *www.lakemoreyresort.com.*

SHOPPING

King Arthur Flour Baker's Store. This shop is a must-see for those who love bread. The shelves are stocked with all the ingredients and tools in the company's *Baker's Catalogue*, including flours, mixes, and local jams, and syrups. The bakery has a viewing area where you can watch products being made, and you can learn to bake them yourself at classes conducted on-site. The store is a fine spot for a quick bite if you're driving along Interstate 91; the timber-frame café serves high-quality pizzas, sandwiches, and baked items. ⊠ *135 U.S. 5 S* ☎ *802/649–3361* ⊕ *www.kingarthurflour.com* ☉ *Daily 7:30–6.*

QUECHEE

11 miles southwest of Norwich, 6 miles west of White River Junction.

A historic mill town, Quechee sits just upriver from its namesake gorge, an impressive 165-foot-deep canyon cut by the Ottauquechee River. Most people view the gorge from U.S. 4. To escape the crowds, hike along the gorge or scramble down one of several trails to the river.

EXPLORING

FAMILY Fodor'sChoice ★ **Simon Pearce.** A restored woolen mill by a waterfall holds Quechee's main attraction, this marvelous glassblowing factory, store, and restaurant. Water power still drives the factory's furnace; take a free self-guided tour of the downstairs factory floor, and see the amazing glassblowers at work. The store sells beautifully crafted contemporary glass and ceramic tableware. An excellent, sophisticated restaurant with outstanding views of the falls uses Simon Pearce glassware and is justifiably popular. ✉ *The Mill, 1760 Quechee Main St.* ☎ *802/295–2711* 🌐 *www.simonpearce.com* 🕒 *Daily 10–9.*

FAMILY **Vermont Institute of Natural Science Nature Center.** Next to Quechee Gorge, this science center has 17 raptor exhibits, including bald eagles, peregrine falcons, and owls. All caged birds have been found injured and are unable to survive in the wild. Raptors Up Close, a 30-minute live bird program, starts daily at 1:30. ✉ *6565 Woodstock Rd.* ☎ *802/359–5000* 🌐 *www.vinsweb.org* 🎟 *$13.50* 🕒 *Mid-Apr.–Oct., daily 10–5; Nov.–mid-Apr., daily 10–4.*

WHERE TO EAT AND STAY

$$$ AMERICAN Fodor'sChoice ★ 🍴 **Simon Pearce.** Sparkling glassware from the studio downstairs, exposed brick, flickering candles, and large windows overlooking the falls of the roaring Ottauquechee River create an ideal setting for contemporary American cuisine. The food here is worthy of a pilgrimage: horseradish-crusted blue cod with crispy leeks, herbed mashed potatoes, and a balsamic shallot reduction is a house specialty, as is roast duck with mango chutney sauce. The wine cellar holds several hundred labels. [$] *Average main: $28* ✉ *The Mill, 1760 Main St.* ☎ *802/295–1470* 🌐 *www.simonpearce.com.*

$$ B&B/INN 🏨 **The Parker House Inn.** This beautiful 1857 house on the National Historic Register once belonged to Senator Joseph Parker, who also owned the textile mill next door. **Pros:** riverfront location; spacious rooms. **Cons:** no yard. [$] *Rooms from: $245* ✉ *1792 Main St.* ☎ *802/295–6077, 800/295–6077* 🌐 *www.theparkerhouseinn.com* 🛏 *7 rooms* 🍽 *Breakfast.*

$$ B&B/INN 🏨 **Quechee Inn at Marshland Farm.** Each room in this handsomely restored 1793 country home has Queen Anne–style furnishings and period antiques. **Pros:** historic house; spacious grounds. **Cons:** some bathrooms are dated; fills up with weddings. [$] *Rooms from: $287* ✉ *1119 Main St.* ☎ *802/295–3133, 800/235–3133* 🌐 *www.quecheeinn.com* 🛏 *22 rooms, 3 suites* 🍽 *Breakfast.*

Simon Pearce is a glassblowing factory, store, and restaurant; the factory's furnace is still powered by hydroelectricity from Quechee Falls.

SPORTS AND THE OUTDOORS

Wilderness Trails and Vermont Fly Fishing School. In summer, Wilderness Trails leads fly-fishing workshops; rents bikes, canoes, kayaks, and paddleboards; and arranges guided canoe, kayaking, and hiking trips. In winter, the company conducts cross-country skiing and snowshoeing treks. ⊠ *1119 Quechee Main St.* ☎ *802/295–7620* ⊕ *www.wildernesstrailsvermont.com.*

SHOPPING

FAMILY **Quechee Gorge Village.** Hundreds of dealers sell their wares at this antiques and crafts mall in a reconstructed barn that also houses a country store and a classic diner. Outlets for Cabot and Danforth Pewter neighbor an ice cream shop and a toy and train museum, where a merry-go-round and a small-scale working railroad operate when weather permits. ⊠ *573 Woodstock Rd., off U.S. 4* ☎ *802/295–1550* ⊕ *www.quecheegorge.com.*

Scotland by the Yard. This store sells all things Celtic, from kilts to argyle jackets and tartan ties. ⊠ *8828 Woodstock Rd.* ☎ *802/295–5351* ⊕ *www.scotlandbytheyard.com.*

WOODSTOCK

4 miles west of Quechee.

Woodstock is a Currier & Ives print come to life. Well-maintained Federal-style houses surround the tree-lined village green, which is not far from a covered bridge. The town owes much of its pristine appearance to the Rockefeller family's interest in historic preservation and land conservation and to native George Perkins Marsh, a congressman, diplomat, and conservationist who wrote the pioneering book *Man and Nature* (1864) about humanity's use and abuse of the land. Only busy U.S. 4 mars the tableau.

ESSENTIALS

Visitor Information Woodstock Vermont Area Chamber of Commerce. ⊠ *59 Central St.* ☎ *802/457–3555, 888/496–6378* ⊕ *www.woodstockvt.com.*

EXPLORING

FAMILY **Billings Farm and Museum.** Founded by Frederick H. Billings in 1871, this is one of the oldest operating dairy farms in the country. In addition to watching the herds of Jersey cows, horses, and other farm animals at work and play, you can tour the restored 1890 farmhouse, and in the adjacent barns learn about 19th-century farming and domestic life. The biggest takeaway, however, is a renewed belief in sustainable agriculture and stewardship of the land. Pick up some raw-milk cheddar while you're here. ⊠ *5302 River Rd., ½ mile north of Woodstock* ☎ *802/457–2355* ⊕ *www.billingsfarm.org* 🎫 *$14* ⊙ *May–Oct., daily 10–5; Nov.–Feb., weekends 10–4.*

Marsh-Billings-Rockefeller National Historical Park. Vermont's only national park is the nation's first to focus on conserving natural resources. The pristine 555-acre spread includes the mansion, gardens, and carriage roads of Frederick H. Billings (1823–1890), a financier and the president of the Northern Pacific Railway. The entire property was the gift of Laurance S. Rockefeller (1910–2004), who lived here with his wife, Mary (Billings's granddaughter). You can learn more at the visitor center, tour the residential complex with a guide every hour on the hour, and explore the 20 miles of trails and old carriage roads that climb Mt. Tom. ⊠ *54 Elm St.* ☎ *802/457–3368* ⊕ *www.nps.gov/mabi* 🎫 *Tour $8* ⊙ *Mansion and garden tours: late May–Oct., daily 10–5. Grounds daily sunrise–sunset.*

WHERE TO EAT

$$$$ ✕ **Barnard Inn Restaurant and Max's Tavern.** The dining room in this 1796 AMERICAN brick farmhouse exudes 18th-century charm, but the food is decidedly 21st century. Former San Francisco restaurant chef-owner Will Dodson creates inventive three-course prix-fixe menus with specialties like seafood curry and Wiener schnitzel with lemon-caper sauce. In the back is a relaxed local favorite, Max's Tavern, which serves some of the same dishes à la carte, along with upscale pub fare. 💲 *Average main: $65* ⊠ *5518 Rte. 12, 8 miles north of Woodstock, Barnard* ☎ *802/234–9961* ⊕ *www.barnardinn.com* ⊙ *Closed Sun. and Mon. No lunch* 🍴 *Reservations essential.*

$$$$ ✕ **Cloudland Farm.** With the table literally on the farm, this restaurant AMERICAN delivers a unique farm-to-table experience that makes it worth the short drive from Woodstock. Prix-fixe dinners ($45) are served on Friday, Saturday, and most Thursdays. All ingredients for the seasonal menu come fresh from the farm or from other growers; Cloudland's own pork and beef figure in such main dishes as maple-glazed ham with apple-and-onion compote, and beef shank osso bucco with sautéed kale and beef bacon. The desserts—among them homemade carrot cake with

8

red wine caramel and carrot jam—are delicious. Bring your own wine or beer, and the restaurant will provide glassware and a corkscrew for a small corkage. $ *Average main: $45 ✉ 1101 Cloudland Rd., North Pomfret* ☎ *802/457–2599 ⊕ www.cloudlandfarm.com ⊗ Closed Sun.– Wed., and Mar. No lunch ⌂ Reservations essential.*

$$ ✕ **Keeper's Café.** Creatively prepared, moderately priced fare draws cus-
CAFÉ tomers from all over the region to chef Chris Loucka's café. The organic dishes he prepares include char-grilled kielbasa and an arugula-and-beet salad. Located in a former general store, the three dining rooms feel relaxed, with locals table-hopping to chat with friends. $ *Average main: $22 ✉ 3685 Rte. 106, 12 miles south of Woodstock, Reading* ☎ *802/484–9090 ⊕ www.keeperscafe.com ⊗ Closed Sun. and Mon. No lunch.*

$$ ✕ **Pane e Saluto.** Don't let the size fool you: meals at this little upstairs
ITALIAN restaurant are exciting and memorable, thanks to young couple Deir-
Fodor's Choice dre Heekin and Caleb Barker. Hip decor, an intimately small space,
★ and Heekin's discreetly passionate front-of-house direction all come together to complement Barker's slow food–inspired dishes. Try *ragù d'agnello e maiale* (spaghetti with a ragù of roasted lamb and pork) followed by *cotechino e lenticchie* (garlic sausage with lentils). Reserve well in advance, as this tiny osteria fills up fast. The couple also run a farm and winery in Barnard, a consuming endeavor that often results in them closing the restaurant for weeks at a time; it's wise to call ahead before coming to make sure it's open. $ *Average main: $22 ✉ 61 Central St.* ☎ *802/457–4882 ⊕ www.osteriapaneesalute.com ⊗ Closed Mon.–Thurs., and Apr., Sept.–mid-Oct., and late Nov. No lunch ⌂ Reservations essential.*

$$ ✕ **The Prince and the Pauper.** Modern French and American fare with a
FRENCH Vermont accent is the focus of this candlelit Colonial restaurant off the town green. The grilled duck breast might have an Asian five-spice sauce, and the boneless rack of lamb is wrapped in puff pastry and splashed with bordelaise sauce. Three-course prix-fixe meals cost $51; a less expensive bistro menu is available in the lounge. If you like the artwork hanging above your table, you can purchase it. $ *Average main: $21 ✉ 24 Elm St.* ☎ *802/457–1818 ⊕ www.princeandpauper. com ⊗ No lunch.*

$ ✕ **Worthy Kitchen.** Be sure to consult the chalkboard near the entrance,
AMERICAN so you can place your order for small bites, sandwiches, sides, and
FAMILY perhaps a craft beer at the bar. Then, grab a seat at a booth under the lofty, wood-beam ceilings in the dining room or at a table outside on the patio. Your meal will be ready in just a few minutes. The owners describe their eatery as a "farm diner," an apt description for a place serving locally sourced comfort food that's by turns decadent, familiar, and fresh. Go with anything fried, from buttermilk chicken to dough-nuts. Up the road in South Royalton, the same people run the immensely popular Worthy Burger. $ *Average main: 10 ✉ 442 Woodstock Rd.* ☎ *802/457–7281 ⊕ www.worthyvermont.com ⊗ No lunch weekdays.*

The upscale Woodstock area is known as Vermont's horse country.

WHERE TO STAY

$$
B&B/INN
Fodor's Choice
★

The Fan House Bed and Breakfast. If you're searching for an authentic inn in the heart of a textbook Vermont town, consider this Colonial dating to 1840. **Pros:** center of old town; plenty of creature comforts; good library; real sense of home. **Cons:** upstairs rooms can be cool in winter. *$ Rooms from: $200 ✉ 6297 Rte. 12 N ☎ 802/234–6704 ⊕ www.thefanhouse.com ▭ No credit cards ☾ Closed Apr. ⬐ 2 rooms, 1 suite ⦿ Breakfast.*

$$
B&B/INN

Kedron Valley Inn. You're likely to fall in love at first sight with the main 1828 three-story brick building here, the centerpiece of a 15-acre retreat. **Pros:** good food; quiet setting; handsome main building. **Cons:** 5 miles south of Woodstock. *$ Rooms from: $259 ✉ 4778 South Rd., South Woodstock ☎ 802/457–1473, 800/836–1193 ⊕ www.kedronvalleyinn.com ☾ Closed Apr. ⬐ 24 rooms, 1 suite ⦿ Breakfast.*

$
HOTEL

The Shire Riverview Motel. Many rooms in this immaculate motel have decks, and most have fabulous views of Ottauquechee River, which runs right along the building. **Pros:** inexpensive access to the heart of Woodstock; views. **Cons:** basic rooms; unexciting exterior. *$ Rooms from: $175 ✉ 46 Pleasant St. ☎ 802/457–2211 ⊕ www.shiremotel.com ⬐ 42 rooms ⦿ No meals.*

$$$$
RESORT
Fodor's Choice
★

Twin Farms. Let's just get it out there: Twin Farms is the best lodging in Vermont; if you can afford it (stays begin at well more than $1,000 a night), you'll want to experience it. **Pros:** impeccable service; gorgeous rooms; sensational meals. **Cons:** steep prices. *$ Rooms from: $1900 ✉ 452 Royalton Tpke., Barnard ☎ 802/234–9999 ⊕ www.twinfarms.com ☾ Closed Apr. ⬐ 10 rooms and suites, 10 cottages ⦿ All-inclusive.*

8

$$$ RESORT Fodor's Choice ★ **The Woodstock Inn and Resort.** Far from the main road but still on Woodstock's gorgeous green, this resort has a hard-to-beat location. **Pros:** attractive historic property; numerous amenities; soothing spa. **Cons:** can lack intimacy. [$] *Rooms from: $315* ✉ *14 The Green* ☎ *802/332–6853, 888/338–2745* 🌐 *www.woodstockinn.com* 🛏 *135 rooms, 7 suites* 🍴 *No meals.*

SPORTS AND THE OUTDOORS

GOLF

Woodstock Inn and Resort Golf Club. Robert Trent Jones Sr. designed the resort's challenging course. ✉ *76 South St.* ☎ *802/457–6674, 888/338–2745* 🌐 *www.woodstockinn.com/golf-club* 🎫 *$59 for 9 holes, $79 for 18 holes, weekdays; $79 for 9 holes, $125 for 18 holes, weekends* ⛳ *18 holes, 6000 yards, par 70.*

SHOPPING

ART GALLERIES

Gallery on the Green. This corner gallery in one of Woodstock's oldest buildings showcases paintings by New England artists depicting regional landscapes. ✉ *1 The Green* ☎ *802/457–4956* 🌐 *www.galleryonthegreen.com.*

CRAFTS

Collective. This funky and attractive shop sells local jewelry, glass, pottery, and clothing. ✉ *47 Central St.* ☎ *802/457–1298* 🌐 *www.collective-theartofcraft.com.*

FOOD

Sugarbush Farm. Take the Taftsville Covered Bridge to this farm, where you can learn how maple sugar is made and can sample as much maple syrup as you'd like. The farm also makes excellent cheeses. ✉ *591 Sugarbush Farm Rd., off U.S. 4* ☎ *802/457–1757, 800/281–1757* 🌐 *www.sugarbushfarm.com.*

Taftsville Country Store. East of town, the store sells Vermont cheeses, moderately priced wines, and Vermont-made specialty foods. ✉ *404 U.S. 4, Taftsville* ☎ *802/457–1135* 🌐 *www.taftsville.com.*

Village Butcher. This emporium of Vermont edibles has great sandwiches, cheeses, local beers, and delicious baked goods—perfect for a picnic or for lunch on the go. ✉ *18 Elm St.* ☎ *802/457–2756* 🌐 *www.thebutcher.biz.*

Woodstock Farmers' Market. The market is a year-round buffet of local produce, fresh fish, and excellent sandwiches and pastries. The maple-walnut scones go fast, so get there early. ✉ *468 Woodstock Rd., aka U.S. 4* ☎ *802/457–3658* 🌐 *www.woodstockfarmersmarket.com* 🕒 *Closed Mon.*

SPAS

Out of the Woods Spa at Twin Farms. A visit to Twin Farms is a trip to another world, and a spa treatment here completes the getaway. The spa at the luxury lodging expounds a philosophy of wellness that goes beyond the realm of massages and skin treatments. Employing an organic product line by Vermont-based Tata Harper and Lunaroma, the spa offers facials, polishes, aromatherapy, massages, and mud wraps that administer a heavenly reboot to your skin and muscles. ⊠ *Twin Farms, 452 Royalton Tpke., Barnard* ☎ *802/234–9999* ⊕ *www. twinfarms.com/experience/spa.*

Spa at the Woodstock Inn and Resort. A mesmerizing, 10,000-square-foot, nature-inspired facility, this LEED-certified spa has 10 treatment rooms, a full-service salon, and a sophisticated shop devoted to wellness and relaxation. Elegant, minimalist design accentuates the beautiful setting: natural light pours into sparkling dressing rooms and the firelit Great Room, and an outdoor meditation courtyard has a soaking pool and a Scandinavian-style sauna that face the sky. The mood is serene, the treatments varied: opt for The Works, and you'll receive a massage, a facial, a manicure, and a pedicure over the course of five or six hours. ⊠ *Woodstock Inn and Resort, 14 The Green* ☎ *802/457–6697, 888/338–2745* ⊕ *www.woodstockinn.com/spa.*

KILLINGTON

15 miles east of Rutland.

With only a gas station, a post office, a motel, and a few shops at the intersection of U.S. 4 and Route 100, it doesn't quite feel like the East's largest ski resort is nearby. The village of Killington has suffered from unfortunate strip development along the access road to the ski resort, but the 360-degree views atop Killington Peak, accessible via the resort's gondola, make it worth the drive.

WHERE TO STAY

$$
B&B/INN
☷ **Birch Ridge Inn.** A slate-covered carriageway about a mile from the Killington ski resort leads to one of the area's most popular off-mountain stays, a former executive retreat in two renovated A-frames. **Pros:** quirky design; well-maintained property; tasty cuisine. **Cons:** oddly furnished; outdated style. Ⓢ *Rooms from: $200* ⊠ *37 Butler Rd.* ☎ *802/422–4293, 800/435–8566* ⊕ *www.birchridge.com* ۞ *Closed May* ⤳ *10 rooms* ⦿*Breakfast.*

$$
RESORT
FAMILY
☷ **The Mountain Top Inn & Resort.** This cross-country skiing and horseback riding haven has stunning views and laid-back yet luxurious accommodations. **Pros:** family-friendly vibe; great spot for outdoor activities. **Cons:** fees for activities can add up. Ⓢ *Rooms from: $275* ⊠ *195 Mountain Top Rd., Chittenden* ☎ *802/483–2311* ⊕ *www.mountaintopinn. com* ⤳ *32 rooms, 4 cabins, 4 cottages, 18 rental homes and condos* ⦿ *No meals.*

$$
RESORT
☷ **The Woods Resort & Spa.** Not a traditional hotel or resort, the Woods is a collection of upscale two- and three-bedroom town houses on wooded lots along a winding road. **Pros:** contemporary facility; spacious rooms; access to spa, pool, and tennis courts; private shuttle to ski area. **Cons:** lacks traditional Vermont feel; several management companies handle the units. Ⓢ *Rooms from: $250* ⊠ *53 Woods La.* ☎ *802/422–3100* ⊕ *www.woodsresort.net* ⤳ *107 units* ⦿ *No meals.*

8

NIGHTLIFE

McGrath's Irish Pub. On weekends, listen to live Irish music and sip Guinness draft at the Inn at Long Trail's pub. ⊠ 709 U.S. 4 ☎ 802/755–7181 ⊕ www.innatlongtrail.com.

Pickle Barrel Night Club. During ski season, this club has live music on Friday and Saturday. After 8, the crowd moves downstairs for dancing, sometimes to big-name bands. ⊠ 1741 Killington Rd. ☎ 802/422–3035 ⊕ www.picklebarrelnightclub.com.

Wobbly Barn. Twentysomethings dance at the Wobbly Barn nightclub, open during ski season, and families dig into giant steaks and graze at the salad bar in the restaurant. ⊠ 2229 Killington Rd. ☎ 802/422–6171 ⊕ www.wobblybarn.com.

SPORTS AND THE OUTDOORS

BIKING

True Wheels Bike Shop. Part of the Basin Sports complex, this shop rents bicycles and has information about local routes. ⊠ 2886 Killington Rd. ☎ 802/422–3234, 877/487–9972 ⊕ www.basinski.com/our-stores/true-wheels.

CROSS-COUNTRY SKIING

The Mountain Top Inn & Resort. This resort has 37 miles of hilly trails groomed for cross-country skiing, 24 miles of which can be used for skate skiing. You can also enjoy snowshoeing, ice-skating, and snowmobile and sleigh rides. Summer activities include horseback riding, clay-bird shooting, fishing, hiking, sand volleyball, and water sports. ⊠ 195 Mountaintop Rd., Chittenden ☎ 802/483–2311 ⊕ www.mountaintopinn.com 🎟 Trail pass $18 per half day, $22 per day for guests not staying overnight.

FISHING

Gifford Woods State Park. This state park's Kent Pond is a terrific fishing spot. ⊠ 34 Gifford Woods Rd., ½ mile north of U.S. 4 ☎ 802/775–5354 ⊕ www.vtstateparks.com/htm/gifford.htm ☉ Facilities closed late Oct.–mid-May.

GOLF

Killington Golf Course. At its namesake resort, the course has a challenging layout. ⊠ 4763 Killington Rd. ☎ 802/422–6700 ⊕ www.killington.com/summer/golf_course 🎟 $30 for 9 holes and $50 for 18 holes, weekdays; $40 for 9 holes and $65 for 18 holes, weekends �🏌 18 holes, 6186 yards, par 72 ☉ Closed mid-Oct.–mid-May.

HIKING

Deer Leap Trail. This 3-mile round-trip hike begins near the Inn at Long Trail and leads to a great view overlooking Sherburne Gap and Pico Peak. ⊠ Trailhead off U.S. 4, just east of Inn at Long Trail, Rutland.

SKI AREAS

FAMILY
Fodor's Choice
★

Killington. "Megamountain" aptly describes Killington. Thanks to its extensive snowmaking capacity, the resort typically opens in early November, and the lifts often run into late April or early May. Skiing includes everything from Outer Limits, the East's steepest and longest mogul trail, to the 6½-mile Great Eastern. The 22-foot Superpipe is one of the best rated in the East. There are also acres of glades. Après-ski activities are plentiful, and Killington ticket holders can also ski Pico Mountain—a shuttle connects the two areas. Summer activities at Killington–Pico include mountain biking, hiking, and golf. **Facilities:** 155 trails; 1,509 acres; 3,050-foot vertical drop; 22 lifts. ■**TIP**➔ **Park at the base of the Skyeship Gondola to avoid the more crowded access road.** ✉ *4763 Killington Rd.* ☎ *802/422–3261 for snow conditions, 802/621–6867* ⊕ *www.killington.com* ☕ *Lift ticket: $96.*

Pico. When weekend hordes descend upon Killington, locals head to Pico. One of Killington's "seven peaks," Pico is physically separated from its parent resort. Trails range from elevator-shaft steep to challenging intermediate runs near the summit. Easier terrain can be found near the bottom of the mountain's nearly 2,000-foot vertical drop, and the learning slope is separated from the upper mountain, so hotshots won't bomb through it. The lower express quad can get crowded, but the upper one rarely has a line. **Facilities:** 57 trails; 468 acres; 1,967-foot vertical drop; 7 lifts. ✉ *73 Alpine Dr., Mendon* ☎ *802/422–6200, 802/422–1200 for snow conditions* ⊕ *www.picomountain.com* ☕ *Lift ticket: $69.*

SNOWMOBILE TOURS

Snowmobile Vermont. Blazing down forest trails on a snowmobile is one way Vermonters embrace the winter landscapes. Rentals are available through Snowmobile Vermont at several locations, including Killington and Okemo. Both have hour-long guided tours across groomed ski trails ($99). If you're feeling more adventurous, take the two-hour backcountry tour through 25 miles of Calvin Coolidge State Forest ($154). ✉ *170 Rte. 100, Bridgewater Corners* ☎ *802/422–2121* ⊕ *www.snowmobilevermont.com.*

8

RUTLAND

15 miles southwest of Killington, 32 miles south of Middlebury.

The strip malls and seemingly endless row of traffic lights on and around U.S. 7 in Rutland are very un-Vermont. Two blocks west, however, stand the mansions of marble magnates. In Rutland you can grab a bite and see some interesting marble, and Depot Park hosts the county farmers' market Saturday 9–2. This isn't a place to spend too much time sightseeing, though.

ESSENTIALS

Visitor Information Rutland Region Chamber of Commerce. ✉ *50 Merchants Row* ☎ *802/773–2747, 800/756–8880* ⊕ *www.rutlandvermont.com.*

EXPLORING

Chaffee Art Center. Housed in a beautiful mansion, the center exhibits the work of more than 200 Vermont artists. A second location is open downtown on Merchants Row. ✉ *16 S. Main St.* ☎ *802/775–0356* ⊕ *www.chaffeeartcenter.org* ☕ *Free* ⊙ *Thurs. and Fri. noon–6, Sat. noon–4.*

New England Maple Museum. Maple syrup is Vermont's signature product, and this museum north of Rutland explains the history and process of

turning sap into syrup. If you don't get a chance to visit a sugarhouse, this is a fine place to sample the different grades and pick up some souvenirs. ✉ *4578 U.S. 7, 9 miles south of Brandon, Pittsford* ☎ *802/483–9414* 🌐 *www.maplemuseum.com* 🎟 *Museum $5* 🕒 *Daily 10–4.*

Paramount Theatre. The highlight of downtown Rutland is this 838-seat gilded playhouse, an architectural gem dating to 1913. The gorgeous theater presents music, theater, films, and stand-up comedy. ✉ *30 Center St.* ☎ *802/775–0570* 🌐 *www.paramountvt.org.*

Vermont Marble Museum. This monument to marble highlights one of the main industries in this region. The hall of presidents has a carved bust of each U.S. president, and in the marble chapel is a replica of Leonardo da Vinci's *Last Supper.* Elsewhere, you can watch a sculptor-in-residence at work, compare marble from around the world, learn about the geological history of the Earth, and check out the Vermont Marble Company's original "stone library." A short walk away is the original quarry, which helped finish the U.S. Supreme Court. ✉ *52 Main St., off Rte. 3, Proctor* ☎ *800/427–1396, 802/459–2750* 🌐 *www.vermont-marble.com* 🎟 *$7* 🕒 *Mid-May–Oct., daily 10–5.*

Wilson Castle. Completed in 1867, this 32-room mansion was built over the course of eight years by a Vermonter who married a British aristocrat. Within the opulent setting are 84 stained-glass windows (one inset with 32 Australian opals), hand-painted Italian frescoes, and 13 fireplaces. The place is magnificently furnished with European and Asian objets d'art. October evenings bring haunted castle tours. ✉ *2708 West St., Proctor* ☎ *802/773–3284* 🌐 *www.wilsoncastle.com* 🎟 *$10* 🕒 *Late May–late Oct., daily 9–5; last tour at 5.*

WHERE TO EAT

$$ ECLECTIC 🍴 **Little Harry's.** Laminated photos of regular customers adorn the tabletops of this restaurant, which locals have packed since 1997, when chef-owners Trip Pearce and Jack Mangan brought Vermont-cheddar ravioli and lamb lo mein to downtown Rutland. If you have a big appetite on a small budget, try the signature pad thai. The place is "little" compared to the bigger Harry's, near Ludlow. [$] *Average main: $20* ✉ *121 West St.* ☎ *802/747–4848* 🌐 *www.littleharrys.com* 🕒 *No lunch.*

SPORTS AND THE OUTDOORS

BOATING

Woodard Marine. Rent pontoon boats, speedboats, stand-up paddleboards, and kayaks at the Lake Bomoseen Marina. ✉ *145 Creek Rd., off Rte. 4A, Castleton* ☎ *802/265–3690* 🌐 *www.woodardmarine.com.*

HIKING

Mountain Travelers. This place sells hiking, sporting, and boating equipment; gives advice on local hikes; and rents skis. ✉ *147 U.S. 4 E* ☎ *802/775–0814* 🌐 *www.mtntravelers.com.*

BRANDON

15 miles northwest of Rutland.

Thanks to an active group of artists, tiny Brandon is making a name for itself. In 2003 the Brandon Artists Guild, led by American folk artist

Warren Kimble, auctioned off 40 life-size fiberglass pigs painted by local artists. The "Really Really Pig Show" raised money for the guild, and has since brought small-town fame to this community through its annual shows. Brandon is also home to the Basin Bluegrass Festival, held in July.

ESSENTIALS

Visitor Information Brandon Visitor Center. ✉ *4 Grove St.* ☎ *802/247–6401* 🌐 *www.brandon.org.*

EXPLORING

Brandon Artists Guild. The guild exhibits and sells affordable paintings, sculpture, and pottery by more than 50 local member artists. ✉ *7 Center St.* ☎ *802/247–4956* 🌐 *www.brandonartistsguild.org/the-gallery* 🎟 *Free* ⏲ *Daily 10–7.*

Brandon Museum at the Stephen A. Douglas Birthplace. The famous statesman was born in this house in 1813. He left 20 years later to establish himself as a lawyer, becoming a three-time U.S. senator and arguing more cases before the U.S. Supreme Court than anyone else. This museum recounts the early Douglas years, early town history, and the antislavery movement in Vermont, the first state to abolish slavery. ✉ *4 Grove St., at U.S. 7* ☎ *802/247–6401* 🌐 *www.brandon.org* 🎟 *Free* ⏲ *Mid-May–mid-Oct., daily 11–4.*

WHERE TO EAT AND STAY

$$ CAFÉ 🍴 **Café Provence.** Robert Barral, the former director of the New England Culinary Institute, graces Brandon with this informal eatery one story above the main street. Flowered seat cushions, dried-flower window valences, and other hints of Barral's Provençal birthplace abound. His café specializes in eclectic farm-fresh dishes: the goat-cheese cake with mesclun greens, braised veal cheeks, and caramelized endive, and the portobello pizza from the restaurant's hearth oven both count among recent favorites. Sunday brunch offerings include buttery pastries, eggs Benedict, and breakfast pizza. There's outdoor seating under large umbrellas. [$] *Average main: $20* ✉ *11 Center St.* ☎ *802/247–9997* 🌐 *www.cafeprovencevt.com* ⏲ *Closed Mon. in winter.*

$$ B&B/INN Fodor's Choice ★ 🏨 **Blueberry Hill Inn.** In the Green Mountain National Forest, 5½ miles off a mountain pass on a dirt road, you'll find this secluded inn with lush gardens and a pond with a wood-fired sauna on its bank. **Pros:** peaceful setting within the national forest; lots of activities; great food. **Cons:** fills up with wedding parties. [$] *Rooms from: $269* ✉ *1245 Goshen–Ripton Rd., Goshen* ☎ *802/247–6735* 🌐 *www.blueberryhillinn.com* 🛏 *12 rooms* 🍽 *Some meals.*

$$ B&B/INN 🏨 **The Lilac Inn.** The best bed-and-breakfast in town has cheery, comfortable guest rooms in a central setting half a block from the heart of Brandon. **Pros:** big manor house; within walking distance of town; cheery rooms. **Cons:** busy in summer with weddings. [$] *Rooms from: $210* ✉ *53 Park St.* ☎ *802/247–5463, 800/221–0720* 🌐 *www.lilacinn.com* 🛏 *8 rooms, 1 suite* 🍽 *Breakfast.*

8

SPORTS AND THE OUTDOORS

GOLF

Neshobe Golf Club. This bent-grass course has terrific views of the Green Mountains. Several local inns offer golfing packages. ✉ *224 Town Farm Rd.* ☎ *802/247–3611* ⊕ *www.neshobe.com* 🖃 *$35 for 9 holes, $60 for 18 holes* 🏌 *18 holes, 6500 yards, par 72.*

HIKING

Branbury State Park. A large turnout on Route 53 marks the trailhead for a moderate hike to the Falls of Lana, a highlight of this park on the shores of Lake Dunmore near the Moosalamoo National Recreation Area. ✉ *3570 Lake Dunmore Rd.* ⊕ *www.vtstateparks.com/htm/ branbury.htm* 🖃 *$4* ⊘ *Facilities closed late Oct.–late May.*

Mt. Horrid. For great views from a vertigo-inducing cliff, hike up the Long Trail to Mt. Horrid. The steep, hour-long hike starts at the top of Brandon Gap. ✉ *Trailhead at Brandon Gap Rte. 73 parking lot, about 8 miles east of Brandon* ⊕ *www.fs.usda.gov/main/gmfl.*

Mt. Independence State Historic Site. West of Brandon, four trails—two short ones of less than a mile each and two longer ones—lead to some abandoned Revolutionary War fortifications. ✉ *28 Shoales Dr., off Mt. Independence Rd. just west of Orwell, Orwell* ⊹ *Parking lot is at top of hill* ☎ *802/948–2000* ⊕ *historicsites.vermont.gov/directory/mount_ independence* 🖃 *$5* ⊘ *Closed mid-Oct.–late May.*

PARKS

Moosalamoo National Recreation Area. Covering more than 15,000 acres of the Green Mountain National Forest, this area northeast of Brandon attracts hikers, mountain bikers, and cross-country skiers who enjoy the 70-plus miles of trails through wondrous terrain. If there is anywhere to stop and smell the flowers in Vermont, this is it. ✉ *Off Rtes. 53 and 73* ⊕ *www.moosalamoo.org.*

MIDDLEBURY

17 miles north of Brandon, 34 miles south of Burlington.

In the late 1800s Middlebury was the largest Vermont community west of the Green Mountains, an industrial center of river-powered wool and grain mills. This is Robert Frost country: Vermont's late poet laureate spent 23 summers at a farm east of Middlebury. Still a cultural and economic hub amid the Champlain Valley's serene pastoral patchwork—and the home of top-notch Middlebury College—the town and rolling countryside invite a day of exploration.

EXPLORING

TOP ATTRACTIONS

Edgewater Gallery. This gallery sits alongside picturesque Otter Creek, and the paintings, jewelry, ceramics, and pieces of furniture inside are just as arresting. Exhibitions in the bright, airy space change regularly, demonstrating the owner's ambition to be more gallery than shop, though all pieces are for sale. A second gallery is across the creek in the Battell Building. ✉ *1 Mill St.* ☎ *802/458–0098* ⊕ *www.edgewatergallery-vt.com* 🖃 *Free* ⊘ *Tues.–Sat. 10–5, Sun. and Mon. 11–4.*

Middlebury College. Founded in 1800, this college was conceived as a more godly alternative to the worldly University of Vermont, though it has no religious affiliation today. The postmodern architecture of the **Mahaney Center for the Arts,** which offers music, theater, and dance performances throughout the year, stands in provocative contrast to the early-19th-century stone buildings in the middle of town. ✉ *131 College St.* ☎ *802/443–5000* 🌐 *www.middlebury.edu.*

Robert Frost Interpretive Trail. Plaques along this easy 1.2-mile wooded trail bear quotations from Frost's poems. A picnic area is located across the road from the trailhead. ✉ *Trailhead on Rte. 125, 10 miles east of downtown* 🌐 *www.fs.usda.gov/main/gmfl.*

WORTH NOTING

FAMILY **University of Vermont Morgan Horse Farm.** The Morgan horse, Vermont's official state animal, has an even temper, high stamina, and slightly truncated legs in proportion to its body. This farm, about 2½ miles west of Middlebury, is a breeding and training center where in summer you can tour the stables and paddocks. ✉ *74 Battell Dr., off Morgan Horse Farm Rd., Weybridge* ☎ *802/388–2011* 🌐 *www.uvm.edu/morgan* 🎟 *$5* 🕘 *May–Oct., daily 9–4.*

Vermont Folklife Center. The redbrick center's exhibits include photography, antiques, folk paintings, manuscripts, and other artifacts and contemporary works that examine various facets of Vermont life. ✉ *88 Main St.* ☎ *802/388–4964* 🌐 *www.vermontfolklifecenter.org* 🎟 *Donations accepted* 🕘 *Tues.–Sat. 10–5.*

WHERE TO EAT

$$ PIZZA 🍴 **American Flatbread Middlebury Hearth.** On weekends this is the most happening spot in town, and it's no wonder: the pizza is extraordinary, and the attitude is pure Vermont. Wood-fired clay domes create masterful thin crusts from organically grown wheat. If you love pizza, you're in for a treat. Besides the innovative, delicious pizzas, try an organic mesclun salad tossed in the house ginger-tamari vinaigrette. There are also locations in Waitsfield and Burlington. [$] *Average main: $20* ✉ *137 Maple St.* ☎ *802/388–3300* 🌐 *www.americanflatbread.com* 🕘 *Closed Sun. and Mon. No lunch Tues.–Fri.* ✍ *Reservations not accepted.*

$$ AMERICAN 🍴 **The Bobcat Cafe & Brewery.** Worth the drive from Middlebury to the small town of Bristol, the Bobcat is fun, funky, and hip—suitable for a date but casual enough for the whole family. Comfort food served here ranges from locally sourced burgers to clever takes on fried fish, meat loaf, and tacos. Wash your meal down with excellent house-brewed beer, and save room for a rich dessert, like the peach upside-down cake. [$] *Average main: $20* ✉ *5 Main St., Bristol* ☎ *802/453–3311* 🌐 *www.thebobcatcafe.com* 🕘 *No lunch.*

$$ AMERICAN FAMILY 🍴 **Fire & Ice Restaurant.** It's hard not to have a good time at this restaurant constructed around a vintage boat. This self-described "museum of Vermont" has nine themed rooms, including a library and a college nostalgia room. Choose from prime rib, steak, fish, and a 55-item salad bar (including peel-and-eat shrimp). Families may wish to request a table next to the "children's theater," where kids can watch movies. Sunday dinner begins at 1 pm. Locals gravitate towards the Big

Moose Pub section. $ *Average main: $24* ✉ *26 Seymour St.* ☎ *802/388–7166, 800/367–7166* ⊕ *www.fireandicerestaurant.com* ☾ No *lunch Mon.–Thurs.*

$$$
AMERICAN
Fodor's Choice
★

✕ **Mary's at Baldwin Creek.** People drive from the far reaches of Vermont to dine at this restaurant just beyond Bristol, 13 miles northeast of Middlebury. Allow a little extra time to visit the sprawling gardens around the beautiful property; they represent the slow approach to cooking that earned this restaurant its stellar reputation. Hearty fare includes the summer lasagna packed with vegetables and the near-legendary garlic soup, a creamy year-round staple that seems calculated to please. Desserts can be hit-or-miss. $ *Average main: $25* ✉ *1868 N. Rte. 116, Bristol* ☎ *802/453–2432* ⊕ *www.innatbaldwincreek.com* ☾ *Closed Mon. and Tues.*

$$
MODERN
AMERICAN

✕ **The Storm Cafe.** There's no setting in town quite like this restaurant's deck, which overlooks Otter Creek Falls at one end of a long footbridge. Even if you're not here in summer, the eclectic, ever-changing menu makes this small café a worthy stop at any time of year. Spicy calamari and vegetable curry are recent dinner favorites, and large salads and diverse sandwiches make for satisfying lunches. $ *Average main: $19* ✉ *Frog Hollow Mill, 3 Mill St.* ☎ *802/388–1063* ⊕ *www.thestormcafe. com* ☾ *Closed Mon. No dinner Tues. and Wed.*

WHERE TO STAY

$
B&B/INN

🏠 **Inn on the Green.** Listed on the National Register of Historic Places, this 1803 inn and its carriage house sit in the center of bucolic Middlebury near the college campus. **Pros:** ideal location; great breakfast. **Cons:** some rooms small and close together. $ *Rooms from: $169* ✉ *71 S. Pleasant St.* ☎ *802/388–7512, 888/244–7512* ⊕ *www.innonthegreen. com* ↩ *9 rooms, 2 suites* ⦿ *Breakfast.*

$
B&B/INN

🏠 **Swift House Inn.** The 1814 Georgian home of a 19th-century governor has white-panel wainscoting, mahogany furnishings, and marble fireplaces. **Pros:** attractive, spacious, well-kept rooms; professionally run. **Cons:** not quite in the heart of town. $ *Rooms from: $179* ✉ *25 Stewart La.* ☎ *866/388–9925* ⊕ *www.swifthouseinn.com* ↩ *20 rooms* ⦿ *Breakfast.*

SHOPPING

Danforth Pewter Workshop & Store. In addition to its handcrafted pewter vases, lamps, and jewelry, this store offers you a front-row seat to the art of pewter spinning in the back workshop. There's also a small museum. ✉ *52 Seymour St.* ☎ *802/388–0098* ⊕ *www.danforthpewter.com.*

Historic Marble Works. This renovated marble manufacturing facility has a collection of shops and eateries set amid quarrying equipment and factory buildings. ✉ *2 Maple St.* ☎ *802/388–3701* ⊕ *www. thehistoricmarbleworks.com.*

WAITSFIELD AND WARREN

32 miles northeast (Waitsfield) and 25 miles east (Warren) of Middlebury.

Skiers first discovered the high peaks overlooking the pastoral Mad River Valley in the 1940s. Today, this valley and its two towns,

Waitsfield and Warren, attract the hip, the adventurous, and the low-key. Warren in particular is tiny and adorable, with a general store popular with tour buses. The gently carved ridges cradling the valley and the swell of pastures and fields lining the river seem to keep notions of ski-resort sprawl at bay. With a map from the Sugarbush Chamber of Commerce you can investigate back roads off Route 100 that have exhilarating valley views.

ESSENTIALS

Visitor Information Mad River Valley Chamber of Commerce. ✉ *4061 Main St., Waitsfield* ☎ *802/496–3409, 800/828–4748* 🌐 *www.madrivervalley.com.*

WHERE TO EAT

$$ PIZZA Fodor's Choice ★ 🍴 **American Flatbread Waitsfield.** Is this among the best pizza experiences in the world? It may well be. The organically grown flour and vegetables—and the wood-fired clay ovens that unite them—take the pizza here to another level. Local favorites include the maple–fennel sausage pie topped with sun-dried tomatoes, caramelized onions, cheese, and herbs—it's a dream, and so are the more traditional flavors. This is the original American Flatbread location. In summer, you can dine outside around fire pits in the beautiful valley. Seats can be hard to come by, but if you stay at the adjoining inn, they're reserved. [$] *Average main: $20* ✉ *46 Lareau Rd., off Rte. 100, Waitsfield* ☎ *802/496–8856* 🌐 *www.americanflatbread.com* ⏲ *Closed Mon.–Wed. No lunch* ✍ *Reservations not accepted.*

$$$ MODERN AMERICAN 🍴 **Common Man.** This restaurant is situated in a big 1800s barn with hand-hewn rafters and crystal chandeliers. That's the Common Man for you: fancy and après-ski all at once. Bottles of Moët & Chandon signed by the customers who ordered them sit atop the beams. The eclectic, sophisticated new American cuisine showcases locally sourced produce and meats; the menu may include grilled octopus with sticky rice and bok choy, orecchiette with pork and fennel sausage, or roast chicken with red onion jam. Seven-course tasting menus are available by request. Dinner is served by candlelight. Couples sit by the big fireplace. [$] *Average main: $25* ✉ *3209 German Flats Rd., Warren* ☎ *802/583–2800* 🌐 *www.commonmanrestaurant.com* ⏲ *Closed Sun.–Wed. No lunch.*

WHERE TO STAY

$$ B&B/INN 🏨 **The Inn at Round Barn Farm.** A Shaker-style round barn—one of only five in Vermont—is the centerpiece of this bed-and-breakfast, but what you'll remember when you leave is how comfortable your stay was. **Pros:** great trails, gardens, and rooms; tasty breakfasts; unique architecture. **Cons:** no restaurant; fills up for wedding parties. [$] *Rooms from: $205* ✉ *1661 E. Warren Rd., Waitsfield* ☎ *802/496–2276* 🌐 *www.theroundbarn.com* 🛏 *11 rooms, 1 suite* 🍽 *Breakfast.*

$$$$ B&B/INN Fodor's Choice ★ 🏨 **The Pitcher Inn.** "Sublime" is the word that comes to mind when thinking about a night at the elegant Pitcher Inn, one of Vermont's trio of Relais & Châteaux properties. **Pros:** exceptional service; fabulous restaurant; beautiful location. **Cons:** at some point, you have to go home. [$] *Rooms from: $450* ✉ *275 Main St., Warren* ☎ *802/496–6350* 🌐 *www.pitcherinn.com* 🛏 *9 rooms, 2 suites* 🍽 *Breakfast.*

Sheep's-milk cheese is just one of the many food products that contribute to great fresh local meals in Vermont.

NIGHTLIFE AND PERFORMING ARTS

NIGHTLIFE

Fodor's Choice ★ **Tracks.** Downstairs at the Pitcher Inn, this comfortable tavern has a tasteful lodge-style setting complete with a crackling fireplace. The bar menu is terrific—featuring items like seared scallops over sweet potatoes and bacon, and skirt steak with chimichurri—and the selection of wines and beers is excellent. There are billiards tables, dartboards, and table shuffleboard. ⊠ *Pitcher Inn, 275 Main St., Warren* ☎ *802/493–6350* ⊕ *www.pitcherinn.com.*

PERFORMING ARTS

Green Mountain Cultural Center. The center hosts concerts, art exhibits, and educational workshops in the historic Round Barn. ⊠ *Inn at the Round Barn Farm, 1661 E. Warren Rd., Waitsfield* ☎ *802/496–7722* ⊕ *www.greenmountainculturalcenter.org.*

SPORTS AND THE OUTDOORS

GOLF

Sugarbush Resort Golf Club. Great views and challenging play are the hallmarks of this mountain course designed by Robert Trent Jones Sr. ⊠ *Sugarbush, 1840 Sugarbush Access Rd., Warren* ☎ *802/583–6725* ⊕ *www.sugarbush.com* ⊡ *$95 for 18 holes, weekdays; $110 for 18 holes, weekends* ⅄ *18 holes, 6464 yards, par 71.*

MULTISPORT OUTFITTER

Clearwater Sports. This outfitter rents canoes and kayaks, and leads guided river trips in warmer months. When the weather turns cold, it offers snowshoeing and backcountry skiing tours. ⊠ *4147 Main St., Waitsfield* ☎ *802/496–2708* ⊕ *www.clearwatersports.com.*

SKI AREAS

Blueberry Lake Cross Country and Snowshoeing Center. This ski area has 18 miles of trails through thickly wooded glades. ⊠ *424 Plunkton Rd., East Warren* ☎ *802/496–6687* ⊕ *www.blueberrylakeskivt.com* ⊠ *Trail pass: $13.*

Mad River Glen. A pristine alpine experience, Mad River attracts rugged individualists looking for less polished terrain. The area was developed in the late 1940s and has changed relatively little since then. It remains one of only three resorts in the country that ban snowboarding, and it's the only one that still has a single-chair lift. Mad River is steep, with slopes that follow the mountain's fall lines. The terrain changes constantly on the interconnected trails of mostly natural snow (expert trails are never groomed). Telemark skiing and snowshoeing are also popular. **Facilities:** 45 trails; 125 acres; 2,036-foot vertical drop; 5 lifts. ⊠ *62 Mad River Resort Rd., off Rte. 17, Waitsfield* ☎ *802/496–3551* ⊕ *www.madriverglen.com* ⊠ *Lift ticket: $79.*

FAMILY **Sugarbush.** A true skier's mountain, Sugarbush has plenty of steep, natural snow glades and fall-line drops. Not as rough around the edges as Mad River Glen, the resort has an extensive computer-controlled system for snowmaking and many groomed trails between its two mountain complexes. This a great choice for intermediate skiers, who will find top-to-bottom runs all over the resort; there are fewer options for beginners. Programs for kids include the enjoyable Sugarbear Forest, a terrain garden full of fun bumps and jumps. At the base of the mountain are condominiums, restaurants, shops, bars, and a health and racquet club. **Facilities:** 111 trails; 484 acres; 2,600-foot vertical drop; 16 lifts. ⊠ *102 Forest Dr., Warren* ⊹ *From Rte. 17, take German Flats Rd. south; from Rte. 100, take Sugarbush Access Rd. west* ☎ *802/583–6300, 802/583–7669* ⊕ *www.sugarbush.com* ⊠ *Lift ticket: $91.*

SHOPPING

All Things Bright and Beautiful. This eccentric Victorian house is filled to the rafters with stuffed animals of all shapes, sizes, and colors, as well as folk art, European glass, and Christmas ornaments. ⊠ *27 Bridge St., Waitsfield* ☎ *802/496–3997* ⊕ *www.allthingsbright.com.*

The Warren Store. This general store has everything you'd hope to find in tiny but sophisticated Vermont: a nice selection of local beer and wine, cheeses, baked goods, strong coffee, and delicious sandwiches and prepared foods. In summer, grab a quick lunch on the small deck by the water; in winter, warm up at the wood stove. Warm, woolly clothing and accessories can be found upstairs. ⊠ *284 Main St., Warren* ☎ *802/496–3864* ⊕ *www.warrenstore.com.*

NORTHERN VERMONT

Vermont's northernmost region presents the state's greatest contrasts. To the west, Burlington and its suburbs have grown so rapidly that rural wags now say that Burlington's main advantage is that it's "close to Vermont." The north country also contains Vermont's tiny capital, Montpelier, and its highest mountain, Mt. Mansfield, site of the famous

Stowe and Smugglers' Notch ski resorts. Northeast of Montpelier is a sparsely populated and heavily wooded territory, which former Senator George Aiken dubbed the "Northeast Kingdom"—the domain of loggers, farmers, and avid outdoors enthusiasts.

MONTPELIER

38 miles southeast of Burlington, 115 miles north of Brattleboro.

With only about 8,000 residents, little Montpelier is the country's smallest capital city, but it has a youthful energy—and certainly an independent spirit—that makes it seem almost as large as Burlington. The well-preserved downtown area bustles with state and city workers walking to meetings and restaurants, and students heading to funky coffee shops.

EXPLORING

Hope Cemetery. Barre, the "Granite Capital of the World," lies 7 miles southeast of Montpelier, and many of this cemetery's superbly crafted tombstones were carved by local stonecutters to demonstrate their skill. A few embrace the avant-garde, while others take defined shapes like a race car, a biplane, and a soccer ball. ⊠ *201 Maple Ave., Barre* ☎ *802/476-6245.*

FAMILY

Fodor'sChoice

★

Morse Farm Maple Sugarworks. With eight generations of sugaring, the Morses may be the oldest maple family in existence, so you're sure to find an authentic experience at their farm. Burr Morse heads up the operation now, along with his son Tom, but you can still see Burr's father playing the role of the curmudgeon in the dated video that screens in the Woodshed Theater. More than 5,000 trees produce the sap used for syrup (you can sample all the grades), candy, cream, and sugar—all sold in the gift shop. Grab a creemee (soft-serve ice cream), take a seat on a swing, and stay awhile. Surrounding trails offer pleasant strolls in summer and prime cross-country skiing in winter. ⊠ *1168 County Rd.* ☎ *800/242-2740* ⊕ *www.morsefarm.com* ⊠ *Free.*

OFF THE
BEATEN
PATH

Rock of Ages Granite Quarry. Attractions here range from the awe-inspiring (the quarry resembles the Grand Canyon in miniature) to the mildly ghoulish (you can consult a directory of tombstone dealers throughout the country) to the whimsical (an outdoor granite bowling alley). At the crafts center, skilled artisans sculpt monuments and blast stone, while at the quarries themselves, workers who clearly earn their pay cut 25-ton blocks of stone from the sheer 475-foot walls. (You may recognize these walls from a chase scene in the 2009 *Star Trek* movie.) ⊠ *560 Graniteville Rd., off I–89, Graniteville* ☎ *802/476–3119* ⊕ *www.rockofages. com* ⊠ *Tours $6* ⊙ *Visitor center: mid-May–Aug., Mon.–Sat. 9–5; Sept. and Oct., daily 9–5.*

Vermont History Museum. The collection here, begun in 1838, focuses on all things Vermont—from a catamount (the now-extinct local cougar) to Ethan Allen's shoe buckles. The museum store stocks fine books, prints, and gifts. A second location in Barre, the Vermont History Center, has three rotating exhibits with notable photographs and artifacts. ⊠ *109 State St.* ☎ *802/828–2291* ⊕ *www.vermonthistory.org* ⊠ *$5* ⊙ *Tues.–Sat. 10–4.*

8

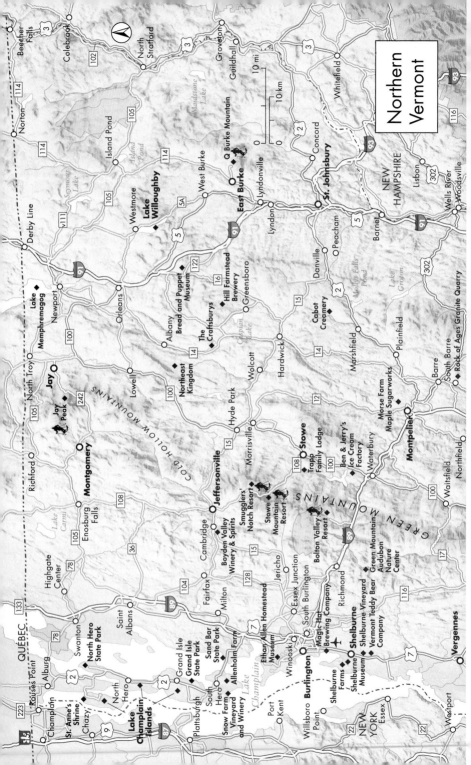

Northern Vermont

QUICK BITES

La Brioche Bakery. New England Culinary Institute students are up at 5 am preparing breads for the thankful patrons of this super breakfast and lunch stop. Soups, salads, and sandwiches are all on the menu, but the pastries are the most tempting. ✉ ***89 Main St.*** ☎ ***802/229–0443*** 🌐 ***www.neci.edu/labrioche.***

Vermont State House. The regal capitol building surrounded by forest is emblematic of this proudly rural state. With a gleaming dome topped by the goddess of agriculture and columns of Barre granite measuring 6 feet in diameter, the state house is home to the country's oldest legislative chambers still in their original condition. A half-hour tour takes you through the governor's office and the house and senate chambers. Interior paintings and exhibits make much of Vermont's sterling Civil War record. ✉ *115 State St.* ☎ *802/828–2228* 🎟 *Donations accepted* 🕘 *Weekdays 7–4. Tours every ½ hr: July–mid-Oct., weekdays 10–3:30, Sat. 11–3.*

WHERE TO EAT

$$$ ECLECTIC 🍴 **Ariel's.** Well off the beaten path, this small restaurant overlooking a lake is worth the drive down a dirt road. The chef prepares small, medium, and large plates of New England–inspired cuisine based on local sources. Favorites include herb-crusted lamb loin and line-caught swordfish. Don't leave without ordering a board of Vermont cheeses, which pair especially well with the excellent wines. [$] *Average main: $26* ✉ *29 Stone Rd., 18 miles south of Montpelier, Brookfield* ☎ *802/276–3939* 🌐 *www.arielsrestaurant.com* 🕘 *Closed Mon. and Tues., and Nov.–Mar. No lunch.*

$ SOUTHERN FAMILY 🍴 **Down Home Kitchen.** Barbecue isn't hard to track down in Vermont, but there aren't many places serving the down-home Southern cuisine found at this breakfast and lunch spot. Biscuits, gravy, and fried chicken and catfish are the specialties, but it's the atmosphere that really sells the place. Plop down at the long soda fountain and sip a float or mint julep, or pull up a blue painted chair to the communal wooden table dressed with fresh flowers in mason jars and settle in for a leisurely and social brunch. The on-site bakery cranks out muffins, cupcakes, and peach and pecan pies, so you won't lack for baked goods. The food may be locally sourced, but the attitude and flavors are all North Carolina—the owner's original home. [$] *Average main: $15* ✉ *100 Main St.* ☎ *802/225–6665* 🌐 *www.downhomekitchenvt.com* 🕘 *Closed Tues. No dinner.*

$$ AMERICAN 🍴 **NECI on Main.** Nearly everyone working at this restaurant is a student at the New England Culinary Institute, but the quality and inventiveness of the food is anything but beginner's luck. The menu changes seasonally, but the soups and Misty Knoll Farm free-range chicken are reliable winners. The lounge downstairs offers the same menu in a more casual atmosphere. Reservations are strongly recommended for the popular Sunday brunch. [$] *Average main: $20* ✉ *118 Main St.* ☎ *802/223–3188* 🌐 *www.neci.edu* 🕘 *Closed Mon. No dinner Sun.*

$ CAFÉ 🍴 **Red Hen Baking Co.** If you're a devotee of artisanal bakeries, it'd be a mistake not to trek the 7-plus miles from Montpelier (15 from Stowe) to have lunch, pick up freshly baked bread, or sample a sweet treat here.

Try the ham-and-cheese croissants, sticky buns, homemade soups, and savory sandwiches. Red Hen supplies bread to some of the state's best restaurants, including Hen of the Wood, and has varied offerings every day. $ *Average main: $8* ⊠ *961B U.S. 2, Middlesex* ☎ *802/223–5200* ⊕ *www.redhenbaking.com* ⊘ *No dinner* ⌂ *Reservations not accepted.*

$
ITALIAN
✕ **Sarducci's.** Legislative lunches have become a lot more leisurely since Sarducci's came along to fill the trattoria void in Vermont's capital. The bright, cheerful rooms here alongside the Winooski River are a local favorite for pizza served fresh from wood-fired ovens, wonderfully textured homemade Italian breads, and imaginative dishes like pasta *pugliese,* which marries penne with basil, black olives, roasted eggplant, portobello mushrooms, and sun-dried tomatoes. $ *Average main: $17* ⊠ *3 Main St.* ☎ *802/223–0229* ⊕ *www.sarduccis.com* ⊘ *No lunch Sun.*

$
CAFÉ
✕ **The Skinny Pancake.** This dine-in creperie makes a great stop for breakfast, lunch, or an easy dinner. The Breakfast Monster, made with eggs and local Cabot cheddar, is a winner. For lunch, try the spinach and feta crêpe, the Veggie Monster (spinach, roasted red peppers, caramelized onions, and cheddar), or the Lamb Fetatastic (local lamb sausage, baby spinach, feta, and kalamata olives). If you're in the mood for dessert, sample the Nutella crêpe or the Pooh Bear, served with warm local honey and cinnamon. $ *Average main: $9* ⊠ *89 Main St.* ☎ *802/262–2253* ⊕ *www.skinnypancake.com.*

$
ECLECTIC
Fodor'sChoice
★
✕ **Three Penny Taproom.** This lively taproom is quickly becoming one of the best in Vermont. The Three Penny serves many craft beers, including the justly celebrated Hill Farmstead. Now featuring a full menu and expanded seating, the pub has become a dining destination as well, sharing an award for the state's best burger. The vibe feels straight out of an artsy neighborhood in Brussels, but with the earthiness of Vermont. $ *Average main: $15* ⊠ *108 Main St.* ☎ *802/223–8277* ⊕ *www.threepennytaproom.com.*

WHERE TO STAY

$
B&B/INN
⌂ **Inn at Montpelier.** The capital's most charming lodging option, this lovingly tended inn dating to 1830 has rooms filled with antique four-poster beds and Windsor chairs—all have private (if small) baths. **Pros:** beautiful home; relaxed central setting; amazing porch. **Cons:** some rooms are small. $ *Rooms from: $170* ⊠ *147 Main St.* ☎ *802/223–2727* ⊕ *www.innatmontpelier.com* ⇥ *19 rooms* ⌾ *Breakfast.*

SHOPPING

Artisans Hand Craft Gallery. For more than 30 years, Maggie Neale has been celebrating and supporting Vermont's craft community. Her store sells jewelry, textiles, sculptures, and paintings by many local artists. ⊠ *89 Main St.* ☎ *802/229–9492* ⊕ *www.artisanshand.com.*

Vermont Creamery. A leader in the artisanal cheese movement, this creamery invites aficionados to visit its 4,000-square-foot production facility, where goat cheeses such as Bonne Bouche—a perfectly balanced, cloudlike cheese—are made on weekdays. The creamery is in Websterville, southwest of Montpelier. ⊠ *20 Pitman Rd., Websterville* ☎ *800/884–6287, 802/479–9371* ⊕ *www.vermontcreamery.com* ⊘ *Closed weekends.*

Zutano. Head here for hip newborn, baby, and toddler clothing designed in Vermont. ✉ *79 Main St.* ☎ *802/223–2229* ⊕ *www.zutano.com.*

EN
ROUTE

Ben & Jerry's Ice Cream Factory. The 30-minute tours at the famous brand's factory are unabashedly corny and only skim the surface of the behind-the-scenes goings-on, but this flaw is almost forgiven when the samples are dished out. To see the machines at work, visit on a weekday but call ahead to confirm if they will indeed be in operation. ✉ *1281 Waterbury–Stowe Rd., 1 mile north of I–89, Waterbury* ☎ *802/846–1500* ⊕ *www.benjerry.com* 🎟 *Tour $4* ⊙ *Late Oct.–June, daily 10–6; July–mid-Aug., daily 9–9; mid-Aug.–late Oct., daily 9–7. Tours every ½ hr.*

Cabot Creamery. The state's biggest cheese producer has a visitor center with displays about the dairy co-op that provides milk for its famous products. The informative tour is worthwhile at any time, though it's best to arrive on a cheese-making day, so call ahead and adjust your schedule if possible. Either way, you may never leave the gift shop, where samples are diverse and plentiful. ✉ *2878 Main St., 5 miles north of U.S. 2, Cabot* ☎ *800/837–4261* ⊕ *www.cabotcheese.coop* 🎟 *$3* ⊙ *May–Oct., daily 9–5; Nov. and Dec., daily 10–4; Jan.–Apr., Mon.–Sat. 10–4.*

STOWE

22 miles northwest of Montpelier, 36 miles east of Burlington.

Fodor's Choice ★ Long before skiing came to Stowe in the 1930s, the rolling hills and valleys beneath Vermont's highest peak, 4,395-foot Mt. Mansfield, attracted summer tourists looking for a reprieve from city heat. Most stayed at one of two inns in the village of Stowe. When skiing made the town a winter destination, visitors outnumbered hotel beds, so locals took them in. This spirit of hospitality continues, and many of these homes are now country inns. The village itself is tiny—just a few blocks of shops and restaurants clustered around a picture-perfect white church with a lofty steeple—but it serves as the anchor for Mountain Road, which leads north past restaurants, lodges, and shops on its way to Stowe's fabled slopes.

8

ESSENTIALS

Visitor Information Stowe Area Association. ✉ *51 Main St.* ☎ *802/253–7321, 877/467–8693* ⊕ *www.gostowe.com.*

EXPLORING

Trapp Family Lodge. Built by the Von Trapp family (of *The Sound of Music* fame), this Tyrolean lodge and its grounds are the site of a popular outdoor music series in summer. You can hike the trails in warm weather, or go cross-country skiing in winter; a ski-in cabin serves homemade soups, sandwiches, and hot chocolate. There's a fine-dining restaurant, and the lodge's café serves tasty food over a breathtaking mountain vista. Finally, an on-site brewery produces Austrian lagers, a welcome change of pace from all the local craft ales. ✉ *700 Trapp Hill Rd.* ☎ *802/253–8511, 800/826–7000* ⊕ *www.trappfamily.com.*

Vermont Ski and Snowboard Museum. The state's skiing and snowboarding history is documented here. Exhibits cover subjects such as the 10th

Mountain Division of World War II, the national ski patrol, Winter Olympians, and the evolution of equipment. An early World Cup trophy is on loan, and one of the most memorable mobiles you'll ever see, made from a gondola and ski-lift chairs, hangs from the ceiling. One recent exhibit, Slope Style, focused on ski fashion from 1930 to 2014. ✉ *1 S. Main St.* ☎ *802/253–9911* ⊕ *www.vtssm.com* 🖃 *$5* ⊗ *Wed.– Mon. noon–5.*

WHERE TO EAT

$$
AMERICAN

✕ **Harrison's Restaurant.** For an excellent dinner at a warm and unpretentious American bistro, head to Harrison's, tucked away in downtown Stowe. A lively locals' scene, booths by the fireplace, and creative cuisine paired with well-chosen wines and regional brews make this place perfect for couples and families alike. Stop in for braised short ribs in blackberry-chipotle barbecue sauce, sirloin bistro steak, or lobster mac 'n' cheese made with Cabot cheddar. The inviting bar is a good spot to dine alone or to chat with a regular. $ *Average main: $23* ✉ *25 Main St., behind TD Bank* ☎ *802/253–7773* ⊕ *www.harrisonsstowe. com* ⊗ *No lunch* 🍴 *Reservations essential.*

$$$
ECLECTIC
Fodor'sChoice
★

✕ **Hen of the Wood.** Ask Vermont's great chefs where they go for a tremendous meal, and Hen of the Wood inevitably tops the list. The setting is riveting: a converted 1835 gristmill beside a waterfall. On the mill's underground level, supported by thick wooden beams, the sunken millstone pit holds tables surrounded by uneven stone walls dotted with tiny candles—it's utterly romantic. Sophisticated dishes showcase an abundance of local produce, meat, and cheese. The daily changing menu might include goat's milk dumplings, local farm pork loin, grass-fed rib eye, or wild Alaskan halibut. When it's warm outside, angle for a coveted patio table overlooking a dramatic series of falls. The restaurant has a second location in Burlington. $ *Average main: $26* ✉ *92 Stowe St., Waterbury* ☎ *802/244–7300* ⊕ *www.henofthewood.com* ⊗ *Closed Sun. and Mon. No lunch* 🍴 *Reservations essential.*

$$$
EUROPEAN

✕ **Michael's on the Hill.** Swiss-born chef Michael Kloeti trained in Europe and New York City before opening this establishment in a 19th-century farmhouse outside Stowe. The seasonal three-course prix-fixe menus ($45 and $67) blend European cuisine with farm-to-table earthiness, exemplified by dishes such as spice-roasted duck breast and venison *navarin* (ragout). You can also order à la carte. $ *Average main: $32* ✉ *4182 Stowe-Waterbury Rd., 6 miles south of Stowe, Waterbury Center* ☎ *802/244–7476* ⊕ *www.michaelsonthehill.com* ⊗ *Closed Tues. No lunch.*

$
AMERICAN
Fodor'sChoice
★

✕ **Prohibition Pig.** This restaurant and brewery in downtown Waterbury is always packed for a reason: fabulous craft beers, sandwiches, salads, and barbecue served in an airy and friendly bar and dining room. Preparations can be decadent—case in point: the duck-fat fries—yet the flavors are more nuanced than the low prices imply. The house burger with pimento cheese and fried green tomato is a winner, as are the roasted brisket and pit-smoked chicken. If you just want a quick bite and a draft, belly up to the tasting room bar at the brewery in the back. For more suds, pop across the street to the Craft Beer Cellar, one

Continued on page 497

LET IT SNOW

WINTER ACTIVITIES IN VERMONT

by Elise Coroneos

SKIING AND SNOWBOARDING IN VERMONT

Less than 5 miles from the Canadian border, Jay Peak is Vermont's northernmost ski resort.

Ever since America's first ski tow opened in a farmer's pasture near Woodstock in January 1934, skiers have headed en masse to Vermont in winter. Today, 19 alpine and 30 nordic ski areas range in size and are spread across the state, from Mount Snow in the south to Jay Peak near the Canadian border. The snow-making equipment has also become more comprehensive over the years, with more than 80% of the trails in the state using man-made snow. Here are some of the best ski areas by various categories:

GREAT FOR KIDS Smugglers' Notch, Okemo, and **Bromley Mountain** all offer terrific kids' programs, with classes organized by age categories and by skill level. Kids as young as 3 (4 at some ski areas) can start learning. Child care, with activities like stories, singing, and arts and crafts, are available for those too young to ski; some ski areas, like Smuggler's Notch, offer babysitting with no minimum age daytime and evening.

BEST FOR BEGINNERS Beginner terrain makes up nearly half of the mountain at **Stratton**, where options include private and group lessons for first-timers. Also good are small but family-friendly **Bolton Valley** and **Bromley Mountains,** which both designate a third of their slopes for beginners.

EXPERT TERRAIN The slopes at **Jay Peak** and massive **Killington** are most notable for their steepness and pockets of glades. About 40% of the runs at these two resorts are advanced or expert. Due to its far north location, Jay Peak tends to get the most snow, making it ideal for powder days. Another favorite with advanced skiers is Central Vermont's **Mad River Glen**, where many slopes are ungroomed (natural) and the motto is "Ski it if you can." In addition, **Sugarbush, Stowe,** and **Smugglers' Notch** are all revered for their challenging untamed side country.

Mount Mansfield is better known as Stowe.   Stratton Mountain clocktower

NIGHT SKIING Come late afternoon, **Bolton Valley** is hopping. That's because it's the only location in Vermont for night skiing. Ski and ride under the lights from 4 until 8 Wednesday through Saturday, followed by a later après-ski scene.

APRÈS-SKI The social scenes at **Killington**, **Sugarbush**, and **Stowe** are the most noteworthy (and crowded). Book a seat on the Snowcat that takes intrepid partiers to the Motor Room Bar in Killington, or stop by the always popular Wobbly Barn. For live music, try Castlerock Pub in Sugarbush or the Matterhorn Bar in Stowe.

SNOWBOARDING Boarders (and some skiers) will love the latest features for freestyle tricks in Vermont. **Stratton** has four terrain parks for all abilities, one of which features a boarder cross course. **Mount Snow's** Carinthia Peak is an all-terrain park–dedicated mountain, the only of its kind in New England. Head to **Killington** for Burton Stash, another beautiful all-natural features terrain park. **Okemo** has a superpipe and eight terrain parks and a gladed park with all-natural features. Note that snowboarding is not allowed at skiing cooperative **Mad River Glen.**

CROSS-COUNTRY To experience the best of cross-country skiing in the state, simply follow the Catamount Trail, a 300-mile nordic route from southern Vermont to Canada. **The Trapp Family Lodge** in Stowe has 37 miles of groomed cross-country trails and 62 miles of back-country trails. Another top option is **The Mountain Top Inn & Resort,** just outside of Killington. Its Nordic Ski and Snowshoe Center provides instruction for newcomers, along with hot drinks and lunches when it is time to take a break and warm up.

TELEMARK Ungroomed snow and tree skiing are a natural fit with free-heel skiing at **Mad River Glen. Bromley** and **Jay Peak** also have telemark rentals and instruction.

MOUNTAIN-RESORT TRIP PLANNER

TIMING

■ **Snow Season.** Winter sports time is typically from Thanksgiving through April, weather permitting. Holidays are the most crowded.

■ **March Madness.** Most of the season's snow tends to come in March, so that's the time to go if you want to ski on fresh, nature-made powder. To increase your odds, choose a ski area in the northern part of the state.

■ **Summer Scene.** During summertime, many ski resorts reinvent themselves as prime destinations for golfers, zipline and canopy tours, mountain bikers, and weddings. Other summer visitors come to the mountains to enjoy hiking trails, climbing walls, aquatic centers, chairlift and horseback rides, or a variety of festivals.

■ **Avoid Long Lift Lines.** Try to hit the slopes early—many lifts start at 8 or 9 am, with ticket windows opening a half-hour earlier. Then take a mid-morning break as lines start to get longer and head out again when others come in for lunch.

SAVINGS TIPS

■ **Choose a Condo.** Especially if you're planning to stay for a week, save money on food by opting for a condominum unit with a kitchen. You can shop at the supermarket and cook breakfast and dinner.

■ **Rent Smart.** Consider ski rental options in the villages rather than those at the mountain. Renting right at the ski area may be more convenient, but it may also cost more.

■ **Discount Lift Tickets.** Online tickets are often the least expensive; multi-day discounts and and ski-and-stay packages will also lower your costs. Good for those who can plan ahead, early-bird tickets often go on sale before the ski season even starts.

■ **Hit the Peaks Off-peak.** In order to secure the best deals at the most competitive rates, avoid booking during school holidays. President's Week in February is the busiest, because that's when Northeastern schools have their spring break.

Top left, Killington's six mountains make up the largest ski area in Vermont. Top right, Stratton has a Snowboard-cross course.

THINK WARM THOUGHTS

It can get cold on the slopes, so be prepared. Consider proper face warmth and smart layering, plus ski-specific socks, or purchase a pair each of inexpensive hand and feet warmers that fit easily in your gloves and boots. Helmets, which can also be rented, provide not only added safety but warmth.

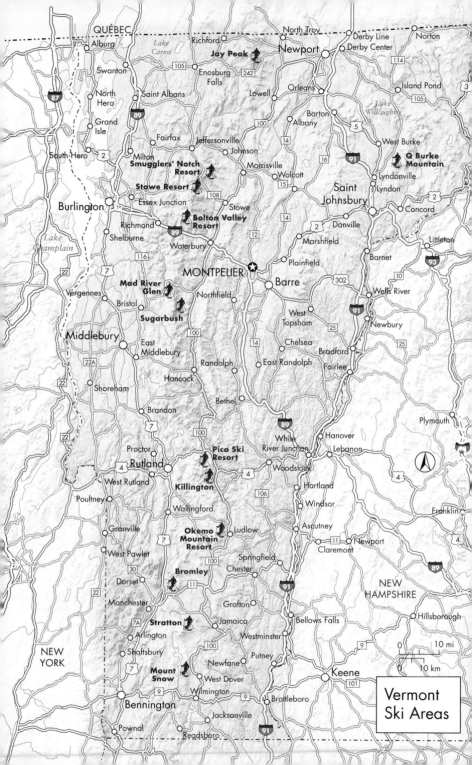

Vermont
Ski Areas

of the state's best beer stores. $ *Average main: $12* ✉ *23 S. Main St., Waterbury* ☎ *802/244–4120* ⊕ *www.prohibitionpig.com* ⊘ *No lunch Tues.–Thurs.*

WHERE TO STAY

$ ⊡ **Field Guide.** A new boutique enterprise just north of Stowe, Field HOTEL   Guide supplies a whimsically stylish alternative to the town's staid resorts and cadre of inns stuck in ski-chalet mold. **Pros:** great location; distinct style; fun attitude. **Cons:** style not for everyone; no elevator. $ *Rooms from: $199* ✉ *433 Mountain Rd.* ☎ *802/253–8088* ⊕ *www. fieldguidestowe.com* ↪ *17 rooms, 10 suites, 3 cottages* ⦿*Breakfast.*

$ ⊡ **Green Mountain Inn.** Welcoming guests since 1833, this classic redbrick B&B/INN   inn puts you within reach of downtown buzz. **Pros:** fun location; lively tavern; lots of character. **Cons:** farther from skiing than other area hotels. $ *Rooms from: $189* ✉ *18 Main St.* ☎ *802/253–7301, 800/253– 7302* ⊕ *www.greenmountaininn.com* ↪ *103 rooms* ⦿*No meals.*

$$ ⊡ **Stone Hill Inn.** A contemporary bed-and-breakfast where classi-B&B/INN   cal music plays in the hallways, the Stone Hill has guest rooms with two-sink vanities and two-person whirlpools in front of double-sided fireplaces. **Pros:** very comfortable rooms; convenient location. **Cons:** grounds could use grooming. $ *Rooms from: $299* ✉ *89 Houston Farm Rd.* ☎ *802/253–6282* ⊕ *www.stonehillinn.com* ↪ *9 rooms* ⦿*Breakfast.*

$ ⊡ **Stowe Motel & Snowdrift.** The accommodations at this family-owned HOTEL   motel on 16 acres range from studios with small kitchenettes and FAMILY   modern two-bedroom suites warmed by their own fireplaces to rental houses that can sleep 10 or more people. **Pros:** inexpensive rates; complimentary bikes; friendly game room. **Cons:** motel-style accommodations. $ *Rooms from: $129* ✉ *2043 Mountain Rd.* ☎ *802/253–7629, 800/829–7629* ⊕ *www.stowemotel.com* ↪ *52 rooms, 4 suites, 6 houses* ⦿*Breakfast.*

$$$ ⊡ **Stowe Mountain Lodge.** At the base of the ski slopes, this lodge would RESORT   be king of the hill for its location alone, but a stay here also affords **Fodor's**Choice   many perks. **Pros:** perfect setting; great concierge; activities galore. **Cons:** ★   somewhat sterile feel; no separate kids' pool. $ *Rooms from: $350* ✉ *7412 Mountain Rd.* ☎ *802/253–3560* ⊕ *www.stowemountainlodge. com* ↪ *312 rooms* ⦿*No meals.*

$$ ⊡ **Stoweflake Mountain Resort and Spa.** With one of the largest spas in the RESORT   area, Stoweflake lets you enjoy an herb-and-flower labyrinth, a fitness center reached via a covered bridge, and a hydrotherapy waterfall that cascades into a hot tub. **Pros:** nice spa; wide range of rooms. **Cons:** mazelike layout can make rooms a bit hard to find. $ *Rooms from: $219* ✉ *1746 Mountain Rd.* ☎ *800/253–2232* ⊕ *www.stoweflake.com* ↪ *120 rooms, 60 town houses* ⦿*No meals.*

$$$ ⊡ **Topnotch Resort.** On 120 acres overlooking Mt. Mansfield, this posh RESORT   property has a contemporary look and an outstanding spa. **Pros:** Mt. FAMILY   Mansfield views; impeccable service; family-friendly atmosphere. **Cons: Fodor's**Choice   boutique style may not be for everyone. $ *Rooms from: $350* ✉ *4000* ★   *Mountain Rd.* ☎ *800/451–8686* ⊕ *www.topnotchresort.com* ↪ *68 rooms and suites, 22 town houses* ⦿*No meals.*

8

NIGHTLIFE AND PERFORMING ARTS
NIGHTLIFE
Doc Ponds. A gastropub from the folks behind the Hen of the Wood restaurant, this place has a diverse beer list. The food's great, too. ⊠ *294 Mountain Rd.* ☎ *802/760–6066* ⊕ *www.docpond.com.*

Matterhorn. This nightspot hosts live music and dancing on weekends during the ski season. If you'd rather just watch, there's a separate martini bar. ⊠ *4969 Mountain Rd.* ☎ *802/253–8198* ⊕ *www. matterhornbar.com* ☽ *Closed Mon.*

Rusty Nail. This bar rocks to live music on weekends. ⊠ *1190 Mountain Rd.* ☎ *802/253–6245* ⊕ *www.rustynailvt.com.*

PERFORMING ARTS
Spruce Peak Performing Arts Center. Part of the Mountain Lodge complex, this state-of-the-art space hosts theater, music, and dance performances. ⊠ *122 Hourglass Dr.* ☎ *802/760–4634* ⊕ *www.sprucepeakarts.org.*

SPORTS AND THE OUTDOORS
CANOEING AND KAYAKING
Umiak Outdoor Outfitters. This full-service outfitter rents canoes and kayaks, organizes tours, and sells equipment. It has seasonal outposts at the Waterbury Reservoir and at North Beach in Burlington. ⊠ *849 S. Main St.* ☎ *802/253–2317* ⊕ *www.umiak.com.*

FISHING
The Fly Rod Shop. This shop provides a guide service, offers introductory classes, and rents tackle and other equipment. ⊠ *2703 Waterbury Rd., 1½ miles south of Stowe* ☎ *802/253–7346* ⊕ *www.flyrodshop.com.*

GOLF
Stowe Country Club. A scenic 18-hole golf course, a driving range, and a putting green are available at this country club. ⊠ *744 Cape Cod Rd.* ☎ *802/760–4653* ⊕ *www.stowe.com/golf/club* 🖃 *$115 for 18 holes* ☽ *18 holes, 6185 yards, par 72.*

HIKING
Mt. Mansfield. Ascending Mt. Mansfield makes for a challenging day hike. Trails lead from Mountain Road to the summit, where they meet the north–south Long Trail. Views encompass New Hampshire's White Mountains, New York's Adirondacks, and southern Québec. The Green Mountain Club publishes a trail guide. ⊠ *Trailheads along Mountain Rd.* ☎ *802/244–7037* ⊕ *www.greenmountainclub.org.*

Fodor'sChoice ★ **Stowe Recreation Path.** An immaculately maintained, paved recreation path begins behind the Community Church in town and meanders about 5 miles along the river valley, with many entry points along the way. Whether you're on foot, skis, bike, or in-line skates, it's a tranquil spot to enjoy the outdoors. In autumn, there's a corn maze, and least four shops along the path rent bikes. ⊠ *Stowe* ⊕ *www.stowerec.org.*

ICE-SKATING
Stowe Arena. Skate rentals are available at this popular rink. Public skating hours change daily, so it's wise to check before coming here. ⊠ *350 Park St.* ☎ *802/253–3054* ⊕ *www.stowerec.org/stowe-arena/about* 🖃 *$5* ☽ *No skating Apr. and May.*

SKI AREA

Stowe Mountain Resort. The name of the village is Stowe, and the name of the mountain is Mt. Mansfield—but to generations of skiers, it's all just plain "Stowe." The area's mystique attracts as many serious skiers as social ones. Stowe is a giant among Eastern ski mountains with intimidating expert runs, but its symmetrical shape allows skiers of all abilities to enjoy long, satisfying runs from the summit. Improved snowmaking capacity, new lifts, and free shuttle buses that gather skiers along Mountain Road have made it all much more convenient. Yet the traditions remain, like the Winter Carnival in January and the Sugar Slalom in April, to name two. Spruce Peak, where you'll find the Adventure Center and the Mountain Lodge, is separate from the main mountain; the peak has a teaching hill and offers a pleasant experience for intermediates and beginners. In the summer, there's a TreeTop Adventure course and an awe-inspiring zip line that extends from the top of the gondola to the bottom in three breathtaking runs. **Facilities:** 116 trails; 485 acres; 2,360-foot vertical drop; 13 lifts. ⊠ *5781 Mountain Rd.* ☎ *802/253–3000, 802/253–3600 for snow conditions* ⊕ *www. stowe.com* ✑ *Lift ticket: $115.*

SLEDDING

FAMILY **Peacepups Dog Sledding.** This one-man (and multiple-dog) company offers two- and four-hour tours with a team of eight Siberian huskies. You can ride inside a padded toboggan, join in the driving using a two-person tandem sled, or learn how to mush and drive on your own. If you prefer to walk the trails yourself, snowshoe rentals are also available. Lake Elmore is a roughly 20-minute drive from Stowe. ⊠ *239 Cross Rd., Lake Elmore* ☎ *802/888–7733* ⊕ *www.peacepupsdogsledding.com* ✑ *$275 for dog sledding tours* ⊗ *Mid-Dec.–Mar., Wed. and Fri.–Sun. at 10, noon, and 2.*

SHOPPING

Cabot Cheese Annex Store. In addition to shelves of Vermont-made jams, mustards, crackers, and maple products, the store features a long central table with samples of a dozen Cabot cheeses. ⊠ *2657 Waterbury–Stowe Rd., 2½ miles north of I–89* ☎ *802/244–6334* ⊕ *www.cabotcheese.coop.*

FAMILY
Fodor'sChoice
★
Cold Hollow Cider Mill. You can watch apples pressed into fabulous cider at this working mill. Its store sells apple butter, jams and jellies, Vermont-made handicrafts, and 50¢ cider doughnuts. Kids get free cider popsicles and will love watching the "doughnut robot" in action. ⊠ *3600 Waterbury–Stowe Rd., 3 miles north of I–89, Waterbury Center* ☎ *800/327–7537* ⊕ *www.coldhollow.com.*

SPAS

Spa and Wellness Center at Stowe Mountain Lodge. This 21,000-square-foot facility has 18 private treatment rooms, a fitness center, and an outdoor pool and hot tub. In addition to the usual array of facials, scrubs, and massages for adults, the spa offers a separate program for kids. ⊠ *Stowe Mountain Lodge, 7412 Mountain Rd.* ☎ *802/760–4782* ⊕ *www.stowemountainlodge.com.*

Spa at Stoweflake. One of the largest spas in New England, the Spa at Stoweflake features a massaging hydrotherapeutic waterfall, a

Hungarian mineral pool, 30 treatment rooms, and 120 services like the Bingham Falls Renewal, named after a local waterfall. This treatment begins with a body scrub and a Vichy shower, followed by an aromatherapy oil massage. The spacious men's and women's sanctuaries have saunas, steam rooms, and whirlpool tubs. ✉ *Stoweflake Mountain Resort and Spa, 1746 Mountain Rd.* ☎ *802/760–1083* 🌐 *www.stoweflake.com.*

Spa at Topnotch. An aura of calm pervades the Spa at Topnotch, with its birchwood doors and accents, natural light, and cool colors. Signature services include the Mount Mansfield Saucha, a three-stage herbal body treatment (scrub, wrap, and massage), and the Little River Stone Massage, which uses the resort's own wood-spice oil. Athletes and skiers might opt for a Thai Massage, while your canine friend will beg for Rover Reiki (really). Locker areas are spacious and spotless, with saunas, steam rooms, and whirlpool tubs. The pool has high ceilings and lots of natural light. Classes in tai chi, yoga, and Pilates are offered throughout the day in the nearby fitness center. ✉ *Topnotch Resort and Spa, 4000 Mountain Rd.* ☎ *802/253–8585* 🌐 *www.topnotchresort.com.*

JEFFERSONVILLE

18 miles north of Stowe.

Jeffersonville is just over Smugglers' Notch from Stowe but miles away in feeling and attitude. In summer, you can drive over the notch road as it curves precipitously around boulders that have fallen from the cliffs above, then pass open meadows and old farmhouses and sugar shacks on the way down to town. Below the notch, Smugglers' Notch Ski Resort is the hub of activity year-round. Downtown Jeffersonville, once home to an artists' colony, is quiet but has excellent dining and nice art galleries.

EXPLORING

Boyden Valley Winery & Spirits. On a beautiful stretch of farmland west of Jeffersonville, this winery conducts tours and tastings and showcases an excellent selection of Vermont specialty products and local handicrafts. The winery's Big Barn Red is full-bodied, but the real fun may be in the ice wines, maple crème liqueur, and hard ice cider. ✉ *Rte. 15 and Rte. 104, Cambridge* ☎ *802/644–8151* 🌐 *www.boydenvalley.com* 🎫 *Tasting $10* 🕒 *June–Oct., daily 10–6; May, Nov., and Dec., daily 10–5; Jan.–Apr., Fri.–Sun 10–5. Tours at 11:30 and 1.*

WHERE TO EAT AND STAY

$ AMERICAN 🍴 **158 Main Restaurant and Bakery.** The best and most popular restaurant in Jeffersonville, 158 Main easily earns its accolades: portions are big, prices are not. For breakfast, locals love the Two Eggs Basic, which comes with two eggs any style, homemade toast, and home fries for $4. Menu selections for dinner range from sesame-seared yellowfin tuna with wok-seared vegetables to hanger steak with a maple-chipotle sauce. Sunday brunch is very popular. [$] *Average main: $17* ✉ *158 Main St.* ☎ *802/644–8100* 🌐 *www.158Main.com* 🕒 *Closed Mon. No dinner Sun.*

$$$ RESORT FAMILY Fodor's Choice ★ **Smugglers' Notch Resort.** With four giant water parks for summer fun and just about every winter activity imaginable, this family resort has amenities other places only dream about. **Pros:** great place for families to learn to ski. **Cons:** not a romantic getaway for couples. [$] *Rooms from: $300* ✉ *4323 Rte. 108 S* ☎ *802/332–6841, 800/419–4615* 🌐 *www.smuggs.com* 🛏 *600 condominiums* 🍴 *No meals.*

SPORTS AND THE OUTDOORS

KAYAKING

Vermont Canoe and Kayak. This outfitter rents canoes and kayaks for use on the Lamoille River, and leads guided canoe trips to Boyden Valley Winery. ✉ *4805 Rte. 15, behind the Family Table* ☎ *802/644–8336* 🌐 *www.vermontcanoeandkayak.com* ⏲ *Closed mid-Sept.–late May.*

LLAMA RIDES

Northern Vermont Llama Co. These llamas carry everything, including snacks and lunches, for half-day treks along the trails of Smugglers' Notch. Reservations are essential. ✉ *766 Lapland Rd., Waterville* ☎ *802/644–2257* 🌐 *www.northernvermontllamaco.com* 🎟 *$60* ⏲ *Closed early Sept.–late May.*

SKI AREA

FAMILY **Smugglers' Notch.** The "granddaddy of all family resorts," Smugglers' Notch (or "Smuggs") receives consistent praise for its family programs. Its children's ski school is one of the best in the country—possibly *the* best—but there are challenges for skiers of all levels, spread over three separate areas. This was the first ski resort in the East to designate a triple–black diamond run: the Black Hole. There's ice-skating, tubing, five terrain parks, Nordic skiing, snowshoe trails, and a snowboarding area for kids ages three–six. Summer brings waterslides, treetop courses, zip lines, and crafts workshops—in other words, something for everyone. **Facilities:** 78 trails; 300 acres; 2,610-foot vertical drop; 8 lifts. ✉ *4323 Rte. 108 S* ☎ *802/332–6841, 800/419–4615* 🌐 *www.smuggs.com* 🎟 *Lift ticket: $72.*

SHOPPING

ANTIQUES

Route 15 between Jeffersonville and Johnson is dubbed the "antiques highway."

Buggy Man. This store sells all sorts of collectibles, including horse-drawn vehicles. ✉ *853 Rte. 15, 7 miles east of Jeffersonville* ☎ *802/635–2110.*

Smugglers' Notch Antiques. In a rambling barn, this shop sells antiques, collectibles, and custom-made furniture from 60 dealers. ✉ *906 Rte. 108 S* ☎ *802/644–2100* 🌐 *www.smugglersnotchantiques.com* ⏲ *Closed Mon.–Wed.*

CLOTHING

Fodor's Choice ★ **Johnson Woolen Mills.** This factory store has great deals on woolen blankets, household goods, and the famous Johnson outerwear. ✉ *51 Lower Main St. E, 9 miles east of Jeffersonville, Johnson* ☎ *802/635–2271* 🌐 *www.johnsonwoolenmills.com.*

8

BURLINGTON

31 miles southwest of Jeffersonville, 76 miles south of Montreal, 349 miles north of New York City, 223 miles northwest of Boston.

Fodor's Choice ★ As you drive along Main Street toward downtown Burlington, it's easy to see why this four-college city is often called one of the most livable small cities in the United States. Downtown Burlington is filled with hip restaurants and bars, art galleries, and the Church Street Marketplace, a bustling pedestrian mall with trendy shops, crafts vendors, street performers, and sidewalk cafés. Just beyond, Lake Champlain shimmers beneath the towering Adirondacks on the New York shore. The revitalized Burlington waterfront teems with outdoors enthusiasts who bike or stroll along its recreation path, picnic on the grass, and ply the waters in sailboats and motor craft in summer.

EXPLORING

TOP ATTRACTIONS

Fodor's Choice ★ **Burlington Farmers' Market.** Burlington's Saturday farmers' market is an absolute must-see when visiting in summer or fall. Set up in the center of town, the market is jam-packed with local farmers selling a colorful array of organic produce, flowers, baked goods, maple syrup, meats, cheeses, and prepared foods. Local artisans also sell their wares. There's live music on the green, fresh cider and doughnuts in the fall, and always superb people-watching. From November to March, the market is held every other Saturday at Memorial Auditorium. ✉ *City Hall Park, College and St. Paul Sts.* ☎ *802/310–5172* ⊕ *www.burlingtonfarmersmarket.org* ✉ *Free* ⊙ *Late May–Oct., Sat. 8:30–2.*

FAMILY
Fodor's Choice ★ **Church Street Marketplace.** For more than 30 years, this pedestrian-only thoroughfare has served as Burlington's center of commerce and activity, with boutiques, cafés, restaurants, and street vendors the focus by day, and a lively bar and live-music scene at night. On sunny days, there are few better places to be in Burlington. ✉ *2 Church St.* ☎ *802/863–1648* ⊕ *www.churchstmarketplace.com.*

Ethan Allen Homestead Museum. When Vermont hero Ethan Allen retired from his Revolutionary activities, he purchased 350 acres along the Winooski River and built this modest cabin in 1787. The original structure is a real slice of 18th-century life, including such frontier hallmarks as saw-cut boards and an open hearth for cooking. The kitchen garden resembles the one the Allens would have had. There's also a visitor center and miles of biking and hiking trails. In warmer months, climb Ethan Allen Tower at the west end of the property for stupendous views of Lake Champlain and the Green Mountains. Don't forget mosquito repellent. ✉ *1 Ethan Allen Homestead, off Rte. 127* ☎ *802/865–4556* ⊕ *www.ethanallenhomestead.org* ✉ *$8* ⊙ *May–Oct., daily 10–4.*

WORTH NOTING

FAMILY
ECHO Leahy Center for Lake Champlain. Kids and adults can explore the geology and ecology of the Lake Champlain region through the center's more than 100 interactive exhibits, including the newest additions at the Action Lab. The lab's 3D Water Projection Sandbox manages to make learning about watersheds exciting. You can also get an up-close look

BURLINGTON'S LOCAL FOOD MOVEMENT

Burlington is exploding on the national food scene as one of the hubs of the local food movement. Known for its excellent soil and abundance of organic farms—as showcased in its huge weekly farmers' market (Saturday May–October) and popular outdoor summertime farm suppers—this health-conscious and liberal city is home to restaurants and markets with a focus on fresh, high-quality ingredients rivaling those of a much larger city. Burlington residents are likely to be seen biking to pick up their weekly CSA (Community Supported Agriculture) share at the Intervale, the city's huge web of community gardens, doing some weeding in their own urban garden plots, or stopping by one of the farms to pick berries or flowers on their way to a dinner party.

at 70 species of indigenous animals. ⊠ *1 College St.* ☎ *802/864–1848* ⊕ *www.echovermont.org* ⌨ *$13.50* ⊙ *Daily 10–5.*

OFF THE BEATEN PATH

Green Mountain Audubon Nature Center. This is a wonderful place to discover Vermont's outdoor wonders. The center's 255 acres of diverse habitats are a sanctuary for all things wild, and the 5 miles of trails provide an opportunity to explore the workings of differing natural communities. Events include bird-monitoring walks, wildflower rambles, nature workshops, and educational activities for children and adults. ⊠ *255 Sherman Hollow Rd., 18 miles southeast of Burlington, Huntington* ☎ *802/434–3068* ⊕ *vt.audubon.org* ⌨ *Donations accepted* ⊙ *Visitor center, weekdays 8:30–4:30; trails, daily sunrise–sunset.*

Magic Hat Brewing Company. You can take a self-guided tour of the brewery, which puts out hundreds of bottles per minute. Head up the ramp past paintings by local artists and look down on the factory floor. When you're finished, try free beer samples and hang out at the Growler Bar, which has eight or more beers on tap. ⊠ *5 Bartlett Bay Rd., South Burlington* ☎ *802/658–2739* ⊕ *www.magichat.net* ⌨ *Free* ⊙ *Late May–mid-Oct., Mon.–Sat. 10–7, Sun. noon–5; mid-Oct.–late May, Mon.–Thurs. 10–6, Fri. and Sat. 10–7, Sun. noon–5.*

University of Vermont. Crowning the hilltop above Burlington is the University of Vermont, known as UVM for the abbreviation of its Latin name, Universitas Viridis Montis, meaning the University of the Green Mountains. With more than 10,000 students, this is the state's principal institution of higher learning. The most architecturally impressive buildings face the green and have gorgeous lake views, as does the statue of founder Ira Allen, Ethan's brother. ⊠ *85 S. Prospect St.* ☎ *802/656–3131* ⊕ *www.uvm.edu.*

WHERE TO EAT

$$
PIZZA
Fodor's Choice
★

✕ **American Flatbread Burlington.** It might be worth going to college in Burlington just to be able to gather with friends at this wildly popular organic pizza place. Seating is first-come, first-served, and the scene is bustling with locals and visitors sipping house-made brews. The wood-fired clay dome is where the cooks create delicious pies like the Punctuated Equilibrium, which has kalamata olives, roasted red peppers, goat

CLOSE UP

Vermont by Bike

Vermont has more than 14,000 miles of roads, and almost 80% of them are town roads that see little high-speed traffic, making them ideal for scenic bike rides. More than half are dirt roads, which means they're especially suitable for mountain biking. Although mountain-bike trails and old farm and logging roads wind through the Green Mountain State, most are on private property and therefore uncharted. Several mountain-biking centers around the state have extensive trail networks (and maps) that will keep avid fat-tire fans happy for a few hours or a few days. To road bike in Vermont, you'll want a map and preferably a bicycle with at least 10 gears. The only roads that prohibit cycling are four-lane highways and U.S. 7 and U.S. 4 in Rutland.

TOP ROAD BIKING ROUTES:
For a relatively easy 16-mile loop, begin at the blinker on U.S. 7 in **Shelburne** and follow Mt. Philo Road south to Hinesburg Road, then west to Charlotte. Lake Road and Orchard Road go past orchards and berry fields; Bostwick Road will take you back to U.S. 7.

In the heart of the central Green Mountains is a moderate 18-mile loop on U.S. 4, Route 100, and Route 100A that passes Calvin Coolidge's home in **Plymouth Notch.**

West of **Rutland** is a beautiful 27-mile ride on Routes 140, 30, and 133 that passes swimming holes, then hugs the shore of Lake St. Catherine. Start in Middletown Springs.

A scenic 43-mile ride in the **Northeast Kingdom** passes through pleasant Peacham and the birches and maples of Groton State Forest. Start in Danville and follow Peacham Road, then Routes 302 and 232, and U.S. 2.

For a real test, try the 48-mile ride over **Middlebury and Brandon Gaps** on Routes 125 and 73, which connect via Routes 153 and 100.

cheese, fresh rosemary, red onions, mozzarella, and garlic. Fresh salads topped with locally made cheese are also popular. Here's to the college life! [$] *Average main: $20* ✉ *115 St. Paul St.* ☎ *802/861–2999* 🌐 *www.americanflatbread.com* ✍ *Reservations not accepted.*

$$ AMERICAN Fodor's Choice ★ 🍴 **Farmhouse Tap and Grill.** This is one of the most popular restaurants in town, so don't be put off by the line on a typical weekend night. Known for using only local beef, cheese, and produce, this farm-to-table enterprise is laid-back in style but provides one of the finest meals in the area. Specialties include burgers, chicken and biscuits, and local cheese and charcuterie plates, and there's a great wine and craft-beer selection. **TIP→ Put your name on the list and have a drink at the downstairs Tap Room or the outdoor beer garden while you wait.** If the wait feels too long, try El Cortijo, the same owners' small taqueria down the street, for locally raised beef or chicken tacos and terrific margaritas. [$] *Average main: $18* ✉ *160 Bank St.* ☎ *802/859–0888* 🌐 *www.farmhousetg.com.*

$$$$ STEAKHOUSE 🍴 **Guild Tavern.** Vermont's best steak can be found roasting over hardwood coals in the tavern's open kitchens. All meat is sourced from local farms, dry-aged a minimum of 21 days, and cooked to absolute perfection. The space itself is also a treat, with antique chicken feeders serving

as light fixtures and a soapstone-topped bar in the center. Lighter fare is available, but make sure at least one person in your party orders the rib eye. [$] *Average main: $45* ✉ *1633 Williston Rd.* ☎ *802/497–1207* 🌐 *www.guildtavern.com* 🕑 *No lunch.*

$$$ MODERN AMERICAN Fodor's Choice ★ 🍴 **Hen of the Wood Burlington.** Arguably Vermont's best restaurant, Hen of the Wood has acquiesced to the desires of its ravenous fans and opened a branch in Burlington. With a more urban feel than that of the original location in Waterbury, the restaurant serves the same inventive yet down-to-earth cuisine that sets diners' hearts aflutter and tongues wagging. Drop your finger anywhere on the menu and you can't go wrong, especially with dishes like brown butter crêpes stuffed with chanterelles, and smoked bluefish toast in buttermilk. If you ever need to say "I love you," this is the place. [$] *Average main: $27* ✉ *55 Cherry St.* ☎ *802/540–0534* 🌐 *www.henofthewood.com* 🕑 *No lunch.*

$$$ MODERN AMERICAN 🍴 **Juniper.** The Hotel Vermont has generated excitement not only for its new-school accommodations, but also its ground-floor restaurant and bar. Juniper's delightful design—a perfect blend of boutique chic and real Vermont, with reclaimed antique red-oak floors, black granite walls, and a free-flowing layout—is only part of the fun. The rest is in the inventive menu, which dazzles with items such as juniper-roasted quail and applewood-smoked pickled eggs. The cocktails lineup is among the best in town. Weather permitting, you can stay toasty on the outdoor patio with its central fire pit. [$] *Average main: $29* ✉ *41 Cherry St.* ☎ *802/651–5027* 🌐 *www.hotelvt.com/dining-drinking.*

$$$ CAFÉ 🍴 **Leunig's Bistro and Cafe.** This popular café delivers alfresco bistro cuisine, a friendly European-style bar, and live jazz. Favorite entrées include salade niçoise, *soupe au pistou* (vegetable and white bean soup with Asiago and pesto), and beef bourguignon. Fans of crème brûlée: this place makes the best in town. A prix-fixe dinner for two goes for $35: it's one of the city's best bargains. An expanded upstairs lounge offers cocktails, a smart wine selection, and local cheese plates and other light fare. This is a great spot for weekend brunch. [$] *Average main: $28* ✉ *115 Church St.* ☎ *802/863–3759* 🌐 *www.leunigsbistro.com.*

$ AMERICAN FAMILY 🍴 **Penny Cluse Cafe.** This popular breakfast and brunch spot is often buzzing with activity. Weekend lines can be long, but locals think it's worth the wait for the famous gingerbread-blueberry pancakes, warm biscuits with herb gravy, huevos rancheros, and homemade banana bread. [$] *Average main: $10* ✉ *169 Cherry St.* ☎ *802/651–8834* 🌐 *www.pennycluse.com* 🕑 *No dinner.*

$$ CHINESE 🍴 **A Single Pebble.** The creative, authentic Chinese fare served on the first floor of this residential row house includes traditional clay-pot dishes as well as wok specialties like beef with baby bok choy and chicken with peanuts and chili peppers. The dry-fried green beans, sautéed with flecks of pork, black beans, preserved vegetables, and garlic, are a house specialty, as is the "mock eel" (braised shiitake mushrooms) served in a crispy ginger sauce. Any dish can be made without meat. **■ TIP→ Try the dim sum on Sunday 11:30–1:45.** [$] *Average main: $22* ✉ *133 Bank St.* ☎ *802/865–5200* 🌐 *www.asinglepebble.com* ✍ *Reservations essential.*

$$$ ITALIAN 🍴 **Trattoria Delia.** If you didn't make that trip to Umbria this year, the next best thing is this Italian country eatery around the corner from

City Hall Park. Seafood, beef, and fresh produce are the stars; go for the braised or wood-grilled items on the menu. In winter, try to reserve a table near the fire. The husband-and-wife owners also run an adjoining wine bar called Sotto. $ *Average main: $25* ⊠ *152 St. Paul St.* ☎ *802/864–5253* ⊕ *www.trattoriadelia.com* ⊗ *No lunch* ⚖ *Reservations essential.*

$$
AMERICAN
✕ **Waterworks Food + Drink.** The converted Champlain Mill houses one of the most popular restaurants in Winooski, Burlington's hip, more diverse neighbor to the north. Come for the expansive bar and dining room, with its lofty wood-beam ceilings and exposed brick, and be wowed by the river views—pure drama in winter. Dishes can be pricey, but there's a good burger with garlicky fries, and you can order flatbread topped with eclectic ingredients that include duck confit, lobster, and sweet corn. Waterworks hosts live music on many weekend nights, brunch on Sunday, and upstairs you can visit the Winooski Historical Society Museum. $ *Average main: $20* ⊠ *20 Winooski Falls Way, Winooski* ☎ *802/497–3525* ⊕ *www.waterworksvt.com.*

$
AMERICAN
✕ **Zabby and Elf's Stone Soup.** A perfect place to stop for a delicious and healthful lunch or early dinner, Stone Soup offers all-local produce and organic ingredients showcased in fresh sandwiches, wonderful soups, homemade breads, and a wide array of baked goods. There are many veggie and vegan options, as well as popular daily specials and a small salad bar. $ *Average main: $12* ⊠ *211 College St.* ☎ *802/862–7616* ⊕ *www.stonesoupvt.com* ⊗ *Closed Sun.*

WHERE TO STAY

$$$
HOTEL
Fodor's Choice
★
🛏 **Hotel Vermont.** Ever since the Hotel Vermont opened its doors in 2013, guests have been stepping inside with acute curiosity and walking out with effusive praise. **Pros:** destination restaurant; gorgeous rooms; unbelievable service. **Cons:** luxury doesn't come cheap. $ *Rooms from: $309* ⊠ *41 Cherry St.* ☎ *802/651–0080* ⊕ *www.hotelvt.com* ⤴ *120 rooms, 5 suites* ⊗ *No meals.*

$$
B&B/INN
🛏 **The Lang House on Main Street.** Within walking distance of downtown in the historic hill section of town, this grand 1881 Victorian home charms completely with its period furnishings, fine woodwork, plaster detailing, and stained-glass windows. **Pros:** family-friendly vibe; interesting location; well run. **Cons:** no elevator. $ *Rooms from: $209* ⊠ *360 Main St.* ☎ *802/652–2500, 877/919–9799* ⊕ *www.langhouse.com* ⤴ *11 rooms* ⊗ *Breakfast.*

$
B&B/INN
🛏 **Willard Street Inn.** High in the historic hill section of Burlington, this ivy-covered house with an exterior marble staircase and English gardens incorporates elements of Queen Anne and Georgian Revival styles. **Pros:** innkeepers passionate about their job; lots of friendly attention. **Cons:** a tad old-fashioned; walk to downtown can be a drag in winter. $ *Rooms from: $150* ⊠ *349 S. Willard St.* ☎ *802/651–8710, 800/577–8712* ⊕ *www.willardstreetinn.com* ⤴ *14 rooms* ⊗ *Breakfast.*

Burlington's pedestrian-only Church Street Marketplace and the nearby shores of Lake Champlain are great for exploring.

NIGHTLIFE AND PERFORMING ARTS

NIGHTLIFE

Higher Ground. When you feel like shaking it up to live music, come to Higher Ground—it gets the lion's share of local and national musicians. ✉ *1214 Williston Rd., South Burlington* ☎ *802/652–0777* ⊕ *www.highergroundmusic.com.*

Nectar's. Jam band Phish got its start at Nectar's, which is always jumping to the sounds of local bands and never charges a cover. Don't leave without a helping of the bar's famous fries and gravy. ✉ *188 Main St.* ☎ *802/658–4771* ⊕ *www.liveatnectars.com.*

Radio Bean. For some true local flavor, head to this funky place for nightly live music, an artsy vibe, and a cocktail. Tuesday is the most fun, as the house band Honkey Tonk blazes through covers of Gram Parsons, Wilco, and the like—all of which goes down especially well with chicken and waffles. ✉ *8 N. Winooski Ave.* ☎ *802/660–9346* ⊕ *www.radiobean.com.*

Vermont Pub & Brewery. Vermont's first brewpub still makes its own beer and remains a popular spot—especially in warm weather, when locals head to the outdoor patio. Folk musicians play here regularly. ✉ *144 College St.* ☎ *802/865–0500* ⊕ *www.vermontbrewery.com.*

PERFORMING ARTS

Fodor'sChoice
★

Flynn Center for the Performing Arts. A grandiose art-deco gem, the Flynn Theatre is the cultural heart of Burlington. In addition to being home to Vermont's largest musical theater company, it hosts the Vermont Symphony Orchestra, as well as big-name acts like Neko Case and

8

Elvis Costello. The adjacent Flynn Space is a coveted spot for more offbeat, experimental performances. ✉ *153 Main St.* ☎ *802/863–5966* ⊕ *www.flynncenter.org.*

SPORTS AND THE OUTDOORS

BEACHES

FAMILY **North Beach.** Along Burlington's "new" North End a long line of beaches stretches to the Winooski River delta, beginning with North Beach, which has a grassy picnic area, a snack bar, and boat rentals. Neighboring Leddy Park offers a more secluded beach. **Amenities:** food and drink; lifeguards; parking (fee); showers; toilets. **Best for:** partiers; swimming; walking; windsurfing. ✉ *North Beach Park, 52 Institute Rd., off North Ave.* ☎ *802/865–7247* ⊕ *www.enjoyburlington.com/venue/north-beach* 🅿 *Parking $8 (May–Oct.)* ☉ *Daily sunrise–sunset.*

BIKING

FAMILY **Burlington Bike Path.** Anyone who's put the rubber to the road on the
Fodor's Choice 7½-mile Burlington Bike Path and its almost equally long northern
★ extension on the Island Line Trail sings its praises. Along the way there are endless postcard views of Lake Champlain and the Adirondack Mountains. The northern end of the trail is slightly more rugged and windswept, so dress accordingly. ✉ *Burlington* ☎ *802/864–0123* ⊕ *www.enjoyburlington.com/venue/burlington-bike-path.*

North Star Sports. In addition to stocking an extensive supply of sports apparel and accessories, this family-owned shop rents bikes and provides cycling maps. ✉ *100 Main St.* ☎ *802/863–3832* ⊕ *www.northstarsportsvt.com.*

Ski Rack. Burlington's one-stop shop for winter sports equipment, the Ski Rack also rents bikes and sells running gear throughout the year. ✉ *85 Main St.* ☎ *802/658–3313, 800/882–4530* ⊕ *www.skirack.com.*

BOATING

Burlington Community Boathouse. This boathouse administers the city's marina as well as a summertime watering hole called Splash, one of the best places to watch the sun set over the lake. ✉ *Burlington Harbor, College St.* ☎ *802/865–3377* ⊕ *www.enjoyburlington.com/venue/community-boathouse-marina.*

FAMILY **Community Sailing Center.** Dinghies, keelboats, and kayaks are available for rent here, and the center offers classes for all experience levels. ✉ *1 Lake St.* ☎ *802/864–2499* ⊕ *www.communitysailingcenter.org* ☉ *Closed mid-Oct.–mid-May.*

Lake Champlain Shoreline Cruises. The trilevel *Spirit of Ethan Allen III,* a 363-passenger vessel, offers narrated cruises, theme dinners, and sunset sails with breathtaking Adirondacks and Green Mountains views. The standard 1½-hour cruise runs four times a day; evening cruises leave at 6:30. ✉ *Burlington Boat House, 1 College St.* ☎ *802/862–8300* ⊕ *www.soea.com* 🅿 *$16* ☉ *Late May–mid-Oct., daily 10–9.*

True North Kayak Tours. This company conducts two- and five-hour guided kayak tours of Lake Champlain that include talks about the region's natural history. It also offers customized lessons and runs a kayak camp for kids. ✉ *25 Nash Pl.* ☎ *802/238–7695* ⊕ *www.vermontkayak.com.*

SKI AREA

Bolton Valley Resort. About 25 miles from Burlington, this ski area is a family favorite. In addition to downhill trails—more than half rated for intermediate and beginner skiers—Bolton offers 62 miles of cross-country and snowshoe trails, night skiing, and a sports center. **Facilities:** 71 trails; 300 acres; 1,704-foot vertical drop; 5 lifts. ✉ *4302 Bolton Valley Access Rd., north off U.S. 2, Bolton* ☎ *802/434–3444, 877/926–5866* ⊕ *www.boltonvalley.com* ⌨ *Lift ticket: $59.*

SHOPPING

With each passing year, Burlington's industrial South End attracts ever greater numbers of artists and craftspeople, who set up studios, shops, and galleries in former factories and warehouses along Pine Street. The district's annual "Art Hop" is the city's largest arts celebration—and a roaring good time.

CLOTHING

April Cornell. The Vermont designer's flagship store stocks her distinctive floral-print dresses and linens. ✉ *131 Battery St.* ☎ *802/863–0060* ⊕ *www.aprilcornell.com.*

CRAFTS

Bennington Potters North. Along with the popular pottery line, this store stocks interesting kitchen items. ✉ *127 College St.* ☎ *802/863–2221* ⊕ *www.benningtonpotters.com.*

Frog Hollow. This nonprofit collective and gallery sells contemporary and traditional crafts, paintings, and photographs by more than 200 Vermont artists and artisans. ✉ *85 Church St.* ☎ *802/863–6458* ⊕ *www.froghollow.org.*

FOOD

Lake Champlain Chocolates. This chocolatier makes sensational truffles, caramels, candies, fudge, and hot chocolate. The chocolates are all-natural, made in Vermont, and make a great edible souvenir. ✉ *750 Pine St.* ☎ *800/465–5909* ⊕ *www.lakechamplainchocolates.com.*

SPORTING GOODS

Burton. The folks who helped start snowboarding—a quintessential Vermont company—sell equipment and clothing at their flagship store. ✉ *80 Industrial Pkwy.* ☎ *802/660–3200* ⊕ *www.burton.com.*

8

SHELBURNE

5 miles south of Burlington.

A few miles south of Burlington, the Champlain Valley gives way to fertile farmland, affording views of the rugged Adirondacks across the lake. In the middle of this farmland is the village of Shelburne (and just farther south, beautiful and more rural Charlotte), chartered in the mid-18th century and partly a bedroom community for Burlington.

Shelburne Farms is worth at least a few hours of exploring, as are Shelburne Orchards in fall, when you can pick your own apples and drink fresh cider while admiring breathtaking views of the lake and mountains beyond.

GETTING HERE AND AROUND

Shelburne is south of Burlington after the town of South Burlington, notable for its very un-Vermont traffic congestion and a commercial and fast food–laden stretch of U.S. 7. It's easy to confuse Shelburne Farms (2 miles west of town on the lake) with Shelburne Museum, which is right on U.S. 7 just south of town, but you'll want to make time for both.

EXPLORING

Fiddlehead Brewing Company. There isn't much to the tasting room here, but there doesn't need to be: Fiddlehead only occasionally cans its celebrated beer, making this the best place outside of a restaurant to sample it on tap (and for free). Decide which one you like best and buy a growler to go—or, better yet, take it to Folino's Pizza next door. The pizzeria may be short on atmosphere, but the pies are mighty fine. ⊠ *6305 Shelburne Rd.* ☏ *802/399–2994* ⊕ *www.fiddleheadbrewing. com* ⌚ *Free* ☉ *Sun. and Mon.–Wed. noon–8, Thurs. and Fri. noon–9, Sat. 11–9.*

FAMILY
Fodor's Choice
★

Shelburne Farms. Founded in the 1880s as a private estate for two very rich New Yorkers, this 1,400-acre farm is much more than an exquisite landscape: it's an educational and cultural resource center with a working dairy farm, an award-winning cheese producer, an organic market garden, and a bakery whose aroma of fresh bread and pastries is an olfactory treat. It's a brilliant place for parents to expose their kids to the dignity of farm work and the joys of compassionate animal husbandry—indeed, children and adults alike will get a kick out of hunting for eggs in the oversize coop, milking a cow, and watching the chicken parade. There are activities every half hour 10–4, and a lunch cart serves up fresh-from-the-farm soups, salads, and sandwiches. Frederick Law Olmsted, the co-creator of New York City's Central Park, designed the magnificent grounds overlooking Lake Champlain; walk to Lone Tree Hill for a splendid view. If you fall in love with the scenery, arrange a romantic dinner at the lakefront mansion, or spend the night. ⊠ *1611 Harbor Rd., west of U.S. 7* ☏ *802/985–8498* ⊕ *www.shelburnefarms. org* ⌚ *$8* ☉ *Visitor center: mid-May–mid-Oct., daily 9–5:30; mid-Oct.– mid-May, daily 10–5.*

FAMILY
Fodor's Choice
★

Shelburne Museum. You can trace much of New England's history simply by wandering through the 45 acres and 38 buildings of this museum. Some 25 buildings were relocated here, including an old-fashioned jail, an 1871 lighthouse, and a 220-foot steamboat, the *Ticonderoga*. The outstanding 150,000-object collection of art, design, and Americana consists of antique furniture, fine and folk art, quilts, trade signs, and weather vanes; there are also more than 200 carriages and sleighs. The Pizzagalli Center for Art and Education is open year-round with changing exhibitions and programs for kids and adults. ⊠ *6000 Shelburne Rd.* ☏ *802/985–3346* ⊕ *www.shelburnemuseum.org* ⌚ *$22* ☉ *May–Dec., daily 10–5; Jan.–Apr., Tues.–Sun. 10–5.*

Shelburne Vineyard. From U.S. 7, you'll see rows and rows of organically grown vines. Visit the attractive tasting room and learn how wine is made. ✉ *6308 Shelburne Rd.* ☎ *802/985–8222* 🌐 *www.shelburnevineyard.com* 🎟 *Tasting $7, tour free* 🕒 *Tasting room: May–Oct., daily 11–6; Nov.–Apr., daily 11–5. Tours: May–Oct., daily at 1, 2, 3, and 4; Nov.–Apr., Sat. at 1, 2, 3, and 4.*

FAMILY **Vermont Teddy Bear Company.** On the 30-minute tour of this fun-filled factory you'll hear more puns than you ever thought possible, while learning how a few homemade bears sold from a cart on Church Street have turned into a multimillion-dollar business. Patrons and children can relax, eat, and play under a large canvas tent in summer, or wander the beautiful 57-acre property. ✉ *6655 Shelburne Rd.* ☎ *802/985–3001* 🌐 *www.vermontteddybear.com* 🎟 *Tour $4* 🕒 *July–mid-Oct., daily 9:30–5 (tours every ½ hr); mid-Oct.–June, daily 10–4 (tours on the hr).*

WHERE TO EAT

$$ ECLECTIC 🍴 **The Bearded Frog.** This is the top restaurant in the Shelburne area, perfect for a casual dinner in the bar or a more sophisticated experience in the attractive dining room. At the bar, try the soups, burgers, and terrific cocktails; the dining room serves fresh salads, seared seafood, roasted poultry, grilled steaks, and decadent desserts. [$] *Average main: $20* ✉ *5247 Shelburne Rd.* ☎ *802/985–9877* 🌐 *www.thebeardedfrog.com* 🕒 *No lunch.*

$$$ AMERICAN Fodor's Choice ★ 🍴 **The Dining Room at the Inn at Shelburne Farms.** Dinner here will make you dream of F. Scott Fitzgerald. Piano music wafts in from the library as you carry a drink through the rooms of this 1880s mansion, gazing across a long lawn and formal gardens on the shore of dark Lake Champlain—you'll swear Jay Gatsby is about to come down the stairs. Count on just-grown ingredients that come from market gardens, as well as flavorful locally grown venison, beef, pork, and chicken. On weekends a spread of produce is set up next to a cocktail bar with fresh specialties, and Sunday brunch is the area's best. The dining room overlooks the lake. [$] *Average main: $32* ✉ *Inn at Shelburne Farms, 1611 Harbor Rd.* ☎ *802/985–8498* 🌐 *www.shelburnefarms.org* 🕒 *Closed mid-Oct.–mid-May.*

$$ AMERICAN 🍴 **Rustic Roots.** Wednesday through Sunday, this downtown restaurant inside a converted farmhouse serves a hearty brunch. Scuffed wood floors and chunky country tables bring the "rustic," but not too much so: an intimate bar and maroon walls adorned with woodcrafts and art add a touch of elegance, and the food is carefully prepared. If your dish doesn't come with the coffee-maple sausage or popovers, order them on the side. There are only seven tables, so reservations are essential for the French-inspired dinners, served on weekend nights only. [$] *Average main: $19* ✉ *195 Falls Rd.* ☎ *802/985–9511* 🌐 *www.rusticrootsvt.com* 🕒 *Closed Mon. and Tues. No dinner Wed., Thurs., and Sun.* ✍ *Reservations essential.*

WHERE TO STAY

$$ B&B/INN 🏨 **Heart of the Village Inn.** Each of the elegantly furnished rooms at this bed-and-breakfast in an 1886 Queen Anne Victorian provides coziness and tastefully integrated modern conveniences. **Pros:** adorable village

Shelburne Museum's many attractions include the *Ticonderoga* steamship and other pieces from New England's past.

inn; elegant; well run; easy walk to shops and restaurants. **Cons:** near to but not within Shelburne Farms. $ *Rooms from: $200* ⊠ *5347 Shelburne Rd.* ☎ *802/985–9060* ⊕ *www.heartofthevillage.com* ⇱ *7 rooms, 2 suites* ⦿ *Breakfast.*

$ ⛳ **The Inn at Shelburne Farms.** It's hard not to feel like an aristocrat at
B&B/INN this exquisite turn-of-the-20th-century Tudor-style inn, one of the most
Fodor's Choice memorable properties in the country. **Pros:** stately lakefront setting in a
★ fantastic historic mansion; great service; wonderful value; romantic restaurant. **Cons:** lowest-priced rooms have shared baths; closed in winter; must book far in advance. $ *Rooms from: $170* ⊠ *1611 Harbor Rd.* ☎ *802/985–8498* ⊕ *www.shelburnefarms.org* ⊘ *Closed mid-Oct.–mid-May* ⇱ *24 rooms (17 with bath), 2 cottages, 2 houses* ⦿ *No meals.*

$$ ⛳ **Mt. Philo Inn.** If you've grown tired of the floral wallpaper of so many
B&B/INN traditional New England inns, Jane and Dave Garbose's Mt. Philo Inn
Fodor's Choice may be for you. **Pros:** space, and lots of it; elegant rooms; great art col-
★ lection. **Cons:** a bit remote. $ *Rooms from: $280* ⊠ *27 Inn Rd., Charlotte* ☎ *802/425–3335* ⊕ *www.mtphiloinn.com* ⇱ *4 suites* ⦿ *No meals.*

SHOPPING

The Flying Pig Bookstore. It should come as no surprise that this bookstore is notable for its whimsy and carefully curated children's section: one of the owners is a stand-up comedian, and the other is a picture-book author. ⊠ *5247 Shelburne Rd.* ☎ *802/985–3999* ⊕ *www.flyingpigbooks.com.*

The Shelburne Country Store. As you enter this store, you'll feel as though you've stepped back in time. Walk past the potbelly stove and take in the aroma emanating from the fudge neatly piled behind huge antique glass cases, alongside a vast selection of penny candies and chocolates. There are creemees, of course, but here the specialties are candles, weather vanes, glassware, and local foods. ✉ *29 Falls Rd., off U.S. 7* ☎ *800/660–3657* 🌐 *www.shelburnecountrystore.com.*

VERGENNES

12 miles south of Shelburne.

Vermont's oldest city, founded in 1788, has a compact downtown area of restored Victorian homes and public buildings, with a few good eateries sprinkled throughout. Main Street slopes down to Otter Creek Falls, where cannonballs were made during the War of 1812. The statue of Thomas Macdonough on the green immortalizes the victor of the Battle of Plattsburgh (1814).

ESSENTIALS

Visitor Information Addison County Chamber of Commerce. ✉ *93 Court St., Middlebury* ☎ *802/388–7951* 🌐 *www.addisoncounty.com.*

EXPLORING

OFF THE BEATEN PATH

Lake Champlain Maritime Museum. This museum documents centuries of activity on the historically significant lake. Climb aboard a replica of Benedict Arnold's Revolutionary War gunboat moored in the lake, learn about shipwrecks, watch craftsmen work at traditional boatbuilding and blacksmithing, or take a course—for an hour or all day—in boatbuilding, rowing, blacksmithing, or other endeavors. ✉ *4472 Basin Harbor Rd., 7 miles west of Vergennes* ☎ *802/475–2022* 🌐 *www.lcmm.org* 🎟 *$12* 🕓 *May–mid-Oct., daily 10–5.*

Rokeby Museum. A Quaker family farm for nearly two centuries, this National Historic Landmark served as a safe haven for runaway slaves during the days of the Underground Railroad. Join one of the guided house tours, explore the grounds and the historic farm buildings, or set off on the 50 acres of hiking trails. ✉ *4334 U.S. 7, Ferrisburgh* ☎ *802/877–3406* 🌐 *www.rokeby.org* 🎟 *$10* 🕓 *Grounds: mid-May–late Oct., daily 10–5. House tours: mid-May–late Oct., Fri.–Mon. at 11 and 2.*

WHERE TO EAT AND STAY

$$$ ECLECTIC

🍴 **Starry Night Café.** This chic restaurant is one of the hottest spots around. The proprietors serve seasonal, farm-to-table cuisine, like grilled organic pork loin and fennel-pollen-scented seared salmon, among handcrafted tableware and furniture. A rotating display of works by local artists graces the walls, and the fireside porch, with its views of gardens and trees, is open at least three seasons of the year. [$] *Average main: $28* ✉ *5371 U.S. 7, 5 miles north of Vergennes, Ferrisburgh* ☎ *802/877–6316* 🌐 *www.starrynightcafe.com* 🕓 *Closed Mon. and Tues. No lunch* ✍ *Reservations essential.*

$ BAKERY

🍴 **Vergennes Laundry.** Though its decor is minimalist, this bakery is full of delights. The morning buns and cardamom buns are worth a stop alone, but there's so much more—including a rotating selection of delicious breads, pastries, and cookies, along with sandwiches on fresh baguettes, artisanal cheeses, gazpacho, and raw oysters. Pair whatever you order with a fresh-squeezed juice or espresso, and you'll be more than satisfied. $ *Average main: $8* ✉ *247 Main St.* ☎ *802/870–7157* ⊕ *vergenneslaundry.squarespace.com* ☉ *Closed Mon.–Wed., and Sept.*

$$

RESORT

FAMILY

Fodor's Choice

★

Basin Harbor Club. Set amid 700 acres overlooking Lake Champlain, this ultimate family resort provides luxurious accommodations and a full roster of amenities, including an 18-hole golf course, various boating options, and morning and evening children's programs. **Pros:** gorgeous lakeside property; activities galore; wonderful for families. **Cons:** open only half the year; pricey; often booked by corporate groups. $ *Rooms from: $270* ✉ *4800 Basin Harbor Rd.* ☎ *802/475–2311, 800/622–4000* ⊕ *www.basinharbor.com* ☉ *Closed mid-Oct.–mid-May* ⌁ *47 rooms, 73 cottages* ◉ *Breakfast.*

SHOPPING

Dakin Farm. Cob-smoked ham, aged cheddar cheese, maple syrup made on-site, and other well-crafted specialty foods can be sampled here. You can also visit the smokehouse and watch the waxing and sealing of cheeses. ✉ *5797 U.S. 7, 5 miles north of Vergennes* ☎ *800/993–2546* ⊕ *www.dakinfarm.com.*

LAKE CHAMPLAIN ISLANDS

Lake Champlain stretches more than 100 miles south from the Canadian border and forms the northern part of the boundary between New York and Vermont. Within it is an elongated archipelago comprising several islands—Isle La Motte, North Hero, Grand Isle, and South Hero—and the Alburg Peninsula. Enjoying a temperate climate, the islands hold several apple orchards and are a center of water recreation in summer and ice fishing in winter. A scenic drive through the islands on U.S. 2 begins at Interstate 89 and travels north to Alburg Center; Route 78 takes you back to the mainland.

ESSENTIALS

Visitor Information Lake Champlain Islands Chamber of Commerce. ✉ *3501 U.S. 2, Suite 100, North Hero* ☎ *802/372–8400, 800/262–5226* ⊕ *www.champlainislands.com.* **Lake Champlain Regional Chamber of Commerce.** ✉ *60 Main St., Suite 100, Burlington* ☎ *802/863–3489, 877/686–5253* ⊕ *www.vermont.org.*

EXPLORING

Allenholm Farm. The pick-your-own apples at this farm are amazingly tasty—if you're here at harvesttime, don't miss out. The farm also has a petting area with donkeys, miniature horses, sheep, goats, and other animals. At the store, you can buy cheeses, dried fruit, homemade pies, and maple syrup creemees. ✉ *111 South St., South Hero* ☎ *802/372–5566* ⊕ *www.allenholm.com* ☲ *Free* ☉ *Mid-May–Dec., daily 9–5.*

Snow Farm Vineyard and Winery. Vermont's first vineyard was started here in 1996; today, the winery specializes in nontraditional botanical hybrid grapes designed to withstand the local climate. Take a self-guided tour and sip some samples in the tasting room—dessert wines are their strong suit. On Thursday evening, mid-June–early September, you can picnic and enjoy the free concerts on the lawn. ✉ *190 W. Shore Rd., South*

Hero ☎ *802/372–9463* 🌐 *www.snowfarm.com* 🎟 *Free* ⏲ *May–Dec., daily 11–5; Jan.–Apr., Fri. 5–9, weekends 11–4.*

St. Anne's Shrine. This spot marks the site where, in 1665, French soldiers and Jesuits put ashore and built a fort, creating Vermont's first European settlement. The state's first Roman Catholic Mass was celebrated here on July 26, 1666. ✉ *92 St. Anne's Rd., Isle La Motte* ☎ *802/928–3362* 🌐 *www.saintannesshrine.org* 🎟 *Free* ⏲ *Mid-May–mid-Oct., daily 9–4; Nov.–Apr., hrs vary.*

WHERE TO STAY

$ B&B/INN FAMILY 🏨 **North Hero House Inn and Restaurant.** This inn has four buildings right on Lake Champlain, among them the 1891 Colonial Revival main house with nine guest rooms, a restaurant, a pub room, a library, and a sitting room. **Pros:** relaxed complex; superb lakefront setting. **Cons:** closed in winter. [$] *Rooms from: $140* ✉ *3643 U.S. Rural Rte. 2, North Hero* ☎ *802/372–4732, 888/525–3644* 🌐 *www.northherohouse.com* ⏲ *Closed Nov.–Mar.* 🛏 *23 rooms, 3 suites* 🍴 *Breakfast.*

$ HOTEL 🏨 **Ruthcliffe Lodge & Restaurant.** Good food and splendid scenery make this off-the-beaten-path motel directly on Lake Champlain a great value. **Pros:** inexpensive rates; serene setting; laid-back vibe. **Cons:** rooms simple, not luxurious. [$] *Rooms from: $142* ✉ *1002 Quarry Rd., Isle La Motte* ☎ *802/928–3200* 🌐 *www.ruthcliffe.com* ⏲ *Closed mid-Oct.–mid-May* 🛏 *7 rooms* 🍴 *Breakfast.*

SPORTS AND THE OUTDOORS

Alburg Dunes State Park. This park has one of the longest sandy beaches on Lake Champlain and some fine examples of rare flora and fauna along the hiking trails. ✉ *151 Coon Point Rd., off U.S. 2, Alburg* ☎ *802/796–4170* 🌐 *www.vtstateparks.com/htm/alburg.htm* 🎟 *$4* ⏲ *Mid-May–early Sept., daily sunrise–sunset.*

Apple Island Resort. The resort's marina rents pontoon boats, rowboats, canoes, kayaks, and pedal boats. ✉ *71 U.S. 2, South Hero* ☎ *802/372–3922* 🌐 *www.appleislandresort.com.*

Grand Isle State Park. You'll find hiking trails, boat rentals, and shore fishing at Grand Isle. ✉ *36 E. Shore S, off U.S. 2, Grand Isle* ☎ *802/372–4300* 🌐 *www.vtstateparks.com/htm/grandisle.htm* 🎟 *$4* ⏲ *Mid-May–mid-Oct., daily sunrise–sunset.*

Hero's Welcome. This general store rents bikes, canoes, kayaks, and paddleboards; come winter, they switch to ice skates, cross-country skis, and snowshoes. ✉ *3643 U.S. 2, North Hero* ☎ *802/372–4161, 800/372–4376* 🌐 *www.heroswelcome.com.*

Missisquoi National Wildlife Refuge. Located on the mainland east of the Alburg Peninsula, the refuge consists of 6,729 acres of federally protected wetlands, meadows, and woods. It's a beautiful area for bird-watching, canoeing, and walking nature trails. ✉ *29 Tabor Rd., 36 miles north of Burlington, Swanton* ☎ *802/868–4781* 🌐 *www.fws.gov/refuge/missisquoi.*

North Hero State Park. The 399-acre North Hero has a swimming beach and nature trails. It's open to rowboats, kayaks, and canoes. ✉ *3803*

DID YOU KNOW?

Long and skinny Lake Champlain is sometimes called the sixth Great Lake. Several small and scenic islands, like Grand Isle, are popular seasonal getaways in warm weather.

Lakeview Dr., North Hero ☎ *802/372–8727* 🌐 *www.vtstateparks.com/htm/northhero.htm* 🎟 *$4* 🕒 *Mid-May–early Sept., daily sunrise–sunset.*

Sand Bar State Park. One of Vermont's best swimming beaches is at Sand Bar State Park, along with a snack bar, a changing room, and boat rentals. ✉ *1215 U.S. 2, South Hero* ☎ *802/893–2825* 🌐 *www.vtstateparks.com/htm/sandbar.htm* 🎟 *$4* 🕒 *Late May–early Sept., daily 10–9.*

MONTGOMERY AND JAY

51 miles northeast of Burlington.

Montgomery is a small village near the Jay Peak ski resort and the Canadian border. Amid the surrounding countryside are seven covered bridges.

GETTING HERE AND AROUND

Montgomery lies at the junction of Routes 58, 118, and 242. From Burlington, take Interstate 89 north to Routes 105 and 118 east. Route 242 connects Montgomery and, to the northeast, the Jay Peak Resort.

EXPLORING

OFF THE BEATEN PATH

Lake Memphremagog. Vermont's second-largest body of water, Lake Memphremagog extends 33 miles north from Newport into Canada. Prouty Beach in Newport has tennis courts, boat rentals, and a 9-hole disc-golf course. Watch the sun set from the deck of the East Side Restaurant, which serves excellent burgers and prime rib. ✉ *242 Prouty Beach Rd., Newport* ☎ *802/334–6345* 🌐 *www.newportrecreation.org.*

WHERE TO STAY

$$ B&B/INN Fodor's Choice ★

🏨 **The INN.** Innkeepers Nick Barletta and Scott Pasfield have transformed this older property into a smart chalet-style lodging with tons of character. **Pros:** Trout River views from back rooms; within walking distance of shops and supplies. **Cons:** noise from bar can seep into nearby rooms. [$] *Rooms from: $209* ✉ *241 Main St.* ☎ *802/326–4391* 🌐 *www.theinn.us* 🛏 *11 rooms* 🍴 *Breakfast.*

$$ HOTEL FAMILY

🏨 **Jay Peak Resort.** Accommodations at Jay Peak include standard hotel rooms, suites, condominiums, town houses, and new cottage and clubhouse suites near the golf course. **Pros:** great for skiers; wide range of accommodations; kids 14 and under stay and eat free. **Cons:** can get noisy; not very intimate; service isn't always helpful. [$] *Rooms from: $264* ✉ *4850 Rte. 242* ☎ *802/988–2611* 🌐 *www.jaypeakresort.com* 🛏 *321 rooms, studios, and suites; 94 condominiums; 100 cottage suites* 🍴 *Some meals.*

$ B&B/INN

🏨 **Phineas Swann Bed & Breakfast Inn.** The top-hatted bulldog on the sign of this 1880 farmhouse isn't just a mascot: it reflects the hotel's welcoming attitude to pet owners. **Pros:** walking distance from shops and supplies; lots of dogs. **Cons:** decor is a tad old-fashioned; lots of dogs. [$] *Rooms from: $189* ✉ *195 Main St.* ☎ *802/326–4306* 🌐 *www.phineasswann.com* 🛏 *3 rooms, 6 suites* 🍴 *Breakfast.*

SPORTS AND THE OUTDOORS

ICE-SKATING

FAMILY **Ice Haus Arena.** The sprawling arena contains a professional-size hockey rink and seating for 400 spectators. You can practice your stick-handling, and the rink is open to the public for skating several times a week. There are tournaments throughout the year. ✉ *830 Jay Peak Rd., Jay* ☎ *802/988–2611* ⊕ *www.jaypeakresort.com* 💲 *$6.*

SKI AREAS

Hazen's Notch Cross Country Ski Center and B&B. Delightfully remote at any time of the year, this center has 40 miles of marked and groomed trails and rents equipment and snowshoes. ✉ *1419 Hazen's Notch Rd.* ☎ *802/326–4799* ⊕ *www.hazensnotch.org* 💲 *Trail pass: $12.*

Jay Peak. Sticking up out of the flat farmland, Jay Peak averages 380 inches of snow per year—more than any other Vermont ski area—and it's renowned for its glade skiing and powder. There are two interconnected mountains, the highest reaching nearly 4,000 feet. The smaller mountain has straight-fall-line, expert terrain that eases mid-mountain into an intermediate pitch. Beginners should stay near the bottom on trails off the Metro quad lift. There are also four terrain parks, snowshoeing, telemark skiing, and a state-of-the art ice arena for hockey, figure skating, and curling. The Pump House, an indoor water park with pools and slides, is open year-round. **Facilities:** 78 trails; 385 acres; 2,153-foot vertical drop; 9 lifts. ✉ *830 Jay Peak Rd., Jay* ☎ *802/988–2611* ⊕ *www.jaypeakresort.com* 💲 *Lift ticket: $79.*

EN ROUTE   **Northeast Kingdom.** Routes 14, 5, 58, and 100 make for a scenic drive around the Northeast Kingdom, so named for the remoteness and stalwart independence that have helped preserve its rural nature. You can extend the loop and head east on Route 105 to the city of Newport on Lake Memphremagog. Some of the most unspoiled areas in all Vermont are on the drive south from Newport on either U.S. 5 or Interstate 91 (the latter is faster, but the former is prettier). ✉ *Montgomery.*

LAKE WILLOUGHBY

30 miles southeast of Montgomery (summer route; 50 miles by winter route), 28 miles north of St. Johnsbury.

The jewel of the Northeast Kingdom is clear, deep, and chilly Lake Willoughby, edged by shear cliffs and surrounded by state forest. The only town on its shores is tiny Westmore, which has a beach and a few shops that cater to campers and seasonal residents.

EXPLORING

FAMILY **Bread and Puppet Museum.** This ramshackle barn houses a surrealistic collection of props used by the world-renowned Bread and Puppet Theater. The troupe has been performing social and political commentary with the towering (they're supported by people on stilts) and eerily expressive puppets for 50 years. In July and August, there are performances on Saturday night and Sunday afternoon, with museum tours before Sunday shows. ✉ *753 Heights Rd., 1 mile east of Rte. 16, Glover*

☎ *802/525–3031* 🌐 *www.breadandpuppet.org* 🎟 *Donations accepted* 🕑 *June–Oct., daily 10–6.*

OFF THE BEATEN PATH

Hill Farmstead Brewery. Recognized as one of the country's leading craft-beer producers, Shaun Hill runs his brewery out of a bucolic Greensboro farm. Though it's off the beaten path down a relatively empty dirt road, beer lovers find their way here to sample and buy whatever is available. Area restaurants serve some of Hill's offerings, but this is the only place to buy bottles of the coveted brews. The selections change regularly—check the website for details—and Hill loves trying out new recipes, so you'll always find something interesting and different. This one's a must for microbrew aficionados. ✉ *403 Hill Rd., 21 miles southwest of Lake Willoughby, off Rte. 16, Greensboro* ✥ *From Rte. 16 take Taylor Rd. northwest to Jaffin Flat north to Hill Rd. west* ☎ *802/533–7450* 🌐 *www.hillfarmstead.com* 🎟 *Tasting $5* 🕑 *Wed.–Sat. noon–5.*

Lake Willoughby. The cliffs of Mt. Pisgah and Mt. Hor drop to the edge of Lake Willoughby on opposite shores, giving this beautiful, deep, glacially carved lake a striking resemblance to a Norwegian fjord. The trails to the top of Mt. Pisgah reward hikers with glorious views. Take note: the beach on the southern end is Vermont's most famous nude beach. ✉ *Westmore.*

EAST BURKE

17 miles south of Lake Willoughby.

Once a sleepy village, East Burke is now the Northeast Kingdom's outdoor-activity hub. The Kingdom Trails attract thousands of mountain bikers in summer and fall; many of them are groomed for cross-country skiing in winter.

GETTING HERE AND AROUND

From U.S. 5 in Lyndon, take Route 114 northeast 4¾ miles to get to East Burke. (Lyndon is 2 miles southeast of Interstate 91 on Route 122, which becomes Route 114.)

WHERE TO STAY

$$ B&B/INN

🏨 **Inn at Mountain View Farm.** Animal lovers will jump at the chance to stay at this 440-acre estate, home to a farm animal sanctuary. **Pros:** family friendly; incredible scenery and setting. **Cons:** no dinner; fills up with weddings. [$] *Rooms from: $215* ✉ *1 E. Darling Hill Rd.* ☎ *802/626–9924, 800/572–4509* 🌐 *www.innmtnview.com* 🕑 *Closed Nov.–mid-May* 🛏 *9 rooms, 5 suites* 🍴 *Breakfast.*

SPORTS AND THE OUTDOORS

BIKING

East Burke Sports. This shop rents, sells, and repairs mountain bikes, kayaks, skis, snowboards, and snowshoes. The owners are among the key developers of Kingdom Trails. ✉ *439 Rte. 114* ☎ *802/626–3215* 🌐 *www.eastburkesports.com.*

Kingdom Trails. Locals maintain this 110-mile network of trails for mountain biking and hiking in the summer, 37 miles of which are groomed

Catch a show and some social commentary at the Bread and Puppet Theater in summer, or visit the museum year-round.

for snowshoeing and cross-country skiing in the winter. ✉ *478 Rte. 114* ☎ *802/626–0737* ⊕ *www.kingdomtrails.com.*

Village Sport Shop. This shop rents bikes, canoes, kayaks, paddleboats, skis, and snowshoes. There's a satellite store on Darling Hill Road. ✉ *511 Broad St., Lyndonville* ☎ *802/626–8448* ⊕ *www.villagesportshop.com.*

SKI AREA

Q Burke Mountain. About an hour's drive from Montpelier, Q Burke is a quiet playground compared to the big resorts of the north. A lower slope of beginner trails is served by separate lifts; the upper slope has exclusively intermediate and expert runs. In the summer, you can mountain bike down from the summit. A new hotel and convention center welcomes guests at the base. **Facilities:** 52 trails; 270 acres; 2,111-foot vertical drop; 6 lifts. ✉ *1 Mountain Rd.* ☎ *802/626–7300* ⊕ *www. skiburke.com* ✉ *Lift ticket: $64.*

ST. JOHNSBURY

16 miles south of East Burke, 39 miles northeast of Montpelier.

St. Johnsbury, the southern gateway to the Northeast Kingdom, was chartered as early as 1786, but really only came into its own after 1830, when Thaddeus Fairbanks invented the platform scale, a device that revolutionized weighing methods. The Fairbanks family's subsequent philanthropic efforts left the city with a strong cultural and architectural imprint. Today "St. J," as locals call it, is the friendly, adventure sports–happy hub of the Northeast Kingdom.

EXPLORING
TOP ATTRACTIONS

FAMILY

Fodor'sChoice

★

Dog Mountain. The late Stephen Huneck, an artist and the creator of Dog Mountain, was famous for his colorful folk art sculptures and paintings of dogs. Much more than an art gallery–gift shop, this deeply moving spot even has a chapel, where animal lovers can reflect on their beloved pets. With hiking trails and a swimming pond, this is, first and foremost, a place to spend time with your dog. ⊠ *143 Parks Rd., off Spaulding Rd.* ☎ *800/449–2580* ⊕ *www.dogmt.com* ⊠ *Free* ⊗ *Mid-May–Oct., daily 10–5; Nov.–mid-May, Thurs.–Mon. 11–4. Chapel daily sunrise–sunset.*

FAMILY

Fodor'sChoice

★

Fairbanks Museum and Planetarium. This odd and deeply thrilling museum displays the eccentric collection of Franklin Fairbanks, who surely had one of the most inquisitive minds in American history. He built this magnificent barrel-vaulted gallery in 1889 to house the specimens of plants, animals, birds, and reptiles, and the collections of folk art and dolls—and a seemingly unending variety of beautifully mounted curios—he picked up around the world. The museum showcases over 175,000 items, but it's surprisingly easy to feast your eyes on everything here without getting a museum headache. The popular 45-seat planetarium is Vermont's only public planetarium, and there's also the Eye on the Sky Weather Gallery, home to live NPR weather broadcasts. ⊠ *1302 Main St.* ☎ *802/748–2372* ⊕ *www.fairbanksmuseum. org* ⊠ *Museum $8, planetarium $3–$5* ⊗ *Daily 9–5.*

WORTH NOTING

Catamount Arts. At the Northeast Kingdom's art hub you can catch a movie, check out an art exhibit, attend a concert, or take a class. Catamount also stages performances at larger regional venues. ⊠ *115 Eastern Ave.* ☎ *802/748–2600* ⊕ *www.catamountarts.org.*

OFF THE
BEATEN
PATH

Peacham. Tiny Peacham, 10 miles southwest of St. Johnsbury, is on almost every tour group's list of "must-sees." With views extending to the White Mountains of New Hampshire and a white-steeple church, Peacham is perhaps the most photographed town in New England. The movie adaptation of *Ethan Frome,* starring Liam Neeson, was filmed here. The soups and stews are especially tasty at **Peacham Café,** which serves breakfast and lunch. Next door, the **Peacham Corner Guild** sells local handicrafts. ⊠ *Peacham* ⊕ *www.peacham.net.*

Fodor'sChoice

★

St. Johnsbury Athenaeum. With its polished Victorian woodwork, dramatic paneling, and ornate circular staircases, this building is both the town library—one of the nicest you're likely to ever come across—and one of the oldest art galleries in the country, housing more than 100 original works, mainly from the Hudson River school. Albert Bierstadt's enormous *Domes of Yosemite* dominates the beautiful painting gallery. ⊠ *1171 Main St.* ☎ *802/748–8291* ⊕ *www.stjathenaeum.org* ⊠ *Free* ⊗ *Mon., Wed., and Fri. 10–5:30, Tues. and Thurs. 2–7, Sat. 10–3.*

WHERE TO EAT AND STAY

$

AMERICAN

✕ **Dylan's Café.** Inside St. Johnsbury's redbrick former post office, this sparsely decorated gallery space and restaurant offers a reliable lineup of fresh soups, salads, and sandwiches for lunch. Heartier fare is served

8

for dinner, like the mahimahi tacos and grilled short ribs—the cheddar-bacon burger is popular. So is brunch, where you can get fine eggs Benedict or huevos rancheros. There are also baked goods and daily specials, and in good weather you can sit outside. [$] *Average main: $15* ✉ *139 Eastern Ave.* ☎ *802/748–6748* ⏲ *No dinner Sun.–Tues.*

$ B&B/INN 🏨 **Emergo Farm.** Bebo and Lori Webster rent out three guest rooms and a suite in their 1890 farmhouse on a 240-acre working dairy farm that has been in their family for six generations (counting their son Justin, who works on the farm). **Pros:** simple but clean; peaceful setting. **Cons:** very remote; only open seasonally. [$] *Rooms from: $120* ✉ *261 Webster Hill Rd., 8 miles west of St. Johnsbury, Danville* ☎ *802/684–2215, 888/383–1185* 🌐 *www.emergofarm.com* ⏲ *Closed Nov.–Apr.* 🛏 *3 rooms, 1 suite* 🍴 *Breakfast.*

$$ B&B/INN 🏨 **Rabbit Hill Inn.** Few inns in New England garner the word-of-mouth buzz that Rabbit Hill seems to from its satisfied guests. **Pros:** attractive, spacious rooms; romantic; gardens and trails; good food. **Cons:** might be too quiet a setting for some. [$] *Rooms from: $215* ✉ *48 Lower Waterford Rd., 11 miles south of St. Johnsbury, Lower Waterford* 🌐 *www.rabbithillinn.com* ⏲ *Closed Apr. and 1st 2 wks of Nov.* 🛏 *18 rooms, 1 suite* 🍴 *Breakfast.*

NEW HAMPSHIRE

WELCOME TO NEW HAMPSHIRE

TOP REASONS TO GO

★ **The White Mountains:** Great for hiking and skiing, these dramatic peaks and notches are unforgettable.

★ **Lake Winnipesaukee:** Water parks, arcades, boat cruises, and classic summer camps fuel a whole season of family fun.

★ **Fall Foliage:** Head to the Kancamagus Highway in autumn for one of America's best drives, or seek out a less-trafficked route that's equally stunning.

★ **Portsmouth:** Less than an hour's drive from Boston, this great American city has coastline allure, colorful Colonial architecture, romantic dining, and fine arts and crafts.

★ **Pristine Towns:** Jaffrey Center, Walpole, Tamworth, Center Sandwich, and Jackson are among the most charming tiny villages in New England.

1 The Seacoast. You can find historical sites, hopping bars, beaches, and both whale-watching and deep-sea fishing opportunities along New Hampshire's 18 miles of coastline. Hampton Beach is the center of summertime activities, while Portsmouth is a hub of nightlife, dining, art, and Colonial history.

2 Lakes Region. Throughout central New Hampshire are lakes and more lakes. The largest, Lake Winnipesaukee, has 240 miles of coastline and attracts all sorts of water-sports enthusiasts, but there are many quiet, secluded lakes with enchanting B&Bs where relaxation is the main activity.

3 The White Mountains. Skiing, snowshoeing, and snowboarding in the winter; hiking, biking, and riding scenic railways in the summer: the Whites, as locals call their mountains, have plenty of natural wonders—some just a stone's throw from the road, others a lung-busting hike through the backcountry. Mt. Washington, the tallest mountain in the Northeast, can be conquered by trail, train, or car.

4 Lake Sunapee. Quiet villages can be found throughout the Lake Sunapee region. Many seem barely removed from Colonial times, and others thrive as centers of arts and education, filled with quaint shops. Hanover, home to Dartmouth College (founded 1769), retains that true New England college-town feel, with ivy-draped buildings and cobblestone walkways. Lake Sunapee itself is a wonderful place to swim, fish, or enjoy a cruise.

Lisbon
302
Woodsville
91
25
Warren
25A
Wentworth
10
118
Hanover
Enfield
89
Lebanon 4
Plainfield Grafton
Grantham 4
Georges Mills Lake Sunapee
Claremont
11
Newport North Sutton
11
Goshen
Charlestown
10
91
Hillsboro
Walpole Stoddard
Antrim
Gilsum 9
Bennington
Keene Peterborough
101 Marlborough ▲ Mt. Monadnock
Hinsdale Troy 5
Jaffrey Jaffrey
91 Winchester Center 202

MASSACHUSETTS

VERMONT

5 The Monadnocks
and Merrimack Valley.
New and old coexist
in the Granite State's
southwestern region,
where high-tech firms
have helped reshape the
cities of Manchester and
Nashua while small towns
in the hills surrounding
Mt. Monadnock celebrate
tradition and history.

GETTING ORIENTED

Although New Hampshire
has three interstates (I–95,
I–93, and I–89), most of its
regions are accessible only
by smaller, rural roads. From
Boston or Portland, Maine,
Interstate 95 provides access
to Portsmouth and beaches,
though many people like
the drive along Route 1A,
which runs parallel to the
coast. North of Portsmouth,
Route 16 leads to the
White Mountains and the
lakes region, home to Lake
Winnipesaukee. From
there, Interstate 93 cuts
north toward Franconia
and Littleton and south into
Concord, Manchester, and
Nashua. State roads east
and north of Interstate 93
lead to Dixville Notch and
the Connecticut Lakes.
Following the Connecticut
River takes you to Hanover,
Claremont, Charleston,
Walpole, and Keene.
From Concord, travelers
head west to reach the
Monadnock Region.

Updated by
Debbie Hagan

New Hampshire's mountain peaks, clear air, and sparkling lakes have attracted trailblazers and artists (and untold numbers of tourists) for centuries. The state's varied geography—not to mention the range of outdoor activities its mountains, lakes, and forests support—is part of the attraction, but hospitality and friendliness are major factors, too: visitors tend to feel quickly at home in this place of beauty and history. Whether you're an outdoors enthusiast seeking adventure or just want to enjoy a good book on the porch swing of a century-old inn, you'll find plenty of opportunities to fulfill your heart's desire.

Ralph Waldo Emerson, Henry David Thoreau, Nathaniel Hawthorne, and Louisa May Alcott all visited and wrote about the state, sparking a fervent literary tradition that continues today. It also has a strong political history: this was the first colony to declare independence from Great Britain, the first to adopt a state constitution, and the first to require its constitution be referred to the people for approval.

The state's diverse terrain makes it popular with everyone from avid adventurers to young families looking for easy access to nature. You can hike, climb, ski, snowboard, snowshoe, and fish, as well as explore on snowmobiles, sailboats, and mountain bikes. New Hampshirites have no objection to others enjoying the beauty here as long as they leave a few dollars behind: the state has long resisted both sales and income taxes, so tourism brings in much-needed revenue.

With a number of cities consistently rated among the most livable in the nation, New Hampshire has seen considerable growth over the past decade. Longtime residents worry that the state will soon develop two distinct personalities: one characterized by rapid urbanization in the southeast and the other by quiet village life in the west and north.

Although newcomers have brought change, the free-spirited sensibility of the Granite State remains intact, as does its natural splendor.

PLANNING

WHEN TO GO

Summer and fall are the best times to visit most of New Hampshire. Winter is a great time to travel to the White Mountains, but most other tourist sights in the state, including museums in Portsmouth and many attractions in the Lakes Region, are closed due to snow and cold weather. In summer people flock to beaches, mountain trails, and lakeside boat launches; in the cities, festivals showcase music, theater, and crafts. Fall brings leaf peepers, especially to the White Mountains and along the Kancamagus Highway (Route 112). Skiers and snowboarders take to the slopes in winter, when Christmas lights and carnivals brighten the long, dark nights. Spring's unpredictable weather—along with April's mud and late May's black flies—tends to deter visitors. Still, the season has its joys, not the least of which is the appearance, mid-May–early June, of the state flower, the purple lilac, soon followed by the blooming of colorful rhododendrons.

PLANNING YOUR TIME

Some people come to New Hampshire to hike or ski the mountains, fish and sail the lakes, or cycle along backcountry roads. Others prefer to drive through scenic towns, stopping at museums and shops along the way. Although New Hampshire is a small state, roads curve around lakes and mountains, making distances longer than they appear on a map. You can get a taste of the coast, lake, and mountain areas in three to five days; eight days will give you time to make a more complete loop.

GETTING HERE AND AROUND

AIR TRAVEL

Manchester Boston Regional Airport, the state's largest airport, has nonstop service from more than a dozen cities. The drive from Boston's Logan Airport to most places in New Hampshire takes one–three hours; the same is true for Bradley International Airport in Hartford, Connecticut.

BIKE TRAVEL

A safe, scenic route along New Hampshire's seacoast is the bike path along Route 1A, where you can park at Odiorne Point and follow the road 14 miles south to Seabrook. Another pretty route runs from Newington Town Hall to the Great Bay Estuary. White Mountains routes are detailed in the *White Mountain Ride Guide,* which is sold at area sporting-goods stores and bookshops and online at Amazon.com. There's also a bike path in Franconia Notch State Park, and a mountain-biking center, Great Glen Trails, at the base of Mt. Washington. Many ski areas offer lift services to mountain bikers in summer.

Maps, Routes, Tours, Information
Bike New England. ⊕ *www.bikenewengland.com.*

CAR TRAVEL

New Hampshire is an easy drive north from Boston and serves as a good base for exploring northern New England. Many destinations are near major highways, so getting around by car is a great way to travel. Interstate 93 stretches from Boston to Littleton and on into neighboring Vermont. Interstate 89 will get you from Concord to Hanover and eventually to Burlington, Vermont. To the east, Interstate 95 (a toll road) passes through southern New Hampshire's coastal area on its way from Massachusetts to Maine. Throughout the state are quiet backcountry lanes and winding roads that might take a little longer but can make for some of the best parts of the journey.

The speed limit on interstate and limited-access highways is usually 65 mph, except in heavily settled areas, where 55 mph is the norm. On state and U.S. routes, speed limits vary considerably. On any given stretch, the limit may be anywhere from 25 mph to 55 mph, so watch the signs carefully. Right turns on red lights are permitted unless otherwise indicated. The website of the **New Hampshire Department of Transportation** (⊕ *hb.511nh.com*) has up-to-the-minute information about traffic and road conditions.

TRAIN TRAVEL

Amtrak's *Downeaster* passenger train operates between Boston and Portland, Maine, with New Hampshire stops in Exeter, Durham, and Dover.

RESTAURANTS

New Hampshire prides itself on its seafood: not only lobster, but also salmon pie, steamed mussels, fried clams, and seared tuna. Across the state you'll find country taverns with upscale Continental and American menus, many of them emphasizing regional ingredients. Alongside a growing number of contemporary restaurants are such state traditions as greasy-spoon diners, pizzerias, and pubs that serve hearty comfort fare. No matter where you go, reservations are seldom required, and dress is casual. *Restaurant prices are the average cost of a main course at dinner or, if dinner is not served, at lunch.*

HOTELS

In the mid-19th century, wealthy Bostonians retreated to imposing New Hampshire country homes in the summer. Grand hotels were built across the state, especially in the White Mountains, which at that time competed with Saratoga Springs, Newport, and Bar Harbor to draw the nation's elite vacationers. A handful of these hotel-resorts survive, with their large kitchen staffs and their tradition of top-notch service. And many of those country houses have since been converted into inns. The smallest have only a couple of rooms and are typically done in period style; the largest contain 30 or more rooms and suites and have in-room fireplaces and even hot tubs. You'll also find a great many well-kept, often family-owned motor lodges, particularly in the White Mountains and Lakes regions. In ski areas, expect the usual ski condos and lodges. In the Merrimack River valley, as well as along major highways, chain hotels and motels predominate. The state's numerous campgrounds accommodate RVers and tent campers alike. The White Mountains provide an excellent base for camping and hiking.

OUTDOOR ACTIVITIES

Skiing: Ski areas abound in New Hampshire, among them Bretton Woods, Mt. Sunapee, Waterville Valley, and Cannon Mountain. For cross-country skiing, nothing beats Gunstock Mountain Resort, with 32 miles of trails, also open for snowshoeing. Or visit Franconia Village, which has 37 miles of cross-country trails.

Biking: Many ski resorts in the White Mountains offer mountain-biking opportunities, providing chairlift rides to the mountaintop and trails for all skill levels at the bottom. Some of the state's best road biking can be found along the Kancamagus Highway and around Lake Sunapee.

Hiking: For the adventurous, hiking the White Mountains or along the Appalachian Trail is the reason for visiting. For those interested in less arduous treks, there are plenty of day hikes in the White Mountain National Forest and in state parks like Pisgah in Cheshire County, the Crawford Notch and Franconia Notch state parks in the Whites, and Mt. Monadnock.

Hotel prices are the lowest cost of a standard double room in high season. Some inns add a 15%–18% service charge. Hotel reviews have been shortened. For full information, visit Fodors.com.

WHAT IT COSTS			
	$	**$$**	**$$$**	**$$$$**
Restaurants	under $18	$18–$24	$25–$35	over $35
Hotels	under $200	$200–$299	$300–$399	over $399

VISITOR INFORMATION

Contacts New Hampshire State Parks. ✉ Concord ☎ 603/271–3556 ⊕ www.nhstateparks.org. **Visit New Hampshire.** ✉ Concord ☎ 603/271–2665, 800/386–4664 *for vacation kit (also available via website)* ⊕ www.visitnh.gov.

9

THE SEACOAST

New Hampshire's 18-mile stretch of coastline packs in a wealth of scenery and diversions. The honky-tonk of Hampton Beach gets plenty of attention—good and bad—but first-timers are often surprised by the significant portion of the shoreline that remains pristine, especially through the town of Rye. This section begins in the regional hub, Portsmouth, cuts down the coast to the beaches, branches inland to the prep-school town of Exeter, and runs back up north through Dover, Durham (home to the University of New Hampshire), and Rochester; from here it's a short drive to the Lakes Region.

ESSENTIALS

Visitor Information Seacoast New Hampshire & South Coast Maine.
☎ 603/427–2020 ⊕ www.seacoastnh.com.

PORTSMOUTH

47 miles southeast of Concord; 50 miles southwest of Portland, Maine; 56 miles north of Boston.

Fodor's Choice ★

More than a quaint harbor town with a long, colorful history, Portsmouth is an upscale community with trendy farm-to-table restaurants, contemporary art galleries, and cultural venues that host nationally recognized speakers and performers. Swank cocktail bars, jumping live music, and late-night eateries create a convivial evening buzz in downtown's Market Square. Settled in 1623 as Strawbery Banke, Portsmouth grew into a prosperous port before the Revolutionary War, during which it harbored many Tory sympathizers. These days, this city of 22,000 has many grand residences from the 18th to the early 20th century; some of them can be found among the restored buildings that make up the Strawbery Banke Museum.

GETTING HERE AND AROUND

Both Interstate 95 and Route 1 run through Portsmouth. From the west, take Route 101 and from the north take Route 16. Amtrak runs through Durham, which is a short drive from the coast. Downtown Portsmouth is walkable, though you'll need a car for attractions farther afield.

ESSENTIALS

Bus and Trolley COAST Bus. ☏ *603/743–5777* ⊕ *www.coastbus.org.*

Taxi Anchor Taxi. ☏ *603/436–1888* ⊕ *www.anchortaxicab.com.*
Annie's Taxi. ⊠ *Portsmouth* ☏ *603/531–9955* ⊕ *www.anniestaxi.com.*

Visitor Information Greater Portsmouth Chamber of Commerce. ⊠ *500 Market St.* ☏ *603/610–5510* ⊕ *www.portsmouthchamber.org.*

FESTIVALS

FAMILY **Prescott Park Arts Festival.** This outdoor festival presents theater, dance, and music events June–August. ⊠ *105 Marcy St.* ☏ *603/436–2848* ⊕ *www.prescottpark.org.*

BOAT TOURS

FAMILY **Gundalow Company.** Sail the Piscataqua River in a flat-bottom gundalow (a type of barge) built at Strawbery Banke. Help the crew set sail, steer the vessel, and trawl for plankton while learning about the region's history from an onboard educator. Passengers are welcome to bring food and beverages on the boat. ⊠ *60 Marcy St.* ☏ *603/433–9505* ⊕ *www.gundalow.org* ⊑ *From $20* ⊗ *Closed Nov.–late May.*

FAMILY **Isles of Shoals Steamship Company.** This company runs cruises aboard the *Thomas Laighton,* a replica of a Victorian steamship. Cruises take you to the Isles of Shoals, Portsmouth Harbor, or the nearby lighthouses. Lunches and light snacks are available on board, or you can bring your own. ⊠ *Barker Wharf, 315 Market St.* ☏ *603/431–5500, 800/441–4620* ⊕ *www.islesofshoals.com* ⊑ *From $24* ⊗ *Closed Nov.–Apr.*

Portsmouth Harbor Cruises. Tours of Portsmouth Harbor and the Isles of Shoals, inland-river foliage trips, and sunset cruises are all in this company's repertoire. ⊠ *64 Ceres St.* ☏ *603/436–8084, 800/776–0915* ⊕ *www.portsmouthharbor.com* ⊑ *From $18* ⊗ *Closed Nov.–Apr.*

FAMILY **Portsmouth Kayak Adventures.** Explore the Piscataqua River Basin and the New Hampshire coastline on a guided kayak or stand-up paddle-board tour. Beginners are welcome (instruction included). ⊠ *185 Wentworth Rd.* ☎ *603/559–1000* ⊕ *www.portsmouthkayak.com* ✉ *From $45* ⊘ *Closed mid-Oct.–May.*

WALKING TOURS

FAMILY **Discover Portsmouth.** The Portsmouth Historical Society operates this combination visitor center–museum, where you can pick up maps, get the scoop on what's happening while you're in town, and view cultural and historical exhibits. Discover Portsmouth is also the place to learn about self-guided historical tours and to sign up for guided ones. ⊠ *10 Middle St.* ☎ *603/436–8433* ⊕ *www.portsmouthhistory.org* ✉ *Tours from $12* ⊘ *Apr.–late Dec., daily 10–5.*

FAMILY **Portsmouth Black Heritage Trail.** Important local sites in African American history can be seen on the 90-minute guided Sankofa Tour. Included are the African Burying Ground and historic homes of local slave traders and abolitionists. Tours, which begin at Strawbery Banke, are conducted on Saturday throughout the summer. ⊠ *Discover Portsmouth, 10 Middle St.* ☎ *603/380–1231* ⊕ *www.portsmouthhistory.org* ✉ *$15.*

EXPLORING
TOP ATTRACTIONS

Albacore Park. Built in Portsmouth in 1953, the USS *Albacore* is the centerpiece of Albacore Park. You can board this prototype submarine, which served as a floating laboratory to test an innovative hull design, dive brakes, and sonar systems for the Navy. The visitor center exhibits *Albacore* artifacts, and the nearby Memorial Garden is dedicated to those who have lost their lives in submarine service. ⊠ *600 Market St.* ☎ *603/436–3680* ⊕ *www.ussalbacore.org* ✉ *$7* ⊘ *Late May–mid-Oct., daily 9:30–5; mid-Oct.–late May, Thurs.–Mon. 9:30–4:30.*

FAMILY **Great Bay Estuarine National Research Reserve.** Just inland from Portsmouth is one of southeastern New Hampshire's most precious assets. In this 10,235 acres of open and tidal waters, you can spot blue herons, ospreys, and snowy egrets, particularly during the spring and fall migrations. The Great Bay Discovery Center has indoor and outdoor exhibits, a library and bookshop, and a 1,700-foot boardwalk, as well as other trails, which wind through mudflats and upland forest. ⊠ *89 Depot Rd., Greenland* ☎ *603/778–0015* ⊕ *www.greatbay.org* ✉ *Free* ⊘ *Visitor center: May–Sept., Wed.–Sun. 10–4; Oct., weekends 10–4.*

FAMILY **John Paul Jones House.** Revolutionary War hero John Paul Jones lived at this boardinghouse while he supervised construction of the USS *America* for the Continental Navy. The 1758 hip-roof building displays furniture, costumes, glass, guns, portraits, and documents from the late 18th century. The collection's specialty is textiles, among them some extraordinary early-19th-century embroidery samplers. ⊠ *43 Middle St.* ☎ *603/436–8420* ⊕ *www.portsmouthhistory.org* ✉ *$6* ⊘ *May–Nov., daily 11–5.*

9

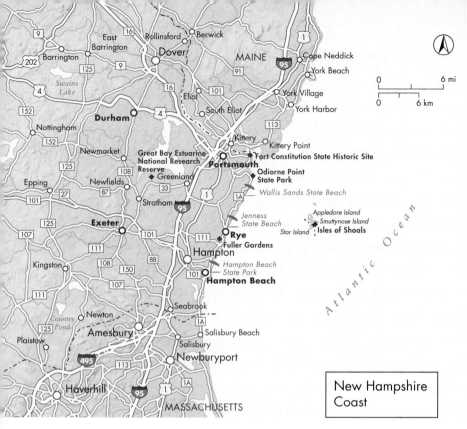

New Hampshire Coast

QUICK BITES

Breaking New Grounds. If you're going out to dinner, consider skipping the coffee and dessert and instead head here for a hot beverage and a pastry, gelato, or other sweet treat. In nice weather, sit outside and soak up the street entertainment. ⌧ *14 Market Sq.* ☎ *603/436–9555* ⊕ *www.bngcoffee.com.*

Redhook Ale Brewery. Guided tours of this brewery take just under an hour and end with a beer tasting; participants receive a souvenir tasting glass. You can also stop at the Cataqua Public House for a mug of ale and a bite to eat. The grounds host many summer events, including August's outdoor multiband concert, Hookfest. ⌧ *Pease International Tradeport, 1 Redhook Way* ☎ *603/430–8600* ⊕ *www.redhook.com* ⌧ *$5* ☽ *Sun.–Thurs. 1–5, Fri. and Sat. noon–6.*

FAMILY
Fodor's Choice
★
Strawbery Banke Museum. The first English settlers named the area around today's Portsmouth for the wild strawberries along the shores of the Piscataqua River. The name survives in this 10-acre outdoor history museum, one of the largest in New England. The compound has 38 homes and other structures dating from 1695 to 1820, some restored and furnished to a particular period, others used for historical exhibits. Half of the interior of the Shapley-Drisco House (built in 1795) depicts its use as a dry-goods store in Colonial times; its living room and kitchen are decorated as they were in the 1950s, showing

how buildings were adapted over time. The Shapiro House has been restored to reflect the life of the Russian-Jewish immigrant family who lived there in the early 1900s. Perhaps the most opulent house, done in decadent Victorian style, is the 1860 Goodwin Mansion, former home of Governor Ichabod Goodwin. ⊠ *14 Hancock St.* ☎ *603/433–1100* ⊕ *www.strawberybanke.org* ⌷ *$20* ⊘ *May–Oct., daily 10–5.*

WORTH NOTING

FAMILY **Fort Constitution State Historic Site.** The original military outpost on the island of New Castle was built on this site in 1631 and rebuilt in 1666 as Fort William and Mary, a British stronghold overlooking Portsmouth Harbor. The fort earned its fame in 1774, when patriots raided in one of Revolutionary America's first overtly defiant acts against King George III. Munitions captured here were used against the British at the Battle of Bunker Hill. The structure was renamed Fort Constitution in 1791; the current ruins date to 1808. The fort commands a great view of nearby Portsmouth Lighthouse. ⊠ *25 Wentworth Rd., off Rte. 1B* ✢ *Park at Battery Farnsworth and walk into Coast Guard Station* ☎ *603/436–1552* ⊕ *www.nhstateparks.org* ⌷ *Free* ⊘ *Daily 8–4.*

FAMILY **Moffatt-Ladd House and Garden.** The period interior of this 1763 home tells the story of Portsmouth's merchant class through portraits, letters, and furnishings. The Colonial Revival garden includes a horse chestnut tree planted by General William Whipple when he returned home after signing the Declaration of Independence in 1776. ⊠ *154 Market St.* ☎ *603/436–8221* ⊕ *www.moffattladd.org* ⌷ *$7 garden and house, $2 garden only* ⊘ *Early June–mid-Oct., Mon.–Sat. 11–5, Sun. 1–5.*

QUICK BITES
Annabelle's Natural Ice Cream. Drop by Annabelle's for a dish of maple-walnut ice cream or rich French vanilla, made with golden egg yolks. ⊠ 49 Ceres St. ☎ 603/436–3400 ⊕ www.annabellesicecream.com.

Warner House. The highlight of this circa 1716 gem is the curious folk-art murals lining the hall staircase, which may be the oldest-known murals in the United States still gracing their original structure. The house, a notable example of Georgian architecture, contains original art, furnishings, and extraordinary examples of area craftsmanship. The west-wall lightning rod is believed to have been installed in 1762 under the supervision of Benjamin Franklin. ⊠ *150 Daniel St.* ☎ *603/436–5909* ⊕ *www.warnerhouse.org* ⌷ *$7* ⊘ *June–mid-Oct., Wed.–Mon. 11–4.*

FAMILY **Wentworth-Coolidge Mansion Historic Site.** A National Historic Landmark now part of Little Harbor State Park, this was originally the residence of Benning Wentworth, New Hampshire's first royal governor (1741–67). Notable among its period furnishings is the carved pine mantelpiece in the council chamber. Wentworth's imported lilac trees bloom each May. Call ahead for house tours, offered on the hour until 3. Also worth a look is the Drift Gallery, which exhibits contemporary art in the adjacent visitor center. ⊠ *375 Little Harbor Rd., near South Street Cemetery* ☎ *603/436–6607* ⊕ *www.nhstateparks.org* ⌷ *$5* ⊘ *May and Sept.–mid-Oct., Fri.–Sun. 10–4; June–early Sept., Wed.–Sun. 10–4.*

9

Strawbery Banke Museum includes period gardens and 38 historic buildings.

OFF THE BEATEN PATH

Isles of Shoals. Four of the nine, small rocky Isles of Shoals belong to New Hampshire (the other five belong to Maine), many of them still known by the earthy names—Hog and Smuttynose, to cite but two—17th-century fishermen bestowed on them. A history of piracy, murder, and ghosts suffuses the archipelago, long populated by an independent lot who, according to one writer, hadn't the sense to winter on the mainland. Celia Thaxter, a native islander, romanticized these islands with her poetry in *Among the Isles of Shoals* (1873). In the late 19th century, **Appledore Island** became an offshore retreat for Thaxter's coterie of writers, musicians, and artists. **Star Island** contains a small museum, the Rutledge Marine Lab, with interactive family exhibits. From May to late October you can take a narrated history cruise of the Isles of Shoals, a day trip to Star Island, or a walking tour of Star Island with Isles of Shoals Steamship Company. ⊠ *315 Market St.* ☎ *800/441–4620* ⊕ *www.islesofshoals.com* ⊠ *4-hr trip $42, 1-hr guided walk $35.*

OFF THE BEATEN PATH

Prescott Park. Picnicking is popular at this waterfront park, whose large formal garden with fountains is perfect for whiling away an afternoon. The park contains Point of Graves, Portsmouth's oldest burial ground, and two 17th-century warehouses. The summerlong Prescott Park Arts Festival features concerts, outdoor movies, and food-related events. ⊠ *105 Marcy St.* ☎ *603/436–2848* ⊕ *www.prescottpark.org.*

WHERE TO EAT

$$$

INTERNATIONAL

Fodor's Choice

★

✕ **Black Trumpet Bistro.** Award-winning chef Evan Mallett brings the bold flavors of Latin America, North Africa, Turkey, and Mexico to bear on the eclectic fare of this romantic harbor-view restaurant. The menu is constantly changing, offering such delights as roasted allium soup, rabbit-and-mushroom enchiladas, and potato-and-cheese pierogi with smoked-corn bisque and a salad with sautéed kale and blueberries. Mallett belongs to the Heirloom Harvest Project and brings unusual vegetables—sometimes in surprising colors—to the table. Vegetarians will always find out-of-the-ordinary entrées. On busy nights, walk-ins might find a table in the upstairs wine bar. $ *Average main: $25* ✉ *29 Ceres St.* ☎ *603/431–0887* ⊕ *www.blacktrumpetbistro.com* ☽ *No lunch.*

$$
CARIBBEAN
FAMILY

✕ **Blue Mermaid Island Grill.** This fun, colorful place is good for seafood, sandwiches, and quesadillas. Specialties include plantain-encrusted cod topped with a grilled mango vinaigrette and served with grilled banana–sweet potato hash, and short ribs braised in a guava-soy reduction and accompanied by garlic–green onion mashed potatoes. In summer you can eat on a deck that overlooks adorable Colonial homes. There's live music on most nights of the week. $ *Average main: $20* ✉ *409 The Hill* ☎ *603/427–2583* ⊕ *www.bluemermaid.com.*

$
AMERICAN
FAMILY

✕ **The Friendly Toast.** In this 1950s-era throwback, furnished with chrome dinette sets and adorned with atomic-age memorabilia, you might expect molded Jell-O salad on the menu—but you'd be wrong. Instead, you'll find the biggest and best breakfasts featuring hefty omelets, Coconut Cakes (buttermilk pancakes made with chocolate chips, coconut, and cashews), and Drunkard French toast (with a Grand Marnier–raspberry sauce). The homemade breads and muffins are worth trying, too, and the cheese fries—topped with blue cheese and served with a raspberry-habanero dipping sauce—are completely addictive. This is also a great stop for lunch, dinner, or a quick snack. $ *Average main: $13* ✉ *113 Congress St.* ☎ *603/430–2154* ⊕ *www.thefriendlytoast.net.*

$$$
SEAFOOD

✕ **Jumpin' Jay's Fish Cafe.** A wildly popular downtown spot, this offbeat, dimly lighted eatery has a changing menu of fresh seafood from as far away as Iceland and Costa Rica. Try the steamed Prince Edward Island mussels with jalapeños, spicy ginger, and saffron sauce, or the haddock with lemon, white wine, and capers. Or go with one of the fresh catches, topped with one of seven different sauces. Singles like to gather at the central bar for dinner and furtive glances. $ *Average main: $25* ✉ *150 Congress St.* ☎ *603/766–3474* ⊕ *www.jumpinjays.com.*

$$$
STEAKHOUSE

✕ **Library Restaurant.** Bibliophiles may find themselves fully enraptured while dining in this historic library whose hand-carved ceiling was constructed by the Pullman Car woodworkers in 1889. The paneling is Spanish mahogany, and the original lighting fixtures are by Shreve, Crump & Low of Boston. Although the kitchen offers light dishes, such as jumbo crab cakes and crispy fried shrimp served with a sweet chili sauce, the mainstays are thick-cut, juicy steaks and chops. (The crushed-peppercorn steak is meat heaven.) Choose from six different rich, creamy sauces, including hollandaise and Gorgonzola, plus an array of fresh vegetables. The English-style pub serves nearly 100 martinis made from more than 250 brands of international vodkas. Sunday brunch is popular here. $ *Average main: $34* ✉ *401 State St.* ☎ *603/431–5202* ⊕ *www.libraryrestaurant.com.*

$
LATIN AMERICAN

✕ **Poco's Bow Street Cantina.** This casual but contemporary eatery turns out exceptional Southwestern and Latin American cuisine. Cajun red snapper tacos, fried calamari, and lobster quesadillas are among the best

9

choices. Most tables have views of the Piscataqua River. The downstairs bar and spacious outdoor deck are local hangouts—try one of the craft cocktails, perhaps a cucumber martini. $ *Average main: $14* ⊠ *37 Bow St.* ☎ *603/431–5967* ⊕ *www.pocosbowstreetcantina.com* ⌲ *Reservations not accepted.*

WHERE TO STAY

$
HOTEL
🏨 **Ale House Inn.** Talk about prime location: this urban-style hotel is steps from the city's historic houses, boutiques, and restaurants. **Pros:** welcome beers from local breweries upon arrival; complimentary tickets to local theater; bicycles for local jaunts. **Cons:** no breakfast; 12 steps to enter hotel. $ *Rooms from: $199* ⊠ *121 Bow St.* ☎ *603/431–7760* ⊕ *www.alehouseinn.com* ➷ *10 rooms* ⦿ *No meals.*

$$
HOTEL
🏨 **Hotel Portsmouth.** John E. Sise, a wealthy ship merchant, built this downtown hotel's main Queen Anne Victorian structure in 1881, and it retains its original architectural beauty and charm. **Pros:** downtown location near most attractions; free parking; lounge serving wine, beer, and small bites. **Cons:** light Continental breakfast; no desks in guest rooms. $ *Rooms from: $249* ⊠ *40 Court St.* ☎ *603/433–1200* ⊕ *www.thehotelportsmouth.com* ➷ *28 rooms, 4 suites* ⦿ *Breakfast.*

$
B&B/INN
🏨 **Martin Hill Inn.** You may fall in love with this yellow 1815 house surrounded by flower-filled gardens, a 10- to 15-minute walk from the historic district and the waterfront. **Pros:** refrigerators in rooms; central location; furnished with antiques; off-street parking. **Cons:** not in historic district. $ *Rooms from: $190* ⊠ *404 Islington St.* ☎ *603/436–2287* ⊕ *www.martinhillinn.com* ➷ *7 rooms* ⦿ *Breakfast.*

$$$
RESORT
Fodor's Choice
★
🏨 **Wentworth by the Sea.** What's not to love about this white colossus overlooking the sea on New Castle Island? Built in 1874 as a summer resort and popular with East Coast socialites, wealthy patrons, and former presidents, the hotel, run by Marriott, retains its grand feel. **Pros:** great spa; spectacular Sunday brunch; new tennis court (rackets and balls available); marina with charters for harbor cruises and deep-sea fishing. **Cons:** not in downtown Portsmouth. $ *Rooms from: $339* ⊠ *588 Wentworth Rd., New Castle* ☎ *603/422–7322, 866/384–0709* ⊕ *www.wentworth.com* ⛳ *18-hole championship course* ➷ *161 rooms, 31 suites* ⦿ *Some meals.*

NIGHTLIFE AND PERFORMING ARTS
PERFORMING ARTS

FAMILY **Music Hall.** Beloved for its acoustics, the 1878 hall brings presents top-drawer music concerts, from pop to classical, along with dance and theater. The more intimate Music Hall Loft, around the corner, screens art films and hosts lectures by leading writers and artists. ⊠ *28 Chestnut St.* ☎ *603/436–2400* ⊕ *www.themusichall.org.*

NIGHTLIFE

BARS **Two Ceres Street.** This artsy bar serves original martinis, like the Lumberjack (Maker's Mark and maple syrup) and the Hammer and Sickle (Grey Goose vodka, peperoncini, and olive juice), plus small plates. ⊠ *2 Ceres St.* ☎ *603/433–2373* ⊕ *www.twocerestreet.com.*

Four of the nine rocky Isles of Shoals belong to New Hampshire; the other five belong to Maine.

MUSIC **Portsmouth Gas Light Co.** This brick-oven pizzeria hosts local rock bands in its lounge, courtyard, and slick upstairs space. ✉ *64 Market St.* ☎ *603/430–9122* ⊕ *www.portsmouthgaslight.com.*

The Press Room. People come from Boston and Portland just to hang out at the Press Room, which showcases folk, jazz, blues, and bluegrass performers nightly. ✉ *77 Daniel St.* ☎ *603/431–5186* ⊕ *www.pressroomnh.com.*

The Red Door Lounge. Discover the local music scene at the Red Door. Indie music fans shouldn't miss Monday night's Hush Hush Sweet Harlot live music series. ✉ *107 State St.* ⊕ *www.reddoorportsmouth.com.*

SHOPPING

Market Square, in the center of town, has gift and clothing boutiques, book and gourmet food shops, and exquisite crafts stores.

Byrne & Carlson. Watch elegant chocolates being made in the European tradition at this small shop. ✉ *121 State St.* ☎ *888/559–9778* ⊕ *www.byrneandcarlson.com.*

Nahcotta. Stylish ceramics, jewelry, glassware, and art fill this contemporary design boutique. ✉ *110 Congress St.* ☎ *603/433–1705* ⊕ *www.nahcotta.com.*

N.W. Barrett Gallery. Marine paintings and handmade jewelry, pottery, and glass are featured in this gallery. You'll also find one-of-a-kind lamps and rocking chairs. ✉ *53 Market St.* ☎ *603/431–4262* ⊕ *www.nwbarrett.com.*

Piscataqua Fine Arts. This gallery mainly shows works by master woodcutter Don Gorvett, who creates spellbinding scenes of New England's coast, particularly the Portsmouth area. There are also works by some of New England's finest printmakers, including Sidney Hurwitz, Alex deConstant, and Sean Hurley. ✉ *123 Market St.* ☏ *603/436–7278* ⊕ *www.dongorvettgallery.com.*

RYE

8 miles south of Portsmouth.

On Route 1A, as it winds south through Rye, you'll pass a group of late-19th- and early-20th-century mansions known as **Millionaires' Row**. Because of the way the road curves, the drive south along this route is breathtaking. In 1623 the English established a settlement at Odiorne Point in what is now the largely undeveloped and picturesque town of Rye, making it the birthplace of New Hampshire. Today, the area's main draws include a lovely state park, beaches, and the views from Route 1A. Strict town laws have prohibited commercial development in Rye, creating a dramatic contrast with its frenetic neighbor, Hampton Beach.

GETTING HERE AND AROUND
Interstate 95 and U.S. 1, both west of town, provide the easiest access, but Rye shows its best face from Route 1A, which leads north from Hampton Beach and south from Portsmouth along the coast.

EXPLORING

FAMILY
Fodor'sChoice
★

Odiorne Point State Park. These 135 acres of protected seaside land are where David Thompson established the first permanent English settlement in what is now New Hampshire. Several nature trails from which you can enjoy vistas of the nearby Isles of Shoals have informative panels describing the park's military history. The rocky shore's tidal pools shelter crabs, periwinkles, and sea anemones. Throughout the year, the **Seacoast Science Center** hosts exhibits on the area's natural history. Its tidal-pool touch tank and 1,000-gallon Gulf of Maine deepwater aquarium are popular with kids. There are also guided nature walks. ✉ *570 Ocean Blvd.* ☏ *603/436–8043* ⊕ *www.seacoastsciencecenter.org* 🎟 *$10* ⊗ *Science center: Mar.–Oct., daily 10–5; Nov.–Feb., Sat.–Mon. 10–5.*

BEACHES

Jenness State Beach. Good for swimming and sunbathing, this long, sandy beach is a favorite among locals who enjoy its light crowds and nice waves for bodysurfing. Wide and shallow, Jenness Beach is a great place for kids to run and build sand castles. **Amenities:** lifeguards; parking (fee); showers; toilets. **Best for:** surfing; swimming; walking. ✉ *2280 Ocean Blvd.* ☏ *603/436–1552* ⊕ *www.nhstateparks.org* 🎟 *Parking $2/ hr May–Sept.*

FAMILY
Wallis Sands State Beach. This family-friendly swimmers' beach has bright white sand, a picnic area, a store, and beautiful views of the Isles of Shoals. **Amenities:** food and drink; lifeguards; parking (no fee); showers; toilets. **Best for:** swimming; walking. ✉ *1050 Ocean Blvd.* ☏ *603/436– 9404* ⊕ *www.nhstateparks.org* 🎟 *$15 per car* ⊗ *Mid-June–early Sept., weekdays 8–6, weekends 8–7.*

WHERE TO EAT

$$$ AMERICAN 🍴 **The Carriage House.** Across from Jenness Beach, this elegant cottage serves innovative dishes with a Continental flair. Standouts include creative curries, penne chock full of fresh seafood, and steak with peppercorns. Savor a hot-fudge ice-cream croissant for dessert. Upstairs is a wood-panel tavern with ocean views. [$] *Average main: $28* ✉ *2263 Ocean Blvd.* ☎ *603/964–8251* 🌐 *www.carriagehouserye.com* 🕒 *No lunch.*

SPORTS AND THE OUTDOORS

FISHING AND WHALE-WATCHING

FAMILY **Atlantic Whale Watch.** Captain Brad Cook takes the *Atlantic Queen II* out on half-day whale-watching trips and helms the vessel on fishing excursions. ✉ *1870 Ocean Blvd.* ☎ *603/964–5220, 800/942–5364* 🌐 *www.atlanticwhalewatch.com* 🎟 *$36* 🕒 *Closed mid-Oct.–mid-May.*

FAMILY **Granite State Whale Watch.** This outfit conducts naturalist-led whale-watching tours aboard the 100-passenger *Granite State.* ✉ *Rye Harbor State Marina, 1860 Ocean Blvd.* ☎ *603/964–5545, 800/964–5545* 🌐 *www.granitestatewhalewatch.com* 🎟 *$36* 🕒 *Closed mid-Oct.–mid-May.*

HAMPTON BEACH

8 miles south of Rye.

This is an authentic seaside amusement center, the domain of fried-dough stands, loud music, arcade games, palm readers, parasailing, and bronzed bodies. The 3-mile-long boardwalk, where kids play games and watch saltwater taffy being made, looks like a relic of the 1940s—indeed, the whole community remains remarkably free of modern franchises. Free outdoor concerts are held on many a summer evening, and once a week there's a fireworks display. An estimated 150,000 people visit the town and its free public beach on the 4th of July, and it draws plenty of people through late September, when its season ends.

9

GETTING HERE AND AROUND

Interstate 95 is the fastest way to get to Hampton, but the town is best seen by driving along Route 1A, which follows the coast and passes several beaches. Once here, you'll find that Route 1 is the quickest way to get around, but be prepared for strip malls and stoplights.

ESSENTIALS

Visitor Information Hampton Area Chamber of Commerce. ✉ *160 Ocean Blvd.* ☎ *603/926–8718* 🌐 *www.hamptonchamber.com.*

EXPLORING

Fuller Gardens. Arthur Shurtleff, a noted landscape architect from Boston, designed this late-1920s estate garden in the Colonial Revival style. Away from the beach crowds, it encompasses 1,700 rosebushes, hosta and Japanese gardens, and a tropical conservatory. ✉ *10 Willow Ave., North Hampton* ☎ *603/964–5414* 🌐 *www.fullergardens.org* 🎟 *$9* 🕒 *Mid-May–mid-Oct., daily 10–5:30.*

BEACHES

FAMILY **Hampton Beach State Park.** A long, sandy strand at the mouth of the Hampton River, this beach has a boardwalk edged by restaurants, attractions, and hotels. There's a visitor center (open year-round), along with multiple picnic areas and a store (seasonal). **Amenities:** food and drink; lifeguards; parking (fee); showers; toilets. **Best for:** swimming. ⊠ *160 Ocean Blvd.* ☎ *603/227–8722* ⊕ *www.nhstateparks.org* ⬅ *Parking $15.*

WHERE TO EAT AND STAY

$$$ ✕ **Ron's Landing.** Diners enjoy sweeping ocean views from many tables
AMERICAN at this casually elegant restaurant. The seared ahi tuna with a citrus, chili, and soy glaze is a tasty starter. Outstanding entrées include the oven-roasted salmon with cream sauce, slivered almonds, and sliced apples. Another winner is the baked haddock stuffed with scallops and lobster. Sunday brunch (November–April) is popular here. $ *Average main: $30* ⊠ *379 Ocean Blvd.* ☎ *603/929–2122* ⊕ *www.ronslanding. com* ⊗ *Closed Mon., and Tues. early Sept.–late May. No lunch Mon.–Sat., no lunch Sun. May–Oct.*

$ 🏨 **Ashworth by the Sea.** Even though this hotel across from the beach
HOTEL has been around for a century, you'll be surprised how contemporary it feels. **Pros:** center-of-town location; comfortable rooftop bar; open year-round. **Cons:** breakfast not included; very busy. $ *Rooms from: $139* ⊠ *295 Ocean Blvd.* ☎ *603/926–6762, 800/345–6736* ⊕ *www. ashworthhotel.com* ⇌ *98 rooms, 7 suites* ⑩ *No meals.*

NIGHTLIFE

Hampton Beach Casino Ballroom. Despite its name, the ballroom isn't a gambling establishment but rather an 1,800-seat late-19th-century auditorium that has hosted the likes of Duke Ellington and Janis Joplin to Trace Adkins and Dweezil Zappa. ⊠ *169 Ocean Blvd.* ☎ *603/929–4100* ⊕ *www.casinoballroom.com* ⊗ *Closed Dec.–Mar.*

SPORTS AND THE OUTDOORS

FISHING AND WHALE-WATCHING

Several companies conduct whale-watching excursions as well as half-day, full-day, and nighttime cruises. Most leave from the Hampton State Pier on Route 1A.

FAMILY **Al Gauron Deep Sea Fishing.** This company maintains a fleet of three boats for whale-watching cruises and fishing charters. ⊠ *State Pier, 1 Ocean Blvd.* ☎ *603/926–2469, 800/905–7820* ⊕ *www.algauron.com* ⬅ *From $33.*

FAMILY **Eastman's Docks.** This company offers whale-watching excursions and fishing charters. ⊠ *River St., Seabrook* ☎ *603/474–3461* ⊕ *www. eastmansdocks.com* ⬅ *From $33.*

FAMILY **Smith & Gilmore.** Enjoy half-day and full-day deep-sea fishing expeditions with Smith & Gilmore. ⊠ *State Pier, Ocean Blvd.* ☎ *603/926–3503, 877/272–4005* ⊕ *www.smithandgilmore.com* ⬅ *From $33.*

EN ROUTE **Applecrest Farm Orchards.** At this 400-acre farm, you can pick your own apples and berries or buy freshly baked fruit pies and cookies, homemade ice cream, and many other treats. Fall brings cider pressing, hayrides, pumpkins, and music on weekends. Author John Irving worked here as a teenager, and his experiences inspired the book *The Cider House Rules.* ⊠ *133 Exeter Rd., Hampton Falls* ☎ *603/926–3721* ⊕ *www.applecrest.com* ⊙ *Daily 8–6.*

EXETER

9 miles northwest of Hampton, 52 miles north of Boston, 47 miles southeast of Concord.

Fodor's Choice
★ During the Revolutionary War, Exeter was the state capital, and it was here amid intense patriotic fervor that the first state constitution and the first Colonial Declaration of Independence from Great Britain were put to paper. These days Exeter shares more in appearance and personality with Boston's blue-blooded satellite communities than the rest of New Hampshire—indeed, plenty of locals commute to Beantown. Cheerful cafés, coffeehouses, and shops with artisanal wares make up this bustling town center.

GETTING HERE AND AROUND
Amtrak's *Downeaster* service stops here between Boston and Portland, Maine. On the road, Exeter is 9 miles northwest of Hampton on Route 111. Route 101 is also a good way to get to Exeter from the east or west. The town itself is easy to walk around.

ESSENTIALS
Visitor Information Exeter Area Chamber of Commerce. ⊠ *24 Front St., Suite 101* ☎ *603/772–2411* ⊕ *www.exeterarea.org.*

EXPLORING
American Independence Museum. This museum celebrates the birth of the nation. The story unfolds over the course of a guided tour, which focuses on the Gilman family, who lived in the house during the Revolutionary War era. See drafts of the U.S. Constitution and the first Purple Heart, as well as letters and documents written by George Washington and the household furnishings of John Taylor Gilman, one of New Hampshire's early governors. In July, the museum hosts the American Independence Festival. ⊠ *Ladd-Gilman House, 1 Governor's La.* ☎ *603/772–2622* ⊕ *www.independencemuseum.org* ⊠ *$6* ⊙ *May–Nov., Tues.–Sat. 10–4.*

Phillips Exeter Academy. The 1,000-plus students of this elite high school give Exeter a certain youthful energy. The grounds, open to the public, resemble an Ivy League university campus. The school's library is one of the masterworks of modernist architect Louis I. Kahn. The Lamont Gallery, in the Frederick R. Mayer Art Center, mounts free contemporary art exhibitions. ⊠ *20 Main St.* ☎ *603/772–4311* ⊕ *www.exeter.edu.*

WHERE TO EAT
$ ✕ **The Green Bean.** All the soups at this self-serve restaurant are made
AMERICAN   fresh daily, and the sandwiches are perfect for dunking. Soups commonly include curried butternut squash, spicy corn chowder, and tarragon potato with peas; often on the sandwich menu are vegetables

9

and walnut pesto and turkey with cranberry and stuffing. Salads with an array of toppings are another lunch option. Breakfast burritos star in the early morning along with French toast and ham and eggs. The Green Bean is a popular spot for those on the go, but if you have the time, sit in the little courtyard for a quiet view of the town. $ *Average main: $7* ☒ *33 Water St.* ☎ *603/778–7585* ⊕ *www.nhgreenbean.com* ⊗ *No dinner.*

$$$ ✕ **The Tavern At River's Edge.** A convivial downtown gathering spot on
AMERICAN the Exeter River, this downstairs tavern pulls in college students, suburbanites, and parents of prep-school kids. The place may be informal, but the kitchen turns out sophisticated meals. Start with sautéed ragout of mushrooms stewed in a marsala cream sauce with sun-dried tomatoes, roasted shallots, garlic, and Asiago cheese, then move on to Moroccan salmon marinated in yogurt and fresh herbs. The bar serves lighter fare. $ *Average main: $25* ☒ *163 Water St.* ☎ *603/772–7393* ⊕ *www.tavernatriversedge.com.*

WHERE TO STAY

$ 🏨 **The Exeter Inn.** This elegant, Georgian-style red-brick inn on the Phil-
HOTEL lips Exeter campus has been the choice of visiting parents since it opened in the 1930s. **Pros:** well-designed rooms; elegant feel; near the center of town. **Cons:** some distance to shops. $ *Rooms from: $139* ☒ *90 Front St.* ☎ *603/772–5901,* ⊕ *www.theexeterinn.com* ⇝ *46 rooms, 3 suites* ⦿ *Breakfast.*

$ 🏨 **Inn by the Bandstand.** This bed-and-breakfast in the heart of town
B&B/INN exudes character and comfort. **Pros:** in-town location; bikes available;
Fodor's Choice friendly staff. **Cons:** no lunch or dinner. $ *Rooms from: $189* ☒ *6 Front*
★ *St.* ☎ *603/772–6352, 877/239–3837* ⊕ *www.innbythebandstand.com* ⇝ *9 rooms, 4 suites* ⦿ *Breakfast.*

SHOPPING

Exeter Fine Crafts. Fine creations by more than 300 of northern New England's top pottery, painting, jewelry, textile, glassware, and other artisans are on display and available for sale here. ☒ *61 Water St.* ☎ *603/778–8282* ⊕ *www.exeterfinecrafts.com.*

A Picture's Worth a Thousand Words. A destination for bibliophiles, this shop sells rare books, town histories, old maps, and antique and contemporary prints. ☒ *65 Water St.* ☎ *603/778–1991* ⊕ *www.apwatw.com.*

Willow. This creative shop stocks finely stitched linens, handcrafted jewelry, woven throws, organic teas, gardening accessories, and gorgeous bags. ☒ *183 Water St.* ☎ *603/773–9666.*

DURHAM

12 miles north of Exeter, 11 miles northwest of Portsmouth.

Settled in 1635 and later the home of General John Sullivan, a Revolutionary War hero and three-time New Hampshire governor, Durham was where Sullivan and his band of rebel patriots stored the gunpowder they captured from Fort William and Mary in New Castle. Easy access to Great Bay via the Oyster River made Durham a maritime hub in the 19th century. Among its lures today are the water, nearby farms that welcome visitors, and the University of New Hampshire, which occupies much of the town's center.

GETTING HERE AND AROUND

By car, Durham can be reached on Route 108 from the north or south and Route 4 from Portsmouth in the east or Concord in the west. The *Downeaster* Amtrak train stops here between Boston and Portland, Maine.

ESSENTIALS

Visitor Information University of New Hampshire. ⊠ *Durham* ☎ *603/862–1234* ⊕ *www.unh.edu.*

EXPLORING

Museum of Art. Notable items in this gallery's collection include 19th-century Japanese wood-block prints, Boston expressionist works, and art of New England. ⊠ *Paul Creative Arts Center, University of New Hampshire, 30 College Rd.* ☎ *603/862–3712* ⊕ *www.unh.edu/moa* 🕮 *Free* ☉ *Sept.–May, Mon.–Wed. 10–4, Thurs. 10–8, weekends 1–5.*

WHERE TO EAT AND STAY

$$$

AMERICAN

FAMILY

✗ **ffrost Sawyer Tavern.** That's not a typo, but an attempt to duplicate the quirky, obsolete rendering of the name of a former owner of this hilltop house. The eccentric stone basement tavern has its original wooden beams, from which hang collections of mugs, hats, and—no way around it—bedpans. Choose from fine dinner fare, such as grilled rib-eye steak with cippolini onions or potato-encrusted haddock. Lunch standards include burgers, pizza, and fish-and-chips. There's a terrific old bar. $ *Average main: $25* ⊠ *Three Chimneys Inn, 17 Newmarket Rd.* ☎ *603/868–7800* ⊕ *www.threechimneysinn.com.*

$

B&B/INN

🛏 **Three Chimneys Inn.** This stately yellow structure has graced a hill overlooking the Oyster River since 1649. **Pros:** intimate inn experience; room rate includes breakfast. **Cons:** have to walk or drive into town. $ *Rooms from: $189* ⊠ *17 Newmarket Rd.* ☎ *603/868–7800, 888/399–9777* ⊕ *www.threechimneysinn.com* 🛏 *23 rooms* 🍽 *Some meals.*

NIGHTLIFE

Stone Church. Music aficionados head to the Stone Church—an 1835 former Methodist church—for its craft beers, pub grub, and live rock, jazz, blues, reggae, soul, and folk music. ⊠ *5 Granite St., Newmarket* ☎ *603/659–7700* ⊕ *www.stonechurchrocks.com.*

SPORTS AND THE OUTDOORS

FAMILY **Wagon Hill Farm.** You can hike several trails and picnic at this 130-acre farm that overlooks the Oyster River. The old farm wagon on the top of a hill is one of the most photographed sights in New England. Park next to the farmhouse and follow walking trails to the wagon and through the woods to the picnic area by the water. Sledding and cross-country skiing are winter activities. ⊠ *U.S. 4, across from Emery Farm.*

SHOPPING

FAMILY **Emery Farm.** In the same family for 11 generations, Emery Farm sells produce in summer (including pick-your-own blueberries), pumpkins in fall, and Christmas trees in winter. The farm shop carries breads, pies, and local crafts. Pumpkin-patch hayrides take place on some weekends

9

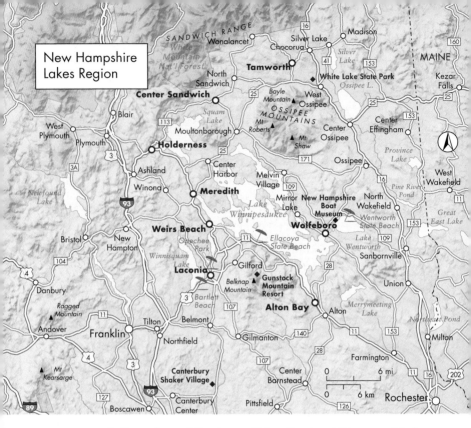

New Hampshire Lakes Region

in September and October, and May–October children can visit the petting barn. ⊠ *135 Piscataqua Rd.* ☎ *603/742–8495* ⊕ *www.emeryfarm. com* ⊙ *Daily 9–6.*

LAKES REGION

Lake Winnipesaukee, a Native American name for "smile of the great spirit," is the largest of the dozens of lakes scattered across the eastern half of central New Hampshire. With about 240 miles of shoreline dotted with inlets and coves, it's the state's largest lake. Some claim Winnipesaukee has an island for each day of the year—the total, though impressive, falls short: 274.

In contrast to Winnipesaukee, which bustles all summer long, stands the more secluded Squam Lake. Its tranquillity is no doubt what attracted the producers of *On Golden Pond*: several scenes of the Academy Award–winning film were shot here. Nearby Lake Wentworth is named for the state's first royal governor, who, in building his country manor here, established North America's first summer resort.

Well-preserved Colonial and 19th-century villages are among the region's many landmarks, and you'll find hiking trails, good antiques shops, and myriad water-oriented activities. This section begins at

Wolfeboro and more or less circles Lake Winnipesaukee clockwise, with several possible side trips.

ESSENTIALS

Visitor Information Lakes Region Association. ✉ *Behind Tilt'n Diner, 61 Laconia Rd., Tilton* ☎ *603/286–8008, 800/605–2537* ⊕ *www.lakesregion.org.*

WOLFEBORO

40 miles northeast of Concord, 49 miles northwest of Portsmouth.

Quietly upscale and decidedly preppy Wolfeboro has been a resort since Royal Governor John Wentworth built his summer home on the shore of the lake in 1768. The town bills itself as the oldest summer resort in the country, and its center, bursting with tony boutiques, fringes Lake Winnipesaukee and sees a major population increase each summer. The century-old, white clapboard buildings of the Brewster Academy prep school bracket the town's southern end. Wolfeboro marches to a steady, relaxed beat, comfortable for all ages.

GETTING HERE AND AROUND

Enter on the west side of Lake Winnipesaukee on Route 28. Be prepared for lots of traffic in the summertime.

ESSENTIALS

Visitor Information Wolfeboro Area Chamber of Commerce. ✉ *32 Central Ave.* ☎ *603/569–2200* ⊕ *www.wolfeborochamber.com.*

EXPLORING

FAMILY **New Hampshire Boat Museum.** Two miles northeast of the town center, this museum celebrates New Hampshire's maritime legacy with displays of vintage wooden boats, models, antique engines, racing photography, trophies, and vintage marina signs. You can also take a 45-minute narrated ride on the lake in a reproduction of a 1928 triple-cockpit HackerCraft (call for details). ✉ *399 Center St.* ☎ *603/569–4554* ⊕ *www. nhbm.org* 🎫 *$7* ☉ *Late May–mid-Oct., Mon.–Sat. 10–4, Sun. noon–4.*

FAMILY **Wright Museum.** Uniforms, vehicles, and other artifacts at this museum illustrate the contributions of those on the home front to the U.S. World War II effort. ✉ *77 Center St.* ☎ *603/569–1212* ⊕ *www.wrightmuseum. org* 🎫 *$10* ☉ *May–Oct., Mon.–Sat. 10–4, Sun. noon–4.*

QUICK
BITES

Kelly's Yum Yum Shop. Picking up freshly baked breads, pastries, cookies, and other sweets at Kelly's has been a tradition since 1948. The buttercrunch cookies are highly addictive. ✉ **16 N. Main St.** ☎ **603/569–1919** ⊕ **www.yumyumshop.net** ☉ **Closed mid-Oct.–Apr.**

BEACHES

FAMILY **Wentworth State Beach.** Away from the hustle and bustle of Wolfeboro, this no-frills park features a quiet beach with good fishing, picnic tables and grills, and ballfields. **Amenities:** parking (no fee); showers; toilets. **Best for:** swimming; walking. ✉ *297 Governor Wentworth Hwy.* ☎ *603/569–3699* ⊕ *www.nhstateparks.org* 🎫 *$4.*

9

With 240 miles of shoreline, Lake Winnipesaukee has something for everyone.

WHERE TO EAT AND STAY

$$
PHILIPPINE
FAMILY

✕ **East of Suez.** In a countrified lodge on the south side of town, this friendly restaurant serves creative Asian cuisine, with an emphasis on Philippine fare, such as *lumpia* (pork-and-shrimp spring rolls with a sweet-and-sour fruit sauce) and *pancit canton* (panfried egg noodles with sautéed shrimp and pork and Asian vegetables with a sweet oyster sauce). You can also sample Thai red curries, Japanese tempura, and Korean-style flank steak. Gluten-free and vegan options are available. $ *Average main: $19* ✉ *775 S. Main St.* ☎ *603/569–1648* ⊕ *www.eastofsuez.com* ⊘ *Closed early Sept.–late May.*

$
B&B/INN

🏠 **Topsides Bed & Breakfast.** Each of the rooms at this stylish retreat captures the allure of a particular region, from Martha's Vineyard to coastal France to British fox-hunting country. **Pros:** close to downtown; appealing rooms; great service. **Cons:** some rooms are upstairs. $ *Rooms from: $185* ✉ *209 S. Main St.* ☎ *603/569–3834* ⊕ *www.topsidesbb.com* 🛏 *5 rooms* ⏷ *Breakfast.*

$$
B&B/INN

🏠 **The Wolfeboro Inn.** This 1812 inn with a commanding lakefront location is a perennial favorite for Lake Winnipesaukee visitors. **Pros:** lakefront setting; interesting pub. **Cons:** breakfast not included. $ *Rooms from: $279* ✉ *90 N. Main St.* ☎ *603/569–3016* ⊕ *www.wolfeboroinn.com* 🛏 *41 rooms, 3 suites* ⏷ *Breakfast.*

SPORTS AND THE OUTDOORS

HIKING

FAMILY

Abenaki Tower. A quarter-mile hike to the 100-foot post-and-beam Abenaki Tower, followed by a more rigorous climb to the top, rewards you with a view of Lake Winnipesaukee and the Ossipee mountain range.

The setting is particularly photogenic at sunset. ✉ *Trailhead on Rte. 109, Tuftonboro.*

WATER SPORTS

Scuba divers can explore *The Lady,* a 125-foot-long cruise ship that sank in 30 feet of water off Glendale in 1895.

Dive Winnipesaukee Corp. This corporation runs charters out to wrecks, rents boats, and offers scuba equipment rentals, repairs, and sales. ✉ *Wolfeboro Bay, 4 N. Main St.* ☎ *603/569–8080* 🌐 *www.divewinnipesaukee.com.*

SHOPPING

FAMILY **The Country Bookseller.** You'll find an excellent regional-history section and plenty of children's titles at this independent bookstore, where you can do a little reading in the small café. ✉ *23A N. Main St.* ☎ *603/569–6030* 🌐 *www.thecountrybookseller.com.*

Hampshire Pewter. The artisans at Hampshire Pewter use 16th-century techniques to make pewter tableware, accessories, and gifts. ✉ *9 Railroad Ave.* ☎ *603/569–4944* 🌐 *www.hampshirepewter.com.*

ALTON BAY

10 miles south of Wolfeboro.

Lake Winnipesaukee's southern shore is alive with visitors from the moment the first flower blooms until the last maple sheds its leaves. Two mountain ridges hold 7 miles of the shoreline in Alton Bay, which is the name of both the inlet and the town at its tip. Cruise boats dock here, and small planes land year-round on the water and the ice. There's a dance pavilion, along with miniature golf, a public beach, and a Victorian-style bandstand.

GETTING HERE AND AROUND

To get to Alton Bay from Wolfeboro, head south on Route 28, also signed as Wolfeboro Highway, departing at Route 28A, which winds along the bays eastern shoreline. Head briefly west at Route 11 to the dock and small business district.

EXPLORING

FAMILY **Mt. Major.** About 5 miles north of Alton Bay, Mt. Major has a 3-mile trail up a series of challenging cliffs. At the top you'll find a four-sided stone shelter built in 1925, but the real reward is the spectacular view of Lake Winnipesaukee. ✉ *Rte. 11.*

WHERE TO EAT

$$$$ AMERICAN Fodor's Choice ★ 🍴 **The Crystal Quail.** With just four tables tucked inside an 18th-century farmhouse, this restaurant is worth the drive for its sumptuous meals. Longtime proprietors Harold and Cynthia Huckaby use free-range meats and mostly organic produce and herbs in their cooking. Their prix-fixe menu changes daily but may include saffron-garlic soup, a house pâté, mushroom and herb quail, or goose confit with apples and onions. Credit cards are not accepted. [$] *Average main: $75* ✉ *202 Pitman Rd., 12 miles south of Alton Bay, Center Barnstead*

9

☎ *603/269–4151* ⊕ *www.crystalquail.com* ▭ *No credit cards* ⊘ *Closed Mon. and Tues. No lunch* ⌲ *Reservations essential* ⌂ *BYOB.*

WEIRS BEACH

17 miles northwest of Alton Bay.

Weirs Beach is Lake Winnipesaukee's center for summertime arcade activity, with souvenir shops, fireworks, waterslides, and hordes of children—there's even a drive-in theater. Cruise boats also depart from here.

GETTING HERE AND AROUND

Weirs Beach is just north of Laconia and south of Meredith on U.S. 3.

EXPLORING

FAMILY   **Funspot.** The mothership of Lake Winnipesaukee's family-oriented amusement parks, Funspot claims that its more than 500 video games make it the world's largest arcade. You can also work your way through a miniature golf course, a driving range, an indoor golf simulator, and 20 lanes of bowling. Some outdoor attractions are closed in winter. ⊠ *579 Endicott St. N* ☎ *603/366–4377* ⊕ *www.funspotnh.com* ⊘ *Mid-June–early Sept., daily 9 am–11 pm; early Sept.–mid-June, Sun.–Thurs. 10–10, Fri. and Sat. 10 am–11 pm.*

FAMILY   **M/S Mount Washington.** The 230-foot M/S *Mount Washington* offers
Fodor's Choice   2½-hour scenic cruises of Lake Winnipesaukee, departing Weirs Beach
★   with stops at Wolfeboro, Alton Bay, Center Harbor, and Meredith depending on the day. Sunset cruises include live music and a buffet dinner, and the Sunday Champagne brunch cruise includes plenty of bubbly. The same company operates the *Sophie C.* ($27), which has been the area's floating post office for more than a century. The boat departs from Weirs Beach with mail and passengers, passing through parts of the lake not accessible to larger ships. The M/V *Doris E.* ($19) has one- and two-hour scenic cruises into Meredith Bay throughout the summer. ⊠ *211 Lakeside Ave., Laconia* ☎ *603/366–5531, 888/843–6686* ⊕ *www.cruisenh.com* ◰ *$30* ⊘ *Mid-May–late Oct., departure times vary.*

FAMILY   **Winnipesaukee Scenic Railroad.** You can board this scenic railroad's restored cars at Weirs Beach or Meredith for one- or two-hour rides along the shoreline. Special excursions include fall foliage and the Santa train. ⊠ *154 Main St., Meredith* ☎ *603/745–2135* ⊕ *www.hoborr.com* ◰ *$16* ⊘ *July and Aug., daily; late May–late June and early Sept.–late Oct., weekends.*

BEACHES

FAMILY   **Ellacoya State Beach.** Families enjoy this secluded 600-foot sandy beach and park on the southwestern shore of Lake Winnipesaukee. Ellacoya, with views of the Sandwich and Ossipee mountains, is never crowded, and its shallow beach is safe for small children. It has sheltered picnic tables and a small campground. **Amenities:** parking (no fee); toilets. **Best for:** solitude; swimming. ⊠ *266 Scenic Rd., Gilford* ☎ *603/293–7821* ⊕ *www.nhstateparks.org* ◰ *$5* ⊘ *Late May–mid-June, weekends 9–5; mid-June–early Sept., daily 9–5.*

NIGHTLIFE AND PERFORMING ARTS

New Hampshire Music Festival. From early July to early August, this festival presents chamber music on Tuesday and classical orchestra on Thursday. ⊠ *Hanaway Theater, Silver Center for the Arts, 7 Main St., Plymouth* ☎ *603/535–2787 for box office* ⊕ *www.nhmf.org.*

SPORTS AND THE OUTDOORS

BOATING

Thurston's Marina. This marina rents boats and equipment and has a gas dock. ⊠ *18 Endicott St. N* ☎ *603/366–4811* ⊕ *www.thurstonsmarina.com.*

GOLF

Pheasant Ridge Golf Club. In a bucolic setting frequented by amazing waterfowl, the course here offers great farm and mountain views. ⊠ *140 Country Club Rd., Gilford* ☎ *603/524–7808* ⊕ *www.playgolfne.com* ⌦ *$30–$44* ⚑ *18 holes, 6044 yards, par 71.*

SKI AREA

FAMILY **Gunstock Mountain Resort.** High above Lake Winnipesaukee, this ski resort has invested millions to increase its snowmaking capacity, introduce more options for beginners, and add slope-side dining. Thrill Hill, a snow-tubing park, has five runs, a lift service, and 21 acres of terrain park. The ski area has 55 trails (24 of them open for night skiing) and 32 miles of cross-country and snowshoeing trails. In summer, the Mountain Adventure Park offers an adrenaline rush with 22 zip lines—the longest at 3,981 feet—an aerial obstacle course, and scenic chairlift rides. There are also mountain-bike trails, Segway tours, and paddleboats. **Facilities:** 55 trails; 2,200 acres; 1,400-foot vertical drop; 8 lifts. ⊠ *719 Cherry Valley Rd., Gilford* ☎ *603/293–4341* ⊕ *www.gunstock.com* ⌦ *Lift ticket $70.*

SHOPPING

FAMILY **Pepi Herrmann Crystal.** Watch artists at work crafting hand-cut crystal glasses, as well as contemporary tableware, ornaments, and jewelry. ⊠ *3 Waterford Pl., Gilford* ☎ *603/528–1020* ⊕ *www.handcut.com* ⊗ *Closed Sun. and Mon.*

LACONIA

4 miles west of Gilford, 27 miles north of Concord.

The arrival of the railroad in 1848 turned the sleepy hamlet of Laconia—then called Meredith Bridge—into the Lakes Region's chief manufacturing hub. Even today it acts as the area's supply depot, a perfect role given its accessibility to both Winnisquam and Winnipesaukee lakes, as well as to Interstate 93. In June the town draws bikers from around the world for Laconia Motorcycle Week.

GETTING HERE AND AROUND

The best way to Laconia is on Route 3 or Route 11. Scenic rides from the south include Route 106 and Route 107.

EXPLORING

FAMILY **Belknap Mill.** Inside this 1823 textile mill, you can see how cloth and clothing were made almost two centuries ago. Belknap Mill contains operational knitting machines, a 1918 hydroelectric power system, and changing exhibits. ⊠ *Mill Plaza, 25 Beacon St. E* ☎ *603/524–8813* ⊕ *www.belknapmill.org* ⊠ *Free* ☉ *Call for hrs.*

OFF THE
BEATEN
PATH

Canterbury Shaker Village. Established in 1792, this village flourished in the 1800s and practiced equality of the sexes and races, common ownership, celibacy, and pacifism. The last member of the religious community passed away in 1992. Shakers invented such household items as the clothespin and the flat broom and were known for the simplicity and integrity of their designs. Engaging tours pass through some of the 694-acre property's more than 25 restored buildings, many of them with original furnishings. Crafts demonstrations take place daily. Ask the admissions desk for a map of the many nature trails. The Shaker Box Lunch and Farm Stand offers salads, soups, and baked goods, and sells seasonal vegetables and locally produced maple syrup. A shop sells handcrafted items. ⊠ *288 Shaker Rd., 15 miles south of Laconia via Rte. 106, Canterbury* ☎ *603/783–9511* ⊕ *www.shakers.org* ⊠ *$17* ☉ *Museum and tours: mid-May–late Oct., daily 10–5; Nov., weekends 10–4. Store: mid-May–late Oct., daily 10–5; late Oct.–Dec. 23, daily 10–4.*

BEACHES

FAMILY **Bartlett Beach.** On Lake Winnisquam, this small but pleasant city-run park has a 600-foot-long sand beach. Picnic tables and a playground make Bartlett Beach ideal for families, particularly those with small children. **Amenities:** lifeguards; parking (no fee); toilets. **Best for:** swimming. ⊠ *99 Winnisquam Ave.* ⊠ *Free.*

FAMILY **Opechee Park.** Nestled in a quiet cove, this medium-size, family-friendly beach has a playground, a baseball field, tennis courts, and picnic areas. **Amenities:** parking (no fee); toilets. **Best for:** swimming. ⊠ *N. Main St.* ⊠ *Free.*

WHERE TO EAT AND STAY

$ ✕ **Tilt'n Diner.** Lakes Region travelers have long been familiar with the AMERICAN flashy pink exterior and neon signage of this convivial 1950s-style res-
FAMILY taurant. Specialties include omelets served every possible way, Reuben sandwiches, shepherd's pie, and Southern breakfasts (sausage gravy, biscuits, and baked beans with two eggs). Breakfast is served all day, and there's free Wi-Fi. $ *Average main:* ⊠ *61 Laconia Rd., Tilton* ☎ *603/286–2204* ⊕ *www.thecman.com.*

$ ⊡ **The Lake House at Ferry Point.** Four miles southwest of Laconia, this B&B/INN home across the street from Lake Winnisquam is a quiet retreat with a dock and a small beach. **Pros:** affordable; lovely setting. **Cons:** away from main attractions. $ *Rooms from: $185* ⊠ *100 Lower Bay Rd., Sanbornton* ☎ *603/637–1758* ⊕ *www.lakehouseatferrypoint.com* ⊠ *8 rooms, 1 suite* ⊙*Breakfast.*

MEREDITH

11 miles north of Laconia.

Meredith is a favored spot for water-sports enthusiasts and anglers. For a true taste of Meredith, take a walk down Main Street (just one block from busy Route 3), which is dotted with intimate coffee shops, salons and barber shops, family restaurants, redbrick buildings, and antiques stores. You can pick up area information at a kiosk across from the town docks. One caveat: on busy weekends getting into town from the west can mean sitting in traffic for 30 minutes or more.

ESSENTIALS

Visitor Information Meredith Area Chamber of Commerce. ☎ *877/279–6121* ⊕ *www.meredithareachamber.com.*

WHERE TO EAT AND STAY

$$$
AMERICAN

✕ **Lakehouse Grille.** Come to this upscale lodge for some of the best lake views of any restaurant in the region. The chef hand-selects steaks from Creekstone Farm and serves them with applewood bacon and cheddar potato cakes. There's a fine assortment of seafood dishes, and the house specialties include duck, roasted chicken, and gnocchi. Breakfast is served daily, with brunch on Sunday. Ⓢ *Average main: $25* ✉ *Church Landing, 281 Daniel Webster Hwy.* ☎ *603/279–5221* ⊕ *www.thecman.com.*

$
HOTEL
Fodor'sChoice
★

🏨 **Mill Falls at the Lake.** You have your choice of four lodgings here: relaxing Church Landing and Bay Point are both on the shore of Lake Winnipesaukee; convivial Mill Falls, across the street, has a swimming pool and a 19th-century mill that now houses more than a dozen unique shops; and Chase House, also across the street, has 21 rooms, all with fireplaces and lake views. **Pros:** many lodging choices and prices; lakefront rooms; fun environment. **Cons:** rooms with views are expensive; two buildings are not on the lake. Ⓢ *Rooms from: $185* ✉ *312 Daniel Webster Hwy., at Rte. 25* ☎ *603/279–7006, 800/622–6455* ⊕ *www.millfalls.com* ⇱ *172 rooms, 15 suites* ⧉ *Breakfast.*

PERFORMING ARTS

FAMILY **Interlakes Summer Theatre.** During its 10-week season of summer stock, the theater presents Broadway musicals like *42nd Street, Godspell,* and *West Side Story.* ✉ *Interlakes Auditorium, 1 Laker La., off Rte. 25* ☎ *603/707–6035* ⊕ *www.interlakestheatre.com.*

SPORTS AND THE OUTDOORS

BOATING

Meredith is near the quaint village of Center Harbor, another boating hub that's in the middle of three bays at the northern end of Lake Winnipesaukee.

FAMILY **Meredith Marina.** Between May and October, you can rent powerboats and other vessels at this marina. ✉ *2 Bayshore Dr.* ☎ *603/279–7921* ⊕ *www.meredithmarina.com.*

FAMILY **Wild Meadow Canoes & Kayaks.** Canoes and kayaks are available here. ✉ *6 Whittier Hwy., Center Harbor* ☎ *603/253–7536, 800/427–7536* ⊕ *www.wildmeadowcanoes.com.*

HIKING

FAMILY **Red Hill.** Off Route 25, Red Hill really does turn red in autumn. The reward at the end of this hiking trail is a fire tower and a view of Squam Lake and the mountains. ✉ *Trailhead on Old Red Hill Rd., 9 miles northeast of Meredith, Moultonborough.*

9

What's your vessel of choice for exploring New Hampshire's Lakes Region: kayak, canoe, powerboat, or sailboat?

SHOPPING

Home Comfort. The owners of Lavinia's Relaxed Dining next door operate this three-floor showroom of designer furnishings, antiques, and accessories. ⊠ *Senters Market, Rte. 25B, Center Harbor* ☎ *603/253–6660* ⊕ *www.homecomfortnh.com.*

Keepsake Quilting. Reputedly America's largest quilting shop, this store contains 5,000 bolts of fabric, hundreds of quilting books, and plenty of supplies. There are also gorgeous handmade quilts. ⊠ *Senters Market, 12 Main St., Center Harbor* ☎ *603/253–4026, 800/525–8086* ⊕ *www.keepsakequilting.com.*

League of New Hampshire Craftsmen. Here you'll find works by more than 250 area artisans who regularly demonstrate their skills. There are other branches in Littleton, Hanover, North Conway, and Concord. ⊠ *279 U.S. 3, next to the Inn at Church Landing* ☎ *603/279–7920* ⊕ *www.nhcrafts.org/meredith.*

Old Print Barn. This shop carries rare prints—Currier & Ives, antique botanicals, and more—from around the world. ⊠ *343 Winona Rd., New Hampton* ☎ *603/279–6479.*

HOLDERNESS

8 miles northwest of Meredith.

The prim small town of Holderness sits between Squam and Little Squam lakes. *On Golden Pond,* starring Katharine Hepburn and Henry Fonda, was filmed on Squam, whose quiet beauty attracts nature lovers.

GETTING HERE AND AROUND

Routes 25B and 25 lead to Holderness.

EXPLORING

FAMILY Fodor's Choice ★ **Squam Lakes Natural Science Center.** This 230-acre property includes a ¾-mile nature trail that passes by trailside exhibits of black bears, bobcats, otters, mountain lions, red and gray fox, and other native wildlife. A pontoon boat cruise, one of the center's main attractions, is the best way to tour the waterfront. Naturalists talk about the animals that make their home here, and give fascinating facts about the loon. Children's activities include learning about bugs and wilderness survival skills. ✉ *23 Science Center Rd.* ☎ *603/968–7194* 🌐 *www.nhnature.org* 🎟 *Trail $17, lake cruise $25* 🕒 *May–Nov., daily 9:30–4:30.*

WHERE TO EAT

$$$ AMERICAN 🍴 **Manor on Golden Pond Restaurant.** Leaded-glass panes and wood paneling set a decidedly romantic tone at this wonderful inn overlooking Squam Lake. The main dining room is in the manor's original billiards room and retains woodwork from 1904. Two others have very different looks: one has white linens, fresh flowers, and candlelight; the other is in the style of a Parisian bistro. The menu changes weekly, but might include lobster risotto, filet mignon, quail, or monkfish. Ask about the fabulous seven-course tasting menu. Breakfast is also served. [$] *Average main: $35* ✉ *31 Manor Dr., at U.S. 3 and Shepard Dr.* ☎ *603/968–3348* 🌐 *www.manorongoldenpond.com* ✍ *Reservations essential.*

$$ AMERICAN 🍴 **Walter's Basin.** A former bowling alley in the heart of Holderness makes an unlikely but charming setting for meals overlooking Little Squam Lake—local boaters dock right beneath the dining room. Among the specialties on the seafood-intensive menu are toasted orzo with pan-fried rainbow trout and lobster macaroni and cheese. Sandwiches and salads are good choices for those looking for lighter fare. [$] *Average main: $22* ✉ *859 U.S. 3* ☎ *603/968–4412* 🌐 *www.waltersbasin.com.*

WHERE TO STAY

$ B&B/INN 🏨 **Glynn House.** Pam, Ingrid, and Glenn Heidenreich operate this beautifully restored 1890s Queen Anne–style Victorian and, next door, a handsome 1920s carriage house. **Pros:** luxurious rooms; complimentary afternoon hors d'oeuvres; social atmosphere. **Cons:** not much to do in town. [$] *Rooms from: $179* ✉ *59 Highland St., Ashland* ☎ *603/968–3775* 🌐 *www.glynnhouse.com* 🛏 *6 rooms, 6 suites* 🍽 *Breakfast.*

$ B&B/INN FAMILY 🏨 **Inn on Golden Pond.** Sweet-as-pie Bill and Bonnie Webb run this comfortable and informal bed-and-breakfast a short distance from Squam Lake, to which they provide hiking trail maps. **Pros:** friendly innkeepers; comfortable rooms and common spaces. **Cons:** not directly on the lake; not luxurious. [$] *Rooms from: $160* ✉ *1080 U.S. 3* ☎ *603/968–7269* 🌐 *www.innongoldenpond.com* 🛏 *6 rooms, 2 suites* 🍽 *Breakfast.*

$$$ B&B/INN Fodor's Choice ★ 🏨 **The Manor on Golden Pond.** A name like this is a lot to live up to, but the Manor succeeds: it's the Lakes Region's most charming inn. **Pros:** wood fireplaces; comfortable sitting rooms; great food; welcoming hosts. **Cons:** expensive. [$] *Rooms from: $310* ✉ *31 Manor Rd., off Shepard Hill Rd.* ☎ *603/968–3348, 800/545–2141* 🌐 *www.manorongoldenpond.com* 🛏 *22 rooms, 2 suites* 🍽 *Breakfast.*

$ B&B/INN **Squam Lake Inn.** Graceful Victorian furnishings fill the nine stylish rooms at this peaceful farmhouse inn a short stroll from Squam Lake. **Pros:** quiet setting; comfortable beds; big breakfasts. **Cons:** short walk to lake. $ *Rooms from: $159* ✉ *28 Shepard Hill Rd.* ☎ *603/968–4417, 800/839–6205* 🌐 *www.squamlakeinn.com* 🕐 *Closed late Oct.–May* 🛏 *9 rooms* 🍴 *Breakfast.*

CENTER SANDWICH

12 miles northeast of Holderness.

With Squam Lake to the west and the Sandwich Mountains to the north, Center Sandwich claims one of the prettiest settings of any Lakes Region community. So appealing are the town and its views that John Greenleaf Whittier used the Bearcamp River as the inspiration for his poem "Sunset on the Bearcamp." The town attracts artisans—crafts shops abound among its clutch of charming 18th- and 19th-century buildings.

ESSENTIALS

Visitor Information Squam Lake Area Chamber of Commerce. ✉ *Ashland* ☎ *603/968–4494* 🌐 *www.visitsquam.com.* **Sandwich Historical Society.** ✉ *4 Maple St.* ☎ *603/284–6269* 🌐 *www.sandwichhistorical.org.*

EXPLORING

FAMILY **Castle in the Clouds.** Looking for all the world like a fairy-tale castle, this wonderful mountaintop estate was finished in 1914. The elaborate mansion has 16 rooms, eight bathrooms, and doors made of lead. Owner Thomas Gustave Plant spent $7 million—the bulk of his fortune—on this project and died penniless in 1941. A tour includes the mansion and the Castle Springs water facility on this high Ossipee Mountain Range property overlooking Lake Winnipesaukee; hiking and pony and horse rides also take place here. ✉ *455 Old Mountain Rd., Moultonborough* ☎ *603/476–5900* 🌐 *www.castleintheclouds.org* 🎟 *$16* 🕐 *Early May–early June, weekends 10–4; early June–late Oct., daily 10–5:30.*

FAMILY **Loon Center.** Recognizable for its eerie calls and striking black-and-white coloring, the loon resides on many New Hampshire lakes but is threatened by the gradual loss of its habitat. Two trails wind through the 200-acre Loon Center; vantage points on the Loon Nest Trail overlook the spot resident loons sometimes occupy in late spring and summer. ✉ *183 Lee's Mills Rd., Moultonborough* ☎ *603/476–5666* 🌐 *www.loon.org* 🎟 *Free* 🕐 *Mid-Oct.–mid-May, Thurs.–Sat. 9–5; mid-May–June, Mon.–Sat. 9–5; July–mid-Oct., daily 9–5.*

WHERE TO EAT

$$ AMERICAN ✕ **Corner House Inn.** In a converted barn adorned with paintings by local artists, this restaurant dishes up classic American fare. Salads made with local greens are a house specialty, but don't overlook the chef's lobster-and-mushroom bisque or the shellfish sauté. Storytelling often takes place on Thursday evening, on Friday night there's live music, and brunch is served on Sunday. $ *Average main: $21* ✉ *22 Main St.* ☎ *603/476–3060* 🌐 *www.cornerhouseinn.com* 🕐 *Closed Tues. No lunch Mon., and Wed.–Sun. mid-Oct.–June.*

View simple yet functional furniture, architecture, and crafts at Canterbury Shaker Village.

9

$$$
AMERICAN

✗ **Lavinia's Relaxed Dining.** Talk about relaxing: that's exactly what you'll want to do in this splendidly restored mansion, built in 1820 by John Coe for his bride, Lavinia. Enjoy a glass of wine on the veranda, then sink into a plush chair in the dining room, where the original French wallpaper depicts the Seven Wonders of the World. The chef offers new twists on New England comfort foods with such dishes as pumpkin-and-mascarpone ravioli and Gorgonzola-stuffed artichoke hearts. Two good entrées are the lobster potpie and the grilled red snapper with pineapple pico de gallo. Lighter fare can be ordered in the upstairs lounge. For an unforgettable romantic evening, reserve the cupola—it seats only two. $ *Average main: $26* ⊠ *18 Main St., Center Harbor* ☎ *603/253–8617* ⊕ *www.laviniasdining.com* ⊗ *No lunch.*

SHOPPING

FAMILY **Old Country Store and Museum.** The store has been selling maple syrup, aged cheeses, jams, molasses, penny candy, and other items since 1781. Much of the equipment used in the store is antique, and the free museum displays old farming and forging tools. ⊠ *1011 Whittier Hwy.* ☎ *603/476–5750* ⊕ *www.nhcountrystore.com.*

TAMWORTH

13 miles east of Center Sandwich, 20 miles southwest of North Conway.

President Grover Cleveland summered in what remains a place of almost unreal quaintness: Tamworth is equally photogenic in verdant summer, during the fall foliage season, or under a blanket of winter snow. Cleveland's son, Francis, returned and founded the acclaimed

Barnstormers Theatre in 1931. One of America's first summer theaters, it continues to this day. Tamworth has a clutch of villages within its borders. At one of them—Chocorua—the view through the birches of Chocorua Lake has been so often photographed that you may experience déjà vu. Rising above the lake is Mt. Chocorua (3,490 feet), which has many good hiking trails.

GETTING HERE AND AROUND

The five villages of Tamworth boast six churches, which are worth a half-day's casual drive to admire their white clapboard elegance. Downtown Tamworth is tiny and can be strolled in a few minutes, but you might linger in the hope of meeting one of the town's many resident poets and artists.

EXPLORING

FAMILY **Remick Country Doctor Museum and Farm.** For 99 years (1894–1993) Dr. Edwin Crafts Remick and his father provided medical services to the Tamworth area and operated a family farm. After the younger Remick died, these two houses were turned into the Remick Country Doctor Museum and Farm. The second floor of the house has been kept as it was when Remick passed away; it's a great way to see the life of a country doctor. Each season, the still-working farm features a special activity such as maple-syrup making. The farm also has hiking trails and picnicking areas. ✉ *58 Cleveland Hill Rd.* ☎ *603/323–7591, 800/686–6117* 🌐 *www.remickmuseum.org* 🎟 *$5* 🕒 *Early Sept.–mid-June, weekdays 10–4; mid-June–early Sept., weekdays 10–5, Sat. 10–4.*

WHERE TO EAT

$ SEAFOOD FAMILY 🍴 **Jake's Seafood and Grill.** Oars and other nautical trappings adorn the wood-panel walls at this stop between West and Center Ossipee, about 8 miles southeast of Tamworth. The kitchen serves some of eastern New Hampshire's freshest and tastiest seafood, notably lobster pie, fried clams, and seafood casserole. Other choices include steak, ribs, and chicken dishes. [$] *Average main: $17* ✉ *2055 Rte. 16, West Ossipee* ☎ *603/539–2805* 🌐 *www.jakesseafoodco.com* 🕒 *Closed Apr. and Nov.*

$$ BARBECUE FAMILY 🍴 **Yankee Smokehouse.** This down-home barbecue joint's logo depicting a happy pig foreshadows the gleeful enthusiasm with which patrons dive into the hefty sandwiches of sliced pork and smoked chicken and the immense platters of baby back ribs and smoked sliced beef. Ample sides of slaw, beans, fries, and garlic toast complement the hearty fare. Even Southerners have come away impressed. The restaurant serves gluten-free items, too. [$] *Average main: $20* ✉ *Rtes. 16 and 25, about 5 miles southeast of Tamworth* ☎ *603/539–7427* 🌐 *www.yankeesmokehouse.com.*

PERFORMING ARTS

FAMILY **Arts Council of Tamworth.** The council sponsors artist residencies and children's programs, hosts lectures, presents dancers, storytellers, musicians of various genres, and other performers, and produces an art show and sale in late July. ✉ *77 Main St.* ☎ *603/323–0104* 🌐 *www.artstamworth.org.*

FAMILY **Barnstormers Theatre.** Founded in 1931, this theater company presents dramas and comedies June–August. ✉ *104 Main St.* ☎ *603/323–8500* 🌐 *www.barnstormerstheatre.org.*

SPORTS AND THE OUTDOORS

FAMILY **White Lake State Park.** The 72-acre stand of native pitch pine here is a National Natural Landmark. The park has a picnic area and a sandy beach, trails you can hike, trout you can fish for, and canoes you can rent. ⊠ *98 State Park Rd.* ☎ *603/323–7350* ⊕ *www.nhstateparks.org* ⊒ *$5* ⊗ *Late May–early Sept., daily 9–sunset; early Sept.–mid-Oct., weekends 8:30–sunset.*

THE WHITE MOUNTAINS

Sailors approaching East Coast harbors frequently mistake the pale peaks of the White Mountains—the highest range in the northeastern United States—for clouds. It was 1642 when explorer Darby Field could no longer contain his curiosity about one mountain in particular. He set off from his Exeter homestead and became the first European to climb what would later be called Mt. Washington. The 6,288-foot peak must have presented Field with formidable obstacles—its summit claims the highest wind velocity in the world ever recorded (231 mph in 1934) and can see snow every month of the year.

Today an auto road and a cog railway lead to the top of Mt. Washington, and people come by the tens of thousands to hike and climb, photograph the vistas, and ski. The peak is part of the Presidential Range, whose peaks are named after early presidents, and part of the White Mountain National Forest, which has roughly 770,000 acres that extend from northern New Hampshire into southwestern Maine. Among the forest's scenic notches (deep mountain passes) are Pinkham, Kinsman, Franconia, and Crawford. In these notches, you'll find trailheads for short hikes and multiday adventures; they are also excellent spots for photographing the majestic White Mountains.

This section of the guide begins in Waterville Valley, off Interstate 93, and continues to North Woodstock. It then follows portions of the White Mountains Trail, a 100-mile loop designated as a National Scenic and Cultural Byway.

9

ESSENTIALS

Visitor Information Bike the Whites. ☎ *603/356–9025* ⊕ *www.bikethewhites. com.* **Ski New Hampshire.** ☎ *603/745–9396* ⊕ *www.skinh.com.* **White Mountain National Forest.** ⊠ *71 White Mountain Dr., Campton* ☎ *603/536–6100* ⊕ *www.fs.fed.us.* **White Mountains Visitors Bureau.** ⊠ *200 Kancamagus Hwy., off I-93, North Woodstock* ☎ *603/745–8720* ⊕ *www.visitwhitemountains.com.*

WATERVILLE VALLEY

60 miles north of Concord.

Visitors began to arrive in Waterville Valley as early as 1835. A 10-mile cul-de-sac follows the Mad River, surrounded by mountains. The valley was first a summer resort and then became more of a ski area. Although it's now a year-round getaway, it still has a small-town charm. There are inns, condos, restaurants, shops, conference facilities, a grocery store, and a post office.

GETTING HERE AND AROUND

Depot Camp is a great starting point for hiking, snowshoeing, and cross-country skiing. In town, the Schuss bus has regular stops at the shops in Village Square, the lodges and condos, the Waterville Valley Conference Center, and the ski area. There's enough to do in this small village to keep outdoors enthusiasts busy for several days.

WHERE TO STAY

$$ RENTAL **Black Bear Lodge.** This family-friendly property has one-bedroom suites that sleep up to six people. **Pros:** affordable rates; perfect for families. **Cons:** basic in decor and services. [$] *Rooms from: $200* ✉ *3 Village Rd.* ☎ *603/236–4501, 800/349–2327* 🌐 *www.blackbearlodgenh.com* 🛏 *107 suites* 🍴 *No meals.*

$ HOTEL FAMILY **Golden Eagle Lodge.** Waterville's premier condominium property, its steep roof punctuated by dozens of gabled dormers, recalls the grand hotels of an earlier era. **Pros:** plenty of elbow room; kitchens. **Cons:** unremarkable architecture and decor. [$] *Rooms from: $129* ✉ *28 Packard's Rd.* ☎ *888/703–2453* 🌐 *www.goldeneaglelodge.com* 🛏 *139 condos* 🍴 *No meals.*

$ HOTEL **Snowy Owl Inn & Resort.** On weekends, visitors are treated to afternoon wine and cheese in this hotel's atrium lobby, which has a three-story fieldstone fireplace and wonderful watercolors of its namesake raptor. **Pros:** affordable; rate includes Continental breakfast. **Cons:** guests must pay for access to nearby gym. [$] *Rooms from: $104* ✉ *41 Village Rd.* ☎ *603/236–8383, 800/766–9969* 🌐 *www.snowyowlinn.com* 🛏 *85 rooms* 🍴 *Breakfast.*

SPORTS AND THE OUTDOORS

FAMILY **Waterville Valley Resort.** Tom Corcoran, a former U.S. ski-team star, designed this family-oriented resort. The lodgings and various amenities are about a mile from the slopes, but a shuttle renders a car unnecessary. This ski area has hosted more World Cup races than any other in the East, so most advanced skiers can look forward to a challenge. Most of the 50 trails are intermediate: straight down the fall line, wide, and agreeably long. About 20 acres of tree-skiing add heart-pounding stimulus. Complete snowmaking coverage ensures good skiing even when nature doesn't cooperate. The Waterville Valley cross-country network, with the ski center in the town square, provides over 43 miles of groomed trails. **Facilities:** 50 trails; 500 acres; 2,020-foot vertical drop; 11 lifts. ✉ *1 Ski Area Rd.* ☎ *603/236–8311, 800/468–2553 for snow conditions, 800/468–2553 for lodging* 🌐 *www.waterville.com* 🎟 *Lift ticket $77.*

LINCOLN AND NORTH WOODSTOCK

64 miles north of Concord.

These neighboring towns at the southwestern end of the White Mountains National Forest and one end of the Kancamagus Highway (Route 112) form a lively resort area, especially for Bostonian families who can make an easy day trip straight up Interstate 93 to Exit 32. Festivals such as the New Hampshire Scottish Highland Games in mid-September keep Lincoln swarming with people year-round. The town itself is not

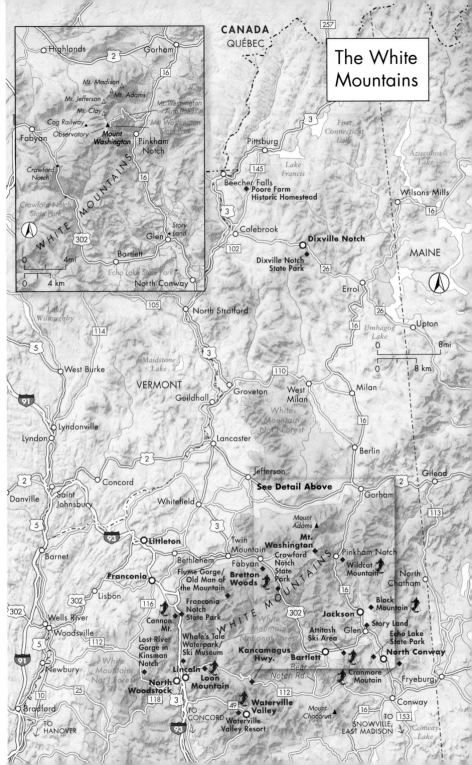

The White Mountains

CANADA
QUÉBEC

MAINE

VERMONT

Detail Inset (Upper Left)

Highlands
Gorham
Mt. Madison
Mt. Jefferson — Mt. Adams
Mt. Clay
Mt. Washington Auto Road
Cog Railway
Observatory
Mount Washington
Mt. Washington State Park
Fabyan
Pinkham Notch
Crawford Notch
Crawford Notch State Park
Glen
Story Land
Bartlett
Echo Lake State Park
North Conway

WHITE MOUNTAINS

0   4mi
0   4 km

Main Map

First Connecticut Lake
Aziscohos Lake
Wilsons Mills
Pittsburg
Lake Francis
Beecher Falls
Poore Farm Historic Homestead
Colebrook
Dixville Notch
Dixville Notch State Park
Errol
Upton
Umbagog Lake

North Stratford
North Stratford

Lake Willoughby
West Burke
Maidstone Lake
Groveton
West Milan
Milan
Lyndonville
Lyndon
Guildhall
Berlin
Lancaster
White Mountain Nat'l Forest
Concord
Jefferson
See Detail Above
Gilead
Danville
Saint Johnsbury
Whitefield
Gorham
Barnet
Littleton
Bethlehem
Twin Mountain
Mt. Washington
Crawford Notch State Park
Pinkham Notch
Mount Adams
Wildcat Mountain
North Chatham
Franconia
Fabyan
Bretton Woods
Flume Gorge/ Old Man of the Mountain
Black Mountain
Lisbon
Wells River
Woodsville
Franconia Notch State Park
Jackson
Story Land
Cannon Mt.
White Mountain National Forest
Attitash Ski Area
Glen
Echo Lake State Park
Lost River Gorge in Kinsman Notch
Whale's Tale Waterpark/ Ski Museum
Kancamagus Hwy.
Bartlett
North Conway
Newbury
Lincoln
Loon Mountain
Bear Notch Rd.
Cranmore Mountain
Fryeburg
North Woodstock
TO CONCORD
Waterville Valley
Waterville Valley Resort
Mount Chocorua
Conway
TO HANOVER
Bradford
SNOWVILLE, EAST MADISON
TO
Conway Lake

WHITE MOUNTAINS

0   8mi
0   8 km

much of an attraction. Tiny North Woodstock maintains more of a village feel.

GETTING HERE AND AROUND

Lincoln and North Woodstock are places to spend a day shopping in their quaint shops, which are within easy walking distance of each other. It's a pleasant 1-mile stroll between the two towns. On Route 112, which connects the two villages, there is a state visitor center.

ESSENTIALS

Visitor Information Lincoln–Woodstock Chamber of Commerce. ⊠ *126 Main St., North Woodstock* ☎ *603/745–6621* ⊕ *www.lincolnwoodstock.com.*

TOURS

FAMILY **Hobo Railroad.** Restored vintage train cars take you along the scenic shores of the Pemigewassett River. Tours take 80 minutes. The Santa Express runs late November–late December. ⊠ *64 Railroad St., off Kancamagus Hwy., Lincoln* ☎ *603/745–2135* ⊕ *www.hoborr.com* ⊠ *$16* ⊙ *Late June–Aug., tours daily at 11, 1, and 3; Sept.–early June, days and hrs vary.*

EXPLORING

FAMILY **Clark's Trading Post.** Chock-full of hokum, this old-time amusement park is a favorite with families. There are half-hour train rides over a 1904 covered bridge, a museum of Americana inside an 1880s firehouse, a restored gas station filled with antique cars, circus performers, and an Old Man of the Mountain rock-climbing tower—there's even a mining sluice where you can pan for gems. Tour guides tell tall tales, and vendors sell popcorn, ice cream, and pizza. The ensemble also includes a mammoth gift shop and a penny-candy store. ⊠ *110 Daniel Webster Hwy., off I–93, Lincoln* ☎ *603/745–8913* ⊕ *www.clarkstradingpost. com* ⊠ *$20* ⊙ *Mid-May–mid-June and mid-Sept., weekends 10–4:30; mid-June and early Sept., daily 9:30–5; July and Aug., daily 9:30–5:30.*

FAMILY **Lost River Gorge in Kinsman Notch.** Parents can enjoy the looks of wonder on their children's faces as they negotiate wooden boardwalks and stairs leading through a granite gorge formed by the roaring waters of the Lost River. One of the 10 caves they can explore is called the Lemon Squeezer (and it's a tight fit). Kids can also pan for gems and search for fossils, while grown-ups might prefer the attractions in the snack bar, gift shop, and nature garden. The park offers weekend lantern tours. ⊠ *1712 Lost River Rd., North Woodstock* ☎ *603/745–8720, 800/346–3687* ⊕ *www.lostrivergorge.com* ⊠ *$18* ⊙ *May, June, Sept. and Oct., daily 9–5; July and Aug., daily 9–6.*

FAMILY **Whale's Tale Waterpark.** You can float on an inner tube along a gentle river, plunge down one of five waterslides, or bodysurf in the large wave pool at Whale's Tale. There's plenty here for toddlers and small children. ⊠ *491 Daniel Webster Hwy., off I–93, Lincoln* ☎ *603/745–8810* ⊕ *www.whalestalewaterpark.net* ⊠ *$35* ⊙ *Mid-June, daily 10–4; late June–mid-Aug., daily 10–6; late Aug.–early Sept., daily 11–5.*

WHERE TO EAT AND STAY

$ ✕ **Sunny Day Diner.** Up in the skiing and hiking haven of Lincoln, this
AMERICAN   cozy, handsomely restored late-1950s diner is a popular stop for break-
FAMILY   fast or coffee and dessert. The banana-bread French toast and cherry
pie à la mode are two local favorites. $ *Average main:* ✉ *90 U.S. 3, off
I–93, Lincoln* ☎ *603/745–4833* ▭ *No credit cards.*

$$ ✕ **Woodstock Inn, Station & Brewery.** If you like restaurants loaded with
AMERICAN   character, don't miss this one inside North Woodstock's late-1800s train
FAMILY   station. The walls are decorated with old maps, historic photographs,
and local memorabilia; there are also fun curiosities, such as an old
phone booth. The menu offers gluten-free items as well as standard pub
fare: pizza, burgers, steaks, and seafood. Gourmet breakfasts are served
daily. The on-site brewery makes 17 different kinds of beer; ask your
server which are on tap. Kids will find a small game room. $ *Average
main: $20* ✉ *135 Main St., off I–93, North Woodstock* ☎ *603/745–
3951* ⊕ *www.woodstockinnnh.com.*

$ ⛺ **Indian Head Resort.** The resort's inexpensive and spacious rooms make
RESORT   this a good choice for families on a budget. **Pros:** great prices; fun for
FAMILY   the whole family; near kid-friendly attractions. **Cons:** can be crowded;
sometimes hard to get a reservation. $ *Rooms from: $169* ✉ *664
U.S. 3, 5 miles north of North Woodstock, Lincoln* ☎ *603/745–8000,
800/343–8000* ⊕ *www.indianheadresort.com* ➾ *98 rooms, 40 cottages*
⦿| *Some meals.*

$$ ⛺ **Mountain Club on Loon.** If you want a ski-in, ski-out stay on Loon
RESORT   Mountain, this lodge centered around a lobby with a large stone fire-
FAMILY   place is your only option. **Pros:** within walking distance of the lifts;
full-service spa; close to the national forest. **Cons:** very busy in winter.
$ *Rooms from: $237* ✉ *90 Loon Mountain, off Kancamagus Hwy.,
Lincoln* ☎ *603/745–2244, 800/229–7829* ⊕ *www.mtnclub.com* ➾ *117
rooms, 117 suites* ⦿| *No meals.*

NIGHTLIFE AND PERFORMING ARTS

NIGHTLIFE

Black Diamond Pub. For après-ski socializing, skiers head to this often
bustling ski-resort hangout. ✉ *Mountain Club on Loon, 90 Loon
Mountain Rd., Lincoln* ☎ *603/745–2244* ⊕ *www.mtnclub.com.*

FAMILY   **Thunderbird Lounge.** Live music, a large dance floor, and great lake views
make this a year-round hot spot. ✉ *Indian Head Resort, 664 U.S. 3,
Lincoln* ☎ *603/745–8000* ⊕ *www.indianheadresort.com.*

PERFORMING ARTS

FAMILY   **Jean's Playhouse.** The area's year-round stage for comedy, theater, music,
and other performances is a popular venue. ✉ *34 Papermill Dr., Lincoln*
☎ *603/745–2141* ⊕ *www.jeans-playhouse.com.*

SPORTS AND THE OUTDOORS

FAMILY   **Loon Mountain.** Wide, straight, and consistent intermediate ski trails prevail at Loon, a modern resort on the western edge of the Pemigewasset
River. The most advanced runs are grouped on the North Peak section,
with 2,100 feet of vertical skiing. Beginner trails are set apart. There's
snow tubing on the lower slopes, and eight terrain parks suitable for
all ages and ability levels. In the base lodge are the usual dining and

9

lounging facilities. There are 13 miles of cross-country trails, ice-skating on an outdoor rink, snowshoeing and snowshoeing tours, and a rock-climbing wall. **Facilities:** 61 trails; 370 acres; 2,100-foot vertical drop; 12 lifts. ⊠ *60 Loon Mountain Rd., off the Kancamagus Hwy., Lincoln* ☎ *603/745–8111* ⊕ *www.loonmtn.com* ✆ *Lift ticket $85.*

FAMILY **Pemi Valley Moose Tours.** If you're eager to see a mighty moose, embark on a moose-watching bus tour into the northernmost White Mountains. The three-hour trips depart at 8:30 pm May to mid-October for the best wildlife-sighting opportunities. ⊠ *136 Main St., off I–93, Lincoln* ☎ *603/745–2744* ⊕ *www.moosetoursnh.com* ✆ *$30.*

FRANCONIA

16 miles northwest of Lincoln/North Woodstock.

Travelers have long passed through the White Mountains via the spectacular Franconia Notch, and in the late 18th century a town evolved just to the north. It and the region's jagged rock formations and heavy coat of evergreens stirred the imaginations of Washington Irving, Henry Wadsworth Longfellow, and Nathaniel Hawthorne, who penned a short story about the craggy cliff known as the Old Man of the Mountain. There is almost no town proper to speak of here, just a handful of stores near Interstate 93, aka the Franconia Notch Parkway.

Four miles west of Franconia, Sugar Hill is a town of about 500 people. It's famous for its spectacular sunsets and views of the Franconia Mountains, best seen from Sunset Hill, where a row of grand hotels and mansions once stood.

GETTING HERE AND AROUND
Franconia is a small town with not much to offer tourists, but it is an access point for many ski areas and the villages of Sugar Hill, Easton, Bethlehem, Bretton Woods, Littleton, Lincoln, and North Woodstock—towns replete with general stores, country inns, picturesque farms, and churches with white steeples.

ESSENTIALS
Visitor Information Franconia Notch Chamber of Commerce. ☎ *603/823–5661* ⊕ *www.franconianotch.org.*

EXPLORING
FAMILY **Flume Gorge.** This 800-foot-long chasm has narrow walls that cause an eerie echo from the gorge's running water. A long wooden boardwalk and a series of stairways lead to the top of the falls that thunder down the gorge. The 2-mile loop takes about an hour to complete. The boardwalk begins at the visitor center, which also has a gift shop, a cafeteria, and a small museum. ⊠ *Franconia Notch State Park, 852 Daniel Webster Hwy.* ☎ *603/745–8391* ⊕ *www.nhstateparks.org* ✆ *$16* ☉ *Early May–late Oct., daily 9–5.*

The Frost Place Museum. Robert Frost's year-round home from 1915 to 1920, this is where the poet soaked up the New England life. The place is imbued with the spirit of his work, down to the rusted mailbox in front that's painted "R. Frost" in simple lettering. Two rooms contain

Continued on page 572

HIKING THE APPALACHIAN TRAIL

Tucked inside the nation's most densely populated corridor, a simple footpath in the wilderness stretches more than 2,100 miles, from Georgia to Maine. The Appalachian Trail passes through some of New England's most spectacular regions, and daytrippers can experience the area's beauty on a multitude of accessible, rewarding hikes.   *By Melissa Kim*

Running along the spine of the Appalachian Mountains, the trail was fully blazed in 1937 and designed to connect anyone and everyone with nature. Within a day's drive of two-thirds of the U.S. population, it draws an estimated two to three million people every year. Through-hikers complete the whole trail in one daunting six-month season, but all ages and abilities can find renewal and perspective here in just a few hours. One-third of the AT passes through New England, and it's safe to say that the farther north you go, the harder the trail gets. New Hampshire and Maine challenge experienced hikers with windy, cold, and isolated peaks.

Top, hiking in New Hampshire's White Mountains. Above, autumn view of Profile Lake, Pemigewasset, NH.

ON THE TRAIL

New England's prime hiking season is in late summer and early fall, when the blaze of foliage viewed from a high peak is unparalleled. Popular trails see high crowds; if you seek solitude, try hiking at sunrise, a peaceful time that's good for wildlife viewing. You'll have to curb your enthusiasm in spring and early summer to avoid mud season in late April and black flies in May and June.

With the right gear, attitude, and preparation, winter can also offer fine opportunities for hiking, snowshoeing, and cross-country skiing.

FOLLOW THE TRAIL

Most hiking trails are marked with blazes, blocks of colored paint on a tree or rock. The AT, and only the AT, is marked by vertical, rectangular 2- by 6-inch white blazes. Two blazes mark route changes; turn in the direction of the top blaze. At higher elevations, you might also see cairns, small piles of rocks carefully placed by trail rangers to show the way when a blaze might be obscured by snow or fog.

Scenic U.S. 302—and the AT—pass through Crawford Notch, a spectacular valley in New Hampshire's White Mountains.

Hikers gather outside Lakes of the Clouds Hut, near the peak of Mount Washington.

TRIP TIPS

WHAT TO WEAR: For clothes, layer with a breathable fabric like polypropylene, starting with a shirt, a fleece, and a wind- or water-resistant shell. Bring gloves, a hat, and a change of socks.

WHAT TO BRING: Carry plenty of water and lightweight high-energy food. Don't forget sunscreen and insect repellent. Bring a map and compass. Just in case: a basic first-aid kit, a flashlight or headlamp, whistle, multi-tool, and matches.

PLAN AHEAD: In your car, leave a change of clothing, especially dry socks and shoes, as well as extra water and food.

PLAY IT SAFE: Tell someone your hiking plan and take a hiking partner. Carry a rescue card with emergency contact information and allergy details.

BE PREPARED: Plan your route and check the weather forecast in advance.

REMEMBER YOUR BEGINNINGS: Look back at the trail especially at the trailhead and at tricky junctions. If you've got a digital camera, photograph trail maps posted at the trailhead or natural landmarks to help you find your way.

WHERE TO STAY

Day hikers looking to extend the adventure can also make the experience as hard or as soft as they choose. Through-hikers combine camping with overnight stays in primitive shelters, mountain huts, comfortable lodges, and resorts just off the trail.

Rustic cabins and lean-tos provide basic shelter in Maine's Baxter State Park. In Maine and New Hampshire, the Appalachian Mountain Club runs four-season lodges as well as a network of mountain huts for backcountry hikers. A hiker code of camaraderie and conviviality prevails in these huts. Experience a night and you might just find yourself dreaming of a through-hike.

FOR MORE INFORMATION

Appalachian Trail Conservancy
(⊕ www.appalachiantrail.org)

Appalachian National Scenic Trail
(⊕ www.nps.gov/appa)

Appalachian Mountain Club
(⊕ www.outdoors.org)

ANIMALS ALONG THE TRAIL

❶ Black bear

Black bears are the most common—and smallest—bear in North America. Clever and adaptable, these adroit mammals will eat whatever they can (though they are primarily vegetarian, favoring berries, grasses, roots, blossoms, and nuts). Not naturally aggressive, black bears usually make themselves scarce when they hear hikers. The largest New England populations are in New Hampshire and Maine.

❷ Moose

Spotting a moose in the wild is unforgettable: their massive size and serene gaze are truly humbling. Treasure the moment, then slowly back away. At more than six feet tall, weighing 750 to 1,000 pounds, a moose is not to be trifled with, particularly during rutting and calving seasons (fall and spring, respectively). Dusk and dawn are the best times to spot the iconic animal; you're most likely to see one in Maine, especially in and around ponds.

⚠ Black flies

Especially fierce in May and June, these pesky flies can upset the tranquility of a hike in the woods as they swarm your face and bite your neck. To ward them off, cover any exposed skin and wear light colors. You'll get some relief on a mountain peak; cold weather and high winds also keep them at bay.

❸ Bald eagles

Countless bird species can be seen and heard along the AT, but what could be more exciting than to catch a glimpse of our national bird as it bounces back from near extinction? Now it's not uncommon to see the majestic bald eagle with its tremendous wing span, white head feathers, and curved yellow beak. The white head and tail distinguish the bald from the golden eagle, a bit less rare but just as thrilling to see. Most of New England's bald eagles are in Maine, but they are now present—albeit in small numbers—in all six states.

WILDFLOWERS ALONG THE TRAIL

❹ Mountain laurel

The clusters of pink and white blooms of the mountain laurel look like bursts of fireworks. Up close, each one has the delicate detail of a lady's parasol. Blooms vary in color, from pure white to darker pink, and have different amounts of red markings. Connecticut's state flower, mountain laurel flourishes in rocky woods, blooming in May and June. Look for the shrub in southern New England; it's rare along the Appalachian trail in Vermont and Maine.

❺ Mountain avens

A member of the rose family, these showy yellow flowers abound in New Hampshire's White Mountains. You can't miss the large buttercup-like blooms on long green stems when they are in bloom from June through August. So common here, yet extremely rare: the only other place in the whole world where you can find mountain avens is on an island off the coast of Nova Scotia.

❻ Painted trillium

You might smell a trillium before you see it; these flowers have an unpleasant odor that may attract the flies that pollinate it. To identify this impressive flower, look for sets of three: three large pointed blue-green leaves, three sepals (small leaves beneath the petals), and three white petals with a brilliant magenta center. It can take four or five years for a trillium to produce one flower, which blooms in May and June in wet woodlands.

❼ Pink lady slippers

These delicate orchids can grow from 6 to 15 inches high and favor specific wet wooded areas in dappled sunlight. The slender stalk rises from a pair of green leaves, then bends a graceful neck to suspend the paper-thin pale pink closed flower. The slow-growing plant needs help from fungus and bees to survive and can live to be 20 years old. New Hampshire's state wildflower, the pink lady slipper blooms in June throughout New England.

● = Somewhat Common   ● = Rare

CHOOSE YOUR DAY HIKE

MAINE

GULF HAGAS, Greenville
Difficult, 8-plus miles round-trip, 6–7 hours

This National Natural Landmark in the North Maine Woods is a spectacular sight for the adventurous day hiker. It involves a long drive on logging roads east from Greenville (see Inland Maine section) to a remote spot and a slippery, sometimes treacherous 8-mile hike around the rim of what's been dubbed Maine's Grand Canyon. Swimming in one of the sparkling pools under a 30-foot-high waterfall and admiring the views of cliffs, cascades, gorges, and chasms in this slate canyon, otherwise unthinkable in New England, will take your breath away.

TABLE ROCK, Bethel
Medium, 2.4 miles round-trip, 2 hours

Maine's Mahoosuc Range is thought to be one of the most difficult stretches of the entire AT, but north of Bethel at Grafton Notch State Park, day hikes range from easy walks in to cascading waterfalls to strenuous climbs up Old Speck's craggy peak. The Table Rock trail offers interesting sights—great views of the notch from the immense slab of granite that gives this trail its name, as well as one of the state's largest system of slab caves—narrow with tall openings unlike underground caves.

NEW HAMPSHIRE

ZEALAND TRAIL, Berlin
Easy, 5.6 miles round-trip, 3.5–4 hours

New Hampshire's Presidential range gets so much attention and traffic that sometimes the equally spectacular Pemigewasset Wilderness, just to its west, gets overlooked. Follow State Route 302 to the trailhead on Zealand Rd. near Bretton Woods. For an easy day hike to one of the Appalachian Mountain Club's excellent overnight huts, take the mostly flat Zealand Trail over bridges and past a beaver swamp to Zealand Pond. The last tenth of a mile is a steep ascent to the mountain retreat, where you might spot an AT through-hiker taking a well-deserved rest. (Most north-bound through-hikers reach this section around July or August.) In winter, you can get here by a lovely cross-country ski trip.

TRAIL NAMES

For through-hikers, doing the AT can be a life-altering experience. One of the trail's most respected traditions is taking an alter ego: a trail name. Lightning Bolt: fast hiker. Pine Knot: tough as one. Bluebearee: because a bear got all her food on her very first night on the trail.

VERMONT

HARMON HILL, Bennington

Medium to difficult, 3.6 miles round-trip, 3–4 hours

This rugged hike in the Green Mountains goes south along the AT where it coincides with the Long Trail, Vermont's century-old "footpath in the wilderness." From the trailhead on Route 9 just east of Bennington, the first half mile or so is strenuous, with some rock and log staircases and hairpins. The payback is the sweeping view from the top; you'll see Mount Anthony, Bennington and its iconic war monument, and the rolling green hills of the Taconics to the west.

STRATTON MOUNTAIN, Stratton

Difficult, 6.6 miles round-trip, 5–6 hours

A steep and steady climb from the trailhead on Kelly Stand Rd. (between West Wardsboro and Arlington) up the 3,936-foot-high Stratton Mountain follows the AT and Long Trail through mixed forests. It's said that this peak is where Benton MacKaye conceived of the idea for the Appalachian Trail in 1921. An observation tower at the summit gives you a great 360-degree view of the Green Mountains. From July to October, you can park at Stratton resort and ride the gondola up (or down) and follow the .75-mile Fire Tower Trail to the southern true peak.

MASSACHUSETTS

MOUNT GREYLOCK, North Adams

Easy to difficult, 2 miles round-trip, less than 1 hour

There are many ways to experience Massachusetts's highest peak. From North Adams, follow Route 2 to the Notch Rd. trailheads. For a warm-up, try the Rounds Rock trail (Easy, 0.7 mi) for some spectacular views. Or drive up the 8-mile-long summit road and hike down the Robinson's Point trail (Difficult, 0.8 miles) for the best view of the Hopper, a glacial cirque that's home to an old-growth red spruce forest. At the summit, the impressive **Bascom Lodge**, built in the 1930s by the Civilian Conservation Corps, provides delicious meals and overnight stays (⊕ www.bascomlodge.net).

CONNECTICUT

LION'S HEAD, Salisbury

Medium, 4.6 miles round-trip, 3.5–4 hours

The AT's 52 miles in Connecticut take hikers up some modest mountains, including Lion's Head in Salisbury. From the trailhead on State Route 41, follow the white blazes of the AT for two easy miles, then take the blue-blazed Lion's Head Trail for a short, steep push over open ledges to the 1,738-foot summit with its commanding views of pastoral southern New England. Try this in summer when the mountain laurels—Connecticut's state flower—are in bloom.

EXPERIENCE MOUNT WASHINGTON

Looking at Mt. Washington from Mt. Bond in the Pemigewasset Wilderness Area, New Hampshire.

Mount Washington is the Northeast's peak of superlatives: worst weather in the world, highest spot in the northeast, windiest place on Earth. It snows in the summer, there are avalanches in winter, and it's foggy 60 percent of the time. Strong 35-mile-per-hour winds are the average, and extreme winds of 100 miles per hour with higher gusts blow year-round. Here, you can literally get blown away.

Explorers, scientists, artists, and botanists have been coming to the mountain for hundreds of years, drawn by its unique geologic features, unusual plants, and exceptional climate.

WHY SO WINDY? The 6,288-foot-high treeless peak is the highest point for miles around, so nothing dampens the force of the wind. Also, the sharp vertical rise causes wind to accelerate. Dramatic changes in air pressure also cause strong, high winds. Add to that the fact that three major storm tracks converge here, and you've got a mountain that has claimed more than 135 lives in the past 150 years.

GOING UP THE MOUNTAIN

An ascent up Mount Washington is for experienced hikers who are prepared for severe, unpredictable weather. Even in summer, cold, wet, foggy, windy conditions prevail. The most popular route to the top is on the eastern face up the Tuckerman Ravine Trail. But countless trails offer plenty of moderate day hikes, like the Alpine Garden Trail, as an alternative to a summit attempt. Start at the Pinkham Notch Visitor Center on Route 16 to review your options.

BACKPACKING ON THE MOUNTAIN

Lakes of the Clouds Hut perches 5,050 feet up the southern shoulder, providing bunkrooms and meals in summer; reservations are required. On the eastern face, the **Hermit Lake Shelter Area** has shelters and tent platforms; to camp here you'll need a first-come, first-served permit from the Visitors Center. Both are operated by the **AMC** (☎ 603/466-2727; ⊕ www.outdoors.org).

NON-HIKING ALTERNATIVES

In the summer, the **Auto Road** (☎ 603/466-3988 ⊕ mtwashingtonautoroad. com) and the **Cog Railway** (☎ 800/922-8825 ⊕ www. thecog.com) present alternate ways up the mountain; both give you a real sense of the mountain's grandeur. In winter, a **SnowCoach** (☎ 603/466-2333 ⊕ www. greatglentrails.com) hauls visitors 4.5 miles up the Auto Road with an option to cross-country ski, telemark, snowshoe, or ride the coach back down.

memorabilia and signed editions of his books. Out back, you can follow short trails marked with lines from his poetry. This place will slow you down and remind you of the intense beauty of the surrounding countryside. Poetry readings are scheduled on many summer evenings. ✉ *158 Ridge Rd.* ☎ *603/823–5510* ⊕ *www.frostplace.org* 🎫 *$5* ☉ *June, daily 1–5; July–early Sept., Wed.–Mon. 1–5; mid-Sept.–Oct., Wed.–Mon. 10–5.*

FAMILY **New England Ski Museum.** This small museum lets you travel back in time to see how skiing began as a sport, particularly in New England. Here you can examine artifacts, clothing, and equipment, as well as Bode Miller's five Olympic medals. For lifelong ski enthusiasts, the trip down memory lane will likely evoke warm smiles. ✉ *Franconia Notch State Park, 135 Tramway Dr., next to Cannon Mountain Tramway* ⊕ *www.skimuseum.org* 🎫 *Free* ☉ *Late Sept.–Apr., daily 10–5.*

FAMILY **Old Man of the Mountain.** This somber profile in the rock high above Franconia Notch crumbled somewhat unexpectedly in 2003. The iconic image had defined New Hampshire, and the Old Man's "death" stunned and saddened residents. You can see photographs and learn about the history of the Old Man at the visitor center at Flume Gorge. Better yet, follow signs to a small Old Man of the Mountain Park. There you can view the mountain face through newly installed steel rods that seem to literally put the beloved visage back on the mountain. ✉ *Franconia Notch State Park, U.S. 3* ⊕ *www.oldmannh.org* 🎫 *Free* ☉ *Daily 9–5.*

WHERE TO EAT AND STAY

$ **✕ Polly's Pancake Parlor.** In the Dexter family for three generations, Pol-
AMERICAN ly's has been serving up pancakes and waffles (from its own original
FAMILY recipe) since the 1930s. Smoked bacon and ham, sandwiches on homemade bread, delicious baked beans, and, more recently, gluten-free items have since been added to the menu. Desserts include raspberry pie. Much of the food is made from grains ground on-site. The gift shop sells maple products. In 2015, a new dining room was built, though all the antiques and country charm remain. $ *Average main: $10* ✉ *672 Rte. 117* ☎ *603/823–5575* ⊕ *www.pollyspancakeparlor.com* ☉ *Closed Mon.–Wed. Nov.–early Mar.*

$$$$ **✕ Sugar Hill Inn.** Inside this romantic 1789 farmhouse you'll find a very
AMERICAN elegant dining room where memorable prix-fixe meals ($68) are pre-
Fodor's Choice pared by chef Val Fortin. Start with a trio of his favorite soups or a
★ butternut squash risotto, followed by a beet-and-anise garden salad. Entrées may include peppercorn-crusted sirloin steak with grilled mushrooms and truffle oil, or free-range duck served three ways: breast with a bittersweet chocolate sauce, braised leg, and foie-gras ravioli. The apple dumpling with pumpkin ice cream and the goat cheese crème brûlée with fruit are among the creative homemade desserts. $ *Average main: $68* ✉ *116 Rte. 117* ☎ *603/823–5621* ⊕ *www.sugarhillinn.com* ☉ *Closed Wed. No lunch* 🍴 *Reservations essential.*

$ **🛏 Franconia Inn.** At this 100-acre family-friendly resort, you can play
RESORT tennis on four clay courts, soak in the outdoor heated pool or hot tub,
FAMILY hop on a mountain bike, or soar in a glider. **Pros:** good for kids; amazing views; outdoor heated pool. **Cons:** may be too remote for some.

$ Rooms from: $149 ⊠ 1172 Easton Rd. ☎ 603/823–5542, 800/473–5299 ⊕ www.franconiainn.com ⊗ Closed Apr.–mid-May ⤳ 34 rooms, 3 suites, 1 cottage with 2 units with kitchens ⦿ Some meals.

SPORTS AND THE OUTDOORS

SKI AREAS

FAMILY **Cannon Mountain.** The first aerial tramway in North America was built here in 1938, and the view from the top of the 4,080-foot summit is spectacular on a clear day. The ride is free with a ski lift ticket; otherwise it's $17. In winter, you'll find classic New England ski terrain that runs the gamut from steep pitches off the peak to gentle blue cruisers. Beginners may want to head over to the separate Tuckerbrook family area, which offers 13 trails and four lifts. Adventurous types will want to try out the Mittersill area, which has 86 acres of lift-accessed "side country" trails and glades where the snow is au naturel. **Facilities:** 81 trails; 282 acres; 2,180-foot vertical drop; 10 lifts. ⊠ *9 Franconia Notch State Park, off U.S. 3* ☎ *603/823–8800, 603/823–7771 for snow conditions* ⊕ *www.cannonmt.com* ⊡ *Lift ticket $75.*

FAMILY **Franconia Village Cross-Country Ski Center.** The cross-country ski center at the Franconia Inn has more than 40 miles of groomed and backcountry trails and rents skis, boots, and poles. One popular route leads to Bridal Veil Falls, a great spot for a picnic lunch. You can also enjoy horse-drawn sleigh rides, snowshoeing, snow tubing, and ice-skating on a lighted rink. ⊠ *Franconia Inn, 1172 Easton Rd.* ☎ *603/823–5542, 800/473–5299* ⊕ *www.franconiainn.com/cross_country_ski_center.php* ⊡ *$12.*

SHOPPING

FAMILY **Sugar Hill Sampler.** In this 1815 barn set high on a hill, you'll find an old-fashioned general store filled with quilts, lamps, candles, ornaments, and other crafts, along with gourmet jams, sauces, and condiments. In the back, owner Barbara Serafini has set up a folksy museum with local photos, newspaper clippings, and curiosities—Bette Davis's will among them. ⊠ *22 Sunset Rd., Sugar Hill* ☎ *603/823–8478* ⊕ *www. sugarhillsampler.com.*

LITTLETON

7 miles north of Franconia, 86 miles north of Concord.

One of northern New Hampshire's largest towns (this isn't saying much, mind you) is on a granite shelf along the Ammonoosuc River, whose swift current and drop of 235 feet enabled the community to flourish as a mill center in its early days. The railroad came through some time later, and Littleton grew into the region's commercial hub. In the minds of many, it's more a place to stock up on supplies than a real destination itself, but few communities have worked harder at revitalization. Intriguing shops and eateries line Main Street, whose tidy 19th- and early-20th-century buildings suggest a set in a Jimmy Stewart movie.

GETTING HERE AND AROUND

Littleton sits just off Interstate 95. Take Exit 41 and follow Cottage Street north to Main Street, portions of which are also signed as Route 116, Route 18, and U.S. 302.

EXPLORING

FAMILY **The Rocks Estate.** The estate of John Jacob Glessner (1843–1936), one of the founders of International Harvester, now serves as the 1,400-acre North Country Conservation and Education Center for the Forest Society. Some of the most striking restored buildings here are in the Shingle style. The property is named for the many surface boulders on the estate when Glessner bought it—some were used to erect its rambling rock walls. Open year-round, the Rocks presents natural-history programs and has self-guided tours and hiking trails with excellent views of the Presidential Range. Come winter, cross-country ski trails and a select-your-own-Christmas-tree farm open up. In spring, watch syrup being made in the New Hampshire Maple Experience Museum. ⊠ *4 Christmas Tree La., Bethlehem* ☎ *603/444–6228* ⊕ *www.therocks.org.*

QUICK BITES **Miller's Cafe & Bakery.** Next to the Riverwalk Covered Bridge, this great stop for breakfast or lunch serves salads, sandwiches, and fabulous baked goods like the chocolate-pecan pie. On a nice day, enjoy the Ammonoosuc River views from the deck. If staying in the area, order a meal to go or have it delivered. ⊠ *16 Mill St.* ☎ *603/444–2146* ⊕ *www.millerscafeandbakery. com* ⊗ *No dinner.*

FAMILY **Thayers Inn.** A former grande-dame hotel and still a working inn, Thayers also functions as an informal museum. Many of the rooms have been recently renovated with new paint, linens, and furniture, but enough antiques remain to lend it yesteryear charm. In the lobby and lining the hall are photos and memorabilia from movie star Bette Davis's huge birthday bash and artifacts of other illustrious guests, including Ulysses S. Grant, Henry Ford, P. T. Barnum, and Richard Nixon. Request a key to climb up to the cupola for 360-degree view of the town. Two rooms are open to the public: one set up as a guest room from the 1840s, and the other a scene from *Pollyanna,* written by Littleton native Eleanor Hodgman Porter (born 1868). ⊠ *111 Main St.* ☎ *603/444–6469* ⊕ *www.thayersinn.com.*

OFF THE BEATEN PATH **Whitefield.** About 11 miles northeast of Littleton, the small village of Whitefield became a prominent summer resort in the late 19th century, when wealthy industrialists flocked to this rolling valley to play golf and hobnob with each other. The yellow clapboard Mountain View Grand Hotel, which first opened in 1865, is once again one of New England's grandest resorts. It's worth driving through the courtly Colonial center of town and up Route 116 just beyond to see this magnificent structure atop a bluff overlooking the Presidentials. ⊠ *Whitefield* ⊕ *www.whitefieldnh.org.*

WHERE TO EAT AND STAY

$$$
AMERICAN ✕ **Tim-bir Alley.** Here's a rare find in New Hampshire: an independent restaurant in a contemporary setting that's been serving customers for decades yet still takes its food seriously. If you're in town, don't miss

it. Tim Carr's menu changes weekly and uses regional American ingredients in creative ways. Entrées may include an eggplant pâté with feta cheese, red pepper, and a tomato-herb marmalade, or basil-and-olive-oil salmon with a spinach-Brie-pecan pesto. Save room for white chocolate–coconut cheesecake and other desserts. [$] *Average main: $25* ✉ *7 Main St.* ☎ *603/444–6142* ▭ *No credit cards* ⏲ *Closed Jan.–Apr., and Mon. and Tues. No lunch.*

$$ B&B/INN Fodor's Choice ★ 🏨 **Adair Country Inn and Restaurant.** An air of yesteryear refinement suffuses Adair, a three-story Georgian Revival home that attorney Frank Hogan built as a wedding present for his daughter in 1927. **Pros:** refined, book-filled spaces; rates include a gourmet breakfast; cross-country skiing. **Cons:** removed from town. [$] *Rooms from: $229* ✉ *80 Guider La., off I–93, Bethlehem* ☎ *603/444–2600, 888/444–2600* 🌐 *www.adairinn.com* ⏲ *Closed mid-Nov. and Apr.* 🛏 *11 rooms* 🍴 *Some meals.*

SHOPPING

FAMILY **Little Village Toy and Book Stop.** If you're looking for hiking maps or good books about the history of the area, you'll find them here, along with unusual children's toys and many adult fiction and nonfiction titles. On the lower level is the League of New Hampshire Craftsmen's shop, featuring glass, prints, ceramics, fiber, and more. ✉ *81 Main St.* ☎ *603/444–5263.*

Potato Barn Antiques Center. Ten dealers operating out of an old potato-storage barn sell antique lamps, vintage clothing and hats, costume jewelry, books, railroad lanterns, signs, and old tools. ✉ *960 Lancaster Rd., 6 miles north of Lancaster, Northumberland* ☎ *603/636–2611* 🌐 *www.potatobarnantiques.com.*

BRETTON WOODS

14 miles southeast of Bethlehem; 28 miles northeast of Lincoln/Woodstock.

In the early 1900s private railcars brought the elite from New York and Philadelphia to the Omni Mount Washington Hotel, the jewel of the White Mountains. A visit to the hotel, which was the site of the 1944 United Nations conference that created the International Monetary Fund and the International Bank for Reconstruction and Development (and the birth of many conspiracy theories), is not to be missed. The area is also known for its cog railway and the Bretton Woods ski resort.

GETTING HERE AND AROUND

Bretton Woods is in the heart of the White Mountains on U.S. 302. A free shuttle makes it easy to get around the resort's various facilities. Helpful advice on how to enjoy your stay can be found at the concierge and activities desk in the main lobby of the Omni Mount Washington Hotel.

EXPLORING

FAMILY Fodor's Choice ★ **Mount Washington Cog Railway.** In 1858, Sylvester Marsh petitioned the state legislature for permission to build a steam railway up Mt. Washington. One politico retorted that Marsh would have better luck building a railroad to the moon, but 11 years later the Mount Washington

Cog Railway chugged its way up to the summit along a 3-mile track on the mountain's west side. Today it's one of the state's most beloved attractions—a thrill in either direction. A small museum at the base has exhibits about the cog rail. The full trip takes three hours including an hour spent at the summit. ⊠ *3168 Base Station Rd., 6 miles northeast of Bretton Woods* ☎ *603/278–5404, 800/922–8825* ⊕ *www.thecog.com* ⊠ *$68* ⊗ *May–early Dec., departures vary.*

WHERE TO EAT

$$$
AMERICAN
✕**Bretton Arms Dining Room.** You're likely to have the best meal in the area at this intimate restaurant. Though the same chef oversees the Omni Mount Washington Hotel's Main Dining Room, the latter is vast, and the Bretton Arms much cozier. The menu is seasonal and might include Georges Bank scallops with pureed celery root, baby bok choy, and cippolini onions. Locally sourced food features prominently in all dishes. ⓢ *Average main: $30* ⊠ *310 Mt. Washington Rd.* ☎ *603/278–1000* ⊕ *www. omnihotels.com/hotels/bretton-woods-bretton-arms/dining* ⊗ *No lunch.*

$$
AMERICAN
FAMILY
✕**Fabyan's Station.** A model train circles the dining room, a nod to the late 19th century, when 60 trains stopped at this former railroad station every day. If you're looking for an easygoing meal, Fabyan's cooks up delicious clam chowder in a bread bowl and house-smoked ribs with coleslaw. There's a kids' menu, too. ⓢ *Average main: $20* ⊠ *U.S. 302, 1 mile north of ski area* ☎ *603/278–2222* ⊕ *www.brettonwoods.com* ⚍ *Reservations not accepted.*

$$$$
AMERICAN
✕**Main Dining Room.** You'd be hard-pressed to find a larger or grander space in New Hampshire than the Omni Mount Washington Hotel's enormous octagonal Main Dining Room, which has massive windows that open onto spectacular views of the Presidential Range. Subtle renovations have brought the place, built in 1902, into the 21st century. Seasonal classics with a twist use ingredients sourced from local New Hampshire farms and suppliers. On the constantly changing menu you may find wild salmon wrapped in buttery pastry served over lobster succotash or a rosemary-scented rack of lamb with candied beets. ■**TIP→** **Appropriate evening wear is expected, meaning no shorts or sneakers.** ⓢ *Average main: $36* ⊠ *Omni Mount Washington Hotel, 310 Mt. Washington Rd.* ☎ *603/278–1000* ⊕ *www.mountwashingtonresort. com* ⊗ *No lunch* ⚍ *Reservations essential* ⌂ *Jacket required.*

WHERE TO STAY

$
HOTEL
☷**The Lodge.** Rooms at this inexpensive roadside motel have private balconies that overlook the Presidential Range. **Pros:** inexpensive; access to many amenities; free ski shuttle. **Cons:** across street from resort amenities; Continental breakfast only. ⓢ *Rooms from: $159* ⊠ *99 Ski Area Rd.* ☎ *603/278–1000, 800/680–6600* ⊕ *www.brettonwoods.com* ⇖ *50 rooms* ⏐⊙⏐ *Breakfast.*

$$
B&B/INN
Fodor's Choice
★
☷**The Notchland Inn.** Built in 1862 by Sam Bemis, America's grandfather of landscape photography, the house conveys mountain charm on a scale unmatched in New England. **Pros:** middle-of-the-forest setting; marvelous house and common rooms; good dinners. **Cons:** may seem too isolated for some. ⓢ *Rooms from: $295* ⊠ *2 Morey Rd., Hart's Location* ☎ *603/374–6131* ⊕ *www.notchland.com* ⇖ *8 rooms, 5 suites, 2 cottages* ⏐⊙⏐ *Breakfast.*

$$$ RESORT FAMILY Fodor's Choice ★ **Omni Mount Washington Hotel.** The two most memorable sights in the White Mountains would have to be Mt. Washington and the Omni Mount Washington Hotel. **Pros:** beautiful resort; loads of activities; free shuttle to skiing and activities. **Cons:** kids love to run around the hotel. [$] *Rooms from: $395* ✉ *310 Mt. Washington Hotel Rd., off U.S. 302* ☎ *603/278–1000* 🌐 *www.mountwashingtonresort.com* 🛏 *175 rooms, 25 suites* 🍴 *Some meals.*

SPORTS AND THE OUTDOORS

SKI AREA

FAMILY Fodor's Choice ★ **Bretton Woods.** New Hampshire's largest ski area is also one of the country's best family ski resorts. The views of Mt. Washington alone are worth the visit, and the scenery is especially beautiful from the Latitude 44 restaurant, open during ski season.

The resort has something for everyone. Steeper pitches, near the top of the 1,500-foot vertical, and glades will keep experts busy, and snowboarders will enjoy the three terrain parks. The Nordic trail system has 62 miles of cross-country ski trails. Both night skiing and snowboarding are available on weekends and holidays. Bretton Woods is also a great place to learn to ski. Trails appeal mostly to novice and intermediate skiers, including two magic carpet lifts for beginners. The Hobbit Ski and Snowplay program, for ages 3–5, is an introduction to skiing, and the Hobbit Ski and Snowboard School, for ages 4–12, has full- and half-day lessons. The complimentary Kinderwoods Winter Playground has a sled carousel, igloos, and a zip line. A snowmobile park at the base area is fun for kids ages 4–13. Parents can purchase interchangeable family tickets that allow them to take turns skiing while the other watches the kids—both passes come for the price of one. The ski area also offers an adaptive program for anyone with disabilities.

One recent addition is the year-round Canopy Tour ($110), which has nine zip lines, two sky bridges, and three rappelling stations. Small groups are led by experienced guides. The tour is an exhilarating introduction to flora and fauna of the White Mountains. **Facilities:** 62 trails; 464 acres, 1,500-foot vertical drop; 10 lifts. ✉ *99 Ski Area Rd.* ☎ *603/278–3320, 603/278–1000 for weather conditions* 🌐 *www.brettonwoods.com* 🎫 *Lift ticket $89.*

EN ROUTE **Crawford Notch State Park.** Scenic U.S. 302 winds southeast of Bretton Woods through the steep, wooded mountains on either side of spectacular Crawford Notch, passing through Crawford Notch State Park, where you can picnic and take a short hike to Arethusa Falls, the longest drop in New England, or to the Silver and Flume cascades. The 5,775-acre park has a number of roadside photo opportunities. Its visitor center has a gift shop, a snack bar, and a picnic area. ✉ *1464 U.S. 302, Hart's Location* ☎ *603/374–2272* 🌐 *www.nhstateparks.org* 🕘 *Visitor center late May.–late Oct., daily 9:30–5.*

BARTLETT

18 miles southeast of Bretton Woods.

With Bear Mountain to its south, Mt. Parker to its north, Mt. Cardigan to its west, and the Saco River to its east, Bartlett, incorporated in 1790, has an unforgettable setting. Lovely Bear Notch Road (closed in winter) has the only midpoint access to the Kancamagus Highway. There isn't much town to speak of: the dining options listed are actually in Glen. It's best known for the Attitash Ski Resort, within walking distance.

GETTING HERE AND AROUND

U.S. 302 passes though Bartlett, southeast from Bretton Woods and west from Glen. Attitash Ski Resort is south of U.S. 302 in Bartlett, signed in town as Crawford Notch Road.

WHERE TO EAT

$$ SOUTHWESTERN FAMILY 🍴 **Margarita Grill.** Après-ski types like to congregate on the Margarita Grill's enclosed heated patio and unwind with a margarita. Tex-Mex and Southwestern specialties served here include homemade salsas, wood-fired steaks, ribs, chicken, and burgers. All ingredients are local and fresh, this being a New Hampshire farm-to-table-certified restaurant. [$] *Average main: $22* ✉ *78 U.S. 302, Glen* ☎ *603/383–6556* 🌐 *www.margaritagrillnh.com* 🕒 *No lunch weekdays.*

$$ AMERICAN FAMILY 🍴 **Red Parka Steakhouse & Pub.** This downtown pub has been an institution for nearly 40 years. Highlights of the family-oriented menu include hand-cut steaks and barbecue ribs, and there's a locally sourced all-you-can-eat salad bar. The barbecue sauce is made on-site, and beer is served in mason jars. Plan to spend some time reading the dozens and dozens of license plates that adorn the walls of the downstairs pub. Open-mike night takes place on Monday, live entertainment on Friday and Saturday. [$] *Average main: $24* ✉ *3 Station St., off U.S. 302, Glen* ☎ *603/383–4344* 🌐 *www.redparkapub.com* 🕒 *No lunch* ✍ *Reservations not accepted.*

WHERE TO STAY

$$ HOTEL FAMILY 🏨 **Attitash Grand Summit Hotel & Conference Center.** If ski-in, ski-out convenience at Attitash is a must, book your stay at the resort's hotel at the base of Bear Peak. **Pros:** great location; outdoor pool and hot tubs; ski-package discounts; kitchenettes in all rooms. **Cons:** generally bland accommodations; facility could use sprucing up. [$] *Rooms from: $259* ✉ *104 Grand Summit Rd.* ☎ *603/374–1900, 888/554–1900* 🌐 *www.attitash.com* 🛏 *143 rooms* 🍽 *No meals.*

$ HOTEL FAMILY 🏨 **Attitash Mountain Village Resort.** Hidden in a cluster of pine trees across from the ski area is a resort with guest rooms—a few of them actually slope-side—that crest the top of this mountain. **Pros:** simple family place; fitness room; nice pools. **Cons:** more functional than posh. [$] *Rooms from: $159* ✉ *784 U.S. 302* ☎ *603/374–6501, 800/862–1600* 🌐 *www.attitashmtvillage.com/lodging* 🛏 *350 units* 🍽 *No meals.*

SPORTS AND THE OUTDOORS

SKI AREA

FAMILY **Attitash Ski Resort.** With a vertical drop of 1,750 feet, Attitash Mountain has dozens of trails to explore, and there are more on the adjacent Attitash Bear Peak (vertical drop 1,450 feet). You'll find traditional New England ski runs and challenging terrain alongside wide-open cruisers that suit all skill levels. There are acres of glades, plus a progressive freestyle terrain park. The Attitash Adventure Center has a rental shop, and also offers lessons and children's programs. **Facilities:** 68 trails; 311 acres; 1,750-foot vertical drop; 11 lifts. ⊠ *775 U.S. 302* ☎ *800/223–7669* ⊕ *www.attitash.com* ⊠ *Lift ticket $75 weekdays, $79 weekends.*

JACKSON

7 miles northeast of Bartlett.

Fodor'sChoice Just off Route 16 via a red covered bridge, Jackson has retained its
★ storybook New England character. Art and antiques shopping, tennis, golf, fishing, and hiking to waterfalls are among the draws. When the snow falls, Jackson becomes the state's cross-country skiing capital, and there are also four downhill ski areas nearby—hotels and inns provide ski shuttles. Visit Jackson Falls for a wonderful photo opportunity.

ESSENTIALS

Visitor Information Jackson Area Chamber of Commerce. ☎ *603/383–9356* ⊕ *www.jacksonnh.com.*

EXPLORING

FAMILY **Story Land.** This theme park with life-size storybook and nursery-rhyme characters is geared to kids (ages 2–12). The 23 rides include a flumer, a river raft, and the Roar-O-Saurus and Polar Coaster roller coasters. Play areas and magic shows provide additional entertainment. ⊠ *850 Rte. 16, Glen* ☎ *603/383–4186* ⊕ *www.storylandnh.com* ⊠ *$33* ☉ *July–late Aug., daily 9:30–6; last 2 wks of June and late Aug.–early Sept., daily 9:30–5; late May–mid-June and early Sept.–mid-Oct., weekends and some Fri. 9:30–5.*

WHERE TO EAT

$$ ✕ **Red Fox Bar & Grille.** Some say this big family restaurant overlooking
AMERICAN the Wentworth Golf Club gets its name from a wily fox with a pen-
FAMILY chant for stealing golf balls off the nearby fairway. Burgers, barbecue ribs, and wood-fired pizzas are on the dinner menu, along with more refined dishes such as seared sea scallops and bourbon steak tips. Lunch is served on Saturday, and there's a popular Sunday breakfast buffet. Younger kids will enjoy the playroom, especially if there's a wait for a table. $ *Average main: $20* ⊠ *49 Rte. 16* ☎ *603/383–4949* ⊕ *www.redfoxbarandgrille.com* ☉ *No lunch weekdays.*

$$ ✕ **Thorn Hill.** This famous inn serves up memorable meals in a roman-
AMERICAN tic atmosphere, with dim lighting and piano music trickling in from
Fodor'sChoice the lounge. Many people enjoy dining on the heated porch, which
★ has views of the Presidential Range. The flavorful dishes include pan-seared trout, Peking duck on a scallion pancake with sesame bok choy, and New York sirloin in a blue cheese demi-glace. $ *Average*

9

main: $26 ✉ *42 Thorn Hill Rd.* ☎ *603/383–4242, 800/289–8990* 🌐 *www.innatthornhill.com* 🕘 *No lunch.*

WHERE TO STAY

$ B&B/INN FAMILY 🏨 **Christmas Farm Inn and Spa.** Despite its wintery name, this 1778 inn is an all-season retreat. **Pros:** kids are welcome; indoor and outdoor pools; very close to ski area; room rate includes a full breakfast. **Cons:** can get busy with kids. [$] *Rooms from: $169* ✉ *3 Blitzen Way, off Rte. 16B* ☎ *603/383–4313, 800/443–5837* 🌐 *www.christmasfarminn.com* 🛏 *18 rooms, 16 suites, 7 cottages* 🍴 *Breakfast.*

$ B&B/INN Fodor's Choice ★ 🏨 **Inn at Jackson.** This bright bed-and-breakfast is impeccably maintained and charmingly furnished. **Pros:** exceptional rooms; peaceful setting; wonderful breakfasts. **Cons:** top-floor rooms lack fireplaces. [$] *Rooms from: $189* ✉ *Thorn Hill Rd. and Main St.* ☎ *603/383–4321, 800/289–8600* 🌐 *www.innatjackson.com* 🛏 *14 rooms* 🍴 *Breakfast.*

$$ B&B/INN Fodor's Choice ★ 🏨 **The Inn at Thorn Hill & Spa.** With a large reception room and sweeping staircase, this inn—after an 1891 Victorian designed by Stanford White—is breathtaking throughout. **Pros:** romantic setting; soothing spa; full breakfast included; relaxed elegance. **Cons:** Wi-Fi works on main floor, but not in the rooms. [$] *Rooms from: $219* ✉ *42 Thorn Hill Rd.* ☎ *800/289–8990, 800/289–8990* 🌐 *www.innatthornhill.com* 🛏 *17 rooms, 5 suites, 3 cottages* 🍴 *Some meals.*

SPORTS AND THE OUTDOORS

SKI AREAS

FAMILY **Black Mountain.** Friendly, informal Black Mountain has a warming southern exposure. The Family Passport allows two adults and two kids to ski at highly discounted rates both during the week ($129) and on weekends ($159)—a great deal, even with regular rates considered among the lowest in the Mt. Washington Valley. The trails and glades on the 3,303-foot mountain (highest skiable elevation 2,350 feet) are evenly divided among beginner, intermediate, and expert ability levels. There's a nursery for kids over six months old. Enjoy guided horseback riding from spring through fall. **Facilities:** 45 trails; 143 acres; 1,100-foot vertical drop; 4 lifts. ✉ *373 Black Mountain Rd.* ☎ *603/383–4490, 800/475–4669 for snow conditions* 🌐 *www.blackmt.com* 🎟 *Lift ticket $40 weekdays, $55 weekends and holidays.*

FAMILY Fodor's Choice ★ **Jackson Ski Touring Foundation.** Experts rate this the best-run cross-country ski operation in the country. That's due to the great advice you get from the attentive staff, and to the 60 miles of groomed trails for skiing, skate skiing, and snowshoeing. The varied terrain offers something for all abilities. Jackson Ski Touring's 80 trails wind through covered bridges and into the picturesque village of Jackson, where you can warm up in cozy trailside restaurants. Lessons and rentals are available. ✉ *153 Main St.* ☎ *603/383–9355* 🌐 *www.jacksonxc.org.*

MT. WASHINGTON

20 miles northwest of Jackson.

At 6,288 feet, Mt. Washington is the highest peak in the northeastern United States. The world's highest winds, 231 mph, were recorded here in 1934. You can take a guided bus tour, a drive, or a hike to the summit. A number of trails circle the mountain and the other peaks in the Presidential Range, but all of them are strenuous. It gets cold up here: even in the summer, you'll want a jacket.

GETTING HERE AND AROUND

Mt. Washington Road heads west from Route 16 about 2 miles north of Wildcat Mountain ski resort and 8 miles south of Gorham.

EXPLORING

FAMILY

Fodor's Choice

★

Mt. Washington Auto Road. The drive to the top of the imposing Mt. Washington is among the most memorable White Mountains experiences. Your route: the narrow, curving Mt. Washington Auto Road, which climbs 4,600 feet in a little more than 7 miles. Upon admission to this private road, drivers receive a CD with a narrated tour, along with a bumper sticker that reads, "This car climbed Mt. Washington." The narration is fascinating, and the views are breathtaking. Once at the top, check out **Extreme Mount Washington,** an interactive museum dedicated to science and weather. ✉ *1 Mt. Washington Auto Rd., at Rte. 16, Pinkham Notch* ☎ *603/356–2137* ⊕ *www.mountwashington. org* 🚗 *Car and driver $28, plus $8 per additional adult; museum $5 (free with auto tour)* ⊙ *Mid-May–late Oct., daily 9–4.*

SPORTS AND THE OUTDOORS

All trails to Mt. Washington's peak are rough and take considerable time. Perhaps the most famous is the **Tuckerman Ravine Trail,** the path used by extreme skiers who risk life and limb to fly down the face of the steep ravine. The hike to the top can easily take five–nine hours round-trip. Because the weather here is so erratic, it's critical to check weather conditions, to be prepared, and to keep in mind that Mt. Washington's summit is much colder than its base. The average year-round temperature is below freezing, and the average wind velocity is 35 mph.

FAMILY

Great Glen Trails Outdoor Center. This outdoor center at the foot of Mt. Washington is the base for year-around outdoor activities. Renowned for its dramatic 25-mile cross-country trail system, Great Glen provides access to more than 1,100 acres of backcountry. Trees shelter most of the trails, so Mt. Washington's infamous weather isn't such a concern. You can travel to the mountain's upper reaches in a Mt. Washington SnowCoach, a nine-passenger van refitted with triangular snowmobile-like treads. You have the option of skiing or snowshoeing down or just enjoying the magnificent winter view. The center has a huge ski and sports shop, a food court, a climbing wall, and an observation deck. In summer it's the base for hiking and biking and has programs in canoeing, kayaking, and fly-fishing. ✉ *1 Mt. Washington Auto Rd., at Rte. 16, Pinkham Notch* ☎ *603/466–2333* ⊕ *www.greatglentrails.com* 🚗 *Trail pass $20, SnowCoach $49.*

Pinkham Notch. Although not a town per se, scenic Pinkham Notch covers Mt. Washington's eastern side and has several ravines, including the famous Tuckerman Ravine. The Appalachian Mountain Club operates a visitor center that provides year-around trail information to hikers. Guided hikes leave from the center, and you can take outdoor skills workshops there. On-site are an outdoors shop and a

9

The highest peak in New England, Mt. Washington rewards those who drive or hike to the top with spectacular views.

cafeteria. ⊠ *Visitor center, 361 Rte. 16, Pinkham Notch* ☎ *603/466–2721* ⊕ *www.pinkhamnotchnh.com* ☉ *Daily 6:30 am–9 pm.*

FAMILY **Wildcat Mountain.** Glade skiers will love Wildcat and its 28 acres of designated tree skiing. Runs include some stunning double–black diamond trails; experts can really zip down the Lynx. Skiers who can hold a wedge should check out the 2½-mile-long Polecat, which offers excellent views of the Presidential Range. The trails are classic New England—narrow and winding—and the views are stunning. Beginners will find gentle terrain and a broad teaching slope. For an adrenaline rush, there's a terrain park. In summer you can dart to the top on the four-passenger gondola, hike the many well-kept trails, and fish in the crystal clear streams. **Facilities:** 48 trails; 225 acres; 2,112-foot vertical drop; 5 lifts. ⊠ *Rte. 16, Pinkham Notch* ☎ *603/466–3326, 888/754–9453 for snow conditions* ⊕ *www.skiwildcat.com* ✉ *Lift ticket $75 weekdays, $79 weekends.*

DIXVILLE NOTCH

63 miles north of Mt. Washington, 66 miles northeast of Littleton, 149 miles north of Concord.

Just 12 miles from the Canadian border, this tiny community is known for the fact that it and another New Hampshire community, Hart's Location, are the first election districts in the nation to vote in presidential general elections.

GETTING HERE AND AROUND

Dixville Notch is along Route 26, 12 miles west of Route 16 and 11 miles east of U.S. 3.

EXPLORING

FAMILY **Poore Farm Historic Homestead.** Maybe you've visited farm museums before, but certainly not one like this. Established in 1825, this farm has survived almost perfectly intact because the Poore family never installed electricity or other modern conveniences. They lived here for a century and a half, and apparently saved everything. The house, barn, outbuildings, and gardens provide a rare opportunity to see how rural New Englanders actually lived, dressed, ate, farmed, and socialized. It's the perfect backdrop for farming demonstrations, music festivals, and discussions about farm life. ✉ *629 Hollow Rd., 7 miles north of Colebrook, Stewartstown* ⊕ *www.poorefarm.org* ✉ *$10* ⊙ *June–Sept., Fri.–Sun. 11–3.*

OFF THE BEATEN PATH **Pittsburg.** In the Great North Woods, Pittsburg contains the springs that form the Connecticut River. The state's northern tip—a chunk of about 250 square miles—lies within the town's borders. Remote though it is, this frontier town teems with hunters, boaters, fishermen, hikers, and photographers from early summer through winter. Moose sightings are common, especially in the colder months. The town has more than a dozen lodges and several informal eateries. It's about a 90-minute drive from Littleton and 40 minutes from Dixville Notch. ✉ *U.S. 3 and Rte. 145* ✛ *From Dixville Notch take Rte. 26 west 11 miles and Rte. 145 north 13 miles.*

WHERE TO EAT AND STAY

$
FRENCH
Fodor'sChoice
★
✕ **Le Rendez Vous.** You might not expect to find an authentic French pastry shop in the workaday village of Colebrook, 11 miles west of Dixville Notch, but Le Rendez Vous serves fabulous tarts and treats—understandably, with Parisian owners. Drop in to this quaint café, furnished with several tables and armchairs, for hand-dipped Belgian chocolates, buttery croissants, freshly baked breads, and gourmet food items. Ⓢ *Average main: $5* ✉ *121 Main St., Colebrook* ☎ *603/237–5150* ⊕ *www.lerendezvousbakerynh.com* ⊙ *Closed Sun. and Mon.*

$$
AMERICAN
FAMILY
✕ **Rainbow Grille.** Everyone loves the Rainbow Grille for one reason or another: the moose antlers hanging on the pine paneling, the sunset views over Black Lake, or the lumberjack-size meals. The restaurant is known for its trout and salmon dishes and mesquite-grilled prime rib. The perfect finish to any meal is a slice of bread pudding. Plan ahead to visit this out-of-the-way place worth checking out; some patrons reserve months in advance. Ⓢ *Average main: $24* ✉ *Tall Timbers Lodge, 609 Beach Rd., Pittsburg* ☎ *603/538–9556, 800/563–5633* ⊕ *www.rainbowgrille.com* ⊙ *Closed 1st 2 wks in Dec.* ⚲ *Reservations essential.*

$
HOTEL
FAMILY
▦ **Cabins at Lopstick.** In business since 1929, the Cabins at Lopstick have long appealed to outdoors enthusiasts. **Pros:** great views of First Connecticut Lake; full kitchens; good summer and winter sports. **Cons:** no on-site restaurants; some older cabins are more rustic than homey. Ⓢ *Rooms from: $115* ✉ *45 Stewart Young Rd., Pittsburg* ☎ *800/538–6659* ⊕ *www.cabinsatlopstick.com* ⤳ *53 cabins* ❘⊙❘ *No meals.*

9

SPORTS AND THE OUTDOORS

Dixville Notch State Park. In the northernmost notch of the White Mountains, the park has a waterfall, two mountain brooks, hiking trails, picnic areas, and restrooms. ✉ *1212 W. Rte. 26* ☎ *603/538–6707* ⊕ *www.nhstateparks.org.*

NORTH CONWAY

76 miles south of Dixville Notch; 7 miles south of Glen; 41 miles east of Lincoln/North Woodstock.

Before the arrival of outlet stores, this town drew visitors for its inspiring scenery, ski resorts, and access to White Mountain National Forest. Today, however, the feeling of natural splendor is gone. Shopping is the big sport, and businesses line Route 16 for several miles. You'll get a close look at them as traffic slows to a crawl here. Take the scenic West Side Road from Conway to Intervale to circumvent the traffic and take in splendid views.

GETTING HERE AND AROUND

Park near the fire station on Main Street and spend half a day visiting the unique shops and restaurants in this part of town. Taxis can get you around between Conway, North Conway, and Jackson.

ESSENTIALS

Visitor Information North Country Chamber of Commerce. ☎ *603/237–8939* ⊕ *www.northcountrychamber.org.*

EXPLORING

FAMILY **Conway Scenic Railroad.** Departing from historic North Conway Station, the railroad operates various trips aboard vintage trains. The Notch Train to Crawford Depot (5 hours round-trip) or to Fabyan Station (5½ hours) travels through rugged territory yielding wonderful views. The First Class package includes a three-course lunch in the dining car. The Valley Train overlooks Mt. Washington during a 55-minute round-trip journey to Conway or a 1¾-hour excursion to Bartlett. The 1874 station displays lanterns, old tickets and timetables, and other artifacts. Reserve your spot early during foliage season. ✉ *38 Norcross Cir.* ☎ *603/356–5251, 800/232–5251* ⊕ *www.conwayscenic.com* ✍ *$16.50–$115* ⊙ *Early Apr.–Dec; departure times vary.*

FAMILY **Hartmann Model Railroad Museum.** All aboard! You can ride a miniature outdoor train at this museum, which also has 10 operating train layouts in scales from G to Z. A hobby shop and a snack bar are also on the premises. ✉ *15 Town Hall Rd., at Rte. 16, Intervale* ☎ *603/356–9922* ⊕ *www.hartmannrr.com* ✍ *$6* ⊙ *July and Aug., daily 10–5; Sept.–June, Fri.–Mon. 10–5.*

FAMILY **Weather Discovery Center.** Ever wonder what it's like to be in a cabin at the summit of Mt. Washington while 200 mph winds shake the rafters? Find out at this fun, interactive museum, where you can experience simulations of different weather conditions and learn about how weather affects our lives. There's a twice-daily video link with scientists hard at work at Mount Washington Observatory. ✉ *2779 Main St.* ☎ *603/356–2137* ⊕ *www.mountwashington.org* ✍ *$2* ⊙ *Daily 10–5.*

WHERE TO EAT

$$
AMERICAN
FAMILY

✕ **Delaney's Hole in the Wall.** This casual tavern has a real fondness for ski history, displaying early photos of local ski areas, old signs and placards, and odd bits of lift equipment. Entrées range from fajitas that come sizzling out of the kitchen to mussels and scallops sautéed with spiced sausage and Louisiana seasonings. There's an entirely separate menu devoted to sushi. $ *Average main: $20* ✉ *2966 White Mountain Hwy., ¼ mile north of North Conway Village* ☎ *603/356–7776* ⊕ *www. delaneys.com.*

$
AMERICAN
FAMILY

✕ **Muddy Moose Restaurant & Pub.** This family restaurant buzzes with the sound of happy kids. The mac 'n' cheese, blueberry-glazed ribs, and hearty burgers are all hits with the young ones, though grown-ups may prefer the pasta and seafood dishes. One unique carrot side has a pleasantly surprising hint of maple syrup. The Muddy Moose Pie, made of ice cream, fudge, and crumbled Oreos, can feed a family of four. $ *Average main: $17* ✉ *2344 White Mountain Hwy.* ☎ *603/356–7696* ⊕ *www.muddymoose.com* ⌦ *Reservations not accepted.*

WHERE TO STAY

$
B&B/INN

🏨 **The Buttonwood Inn.** A tranquil oasis in a busy resort area, the Buttonwood sits on Mt. Surprise, 2 miles northeast of North Conway Village. **Pros:** good bedding and amenities; tranquil setting; 6 acres of grounds. **Cons:** unexciting for those not wanting a remote getaway. $ *Rooms from: $169* ✉ *64 Mt. Surprise Rd.* ☎ *603/356–2625, 800/258–2625* ⊕ *www.buttonwoodinn.com* ⌦ *10 rooms* ❶❶ *Breakfast.*

$
B&B/INN

🏨 **Darby Field Inn.** Most rooms in this unpretentious 1826 farmhouse at the entrance to White Mountain National Park have stunning views, and several also have fireplaces. **Pros:** romantic setting; away-from-it-all feel. **Cons:** better for couples than families. $ *Rooms from: $165* ✉ *185 Chase Hill, Albany* ☎ *603/447–2181, 800/426–4147* ⊕ *www. darbyfield.com* ⌦ *13 rooms* ❶❶ *Breakfast.*

$
B&B/INN

🏨 **Snowville Inn.** The finest room in the Snowville's main gambrel-roof house (built in 1916) has 12 windows that look out over the Presidential Range, and many guest rooms have fireplaces. **Pros:** spectacular views; fine dining; full breakfast. **Cons:** off the beaten path. $ *Rooms from: $179* ✉ *136 Stewart Rd., 6 miles southeast of Conway, Eaton Center* ☎ *603/447–2818* ⊕ *www.snowvillageinn.com* ⌦ *16 rooms, 1 suite* ❶❶ *Breakfast.*

$
RESORT
FAMILY

🏨 **White Mountain Hotel and Resort.** Rooms in this hotel at the base of Whitehorse Ledge have splendid mountain views, and the proximity to White Mountain National Forest and Echo Lake State Park makes you feel farther away from the outlet malls than you actually are. **Pros:** scenic setting close to shopping; free fitness center and spa. **Cons:** two-night minimum on summer weekends. $ *Rooms from: $189* ✉ *2560 West Side Rd.* ☎ *800/533–6301, 603/356–7100* ⊕ *www.whitemountainhotel. com* ⌦ *69 rooms, 11 suites* ❶❶ *Some meals.*

9

Sit back and enjoy the view on the Conway Scenic Railroad.

SPORTS AND THE OUTDOORS

CANOEING AND KAYAKING

FAMILY **Outdoors Saco Bound.** This outfitter rents stand-up paddleboards, canoes, and kayaks and will even provide transportation for you and your inner tubes for gentle floats down the Saco River. ⊠ *2561 E. Main St., Center Conway* ☎ *888/447–2177* ⊕ *www.sacobound.com.*

FISHING

North Country Angler. One of the best tackle shops in the state, North Country offers casting clinics and guided fly-fishing trips throughout the region. ⊠ *2888 White Mountain Hwy.* ☎ *603/356–6000* ⊕ *www. northcountryangler.com.*

PARK

FAMILY **Echo Lake State Park.** You don't have to be a rock climber to enjoy the views from the 700-foot White Horse and Cathedral ledges. From the top, you'll see the entire valley, including Echo Lake, which offers fishing, swimming, boating, and, on quiet days, an excellent opportunity to shout for echoes. ⊠ *68 Echo Lake Rd., off U.S 302, Conway* ☎ *603/356–2672* ⊕ *www.nhstateparks.org* ⊠ *$4* ⊙ *Memorial Day–mid-Oct., daily 9–sunset.*

SKI AREAS

FAMILY **Cranmore Mountain Adventure Park.** This fun-to-ski area has been a favorite with families since it opened in 1938. Most runs are naturally formed intermediates that weave in and out of glades. Beginners have several slopes and routes from the summit; experts must be content with a few short, steep pitches. Snowboarders can explore five different terrain parks. Snow tubing, a mountain coaster, a giant swing, and a zip line provide additional entertainment. Twilight skiing is offered on Saturday and holidays. **Facilities:** 56 trails; 170 acres; 1,200-foot vertical drop; 9 lifts. ✉ *1 Skimobile Rd.* ☎ ⊕ *www.cranmore.com* ✆ *Lift ticket $70.*

FAMILY **King Pine Ski Area at Purity Spring Resort.** About 9 miles south of Conway, this family-run ski area has been going strong since 1962. King Pine's gentle trails are ideal for beginner and intermediate skiers; experts won't be challenged except for a brief section of the Pitch Pine trail. There are 9 miles of cross-country ski trails. Indoors, you can enjoy a pool and fitness complex and go ice-skating. In summer the resort has every outdoor activity imaginable, including archery, waterskiing, kayaking, loon-watching, tennis, hiking, mountain biking, and fishing. **Facilities:** 17 trails; 48 acres; 350-foot vertical drop; 6 lifts. ✉ *1251 Eaton Rd. (Rte. 153), East Madison* ☎ *603/367–8896* ⊕ *www.kingpine.com* ✆ *Lift ticket $52.*

Mt. Washington Valley Ski Touring and Snowshoe Foundation. Nearly 30 miles of groomed cross-country trails weave through the North Conway countryside, maintained by this foundation. Membership to the Mt. Washington Valley Ski Touring Club is required; it can be purchased by the day or year. Equipment rentals are available. ✉ *279 Rte. 16/U.S. 302, Intervale* ☎ *603/356–9920* ⊕ *www.mwvskitouring.org* ✆ *$10 half day, $15 full day.*

SHOPPING

ANTIQUES

Richard M. Plusch Antiques. This shop deals in period furniture and accessories, including glass, sterling silver, Oriental porcelains, rugs, and paintings. ✉ *2584 White Mountain Hwy.* ☎ *603/356–3333* ⊕ *www. conwayantiquesandappraisals.com.*

CLOTHING

Joe Jones' Sun & Ski Sports. You'll find outdoor clothing and gear here, as well as that bathing suit you forgot to pack for the hot tub. Joe Jones' also rents gear and clothing. ✉ *2709 White Mountain Hwy.* ☎ *603/356–9411* ⊕ *www.joejonessports.com.*

CRAFTS

Handcrafters Barn. This place stocks the work of 150 area artists and artisans. ✉ *2473 White Mountain Hwy.* ☎ *603/356–8996* ⊕ *www. handcraftersbarn.com.*

FAMILY **Zeb's General Store.** This old-fashioned country store sells specialty foods, crafts, and clothing, as well as a range of products made in New England. ✉ *2675 Main St.* ☎ *800/676–9294* ⊕ *www.zebs.com.*

EN ROUTE One great place to settle into the White Mountains, take in one of the greatest panoramic views of the mountains, and get visitor info is at the **Intervale Scenic Vista.** The stop, off Route 16 a few miles north of North Conway, has a helpful volunteer staff, features a wonderful large topographical map, and has terrific bathrooms.

9

KANCAMAGUS HIGHWAY

36 miles between Conway and Lincoln/North Woodstock.

In 1937, two old town roads were connected to create this remarkable 35-mile stretch of roadway, winding through some of the state's most unspoiled mountain scenery. Kancamagus (pronounced kank-ah-MAH-gus) was one of the first roads in the nation to be designated a National Scenic Byway. No gas stations, hotels, gift shops, or billboards mar the vistas. You'll see one great view after another: the White Mountains, the Swift River, Sabbaday Falls, Lower Falls, and Rocky Gorge. The highest point is just under 3,000 feet, on the flank of Mt. Kancamagus, near Lincoln.

EXPLORING

Fodor's Choice **Kancamagus Highway.** Interstate 93 is the fastest way to the White Mountains, but it's hardly the most appealing. The section of Route 112 known as the Kancamagus Highway passes through some of the state's most unspoiled mountain scenery—it was one of the first roads in the nation to be designated a National Scenic Byway. The Kanc, as it's called by locals, is punctuated by overlooks and picnic areas, and erupts into fiery color each fall, when photo-snapping drivers really slow things down. In bad weather, check with the White Mountains Visitors Bureau for road conditions. ⊕ *www.kancamagushighway.com.*

SPORTS AND THE OUTDOORS

FAMILY **Lincoln Woods Trail.** This hiking trail off the Kancamagus Highway greatly rewards relatively little effort. Find the trailhead in the large parking lot of the Lincoln Woods Visitor Center, 5 miles east of Lincoln. On-site or online you can purchase a parking pass ($5 per week) for White Mountain National Forest lots and overlooks. (Stopping briefly to take photos or to use the restrooms at the visitor center is permitted without a pass.) The trail crosses a suspension bridge over the Pemigewasset River and follows an old railroad bed for 3 miles along the river. ⊠ *Trailhead on Kancamagus Hwy., 5 miles east of I–93, Exit 32* ☎ *603/530–5190* ⊕ *www.fs.usda.gov/whitemountain.*

FAMILY **Sabbaday Falls.** The parking and picnic area for Sabbaday Falls, about 15 miles west of Conway, is the trailhead for an easy ½-mile route to this multilevel cascade that plunges through two potholes and a flume. Swimming is not allowed. There are restrooms on-site. ⊠ *Trailhead on Kancamagus Hwy., 20 miles east of Lincoln, 16 miles west of Conway* ⊕ *www.kancamagushighway.com.*

LAKE SUNAPEE

In the west-central part of the state, the towns around prestigious Dartmouth College and rippling Lake Sunapee vary from sleepy, old-fashioned outposts that haven't changed much in decades to bustling, sophisticated towns filled with cafés, art galleries, and boutiques. Among the latter, Hanover and New London are the area's main hubs, both of them increasingly popular vacation destinations. Although distinctly removed from the Lakes Region, greater Lake Sunapee quite

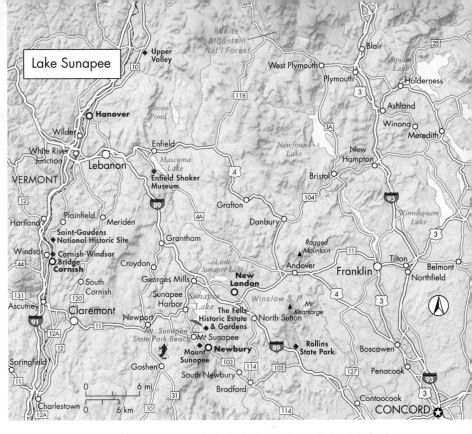

resembles a miniature Lake Winnipesaukee, albeit with far less commercial development. This part of the state, along with the even quieter Monadnock area to the south, has long been an informal artists' colony where people come to write, paint, and weave in solitude.

For a great drive, follow the Lake Sunapee Scenic and Cultural Byway, which runs about 25 miles from Georges Mills (a bit northwest of New London) down into Warner, tracing much of the Lake Sunapee shoreline.

ESSENTIALS

Visitor Information Lake Sunapee Region Chamber of Commerce.
☎ 603/526-6575, 877/526-6575 ⊕ www.sunapeevacations.com.

NEW LONDON

16 miles northwest of Warner, 25 miles west of Tilton.

New London, the home of Colby-Sawyer College (1837), is a good base for exploring the Lake Sunapee region. A campus of stately Colonial-style buildings abuts the vibrant commercial district, where you'll find several cafés and boutiques.

GETTING HERE AND AROUND

From the south, take Interstate 93's Exit 11 to Crockett Corner and then head north on Route 114. From the north, take Exit 12 and travel south on Route 114. Mount Sunapee Ski Area offers a ski shuttle to and from many area hotels and inns.

WHERE TO EAT AND STAY

$$ AMERICAN 🍴 **Flying Goose Brew Pub & Grille.** Offering a regular menu of 11 handcrafted beers—as well as a few seasonal varieties—made with hops grown on-site, this restaurant, pub, and solar-powered brewery is a hit with beer connoisseurs. Diners go for the juicy ribs, paper-thin onion rings, fresh-cut steaks, and the burger topped with blue cheese and bacon. Enjoy live music on Thursday evening. [$] *Average main: $20* ✉ *40 Andover Rd., at Rtes. 11 and 114* ☎ *603/526–6899* 🌐 *www.flyinggoose.com.*

$ B&B/INN 🏨 **Follansbee Inn.** Built in 1840, this country inn on the shore of Kezar Lake is the kind of place that almost automatically turns strangers into fast friends. **Pros:** relaxed lakefront setting; free use of canoes, kayaks, sailboats, rowboats, and bicycles; nice breakfast. **Cons:** not all rooms have lake views; some Wi-Fi dead zones. [$] *Rooms from: $170* ✉ *2 Keyser St., North Sutton* ☎ *603/927–4221, 800/626–4221* 🌐 *www.follansbeeinn.com* 🛏 *18 rooms* 🍽 *Breakfast.*

$ B&B/INN 🏨 **The Inn at Pleasant Lake.** Across Pleasant Lake from majestic Mt. Kearsarge, this 1790s inn has spacious rooms filled with country antiques. **Pros:** lakefront with a small beach; kayaks and stand-up paddleboards available; room rate includes a full breakfast and afternoon tea. **Cons:** away from town; no mobile phone reception. [$] *Rooms from: $139* ✉ *853 Pleasant St.* ☎ *603/526–6271, 800/626–4907* 🌐 *www.innatpleasantlake.com* 🛏 *10 rooms* 🍽 *Breakfast.*

SPORTS AND THE OUTDOORS

FAMILY **Rollins State Park.** A 3½-mile scenic auto route through Rollins State Park snakes up the southern slope of Mt. Kearsarge, where you can hike a ½-mile trail to the summit. The road often closes in winter due to hazardous conditions. ✉ *1066 Kearsarge Rd., off Rte. 103, Warner* ☎ *603/456–3808* 🌐 *www.nhstateparks.org* 🎟 *$4.*

NEWBURY

8 miles southwest of New London.

Newbury is on the edge of Mt. Sunapee State Park. The sparkling lake and the mountain, which rises to an elevation of nearly 3,000 feet, serve as the region's outdoor recreation centers. The popular League of New Hampshire Craftsmen's Fair, the oldest crafts fair in the nation, is held at the base of Mt. Sunapee each August.

GETTING HERE AND AROUND

From New London, take Route 114 West to Route 103A South, which follows the eastern coast of Lake Sunapee to Newbury.

EXPLORING

The Fells Historic Estate & Gardens. John M. Hay, who served as private secretary to Abraham Lincoln, built the Fells on Lake Sunapee as a summer home in 1890. House tours offer a glimpse of early-20th-century life on a New Hampshire estate. The grounds, a gardener's delight, include a 100-foot-long perennial garden and a rock garden with a brook flowing through it. Miles of hiking trails can also be accessed from the estate. The 40-minute guided house and garden tour costs an additional $6. ✉ *456 Rte. 103A* ☎ *603/763–4789* 🌐 *www.thefells.org* 🎟 *Apr.–Nov., $10 when house open, $8 when house closed; Dec.–Mar., $5 per household* 🕒 *Shop and Main House: late May–late June, weekends and holiday Mon. 10–4; late June–early Sept., Wed.–Sun. 10–4; early Sept.–mid-Oct., weekends and holiday Mon. 10–4. Gardens and trails daily 9–5.*

FAMILY **Sunapee Harbor.** On the west side of Lake Sunapee, this old-fashioned summer resort community has a large marina, a handful of restaurants and shops on the water, a tidy village green with a gazebo, and a small museum. A plaque on Main Street outside the Wild Goose Country Store details some of Lake Sunapee's attributes: it's one of the highest lakes in New Hampshire, for example, and one of the cleanest. Lake Sunapee is home to brook and lake trout, salmon, smallmouth bass, perch, and pickerel. ✉ *Sunapee* 🌐 *www.sunapeevacations.com.*

BEACHES

FAMILY **Mt. Sunapee State Park Beach.** A great family spot, this beach has picnic areas, fishing, and a bathhouse. You can also rent canoes and kayaks, and there's a campground on-site. **Amenities:** lifeguards; parking (fee); showers; toilets. **Best for:** swimming; walking. ✉ *86 Beach Access Rd.* ☎ *603/763–5561* 🌐 *www.nhstateparks.org* 🎟 *$5* 🕒 *Late May–early Sept., daily 9–5.*

WHERE TO EAT AND STAY

$ AMERICAN FAMILY 🍴 **Anchorage at Sunapee Harbor.** Fans of this long, gray restaurant with a sprawling deck overlooking Sunapee Harbor's marina come as much for the great views as for the dependable—and occasionally creative—American chow. It's as likely a place for a burger or a fried seafood platter as for homemade lobster spring rolls. There's live entertainment Friday–Sunday. This is where the founding members of Aerosmith first met back in the early 1970s. [$] *Average main: $18* ✉ *71 Main St., Sunapee Harbor* ☎ *603/763–3334* 🌐 *www.theanchorageatsunapeeharbor.com* 🕒 *Closed Oct.–mid-May.*

$$ RENTAL 🏨 **Sunapee Harbor Cottages.** The six charming cottages here are within a stone's throw of Sunapee Harbor. **Pros:** spacious units; free beach passes. **Cons:** no maid service; little clothes storage. [$] *Rooms from: $225* ✉ *4 Lake Ave., Sunapee Harbor* ☎ *603/763–5052, 888/763–5052* 🌐 *www.sunapeeharborcottages.com* 🛏 *6 cottages* 🍽 *No meals.*

SPORTS AND THE OUTDOORS

BOAT TOURS

Sunapee Cruises. This company operates afternoon and dinner cruises of Lake Sunapee narrated by the captains from June to mid-October. Ninety-minute afternoon cruises on the M/V *Mt. Sunapee* focus on

Lake Sunapee's history and the mountain scenery. A buffet dinner is included on the two-hour sunset cruises aboard the M/V *Kearsarge*. The boats operate daily in summer and on weekends in late spring and early fall. ⊠ *Town Dock, 81 Main St., Sunapee Harbor* ☎ *603/938–6465* ⊕ *www.sunapeecruises.com* ☞ *$20–$40.*

SKI AREA

FAMILY **Mount Sunapee.** This family-friendly resort is one of New England's best-kept secrets. The owners have spent millions upgrading their snow machines and grooming equipment and turning this into a four-seasons resort. Mount Sunapee offers over 1,500 vertical feet of downhill excitement, 11 lifts (including three quads), and 66 trails and slopes for all abilities. There are four terrain parks and nine glade trails. In summer, the adventure park features a canopy zip-line tour, an aerial challenge course, an 18-hole disc-golf course, miniature golf, and numerous hiking trails. **Facilities:** 66 trails; 233 acres; 1,500-foot vertical drop; 11 lifts. ⊠ *1398 Rte. 103* ☎ *603/763–3500* ⊕ *www.mtsunapee.com* ☞ *Lift ticket $72 midweek, $82 weekends and holidays.*

HANOVER

12 miles northwest of Enfield; 62 miles northwest of Concord.

Eleazar Wheelock founded Hanover's Dartmouth College in 1769 to educate the Abenaki "and other youth." When he arrived, the town consisted of about 20 families. Over time the college and the town grew symbiotically, with Dartmouth eventually becoming the northernmost Ivy League school. Hanover is still synonymous with Dartmouth, but it's also a respected medical and cultural center for the upper Connecticut River Valley.

Plan on spending a day visiting Hanover and to see all the sights on the Dartmouth campus. Shops, mostly of the independent variety but with a few upscale chains sprinkled in, line Hanover's main street. The commercial district blends almost imperceptibly with the Dartmouth campus. West Lebanon, south of Hanover on the Vermont border, has many more shops.

GETTING HERE AND AROUND

Lebanon Municipal Airport, near Dartmouth College, is served by Cape Air. By car, Interstate 91 North and Interstate 89 are the best ways to get to Lebanon, Hanover, and the surrounding area.

ESSENTIALS

Airport Lebanon Municipal Airport. ⊠ *5 Airpark Rd., West Lebanon* ☎ *603/298–8878* ⊕ *www.flyleb.com.*

Visitor Information Hanover Area Chamber of Commerce. ⊠ *Nugget Arcade Bldg., 53 S. Main St., Suite 208* ☎ *603/643–3115* ⊕ *www.hanoverchamber.org.*

EXPLORING

Dartmouth College. The poet Robert Frost spent part of a brooding freshman semester at this Ivy League school before giving up college altogether, but the school counts politician Nelson Rockefeller, actor Mindy Kaling, and author Theodor ("Dr.") Seuss Geisel among its many illustrious grads. The buildings clustered around the green include the **Baker Memorial Library,** which houses such literary treasures as 17th-century editions of William Shakespeare's works. The library is also well-known for Mexican artist José Clemente Orozco's 3,000-square-foot murals that depict the story of civilization in the Americas. Free campus tours are available on request. ✉ *N. Main and Wentworth Sts.* ☎ *603/646–1110* ⊕ *www.dartmouth.edu.*

QUICK BITES

Dirt Cowboy Cafe. Take a respite from museum-hopping with a cup of espresso, a ham-and-cheese scone, or a freshly baked brownie at this café across from the green next to a used-book store. ✉ *7 S. Main St.* ☎ *603/643–1323* ⊕ *www.dirtcowboycafe.com.*

FAMILY **Enfield Shaker Museum.** In 1782, two Shaker brothers from Mount Lebanon, New York, arrived on Lake Mascoma's northeastern side, about 12 miles southeast of Hanover. Eventually, they formed Enfield, the ninth of 18 Shaker communities in the United States, and moved it to the lake's southern shore, where they erected more than 200 buildings. The Enfield Shaker Museum preserves the legacy of the Shakers, who numbered 330 members at the village's peak. By 1923, interest in the society had waned, and the last 10 members joined the Canterbury community, south of Laconia. A self-guided walking tour takes you through 13 of the remaining buildings, among them an 1849 stone mill. Demonstrations of Shaker crafts techniques and numerous special events take place year-round. ✉ *447 Rte. 4A, Enfield* ☎ *603/632–4346* ⊕ *www.shakermuseum.org* 🔖 *$12* ☉ *Mon.–Sat. 10–4, Sun. noon–4.*

FAMILY **Hood Museum of Art.** Dartmouth's art museum owns Picasso's *Guitar on a Table,* silver by Paul Revere, a set of Assyrian reliefs from the 9th century BC, along with other noteworthy examples of African, Peruvian, Oceanic, Asian, European, and American art. The range of contemporary works—including pieces by John Sloan, William Glackens, Mark Rothko, Fernand Léger, and Joan Miró—is particularly notable. Rivaling the collection is the museum's architecture: a series of austere, copper-roof, redbrick buildings arranged around a courtyard. ✉ *Dartmouth College, Wheelock St.* ☎ *603/646–2808* ⊕ *hoodmuseum. dartmouth.edu* ☉ *Tues. and Thurs.–Sat. 10–5, Wed. 10–9, Sun. noon–5.*

Hopkins Center for the Arts. If the towering arcade at the entrance to the center appears familiar, it's probably because it resembles the project that architect Wallace K. Harrison completed just after designing it: New York City's Metropolitan Opera House at Lincoln Center. The complex includes a 900-seat theater for concerts and film screenings, a 480-seat theater for plays, and a black-box theater for new plays. This is the home of the Dartmouth Symphony Orchestra. ✉ *Dartmouth College, 2 E. Wheelock St.* ☎ *603/646–2422 for box office* ⊕ *hop.dartmouth.edu.*

OFF THE BEATEN PATH

Upper Valley. From Hanover, you can make the 60-mile drive up Route 10 all the way to Littleton for a highly scenic tour of the upper Connecticut River valley. You'll have views of the river and Vermont's Green Mountains from many points along the way. The road passes through groves of evergreens, over leafy ridges, and through delightful hamlets.

9

DID YOU KNOW?

The Baker Memorial Library was modeled after Independence Hall in Philadelphia. Today it is the heart of the Dartmouth College campus in Hanover.

Grab gourmet picnic provisions at the general store on Lyme's village common and stop at the bluff-top village green in historical Haverhill (28 miles north of Hanover) for a picnic amid the panorama of classic Georgian- and Federal-style mansions and faraway farmsteads. ⊠ *Hanover* ⊕ *www.uppervalleychamber.com.*

WHERE TO EAT

$$ ✕**Canoe Club.** Bedecked with canoes, paddles, and classic Dartmouth paraphernalia, this festive spot presents live jazz and folk music on most nights. The mood may be casual, but the kitchen offers imaginative preparations, including memorable starters like a roasted beet medley with a spiced chocolate sauce and an orange glaze, and steamed mussels in a delectable garlic-and-herb sauce. Among the main courses, the Malay curry shrimp with cucumbers, peanuts, and coconut curry is a favorite. There's also a lighter, late-night menu. $ *Average main: $19* ⊠ *27 S. Main St.* ☎ *603/643–9660* ⊕ *www.canoeclub.us.*

AMERICAN

$ ✕**Lou's Restaurant.** A Hanover tradition since 1948, this diner-cum-café-cum-bakery serves possibly the best breakfast in the valley. The blueberry-cranberry buttermilk pancakes really satisfy, and a plate of *migas* (eggs, cheddar, salsa, and guacamole mixed with tortilla chips) can fill you up for the better part of the day. Or just grab a seat at the old-fashioned soda fountain for an ice-cream sundae. Lou's can accommodate diners on gluten-free diets, too. One of the few spots in town where students and locals really mix, this place is hard to resist. $ *Average main: $9* ⊠ *30 S. Main St.* ☎ *603/643–3321* ⊕ *www.lousrestaurant. net* ⊘ *No dinner.*

AMERICAN
FAMILY

$$ ✕**Lui Lui.** The creatively topped thin-crust pizzas and huge portions of pasta are only part of the draw at this chatter-filled eatery; the other is its dramatic setting inside a former power station on the Mascoma River. Pizza picks include the Zeppo (pepperoni, mozzarella, tomato sauce) and di Carni, with house-made meatballs. Pasta fans should dive into a bowl of linguine with homemade clam sauce. $ *Average main: $18* ⊠ *8 Glen Rd., West Lebanon* ☎ *603/298–7070* ⊕ *www.luilui.com.*

ITALIAN
FAMILY

$$ ✕**Murphy's On the Green.** Students, visiting alums, and locals regularly descend on this wildly popular pub, which has walls lined with shelves of old books. The varied menu features burgers and salads as well as meat loaf, crusted lamb sirloin, and vegetarian dishes like eggplant stuffed with tofu. Check out the extensive beer list. $ *Average main: $20* ⊠ *5 Main St.* ☎ *603/643–7777* ⊕ *www.murphysonthegreen.com.*

ECLECTIC

$ ✕**Sunny Day Diner.** Up in the skiing and hiking haven of Lincoln, this cozy, handsomely restored late-1950s diner is a popular stop for breakfast or coffee and dessert. The banana-bread French toast and cherry pie à la mode are two local favorites. $ *Average main:* ⊠ *90 U.S. 3, off I–93, Lincoln* ☎ *603/745–4833* ⚏ *No credit cards.*

AMERICAN
FAMILY

WHERE TO STAY

$$$ 🛏 **The Hanover Inn.** If you're in town for a Dartmouth event, you'll want to stay on the college's—and the town's—main square, above which this sprawling Georgian-style brick structure rises five white-trimmed stories. **Pros:** center of campus and town; great service; handy fitness center. **Cons:** rates do not include breakfast; pricey. $ *Rooms from:*

HOTEL
FAMILY

9

The Cornish–Windsor Bridge is the second-longest covered bridge in the United States, at 460 feet.

$319 ✉ *The Green, 2 E. Wheelock St.* ☎ *603/643–4300, 800/443–7024* ⊕ *www.hanoverinn.com* ⇆ *93 rooms, 15 suites* ¹⊙¹ *No meals.*

\$\$
 B&B/INN 🏠 **Trumbull House.** The rooms at this white Colonial-style house on 16 acres on Hanover's outskirts have king- and queen-size beds, feather pillows, writing desks, and other comfortable touches, as well as Wi-Fi access. **Pros:** many activities on-site; lovely home; big breakfast. **Cons:** 3 miles east of town. $ *Rooms from: $230* ✉ *40 Etna Rd.* ☎ *603/643–2370, 800/651–5141* ⊕ *www.trumbullhouse.com* ⇆ *4 rooms, 1 suite, 1 cottage* ¹⊙¹ *Breakfast.*

SPORTS AND THE OUTDOORS

FAMILY **Ledyard Canoe Club.** On the banks of the Connecticut River, the Ledyard Canoe Club of Dartmouth rents canoes, kayaks, and stand-up paddleboats by the hour. The club also rents rustic cabins. ✉ *9 Boathouse Rd., below Ledyard Bridge ✛ East side of Connecticut River; parking lot past pillars* ☎ *603/643–6709* ⊕ *www.ledyardcanoeclub.org.*

CORNISH

22 miles south of Hanover.

Today Cornish is best known for its covered bridges and for being the home of the late reclusive author J. D. Salinger, but at the turn of the 20th century the village was known primarily as the home of the country's then-most-popular novelist, Winston Churchill (no relation to the British prime minister). His novel *Richard Carvel* sold more than a million copies. Churchill was such a celebrity that he hosted Theodore Roosevelt during the president's 1902 visit. At that time Cornish was an artistic enclave: painter Maxfield Parrish lived and worked here, and sculptor Augustus Saint-Gaudens set up his studio here, where he created the heroic bronzes for which he is known.

GETTING HERE AND AROUND

About 5 miles west of town on Route 44, the Cornish–Windsor Bridge crosses the Connecticut River between New Hampshire and Vermont. The Blacksmith Shop covered bridge is 2 miles east of Route 12A on Town House Road, and the Dingleton Hill covered bridge is 1 mile east of Route 12A on Root Hill Road. Cornish itself is small enough to see in one morning.

EXPLORING

FAMILY **Cornish-Windsor Bridge.** This 460-foot bridge, 1½ miles south of the Saint-Gaudens National Historic Site, connects New Hampshire to Vermont across the Connecticut River. Erected in 1866, it is the longest covered wooden bridge in the United States. The notice on the bridge reads, "Walk your horses or pay two dollar fine." ⊠ *Bridge St.* ⊕ *www.nh.gov/nhdhr/bridges/p39.html.*

FAMILY **Saint-Gaudens National Historic Site.** Just south of Plainfield, a small road

Fodor's Choice leads to this historic site that celebrates the life and artistry of Augustus

★ Saint-Gaudens, a leading 19th-century sculptor with major works on Boston Common and in Manhattan's Central Park. You can tour his house (with original furnishings), studio, and gallery, as well as 150 acres of grounds and gardens, scattered throughout which are casts of his works. The property has two hiking trails, the longer of which is the Blow-Me-Down Trail. Concerts are held at 2 pm on Sunday in July and August. ⊠ *139 Saint-Gaudens Rd., off Rte. 12A* ☎ *603/675–2175* ⊕ *www.nps.gov/saga* ⊠ *$7* ⊙ *Late May–Oct., daily 9–4:30.*

SPORTS AND THE OUTDOORS

North Star Canoe Rentals. Rent a canoe, a kayak, or an inner tube and enjoy a lazy trip down the Connecticut River, with stops en route for swimming and sunbathing. Afterward, North Star Canoe will bring you back to your car. For a bigger adventure, join one of the half-day, full-day, or overnight trips. ⊠ *1356A Rte. 12A* ☎ *603/542–6929* ⊕ *www.kayak-canoe.com* ⊠ *From $25 for kayak.*

9

THE MONADNOCKS AND MERRIMACK VALLEY

Southwestern and south-central New Hampshire mix village charm with city hustle and bustle across two distinct regions. The Merrimack River Valley has the state's largest and fastest-growing cities: Nashua, Manchester, and Concord. To the west, in the state's sleepy southwestern corner, is the Monadnock region, one of New Hampshire's least developed and most naturally stunning parts. Here you'll find plenty of hiking trails, as well as peaceful hilltop hamlets that appear to have barely changed in the past two centuries. Mt. Monadnock, southern New Hampshire's largest peak, stands guard over the region, which has more than 200 lakes and ponds. Rainbow trout, smallmouth and largemouth bass, and some northern pike swim in Chesterfield's Spofford Lake. Goose Pond, just north of Keene, holds smallmouth bass and white perch.

NASHUA

98 miles south of Lincoln/North Woodstock; 48 miles northwest of Boston; 36 miles south of Concord; 50 miles southeast of Keene.

Once a prosperous manufacturing town that drew thousands of immigrant workers in the late 1800s and early 1900s, Nashua fell into decline following World War II, as many factories shut down or moved in search of cheaper labor. Since the 1970s, however, the metro area has jumped in population, developing into a charming community. In its low-key downtown area, classic redbrick buildings line the Nashua River, a tributary of the Merrimack. Though not as popular with tourists as other communities in the region, Nashua (population 90,000) has some good restaurants and a few major shopping centers.

GETTING HERE AND AROUND

A good place to start exploring Nashua is at Main and High streets, where a number of fine restaurants and shops are located. Downtown Nashua has free Wi-Fi.

ESSENTIALS

Taxi SK Taxi. ✉ *Nashua* ☎ *603/882–5155* 🌐 *www.sktaxi.com.*

EXPLORING

Florence Hyde Speare Memorial Museum. The city's impressive industrial history is retold here, the home of the Nashua Historical Society. In this two-story museum, you'll find artifacts, early furnishings, photos, a vintage printing press, and a research library. Adjacent to the museum is the Federal-style **Abbot-Spalding House,** furnished with 18th- and 19th-century antiques, art, and household items. ✉ *5 Abbott St.* ☎ *603/883–0015* 🌐 *www.nashuahistoricalsociety.org/spearemuseum* 🎟 *Free (donations accepted)* 🕒 *Mar.–late Nov., Tues.–Thurs. 9:30–3:30.*

WHERE TO EAT

$$$ BISTRO FRENCH Fodor's Choice ★

🍴 **MT's Local Kitchen and Wine Bar.** Part hip bistro, part jazzy wine bar, MT's is so popular that foodies from across the state make a beeline for this hot spot. The regularly changing menu highlights local products and might include pork scaloppine with a cognac-soaked raisin sauce or wood-grilled Vermont chicken with marinated mushrooms. The pesto fries are legendary. Wood-fired pizzas are also a specialty—try the one topped with Green Mountain smoked pepperoni and MT's own pickled jalapeños. [$] *Average main: $27* ✉ *212 Main St.* ☎ *603/595–9334* 🌐 *www.mtslocal.com.*

MANCHESTER

18 miles north of Nashua, 53 miles north of Boston.

With 108,000-plus residents, Manchester is New Hampshire's largest city. The town grew up around the Amoskeag Falls on the Merrimack River, which drove small textile mills through the 1700s. By 1828 Boston investors had bought the rights to the Merrimack's water power and built the Amoskeag Mills, which became a testament to New England's manufacturing capabilities. In 1906 the mills employed 17,000 people and churned out more than 4 million yards of cloth weekly. This vast

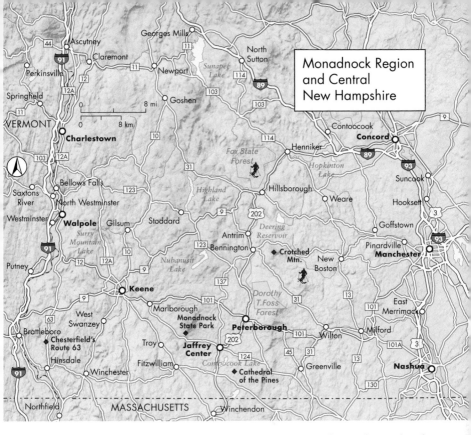

Monadnock Region and Central New Hampshire

enterprise served as Manchester's entire economic base; when it closed in 1936, the town was devastated.

Today Manchester is mainly a banking and business center. The old mill buildings have been converted into warehouses, classrooms, restaurants, museums, and office space. The city has the state's major airport, as well as the Verizon Wireless Arena, which hosts minor-league hockey matches, concerts, and conventions.

GETTING HERE AND AROUND
Manchester Airport, the state's largest airport, is a cost-effective, hassle-free alternative to Boston's Logan Airport, with nonstop service from 16 cities. Manchester can be hard to get around, but there are several taxi companies.

ESSENTIALS
Airport Manchester-Boston Regional Airport. ⊠ *1 Airport Rd.* ☎ *603/624–6539* ⊕ *www.flymanchester.com.*

Taxi Manchester Taxi. ⊠ *Manchester* ☎ *603/623–2222.* **Queen City Taxi.** ☎ *603/622–0008.*

Visitor Information Greater Manchester Welcome Center. ⊠ *Elm St. and Merrimack St., northwest corner Veterans Memorial Park* ☎ *603/666–6600* ⊕ *www.manchester-chamber.org.*

EXPLORING

FAMILY **Amoskeag Fishways.** From May to mid-June, salmon, shad, and river herring "climb" the 54-step fish ladder at this spot near the Amoskeag Dam. The visitor center has an underwater viewing window, and there are interactive exhibits and programs about the aquatic wildlife of the Merrimack River. ✉ *4 Fletcher St., off I–293/Rte. 3A* ☎ *603/626–3474* 🌐 *www.amoskeagfishways.org* 🎟 *Free ($2 suggested donation)* 🕒 *May and June, daily 9–5; July–Apr., Mon.–Sat. 9–5.*

Fodor's Choice ★ **Currier Museum of Art.** The Currier maintains an astounding permanent collection of works by European and American masters, among them Claude Monet, Edward Hopper, Winslow Homer, John Marin, Andrew Wyeth, and Childe Hassam, and it presents changing exhibits of contemporary art. The museum also arranges guided tours of the nearby Zimmerman House. Completed in 1950, it's New England's only Frank Lloyd Wright–designed residence open to the public. Wright called this sparse, utterly functional living space "Usonian," an invented term used to describe several dozen similar homes based on his vision of distinctly American architecture. ✉ *150 Ash St.* ☎ *603/669–6144, 603/669–6144 ext. 108 for house tours* 🌐 *www.currier.org* 🎟 *$12; $20 with Zimmerman House* 🕒 *Sun., Mon., and Wed.–Fri. 11–5, Sat. 10–5.*

Millyard Museum. In the Amoskeag Mills building, state-of-the-art exhibits depict the region's history from when Native Americans lived here and fished the Merrimack River to when the machines of Amoskeag Mills wove cloth. The museum also offers lectures and walking tours, and has a Discovery Gallery and a gift shop. ✉ *200 Bedford St.* ☎ *603/622–7531* 🌐 *www.manchesterhistoric.org* 🎟 *$8* 🕒 *Tues.–Sat. 10–4.*

FAMILY Fodor's Choice ★ **SEE Science Center.** The world's largest permanent LEGO installation at minifigure scale, depicting Amoskeag Millyard and Manchester as they were a century ago, is the star attraction at this hands-on science lab and children's museum. The mind-blowing exhibit, covering 2,000 square feet, is made up of about 3 million LEGO bricks. It conveys the massive size and importance of the mills, which ran a mile on each side of the Merrimack. The museum also offers daily science demonstrations, as well as changing exhibits. ✉ *200 Bedford St.* ☎ *603/669–0400* 🌐 *www.see-sciencecenter.org* 🎟 *$8* 🕒 *Weekdays 10–4, weekends 10–5.*

WHERE TO EAT

$$ AMERICAN 🍴 **Cotton.** Mod lighting and furnishings lend this restaurant inside an old Amoskeag Mills building a swanky atmosphere. For warm weather there's also a patio set in an arbor. Chef Jeffrey Paige, a leader in the farm-to-table movement, puts a winning new spin on comfort food. Start with pan-seared crab cakes or a kale and blueberry salad. The menu changes four times a year but might include an all-natural Delmonico steak or wood-grilled scallops with sweet-potato corn hash. The martinis here have won awards for good reason. [$] *Average main: $24* ✉ *75 Arms St.* ☎ *603/622–5488* 🌐 *www.cottonfood.com* 🕒 *No lunch weekends.*

At the Currier Museum of Art, you can enjoy European and American classics, or visit a nearby Frank Lloyd Wright house.

$ ✕ **Red Arrow Diner.** Once listed among the country's "top 10 diners,"
AMERICAN this bustling downtown diner caters to politicians, students, artists, and
Fodor's Choice everyone in between. The 1922 restaurant, open around the clock, is
★ a friendly place with fresh daily specials sized for the famished. Menu classics include kielbasa and cheese omelets and triple-bun Dinahmoe burgers. Order a house-brewed root beer or cream soda to round out the nostalgic dining experience. $ *Average main: $9* ✉ *61 Lowell St.* ☎ *603/626–1118* ⊕ *www.redarrowdiner.com.*

WHERE TO STAY

$ ⌂ **Ash Street Inn.** This five-room bed-and-breakfast is one of many strik-
B&B/INN ing Victorian homes in its residential neighborhood. **Pros:** nicely deco-rated rooms; within walking distance of Currier Museum. **Cons:** not a full-service hotel. $ *Rooms from: $189* ✉ *118 Ash St.* ☎ *603/668–9908* ⊕ *www.ashstreetinn.com* ⊅ *5 rooms* ❙❂❙ *Breakfast.*

$$$ ⌂ **Bedford Village Inn.** If you've decided to sacrifice downtown conve-
B&B/INN niences and venture a few miles southwest of Manchester to this lovely manor, you'll be rewarded by comfort and beauty. **Pros:** tuck down with homemade cookies; exceptional grounds; great restaurant. **Cons:** outside town. $ *Rooms from: $319* ✉ *2 Olde Bedford Way, Bedford* ☎ *603/472–2001, 800/852–1166* ⊕ *www.bedfordvillageinn.com* ⊅ *12 suites, 2 apartments, 1 cottage* ❙❂❙ *Some meals.*

$ ⌂ **Radisson Hotel Manchester Downtown.** Of Manchester's many chain
HOTEL properties, the 12-story Radisson has the most central location: a short walk from Amoskeag Mills and the great dining along Elm Street. **Pros:** downtown location; free airport shuttle; pets welcome. **Cons:**

9

fee for parking; unexciting decor. $ *Rooms from: $159* ✉ *700 Elm St.* ☎ *603/625–1000, 800/333–3333* ⊕ *www.radisson.com/manchester-hotel-nh-03101/nhmanch* ⌁ *244 rooms, 6 suites* ⦿ *No meals.*

NIGHTLIFE AND PERFORMING ARTS

PERFORMING ARTS
The Palace Theatre. The century-old Palace, a former vaudeville house, presents musicals and plays, comedy, and concerts throughout the year. ✉ *80 Hanover St.* ☎ *603/668–5588* ⊕ *www.palacetheatre.org.*

NIGHTLIFE
Midnight Rodeo Bar. On Saturday night, country-music lovers swarm to the bar at the Yard Restaurant for line-dancing lessons, followed by live music and mechanical-bull riding. ✉ *1211 S. Mammoth Rd.* ☎ *603/623–3545* ⊕ *www.midnightrodeobar.com* ⛟ *$10.*

SHOPPING
FAMILY **Bedford Farmers' Market.** Just outside Manchester, this market hosts a rich mix of local growers and food purveyors selling seasonal jams, pasture-raised lamb and chicken, homemade treats for dogs and cats, goats' milk soaps and balms, and even New Hampshire wines. There's usually live music, along with activities for children. ✉ *St. Elizabeth Seton Parish parking lot, 190 Meetinghouse Rd., 5 miles south of downtown Manchester off I–293, Bedford* ☎ *603/203–8440* ⊕ *www. bedfordfarmersmarket.org* ⊗ *June–Oct., Tues. 3–6.*

CONCORD

20 miles northwest of Manchester, 67 miles northwest of Boston, 46 miles northwest of Portsmouth.

New Hampshire's capital (population 42,000) is a quiet town that tends to state business and little else—the sidewalks roll up promptly at 6. Stop in town to get a glimpse of New Hampshire's State House, which is crowned by a gleaming, eagle-topped gold dome.

GETTING HERE AND AROUND
Interstate 93 bisects Concord north–south. Coming from the west, reach the city by Interstate 89; from the east use U.S. 202, which becomes Interstate 393 near the city line. Taxis can help get you around town, though Main Street near the State House is walkable.

ESSENTIALS
Taxi Concord Cab. ✉ *Concord* ☎ *603/225–4222.*

Visitor Information Greater Concord Chamber of Commerce. ✉ *49 S. Main St.* ☎ *603/224–2508* ⊕ *www.concordnhchamber.com.*

TOURS
FAMILY **Concord on Foot.** This walking trail winds past 62 points of interest throughout the historic district. Download the map online for free or pick up a printed copy ($2) at the chamber of commerce or at stores along the trail. ✉ *Greater Concord Chamber of Commerce, 49 S. Main St.* ⊕ *www.concordnhchamber.com/visitor_info.html.*

EXPLORING

FAMILY **McAuliffe-Shepard Discovery Center.** New England's only air-and-space center offers a full day of activities focused mostly on the heavens. See yourself in infrared light, learn about lunar spacecraft, examine a replica of the Mercury-Redstone rocket, or experience what it's like to travel in space—you can even try your hand at being a television weather announcer. There's also a café and a gift shop. ✉ *2 Institute Dr.* ☎ *603/271–7827* 🌐 *www.starhop.com* 🎟 *$10* 🕒 *July and Aug., daily 10:30–4; Sept.–June, Fri.–Sun. 10:30–4; 1st Fri. evening of month year-round also 6:30–9.*

New Hampshire Historical Society. Steps from the state capitol, this museum is a great place to learn about the Concord coach, a popular mode of transportation before railroads. Temporary exhibitions might include locally made quilts or historical portraits of residents. ✉ *6 Eagle Sq.* ☎ *603/228–6688* 🌐 *www.nhhistory.org* 🎟 *$7* 🕒 *Tues.–Sat. 9:30–5.*

Pierce Manse. Franklin Pierce lived in this Greek Revival home before he moved to Washington to become the 14th U.S. president. He's buried nearby. A guided tour covers his life in mid-19th-century historical context. ✉ *14 Horseshoe Pond La.* ☎ *603/225–4555* 🌐 *www.piercemanse.org* 🎟 *$7* 🕒 *Mid-June–early Sept., Tues.–Sat. 11–3; mid-Sept.–mid-Oct., Fri. and Sat. noon–3.*

FAMILY
Fodor's Choice ★
State House. The gilded-dome state house, built in 1819, is the nation's oldest capitol building in which the legislature still uses the original chambers. From January through June, you can watch the two branches in action. The Senate has 24 members, and the House house has 400—a ratio of 1 representative per 3,500 residents (a world record). The visitor center coordinates guided and self-guided tours, bookable online or on-site. The center also has history exhibits and paraphernalia from presidential primaries. ✉ *Visitor center, 107 N. Main St.* ☎ *603/271–2154* 🌐 *www.gencourt.state.nh.us/nh_visitorcenter/default.htm* 🎟 *Free* 🕒 *Weekdays 8–4.*

9

WHERE TO EAT AND STAY

$ AMERICAN FAMILY
🍴 **Arnie's Place.** If you need a reason to make the 1½-mile detour from Interstate 93, the selection of more than 50 kinds of homemade ice cream at Arnie's should do it: try the raspberry, vanilla, or toasted coconut. Chocoholics will love the shakes, and the lemon freeze will give you a headache in no time (it's worth it). A small dining room serves hamburgers, hot dogs, and a barbecue platter, but the five walk-up windows are the way to go: grab some grub and head to one of the picnic tables. [$] *Average main: $12* ✉ *164 Loudon Rd., off I–93, Concord Heights* ☎ *603/228–3225* 🌐 *www.arniesplace.com* 🕒 *Closed mid-Oct.–late Feb.*

$$ ECLECTIC
🍴 **Barley House.** A lively, old-fashioned tavern with Irish overtones, the Barley House is often abuzz with a mix of politicos, businessfolk, and tourists. The impressive melting pot of a menu includes chorizo-topped pizzas, burgers smothered with a peppercorn-whiskey sauce, chicken potpies, beer-braised bratwurst, and Mediterranean chicken salad—all reliably prepared. The bar serves dozens of interesting beers, on tap and by the bottle, and the wine list is decent. On Tuesday night, musicians play traditional Irish tunes. [$] *Average main: $20* ✉ *132 N. Main St.* ☎ *603/228–6363* 🌐 *www.thebarleyhouse.com* 🕒 *Closed Sun.* ✍ *Reservations not accepted.*

$ ✕ **Siam Orchid Thai Bistro.** This Thai restaurant recently moved closer to
THAI   the capitol building and now has outdoor seating in the summer. It's
FAMILY known for serving spicy and reasonably authentic dishes prepared with
flair, and attracts a stately weekday lunch crowd. $ *Average main: $16*
✉ *12 N. Main St.* ☎ *603/228–3633* ⊕ *www.siamorchid.net.*

$ 🛏 **The Centennial.** The most modern hotel in New Hampshire, the Cen-
HOTEL tennial is fittingly home to Granite, the state's most contemporary
restaurant and bar, making it a draw for politicians and those doing
business here. **Pros:** sleek redesign of historic structure; very comfortable
and clean rooms; great bar and restaurant. **Cons:** busy. $ *Rooms from:*
$199 ✉ *96 Pleasant St.* ☎ *603/227–9000* ⊕ *www.thecentennialhotel.*
com ⤳ *27 rooms, 5 suites* ❚◯❚ *Some meals.*

NIGHTLIFE AND PERFORMING ARTS

FAMILY **Capitol Center for the Arts.** The Egyptian-motif artwork, part of the
original 1927 decor, has been restored in the former Capitol Theatre.
Now the Capitol Center for the Arts, it hosts touring Broadway shows,
dance companies, and musical acts. ✉ *44 S. Main St.* ☎ *603/225–1111*
⊕ *www.ccanh.com.*

SHOPPING

Capitol Craftsman Jewelers. Fine jewelry, pottery, hand-painted glassware,
and hand-tooled leather goods are among the specialties here. ✉ *16 N.*
Main St. ☎ *603/224–6166* ⊕ *www.capitolcraftsman.com.*

Mark Knipe Goldsmiths. The designers at this shop near the capitol create
highly original rings, pendants, earrings, bracelets, and other jewelry.
✉ *2 Capitol Plaza, Main St.* ☎ *603/224–2920* ⊕ *www.knipegold.com.*

CHARLESTOWN

70 miles northwest of Concord.

Charlestown boasts the state's largest historic district, with about 60
homes—all handsome examples of Federal, Greek Revival, and Gothic
Revival architecture (and 10 built before 1800)—clustered about the
town center. Several merchants on the main street distribute brochures
that describe an interesting walking tour of the district.

GETTING HERE AND AROUND

You can reach Charlestown from Interstate 91, but it's best to follow
Route 12 North from Keene for the gorgeous scenery. Walking downtown Charlestown should take only 15 minutes of your day, but it's
worth admiring the buildings in the town center. The Fort at No. 4 is
less than 2 miles out of town, north on Route 11.

EXPLORING

FAMILY **Fort at No. 4.** In 1747, this fort 1½ miles north of downtown Charlestown was an outpost on the periphery of Colonial civilization. That
year fewer than 50 militiamen at the fort withstood an attack by 400
French soldiers, ensuring that northern New England remained under
British rule. Today, costumed interpreters at this living-history museum
cook dinner over an open hearth and demonstrate weaving, gardening,
and candle making. Each year the museum holds reenactments of militia

musters and the battles of the French and Indian War. ✉ *267 Springfield Rd. (Rte. 11), off Rte. 12A* ☎ *603/826–5700* 🌐 *www.fortat4.com* 🎟 *$10* 🕒 *May–Oct., Wed.–Sat. 10–4:30, Sun. 10–3:30.*

SPORTS AND THE OUTDOORS

FAMILY **Morningside Flight Park.** Here's a place for the adrenaline junkie: laser tag, zip-lining, paragliding, and hang gliding are all on the menu at Morningside Flight Park, where lessons are also available for the uninitiated. Morningside is considered among the best flying areas in the country, so even if you have a fear of flying, stop and watch the bright colors of the gliders as they take off from the 450-foot peak. ✉ *357 Morningside La., off Rte. 12* ☎ *603/542–4416* 🌐 *flymorningside.kittyhawk.com.*

WALPOLE

13 miles south of Charlestown.

Walpole possesses one of the state's most perfect town greens. Bordered by Elm and Washington streets, it's surrounded by homes dating to 1790 or so, when the townsfolk constructed a canal around the Great Falls of the Connecticut River, bringing commerce and wealth to the area. The town now has 3,200 inhabitants, more than a dozen of whom are millionaires. Walpole is also home to Florentine Films, documentarian Ken Burns's production company.

GETTING HERE AND AROUND

Walpole is a short jaunt off Route 12, north of Keene. The small downtown area is especially photogenic.

WHERE TO EAT

$ FRENCH Fodor's Choice ★ 🍴 **The Restaurant at L. A. Burdick Handmade Chocolates.** Famous candyman Larry Burdick, who sells his hand-filled, hand-cut chocolates to top restaurants around the Northeast, is a Walpole resident. The restaurant next door to his shop has the easygoing sophistication of a Parisian café and may tempt you to linger over an incredibly rich hot chocolate. The French-inspired menu utilizes fresh, often local, ingredients and changes daily. For dinner, you might start with a selection of grilled octopus, followed by the house beef stew or honey-roasted duck breast. Naturally, dessert is a big treat here, and features Burdick's own chocolates and pastries. [$] *Average main: $17* ✉ *47 Main St.* ☎ *603/756–9058* 🌐 *www.burdickchocolate.com.*

SHOPPING

FAMILY **Boggy Meadow Farm.** At this farm, you can watch the cheese-making process unfold, from the 200 cows being milked to the finer process of cheese making. Boggy Meadow cheeses can be sampled in the store and are available for purchase, as are cheese boards, cider doughnuts, and root vegetables. It's worth the trip just to see the beautiful 400-acre farm. ✉ *13 Boggy Meadow La.* ☎ *603/756–3300, 877/541–3953* 🌐 *www.boggymeadowfarm.com.*

KEENE

17 miles southeast of Walpole; 20 miles northeast of Brattleboro, Vermont; 56 miles southwest of Manchester.

Keene is the largest city in the state's southwestern corner. Its gentrified main street, with several engaging boutiques and cafés, is America's widest (132 feet); you can spend a fun few hours strolling along it. Even though settlers first arrived as far back as 1735, the city's atmosphere remains youthful, with its funky crafts stores and eclectic entertainment, like the Monadnock International Film Festival, held in April.

ESSENTIALS

Visitor Information Greater Keene Chamber of Commerce. ✉ *48 Central Sq.* ☎ *603/352–1303* 🌐 *www.keenechamber.com.* **Monadnock Travel Council.** ☎ 🌐 *www.monadnocktravel.com.*

EXPLORING

FAMILY **Keene State College.** The hub of the local arts community is this bustling college. The permanent collection of the Thorne-Sagendorph Art Gallery includes works by Richard Sumner Meryman, Abbott Handerson Thayer, and Robert Mapplethorpe. ✉ *Thorne-Sagendorph Art Gallery, 229 Main St.* ☎ *603/358–2720* 🌐 *www.keene.edu* 🕒 *Sat.–Wed. noon–5, Thurs. and Fri. noon–7.*

QUICK BITES

Prime Roast Coffee Company. Serving up fine coffee and pastries alongside fine art (covering the walls and tables), Prime Roast is a sensory experience; the beans are roasted and ground on-site, so the air is filled with the scent of delicious coffee. The café is two blocks from Keene State College. ✉ ***16 Main St.*** ☎ ***603/352–7874*** 🌐 ***www.primeroastcoffee.com.***

OFF THE BEATEN PATH

Chesterfield's Route 63. If you're in the mood for a country drive, head west from Keene along Route 9 to Route 63 (about 11 miles) and turn left toward the hilltop town of Chesterfield. This is an especially rewarding journey at sunset: from many points along the road you can see west out over the Connecticut River valley and into Vermont. The village center itself consists of little more than a handful of dignified granite buildings and a small general store. ✉ *Chesterfield.*

WHERE TO EAT AND STAY

$$ MEDITERRANEAN Fodor's Choice ★ 🍴 **Luca's Mediterranean Café.** A deceptively simple storefront bistro overlooking Keene's graceful town square, Luca's dazzles with epicurean creations influenced by Italy, France, Greece, Spain, and North Africa. Enjoy sautéed shrimp with cilantro pesto and plum tomatoes, three-cheese ravioli with artichoke hearts, or grilled salmon marinated in cumin and coriander. Don't forget to order the locally made gelato or sorbet for dessert. Luca's Market, next door, offers many of the same flavors in wraps, salads, and panini. [$] *Average main: $23* ✉ *10 Central Sq.* ☎ *603/358–3335* 🌐 *www.lucascafe.com.*

$ B&B/INN 🏨 **Chesterfield Inn.** With views of the hill in the distance, the Chesterfield Inn is nestled on a 10-acre farm. **Pros:** attractive gardens; close to Connecticut River; room rate includes full breakfast. **Cons:** no dinner on Sunday. [$] *Rooms from: $149* ✉ *20 Cross Rd., West Chesterfield*

DID YOU KNOW?

From 1991 to 2014, Keene hosted an annual Pumpkin Festival, a celebration that culminated in a fireworks display. In 2015, Laconia hosted the event.

☎ *603/256–3211, 800/365–5515* ⊕ *www.chesterfieldinn.com* ⇨ *13 rooms, 2 suites* ⦿ *Breakfast.*

$
HOTEL
🍽 **Fairfield Inn and Suites Keene Downtown.** You get a rare urban touch in the sleepy Monadnocks at this upscale property in the middle of Main Street. **Pros:** spacious and comfortable rooms; center of town. **Cons:** no pool. $ *Rooms from: $199* ⊠ *30 Main St.* ☎ *603/357–7070, 888/300–5056* ⊕ *www.fairfieldinnkeene.com* ⇨ *33 rooms, 7 suites* ⦿ *Breakfast.*

$
RESORT
FAMILY
🍽 **The Inn at East Hill Farm.** For those with kids who like animals, East Hill Farm is heaven: a family resort with daylong children's programs on a 160-acre farm overlooking Mt. Monadnock. **Pros:** rare agritourism and family resort; activities galore; beautiful setting; no TVs. **Cons:** remote location; noisy mess-hall dining. $ *Rooms from: $135* ⊠ *460 Monadnock St., 10 miles southeast of Keene, Troy* ☎ *603/242–6495, 800/242–6495 for reservations* ⊕ *www.east-hill-farm.com* ⇨ *65 rooms* ⦿ *All meals.*

NIGHTLIFE AND PERFORMING ARTS

ARTS VENUES

Colonial Theatre. This renovated 1924 vaudeville theater now shows art-house movies on the largest screen in town, and also hosts comedy, music, and dance performances. ⊠ *95 Main St.* ☎ *603/352–2033* ⊕ *www.thecolonial.org.*

BREWPUB

FAMILY **Elm City Restaurant & Brewery.** This microbrewery is an affordable hangout for everyone from college students to families. Burgers, steaks, and seafood are all on the menu. The beers range from light golden ales to dark and heavy porters and stouts. ⊠ *Colony Mill, 222 West St.* ☎ *603/355–3335* ⊕ *www.elmcitybrewing.com.*

SHOPPING

Fairgrounds Antiques. If you're not afraid of a little dust, there's no telling what kind of treasure you'll find at this longtime collection of several dozen dealers. Vintage furniture, prints and paintings, collectibles, ephemera, and much more are for sale. ⊠ *Cheshire Fairgrounds, 249 Monadnock Hwy., 3 miles southeast of downtown, East Swanzey* ☎ *603/352–4420.*

JAFFREY CENTER

16 miles southeast of Keene.

Novelist Willa Cather came to Jaffrey Center in 1919 and stayed in the Shattuck Inn, which is now the Shattuck Golf Club. Not far from here, she pitched the tent in which she wrote several chapters of *My Ántonia*. She returned nearly every summer thereafter until her death and was buried in the Old Burying Ground, also the resting place of Amos Fortune, a former slave who bought his freedom in 1863 and moved to town when he was 71. Fortune, who was a tanner, also bought the freedom of his two wives.

GETTING HERE AND AROUND

Jaffrey Center's historic district is on Route 124 and is home to a number of brick buildings. It should take less than an hour to view it in its entirety. The Old Burying Ground is 2 miles east of town on Route 124, behind the Old Meeting House.

ESSENTIALS

Visitor Information Jaffrey Chamber of Commerce. ☎ *603/532-4549* 🌐 *www.jaffreychamber.com.*

EXPLORING

FAMILY **Cathedral of the Pines.** This outdoor memorial pays tribute to Americans who have sacrificed their lives in service to their country. There's an inspiring view of Mt. Monadnock and Mt. Kearsarge from the Altar of the Nation, which is composed of rock from every U.S. state and territory. All faiths are welcome; organ music for meditation is played at midday Tuesday–Thursday in July and August. The Memorial Bell Tower, with a carillon of bells from around the world, is built of native stone. Norman Rockwell designed the bronze tablets over the four arches. Flower gardens, an indoor chapel, and a museum of military memorabilia share the hilltop. ✉ *10 Hale Hill Rd., off Rte. 119, 8 miles southeast of Jaffrey Center, Rindge* ☎ *603/899-3300* 🌐 *www.cathedralofthepines.org* 🕒 *May–Oct., daily 9–5.*

WHERE TO EAT AND STAY

$$ AMERICAN 🍴 **J.P. Stephens Restaurant and Tavern.** An appealing choice for lunch or dinner, this rustic, timber dining room overlooks a small mill pond in Rindge. The 1790 building used to house a sawmill, a gristmill, a forge, and a blacksmith. Now it's an all-around good restaurant with live music on weekends. Try the flavorful Cajun-style sirloin or the savory-sweet apple-brandy-and-walnut chicken. [$] *Average main: $22* ✉ *377 U.S. 202, 5 miles south of Jaffrey Center, Rindge* ☎ *603/899-3322* 🌐 *www.jpstephensrestaurant.com.*

$ B&B/INN 🏨 **Benjamin Prescott Inn.** Thanks to the dairy farm surrounding this 1853 Colonial house—with its stenciling and wide pine floors—you'll feel as though you're miles out in the country rather than just minutes from Jaffrey Center. **Pros:** inexpensive; homey and comfortable. **Cons:** not many amenities. [$] *Rooms from: $129* ✉ *433 Turnpike Rd.* ☎ *603/532-6637* 🌐 *www.benjaminprescottinn.com* 🛏 *7 rooms, 3 suites* 🍽 *Breakfast.*

$ B&B/INN 🏨 **The Fitzwilliam Inn.** Once a stagecoach stop, the Fitzwilliam Inn has graced this picturesque town green since 1786. **Pros:** affordable; friendly staff; full country breakfast. **Cons:** stair access issues. [$] *Rooms from: $127* ✉ *Town Common, 62 Rte. 119 W, Fitzwilliam* ☎ *603/585-9000* 🌐 *www.fitzwilliaminn.com* 🛏 *10 rooms* 🍽 *Breakfast.*

$ B&B/INN 🏨 **The Monadnock Inn.** Rooms in this 1830s home are painted in lively lavenders, yellows, and peaches, lending it a cheery air in the heart of pristine Jaffrey Center—a perfect place to get away from it all. **Pros:** well-lit rooms with lacy curtains; feels cozy, like grandma's house. **Cons:** limited amenities. [$] *Rooms from: $110* ✉ *379 Main St.* ☎ *603/532-7800* 🌐 *www.monadnockinn.com* 🛏 *11 rooms, 2 suites* 🍽 *Some meals.*

9

$ B&B/INN FAMILY 🏨 **Woodbound Inn.** A favorite of families and outdoors enthusiasts, this 1819 farmhouse became an inn in 1892. **Pros:** scenic lakefront location; focus on food; private beach. **Cons:** older property; simple furnishings. [$] *Rooms from: $159* ✉ *247 Woodbound Rd., Rindge* ☎ *603/532–8341, 855/966–3268* 🌐 *www.woodboundinn.com* 🛏 *44 rooms, 11 cabins* 🍴 *Breakfast.*

SPORTS AND THE OUTDOORS

FAMILY **Monadnock State Park.** The oft-quoted statistic about Mt. Monadnock is that it is America's most-climbed mountain—third in the world after Japan's Mt. Fuji and China's Mt. Tai. Whether this is true or not, locals agree that it's never lonely at the top: some days, more than 400 people crowd its bald peak. However, when the parking lot fills up, rangers close the park. Thus, an early morning start, especially during fall foliage, is recommended. Monadnock rises to 3,165 feet, and on a clear day the hazy Boston skyline is visible. Five trailheads branch out into more than two dozen trails of varying difficulty (though all rigorous) that wend their way to the top. Allow three–four hours for any round-trip hike. The visitor center has free trail maps as well as exhibits documenting the mountain's history. In winter, you can cross-country ski along roughly 12 miles of groomed trails on the lower elevations. ✉ *116 Poole Rd., off Rte. 124* ☎ *603/532–8862* 🌐 *www.nhstateparks.org* 🎟 *$5* 🕒 *Daily sunrise–sunset* ☞ *No pets.*

SHOPPING

Bloomin' Antiques. Fine art and unusual antiques abound in this quaint shop overlooking the town green. ✉ *3 Templeton Pike, Village Green, Fitzwilliam* ☎ *603/585–6688.*

PETERBOROUGH

9 miles northeast of Jaffrey Center, 30 miles northwest of Nashua.

Thornton Wilder's play *Our Town* was based on Peterborough. The nation's first free public library opened here in 1833. The town, which was the first in the region to be incorporated (1760), is still a commercial and cultural hub.

GETTING HERE AND AROUND

Parking can be found just off Main Street, with shopping, coffee, and food all close by. Stand on the bridge and watch the roiling waters of the Nubanusit River at the north end of Main Street.

ESSENTIALS

Visitor Information Greater Peterborough Chamber of Commerce. ☎ *603/924–7234* 🌐 *www.peterboroughchamber.com.*

EXPLORING

FAMILY **Mariposa Museum.** You can play instruments or try on costumes from around the world and indulge your cultural curiosity at this nonprofit museum dedicated to hands-on exploration of international folk art. The three-floor museum is housed inside a historic Baptist church, across from the Universalist church in the heart of town. The museum hosts workshops and presentations on dance and arts and crafts.

Charming Peterborough was the inspiration for the fictional Grover's Corners in Thornton Wilder's *Our Town*.

✉ *26 Main St.* ☎ *603/924–4555* 🌐 *www.mariposamuseum.org* 🎟 *$6* 🕑 *Tues.–Sun. 11–5.*

WHERE TO STAY

$ B&B/INN 🏨 **Birchwood Inn.** Henry David Thoreau slept here, probably on his way to climb Monadnock or to visit Jaffrey or Peterborough. **Pros:** nice tavern; pleasant rooms; inexpensive. **Cons:** remote small town. [$] *Rooms from: $109* ✉ *340 Rte. 45, Temple* ☎ *603/878–3285* 🌐 *www.thebirchwoodinn.com* 🛏 *3 rooms, 3 suites* 🍴 *Breakfast.*

$$ B&B/INN 🏨 **The Hancock Inn.** This Federal-style 1789 inn is the real deal—the oldest in the state and the pride of this idyllic town 8 miles north of Peterborough. **Pros:** quintessential Colonial inn in a perfect New England town; cozy rooms. **Cons:** remote. [$] *Rooms from: $209* ✉ *33 Main St., Hancock* ☎ *603/525–3318* 🌐 *www.hancockinn.com* 🛏 *13 rooms* 🍴 *Breakfast.*

PERFORMING ARTS

Monadnock Music. From early July to late August, Monadnock Music sponsors a series of solo recitals, chamber music concerts, and orchestra and opera performances by renowned musicians. Events take place throughout the area Wednesday–Saturday evening and on Sunday afternoon. Many of the offerings are free. ✉ *2A Concord St.* ☎ *603/924–7610* 🌐 *www.monadnockmusic.org.*

Peterborough Folk Music Society. The Music Society presents folk concerts by artists such as John Gorka, Greg Brown, and Cheryl Wheeler. Concerts are held in the Peterborough Players Theatre, a fantastic repurposed old barn. ✉ *55 Hadley Rd., off Middle Hancock Rd.* ☎ *603/827–2905* 🌐 *www.pfmsconcerts.org.*

FAMILY **Peterborough Players.** This theater troupe has been performing since 1933, these days presenting seven main-stage productions in a converted 18th-century barn throughout the summer. The Players also present children's shows in July and August. ✉ *55 Hadley Rd., off Middle Hancock Rd.* ☎ *603/924–7585* ⊕ *www.peterboroughplayers. org* ⊘ *Closed mid-Sept.–late June.*

SPORTS AND THE OUTDOORS

GOLF

Crotched Mountain Golf Club. Donald Ross, one of golf's earliest stars of course architecture, designed this club's hilly, rolling 18-hole layout here. The course has a nice view of the Monadnocks. ✉ *740 Francestown Rd., Francestown* ☎ *603/588–2923* ⊕ *www.crotchedmountaingolfclub. com* 🖃 *$39 weekdays, $49 weekends* 🏌 *18 holes, 6111 yards, par 71.*

SKI AREA

FAMILY **Crotched Mountain.** New Hampshire's southernmost skiing and snowboarding facility has 25 trails, almost half of them intermediate, and the rest divided pretty evenly between beginner and expert. There are four glade areas. Ample snowmaking capacity ensures good skiing all winter long. Crotched Mountain is famous for its night skiing: if you can stay up, you will save on a lift ticket and maybe hear a few good bands, too. Other facilities include a 40,000-square-foot lodge with a couple of restaurants, a ski school, and a snow camp for youngsters. **Facilities:** 25 trails; 100 acres; 1,000-foot vertical drop; 5 lifts. ✉ *615 Francestown Rd., Bennington* ☎ *603/588–3668* ⊕ *www.crotchedmountain. com* 🖃 *Lift ticket $52 midweek, $64 weekends and holidays.*

INLAND MAINE

WELCOME TO INLAND MAINE

TOP REASONS TO GO

★ **Baxter State Park:** Mt. Katahdin, the state's highest peak, stands sentry over Baxter's forestland in its "natural wild state."

★ **Moosehead Lake:** Surrounded by mountains, Maine's largest lake—dotted with islands and chiseled with inlets and coves—retains the rugged beauty that so captivated author Henry David Thoreau in the mid-1800s.

★ **Water Sports:** It's easy to get out on the water on scheduled cruises of large inland lakes; guided or self-guided boating, canoeing, and kayaking trips; and white-water rafting excursions on several rivers.

★ **Winter Pastimes:** Downhill skiing, snowmobiling, snowshoeing, cross-country skiing, and dogsledding are all popular winter sports.

★ **Foliage Drives:** Maine's best fall foliage is inland, where hardwoods outnumber spruce, fir, and pine trees in many areas.

1 Western Lakes and Mountains. Lakes both quiet and busy, classic New England villages, and ski resorts fit perfectly into the forested landscape. Snowmobiling and snowshoeing are popular in winter, while the woods and water draw summer vacationers for a cool escape. Spectacular fall foliage invites exploration of the region's national forest, state parks, and scenic byways. Crowds are thinner in spring, but fishermen, white-water rafters, kayakers, and canoeists still find their way here.

2 The North Woods. Much of the North Woods is best experienced by canoeing or kayaking, fishing, hiking, snowshoeing, or snowmobiling. Baxter State Park and Allagash Wilderness Waterway are premier wilderness destinations, and commercial forestland is open for public recreation. The woodsy town of Greenville, on Moosehead Lake, is a good base for day trips—take a drive (go slow!) down a "moose alley."

Madawaska
Fort Kent
Van Buren
161
Allagash
161
11
Caribou
Fort Fairfield
Allagash Wilderness Waterway
Presque Isle
Ashland
163
11
2
Baxter State Park
Mt. Katahdin ▲
Houlton
Sherman
ckwood
Kokadjo
Grindstone
95
Millinocket
Medway
2
6
Moosehead Lake
11
Greenville
Brownville Junction
Dover-Foxcroft
11
Passadumkeag
ld
7
15
Old Town
Newport
Orono
vhegan
95
Bangor
Waterville
Augusta
Gardiner

CANADA

NEW BRUNSWICK

0 — 20 mi
0 — 20 km

GETTING ORIENTED

Though Maine is well known for its miles of craggy coastline, the inland part of the state is surprisingly vast and far less populated. Not one hour's drive from the bays and ocean, huge swaths of forestland are punctuated by lakes (sometimes called ponds, despite their size). Summer camps, ski areas, and small villages populate the mountainous western part of the state, which stretches north along the New Hampshire border to Québec. In the remote North Woods, wilderness areas beckon outdoors lovers.

10

Updated by
Mary Ruoff

Unlike the state's higher-profile coastline, inland Maine is a four-season destination. Natural beauty is abundant here, in the form of mountains, lakes, rivers, and hilly pastoral stretches, and there's an ample supply of classic New England villages. Spring is the slow season, to be sure, though canoeists, kayakers, fishermen, and white-water rafters all venture inland at this time of year.

Sebago and Long lakes, north of Portland and the gateway to the Western Lakes and Mountains region, hum with boaters and watercraft in the summer. Mt. Katahdin, Maine's highest peak and the terminus of the Appalachian Trail, rises in 210,000-acre Baxter State Park, outside Millinocket in the North Woods.

Come winter, ski resorts—including Maine's largest, Sugarloaf and Sunday River, both in the state's western section—wait for large snowfalls (and make it themselves in between). Maine often receives snow when the rest of New England doesn't and vice versa, so track the weather if you're coming for winter sports or to bask in the serenity of a good snowfall.

Rangeley, in western Maine, has been a haven for anglers since the 19th century, but these days this lakes-strewn area is also known for hiking and winter sports. Remote forestland lines most of Moosehead Lake, the biggest natural lake east of the Mississippi River within a single state. Greenville, at its southern end, is a hub for visitors who come to enjoy the lake and explore nearby wilderness locales.

Wealthy urban "rusticators" began flocking to inland Maine on vacation in the mid-1800s. The legacy of the rusticators and the locals who catered to them lives on at sporting camps still found—albeit in smaller numbers than in days past—on remote lakes and rivers, and through Maine's unique system of licensed outdoor guides. Known as Registered Maine Guides, these well-qualified practitioners lead excursions that might involve kayaking, white-water rafting, hiking, fishing, hunting, canoeing, and moose spotting.

PLANNING

WHEN TO GO

As a rule, inland Maine's most popular hiking trails and lakeside beaches get busier when the weather gets warmer, but if splendid isolation is what you crave, you can still find it. Summertime is when lodging rates peak and traffic picks up—though rarely jams, outside of a few spots—but the weather makes it a beautiful time of year to visit. Inland Maine gets hotter than the coast in July and August; lakes and higher elevations are naturally cooler. September is a good bet: the weather is more moderate, and the crowds thinner.

Western Maine is the state's premier destination for leaf peepers—hardwoods are more abundant here than on the coast. Peak foliage season runs late September–mid-October.

Maine's largest ski areas can make their own snow—at least one of them opens its doors in mid-November and remains open until May. Inland Maine typically has snow cover by Christmas, so cross-country skiing, snowshoeing, and snowmobiling are in full swing by the end of the year. In ski towns, lodging rates peak in winter.

Early spring snowmelt ushers in mud season, which leads to black fly season mid-May–mid-June. The flies are especially pesky in the woods but less bothersome in town. Spring is prime time for canoeing and fishing.

PLANNING YOUR TIME

Visitors to inland Maine often spend their entire vacation in the region. That's certainly true of those who come to ski at a resort, fish at a remote sporting camp, or just relax at a lakeside cabin. After a day hike on a mountain trail reached by driving gravel logging roads, visitors are unlikely to hurry along to another town. Vacation rental homes and cottages often require a week's stay, minimum, as do lakeside cottage resorts. And generally speaking, the farther inland you go, the farther it is between destinations.

GETTING HERE AND AROUND

AIR TRAVEL

Two primary airports serve Maine: Portland International (PWM) and Bangor International (BGR). Portland is closer to the Western Lakes and Mountains area; Bangor is more convenient to the North Woods. Regional flying services, operating from regional and municipal airports, provide access to remote lakes and wilderness areas and offer scenic flights.

CAR TRAVEL

Because Maine is large and rural, a car is essential. U.S. 2 is the major east–west thoroughfare in Western Maine, winding from Bangor to New Hampshire. Interstate 95 is a departure point for many visitors to inland Maine, especially the North Woods. The highway heads inland at Brunswick and becomes a toll road (the Maine Turnpike) from the New Hampshire border to Augusta. Because of the hilly terrain and abundant lakes and rivers, inland Maine can get curvy. Traffic rarely

10

gets heavy, though highways often pass right through instead of around the larger towns, which can slow your trip a bit.

There are few public roads in Maine's North Woods, but private logging roads there are often open to the public (sometimes by permit and fee). When driving these roads, always give lumber-company trucks the right-of-way; loggers must drive in the middle of the road and often can't move over or slow down for cars. Be sure to have a full tank of gas before heading onto private roads in the region.

RESTAURANTS

Fear not, lobster lovers: this succulent, emblematic Maine food is on the menu at many inland restaurants, from fancier establishments to roadside places. Dishes containing lobster are more common than boiled lobster dinners, but look for daily specials. Shrimp, scallops, and other seafood are also menu mainstays, and you may find surprises like bison burgers or steaks from a nearby farm. Organic growers and natural foods producers do business throughout the state and often sell their products to inland restaurants. Pumpkins, blackberries, strawberries, and other seasonal foods make their way into homemade desserts, as do Maine's famed blueberries. Many lakeside resorts and sporting camps have a reputation for good food—some of the latter will even cook the fish you catch. *Prices in the reviews are the average cost of a main course at dinner or, if dinner is not served, at lunch.*

HOTELS

Well-run inns, bed-and-breakfasts, and motels can be found throughout inland Maine, including some more sophisticated lodgings. At places near ski resorts, peak-season rates may apply in winter and summer. Both hotel rooms and condo units are among the options at the two largest ski resorts, Sunday River and Sugarloaf. Greenville has the largest selection of lodgings in the North Woods region, with elaborate and homey accommodations alike. Lakeside sporting camps, from the primitive to the upscale, are popular around Rangeley and the North Woods; many have cozy cabins heated with wood stoves and serve three hearty meals a day. Conservation organizations also operate wilderness retreats. In Maine's mountains, as on its coast, many small inns don't have air-conditioning. *Prices in the reviews are the lowest cost of a standard double room in high season. Hotel reviews have been shortened. For full reviews visit Fodors.com.*

Maine Campground Owners Association. The association's helpful membership directory is available by mail and on its website, which also has an interactive campground map. Many campgrounds have RV spaces and cabin rentals. ☎ *207/782–5874* ⊕ *www.campmaine.com.*

Maine State Parks Campsite Reservations Service. You can get information about and make reservations for 12 state park campgrounds through this service. Note: reservations for Baxter State Park, which is administered separately, are not handled by the service. ☎ *207/624–9950, 800/332–1501 in Maine* ⊕ *www.campwithme.com.*

WHAT IT COSTS				
	$	$$	$$$	$$$$
Restaurants	under $18	$18–$24	$25–$35	over $35
Hotels	under $200	$200–$299	$300–$399	over $399

VISITOR INFORMATION
Maine Office of Tourism. ☎ 888/624–6345 ⊕ *www.visitmaine.com.*
Maine Tourism Association. ☎ *207/623–0363, 800/767–8709*
⊕ *www.mainetourism.com.*

WESTERN LAKES AND MOUNTAINS

From Sebago Lake, less than 20 miles northwest of Portland, the sparsely populated Western Lakes and Mountains region stretches north and west, bordered by New Hampshire and Québec. Each season offers different outdoor highlights: you can choose from snow sports, hiking, mountain biking, leaf peeping, fishing, swimming, and paddling. The Sebago Lake area bustles with activity in summer. Bridgton is a classic New England town, as is Bethel, in the valley of the Androscoggin River. Sunday River, a major ski resort nearby, also offers a host of summer activities. The more rural Rangeley Lakes area contains long stretches of pine, beech, spruce, and sky, and more classic inns. Just north of Kingfield is Sugarloaf Mountain Resort, Maine's other big ski resort, which has plenty to offer year-round.

SEBAGO LAKE AREA

20 miles northwest of Portland.

The shores of sprawling Sebago Lake and fingerlike Long Lake are popular with water-sports enthusiasts, as are Brandy Pond and many other bodies of water in the area. Several rivers flow into Sebago Lake, linking nearby lakes and ponds to form a 43-mile waterway. Naples, on the causeway separating Long Lake from Brandy Pond, pulses with activity in the summer, when the area swells with seasonal residents and weekend visitors. Open-air cafés overflow with patrons, boats buzz along the water, and families parade along the sidewalk edging Long Lake. On clear days the view includes snowcapped Mt. Washington.

10

GETTING HERE AND AROUND
Sebago Lake, gateway to Maine's Western Lakes and Mountains, is less than 20 miles from Portland on U.S. 302.

ESSENTIALS
Vacation Rentals Krainin Real Estate. ✉ *1539 Roosevelt Tr., Raymond* ☎ *207/655–3811* ⊕ *www.krainin.com.*

Visitor Information Sebago Lakes Region Chamber of Commerce. ✉ *747 Roosevelt Tr., Windham* ☎ *207/892–8265* ⊕ *www.sebagolakeschamber.com.*

Inland Maine Outdoor Activities

People visit inland Maine year-round for hiking, biking, camping, fishing, canoeing, kayaking, downhill and cross-country skiing, snowshoeing, and snowmobiling. During the summer, mountain biking is big at some ski resorts.

The Kennebec and Dead rivers, which converge at The Forks in Western Maine, and the West Branch of the Penobscot River, near Millinocket in the North Woods, provide thrilling white-water rafting. Boating, canoeing, and kayaking are popular on inland Maine's many lakes and rivers.

BICYCLING
Bicycle Coalition of Maine. The coalition provides information about biking in the state. ☎ 207/623–4511 ⊕ www.bikemaine.org.

FISHING
Maine Department of Inland Fisheries and Wildlife. You can get information about and purchase fishing and hunting licenses by phone and online through this state agency. ☎ 207/287–8000 ⊕ www.mefishwildlife.com.

HIKING
Maine Appalachian Trail Club. The club publishes seven Appalachian Trail maps ($8), all of which are bound together in its Maine trail guide ($30).

Its interactive online map divides the AT in Maine into 30-plus sections, with photos and information on each. ⊕ www.matc.org.

Maine Trail Finder. Visitors can find Maine trails to hike, mountain bike, paddle, snowshoe, and cross-county ski on this website, which includes trail descriptions, photos, user comments, directions, links to maps, weather conditions, and more. ⊕ www.mainetrailfinder.com.

RAFTING
Maine Professional Guides Association. The association can help you find a state-licensed guide to lead a fishing, kayaking, canoeing, white-water rafting, or wildlife-watching trip. ⊕ www.maineguides.org.

SKIING
Ski Maine. For alpine and cross-country skiing information, contact Ski Maine. ☎ 207/773–7669 ⊕ www.skimaine.com.

SNOWMOBILING
Maine Snowmobile Association. The association's excellent statewide map of about 3,500 miles of interconnected trails is available online and by mail. Their website also has contacts and links for 11,000 miles of local and regional trails. ☎ 207/622–6983 ⊕ www.mesnow.com.

EXPLORING

Sebago Lake. Year-round and seasonal dwellings, from simple camps to sprawling showplaces, line the shores of Maine's second-largest lake, the source of Greater Portland's drinking water. ✉ *Windham* ☎ 207/892–8265 ⊕ *www.sebagolakeschamber.com.*

FAMILY   **Sebago Lake State Park.** This 1,400-acre expanse on the north shore of Sebago Lake is a great spot for swimming, boating, and fishing for both salmon and togue. Its 250-site campground is the largest of any of the Maine state parks. Songo Lock State Historic Site, an operational lock along the twisting, narrow Songo River, is pleasant picnic

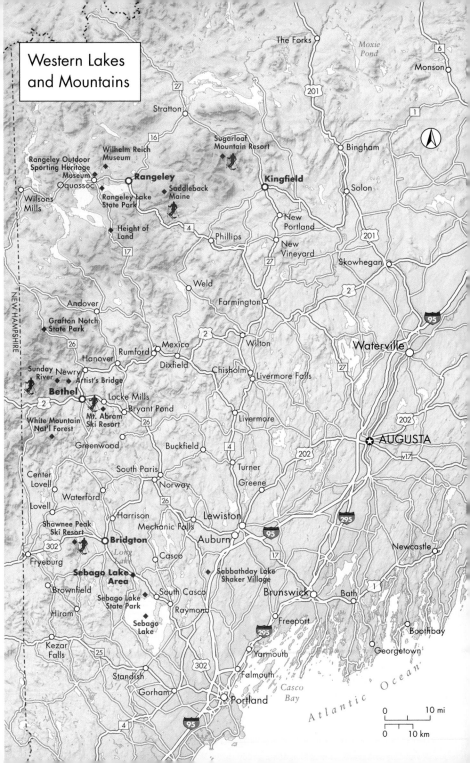

Western Lakes and Mountains

The Forks

Moxie Pond

Monson

6

201

27

Stratton

Bingham

16

Sugarloaf
Mountain Resort

Kingfield

Solon

Wilhelm Reich
Museum

Rangeley

Saddleback
Maine

Rangeley Outdoor
Sporting Heritage
Museum

Oquossoc

New
Portland

201

Rangeley Lake
State Park

1

Wilsons
Mills

Height of
Land

New
Vineyard

Skowhegan

4

Phillips

27

17

Weld

Farmington

2

Andover

Waterville

Grafton Notch
State Park

Rumford

Mexico

Wilton

95

26

Hanover

Dixfield

Chisholm

27

Sunday
River

Newry

Artist's Bridge

Livermore Falls

Bethel

Locke Mills

2

Mt. Abram
Ski Resort

Bryant Pond

Livermore

White Mountain
Nat'l Forest

26

202

Greenwood

Buckfield

4

AUGUSTA

South Paris

Turner

202

Center
Lovell

Norway

Greene

v17

Lovell

26

Waterford

Shawnee Peak
Ski Resort

Harrison

Lewiston

295

Mechanic Falls

302

Bridgton

Auburn

Newcastle

Fryeburg

Long
Lake

Casco

95

17

Sebago Lake
Area

Sabbathday Lake
Shaker Village

Brownfield

South Casco

Brunswick

Bath

Sebago Lake
State Park

Raymond

1

Hiram

Sebago
Lake

Freeport

Boothbay

Kezar
Falls

295

Georgetown

25

Yarmouth

Standish

Falmouth

Atlantic Ocean

Gorham

302

Casco
Bay

Portland

4

95

0   10 mi

0   10 km

NEW HAMPSHIRE

area. Bicycling along the park's roads is a popular pastime in warm weather. Come winter, the 6 miles of hiking trails here are groomed for cross-country skiing. ✉ *11 Park Access Rd., Casco* ☎ *207/693–6231* 🌐 *www.parksandlands.com* 🎟 *$6.50* 🕒 *Daily 9–sunset.*

OFF THE BEATEN PATH

Sabbathday Lake Shaker Village. Established in the late 18th century, this is the last active Shaker community in the world. Several buildings with Shaker furniture, folk art, tools, farm implements, and crafts from the 18th to the early 20th century are open for guided hour-long tours. The structures include the 1794 Meetinghouse, the 1839 Ministry's Shop, where the elders and eldresses lived until the early 1900s, and the 1821 Sister's Shop, where household goods and candies were made. The 1850 Boys' Shop has a free exhibit about Shaker childhood. A changing exhibit in the 1816 Granary is included with the tour, but tickets are also sold separately. The same is true for the herb garden tours on Tuesday and Thursday afternoons July–early September. The Shaker Store sells community-produced foods and goods as well as handicrafts by area artisans. If you're visiting the village in late August, don't miss the popular Maine Native American Summer Market and Demonstration. ✉ *707 Shaker Rd., near Rte. 26, New Gloucester* ☎ *207/926–4597* 🌐 *www.maineshakers.com* 🎟 *Tour $10, granary exhibit $7, herb garden tour $7* 🕒 *Late May–mid-Oct., Mon.–Sat. 10–4:30.*

WHERE TO STAY

$$$$ RESORT FAMILY

🏨 **Migis Lodge.** Scattered under a canopy of trees along Sebago Lake, the classy pine-panel cottages at this 125-acre resort have fieldstone fireplaces and are furnished with colorful rugs and handmade quilts. **Pros:** many water sports included; picnicking on resort's private island; evening cocktail hour. **Cons:** pricey; credit cards not accepted. [$] *Rooms from: $688* ✉ *30 Migis Lodge Rd., off U.S. 302, South Casco* ☎ *207/655–4524* 🌐 *www.migis.com* 💳 *No credit cards* 🕒 *Closed mid-Oct.–mid-June* 🛏 *35 cottages, 6 rooms* 🍴 *All meals.*

SPORTS AND THE OUTDOORS

Sebago and Long lakes are popular areas for sailing, fishing, and motorboating. As U.S. 302 cuts through the center Naples, at the Naples causeway you'll find rental craft for fishing or cruising.

FAMILY

Songo River Queen II. Departing from the Naples causeway, the *Songo River Queen II,* a 93-foot stern-wheeler, takes passengers on one- and two-hour cruises on Long Lake. ✉ *841 Roosevelt Tr., Naples* ☎ *207/693–6861* 🌐 *www.songoriverqueen.net* 🎟 *$15–$25* 🕒 *July–early Sept., daily; late May–June and early Sept.–mid-Oct., weekends; hrs vary.*

BRIDGTON

8 miles north of Naples, 30 miles south of Bethel.

U.S. 302 becomes Main Street in picturesque Bridgton, whose 10 lakes are popular for boating and fishing. Steps from the tree-lined downtown with its restaurants, galleries, and shops, a covered pedestrian bridge leads to 66-acre Pondicherry Park, a nature preserve with wooded trails and two streams. On hot summer days, kids dive off the dock at the town's Highland Lake Beach, just north of Main Street at the lake's southern end. Come winter, visitors hit the slopes at Shawnee Peak.

The surrounding countryside is a good choice for leaf peepers and outdoors lovers. A few miles north, Harrison anchors the northern end of Long Lake. In fall, Fryeburg, 15 miles west on the New Hampshire border, is home to the Fryeburg Fair (🌐 *www.fryeburgfair.com*), the region's largest agricultural fair.

GETTING HERE AND AROUND

From Portland, U.S. 302 runs northwest to Bridgton along the east side of Sebago Lake and the west side of Long Lake. From there it continues west to Fryeburg, where you can take Route 5 north to Center Lovell.

ESSENTIALS

Vacation Rentals Maine Lakeside Getaways. ✉ *1 Mountain Rd., Suite 1* ☎ *207/647–4000, 866/647–8557* 🌐 *www.mainelakesidegetaways.com.*

Visitor Information Greater Bridgton Lakes Region Chamber of Commerce. ✉ *101 Portland Rd.* ☎ *207/647–3472* 🌐 *www.mainelakeschamber.com.*

EXPLORING

Rufus Porter Museum. Local youth Rufus Porter became a leading folk artist in the early 1800s, painting landscape and harbor murals on the walls of New England homes, like this museum's red Cape Cod–style house, which bears unsigned murals by Porter (or one of his apprentices). Also an inventor, Porter founded *Scientific American* magazine. Early issues are on display, as are some of his inventions and miniature portraits. By 2016, the museum plans to include an 1840s-era house at 121 Main Street. ✉ *67 N. High St.* ☎ *207/647–2828* 🌐 *www.rufusportermuseum.org* 🎫 *$8* ⏲ *Mid-June–mid-Oct., Wed.–Sat. noon–4.*

WHERE TO STAY

$ B&B/INN 🏨 **Noble House Inn.** On a quiet road, this 1903 estate above Highland Lake offers a convenient location, plenty of creature comforts, and a relaxing atmosphere. **Pros:** bottomless cookie jar; skiing and golfing packages; distinctive suites. **Cons:** limited lake views; only suites have TVs. [$] *Rooms from: $175* ✉ *81 Highland Rd.* ☎ *207/647–3733, 888/237–4880* 🌐 *www.noblehouseinn.com* 🛏 *4 rooms, 4 suites* 🍴 *Breakfast.*

SPORTS AND THE OUTDOORS

FAMILY **Shawnee Peak.** Just a few miles from Bridgton, Shawnee Peak appeals to families and to those who enjoy nighttime skiing—trails are lighted most evenings. Three terrain parks and seven glade areas offer alternatives to trails and downhill runs. The main base lodge has a restaurant with an expansive deck; the smaller East Lodge has a second-floor bunkhouse. Lodging choices also include Shawnee Peak House, slope-side condos, and a mountaintop yurt and cabin. Summer visitors can hike and pick blueberries. **Facilities:** 41 trails; 249 acres; 1,300-foot vertical drop; 5 lifts. ✉ *119 Mountain Rd., off U.S. 302* ☎ *207/647–8444* 🌐 *www.shawneepeak.com* 🎫 *Lift ticket $63.*

BETHEL

27 miles north of Bridgton; 65 miles north of Portland.

Bethel is pure New England: a town with white clapboard houses, white-steeple churches, and a mountain vista at the end of every street. The campus of Gould Academy, a college prep school founded in 1836, anchors the east side of downtown. In winter, this is ski country—Sunday River, one of Maine's big ski resorts, is only a few miles north in Newry. On the third weekend in July, MollyOckett Day, which includes a parade, fireworks, and a frog-jumping contest, honors a Pequawket Indian renowned for her medicinal cures in the early days of white settlement.

GETTING HERE AND AROUND

From the south, both Routes 35 and 5 lead to Bethel, overlapping several miles south of town. Route 5 from Bethel to Fryeburg is especially pretty come fall, with long stretches of overhanging trees. Kezar Lake can be glimpsed as the road passes through tiny Center Lovell. If you're coming to Bethel from the west on U.S. 2, you'll pass White Mountain National Forest.

ESSENTIALS

Vacation Rentals Four Seasons Realty & Rentals. ✉ *32 Parkway Plaza, Suite 1* ☎ *207/824–3776* ⊕ *www.fourseasonsrealtymaine.com.*

Visitor Information Bethel Area Chamber of Commerce. ✉ *8 Station Pl., off Cross St.* ☎ *207/824–2282, 800/442–5826* ⊕ *www.bethelmaine.com.*

EXPLORING

FAMILY **Grafton Notch State Park.** Route 26 runs through Grafton Notch, a favorite destination for viewing fall foliage that stretches along the Bear River Valley 14 miles north of Bethel. It's an easy walk from roadside parking areas to Mother Walker Falls, Moose Cave, and spectacular Screw Auger Falls. The Table Rock Loop Trail (about 2 miles round-trip) rewards hikers with views of the mountainous terrain. For more of a challenge, make the 7.6-mile round-trip trek along the Appalachian Trail to the viewing platform atop Old Speck Mountain, the state's third-highest peak. The AT also traverses the 9,993-acre Mahoosuc Public Reserved Land—its two tracts sandwich the park—whose trails offer stunning, if strenuous, backcountry hiking (there are backcountry campsites). In winter, a popular snowmobile trail follows the river through the park. ✉ *1941 Bear River Rd., Newry* ☎ *207/824–2912 Mid-May–mid-Oct. only, 207/624–6080* ⊕ *www.parksandlands.com* ✑ *$3* ⊙ *Daily 9–sunset.*

Museums of the Bethel Historical Society. Start your stroll in Bethel here, across from the Village Common. The center's campus comprises two buildings: the 1821 O'Neil Robinson House and the 1813 Dr. Moses Mason House, both listed on the National Register of Historic Places. The O'Neil Robinson House has changing and permanent exhibits pertaining to the region's history. One parlor room serves as a gift shop with a nice book selection. The Moses Mason House has nine period rooms, and the front hall and stairway are decorated with Rufus Porter School folk art murals. The barn gallery has changing and traveling exhibits. ✉ *10 Broad St.* ☎ *207/824–2908, 800/824–2910* ⊕ *www.bethelhistorical.org* 💲 *O'Neil Robinson free, Moses Mason $3* 🕙 *O'Neil Robinson: late Nov.–June, Sept., and Oct., Tues.–Fri. 10–4; July and Aug., Tues.–Fri. 10–4, Sat. 1–4. Moses Mason: July and Aug., Thurs.–Sat. 1–4; Sept.–June, by appointment (barn gallery open in Sept., hrs vary).*

FAMILY **White Mountain National Forest.** This forest straddles New Hampshire and Maine, with the highest peaks on the New Hampshire side. The Maine section, though smaller, has magnificent rugged terrain. Hikers can enjoy everything from hour-long nature loops to a day hike up Speckled Mountain. The mountain is part of the 11,000-acre Caribou-Speckled Mountain Wilderness Area, one of several in the forest, but the only one entirely contained within Maine. The most popular Maine access to the national forest is via Route 113, which runs south from its terminus at U.S. 2 in Gilead, 10 miles from downtown Bethel. Most of the highway is the Pequawket Trail Maine Scenic Byway, and the section through the forest is spectacular come fall. This stretch is closed in winter but is used by snowmobilers and cross-country skiers. Two of the forest's campgrounds are in Maine; backcountry camping is allowed. ✉ *Rte. 113, off U.S. 2, Gilead* ☎ *603/466–2713* ⊕ *www.fs.usda.gov/ whitemountain* 💲 *Day pass $3 per car, weekly $7.*

WHERE TO STAY

$ 🛏 **Holidae House.** New owners took over this affordable downtown B&B/INN bed-and-breakfast in 2015, and they have embraced the welcoming hospitality that keeps guests returning year after year. **Pros:** courtesy cordials in parlor; fresh-baked treats in afternoon; blow-up mattresses available. **Cons:** little outdoor space. 💲 *Rooms from: $139* ✉ *85 Main St.* ☎ *207/824–3400, 877/224–3400* ⊕ *www.holidaehouse.com* 🛏 *7 rooms* 🍽 *Breakfast.*

EN
ROUTE
Artist's Bridge. The most painted and photographed of Maine's nine covered bridges can be found on a detour from Newry. Head south on U.S. 2 and then northwest on Sunday River Road (stay to the right at "Y" intersections). ✉ *Sunday River Rd., 4 miles northwest of U.S. 2, Newry.*

Height of Land. The most direct route from Bethel to Rangeley is a stunning 67-mile drive, much of it along Rangeley Lakes National Scenic Byway. Take U.S. 2 east to Mexico and head north on Route 17, which winds through the Swift River Valley before ascending to Height of Land, with unforgettable views of mountains and lakes. In Oquossoc, continue on Route 4 to Rangeley. ✉ *Rte. 17, Rangeley.*

SPORTS AND THE OUTDOORS
CANOEING AND KAYAKING

FAMILY **Bethel Outdoor Adventure.** On the Androscoggin River, this outfitter rents canoes, kayaks, tubes, paddleboards, and drift boats; leads guided fishing and boating trips; and operates a shuttle service and campground. Maine Mineralogy Expeditions is based here, with an open-air facility where you can sluice for precious gems. ✉ *121 Mayville Rd.* ☎ *207/824–4224* ⊕ *www.betheloutdooradventure.com.*

10

One of the Rangeley Lakes, Mooselookmeguntic is said to mean "portage to the moose feeding place" in the Abenaki language.

DOGSLEDDING

Mahoosuc Guide Service. This acclaimed guide company leads dogsledding expeditions in the Umbagog National Wildlife Refuge on the Maine–New Hampshire border and in northern Maine and Canada. Canoe trips in the refuge and elsewhere in Maine take place in the summer. The company has lodging for customers and groups. ⊠ *1513 Bear River Rd., Newry* ☎ *207/824–2073* ⊕ *www.mahoosuc.com* ⊠ *From $280.*

SKI AREAS

FAMILY **Carter's Cross-Country Ski Center.** This cross-country ski center offers about 30 miles of trails for all levels of skiers. Snowshoes, skis, and sleds to pull children are all available for rental. The place also rents lodge rooms and ski-in cabins. Carter's has another ski center in Oxford. ⊠ *786 Intervale Rd.* ☎ *207/824–3880, 207/539–4848* ⊕ *www.cartersxcski.com* ⊠ *$15.*

FAMILY **Mt. Abram.** Family-friendly and affordable, Mt. Abram is open Thursday–Sunday during ski season, with night skiing on Saturday. It allows off-trail "boundary-to-boundary" skiing, and has a tubing area and two terrain parks. Westside, the popular lift-served beginner area, has its own base lodge. The main lodge is home to the Loose Boots Lounge, which features live music on Saturday night. **Facilities:** 51 trails; 250 acres; 1,150-foot vertical drop; 5 lifts. ⊠ *308 Howe Hill Rd., off Rte. 26, Greenwood* ☎ *207/875–5000* ⊕ *www.skimtabram.com* ⊠ *Lift ticket $55.*

Whoopie Pies

When a bill aiming to make the whoopie pie Maine's official dessert was debated in state legislature, some lawmakers countered that the blueberry pie (made with Maine wild blueberries, of course) should have the honor. The blueberry pie won out, but what might have erupted into civil war instead ended civilly, with whoopie pies designated the official state "treat." Spend a few days anywhere in Maine and you'll notice just how popular it really is.

The name is misleading: it's a "pie" only in the sense of a having a filling between two "crusts"—namely, a thick layer of sugary frosting sandwiched between two saucers of rich cake, usually chocolate. It may have acquired its distinctive moniker from the jubilant yelp farmers emitted after discovering it in their lunchboxes. The whoopie pie is said to have Pennsylvania Dutch roots, but many Mainers insist that it originated here. Typically, the filling is made with butter or shortening; some recipes add Marshmallow Fluff. Many bakers have indulged the temptation to experiment with flavors and ingredients, particularly in the filling but also in the cake, offering pumpkin, raspberry, oatmeal cream, red velvet, peanut butter, and more.

FAMILY
Fodor's Choice
★

Sunday River. Once-sleepy Sunday River has evolved into a sprawling resort that attracts skiers from around the world. Stretching for 3 miles, it encompasses eight trail-connected peaks, six terrain parks, a super-pipe, and multiple glade areas. There's night skiing on midwinter weekends. Sunday River has three base areas and several lodging choices, including condos and two slope-side hotels: the family-friendly Grand Summit, at one of the mountain bases, and the more upscale Jordan Grand, near a summit at the resort's western end. (It's really up there, several miles by vehicle from the base areas, but during ski season there's a shuttle, or you can ski over for lunch.) From the less costly Snow Cap Inn, it's a short walk to the slopes. Maine Adaptive Sports & Recreation, which serves skiers with disabilities, is at the resort, whose summer hub, the main South Ridge Base Lodge, hosts activities that include zip-lining and mountain biking. **Facilities:** 135 trails; 870 acres; 2,340-foot vertical drop; 15 lifts. ⊠ *15 S. Ridge Rd., off U.S. 2, Newry* ☎ *207/824–3000, 207/824–5200 for snow conditions, 800/543–2754 for reservations* ⊕ *www.sundayriver.com* ⛷ *Lift ticket $89.*

10

RANGELEY

66 miles north of Bethel.

Situated on the north side of Rangeley Lake along Route 4, Rangeley has long attracted anglers and winter-sports enthusiasts. The vastly forested Rangeley Lakes region has 100-plus lakes and ponds linked by rivers and streams. Right behind Main Street, Lakeside Park ("Town Park" to locals) has a large swimming area, a playground, and a boat launch. Equally popular in summer and winter, Rangeley has a rough, wilderness feel. In late January, the Rangeley Lakes Snowmobile Club's

Snodeo offers thrilling snowmobile acrobatics, fireworks, a parade, and a cook-off for which area restaurants enter their chilies and chowders. Family-friendly Saddleback ski resort is several miles from town on its namesake mountain.

GETTING HERE AND AROUND

To reach Rangeley on a scenic drive through Western Maine, take Route 17 north from U.S. 2 in Mexico to Route 4 in Oquossoc, then head east into town. Route 16 soon joins the highway and from Rangeley continues east to Sugarloaf ski resort and Kingfield.

ESSENTIALS

Vacation Rentals Morton and Furbish Vacation Rentals. ✉ *2478 Main St.* ☎ *207/864–9065, 888/218–4882* ⊕ *www.rangeleyrentals.com.*

Visitor Information Rangeley Lakes Chamber of Commerce. ✉ *6 Park Rd., off Main St.* ☎ *207/864–5364, 800/685–2537* ⊕ *www.rangeleymaine.com.*

EXPLORING

FAMILY   **Rangeley Lake State Park.** On the south shore of Rangeley Lake, this 869-acre park has superb lakeside scenery, swimming, picnic tables, a playground, a few short hiking trails, a boat ramp, and a campground. ✉ *S. Shore Dr., off Rte. 17 or Rte. 4* ☎ *207/864–3858 May–mid-Oct. only, 207/624–6080 for regional state parks office* ⊕ *www.parksandlands.com* 🗺 *$4.50* ⊙ *Daily 9–sunset (gate closed, no staff or facilities mid-Oct.–Apr.).*

FAMILY   **Rangeley Outdoor Sporting Heritage Museum.** Spruce railings and siding on the museum's facade replicate a local taxidermy shop from about 1900. The welcome center inside is an authentic log-built sporting camp from the same period, when grand hotels and full-service sporting lodges drew well-to-do "rusticators" on long stays. One of the big draws is the exhibit on local flytier Carrie Stevens, whose famed streamer flies increased the region's fly-fishing fame in the 1920s. Displays also include vintage watercraft and Native American birch-bark canoes. ✉ *8 Rumford Rd., Oquossoc* ☎ *207/864–3091* ⊕ *www.rangeleyoutdoormuseum.org* 🗺 *$5* ⊙ *May and 1st half of Oct., Thurs.–Sun. 10–4; June and Sept., Wed.–Sun. 10–4; July and Aug., daily 10–4.*

FAMILY   **Wilhelm Reich Museum.** The museum showcases the life and work of the Austrian physician and scientist Wilhelm Reich (1897–1957), who believed that all living matter and the atmosphere contained a force called orgone energy. The hilltop Orgone Energy Observatory exhibits biographical materials, inventions, and equipment used in his experiments, whose results were disputed by the Food and Drug Administration and other government agencies. The observatory deck has magnificent countryside views. In July and August, the museum presents engaging nature programs; trails lace the largely forested 175-acre property, which has two vacation rental cottages. Reich's tomb sits next to one of his inventions. ✉ *19 Orgonon Cir., off Rte. 4* ☎ *207/864–3443* ⊕ *www.wilhelmreichtrust.org* 🗺 *Museum $8, grounds free* ⊙ *Museum: July and Aug., Wed.–Sun. 1–5; Sept., Sat. 1–5. Grounds daily 9–5.*

WHERE TO EAT AND STAY

$$
AMERICAN

✗**Gingerbread House Restaurant.** With a fieldstone fireplace in the main dining room, tables scattered around the deck, and an antique marble soda fountain, there are lots of reasons to stop at what really does look like a giant gingerbread house at the edge of the woods. Sandwiches and burgers at lunch give way at dinnertime to crab cake appetizers big enough for a meal and entrées that include lobster mac 'n' cheese and barbecued ribs with a blueberry-chipotle sauce. Locals also come for the baked goods and the ice cream. $ *Average main: $22 ⊠ 55 Carry Rd., Oquossoc* ☎ *207/864–3602* ⊕ *www.gingerbreadhouserestaurant. net* ⊙ *Closed late Oct.–Nov. and Apr.; Mon.–Thurs. Dec.–Mar.; Mon. and Tues. May–late June; and Mon. early Sept.–late Oct.*

$
B&B/INN
FAMILY

⛳ **Country Club Inn.** Built in 1920 as the country club for the adjacent Mingo Springs Golf Course, this hilltop retreat has sweeping mountain and lake views and plenty of charm. **Pros:** super-helpful staff; discount coupons for neighboring golf course; pool and sledding hill. **Cons:** rooms in main building are smaller; no TV in rooms. $ *Rooms from: $169 ⊠ 56 Country Club Rd., off Rte. 4* ☎ *207/864–3831* ⊕ *www. countryclubinnrangeley.com* ⊙ *Closed Nov.–late Dec. and mid-Apr.– mid-May* ⤳ *19 rooms* ❏|*Some meals.*

$
HOTEL

⛳ **The Rangeley Inn.** Painted eggshell blue, this historic downtown hotel was built around 1900 for wealthy urbanites on vacation. **Pros:** Continental breakfast in elegant original dining room; impressive baths (some with claw-foot tubs); canoeing and kayaking on Hayley Pond. **Cons:** no elevator; restaurant open only for dinner. $ *Rooms from: $145 ⊠ 2443 Main St.* ☎ *207/864–3341* ⊕ *www.therangeleyinn.com* ⊙ *Closed Nov. and late Apr.* ⤳ *41 rooms, 4 suites* ❏|*Breakfast.*

SPORTS AND THE OUTDOORS

BOATING AND FISHING

Rangeley and Mooselookmeguntic lakes are good for canoeing, kayaking, sailing, fishing, and motorboating. Several outfits rent equipment and provide guide service if needed. Lake fishing for brook trout and landlocked salmon is at its best in May, June, and September. The Rangeley area's rivers and streams are especially popular with fly-fishers, who enjoy the sport May–October.

GOLF

Mingo Springs Golf Course. This popular course is known for its mountain and water views. The course is short but challenging, with very angled drives. The front 9 holes are the hilliest; the back 9 holes the longest. You can also take in the views and spot wildlife on the Mingo Springs Trail & Bird Walk, an easy 3-mile loop trail through the woods along the course. ⊠ *43 Country Club Rd.* ✛ *From Rte. 4 head south on Proctor Rd.* ☎ *207/864–5021* ⊕ *www.mingosprings.com* ✉ *$32 for 9 holes, $44 for 18 holes* ⅃ *18 holes, 6024 yards, par 71.*

SEAPLANES

Acadian Seaplanes. In addition to 15- to 90-minute scenic flights high above the mountains by seaplane or helicopter, this operator offers enticing "fly-in" excursions. You can travel by seaplane to wilderness locales to fish, dine at a sporting camp, spot moose in their natural

10

habitat, observe nature, or go white-water rafting on the remote Rapid River. Arcadian also provides charter service between Rangeley and Portland, Boston, and New York. ⊠ *2640 Main St.* ☎ *207/864–5307* ⊕ *www.acadianseaplanes.com* ✉ *From $99.*

SKI AREAS

Rangeley Lakes Trails Center. About 35 miles of groomed cross-country and snowshoe trails stretch along the side of Saddleback Mountain. The trail network is largely wooded and leads to Saddleback Lake. A yurt lodge has ski and snowshoe rentals and a snack bar known for tasty soups. In warmer weather, the trails are popular with mountain bikers, hikers, and runners. ⊠ *524 Saddleback Mountain Rd., off Rte. 4, Dallas* ☎ *207/864–4309* ⊕ *www.rangeleylakestrailscenter.com* ✉ *$19 ($9 for snowshoe).*

FAMILY **Saddleback Maine.** A family atmosphere prevails at this resort that entices many return visitors with its relatively thin crowds, affordable prices, and spectacular valley views. The beginner ski area is one of New England's best, partly because it is *below* the base lodge. At the other end of the spectrum, it's black diamonds all the way down at Kennebago Steeps!, touted as the East's largest steep-skiing area. Saddleback also has several glade areas and three terrain parks. A fieldstone fireplace keeps things warm in the post-and-beam base lodge, which has a second-story pub with views of Saddleback Lake. Lodging choices include ski-in, ski-out homes and trailside condos. Summer guests enjoy hiking. At time of writing a sale of the property was being negotiated, with the prospective new owners likely to initiate major upgrades. **Facilities:** 66 trails; 220 acres; 2,000-foot vertical drop; 5 lifts. ⊠ *976 Saddleback Mountain Rd., off Rte. 4, Dallas* ☎ *207/864–5671, 866/918–2225* ⊕ *www.saddlebackmaine.com* ✉ *Lift ticket $69.*

KINGFIELD

38 miles east of Rangeley.

In the shadows of Mt. Abraham ("Mt. Abram" to locals) and Sugarloaf Mountain, home to the eponymous ski resort, Kingfield has everything a "real" New England town should have: a general store, historic inns, and white clapboard churches.

ESSENTIALS

Visitor Information Franklin County Chamber of Commerce. ⊠ *615 Wilton Rd., Farmington* ☎ *207/778–4215* ⊕ *www.franklincountymaine.org.*

EXPLORING

Stanley Museum. Original Stanley Steamer cars built by twin brothers Francis and Freelan Stanley—Kingfield's most famous natives—are the main draw at this museum inside a 1903 Georgian-style former school. Also worth a look are the exhibits about the glass-negative photography business the twins sold to Eastman Kodak, and the well-composed photographs, taken by their sister, Chansonetta Stanley Emmons, of everyday country life at the turn of the 20th century. ⊠ *40 School St.* ☎ *207/265–2729* ⊕ *www.stanleymuseum.org* ✉ *$4* ☉ *June–Oct., Tues.–Sun. 11–4; Nov.–May, Tues.–Fri. 11–4; by appt. at other times.*

SPORTS AND THE OUTDOORS
SKI AREAS

FAMILY **Sugarloaf Mountain Resort.** An eye-catching setting, abundant natural snow, and the only above-the-tree line lift-service skiing in the East have made Sugarloaf one of Maine's best-known ski resorts. Glade areas, three terrain parks, a border-cross track, and a super pipe amp up the skiing options. There are two slope-side hotels and hundreds of slope-side condos with ski-in, ski-out access. Sugarloaf Mountain Hotel is in the ski village; the smaller, more affordable Sugarloaf Inn is a bit down the mountain. The Outdoor Center has more than 90 miles of cross-country ski trails, and you can snowshoe and ice-skate. Indoor skateboarding and trampolining are among the many kids-oriented activities. Once at Sugarloaf, you'll find a car unnecessary—a shuttle connects all mountain operations. The ski season runs November–May. Summer is much quieter, but you can mountain bike, hike, zip-line, take a moose safari, or play a round of golf. **Facilities:** 122 trails; 1,240 acres; 2,820-foot vertical drop; 14 lifts. ✉ *5092 Access Rd., Carrabassett Valley* ☎ *207/237–2000, 800/843–5623 for reservations* ⊕ *www.sugarloaf. com* ✉ *Lift ticket $86.*

THE NORTH WOODS

Moosehead Lake, Baxter State Park, the Allagash Wilderness Waterway, and the four-season resort town of Greenville are dispersed within Maine's remote North Woods. This vast area in the state's north-central section is best experienced by canoe, kayak, or white-water raft; along the hiking, snowshoeing, cross-country-skiing, or snowmobiling trails; or on a fishing trip. As Maine's largest lake, Moosehead supplies more in the way of rustic camps, guides, and outfitters than any other northern locale. Its 400-plus miles of shorefront, three-quarters of which is owned by lumber companies or the state, are virtually uninhabited.

GREENVILLE

155 miles northeast of Portland; 70 miles northwest of Bangor.

Greenville, tucked at the southern end of island-dotted, mostly forest-lined Moosehead Lake, is an outdoors lover's paradise. Boating, fishing, and hiking are popular in summer, snowmobiling and ice fishing in winter. The town has the best selection of shops, restaurants, and inns in the North Woods region. Restaurants and lodgings are also clustered 20 miles north in Rockwood, where the Moose River flows through the village and—across from Mt. Kineo's majestic cliff face—into the lake.

GETTING HERE AND AROUND

To reach Greenville from Interstate 95, get off at Exit 157 in Newport and head north, successively, on Routes 7, 23, and 15.

ESSENTIALS

Vacation Rentals Northwoods Camp Rentals. ✉ *14 Lakeview St.* ☎ *800/251–8042, 207/695–4300* ⊕ *www.mooseheadrentals.com.*

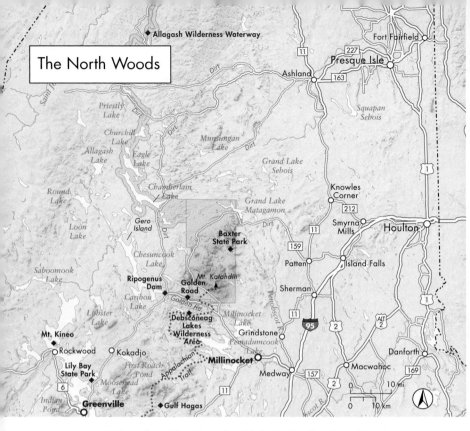

The North Woods

- Allagash Wilderness Waterway
- Fort Fairfield
- Presque Isle
- Ashland
- Priestly Lake
- Squapan Sebois
- Churchill Lake
- Munsungan Lake
- Allagash Lake
- Eagle Lake
- Grand Lake Sebois
- Round Lake
- Chamberlain Lake
- Knowles Corner
- Loon Lake
- Gero Island
- Grand Lake Matagamon
- Smyrna Mills
- Houlton
- Chesuncook Lake
- Baxter State Park
- Saboomook Lake
- Patten
- Island Falls
- Ripogenus Dam
- Mt. Katahdin
- Golden Road
- Sherman
- Caribou Lake
- Golden Rd.
- Lobster Lake
- Millinocket Lake
- Mt. Kineo
- Debsconeag Lakes Wilderness Area
- Grindstone
- Rockwood
- Kokadjo
- Pemadumcook Lake
- Danforth
- Lily Bay State Park
- First Roach Pond
- Millinocket
- Macwahoc
- Moosehead Lake
- Medway
- Greenville
- Gulf Hagas
- Indian Pond

Visitor Information Moosehead Lake Region Chamber of Commerce. ⊠ 480 Moosehead Lake Rd. ☎ 207/695–2702 ⊕ www.mooseheadlake.org.

EXPLORING

FAMILY **Lily Bay State Park.** Nine miles northeast of Greenville on Moosehead Lake, this park has good lakefront swimming, a 1.6-mile walking trail with water views, two boat-launching ramps, a playground, and two campgrounds with a total of 90 sites. In winter, the entrance road is plowed to access the groomed cross-country ski trails and the lake for ice fishing and snowmobiling. ⊠ *State Park Rd. and Lily Bay Rd., Beaver Cove* ☎ *207/695–2700 mid-May–mid-Oct. only, 207/941–4014 for regional parks bureau office* ⊕ *www.parksandlands.com* ☝ *$4.50* ⊗ *Daily 9–sunset (no staff mid-Oct.–mid-May; limited road access during snow season).*

FAMILY **Moosehead Historical Society & Museums.** Guides in period costume lead
Fodor's Choice tours of the Eveleth-Crafts-Sheridan House, a late-19th-century Victo-
★ rian mansion filled with antiques, most of them original to the home. The Lumberman's Museum, with exhibits about the region's logging history, is in the carriage house, and the barn next door houses a re-creation of a one-room schoolhouse and a general-store display. You can savor lunch and the architecture of these meticulously main-tained buildings from the art-accented Sunken Garden. A mile away

CLOSE UP

Rafting in the North Woods

Virtually all of Maine's white-water rafting takes place between the dam-controlled Kennebec and Dead rivers, which meet at The Forks in Western Maine, and on the West Branch of the Penobscot River, near Millinocket in the North Woods. Guided single- or multiday excursions run rain or shine daily from spring (late April on the Kennebec, early May on the Dead, and mid-May on the Penobscot) to mid-October.

Maine is New England's premier destination for the sport, which is why thousands of people come here every year to ride the waves. The Kennebec is known for abundant big waves and splashes; the Dead has New England's longest stretch of continuous white water, some 16 miles. The most challenging rapids are on the West Branch of the Penobscot River, a Class V river on the southern border of Baxter State Park outside Millinocket.

Many rafting outfitters operate resort facilities in their base towns. It's not uncommon for outfitters to run trips in both the Millinocket region and The Forks. On family-friendly rafting trips you can explore some of the gentler stretches of these mighty rivers. North Country Rivers, based south of The Forks in Bingham, and New England Outdoor Center, outside Millinocket, are leading white-water-rafting outfitters. The website of **Raft Maine** (⊕ *www.raftmaine.com*), an association of licensed outfitters, has answers to basic questions about everything from what happens on white-water trips to what to wear and when to go. Many companies offer packages that include lodging.

---

in downtown Greenville, the former Universalist Church houses the Center for Moosehead History and Moosehead Lake Aviation Museum. The former has a fine exhibit of Native American artifacts from the Moosehead Lake region, dating from 9,000 BC to the 1700s. The latter focuses on the impact of aviation on the area, from early bush pilots to Greenville's annual International Seaplane Fly-in. ✉ *444 Pritham Ave., Greenville Junction* ☎ *207/695–2909* ⊕ *www.mooseheadhistory.org* ✉ *Eveleth-Crafts-Sheridan House $5, other museums free* ⊗ *Eveleth-Crafts-Sheridan House: mid-June–early Oct., Wed.–Fri. 1–4; Lumberman's Museum Tues.–Fri. 9–4; Center for Moosehead History and Moosehead Lake Aviation Museum: mid-June–mid-Oct., Thurs.–Sun. 10–4.*

10

OFF THE BEATEN PATH

Mt. Kineo. Accessible primarily by steamship, Mt. Kineo House was a thriving upscale summer resort set below its namesake's 700-foot cliff on an islandlike peninsula jutting into Moosehead Lake. The last of three successive hotels with this name was built in 1884 and became America's largest inland waterfront hotel. It was torn down in 1938, but Kineo remains a pleasant day trip. Mt. Kineo State Park occupies most of the 1,200-acre peninsula, with trails to the summit of the spectacular landmark. You can also play a round on Mt. Kineo Golf Course, one of the oldest courses in New England. There is no road access, but you can take a 15-minute boat trip from Rockwood on the golf course's seasonal shuttle. ✉ *Kineo Dock, Village Rd., Rockwood*

☎ *207/534–9012 for golf course and shuttle, 207/941–4014 for park regional office* 🌐 *www.parksandlands.com* 🎟 *$3* 🕒 *Daily 9–sunset.*

WHERE TO STAY

$$$ RESORT FAMILY Fodor's Choice ★ 🏨 **Appalachian Mountain Club Maine Wilderness Lodges.** When you want to get away from it all, head to the Appalachian Mountain Club's 70,000 acres in Maine's 100-Mile Wilderness, where you can choose between two historic sporting-camp retreats: Gorman Chairback and Little Lyford. **Pros:** great for outdoors lovers; sauna; made-to-order trail lunch. **Cons:** winter access only by cross-country skis or snowmobile transport (fee). [$] *Rooms from: $374* ✉ *Off Katahdin Iron Works Rd.* ☎ *603/466–2727* 🌐 *www.outdoors.org/lodging/mainelodges* 🕒 *Closed mid-Mar.–mid-May and late Oct.–late Dec.* 🛏 *Gorman Chairback: 12 cabins, 1 bunkhouse (sleeps 10); Little Lyford: 10 cabins, 1 bunkhouse (sleeps 12)* 🍴 *All meals.*

$$$ B&B/INN Fodor's Choice ★ 🏨 **Blair Hill Inn.** Beautiful gardens and a hilltop location with marvelous views over the lake distinguish this 1891 country estate, one of New England's top inns. **Pros:** free concierge plans outdoor excursions; amazing restaurant; 15-acre property with stone paths, wooded picnic area, and trout pond; lake view views from all but one room. **Cons:** pricey; no direct lake access. [$] *Rooms from: $399* ✉ *351 Lily Bay Rd.* ☎ *207/695–0224* 🌐 *www.blairhill.com* 🕒 *Closed mid-Oct.–Apr.* 🛏 *8 rooms, 1 suite* 🍴 *Breakfast.*

SPORTS AND THE OUTDOORS

Togue (lake trout), landlocked salmon, smallmouth bass, and brook trout attract anglers to the region from ice-out in mid-May until September; the hardiest return in winter to ice fish.

MULTI-SPORT OUTFITTERS

Moose Country Safaris & Eco Tours. This outfit leads moose-spotting and bird-watching excursions; snowshoe, hiking, and canoe trips; and tours highlighting waterfalls, late-summer meteor showers, and an ice cave near Baxter State Park. ✉ *191 N. Dexter Rd., Sangerville* ☎ *207/876–4907* 🌐 *www.moosecountrysafaris.com* 🎟 *From $88.*

Northwoods Outfitters. You can rent canoes, kayaks, camping equipment, ATVs, bikes, snowmobiles, snowshoes, skates, ski equipment, snowboards, and winter clothing here. Northwoods organizes a host of outdoor trips, including fishing and moose-watching (by land or water), and operates a shuttle to remote areas. At the base in downtown Greenville, you can pick up sporting goods, get trail advice, or kick back in the Internet café. ✉ *5 Lily Bay Rd.* ☎ *207/695–3288, 866/223–1380* 🌐 *www.maineoutfitter.com.*

BOATING

Allagash Canoe Trips. Run by a husband and wife, both championship paddlers and Registered Maine Guides, Allagash offers single-day, overnight, and weeklong canoe trips on the Allagash Wilderness Waterway, the Moose and St. John rivers, and the East and West branches of the Penobscot River. White-water canoe and kayak trips are run on the Kennebec and Dead rivers. The company also conducts clinics on white-water paddling and kayaking and canoe poling. ✉ *156 Scammon Rd.* ☎ *207/280–1551, 207/280–0191* 🌐 *www.allagashcanoetrips.com* 🎟 *From $225.*

SEAPLANES

Currier's Flying Service. You can take sightseeing flights over the Moosehead Lake region with Currier's from ice-out until mid-October. ✉ *447 Pritham Ave., Greenville Junction* ☎ *207/695–2778* ⊕ *www. curriersflyingservice.com* 💲 *From $40.*

TOURS

Katahdin Cruises. The Moosehead Marine Museum runs 3- and 4½-hour afternoon trips on Moosehead Lake aboard the *Katahdin,* a 115-foot 1914 steamship converted to diesel. (The longer trip skirts Mt. Kineo's cliffs.) Also called the *Kate,* this ship carried resort guests to Mt. Kineo until 1938; the logging industry then used it until 1975. The boat and the free shore-side museum have displays about these steamships, which transported people and cargo on Moosehead Lake for a century starting in the 1830s. ✉ *12 Lily Bay Rd.* ☎ *207/695–2716* ⊕ *www.katahdincruises.com* 💲 *From $33* ☽ *Cruises: late June–mid-Oct., Tues.–Sat. at 12:30. Museum: late June–mid-Oct., Sun. and Mon. noon–4, Tues.–Sat. 10–4.*

OFF THE BEATEN PATH

Gulf Hagas. Called the "Grand Canyon of the East," this National Natural Landmark has chasms, cliffs, four major waterfalls, pools, exotic flora, and intriguing rock formations. Part of the Appalachian Trail Corridor, the slate-walled gorge east of Greenville is located in a remote, privately owned commercial forest, KI Jo-Mary, which allows access to it via gravel logging roads (always yield to trucks). A fee is usually charged at forest checkpoints, where you can also get trail maps and hiking information.

From either parking area you can hike to one of the showcase falls and mostly avoid the difficult rim trail. Start at Head of Gulf parking area for a 3½-mile round-trip hike, a good choice for families with young children, to Stair Falls on the gorge's western end. From the Gulf Hagas parking area, a 3-mile round-trip hike takes you to spectacular Screw Auger Falls on the gulf's eastern end. Gulf hikers who start from this parking area must ford the Pleasant River—easily done in summer, but dangerous in high water—and pass through the Hermitage, a stand of old pines and hemlock. A loop route that follows the rim and the less difficult Pleasant River Tote Trail is an 8- to 9-mile trek; there are shorter loops as well. Slippery rocks and rugged terrain make for challenging progress along the rim trail. ✉ *Greenville* ✛ *From Greenville, travel 11 miles east via Pleasant St., which eventually becomes Katahdin Iron Works Rd., to the Hedgehog checkpoint. Follow signs to the parking areas: Head of Gulf, 2½ miles; Gulf Hagas, 6½ miles* ⊕ *www.northmainewoods.org.*

10

MILLINOCKET

67 miles north of Bangor, 88 miles northwest of Greenville.

Millinocket, a former paper-mill town with a population of about 4,000, is a gateway to Baxter State Park and Maine's North Woods. Millinocket is the place to stock up on supplies, fill your gas tank, and grab a hot meal or shower before heading into the wilderness. Numerous rafting and canoeing outfitters and guides are based in the region.

GETTING HERE AND AROUND

From Interstate 95, take Route 157 (Exit 244) west to Millinocket. From here follow signs to Baxter State Park (Millinocket Lake Road becomes Baxter Park State Road), 18 miles from town.

ESSENTIALS

Visitor Information Katahdin Area Chamber of Commerce. ⊠ *1029 Central St.* ☎ *207/723–4443* ⊕ *www.katahdinmaine.com.*

EXPLORING

Allagash Wilderness Waterway. A spectacular 92-mile corridor of lakes, ponds, streams, and rivers, the waterway park cuts through vast commercial forests, beginning near the northwestern corner of Baxter State Park and running north to the town of Allagash, 10 miles from the Canadian border. From May to mid-October, the Allagash is prime canoeing and camping country. The Maine Bureau of Parks and Lands has campsites along the waterway, most not accessible by vehicle. The complete 92-mile course, part of the 740-mile Northern Forest Canoe Trail, which runs from New York to Maine, requires 7–10 days to canoe. Novices may want hire a guide, as there are many areas with strong rapids. A good outfitter can help plan your route and provide equipment and transportation. ⊠ *Millinocket* ☎ *207/941–4014 for regional parks bureau office* ⊕ *www.parksandlands.com.*

FAMILY

Fodor's Choice

★

Baxter State Park. A gift from Governor Percival Baxter, this is the jewel in the crown of northern Maine: a 210,000-acre wilderness area that surrounds **Mt. Katahdin,** Maine's highest mountain and the terminus of the Appalachian Trail. Every year, the 5,267-foot Katahdin draws thousands of hikers to make the daylong summit, rewarding them with stunning views of forests, mountains, and lakes. There are three parking-lot trailheads for Katahdin, including the one for Abol Trail (closed since 2014 because of landslide activity but likely to reopen in 2016). Depart from the Roaring Branch trailhead for a route that includes the hair-raising Knife Edge Ridge. ■TIP➔ Reserve a day-use parking space at the trailheads May 15–October 15.

The crowds climbing Katahdin can be formidable on clear summer days and fall weekends, so if it's solitude you crave, tackle one of the park's many other mountains. All are accessible from the extensive trail network, and 14 peaks exceed an elevation of 3,000 feet. The Brothers and Doubletop Mountain are challenging daylong hikes; the Owl takes about six hours; and South Turner can be climbed in a morning—its summit has a great view across the valley. A trek around Daicey Pond, or from the pond to Big and Little Niagara Falls, are good options for families with young kids. Another option if you only have a couple of hours is renting a canoe at Daicey or Togue ponds. Park roads are unpaved, narrow, and winding, and there are no pay phones, gas stations, or stores. Camping is primitive and reservations are required; there are 10 campgrounds plus backcountry sites. ⊠ *Baxter State Park Rd.* ⊹ *Togue Pond Gate (park's southern entrance) is 18 miles northwest of Millinocket; follow signs from Rte. 157* ☎ *207/723–5140, 207/723–4636 for hiking hotline* ⊕ *www. baxterstateparkauthority.com* ⊠ *$14 per vehicle* ☉ *Mid-May–mid-Oct., daily 6 am–10 pm; mid-Oct.–mid-May, daily sunrise–sunset.*

Debsconeag Lakes Wilderness Area. Bordering the south side of the Golden Road below Baxter State Park, the Nature Conservancy's 46,271-acre Debsconeag Lakes Wilderness Area is renowned for its rare ice cave, old forests, abundant pristine ponds, and views of Mt. Katahdin. The access road for the Ice Cave Trail (2 miles round-trip) and Hurd Pond is 17 miles northwest of Millinocket, just west of the Golden Road's Abol Bridge. Near here the Appalachian Trail exits the conservancy land, crossing the bridge en route to Baxter. Before hiking, paddling, fishing, or camping in the remote preserve (no fees or reservations required) visit the conservancy's website for directions and other information. The Golden Road accesses are marked, but the signs aren't large. There are trail kiosks and marked trailheads within the preserve. ⊠ *Golden Rd.* ⊕ *www.nature.org/maine.*

SCENIC DRIVE

Golden Road. For a scenic North Woods drive, set off on the roughly 20-mile stretch of this private east–west logging road near Baxter State Park northwest of Millinocket. Have patience with ruts and bumps, and yield to logging trucks (keep right!). From Millinocket follow the signs for Baxter State Park from Route 157. This scenic drive begins about 9 miles from town, at the crossover from Millinocket Lake Road to the Golden Road, the latter named for the huge sum a paper company paid to build it.

The North Woods Trading Post, a great stop for takeout and souvenirs and the last place to gas up before Baxter, is at this junction, across from Ambajejus Lake. From here it's about 9 miles on the Golden Road to one-lane Abol Bridge, which has parking areas on both sides. Take photos of Baxter's Mt. Katahdin from the footbridge alongside the bridge: this view is famous. Abol Bridge Campground, with a restaurant and store, is right before the bridge. Just beyond it is an access road for Debsconeag Lakes Wilderness Area. From here the road flows alongside the West Branch of the Penobscot River.

At the western end of the drive, the river drops 70-plus feet per mile through Ripogenus Gorge, giving white-water rafters a thrilling ride during scheduled releases from Ripogenus Dam. The Crib Works Rapid (Class V) overlook is off the Golden Road about 10 miles from Abol Bridge. (Turn right on Telos Road; parking is on the right after the bridge.) To drive across the dam on Ripogenus Lake and view the gorge, return to the Golden Road and continue west to Rip Dam Road, which veers right about a mile after Telos Road. Returning to the crossover at the North Woods Trading Post, turn left for Baxter or right for Millinocket. ⊠ *Golden Rd.*

10

SPORTS AND THE OUTDOORS
MULTI-SPORT OUTFITTERS
Katahdin Outfitters. This company provides gear and shuttles for overnight canoe and kayak expeditions on the Allagash Wilderness Waterway, the West Branch of the Penobscot River, and the St. John River. They also rent canoes and kayaks from their location just outside

Millinocket at the base of Wilderness Edge Campground. ⊠ *Millinocket* ☎ *207/723–5700* ⊕ *www.katahdinoutfitters.com* ⊠ *Call for prices.*

FAMILY
Fodor's Choice
★
New England Outdoor Center (*NEOC*). With Baxter State Park's Mt. Katahdin rising above the shore opposite both its locations, this business helps visitors enjoy the North Woods. Its year-round home base, NEOC/Twin Pines on Millinocket Lake, 8 miles from the park's southern entrance, has rental cabins and a restaurant and conducts many guided trips, some within the park. Older log cabins (and a few newer ones) sit beneath tall pines on a grassy nub of land that juts into Millinocket Lake; upscale "green" units (spacious lodges and cozy cabins) are tucked among trees on a cove. Amenities include kayaks and canoes for use on the lake and a recreation center with a sauna.

At the deservedly popular **River Driver's Restaurant,** wood for the trim, wainscoting, bar, and floors was milled from old logs salvaged from local waters. Diners enjoy views of Katahdin from behind rows of windows or from the patio, and your dish may feature farm-to-table fare from the center's own gardens.

In addition to offering a full slate of guided snowmobiling, fishing, canoe, kayak, hiking, and moose-spotting trips, NEOC rents canoes, kayaks, and paddleboards, gives paddling lessons, and rents snowmobiles. Trails for hiking, cross-country skiing (11 miles, groomed), and mountain biking are right on the 1,400-acre property. About 2 miles from Baxter, the seasonal Penobscot Outdoor Center is the base for white-water rafting trips on the West Branch of the Penobscot River. The center also has a wooded campground on Pockwockamus Pond. There are tent sites as well as canvas tents and simple wood-frame cabins with cots or bunks. A circular fireplace anchors the open-plan base lodge, which has a snack bar, a pub area, a hot tub, pool tables, and a communal outdoor fire pit. A towering window wall reveals glimpses of water through trees, and there are campsites near the water with Katahdin views. ■ TIP→ Nonguests can use showers for $2 after hiking or camping at Baxter. ⊠ *30 Twin Pines Rd.* ✛ *From Millinocket Lake Rd., take Black Cat Rd. east 1 mile* ☎ *207/723–5438, 800/766–7238* ⊕ *www.neoc.com.*

North Country Rivers. From spring to fall, North Country Rivers runs white-water rafting trips on the Dead and Kennebec rivers in The Forks in western Maine, and on the West Branch of Penobscot River outside Millinocket in the North Woods. North Country's 55-acre resort south of The Forks in Bingham has cabin and cottage rentals, a restaurant, pub, and store; its Millinocket base is the Big Moose Inn. The outfitter also offers moose and wildlife safaris and rents snowmobiles, mountain and trail bikes, and kayaks. ⊠ *36 Main St., Bingham* ☎ *207/672–4814, 800/348–8871* ⊕ *www.northcountryrivers.com.*

MAINE COAST

WELCOME TO MAINE COAST

TOP REASONS TO GO

★ **Lobster and Wild Maine Blueberries:** It's not a Maine vacation unless you don a bib and dig into a steamed lobster with drawn butter, and finish with a wild blueberry pie for dessert.

★ **Boating:** The coastline of Maine was made for boaters: whether it's your own boat, a friend's, or a charter, make sure you get out on the water.

★ **Hiking the Bold Coast:** Miles of unspoiled coastal and forest paths Down East make for a hiker's (and a bird-watcher's) dream.

★ **Cadillac Mountain:** Drive a winding 3½ miles to the 1,530-foot summit in Acadia National Park for the sunrise.

★ **Dining in Portland:** With over 250 restaurants and counting, Forest City is a foodie haven with one of the highest per-capita restaurant densities in the U.S.

1 The Southern Coast. Stretching north from Kittery to just outside Portland, this is Maine's most visited region; miles of sandy expanses and shore towns cater to summer visitors. Kittery, the Yorks, Wells, and the Kennebunks offer low-key getaways, while Biddeford—a stone's throw from Portland—is on the rise, with charming boutiques and top-notch restaurants.

2 Portland. Maine's largest and most cosmopolitan city, Portland balances its historic role as a working harbor with its newer identity as a foodie mecca and the center of a thriving arts community.

3 The Mid-Coast Region. North of Portland, from Brunswick to Monhegan Island, the craggy coastline winds its way around pastoral peninsulas. Its villages boast maritime museums, innovative restaurants, antiques shops, and beautiful architecture.

(Map showing the Maine coast with locations including Waterville, Augusta, Lewiston, Auburn, Waldoboro, Newcastle, Damariscotta, Brunswick, Freeport, Bath, Boothbay, Phippsburg, Georgetown, Yarmouth, Falmouth, Portland, Casco Bay, Saco, Old Orchard Beach, Sanford, Biddeford, Kennebunk, Kennebunkport, Wells, Ogunquit, York, Kittery, Portsmouth, NEW HAMPSHIRE. Scale: 0–20 mi, 0–20 km.)

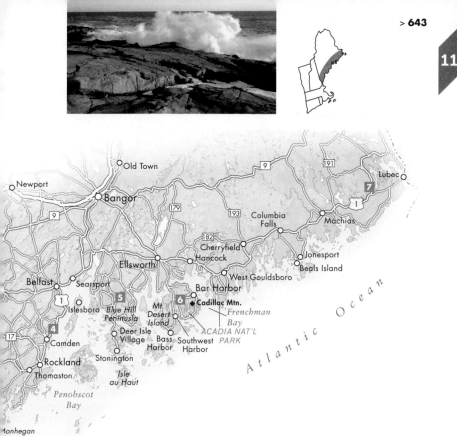

4 Penobscot Bay. This region's dramatic natural scenery highlights its lively coastal towns, and Camden is one of Maine's most picture-perfect, with pointed church steeples, historic homes, a cozy harbor, and celebrated windjammer fleet.

5 The Blue Hill Peninsula. Art galleries are plentiful here, and the entire region is ideal for biking, hiking, kayaking, and boating. For many, the peninsula epitomizes the silent beauty of the Maine Coast.

6 Acadia National Park and Mount Desert Island. Millions come to enjoy Acadia National Park's stunning peaks and vistas. Bar Harbor is fun to explore, with its many gift shops and restaurants, while Southwest Harbor and Bass Harbor offer quieter retreats.

7 Way Down East. The "real Maine," as some call it, unfurls in thousands of acres of wild blueberry barrens, congestion-free coastlines, vast wilderness preserves, and a tangible sense of rugged endurance.

GETTING ORIENTED

Much of the appeal of the Maine Coast lies in geographical contrasts—from its long stretches of swimming and walking beaches in the south to the rugged, rocky cliffs in the north. As the shoreline physically evolves, so each town along the way reveals a distinct character.

Updated by
Grace-Yvette
Gemmell

As you drive across the border into Maine, a sign reads, "The way life should be." It's a slogan that's hard to argue with once you've spent some time in the Pine Tree State. Here, time stays in step with you, and Mainers take their play just as seriously as their work.

Romantics thrill at the wind and salt spray in their faces on a historic windjammer. Birders fill their notebooks to the brim with new field notes. Families love the unspoiled beaches and sheltered inlets dotting the shoreline—not to mention the numerous homemade-ice-cream stands. Foodies revel in greater Portland's booming restaurant scene, while artists and art lovers find inspiration both on and off the canvas amid art galleries and museums or along the craggy seaboard. Adventure-seekers find many opportunities to kayak and cycle at the Bold Coast and Acadia National Park, whose trails invigorate hikers with their natural beauty. At night, the sky is dark enough to spot rare constellations and experience the magic of auroras.

The Maine Coast is several places in one. Classic New England townscapes with picturesque downtowns mingle with rocky shorelines punctuated by sandy beaches and secluded coves with sweeping views of lighthouses, forested islands, and the wide-open sea. So, no matter what strikes your fancy—a spontaneous picnic on the beach or a sunset cruise with a bottle of local wine, an afternoon exploring hidden tide pools or a dose of culture followed by shopping and dining in town—there's something to suit every disposition.

Counting all its nooks, crannies, and crags, Maine's coast would stretch thousands of miles if you could pull it straight, which means there's always some new, undiscovered territory awaiting you. Stretching north from Kittery to just outside Portland, the Southern Coast is the most popular area, with many top-notch restaurants, museums, and wineries. Don't let that stop you from heading further Down East (Maine-speak for "way up the coast"), where you'll be rewarded with the majestic mountains and rugged coastline of Acadia National Park, as well as the unspoiled, dramatic scenery of the Bold Coast.

PLANNING

WHEN TO GO

Maine's dramatic coastline and pure natural beauty welcome visitors year-round, but note that many smaller museums and attractions are open only in high season (Memorial Day–mid-October), as are many waterside attractions and eateries.

Summer begins in earnest on July 4th, and you'll find that many smaller inns, B&Bs, and hotels from Kittery on up to Bar Harbor are booked a month or two in advance for dates through August. That's also the case come fall, when the fiery foliage draws leaf peepers. After Halloween, hotel rates drop significantly until ski season begins around Thanksgiving. Bed-and-breakfasts that stay open year-round but are not near ski slopes will often rent rooms at far lower prices than in summer.

In spring, the fourth Sunday in March is designated as Maine Maple Sunday, and farms throughout the state open their doors to visitors not only to watch sap turn into golden syrup but to sample the sweet results.

PLANNING YOUR TIME

You could easily spend a lifetime's worth of vacations along the Maine Coast and never truly see it all. But if you are determined to travel the coast end-to-end, allot at least two weeks at a comfortable pace. Count on longer transit time getting from place to place in summer, as traffic along Route 1 can be agonizing in high season, especially in the areas around Wiscasset and Acadia National Park.

Driving in Coastal Maine		
	Miles	Time
Boston–Portland	112	2 hours
Kittery–Portland	50	50 minutes
Portland–Freeport	18	20 minutes
Portland–Camden	80	2 hours
Portland–Bar Harbor	175	3 hours, 20 minutes

GETTING HERE AND AROUND

AIR TRAVEL

Maine has two major international airports, Portland International Jetport and Bangor International Airport, to get you to or close to your coastal destination. Manchester–Boston Regional Airport in New Hampshire is about 45 minutes away from the southern end of the Maine coastline. Boston's Logan Airport is the only truly international airport in the region; it's about 90 minutes south of the Maine border.

CAR TRAVEL

Once you are here the best way to experience the winding back roads of the craggy Maine Coast is in a car. There are miles and miles of roads far from the larger towns that have no bus service, and you won't want to miss the chance to discover your own favorite ocean vista while on a scenic drive.

BUS TRAVEL

The Shoreline Explorer links seasonal trolleys in southern Maine beach towns from the Yorks to the Kennebunks, allowing you to travel between towns without a car. Concord Coach Lines has express service between Portland and Boston's Logan Airport and South Station. Concord operates out of the Portland Transportation Center (⊠ *100 Thompson's Point Rd.*).

FAMILY **Shoreline Explorer.** Running late June–Labor Day, the Shoreline Explorer offers seasonal trolley and shuttle service along the southern Maine coast. With links to private trolley operators in Kennebunkport, Ogunquit, and York, the service also provides access to the Amtrak Downeaster at Wells, as well as to the Sanford Regional Airport. Many lines have bicycle racks and wheelchair lifts, as well as stops close to trailheads for hiking. The Shoreline Explorer's Orange Line 5 offers year-round shuttle service with a bike rack from Sanford to Wells. A Day Pass or Multipass can be purchased from the driver. ☎ *207/459–2932* ⊕ *www.shorelineexplorer.com.*

TRAIN TRAVEL

Amtrak offers regional service from Boston to Portland via its Downeaster line, which originates at Boston's North Station and makes six stops in Maine: Wells, Saco, Old Orchard Beach (seasonal), Portland, Freeport, and Brunswick.

RESTAURANTS

Many breakfast spots along the coast open as early as 6 am to serve the working crowd, as early as 4 am for fishermen. Lunch generally runs 11–2:30; dinner is usually served 5–9. Only in larger cities will you find full dinners offered much later than 9, although in larger towns you can usually find a bar or bistro with a limited menu available late into the evening.

Many restaurants in Maine are closed Monday. Resort areas take exception to this in high season, but these eateries often shut down altogether in the off-season. *Unless otherwise noted in reviews, restaurants are open daily for lunch and dinner.*

Credit cards are generally accepted at restaurants throughout Maine, even in more modest establishments, but it's still a good idea to have cash on hand wherever you go, just in case.

The one signature meal on the Maine Coast is, of course, the lobster dinner. It typically includes a whole boiled lobster with drawn butter for dipping, a clam or seafood chowder, corn on the cob, coleslaw, and a bib. Lobster prices vary from day to day, but generally a full lobster dinner should cost around $25–$30, or about $18–$20 without all the extras. *Prices in the reviews are the average cost of a main course at dinner or, if dinner is not served, at lunch.*

HOTELS

Beachfront and roadside motels, historic-home B&Bs and inns, as well as a handful of newer boutique hotels, make up the majority of lodging along the Maine Coast. There are a few larger luxury resorts, such as the Samoset Resort in Rockport or the Bar Harbor Inn in Bar Harbor, but most accommodations are simple, comfortable, and relatively inexpensive. You will find some chain hotels in larger cities and towns, including major tourist destinations like Portland, Freeport, and Bar Harbor. Many properties close during the off-season (mid-October–mid-May); those that stay open year-round often drop their rates dramatically after high season. (It is often possible to negotiate a nightly rate with smaller establishments during low season.) There is a 9% state hospitality tax on all room rates. *Prices in the reviews are the lowest cost of a standard double room in high season. Hotel reviews have been shortened. For full reviews visit Fodors.com.*

WHAT IT COSTS			
$	**$$**	**$$$**	**$$$$**
Restaurants	under $18	$18–$24	$25–$35	over $35
Hotels	under $200	$200–$299	$300–$399	over $399

OUTDOOR ADVENTURES

No visit to the Maine Coast is complete without some outdoor activity—on two wheels, two feet, two paddles, or pulling a bag full of clubs.

BICYCLING

Both the Bicycle Coalition of Maine and Explore Maine by Bike are excellent resources for trail maps and other riding information.

FAMILY **Bicycle Coalition of Maine.** The well-regarded Bicycle Coalition of Maine provides cyclists with essential touring information like cycling routes, safety tips, where to rent and repair bikes, and annual events. ✉ *34 Preble St., Portland* ☎ *207/623–4511* ⊕ *www.bikemaine.org.*

Explore Maine by Bike. Run by the Maine Department of Transportation, this helpful website includes an exhaustive list of the state's most popular bike routes, as well as other valuable cycling resources. ☎ *207/624–3300* ⊕ *www.exploremaine.org/bike.*

HIKING

Exploring the Maine Coast on foot is a quick way to acclimate yourself to the relaxed pace of life here—and sometimes the only way to access some of the best coastal spots. Many privately owned lands are accessible to hikers, especially way Down East. Inquire at a local establishment about hikes that may not appear on a map.

Healthy Maine Walks. The Healthy Maine Walks website has comprehensive listings and a searchable database for statewide walks that can be done in an hour or less, from park paths to routes that follow roads and streets. ⊕ *www.healthymainewalks.com.*

KAYAKING

Nothing gets you literally off the beaten path like plying the salt waters in a graceful sea kayak.

Maine Association of Sea Kayaking Guides and Instructors. This association lists state-licensed guides and offers information about instructional classes, guided tours, and trip planning. ⊕ *www.mainepaddlesports.org.*

Maine Island Trail Association. Seasoned paddlers can join the Maine Island Trail Association ($45 individual, $65 family) for a map of and full access to Maine's famous sea trail: more than 200 islands and mainland sites—most privately owned but open to members—on a 375-mile path from the southernmost coast to the Canadian Maritimes. Member benefits include discounts at outfitters and retailers. ⊠ *58 Fore St., Suite 30-3, Portland* ☎ *207/761–8225* ⊕ *www.mita.org.*

THE SOUTHERN COAST

The Maine Coast's southernmost stretch—including Kittery, the Yorks, Ogunquit, the Kennebunks, and Biddeford—features miles and miles of inviting sandy beaches and beautifully preserved historic towns and charming lighthouses. There is something for everyone here, whether you seek solitude in a kayak or the infectious conviviality of locals and fellow vacationers alike.

North of Kittery, long stretches of hard-packed white-sand beach are closely crowded by nearly unbroken ranks of beach cottages, motels, and oceanfront restaurants. The summer colonies of York Beach and Wells brim with family crowds, T-shirt and gift shops, and shorefront development; nearby wildlife refuges and land preserves promise an easy quiet escape. York Village's acclaimed historic district evokes the New England of yesteryear, while Ogunquit attracts visitors with its array of boutiques and art galleries and its paved cliff-side walk.

More than any other region south of Portland, the Kennebunks—and especially Kennebunkport—provide the complete Maine Coast experience: classic townscapes where white-clapboard houses rise from manicured lawns and gardens; rocky shorelines punctuated by sandy beaches; quaint downtown districts packed with gift shops, ice cream stands, and spas; harbors with lobster boats bobbing alongside stately yachts; and both five-star restaurants and rustic, picnic-table eateries serving fresh lobster and fried seafood.

KITTERY

65 miles north of Boston; 3 miles north of Portsmouth, New Hampshire.

Known as the "Gateway to Maine," Kittery has become primarily a major shopping destination thanks to its massive complex of factory outlets. Flanking both sides of U.S. 1 are more than 120 stores, which attract serious shoppers year-round. But Kittery has more to offer than just retail therapy: head east on Route 103 to the area around **Kittery Point** to experience the great outdoors. Here you'll find hiking and biking trails, as well as fantastic views of Portsmouth, New Hampshire, Whaleback Ledge Lighthouse, and the nearby Isles of Shoals. The isles and the light, along with two others, can be seen from two forts near this winding stretch of Route 103: Fort McClary State Historic Site and Fort Foster, a town park (both closed to vehicles off-season).

GETTING HERE AND AROUND

Three bridges—on U.S. 1, U.S. 1 Bypass, and Interstate 95—cross the Piscataqua River from Portsmouth, New Hampshire to Kittery. Interstate 95 has three Kittery exits. Route 103 is a scenic coastal drive through Kittery Point to York.

ESSENTIALS

VISITOR INFORMATION

Greater York Region Chamber of Commerce. This is a good resource for exploring all that the region has to offer, including York Village, York Harbor, York Beach, Cape Neddick, Kittery, Eliot, and South Berwick. ✉ *1 Stonewall La., off U.S. 1, York* ☎ *207/363–4422* 🌐 *www.gatewaytomaine.org.*

Kittery Visitor Information Center. The Kittery Visitor Information Center is an excellent place to get information for mapping out your tour of Maine (and for a quick photo op with Smokey the Bear). Sometimes local organizations are on hand selling delicious homemade goodies for the road. ✉ *U.S. 1 and I–95* ☎ *800/767–8709* 🌐 *www.mainetourism.com.*

WHERE TO EAT

$$ SEAFOOD FAMILY

🍴 **Chauncey Creek Lobster Pier.** From the road you can barely see the red roof hovering below the trees, but chances are you can see the line of cars parked at this popular outdoor restaurant that has been serving up fresh lobster for over 70 years. Brightly colored picnic tables fill the deck and enclosed eating areas atop the high banks of the tidal river, beside a working pier. The menu has lots of fresh lobster choices, as well as a raw bar. Bring your own beer or wine, if you like; you can pick up a growler of local, handcrafted suds at the Tributary Brewing Company just around the corner on Shapleigh Road off Highway 103. You can also bring sides and desserts that aren't on the menu. [$] *Average main: $22* ✉ *16 Chauncey Creek Rd.* ☎ *207/439–1030* 🌐 *www.chaunceycreek.com* 🕒 *Closed Columbus Day–mid-May, and Mon. Labor Day–Columbus Day.*

$ ASIAN FUSION

🍴 **Anju Noodle Bar.** With a cozy, open-plan dining area and a laid-back atmosphere, Anju Noodle Bar serves up free-style Asian dishes such as house-made shredded pork buns packed with hoisin, cucumbers, kimchi mayo and pickled red onion, spicy miso ramen, and inspired local seafood dishes. This is one of the few places in the Pine Tree State outside Portland where you'll find fresh and innovative Asian-inspired cuisine done really well. You'll likely be eating lobster and fried seafood for every meal the farther north you go in Maine, so it's well worth stopping here en route Down East, or on the ride home, for a (delicious) palate cleanser. [$] *Average main: $14* ✉ *7 Wallingford Sq., Unit 102* ☎ *207/703-4298* 🌐 *www.anjunoodlebar.com* 🕒 *Closed Mon.*

SPORTS AND THE OUTDOORS

HIKING AND WALKING

Cutts Island Trail. For a peek into the Rachel Carson National Wildlife Refuge, this scenic 1.8-mile upland trail leads into the 800-acre Brave Boat Harbor Division and is a prime bird-watching area. There's a restroom and an information kiosk at the trailhead. The trail is open dawn–dusk year-round; dogs are not allowed. ✉ *Seapoint Rd.* ☎ *207/646–9226* 🌐 *www.fws.gov/refuge/rachel_carson.*

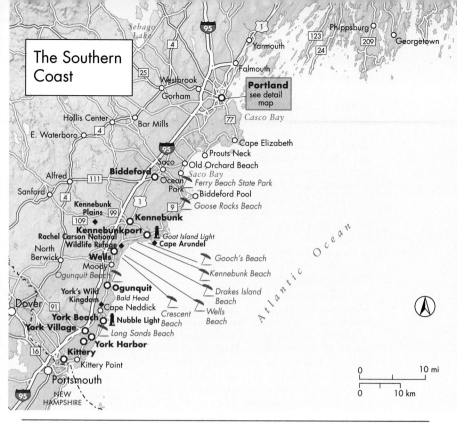

The Southern Coast

Sebago Lake
95
1
Phippsburg
123 Yarmouth 209 Georgetown
4 24
25 Falmouth
Westbrook
Gorham
Portland
see detail
map
Casco Bay
77
Hollis Center
Bar Mills
E. Waterboro
4 Cape Elizabeth
Prouts Neck
95 Old Orchard Beach
Saco Saco Bay
Alfred 111 Ocean Ferry Beach State Park
Biddeford Park
Sanford Biddeford Pool
4 Kennebunk 9 Goose Rocks Beach
Plains 99
109 Kennebunk
Kennebunkport
Rachel Carson National Goat Island Light
North Wildlife Refuge Cape Arundel
Berwick Wells
Moody Gooch's Beach
Ogunquit Beach Kennebunk Beach

York's Wild Drakes Island
Kingdom Ogunquit Beach
Dover Bald Head
91 Cape Neddick Wells
York Beach Crescent Beach
York Village Nubble Light Beach
Long Sands Beach

16 York Harbor
Kittery
Kittery Point
Portsmouth
95 NEW
HAMPSHIRE

Atlantic Ocean

0   10 mi
0   10 km

YORK VILLAGE

8 miles north of Kittery via I–95, U.S. 1, and U.S. 1A.

Spending an afternoon in York village is like going back in time—and you really only need a couple of hours here to roam the historic streets of this pint-size but worthwhile town. One of the first permanent settlements in Maine, the village museums detail the area's rich history. York is also home to the flagship store of Stonewall Kitchen, one of Maine's signature gourmet-food purveyors; the store has a café and a cooking school. There's also a cluster of vibrant contemporary-art galleries.

GETTING HERE AND AROUND

York is Exit 7 off Interstate 95; follow signs to U.S. 1, the modern commercial strip. From here, U.S. 1A will take you to the village center and on to York Harbor and York Beach before looping back up to U.S. 1 in Cape Neddick.

EXPLORING

George Marshall Store Gallery. The storefront windows and beadboard trim at the George Marshall Store Gallery (built in 1867) pay homage to its past as a general store, but the focus here is on the present. Changing exhibits, installations, and educational programs focus on prominent and up-and-coming regional artists. ✉ *140 Lindsay Rd.*

☏ *207/351–1083* ⊕ *www.georgemarshallstoregallery.com* ⊙ *Thurs.–Sat. 10–4, Sun. 1–4, and by appt. Call in advance in the off-season.*

Museums of Old York. Nine historic 18th- and 19th-century buildings, clustered on York Street and along Lindsay Road and the York River, highlight York's rich history, which dates back to early Colonial times. The Old York Gaol (1719) was once the King's Prison for the Province of Maine; inside are dungeons, cells, and the jailer's quarters. The many period rooms in the Emerson-Wilcox House, the main part of which was built in 1742, display items from daily life here in centuries past, including furniture from the 1600s and an impressive ceramic dishware collection. The 1731 Elizabeth Perkins House reflects the Victorian style of its last occupants, the prominent Perkins family. Start your visit at the museum's Visitor Center, located at 3 Lindsay Road in the Remick Barn at the corner of Route 1A and Lindsay Road in York. ✉ *Visitor Center, 3 Lindsay Rd.* ☏ *207/363–4974* ⊕ *www.oldyork.org* 🖃 *$5 single-museum entry, $12 for all* ⊙ *Memorial Day–Labor Day, Tues.–Sat. 10–5, Sun. 1–5; Labor Day–Columbus Day, Thurs.–Sat. 10–5, Sun. 1–5.*

Stonewall Kitchen. You've probably seen the kitchen's smartly labeled jars of gourmet chutneys, jams, jellies, salsas, and sauces in specialty stores back home. This complex houses the expansive flagship company store, which has a viewing area of the bottling process and stunning gardens. Sample all the mustards, salsas, and dressings you can stand, or have lunch at the café and take-out restaurant. The campus also houses a cooking school where you can join in evening or daytime courses. Reservations are required; most classes are shorter than two hours and cost $45–$80. ✉ *2 Stonewall La., off U.S. 1* ☏ *207/351–2712* ⊕ *www.stonewallkitchen.com/yorkstore.html* ⊙ *Mon.–Sat. 8–7, Sun. 9–6.*

SHOPPING

Gateway Farmers' Market. Bring your own bag for morning shopping at the Gateway Farmers' Market, held in the back lot at the Greater York Region Chamber of Commerce in summer, and in the First Parish Church Fellowship Hall (180 York Street) in winter. You'll find fresh local produce, lots of baked goods and artisanal breads, local seafood and meat, fresh flowers, and handcrafted items like soaps and candles. It's a good place to gather the makings for a beach picnic or to stock up on holiday gifts. The summer market is open on Saturday 9–1, June–October, as well as on Thursday 9–1, July and August; the winter market is open on Saturday 9–1, November–April. ✉ *1 Stonewall La., off U.S. 1, York* ☏ *207/363–4422* ⊕ *www.gatewayfarmersmarket.com.*

Ocean Fire Pottery. This artist-owned and -operated studio and gallery features unique wheel-thrown stoneware. Live demonstrations are available daily; call ahead to make sure the studio is open during the off-season. ✉ *23 Woodbridge Rd.* ☏ *207/361–3131* ⊕ *www.oceanfirepottery.com.*

YORK HARBOR

1 mile from York Village via U.S. 1A.

A short distance from the village proper, York Harbor opens to the water and offers many places to linger and explore. The harbor itself is busy with boats of all kinds, while the sandy harbor beach is good for swimming. Much quieter and more formal than York Beach to the north, this area has a somewhat exclusive air. Perched along the cliffs on the north side of the harbor are huge "cottages" built by wealthy summer residents in the late 1800s, when the area became a premier seaside resort destination with several grand hotels.

GETTING HERE AND AROUND

After passing through York Village to York Harbor (originally called Lower Town), U.S. 1A winds around and heads north to York Beach's village center, a 4-mile trip.

EXPLORING

Sayward-Wheeler House. Built in 1718, the waterfront home was remodeled in the 1760s by Jonathan Sayward, a local merchant who had prospered in the West Indies trade. By 1860 his descendants had opened the house to the public to share the story of their Colonial ancestors. Accessible only by guided tour, the house reveals the decor of a prosperous New England family at the outset of the Revolutionary War. The parlor—considered one of the country's best preserved Colonial interiors, with a tall clock and mahogany Chippendale-style chairs—looks pretty much as it did when Sayward lived here. ✉ *9 Barrell La. Ext.* ☎ *207/384–2454* 🌐 *www.historicnewengland.org* 🎟 *$5* 🕓 *June–mid-Oct., 2nd and 4th Sat. of month 11–5; tours on the hr (last tour at 4 pm).*

WHERE TO EAT

$$$ SEAFOOD 🍴 **Dockside Restaurant.** On an islandlike peninsula overlooking York Harbor, this restaurant has plenty of seafood on the menu. Popular dishes include haddock stuffed with Maine shrimp, and "drunken" lobster (sautéed lobster, scallops, shallots, and herbs in an Irish-whiskey cream), as well as beef tenderloin, slow-roasted duckling, seafood chowder, or cakes of native crab and wild mushrooms. Lighter fare is served in the cozy mahogany bar. Floor-to-ceiling windows in the stepped modern dining space transport diners to the water beyond—every seat has a water view. The Dockside Restaurant is part of a 7-acre property with guest rooms and suites in several buildings, from a grand 1895 summer home to condo-style quarters. [$] *Average main: $25* ✉ *22 Harris Island Rd., off Rte. 103* ☎ *207/363–2722* 🌐 *www.dockside-restaurant.com* 🕓 *Closed late Oct.–late May, and Tues. in June and Sept.*

$$$ SEAFOOD 🍴 **Foster's Downeast Clambake.** Save your appetite for this one. Specializing in the traditional Maine clambake—a feast consisting of rich clam chowder, a pile of mussels and steamers, Maine lobster with drawn butter for dipping, corn on the cob, roasted potatoes and onions, and Maine blueberry crumb cake (phew!)—this massive complex provides musical entertainment to go with its belly-busting meals. There are also several barbecue offerings. [$] *Average main: $28* ✉ *5 Axholme Rd.,*

at U.S. 1A ☎ 207/363–3255, 800/552–0242 🌐 www.fostersclambake.com ⏲ Closed early Sept.–late May, and weekdays late May–mid-June.

WHERE TO STAY

$ B&B/INN 🏨 **Inn at Tanglewood Hall.** The inn's artfully painted floors, lush wallpaper, and meticulous attention to detail are the fruits of a former designation as a designers' showcase home. **Pros:** authentic historic lodging; short walk to beaches. **Cons:** no water views. [$] *Rooms from: $185 ✉ 611 York St., York ☎ 207/351–1075 🌐 www.tanglewoodhall.com 🛏 4 rooms, 2 suites 🍴 Breakfast.*

$$$ B&B/INN 🏨 **Stage Neck Inn.** Built in the 1970s, this 58-room resort hotel takes full advantage of its harborside location, with chaise lounges and a fire pit on the surrounding lawns, water views from most guest rooms, floor-to-ceiling windows in the Harbor Porches and Sandpiper Grille restaurants, and outdoor dining in season. **Pros:** elaborate full-breakfast buffet with scrumptious baked goods; poolside service and snack bar in season; rooms have balconies or deck areas and most have water views. **Cons:** no suites. [$] *Rooms from: $345 ✉ 8 Stage Neck Rd., off U.S. 1A ☎ 800/340–1130, 207/363–3850 🌐 www.stageneck.com ⏲ Closed 1st 2 wks in Jan. 🛏 58 rooms 🍴 Breakfast.*

$ B&B/INN 🏨 **York Harbor Inn.** A mid-17th-century fishing cabin with dark timbers and a fieldstone fireplace forms the heart of this historic inn, which now includes several neighboring buildings. **Pros:** many rooms have harbor views; close to beaches, scenic walking trails. **Cons:** rooms vary greatly in style, size, and appeal. [$] *Rooms from: $189 ✉ 480 York St. ☎ 207/363–5119 🌐 www.yorkharborinn.com 🛏 61 rooms 🍴 Breakfast.*

SPORTS AND THE OUTDOORS

BIKING

Berger's Bike Shop. This former auto garage and full-service bike shop rents hybrid bikes for local excursions and sells bikes of all kinds. *✉ 241 York St., York ☎ 207/363–4070 🌐 www.bergersbikeshop.com.*

FISHING

For a list of fishing charters, check the directory on the Maine Fishing Guides website (*🌐 www.maineguides.com/activity/fishing-guides*).

Shearwater Charters. Shearwater Charters offers light tackle and fly-fishing charters in the York River and along the shoreline from Kittery to Ogunquit. Bait-fishing trips are also available. Departures are from Town Dock #2 in York Harbor. *✉ Town Dock #2, 20 Harris Island Rd., York ☎ 207/363–5324 🌐 www.mainestripers.net.*

HIKING AND WALKING

Cliff Walk and Fisherman's Walk. Two walking trails begin near Harbor Beach. Starting in a small nearby park, the Cliff Walk ascends its granite namesake and passes the summer "cottages" at the harbor entrance. There are some steps, but, as signs caution, tread carefully because of erosion. Fisherman's Walk, on the other hand, is an easy stroll. Starting across Stage Neck Road from the beach, it passes waterfront businesses, historic homes, and rocky harbor beaches on the way to York's beloved Wiggly Bridge. This pedestrian suspension bridge alongside Route 103 (there is minimal parking here) leads to Steedman Woods, a public preserve with a shaded loop trail along the York River estuary's ambling waters. You can also enter the preserve near the George Marshall Store in York Village ✉ *Stage Neck Rd., off U.S. 1A, York.*

YORK BEACH

6 miles north of York Harbor via U.S. 1A.

Like many shorefront towns in Maine, York Beach has a long history entertaining summer visitors. Take away today's bikinis and smart-phones, and it's easy to imagine these squealing tourists adorned in the full-length bathing garb of the late 19th century. Just as they did back then, visitors still come here to eat ice cream, enjoy carnival-like novelties, and indulge in the sun and salty sea air.

York Beach is a real family destination, devoid of all things staid and stuffy—children are meant to be both seen and heard here. Just beyond the sands of Short Sand Beach are a host of amusements, from bowling to indoor minigolf and the Fun-O-Rama arcade. Nubble Light is at the tip of the peninsula separating Long Sands and Short Sands beaches. The latter is mostly lined with unpretentious seasonal homes, with motels and restaurants mixed in.

GETTING HERE AND AROUND

It's a scenic 6 miles to York Beach via the loop road, U.S. 1A, from its southern intersection with U.S. 1. Although 2 miles longer, it's generally faster to continue north on U.S. 1A to Cape Neddick and then U.S 1A south to the village center, home to Short Sands Beach. Here U.S. 1A is known as Ocean Avenue as it heads north from York Harbor along Long Sands Beach en route to York Beach village and Short Sands Beach.

A trolley along U.S. 1 links the beaches in summer. You can also get from beach to beach on a series of residential streets that wind around Nubble Point between these beaches.

York Trolley Co. From late June through Labor Day, these bright-red trolleys link Short Sands Beach in York Beach village and nearby Long Sands Beach, running along U.S. 1A, making a number of stops. Maps can be picked up throughout York; fares are $2 one way, $4 round-trip, cash only (payable to driver upon boarding). You can also connect with a shuttle service to Ogunquit. ✉ *York* ☎ *207/363–9600* ⊕ *www.yorktrolley.com.*

EXPLORING

Fodor'sChoice **Nubble Light.** On a small island just off the tip of the cape jutting dra-
★ matically into the Atlantic Ocean between Long Sands Beach and Short Sands Beach, Nubble Light is one of the most photographed lighthouses on the globe. Direct access is prohibited, but the small Sohier Park right across from the light has parking, historical placards, benches, and a seasonal information center that shares the 1879 light's history. ✉ *End of Nubble Rd., off U.S. 1A, York* ☎ *207/363–3569 (Memorial Day weekend–Labor Day)* ⊕ *www.nubblelight.org* ⊗ *Park daily dawn to dusk. Information center: mid-Apr.–mid-May, daily 9–4; mid-May–late Oct., daily 9–7.*

FAMILY **York's Wild Kingdom.** Surrounded by forest, this popular zoo has an impressive variety of exotic animals and is home to the state's only white Bengal tiger. There's a nostalgic charm to the amusement park, which offers discounts for kids under 13—the target market, as there are no large thrill rides. Many York Beach visitors come just to enjoy the ocean views from the Ferris wheel and share what's advertised as the "seaboard's largest fried dough." ✉ *1 Animal Park Rd., off U.S. 1* ☎ *207/363–4911* 🌐 *www.yorkzoo.com* 🎟 *Zoo $14.74, zoo and rides $22.25* 🕒 *Zoo: late May–late Sept. daily 10–5. Amusement park hrs vary.*

WHERE TO EAT AND STAY

$ AMERICAN FAMILY 🍴 **The Goldenrod.** People line the windows to watch Goldenrod Kisses being made the same way they have since 1896—and some 50 tons are made every year. Aside from the famous taffy (there's penny candy, too), this eatery is family oriented, very reasonably priced, and a great place to get ice cream from the old-fashioned soda fountain. Breakfast is served all day, while the simple lunch menu of sandwiches and burgers does just as well for dinner, with the addition of a handful of entrées, like baked haddock and meat loaf. [$] *Average main: $10* ✉ *2 Railroad Ave.* ☎ *207/363–2621* 🌐 *www.thegoldenrod.com* 🕒 *Closed mid-Oct.–mid-May.*

$$ B&B/INN FAMILY 🏨 **Atlantic House Inn.** In a nicely renovated 1888 beauty, this inn's standard guest rooms feel fresh with designer fabrics, gas fireplaces, and whirlpool tubs. **Pros:** lots of amenities; walk to beach, shops; suites are good choice for weekly stay; some ocean views. **Cons:** not on beach; lacks public spaces; some rooms have a two-night minimum. [$] *Rooms from: $269* ✉ *2 Beach St.* ☎ *207/361–6677* 🌐 *www.atlantichouseinn.com* 🕒 *Closed Nov.–Apr.* 🛏 *7 rooms, 9 suites* 🍽 *No meals.*

$$ HOTEL 🏨 **Union Bluff Hotel.** This massive, turreted structure still looks much the same as it did when it opened in the mid-19th century. **Pros:** many spectacular ocean views; in the middle of the action. **Cons:** rooms lack any charm or character befitting of inn's origins; not for those looking for a quiet getaway. [$] *Rooms from: $229* ✉ *8 Beach St.* ☎ *207/363–1333, 800/833–0721* 🌐 *www.unionbluff.com* 🛏 *65 rooms, 6 suites* 🍽 *No meals.*

NIGHTLIFE

Inn on the Blues. This hopping music club attracts nationally known bands playing funk, jazz, and reggae, as well as blues. It's open April–December and weekends only in the shoulder seasons. ✉ *7 Ocean Ave., York* ☎ *207/351–3221* 🌐 *www.innontheblues.com.*

OGUNQUIT

8 miles north of the Yorks via U.S. 1.

A resort village since the late 19th century, Ogunquit made a name for itself as an artists' colony. Today it has become a mini Provincetown, with a gay population that swells in summer, and many inns and small clubs cater to a primarily gay and lesbian clientele. The nightlife in Ogunquit revolves around the precincts of Ogunquit Square and Perkins Cove, where people stroll, often enjoying an after-dinner ice cream cone

Ogunquit's Perkins Cove is a pleasant place to admire the boats (and wonder at the origin of their names).

or espresso. For a scenic drive, take Shore Road from downtown to the 175-foot Bald Head Cliff; you'll be treated to views up and down the coast. On a stormy day the surf can be quite wild here.

GETTING HERE AND AROUND

Parking in the village and at the beach is costly and limited, so leave your car at the hotel or in a public parking space and hop the trolley. It costs $1.50 per trip and runs Memorial Day weekend–Columbus Day, with weekend-only service during the first few weeks. From Perkins Cove, the trolley runs through town along Shore Road and then down to Ogunquit Beach; it also stops along U.S. 1.

ESSENTIALS

Transportation Information Ogunquit Trolley. ☎ *207/646–1411* ⊕ *www.ogunquittrolley.com.*

Visitor Information Ogunquit Chamber of Commerce. ⊠ *36 Main St.* ☎ *207/646–2939* ⊕ *www.ogunquit.org.*

EXPLORING

Perkins Cove. This neck of land off Shore Road in the lower part of Ogunquit village has a jumble of sea-weathered fish houses and buildings that were part of an art school. These have largely been transformed by the tide of tourism into shops and restaurants. When you've had your fill of browsing, stroll out along **Marginal Way,** a mile-long, paved footpath that hugs the shore of a rocky promontory known as Israel's Head. Benches allow you to appreciate the open sea vistas. Expect heavy foot traffic along the path, even in the off-season. ⊠ *Perkins Cove Rd., off Shore Rd.*

WHERE TO EAT

$ ✕ **Amore Breakfast.** You could hardly find a more satisfying, heartier
AMERICAN   breakfast than at this smart and busy joint just shy of the entrance to
Perkins Cove. A lighthearted mix of retro advertising signs adorns the
walls of this bright, open, and bustling dining room. You won't find
tired standards here—the only pancakes are German potato, and the
Oscar Madison omelet combines crabmeat with asparagus and Swiss,
topped with a béarnaise sauce. For a really decadent start, opt for
the Banana Foster: pecan-coated, cream cheese–stuffed French toast
with a side of sautéed bananas in rum syrup. Next door, at the Cafe
Amore, you can pick up sandwiches and other light fare. $ *Average
main: $10 ⊠ 309 Shore Rd. ☎ 207/646–6661 ⊕ www.amorebreakfast.
com ⊙ Closed mid-Dec.–early Apr. No dinner.*

$$ ✕ **The Velveteen Habit.** With an on-site microgarden, which supplies
AMERICAN   most of the ingredients used in the restaurant's dishes, The Velveteen
Habit takes farm-to-table to a new level. House-cured meats and
pickled veggies are served alongside fresh and smoked seafood and
craft cocktails in a cozy, refurbished farmhouse with tables look-
ing out over the kitchen garden. $ *Average main: $20 ⊠ 37 Ogun-
quit Rd., 3 miles outside Ogunquit, Cape Neddick ☎ 207/216–9884
⊕ www.thevelveteenhabit.com ⊟ No credit cards.*

WELLS

5 miles north of Ogunquit via U.S. 1.

Lacking any kind of discernible village center, Wells could be eas-
ily overlooked as nothing more than a commercial stretch of U.S. 1
between Ogunquit and the Kennebunks. But look more closely: this is
a place where people come to enjoy some of the best beaches on the
coast. Until 1980 the town of Wells incorporated Ogunquit, and today
this family-oriented beach community has 7 miles of densely popu-
lated shoreline, along with nature preserves, where you can explore
salt marshes and tidal pools.

GETTING HERE AND AROUND

Just $2 per trip, the seasonal Shoreline Trolley serves Wells Beach and
Crescent Beach and has many stops along U.S. 1 at motels, camp-
grounds, restaurants, and so on. You can also catch it at the Wells
Transportation Center when Amtrak's *Downeaster* pulls in.

ESSENTIALS

Transportation Information Shoreline Trolley. ☎ *207/324–5762
⊕ www.shorelineexplorer.com.*

Visitor Information Wells Chamber of Commerce. ⊠ *136 Post Rd.
☎ 207/646–2451 ⊕ www.wellschamber.org.*

EXPLORING

FAMILY   **Rachel Carson National Wildlife Refuge.** At the headquarters of the Rachel
Carson National Wildlife Refuge, which has 11 divisions from Kit-
tery to Cape Elizabeth, is the Carson Trail, a 1-mile loop. The trail
traverses a salt marsh and a white-pine forest where migrating birds
and waterfowl of many varieties are regularly spotted, and it borders

Branch Brook and the Merriland River. ✉ *321 Port Rd.* ☎ *207/646–9226* ⊕ *www.fws.gov/northeast/rachelcarson* ☉ *Daily sunrise–sunset.*

Congdon's Doughnuts. These superior doughnuts have been made by the same family since 1945. Congdon's has about 40 different varieties, though the plain variety really gives you an idea of just how good these doughnuts are: it's the biggest seller, along with the honey dipped and black raspberry jelly. You're welcome to sit inside for breakfast or lunch, but waits can be long in summer. There are also drive-through and take-out windows. ✉ *1090 Post Rd.* ☎ *207/646–4219* ⊕ *www.congdons.com* ☉ *Closed Mon.– Wed. No dinner.*

BEACHES

With its thousands of acres of marsh and preserved land, Wells is a great place to spend time outdoors. Nearly 7 miles of sand stretch along the boundaries of Wells, making beachgoing a prime occupation. Tidal pools sheltered by rocks are filled with all manner of creatures awaiting discovery. During the summer season a pay-and-display parking system (no quarters, receipt goes on dashboard) is in place at the public beaches.

A summer trolley serves **Crescent Beach,** along Webhannet Drive, and **Wells Beach,** at the end of Mile Road off U.S. 1. There is another parking lot, but no trolley stop, at the north end of Atlantic Avenue, which runs north along the shore from the end of Mile Road. Stretching north from the jetty at Wells Harbor is **Drakes Island Beach** (end of Drakes Island Road off U.S. 1). Lifeguards are on hand at all beaches, and all have public restrooms.

FAMILY **Crescent Beach.** Lined with summer homes, this sandy strand is busy in the summer, but the beach and the water are surprisingly clean, considering all the traffic. The swimming's good, and beachgoers can also explore tidal pools and look for seals on the sea rocks nearby. **Amenities:** food and drink; lifeguards; parking (fee); toilets. **Best for:** swimming. ✉ *Webhannet Dr., south of Mile Rd.* ☎ *207/646–5113.*

FAMILY **Drakes Island Beach.** Smaller and quieter than the other two beaches in Wells, Drakes Island Beach is also a little more natural, with rolling sand dunes and access to salt-marsh walking trails at an adjacent estuary. The ice-cream truck swings by regularly in the summer. **Amenities:** lifeguards; parking (fee); toilets. **Best for:** walking. ✉ *Island Beach Rd., 1 mile southwest of U.S. 1* ☎ *207/646–5113.*

FAMILY **Wells Beach.** The northern end of a 2-mile stretch of golden sand, Wells Beach is popular with families and surfers, who line up in the swells and preen on the boardwalk near the arcade and snack shop. The beach's northern tip is a bit quieter, with a long rock jetty perfect for strolling. **Amenities:** food and drink; lifeguards; parking (fee); toilets. **Best for:** surfing; walking. ✉ *Atlantic Ave., north of Mile Rd.* ☎ *207/646–5113.*

Wheels and Waves. Rent bikes, surfboards, wet suits, boogie boards, kayaks, and all sorts of outdoor gear at Wheels and Waves. ✉ *365 Post Rd., Rte. 1* ☎ *207/646–5774* ⊕ *www.wheelsnwaves.com.*

WHERE TO EAT AND STAY

$ SEAFOOD 🍴 **Billy's Chowder House.** Locals and vacationers head to this classic roadside seafood restaurant in the midst of a salt marsh en route to Wells Beach. They come for the generous lobster rolls, haddock sandwiches, and chowders, but there are plenty of non-seafood choices, too. Big windows in the bright dining rooms overlook the marsh, part of the Rachel Carson National Wildlife Refuge. [$] *Average main: $15* ✉ *216 Mile Rd.* ☎ *207/646–7558* 🌐 *www.billyschowderhouse.com* 🕓 *Closed mid-Dec.–mid-Jan.*

$ AMERICAN DINER 🍴 **Maine Diner.** One look at the 1953 exterior, and you'll start craving diner food. Here, you'll get a little more than you bargained for: after all, how many greasy spoons make an award-winning lobster pie? It's a house favorite, along with a heavenly seafood chowder. There's plenty of fried seafood in addition to the usual diner fare, and breakfast is served all day. Check out the adjacent gift shop, Remember the Maine. [$] *Average main: $15* ✉ *2265 Post Rd.* ☎ *207/646–4441* 🌐 *www.mainediner.com* 🕓 *Closed at least 1 wk in Jan.*

$$ B&B/INN Fodor's Choice ★ 🏨 **Haven by the Sea.** Once the summer mission of St. Martha's Church in Kennebunkport, this exquisite inn has retained many original details from its former life as a seaside church, including cathedral ceilings and stained-glass windows. **Pros:** unusual structure with elegant appointments; tucked-away massage room. **Cons:** not an in-town location. [$] *Rooms from: $250* ✉ *59 Church St.* ☎ *207/646–4194* 🌐 *www.havenbythesea.com* 🛏 *7 rooms, 2 suites, 1 apartment* 🍽 *Breakfast.*

KENNEBUNK AND KENNEBUNKPORT

5 miles north of Wells via U.S. 1.

The town centers of Kennebunk and Kennebunkport are separated by 5 miles and two rivers, but united by a common history and a laid-back seaside vibe. Perhaps best described as the Hamptons of the Pine Tree State, Kennebunkport has been a resort area since the 19th century. Its most recent residents have made it even more famous: the dynastic Bush family is often in residence on its immense estate here, which sits dramatically out on Walker's Point on Cape Arundel. Newer homes have sprung up alongside the old, and a great way to take them all in is with a slow drive out Ocean Avenue along the cape.

Sometimes bypassed on the way to its sister town, Kennebunk has its own appeal. Once a major shipbuilding center, Kennebunk today retains the feel of a classic New England small town, with an inviting shopping district, steepled churches, and fine examples of 18th- and 19th-century brick and clapboard homes. There are also plenty of natural spaces for walking, swimming, birding, and biking, and the Kennebunks' major beaches are here.

GETTING HERE AND AROUND

Kennebunk's main village sits along U.S. 1, extending west from the Mousam River. The Lower Village is along Routes 9 and 35, 4 miles down Route 35 from the main village, and the drive between the two keeps visitors agog with the splendor of the area's mansions, spread out on both sides of Route 35. To get to the grand and gentle beaches of

Kennebunk, continue straight (the road becomes Beach Avenue) at the intersection with Route 9. If you turn left instead, Route 9 will take you across the Kennebunk River, into Kennebunkport's touristy downtown, called Dock Square (or sometimes just "the Port"), a commercial area with restaurants, shops, boat cruises, and galleries. Here you'll find the most activity (and crowds) in the Kennebunks.

Take the Intown Trolley for narrated 45-minute jaunts that run daily from Memorial Day weekend through Columbus Day. The $16 fare is valid for the day, so you can hop on and off—or start your journey—at any of the stops. The route includes Kennebunk's beaches and Lower Village and as well as neighboring Kennebunkport's scenery and sights. The main stop is at 21 Ocean Avenue in Kennebunkport, around the corner from Dock Square.

ESSENTIALS

Visitor Information Intown Trolley. ☎ *207/967–3686* ⊕ *www.intowntrolley. com.* **Kennebunk-Kennebunkport Chamber of Commerce.** ✉ *16 Water St.* ☎ *207/967–0857* ⊕ *www.gokennebunks.com.*

WALKING TOURS

To take a little walking tour of Kennebunk's most notable structures, begin at the Federal-style Brick Store Museum at 117 Main Street. Head south on Main Street (turn left out of the museum) to see several extraordinary 18th- and early-19th-century homes, including the **Lexington Elms** at No. 99 (1799), the **Horace Porter House** at No. 92 (1848), and the **Benjamin Brown House** at No. 85 (1788).

When you've had your fill of historic homes, head back up toward the museum, pass the 1773 **First Parish Unitarian Church** (its Asher Benjamin–style steeple contains an original Paul Revere bell), and turn right onto **Summer Street.** This street is an architectural showcase, revealing an array of styles from Colonial to Federal. Walking past these grand beauties will give you a real sense of the economic prowess and glamour of the long-gone shipbuilding industry.

For a guided 90-minute architectural walking tour of Summer Street, contact the museum at ☎ *207/985–4802.* You can also purchase a $4.95 map that marks historic buildings or a $15.95 guidebook, *Windows on the Past.*

For a dramatic walk along Kennebunkport's rocky coastline and beneath the views of Ocean Avenue's grand mansions, head out on the **Parson's Way Shore Walk,** a paved 4.8-mile round-trip. Begin at Dock Square and follow Ocean Avenue along the river, passing the Colony Hotel and St. Ann's Church, all the way to Walker's Point. Simply turn back from here.

EXPLORING

FAMILY **Brick Store Museum.** The cornerstone of this block-long preservation of early-19th-century commercial and residential buildings is William Lord's Brick Store. Built as a dry-goods store in 1825 in the Federal style, the building has an openwork balustrade across the roofline, granite lintels over the windows, and paired chimneys. Exhibits chronicle the Kennebunk area's history and Early American decorative and fine arts. Museum staff lead architectural walking tours of Kennebunk's National Historic District by appointment late May–September. ⊠ *117 Main St., Kennebunk* ☎ *207/985–4802* ⊕ *www.brickstoremuseum.org* ⊠ *$7.50* ⊙ *Tues.–Fri. 10–4:30, Sat. 10–1.*

Dock Square. Clothing boutiques, T-shirt shops, art galleries, and restaurants line this bustling square, spreading out along the nearby streets and alleys. Walk onto the drawbridge to admire the tidal Kennebunk River; cross to the other side and you are in the Lower Village of neighboring Kennebunk. ⊠ *Dock Sq., Kennebunkport.*

FAMILY **First Families Kennebunkport Museum.** Also known as White Columns, the imposing Greek Revival mansion with Doric columns is furnished with the belongings of four generations of the Perkins-Nott family. From mid-July through mid-October, the 1853 house is open for guided tours and also serves as a gathering place for village walking tours. It is owned by the Kennebunkport Historical Society, which has several other historical buildings a mile away at 125–135 North Street, including an old jail and schoolhouse. ⊠ *8 Maine St., Kennebunkport* ☎ *207/967–2751* ⊕ *www.kporthistory.org* ⊠ *$10* ⊙ *Mid-July–mid-Oct., Mon.–Sat. 11–5.*

FAMILY **First Parish of Kennebunk Unitarian Universalist Church.** Built in 1773, just before the American Revolution, this stunning church is a marvel. The 1804 Asher Benjamin–style steeple stands proudly atop the village, and the sounds of the original Paul Revere bell can be heard for miles. The church holds Sunday service at 9:30 am in the summer (at 10:30 the rest of the year). ⊠ *114 Main St., Kennebunk* ☎ *207/985–3700* ⊕ *www.uukennebunk.org.*

FAMILY **Kennebunk Plains.** For an unusual experience, visit this 135-acre grasslands habitat that is home to several rare and endangered species. Locals call it Blueberry Plains, and a good portion of the area is abloom with the hues of ripening wild blueberries in late July; after August 1, you are welcome to pick and eat all the berries you can find. The area is maintained by the Nature Conservancy. ⊠ *Webber Hill Rd., 4½ miles northwest of town, Kennebunk* ☎ *207/729–5181* ⊕ *www.nature.org* ⊙ *Daily sunrise–sunset.*

FAMILY **Seashore Trolley Museum.** Streetcars were built here from 1872 to 1972, including trolleys for major metropolitan areas—from Boston to Budapest, New York to Nagasaki, and San Francisco to Sydney. Many of them are beautifully restored and displayed. Best of all, you can take a nearly 4-mile ride on the tracks of the former Atlantic Shoreline trolley line, with a stop along the way at the museum restoration shop, where trolleys are transformed from junk into gems. The outdoor museum is self-guided. ⊠ *195 Log Cabin Rd., Kennebunkport* ☎ *207/967–2712* ⊕ *www.trolleymuseum.org* ⊠ *$10* ⊙ *Memorial Day–Columbus Day, daily 10–5.*

BEACHES

FAMILY **Gooch's Beach.** Kennebunk has three beaches, one after another, along Beach Avenue, which is lined with cottages and old Victorians. The most northerly, and the closest to downtown Kennebunkport, is Gooch's Beach, the main swimming beach. Next is stony Kennebunk Beach, followed by Mother's Beach, which is popular with families. There's a small playground and tidal puddles for splashing; rock outcroppings lessen the waves. **Amenities:** lifeguards; parking (fee); toilets. **Best for:** walking; swimming. ✉ *Beach Ave., south of Hwy. 9, Kennebunk.*

Goose Rocks Beach. Three-mile-long Goose Rocks, a 10-minute drive north of town, has a good long stretch of smooth sand and plenty of shallow pools for exploring. It's a favorite of families with small children. Pick up a $15 daily permit at the Kennebunkport Town Hall. Dogs are allowed, but only before 8 am and after 6 pm. No facilities are available at the beach. **Amenities:** parking (fee). **Best for:** walking. ✉ *Dyke Rd., off Rte. 9, Kennebunkport* 🌐 *www.visitmaine.com.*

WHERE TO EAT

The Kennebunks are chock-full of restaurants and cafés vying for attention. Service and food can be hit-or-miss in this area; often the best meals are those that you pack yourself into a picnic basket to enjoy on one of the area's many sandy beaches.

$ AMERICAN

🍴 **Duffy's Tavern & Grill.** Every small town needs its own lively and friendly tavern, and this bustling spot is Kennebunk's favorite, housed in a former shoe factory, with exposed brick, soaring ceilings, and hardwood floors. Right outside are the tumbling waters of the Mousam River as it flows from the dam. There's a large bar with overhead televisions and plenty of seating in the main room, plus a less captivating rear section. You'll find lots of comfortable standards, like burgers, pizza, and the popular fish 'n' chips. The tasty onion rings are hand dipped. [$] *Average main: $16* ✉ *4 Main St., Kennebunk* ☎ *207/985–0050* 🌐 *www.duffyskennebunk.com.*

$ AMERICAN

🍴 **Federal Jack's.** Run by the Kennebunkport Brewing Company, this two-story complex is near the bridge from Lower Village into Kennebunkport. All beers are handcrafted on-site, including the Blue Fin Stout and Goat Island Light—try the sampler if you can't decide. In the upstairs restaurant, an American pub-style menu includes plenty of seafood; the clam chowder is rich and satisfying. The restaurant has two dining rooms and a huge deck that packs in the crowds in the summer. There's a brunch buffet on Sunday, and live entertainment Thursday–Saturday (Sunday, too, in summer). [$] *Average main: $14* ✉ *8 Western Ave., Kennebunk* ☎ *207/967–4322* 🌐 *www.federaljacks.com.*

$$$ SEAFOOD FAMILY

🍴 **Mabel's Lobster Claw.** Since the 1950s, Mabel's has been serving lobsters, homemade pies, and lots of seafood for lunch and dinner in this tiny dwelling out on Ocean Avenue. The decor includes paneled walls, wooden booths, and autographed photos of various TV stars (and members of the Bush family). There's outside seating, and paper place mats with illustrated instructions on how to eat a Maine lobster. The house favorite is the Lobster Savannah: split and filled with scallops, shrimp, and mushrooms, and baked in a Newburg sauce. Save room for the peanut-butter ice-cream pie. There's also a take-out window where you can order ice cream and food. [$] *Average main: $25* ✉ *124 Ocean Ave., Kennebunkport* ☎ *207/967–2562* 🌐 *www.mabelslobster.com* 🕒 *Closed Nov.–early Apr.*

$$$ AMERICAN

🍴 **Pier 77 Restaurant.** The view takes center stage at this restaurant and bar. Located on the ground level, the restaurant, Pier 77, serves sophisticated fare with an emphasis on meats and seafood. There are large windows overlooking the harbor, and every seat has a nice view. The place is vibrant, with live music in summer—a great place for cocktails on the water. Tucked down below, the tiny but oh-so-funky-and-fun Ramp Bar & Grill pays homage to a really good burger, fried seafood, and other pub-style classics. $ *Average main: $25* ✉ *77 Pier Rd., Cape Porpoise* ☎ *207/967–8500* ⊕ *www.pier77restaurant.com.*

WHERE TO STAY

$

B&B/INN

⛉ **Bufflehead Cove Inn.** On the Kennebunk River, this gray-shingled B&B sits at the end of a winding dirt road amid fields and apple trees. **Pros:** pastoral setting; riverfront location; perfect for a serene getaway. **Cons:** two-night minimum stay on weekends. $ *Rooms from: $190* ✉ *18 Bufflehead Cove Rd., Kennebunk* ☎ *207/967–3879* ⊕ *www.buffleheadcove.com* ⊙ *Closed mid-Nov.–Apr.* ⬦ *4 rooms, 1 suite, 1 cottage* ⑂ *Breakfast.*

$$

B&B/INN

⛉ **Cape Arundel Inn.** This shingle-style 19th-century mansion, originally one of the area's many summer "cottages," commands a magnificent ocean view that takes in the Bush estate at Walker's Point. **Pros:** extraordinary views from most rooms; across the road from rockbound coast. **Cons:** not for the budget-minded. $ *Rooms from: $294* ✉ *208 Ocean Ave., Kennebunkport* ☎ *855/346–5700* ⊕ *www.capearundelinn.com* ⊙ *Closed late Dec.–late Feb.* ⬦ *14 rooms, 1 suite* ⑂ *Breakfast.*

$$$

B&B/INN

Fodor'sChoice

★

⛉ **Captain Fairfield Inn.** With its inviting common spaces, tastefully designed rooms, central location, and delicious, healthy breakfast, this boutique inn makes for an excellent stay. **Pros:** wide selection of rooms, all well-appointed with modern updates; fireplaces in many rooms and communal spaces; friendly, generous service. **Cons:** short walk to the water. $ *Rooms from: $339* ✉ *8 Pleasant St., Kennebunkport* ☎ *207/967–4454* ⊕ *www.captainfairfield.com* ⬦ *7 rooms, 2 suites* ⑂ *Breakfast.*

$$$

B&B/INN

Fodor'sChoice

★

⛉ **The Captain Lord Mansion.** Of all the mansions in Kennebunkport's historic district that have been converted to inns, the 1814 Captain Lord Mansion is the stateliest and most sumptuously appointed. **Pros:** beautiful landscaped grounds; bikes for guests; putting green. **Cons:** not a beachfront location. $ *Rooms from: $329* ✉ *6 Pleasant St., Kennebunkport* ☎ *207/967–3141, 800/522–3141* ⊕ *www.captainlord.com* ⬦ *18 rooms, 2 suites* ⑂ *Breakfast.*

$$

RESORT

FAMILY

Fodor'sChoice

★

⛉ **The Colony Hotel.** You can't miss this place: it's grand, white, and incredibly large, set majestically atop a rise overlooking the ocean. **Pros:** private beach; heated saltwater swimming pool; activities and entertainment for all ages. **Cons:** not intimate. $ *Rooms from: $245* ✉ *140 Ocean Ave., Kennebunkport* ☎ *207/967–3331, 800/552–2363* ⊕ *www.colonymaine.com* ⊙ *Closed Nov.–mid-May* ⬦ *112 rooms, 11 suites, 2 cottages* ⑂ *Breakfast.*

$$

HOTEL

FAMILY

⛉ **The Seaside.** This handsome seaside property has been in the hands of the Severance family since 1667. **Pros:** great ocean views from upper-floor rooms; tasty breakfast; rates drop significantly in winter. **Cons:** motel-style rooms; not an in-town location. $ *Rooms from: $259* ✉ *80 Beach Ave., Kennebunk* ☎ *207/967–4461, 800/967–4461* ⊕ *www.kennebunkbeachmaine.com* ⬦ *22 rooms* ⑂ *Breakfast.*

Kennebunk is a classic New England town, while Kennebunkport (pictured) has more upscale inns and shopping.

$
B&B/INN
🏨 **Waldo Emerson Inn.** The home itself is a historical gold mine, made grand with unusual maritime architectural touches by a shipbuilder in 1784. **Pros:** good base for exploring Kennebunk and Kennebunkport; authentic historic lodging; complimentary afternoon tea. **Cons:** some steep stairs; no water views or beachfront; not in town. $ *Rooms from: $175* ✉ *108 Summer St., Kennebunk* ☎ *207/985–4250, 877/521–8776* ⊕ *www.waldoemersoninn.com* ⇨ *6 rooms* ○ *Breakfast.*

$$$
B&B/INN
🏨 **White Barn Inn.** For a romantic, indulgent overnight stay, look no further than the exclusive White Barn Inn, known for its attentive, old-school service and intimate atmosphere. **Pros:** 10-minute walk to the beach; elegant spa offers it all; over-the-top service. **Cons:** prices are steep. $ *Rooms from: $340* ✉ *37 Beach Ave., Kennebunk* ☎ *207/967–2321* ⊕ *www.whitebarninn.com* ⇨ *13 rooms, 9 suites, 5 cottages* ○ *Breakfast.*

SPORTS AND THE OUTDOORS
FISHING

FAMILY
Cast-Away Fishing Charters. Find and catch fish with Cast-Away Fishing Charters. The captain also offers a lobstering trip that's fun for kids, who can help haul in the traps. ✉ *Performance Marine, 4-A Western Ave., Kennebunk* ☎ *207/284–1740* ⊕ *www.castawayfishingcharters.com.*

FAMILY
Rugosa. Lobster-trap hauling trips aboard the *Rugosa* in the scenic waters off the Kennebunks run daily, Memorial Day weekend– early October. ✉ *Nonantum Resort, 95 Ocean Ave., Kennebunkport* ☎ *207/468–4095* ⊕ *www.rugosalobstertours.com.*

WHALE-WATCHING

FAMILY   **First Chance.** This company leads whale-watching cruises on 85-foot *Nick's Chance.* If you don't see a whale, you get a ticket for a free trip. Scenic lobster cruises are also offered aboard 65-foot *Kylie's Chance.* Trips run daily in summer and on weekends in the shoulder season. ⊠ *Performance Marine, 4-A Western Ave., Kennebunk* ☎ *207/967–5507* ⊕ *www.firstchancewhalewatch.com.*

SHOPPING

Abacus. This shop sells eclectic crafts, jewelry, and furniture. It's a good place to pick up gifts. ⊠ *2 Ocean Ave., at Dock Sq., Kennebunkport* ☎ *800/206–2166* ⊕ *www.abacusgallery.com.*

Fodor'sChoice   **Daytrip Society.** The impossibly hip and well-selected array of goods that ★ this modern-design shop stocks makes it an excellent place for both window-shopping and finding gifts for just about anyone on your list (including yourself). A refreshing departure from the rest of the somewhat stodgy gift shops in the village, this boutique is chock-full of eye candy, most of which is also very functional. There are many locally sourced and decidedly contemporary products, from hats and jewelry to novelty books, home decor, and scents. Check out Daytrip Jr., their equally hip children's store around the corner. ⊠ *4 Dock Sq., Kennebunkport* ☎ *207/967–4440* ⊕ *www.daytripsociety.com.*

Maine Art. Showcasing works by artists from Maine and New England, Maine Art has a two-story gallery with a sculpture garden. There's another gallery space on Western Avenue. ⊠ *14 Western Ave., Kennebunk* ☎ *207/967–2803* ⊕ *www.maine-art.com.*

Mast Cove Galleries. Since 1979, Mast Cove Galleries has been selling paintings and sculpture by artists from New England and beyond. It occupies the barn and first floor of the owner's 1851 village home, which has a sculpture garden. The gallery hosts indoor jazz and blues concerts year-round. ⊠ *2 Mast Cove La., at Main St., Kennebunkport* ☎ *207/967–3453* ⊕ *www.mastcove.com.*

▌EN
ROUTE
For a rewarding drive that goes into the reaches of the coastline on the way to Old Orchard Beach, head out of Kennebunkport on Route 9. You'll soon come to the fishing village of Cape Porpoise, where the pier has wondrous views. Continuing on Route 9, plan to do some beach walking at Goose Rocks Beach or Fortunes Rocks Beach, both ideal for stretching your legs or for just looking for shells or critters in the tide pools. (Pick up a parking permit first.) Route 9 winds through wooded areas, then heads past the charming resort villages of Camp Ellis and Ocean Park. You could pack a picnic and spend some time at Ferry Beach State Park. The varied landscapes here include forested sections, swamp, beach, a rare stand of tupelo (black gum) trees, and lots of dunes. There are a few miles of marked trails to hike.

BIDDEFORD

11 miles north of Kennebunkport; 18 miles south of Portland.

Biddeford is waking from a deep sleep, having devolved into something of a ghost town for a good deal of the past half century. It's a ghost town no more, thanks to chefs and small-business owners who have relocated from Portland; they are giving Biddeford's beautiful old-mill-town architecture a new lease on life. Developers have taken note as well, revamping many of the mill district's historic buildings, including the town's imposing 233,000-square-foot Lincoln Mill. Today, Biddeford is filled with art galleries and quirky boutiques, a distillery, an art school, and top-notch restaurants.

GETTING HERE AND AROUND

From Interstate 95, get off at Exit 2A. U.S. 1 runs right through town.

Visitor Information Biddeford-Saco Chamber of Commerce. ⊠ *28 Water St., Biddeford* ☎ *207/282–1567* ⊕ *www.biddefordsacochamber.org.*

EXPLORING

Round Turn Distilling. There's a reason why all the good craft cocktail bars in Maine stock Bimini Gin, the flagship spirit of this distillery, located in a 150-year-old textile mill on the Saco River. Learn more about the best small-batch gin in the Pine Tree State, and be sure to take a peek at the production area: the distillery uses steam to power its modern steel-and-copper still. The Tasting Room is open Friday 4–9, Saturday 2–8, and otherwise by appointment. ⊠ *32 Maine St., Bldg. 13W, Suite 103, Biddeford* ☎ *207/370–9446* ⊕ *www.roundturndistilling.com.*

EN ROUTE **Ocean Park.** Ten miles east of Biddeford lies Ocean Park, a vacation community founded in 1881 by Free Will Baptist leaders as a summer assembly with both religious and educational purposes, following the example of Chautauqua, New York. The 1881 Temple, in an unusual octagon shape, is on the National Register of Historic Places. Today the community hosts an impressive variety of cultural events, from concerts to sand-sculpture contests. There's even a public shuffleboard area for vacationers not interested in the neon carnival attractions in Old Orchard Beach just up the road. Get an old-fashioned raspberry-lime rickey at the Ocean Park Soda Fountain, at Furber Park. ⊠ *14 Temple Ave., Ocean Park* ☎ *207/934–9068* ⊕ *www.oceanpark.org.*

WHERE TO EAT

$
AMERICAN
✕ **Custom Deluxe.** In a cozy space with exposed-brick walls and high pressed-tin ceilings that can only accommodate 28 diners, Custom Deluxe serves unassuming but creative bistro dishes, like rich mushroom soup topped with toasted benne seeds, roasted chicken on rye bread with jardiniere relish and miso mayo, or crispy fries with garlic oil and black pepper. And desserts don't disappoint either—with treats like a perfectly divine fresh-yeast doughnut with maple-smoked cheddar and maple mousse, you'll be tempted to eat dessert first. $ *Average main: $12* ⊠ *140 Main St., Biddeford* ☎ *207/494–7110* ⊗ *Closed Sun. and Mon.*

$
CAFÉ
✕ **Elements: Books, Coffee, Beer.** You could easily while away an entire day at this cozy spot that's part café, part bookstore, and part pub, starting with coffee in the morning to fuel an afternoon of reading, followed by a satisfying brew in the early evening. Pop by for any combination of the three, plus the occasional poetry reading or evening of live local music. $ *Average main: $10* ⊠ *265 Main St., Biddeford* ☎ *207/710–2011* ⊕ *www.elementsbookscoffeebeer.com.*

$ ✕ **Palace Diner.** Located in an old-fashioned train car just off of Main
AMERICAN   Street, everything about this diner is retro except the food. Hop on a
Fodor'sChoice   stool at the counter (that's all there is), enjoy the Motown tunes, and
★   tuck into one of their deluxe sandwiches with applewood bacon, egg,
jalapeño, and cheddar, or the challah French toast with Maine maple
syrup, with a side of caramelized grapefruit for breakfast. At lunch
you'll do well to order the delicious fried-chicken sandwich with cabbage slaw and french fries. $ *Average main: $10* ✉ *18 Franklin St., Bid-*
deford ☎ *207/284–0015* ⊕ *www.palacedinerme.com* ▭ *No credit cards.*

SHOPPING

Farrell & Co. At Farrell & Co. you can find fine, hand-dyed leather
goods, such as wallets, purses, and belts. Everything is individually
handcrafted by owner Meg Farrell. ✉ *22 Pearl St., Biddeford* ☎ *No*
phone ⊕ *www.farrellandcompany.com.*

Fodor'sChoice   **Rabelais Books.** Recently relocated from their longtime Portland location,
★   Rabelais Books, whose cheeky slogan is "Thought for Food," is an ode
to the art of cooking, drinking, and eating (and writing about it). Get
lost in one of the many recipe reference tomes, many of which are very
rare, or pick up a book or two for your favorite foodie. Rabelais is
located in the massive North Dam Mill complex, which houses a bevy
of unique local shops, many featuring products made by local artisans.
✉ *North Dam Mill Building 18, 2 Main St., Biddeford* ☎ *207/602–6246*
⊕ *www.rabelaisbooks.com.*

PORTLAND

Fodor'sChoice   *28 miles from Kennebunk via I–95 and I–295.*
★
Maine's largest city may be considered small by national standards—its
population is just 66,000—but its character, spirit, and appeal make it
feel much larger. It's well worth at least a day or two of exploration,
even if all you do is spend the entire time eating and drinking at the
many phenomenal restaurants, bakeries and specialty dessert shops,
craft cocktail bars, and microbreweries scattered across the city. Work
up your appetite roaming the working waterfront and strolling the
Eastern Promenade, shopping in the boutiques lined up along the brick
streets of the Old Port, or sauntering through the galleries of its top-
notch art museum.

A city of many names throughout its history, including Casco and Falmouth, Portland has survived many dramatic transformations, the most
recent of which is the massive influx of hipsters and foodies who have
opened up artisanal bars and quirky boutiques that are rapidly changing the city's character. Sheltered by the nearby Casco Bay Islands and
blessed with a deep port, Portland was a significant settlement right
from its start in the early 17th century. Settlers thrived on fishing and
lumbering, repeatedly building up the area while the British, French, and
Native Americans continually sacked it. Many considered the region
a somewhat dangerous frontier, but its potential for prosperity was so
apparent that settlers came anyway to tap its rich natural resources.

Portland's busy harbor is full of working boats, pleasure craft, and ferries headed to the Casco Bay Islands.

In 1632 Portland's first home was built on the Portland Peninsula in the area now known as Munjoy Hill. The British burned the city in 1775, when residents refused to surrender arms, but it was rebuilt and became a major trading center. Much of Portland was destroyed again in the Great Fire on July 4, 1866, when a flicked ash or perhaps a celebratory firecracker started a fire in a boatyard that grew into conflagration; 1,500 buildings burned to the ground.

GETTING HERE AND AROUND

From Interstate 95, take Interstate 295 to get to the Portland Peninsula and downtown. Commercial Street runs along the harbor, Fore Street is in one block up in the heart of the Old Port, and the Arts District stretches along diagonal Congress Street. Munjoy Hill is on the eastern end of the peninsula and the West End on the opposite side.

ESSENTIALS

Contacts Downtown Portland. ✉ *549 Congress St.* ☎ *207/772-6828* ⊕ *www.portlandmaine.com.* **Greater Portland Convention and Visitors Bureau.** ✉ *Visitor Information Center, 14 Ocean Gateway Pier* ☎ *207/772-5800* ⊕ *www.visitportland.com.*

TOURS

BUS TOURS

Portland Discovery Land & Sea Tours. The informative trolley tours of Portland Discovery detail the city's historical and architectural highlights, Memorial Day–October. Options include combining a city tour with a bay or lighthouse cruise. ✉ *Long Wharf, 170 Commercial St.* ☎ *207/774-0808* ⊕ *www.portlanddiscovery.com* 🎫 *From $14.*

WALKING TOURS

Greater Portland Landmarks. Take 1½-hour walking tours of Portland's historic West End on Friday, July–September, with Greater Portland Landmarks. Tours past the neighborhood's Greek Revival mansions and grand Federal-style homes begin at the group's headquarters and cost $10. You can also pick up maps for self-guided tours of the Old Port or the Western Promenade. ⌧ *93 High St.* ☎ *207/774–5561* ⊕ *www.portlandlandmarks.org* ✆ *From $10* ☉ *Tour at 11.*

Maine Foodie Tours. Learn about Portland's culinary history and sample local delights like lobster hors d'oeuvres, organic cheese, and the famous Maine whoopie pie. The culinary foot tours include stops at fishmongers, bakeries, and cheese shops that provide products to Portland's famed restaurants. From summer into early fall, you can also take a chocolate tour, a bike-and-brewery tour, or a trolley tour with a stop at a microbrewery. Tours begin at various locales in the Old Port. ☎ *207/233–7485* ⊕ *www.mainefoodietours.com* ✆ *From $55.*

Portland Freedom Trail. The Portland Freedom Trail offers a self-guided tour of sites associated with the Underground Railroad and the antislavery movement. ⌧ *Portland* ☎ *207/591–9980* ⊕ *www. portlandfreedomtrail.org* ✆ *Free.*

THE OLD PORT

Fodor'sChoice ★ A major international port and a working harbor since the early 17th century, the Old Port bridges the gap between the city's historical commercial activities and those of today. It is home to fishing boats docked alongside whale-watching charters, luxury yachts, cruise ships, and oil tankers from around the globe. Commercial Street parallels the water and is lined with brick buildings and warehouses that were built following the Great Fire of 1866. In the 19th century, candle makers and sail stitchers plied their trades here; today specialty shops, art galleries, and restaurants have taken up residence.

As with much of the city, it's best to park your car and explore the Old Port on foot. You can park at the city garage on Fore Street (between Exchange and Union streets) or opposite the U.S. Custom House at the corner of Fore and Pearl streets. A helpful hint: look for the "Park & Shop" sign on garages and parking lots, and get one hour of free parking for each stamp collected at participating shops. Allow a couple of hours to wander at leisure on Market, Exchange, Middle, and Fore streets. The city is very pedestrian-friendly. Maine state law requires vehicles to stop for pedestrians in crosswalks.

Harbor Fish Market. A Portland favorite since 1968, this freshest-of-the-fresh seafood market ships lobsters and other Maine delectables almost anywhere in the country. A bright-red facade on a working wharf opens into a bustling space with bubbling lobster tanks and fish, clams, and other shellfish on ice; employees are as skilled with a fillet knife as sushi chefs. There is also a small retail store. ⌧ *9 Custom House Wharf* ☎ *207/775–0251* ⊕ *www.harborfish.com* ✆ *Free.*

FAMILY **Maine Narrow Gauge Railroad Museum.** Whether you're crazy about old trains or just want to see the sights from a different perspective, the railroad museum has an extensive collection of locomotives and rail coaches, and offers scenic tours on narrow-gauge railcars. The 3-mile jaunts run on the hour and take you along Casco Bay, at the foot of the Eastern Promenade. The operating season caps off with a fall harvest ride (complete with cider), and during the Christmas season there are special Polar Express rides, based on the popular children's book. ⊠ *58 Fore St.* ☎ *207/828–0814* ⊕ *www.mainenarrowgauge.org* ⊠ *Museum $3, train rides $10* ⊗ *May–Oct., daily 10–4.*

NEED A BREAK?

Two Fat Cats Bakery. This bakery's whoopie pies are delicately proportioned, with a smooth and light marshmallow-cream filling, and a conservative selection of flavors (no mint-chocolate-chip pies to be found here). ⊠ *47 India St.* ☎ *207/347–5144* ⊕ *www.twofatcatsbakery.com.*

Portland Fish Exchange. You may want to hold your nose as you take a dip into the Old Port's active fish business at the 20,000-square-foot Portland Fish Exchange. Peek inside coolers teeming with cod, flounder, and monkfish, and watch fishermen repairing nets outside. ⊠ *6 Portland Fish Pier* ☎ *207/773–0017* ⊕ *www.pfex.org* ⊠ *Free* ⊗ *Daily 7–3.*

THE ARTS DISTRICT

This district starts at the top of Exchange Street, near the upper end of the Old Port, and extends west past the Portland Museum of Art. The district's central artery is Congress Street, which is lined with art galleries, specialty stores, and a score of restaurants and cafés. Parking is tricky; two-hour meters dot the sidewalks, but there are several garages nearby.

TOP ATTRACTIONS

FAMILY **Children's Museum & Theatre of Maine.** Kids can pretend they are lobstermen, veterinarians, shopkeepers, or actors in a play at Portland's small but fun Children's Museum. Most exhibits, many of which have a Maine theme, are hands-on and best for kids 10 and younger. Have a Ball! teaches about the science of motion, letting kids build ramps that make balls speed up, slow down, and leap across tracks. Don't miss the life-size inflatable humpback whale rising to the ceiling at the whale exhibit. The outdoor pirate-ship play area is a great place for a picnic lunch. Camera Obscura, an exhibit about optics, provides fascinating panoramic views of the city; it's aimed at adults and older children, and admission is therefore separate. ⊠ *142 Free St.* ☎ *207/828–1234* ⊕ *www.kitetails.org* ⊠ *Museum $10, Camera Obscura $4 ($2 on 1st Fri. of the month)* ⊗ *Memorial Day–Labor Day, daily 10–5; Labor Day–Memorial Day, Mon.–Sat. 10–5.*

Longfellow House and Garden. The boyhood home of the famous American poet was the first brick house in Portland and the oldest building on the peninsula. It's particularly interesting, because most of the furnishings, including the young Longfellow's writing desk, are original. Wallpaper, window coverings, and a vibrant painted carpet are period reproductions. Built in 1785, the large dwelling (a third floor was added in 1815) sits back from the street and has a small portico over its entrance and four chimneys surmounting the roof. It's part

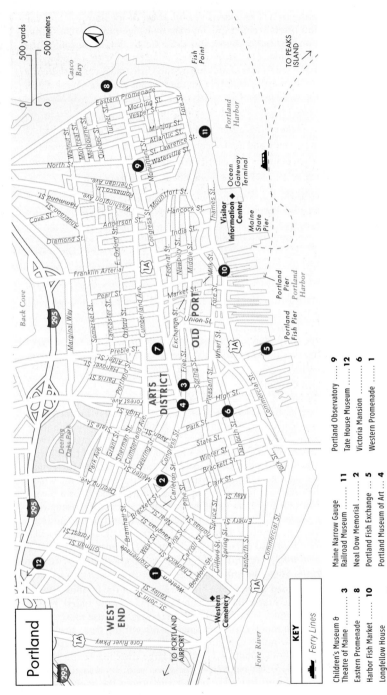

Portland

KEY

⛴ Ferry Lines

Children's Museum &
Theatre of Maine **3**
Eastern Promenade **8**
Harbor Fish Market **10**
Longfellow House
and Garden **7**

Maine Narrow Gauge
Railroad Museum **11**
Neal Dow Memorial **2**
Portland Fish Exchange ... **5**
Portland Museum of Art ... **4**

Portland Observatory **9**
Tate House Museum **12**
Victoria Mansion **6**
Western Promenade **1**

of the Maine Historical Society, which includes an adjacent research library and a museum with exhibits about Maine life. After your guided tour, stay for a picnic in the Longfellow Garden; it's open to the public during museum hours. ⊠ *489 Congress St.* ☎ *207/774–1822* ⊕ *www. mainehistory.org* ☜ *House and museum $15, gardens free* ⊗ *May–Oct., Mon.–Sat. 1st tour at 10:30–last tour at 4, Sun. 1st tour at noon–last tour at 4. Garden: May–Oct., daily 10–5.*

Fodor's Choice ★ **Portland Museum of Art.** Maine's largest public art institution's collection includes fine seascapes and landscapes by Winslow Homer, John Marin, Andrew Wyeth, Edward Hopper, Marsden Hartley, and other American painters. Homer's *Weatherbeaten,* a quintessential Maine Coast image, is here, and the museum owns and displays, on a rotating basis, 16 more of his paintings, plus more than 400 of his illustrations. The museum has works by Monet and Picasso, as well as Degas, Renoir, and Chagall. I. M. Pei designed the strikingly modern Charles Shipman Payson building, which fittingly displays modern art. The nearby L. D. M. Sweat Galleries showcase the collection of 19th-century American art. Special events are held in the gorgeous Federal-style 1801 McLellan House. ⊠ *7 Congress Sq.* ☎ *207/775–6148* ⊕ *www.portlandmuseum. org* ☜ *$12 (free Fri. 5–9)* ⊗ *Late May–mid-Oct., Mon.–Thurs. and weekends 10–5, Fri. 10–9; mid-Oct.–late May, Tues.–Thurs. and weekends 10–5, Fri. 10–9.*

Victoria Mansion. Built between 1858 and 1860, this Italianate mansion is widely regarded as the most sumptuously ornamented dwelling of its period remaining in the country. Architect Henry Austin designed the house for hotelier Ruggles Morse and his wife, Olive. The interior design—everything from the plasterwork to the furniture (much of it original)—is the only surviving commission of New York designer Gustave Herter. Behind the elegant brownstone exterior of this National Historic Landmark are colorful frescoed walls and ceilings, ornate marble mantelpieces, gilded gas chandeliers, a magnificent 6-foot-by-25-foot stained-glass ceiling window, and a freestanding mahogany staircase. A guided tour runs about 45 minutes and covers all the architectural highlights. Victorian era–themed gifts and art are sold in the museum shop, and the museum often has special themed events. ⊠ *109 Danforth St.* ☎ *207/772–4841* ⊕ *www.victoriamansion. org* ☜ *$15* ⊗ *May–Oct., Mon.–Sat. 10–4, Sun. 1–5. Christmas tours, day after Thanksgiving–Jan. 3, daily 11–5.*

WORTH NOTING

FAMILY **Eastern Promenade.** Between the city's two promenades, this one, often overlooked by tourists, has by far the best view. Gracious Victorian homes, many now converted to condos and apartments, border one side of the street. On the other is 68 acres of hillside parkland that includes Ft. Allen Park and, at the base of the hill, the Eastern Prom Trail and tiny East End Beach and Boat Launch. On a sunny day the Eastern Prom is a lovely spot for picnicking and people-watching. ⊠ *Washington Ave. to Fore St.*

Neal Dow Memorial. The mansion, once a stop on the Underground Railroad, was the home of Civil War general Neal Dow, who became known as the "Father of Prohibition." He was responsible for Maine's adoption of the anti-alcohol bill in 1851, which spurred a nationwide temperance movement. Now a museum, this majestic 1829 Federal-style home is open for guided tours that start on the hour. ⊠ *714 Congress St.* ☎ *207/773–7773* 🖃 *$5* ⊘ *May–Dec., Mon.–Sat. 11–4; Jan.–Apr., by appt.*

FAMILY **Portland Observatory.** This octagonal observatory on Munjoy Hill was built in 1807 by Captain Lemuel Moody, a retired sea captain, as a maritime signal tower. Moody used a telescope to identify incoming ships, and flags to signal to merchants where to unload their cargo. Held in place by 122 tons of ballast, it's the last remaining historic maritime signal station in the country. The guided tour leads all the way to the dome, where you can step out on the deck and take in views of Portland, the islands, and inland towards the White Mountains. ⊠ *138 Congress St.* ☎ *207/774–5561* ⊕ *www.portlandlandmarks.org* 🖃 *$9* ⊘ *Memorial Day weekend–Columbus Day, daily 10–5. Sunset tours: mid-July–early Sept., Thurs. 5–8.*

OFF THE
BEATEN
PATH
Tate House Museum. Built astride rose-granite steps and a period herb garden overlooking the Stroudwater River on the outskirts of Portland, this magnificent 1755 house was built by Captain George Tate. Tate had been commissioned by the English Crown to organize "the King's Broad Arrow"—the marking and cutting down of gigantic trees, which were shipped to England to be fashioned as masts for the British Royal Navy. The house has several period rooms, including a sitting room with some fine English Restoration chairs. With its clapboard siding still gloriously unpainted, its impressive Palladian doorway, dogleg stairway, unusual clerestory, and gambrel roof, this house will delight all lovers of Early American decorative arts. ⊠ *1267 Westbrook St.* ☎ *207/774–6177* ⊕ *www.tatehouse.org* 🖃 *$12* ⊘ *Early June–mid-Oct., Wed.–Sat. 10–4, Sun. 1–4. Tours on the hr (last tour at 3 pm).*

THE WEST END

A leisurely walk through Portland's West End, beginning at the top of the Arts District, offers a real treat to historic architecture buffs. The quiet and stately neighborhood, on the National Register of Historic Places, presents an extraordinary display of architectural splendor, from High Victorian Gothic to lush Italianate, Queen Anne, and Colonial Revival.

Western Promenade. A good place to start is at the head of the Western Promenade, which has benches and a nice view. From the Old Port, take Danforth Street all the way up to Vaughn Street; take a right on Vaughn and then an immediate left onto Western Promenade. Pass by the Western Cemetery, Portland's second official burial ground, laid out in 1829—inside is the ancestral plot of poet Henry Wadsworth Longfellow—and look for street parking. ⊠ *Danforth St. to Bramhall St.*

WHERE TO EAT

America's "Foodiest Small Town" is how one magazine described Portland, which is practically bursting at the seams with fabulous restaurants to rival those of a major metropolis. It's worth it to splurge and try as many as possible while visiting. Fresh seafood, including the famous Maine lobster, is still popular and prevalent, but it is being served up in unexpected ways that are a far cry from the usual bib and butter. There is a broad spectrum of cuisines to be enjoyed, and many chefs are pushing the envelope in their reinventions of traditional culinary idioms. More and more restaurants are using local meats, seafood, and organic produce as much as possible; changing menus reflect what is available in the region at the moment. Even the many excellent food trucks that have popped up across the city—several of which remain open in the off-season—reflect this trend. As sophisticated as many of these establishments have become in the way of food and service, the atmosphere is generally laid-back; with a few exceptions, you can leave your jacket and tie at home—just not your appetite.

Smoking is banned in all restaurants, taverns, and bars in Maine.

$ ✕**BaoBao Dumpling House.** Situated in a historic town house with traditional Asian decor in Portland's quaint West End, this dumpling house serves deeply satisfying Asian-inspired comfort food in an intimate setting. Start with their crispy braised chicken skin with ponzu, cucumber, scallion, and *togarashi* chili, then move on to one of their satisfying dumpling dishes with fillings like lamb, black-bean chili, and peanuts, or thread-cut hake with burdock. ⓢ *Average main: $10* ✉ *133 Spring St., at Park St. in Portland's West End* ☎ *207/772–8400* ⊕ *www.baobaodumplinghouse.com* ⊙ *Closed Mon. and Tues.*

ASIAN
FAMILY

$ ✕**Becky's Diner.** You won't find a more local or unfussy place—or one more abuzz with conversation at 4 am—than this waterfront institution way down on the end of Commercial Street. The food is cheap, generous in proportion, and has that satisfying, old-time-diner quality. Sitting next to you at the counter or in a neighboring booth could be rubber-booted fishermen back from sea, college students soothing a hangover, or suited business folks with BlackBerrys. From the upstairs deck you can watch the working waterfront in action. ⓢ *Average main: $14* ✉ *390 Commercial St.* ☎ *207/773–7070* ⊕ *www.beckysdiner.com.*

DINER
FAMILY

$ ✕**Duckfat.** Even in midafternoon, this small, hip sandwich shop in the Old Port is packed. The focus here is everyday farm-to-table fare: the signature Belgian fries are made with Maine potatoes cooked, yes, in duck fat and served in paper cones. Sandwiches are made with panini bread; choices like tuna melt with Thai chili mayo change seasonally, but the meat loaf and B.G.T. (bacon, goat cheese, tomato) are standards. Drink choices include gelato milk shakes, French-press coffee, lime-mint fountain sodas, beer, and wine. ⓢ *Average main: $12* ✉ *43 Middle St.* ☎ *207/774–8080* ⊕ *www.duckfat.com* ⌁ *Reservations not accepted.*

MODERN
AMERICAN

Lobster Shacks

If it's your first time to the Maine Coast, it won't be long before you stumble upon that famous and quintessentially Maine seaside eatery: the lobster shack. Also known as a lobster "pound" (especially elsewhere in New England), lobster shacks are essentially wooden huts with picnic tables set around the waterfront. The menu is simplicity itself: steamed lobster or clams by the pound, or a lobster roll; sides may include potato chips, coleslaw, or corn on the cob. Some pounds are even BYOB—no, not "bring your own bib" (those are usually provided)—but "bring your own beer" or refreshments.

One signature item at a lobster shack is the lobster dinner. Although it can vary from pound to pound, generally this means the works: a whole steamed lobster, steamed clams, corn on the cob, and potato chips. If the lobster dinner sounds like a bit much, then go for the classic lobster roll, a buttered New England–style hot-dog roll filled with chunks of lobster meat and a bit of mayo. Some pounds will serve it with lemon, some will serve it with butter, and some with even a touch of lettuce or herbs. Purists will serve no toppings at all—and why bother, when the unadulterated taste of fresh, sweet lobster meat can't be beat. Most shacks will even have a tank with live lobsters; a few will let you pick your own.

We can say this much: the best place to get a lobster dinner or lobster roll is at a shack, and the only authentic pounds are the simplest: a wooden shack, right on the water, with wooden picnic tables and—perhaps most important of all—a beautiful unobstructed view of working lobster boats in a scenic Maine harbor.

Maine Lobster Marketing Collaborative. You can find out more about Maine lobster from the Maine Lobster Marketing Collaborative. ⊠ 2 Union St., Suite 204 ☎ 207/541–9310 ⊕ www.lobsterfrommaine.com.

$$ ✕ **East Ender.** It doesn't get much better than the Maine lobster melt with
AMERICAN bacon jam and peppadew relish served at this pint-size restaurant; once
FAMILY you've had it, you may find it hard to go back to lobster merely dressed
Fodor's Choice in mayo on buttery bread. You'd also do well to try dishes like grilled
★ escarole and radicchio with poached egg and Parmesan, fried brussels sprouts and chili-lime vinaigrette, or pork-belly chili-cheese fries, washed down with a delicious craft cocktail. The emphasis is on the food rather than the atmosphere, which isn't surprising, given that the owners formerly served their tasty fare from a truck. $ *Average main: $24* ⊠ *47 Middle St.* ☎ *207/879–7669* ⊕ *www.eastenderportland.com.*

$ ✕ **El Rayo Taqueria.** For some of the best Mexican food in town, head to
MEXICAN this hip spot housed in a former gas station. The flavors are as vibrant as the turquoise, yellow, and fuchsia decor. The guacamole and salsas are made fresh daily. Pull up a stool at the counter, or grab a bright oilcloth-covered picnic table out front. Wash down achiote-seasoned fish tacos or a citrus-and-cumin-marinated chicken burrito with a lemon-hibiscus *refresca* (cold drink) or a house margarita. $ *Average main: $10* ⊠ *101 York St., at High St.* ☎ *207/780–8226* ⊕ *www.elrayotaqueria.com.*

For the full "Maine" experience, try a classic lobster dinner.

$
BURGER
✕ **Elevation Burger.** There's nothing like tucking into a nice, juicy burger; it's even better when you can do so with a clear conscience. Elevation Burger serves up simple, delicious fare made from high-quality ingredients, most of which are sustainably sourced, like their organic, grass-fed, free-range beef. The crispy french fries here are cooked in 100% olive oil and a tasty organic veggie burger means that grass-fed visitors don't have to miss out on the fun. $ *Average main: $10* ✉ *205 Commercial St.* ☎ *207/775–6800* ⊕ *www.elevationburger.com.*

$
SEAFOOD
Fodor's Choice
★
✕ **Eventide Oyster Co.** Eventide is not just any old oyster bar. Not only do they have fresh and tasty oysters artfully prepared with novel accoutrements like kimchi and ginger ices and cucumber-champagne mignonette, they also serve a delicious scallop crudo with blood orange and chili miso, and smoked arctic char with cucumber and Pernod. If seafood isn't exactly your cup of tea, they also have good alternatives like house-cured corned beef and a fried-chicken sandwich with pickled watermelon. The menu constantly changes, depending on what's in season, so it's best to order a handful of small plates, a glass of bubbly, or one of their signature tiki-style cocktails, and, of course, a dozen oysters. $ *Average main: $15* ✉ *86 Middle St.* ☎ *207/774–8538* ⊕ *www.eventideoysterco.com.*

$$$
MODERN
AMERICAN
✕ **Five Fifty-Five.** Classic dishes are cleverly updated at this classy and very popular Congress Street spot. The menu changes seasonally to reflect ingredients available from local waters, organic farms, and food purveyors, but seared local diver scallops, served in a buttery carrot-vanilla emulsion, are an exquisite mainstay. So is the mac 'n' cheese, which boasts artisanal cheeses and shaved black truffles. You may also

find dishes such as milk-braised rabbit with Himalayan red rice and lemon-dressed local greens. Try the tasting menus, which start at $70, or come for Sunday brunch. The space, with exposed brick and copper accents, is a former 19th-century firehouse. A sister restaurant, Petite Jacqueline bistro in Longfellow Square, has also earned accolades and fans. [$] *Average main: $30* ✉ *555 Congress St.* ☎ *207/761–0555* 🌐 *www.fivefifty-five.com* 🕒 *No lunch.*

$ PIZZA FAMILY 🍴 **Flatbread.** Families, students, and bohemian types gather at this popular New England chain flatbread-pizza place. Two massive wood-fire ovens are the heart of the soaring, warehouselike space; in summer, you can escape the heat by dining on the deck overlooking the harbor. The menu has eight signature pizzas made with fresh, local ingredients, plus weekly veggie and meat specials; everything is homemade, organic, and nitrate-free. Be sure to order the delicious house salad with toasted sesame seeds, seaweed, blue or goat cheese, and ginger-tamarind vinaigrette, and don't neglect to gulp down one of the delicious microbrews on tap. **■ TIP→ Waits can be long on weekends and in summer, but you can call a half-hour ahead to put your name on the list, or grab a drink from the bar and wait outside with a view of the harbor.** [$] *Average main: $15* ✉ *72 Commercial St.* ☎ *207/772–8777* 🌐 *www.flatbreadcompany.com.*

$$$ MODERN AMERICAN Fodor's Choice ★ 🍴 **Fore Street.** One of Maine's best chefs, Sam Hayward, opened this restaurant in a renovated warehouse on the edge of the Old Port in 1996. The menu changes daily to reflect the freshest ingredients from Maine's farms and waters, as well as the tremendous creativity of the staff. Every copper-top table in the main dining room has a view of the enormous brick oven and soapstone hearth that anchor the open kitchen, where sous-chefs seem to dance as they create such dishes as turnspit-roasted dry-rubbed pork loin, wood-grilled Maine-island lamb chop with sunroot purée, and Maine mussels oven roasted in garlic and almond butter. Desserts include artisanal cheeses, homemade chocolate truffles, and pastries. In July or August, book two months in advance; otherwise, a week is usually fine. **■ TIP→ Last-minute planners take heart: a third of the tables are reserved for walk-ins.** [$] *Average main: $30* ✉ *288 Fore St.* ☎ *207/775–2717* 🌐 *www.forestreet.biz* 🕒 *No lunch* ✍ *Reservations essential.*

$ CAFÉ FAMILY Fodor's Choice ★ 🍴 **Gelato Fiasco.** Proper Italian gelato and sorbetto here comes in traditional flavors, as well as more offbeat varieties like molasses peppermint stick, Wild Turkey bourbon, Girl Scout cookie, Vietnamese coffee, and spiked eggnog. There are new flavors everyday, along with espresso and other hot drinks. If you can't make a decision from the impossible selection, they also sell mystery pints that make that selection for you. [$] *Average main: $5* ✉ *425 Fore St.* ☎ *207/699–4314* 🌐 *www.gelatofiasco.com.*

$$ SEAFOOD FAMILY 🍴 **Gilbert's Chowder House.** This is the real deal, as quintessential as Maine dining can be. Clam rakes and nautical charts hang from the walls of this unpretentious waterfront diner. The flavors are from the depths of the North Atlantic, prepared and presented simply: fried shrimp, haddock, clam strips, extraordinary clam cakes, and fish, clam, and seafood chowders (corn, too). A chalkboard of daily specials often

features fish 'n' chips. Don't miss out on the lobster roll: a toasted hot-dog bun bursting with claw and tail meat lightly dressed with mayo but otherwise unadulterated. It's classic Maine, fuss-free, and presented on a paper plate. $ *Average main: $19* ⊠ *92 Commercial St.* ☎ *207/871–5636* ⊕ *www.gilbertschowderhouse.com.*

$ ✕ **The Holy Donut.** Even if you're a health freak, you'll love the doughnuts
CAFÉ at this place. Sweet and savory all-natural, potato-based doughnuts are
FAMILY glazed in flavors such as dark chocolate sea salt, maple, pomegranate, coffee brandy, and chai, or stuffed with delicious fillings like Maine wild blueberries, bacon cheddar, or ricotta. And if those aren't adventurous enough for you, they're always coming up with new inventions, like the preposterously wonderful lobster-stuffed doughnut. Many vegan and gluten-free options are available regularly, and the shop closes once all the doughnuts are sold for the day. $ *Average main: $5* ⊠ *7 Exchange St.* ☎ *207/874–7774* ⊕ *www.theholydonut.com.*

$ ✕ **Home Catering Company.** Nestled in a former grocer's shop in Port-
DELI land's West End, this deli has all the fixings you need for an impromptu picnic, a cozy night in, or just chowing down on the bench outside. Order a delicious sandwich with their famous candied bacon, or try one of their decadent French onion grilled cheeses. You can also grab a bottle of good wine, craft beer, or an artisanal soft drink from their coolers, as well as a bag of specialty chips and maybe a dessert (or two). $ *Average main: $10* ⊠ *129 Spring St.* ☎ *207/536–0260* ⊕ *www.homecateringcompany.com* ☽ *Closed Sun.*

$ ✕ **The Honey Paw.** Come for the salty wontons, piping-hot broths, and
ASIAN FUSION wok-fried noodles; stay for the turntable music, the well-stocked cock-tail bar, and the soft-serve ice cream that comes in flavors like honey-comb, magic shell, or caramelized honey. If you order one thing here, make it the lobster tartine, topped with a cilantro emulsion, radish, and hijiki. Slurp down some oysters and bubbly next door at their sister restaurant, Eventide Oyster Co., and then skip over here for something more substantial. $ *Average main: $15* ⊠ *7 Middle St.* ☎ *207/774–8538* ⊕ *www.thehoneypaw.com* ☽ *Closed Tues.*

$$$$ ✕ **Hugo's.** Serving the freshest local organic foods is a high priority at
ECLECTIC Hugo's, and your server is sure to know everything about their various purveyors. Updated daily, the menu at this stylish eatery is made up of smartly prepared, seasonally inspired dishes like crispy-skin pork belly and crêpe-wrapped arctic char. You can choose five courses for $90, or go light with two courses for $45. A 2013 renovation added an open kitchen, a handsome curved bar, and an airy, open-concept dining room. $ *Average main: $45* ⊠ *88 Middle St.* ☎ *207/774–8538* ⊕ *www.hugos.net* ☽ *Closed Sun. No lunch.*

$$ ✕ **Local 188.** There's an infectious vibe at this eclectic, Spanish-inspired
SPANISH Arts District eatery, a foodie hot spot as well as a longtime local favor-
Fodor's Choice ite. The 2,000-square-foot space has lofty tin ceilings and worn maple
★ floors; mismatched chandeliers dangle over the dining area, and a pair of antlers crowns the open kitchen. Regulars chat with servers about which just-caught seafood will decorate the paella or which organic veggies will star in the tortillas, one of several tapas choices. You'll find entrées like Casco Bay hake with herb salsa verde, poached purple

potatoes, smoked aioli, and beets. Many of the 10 or so draft brews are Maine crafted; there are some 150 wines (mostly European). Reservations aren't taken for the large bar area. [$] *Average main: $23* ✉ *685 Congress St.* ☎ *207/761–7909* 🌐 *www.local188.com* 🕘 *No lunch.*

$$$ TAPAS 🍴 **Lolita.** Perched on Munjoy Hill near the Portland Observatory, Lolita has a sophisticated bodega vibe, where wood-fired dishes like scallops with hazelnuts and roasted clams are offered alongside charcuterie and cheese boards and plenty of robust wine—the intimate setting makes for a great date night. Or come for a midday snack alone or with a group of friends and pass around a bevy of the many small, tapas-style dishes. [$] *Average main: $30* ✉ *90 Congress St.* ☎ *207/775–5652* 🌐 *www.lolita-portland.com.*

$ FRENCH FAMILY Fodor's Choice ★ 🍴 **Portland Pâtisserie and Grand Café.** This is the perfect spot for a quick, delicious bite any time of day, but early risers will be rewarded with a wider selection of pastries at this chic patisserie, with floor-to-ceiling picture windows that allow for superb people-watching. Whether you're in the mood for a frothy café au lait and a macaron, or a decadent duck-confit-and-Gruyère-filled crêpe, Portland Pâtisserie does not disappoint. Don't shy away from sharing a couple of different desserts, or taking some for the road. [$] *Average main: $10* ✉ *46 Market St.* ☎ *207/553–2555* 🌐 *www.portlandpatisserie.com.*

$$$$ ASIAN FUSION 🍴 **Tempo Dulu.** Probably the only place in Maine that focuses exclusively on top-notch Southeast Asian cuisine, Tempo Dulu offers both three-course and tasting menus with outstanding service. This tastefully appointed restaurant and bar has refined decor that includes special touches like a hollowed-out lamp-shade topiary, a bevy of giant golden eggs, and shimmering chandeliers. The exceptional cocktail bar serves drinks concocted with exotic ingredients like smoked Chinese spices, absinthe mist, jasmine-infused Plymouth gin, and rose air. Splurge and try the lobster tasting menu, or order the Indonesian *rijsttafel,* with many small dishes that are well suited to both a family-style meal and a more adventurous palate. [$] *Average main: $67* ✉ *Danforth Inn, 163 Danforth St.* ☎ *207/879–8755* 🌐 *www.tempodulu.restaurant.*

$$$ AMERICAN FAMILY 🍴 **Union.** Located in the newly minted Press Hotel, Union Restaurant has a sophisticated (but not stuffy) air that is reflected in its menu, which focuses on local ingredients, many of which are foraged and fished. Most dishes are modern comfort food, like the local venison carpaccio with toasted hazelnuts, juniper, spruce-bud oil, and endive drizzled with white-truffle emulsion, or the caramelized brussels sprouts with orange aioli and smoked almonds. Breakfast is also a treat: you'll find maple *pain perdu* served alongside smoked-salmon tartines and classic dishes like eggs Benedict. [$] *Average main: $30* ✉ *Press Hotel, 390 Congress St.* ☎ *207/808–8700* 🌐 *www.unionportland.com.*

$$$ ECLECTIC 🍴 **Walter's.** A fixture in the Old Port since the late 1980s, this relaxed, busy place with a chic modern interior is popular with suits and tourists alike. The seasonal menu nicely balances local seafood and meats with Asian and other international flavors. You'll find appetizers like calamari dressed with lemon-and-cherry-pepper aioli and such entrées as crispy duck breast served with spaetzle, baby bok choy, and plum sauce. An inviting bar has a lighter menu; try the mussels or the Greek

lamb sliders. $ *Average main: $28* ⊠ *2 Portland Sq.* ☎ *207/871–9258* ⊕ *www.waltersportland.com* ⊙ *Closed Sun. No lunch Sat.*

WHERE TO STAY

As Portland's popularity as a vacation destination has increased, so have its options for overnight visitors. Though several large hotels—geared toward high-tech, amenity-obsessed guests—have been built in the Old Port, they have in no way diminished the success of smaller, more intimate lodgings. Inns and B&Bs have taken up residence throughout the West End, often giving new life to the grand mansions of Portland's wealthy 19th-century merchants. For the least expensive accommodations, you'll find chain hotels near the interstate and the airport.

Expect to pay at least $150 or so per night for a pleasant room (often with complimentary breakfast) within walking distance of the Old Port during high season, and more than $400 for the most luxurious of suites. At the height of summer, many places are booked; make reservations well in advance, and ask about off-season specials.

$$
B&B/INN
The Danforth. A stunning showpiece, this stylish inn was one of Portland's grandest Federal-style dwellings when it was built in 1823. **Pros:** gorgeous rooms; basement billiards room; city views from cupola. **Cons:** small windows in some third-floor rooms. $ *Rooms from: $298* ⊠ *163 Danforth St.* ☎ *207/879–8755, 800/879–8755* ⊕ *www.danforthinn. com* ⇨ *9 rooms* ¶⊙¶ *Breakfast.*

$
B&B/INN
FAMILY
Inn on Carleton. This 1869 Victorian has a curved mahogany staircase to the third floor, a bay window overlooking the street from the front parlor, and gleaming pumpkin-pine floors. **Pros:** most rooms have electric fireplaces; English garden with fountain; attentive resident innkeeper. **Cons:** no elevator. $ *Rooms from: $195* ⊠ *46 Carleton St.* ☎ *207/775–1910, 800/639–1779* ⊕ *www.innoncarleton.com* ⇨ *6 rooms* ¶⊙¶ *Breakfast.*

$
B&B/INN
FAMILY
Morrill Mansion. This 19th-century town house has tastefully appointed rooms with well-executed color schemes—blue is a favorite hue here. **Pros:** close to arts district; parlors on each floor for relaxing. **Cons:** not on a grand block. $ *Rooms from: $169* ⊠ *249 Vaughan St.* ☎ *207/774–6900, 888/566–7745* ⊕ *www.morrillmansion.com* ⇨ *6 rooms, 2 suites* ¶⊙¶ *Breakfast.*

$$
B&B/INN
Fodor's Choice
★
Pomegranate Inn. The classic facade of this handsome 1884 Italianate in the architecturally rich Western Promenade area gives no hint of the splashy, modern, but cozy surprises within. **Pros:** funky, modern decor; many rooms have gas fireplaces; close to Western Promenade. **Cons:** 15- to 20-minute walk to the Old Port. $ *Rooms from: $299* ⊠ *49 Neal St.* ☎ *207/772–1006, 800/356–0408* ⊕ *www.pomegranateinn.com* ⇨ *7 rooms, 1 suite* ¶⊙¶ *Breakfast.*

$$
HOTEL
The Portland Regency Hotel & Spa. Not part of a chain despite the "Regency" name, this brick building in the center of the Old Port served as Portland's armory in the late 19th century. **Pros:** easy walk to sites; lots of room variety for a hotel. **Cons:** lower-than-standard ceilings in many rooms. $ *Rooms from: $284* ⊠ *20 Milk St.* ☎ *207/774–4200, 800/727–3436* ⊕ *www.theregency.com* ⇨ *95 rooms, 10 suites* ¶⊙¶ *No meals.*

$$$
HOTEL
FAMILY
Fodor's Choice
★

The Press Hotel. Housed in a former newspaper building, this boutique hotel is part of the Marriott group—though you'd never guess it. **Pros:** excellent views of the water from the top two floors; sparkling-clean rooms with a modern-design feel; art gallery and excellent public spaces with tasteful furnishings; Frette bed linens and Maine-made Cuddledown comforters and bed throws. **Cons:** right next to the fire department. $ *Rooms from: $332* ✉ *119 Exchange St.* ☎ *877/890–5641* ⊕ *www.thepresshotel.com* ⇆ *110 rooms* ◉ *No meals.*

$
B&B/INN
FAMILY

West End Inn. Set among the glorious homes of the Western Promenade, this 1871 Georgian displays much of the era's grandeur, with high pressed-tin ceilings, intricate moldings, ceiling medallions, and a dramatic ruby-red foyer. **Pros:** fireplace library is a cozy place to relax; just heading out for the paper is a historic walking tour. **Cons:** 15-to 20-minute walk downtown. $ *Rooms from: $189* ✉ *146 Pine St.* ☎ *800/338–1377* ⊕ *www.westendbb.com* ⇆ *6 rooms* ◉ *Breakfast.*

NIGHTLIFE AND PERFORMING ARTS

NIGHTLIFE

Portland's nightlife scene is largely centered on the bustling Old Port and a few smaller, artsy spots on Congress Street. There's a great emphasis on live music from local bands and pubs serving award-winning local microbrews. Several hip bars have cropped up, serving appetizers along with a full array of specialty wines and serious craft cocktails. Portland is a fairly sleepy city after midnight, but you can usually find a couple of bars and restaurants open, even after the clock strikes 12.

The Bearded Lady's Jewelbox. This hip, craft cocktail–centric hole-in-the-wall has tons of charm and a speakeasy vibe (indeed, there's no sign on the door). Sip a dainty glass of potent French absinthe, or one of the many creative concoctions on the ever-changing cocktail list. Rotating bar snacks include things like house meatballs, turmeric pickles, and candied popcorn with bacon butter and cayenne pepper. Check out the massive, hand-painted mural on the wall that depicts—you guessed it—some elegant bearded ladies. ✉ *644 Congress St.* ☎ *207/747–5384* ⊕ *www.thebeardedladysjewelbox.com.*

Bull Feeney's. For nightly specials, plenty of Guinness, and live entertainment, head to Bull Feeney's, a lively two-story Irish pub and restaurant. ✉ *375 Fore St.* ☎ *207/773–7210.*

Gritty McDuff's Portland Brew Pub. Maine's original brewpub serves fine ales, British pub fare, and seafood dishes. There are between six and eight rotating ales on tap, and there's always a seasonal offering. Come on Tuesday, Saturday, and Sunday nights for live music. ✉ *396 Fore St.* ☎ *207/772–2739* ⊕ *www.grittys.com.*

Fodor's Choice
★

Novare Res Bier Café. At tucked-away Novare Res Bier Café, choose from some three dozen rotating drafts and more than 300 bottled brews. Relax on an expansive deck, munch on antipasti, or share a meat-and-cheese plate. Maine craft beers occupy at least eight of the taps at any given time, and the rest span the globe, with an emphasis on Belgian

WHAT'S ON TAP: MICROBREWERIES

One of the nation's craft-beer hotbeds, Maine is home to around 40 breweries, and several of the larger ones—Allagash, Geary's, and Shipyard—are in and around Portland. These breweries are open for tours and tastings, but beer lovers may prefer the smaller brewpubs that make their own beer and serve it fresh from their own taps in neighborhood taverns. In the Old Port you'll find Gritty McDuff's, Sebago Brewing Company, and Liquid Riot Bottling Company. In Bayside there's Rising Tide and Bunker Brewing Company. Sign up for one of the excellent sudsy tours offered by Maine Beer Tours (⊕ www.mainebeertours.com), and if you're in town in November, check out the Maine Brewer's Festival (⊕ www.mainebrewersfestival. com). Or pick up a Maine Beer Trail map from the Maine Brewers' Guild (⊕ www.mainebrewersguild.org).

and Trappist ales. ⊠ *4 Canal Plaza, off Exchange St.* ☎ *207/761–2437* ⊕ *www.novareresbiercafe.com.*

Fodor's Choice ★ **Portland Hunt and Alpine Club.** Scandinavian-inspired small bites and serious craft cocktails drive this hip new locale that includes delicious negronis on tap and excellent charcuterie and seafood boards in an intimate Alpine-style hut. Go for the excellent happy hour, on Monday 3–6 or on Friday 1–6. ⊠ *75 Market St.* ☎ *207/747–4754* ⊕ *www. huntandalpineclub.com.*

Rí Rá. This happening Irish pub has live music Thursday–Saturday nights and a pub quiz on Tuesday. For a more mellow experience, settle into a couch at the upstairs bar. ⊠ *72 Commercial St.* ☎ *207/761–4446* ⊕ *www.rira.com.*

Sonny's. In a Victorian-era bank building with arched windows overlooking an Old Port square, this stylish bar and lounge packs in the late-night crowd. It has quite a list of cocktails, many of which use house-infused liquors—try the chili tequila. Bluegrass and funk bands play on Thursday, and there's a DJ on Saturday. Their Latin American cuisine is a winner, too; at night you can order lighter fare like a poblano cheeseburger with yam fries, as well as entrées like the braised brisket enchilada. On weekends, brunch is served 10–3, and the kitchen stays open until 10:30 pm. ⊠ *83 Exchange St.* ☎ *207/772–7774* ⊕ *www. sonnysportland.com.*

Fodor's Choice ★ **Vena's Fizz House.** The old-fashioned soda fountain gets a modern update at Vena's Fizz House, where flavors like raspberry mint, chocolate-covered cherry cordial, and frothy blood orange go into delicious, fizzy "mocktails," while their cocktails feature artisanal ingredients such as peppercorn-bacon bitters, saffron, and ghost pepper. ⊠ *345 Fore St.* ☎ *207/747–4901* ⊕ *www.venasfizzhouse.com.*

PERFORMING ARTS

Art galleries and studios have spread throughout the city, infusing many abandoned, yet beautiful, old buildings and shops with new life. Many are concentrated along the Congress Street downtown corridor; others are hidden amid the boutiques and restaurants of the Old Port and the East End. A great way to get acquainted with the city's artists is to participate in the First Friday Art Walk, a free self-guided tour of galleries, museums, and alternative-art venues that happens—you guessed it—on the first Friday of each month.

FAMILY **Mayo Street Arts.** An alternative arts venue for the innovative and up-and-coming, Mayo Street Arts often features intimate concerts, contemporary exhibitions, and offbeat puppet shows in a repurposed church. ⊠ *10 Mayo St.* ☎ *207/879–4629* ⊕ *www.mayostreetarts.org.*

FAMILY **Merrill Auditorium.** This soaring concert hall hosts numerous theatrical and musical events, including performances by the Portland Symphony Orchestra and the Portland Opera Repertory Theatre. Ask about organ recitals on the auditorium's huge 1912 Kotzschmar Memorial Organ. ⊠ *20 Myrtle St.* ☎ *207/842–0800* ⊕ *www.merrillauditorium.net.*

FAMILY **Portland Stage.** This company mounts theatrical productions on its two stages September–May. ⊠ *25-A Forest Ave.* ☎ *207/774–0465* ⊕ *www. portlandstage.org.*

FAMILY **Space Gallery.** Space Gallery sparkles as a contemporary art gallery and alternative arts venue, opening its doors to everything from poetry readings and art fairs to live music to documentary films. The gallery is open Wednesday–Saturday. ⊠ *538 Congress St.* ☎ *207/828–5600* ⊕ *www.space538.org.*

SPORTS AND THE OUTDOORS

When the weather's good, everyone in Portland heads outside, whether for boating on the water, lounging on a beach, or walking and biking the promenades. There are also many green spaces nearby Portland, including Crescent Beach State Park, Two Lights State Park, and Fort Williams Park, home to Portland Head Light. All are on the coast south of the city in suburban Cape Elizabeth and offer walking trails, picnic facilities, and water access. Bradbury Mountain State Park, in Pownal, has incredible vistas from its easily climbed peak. In Freeport is Wolfe's Neck Woods State Park, where you can take a guided nature walk and see nesting ospreys. Both are north of Portland.

BICYCLING

FAMILY **Bicycle Coalition of Maine.** For state bike trail maps, club and tour listings, or hints on safety, contact the Bicycle Coalition of Maine. Maps are available at the group's headquarters in the Arts District. ⊠ *34 Preble St.* ☎ *207/623–4511* ⊕ *www.bikemaine.org.*

FAMILY **Cycle Mania.** Rent bikes downtown at Cycle Mania. The $25 per day rate includes a helmet and lock. ⊠ *65 Cove St.* ☎ *207/774–2933* ⊕ *www.cyclemania1.com.*

FAMILY **Gorham Bike and Ski.** You can rent several types of bikes, including hybrid and tandem models, starting at $35 per day. ⊠ *693 Congress St.* ☎ *207/773–1700* ⊕ *www.gorhambike.com.*

FAMILY **Portland Trails.** For local biking and hiking information, contact Portland Trails. The staff can tell you about designated paved and unpaved

CLOSE UP

The Eastern Prom Trail

To experience the city's busy shoreline and take in the grand views of Casco Bay, walkers, runners, and cyclists head out on the 2.1-mile Eastern Prom Trail.

Beginning at the intersection of Commercial and India streets, this paved trail runs along the water at the bottom of the Eastern Promenade, following an old rail bed alongside the still-used railroad tracks of the Maine Narrow Gauge Railroad Co. & Museum. There are plenty of places with benches and tables for a picnic break along the way. From the trailhead, it's about 1 mile to the small East End Beach.

Continuing along the trail, you'll pass underneath busy Interstate 295, and emerge at the Back Cove Trail, a popular 3½-mile loop you can connect with for a long trek. To return to the Old Port, backtrack along the

trail or head up the steep path to the top of the promenade. Here you can continue along the promenade sidewalk or take the trails through this 68-acre stretch of parkland to the lovely picnic area and playground.

Continuing along the sidewalk toward the Old Port, a gazebo and several old cannons to your left indicate you're at the small Fort Allen Park. Use one of the coin-operated viewing scopes to view Civil War–era Fort Gorges, which never saw action.

Where the Eastern Prom becomes Fore Street, continue on for a few blocks to India Street and take a left, which will bring you back to where you started. Or, continue into the Old Port.

Plan at least an hour to walk the trail with brief stops, or two if you continue along the Back Cove Trail. But if can, make time for the Prom— it's truly an urban jewel.

---

routes that wind along the water, through parks, and beyond. ⊠ *305 Commercial St.* ☎ *207/775–2411* ⊕ *www.trails.org.*

BOATING

Various Portland-based skippers offer whale-, dolphin-, and seal-watching cruises; excursions to lighthouses and islands; and fishing and lobstering trips. Board the ferry to see nearby islands. Self-navigators can rent kayaks or canoes.

FAMILY **Casco Bay Lines.** Casco Bay Lines operates ferry service to the seven bay islands with year-round populations. Summer offerings include music cruises, lighthouse excursions, and a trip to Bailey Island with a stopover for lunch. ⊠ *Maine State Pier, 56 Commercial St.* ☎ *207/774–7871* ⊕ *www.cascobaylines.com.*

FAMILY **Lucky Catch Cruises.** Set sail in a real lobster boat: this company gives you the genuine experience, which includes hauling traps and the chance to purchase the catch. ⊠ *Long Wharf, 170 Commercial St.* ☎ *207/761– 0941* ⊕ *www.luckycatch.com.*

FAMILY **Odyssey Whale Watch.** From mid-May to mid-October, Odyssey Whale Watch leads whale-watching and deep-sea-fishing excursions. ⊠ *Long Wharf, 170 Commercial St.* ☎ *207/775–0727* ⊕ *www. odysseywhalewatch.com.*

FAMILY **Portland Discovery Land & Sea Tours.** For tours of the harbor and Casco Bay in a boat or on a trolley, including an up-close look at several lighthouses, try Portland Discovery Land & Sea Tours. ⊠ *Long Wharf, 170 Commercial St.* ☎ *207/774–0808* ⊕ *www.portlanddiscovery.com.*

FAMILY **Portland Paddle.** Run by a pair of Registered Maine Guides, Portland Paddle leads introductory sea kayaking clinics along with guided trips between the Casco Bay islands June through September. Two-hour sunset paddles ($38) are a fave, but the most unique offering involves a four-hour paddle to the abandoned island military installation of Fort Gorges ($65), where you'll enjoy a short acoustic concert before heading back. Kayak and paddleboard rentals are available. ⊠ *Eastern Promenade, East End Beach, off Cutter St.* ☎ *207/370–9730* ⊕ *www. portlandpaddle.net* ⊙ *Closed Nov.–May. Oct. by appt. only.*

FAMILY **Portland Schooner Co.** May through October this company offers daily windjammer cruises aboard the vintage schooners *Bagheera* and *Wendameen.* You can also arrange overnight trips. ⊠ *Maine State Pier, 56 Commercial St.* ☎ *207/766–2500* ⊕ *www.portlandschooner.com.*

HOT-AIR-BALLOON RIDES

FAMILY **Hot Fun First Class Balloon Flights.** Hot Fun First Class Balloon Flights flies mainly sunrise trips and can accommodate two people. The price of $325 per person includes a postflight champagne toast, snacks, and shuttle to the liftoff site. Additional passengers can sometimes be accommodated, especially children. ⊠ *Portland* ☎ *207/799–0193* ⊕ *www.hotfunballoons.com.*

SHOPPING

Exchange Street is great for arts and crafts and boutique browsing, while Commercial Street caters to the souvenir hound—gift shops are packed with nautical items, and lobster and moose emblems are emblazoned on everything from T-shirts to shot glasses.

ART AND ANTIQUES

Abacus. This appealing crafts gallery has gift items in glass, wood, and textiles, as well as fine modern jewelry. ⊠ *44 Exchange St.* ☎ *207/772–4880* ⊕ *www.abacusgallery.com.*

Greenhut Galleries. The contemporary art at this gallery changes with the seasons. Artists represented include David Driskell, an artist and leading art scholar. ⊠ *146 Middle St.* ☎ *207/772–2693, 207/772–2693* ⊕ *www.greenhutgalleries.me.*

Portland Architectural Salvage. A fixer-upper's dream, Portland Architectural Salvage has four floors of unusual finds from old buildings, including fixtures, hardware, and stained-glass windows, as well as assorted antiques. ⊠ *131 Preble St.* ☎ *207/780–0634* ⊕ *www.portlandsalvage.com.*

FAMILY **Portland Flea-for-All.** Friday through Sunday, head to the city's Bayside neighborhood for the Portland Flea-for-All, where you'll find all sorts of vintage eye candy from an-ever rotating array of antiques and artisan vendors—a fun excursion, whether or not you actually buy anything. ⊠ *125 Kennebec St.* ☎ *207/370–7570* ⊕ *www.portlandfleaforall.com.*

BOOKS

Longfellow Books. This shop is known for its good service, author readings, and excellent selection of new and used books and magazines. Even if you go in looking for something specific, you'll almost certainly stumble on something even better you didn't know about before. ⊠ *1 Monument Way* ☎ *207/772–4045* ⊕ *www.longfellowbooks.com.*

Fodor's Choice
★ **Sherman's Books and Stationery.** Open since 1886, Sherman's is Maine's oldest bookstore chain. The Portland store has an impressive stock of well-selected books interspersed with excellent gift choices, such as stationery, candles, and holiday decor, as well as a fun array of toys. It's a good place to spend a cold or rainy day perusing the selection. ⊠ *49 Exchange St.* ☎ *207/773–4100* ⊕ *www.shermans.com.*

CLOTHING

Bliss. Hip boutique Bliss stocks clothing and accessories by cutting-edge designers, plus jeans by big names like J Brand and Mother. There's also a great selection of Frye boots. ⊠ *58 Exchange St.* ☎ *207/879–7129* ⊕ *www.blissboutiques.com.*

Fodor's Choice
★ **Judith.** Owned and operated by a former fashion designer, this stunning, well-curated concept boutique features women's apparel, shoes, accessories, and contemporary housewares. ⊠ *3 Market St.* ☎ *207/747–4778* ⊕ *www.shopjudith.com* ⊗ *Closed Tues.*

Sea Bags. At Sea Bags, totes made from recycled sailcloth and decorated with bright, graphic patterns are sewn right in the store. ⊠ *25 Custom House Wharf* ☎ *207/780–0744* ⊕ *www.seabags.com.*

HOUSEHOLD ITEMS/FURNITURE

Angela Adams. Maine islander Angela Adams specializes in simple but bold geometric motifs parlayed into dramatic rugs (custom, too), canvas totes, bedding, and other home accessories. The shop also carries sleek wood furniture from her husband's wood shop. ⊠ *131 Middle St.* ⊕ *www.angelaadams.com.*

Asia West. For reproduction and antique furnishings with a Far East feel, head to this stylish showroom on the waterfront. ⊠ *219 Commercial St.* ☎ *207/775–0066* ⊕ *www.asiawest.net.*

Fodor's Choice
★ **More & Co.** Each month this peppy design store stocks a new collection centered on a certain theme, featuring a wide selection of well-designed and charming items that range from unique ceramics and glassware to children's clothing. It's excellent for gift shopping and window-shopping alike. ⊠ *112 High St.* ☎ *207/747–4730* ⊕ *www.alittlemorelikethis.com.*

TOYS

FAMILY
Fodor's Choice
★ **Treehouse Toys.** An instant mood-lifter, this shop is chock-full of offbeat toys and novelty items that are certain to delight children of all ages. ⊠ *47 Exchange St.* ☎ *207/775–6133* ⊕ *www.treehousetoys.us.*

SIDE TRIPS FROM PORTLAND

CASCO BAY ISLANDS

The islands of Casco Bay are also known as the Calendar Islands, because an early explorer mistakenly thought there was one for each day of the year (in reality there are only 140 or so). These islands range from ledges visible only at low tide to populous Peaks Island, a suburb of Portland. Some are uninhabited; others support year-round communities, as well as stores and restaurants. Fort Gorges commands Hog Island Ledge, and Eagle Island is the site of Arctic explorer Admiral Robert Peary's home. The brightly painted ferries of Casco Bay Lines are the islands' lifeline. There is frequent service to the most populated ones, including Peaks, Long, Little Diamond, and Great Diamond.

There is little in the way of overnight lodging on the islands—the population swells during the warmer months due to summer residents—and there are few restaurants or organized attractions other than the natural beauty of the islands themselves. Meandering about by bike or on foot is a good way to explore on a day trip.

GETTING HERE AND AROUND

Casco Bay Lines provides ferry service from Portland to the islands of Casco Bay.

ESSENTIALS

Transportation Information Casco Bay Lines. ⊠ *56 Commercial St., Portland* ☎ *207/774–7871* ⊕ *www.cascobaylines.com.*

CAPE ELIZABETH

Winslow Homer painted many of his famous oceanscapes from a tiny studio on the rocky peninsula known as Prout's Neck, 12 miles south of Portland. Visitors today navigate a neighborhood of summer homes and a sprawling country-club property for a glimpse of the same dramatic coastline. Follow Highway 77 through South Portland (sometimes called "SoPo"), stopping off for bagels and coffee in its hipper residential neighborhoods. In the affluent bedroom community of Cape Elizabeth, a detour along the two-lane Shore Road shows off the famed Portland Head Light and quite a few stunning oceanfront homes.

EXPLORING

FAMILY **Cape Elizabeth Light.** This was the first twin lighthouse erected on the Maine coast in 1828—and locals still call it Two Lights—but half of the Cape Elizabeth Light was dismantled in 1924 and converted into a private residence. The other half still operates, and you can get a great photo of it from the end of Two Lights Road in the surrounding state park of the same name. The lighthouse itself is closed to the public, but you can explore the tidal pools at its base for small, edible snails known as periwinkles, or just "wrinkles," as they're sometimes referred to in Maine. Picnic tables are also available. ⊠ *7 Tower Dr.* ☎ *207/799–5871* ⊕ *www.maine.gov/twolights* ☜ *$4.50* ☉ *Daily 9–sunset.*

FAMILY **Portland Head Light.** Familiar to many from photographs and the Edward
Fodor'sChoice Hopper painting *Portland Head-Light* (1927), this lighthouse was
★ commissioned by George Washington in 1790. The towering, white-stone structure stands over the keeper's quarters, a white home with

a blazing red roof, today the Museum at Portland Head Light. The lighthouse is in 90-acre Fort Williams Park, a sprawling green space with walking paths, picnic facilities, a beach and—you guessed it—a cool old fort. ⊠ *Museum, 1000 Shore Rd.* ☎ *207/799–2661* ⊕ *www.portlandheadlight.com* ✉ *$2* ⊙ *Memorial Day–mid-Oct., daily 10–4; Apr., May, Nov., and Dec., weekends 10–4.*

FAMILY **Scarborough Marsh Audubon Center.** You can explore this Maine Audubon Society–run nature center by foot or canoe, on your own or by signing up for a guided walk or paddle. Canoes and kayaks are available to rent and come with a life jacket and map. The salt marsh is Maine's largest and is an excellent place for bird-watching and peaceful paddling along its winding ways. The center has a discovery room for kids, programs for all ages ranging from basket making to astronomy, and a good gift shop. Tours include birding walks. ⊠ *Pine Point Rd., Scarborough* ☎ *207/883–5100 (May–Sept.), 207/781–2330 (Oct.–Apr.)* ⊕ *www.maineaudubon.org* ✉ *Free, guided tours from $5* ⊙ *Visitor center: mid-June–Labor Day, daily 9:30–5:30; Memorial Day–mid-June and Labor Day–Sept., weekends 9:30–5:30.*

FAMILY **Winslow Homer Studio.** The great American landscape painter created many of his best-known works in this seaside home between 1883 until his death in 1910. It's easy to see how this rocky, jagged peninsula might have been inspiring. The only way to get a look is on a tour with the Portland Museum of Art, which leads 2½-hour strolls through the historic property. ⊠ *5 Winslow Homer Rd., Scarborough* ☎ *207/775–6148* ⊕ *www.portlandmuseum.org* ✉ *$55* ⊙ *June–Oct., hrs vary.*

WHERE TO EAT AND STAY

$$ ✕ **The Lobster Shack at Two Lights.** You can't beat the location—right on the water, below the lighthouse pair that gives Two Lights State Park its name—and the food's not bad either. Enjoy fresh lobster whole or piled into a hot-dog bun with a dollop of mayo. Other menu musts include chowder, fried clams, and fish 'n' chips. It's been a classic spot since the 1920s. Eat inside or out. $ *Average main: $18* ⊠ *225 Two Lights Rd.* ☎ *207/799–1677* ⊕ *www.lobstershacktwolights.com* ⊙ *Closed late Oct.–late Mar.*

SEAFOOD
FAMILY

$$$$ ⊞ **Black Point Inn.** Toward the tip of the peninsula that juts into the ocean at Prout's Neck stands this stylish, tastefully updated 1878 resort inn with spectacular views up and down the coast. **Pros:** dramatic setting; geothermally heated pool; discounts in shoulder seasons. **Cons:** "guest service charge" is tacked onto room rate. $ *Rooms from: $500* ⊠ *510 Black Point Rd., Scarborough* ☎ *207/883–2500* ⊕ *www.blackpointinn.com* ⊙ *Closed late Oct.–early May* ⤳ *20 rooms, 5 suites* ⍟ *Some meals.*

RESORT
FAMILY

FREEPORT

17 miles north of Portland via I–295.

Those who flock straight to L.L. Bean and see nothing else of Freeport are missing out. The city's charming backstreets are lined with historic buildings and old clapboard houses, and there's a pretty little harbor on the south side of the Harraseeket River. It's true that many who come to the area do so simply to shop: L.L. Bean is the store that put Freeport on the map, and plenty of outlets and some specialty stores have settled

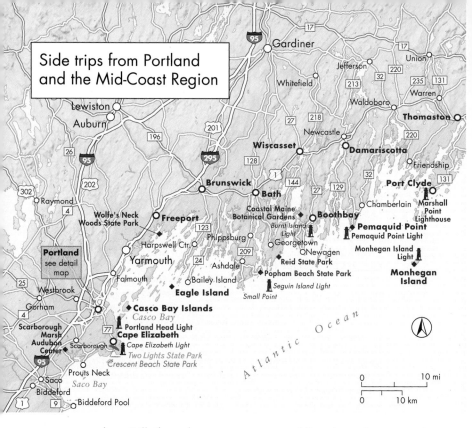

Side trips from Portland and the Mid-Coast Region

here. Still, if you choose, you can stay a while and experience more than fabulous bargains; beyond the shops are bucolic nature preserves with miles of walking trails and plenty of places for leisurely ambling that don't require the overuse of your credit cards.

GETTING HERE AND AROUND

Interstate 295 has three Freeport exits and passes by on the edge of the downtown area. U.S. 1 is Main Street here.

EXPLORING

FAMILY **Freeport Historical Society.** Pick up a village walking map and check out the historical exhibits at the Freeport Historical Society, located in Harrington House, a hybrid Federal- and Greek Revival–style home built in the 1830s. Always call ahead when planning a visit. ⊠ *45 Main St.* ☎ *207/865–3170* ⊕ *www.freeporthistoricalsociety.org* ☉ *Memorial Day–Columbus Day, Mon.–Sat. 9–5; Columbus Day–Memorial Day, Tues.–Fri. 10–4.*

Pettengill Farm. The grounds of the Freeport Historical Society's saltwater Pettengill Farm—140 beautifully tended acres along an estuary of the Harraseeket River—are open to the public. It's about a 15-minute walk from the parking area down a farm road to the circa-1800 saltbox farmhouse, which is open by appointment. Little has changed since it was built, and it has rare etchings (called sgraffitti) of ships and sea monsters on three bedroom walls. ✉ *Pettengill Rd.* ☎ *207/865–3170* 🌐 *www.freeporthistoricalsociety.org* 🎟 *Free (donations appreciated)* 🕘 *Daily dawn–dusk.*

WHERE TO EAT AND STAY

$$ SEAFOOD FAMILY 🍴 **Harraseeket Lunch & Lobster Co.** Seafood baskets and lobster dinners are the focus at this popular, bare-bones place beside the town landing in South Freeport. Order at the counter, find a seat inside or out, and expect long lines in summer. [$] *Average main: $18* ✉ *36 S. Main St., South Freeport* ☎ *207/865–4888* 🌐 *www.harraseeketlunchandlobster.com* 💳 *No credit cards* 🕘 *Closed mid-Oct.–Apr.* ✍ *Reservations not accepted.*

$$ HOTEL FAMILY Fodor's Choice ★ 🏨 **Harraseeket Inn.** Despite some modern appointments, this large hotel has a country-inn ambience throughout. **Pros:** full breakfast and afternoon tea; elevators and other modern touches; walk to shopping district. **Cons:** additions have diminished some authenticity. [$] *Rooms from: $235* ✉ *162 Main St.* ☎ *207/865–9377, 800/342–6423* 🌐 *www.harraseeketinn.com* 🛏 *82 rooms, 2 suites, 9 town houses* 🍽 *Breakfast.*

NIGHTLIFE AND PERFORMING ARTS

FAMILY **L.L. Bean Summer Concert Series.** Throughout the summer, L.L.Bean hosts free activities, including concerts, at the L.L. Bean Discovery Park. It's set back from Main Street, along a side street the runs between the company's flagship and home furnishings stores. ✉ *L.L. Bean Discovery Park, 95 Main St.* ☎ *877/755–2326* 🌐 *www.llbean.com.*

SPORTS AND THE OUTDOORS

FAMILY **L.L. Bean Outdoor Discovery Schools.** It shouldn't come as a surprise that one of the world's largest outdoor outfitters also provides its customers with instructional adventures to go with its products. L.L. Bean's year-round Outdoor Discovery Schools offer courses in canoeing, biking, kayaking, fly-fishing, snowshoeing, cross-country skiing, and other outdoor sports. ✉ *95 Main St.* ☎ *888/552–3261* 🌐 *www.llbean.com/ods.*

SHOPPING

The *Freeport Visitors Guide* lists the more than 200 stores on Main Street, Bow Street, and elsewhere, including Coach, Brooks Brothers, Banana Republic, J. Crew, and Cole Haan. You can pick it up around town.

Edgecomb Potters. Nationally known Edgecomb Potters produces vibrantly colored, hand-thrown porcelain tableware finished with an unusual crystalline glaze. It also sells jewelry, glassware, glass sculptures, and gifts for the home, almost all made by American artisans. ✉ *8 School St.* ☎ *207/865–1705* 🌐 *www.edgecombpotters.com.*

FAMILY Fodor's Choice ★ **L.L. Bean.** Founded in 1912 as a mail-order merchandiser after its namesake invented a hunting boot, L.L. Bean's giant flagship store attracts more than 3 million shoppers annually and is open 365 days a year in the heart of Freeport's outlet shopping district. You can still find the original hunting boots, along with cotton and wool sweaters; outerwear of all kinds; casual clothing, boots, and shoes for men, women, and kids; and camping equipment. Nearby are the company's home furnishings store; bike, boat, and ski store; and outlet. ✉ *95 Main St.* ☎ *877/755–2326* 🌐 *www.llbean.com.*

R. D. Allen Freeport Jewelers. This shop specializes in brightly colored tourmaline and other gemstones mined in Maine. Most of the pieces are the work of Maine artisans. Watermelon tourmaline is a specialty. ✉ *13 Middle St., Suite 1* ☎ *207/865–1818, 877/837–3835* ⊕ *www. rdallen.com.*

Thos. Moser Cabinetmakers. Famed local furniture company Thos. Moser Cabinetmakers sells artful, handmade wood pieces with clean, classic lines. The store has information on tours at the workshop 30 minutes away in Auburn (by appointment only). ✉ *149 Main St.* ☎ *207/865–4519* ⊕ *www.thosmoser.com.*

THE MID-COAST REGION

Lighthouses dot the headlands of Maine's Mid-Coast region, where thousands of miles of coastline wait to be explored. Defined by chiseled peninsulas stretching south from U.S. 1, this area has everything from the sandy beaches and sandbars of Popham Beach to the jutting cliffs of Monhegan Island. If you are intent on hooking a trophy-size fish or catching a glimpse of a whale, there are plenty of opportunities. If you want to explore deserted beaches and secluded coves, kayaks are your best bet; put in at the Harpswells, or on the Cushing and Saint George peninsulas, or simply paddle among the lobster boats and other vessels that ply the waters here.

Tall ships often visit Maine, sometimes sailing up the Kennebec River for a stopover at Bath's Maine Maritime Museum, on the site of the old Percy & Small Shipyard. Next door to the museum, the Bath Iron Works still builds the U.S. Navy's Aegis-class destroyers.

Along U.S. 1, charming towns, each unique, have an array of attractions. Brunswick, while a bigger, more commercial city, has rows of historic brick and clapboard homes and is home to Bowdoin College. Bath is known for its maritime heritage. Wiscasset has arguably the best antiques shopping in the state. On its waterfront you can choose from a variety of seafood shacks competing for the best lobster rolls. Damariscotta, too, is worth a stop for its good seafood restaurants, and you'd be hard-pressed to find better-tasting oysters than those from the Damariscotta River.

South along the peninsulas, the scenery opens to glorious vistas of working lobster harbors and marinas. It's here you find the authentic lobster pounds, where you can watch your lunch come right out of the traps. Boothbay Harbor and Camden are two of the quaintest towns in the Mid-Coast—and busy tourist destinations come summer, with lots of little stores that are perfect for window-shopping. Boothbay Harbor is one of three towns from which you can take a ferry to Monhegan Island, which seems to be inhabited exclusively by painters at their easels, intent on capturing the windswept cliffs and weathered homes with colorful gardens.

ESSENTIALS
Visitor Information Southern Midcoast Maine Chamber. ⊠ *Maine
Technology Institute Bldg., 8 Venture Ave., Brunswick* ☎ *207/725-8797*
⊕ *www.midcoastmaine.com.* **State of Maine Visitor Information Center.**
⊠ *1100 U.S. 1, off I–295 (Exit 17), Yarmouth* ☎ *207/846-0833, 888/624-6345*
for Maine Office of Tourism ⊕ *www.mainetourism.com.*

BRUNSWICK

10 miles north of Freeport via U.S. 1.

Lovely brick and clapboard buildings are the highlight of Brunswick's
Federal Street Historic District, which includes Federal Street and Park
Row and the stately campus of Bowdoin College. From the intersection
of Pleasant and Maine streets, in the center of town, you can walk in
any direction and discover an impressive array of restaurants, as well
as bookstores, gift shops, boutiques, and jewelers.

Below Brunswick are Harpswell Neck and the more than 40 islands
that make up the town of Harpswell, known collectively as the Harpswells. Route 123 runs down Harpswell Neck, where small coves shelter
lobster boats, and summer cottages are tucked away among birch and
spruce trees. On your way down from Cook's Corner to Land's End at
the end of Route 24, you cross Sebascodegan Island. Heading east here
leads to East Harpswell and Cundy's Harbor. Continuing straight south
down Route 24 leads to Orr's Island. Stop at Mackerel Cove to see a
real fishing harbor; there are a few parking spaces, where you can stop
to picnic and look for beach glass or put in your kayaks. Inhale the salt
breeze as you cross the world's only cribstone bridge (designed so that
water flows freely through gaps between the granite blocks) on your
way to Bailey Island, home to a lobster pound made famous thanks in
part to a Visa commercial.

GETTING HERE AND AROUND

From Interstate 295 take the Coastal Connector to U.S. 1 in Brunswick. From here Route 24 runs to Bailey Island and Route 123 down
Harpswell Neck.

EXPLORING

FAMILY

Fodor'sChoice

★

Bowdoin College Museum of Art. This small museum housed in a stately
building on Bowdoin's main quad features one of the oldest permanent collections of art in the United States, comprising paintings, sculpture, decorative arts, and works on paper. The museum often mounts
well-curated, rotating exhibitions and has stellar programs for getting
children excited about art. ⊠ *245 Maine St.* ☎ *207/725–3275* ⊕ *www.
bowdoin.edu/art-museum* 🎟 *Free.*

WHERE TO EAT

$$

SEAFOOD

FAMILY

Fodor'sChoice

★

✕ Cook's Lobster House. What began as a lobster shack on Bailey's Island
in 1955 has grown into a huge, internationally famous family-style
restaurant with a small gift shop. The restaurant still catches its own
seafood, so you can count on the lobster casserole and the haddock
sandwich to be delectable. A shore dinner will still set you back close
to $50, but you won't leave hungry after a 1¼-pound lobster with

Low tide is the perfect time to explore tidal flats, tide pools, or fish from the shore at Popham Beach State Park.

coleslaw, potato, chowder, and mussels or clams. Whether you choose indoor or deck seating, you can watch the activity on the water as people check lobster pots and kayakers fan across the bay. $\boxed{\$}$ *Average main: $24 ⊠ 68 Garrison Cove Rd., Bailey Island* ☎ *207/833–2818* ⊕ *www.cookslobster.com* ⊘ *Closed early Jan.–mid-Feb.*

SPORTS AND THE OUTDOORS

H2Outfitters. The coast near Brunswick is full of hidden nooks and crannies waiting to be explored by kayak. H2Outfitters, at the southern end of Orr's Island just before the cribstone bridge, is the place in Harpswell to get on the water. It provides top-notch kayaking instruction and also offers half-day, full-day, bed-and-breakfast, and camping trips in the waters off its home base and elsewhere in Maine. ⊠ *1894 Harpswell Island Rd., Orrs Island* ☎ *207/833–5257, 800/205–2925* ⊕ *www.h2outfitters.com.*

BATH

11 miles north of Brunswick via U.S. 1.

Bath has been a shipbuilding center since 1607. The result of its prosperity can be seen in its handsome mix of Federal, Greek Revival, and Italianate homes along Front, Centre, and Washington streets. In the heart of Bath's historic district are some charming 19th-century homes, including the 1820 Federal-style home at 360 Front Street; the 1810 Greek Revival mansion at 969 Washington Street, covered with gleaming white clapboards; and the Victorian gem at 1009 Washington Street, painted a distinctive shade of raspberry. All three operate as inns. One easily overlooked site is the town's City Hall; the bell in its tower was cast by Paul Revere in 1805.

The venerable Bath Iron Works completed its first passenger ship in 1890. During World War II, BIW (as it's locally known) launched a new ship every 17 days. Not only is it still in production today, BIW is one of the state's largest employers, with about 5,600 workers, who turn out destroyers for the U.S. Navy. (It's a good idea to avoid U.S. 1 on weekdays 3:15–4:30 pm, when a major shift change takes place.) You can tour BIW through the Maine Maritime Museum.

GETTING HERE AND AROUND
U.S. 1 passes through downtown and across the Kennebec River at Bath. Downtown is on the north side of the highway along the river.

EXPLORING

FAMILY
Fodor'sChoice
★

Maine Maritime Museum. No trip to Bath is complete without a visit to this cluster of buildings that once made up the historic Percy & Small Shipyard. Plan on at least half a day—indeed, tickets are good for two: there's just that much to see at this museum, which examines the world of shipbuilding and which is the only way to tour Bath Iron Works (June–mid-Oct.) From mid-June through Columbus Day, five nature and lighthouse boat tours cruise the scenic Kennebec River—one takes in 10 lights. The 142-foot Grand Banks fishing schooner *Sherman Zwicker* docks here during the same period. Hour-long tours of the shipyard show how these massive wooden ships were built. In the boat shop, you can watch boatbuilders wield their tools. Inside the main museum building, exhibits use ship models, paintings, photographs, and historical artifacts to tell the maritime history of the region. A separate historic building houses a fascinating lobstering exhibit; it's worth coming here just to watch the 18-minute video on lobstering written and narrated by E. B. White. A gift shop and bookstore are on the premises, and you can grab a bite to eat in the café or bring a picnic to eat on the grounds. ■ TIP→ Kids ages six and younger get in free. ⊠ *243 Washington St.* ☎ *207/443–1316* ⊕ *www.mainemaritimemuseum.org* ⊠ *$15, good for 2 days within 7-day period* ⊙ *Daily 9:30–5.*

OFF THE BEATEN PATH

Popham Beach State Park. This park has bathhouses and picnic tables. At low tide you can walk several miles of tidal flats and also out to a nearby island, where you can explore tide pools or fish off the ledges. It's on a peninsula facing the open Atlantic, between the mouths of the Kennebec and Morse rivers. About a mile from Popham Beach State Park, the road ends at the Civil War–era Fort Popham State Historic Site, an unfinished semicircular granite fort on the sea. Enjoy the beach views at nearby Spinney's Restaurant, or grab a quick bite next door at Percy's Store, which has picnic tables and a path to the beach. **Amenities:** food and drink; lifeguards; parking (no fee); showers; toilets. **Best for:** swimming; walking. ⊠ *10 Perkins Farm La., off Rte. 209, Phippsburg* ☎ *207/389–1335* ⊕ *www.maine.gov/pophambeach* ⊠ *$6* ⊙ *Daily 9–sunset.*

Continued on page 703

MAINE'S LIGHTHOUSES
GUARDIANS OF THE COAST By John Blodgett

Perched high on rocky ledges, on the tips of wayward islands, and sometimes seemingly on the ocean itself are the more than five dozen lighthouses standing watch along Maine's craggy and ship-busting coastline.

Marshall Point Light

LIGHTING THE WAY: A BIT OF HISTORY

Portland Head Light

Most lighthouses were built in the first half of the 19th century to protect vessels from running aground at night or when the shoreline was shrouded in fog. Along with the mournful siren of the foghorn and maritime lore, these practical structures have come to symbolize Maine throughout the world.

SHIPWRECKS AND SAFETY

These alluring sentinels of the eastern seaboard today have more form than function, but that certainly was not always the case. Safety was a strong motivating factor in the erection of the lighthouses. Commerce also played a critical role. For example, in 1791 Portland Head light was completed, partially as a response to local merchants' concerns about the rocky entrance to Portland Harbor and the varying depths of the shipping channel, but approval wasn't given until a terrible accident in 1787 in which a 90-ton sloop wrecked. In 1789, the federal government created the U.S. Lighthouse Establishment (later the U.S. Lighthouse Service) to manage them. In 1939 the U.S. Coast Guard took on the job.

Some lighthouses in Maine were built in a much-needed venue, but the points and islands upon which they sat were prone to storm damage. Along with poor construction, this meant that over the years many lighthouses had to be rebuilt or replaced.

LIGHTHOUSES TODAY

In modern times, many of the structures still serve a purpose. Technological advances, such as GPS and radar, are mainly used to navigate through the choppy waters, but a lighthouse or its foghorns are helpful secondary aids, and sometimes the only ones used by recreational boaters. The numerous channel-marking buoys still in existence also are testament to the old tried-and-true methods.

Of the 66 lighthouses along this far northeastern state, 55 are still working, alerting ships (and even small aircraft) of the shoreline's rocky edge. Government agencies, historic preservation organizations, and mostly private individuals own the decommissioned lights.

KEEPERS OF THE LIGHT

Some keepers also used bells and sirens, like this Fog Signal Station on Manana Island in 1898.

Pemaquid Point's fourth-order Fresnel lens

LIFE OF A LIGHTKEEPER

One thing that has changed with the modern era is the disappearance of the lighthouse keeper. In the early 20th century, lighthouses began the conversion from oil-based lighting to electricity. A few decades later, the U.S. Coast Guard switched to automation, phasing out the need for an on-site keeper.

While the keepers of tradition were no longer needed, the traditions of these stalwart, 24/7 employees live on through museum exhibits and retellings of Maine's maritime history, legends, and lore. The tales of a lighthouse keeper's life are the stuff romance novels are made of: adventure, rugged but lonely men, and a beautiful setting along an unpredictable coastline.

The lighthouse keepers of yesterday probably didn't see their own lives so romantically. Their daily narrative was one of hard work and, in some cases, exceptional solitude. A keeper's primary job was to ensure that the lamp was illuminated all day, every day. This meant that oil (whale or coal oil and later kerosene) had to be carried about and wicks trimmed on a regular basis. When fog shrouded the coast, they sounded the solemn horn to pierce through the damp darkness that hid their light. Their quarters were generally small and often attached to the light tower itself. The remote locations of the lights added to the isolation a keeper felt, especially before the advent of radio and telephone, let alone the Internet. Though some brought families with them, the keepers tended to be men who lived alone.

THE LIGHTS 101

Over the years, Fresnel (fray-NELL) lenses were developed in different shapes and sizes so that ship captains could distinguish one lighthouse from another. Invented by Frenchman Augustin Fresnel in the early 19th century, the lens design allows for a greater transmission of light perfectly suited for lighthouse use. Knowing which lighthouse they were near helped captains know which danger was present, such as a submerged ledge or shallow channel. Some lights, such as those at Seguin Island Light, are fixed and don't flash. Other lights are colored red.

DID YOU KNOW?

A lighthouse's personality shines through its flash pattern. For example, Bass Harbor Light (pictured) blinks red every four seconds. Some lights, such as Seguin Island Light, are fixed and don't flash.

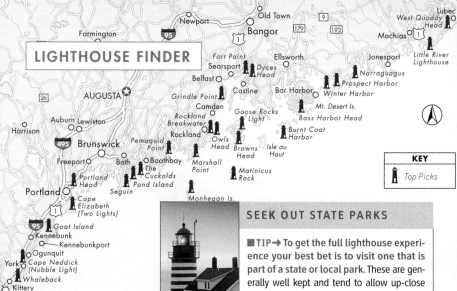

LIGHTHOUSE FINDER

Lubec
West Quoddy Head
Old Town
Newport
Bangor
Machias
Farmington
Little River Lighthouse
Fort Point
Ellsworth
Jonesport
Searsport
Dyces Head
Narraguagus
Belfast
Prospect Harbor
Castine
Bar Harbor
Winter Harbor
AUGUSTA
Grindle Point
Camden
Goose Rocks Light
Mt. Desert Is.
Auburn Lewiston
Rockland Breakwater
Bass Harbor Head
Harrison
Rockland
Burnt Coat Harbor
Brunswick
Pemaquid Point
Owls Head
Browns Head
Isle au Haut
Freeport
Bath
Boothbay
Marshall Point
The Cuckolds
Matinicus Rock
Portland
Pond Island
Seguin
Monhegan Is.
Cape Elizabeth (Two Lights)
Goat Island
Kennebunk
Kennebunkport
Ogunquit
York
Cape Neddick (Nubble Light)
Whaleback
Kittery
Portsmouth

KEY

🚨 Top Picks

West Quoddy Head

SEEK OUT STATE PARKS

■ TIP→ To get the full lighthouse experience your best bet is to visit one that is part of a state or local park. These are generally well kept and tend to allow up-close approach, though typically only outside. While you're at the parks you can picnic or stroll on the trails. Wildlife is often abundant in and near the water; you might spot sea birds and even whales in certain locations (try West Quoddy Head, Portland Head, or Two Lights).

VISITING MAINE'S LIGHTHOUSES

As you travel along the Maine Coast, you won't see lighthouses by watching your odometer—there were no rules about the spacing of lighthouses. The decision as to where to place a lighthouse was a balance between a region's geography and its commercial prosperity and maritime traffic.

Lighthouses dot the shore from as far south as York to the country's easternmost tip at Lubec. Accessibility varies according to location and other factors. A handful are so remote as to be outright impossible to reach (except perhaps by kayaking and rock climbing). Some don't allow visitors according to Coast Guard policies, though you can enjoy them through the zoom lens of a camera. Others you can walk right up to and, occasionally, even climb to the top. Lighthouse enthusiasts and preservation groups restore and maintain many of them. All told, approximately 30 lighthouses allow some sort of public access.

MUSEUMS, TOURS, AND MORE

Most keeper's quarters are closed to the public, but some of the homes have been converted to museums, full of intriguing exhibits on lighthouses, the famous Fresnel lenses used in them, and artifacts of Maine maritime life in general. Talk to the librarians at the **Maine Maritime Museum** in Bath (⊕ *www.mainemaritimemuseum.org*) or sign up for one of the museum's daily lighthouse cruises to pass by no fewer than ten on the Lighthouse Lovers Cruise. In Rockland, the **Maine Lighthouse Museum** (⊕ *www.mainelighthousemuseum.org*) has the country's largest display of Fresnel lenses. The museum also displays keepers' memorabilia, foghorns, brassware, and more. Maine Open Lighthouse Day is the second Saturday after Labor Day; you can tour and even climb lights usually closed to the public.

For more information, check out the lighthouse page at Maine's official tourism site: ⊕ *visitmaine.com*.

SLEEPING LIGHT: STAYING OVERNIGHT

Goose Rocks, where you can play lighthouse keeper for a week.

Want to stay overnight in a lighthouse? There are several options to do so. ■ TIP→ Book lighthouse lodgings as far in advance as possible, up to one year ahead.

Our top pick is **Pemaquid Point Light** (*Newcastle Square Vacation Rentals* ☎ *207/563–6500* ⊕ *www.mainecoast-cottages.com*) because it has one of the most dramatic settings on the Maine coast. Two miles south of **New Harbor**, the second floor of the lighthouse keeper's house is rented out on a weekly basis early May through mid-November to support upkeep of the grounds. When you aren't enjoying the interior, head outdoors: the covered front porch has a rocking-chair view of the ocean. The one-bedroom, one-bath rental sleeps up to a family of four.

Situated smack dab in the middle of a major maritime thoroughfare between two Penobscot Bay islands, **Goose Rocks Light** (☎ *203/400–9565* ⊕ *www.beaconpreservation.org*) offers lodging for the adventuresome—the 51-foot "spark plug" lighthouse is completely surrounded by water. Getting there requires a ferry ride from Rockland to nearby **North Haven**, a 5- to 10-minute ride by motorboat, and then a climb up an iron-rung ladder from the pitching boat—all based on high tide and winds, of course. There's room for up to eight people. It's a bit more cushy experience than it was for the original keepers: there's a flat-screen tv with DVD player and a selection of music and videos for entertainment. In addition, a hammock hangs on the small deck that encircles the operational light; it's a great place from which to watch the majestic wind-jammers and the fishing fleet pass by.

Little River Lighthouse (☎ *877/276–4682* ⊕ *www.littleriverlight.org*), along the far northeastern reaches of the coast in **Cutler**, has three rooms available for rent in July and August. You're responsible for food and beverages, linens, towels, and other personal items (don't forget the bug spray), but kitchen and other basics are provided. The lighthouse operators will provide a boat ride to the island upon which the lighthouse sits.

TOP LIGHTHOUSES TO VISIT

BASS HARBOR LIGHT
Familiar to many as the subject of countless photographs is Bass Harbor Light, at the southern end of **Mount Desert Island.** It is within Acadia National Park and 17 miles from the town of Bar Harbor. The station grounds are open year-round.

CAPE ELIZABETH LIGHT
Two Lights State Park is so-named because it's next to two lighthouses. Both of these **Cape Elizabeth** structures were built in 1828. The western light was converted into a private residence in 1924; the eastern light, Cape Elizabeth Light, still projects its automated cylinder of light. The grounds surrounding the building and the lighthouse itself are closed to the public, but the structure is easily viewed and photographed from nearby at the end of Two Lights Road.

Cape Neddick

CAPE NEDDICK LIGHT
More commonly known as Nubble Light for the smallish offshore expanse of rock it rests upon, Cape Neddick Light sits a few hundred feet off a rock point in **York Beach.** With such a precarious location, its grounds are inaccessible to visitors, but close enough to be exceptionally photogenic, especially during the Christmas season.

MONHEGAN ISLAND LIGHT
Only the adventuresome and the artistic see this light, because **Monhegan Island** is accessible by an approximately one-hour ferry ride. To reach the lighthouse, you have an additional half-mile walk uphill from the ferry dock. The former keeper's quarters is home to the Monhegan Museum, which has exhibits about the island. The tower itself is closed to the public.

Portland Head

PORTLAND HEAD LIGHT
One of Maine's most photographed lighthouses (and its oldest), the famous Portland Head Light was completed in January 1791. At the edge of Fort Williams Park, in **Cape Elizabeth,** the towering white stone lighthouse stands 101 feet above the sea. The Coast Guard operates it and it is not open for tours. However the adjacent keeper's dwelling is now a museum.

WEST QUODDY HEAD LIGHT
Originally built in 1808 by mandate of President Thomas Jefferson, West Quoddy Head Light sits in **Lubec** on the easternmost tip of land in the mainland United States. The 49-foot-high lighthouse with distinctive red and white stripes, is part of Quoddy Head State Park.

West Quoddy Head

11

WHERE TO EAT AND STAY

$ ✕ **Beale Street Barbecue.** Ribs are the thing at one of Maine's oldest
BARBECUE barbecue joints, opened in 1996. Hearty eaters should ask for one of
the platters piled high with pulled pork, pulled chicken, or shredded
beef. Fried calamari with habanero mayo served with corn bread is a
popular appetizer. Enjoy a Maine microbrew at the bar while you wait
for your table. $ *Average main: $15* ⌧ *215 Water St.* ☎ *207/442–9514*
⊕ *www.mainebbq.com.*

$$ ⊞ **Sebasco Harbor Resort.** A family-friendly resort spread over 575 acres
RESORT on the water near the foot of the Phippsburg Peninsula, this place has a
FAMILY golf course, tennis courts, and even a lawn-bowling green and a cricket
Fodor's Choice pitch, among a host of other amenities. **Pros:** good choice for families;
★ perfect location; children's activities; wonderful array of lawn games.
Cons: no sand beach. $ *Rooms from: $289* ⌧ *29 Kenyon Rd., off Rte.*
217, Phippsburg ☎ *207/389–1161, 877/389–1161* ⊕ *www.sebasco.*
com ⊗ *Closed late Oct.–mid-May* ⇌ *107 rooms, 8 suites, 23 cottages*
⊠ *Some meals.*

WISCASSET

10 miles north of Bath via U.S. 1.

Settled in 1663, Wiscasset sits on the banks of the Sheepscot River.
It bills itself "Maine's Prettiest Village," and it's easy to see why: it
has graceful churches, old cemeteries, and elegant sea captains' homes
(many converted into antiques shops or galleries).

There's also a good wine and specialty foods shop called Treats (stock
up here if you're heading north). Pack a picnic and take it down to the
dock on Water Street, where you can watch the fishing boats, or grab
a lobster roll from Red's Eats or the lobster shack nearby. Wiscasset
has expanded its wharf, and this is a great place to catch a breeze on
a hot day.

GETTING HERE AND AROUND

U.S. 1 becomes Main Street, and traffic often slows to a crawl come
summer. You'll likely have success parking on Water Street rather than
Main. It's a good idea to do your driving around Wiscasset very early
in the morning and after 7 in the evening when traffic eases a bit. The
best way to get around here is on foot.

WHERE TO EAT

$ ✕ **Red's Eats.** It's hard to miss the long line of hungry customers outside
FAST FOOD this little red shack on the Wiscasset side of the bridge. Red's is a local
FAMILY landmark famous for its hamburgers, hot dogs, lobster and crab rolls,
and crispy onion rings and clams fried in their own house-made batters.
Maine-made Round Top ice cream is also sold (try blueberry or black
raspberry). Enjoy views of the tidal Sheepscot River from picnic tables
on the bi-level deck or down on the grass by the water. $ *Average main:*
$12 ⌧ *41 Water St.* ☎ *207/882–6128* ▭ *No credit cards* ⊗ *Closed mid-*
Oct.–mid-Apr. ⊜ *Reservations not accepted.*

SHOPPING

Edgecomb Potters. Edgecomb Potters is not to be missed: they make vibrantly colored, exquisitely glazed porcelain known all around the country. The store also carries jewelry, glassware, and glass sculptures. ⊠ *727 Boothbay Rd., Edgecomb* ☎ *207/882–9493* ⊕ *www. edgecombpotters.com.*

In the Clover. There's something charmingly old-school about this pretty boutique with its warm and friendly service and fine displays of women's clothing, accessories, and beauty products. Geared towards elegant but no-fuss women of every age, the shop stocks clothing items such as fine cashmere shawls; pretty but not froufrou lingerie; and sophisticated loungewear as well as a good selection of natural beauty products and fragrances, unique jewelry, and inspiring books. ⊠ *85 Main St.* ☎ *207/882–9435* ⊕ *intercloverbeauty.blogspot.com.*

Fodor'sChoice ★ **Rock Paper Scissors.** Not your run-of-the-mill gift shop, this well-curated boutique stocks offbeat cards and letterpress stationary, local handcrafted goods such as blankets, purses, and ceramics, and beautiful, one-of-a-kind objects for the home and kitchen. Stocked to the brim with charming goodies for anyone on your list (including yourself), this shop is decidedly contemporary, with a Scandinavian bent, and is well worth a stop, if only to peruse the gorgeously arranged array of products on display. ⊠ *68 Main St.* ☎ *207/882–9930.*

Sheepscot River Pottery. This shop boasts beautifully glazed kitchen tiles, as well as kitchenware and home accessories, including sinks. Jewelry and other items by local artisans are also on sale. ⊠ *34 U.S. 1, Edgecomb* ☎ *207/882–9410* ⊕ *www.sheepscot.com.*

BOOTHBAY

10 miles south of Wiscasset via Rte. 27.

The shoreline of the Boothbay Peninsula is a craggy stretch of inlets, where pleasure craft anchor alongside trawlers and lobster boats. The town of Boothbay comprises the village center, Boothbay Harbor, as well as East Boothbay. The harbor is like a smaller version of Bar Harbor—touristy, but friendly and fun—with pretty, winding streets and lots to explore. Commercial Street, Wharf Street, Townsend Avenue, and the By-Way are lined with shops and ice cream parlors. One of the biggest draws here is the stunning Coastal Maine Botanical Gardens, with its beautiful café and gift shop, as well as its famous children's garden.

GETTING HERE AND AROUND

In season, boat trips to Monhegan Island leave from the piers off Commercial Street. Drive out to Ocean Point in East Boothbay for some incredible scenery. Boothbay is 13 miles south of Wiscasset via U.S. 1 and Route 27.

EXPLORING

FAMILY
Fodor'sChoice ★ **Coastal Maine Botanical Garden.** Set aside a couple of hours to stroll among the roses, lupines, and rhododendrons at the 250-acre Coastal Maine Botanical Garden. In the summer, free docent-led tours leave from the

visitor center at 11 and 1 on Thursday and Saturday. The "children's garden" is a wonderland of stone sculptures, rope bridges, small teahouse-like structures with grass roofs, and even a hedge maze. Children and adults alike adore the separate woodland fairy area. The on-site restaurant and café, as well as the bookshop and resource library, are also delightful. It's easy to spend an entire day here and not see everything—be sure to wear comfortable walking shoes. For those less inclined to go by foot, the gardens offer free shuttle service to most spots on the property. ✉ *132 Botanical Gardens Dr., off Rte. 27* ☎ *207/633–8000* 🌐 *www.mainegardens.org* 🎟 *$16* 🕘 *Apr.–Oct., daily 9–5.*

WHERE TO EAT AND STAY

$$ **TAPAS** 🍴 **Boat House Bistro.** The multitier rooftop terrace (complete with an outdoor bar) stays crowded all summer at the Boat House Bistro. Austrian-born chef Karin Guerin dishes up tapas-style small plates ranging from mango empanadas to sweet-potato latkes. For those seeking the full-on Maine experience, there are plenty of seafood options, too, including a different paella each day. The waitstaff are young, friendly, and just as diverse as the menu. [$] *Average main: $21* ✉ *12 By-Way, Boothbay Harbor* ☎ *207/633–0400* 🌐 *www.theboathousebistro.com* 🕘 *Closed mid-Oct.–mid-Apr.*

$$$ **B&B/INN** 🏨 **Topside Inn.** The Adirondack chairs on the immense lawn of this historic hilltop B&B have what is probably the best bay view in town. **Pros:** knockout views; plenty of green space for croquet; easy walk downtown. **Cons:** walls are a bit thin in the annexes. [$] *Rooms from: $300* ✉ *60 McKown St., Boothbay Harbor* ☎ *207/633–5404* 🌐 *www.topsideinn.com* 🕘 *Closed mid-Oct.–mid-May* 🛏 *25 rooms* 🍽 *Breakfast.*

DAMARISCOTTA

8 miles north of Wiscasset via U.S. 1.

The Damariscotta region comprises several communities along the rocky coast. The town itself sits on the water, a lively place filled with attractive shops and restaurants, as well as some of the best oysters around.

Just across the bridge over the Damariscotta River is the town of Newcastle, between the Sheepscot and Damariscotta rivers. Newcastle was settled in the early 1600s. The earliest inhabitants planted apple trees, but the town later became an industrial center, home to several shipyards and a couple of mills. The oldest Catholic church in New England, St. Patrick's, is here, and it still rings its original Paul Revere bell.

Bremen, which encompasses more than a dozen islands and countless rocky outcrops, has many seasonal homes along the water, and the main industries in the small community are fishing and clamming. Nobleboro, a bit north of here on U.S. 1, was settled in the 1720s by Colonel David Dunbar, sent by the British to rebuild the fort at Pemaquid. Neighboring Waldoboro is situated on the Medomak River and was settled largely by Germans in the mid-1700s. You can still visit the old German Meeting House, built in 1772. The Pemaquid Peninsula stretches south from Damariscotta to include Bristol, South Bristol, Round Pond, New Harbor, and Pemaquid.

Lobster trap buoys are popular decorations in Maine; the markings represent a particular lobsterman's claim.

GETTING HERE AND AROUND

In Newcastle, U.S. 1B runs from U.S. 1 across the Damariscotta River to Damariscotta. From this road take Route 129 south to South Bristol and Route 130 south to Bristol and New Harbor. From here you can return to U.S. 1 heading north on Route 32 through Round Pond and Bremen. In Waldoboro, turn off U.S. 1 on Jefferson Street to see the historic village center.

ESSENTIALS

Visitor Information Damariscotta Region Chamber of Commerce. ✉ *67-A Main St.* ☎ *207/563–8340* 🌐 *www.damariscottaregion.com.* 🍴 **Moody's Diner.** ✉ *1885 Atlantic Hwy., Waldoboro* ☎ *207/832–7785* 🌐 *www.moodysdiner.com.*

WHERE TO EAT AND STAY

$$ AMERICAN FAMILY

🍴 **King Eider's Pub & Restaurant.** This classic pub with a supercozy atmosphere right downtown bills itself as having the finest crab cakes in New England. Start with the fresh local oysters that the Damariscotta region is known for, then move on to entrées like steak-and-ale pie, sea-scallop Florentine, or sautéed haddock with chips. With exposed-brick walls and low wooden beams, it's a cozy place to enjoy your favorite ale. Stop by on Thursday night for live music. [$] *Average main: $18* ✉ *2 Elm St.* ☎ *207/563–6008* 🌐 *www.kingeiderspub.com.*

$$ AMERICAN FAMILY Fodor's Choice ★

🍴 **Publick House.** Located in a historic building that has been handsomely renovated, Publick House serves delicious comfort food, including fresh oysters, creative flatbreads, and local craft beers, as well as one of the best French onion soups around. There is often live music, making it a great place for a night out on a date or with the entire family.

$ *Average main: $20* ✉ *52 Main St., Newcastle* ☎ *207/563–3434* ⊕ *www.newcastlepublickhouse.com.*

$$ ✕ **Van Lloyd's Bistro.** Packed with funky decor culled from the owners' travels and local antiquing trips, this lively new restaurant serves an eclectic mix of dishes that lean towards a Mediterranean style. Pop in for the excellent happy hour and stay for dishes like pork-belly tortillas, Welsh rarebit, and Angus beef–stuffed grape leaves, or the fantastic Hunter's Plate, which includes a tasty rabbit porchetta. $ *Average main: $20* ✉ *85 Parking Lot La.* ☎ *207/563–5005* ⊕ *www.vanlloydsbistro. com* ▭ *No credit cards.*

AMERICAN

$ 🛏 **Newcastle Inn.** A riverside location, tasteful decor, and lots of common areas (inside and out) make this a relaxing country inn. **Pros:** guests can order beer or wine; one suitelike room and two suites with sitting areas. **Cons:** short walk into the village. $ *Rooms from: $180* ✉ *60 River Rd., Newcastle* ☎ *207/563–5685* ⊕ *www.newcastleinn.com* ⇨ *12 rooms, 2 suites* ⍾⃝ *Breakfast.*

B&B/INN
FAMILY

PEMAQUID POINT

10 miles south of Damariscotta via U.S. 1, U.S. 1B, and Rte. 130.

Pemaquid Point is the tip of the Pemaquid Peninsula, bordered by Muscongus and Johns bays. It's home to the famous lighthouse of the same name and its attendant fog bell and tiny museum. Also at the bottom of the peninsula, along the Muscongus Bay, is the Nature Conservancy's Rachel Carson Salt Pond Preserve.

GETTING HERE AND AROUND
From U.S. 1, take U.S. 1B into Damariscotta and head south on Route 130 to Pemaquid Point.

EXPLORING

FAMILY
Fodor'sChoice
★

Pemaquid Point Light. At the end of Route 130, this lighthouse at the tip of the Pemaquid Peninsula looks as though it sprouted from the ragged, tilted chunk of granite it commands. Most days in the summer you can climb the tower to the light. The former keeper's cottage is now the Fishermen's Museum, which displays historic photographs, scale models, and artifacts that explore commercial fishing in Maine. Also here are the original fog bell and bell house. The on-site Pemaquid Art Gallery mounts exhibitions by area artists in the summer. There are restrooms and picnic tables. ✉ *3115 Bristol Rd., Pemaquid* ☎ *207/677–2492* ⊕ *www.bristolparks.org* ⌦ *$2* ⊙ *Museum: early May–Oct., daily 9–5.*

WHERE TO EAT AND STAY

$$
SEAFOOD
FAMILY

✕ **Moscungus Bay Lobster Co.** The food here is practically guaranteed to be fresh: lobsters come in off the boat at one end of the pier, and the restaurant is at the other. Grab a picnic table and be careful not to hit your head on the colorful, dangling wooden buoys. It's fun to watch the lobstermen unload their catch over lunch. $ *Average main: $18* ✉ *28 Landing Rd., Round Pond* ☎ *207/529–2251* ⊕ *www.mainefreshlobster. com* ⊙ *Closed mid-May–mid-Oct.*

$$
SEAFOOD

✕ **Round Pond Fisherman's Coop.** Sheltered Moscungus Bay is where you'll find this down-home lobster shack, right on the pier with pleasant views of the water. Competition with the neighboring Moscungus Bay Lobster Co. keeps the prices low for fresh-off-the-boat lobster and steamers. [$] *Average main: $18* ✉ *25 Town Landing Rd., Round Pond* ☎ *207/529–5725* ⏲ *Closed Labor Day–mid-May.*

$ B&B/INN FAMILY 🏨 **Christmas Cove Inn.** If you're traveling with a dog, you'll find few more accommodating spots in Maine than this out-of-the-way place on Rutherford Island. **Pros:** great if you're traveling with dogs; great views from lookout. **Cons:** dogs on premises. [$] *Rooms from: $150* ✉ *53 Coveside Rd., South Bristol* ☎ *207/644–1502, 866/644–1502* 🌐 *www.christmascoveinn.com* 🛏 *7 rooms* 🍽 *No meals.*

SPORTS AND THE OUTDOORS

FAMILY **Hardy Boat Cruises.** Mid-May through mid-October, you can take a cruise to Monhegan with Hardy Boat Cruises. The company also offers seal- and puffin-watching trips and lighthouse and fall coastal cruises. Dogs are welcome on the boat for $5. ✉ *Shaw's Wharf, 132 State Rte. 32, New Harbor* ☎ *207/677–2026, 800/278–3346* 🌐 *www.hardyboat.com.*

THOMASTON

10 miles northeast of Waldoboro, 72 miles northeast of Portland.

Thomaston is a delightful town, full of beautiful sea captains' homes and dotted with antiques and specialty shops. A National Historic District encompasses parts of High, Main, and Knox streets. The town is the gateway to the two peninsulas; you'll see water on both sides as you arrive.

GETTING HERE AND AROUND

U.S. 1 is Main Street through Thomaston. Route 131 runs down the St. George Peninsula from here and Route 97 leads down the Cushing Peninsula and to Friendship.

WHERE TO EAT

$$$ AMERICAN 🍴 **Thomaston Cafe.** This is a great pit stop on the long, slow drive up U.S. 1. Works by local artists adorn the walls of this small downtown café, which uses local ingredients as much as possible. It serves an excellent breakfast, including homemade corned beef hash. For lunch there's scrumptious haddock chowder and delicious sandwiches. Try the sandwich with panfried haddock lightly breaded with panko bread crumbs, or a salad and crab cakes (sold at breakfast, too). Entrées include lobster ravioli and filet mignon with béarnaise sauce. Sunday brunch is popular. [$] *Average main: $30* ✉ *154 Main St.* ☎ *207/354–8589* 🌐 *www.thomastoncafe.com* ⏲ *Closed Mon.–Wed. No dinner Sun.*

$$ SEAFOOD FAMILY 🍴 **Waterman's Beach Lobster.** This place in South Thomaston is authentic, inexpensive, and scenic, overlooking islands in the Atlantic. You can eat lunch or dinner under the pavilions right next to the beach and pier, or get closer to the water at picnic tables. In addition to seafood favorites, Waterman's also sells freshly baked pies and locally made ice cream. It's strictly BYOB. [$] *Average main: $18* ✉ *343 Waterman's Beach Rd., South Thomaston* ☎ *207/596–7819, 207/594–7518* 🌐 *www.watermansbeachlobster.com* ⏲ *Closed Oct.–mid-June.*

PORT CLYDE

5 miles south of Tenants Harbor via Rte. 131.

Sitting at the end of the St. George Peninsula, the sleepy fishing village of Port Clyde is a haven for artists, with a number of galleries and a sweeping vista of the ocean that can't be beat. It's also a good spot to spend time nursing a beer or a coffee while waiting for your boat out to Monhegan. Like many places in Maine, lobster fishing is an economic mainstay here. Marshall Point Lighthouse, right in the harbor, has a small museum.

EXPLORING

FAMILY

Fodor'sChoice

★

Marshall Point Lighthouse. This 31-foot lighthouse, which has been in operation since it was erected in 1858, is perhaps best known as the spot where Forrest Gump concluded his very long cross-country run in the 1994 film adaptation of the book by the same name, Be prepared for sweeping views of the ocean and a resounding "Run, Forrest, run!" coming from visitors taking full advantage of an exceptional photo op. The site also has a small museum and a gift shop, housed in the old lightkeepers' house. ⊠ *Marshall Point Rd.* ☎ *207/372–6450* ⊕ *www. marshallpoint.org.*

MONHEGAN ISLAND

East of Pemaquid Peninsula, 10 miles south of Port Clyde.

If you love rocky cliffs, this is your place. And if you happen to be an artist you might never leave; studios and galleries are all over the island. The village bustles with activity in summer, when many artists open their studios. Several shops are available for browsers. You can escape the crowds on the island's 17 miles of hiking trails, which lead to the lighthouse and to the cliffs. Bring your camera!

GETTING HERE AND AROUND

Three excursion boats dock here. The boat trip out to Monhegan is almost as exhilarating as exploring the island itself. You'll likely pass by the Marshall Point Lighthouse, and be sure to be on the lookout for porpoises, seals, puffins, and small whales en route to the island.

FAMILY **Monhegan Boat Line.** The Port Clyde boat landing is home to the *Elizabeth Ann* and the *Laura B,* the mail boats that serve Monhegan Island, about 10 miles offshore. There are three round-trips daily Memorial Day weekend–Columbus Day, one daily in late fall and early spring, and three weekly in the winter. ⊠ *880 Port Clyde Rd., Port Clyde* ☎ *207/372–8848* ⊕ *www.monheganboat.com.*

EXPLORING

FAMILY **Monhegan Island Light.** Getting a look at this squat stone lighthouse—from land, anyway—requires a slightly steep half-mile walk uphill from the island's ferry dock. The lighthouse was automated in 1959, and the former keeper's quarters became the Monhegan Museum shortly thereafter. Exhibits at the museum have as much to do with life on the island as they do with the lighthouse itself. The tower is open sporadically throughout the summer for short tours. ⊠ *Lighthouse Hill Rd.,*

½ mile east of dock, Monhegan ☎ *207/596–7003* 🕒 *Museum: July and Aug., daily 11:30–3:30; June and Sept., daily 1:30–3:30.*

WHERE TO EAT AND STAY

$$ SEAFOOD 🍴 **Fish House Market.** The menu here is focused on fresh, local seafood prepared simply. Order inside the little hut by the water, and when your meal is ready, eat outside at a table inches from the shoreline, lapping up the view of the bay and the lobster boats moored there. Bring your own wine or beer and savor the outstanding fish chowder or a steamed lobster. [$] *Average main: $18* ✉ *98 Fish Beach La., Monhegan* 💳 *No credit cards.*

$ B&B/INN 🏨 **Island Inn.** This three-story inn, which dates to 1907, has a commanding presence on Monhegan Island's harbor. **Pros:** great food; great view. **Cons:** pricey; no a/c. [$] *Rooms from: $185* ✉ *1 Ocean Ave., Monhegan* ☎ *207/596–0371* 🌐 *www.islandinnmonhegan.com* 🕒 *Closed Columbus Day–Memorial Day* 🛏 *28 rooms (20 with bath), 4 suites* 🍽 *No meals* 💳 *No credit cards.*

PENOBSCOT BAY

Few could deny that Penobscot Bay is one of Maine's most dramatically beautiful regions. Its more than 1,000 miles of coastline is made up of rocky granite boulders, often undeveloped shores, a sprinkling of colorful towns and quaint villages, and views of the sea and islands that are a photographer's (and painter's) dream.

Penobscot Bay stretches 37 miles from Port Clyde in the south to Stonington, the little fishing village at the tip of Deer Isle, in the north. The bay begins near Stockton Springs, where the Penobscot River, New England's second-largest river system, ends, and terminates in the Gulf of Maine, where it is 47 miles wide. It covers an estimated 1,070 square miles and is home to more than 1,800 islands.

Initially, shipbuilding was the primary moneymaker here. In the 1800s, during the days of the great tall ships (or Down Easters, as they were often called), more wooden ships were built in Maine than in any other state in the country, and many were constructed along Penobscot Bay. This golden age of billowing sails and wooden sailing ships came to an end with the development of the steam engine, and by 1900, sailing ships were no longer a viable commercial venture in Maine. However, as you will see when traveling the coast, the tall ships have not entirely disappeared—some, albeit tiny in number compared to their 1800s heyday, have been revived as recreational boats known as windjammers. Today, once again, there are more tall ships along Penobscot Bay than anywhere else in the country.

ROCKLAND

3 miles north of Thomaston via U.S. 1.

This town is considered the gateway to Penobscot Bay and is the first stop on U.S. 1 offering a glimpse of the often-sparkling and island-dotted blue bay. Though once merely a place to pass through on the way to tonier ports like Camden, Rockland now gets attention on its own, thanks to a trio of attractions: the renowned Farnsworth Art Museum, the increasingly popular summer Lobster Festival, and the lively North Atlantic Blues Festival. Specialty shops and galleries line the main street, and one of the restaurants, Primo (between Camden and the little village of Owls Head), has become nationally famous. The town is still a large fishing port and the commercial hub of this coastal area.

Rockland Harbor bests Camden (by one) as home to the largest fleet of Maine windjammers. The best place in Rockland to view these handsome vessels as they sail in and out of the harbor is the mile-long granite breakwater, which bisects the outer portion of Rockland Harbor. To get there, from U.S. 1, head east on Waldo Avenue and then right on Samoset Road; follow this short road to its end.

GETTING HERE AND AROUND

U.S. 1 runs along Main Street here, while U.S. 1A curves through the residential neighborhood west of the business district, offering a faster route if you are passing through.

FESTIVALS **Maine Lobster Festival.** Rockland's annual Maine Lobster Festival, held in
FAMILY early August, is the region's largest annual event. About 10 tons of lobsters are steamed in a huge lobster cooker—you have to see it to believe it. The festival, held in Harbor Park, includes a parade, live entertainment, food booths, and, of course, the crowning of the Maine Sea Goddess. ⊠ *Harbor Park, Main St., south of Rte. 1* ☎ *800/576–7512* ⊕ *www.mainelobsterfestival.com.*

FAMILY **North Atlantic Blues Festival.** About a dozen well-known musicians gather for the North Atlantic Blues Festival, a two-day affair held the first full weekend after July 4th. The show officially takes place at the public landing on Rockland Harbor Park, but it also includes a "club crawl" through downtown Rockland on Saturday night. Admission to the festival is $30 in advance, $40 at the gate. ⊠ *Harbor Park, Main St.* ☎ *207/691–2248* ⊕ *www.northatlanticbluesfestival.com.*

Visitor Information Penobscot Bay Regional Chamber of Commerce.
⊠ *Visitor Center, 1 Park Dr.* ☎ *207/596–0376, 800/562–2529* ⊕ *www.therealmaine.com.*

EXPLORING

FAMILY **Farnsworth Art Museum.** One of the most important small museums in the
Fodor's Choice country, much of the Farnsworth's collection is devoted to Maine-related
★ works of the famous Wyeth family: N. C. Wyeth, an accomplished illustrator whose works were featured in many turn-of-the-20th-century books; his late son Andrew, one of the country's best-known painters; and Andrew's son James, also an accomplished painter, who like his elders before him summers nearby. Galleries in the main building always display some of Andrew Wyeth's works, such as *The Patriot, Witchcraft,* and *Turkey Pond.* The **Wyeth Center,** a former church, shows art by his father and son. The museum's collection also includes works by Fitz Henry Lane, George Bellows, Frank W. Benson, Edward Hopper (as watercolors, they may be "resting"), Louise Nevelson, and Fairfield Porter. Changing exhibits are shown in the **Jamien Morehouse Wing.** The **Farnsworth Homestead,** a handsome circa-1850 Greek Revival dwelling

Penobscot Bay and Blue Hill Peninsula

221
Old Town
15
2
Orono
222
95
Aurora
Amherst
9
179
Bangor
Brewer
East Holden
Waltham
2
95
Dixmont
US 1A
Frankfort
US 1A
Franklin
Unity
139
Thorndike 7
Orland
Ellsworth
Penobscot Narrows
Bridge &
Observatory Tower/
Fort Knox Historic Site
Bucksport
9
Brooks
Hancock
Albion
1
137
175
Surry
3
Trenton
Searsport
Penobscot 172
Bar
Harbor
Belfast
Blue Hill
3
Pripet
ACADIA
NATIONAL
PARK
Liberty
Castine
15
Searsmont
Brooksville
MT.
DESERT
ISLAND
Northport
Sargentville
Sedgwick
Washington
Lincolnville
LITTLE DEER
ISLE
Brooklin
Bass
Harbor
102
ISLESBORO
Deer Isle
Village
Jefferson
17
Dark Harbor
DEER
ISLE 15
Edgar M.
Tennis Preserve
Union
105
Camden
Haystack Mountain
School of Crafts
SWANS
ISLAND
LONG ISLAND
213
32
220
235 131
Rockport
NORTH HAVEN
ISLAND
Stonington
Waldoboro
1
Penobscot
Bay
North Haven
Newcastle
220
Thomaston
131
VINALHAVEN
ISLAND
Isle au Haut
Damariscotta
32
Spruce Head
Rockland
Friendship
Vinalhaven
ACADIA NAT'L PARK
(Isle au Haut unit)
Tenants Harbor
Chamberlain
Port Clyde
Pemaquid Point
MATINICUS
ISLAND
Atlantic Ocean
Monhegan Island
Light
MONHEGAN
ISLAND

Acadia National
Park and Mount
Desert Island
see detail
map

KEY
- - - Ferry Lines

0   10 mi
0   10 km

Windjammer Excursions

CLOSE UP

Nothing defines the Maine coastal experience better than a sailing trip on a windjammer. These vessels were built all along the East Coast in the 19th and early 20th centuries. Designed primarily to carry cargo, these beauties (most are wood hulled) have a rich past: the *Schooner Ladona* served in World War II, while others plied the waters in the lumbering, granite, fishing, and oystering trades or served as pilot boats. They vary in size but can be as small as 46 feet, holding six passengers (plus a couple of crew members), or more than 130 feet, holding 40 passengers and 10 crew members. During a windjammer excursion, passengers are usually able to participate in the navigation, be it hoisting a sail or playing captain at the wheel.

During the Camden Windjammer Festival, held Labor Day weekend, crowds gather to watch the region's fleet sail into the harbor, and most boats are open for tours. The schooner-crew talent show later in the weekend is a bit more irreverent than the majestic arrival ceremony.

A windjammer cruise gives you a chance to admire Maine's dramatic coast from the water. They can run anywhere from one to eight days, and day trips usually involve a tour of the harbor and some lighthouse sightseeing. The price—ranging $230–$1,100, depending on length of trip—includes all meals. Trips leave from Camden, Rockland, and Rockport. You can get information on the fleets by contacting one of two windjammer organizations:

Maine Windjammer Association.
☎ *800/807-9463*
⊕ *www.sailmainecoast.com.*

Maine Windjammer Cruises. A fleet of three handsome vessels offer a variety of cruises. ☎ *207/236-2938, 800/736-7981* ⊕ *www. mainewindjammercruises.com* ⤴ *n/a.*

---

that's part of the museum, retains its original lavish Victorian furnishings and is open late June–mid-October.

In Cushing, a tiny town about 10 miles south of Thomaston on the St. George River, the museum operates the **Olson House,** which is depicted in Andrew Wyeth's famous painting *Christina's World,* as well as in other works by the artist. It's accessible by guided tour only. ⊠ *16 Museum St.* ☎ *207/596–6457* ⊕ *www.farnsworthmuseum.org* ✉ *$12 (July–Sept., free Wed. 5–8)* ⊙ *Jan.–Mar., Wed.–Sun. 10–5; Apr., May, Nov., and Dec., Tues.–Sun. 10–5; June–Oct., Sat.–Tues. and Thurs., 10–5, Wed. and Fri. 10–8.*

FAMILY **Maine Lighthouse Museum.** The lighthouse museum has more than 25 Fresnel lighthouse lenses, as well as a collection of lighthouse artifacts and Coast Guard memorabilia. Permanent exhibits spotlight topics like lighthouse heroines—women who manned the lights when the keepers couldn't—and lightships. ⊠ *1 Park Dr.* ☎ *207/594–3301* ⊕ *www. mainelighthousemuseum.org* ✉ *$8* ⊙ *June–Oct., weekdays 9–5, weekends 10–4; Nov., Dec., and Mar.–May, Thurs. and Fri. 9–5, Sat. 10–4.*

WHERE TO EAT

$$$$
MEDITERRANEAN
Fodor's Choice
★

✕ **Primo.** Award-winning chef Melissa Kelly and her world-class restaurant have been written up in *Gourmet, Bon Appétit,* and *O* magazines. In this restored Victorian home, upstairs seating has a funky vibe; downstairs is fancier. No matter where you sit, it's farm-to-table here: the restaurant raises its own chickens and pigs, cures its own meats, produces its own eggs, and grows its own fruits and vegetables. Combining fresh Maine ingredients with Mediterranean influences, the daily menu includes dishes like kale salad with creamy garlic dressing, house-made pasta with local squid, and duck with sweet-and-sour rhubarb chutney. Pastry chef Price Kushner creates delectable desserts like cannoli featuring crushed pistachios and amarena cherries. $ *Average main: $40* ✉ *2 N. Main St.* ☎ *207/596–0770* ⊕ *www.primorestaurant. com* ☾ *No lunch.*

$
DINER
FAMILY

✕ **Rockland Cafe.** It may not look like much from the outside, but the Rockland Cafe is one of the most popular eateries in town. It's famous for the size of its breakfasts—don't pass up the fish-cake Benedict. If you're a late riser, don't worry: breakfast is served until noon (until 4 November–April). At dinner, the seafood combo of shrimp, scallops, clams, and haddock is excellent, or there's also classic liver and onions. $ *Average main: $15* ✉ *441 Main St.* ☎ *207/596–7556* ⊕ *www.rocklandcafe.com.*

WHERE TO STAY

$
B&B/INN

▣ **Berry Manor Inn.** Originally the residence of Rockland merchant Charles H. Berry, this 1898 shingle-style B&B sits in Rockland's National Historic District. **Pros:** quiet neighborhood; within walking distance of downtown and the harbor; rooms have TVs. **Cons:** not much of a view. $ *Rooms from: $185* ✉ *81 Talbot Ave.* ☎ *207/596–7696, 800/774–5692* ⊕ *www.berrymanorinn.com* ⟿ *12 rooms* ⏽◯⏽ *Breakfast.*

$
B&B/INN

▣ **LimeRock Inn.** In the center of town in Rockland's National Historic District, the LimeRock Inn puts you within easy walking distance of the Farnsworth Museum and many restaurants. **Pros:** all rooms have TVs and DVD players; large in-town lot with gazebo. **Cons:** not on the water. $ *Rooms from: $169* ✉ *96 Limerock St.* ☎ *207/594–2257, 800/546–3762* ⊕ *www.limerockinn.com* ⟿ *8 rooms* ⏽◯⏽ *Breakfast.*

$$$
RESORT
FAMILY
Fodor's Choice
★

▣ **Samoset Resort.** Occupying 230 waterfront acres on the Rockland–Rockport town line, this all-encompassing resort offers luxurious rooms and suites with private balconies overlooking the water or the grounds. **Pros:** full-service spa; children's programs; activities from basketball to croquet. **Cons:** no beach. $ *Rooms from: $339* ✉ *220 Warrenton St., Rockport* ☎ *207/594–2511, 800/341–1650* ⊕ *www.samoset.com* ⟿ *160 rooms, 18 suites, 4 cottages, 72 condos* ⏽◯⏽ *Breakfast.*

SPORTS AND THE OUTDOORS

Schooner Ladona. A handsome racing yacht built in 1922 (and rebuilt in 1971), recently restored from nose to tail, the *Schooner Ladona* leads chartered trips lasting from a single afternoon up to six days. All trips include breakfast and lunch, including a traditional Downeast lobster bake and beach barbecue, as well as a selection of wines and ports every evening. ✉ *Rockland* ☎ *800/999–7352, 207/594–4723* ⊕ *www.schoonerladona.com.*

WALK FROM ROCKPORT TO CAMDEN

For a stunning walk or drive, take the two-lane paved road that winds up and down on its way out of Rockport, with occasional views of the ocean and the village, en route to Camden. Begin at the intersection of U.S. 1 and Pascal Avenue in Rockport. Take a right off U.S. 1 toward Rockport Harbor, then cross the bridge and go up the hill to Central Street. One block later, bear right on Russell Avenue, which becomes Chestnut Street at the Camden town line; take this all the way to downtown Camden.

Lining the way are some of the most beautiful homes in Maine, surrounded by an abundance of flora and fauna. Keep an eye out for views of the sparkling ocean, as well as for Aldermere Farm and its Belted Galloway cows. (These rare cows get their name from the foot-wide white "belt" around their middles.) The walk or drive is beautiful at any time of the year, but in fall it's breathtaking. Like the rest of New England, the coast of Maine gets a large number of fall-foliage "leaf peepers," and the reds and golds of the chestnut, birch, and elm trees along this winding route are especially beautiful.

FAMILY **Schooner Heritage.** The newest windjammer in Maine's fleet offers three- to six-day cruises. Captain Doug Lee is a storyteller and author of nautical histories. ⊠ *North End Shipyard, 11 Front St.* ☎ *207/594–8007, 800/648–4544* ⊕ *www.schoonerheritage.com.*

CAMDEN

8 miles north of Rockland.

More than any other town along Penobscot Bay, Camden is the perfect picture-postcard of a Maine coastal village. It is one of the most popular destinations on the Maine Coast, and June–September the town is crowded with visitors—but don't let that scare you away: Camden is worth it. Just come prepared for busy traffic on the town's Main Street, and make reservations for lodging and restaurants well in advance.

Camden is famous not only for its geography, but also for its large fleet of windjammers—relics and replicas from the age of sailing—with their romantic histories and great billowing sails. At just about any hour during warm months you're likely to see at least one windjammer tied up in the harbor. Excursions, whether for an afternoon or a week, are best June–September.

The town's compact size makes it perfect for exploring on foot: shops, restaurants, and galleries line Main Street, as well as the side streets and alleys around the harbor. But be sure to include Camden's residential area on your walking tour. It is quite charming and filled with many fascinating old period houses from the time when Federal, Greek Revival, and Victorian architectural styles were the rage among the wealthy, and many of them are now B&Bs. The Chamber of Commerce, at the Public Landing, can provide you with a walking map. Humped on the north side of town are the Camden Hills; drive or hike to the summit at the state park to enjoy mesmerizing views of the town, harbor, and island-dotted bay.

GETTING HERE AND AROUND

U.S. 1 becomes Camden's Main Street. Take Route 90 west from U.S. 1 and rejoin it in Warren to bypass Rockland—this is the quickest route south.

ESSENTIALS

Visitor Information Penobscot Bay Regional Chamber of Commerce. ✉ *Visitor Center, 2 Public Landing* ☎ *207/236–4404, 800/562–2529* 🌐 *www.mainedreamvacation.com.*

WORD OF MOUTH

"Camden is an absolute must to visit. A writer for *Yankee* magazine famously declared that the two-plus mile walk between Camden and Rockport is "the most beautiful in the world." Decided to find out for myself, and it is indeed well worth doing."

—bachslunch

FESTIVALS FAMILY **Windjammer Weekend.** One of the biggest and most colorful events of the year is the Camden Windjammer Festival, which takes place over Labor Day weekend. The harbor is packed with historic vessels, and there are lots of good eats. Visitors can tour the ships. ✉ *Camden* ☎ *800/223–5459* 🌐 *www.camdenwindjammerfestival.org.*

WHERE TO EAT

$ AMERICAN FAMILY Fodor's Choice ★ 🍴 **Boynton-McKay Food Co.** At Camden's longtime go-to breakfast and lunch spot, Boynton-McKay's new owners have updated the tried-and-true menu with foodie touches, while staying true to cherished staples. Order one of their ever-changing breakfast skillets, with eggs perched atop veggies and chorizo, say, or a breakfast salad with poached duck egg, bacon, avocado, and hot-sauce vinaigrette. Pop by for lunch to grab a slow-cooked brisket sandwich with a side of quinoa salad and avocado. Try the house-made kombucha or one of their rotating desserts with a cup of coffee made from locally roasted beans. The walls are covered in local historical documents and objects, and this spot has a retro feel to it, having once been a drugstore and soda fountain. [$] *Average main: $10* ✉ *30 Main St.* ☎ *207/236–2465* 🌐 *www.boynton-mckay.com* ⏲ *Closed Mon.*

$ SEAFOOD FAMILY 🍴 **Cappy's Chowder House.** As you might expect from the name, Cappy's clam "chowdah" is the thing to order here—it's been written up in the *New York Times* and *Bon Appétit*—but there are plenty of other worthy seafood specials at this restaurant, and their fish tacos are a real treat. Don't be afraid to bring the kids—they'll love the "Crow's Nest" upper level. [$] *Average main: $13* ✉ *1 Main St.* ☎ *207/236–2254* 🌐 *www.cappyschowder.com* ✍ *Reservations not accepted.*

$ BRITISH FAMILY Fodor's Choice ★ 🍴 **The Drouthy Bear.** The Drouthy ("thirsty" in old Scots) Bear serves up excellent pub food in an intimate, authentic setting. Tuck into the bangers and mash, or a traditional ploughman's lunch with a Branston pickle, or pop in for full afternoon tea, complete with a selection of sandwiches, scones, and of course, a pot of hot tea. [$] *Average main: $10* ✉ *50 Elm St.* ☎ *207/236–2327* 🌐 *www.drouthybear.com.*

The view from Camden Hills is a great way to see Penobscot Bay and the town of Camden.

$ ✕**Long Grain.** It doesn't look like much from the outside, but don't let
ASIAN FUSION that deter you from this cozy Asian-fusion eatery with an emphasis on
Thai curries and house-made noodles. Chef Ravin Nakjaroen was a
James Beard semifinalist for the Best Northeast Chef Award in 2015.
A very popular restaurant with locals and visitors alike, reservations
are essential, though you might be able to squeeze in at the tiny bar
without one if you're dining solo and don't mind a little chaos. $ *Aver-
age main: $12* ✉ *13 Elm St.* ☎ *207/236–9001* ⊗ *Closed Sun. and Mon.*
⚑ *Reservations essential.*

$$$$ ✕**Natalie's Restaurant.** One of the most sought-after dining spots in Cam-
MODERN den, Natalie's is the creation of Dutch owners Raymond Brunyanszki
AMERICAN and Oscar Verest, who brought in chefs to create splurge-worthy dishes
Fodor's Choice in an intimate setting. Located in the cozy and elegant Camden Har-
★ bour Inn, the restaurant is fine dining with a distinctly Maine flair, and
seasonal ingredients set the tone. Choose from two prix-fixe menus
(three courses for $76 or a seven-course chef's tasting menu for $102),
which may feature cabbage-wrapped Maine monkfish or local lamb
with root veggies. There's also a five-course lobster tasting menu ($109)
that may include lobster with peaches and wasabi cream, or Maine
lobster salad with sunchoke, caviar, and foie gras. The service is phenomenal. In the lounge, you can order small tapas-style dishes or enjoy
a pre-dinner cocktail in front of the big fireplace. $ *Average main: $76*
✉ *Camden Harbour Inn, 83 Bay View St.* ☎ *207/236–7008* ⊕ *www.*
nataliesrestaurant.com ⊗ *Closed Sun. Nov.–May. No lunch* ⚑ *Reser-*
vations essential.

WHERE TO STAY

$
B&B/INN

⊡ Camden Hartstone Inn. This 1835 mansard-roofed Victorian home has been turned into a plush, sophisticated retreat and a fine culinary destination. **Pros:** luxury in the heart of town; extravagant breakfasts; some private entrances. **Cons:** not on water. $ *Rooms from: $199 ⊠ 41 Elm St.* ☎ *207/236–4259* ⊕ *www.hartstoneinn.com* ↪ *11 rooms, 11 suites* ⦿ *Breakfast.*

$$
B&B/INN
FAMILY

⊡ Lord Camden Inn. If you want to be in the center of town and near the harbor, look for this handsome brick building with the bright blue-and-white awnings. **Pros:** large Continental breakfast; suitelike "premier" rooms have balconies and sitting areas. **Cons:** traffic noise in front rooms. $ *Rooms from: $259 ⊠ 24 Main St.* ☎ *207/236–4325, 800/336–4325* ⊕ *www.lordcamdeninn.com* ↪ *36 rooms and suites* ⦿ *Breakfast.*

$$
B&B/INN
Fodor's Choice
★

⊡ Norumbega Inn. This welcoming B&B is one of the most photographed pieces of real estate in Maine, and once you get a look at its castlelike facade, you'll understand why. **Pros:** eye-popping architecture; beautiful views; close to town. **Cons:** stairs to climb. $ *Rooms from: $269 ⊠ 63 High St.* ☎ *207/236–4646, 877/363–4646* ⊕ *www.norumbegainn.com* ↪ *9 rooms, 2 suites (including 1 penthouse)* ⦿ *Breakfast.*

$
B&B/INN
FAMILY
Fodor's Choice
★

⊡ Whitehall. Although the oldest part of the Whitehall is an 1834 white-clapboard sea captain's home, the bright and cheery design characteristic of the Lark Hotel group that recently redesigned and renovated the hotel is decidedly contemporary with nostalgic touches here and there. **Pros:** short walk to downtown and harbor; breakfast entrée choices; beautifully renovated with a design focus. **Cons:** no good water views. $ *Rooms from: $189 ⊠ 52 High St.* ☎ *207/236–3391, 800/789–6565* ⊕ *www.whitehall-inn.com* ⊗ *Closed mid-Oct.–mid-May* ↪ *37 rooms, 4 suites* ⦿ *Breakfast.*

SPORTS AND THE OUTDOORS

FAMILY

Angelique. Captain Mike and Lynne McHenry have more than three decades' experience on the high seas. Three- to six-day cruise options aboard the *Angelique* include photography workshops and meteor-watching trips, as well as yoga and wellness excursions. ⊠ *Camden Harbor* ☎ *800/282–9899* ⊕ *www.sailangelique.com.*

FAMILY

Heron. This schooner, which had a cameo in the movie *The Rum Diary*, offers lunchtime sails, wildlife-watching trips, and sunset cruises. ⊠ *Rockport Marine Park, Pascal Ave., Rockport* ☎ *207/236–8605, 800/599–8605* ⊕ *www.sailheron.com.*

FAMILY
Fodor's Choice
★

Mary Day. Sailing for more than 50 years, the *Mary Day* is the first schooner in Maine built specifically for vacation excursions. Meals are cooked on an antique wood-fired stove. ⊠ *Camden Harbor, Atlantic Ave.* ☎ *800/992–2218* ⊕ *www.schoonermaryday.com.*

Olad. Captain Aaron Lincoln runs two-hour trips on both the *Olad* and a smaller sailing vessel, spotting lighthouses, coastal mansions, the occasional seal, and the red-footed puffin cousins known as guillemots. Either boat can also be chartered for longer trips. ⊠ *Camden Harbor, Bay View St.* ☎ *207/236–2323* ⊕ *www.maineschooners.com.*

SHOPPING

Camden's downtown area makes for excellent window-shopping, with lots of adorable and sophisticated boutiques stocking a curated assortment of local products. Most shops and galleries are along Camden's main drag. From the harbor, turn right on Bay View, and walk to Main/High Street. U.S. 1 has lots of names as it runs through Maine. Three are within Camden's town limits—it starts as Elm Street, changes to Main Street, then becomes High Street.

Lily, Lupine & Fern. This full-service florist offers a wonderful array of gourmet foods, chocolates, wines, imported beers, high-quality olive oils, and cheeses. There's a small deck where you can enjoy harbor views and a cup of coffee. ⊠ *11 Main St.* ☎ *207/236–9600* ⊕ *www. lilylupine.com* ☽ *Sun.*

FAMILY **Owl and Turtle Bookshop and Cafe.** This pint-size but well-stocked inde-
Fodor$Choice pendent bookstore has been serving Camden for over 45 years, and has
★ recently added a cozy café. It also hosts author events. It's closed on Monday. ⊠ *33 Bay View St.* ☎ *207/230–7335* ⊕ *www.owlandturtle.com.*

Planet. In this storefront shop you'll find unique clothing, lots of books, and quality toys, many of them made in Maine. ⊠ *10 Main St.* ☎ *207/236–4410.*

Fodor$Choice **Swans Island.** For gorgeous, handmade blankets, throws, and pillows,
★ as well as wraps and scarves, look no further. All products are made in Maine using natural, heirloom-quality yarns—the expert craftsmanship explains the hefty price tag. ⊠ *2 Bayview St.* ☎ *207/706–7926* ⊕ *www.swansislandcompany.com.*

LINCOLNVILLE

6 miles north of Camden via U.S. 1.

Lincolnville's area of most interest is Lincolnville Beach, where you'll find a few restaurants, the ferry to Islesboro, and a swimming beach that attracts folks from neighboring Camden and Belfast. The village is tiny: you could go through it in less than a minute. Still, it has a history going back to the Revolution, and you can see a small cannon on the beach here (never fired), intended to repel the British in the War of 1812.

GETTING HERE AND AROUND

Lincolnville Beach is on U.S. 1, and the town of Lincolnville Center is inland on Route 173.

WHERE TO EAT

$$ ✕ **Lobster Pound Restaurant.** If you're looking for an authentic place to
SEAFOOD enjoy a Maine lobster dinner, this is it. This large restaurant has rustic
FAMILY wooden picnic tables outside, an enclosed patio, and two dining rooms with a gift shop in between. Hundreds of live lobsters swim in tanks out back, so feel free to pick your own. There's a full bar, and the wine list includes some local labels. The classic "shore dinner deluxe" consists of lobster stew or fish chowder, steamed clams or mussels, fried clams, and a 1½-pound lobster, along with sides and dessert. Because this is such a big place, you won't have to wait long, even if it's busy.

Right on U.S. 1, next to a small beach, the restaurant has beautiful views. $ *Average main: $22* ⊠ *2521 Atlantic Hwy.* ☎ *207/789–5550* ⊕ *www.lobsterpoundmaine.com* ⊘ *Closed Nov.–mid-Apr.*

BELFAST

13 miles north of Lincolnville via U.S. 1.

Lots of Maine coastal towns like to think of themselves as the prettiest little town in the state, and any judge would be spoiled for choice. Charming Belfast (originally to be named Londonderry) is a strong contender, with a beautiful waterfront; an old and interesting main street rising from the harbor; a delightful array of B&Bs, restaurants, and shops; and friendly townsfolk. The downtown even has old-fashioned street lamps, which set the streets aglow at night.

GETTING HERE AND AROUND

U.S. 1 runs through Belfast as it travels up the coast. From Interstate 95, take U.S. 3 in Augusta to get here. The highways meet in Belfast, heading north. The information center has a large array of magazines, guidebooks, maps, and brochures that cover the entire Mid-Coast. It also can provide you with a free walking-tour brochure that describes the various historic buildings.

ESSENTIALS

Visitor Information Belfast Area Chamber of Commerce. ⊠ *93 Main St.* ☎ *207/338–1975* ⊕ *www.belfastmaine.org.*

EXPLORING

Belfast is a funky coastal town, where the streets are lined with eclectic boutiques and a decidedly laissez-faire attitude presides. There is still evidence of the wealth of the mid-1800s, when Belfast was home to a number of business magnates, shipbuilders, ship captains, and so on. Their mansions still stand along High Street and in the residential area above it, offering excellent examples of Greek Revival and Federal-style architecture. In fact, the town has one of the best showcases of Greek Revival homes in the state. Don't miss the "White House," where High and Church streets merge several blocks south of downtown.

WHERE TO EAT

$$
AMERICAN
FAMILY

✕ **Darby's Restaurant and Pub.** This charming, old-fashioned restaurant and bar is very popular with locals. With pressed-tin ceilings, it has been a bar or a restaurant since it was built in the 1890s. On the walls are works for sale by local artists and old murals of Belfast scenes. Pad thai and chicken with chili and cashews are signature dishes. The menu also has hearty homemade soups and sandwiches and classic fish 'n' chips. $ *Average main: $23* ⊠ *155 High St.* ☎ *207/338–2339* ⊕ *www. darbysrestaurant.com.*

$$$
SEAFOOD
FAMILY
Fodor's Choice
★

✕ **Young's Lobster Pound.** The corrugated-steel building looks more like a fish cannery than a restaurant, but it's one of the best places for an authentic Maine lobster dinner. It sits right on the water's edge, across the harbor from downtown Belfast. When you first walk in, you'll see numerous tanks of live lobsters of varying size. The traditional meal here is the "shore dinner," consisting of clam chowder or lobster stew, steamed clams or mussels, a 1½-pound boiled lobster, corn on the cob, and chips. Surf-and-turf dinners and hot dogs are popular, too. It's BYOB. Order your dinner at the counter, then find a table inside or on the deck. Don't leave your outdoor table unattended—seagulls *love* lobster. $ *Average main: $25* ⊠ *2 Fairview St., off U.S. 1* ☎ *207/338–1160* ⊕ *youngslobsterpound.webs.com* ⊘ *Takeout only Jan.–Mar.*

NIGHTLIFE

FAMILY **Rollie's Bar & Grill.** Up a bit from the harbor, Rollie's Bar & Grill has been in business since 1972. The vintage bar is from a 19th-century sailing ship. Rollie's is the town's most popular watering hole, especially among sports fans who come to watch the big game. It just may serve the best hamburgers in the state, and you'll see families crop up around dinnertime. Food is served until midnight on Friday and Saturday and there's an excellent happy hour weekdays 3–6. ⊠ *37 Main St.* ☎ *207/338–4502* ⊕ *www.rollies.me.*

SEARSPORT

6 miles north of Belfast via U.S. 1.

Searsport is well-known as the antiques and flea-market capital of Maine, and with good reason: the Antique Mall alone, on U.S. 1 just north of town, is home to some 60 dealers, and flea markets during the visitor season line both sides of U.S. 1.

Searsport also has a rich history of shipbuilding and seafaring. In the early to mid-1800s there were 10 shipbuilding facilities in Searsport, and the population of the town was about 1,000 people more than it is today, and jobs were plentiful. By the mid-1800s Searsport was home to more than 200 sailing-ship captains.

GETTING HERE AND AROUND

Downtown Searsport is right along U.S. 1, as is much of the town, which doesn't have lots of side streets. Just north of here in Stockton Springs, U.S. 1A leads to Bangor.

EXPLORING

FAMILY **Penobscot Marine Museum.** Just off Main Street, this downtown museum
Fodor's Choice explores the maritime culture of the Penobscot Bay region. Exhibits
★ of artifacts and paintings are spread throughout six nearby buildings, most dating to the first half of the 19th century, and one of the former sea captain's homes has period rooms. Outstanding marine art includes a notable collection of works by Thomas and James Buttersworth. There are photos of local sea captains, model ships, lots of scrimshaw, navigational instruments, and tools from the area's history of logging, granite mining, and ice cutting. There are also exhibits just for kids. ⊠ *2 Church St.* ☎ *207/548–2529* ⊕ *www.penobscotmarinemuseum.org* ⊞ *$12* ⊘ *Late May–late Oct., Mon.–Sat. 10–5, Sun. noon–5.*

SHOPPING

Searsport Antique Mall. The area's biggest collection of antiques is in the Searsport Antique Mall, which has more than 60 dealers. ⊠ *149 E. Main St.* ☎ *207/548–2640.*

Learn about Maine's seafaring heritage at the Penobscot Marine Museum.

BUCKSPORT

9 miles north of Searsport via U.S. 1.

The stunning Penobscot Narrows Bridge, spanning the Penobscot River, makes Bucksport, a town founded in 1763, well worth a visit, even if you only stop while passing through to points north. Fort Knox, Maine's largest historic fort, overlooks the town from across the river. There are magnificent views of the imposing granite structure from the pleasant riverfront walkway downtown.

GETTING HERE AND AROUND

After you pass over the spectacular Penobscot Narrows Bridge onto Verona Island driving north on U.S. 1, you cross another bridge into Bucksport; turn left for downtown and right to continue on the highway. Route 15 heads north to Bangor from here.

EXPLORING

FAMILY
Fodor's Choice
★

Penobscot Narrows Bridge & Observatory Tower/Fort Knox Historic Site. An "an engineering marvel" is how experts describe the 2,120-foot-long Penobscot Narrows Bridge, which opened in 2006 and which is taller than the Statue of Liberty. It's certainly beautiful to look at—from the surrounding countryside it pops up on the horizon like the towers of a fairy-tale castle. Spanning the Penobscot River across from Bucksport, the bridge's 437-foot observation tower is the tallest in the world; an elevator shoots you to the top. Don't miss it—the panoramic views, which take in the hilly countryside and the river as it widens into Penobscot Bay, are breathtaking. In summer, the observatory often offers moonrise viewings.

Also here is Fort Knox, the largest historic fort in Maine. It was built between 1844 and 1869, when, despite a treaty with Britain settling boundary disputes, invasion was still a concern—after all, the British controlled this region during both the Revolutionary War and the War of 1812. The fort never saw any real action, but it was used for troop training and as a garrison during the Civil War and the Spanish-American War. Visitors are welcome to explore the many rooms and passageways. Guided tours are given daily during the summer and several days a week in the shoulder seasons. ⊠ *711 Ft. Knox Rd., off U.S. 1, Prospect* ☎ *207/469–6553* ⊕ *www.fortknox.maineguide.com* ☜ *Fort $4.50, fort and observatory $7* ☉ *Observatory: May, June, Sept., and Oct., daily 9–5, July and Aug., daily 9–6. Fort: May–Oct., daily 9–5.*

BANGOR

122 miles north of Portland via I–95, 19 miles north of Bucksport via Rte. 15.

The state's second-largest metropolitan area (Portland is the largest), Bangor is about 20 miles from the coast and is the unofficial capital of northern Maine. Back in the 19th century, the most important product and export of the "Queen City" was lumber from the state's vast North Woods. Now, because of its airport, Bangor has become a gateway to Mount Desert Island, Bar Harbor, and Acadia National Park. Along the revitalized waterfront, the American Folk Festival draws big crowds on the last full weekend in August, and an outdoor stage attracts top bands and musicians throughout the summer.

GETTING HERE AND AROUND
Interstate 95 has five Bangor exits: 45–49. U.S. 1A loops up to Bangor from Stockton Springs and Ellsworth, near Bar Harbor, and connects with Interstate 395 on the western side of the Bangor area.

ESSENTIALS
Visitor Information Greater Bangor Convention & Visitors Bureau. ⊠ *33 Harlow St.* ☎ *207/947–5205, 800/916–6673* ⊕ *www.bangorcvb.org.*

EXPLORING
FAMILY **Maine Discovery Museum.** Three floors with more than 60 interactive exhibits let kids explore the state's ecosystem in Nature Trails, learn about other cultures in TradeWinds, step into classic children's books like *Charlotte's Web*—all written by Maine authors—in Booktown, and unearth dinosaur "bones" in DINO DIG. There's also drop-in art studio and daily programs on art and other topics. ■ TIP→ **Visitors to Acadia National Park often head here on a rainy day.** ⊠ *74 Main St.* ☎ *207/262–7200* ⊕ *www.mainediscoverymuseum.org* ☜ *$7.50* ☉ *June–Sept., Mon.–Sat. 10–5, Sun. noon–5; Oct.–May, Tues.–Sat. 10–5, Sun. noon–5.*

NEED A BREAK?
Friars' Bakehouse. Locals say this place has the best whoopie pies in the Bangor area, and its yeasty breads are equally prized. The bakery and restaurant are run by three Franciscan friars, one of whom spent time in various highly regarded culinary programs. ⊠ *21 Central St.* ☎ *207/947–3770.*

Governor's Restaurant & Bakery. This old family-friendly standby, with six locations including Bangor, is famed for its peanut-butter whoopie pies as well as the classic black-and-white, and can grant any special flavor combinations by request with 24-hour notice. ✉ *643 Broadway* ☎ *207/947–3113* 🌐 *www.governorsrestaurant.com.*

WHERE TO STAY

$ HOTEL **Lucerne Inn.** Nestled in the mountains, the Lucerne Inn overlooks beautiful Phillips Lake. **Pros:** golf course across the road; lake views. **Cons:** most rooms are dated. *Rooms from: $109* ✉ *2517 Main Rd., Dedham* ☎ *207/843–5123, 800/325–5123* 🌐 *www.lucerneinn.com* *21 rooms, 10 suites* *Breakfast.*

SHOPPING

Fodor's Choice ★ **The Rock and Art Shop.** With things like taxidermied bats and terraria filled with tropical plants mixed in among books, stationery, jewelry, and natural history objects this is no ordinary store: it's a veritable cabinet of curiosities, and a delight for the serious shopper and the window-shopper alike. The store has rotating exhibitions of local art that is also for sale. You'll find their other outposts in Bar Harbor, Ellsworth, and just outside Ellsworth off Route 1A. ✉ *36 Central St.* ☎ *207/947–2205* 🌐 *www.therockandartshop.com.*

THE BLUE HILL PENINSULA

If you want to see unspoiled Down East Maine landscapes, explore art galleries, savor exquisite meals, or simply enjoy life at an unhurried pace, you should be quite content on the Blue Hill Peninsula.

The large peninsula juts south into Penobscot Bay. Not far from the mainland are the islands of Little Deer Isle, Deer Isle, and, at the latter's tip, the picturesque fishing town of Stonington. A twisting labyrinth of roads winds through blueberry barrens and around picturesque coves, linking the towns of Blue Hill, Brooksville, Sedgwick, and Brooklin. Blue Hill and Castine are the area's primary business hubs. Painters, photographers, sculptors, and other artists are drawn to the peninsula; you can find more than 20 galleries on Deer Isle and in Stonington and at least half as many on the mainland. With its small inns, charming B&Bs, and outstanding restaurants scattered across the area, the Blue Hill Peninsula may just persuade you to leave the rest of the coastline to the tourists.

VISITOR INFORMATION

Contacts Blue Hill Peninsula Chamber of Commerce. ✉ *16 South St., Suite B, Blue Hill* ☎ *207/374–3242* 🌐 *www.bluehillpeninsula.org.* **Deer Isle–Stonington Chamber of Commerce.** ✉ *Main St., and Rte. 15, Deer Isle* ☎ *207/348–6124* 🌐 *www.deerisle.com.*

CASTINE

18 miles north of Bucksport via U.S. 1 and Rtes. 175 and 166.

A summer destination for more than 100 years, Castine is a well-preserved seaside village that serves as an excellent base for exploring the Blue Hill area and Mount Desert Island.

GETTING HERE AND AROUND

From U.S. 1 in Orland, near Bucksport, Route 175 heads south along the Penobscot River toward Castine. Continue on Route 166 at the crossroads of West Penobscot, and after a bit you have the option of taking Route 166A into the village. Routes 166 and 166A form a loop—taking either will get you to Castine—but the latter is especially scenic, passing expansive Wadsworth Cove at the mouth of the river as it enters its namesake bay.

EXPLORING

Federal- and Greek Revival–style architecture, rich history, and spectacular views of Penobscot Bay make Castine an ideal spot to spend a day or two. Explore its lively harbor front, two small museums (the Wilson Museum and the Castine Historical Society), and the ruins of a British fort. You can't miss the oversize historical signs throughout the village.

An excellent self-guided walking tour is available at local businesses and the historical society. For a nice stroll, park your car at the landing and walk up Main Street toward the white Trinitarian Congregational Church. Turn right on Court Street and go one block to the town common. Among the white-clapboard buildings ringing this green space are the Ives House (once the summer home of poet Robert Lowell), the Adams School, the former Abbott School (home to the historical society), and the Unitarian Church, capped by a whimsical belfry. From lower Main Street, head out Perkins Street on foot or by bike or car. You'll pass summer "cottage" mansions and the Wilson Museum on the way to Dyces Head Lighthouse (private), where a path leads to cliffs (careful here) fronting Penobscot Bay, site of a major Revolutionary War battle. You can return on Battle Avenue to make a loop.

WHERE TO EAT

$$ AMERICAN FAMILY

🍴 **Dennett's Wharf.** Originally built as a sail-rigging loft in the early 1800s, this longtime favorite is a good place for oysters and fresh seafood of all kinds. The waterfront restaurant also serves burgers, sandwiches, and light fare. There are over 20 microbrews on tap, including Dennett's tasty Wharf Rat Ale. Eat in the dining room or outside on the deck: there are covered and open sections, another bar, and Adirondack chairs if you just stop by for a brew. [$] *Average main: $18* ✉ *15 Sea St.* ☎ *207/326–9045* 🌐 *www.dennettswharf.net.*

SPORTS AND THE OUTDOORS

Castine Kayak International Adventures. At Eaton's Wharf, Castine Kayak Adventures operates tours run by owner Karen Francoeur, a Registered Maine Guide. Sign up for a half day of kayaking along the shore, a full day of kayaking in Penobscot Bay, or for nighttime trips—paddling stirs up a type of bioluminescent phytoplankton, causing them to light up like fireflies as they shoot through the water. The company also offers overnight kayak camping trips and rents mountain bikes and kayaks. ⊠ *Eaton's Wharf, 17 Sea St.* ☎ *207/866–3506* ⊕ *www.castinekayak.com.*

BLUE HILL

20 miles east of Castine via Rtes. 166, 175, and 176.

Nestled snugly between 943-foot Blue Hill Mountain and Blue Hill Bay, the village of Blue Hill sits right beside its harbor. About 30 miles from Acadia National Park, Blue Hill makes for a more laid-back base for exploring the Mount Desert Island area, but bear in mind that 30 miles can take at least twice as long to travel with heavy traffic in summertime. Originally known for its granite quarries, copper mines, and shipbuilding, today the town is known for its pottery and galleries, bookstores, antiques shops, and studios that line its streets. The Blue Hill Fair (⊕ *www.bluehillfair.com*), held Labor Day weekend, is a tradition in these parts, with agricultural exhibits, food, rides, and entertainment. A charming little park with a great playground is tucked away near the harbor downtown.

GETTING HERE AND AROUND

From U.S. 1 in Orland, Route 15 heads south to Blue Hill. To continue north on the highway, take Route 172 north to Ellsworth.

WHERE TO EAT AND STAY

$$$

MODERN
AMERICAN

Fodor'sChoice

★

✕ **Arborvine.** Glowing gas fireplaces, period antiques, exposed beams, and hardwood floors covered with Oriental rugs distinguish the four candlelit dining areas in this renovated Cape Cod–style house. Begin with a salad of mixed greens, sliced beets, and pears with blue cheese crumbled on top. For your entrée, choose from seasonal dishes such as crispy duck with rhubarb and lime glaze, or roasted rack of lamb with a basil-and-pine-nut crust—fresh fish dishes are also superb. Save room for dessert; the ice cream is homemade. Return when you're in a more casual mood: like the restaurant, the adjacent nautical-theme DeepWater Brew Pub serves dishes made with organic ingredients to go with its own beer. It's housed in an inviting, historic barn that opens to lawn seating come summer. $ *Average main: $31* ⊠ *33 Tenney Hill* ☎ *207/374–2119* ⊕ *www.arborvine.com* ☉ *No lunch.*

$$

B&B/INN

🛏 **Blue Hill Inn.** One side of this Federal-style inn was built as a home in 1835, but it soon became lodging, adding a wing with a matching facade in the 1850s. **Pros:** plenty of charm; modern suites with kitchens in separate building; 30 miles from Acadia National Park. **Cons:** some narrow stairs and thin walls consistent with historic property. $ *Rooms from: $225* ⊠ *40 Union St.* ☎ *207/374–2844* ⊕ *www.bluehillinn.com* ☉ *Closed Nov.–mid-May, except for the Cape House Suite and the Studio* ⤳ *10 rooms, 3 suites* ❏ *Breakfast.*

SHOPPING

ART GALLERIES

Blue Hill Bay Gallery. This gallery sells oil and watercolor landscapes and seascapes of Maine and New England from the 19th through the 21st century. It also carries the proprietor's own photography. Call ahead in the off-season. ⊠ *11 Tenney Hill* ☎ *207/374–5773* ⊕ *www.bluehillbaygallery.com.*

11

POTTERY

Rackliffe Pottery. In business since 1969, this shop sells colorful pottery made with lead-free glazes. You can choose between water pitchers, serving platters, tea-and-coffee sets, and sets of canisters, among other lovely items. ⊠ *132 Ellsworth Rd.* ☎ *888/631–3321, 207/374–2297* ⊕ *www.rackliffepottery.com.*

WINE

Blue Hill Wine Shop. In a restored barn at the rear of one of Blue Hill's earliest houses, the Blue Hill Wine Shop carries more than 1,200 carefully selected wines. Coffee, tea, cheeses, and prewrapped sandwiches are also available. ⊠ *138 Main St.* ☎ *207/374–2161* ⊕ *www. bluehillwineshop.com.*

DEER ISLE VILLAGE

16 miles south of Blue Hill via Rtes. 176 and 15.

Around Deer Isle Village, thick woods give way to tidal coves. Stacks of lobster traps populate the backyards of shingled houses, and dirt roads lead to secluded summer cottages. This region is prized by artists, and studios and galleries are plentiful.

GETTING HERE AND AROUND

From Sedgwick, Route 15 crosses a 1930s suspension bridge onto Little Deer Isle and continues on to the larger Deer Isle.

EXPLORING

Edgar M. Tennis Preserve. Enjoy several miles of woodland and shore trails at the Edgar M. Tennis Preserve. Look for hawks, eagles, and ospreys and wander among old apple trees, fields of wildflowers, and ocean-polished rocks. ⊠ *Tennis Rd., Deer Isle* ☎ *207/348–2455* ⊕ *www.islandheritagetrust.org* ⊠ *Free* ☉ *Daily dawn–dusk.*

Haystack Mountain School of Crafts. Want to learn a new craft? This school 6 miles from Deer Isle Village offers one- and two-week courses for people of all skill levels in crafts such as blacksmithing, basketry, print-making, and weaving. Artisans from around the world present free evening lectures throughout summer. Tours of the school and studios are available on Wednesday. ⊠ *89 Haystack School Dr., off Rte. 15, Deer Isle* ☎ *207/348–2306* ⊕ *www.haystack-mtn.org* ⊠ *Tours $5* ☉ *Tours: June–Aug., Wed. at 1.*

SHOPPING

Nervous Nellie's Jams and Jellies. Jams and jellies are made right on the property at Nervous Nellie's. There is a tearoom with homemade goodies, and also a fanciful sculpture garden with everything from knights to witches to a lobster and a flamingo. They are the works of sculptor Peter Beerits, who operates Nervous Nellie's with his wife. ⊠ *598 Sunshine Rd., off Rte. 15, Deer Isle* ☎ *207/348–6182, 800/777–6845* ⊕ *www.nervousnellies.com.*

STONINGTON

6 miles south of Deer Isle.

Stonington is at the southern end of Route 15, which has helped it to retain its small-town flavor. The boutiques and galleries lining Main Street cater mostly to out-of-towners, but the village remains a fishing and lobstering community at heart. The principal activity is at the waterfront, where you can watch boats arrive with the day's catch. The sloped island that rises to the south is Isle au Haut, which contains a remote section of Acadia National Park.

GETTING HERE AND AROUND

From Deer Isle village, Route 15 runs all the way to Stonington at the tip of the island. There is a ferry from here to Isle au Haut.

EXPLORING

Deer Isle Granite Museum. This tiny museum documents Stonington's quarrying tradition. The museum's centerpiece is a working model of quarrying operations on Crotch Island and the town of Stonington at the turn of the last century. Granite was quarried here for Rockefeller Plaza in New York City and for the John F. Kennedy Memorial in Arlington National Cemetery, among other well-known structures. ⊠ *51 Main St.* ☎ *207/367–6331 July and Aug. only* ⊕ *deerislegranitemuseum. wordpress.com* ▨ *Free* ☉ *July and Aug., Thurs.–Tues. 9–5.*

SPORTS AND THE OUTDOORS

Old Quarry Ocean Adventures. Departing Webb Cove and passing Stonington Harbor en route to the outer islands, Captain Bill Baker's refurbished lobster boat takes visitors on puffin-watching, whale-watching, sunset, and lighthouse trips. There's also a three-hour Sightseeing and Natural History Eco-Cruise that goes by Crotch Island, which has one of the area's two active stone quarries, and stops at Green Island, where you can take a dip in a water-filled quarry. There are also day trips for biking or kayaking on nearby islands, including Isle au Haut. ⊠ *130 Settlement Rd.* ☎ *207/367–8977* ⊕ *www.oldquarry.com.*

ISLE AU HAUT

6 miles south of Stonington via ferry.

Isle au Haut thrusts its steeply ridged back out of the sea south of Stonington. French explorer Samuel D. Champlain discovered Isle au Haut—or "High Island"—in 1604, but heaps of shells suggest that native populations lived on or visited the island prior to his arrival. The island is accessible only by mail boat, but the 45-minute journey is well worth the effort. Acadia National Park extends to cover part of the island, with miles of trails, and the boat will drop visitors off there in peak season. The island has some seasonal rentals but no inns. With only three stores, you wouldn't think folks would come here to shop, but some do, as the island is home to Black Dinah Chocolatiers (☎ *207/335–5010* ⊕ *www.blackdinahchocolatiers.com*), which makes artful high-end chocolates and has a small café.

GETTING HERE AND AROUND

There's one main road here: it circles the island and goes through the Acadia National Park section. Locals have different names for sections of the road.

Isle au Haut Boat Services (☎ *207/367–5193* ⊕ *www.isleauhaut.com*) operates daily mail-boat ferry service out of Stonington. During the summer season trips increase from two to five Monday–Saturday and from one to two on Sunday. From mid-June until late September, the boat also stops at Duck Harbor, in the island section of Acadia National Park (it will not unload bicycles, kayaks, or canoes). Ferry service is scaled back in the fall, then returns to the regular or "winter" schedule.

QUICK BITES

Maine Lobster Lady. Come summer, this former island innkeeper sells yummy and quick eats, many of them made with fish from local waters and her own organic garden produce. Her "food truck" (actually a tow trailer) is parked near the ranger's station at the Acadia National Park section on Isle au Haut. She sells lobster rolls, naturally, but you might try her shrimp-salad sandwich with paprika-dill mayo on a homemade roll, or shrimp puffs served in a paper cone. ⊠ Off Main Rd., Isle Au Haut ☎ 207/335–5141 in summer, 207/669–2751 ⊕ www.mainelobsterlady.com.

ACADIA NATIONAL PARK AND MOUNT DESERT ISLAND

With some of the most dramatic and varied scenery on the Maine Coast—and home to Maine's only national park—Mount Desert Island (pronounced "dessert" by locals) is Maine's most popular tourist destination, attracting well over 2 million visitors a year. Much of the approximately 12-by-15-mile island belongs to Acadia National Park. You can take a scenic drive along the island's rocky coastline, whose stark cliffs rise from the ocean. A network of old carriage roads lets you explore Acadia's wooded interior, filled with birds and other wildlife, and trails for hikers of all skill levels lead to rounded mountaintops, providing views of Frenchman and Blue Hill bays and beyond. Ponds and lakes beckon you to swim, fish, or boat, and ferries and charter boats provide a different perspective on the island and a chance to explore the outer islands.

Mount Desert Island has four different towns, each with its own personality. The town of Bar Harbor is on the northeastern corner of the island and includes the little villages of Hulls Cove, Salisbury Cove, and Town Hill. Aside from Acadia, Bar Harbor is the major tourist destination here, with plenty of lodging, dining, and shopping. The town of Mount Desert, in the middle of the island, has four main villages: Somesville, Seal Harbor, Otter Creek, and Northeast Harbor, a summer haven for the very wealthy. Southwest Harbor includes the smaller village of Manset south of the village center. Tremont is at the southernmost tip of the island and stretches up the western shore. It includes the villages of Bass Harbor, Bernard, and Seal Cove. Yes, Mount Desert

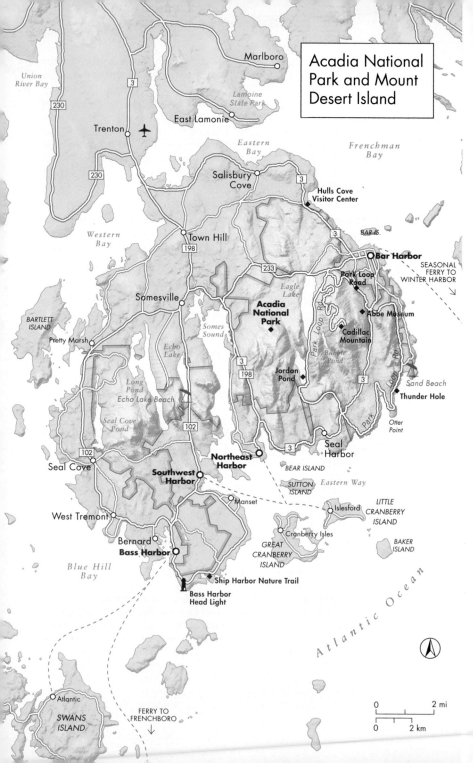

Island is a place with three personalities: the hustling, bustling tourist mecca of Bar Harbor; the "quiet side" on the western half; and the vast natural expanse of Acadia National Park. But though less congested and smaller, Northeast Harbor and Southwest Harbor are home to inns, campgrounds, restaurants, ferries, galleries, and small museums.

ESSENTIALS

VISITOR INFORMATION

Bar Harbor Chamber of Commerce. ⊠ *1201 Bar Harbor Rd., Trenton* ☎ *800/345–4617, 207/288–5103* ⊕ *www.barharborinfo.com.*

Mount Desert Chamber of Commerce. ⊠ *18 Harbor Dr., Northeast Harbor* ☎ *207/276–5040* ⊕ *www.mountdesertchamber.org.*

Mt. Desert Island Information Center at Thompson Island. Sponsored by several Mount Desert Island communities as well as Acadia National Park, the Mt. Desert Island Information Center is along Route 3 just before it crosses to Mount Desert Island. The center is loaded with pamphlets about island tours, restaurants, inns, and attractions, including Acadia National Park. You can buy park passes here, and the staff includes a park ranger. ⊠ *1319 Bar Harbor Rd., Trenton* ☎ *207/288–3411* ⊘ *Mid-May–mid-June, daily 8–5; late June–Aug., daily 8–6; Sept.–mid-Oct., daily 8–5:30.*

BAR HARBOR

34 miles from Blue Hill via Rte. 172 and U.S. 1.

A resort town since the 19th century, Bar Harbor is the artistic, culinary, and social center of Mount Desert Island, and it serves visitors to Acadia National Park with inns, motels, and restaurants. Around the turn of the last century the island was known as a summer haven for the very rich because of its cool breezes. The wealthy built lavish mansions throughout the island, many of which were destroyed in a huge fire that devastated the island in 1947—a good number of those that survived have been converted into businesses. In Bar Harbor, shops are clustered along Main, Mount Desert, and Cottage streets; take a stroll down West Street, a National Historic District, where you can see some fine old houses.

The island and the surrounding Gulf of Maine are home to a great variety of wildlife: whales, seals, eagles, falcons, ospreys, and puffins (though not right offshore here), and forest dwellers such as deer, foxes, coyotes, and beavers.

GETTING HERE AND AROUND

In Ellsworth, Route 3 leaves U.S. 1 and heads to Bar Harbor. In season, free Island Explorer buses (☎ *207/667–5796* ⊕ *www.exploreacadia. com*) take visitors to Acadia National Park and other island towns. There is also a passenger ferry to Winter Harbor across Frenchman Bay.

EXPLORING

FAMILY **Abbe Museum.** This small museum dedicated to Maine's indigenous tribes—collectively known as the Wabanaki—is the state's only Smithsonian-affiliated facility. The year-round archaeology exhibit displays spear points, bone tools, and other artifacts found around Mount Desert

Island. Rotating exhibits often feature contemporary Native American art, and there are frequent demonstrations of everything from boatbuilding to basket weaving. Call on rainy days for impromptu children's activities. A second location, inside the park at Sieur de Monts Spring, open only during the summer, features artifacts from the earliest digs around the island. ✉ *26 Mount Desert St.* ☎ *207/288–3519* 🌐 *www.abbemuseum.org* 🎟 *$8* 🕒 *May–Oct., daily 10–5; Nov.–late Dec., Thurs.–Sat. 10–4.*

THE EARLY BIRD GETS THE SUN

During your visit to Mount Desert, pick a day when you are willing to get up very early, around 4:30 or 5 am. Drive with a friend, or a camera with a timer, to the top of Cadillac Mountain in Acadia National Park, and stand on the highest rock you can find and wait for the sun to come up. When it does, have your friend, or your camera, take a photo of you looking at it and label the photo something like, "The first person in the country to see the sun come up today."

WHERE TO EAT

$$$ SEAFOOD Fodor's Choice ★ 🍴 **Burning Tree.** One of the top restaurants in Maine, this easy-to-miss gem with a festive dining room is on Route 3 between Bar Harbor and Otter Creek. The seasonal menu emphasizes freshly caught seafood, and seven species of fish are offered virtually every day—all from the Gulf of Maine. Monkfish is always on the menu: you may find it sautéed, glazed with sweet chili sauce, and served with Thai-flavored eggplant and coconut rice. Oven-poached cod and stuffed gray sole are two other signature dishes. There are always two or three vegetarian options using organic produce, much of it from the owners' garden. [$] *Average main: $25* ✉ *69 Otter Creek Dr., 5 miles from Bar Harbor, 7 miles from Northeast Harbor, Otter Creek* ☎ *207/288–9331* 🕒 *Closed mid-Oct.–mid-June. No lunch* ✍ *Reservations essential.*

$$ CUBAN Fodor's Choice ★ 🍴 **Havana.** A lively yet intimate spot, Havana serves Latin-inspired dishes paired with robust wines right in the middle of downtown Bar Harbor. In the summer, have a bite on their patio; during winter months, dine in a pleasant indoor space with a modern aesthetic, featuring clean lines and cheery colors. Don't miss the Spanish tortilla, served with a dollop of garlic aioli and chili oil, as well as the excellent seafood paella, which includes lobster, mussels, mahogany clams, shrimp, scallops, chorizo, tomatoes, peppers, and smoked chicken, piled in with fragrant saffron rice. You'd do well to finish off your meal with a serving of affogato made with MDI vanilla-bean ice cream and a side of dulce de leche. [$] *Average main: $24* ✉ *318 Main St.* ☎ *207/288–2822* 🌐 *www.havanamaine.com.*

$ SEAFOOD FAMILY 🍴 **Lazy Lobster.** This breakfast and lunch spot in the middle of town serves some of the freshest lobster around at a reasonable price. The full breakfast here features a fabulous lobster Benedict, as well as lobster omelets and crêpes. At lunch you can go for a whole lobster or a tasty, no-fuss lobster roll, or tuck into their classic clam chowder or lobster bisque. If seafood isn't your thing, they also have nice panini, wraps, and flatbreads, as well as an impressive selection of craft beers. [$] *Average main: $17* ✉ *16 Mount Desert St.* ☎ *207/288–1066.*

Long ramps on Maine's many docks make it easier to access boats at either high or low tide.

$$$ FRENCH FUSION 🍴 **Mâche Bistro.** This lively restaurant serves eclectic French bistro fare in a hip space with dim lighting and a modern aesthetic. Share some tapas-style appetizers, like the black-truffle salami with truffle-whipped brie, the duck-confit tartine, or the roasted beets with burrata cheese, or go for something more substantial like steak frites with truffle fries or seared Atlantic scallops with fennel salad, caper relish, and charred onion. If you're looking for a spot to have an intimate tête-à-tête this isn't the place, given the noise level. [$] *Average main: $28* ✉ *321 Main St.* ☎ *207/288–0447* 🌐 *www.machebistro.com* 🕒 *No lunch.*

WHERE TO STAY

$$ HOTEL 🏨 **Bar Harbor Grand Hotel.** Taking one of the well-appointed, modern rooms in this renovated historic building puts you right in the middle of Bar Harbor, just a stone's throw from lively restaurants, cafés, and gift shops. **Pros:** excellent center-of-town location; breakfast included; good value. **Cons:** street noise; decor could use updates. [$] *Rooms from: $245* ✉ *269 Main St.* ☎ *207/288–5226* 🌐 *www.barharborgrand.com* 🕒 *Closed mid-Nov.–Mar.* 🛏 *71 rooms* 🍽 *Breakfast.*

$$ HOTEL Fodor's Choice ★ 🏨 **Bar Harbor Inn & Spa.** Originally established in the late 1800s as a men's social club, this waterfront inn has rooms spread among three buildings on well-landscaped grounds. **Pros:** views of the beach and harbor; some two-level suites. **Cons:** dated room decor and bathrooms; views often include cruise ships in port; service can be hit or miss. [$] *Rooms from: $229* ✉ *1 Newport Dr.* ☎ *207/288–3351, 800/248–3351* 🌐 *www.barharborinn.com* 🕒 *Closed late Nov.–mid-Mar.* 🛏 *138 rooms, 15 suites* 🍽 *Breakfast.*

$ ⊡ **The Colony Cottages on Frenchman's Bay.** These clean, old-fashioned cot-
HOTEL tages are situated on a sweeping lawn that overlooks Frenchman's Bay.
FAMILY Just a five-minute drive or bus ride away from Bar Harbor and Acadia
National Park, this is an ideal base for exploring Mount Desert Island.
Pros: views of Frenchman's Bay; private beach access; good value. **Cons:**
five-minute drive to center of town and Acadia. *$ Rooms from: $150*
⊠ *20 Rte. 3, Hulls Cove* ☎ *207/288–3383* ⊕ *www.colonyathullscove.*
com ⇌ *31 cottages* ⟨◎⟩ *No meals.*

$ ⊡ **Primrose Place.** Recently renovated guest rooms at Primrose Place
HOTEL have retained their quaint local charm. **Pros:** centrally located. **Cons:**
two-night minimum in high season; basic rooms; renovated motel-style
lodgings are not for everyone. *$ Rooms from: $175* ⊠ *51 Holland Ave.*
☎ *207/288–3771* ⊕ *www.primroseplacebarharbor.com* ⇌ *10 rooms*
⟨◎⟩ *No meals.*

$$ ⊡ **Ullikana Inn.** Nestled in a quiet spot secluded from the chaos of Bar
B&B/INN Harbor proper, this quaint inn has elegant but cozy guest rooms, many
FAMILY of which have fireplaces, snug and sophisticated sitting areas, as well as
Fodor's Choice private balconies overlooking the water. **Pros:** generous gourmet break-
★ fast included; outdoor patio with landscaped gardens; intimate atmo-
sphere; water views; quiet central location. **Cons:** no pool. *$ Rooms*
from: $205 ⊠ *16 The Field* ☎ *207/288 9552* ⊕ *www.ullikana.com* ⇌ *10*
rooms ⟨◎⟩ *Breakfast.*

$ ⊡ **Wonder View Inn.** Situated on 14 sweeping acres just a stone's throw
HOTEL from downtown Bar Harbor and Acadia National Park, the Wonder
View Inn is one of the most pet-friendly properties in town. **Pros:** pet-
friendly. **Cons:** basic rooms; dated interiors; older hotel. *$ Rooms*
from: $150 ⊠ *50 Eden St.* ☎ *207/288–3358* ⊕ *www.wonderviewinn.*
com ⊗ *Closed Nov.–Apr.* ⇌ *15 rooms* ⟨◎⟩ *No meals.*

SPORTS AND THE OUTDOORS

AIR TOURS

Acadia Air Tours. This outfit runs sightseeing flights over Bar Harbor
and Acadia National Park. Most tours run 15 minutes to an hour and
range $150–$450 for two people. The sunset tour is $50 extra. ⊠ *968*
Bar Harbor Rd., Trenton ☎ *207/667–7627* ⊕ *www.acadiaairtours.com.*

BICYCLING

Acadia Bike. Rent mountain bikes and hybrids at Acadia Bike, both good
models for negotiating the carriage roads in Acadia National Park. ⊠ *48*
Cottage St. ☎ *207/288–9605, 800/526–8615* ⊕ *www.acadiabike.com.*

Bar Harbor Bicycle Shop. Rent bikes for anywhere from four hours to a
full day at the Bar Harbor Bicycle Shop. ⊠ *141 Cottage St.* ☎ *207/288–*
3886, 800/824–2453 ⊕ *www.barharborbike.com.*

BOATING

Coastal Kayaking Tours. This outfitter has been leading trips in the sce-
nic waters off Mount Desert Island since 1982. Rentals are provided
through its sister business, Acadia Outfitters, on the same downtown
street. Trips are limited to no more than 12 people. The season is
May–October. ⊠ *48 Cottage St.* ☎ *207/288–9605, 800/526–8615*
⊕ *www.acadiafun.com.*

Downeast Sailing Adventures. Take two-hour sailing trips and sunset cruises for $35 per person with six passengers ($50 per person with fewer), or hire a private charter starting at $100 per hour. Boats depart the Upper Town Dock in Southwest Harbor and several other locations. ⊠ *Upper Town Dock, Clark Point Rd., Southwest Harbor* ☎ *207/288–2216* ⊕ *www.downeastsail.com.*

FAMILY **Margaret Todd.** The 151-foot four-masted schooner *Margaret Todd* operates 1½- to 2-hour trips three times daily among the islands of Frenchman's Bay. The sunset sail has live music, and the 2 pm trip is sometimes narrated by an Acadia National Park ranger. Trips are $39.50 and depart mid-May–mid-October. ⊠ *Bar Harbor Inn pier, Newport Dr.* ☎ *207/288–4585* ⊕ *www.downeastwindjammer.com.*

WHALE-WATCHING

FAMILY **Bar Harbor Whale Watch Co.** This company has four boats, one of them a 140-foot jet-propelled double-hulled catamaran with spacious decks. It's one of two large catamarans used for whale-watching trips, some of which depart at sunset or include a side trip to see puffins. The company also offers lighthouse, lobstering, and seal-watching cruises, as well as a trip to Acadia National Park's Baker Island. ⊠ *1 West St.* ☎ *207/288–2386, 800/942–5374* ⊕ *www.barharborwhales.com.*

SHOPPING
ART
Alone Moose Fine Crafts. The oldest made-in-Maine gallery in Bar Harbor, Alone Moose Fine Crafts offers bronze wildlife sculptures, jewelry, pottery, photography, and watercolors. ⊠ *78 West St.* ☎ *207/288–4229 Mid-May–Oct., 207/288–9428* ⊕ *www.finemainecrafts.com.*

Eclipse Gallery. Eclipse Gallery carries handblown glass, ceramics, wood and metal furniture, and home decor items like mirrors and lamps. The gallery is open mid-May–October. ⊠ *12 Mount Desert St., Suite B* ☎ *207/288–9088, 207/610–2862 off-season* ⊕ *www.eclipsegallery.us.*

Island Artisans. This shop sells basketry, pottery, fiber work, and jewelry created by about 150 Maine artisans. It's open May–December. ⊠ *99 Main St.* ☎ *207/288–4214* ⊕ *www.islandartisans.com.*

Native Arts Gallery. Silver and gold Southwest Indian jewelry is a specialty at Native Arts Gallery, open May–October. ⊠ *99 Main St.* ☎ *207/288–4474* ⊕ *www.nativeartsgallery.com.*

Fodor's Choice ★ **The Rock and Art Shop.** As advertised, there are both "rocks" and "art" for sale at this eclectic family-owned store. There are also taxidermied animals, fossils, home decor and plants, interesting jewelry, and bath products. There are other locations in Bangor, Ellsworth, and just outside Ellsworth off Route 1A; here, they're open May–November. ⊠ *13 Cottage St.* ☎ *207/288–4800* ⊕ *www.therockandartshop.com.*

SPORTING GOODS
Cadillac Mountain Sports. One of the best sporting-goods stores in the state, Cadillac Mountain Sports has developed a following of locals and visitors alike. Here you'll find top-quality climbing, hiking, boating, paddling, and camping equipment, and in winter you can rent

cross-country skis, ice skates, and snowshoes. ⊠ *26 Cottage St.* ☎ *207/288–4532* ⊕ *www.cadillacsports.com.*

ACADIA NATIONAL PARK

3 miles from Bar Harbor via U.S. 3.

Fodor's Choice
★

With about 49,000 acres of protected forests, beaches, mountains, and rocky coastline, Acadia National Park is one of the most visited national parks in America. According to the National Park Service, over 2 million people visit Acadia each year, and the number is steadily rising. The park holds some of the most spectacular scenery on the Eastern Seaboard: a rugged coastline of surf-pounded granite and an interior graced by sculpted mountains, quiet ponds, and lush, deciduous forests. Cadillac Mountain (named after a Frenchman who explored here in the late 1600s and who later founded Detroit)—the highest point of land on the East Coast—dominates the park. Although rugged, the park also has graceful stone bridges, miles of carriage roads (popular with walkers, runners, and bikers as well as horse-drawn carriages), and the Jordan Pond House restaurant (famous for its popovers).

BOOK A CARRIAGE RIDE

Riding down one of the park's scenic carriage roads in a horse-drawn carriage is a truly unique way to experience Acadia. You can book a reservation for a ride, late May–mid-October, with Wildwood Stables, located next to Park Loop Road (☎ *877/276–3622*). One of the carriages can accommodate wheelchairs.

The 27-mile Park Loop Road provides an excellent overview, but to truly appreciate the park you must get off the main road and experience it by walking, hiking, biking, sea kayaking, or taking a carriage ride. Get off the beaten path, and you can find places you'll have practically all to yourself. Mount Desert Island was once a preserve of summer homes for the very rich (and still is for some), and, partly because of this, Acadia is the first national park in the United States largely created by donations of private land. There are two smaller parts of the park: on Isle au Haut, 15 miles away out in the ocean, and on the Schoodic Peninsula, on the mainland across Frenchman Bay from Mt. Desert.

PARK ESSENTIALS
ADMISSION FEE
A user fee is required May–October. The per-vehicle fee is $25 ($20 for motorcycles) for a seven-consecutive-day pass; you can walk or bike in on a $12 individual pass (also good for seven days); or you can use your National Park America the Beautiful Pass, which allows entrance to any national park in the United States. There are also a few fee-free days throughout the year.

ADMISSION HOURS
The park is open 24 hours a day, year-round, but roads are closed December–mid-April, except for the Ocean Drive section of Park Loop Road and a small part of the road with access to Jordan Pond.

PARK CONTACT INFORMATION

Acadia National Park. ⊠ *Acadia National Park* ☎ *207/288–3338* ⊕ *www.nps.gov/acad.*

GETTING HERE AND AROUND

Route 3 leads to the island and Bar Harbor from Ellsworth and circles the eastern part of the island. Route 102 is the major road on the west side.

Island Explorer buses, which serve the park and island villages June 23–Columbus Day, offer transportation to and around the park. In addition to regularly scheduled stops, they also pick up and drop off passengers anywhere in the park it is safe to stop.

Fodor's Choice ★ **Island Explorer.** These free buses transport locals and visitors throughout Acadia National Park on clean propane-powered buses. Eight routes connect the campgrounds, including Bar Harbor, Sand Beach, Southwest Harbor, and others. The bus system operates June 23–Columbus Day, and buses are equipped with bicycle racks. ⊠ *Acadia National Park* ☎ *207/667–5796* ⊕ *www.exploreacadia.com.*

EXPLORING

SCENIC DRIVES AND STOPS

FAMILY Fodor's Choice ★ **Cadillac Mountain.** At 1,530 feet, this is one of the first places in the United States to see the sun's rays at daybreak. It is the highest mountain on the eastern seaboard north of Brazil. Hundreds of visitors make the trek to see the sunrise or—for those less inclined to get up so early— sunset. From the smooth summit you have a stunning 360-degree view of the jagged coastline that runs around the island. The only structures at the top are restrooms and a small gift shop, which sells coffee and snacks. The road up the mountain is closed December–mid-May. ⊠ *Cadillac Summit Rd.* ⊕ *www.nps.gov/acad/.*

FAMILY Fodor's Choice ★ **Park Loop Road.** This 27-mile road provides a perfect introduction to the park. You can drive it in an hour, but allow at least half a day, so that you can explore the many sites along the way. The route is also served by the free Island Explorer buses, which also picks up and drops off passengers anywhere it is safe to stop along the route. Traveling south on Park Loop Road toward Sand Beach, you'll reach a small ticket booth, where, if you haven't already, you will need to pay the park entrance fee (May–October). Traffic is one way from the Route 233 entrance to the Stanley Brook Road entrance south of the Jordan Pond House. The section known as Ocean Drive is open year-round, as is a small section that provides access to Jordan Pond from Seal Harbor. ⊠ *Acadia National Park.*

VISITOR CENTER

FAMILY **Hulls Cove Visitor Center.** This is a great spot to get your bearings. A large 3-D relief map of Mount Desert Island gives you the lay of the land, and a free 15-minute video about everything the park has to offer plays every half hour. You can pick up guidebooks, maps of hiking trails and carriage roads, and recordings for drive-it-yourself tours—don't forget to grab a schedule of ranger-led programs, which includes guided hikes and other interpretive events. Junior-ranger programs for kids, nature hikes, photography walks, tide-pool explorations, and evening talks

Acadia's Best Campgrounds

Acadia National Park's two main campgrounds, Seawall and Black-woods, don't have water views, but the price is right and the ocean is just a 10-minute walk from each. The park added a third campground on the Schoodic Peninsula in 2015.

Blackwoods Campground. Located only 5 miles from Bar Harbor, this is Acadia's most popular campground. It is open year-round and well served by the Island Explorer bus system. ⊠ *Rte. 3, 5 miles south of Bar Harbor* *877/444–6777 for reservations* ⊕ *www.recreation.gov.*

Schoodic Woods Campground. Opened in September 2015, this campground is in the Schoodic Peninsula section of Acadia, meaning you have to take the ferry from Winter Harbor in order to cross over to Mount Desert Island (or drive). It is open May–Columbus Day. ⊠ *Schoodic Loop Road, 1 mile south of Rte. 186, Winter Harbor.*

Seawall Campground. On the quiet western side of the island, Seawall is open late May–September. ⊠ *Rte. 102A, 4 miles south of Southwest Harbor* ☎ *877/444–6777 for reservations* ⊕ *www.recreation.gov.*

are all popular. The Acadia National Park Headquarters, off Route 233 near the north end of Eagle Lake, serves as the park's visitor center during the off-season. ⊠ *Rte. 3, Hulls Cove* ☎ *207/288–3338* ⊕ *www. nps.gov/acad* ☉ *Mid-Apr.–June, Sept., and Oct., daily 8:30–4:30; July and Aug., daily 8–6.*

SPORTS AND THE OUTDOORS

The best way to see Acadia National Park is to get out of your vehicle and explore on foot or by bicycle or boat. There are more than 45 miles of carriage roads that are perfect for walking and biking in the warmer months and for cross-country skiing and snowshoeing in winter. There are 125 miles of trails for hiking, numerous ponds and lakes for canoeing or kayaking, two beaches for swimming, and steep cliffs for rock climbing.

HIKING

Acadia National Park maintains more than 125 miles of hiking trails, from easy strolls around lakes and ponds to rigorous treks with climbs up rock faces and scrambles along cliffs. Although hiking trails are concentrated on the east side of the island, the west side also has some scenic trails. For those wishing for a longer trek, try the trails leading up Cadillac Mountain or Dorr Mountain; you may also try Parkman, Sargeant, and Penobscot mountains. Most hiking is done mid-May–mid-November; snow falls early in Maine, so from as early as late November to the end of March, cross-country skiing and snowshoeing replace hiking. Volunteers groom most of the carriage roads if there's been 4 inches of snow or more. ■ TIP➜ **You can park at one end of any trail and use the free shuttle bus to get back to your starting point.**

Distances for trails are given for round-trips.

11

Fodor's Choice ★ **Acadia Mountain Trail.** If you're up for a challenge, this is one of the area's best trails. The 2.5-mile round-trip climb up Acadia Mountain is a steep and strenuous 700-foot climb, but the payoff views of Somes Sound are grand. If you want a guided trip, look into ranger-led hikes for this trail. ⊠ *Rte. 102* ☎ *207/288–3338* ⊕ *www.nps.gov/acad.*

> **CAUTION**
>
> Every few years, someone falls off one of the park's trails or cliffs and is swept out to sea. There is a lot of loose, rocky gravel along the shoreline, and sea rocks can often be slippery—so watch your step.

Fodor's Choice ★ **Ocean Path Trail.** This easily accessible 4.4-mile round-trip trail runs parallel to the Ocean Drive section of the Park Loop Road from Sand Beach to Otter Point. It has some of the best scenery in Maine: cliffs and boulders of pink granite at the ocean's edge, twisted branches of dwarf jack pines, and ocean views that stretch to the horizon. Be sure to save time to stop at **Thunder Hole**, named for the sound the waves make as they thrash through a narrow opening in the granite cliffs, into a sea cave, and whoosh up and out. Approximately halfway between Sand Beach and Otter Cliff, steps lead down to the water, where you can watch the wave action close-up. Use caution as you descend (access may be limited due to storms), and also if you venture onto the outer cliffs along this walk. ⊠ *Ocean Dr. section of Park Loop Rd.*

SWIMMING

The park has two swimming beaches, Sand Beach and Echo Lake Beach. Sand Beach, along Park Loop Road, has changing rooms, restrooms, and a lifeguard on duty Memorial Day–Labor Day. Echo Lake Beach, on the western side of the island just north of Southwest Harbor, has much warmer water, as well as changing rooms, restrooms, and a lifeguard on duty throughout the summer. This beach is particularly well suited for small children, as the water remains relatively shallow fairly far out.

FAMILY **Echo Lake Beach.** A quiet lake surrounded by woods in the shadow of Beech Mountain, Echo Lake draws swimmers to its sandy southern shore. The lake bottom is bit muckier than the ocean beaches nearby, but the water is considerably warmer. The surrounding trail network skirts the lake and ascends the mountain. The beach is 2 miles north of Southwest Harbor. **Amenities:** lifeguards; toilets. **Best for:** swimming. ⊠ *Echo Lake Beach Rd., off Rte. 102.*

Sand Beach. This pocket beach is hugged by two picturesque rocky outcroppings, and the combination of the crashing waves and the chilly water (peaking at around 55°F) keeps most people on the beach. You'll find some swimmers at the height of summer, but the rest of the year this is a place for strolling and snapping photos. In the shoulder season, you'll have the place to yourself. **Amenities:** lifeguards; parking; toilets. **Best for:** solitude; sunrise; walking. ⊠ *Ocean Dr. section of Park Loop Rd., 3 miles south of Rte. 3.*

NORTHEAST HARBOR

12 miles south of Bar Harbor via Rtes. 3 and 198.

The summer community for some of the nation's wealthiest families, Northeast Harbor has one of the best ports on the coast, which fills with yachts and powerboats during peak season. Some summer residents rebuilt here after the Great Fire of 1947 destroyed their mansions in Bar Harbor. This quiet village has a handful of restaurants, inns, boutiques, and art galleries. It's also a great place to sign up for a cruise around Somes Sound or to the Cranberry Isles.

ACADIA LEAF PEEPING

The fall foliage in Maine can be spectacular. Because of littoral humidity, leaves turn later here—usually around the middle of October—than they do in the interior of the state. The best way to catch the colors along the coast is travel on the Acadia National Park Loop Road. For up-to-date information, go to ⊕ *www.mainefoliage.com*.

WHERE TO STAY

$
B&B/INN
FAMILY
Fodor's Choice
★

🏠 **Asticou Inn.** Overlooking the water in Northeast Harbor, the Asticou Inn is tucked away in a quiet location but still has easy access to Acadia and the Asticou Azalea Garden. **Pros:** near hiking trails; excellent breakfast; manicured grounds with water views; quiet location. **Cons:** located 11 miles southwest of Bar Harbor. $ *Rooms from: $150* ⊠ *15 Peabody Rd., Bar Harbor* ☎ *207/276–3344* ⊕ *www.asticou.com* 🛏 *48 rooms* ⏐◌⏐ *Breakfast.*

SOUTHWEST HARBOR

6 miles south of Somesville via Rte. 102.

Across the water from Northeast Harbor, Southwest Harbor sits on the south side of the entrance to Somes Sound, which cuts up the center of the island. The town makes for a mellower Acadia base camp than Bar Harbor, with handsome yachts and towering sailboats lining the waterfront throughout the summer. Just north of town, trailheads at Echo Lake Beach and Fernald Point access some of the park's less explored territory.

BASS HARBOR

10 miles south of Somesville via Rtes. 102 and 102A.

Bass Harbor is a tiny lobstering village with a relaxed atmosphere and a few accommodations and restaurants. If you're looking to get away from the crowds, consider using this hardworking community as your base. Although Bass Harbor does not draw as many tourists as other villages, the Bass Harbor Head Light in Acadia National Park is one of the region's most popular attractions and is undoubtedly one of the most photographed lighthouses in Maine. From Bass Harbor, you can hike the Ship Harbor Nature Trail or take a ferry to Frenchboro or Swans Island.

GETTING HERE AND AROUND

From Bass Harbor, the Maine State Ferry Service operates the *Captain Henry Lee,* carrying both passengers and vehicles to Swans Island (40 minutes; $17.50 per person round-trip, $49.50 per car with driver) and Frenchboro (50 minutes; $11.25 per person round-trip, $32.25 per car with driver). The Frenchboro ferry doesn't run daily; a passenger-only ferry on a smaller boat (same price) runs on Fridays, April–November. Round-trip excursions (you don't get off the boat) are $10.

ESSENTIALS

Transportation Information Maine State Ferry Service. ✉ *45 Granville Rd.* ☎ *207/244–3254* 🌐 *www.maine.gov/mdot.*

EXPLORING

Fodor's Choice ★ **Bass Harbor Head Light.** Built in 1858, this lighthouse is one of the most photographed lights in Maine. Now automated, it marks the entrance to Bass Harbor and Blue Hill Bay. You can't actually go inside—the grounds and residence are Coast Guard property—but two trails around the facility have excellent views. It's within Acadia National Park, and there is parking. ■**TIP→ The best place to take a picture is from the rocks below—but watch your step, as they can be slippery.** ✉ *Lighthouse Rd., off Rte. 102A* ☎ *207/244–9753* 🎟 *Free* 🕒 *Daily 9–sunset.*

WHERE TO EAT

$$ SEAFOOD 🍴 **Thurston's Lobster Pound.** Right on Bass Harbor, looking across to the village, Thurston's is easy to spot because of its bright yellow awning. You can buy fresh lobsters to go, or you can eat at covered outdoor tables. Order everything from a grilled-cheese sandwich, soup, or hamburger to a boiled lobster served with clams or mussels. [$] *Average main: $20* ✉ *Steamboat Wharf, 9 Thurston Rd., Bernard* ☎ *207/244–7600* 🌐 *www.thurstonslobster.com* 🕒 *Closed mid-Oct.–Memorial Day.*

WAY DOWN EAST

Slogans like "The Real Maine" ring true Way Down East, where raw, mostly undeveloped coast dominates the remote region. Even in summer here you're likely to have rocky beaches and shady hiking trails all to yourself. And the slower pace is as calming as a sea breeze.

One innkeeper relates that visitors who plan to stay a few days often opt for a week after learning more about all the region has to offer, including historic sites; museums on local history, culture, and art; national wildlife refuges; state parks and preserves; and increasingly, conservancy-owned public land. Cutler's Bold Coast, with its dramatic granite headlands, is protected from development. Waters near Eastport have some of the world's highest tides. Lakes perfect for canoeing and kayaking are sprinkled inland, and rivers snake through marshland as they near the many bays. Boulders are strewn on blueberry barrens. Rare plants thrive in coastal bogs and heaths, and dark-purple and pink lupines line roads in late June.

VISITOR INFORMATION

Many chambers of commerce in the region distribute free copies of the pamphlet "Maine's Washington County: Just Off the Beaten Path." It's several cuts above the usual tourist promotion booklet, but chatting with locals is often the best way to find out about lesser-known trails and beaches, as well as which restaurants are worth a stop.

Contacts DownEast and Acadia Regional Tourism. ⊠ *87 Milbridge Rd., Cherryfield* ☎ *207/546–3600, 888/665–3278* ⊕ *www.downeastacadia.com.*

SCHOODIC PENINSULA

25 miles east of Ellsworth via U.S. Rte. 1 and Rte. 186.

The landscape of Schoodic Peninsula's craggy coastline, towering evergreens, and views over Frenchman Bay are breathtaking year-round. A drive through the well-to-do summer community of Grindstone Neck shows what Bar Harbor might have been like before so many of its mansions were destroyed in the Great Fire of 1947. Artists and artisans have opened galleries in and around Winter Harbor. Anchored at the foot of the peninsula, Winter Harbor was once part of Gouldsboro, which wraps around it. The southern tip of the peninsula is home to the Schoodic section of Acadia National Park.

GETTING HERE AND AROUND

From U.S. 1, Route 186 loops around the peninsula. Route 195 runs from U.S. 1 to Prospect Harbor and on to its end in Corea.

Island Explorer. The Island Explorer operates on the Schoodic Peninsula, with bus service from Prospect Harbor, Birch Harbor, and Winter Harbor to anywhere in the Schoodic Peninsula section of the park that's safe to stop. The bus also connects with the Winter Harbor ferry terminal, where you can take a ferry back to Bar Harbor. ⊠ *Winter Harbor* ☎ *207/288–2984* ⊕ *www.exploreacadia.com.*

ESSENTIALS

Visitor Information Schoodic Chamber of Commerce. ⊠ *Winter Harbor* ⊕ *www.acadia-schoodic.org.*

EXPLORING

Within Gouldsboro on the Schoodic Peninsula are several small coastal villages. You drive through Wonsqueak and Birch Harbor after leaving the Schoodic section of Acadia National Park. Near Birch Harbor you can find Prospect Harbor, a small fishing village nearly untouched by tourism. In Corea, there's little to do besides watch fishermen at work, wander along stone beaches, or gaze out at the sea.

Fodor's Choice
★
Acadia National Park—Schoodic Peninsula. The only section of Maine's national park that sits on the mainland is at the southern end of the Schoodic Peninsula in the town of Winter Harbor. The park has a scenic 6-mile loop that edges along the coast, yielding views of Grindstone Neck, Winter Harbor, Winter Harbor Lighthouse, and, across the water, Cadillac Mountain. At the tip of the point, huge slabs of pink granite lie jumbled along the shore, thrashed unmercifully by the crashing surf, and jack pines cling to life amid the rocks. Fraser Point, at the beginning

of the loop, is an ideal place for a picnic. Work off lunch with a hike up Schoodic Head for the panoramic views up and down the coast. During the summer season you can take a passenger ferry ($22 one way, $32 round-trip) to Winter Harbor from Bar Harbor. In Winter Harbor catch the free Island Explorer bus, which stops throughout the park, but you'll need to take the ferry to get back to Bar Harbor. ✉ *End of Moore Rd., off Rte. 186, Winter Harbor* ☎ *207/288–3338* 🌐 *www.nps.gov/acad* 🕒 *Daily 24 hrs.*

Schoodic Education and Research Center. In the Schoodic Peninsula section of Acadia National Park, this center offers lectures, workshops, and kid-friendly events about nature. It's worth a drive by just to see the Rockefeller Building, a massive 1935 French Eclectic and Renaissance-style structure with a stone-and-half-timber facade that served as naval offices and housing. In 2013, the building reopened as a visitor center after an extensive renovation. ✉ *9 Atterbury Circle, Winter Harbor* ☎ *207/288–1310* 🌐 *www.schoodicinstitute.org.*

WHERE TO EAT AND STAY

$ SEAFOOD FAMILY

🍴 **Chase's Restaurant.** This family restaurant has a reputation for serving good, basic fare—and in this region that means a whole lot of fresh fish. There are large and small fried seafood dinners, as well as several more expensive seafood platters. Try the sweet-potato fries as a side. Lunch fare, sold all day, includes wraps and burgers. It's also open for breakfast. [$] *Average main: $10* ✉ *193 Main St., Winter Harbor* ☎ *207/963–7171.*

$ B&B/INN FAMILY

🏨 **Bluff House Inn.** This cozy, modern inn is on a secluded hillside with expansive views of Frenchman's Bay. You can see its granite shores from the wraparound porches on each floor; the downstairs porch is partially screened. **Pros:** good value; largest room has sitting area with pull-out couch. **Cons:** only two rooms have good water views. [$] *Rooms from: $105* ✉ *57 Bluff House Rd., off Rte. 186, Gouldsboro* ☎ *207/963–7805* 🌐 *www.bluffinn.com* 🛏 *9 rooms* 🍽 *Breakfast.*

$ B&B/INN FAMILY Fodor's Choice ★

🏨 **Oceanside Meadows Inn.** A must for nature lovers, this lodging sits on a 200-acre preserve dotted with woods, streams, salt marshes, and ponds. **Pros:** one of region's few sand beaches; staff share info about the area over tea. **Cons:** need to cross road to beach. [$] *Rooms from: $179* ✉ *202 Corea Rd., Prospect Harbor* ☎ *207/963–5557* 🌐 *www.oceaninn.com* 🕒 *Closed mid-Oct.–late May* 🛏 *13 rooms, 2 suites* 🍽 *Breakfast.*

SPORTS AND THE OUTDOORS

KAYAKING

SeaScape Kayaking. Led by a Registered Maine Guide, SeaScape's morning and afternoon kayak tours include an island stop and a blueberry snack. The company also rents canoes, kayaks, and bikes from its location in Birch Harbor and welcomes handicapped kayakers. ✉ *8 Duck Pond Rd., Winter Harbor* ☎ *207/963–5806* 🌐 *www.seascapekayaking.com.*

SHOPPING

ANTIQUES AND MORE

U.S. Bells. Hand-cast bronze doorbells and wind chimes are among the items sold at U.S. Bells. You can also buy finely crafted quilts and wood-fired pottery made by the owner's family. Ask for a tour of the foundry. ✉ *56 W. Bay Rd., Prospect Harbor* ☎ *207/963–7184* 🌐 *www.usbells.com.*

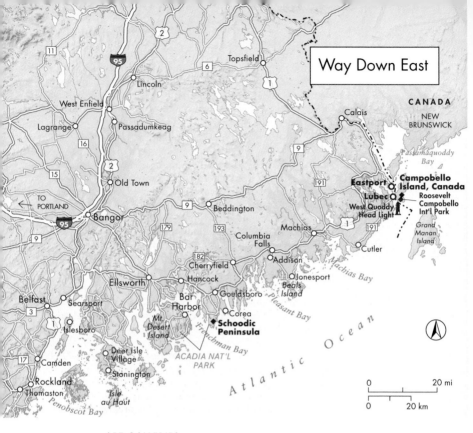

Way Down East

ART GALLERIES

Lee Fusion Art Glass. Window glass is fused in a kiln to create unusual glass dishware. Colorful enamel accents depict birds, lighthouses, flowers, and designs made from doilies. The store is open June–October. ✉ 679 S. Gouldsboro Rd., Rte. 186, Gouldsboro ☎ 207/712–2148 ⊕ *www.leefusionartglass.com.*

LUBEC

28 miles northeast of Machias via U.S. 1 and Rte. 189.

Lubec is one of the first places in the United States to see the sunrise. A popular destination for outdoors enthusiasts, it offers plenty of opportunities for hiking and biking, and the birding is renowned. It's a good base for day trips to New Brunswick's Campobello Island, reached by a bridge—the only one to the island—from downtown Lubec, so don't forget to bring your passport. One of the main attractions there, Roosevelt Campobello International Park, operates a visitor center on the U.S. side of the border, which provides information about the region, generally; it's in a Whiting general store and gas station at the corner of U.S. 1 and Route 189. The village itself is perched at the end of a narrow strip of land at the end of Route 189, so you often see water in three directions in this laid-back, off-the-beaten-path place.

GETTING HERE AND AROUND

From U.S. 1 in Whiting, Route 189 leads to Lubec; it's about 13 miles to the village. You can stock up on groceries in nearby Machias, just before you hit Whiting, en route to Lubec. In summer you can take a water taxi from here to Eastport—about a mile by boat, but 40 miles by the circuitous northerly land route.

EXPLORING

FAMILY Fodor's Choice ★ **West Quoddy Head Light.** The easternmost point of land in the United States is marked by candy-stripe West Quoddy Head Light. In 1806 President Thomas Jefferson signed an order authorizing construction of a lighthouse on this site. You can't climb the tower, but the former lightkeeper's house has a museum with a video with shots of the interior, as well as displays on Lubec's maritime past; a gallery displays works by artists who live or summer in the area. The mystical 2-mile path along the cliffs at Quoddy Head State Park (one of five trails) yields magnificent views of Canada's cliff-clad Grand Manan Island. Whales and seals—as well as the ubiquitous bald eagles—can often be sighted offshore. The 540-acre park has a picnic area with grills, but sometimes the best place to take lunch is perched on a rock overlooking the sea. Don't miss the easy, 0.2-mile bog trail that includes a fascinating array of subarctic vegetation, including carnivorous pitcher plants. ✉ *973 S. Lubec Rd., off Rte. 189* ☎ *207/733–2180* 🌐 *www.westquoddy.com* 🎟 *$3* 🕒 *Daily 9–sunset.*

WHERE TO EAT AND STAY

$ AMERICAN 🍴 **Lubec Brewing Company.** Tucked downtown on Water Street, the Lubec Brewing Company serves up a rotating array of suds. The pub sometimes hosts impromptu potluck dinners—check their Facebook page—and usually has one or two things to fill you up other than beer. [$] *Average main: 8* ✉ *41 Water St.* ☎ *207/733–4555* 🕒 *Closed Mon.–Wed. No lunch.*

$ SEAFOOD FAMILY 🍴 **Uncle Kippy's.** There isn't much of a view from the picture windows, but locals don't mind: they come here for the satisfying seafood—and the occasional ukulele concert. The dining room is large and has a modestly stocked, beer-centric bar. Entrées include seafood dinners and combo platters and some chicken and meat dishes; there are burgers, too, and the pizza is popular. You can order from the lunch or dinner menu. A take-out window and ice-cream bar are open May–September. If you can't get a table in the summer, head directly across the street to Becky's Seafood, an excellent food truck parked in the owner's front yard that serves similar fare, plus locally smoked salmon. Becky's also sells fresh, uncooked seafood to grill yourself. [$] *Average main: $16* ✉ *170 Main St.* ☎ *207/733–2400* 🌐 *www.unclekippys.com.*

$$ SEAFOOD FAMILY 🍴 **Waterstreet Tavern and Inn.** Perched right on the water in downtown Lubec, this favorite local restaurant recently spruced up its menu, which includes some of the sweetest scallops you'll ever eat, a very satisfying burger, and a massive chunk of chocolate cake. It's also a great place to grab a drink or a slice of blueberry pie and a coffee while looking out at the water from the deck or through the picture windows. If you want the lowdown on where to go or what to see in Lubec, this is the place to ask. There's often live music by local performers on Thursday. It

Wild for Blueberries

There's no need to inquire about cheesecake topping in August, when the wild blueberry crop comes in: anything else would be unthinkable.

Way Down East, wild blueberries have long been a favorite food and a key ingredient in cultural and economic life. Maine produces about a third of the commercial harvest, which totals about 80 million pounds annually—Canada supplying virtually all the rest. Washington County yields more than half of Maine's total crop, which is why the state's largest blueberry processors are here: Jasper Wyman & Son and the predecessor of what is now Cherryfield Foods were founded shortly after the Civil War.

Wild blueberries, which bear fruit every other year, thrive in the region's cold climate and sandy, acidic soil. Undulating blueberry barrens stretch for miles in Deblois and Cherryfield (the "Blueberry Capital of the World") and are scattered throughout Washington County. Look for tufts among low-lying plants along roadways. In spring, the fields shimmer as the small-leaf plants turn myriad shades of mauve, honey orange, and lemon yellow. White flowers appear in June. Fall transforms the barrens into a sea of otherworldly red.

Amid Cherryfield's barrens, a plaque on a boulder lauds the late J. Burleigh Crane for helping advance an industry that's not as wild as it used to be: fields are irrigated, honeybees have been brought in to supplement native pollinators, and barrens are burned and mowed to rid plants of disease and insects, reducing the need for pesticides. Most of the barrens in and around Cherryfield are owned by large blueberry processors. About 80% of Maine's crop is now harvested with machinery. That requires moving boulders, so the rest continues to be harvested by hand with blueberry rakes, which resemble large forks and pull the berries off their stems. Years ago, year-round residents did the work; today, migrant workers make up 90% of this seasonal labor force.

Blueberries get their dark color from anthocyanin, believed to act as an antioxidant. Wild blueberries have more of these anti-aging, anticancer compounds than their cultivated cousins; they're also smaller and more flavorful, and therefore mainly used in packaged foods. Less than 1% of the state's crop (about 500,000 pints) is consumed fresh, most of it in Maine. Look for fresh berries (sometimes starting in late July and lasting until early September) at roadside stands, farmers' markets, and supermarkets.

Wild Blueberry Land in Columbia Falls sells everything blueberry, from muffins and candy to socks and books. Find farm stores, stands, and markets statewide, many selling blueberries and blueberry jams and syrups, at ⊕ *www.getrealmaine.com*, a Maine Department of Agriculture site that promotes Maine foods.

DID YOU KNOW?

Atlantic puffin colonies were reintroduced to the Maine Coast by the Maine Audubon Society's Project Puffin. Get a closer look at these seabirds and their distinctive beaks on a seasonal puffin cruise from Cutler to Machias Seal Island, the sovereignty of which remains contested between Canada and the United States.

also offers two cozy suites and three guest rooms, most with good views of the water. $ *Average main: $20* ⊠ *12 Water St.* ☎ *207/733–2477* ⊕ *www.watersttavernandinn.com* ☉ *Closed late-Oct.–Mar.*

$

B&B/INN

Fodor'sChoice

★

⚏ **Peacock House.** Five generations of the Peacock family lived in this 1860 sea captain's home before it was converted to an inn. **Pros:** piano and fireplace in living room; lovely garden off deck; think-of-everything innkeepers direct guests to area's tucked-away spots. **Cons:** not on the water. $ *Rooms from: $105* ⊠ *27 Summer St.* ☎ *207/733–2403, 888/305–0036* ⊕ *www.peacockhouse.com* ☉ *Closed Nov.–Apr.* ⤴ *3 rooms, 4 suites* ⊙| *Breakfast.*

SHOPPING

Monica's Chocolates. Taking in all the appetizing scents in this shop is almost enough, but sinking your teeth into one of Monica's truffles, bonbons, crèmes, or caramels is pure heaven. ⊠ *100 County Rd.* ☎ *207/733–4500* ⊕ *www.monicaschocolates.com.*

CAMPOBELLO ISLAND, CANADA

4 miles northeast of Lubec.

A popular excursion from Lubec, New Brunswick's Campobello Island has two fishing villages, Welshpool and Wilson's Beach. The only land route is the bridge from Lubec, but in summer a car ferry shuttles passengers from Campobello Island to Deer Island, where you can continue on to the Canadian mainland.

GETTING HERE AND AROUND

After coming across the bridge from Lubec, Route 774 runs from one end of the island to the other, taking you through the two villages and to Roosevelt Campobello International Park.

EXPLORING

FAMILY

Fodor'sChoice

★

Roosevelt Campobello International Park. President Franklin Roosevelt and his family spent summers at this estate, which is now an international park with neatly manicured lawns that stretch out to the beach. You can take a self-guided tour of the 34-room Roosevelt Cottage that was presented to Eleanor and Franklin as a wedding gift. The wicker-filled structure looks essentially as it did when the family was in residence. A visitor center has displays about the Roosevelts and Canadian-American relations. Eleanor Roosevelt Teas are held at 11 and 3 daily in the neighboring Hubbard Cottage. A joint project of the American and the Canadian governments, this park is crisscrossed with interesting hiking trails. Groomed dirt roads attract bikers. Eagle Hill Bog has a wooden walkway and signs identifying rare plants. ■TIP→ **Note that the Islands are on Atlantic Time, which is an hour later than Eastern Standard Time.** ⊠ *459 Rte. 774, Welshpool* ☎ *506/752–2922, 877/851–6663* ⊕ *www.fdr.net* ⊡ *Free* ☉ *House and visitor center: Memorial Day weekend–Columbus Day, daily 10–6.*

WHERE TO EAT

$

SEAFOOD

FAMILY

✕ **Family Fisheries.** Seafood lovers know that fried fish doesn't have to be greasy. That's why people keep heading across the international bridge to eat at this family establishment in Wilson's Beach. The freshest seafood is delivered to the restaurant, where you can bring your own wine (corkage $2). Order fried haddock, scallops, shrimp, or clams, alone or as part of a platter. Eat in the large dining room or near the playground at picnic tables or in a screened room. Lobsters are cooked outside and also sold live or steamed to go. You can buy ice cream at the take-out window, and the restaurant also serves breakfast in July and August. $ *Average main: C$15* ⊠ *1977 Rte. 774, Wilson's Beach* ☎ *506/752–2470* ⊕ *www. familyfisheries.com* ☉ *Closed late Oct.–early Apr.*

$$ ✕ **Fireside Restaurant.** Named after FDR's famous "fireside chats," this
CANADIAN   cozy lodge-style restaurant serves fresh seafood dishes and comfort
FAMILY   food, like grilled cheese sandwiches and jumbo hot dogs. Try and get seated close to one of the enormous fireplaces or picture windows. $ *Average main: C$20* ⊠ *610 Rte. 774, Welshpool* ☎ *506/752–6055* ⊕ *www.fdr.net/fireside-restaurant.php*.

EASTPORT

39 miles northeast of Lubec via Rte. 189, U.S. 1, and Rte. 190; 109 miles north of Ellsworth via U.S. 1 and Rte. 190.

Connected by a granite causeway to the mainland at Pleasant Point Reservation, Eastport has wonderful views of the nearby islands, and because the harbor is so deep, you can sometimes spot whales from the waterfront. Known for its diverse architecture, the island city was one of the nation's busiest seaports in the early 1800s.

If you find yourself in town mid- to late summer, you might catch one of a few notable events. For starters, Maine's largest Fourth of July parade takes place in Eastport—be sure to get downtown early to secure a viewing spot. Then, on the weekend of the second Sunday in August, locals celebrate Sipayik Indian Days at the Pleasant Point Reservation; this festival of Passamaquoddy culture includes canoe races, dancing, drumming, children's games, fireworks, and traditional dancing. And on the weekend after Labor Day, the Eastport Pirate Festival brings folks out in pirate attire for a ship race, a parade, fireworks, cutlass "battles" by reenactors, and other events, including a children's breakfast and a schooner ride with pirates.

GETTING HERE AND AROUND

From U.S. 1, Route 190 leads to the Island City. Continue on Washington Street to the water. In the summer, you can also take a water taxi from here to Lubec—a mile or so by boat, but about 40 miles by land.

ESSENTIALS

Visitor Information Eastport Area Chamber of Commerce. ⊠ *64 Water St.* ☎ *207/853–4644* ⊕ *www.eastport.net.*

WHERE TO EAT

$ ✕ **Chowder House.** Just north of downtown Eastport, this expansive
SEAFOOD   waterfront eatery sits on the pier next to the ferry dock. Built atop
FAMILY   the foundation of an old cannery, it has original details such as wood beams and a stone wall. Eat in the downstairs pub, in the upstairs dining room, or on the large deck. House specialties include a smoked fish appetizer and seafood pasta in a wine-and-cheese sauce. Lunch, served

until 4, includes fried seafood plates, burgers, wraps, and sandwiches. $ *Average main: $17* ✉ *167 Water St.* ☎ *207/853–4700* ⊕ *www. eastportchowderhouse.org* ⊗ *Closed mid-Oct.–mid-May.*

$ ✗ **Dastardly Dick's Wicked Good Coffee.** The coffee isn't the only thing
CAFÉ   that's wicked good at this local café; homemade pastries, rich soups,
FAMILY   and tasty sandwiches are all prepared daily, and the hot chocolate and
chai are worth writing home about. $ *Average main: $6* ✉ *62 Water St.* ☎ *207/853–2090* ⊗ *Closed Mon.*

TRAVEL SMART
NEW ENGLAND

GETTING HERE AND AROUND

Boston, New England's largest and most cosmopolitan city, is also the region's major transportation and cultural center. Secondary hubs include Hartford, Connecticut, and Portland, Maine. Your best bet for exploring widely is to travel by car: flying within the region is expensive, and driving distances between most attractions are short. Within most cities, however, public transportation is a viable—and often preferable—means for getting around. Passenger ferry service is available to outlying islands (some vessels accommodate vehicles).

See the Getting Here and Around section at the beginning of each chapter for more transportation information.

▌ AIR TRAVEL

Most travelers visiting New England head for a major gateway, such as Boston, Providence, Hartford/Springfield, Manchester, or even New York City or Albany, and then rent a car to explore the region. The New England states form a fairly compact region, with few important destinations more than six hours apart by car. It's costly and generally impractical to fly within New England, the exceptions being the island resort destinations of Martha's Vineyard and Nantucket in Massachusetts, and Block Island in Rhode Island, which have regular service from Boston and a few other regional airports.

Boston's Logan Airport is one of the nation's most important domestic and international airports, with direct flights arriving from all over North America and abroad. New England's other major airports receive few international flights (mostly from Canada) but receive many direct domestic flights from East Coast and Midwest destinations and, to a lesser extent, from the western United States. Some sample flying times to Boston are: 2½ hours from Chicago, 6½ hours from

London, and 6 hours from Los Angeles. Times from other U.S. cities are similar, if slightly shorter, to Albany and Hartford, assuming you can find direct flights.

AIRPORTS

The main gateway to New England is Boston's Logan International Airport (BOS). Bradley International Airport (BDL), in Windsor Locks, Connecticut (12 miles north of Hartford), is convenient to Western Massachusetts and all of Connecticut. T. F. Green Airport (PVD), just outside Providence, Rhode Island, and Manchester Boston Regional Airport (MHT), in New Hampshire, are other major airports—and alternative approaches to Boston, which is a one-hour drive from each. Additional New England airports served by major carriers include Portland International Jetport (PWM) in Maine and Burlington International Airport (BTV) in Vermont.

Other airports can be found in Albany, New York (ALB, near Western Massachusetts and Vermont); Westchester County, New York (HPN, near Southern Connecticut); Bangor, Maine (BGR); and in Hyannis, Massachusetts (Barnstable Municipal, HYA). You can access Nantucket and Martha's Vineyard via ferries from Hyannis or fly directly to the islands' airports.

Airport Information Albany International Airport. ✉ *737 Albany Shaker Rd., Albany* ☎ *518/242-2200* ⊕ *www.albanyairport. com.* **Bangor International Airport.** ✉ *287 Godfrey Blvd., Bangor* ☎ *207/992-4600* ⊕ *www.flybangor.com.* **Barnstable Municipal Airport.** ✉ *480 Barnstable Rd., Hyannis* ☎ *508/775-2020* ⊕ *www.town.barnstable. ma.us/airport.* **Bradley International Airport.** ✉ *Schoephoester Rd., Windsor Locks* ☎ *860/292-2000* ⊕ *www.bradleyairport.com.* **Burlington International Airport.** ✉ *1200 Airport Dr., South Burlington* ☎ *802/863-2874* ⊕ *www.btv.aero.* **Logan International Airport.** ✉ *1 Harborside Dr., Boston* ☎ *800/235-6426*

⊕ www.massport.com/logan-airport Ⓜ Blue, Silver. **Manchester Boston Regional Airport.** ✉ 1 Airport Rd., Manchester ☎ 603/624–6539 ⊕ www.flymanchester.com. **Martha's Vineyard Airport.** ✉ 71 Airport Rd., West Tisbury ☎ 508/693–7022 ⊕ www.mvyairport.com. **Nantucket Memorial Airport.** ✉ 14 Airport Rd., Nantucket ☎ 508/325–5300 ⊕ www. nantucketairport.com. **Portland International Jetport.** ✉ 1001 Westbrook St., Portland ☎ 207/874–8877 ⊕ www.portlandjetport. org. **T.F. Green Airport.** ✉ 2000 Post Rd., Warwick ☎ 401/691–2471, 888/268–7222 ⊕ www.pvdairport.com. **Westchester County Airport.** ✉ 240 Westchester Airport County Rd., White Plains ☎ 914/995–4850 ⊕ airport. westchestergov.com.

FLIGHTS

American, Delta, Southwest, and United serve airports in Albany, Boston, Hartford, Manchester, Portland, Providence, and (except Southwest) Westchester County. Smaller or discount airlines serving some of these airports and others in New England include Cape Air, JetBlue, and Spirit. Cape Air also provides service from Cape Cod and the islands to Providence and New Bedford, Massachusetts. New England Airlines serves Block Island, with regularly scheduled flights from Westerly, Rhode Island.

Airline Contacts American Airlines. ☎ 800/433–7300 ⊕ www.aa.com. **Cape Air.** ☎ 800/227–3247 ⊕ www.capeair.com. **Delta Airlines.** ☎ 800/221–1212 ⊕ www. delta.com. **JetBlue.** ☎ 800/538–2583 ⊕ www.jetblue.com. **New England Airlines.** ☎ 800/243–2460 ⊕ www.block-island.com/ nea. **Southwest Airlines.** ☎ 800/435–9792 ⊕ www.southwest.com. **Spirit Airlines.** ☎ 801/401–2222 ⊕ www.spirit.com. **United Airlines.** ☎ 800/864–8331 ⊕ www.united.com.

▌BOAT TRAVEL

Principal ferry routes in New England connect New Bedford on the mainland and Cape Cod with Martha's Vineyard and Nantucket, Boston with Provincetown, southern Rhode Island with Block Island, and Connecticut with Block Island and New York's Long Island. Other routes provide access to many islands off the Maine coast. Ferries cross Lake Champlain between Vermont and upstate New York. International service between Portland, Yarmouth, and Bar Harbor, Maine, and Nova Scotia, is also available. With the exception of the Lake Champlain ferries—which are first-come, first-served—reservations are advisable for cars.

▌BUS TRAVEL

With fares starting at just $1 if you reserve early enough, BoltBus runs buses equipped with Wi-Fi and electrical outlets between Boston, New York, Philadelphia, and Washington, D.C. Megabus also offers low fares, and its buses (also with Wi-Fi) serve New York City and many other points on the East Coast. Both BoltBus and Megabus use Boston's South Station.

Once in New England, regional bus service is relatively extensive. It can be a handy and affordable means of getting around, as buses travel many routes that trains do not. Concord Coach runs buses between Boston and Concord, New Hampshire, Portland, Maine, and Bangor, Maine; the company also operates a route between New York City and Portland. C&J sends buses (with Wi-Fi) up the New Hampshire coast to Newburyport, Massachusetts, Dover, New Hampshire, Durham, New Hampshire, and Portsmouth, New Hampshire, and provides service to New York City. Both Concord and C&J leave from Boston's South Station, which is connected to the Amtrak rail station, and Logan Airport.

Information BoltBus. ☎ 877/265–8287 ⊕ www.boltbus.com. **C&J.** ☎ 800/258–7111 ⊕ www.ridecj.com. **Concord Coach.** ☎ 800/639–3317 ⊕ www.concordcoachlines. com. **Megabus.** ☎ 877/462–6342 ⊕ us.megabus.com.

▌ CAR TRAVEL

New England is best explored by car. Inland, especially in Western Massachusetts, Vermont, New Hampshire, and Maine, public transportation options are limited and a car is almost essential. Coastal areas can get congested, however, especially the roads to and from Cape Cod during the summer. Parking can be hard to find or expensive in Boston, Providence, and many smaller resort towns along the coast: you may find it easiest to park at your hotel once in Boston or on Cape Cod and use it as little as possible. Note that Interstate 90, the Massachusetts Turnpike, is a toll road throughout Massachusetts. If you rent a car at Logan International Airport, allow plenty of time to return it—as much as an hour to be on the safe side.

GASOLINE

Gas stations are easy to find along major highways and in most communities throughout the region. Prices vary from station to station within any city. The majority are self-serve with pumps that accept credit cards, though you may find a holdout full-service station here and there (tipping is not expected).

PARKING

In Boston and other large cities, finding a parking space on the street can be time-consuming. Your best bet is to park in a garage, but rates in large cities can top $30 a day. In smaller cities, street parking is usually simpler, though parking garages are still convenient and less expensive than their big-city counterparts. Pay attention to signs: some cities allow only residents to park on certain streets. In most small towns parking is not a problem, though some beach and lake parking areas are reserved for those with resident stickers.

ROAD CONDITIONS

Major state and U.S. routes are generally well maintained, with snowplows at the ready during the winter to salt and plow road surfaces soon after the flakes begin to fall. Traffic is heaviest around Boston, Hartford, and New Haven, especially during rush hour. Secondary state routes and rural roads can be a mixed bag; Route 1, for example, is well maintained, but traffic is slow and can get tied up in even the smallest coastal towns.

ROADSIDE EMERGENCIES

Throughout New England, call ☎ 911 for any travel emergency, such as an accident or a serious health concern. For breakdowns, dial a towing service.

RULES OF THE ROAD

On city streets the speed limit is 30 mph unless otherwise posted; on rural roads the speed limit runs 40–50 mph unless otherwise posted. Interstate speeds run 50–65 mph, depending on how densely populated the area is. Throughout the region, you're permitted to make a right turn on a red light except where posted. Be alert for one-way streets in congested cities like Boston and Providence.

Boston motorists are notorious for driving aggressively. Streets in the Boston area are confusing, so a GPS unit can be very helpful.

You will encounter many traffic circles or rotaries if you drive in New England, especially in the Boston area. Cars entering traffic circles must yield to cars that are already in the circle. Some rotaries have two lanes, which complicates things. If you're leaving the rotary at the next possible exit, enter from the right lane. If you're leaving the rotary at any exit after the first possible exit, enter from the left lane (which becomes the inner lane of the circle); you can also exit the circle directly from this lane—though check your right side so you don't sideswipe a driver who's incorrectly in the right lane.

State law requires drivers and passengers to wear seat belts at all times. The age and weight requirements for safety seats for children vary from state to state; the Governors Highway Safety Association's website lists the requirements for each.

Contact Governors Highway Safety Association. ☎ *202/789–0942* ⊕ *www.ghsa. org/html/stateinfo/laws/childsafety_laws.html.*

CAR RENTAL

A car is the most practical way to get around New England. Major airports serving the region all have on-site car-rental agencies. A few train or bus stations have one or two car-rental agencies on-site.

Rates at Boston's Logan Airport begin at around $50 per day and $200 per week for an economy car with air-conditioning, automatic transmission, and unlimited mileage. The same car might go for around $70 per day and $300 per week at a smaller airport, such as Portland's. These rates do not include state tax on car rentals, which varies depending on the airport but generally runs 12%–15%. It usually costs less to rent a car away from an airport, but be sure to consider how easy or difficult it may be to get to that off-airport location with luggage.

Most agencies won't rent to drivers under the age of 21, and several major agencies won't rent to anyone under 25. When picking up a rental car, non-U.S. residents need a voucher for any prepaid reservation made in their home country, a passport, a driver's license, and a travel policy that covers each driver. Logan Airport is spread out and usually congested, so if returning a rental vehicle there, allow plenty of time to do so before heading to your flight.

Major Rental Agencies
Alamo. ☎ *877/222–9075* ⊕ *www.alamo.com.*
Avis. ☎ *800/331–1212* ⊕ *www.avis.com.*
Budget. ☎ *800/527–0700* ⊕ *www.budget.com.*
Hertz. ☎ *800/654–3131* ⊕ *www.hertz.com.*
National Car Rental. ☎ *877/222–9058* ⊕ *www.nationalcar.com.*

▌ TRAIN TRAVEL

Amtrak offers frequent daily service along its Northeast Corridor route from Washington, D.C., Philadelphia, and New York to Boston. Amtrak's high-speed Acela trains link Boston and Washington, with stops at New York, Philadelphia, and other cities along the way. The *Downeaster* connects Boston and Portland, Maine, with stops in coastal New Hampshire.

Other Amtrak services include the *Vermonter* between Washington, D.C., and St. Albans, Vermont; the *Ethan Allen Express* between New York and Rutland, Vermont; and the *Lake Shore Limited* between Boston and Chicago, with stops at Pittsfield, Springfield, Worcester, and Framingham, Massachusetts.

Several commuter services are handy for travelers. The Massachusetts Bay Transportation Authority (MBTA) connects Boston with outlying areas on the north and south shores of the state. Metro-North Railroad's New Haven Line offers service from New York City along the Connecticut coast up to New Haven. The line also reaches as far north as Danbury and Waterbury.

Information Amtrak. ☎ *800/872–7245* ⊕ *www.amtrak.com.* **Massachusetts Bay Transportation Authority** (*MBTA*). ☎ *617/222–3200, 800/392–6100* ⊕ *www.mbta.com.* **Metro-North Railroad.** ☎ *212/532–4900, 877/690–5114* ⊕ *www.mta.info/mnr.*

ESSENTIALS

■ ACCOMMODATIONS

In New England you can bed down in a basic chain hotel or a luxurious grande dame, but unless you're staying in a city, this is really bed-and-breakfast land. Charming—and sometimes historic—inns, small hotels, and bed-and-breakfasts dot the region and provide a glimpse of local life.

Hotel prices are the lowest cost of a standard double room in high season.

BED-AND-BREAKFASTS

In many less touristy areas, bed-and-breakfasts offer an affordable, homey alternative to chain properties. In most major towns, expect to pay about the same or more for a historic inn. Many of the region's finest restaurants are attached to country inns, so you often don't have to go far for the best meal in town. Quite a few inns serve substantial breakfasts.

Reservation Services BedandBreakfast. com. ☎ *512/322–2710, 800/462–2632* ⊕ *www.bedandbreakfast.com.* **Bed & Breakfast Inns Online.** ☎ *800/215–7365* ⊕ *www.bbonline.com.* **BnBFinder.com.** ☎ *888/469–6663* ⊕ *www.bnbfinder.com.*

HOUSE AND APARTMENT RENTALS

You are most likely to find a house, apartment, or condo rental in areas of New England in which ownership of second homes is common, such as beach resorts and ski country. Home-exchange directories sometimes list rentals alongside exchanges. Another good bet is to contact real-estate agents in the area in which you are interested.

Contacts Home Away. ☎ *512/782–0805* ⊕ *www.homeaway.com.* **Interhome.** ☎ *800/882–6864* ⊕ *www.interhomeusa. com.* **Villas International.** ☎ *415/499–9490, 800/221–2260* ⊕ *www.villasintl.com.*

HOTELS

Major hotel and motel chains are amply represented in New England. The region is also liberally supplied with small, independent motels. Don't overlook these mom-and-pop operations; they frequently offer cheerful, convenient accommodations at lower rates than the chains.

Reservations are always a good idea, particularly in summer and winter resort areas; at college towns in September and at graduation time in spring; and at areas renowned for autumn foliage. Most hotels and motels will hold your reservation until 6 pm; call ahead if you plan to arrive late. All will hold a late reservation for you if you guarantee it with your credit card.

In Massachusetts and Vermont all hotels are no-smoking by state law. All lodgings listed have private baths unless otherwise noted.

Information New England Inns & Resorts Association. ☎ *603/964–6689* ⊕ *www.newenglandinnsandresorts.com.*

■ CHILDREN IN NEW ENGLAND

Favorite destinations for family vacations in New England include Boston, Cape Cod, the White Mountains, Mystic and southeastern Connecticut, and coastal Maine, but in general, the entire region has plenty to offer families. Throughout New England you'll have no problem finding comparatively inexpensive kid-friendly hotels and family-style restaurants, as well as museums, beaches, parks, planetariums, and lighthouses, though some of the quieter and more rural areas lack child-oriented attractions.

LODGING

New England has many family-oriented resorts with lively children's programs. Farms that accept guests can be great fun for children. Rental houses and apartments abound, particularly around ski areas. In the off-season, these can be economical because most have kitchens, saving you the expense of restaurant dining for some or all meals.

Most hotels in New England allow children under a certain age to stay in their parents' room at no extra charge, but others charge for them as extra adults; find out the cutoff age. Bed-and-breakfasts and historic inns are not always suitable for kids, and many flat-out refuse to accommodate them. In Maine, only hotels and inns with five or fewer rooms can put age restrictions on children.

Most lodgings that welcome infants and small children will provide a crib or cot, but remember to provide notice so that one will be available for you. Many family resorts make special accommodations for small children during meals.

TRANSPORTATION

Each New England state has specific requirements regarding age and weight requirements for children in car seats. If you will need a car seat, make sure your rental-car agency can provide one.

▌ COMMUNICATIONS

INTERNET

Most major chain hotels and many smaller motels throughout New England now offer wired or wireless Internet access (often both). Many have a desktop computer available for guest use; access is often free, but be sure to ask about possible fees when you book. Many coffee shops offer Wi-Fi, as do most libraries.

▌ EATING OUT

Although certain ingredients and preparations are common to the region as a whole, New England's cuisine varies greatly from place to place. Urban centers like Boston, Providence, New Haven, and Portland, and upscale resort areas such as the Berkshires, Martha's Vineyard, and Nantucket have stellar restaurants, many of them with culinary luminaries at the helm and a reputation for creative—and occasionally daring—menus.

Elsewhere, restaurant food tends more toward the simple, traditional, and conservative. Towns and cities have a variety of international restaurants, especially excellent Italian, French, Japanese, Indian, and Thai eateries. There are also many diners serving burgers and other comfort food—a few serve breakfast all day.

The proximity to the ocean accounts for the abundance of very fresh seafood, and the area's numerous boutique dairy, meat, and vegetable suppliers account for other choice ingredients. Menus in the more upscale and tourism-driven communities often note which Vermont dairy or Berkshires farm a particular goat cheese or heirloom tomato came from.

For information on food-related health issues, see Health below.

MEALS AND MEALTIMES

For an early breakfast, pick places that cater to a working clientele. City, town, and roadside establishments specializing in breakfast for early workers often open their doors at 5 or 6 am. At country inns, breakfast is seldom served before 8 am; if you need to get an earlier start, ask ahead of time. Lunch generally runs 11 am–2:30 pm; dinner is usually served 6–9 pm, with early-bird specials sometimes beginning at 5. Only in larger cities will you find dinner available much later than 9 pm. Many restaurants in New England close Monday and sometimes Sunday or Tuesday, although this is never true in resort areas during high season. However, resort-town eateries often shut down completely in the off-season.

Unless otherwise noted, the restaurants listed *in this guide* are open daily for lunch and dinner.

PAYING

Credit cards are accepted for meals throughout New England in all but the most modest establishments. *Prices in the reviews are the average cost of a main course at dinner or, if dinner is not served, at lunch.*

RESERVATIONS AND DRESS

It's a good idea to make a reservation if you can. We only mention them specifically when reservations are essential—there's no other way you'll ever get a table—or when they are not accepted. For popular restaurants, book as far ahead as you can, and reconfirm as soon as you arrive. Large parties should always call ahead to check the reservations policy. We mention dress only when men are required to wear a jacket or a jacket and tie.

WINE, BEER, AND SPIRITS

New England is no stranger to microbrews. The granddaddy of New England's independent breweries is the Boston Beer Company, maker of Samuel Adams. Following the Sam Adams lead in offering hearty English-style ales and special seasonal brews are breweries such as Vermont's Long Trail, Maine's Shipyard, and New Hampshire's Smuttynose Brewing Co. Green Mountain Cidery makes Woodchuck hard cider in Middlebury, Vermont.

New England is beginning to earn some respect as a wine-producing region. Cabernet Franc, Vidal, Riesling, and other grape varieties capable of withstanding the region's harsher winters and relatively shorter growing season compared to California and other leading areas have been the basis of promising enterprises such as Rhode Island's Sakonnet Vineyards, Chicama Vineyards on Martha's Vineyard, and Connecticut's Hopkins Vineyard (part of the Connecticut Wine Trail). Even Vermont is getting into the act with the Snow Farm Vineyard in the Lake Champlain Islands and Boyden Valley Winery in Cambridge.

Although a patchwork of state and local regulations affect the hours and locations of places that sell alcoholic beverages (for example, Massachusetts bans "happy hour"), New England licensing laws are fairly liberal. State-owned or -franchised stores sell hard liquor in New Hampshire, Maine, and Vermont. Many travelers have found that New Hampshire offers the region's lowest prices; look for state-run liquor "supermarkets" on interstates in the southern part of the state.

▌ HEALTH

Lyme disease, so named for its having been first reported in the town of Lyme, Connecticut, is a potentially debilitating disease carried by deer ticks. They thrive in dry, brush-covered areas, particularly in coastal areas. Always use insect repellent: the potential for outbreaks of Lyme disease makes it imperative that you protect yourself from ticks from early spring through summer. To prevent bites, wear light-color clothing and tuck pant legs into socks. Look for black ticks about the size of a pinhead around hairlines and the warmest parts of the body. If you have been bitten, consult a physician, especially if you see the telltale bull's-eye bite pattern. Flu-like symptoms often accompany a Lyme infection. Early treatment is imperative.

New England's two greatest insect pests are black flies and mosquitoes. The former are a phenomenon of late spring and early summer and are generally a problem only in the densely wooded areas of the far north. Mosquitoes, however, are a nuisance just about everywhere. The best protection against both pests is repellent containing DEET; if you're camping in the woods during black fly season, you'll also want to use fine mesh screening in eating and sleeping areas and even wear mesh headgear. One pest particular to coastal areas, especially salt marshes, is the greenhead fly, which has a nasty bite and is hard to kill. It is best repelled by a liberal application of Avon Skin So Soft or a similar product.

Coastal waters attract seafood lovers who enjoy harvesting their own clams, mussels, and even lobsters; permits are required, and casual harvesting of lobsters is strictly forbidden. Amateur clammers should be aware that New England shellfish beds are periodically visited by red tides, during which micro-organisms can render shellfish poisonous. To keep abreast of the situation, inquire when you apply for a license (usually at town halls or police stations) and pay attention to red tide postings as you travel.

▌ HOURS OF OPERATION

Hours in New England differ little from those in other parts of the United States. Within the region, shops and other businesses tend to keep slightly later hours in larger cities and along the coast, which is generally more populated than interior New England.

Most major museums and attractions are open daily or six days a week, with Monday being the most likely day of closing. Hours are often shorter on Saturday and especially Sunday, though some prominent museums stay open late one or two nights a week, usually Tuesday, Thursday, or Friday. New England has many small museums—historical societies, art galleries, highly specialized collections—that open only a few days a week and sometimes only by appointment in winter or slow periods.

▌ MONEY

It costs a bit more to travel in most of New England than it does in the rest of the country, the most costly areas being Boston and the coastal resort towns. There are also some posh inns and restaurants in the Berkshires, northwestern Connecticut, and parts of Vermont and New Hampshire. ATMs are plentiful and larger denomination bills (as well as credit cards) are readily accepted in tourist destinations during the high season.

Prices *throughout this guide* are given for adults. Substantially reduced fees are almost always available for children, students, and senior citizens.

CREDIT CARDS

Major credit cards are readily accepted throughout New England, though in rural areas you may encounter difficulties or the acceptance of only MasterCard or Visa. If you'll be making an excursion into Canada, be aware that many outlets there accept Visa but not MasterCard.

Reporting Lost Cards American Express. ☎ *800/528–4800* ⊕ *www.americanexpress. com.* **Diners Club.** ☎ *800/234–6377* ⊕ *www.dinersclub.com.* **Discover.** ☎ *800/347– 2683* ⊕ *www.discover.com.* **MasterCard.** ☎ *800/627–8372* ⊕ *www.mastercard.us.* **Visa.** ☎ *800/847–2911* ⊕ *usa.visa.com.*

▌ PACKING

The principal rule of weather in New England is that there are no rules. A cold, foggy spring morning often warms to a bright, 60°F afternoon. A summer breeze can suddenly turn chilly, and rain often appears with little warning. Thus, the best advice on how to dress is to layer your clothing; that way, you can peel off or add garments as needed for comfort. Even in summer you should bring long pants, a sweater or two, and a waterproof windbreaker, for evenings are often chilly, and sea spray can make things cool. Showers are frequent, so pack a raincoat and umbrella.

Casual sportswear—walking shoes and jeans or khakis—will take you almost everywhere, but swimsuits and bare feet will not: shirts and shoes are required attire at even the most casual venues. Dress in restaurants is generally casual, except at some of the distinguished restaurants of Boston, Newport, and Maine coast towns such as Kennebunkport, a few inns in the Berkshires, and in Litchfield and Fairfield counties in Connecticut. Upscale resorts, at the very least, will require men to wear collared shirts at dinner, and jeans are often frowned upon.

In summer, bring a hat and sunscreen. Remember also to pack insect repellent: to prevent Lyme disease you'll need to guard against ticks from early spring through summer *(Health)*.

▌ SAFETY

Rural New England is one of the country's safest regions, so much so that residents often leave their doors unlocked. In cities—Boston, in particular—observe the usual precautions: avoid out-of-the-way or poorly lighted areas at night; clutch handbags close to your body and don't let them out of your sight; and be on your guard in subways and buses, not only during the deserted wee hours but also during crowded rush hours, when pickpockets are at work. Keep your valuables in hotel safes. Try to use ATMs in busy, well-lighted places such as bank lobbies.

If your vehicle breaks down in a rural area, pull as far off the road as possible, tie a handkerchief to your radio antenna (use flares at night—check if your rental agency can provide them), and stay in your car with the doors locked until help arrives. Don't pick up hitchhikers. If you're planning to leave a car overnight to make use of off-road trails or camping facilities, make arrangements for a supervised parking area if at all possible. Cars left at trailhead parking lots are subject to theft and vandalism.

The universal telephone number for crime and other emergencies throughout New England is 911.

TIPPING GUIDELINES FOR NEW ENGLAND	
Bartender	$1 to $5 per round of drinks, depending on the number of drinks
Bellhop	$1 or $2 per bag, depending on the level of the hotel
Hotel Concierge	$5 or more, if he or she performs a service for you
Hotel Doorman	$1 or $2 if he helps you get a cab
Hotel Maid	$2 to $5 a day depending on the level of the hotel, either daily or at the end of your stay, in cash
Hotel Room-Service Waiter	$2 to $5 per delivery, even if a service charge has been added
Porter at Airport or Train Station	$1 per bag
Skycap at Airport	$2 or $3 per bag checked
Taxi Driver	15% to 20%, but round up the fare to the next dollar amount
Tour Guide	15% of the cost of the tour
Valet Parking Attendant	$3 to $5, but only when you get your car
Waiter	15% to 20%, with 20% being the norm at high-end restaurants; nothing additional if a service charge is added to the bill
Other Attendants	Restroom attendants in expensive restaurants expect some small change or $1. Tip coat-check personnel at least $1 or $2 per item checked unless there is a fee, then nothing.

▌TAXES

Sales taxes in New England are as follows: Connecticut, 6.35%; Maine, 5.5%; Massachusetts, 6.25%; Rhode Island, 7%; Vermont, 6%. No sales tax is charged in New Hampshire. Some states and municipalities levy an additional tax (1%–10%) on lodging or restaurant meals. Alcoholic beverages are sometimes taxed at a higher rate than that applied to food.

▌TIME

New England operates on Eastern Standard Time and follows daylight saving time. When it is noon in Boston, it is 9 am in Los Angeles, 11 am in Chicago, 5 pm in London, and 3 am the following day in Sydney. When taking a ferry to Nova Scotia, remember that the province operates on Atlantic Standard Time and is therefore an hour ahead.

▌TOURS

BICYCLING
Urban Adventours. This bike shop in downtown Boston conducts guided bicycle tours of the city, regional foliage, and other routes. For example, the ambitious 26-mile Paul Revere tour traces the patriot's famous ride. ☎ 617/670–0637 ⊕ www.urbanadventours.com ✉ From $55.

CULINARY
Creative Culinary Tours. Foodies love exploring a new destination through their stomachs, and this outfit aims to please with three- to seven-day tours all over New England. ☎ 888/889–8681 ⊕ www.creativeculinarytours.com ✉ Call for prices.

GENERAL INTEREST
Contiki Vacations. Specializing in vacations for 18- to 35-year-olds, Contiki conducts tours throughout the Northeast, as well as several in New England specifically. ☎ 866/266–8454 ⊕ www.contiki.com ✉ From $2,255.

Insight Vacations. This company offers fall foliage tours and conducts summer tours that take in Boston, Newport, and Cape Cod. These luxurious tours are aimed at travelers who want every detail taken care of, so they can simply enjoy the destination. Local expert guides make sure you don't miss a thing. ☎ 888/680–1241 ⊕ www.insightvacations.com/us ✉ From $2,725.

New England Vacation Tours. This versatile company conducts everything from packages that include flights and tours in luxury coaches to ones that involve cruises and sightseeing excursions on land. All transportation is covered, and every detail is attended to. You can also create a completely customized itinerary to take you wherever your heart desires—the people here are very easy to work with. ☎ 800/742–7669 ⊕ www.newenglandvacationtours.com ✉ Call for prices.

Northeast Unlimited Tours. As the name indicates, Northeast Unlimited's range of itineraries includes New England. The eight-day Taste of New England tour, for example, hits all the highlights from Boston to Maine. ☎ 800/759–6820 ⊕ www.newenglandtours.com ✉ From $1,839.

Wolfe Adventures & Tours. Though Wolfe specializes in group tours, a family can be defined as a group. Themed New England tours include Cape Cod, the American Revolution, and the North Shore. ☎ 888/449–6533 ⊕ www.wolfetours.com ✉ Call for prices.

SKIING
New England Action Sports. Through this outfit you can book day trips, midweek overnights, weekend trips, and weeklong visits to popular ski resorts, including Stowe, Okemo, and Killington. ☎ 800/477–7669 ⊕ www.skitrip.net ✉ From $229.

▮ VISITOR INFORMATION

Contacts Connecticut Commission on Culture and Tourism. ☎ *888/288–4748* ⊕ *www.ctvisit.com.* **Greater Boston Convention & Visitors Bureau.** ☎ *617/536–4100* ⊕ *www.bostonusa.com.* **Maine Office of Tourism.** ☎ *888/624–6345* ⊕ *www.visitmaine. com.* **Massachusetts Office of Travel and Tourism.** ☎ *800/227–6277, 617/973–8500* ⊕ *www.massvacation.com.* **New Hampshire Division of Travel and Tourism Development.** ☎ *603/271–2665* ⊕ *www.visitnh.gov.* **Rhode Island Tourism Division.** ☎ *800/556– 2484* ⊕ *www.visitrhodeisland.com.* **Vermont Department of Tourism and Marketing.** ☎ *800/837–6668* ⊕ *www.vermontvacation.com.*

ONLINE RESOURCES
Online Info Visit New England. ⊕ *www.visitnewengland.com.* **Yankee.** ⊕ *www.yankeemagazine.com/travel.*

INDEX

PHOTO CREDITS

NOTES

ABOUT OUR WRITERS

Former Fodor's production editor **Bethany Cassin Beckerlegge** traveled the highways and byways of her home state of Connecticut for this edition. A native New Englander, Bethany discovered unsung hideaways and revisited old haunts while exploring the Nutmeg State. She frequently writes for other guides such as *Fodor's Boston,* and spends as much time as she can traveling along the shorelines of New Hampshire and Maine.

Seth Brown lives in the beautiful Berkshires, where he writes a humor column for the *Berkshire Eagle.* He is the author of five books including *It Happened In Rhode Island* and *From God To Verse.* In updating the Berkshires and Western Massachusetts chapter of this guide, he especially enjoyed the rich variety of international restaurants the region has to offer.

Liz Boardman is the managing editor of two southern Rhode Island publications, *The Independent,* a weekly newspaper, and *South County Life,* a lifestyle magazine. She is an award-winning journalist, novelist, and playwright who also works as a brand consultant to boutique hotels and upscale inns across New England. She updated the Rhode Island chapter.

Originally a hayseed from the Territories, **Grace-Yvette Gemmell's** incurable wanderlust has led her to hang her hat in a number of different offbeat nooks and crannies across the globe, including a haunted house in the Netherlands, a Celtic enclave in Germany, a shoebox on the tiny island of Manhattan, a certain infamous English-language bookshop on Paris's Left Bank, and most recently, the Pine Tree State. She is a regular contributor to arts, culture, and travel publications, including *Art and Auction, Modern Painters, Down East Magazine, Hyperallergic, This Land Press,* and the *Daily Beast.* She is a gallery focus writer for *Artsy Editorial* and frequently undertakes curatorial work at museums and other cultural institutions, including the Museum of the City of New York and the Currier Museum of Art. Grace-Yvette updated the Maine Coast chapter.

Debbie Hagan is a magazine writer and former editor of *Art New England.* She is an avid international traveler and skier, who has spent most of her adult life exploring ski trails and inns in New England and the Alps. She currently lives in northern Massachusetts and teaches writing classes at New Hampshire Institute of Art in Manchester. She updated the New Hampshire chapter.

Kim Foley MacKinnon, an award-winning Boston-based journalist, loves to explore and write about New England for a number of publications, including *AAA Horizons,* the *Appalachian Mountain Club,* and the *Boston Globe,* among many others. She helped update the *Fodor's Boston* guide and has written or contributed to several other guidebooks about the area. While much of her work is focused in New England, she also goes farther afield for publications such as *Forbes Travel* and *Shermans Cruise.* She updated Experience New England, Best Fall Foliage Drives and Road Trips, and Travel Smart this edition.

As a freelance writer in Belfast, Maine, **Mary Ruoff** covers travel and other subjects. She is an award-winning former newspaper reporter and a graduate of the School of Journalism at the University of Missouri-Columbia. One of her sources on all things Maine is her husband, Michael Hodsdon, a mariner and lifelong Mainer. They enjoy exploring the state with their son, Dima. For this edition, Mary updated the Inland Maine chapter.

Laura V. Scheel updated the Cape Cod, Martha's Vineyard, and Nantucket chapter of this book. She has written frequently for Fodor's since 1999, contributing to multiple guidebooks throughout New England.

Aaron Starmer is a veteran of the travel industry who lives with his wife and daughter in Stowe, Vermont. When he's not updating guidebooks, he's writing novels for young readers, including *The Only Ones, The Riverman,* and *Spontaneous.*

Our Boston coverage was updated by several writers, including Kara Baskin (Experience Boston), Fred Bouchard (Nightlife and Performing Arts and Travel Smart), Megan Johnson (Where to Stay and Side Trips), Kim Foley MacKinnon (Exploring Boston and Sports and the Outdoors), and Victoria Abbott Riccardi (Where to Eat and Shopping).